기출이 답이다

9급 공무원

영어

7개년 기출문제집

시대에듀

9급 공무원 채용 필수체크

❖ 아래 내용은 2024년 국가직 공무원 공개경쟁채용시험 계획 공고를 기준으로 작성되었습니다. 2025년부터 변경되는 세부 사항은 반드시 시행처의 최신 공고를 확인하시기 바랍니다.

✎ 시험방법

- 제1 · 2차 시험(병합실시): 선택형 필기
- 제3차 시험: 면접

※ 교정직 6급 이하 채용시험의 경우, 필기시험 합격자를 대상으로 실기시험(체력검사)을 실시하고 실기시험 합격자에 한하여 면접시험을 실시함

✎ 응시자격

구분	내용
응시연령	• 교정 · 보호직 제외: 18세 이상 • 교정 · 보호직: 20세 이상
학력 및 경력	• 제한 없음

✎ 시험일정(국가직 기준)

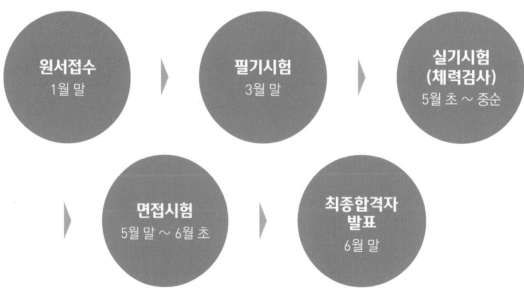

✏ 가산점 적용

구분	가산비율	비고
취업지원대상자	과목별 만점의 10% 또는 5%	• 취업지원대상자 가점과 의사상자 등 가점은 1개만 적용 • 취업지원대상자/의사상자 등 가점과 자격증 가산점은 각각 적용
의사상자 등 (의사자 유족, 의상자 본인 및 가족)	과목별 만점의 5% 또는 3%	
직렬별 가산대상 자격증 소지자	과목별 만점의 3~5% (1개의 자격증만 인정)	

✏ 2025년부터 달라지는 제도

■ 9급 공무원 국어, 영어 과목 출제 기조 전환

지식암기 위주		현장 직무 중심

■ 출제 방향

국어	• 기본적인 국어 능력과 이해, 추론, 비판력 등 사고력 검증 • 배경지식이 없더라도 지문 속 정보를 활용해 문제를 풀 수 있도록 출제
영어	• 실제 업무수행에 필요한 실용적인 영어능력 검증 • 실제 활용도가 높은 어휘와 전자메일, 안내문 등 업무현장에서 접할 수 있는 소재와 형식을 활용한 문제 출제

2024년 영어 출제경향

국가직

작년보다는 다소 어렵게 출제되었다. 특히 독해 영역에서 신화, 과학 등 내용을 빠르게 파악하기 힘든 주제가 제시되었고 문장의 길이가 길어 해석하는 데 시간이 많이 소요되었을 것이다. 2025년부터 반영될 것으로 예상되었던 새로운 문제 유형이 3문항 정도 출제되었으나 난도는 높지 않았다. 각 문제 유형에 맞는 풀이법을 충분히 연습한다면 2025년 시험을 대비하는 데 큰 어려움은 없을 것이다.

■ 출제율 순위

　독해 > 어휘 > 어법 = 표현

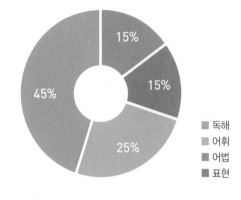

지방직

과년도 기출문제와 유사하게 출제되어 전체적으로 평이했으며, 국가직 시험과 비교했을 때도 높지 않은 난도였다. 그러나 독해 영역에서 다소 고민을 요하는 문제가 출제되었는데, 이는 평소 정량의 단어를 암기하고, 문장 해석 시 글의 핵심을 찾는 연습 등 대비를 충분히 했다면 큰 문제 없이 해결할 수 있었을 것으로 보인다.

■ 출제율 순위

　독해 > 어휘 > 어법 = 표현

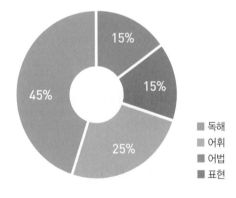

3개년 분석으로 영어 Knock! Knock!

국가직

■ 출제율 순위

독해 > 어휘 > 어법 > 표현

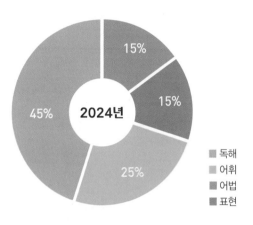

2024년
- 15% 어휘
- 15% 어법
- 25% 표현
- 45% 독해

범례:
- 독해
- 어휘
- 어법
- 표현

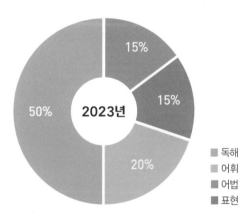

2023년
- 15% 어휘
- 15% 어법
- 20% 표현
- 50% 독해

범례:
- 독해
- 어휘
- 어법
- 표현

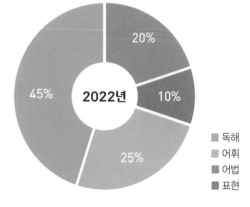

2022년
- 20% 어휘
- 10% 어법
- 25% 표현
- 45% 독해

범례:
- 독해
- 어휘
- 어법
- 표현

지방직

■ 출제율 순위

독해 > 어휘 > 어법 > 표현

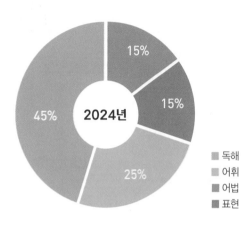

2024년
- 15% 어휘
- 15% 어법
- 25% 표현
- 45% 독해

범례:
- 독해
- 어휘
- 어법
- 표현

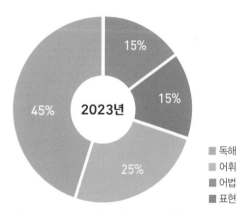

2023년
- 15% 어휘
- 15% 어법
- 25% 표현
- 45% 독해

범례:
- 독해
- 어휘
- 어법
- 표현

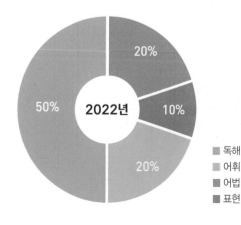

2022년
- 20% 어휘
- 10% 어법
- 20% 표현
- 50% 독해

범례:
- 독해
- 어휘
- 어법
- 표현

이 책의 구성과 특징

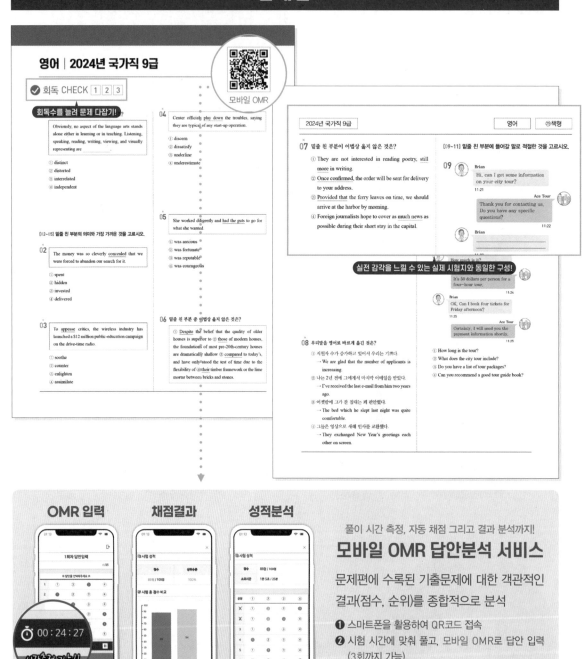

문제편

영어 | 2024년 국가직 9급

모바일 OMR

✅ 회독 CHECK 1 2 3

회독수를 늘려 문제 다잡기!

Obviously, no aspect of the language arts stands alone either in learning or in teaching. Listening, speaking, reading, writing, viewing, and visually representing are _____.

① distinct
② distorted
③ interrelated
④ independent

[02~05] 밑줄 친 부분의 의미와 가장 가까운 것을 고르시오.

02
The money was so cleverly concealed that we were forced to abandon our search for it.

① spent
② hidden
③ invested
④ delivered

03
To appease critics, the wireless industry has launched a $12 million public-education campaign on the drive-time radio.

① soothe
② counter
③ enlighten
④ assimilate

04
Center officials play down the troubles, saying they are typical of any start-up operation.

① discern
② dissatisfy
③ underline
④ underestimate

05
She worked diligently and had the guts to go for what she wanted.

① was anxious
② was fortunate
③ was reputable
④ was courageous

06 밑줄 친 부분 중 어법상 옳지 않은 것은?

① Despite the belief that the quality of older houses is superior to ② those of modern houses, the foundations of most pre-20th-century houses are dramatically shallow ③ compared to today's, and have only ④ stood the test of time due to the flexibility of their timber framework or the lime mortar between bricks and stones.

07 밑줄 친 부분이 어법상 옳지 않은 것은?

① They are not interested in reading poetry, still more in writing.
② Once confirmed, the order will be sent for delivery to your address.
③ Provided that the ferry leaves on time, we should arrive at the harbor by morning.
④ Foreign journalists hope to cover as much news as possible during their short stay in the capital.

08 우리말을 영어로 바르게 옮긴 것은?

① 지원자 수가 증가하고 있어서 우리는 기쁘다.
   · We are glad that the number of applicants is increasing.
② 나는 2년 전에 그에게서 마지막 이메일을 받았다.
   · I've received the last e-mail from him two years ago.
③ 어젯밤에 그가 잔 침대는 꽤 편안했다.
   · The bed which he slept last night was quite comfortable.
④ 그들은 영상으로 새해 인사를 교환했다.
   · They exchanged New Year's greetings each other on screen.

[09~11] 밑줄 친 부분에 들어갈 말로 적절한 것을 고르시오.

09
Brian
Hi, can I get some information on your city tour?
11:21

Ace Tour
Thank you for contacting us. Do you have any specific questions?
11:22

Brian
_____

실전 감각을 느낄 수 있는 실제 시험지와 동일한 구성!

It's 50 dollars per person for a four-hour tour.
11:24

Brian
OK, Can I book four tickets for Friday afternoon?
11:25

Ace Tour
Certainly, I will send you the payment information shortly.
11:25

① How long is the tour?
② What does the city tour include?
③ Do you have a list of tour packages?
④ Can you recommend a good tour guide book?

OMR 입력 채점결과 성적분석

풀이 시간 측정, 자동 채점 그리고 결과 분석까지!

모바일 OMR 답안분석 서비스

문제편에 수록된 기출문제에 대한 객관적인 결과(점수, 순위)를 종합적으로 분석

❶ 스마트폰을 활용하여 QR코드 접속
❷ 시험 시간에 맞춰 풀고, 모바일 OMR로 답안 입력 (3회까지 가능)
❸ 종합적 결과 분석으로 현재 나의 합격 가능성 예측

⏱ 00 : 24 : 27
시간측정 가능!!

QR코드 찍기 ▶ 로그인 ▶ 시작하기 ▶ 응시하기 ▶ 모바일 OMR 카드에 답안 입력 ▶ 채점결과&성적분석 ▶ 내 실력 확인하기

해설편

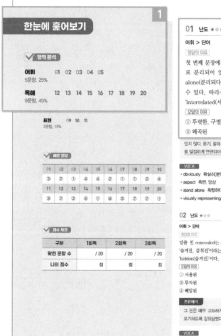

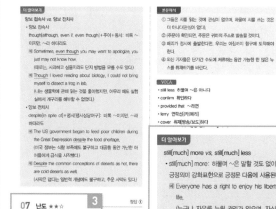

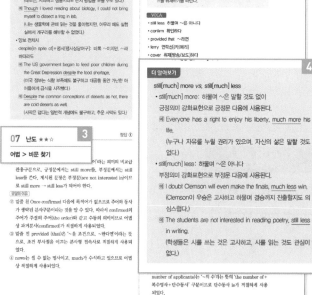

1 한눈에 훑어보기

어떤 영역에서 출제되었었는지 또는 주로 출제되는 영역은 어디인지 한 눈에 확인할 수 있어요!

2 정답의 이유/오답의 이유

각 문제마다 정답의 이유와 오답의 이유를 수록하여 혼자서도 학습이 가능해요!

3 난도와 영역 분석

난도와 문항별 세분화된 출제 영역 분석을 통해 부족한 영역을 확인하고 보충할 수 있어요!

4 더 알아보기

이해도를 높일 수 있도록 문제와 관련된 핵심 이론과 개념을 알기 쉽게 정리했어요!

이 책의 목차

영어

부록

- 2025년 출제기조 전환 예시문제
- 2025년 출제기조 전환 예시문제 해설

[01~03] 밑줄 친 부분에 들어갈 말로 가장 적절한 것을 고르시오.

01

Recently, increasingly _____ weather patterns, often referred to as "abnormal climate," have been observed around the world.

① irregular
② consistent
③ predictable
④ ineffective

02

Most economic theories assume that people act on a _____ basis; however, this doesn't account for the fact that they often rely on their emotions instead.

① temporary
② rational
③ voluntary
④ commercial

03

By the time she _____ her degree, she will have acquired valuable knowledge on her field of study.

① will have finished
② is finishing
③ will finish
④ finishes

[04~05] 밑줄 친 부분 중 어법상 옳지 않은 것을 고르시오.

04

You may conclude that knowledge of the sound systems, word patterns, and sentence structures ① are sufficient to help a student ② become competent in a language. Yet we have ③ all worked with language learners who understand English structurally but still have difficulty ④ communicating.

05

Beyond the cars and traffic jams, she said it took a while to ① get used to have so many people in one place, ② all of whom were moving so fast. "There are only 18 million people in Australia ③ spread out over an entire country," she said, "compared to more than six million people in ④ the state of Massachusetts alone."

[06~07] 밑줄 친 부분에 들어갈 말로 가장 적절한 것을 고르시오.

06

A: Hello. I'd like to book a flight from Seoul to Oakland.

B: Okay. Do you have any specific dates in mind?

A: Yes. I am planning to leave on May 2nd and return on May 14th.

B: Okay, I found one that fits your schedule. What class would you like to book?

A: Economy class is good enough for me.

B: Any preference on your seating?

A: _____

B: Great. Your flight is now booked.

① Yes. I'd like to upgrade to business class.

② No. I'd like to buy a one-way ticket.

③ No. I don't have any luggage.

④ Yes. I want an aisle seat.

07

Kate Anderson

Are you coming to the workshop next Friday?

10:42

Jim Henson

I'm not sure. I have a doctor's appointment that day.

10:42

Kate Anderson

You should come! The workshop is about A.I. tools that can improve out work efficiency.

10:43

Jim Henson

Wow, the topic sounds really interesting!

10:44

Kate Anderson

Exactly. But don't forget to reserve a seat if you want to attend the workshop.

10:45

Jim Henson

How do I do that?

10:45

Kate Anderson

_____
_____

10:46

① You need to bring your own laptop.

② I already have a reservation.

③ Follow the instructions on the bulletin board.

④ You should call the doctor's office for an appointment.

[08~09] 다음 글을 읽고 물음에 답하시오.

To whom it may concern,

I hope this email finds you well. I am writing to express my concern and frustration regarding the excessive noise levels in our neighborhood, specifically coming from the new sports field.

As a resident of Clifton district, I have always appreciated the peace of our community. However, the ongoing noise disturbances have significantly impacted my family's well-being and our overall quality of life. The sources of the noise include crowds cheering, players shouting, whistles, and ball impacts.

I kindly request that you look into this matter and take appropriate steps to address the noise disturbances. Thank you for your attention to this matter, and I appreciate your prompt response to help restore the tranquility in our neighborhood.

Sincerely,
Rachael Beasley

08 윗글의 목적으로 가장 적절한 것은?

① 체육대회 소음에 대해 주민들의 양해를 구하려고
② 새로 이사 온 이웃 주민의 소음에 대해 항의하려고
③ 인근 스포츠 시설의 소음에 대한 조치를 요청하려고
④ 밤시간 악기 연주와 같은 소음의 차단을 부탁하려고

09 밑줄 친 "steps"의 의미와 가장 가까운 것은?

① movements
② actions
③ levels
④ stairs

[10~11] 다음 글을 읽고 물음에 답하시오.

(A)

We're pleased to announce the upcoming City Harbour Festival, an annual event that brings our diverse community together to celebrate our shared heritage, culture, and local talent. Mark your calendars and join us for an exciting weekend!

Details
- Dates: Friday, June 16 - Sunday, June 18
- Times: 10:00a.m. - 8:00p.m. (Friday & Saturday)
          10:00a.m. - 6:00p.m. (Sunday)
- Location: City Harbour Park, Main Street, and surrounding areas

Highlights
- Live Performances
  Enjoy a variety of live music, dance, and theatrical performances on multiple stages throughout the festival grounds.
- Food Trucks
  Have a feast with a wide selection of food trucks offering diverse and delicious cuisines, as well as free sample tastings.

For the full schedule of events and activities, please visit our website at www.cityharbourfestival.org or contact the Festival Office at (552) 234-5678.

---

10 (A)에 들어갈 윗글의 제목으로 가장 적절한 것은?

① Make Safety Regulations for Your Community
② Celebrate Our Vibrant Community Events
③ Plan Your Exciting Maritime Experience
④ Recreate Our City's Heritage

11 City Harbour Festival에 관한 윗글의 내용과 일치하지 않는 것은?

① 일 년에 한 번 개최된다.
② 일요일에는 오후 6시까지 열린다.
③ 주요 행사로 무료 요리 강습이 진행된다.
④ 웹사이트나 전화 문의를 통해 행사 일정을 알 수 있다.

12 Enter-K 앱에 관한 다음 글의 내용과 일치하지 않는 것은?

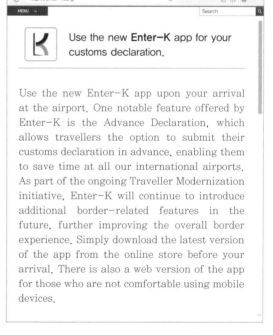

Use the new **Enter-K** app for your customs declaration.

Use the new Enter-K app upon your arrival at the airport. One notable feature offered by Enter-K is the Advance Declaration, which allows travellers the option to submit their customs declaration in advance, enabling them to save time at all our international airports. As part of the ongoing Traveller Modernization initiative, Enter-K will continue to introduce additional border-related features in the future, further improving the overall border experience. Simply download the latest version of the app from the online store before your arrival. There is also a web version of the app for those who are not comfortable using mobile devices.

① It allows travellers to declare customs in advance.
② More features will be added later.
③ Travellers can download it from the online store.
④ It only works on personal mobile devices.

13 Office of the Labor Commissioner에 관한 다음 글의 내용과 일치하는 것은?

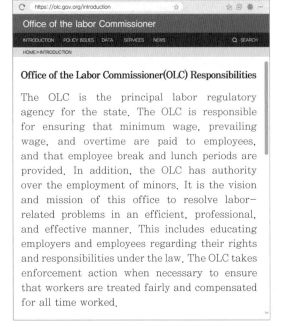

Office of the Labor Commissioner(OLC) Responsibilities

The OLC is the principal labor regulatory agency for the state. The OLC is responsible for ensuring that minimum wage, prevailing wage, and overtime are paid to employees, and that employee break and lunch periods are provided. In addition, the OLC has authority over the employment of minors. It is the vision and mission of this office to resolve labor-related problems in an efficient, professional, and effective manner. This includes educating employers and employees regarding their rights and responsibilities under the law. The OLC takes enforcement action when necessary to ensure that workers are treated fairly and compensated for all time worked.

① It ensures that employees pay taxes properly.

② It has authority over employment of adult workers only.

③ It promotes employers' business opportunities.

④ It takes action when employees are unfairly treated.

14 다음 글의 주제로 가장 적절한 것은?

The Ministry of Food and Drug Safety warned that cases of food poisoning have occurred as a result of cross-contamination, where people touch eggs and neglect to wash their hands before preparing food or using utensils. To mitigate such risks, the ministry advised refrigerating eggs and ensuring they are thoroughly cooked until both the yolk and white are firm. Over the past five years, a staggering 7,400 people experienced food poisoning caused by Salmonella bacteria. Salmonella thrives in warm temperatures, with approximately 37 degrees Celsius being the optimal growth condition. Consuming raw or undercooked eggs and failing to separate raw and cooked foods were identified as the most common causes of Salmonella infection. It is crucial to prioritize food safety measures and adhere to proper cooking practices to minimize the risk of Salmonella-related illnesses.

① Benefits of consuming eggs to the immune system

② Different types of treatments for Salmonella infection

③ Life span of Salmonella bacteria in warm temperatures

④ Safe handling of eggs for the prevention of Salmonella infection

15 다음 글의 요지로 가장 적절한 것은?

Despite ongoing efforts to address educational disparities, the persistent achievement gap among students continues to highlight significant inequities in the education system. Recent data reveal that marginalized students, including those from low-income backgrounds and vulnerable groups, continue to lag behind their peers in academic performance. The gap poses a challenge to achieving educational equity and social mobility. Experts emphasize the need for targeted interventions, equitable resource allocation, and inclusive policies to bridge this gap and ensure equal opportunities for all students, irrespective of their socioeconomic status or background. The issue of continued educational divide should be addressed at all levels of education system in an effort to find a solution.

① We should deal with persistent educational inequities.

② Educational experts need to focus on new school policies.

③ New teaching methods are necessary to bridge the achievement gap.

④ Family income should not be considered in the discussion of education.

16 다음 글의 흐름상 어색한 문장은?

Every parent or guardian of small children will have experienced the desperate urge to get out of the house and the magical restorative effect of even a short trip to the local park. ① There is probably more going on here than just letting off steam. ② The benefits for kids of getting into nature are huge, ranging from better academic performance to improved mood and focus. ③ Outdoor activities make it difficult for them to spend quality time with their family. ④ Childhood experiences of nature can also boost environmentalism in adulthood. Having access to urban green spaces can play a role in children's social networks and friendships.

17 주어진 문장이 들어갈 위치로 가장 적절한 것은?

In particular, in many urban counties, air pollution, as measured by the amount of total suspended particles, had reached dangerous levels.

Economists Chay and Greenstone evaluated the value of cleaning up of air pollution after the Clean Air Act of 1970. (①) Before 1970, there was little federal regulation of air pollution, and the issue was not high on the agenda of state legislators. (②) As a result, many counties allowed factories to operate without any regulation on their pollution, and in several heavily industrialized counties, pollution had reached very high levels. (③) The Clean Air Act established guidelines for what constituted excessively high levels of five particularly dangerous pollutants. (④) Following the Act in 1970 and the 1977 amendment, there were improvements in air quality.

18 주어진 글 다음에 이어질 글의 순서로 가장 적절한 것은?

> Before anyone could witness what had happened, I shoved the loaves of bread up under my shirt, wrapped the hunting jacket tightly about me, and walked swiftly away.

> (A) When I dropped them on the table, my sister's hands reached to tear off a chunk, but I made her sit, forced my mother to join us at the table, and poured warm tea.
>
> (B) The heat of the bread burned into my skin, but I clutched it tighter, clinging to life. By the time I reached home, the loaves had cooled somewhat, but the insides were still warm.
>
> (C) I sliced the bread. We ate an entire loaf, slice by slice. It was good hearty bread, filled with raisins and nuts.

① (A) - (B) - (C)

② (B) - (A) - (C)

③ (B) - (C) - (A)

④ (C) - (A) - (B)

[19~20] 밑줄 친 부분에 들어갈 말로 가장 적절한 것을 고르시오.

19

> Falling fertility rates are projected to result in shrinking populations for nearly every country by the end of the century. The global fertility rate was 4.7 in 1950, but it dropped by nearly half to 2.4 in 2017. It is expected to fall below 1.7 by 2100. As a result, some researchers predict that the number of people on the planet would peak at 9.7 billion around 2064 before falling down to 8.8 billion by the century's end. This transition will also lead to a significant aging of populations, with as many people reaching 80 years old as there are being born. Such a demographic shift _____, including taxation, healthcare for the elderly, caregiving responsibilities, and retirement. To ensure a "soft landing" into a new demographic landscape, researchers emphasize the need for careful management of the transition.

① raises concerns about future challenges

② mitigates the inverted age structure phenomenon

③ compensates for the reduced marriage rate issue

④ provides immediate solutions to resolve the problems

20

Many listeners blame a speaker for their inattention by thinking to themselves: "Who could listen to such a character? Will he ever stop reading from his notes?" The good listener reacts differently. He may well look at the speaker and think, "This man is incompetent. Seems like almost anyone would be able to talk better than that." But from this initial similarity he moves on to a different conclusion, thinking "But wait a minute. I'm not interested in his personality or delivery. I want to find out what he knows. Does this man know some things that I need to know?" Essentially, we "listen with our own experience." Is the speaker to be held responsible because we are poorly equipped to comprehend his message? We cannot understand everything we hear, but one sure way to raise the level of our understanding is to _____.

① ignore what the speaker knows
② analyze the character of a speaker
③ assume the responsibility which is inherently ours
④ focus on the speaker's competency of speech delivery

한눈에 훑어보기

✓ 영역 분석

어휘   01 02 09
3문항, 15%

독해   08 10 11 12 13 14 15 16 17 18 19 20
12문항, 60%

어법   03 04 05
3문항, 15%

표현   06 07
2문항, 10%

✓ 빠른 정답

01	02	03	04	05	06	07	08	09	10
①	②	④	①	①	④	③	③	②	②
11	12	13	14	15	16	17	18	19	20
③	④	④	④	①	③	③	②	①	③

✓ 점수 체크

구분	1회독	2회독	3회독
맞힌 문항 수	/ 20	/ 20	/ 20
나의 점수	점	점	점

---

01 난도 ★☆☆   정답 ①

어휘 > 단어

정답의 이유

weather patterns를 수식하는 often referred to as "abnormal climate"으로 미루어 보아 밑줄 친 부분에는 abnormal climate(이상기후)의 특징을 나타내는 말이 들어가야 함을 유추할 수 있다. 따라서 밑줄 친 부분에 들어갈 말로 가장 적절한 것은 ① 'irregular(불규칙한)'이다.

오답의 이유

② 일관된
③ 예측[예견]할 수 있는
④ 효과[효력] 없는

본문해석

최근, 종종 '이상기후'로 불리는, 갈수록 더 불규칙한 기후 패턴이 세계 곳곳에서 관측되고 있다.

VOCA

• increasingly 점점 더, 갈수록 더
• refer to as ~(이)라고 언급하다
• abnormal climate 이상기후
• observe 관찰[관측/주시]하다

02 난도 ★☆☆   정답 ②

어휘 > 단어

정답의 이유

'however, this doesn't account for the fact that they often rely on their emotions instead(그러나 이것은 그들이 종종 감정에 의존한다는 사실을 설명하지 않는다).'라고 했으므로 밑줄 친 부분에는 'emotions(감정)'와 반대되는 의미의 단어가 들어가야 함을 유추할 수 있다. 따라서 밑줄 친 부분에 들어갈 말로 가장 적절한 것은 ② 'rational(이성적인)'이다.

오답의 이유

① 일시적인, 임시의
③ 자발적인, 임의적인
④ 상업적인

대부분의 경제 이론은 사람들이 <u>이성적인</u> 근거에 따라 행동한다고 가정한다. 그러나 이것은 그들이 종종 감정에 의존한다는 사실을 설명하지 않는다.

VOCA

- assume that ～(이)라 가정하여, ～(이)라 하면
- act on ～에 따라서 행동하다, 따르다
- basis 근거, 기준
- account for ～을 설명하다
- rely on 의존[의지]하다

03 난도 ★☆☆ 　　　　　　　　　정답 ④

어법 > 정문 찾기

정답의 이유

By the time(～할 때까지, ～할 무렵)은 시간 접속사로, 부사절을 이끌고 있다. 시간·조건 부사절에서는 현재시제가 미래시제를 대신하므로, 'By the time+주어+현재동사, 주어+will have p.p.(미래완료)'가 되어야 한다. 따라서 밑줄 친 부분에 들어갈 말로 가장 적절한 것은 현재시제인 ④ 'finishes(마치다)'이다.

본문해석

학위를 마칠 무렵, 그녀는 자신의 연구 분야에 대한 귀중한 지식을 습득하게 될 것이다.

VOCA

- degree 학위
- acquire 습득하다[얻다]
- field 분야

04 난도 ★★☆ 　　　　　　　　　정답 ①

어법 > 비문 찾기

정답의 이유

① are는 명사절(that knowledge of the sound systems ～ in a language)의 주어(knowledge)를 받는 동사인데, knowledge가 단수 명사이므로 are → is가 되어야 한다.

오답의 이유

② 'help+목적어+(to) 동사원형'은 '목적어가 ～하도록 돕다'의 뜻으로, 어법상 준사역동사(help) 다음에 동사원형(become)이 올바르게 사용되었다.

③ all은 명사, 형용사, 부사로 사용되는데, 밑줄 친 all은 have worked 사이에서 부사로 올바르게 사용되었다.

④ 'have difficulty+-ing'는 '～하느라 고생하다'라는 뜻의 동명사의 관용적 표현이므로, 밑줄 친 communicating이 어법상 올바르게 사용되었다.

여러분은 소리 체계와 단어 패턴, 문장 구조에 대한 지식이 학생을 한 언어에 능숙해지도록 돕는 데 충분하다고 판단할지도 모른다. 하지만 우리는 영어를 구조적으로 이해하지만 여전히 의사소통에 어려움을 겪는 언어 학습자들을 연구 대상으로 해왔다.

VOCA

- conclude 결론[판단]을 내리다
- be sufficient to ～하기에 충분하다
- competent 능숙한
- work with ～을 연구[작업] 대상으로 하다
- structurally 구조상, 구조적으로

05 난도 ★☆☆ 　　　　　　　　　정답 ①

어법 > 비문 찾기

정답의 이유

① 'get used to+-ing'는 '～에 익숙해지다'를 의미하는 관용적 표현이므로, get used to have → get used to having이 되어야 한다. 이때 to는 전치사이므로, to 다음에는 명사(구)가 와야 한다. 참고로 'used to+동사원형'은 '～하곤 했다'의 뜻이다.

오답의 이유

② '명사(all)+of whom' 다음에 불완전한 문장이 나오는 문장에서 whom은 선행하는 people을 받는 관계대명사로 전치사(of) 다음에 올바르게 사용되었다.

③ 밑줄 친 spread out은 명사(18 million people)를 수식하는 과거분사로 올바르게 사용되었다.

④ 전치사(in) 다음에 명사(the state of Massachusetts)가 올바르게 사용되었다.

본문해석

그녀는 자동차들과 교통체증을 넘어서, 한 장소에 매우 많은 사람들이 있고, 그들 모두가 아주 바쁘게 이동하고 있는 것에 익숙해지는 데 조금 시간이 걸렸다고 말했다. "매사추세츠주에만 600만 명 이상의 사람들이 있는 것과 비교할 때, 호주에는 나라 전체에 퍼져 있는 1,800만 명의 사람들이 있을 뿐이에요."라고 그녀가 말했다.

VOCA

- traffic jam 교통체증
- it takes a while 조금 시간이 필요하다
- spread out 몸을 뻗다, 넓은 공간을 쓰다[차지하다]
- compared to ～와 비교하여

06 난도 ★☆☆   정답 ④

표현 > 일반회화

정답의 이유

서울에서 오클랜드로 가는 항공편을 예약하는 상황으로, 밑줄 앞에서 B가 'Any preference on your seating(선호하는 좌석이 있으신가요?)'이라고 물었으므로 밑줄 친 부분에 들어갈 A의 답변으로 가장 적절한 것은 ④ 'Yes. I want an aisle seat(네. 통로 쪽 좌석을 원해요.)'이다.

오답의 이유

① 네. 비즈니스석으로 업그레이드하고 싶어요.

② 아니요. 편도로 티켓을 사고 싶어요.

③ 아니요. 짐이 없어요.

본문해석

A: 안녕하세요. 서울에서 오클랜드로 가는 비행기를 예약하고 싶어요.

B: 알겠습니다. 계획하고 있는 날짜가 있으신가요?

A: 네. 5월 2일에 출발해서 5월 14일에 돌아올 예정이에요.

B: 네, 고객님 일정에 맞는 것을 찾았습니다. 어떤 등급 좌석으로 예약하시겠어요?

A: 이코노미 클래스면 충분해요.

B: 원하시는 좌석이 있으신가요?

A: 네. 통로 쪽 좌석을 원해요.

B: 잘됐네요. 항공편이 지금 예약되었어요.

VOCA

• book a flight 비행기 좌석을 예약하다

• fit (의도 · 목적 · 시기 등에) 적합하다

• preference 선호, 애호

07 난도 ★☆☆   정답 ③

표현 > 일반회화

정답의 이유

제시문은 워크숍 참석을 안내하는 문자 메시지이다. 밑줄 앞에서 Kate Anerson이 워크숍에 참석하고 싶다면 좌석 예약하는 것을 잊지 말라고 하자 Jim Henson이 'How do I do that(어떻게 하지요)?'이라고 물었으므로 밑줄에는 워크숍 좌석 예약에 관한 내용이 와야 한다. 따라서 밑줄 친 부분에 들어갈 말로 가장 적절한 것은 ③ 'Follow the instructions on the bulletin board(게시판의 설명대로 따라하세요.)'이다.

오답의 이유

① 노트북을 가지고 오셔야 합니다.

② 이미 예약했어요.

④ 진료실에 전화해서 진료 예약을 해야 해요.

본문해석

Kate Anderson: 다음 주 금요일에 워크숍에 오시나요?

Jim Henson: 잘 모르겠어요. 그날 병원 예약이 있어요.

Kate Anderson: 꼭 오셔야 해요! 워크숍은 업무 효율을 향상시킬 수 있는 인공지능 도구에 관한 것입니다.

Jim Henson: 와우, 주제가 정말 재미있을 거 같아요!

Kate Anderson: 맞아요. 하지만 워크숍에 참석하고 싶다면 좌석 예약하는 것 잊지 마세요.

Jim Henson: 어떻게 하지요?

Kate Anderson: 게시판의 설명대로 따라하세요.

VOCA

• appointment 약속[예약]

• improve 개선하다, 향상시키다

• work efficiency 업무 효율

• reserve 예약하다

08~09

본문해석

관계자 제위,

이 이메일이 귀하에게 잘 닿기를 바랍니다. 저는 이웃의 과도한 소음, 즉 구체적으로 말하면 새 스포츠 시설에서 나오는 소음과 관련된 우려와 불만에 대해 말하려고 합니다.

Clifton 지역 주민의 한 사람으로서, 저는 항상 평화로운 지역 사회에 감사해 왔습니다. 하지만, 계속되는 소음장애가 심각하게 우리 가족의 안녕과 전반적인 삶의 질에 영향을 주었습니다. 소음의 원인은 군중의 응원, 선수들의 함성, 호각 소리, 그리고 공에 의한 충격 등입니다.

이 문제를 주의 깊게 살펴보고 소음장애 문제를 해결하기 위해 적절한 조치를 취해줄 것을 부탁드립니다. 이 문제에 관심을 가져주셔서 감사드리며, 우리 동네의 평온을 되찾는 데 도움이 되도록 신속하게 대응해 주시면 감사하겠습니다.

진심을 담아,

Rachael Beasley

VOCA

• To whom it may concern 관계자 제위[각위]

• frustration 불만, 좌절감

• regarding ~에 관하여[대하여]

• specifically 구체적으로 말하면

• ongoing 계속 진행 중인

• noise disturbance 소음장애

• impact 영향[충격]을 주다

• well-being 행복, 안녕

• overall 종합[전반]적인, 전체의

• source 출처, 원천

• look into 조사하다, 주의깊게 살피다

• step 조치, 걸음

- address 해결하다, 연설하다
- restore 회복하다, 되찾다
- tranquility 고요, 평안

08 난도 ★☆☆   정답 ③

독해 > 대의 파악 > 글의 목적

정답의 이유

두 번째 문장에서 'I am writing to express my concern and frustration regarding the excessive noise levels in our neighborhood, specifically coming from the new sports field(저는 이웃의 과도한 소음, 즉 구체적으로 말하면 새 스포츠 시설에서 나오는 소음과 관련된 우려와 불만에 대해 말하려고 합니다).'라고 했고, 마지막 문단의 첫 문장에서 'I kindly request that you look into this matter and take appropriate steps to address the noise disturbances(이 문제를 주의 깊게 살펴보고 소음장애 문제를 해결하기 위해 적절한 조치를 취해줄 것을 부탁드립니다).'라고 했으므로, 글의 목적으로 적절한 것은 ③ '인근 스포츠 시설의 소음에 대한 조치를 요청하려고'이다.

09 난도 ★☆☆   정답 ②

어휘 > 단어

정답의 이유

밑줄 친 steps 앞에 'appropriate(적절한)'와 다음에 'to address the noise disturbances(소음장애를 해결하다)'로 미루어 문맥상 밑줄 친 steps는 '조치'의 의미로 사용되었음을 유추할 수 있다. 따라서 밑줄 친 steps의 의미와 가장 가까운 것은 ② 'actions(조치, 행동)'이다.

오답의 이유

① 움직임, 이동
③ 수준[단계]
④ 계단

10~11

본문해석

활기찬 지역 공동체 행사 축하하기

우리의 공유 유산과 문화, 지역의 재능을 기념하기 위해 다양한 지역 공동체를 하나로 모으는 연례 행사인 금번 City Harbour Festival을 발표하게 되어 대단히 기쁩니다. 달력 일정에 표시하고, 신나는 주말을 함께해요!

세부 사항

- 날짜: 6월 16일 금요일 – 6월 18일 일요일
- 시간: 오전 10:00 – 오후 8:00 (금, 토)
  오전 10:00 – 오후 6:00 (일)
- 장소: City Harbour Park, Main Street, 주변 지역

주요 행사

- 라이브 공연
  축제장 곳곳의 여러 무대에서 다양한 라이브 음악, 춤, 연극 공연을 즐기세요.
- 푸드 트럭
  무료 시식회뿐만 아니라, 다채롭고 맛있는 음식을 제공하는 엄선된 푸드 트럭의 연회를 벌이세요.

행사 및 활동의 전체 일정은 당사 웹사이트 www.cityharbourfestival.org를 방문하시거나 페스티벌 사무실 전화 (552) 234–5678로 문의하시기 바랍니다.

VOCA

- announce 발표하다, 알리다
- upcoming 다가오는, 곧 있을
- bring together 묶다, 합치다
- multiple 다양한, 복합적인

10 난도 ★☆☆   정답 ②

독해 > 대의 파악 > 제목, 주제

정답의 이유

제시문의 첫 문장에서 '~ the upcoming City Harbour Festival, an annual event that brings our diverse community together to celebrate(~을 기념하기 위해 다양한 지역 공동체를 하나로 모으는 연례 행사인 금번 City Harbour Festival) ~'라고 했고, 라이브 공연과 푸드 트럭 행사를 주요 이벤트로 소개하고 있으므로 글의 제목으로 적절한 것은 ② 'Celebrate Our Vibrant Community Events(활기찬 지역 공동체 행사 축하하기)'이다.

오답의 이유

① 지역 공동체를 위한 안전 규정 만들기
③ 여러분의 신나는 해양 체험 계획하기
④ 우리 도시의 유산 재현하기

11 난도 ★☆☆

정답 ③

독해 > 세부 내용 찾기 > 내용 (불)일치

정답의 이유

③ 주요 행사로 라이브 공연과 푸드 트럭에서 제공하는 '무료 시식 행사(free sample tastings)'를 언급하고 있으므로 글의 내용과 일치하지 않는다.

오답의 이유

① 첫 문장에서 'an annual event(연례 행사)'라고 했으므로 글의 내용과 일치한다.

② 행사 세부 사항에서 '10:00a.m. - 6:00p.m. (Sunday)'라고 나와 있으므로 글의 내용과 일치한다.

④ 마지막 문장에서 'For the full schedule of events and activities, please visit our website at www.cityharbourfestival.org or contact the Festival Office at (552) 234-5678(행사 및 활동의 전체 일정은 당사 웹사이트 www.cityharbourfestival.org를 방문하시거나 페스티벌 사무실 전화 (552) 234-5678로 문의하시기 바랍니다).'라고 했으므로 글의 내용과 일치한다.

12 난도 ★☆☆

정답 ④

독해 > 세부 내용 찾기 > 내용 (불)일치

정답의 이유

④ 개인용 모바일 장치에서만 작동한다. → 마지막 문장에서 'There is also a web version of the app for those who are not comfortable using mobile devices(모바일 장치 사용이 불편한 사람들을 위한 웹 버전의 앱도 있습니다).'라고 했으므로 글의 내용과 일치하지 않는다.

오답의 이유

① 여행자가 미리 세관 신고를 할 수 있다. → 두 번째 문장에서 '~ the Advance Declaration, which allows travellers the option to submit their customs declaration in advance(사전 세관 신고 기능인데, 이는 여행객들이 사전에 세관 신고서를 제출하는 선택권을 제공해서) ~'라고 했으므로 글의 내용과 일치한다.

② 더 많은 기능이 후에 추가될 것이다. → 세 번째 문장에서 '~ Enter-K will continue to introduce additional border-related features in the future, further improving the overall border experience(Enter-K는 향후 국경 관련 기능의 추가 도입을 계속 진행하여 전반적인 국경 체험을 더욱 향상시킬 것입니다).'라고 했으므로 글의 내용과 일치한다.

③ 여행자는 온라인 스토어에서 그것을 다운로드할 수 있다. → 네 번째 문장에서 'Simply download the latest version of the app from the online store before your arrival(여러분이 도착하기 전에 온라인 스토어에서 간단하게 최신 버전 앱을 다운로드하세요).'이라고 했으므로 글의 내용과 일치한다.

세관 신고에 새로운 Enter-K 앱을 사용하세요.

여러분이 공항에 도착하자마자 새로운 Enter-K 앱을 사용하세요. Enter-K에 의해 제공되는 눈에 띄는 한 가지 기능은 사전 세관 신고 기능인데, 이는 여행객들이 사전에 세관 신고서를 제출하는 선택권을 제공해서 여행객들이 모든 국제공항에서 시간을 절약할 수 있게 합니다. 현재 진행 중인 Traveller Modernization initiative의 일환으로, Enter-K는 향후 국경 관련 기능의 추가 도입을 계속 진행하여 전반적인 국경 체험을 더욱 향상시킬 것입니다. 여러분이 도착하기 전에 온라인 스토어에서 간단하게 최신 버전 앱을 다운로드하세요. 모바일 장치 사용이 불편한 사람들을 위한 웹 버전의 앱도 있습니다.

VOCA
- feature 특징, 기능
- submit 제출[제기, 부탁]하다
- additional 추가의, 다른

13 난도 ★☆☆

정답 ④

독해 > 세부 내용 찾기 > 내용 (불)일치

정답의 이유

④ 그것은 직원들이 부당한 대우를 받을 때 조치를 취한다. → 마지막 문장에서 'The OLC takes enforcement action when necessary to ensure that workers are treated fairly and compensated for all time worked(OLC는 근로자들에 대한 공정한 대우와 모든 노동 시간에 대한 보상을 보장하기 위해 필요한 경우 집행 조치를 취한다).'라고 했으므로 글의 내용과 일치한다.

오답의 이유

① 그것은 직원들이 세금을 제대로 납부하도록 보장한다. → 직원들이 세금을 납부하도록 보장한다는 내용은 제시되지 않았다.

② 그것은 성인 근로자의 고용에 대한 권한만 가지고 있다. → 세 번째 문장에서 'In addition, the OLC has authority over the employment of minors(추가로, OLC는 미성년자 고용에 대한 권한도 가지고 있다).'라고 했으므로 글의 내용과 일치하지 않는다.

③ 그것은 고용주의 사업 기회를 장려한다. → 고용주의 사업 기회 장려에 관한 내용은 제시되지 않았다.

노동청장실(OLC) 업무

OLC는 정부의 주요 노동 감독 기관이다. OLC는 최저임금, 직종별 임금, 초과근무수당이 근로자들에게 지급되고, 휴식시간과 점심시간이 근로자들에게 제공되도록 보장할 책임이 있다. 추가로, OLC는 미성년자 고용에 대한 권한도 가지고 있다. 노동 관련 문제의 효율적 · 전문적 · 효과적 방식으로 해결하는 것이 이 사무소(OLC)의 비전이자 사명이다. 이것은 법에 따른 권리와 책임에 대해 고용주와 직원들을 교육하는 것을 포함한다. OLC는 근로자들에 대한 공정한 대우와 모든 노동 시간에 대한 보상을 보장하기 위해 필요한 경우 집행 조치를 취한다.

- principal 주요한, 주된
- regulatory agency 감독 기관
- state 국가, 나라
- ensure 보장하다
- minimum wage 최저 임금
- prevailing wage 일반 직종별 임금
- resolve 해결하다
- manner 방식
- enforcement 집행
- compensate 보상하다

14 난도 ★★☆   정답 ④

독해 > 대의 파악 > 제목, 주제

정답의 이유

제시문의 첫 번째 문장에서 '식품의약품안전처는 조리 시 계란 취급상의 부주의한 위생 문제로 인한 교차오염이 식중독의 원인이라고 경고했다'고 했고, 마지막 문장에서 '살모넬라균과 관련된 질병 위험을 최소화하려면 식품 안전 조치를 우선으로 하고 올바른 조리법을 지키는 것이 중요하다.'라고 했으므로 글의 주제로 가장 적절한 것은 ④ 'Safe handling of eggs for the prevention of Salmonella infection(살모넬라균 감염 예방을 위한 계란의 안전한 취급)'이다.

오답의 이유

① 계란 섭취가 면역체계에 미치는 이점
② 살모넬라균 감염을 위한 다른 유형의 치료제들
③ 따뜻한 온도에서 살모넬라균의 수명

식품의약품안전처는 경고하기를, 계란을 만지고 음식을 준비하거나 도구를 사용하기 전에 손 씻기를 소홀히 하는 곳에 생기는 교차오염의 결과로 식중독 사례가 발생했다고 했다. 이러한 위험을 완화하기 위해 식품의약품안전처가 권장하는 바에 따르면, 계란을 냉장 보관하고 노른자와 흰자가 모두 굳을 때까지 완전히 익혀야 한다. 지난 5년 동안 믿기 어려운 7,400명이라는 사람들이 살모넬라균에 의한 식중독을 겪었다. 살모넬라균은 따뜻한 온도에서 잘 자라는데, 대략 섭씨 37도가 최적의 성장조건이다. 날계란 또는 덜 익은 계란을 섭취하고 조리된 음식을 날계란과 분리하지 않는 것이 살모넬라 감염의 가장 흔한 원인으로 확인되었다. 살모넬라균과 관련된 질병 위험을 최소화하려면 식품 안전 조치를 우선으로 하고 올바른 조리법을 지키는 것이 중요하다.

- the Ministry of Food and Drug Safety 식품의약품안전처
- warn 경고하다, 주의를 주다
- cross-contamination 교차 오염
- utensil 기구[도구]
- mitigate 완화[경감]시키다
- refrigerate 냉장하다[냉장고에 보관하다]
- thoroughly 철저히, 철두철미하게
- yolk (달걀 등의) 노른자
- white (달걀의) 흰자위, 달걀흰자
- staggering 충격적인, 믿기 어려운
- Salmonella bacteria 살모넬라 박테리아
- thrive 번창하다, 잘 자라다
- optimal growth condition 최적 성장조건
- undercooked 설익은
- identify 식별하다, 구분하다, 확인하다
- infection 전염, 감염
- It is crucial to ~하는 것이 결정적으로 중요하다
- prioritize 우선순위를 매기다
- adhere to ~을 고수하다

15 난도 ★★☆   정답 ①

독해 > 대의 파악 > 요지, 주장

정답의 이유

첫 번째 문장에서 교육 격차를 해결하기 위한 지속적인 노력에도 불구하고 학생들 사이의 지속적인 학업성적의 격차로 인해 교육 시스템 내 '상당히 불공평한 사태(significant inequities)'가 계속 부각되고 있다고 했고, 마지막 문장에서 '계속된 교육 격차에 대한 문제가 해결되어야만 한다'고 했으므로 글의 요지로 가장 적절한 것은 ① 'We should deal with persistent educational inequities(우리는 되풀이하여 일어나는 교육 불평등을 처리해야 한다).'이다.

② 교육 전문가들은 새로운 학교 정책에 중점을 두어야 한다.

③ 성취도 격차를 해소하기 위해서 새로운 교수법이 필요하다.

④ 가정의 소득이 교육의 논의에서 고려되어서는 안 된다.

본문해석

교육 격차를 해결하기 위한 지속적인 노력에도 불구하고, 학생들 사이의 지속적인 학업성적의 격차로 인해 교육 시스템 내 상당히 불공평한 사태가 계속 부각되고 있다. 최근 자료에 따르면 저소득 배경과 취약계층 학생들을 포함하는 소외된 학생들이 학업 성취에서 또래들보다 계속 뒤떨어지고 있는 것이 드러난다. 그 차이가 교육적인 형평성과 사회적 유동성 달성의 난제이다. 전문가들은 이 차이를 줄이고 사회 경제적 지위, 배경에 상관없이 모든 학생들을 대상으로 공평한 기회를 보장하기 위해 표적 개입, 공평한 자원 할당, 포용적 정책의 필요성을 강조한다. 지속적인 교육 격차의 문제는 해결책을 찾기 위한 노력으로 교육 시스템의 모든 단계에서 다루어져야 한다.

VOCA

• address 해결하다, 다루다

• disparity (특히 한쪽에 불공평한) 차이

• persistent 끊임없이 지속[반복]되는

• inequity 불공평

• marginalize ～을 (특히 사회의 진보에서) 처지게 하다

• vulnerable (～에) 취약한, 연약한

• lag behind ～보다 뒤떨어지다

• allocation 할당량[액]

• bridge (공백을) 메우다

16 난도 ★★☆   정답 ③

독해 > 글의 일관성 > 무관한 어휘 · 문장

정답의 이유

③의 앞 문장에서 'The benefits for kids of getting into nature are huge, ranging from better academic performance to improved mood and focus(아이들이 자연 속에서 얻는 혜택은 학업 성취도 향상부터 기분과 집중력 향상에 이르기까지 매우 방대하다).'라고 하였고, ③의 다음 문장에서는 'Childhood experiences of nature can also boost environmentalism in adulthood(또한 어린 시절의 자연에 대한 경험이 성인의 환경주의를 북돋울 수 있다).'라고 하며 자연으로부터 얻는 혜택에 대해 말하고 있다. 하지만 ③에서는 '야외 활동은 아이들이 그들의 가족과 귀중한 시간을 함께하는 것을 어렵게 만든다.'라는 단점을 언급하고 있으므로 글의 흐름상 어색한 문장은 ③이다.

본문해석

어린 아이들의 부모나 보호자들은 집 밖으로 나가려는 간절한 충동과 심지어 지역 공원에 잠깐 다녀오는 짧은 여행만으로도 마법 같은 회복 효과를 경험했을 것이다. 아마 여기에는 단지 기분 전환 이상이 있다. 아이들이 자연 속에서 얻는 혜택은 학업 성취도 향상부터 기분과 집중력 향상에 이르기까지 매우 방대하다. 야외 활동은 아이들이 그들의 가족과 귀중한 시간을 함께하는 것을 어렵게 만든다. 또한 어린 시절의 자연에 대한 경험이 성인의 환경주의를 북돋울 수 있다. 도시의 녹지 공간에 접근할 수 있는 것은 아이들의 사회적 관계망과 우정에서 역할을 할 수 있다.

VOCA

• desperate 필사적인, 절실한

• urge 욕구, 충동

• restorative 회복시키는

• let off steam 울분[열기 등]을 발산하다, 기분 풀다

• range from ～에서 (～까지) 걸치다

• boost 북돋우다

• environmentalism 환경 보호주의

• have access to ～에게 접근[출입]할 수 있다

17 난도 ★★★   정답 ③

독해 > 글의 일관성 > 문장 삽입

정답의 이유

주어진 문장은 '특히 도시화된 많은 주에서는 부유입자의 총량으로 측정되는 대기오염이 위험한 수준에 이르렀다.'라는 내용이다. ③ 앞 문장에서 다수의 주에서 오염에 대한 규제 없이 공장 가동을 허락했으며 산업화가 심한 몇몇 주에서는 오염이 매우 높은 단계에 도달했다고 했고, ③ 다음 문장에서 '대기오염 방지법은 특히 과도하게 높은 단계의 다섯 가지 위험한 오염물질에 대한 지침을 제정했다.'라고 했으므로 글의 흐름상 주어진 문장이 들어갈 위치로 적절한 것은 ③이다.

본문해석

경제학자 Chay와 Greenstone은 1970년 대기오염 방지법 이후에 대기오염 정화의 가치를 평가했다. 1970년 이전에는 대기오염에 대한 연방정부의 규제가 거의 없었고, 그 문제는 주 의회 의원들의 중요한 안건이 아니었다. 그 결과, 다수의 주에서 오염에 대한 규제 없이 공장 가동을 허용했고, 산업화가 심한 몇몇 주에서는 오염이 매우 높은 단계에 도달했다. 특히, 도시화된 많은 주에서는 부유입자의 총량으로 측정되는 대기오염이 위험한 수준에 이르렀다. 대기오염 방지법은 특히 과도하게 높은 단계의 다섯 가지 위험한 오염물질에 대한 지침을 제정했다. 1970년 대기오염방지법 제정과 1977년 법 개정에 따라 공기의 질이 개선되었다.

VOCA

• economist 경제학자

• evaluate 평가하다

• the Clean Air Act (미) 대기 오염 방지법

- regulation 규제, 규정
- legislator 입법자, 국회[의회]의원
- suspended particle 부유입자
- constitute ~을 구성하다[이루다]
- pollutant 오염 물질, 오염원
- air quality 공기의 질[청정도]

18 난도 ★★☆　　　　　　　　　　　정답 ②

독해 > 글의 일관성 > 글의 순서

정답의 이유

주어진 글은 글쓴이가 아무도 모르게 빵을 셔츠에 감추고 재빨리 걸어가는 장면으로 끝난다. 따라서 이 다음에는 문맥상 빵을 감추고 재빨리 걸어간 후의 일이 시간순으로 이어지는 전개가 적절하므로 'The heat of the bread burned into my skin(뜨거운 빵의 열기로 피부가 화끈거렸지만)'으로 시작하는 (B)가 오는 게 자연스럽다. (B)의 마지막에서 집에 도착했을 때쯤 빵이 어느 정도 식었지만, 속은 여전히 따뜻했다고 했으므로 (B) 다음에는 'When I dropped them on the table(그것들을 식탁 위에 내려놓자)'로 시작하는 (A)가 이어져야 한다. 어머니와 여동생을 식탁에 앉히고 따뜻한 차를 따라주는 장면으로 끝나는 (A) 다음에는 빵을 썰어서 한 조각씩 먹는 것으로 시작하는 (C)가 오는 게 자연스럽다. 따라서 주어진 글 다음에 이어질 글의 순서로 적절한 것은 ② '(B) - (A) - (C)'이다.

본문해석

무슨 일이 일어났는지 아무도 목격하기 전에, 나는 빵 덩어리를 셔츠 아래에 밀어 넣고, 헌팅 재킷을 단단히 여미고는 재빨리 걸어갔다.
(B) 뜨거운 빵의 열기로 피부가 화끈거렸지만, 나는 필사적으로 그것을 더 꽉 움켜쥐었다. 집에 도착했을 때는 빵이 다소 식었지만 속은 여전히 따뜻했다.
(A) 그것들을 식탁 위에 내려놓자 여동생이 손을 뻗어 빵 덩어리를 뜯으려 했지만, 나는 여동생을 자리에 앉게 하고 어머니가 우리와 함께 하도록 억지로 식탁에 앉힌 다음, 따뜻한 차를 따라주었다.
(C) 나는 빵을 얇게 썰었다. 우리는 빵 한 덩어리를 한 조각 한 조각씩 다 먹었다. 그것은 건포도와 견과류가 듬뿍 들어 있는 푸짐한 빵이었다.

VOCA

- witness 목격하다
- shove 아무렇게나 놓다[넣다]
- wrap (옷 등을) 두르다, 걸치다, 입다
- swiftly 신속히, 빨리
- clutch 움켜잡다
- chunk 덩어리
- slice (얇게) 썰다[자르다/저미다]

19 난도 ★★☆　　　　　　　　　　　정답 ①

독해 > 빈칸 완성 > 단어 · 구 · 절

정답의 이유

제시문은 출산율 하락이 전 세계 국가의 인구 감소로 이어져 인구통계학적 변화를 초래할 것이라는 내용이다. 밑줄이 있는 문장의 주어가 Such a demographic shift(이러한 인구통계학적 변화)이고, 밑줄 다음이 including taxation, healthcare for the elderly, caregiving responsibilities, and retirement(세금, 노인 의료, 돌봄 책임, 은퇴를 포함하는)인 것으로 미루어 보아 밑줄에는 '동사+목적어(~을 …하다)'가 들어가야 함을 유추할 수 있다. 그리고 밑줄 앞 문장에서 'This transition will also lead to a significant aging of populations, ~'라고 했으므로, 문맥상 밑줄에는 부정적인 의미가 들어가야 한다. 따라서 밑줄 친 부분에 들어갈 말로 가장 적절한 것은 ① 'raises concerns about future challenges(미래의 과제에 대한 우려를 자아내다)'이다.

오답의 이유

② 거꾸로 된 연령 구조 현상을 완화하다
③ 혼인율 감소 문제를 보상하다
④ 문제를 해결하기 위해 즉각적인 해결책을 제공하다

본문해석

출산율 하락은 금세기 말까지 거의 모든 국가의 인구 감소를 초래할 것으로 예상된다. 전 세계 출산율은 1950년에 4.7명이었지만 2017년에는 2.4명으로 거의 절반으로 떨어졌다. 2100년에는 1.7명 아래로 떨어질 것으로 예상된다. 그 결과, 일부 연구원들의 예상에 따르면 지구상의 인구는 2064년 즈음에 97억 명으로 정점에 도달한 후 금세기 말에는 88억 명으로 떨어질 것이라고 한다. 이 변화는 또한 인구의 상당한 고령화를 초래하여, 출생 인구만큼의 사람들이 80세에 도달할 것이다. 이러한 인구통계학적 변화는 세금, 노인 의료, 돌봄 책임 및 은퇴를 비롯한 미래의 과제에 대한 우려를 자아낸다. 새로운 인구통계학적 지형으로의 '연착륙'을 보장하기 위해, 연구원들은 그 변화에 대한 신중한 관리의 필요성을 강조한다.

VOCA

- fertility rate 출산율
- project 예상[추정]하다
- shrink 줄어들다[줄어들게 하다]
- peak 절정[최고조]에 달하다
- transition 변이, 전이
- demographic shift 인구통계학적 변화
- taxation 조세, 세수
- healthcare 의료 서비스, 보건
- caregiving 부양
- soft landing 연착륙

독해 > 빈칸 완성 > 단어·구·절

정답의 이유

마지막 부분에서 '본질적으로, 우리는 우리 자신의 경험으로 듣는다.'라고 하며 '우리가 그의 메시지를 이해할 수 있는 준비가 제대로 되어 있지 않다는 이유로 연사가 책임을 져야 할까?'라고 언급하였고, 밑줄이 있는 문장의 앞부분에서 '우리의 이해 수준을 높이는 한 가지 확실한 방법은 ~는 것이다(one sure way to raise the level of our understanding is to ~).'라고 했으므로, 문맥상 밑줄 친 부분에 들어갈 말로 적절한 것은 ③ 'assume the responsibility which is inherently ours(원래부터 우리 것인 책임을 지다)'이다.

오답의 이유

① 연사가 알고 있는 것을 무시하다

② 연사의 성격을 분석하다

④ 연사의 연설 전달력에 초점을 맞추다

본문해석

다수의 청취자들은 마음속으로 "누가 그런 사람의 말을 주의 깊게 들을 수 있었겠어? 과연 그는 원고를 읽기를 멈출 것인가?"라고 생각함으로써 자신들의 부주의를 연사의 탓으로 돌린다. 경청하는 사람은 다르게 반응한다. 그는 연사를 보고 "이 사람은 무능해. 누구라도 그보다는 더 잘 말할 수 있을 것 같아."라고 생각할 수도 있다. 그러나 그는 이러한 초기 유사성에서 다른 결론으로 이동해서, 생각한다. "하지만 잠시만. 나는 그의 성격이나 전달력에는 관심 없어. 나는 그가 무엇을 알고 있는지 알고 싶어. 이 사람이 내가 알아야 할 것들을 알고 있을까?" 본질적으로, 우리는 '우리 자신의 경험으로 듣는다.' 우리가 그의 메시지를 이해할 수 있는 준비가 제대로 되어 있지 않다는 이유로 연사가 책임을 져야 할까? 우리가 듣는 모든 것을 이해할 수는 없지만, 우리의 이해 수준을 높이는 한 가지 확실한 방법은 원래부터 우리 것인 책임을 지는 것이다.

VOCA

• inattention　부주의
• incompetent　무능한[기술이 부족한]
• initial　처음의, 초기의
• move on to　(새로운 일·주제로) 옮기다[넘어가다]
• equipped to　~에 적합한
• comprehend　이해하다

영어

문제편

PART 1

국가직

꼭 읽어보세요!

2025년 영어 과목 출제기조 변화

인사혁신처에서 출제하는 2025년 9급 공무원 시험부터는 문법(어법)이나 어휘 등 암기 영역의 문제가 줄어들고 이해력과 추론력을 평가하는 독해 문제의 비중이 커질 예정입니다. 또한, 실생활에서 많이 사용하는 어휘, 그리고 이메일이나 안내문 등으로 구성된 독해 지문이 많이 출제될 것으로 보입니다.

기출문제 학습 시 유의사항

본서는 2025년 영어 과목 출제기조 변화에 따라 출제 유형에서 벗어나거나 달라지는 문항에 ×표시를 하였습니다. 이는 인사혁신처가 공개한 2025년 출제기조 전환 예시문제를 기준으로 한 것이며, 실제 출제 방향과 다를 수 있다는 점에 유의하시기 바랍니다. 또한, 인사혁신처에서 출제하는 국가직, 지방직 9급 기출문제에만 ×표시를 하였으니 이를 염두에 두고 학습에 임하시기 바랍니다.

×표시를 한 문항은 출제되지 않는 영역이라는 의미가 아닌, 출제기조 변화에 따라 유형이 바뀔 수 있는 문항임을 표시한 것입니다. 어휘 영역은 문맥에 따라 밑줄에 들어갈 단어를 추론하는 유형으로 전환되며, 문법(어법) 영역은 밑줄이나 빈칸이 주어지고 문맥 속에서 묻는 부분이 무엇인지 명확하게 제시하는 방향으로 전환됩니다. 독해도 전자메일이나 안내문 등 업무현장에서 접할 수 있는 소재와 형식을 활용한 지문이 출제됩니다.

출제경향

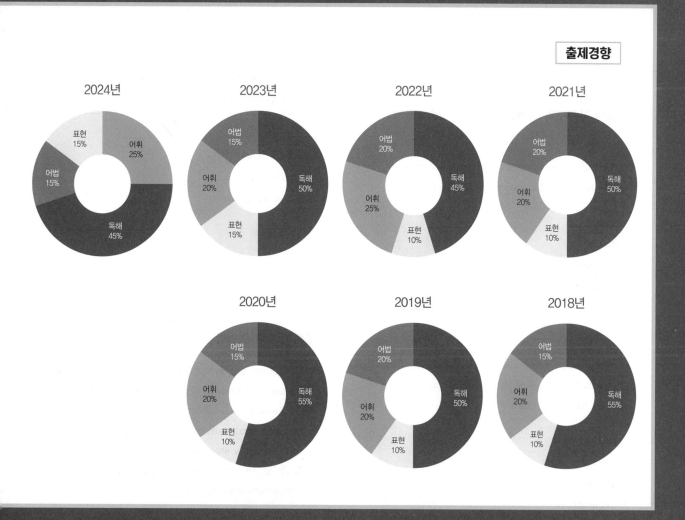

2024년 — 표현 15%, 어휘 25%, 어법 15%, 독해 45%

2023년 — 어법 15%, 어휘 20%, 표현 15%, 독해 50%

2022년 — 어법 20%, 어휘 25%, 표현 10%, 독해 45%

2021년 — 어법 20%, 어휘 20%, 표현 10%, 독해 50%

2020년 — 어법 15%, 어휘 20%, 표현 10%, 독해 55%

2019년 — 어법 20%, 어휘 20%, 표현 10%, 독해 50%

2018년 — 어법 15%, 어휘 20%, 표현 10%, 독해 55%

✔ 회독 CHECK 1 2 3

01 밑줄 친 부분에 들어갈 말로 적절한 것은?

> Obviously, no aspect of the language arts stands alone either in learning or in teaching. Listening, speaking, reading, writing, viewing, and visually representing are _____.

① distinct
② distorted
③ interrelated
④ independent

[02~05] 밑줄 친 부분의 의미와 가장 가까운 것을 고르시오.

02

> The money was so cleverly concealed that we were forced to abandon our search for it.

① spent
② hidden
③ invested
④ delivered

03

> To appease critics, the wireless industry has launched a $12 million public-education campaign on the drive-time radio.

① soothe
② counter
③ enlighten
④ assimilate

04

> Center officials play down the troubles, saying they are typical of any start-up operation.

① discern
② dissatisfy
③ underline
④ underestimate

05

> She worked diligently and had the guts to go for what she wanted.

① was anxious
② was fortunate
③ was reputable
④ was courageous

06 밑줄 친 부분 중 어법상 옳지 않은 것은?

> ① Despite the belief that the quality of older houses is superior to ② those of modern houses, the foundations of most pre-20th-century houses are dramatically shallow ③ compared to today's, and have only stood the test of time due to the flexibility of ④ their timber framework or the lime mortar between bricks and stones.

07 밑줄 친 부분이 어법상 옳지 <u>않은</u> 것은?

① They are not interested in reading poetry, <u>still more</u> in writing.

② <u>Once confirmed</u>, the order will be sent for delivery to your address.

③ <u>Provided that</u> the ferry leaves on time, we should arrive at the harbor by morning.

④ Foreign journalists hope to cover as <u>much news</u> as possible during their short stay in the capital.

08 우리말을 영어로 바르게 옮긴 것은?

① 지원자 수가 증가하고 있어서 우리는 기쁘다.
   → We are glad that the number of applicants is increasing.

② 나는 2년 전에 그에게서 마지막 이메일을 받았다.
   → I've received the last e-mail from him two years ago.

③ 어젯밤에 그가 잔 침대는 꽤 편안했다.
   → The bed which he slept last night was quite comfortable.

④ 그들은 영상으로 새해 인사를 교환했다.
   → They exchanged New Year's greetings each other on screen.

[09~11] 밑줄 친 부분에 들어갈 말로 적절한 것을 고르시오.

09

 Brian
Hi, can I get some information on your city tour?
11:21

Ace Tour
Thank you for contacting us. Do you have any specific questions?
11:22

 Brian
_____
_____
11:22

Ace Tour
It'll take you to all the major points of interest in the city.
11:23

 Brian
How much is it?
11:24

Ace Tour
It's 50 dollars per person for a four-hour tour.
11:24

 Brian
OK. Can I book four tickets for Friday afternoon?
11:25

Ace Tour
Certainly. I will send you the payment information shortly.
11:25

① How long is the tour?

② What does the city tour include?

③ Do you have a list of tour packages?

④ Can you recommend a good tour guide book?

10

A: Thank you. We appreciate your order.

B: You are welcome. Could you send the goods by air freight? We need them fast.

A: Sure. We'll send them to your department right away.

B: Okay. I hope we can get the goods early next week.

A: If everything goes as planned, you'll get them by Monday.

B: Monday sounds good.

A: Please pay within 2 weeks. Air freight costs will be added on the invoice.

B: _____

A: I am afraid the free delivery service is no longer available.

① I see. When will we be getting the invoice from you?

② Our department may not be able to pay within two weeks.

③ Can we send the payment to your business account on Monday?

④ Wait a minute. I thought the delivery costs were at your expense.

11

A: Have you found your phone?

B: Unfortunately, no. I'm still looking for it.

A: Have you contacted the subway's lost and found office?

B: _____.

A: If I were you, I would do that first.

B: Yeah, you are right. I'll check with the lost and found before buying a new phone.

① I went there to ask about the phone

② I stopped by the office this morning

③ I haven't done that yet, actually

④ I tried searching everywhere

12 Northeastern Wildlife Exposition에 관한 다음 글의 내용과 일치하는 것은?

NORTHEASTERN WILDLIFE EXPOSITION(NEWE)
—
Admission ticket for Saturday, March 30th, 2024
■ Price: $40.00
■ Opening hours: 10:00 a.m. – 6:00 p.m.

Kids 10 and under are free. Entry to shows and lectures are first-come, first-served. All venues open rain or shine.

March 20th is the last day to buy tickets online for the 2024 Northeastern Wildlife Exposition.

Please note: Purchasing NEWE tickets in advance is the best way to guarantee entry into all exhibits. NEWE organizers may discontinue in-person ticket sales should any venue reach capacity.

① 10세 어린이는 입장료 40불을 지불해야 한다.

② 공연과 강연의 입장은 선착순이다.

③ 비가 올 경우에는 행사장을 닫는다.

④ 입장권은 온라인으로만 구매할 수 있다.

13 다음 글의 내용과 일치하지 않는 것은?

The tragedies of the Greek dramatist Sophocles have come to be regarded as the high point of classical Greek drama. Sadly, only seven of the 123 tragedies he wrote have survived, but of these perhaps the finest is *Oedipus the King*. The play was one of three written by Sophocles about Oedipus, the mythical king of Thebes (the others being *Antigone* and *Oedipus at Colonus*), known collectively as the Theban plays. Sophocles conceived each of these as a separate entity, and they were written and produced several years apart and out of chronological order. *Oedipus the King* follows the established formal structure and it is regarded as the best example of classical Athenian tragedy.

① A total of 123 tragedies were written by Sophocles.

② *Antigone* is also about the king Oedipus.

③ The Theban plays were created in time order.

④ *Oedipus the King* represents the classical Athenian tragedy.

14 다음 글의 주제로 적절한 것은?

It seems incredible that one man could be responsible for opening our eyes to an entire culture, but until British archaeologist Arthur Evans successfully excavated the ruins of the palace of Knossos on the island of Crete, the great Minoan culture of the Mediterranean was more legend than fact. Indeed its most famed resident was a creature of mythology: the half-man, half-bull Minotaur, said to have lived under the palace of mythical King Minos. But as Evans proved, this realm was no myth. In a series of excavations in the early years of the 20th century, Evans found a trove of artifacts from the Minoan age, which reached its height from 1900 to 1450 B.C.: jewelry, carvings, pottery, altars shaped like bull's horns, and wall paintings showing Minoan life.

① King Minos' successful excavations

② Appreciating artifacts from the Minoan age

③ Magnificence of the palace on the island of Crete

④ Bringing the Minoan culture to the realm of reality

15 다음 글의 제목으로 적절한 것은?

Currency debasement of a good money by a bad money version occurred via coins of a high percentage of precious metal, reissued at lower percentages of gold or silver diluted with a lower value metal. This adulteration drove out the good coin for the bad coin. No one spent the good coin, they kept it, hence the good coin was driven out of circulation and into a hoard. Meanwhile the issuer, normally a king who had lost his treasure on interminable warfare and other such dissolute living, was behind the move. They collected all the good old coins they could, melted them down and reissued them at lower purity and pocketed the balance. It was often illegal to keep the old stuff back but people did, while the king replenished his treasury, at least for a time.

① How Bad Money Replaces Good
② Elements of Good Coins
③ Why Not Melt Coins?
④ What Is Bad Money?

16 다음 글의 흐름상 어색한 문장은?

In spite of all evidence to the contrary, there are people who seriously believe that NASA's Apollo space program never really landed men on the moon. These people claim that the moon landings were nothing more than a huge conspiracy, perpetuated by a government desperately in competition with the Russians and fearful of losing face. ① These conspiracy theorists claim that the United States knew it couldn't compete with the Russians in the space race and was therefore forced to fake a series of successful moon landings. ② Advocates of a conspiracy cite several pieces of what they consider evidence. ③ Crucial to their case is the claim that astronauts never could have safely passed through the Van Allen belt, a region of radiation trapped in Earth's magnetic field. ④ They also point to the fact that the metal coverings of the spaceship were designed to block radiation. If the astronauts had truly gone through the belt, say conspiracy theorists, they would have died.

17 주어진 문장이 들어갈 위치로 적절한 것은?

Tribal oral history and archaeological evidence suggest that sometime between 1500 and 1700 a mudslide destroyed part of the village, covering several longhouses and sealing in their contents.

From the village of Ozette on the westernmost point of Washington's Olympic Peninsula, members of the Makah tribe hunted whales. (①) They smoked their catch on racks and in smokehouses and traded with neighboring groups from around the Puget Sound and nearby Vancouver Island. (②) Ozette was one of five main villages inhabited by the Makah, an Indigenous people who have been based in the region for millennia. (③) Thousands of artifacts that would not otherwise have survived, including baskets, clothing, sleeping mats, and whaling tools, were preserved under the mud. (④) In 1970, a storm caused coastal erosion that revealed the remains of these longhouses and artifacts.

18 주어진 글 다음에 이어질 글의 순서로 적절한 것은?

Interest in movie and sports stars goes beyond their performances on the screen and in the arena.

(A) The doings of skilled baseball, football, and basketball players out of uniform similarly attract public attention.

(B) Newspaper columns, specialized magazines, television programs, and Web sites record the personal lives of celebrated Hollywood actors, sometimes accurately.

(C) Both industries actively promote such attention, which expands audiences and thus increases revenues. But a fundamental difference divides them: What sports stars do for a living is authentic in a way that what movie stars do is not.

① (A) - (C) - (B)   ② (B) - (A) - (C)

③ (B) - (C) - (A)   ④ (C) - (A) - (B)

[19~20] 밑줄 친 부분에 들어갈 말로 적절한 것을 고르시오.

19

_____. Nearly every major politician hires media consultants and political experts to provide advice on how to appeal to the public. Virtually every major business and special-interest group has hired a lobbyist to take its concerns to Congress or to state and local governments. In nearly every community, activists try to persuade their fellow citizens on important policy issues. The workplace, too, has always been fertile ground for office politics and persuasion. One study estimates that general managers spend upwards of 80 % of their time in verbal communication—most of it with the intent of persuading their fellow employees. With the advent of the photocopying machine, a whole new medium for office persuasion was invented—the photocopied memo. The Pentagon alone copies an average of 350,000 pages a day, the equivalent of 1,000 novels.

① Business people should have good persuasion skills

② Persuasion shows up in almost every walk of life

③ You will encounter countless billboards and posters

④ Mass media campaigns are useful for the government

20

It is important to note that for adults, social interaction mainly occurs through the medium of language. Few native-speaker adults are willing to devote time to interacting with someone who does not speak the language, with the result that the adult foreigner will have little opportunity to engage in meaningful and extended language exchanges. In contrast, the young child is often readily accepted by other children, and even adults. For young children, language is not as essential to social interaction. So-called 'parallel play', for example, is common among young children. They can be content just to sit in each other's company speaking only occasionally and playing on their own. Adults rarely find themselves in situations where _____.

① language does not play a crucial role in social interaction

② their opinions are readily accepted by their colleagues

③ they are asked to speak another language

④ communication skills are highly required

영어 | 2023년 국가직 9급

영어

✅ 회독 CHECK 1 2 3

[01~04] 밑줄 친 부분의 의미와 가장 가까운 것을 고르시오.

01
Jane wanted to have a small wedding rather than a fancy one. Thus, she planned to invite her family and a few of her intimate friends to eat delicious food and have some pleasant moments.

① nosy
② close
③ outgoing
④ considerate

02
The incessant public curiosity and consumer demand due to the health benefits with lesser cost has increased the interest in functional foods.

① rapid
② constant
③ significant
④ intermittent

03
Because of the pandemic, the company had to hold off the plan to provide the workers with various training programs.

① elaborate
② release
③ modify
④ suspend

04
The new Regional Governor said he would abide by the decision of the High Court to release the prisoner.

① accept
② report
③ postpone
④ announce

05 밑줄 친 부분 중 어법상 옳지 않은 것은?

While advances in transplant technology have made ① it possible to extend the life of individuals with end-stage organ disease, it is argued ② that the biomedical view of organ transplantation as a bounded event, which ends once a heart or kidney is successfully replaced, ③ conceal the complex and dynamic process that more ④ accurately represents the experience of receiving an organ.

PART 1 | 2023년 국가직 9급 **11**

06 어법상 옳지 않은 것은?

① All assignments are expected to be turned in on time.

② Hardly had I closed my eyes when I began to think of her.

③ The broker recommended that she buy the stocks immediately.

④ A woman with the tip of a pencil stuck in her head has finally had it remove.

07 우리말을 영어로 잘못 옮긴 것은?

① 내 고양이 나이는 그의 고양이 나이의 세 배이다.
  → My cat is three times as old as his.

② 우리는 그 일을 이번 달 말까지 끝내야 한다.
  → We have to finish the work until the end of this month.

③ 그녀는 이틀에 한 번 머리를 감는다.
  → She washes her hair every other day.

④ 너는 비가 올 경우에 대비하여 우산을 갖고 가는 게 낫겠다.
  → You had better take an umbrella in case it rains.

08 다음 글의 내용과 일치하지 않는 것은?

Are you getting enough choline? Chances are, this nutrient isn't even on your radar. It's time choline gets the attention it deserves. A shocking 90 percent of Americans aren't getting enough choline, according to a recent study. Choline is essential to health at all ages and stages, and is especially critical for brain development. Why aren't we getting enough? Choline is found in many different foods but in small amounts. Plus, the foods that are rich in choline aren't the most popular: think liver, egg yolks and lima beans. Taylor Wallace, who worked on a recent analysis of choline intake in the United States, says, "There isn't enough awareness about choline even among health-care professionals because our government hasn't reviewed the data or set policies around choline since the late '90s."

① A majority of Americans are not getting enough choline.

② Choline is an essential nutrient required for brain development.

③ Foods such as liver and lima beans are good sources of choline.

④ The importance of choline has been stressed since the late '90s in the U.S.

09 다음 글의 내용과 일치하는 것은?

Around 1700 there were, by some accounts, more than 2,000 London coffeehouses, occupying more premises and paying more rent than any other trade. They came to be known as penny universities, because for that price one could purchase a cup of coffee and sit for hours listening to extraordinary conversations. Each coffeehouse specialized in a different type of clientele. In one, physicians could be consulted. Others served Protestants, Puritans, Catholics, Jews, literati, merchants, traders, Whigs, Tories, army officers, actors, lawyers, or clergy. The coffeehouses provided England's first egalitarian meeting place, where a man chatted with his tablemates whether he knew them or not.

① The number of coffeehouses was smaller than that of any other business.

② Customers were not allowed to stay for more than an hour in a coffeehouse.

③ Religious people didn't get together in a coffeehouse to chat.

④ One could converse even with unknown tablemates in a coffeehouse.

[10~11] 밑줄 친 부분에 들어갈 말로 알맞은 것을 고르시오.

10

A: I got this new skin cream from a drugstore yesterday. It is supposed to remove all wrinkles and make your skin look much younger.

B: _____

A: Why don't you believe it? I've read in a few blogs that the cream really works.

B: I assume that the cream is good for your skin, but I don't think that it is possible to get rid of wrinkles or magically look younger by using a cream.

A: You are so pessimistic.

B: No, I'm just being realistic. I think you are being gullible.

① I don't buy it.

② It's too pricey.

③ I can't help you out.

④ Believe it or not, it's true.

11

A: I'd like to go sightseeing downtown. Where do you think I should go?

B: I strongly suggest you visit the national art gallery.

A: Oh, that's a great idea. What else should I check out?

B: _____

A: I don't have time for that. I need to meet a client at three.

B: Oh, I see. Why don't you visit the national park, then?

A: That sounds good. Thank you!

① This is the map that your client needs. Here you go.

② A guided tour to the river park. It takes all afternoon.

③ You should check it out as soon as possible.

④ The checkout time is three o'clock.

12 두 사람의 대화 중 자연스럽지 않은 것은?

① A: He's finally in a hit movie!

   B: Well, he's got it made.

② A: I'm getting a little tired now.

   B: Let's call it a day.

③ A: The kids are going to a birthday party.

   B: So, it was a piece of cake.

④ A: I wonder why he went home early yesterday.

   B: I think he was under the weather.

13 다음 글의 제목으로 알맞은 것은?

The feeling of being loved and the biological response it stimulates is triggered by nonverbal cues: the tone in a voice, the expression on a face, or the touch that feels just right. Nonverbal cues—rather than spoken words—make us feel that the person we are with is interested in, understands, and values us. When we're with them, we feel safe. We even see the power of nonverbal cues in the wild. After evading the chase of predators, animals often nuzzle each other as a means of stress relief. This bodily contact provides reassurance of safety and relieves stress.

① How Do Wild Animals Think and Feel?

② Communicating Effectively Is the Secret to Success

③ Nonverbal Communication Speaks Louder than Words

④ Verbal Cues: The Primary Tools for Expressing Feelings

14 다음 글의 주제로 알맞은 것은?

There are times, like holidays and birthdays, when toys and gifts accumulate in a child's life. You can use these times to teach a healthy nondependency on things. Don't surround your child with toys. Instead, arrange them in baskets, have one basket out at a time, and rotate baskets occasionally. If a cherished object is put away for a time, bringing it out creates a delightful remembering and freshness of outlook. Suppose your child asks for a toy that has been put away for a while. You can direct attention toward an object or experience that is already in the environment. If you lose or break a possession, try to model a good attitude ("I appreciated it while I had it!") so that your child can begin to develop an attitude of nonattachment. If a toy of hers is broken or lost, help her to say, "I had fun with that."

① building a healthy attitude toward possessions
② learning the value of sharing toys with others
③ teaching how to arrange toys in an orderly manner
④ accepting responsibility for behaving in undesirable ways

15 다음 글의 요지로 알맞은 것은?

Many parents have been misguided by the "self-esteem movement," which has told them that the way to build their children's self-esteem is to tell them how good they are at things. Unfortunately, trying to convince your children of their competence will likely fail because life has a way of telling them unequivocally how capable or incapable they really are through success and failure. Research has shown that how you praise your children has a powerful influence on their development. Some researchers found that children who were praised for their intelligence, as compared to their effort, became overly focused on results. Following a failure, these same children persisted less, showed less enjoyment, attributed their failure to a lack of ability, and performed poorly in future achievement efforts. Praising children for intelligence made them fear difficulty because they began to equate failure with stupidity.

① Frequent praises increase self-esteem of children.
② Compliments on intelligence bring about negative effect.
③ A child should overcome fear of failure through success.
④ Parents should focus on the outcome rather than the process.

16 밑줄 친 부분에 들어갈 말로 알맞은 것은?

In recent years, the increased popularity of online marketing and social media sharing has boosted the need for advertising standardization for global brands. Most big marketing and advertising campaigns include a large online presence. Connected consumers can now zip easily across borders via the internet and social media, making it difficult for advertisers to roll out adapted campaigns in a controlled, orderly fashion. As a result, most global consumer brands coordinate their digital sites internationally. For example, Coca-Cola web and social media sites around the world, from Australia and Argentina to France, Romania, and Russia, are surprisingly _____. All feature splashes of familiar Coke red, iconic Coke bottle shapes, and Coca-Cola's music and "Taste the Feeling" themes.

① experimental

② uniform

③ localized

④ diverse

17 다음 글의 흐름상 어색한 문장은?

In our monthly surveys of 5,000 American workers and 500 U.S. employers, a huge shift to hybrid work is abundantly clear for office and knowledge workers. ① An emerging norm is three days a week in the office and two at home, cutting days on site by 30% or more. You might think this cutback would bring a huge drop in the demand for office space. ② But our survey data suggests cuts in office space of 1% to 2% on average, implying big reductions in density not space. We can understand why. High density at the office is uncomfortable and many workers dislike crowds around their desks. ③ Most employees want to work from home on Mondays and Fridays. Discomfort with density extends to lobbies, kitchens, and especially elevators. ④ The only sure-fire way to reduce density is to cut days on site without cutting square footage as much. Discomfort with density is here to stay according to our survey evidence.

18 주어진 문장이 들어갈 위치로 알맞은 것은?

> They installed video cameras at places known for illegal crossings, and put live video feeds from the cameras on a Web site.

Immigration reform is a political minefield. (①) About the only aspect of immigration policy that commands broad political support is the resolve to secure the U.S. border with Mexico to limit the flow of illegal immigrants. (②) Texas sheriffs recently developed a novel use of the Internet to help them keep watch on the border. (③) Citizens who want to help monitor the border can go online and serve as "virtual Texas deputies." (④) If they see anyone trying to cross the border, they send a report to the sheriff's office, which follows up, sometimes with the help of the U.S. Border Patrol.

19 주어진 글 다음에 이어질 글의 순서로 알맞은 것은?

> All civilizations rely on government administration. Perhaps no civilization better exemplifies this than ancient Rome.

(A) To rule an area that large, the Romans, based in what is now central Italy, needed an effective system of government administration.

(B) Actually, the word "civilization" itself comes from the Latin word *civis*, meaning "citizen."

(C) Latin was the language of ancient Rome, whose territory stretched from the Mediterranean basin all the way to parts of Great Britain in the north and the Black Sea to the east.

① (A) - (B) - (C)
② (B) - (A) - (C)
③ (B) - (C) - (A)
④ (C) - (A) - (B)

20 밑줄 친 부분에 들어갈 말로 알맞은 것은?

> Over the last fifty years, all major subdisciplines in psychology have become more and more isolated from each other as training becomes increasingly specialized and narrow in focus. As some psychologists have long argued, if the field of psychology is to mature and advance scientifically, its disparate parts (for example, neuroscience, developmental, cognitive, personality, and social) must become whole and integrated again. Science advances when distinct topics become theoretically and empirically integrated under simplifying theoretical frameworks. Psychology of science will encourage collaboration among psychologists from various sub-areas, helping the field achieve coherence rather than continued fragmentation. In this way, psychology of science might act as a template for psychology as a whole by integrating under one discipline all of the major fractions/factions within the field. It would be no small feat and of no small import if the psychology of science could become a model for the parent discipline on how to combine resources and study science _____.

① from a unified perspective

② in dynamic aspects

③ throughout history

④ with accurate evidence

영어 | 2022년 국가직 9급

✅ 회독 CHECK 1 2 3

[01~03] 밑줄 친 부분의 의미와 가장 가까운 것을 고르시오.

01

For years, detectives have been trying to unravel the mystery of the sudden disappearance of the twin brothers.

① solve
② create
③ imitate
④ publicize

02

Before the couple experienced parenthood, their four-bedroom house seemed unnecessarily opulent.

① hidden
② luxurious
③ empty
④ solid

03

The boss hit the roof when he saw that we had already spent the entire budget in such a short period of time.

① was very satisfied
② was very surprised
③ became extremely calm
④ became extremely angry

[04~05] 밑줄 친 부분에 들어갈 말로 가장 적절한 것을 고르시오.

04

A mouse potato is the computer _____ of television's couch potato: someone who tends to spend a great deal of leisure time in front of the computer in much the same way the couch potato does in front of the television.

① technician
② equivalent
③ network
④ simulation

05

Mary decided to _____ her Spanish before going to South America.

① brush up on
② hear out
③ stick up for
④ lay off

06 어법상 옳은 것은?

① A horse should be fed according to its individual needs and the nature of its work.

② My hat was blown off by the wind while walking down a narrow street.

③ She has known primarily as a political cartoonist throughout her career.

④ Even young children like to be complimented for a job done good.

07 다음 글의 내용과 일치하지 않는 것은?

Umberto Eco was an Italian novelist, cultural critic and philosopher. He is widely known for his 1980 novel *The Name of the Rose*, a historical mystery combining semiotics in fiction with biblical analysis, medieval studies and literary theory. He later wrote other novels, including *Foucault's Pendulum* and *The Island of the Day Before*. Eco was also a translator: he translated Raymond Queneau's book *Exercices de style* into Italian. He was the founder of the Department of Media Studies at the University of the Republic of San Marino. He died at his Milanese home of pancreatic cancer, from which he had been suffering for two years, on the night of February 19, 2016.

① *The Name of the Rose* is a historical novel.

② Eco translated a book into Italian.

③ Eco founded a university department.

④ Eco died in a hospital of cancer.

08 밑줄 친 부분 중 어법상 옳지 않은 것은?

To find a good starting point, one must return to the year 1800 during ① which the first modern electric battery was developed. Italian Alessandro Volta found that a combination of silver, copper, and zinc ② were ideal for producing an electrical current. The enhanced design, ③ called a Voltaic pile, was made by stacking some discs made from these metals between discs made of cardboard soaked in sea water. There was ④ such talk about Volta's work that he was requested to conduct a demonstration before the Emperor Napoleon himself.

09 다음 글의 제목으로 가장 적절한 것은?

Lasers are possible because of the way light interacts with electrons. Electrons exist at specific energy levels or states characteristic of that particular atom or molecule. The energy levels can be imagined as rings or orbits around a nucleus. Electrons in outer rings are at higher energy levels than those in inner rings. Electrons can be bumped up to higher energy levels by the injection of energy—for example, by a flash of light. When an electron drops from an outer to an inner level, "excess" energy is given off as light. The wavelength or color of the emitted light is precisely related to the amount of energy released. Depending on the particular lasing material being used, specific wavelengths of light are absorbed (to energize or excite the electrons) and specific wavelengths are emitted (when the electrons fall back to their initial level).

① How Is Laser Produced?

② When Was Laser Invented?

③ What Electrons Does Laser Emit?

④ Why Do Electrons Reflect Light?

10 다음 글의 흐름상 가장 어색한 문장은?

Markets in water rights are likely to evolve as a rising population leads to shortages and climate change causes drought and famine. ① But they will be based on regional and ethical trading practices and will differ from the bulk of commodity trade. ② Detractors argue trading water is unethical or even a breach of human rights, but already water rights are bought and sold in arid areas of the globe from Oman to Australia. ③ Drinking distilled water can be beneficial, but may not be the best choice for everyone, especially if the minerals are not supplemented by another source. ④ "We strongly believe that water is in fact turning into the new gold for this decade and beyond," said Ziad Abdelnour. "No wonder smart money is aggressively moving in this direction."

[11~12] 밑줄 친 부분에 들어갈 말로 가장 적절한 것을 고르시오.

11

A: I heard that the university cafeteria changed their menu.

B: Yeah, I just checked it out.

A: And they got a new caterer.

B: Yes. Sam's Catering.

A: _____?

B: There are more dessert choices. Also, some sandwich choices were removed.

① What is your favorite dessert
② Do you know where their office is
③ Do you need my help with the menu
④ What's the difference from the last menu

12

A: Hi there. May I help you?

B: Yes, I'm looking for a sweater.

A: Well, this one is the latest style from the fall collection. What do you think?

B: It's gorgeous. How much is it?

A: Let me check the price for you. It's $120.

B: _____.

A: Then how about this sweater? It's from the last season, but it's on sale for $50.

B: Perfect! Let me try it on.

① I also need a pair of pants to go with it
② That jacket is the perfect gift for me
③ It's a little out of my price range
④ We are open until 7 p.m. on Saturdays

[13~14] 우리말을 영어로 잘못 옮긴 것을 고르시오.

13

① 우리가 영어를 단시간에 배우는 것은 결코 쉬운 일이 아니다.
  → It is by no means easy for us to learn English in a short time.

② 우리 인생에서 시간보다 더 소중한 것은 없다.
  → Nothing is more precious as time in our life.

③ 아이들은 길을 건널 때 아무리 조심해도 지나치지 않다.
  → Children cannot be too careful when crossing the street.

④ 그녀는 남들이 말하는 것을 쉽게 믿는다.
  → She easily believes what others say.

14 ① 커피 세 잔을 마셨기 때문에, 그녀는 잠을 이룰 수 없다.

→ Having drunk three cups of coffee, she can't fall asleep.

② 친절한 사람이어서, 그녀는 모든 이에게 사랑받는다.

→ Being a kind person, she is loved by everyone.

③ 모든 점이 고려된다면, 그녀가 그 직위에 가장 적임인 사람이다.

→ All things considered, she is the best-qualified person for the position.

④ 다리를 꼰 채로 오랫동안 앉아 있는 것은 혈압을 상승시킬 수 있다.

→ Sitting with the legs crossing for a long period can raise blood pressure.

15 밑줄 친 (A), (B)에 들어갈 말로 가장 적절한 것은?

Beliefs about maintaining ties with those who have died vary from culture to culture. For example, maintaining ties with the deceased is accepted and sustained in the religious rituals of Japan. Yet among the Hopi Indians of Arizona, the deceased are forgotten as quickly as possible and life goes on as usual.　(A)　, the Hopi funeral ritual concludes with a break-off between mortals and spirits. The diversity of grieving is nowhere clearer than in two Muslim societies— one in Egypt, the other in Bali. Among Muslims in Egypt, the bereaved are encouraged to dwell at length on their grief, surrounded by others who relate to similarly tragic accounts and express their sorrow.　(B)　, in Bali, bereaved Muslims are encouraged to laugh and be joyful rather than be sad.

	(A)	(B)
①	However	Similarly
②	In fact	By contrast
③	Therefore	For example
④	Likewise	Consequently

16 밑줄 친 부분에 들어갈 말로 가장 적절한 것은?

Scientists have long known that higher air temperatures are contributing to the surface melting on Greenland's ice sheet. But a new study has found another threat that has begun attacking the ice from below: Warm ocean water moving underneath the vast glaciers is causing them to melt even more quickly. The findings were published in the journal *Nature Geoscience* by researchers who studied one of the many "ice tongues" of the Nioghalvfjerdsfjorden Glacier in northeast Greenland. An ice tongue is a strip of ice that floats on the water without breaking off from the ice on land. The massive one these scientists studied is nearly 50 miles long. The survey revealed an underwater current more than a mile wide where warm water from the Atlantic Ocean is able to flow directly towards the glacier, bringing large amounts of heat into contact with the ice and _____ the glacier's melting.

① separating

② delaying

③ preventing

④ accelerating

17 다음 글의 제목으로 가장 적절한 것은?

Do people from different cultures view the world differently? A psychologist presented realistic animated scenes of fish and other underwater objects to Japanese and American students and asked them to report what they had seen. Americans and Japanese made about an equal number of references to the focal fish, but the Japanese made more than 60 percent more references to background elements, including the water, rocks, bubbles, and inert plants and animals. In addition, whereas Japanese and American participants made about equal numbers of references to movement involving active animals, the Japanese participants made almost twice as many references to relationships involving inert, background objects. Perhaps most tellingly, the very first sentence from the Japanese participants was likely to be one referring to the environment, whereas the first sentence from Americans was three times as likely to be one referring to the focal fish.

① Language Barrier Between Japanese and Americans
② Associations of Objects and Backgrounds in the Brain
③ Cultural Differences in Perception
④ Superiority of Detail-oriented People

18 주어진 문장이 들어갈 위치로 가장 적절한 곳은?

Thus, blood, and life-giving oxygen, are easier for the heart to circulate to the brain.

People can be exposed to gravitational force, or g-force, in different ways. It can be localized, affecting only a portion of the body, as in getting slapped on the back. It can also be momentary, such as hard forces endured in a car crash. A third type of g-force is sustained, or lasting for at least several seconds. (①) Sustained, body-wide g-forces are the most dangerous to people. (②) The body usually withstands localized or momentary g-force better than sustained g-force, which can be deadly because blood is forced into the legs, depriving the rest of the body of oxygen. (③) Sustained g-force applied while the body is horizontal, or lying down, instead of sitting or standing tends to be more tolerable to people, because blood pools in the back and not the legs. (④) Some people, such as astronauts and fighter jet pilots, undergo special training exercises to increase their bodies' resistance to g-force.

19 다음 글의 요지로 가장 적절한 것은?

If someone makes you an offer and you're legitimately concerned about parts of it, you're usually better off proposing all your changes at once. Don't say, "The salary is a bit low. Could you do something about it?" and then, once she's worked on it, come back with "Thanks. Now here are two other things I'd like..." If you ask for only one thing initially, she may assume that getting it will make you ready to accept the offer (or at least to make a decision). If you keep saying "and one more thing...," she is unlikely to remain in a generous or understanding mood. Furthermore, if you have more than one request, don't simply mention all the things you want—A, B, C, and D; also signal the relative importance of each to you. Otherwise, she may pick the two things you value least, because they're pretty easy to give you, and feel she's met you halfway.

① Negotiate multiple issues simultaneously, not serially.

② Avoid sensitive topics for a successful negotiation.

③ Choose the right time for your negotiation.

④ Don't be too direct when negotiating salary.

20 주어진 글 다음에 이어질 글의 순서로 가장 적절한 것은?

Today, Lamarck is unfairly remembered in large part for his mistaken explanation of how adaptations evolve. He proposed that by using or not using certain body parts, an organism develops certain characteristics.

(A) There is no evidence that this happens. Still, it is important to note that Lamarck proposed that evolution occurs when organisms adapt to their environments. This idea helped set the stage for Darwin.

(B) Lamarck thought that these characteristics would be passed on to the offspring. Lamarck called this idea *inheritance of acquired characteristics*.

(C) For example, Lamarck might explain that a kangaroo's powerful hind legs were the result of ancestors strengthening their legs by jumping and then passing that acquired leg strength on to the offspring. However, an acquired characteristic would have to somehow modify the DNA of specific genes in order to be inherited.

① (A) - (C) - (B)

② (B) - (A) - (C)

③ (B) - (C) - (A)

④ (C) - (A) - (B)

영어 | 2021년 국가직 9급

✔ 회독 CHECK ① ② ③

[01~03] 밑줄 친 부분의 의미와 가장 가까운 것을 고르시오.

01

> Privacy as a social practice shapes individual behavior in conjunction with other social practices and is therefore central to social life.

① in combination with
② in comparison with
③ in place of
④ in case of

02

> The influence of Jazz has been so pervasive that most popular music owes its stylistic roots to jazz.

① deceptive
② ubiquitous
③ persuasive
④ disastrous

03

> This novel is about the vexed parents of an unruly teenager who quits school to start a business.

① callous
② annoyed
③ reputable
④ confident

04 밑줄 친 부분에 들어갈 말로 가장 적절한 것은?

> A group of young demonstrators attempted to _____ the police station.

① line up
② give out
③ carry on
④ break into

05 다음 글의 내용과 일치하는 것은?

The most notorious case of imported labor is of course the Atlantic slave trade, which brought as many as ten million enslaved Africans to the New World to work the plantations. But although the Europeans may have practiced slavery on the largest scale, they were by no means the only people to bring slaves into their communities: earlier, the ancient Egyptians used slave labor to build their pyramids, early Arab explorers were often also slave traders, and Arabic slavery continued into the twentieth century and indeed still continues in a few places. In the Americas some native tribes enslaved members of other tribes, and slavery was also an institution in many African nations, especially before the colonial period.

① African laborers voluntarily moved to the New World.
② Europeans were the first people to use slave labor.
③ Arabic slavery no longer exists in any form.
④ Slavery existed even in African countries.

06 어법상 옳은 것은?

① This guide book tells you where should you visit in Hong Kong.
② I was born in Taiwan, but I have lived in Korea since I started work.
③ The novel was so excited that I lost track of time and missed the bus.
④ It's not surprising that book stores don't carry newspapers any more, doesn't it?

07 다음 글의 제목으로 가장 적절한 것은?

Warming temperatures and loss of oxygen in the sea will shrink hundreds of fish species—from tunas and groupers to salmon, thresher sharks, haddock and cod—even more than previously thought, a new study concludes. Because warmer seas speed up their metabolisms, fish, squid and other water-breathing creatures will need to draw more oxygen from the ocean. At the same time, warming seas are already reducing the availability of oxygen in many parts of the sea. A pair of University of British Columbia scientists argue that since the bodies of fish grow faster than their gills, these animals eventually will reach a point where they can't get enough oxygen to sustain normal growth. "What we found was that the body size of fish decreases by 20 to 30 percent for every 1 degree Celsius increase in water temperature," says author William Cheung.

① Fish Now Grow Faster than Ever
② Oxygen's Impact on Ocean Temperatures
③ Climate Change May Shrink the World's Fish
④ How Sea Creatures Survive with Low Metabolism

08 밑줄 친 부분 중 어법상 옳지 않은 것은?

Urban agriculture (UA) has long been dismissed as a fringe activity that has no place in cities; however, its potential is beginning to ① be realized. In fact, UA is about food self-reliance: it involves ② creating work and is a reaction to food insecurity, particularly for the poor. Contrary to ③ which many believe, UA is found in every city, where it is sometimes hidden, sometimes obvious. If one looks carefully, few spaces in a major city are unused. Valuable vacant land rarely sits idle and is often taken over—either formally, or informally—and made ④ productive.

09 주어진 문장이 들어갈 위치로 가장 적절한 것은?

For example, the state archives of New Jersey hold more than 30,000 cubic feet of paper and 25,000 reels of microfilm.

Archives are a treasure trove* of material: from audio to video to newspapers, magazines and printed material—which makes them indispensable to any History Detective investigation. While libraries and archives may appear the same, the differences are important. (①) An archive collection is almost always made up of primary sources, while a library contains secondary sources. (②) To learn more about the Korean War, you'd go to a library for a history book. If you wanted to read the government papers, or letters written by Korean War soldiers, you'd go to an archive. (③) If you're searching for information, chances are there's an archive out there for you. Many state and local archives store public records—which are an amazing, diverse resource. (④) An online search of your state's archives will quickly show you they contain much more than just the minutes of the legislature—there are detailed land grant* information to be found, old town maps, criminal records and oddities such as peddler license applications.

*treasure trove: 귀중한 발굴물(수집물)

*land grant: (대학·철도 등을 위해) 정부가 주는 땅

10 다음 글의 흐름상 가장 어색한 문장은?

The term burnout refers to a "wearing out" from the pressures of work. Burnout is a chronic condition that results as daily work stressors take their toll on employees. ① The most widely adopted conceptualization of burnout has been developed by Maslach and her colleagues in their studies of human service workers. Maslach sees burnout as consisting of three interrelated dimensions. The first dimension—emotional exhaustion—is really the core of the burnout phenomenon. ② Workers suffer from emotional exhaustion when they feel fatigued, frustrated, used up, or unable to face another day on the job. The second dimension of burnout is a lack of personal accomplishment. ③ This aspect of the burnout phenomenon refers to workers who see themselves as failures, incapable of effectively accomplishing job requirements. ④ Emotional labor workers enter their occupation highly motivated although they are physically exhausted. The third dimension of burnout is depersonalization. This dimension is relevant only to workers who must communicate interpersonally with others (e.g. clients, patients, students) as part of the job.

[11~12] 밑줄 친 부분에 들어갈 말로 가장 적절한 것을 고르시오.

11

A: Were you here last night?

B: Yes. I worked the closing shift. Why?

A: The kitchen was a mess this morning. There was food spattered on the stove, and the ice trays were not in the freezer.

B: I guess I forgot to go over the cleaning checklist.

A: You know how important a clean kitchen is.

B: I'm sorry. _____

① I won't let it happen again.

② Would you like your bill now?

③ That's why I forgot it yesterday.

④ I'll make sure you get the right order.

12

A: Have you taken anything for your cold?

B: No, I just blow my nose a lot.

A: Have you tried nose spray?

B: _____

A: It works great.

B: No, thanks. I don't like to put anything in my nose, so I've never used it.

① Yes, but it didn't help.

② No, I don't like nose spray.

③ No, the pharmacy was closed.

④ Yeah, how much should I use?

13 다음 글의 내용과 일치하지 않는 것은?

Deserts cover more than one-fifth of the Earth's land area, and they are found on every continent. A place that receives less than 25 centimeters (10 inches) of rain per year is considered a desert. Deserts are part of a wider class of regions called drylands. These areas exist under a "moisture deficit," which means they can frequently lose more moisture through evaporation than they receive from annual precipitation. Despite the common conceptions of deserts as hot, there are cold deserts as well. The largest hot desert in the world, northern Africa's Sahara, reaches temperatures of up to 50 degrees Celsius (122 degrees Fahrenheit) during the day. But some deserts are always cold, like the Gobi Desert in Asia and the polar deserts of the Antarctic and Arctic, which are the world's largest. Others are mountainous. Only about 20 percent of deserts are covered by sand. The driest deserts, such as Chile's Atacama Desert, have parts that receive less than two millimeters (0.08 inches) of precipitation a year. Such environments are so harsh and otherworldly that scientists have even studied them for clues about life on Mars. On the other hand, every few years, an unusually rainy period can produce "super blooms," where even the Atacama becomes blanketed in wildflowers.

① There is at least one desert on each continent.
② The Sahara is the world's largest hot desert.
③ The Gobi Desert is categorized as a cold desert.
④ The Atacama Desert is one of the rainiest deserts.

[14~15] 우리말을 영어로 가장 잘 옮긴 것을 고르시오.

14 ① 나는 너의 답장을 가능한 한 빨리 받기를 고대한다.
→ I look forward to receive your reply as soon as possible.
② 그는 내가 일을 열심히 했기 때문에 월급을 올려 주겠다고 말했다.
→ He said he would rise my salary because I worked hard.
③ 그의 스마트 도시 계획은 고려할 만했다.
→ His plan for the smart city was worth considered.
④ Cindy는 피아노 치는 것을 매우 좋아했고 그녀의 아들도 그랬다.
→ Cindy loved playing the piano, and so did her son.

15 ① 당신이 부자일지라도 당신은 진실한 친구들을 살 수는 없다.
→ Rich as if you may be, you can't buy sincere friends.
② 그것은 너무나 아름다운 유성 폭풍이어서 우리는 밤새 그것을 보았다.
→ It was such a beautiful meteor storm that we watched it all night.
③ 학위가 없는 것이 그녀의 성공을 방해했다.
→ Her lack of a degree kept her advancing.
④ 그는 사형이 폐지되어야 하는지 아닌지에 대한 에세이를 써야 한다.
→ He has to write an essay on if or not the death penalty should be abolished.

[16~17] 밑줄 친 부분에 들어갈 말로 가장 적절한 것을 고르시오.

16

Social media, magazines and shop windows bombard people daily with things to buy, and British consumers are buying more clothes and shoes than ever before. Online shopping means it is easy for customers to buy without thinking, while major brands offer such cheap clothes that they can be treated like disposable items—worn two or three times and then thrown away. In Britain, the average person spends more than £1,000 on new clothes a year, which is around four percent of their income. That might not sound like much, but that figure hides two far more worrying trends for society and for the environment. First, a lot of that consumer spending is via credit cards. British people currently owe approximately £670 per adult to credit card companies. That's 66 percent of the average wardrobe budget. Also, not only are people spending money they don't have, they're using it to buy things _____.
Britain throws away 300,000 tons of clothing a year, most of which goes into landfill sites.

① they don't need
② that are daily necessities
③ that will be soon recycled
④ they can hand down to others

17

Excellence is the absolute prerequisite in fine dining because the prices charged are necessarily high. An operator may do everything possible to make the restaurant efficient, but the guests still expect careful, personal service: food prepared to order by highly skilled chefs and delivered by expert servers. Because this service is, quite literally, manual labor, only marginal improvements in productivity are possible. For example, a cook, server, or bartender can move only so much faster before she or he reaches the limits of human performance. Thus, only moderate savings are possible through improved efficiency, which makes an escalation of prices _____. (It is an axiom of economics that as prices rise, consumers become more discriminating.) Thus, the clientele of the fine-dining restaurant expects, demands, and is willing to pay for excellence.

① ludicrous
② inevitable
③ preposterous
④ inconceivable

18 주어진 글 다음에 이어질 글의 순서로 가장 적절한 것은?

> To be sure, human language stands out from the decidedly restricted vocalizations of monkeys and apes. Moreover, it exhibits a degree of sophistication that far exceeds any other form of animal communication.

(A) That said, many species, while falling far short of human language, do nevertheless exhibit impressively complex communication systems in natural settings.

(B) And they can be taught far more complex systems in artificial contexts, as when raised alongside humans.

(C) Even our closest primate cousins seem incapable of acquiring anything more than a rudimentary communicative system, even after intensive training over several years. The complexity that is language is surely a species-specific trait.

① (A) - (B) - (C)

② (B) - (C) - (A)

③ (C) - (A) - (B)

④ (C) - (B) - (A)

19 다음 글의 주제로 가장 적절한 것은?

> During the late twentieth century socialism was on the retreat both in the West and in large areas of the developing world. During this new phase in the evolution of market capitalism, global trading patterns became increasingly interlinked, and advances in information technology meant that deregulated financial markets could shift massive flows of capital across national boundaries within seconds. 'Globalization' boosted trade, encouraged productivity gains and lowered prices, but critics alleged that it exploited the low-paid, was indifferent to environmental concerns and subjected the Third World to a monopolistic form of capitalism. Many radicals within Western societies who wished to protest against this process joined voluntary bodies, charities and other non-governmental organizations, rather than the marginalized political parties of the left. The environmental movement itself grew out of the recognition that the world was interconnected, and an angry, if diffuse, international coalition of interests emerged.

① The affirmative phenomena of globalization in the developing world in the past

② The decline of socialism and the emergence of capitalism in the twentieth century

③ The conflict between the global capital market and the political organizations of the left

④ The exploitative characteristics of global capitalism and diverse social reactions against it

20 다음 글에 나타난 Johnbull의 심경으로 가장 적절한 것은?

> In the blazing midday sun, the yellow egg-shaped rock stood out from a pile of recently unearthed gravel. Out of curiosity, sixteen-year-old miner Komba Johnbull picked it up and fingered its flat, pyramidal planes. Johnbull had never seen a diamond before, but he knew enough to understand that even a big find would be no larger than his thumbnail. Still, the rock was unusual enough to merit a second opinion. Sheepishly, he brought it over to one of the more experienced miners working the muddy gash deep in the jungle. The pit boss's eyes widened when he saw the stone. "Put it in your pocket," he whispered. "Keep digging." The older miner warned that it could be dangerous if anyone thought they had found something big. So Johnbull kept shoveling gravel until nightfall, pausing occasionally to grip the heavy stone in his fist. Could it be?

① thrilled and excited
② painful and distressed
③ arrogant and convinced
④ detached and indifferent

✅ 회독 CHECK 1 2 3

[01~04] 밑줄 친 부분의 의미와 가장 가까운 것을 고르시오.

01

> Extensive lists of microwave oven models and styles along with candid customer reviews and price ranges are available at appliance comparison websites.

① frank
② logical
③ implicit
④ passionate

02

> It had been known for a long time that Yellowstone was volcanic in nature and the one thing about volcanoes is that they are generally conspicuous.

① passive
② vaporous
③ dangerous
④ noticeable

03

> He's the best person to tell you how to get there because he knows the city inside out.

① eventually
② culturally
③ thoroughly
④ tentatively

04

> All along the route were thousands of homespun attempts to pay tribute to the team, including messages etched in cardboard, snow and construction paper.

① honor
② compose
③ publicize
④ join

05 어법상 옳은 것은?

① The traffic of a big city is busier than those of a small city.

② I'll think of you when I'll be lying on the beach next week.

③ Raisins were once an expensive food, and only the wealth ate them.

④ The intensity of a color is related to how much gray the color contains.

06 우리말을 영어로 가장 잘 옮긴 것은?

① 몇 가지 문제가 새로운 회원들 때문에 생겼다.
→ Several problems have raised due to the new members.

② 그 위원회는 그 건물의 건설을 중단하라고 명했다.
→ The committee commanded that construction of the building cease.

③ 그들은 한 시간에 40마일이 넘는 바람과 싸워야 했다.
→ They had to fight against winds that will blow over 40 miles an hour.

④ 거의 모든 식물의 씨앗은 혹독한 날씨에도 살아남는다.
→ The seeds of most plants are survived by harsh weather.

07 우리말을 영어로 잘못 옮긴 것은?

① 인간은 환경에 자신을 빨리 적응시킨다.
→ Human beings quickly adapt themselves to the environment.

② 그녀는 그 사고 때문에 그녀의 목표를 포기할 수밖에 없었다.
→ She had no choice but to give up her goal because of the accident.

③ 그 회사는 그가 부회장으로 승진하는 것을 금했다.
→ The company prohibited him from promoting to vice-president.

④ 그 장난감 자동차를 조립하고 분리하는 것은 쉽다.
→ It is easy to assemble and take apart the toy car.

08 다음 글의 요지로 가장 적절한 것은?

Listening to somebody else's ideas is the one way to know whether the story you believe about the world—as well as about yourself and your place in it—remains intact. We all need to examine our beliefs, air them out and let them breathe. Hearing what other people have to say, especially about concepts we regard as foundational, is like opening a window in our minds and in our hearts. Speaking up is important. Yet to speak up without listening is like banging pots and pans together: even if it gets you attention, it's not going to get you respect. There are three prerequisites for conversation to be meaningful: 1. You have to know what you're talking about, meaning that you have an original point and are not echoing a worn-out, hand-me-down or pre-fab argument; 2. You respect the people with whom you're speaking and are authentically willing to treat them courteously even if you disagree with their positions; 3. You have to be both smart and informed enough to listen to what the opposition says while handling your own perspective on the topic with uninterrupted good humor and discernment.

① We should be more determined to persuade others.

② We need to listen and speak up in order to communicate well.

③ We are reluctant to change our beliefs about the world we see.

④ We hear only what we choose and attempt to ignore different opinions.

09 다음 글의 제목으로 가장 적절한 것은?

The future may be uncertain, but some things are undeniable: climate change, shifting demographics, geopolitics. The only guarantee is that there will be changes, both wonderful and terrible. It's worth considering how artists will respond to these changes, as well as what purpose art serves, now and in the future. Reports suggest that by 2040 the impacts of human-caused climate change will be inescapable, making it the big issue at the centre of art and life in 20 years' time. Artists in the future will wrestle with the possibilities of the post-human and post-Anthropocene—artificial intelligence, human colonies in outer space and potential doom. The identity politics seen in art around the #MeToo and Black Lives Matter movements will grow as environmentalism, border politics and migration come even more sharply into focus. Art will become increasingly diverse and might not 'look like art' as we expect. In the future, once we've become weary of our lives being visible online for all to see and our privacy has been all but lost, anonymity may be more desirable than fame. Instead of thousands, or millions, of likes and followers, we will be starved for authenticity and connection. Art could, in turn, become more collective and experiential, rather than individual.

① What will art look like in the future?
② How will global warming affect our lives?
③ How will artificial intelligence influence the environment?
④ What changes will be made because of political movements?

10 다음 글의 내용과 일치하지 않는 것은?

The Second Amendment of the U.S. Constitution states: "A well-regulated Militia, being necessary to the security of a free State, the right of the people to keep and bear Arms, shall not be infringed." Supreme Court rulings, citing this amendment, have upheld the right of states to regulate firearms. However, in a 2008 decision confirming an individual right to keep and bear arms, the court struck down Washington, D.C. laws that banned handguns and required those in the home to be locked or disassembled. A number of gun advocates consider ownership a birthright and an essential part of the nation's heritage. The United States, with less than 5 percent of the world's population, has about 35~50 percent of the world's civilian-owned guns, according to a 2007 report by the Switzerland-based Small Arms Survey. It ranks number one in firearms per capita. The United States also has the highest homicide-by-firearm rate among the world's most developed nations. But many gun-rights proponents say these statistics do not indicate a cause-and-effect relationship and note that the rates of gun homicide and other gun crimes in the United States have dropped since highs in the early 1990's.

① In 2008, the U.S. Supreme Court overturned Washington, D.C. laws banning handguns.
② Many gun advocates claim that owning guns is a natural-born right.
③ Among the most developed nations, the U.S. has the highest rate of gun homicides.
④ Gun crimes in the U.S. have steadily increased over the last three decades.

11 두 사람의 대화 중 가장 어색한 것은?

① A: When is the payment due?

   B: You have to pay by next week.

② A: Should I check this baggage in?

   B: No, it's small enough to take on the plane.

③ A: When and where shall we meet?

   B: I'll pick you up at your office at 8:30.

④ A: I won the prize in a cooking contest.

   B: I couldn't have done it without you.

12 밑줄 친 부분에 들어갈 말로 가장 적절한 것은?

> A: Thank you for calling the Royal Point Hotel Reservations Department. My name is Sam. How may I help you?
>
> B: Hello, I'd like to book a room.
>
> A: We offer two room types: the deluxe room and the luxury suite.
>
> B: _____?
>
> A: For one, the suite is very large. In addition to a bedroom, it has a kitchen, living room and dining room.
>
> B: It sounds expensive.
>
> A: Well, it's $200 more per night.
>
> B: In that case, I'll go with the deluxe room.

① Do you need anything else

② May I have the room number

③ What's the difference between them

④ Are pets allowed in the rooms

13 밑줄 친 (A), (B)에 들어갈 말로 가장 적절한 것은?

> Advocates of homeschooling believe that children learn better when they are in a secure, loving environment. Many psychologists see the home as the most natural learning environment, and originally the home was the classroom, long before schools were established. Parents who homeschool argue that they can monitor their children's education and give them the attention that is lacking in a traditional school setting. Students can also pick and choose what to study and when to study, thus enabling them to learn at their own pace. ____(A)____, critics of homeschooling say that children who are not in the classroom miss out on learning important social skills because they have little interaction with their peers. Several studies, though, have shown that the home-educated children appear to do just as well in terms of social and emotional development as other students, having spent more time in the comfort and security of their home, with guidance from parents who care about their welfare. ____(B)____, many critics of homeschooling have raised concerns about the ability of parents to teach their kids effectively.

	(A)	(B)
①	Therefore	Nevertheless
②	In contrast	In spite of this
③	Therefore	Contrary to that
④	In contrast	Furthermore

14 다음 글의 주제로 가장 적절한 것은?

For many people, work has become an obsession. It has caused burnout, unhappiness and gender inequity, as people struggle to find time for children or passions or pets or any sort of life besides what they do for a paycheck. But increasingly, younger workers are pushing back. More of them expect and demand flexibility—paid leave for a new baby, say, and generous vacation time, along with daily things, like the ability to work remotely, come in late or leave early, or make time for exercise or meditation. The rest of their lives happens on their phones, not tied to a certain place or time—why should work be any different?

① ways to increase your paycheck
② obsession for reducing inequity
③ increasing call for flexibility at work
④ advantages of a life with long vacations

15 주어진 글 다음에 이어질 글의 순서로 가장 적절한 것은?

Past research has shown that experiencing frequent psychological stress can be a significant risk factor for cardiovascular disease, a condition that affects almost half of those aged 20 years and older in the United States.

(A) Does this mean, though, that people who drive on a daily basis are set to develop heart problems, or is there a simple way of easing the stress of driving?

(B) According to a new study, there is. The researchers noted that listening to music while driving helps relieve the stress that affects heart health.

(C) One source of frequent stress is driving, either due to the stressors associated with heavy traffic or the anxiety that often accompanies inexperienced drivers.

① (A) - (C) - (B)
② (B) - (A) - (C)
③ (C) - (A) - (B)
④ (C) - (B) - (A)

16 다음 글의 흐름상 가장 어색한 문장은?

When the brain perceives a threat in the immediate surroundings, it initiates a complex string of events in the body. It sends electrical messages to various glands, organs that release chemical hormones into the bloodstream. Blood quickly carries these hormones to other organs that are then prompted to do various things. ① The adrenal glands above the kidneys, for example, pump out adrenaline, the body's stress hormone. ② Adrenaline travels all over the body doing things such as widening the eyes to be on the lookout for signs of danger, pumping the heart faster to keep blood and extra hormones flowing, and tensing the skeletal muscles so they are ready to lash out at or run from the threat. ③ The whole process is called the fight-or-flight response, because it prepares the body to either battle or run for its life. ④ Humans consciously control their glands to regulate the release of various hormones. Once the response is initiated, ignoring it is impossible, because hormones cannot be reasoned with.

17 주어진 문장이 들어갈 위치로 가장 적절한 것은?

It was then he remembered his experience with the glass flask, and just as quickly, he imagined that a special coating might be applied to a glass windshield to keep it from shattering.

In 1903 the French chemist, Edouard Benedictus, dropped a glass flask one day on a hard floor and broke it. (①) However, to the astonishment of the chemist, the flask did not shatter, but still retained most of its original shape. (②) When he examined the flask he found that it contained a film coating inside, a residue remaining from a solution of collodion that the flask had contained. (③) He made a note of this unusual phenomenon, but thought no more of it until several weeks later when he read stories in the newspapers about people in automobile accidents who were badly hurt by flying windshield glass. (④) Not long thereafter, he succeeded in producing the world's first sheet of safety glass.

18 다음 글의 내용과 일치하지 않는 것은?

Dubrovnik, Croatia, is a mess. Because its main attraction is its seaside Old Town surrounded by 80-foot medieval walls, this Dalmatian Coast town does not absorb visitors very well. And when cruise ships are docked here, a legion of tourists turn Old Town into a miasma of tank-top-clad tourists marching down the town's limestone-blanketed streets. Yes, the city of Dubrovnik has been proactive in trying to curb cruise ship tourism, but nothing will save Old Town from the perpetual swarm of tourists. To make matters worse, the lure of making extra money has inspired many homeowners in Old Town to turn over their places to Airbnb, making the walled portion of town one giant hotel. You want an "authentic" Dubrovnik experience in Old Town, just like a local? You're not going to find it here. Ever.

① Old Town은 80피트 중세 시대 벽으로 둘러싸여 있다.
② 크루즈 배가 정박할 때면 많은 여행객이 Old Town 거리를 활보한다.
③ Dubrovnik 시는 크루즈 여행을 확대하려고 노력해 왔다.
④ Old Town에서는 많은 집이 여행객 숙소로 바뀌었다.

19 밑줄 친 (A), (B)에 들어갈 말로 가장 적절한 것은?

When an organism is alive, it takes in carbon dioxide from the air around it. Most of that carbon dioxide is made of carbon-12, but a tiny portion consists of carbon-14. So the living organism always contains a very small amount of radioactive carbon, carbon-14. A detector next to the living organism would record radiation given off by the carbon-14 in the organism. When the organism dies, it no longer takes in carbon dioxide. No new carbon-14 is added, and the old carbon-14 slowly decays into nitrogen. The amount of carbon-14 slowly 　(A)　 as time goes on. Over time, less and less radiation from carbon-14 is produced. The amount of carbon-14 radiation detected for an organism is a measure, therefore, of how long the organism has been 　(B)　. This method of determining the age of an organism is called carbon-14 dating. The decay of carbon-14 allows archaeologists to find the age of once-living materials. Measuring the amount of radiation remaining indicates the approximate age.

	(A)	(B)
①	decreases	dead
②	increases	alive
③	decreases	productive
④	increases	inactive

20 밑줄 친 부분에 들어갈 말로 가장 적절한 것은?

All creatures, past and present, either have gone or will go extinct. Yet, as each species vanished over the past 3.8-billion-year history of life on Earth, new ones inevitably appeared to replace them or to exploit newly emerging resources. From only a few very simple organisms, a great number of complex, multicellular forms evolved over this immense period. The origin of new species, which the nineteenth-century English naturalist Charles Darwin once referred to as "the mystery of mysteries," is the natural process of speciation responsible for generating this remarkable _____ with whom humans share the planet. Although taxonomists presently recognize some 1.5 million living species, the actual number is possibly closer to 10 million. Recognizing the biological status of this multitude requires a clear understanding of what constitutes a species, which is no easy task given that evolutionary biologists have yet to agree on a universally acceptable definition.

① technique of biologists
② diversity of living creatures
③ inventory of extinct organisms
④ collection of endangered species

영어 | 2019년 국가직 9급

모바일 OMR

✅ 회독 CHECK 1 2 3

[01~02] 밑줄 친 부분의 의미와 가장 가까운 것을 고르시오.

01

Natural Gas World subscribers will receive accurate and reliable key facts and figures about what is going on in the industry, so they are fully able to discern what concerns their business.

① distinguish

② strengthen

③ undermine

④ abandon

02

Ms. West, the winner of the silver in the women's 1,500m event, stood out through the race.

① was overwhelmed

② was impressive

③ was depressed

④ was optimistic

03 두 사람의 대화 중 가장 어색한 것은?

① A: I'm traveling abroad, but I'm not used to staying in another country.

　B: Don't worry. You'll get accustomed to it in no time.

② A: I want to get a prize in the photo contest.

　B: I'm sure you will. I'll keep my fingers crossed!

③ A: My best friend moved to Sejong City. I miss her so much.

　B: Yeah. I know how you feel.

④ A: Do you mind if I talk to you for a moment?

　B: Never mind. I'm very busy right now.

04 밑줄 친 부분에 들어갈 말로 가장 적절한 것은?

A: Would you like to try some dim sum?

B: Yes, thank you. They look delicious. What's inside?

A: These have pork and chopped vegetables, and those have shrimps.

B: And, um, _____?

A: You pick one up with your chopsticks like this and dip it into the sauce. It's easy.

B: Okay. I'll give it a try.

① how much are they

② how do I eat them

③ how spicy are they

④ how do you cook them

[05~06] 우리말을 영어로 잘못 옮긴 것을 고르시오.

05 ① 제가 당신께 말씀드렸던 새로운 선생님은 원래 페루 출신입니다.

→ The new teacher I told you about is originally from Peru.

② 나는 긴급한 일로 자정이 5분이나 지난 후 그에게 전화했다.

→ I called him five minutes shy of midnight on an urgent matter.

③ 상어로 보이는 것이 산호 뒤에 숨어 있었다.

→ What appeared to be a shark was lurking behind the coral reef.

④ 그녀는 일요일에 16세의 친구와 함께 산 정상에 올랐다.

→ She reached the mountain summit with her 16-year-old friend on Sunday.

06 ① 개인용 컴퓨터를 가장 많이 가지고 있는 나라는 종종 바뀐다.

→ The country with the most computers per person changes from time to time.

② 지난 여름 나의 사랑스러운 손자에게 일어난 일은 놀라웠다.

→ What happened to my lovely grandson last summer was amazing.

③ 나무 숟가락은 아이들에게 매우 좋은 장난감이고 플라스틱 병 또한 그렇다.

→ Wooden spoons are excellent toys for children, and so are plastic bottles.

④ 나는 은퇴 후부터 내내 이 일을 해 오고 있다.

→ I have been doing this work ever since I retired.

[07~08] 밑줄 친 부분 중 어법상 옳지 않은 것을 고르시오.

07

Domesticated animals are the earliest and most effective 'machines' ① available to humans. They take the strain off the human back and arms. ② Utilizing with other techniques, animals can raise human living standards very considerably, both as supplementary foodstuffs (protein in meat and milk) and as machines ③ to carry burdens, lift water, and grind grain. Since they are so obviously ④ of great benefit, we might expect to find that over the centuries humans would increase the number and quality of the animals they kept. Surprisingly, this has not usually been the case.

08

A myth is a narrative that embodies—and in some cases ① helps to explain—the religious, philosophical, moral, and political values of a culture. Through tales of gods and supernatural beings, myths ② try to make sense of occurrences in the natural world. Contrary to popular usage, myth does not mean "falsehood." In the broadest sense, myths are stories—usually whole groups of stories—③ that can be true or partly true as well as false; regardless of their degree of accuracy, however, myths frequently express the deepest beliefs of a culture. According to this definition, the *Iliad* and the *Odyssey*, the Koran, and the Old and New Testaments can all ④ refer to as myths.

09 다음 글의 제목으로 가장 적절한 것은?

Mapping technologies are being used in many new applications. Biological researchers are exploring the molecular structure of DNA ("mapping the genome"), geophysicists are mapping the structure of the Earth's core, and oceanographers are mapping the ocean floor. Computer games have various imaginary "lands" or levels where rules, hazards, and rewards change. Computerization now challenges reality with "virtual reality," artificial environments that stimulate special situations, which may be useful in training and entertainment. Mapping techniques are being used also in the realm of ideas. For example, relationships between ideas can be shown using what are called concept maps. Starting from a general or "central" idea, related ideas can be connected, building a web around the main concept. This is not a map by any traditional definition, but the tools and techniques of cartography are employed to produce it, and in some ways it resembles a map.

① Computerized Maps vs. Traditional Maps
② Where Does Cartography Begin?
③ Finding Ways to DNA Secrets
④ Mapping New Frontiers

10 다음 글의 요지로 가장 적절한 것은?

When giving performance feedback, you should consider the recipient's past performance and your estimate of his or her future potential in designing its frequency, amount, and content. For high performers with potential for growth, feedback should be frequent enough to prod them into taking corrective action, but not so frequent that it is experienced as controlling and saps their initiative. For adequate performers who have settled into their jobs and have limited potential for advancement, very little feedback is needed because they have displayed reliable and steady behavior in the past, knowing their tasks and realizing what needs to be done. For poor performers—that is, people who will need to be removed from their jobs if their performance doesn't improve—feedback should be frequent and very specific, and the connection between acting on the feedback and negative sanctions such as being laid off or fired should be made explicit.

① Time your feedback well.
② Customize negative feedback.
③ Tailor feedback to the person.
④ Avoid goal-oriented feedback.

11 다음 글의 내용과 일치하지 않는 것은?

Langston Hughes was born in Joplin, Missouri, and graduated from Lincoln University, in which many African-American students have pursued their academic disciplines. At the age of eighteen, Hughes published one of his most well-known poems, "Negro Speaks of Rivers." Creative and experimental, Hughes incorporated authentic dialect in his work, adapted traditional poetic forms to embrace the cadences and moods of blues and jazz, and created characters and themes that reflected elements of lower-class black culture. With his ability to fuse serious content with humorous style, Hughes attacked racial prejudice in a way that was natural and witty.

① Hughes는 많은 미국 흑인들이 다녔던 대학교를 졸업하였다.
② Hughes는 실제 사투리를 그의 작품에 반영하였다.
③ Hughes는 하층 계급 흑인들의 문화적 요소를 반영한 인물을 만들었다.
④ Hughes는 인종 편견을 엄숙한 문체로 공격하였다.

12 밑줄 친 부분 중 글의 흐름상 가장 어색한 것은?

In 2007, our biggest concern was "too big to fail." Wall Street banks had grown to such staggering sizes, and had become so central to the health of the financial system, that no rational government could ever let them fail. ① Aware of their protected status, banks made excessively risky bets on housing markets and invented ever more complicated derivatives. ② New virtual currencies such as bitcoin and ethereum have radically changed our understanding of how money can and should work. ③ The result was the worst financial crisis since the breakdown of our economy in 1929. ④ In the years since 2007, we have made great progress in addressing the too-big-to-fail dilemma. Our banks are better capitalized than ever. Our regulators conduct regular stress tests of large institutions.

13 다음 글의 주제로 가장 적절한 것은?

Imagine that two people are starting work at a law firm on the same day. One person has a very simple name. The other person has a very complex name. We've got pretty good evidence that over the course of their next 16 plus years of their career, the person with the simpler name will rise up the legal hierarchy more quickly. They will attain partnership more quickly in the middle parts of their career. And by about the eighth or ninth year after graduating from law school the people with simpler names are about seven to ten percent more likely to be partners—which is a striking effect. We try to eliminate all sorts of other alternative explanations. For example, we try to show that it's not about foreignness because foreign names tend to be harder to pronounce. But even if you look at just white males with Anglo-American names—so really the true in-group, you find that among those white males with Anglo names they are more likely to rise up if their names happen to be simpler. So simplicity is one key feature in names that determines various outcomes.

① the development of legal names

② the concept of attractive names

③ the benefit of simple names

④ the roots of foreign names

[14~15] 밑줄 친 부분의 의미와 가장 가까운 것을 고르시오.

14

Schooling is compulsory for all children in the United States, but the age range for which school attendance is required varies from state to state.

① complementary

② systematic

③ mandatory

④ innovative

15

Although the actress experienced much turmoil in her career, she never disclosed to anyone that she was unhappy.

① let on

② let off

③ let up

④ let down

16 밑줄 친 (A), (B)에 들어갈 말로 가장 적절한 것은?

Visionaries are the first people in their industry segment to see the potential of new technologies. Fundamentally, they see themselves as smarter than their opposite numbers in competitive companies—and, quite often, they are. Indeed, it is their ability to see things first that they want to leverage into a competitive advantage. That advantage can only come about if no one else has discovered it. They do not expect, ___(A)___, to be buying a well-tested product with an extensive list of industry references. Indeed, if such a reference base exists, it may actually turn them off, indicating that for this technology, at any rate, they are already too late. Pragmatists, ___(B)___, deeply value the experience of their colleagues in other companies. When they buy, they expect extensive references, and they want a good number to come from companies in their own industry segment.

	(A)	(B)
①	therefore	on the other hand
②	however	in addition
③	nonetheless	at the same time
④	furthermore	in conclusion

17 주어진 문장이 들어갈 위치로 가장 적절한 것은?

Some of these ailments are short-lived; others may be long-lasting.

For centuries, humans have looked up at the sky and wondered what exists beyond the realm of our planet. (①) Ancient astronomers examined the night sky hoping to learn more about the universe. More recently, some movies explored the possibility of sustaining human life in outer space, while other films have questioned whether extraterrestrial life forms may have visited our planet. (②) Since astronaut Yuri Gagarin became the first man to travel in space in 1961, scientists have researched what conditions are like beyond the Earth's atmosphere, and what effects space travel has on the human body. (③) Although most astronauts do not spend more than a few months in space, many experience physiological and psychological problems when they return to the Earth. (④) More than two-thirds of all astronauts suffer from motion sickness while traveling in space. In the gravity-free environment, the body cannot differentiate up from down. The body's internal balance system sends confusing signals to the brain, which can result in nausea lasting as long as a few days.

18 밑줄 친 부분에 들어갈 말로 가장 적절한 것은?

Why bother with the history of everything? _____
_____. In literature classes you don't learn about genes; in physics classes you don't learn about human evolution. So you get a partial view of the world. That makes it hard to find *meaning* in education. The French sociologist Emile Durkheim called this sense of disorientation and meaninglessness *anomie*, and he argued that it could lead to despair and even suicide. The German sociologist Max Weber talked of the "disenchantment" of the world. In the past, people had a unified vision of their world, a vision usually provided by the origin stories of their own religious traditions. That unified vision gave a sense of purpose, of meaning, even of enchantment to the world and to life. Today, though, many writers have argued that a sense of meaninglessness is inevitable in a world of science and rationality. Modernity, it seems, means meaninglessness.

① In the past, the study of history required disenchantment from science

② Recently, science has given us lots of clever tricks and meanings

③ Today, we teach and learn about our world in fragments

④ Lately, history has been divided into several categories

19 다음 글의 내용과 일치하지 않는 것은?

The earliest government food service programs began around 1900 in Europe. Programs in the United States date from the Great Depression, when the need to use surplus agricultural commodities was joined to concern for feeding the children of poor families. During and after World War II, the explosion in the number of working women fueled the need for a broader program. What was once a function of the family—providing lunch—was shifted to the school food service system. The National School Lunch Program is the result of these efforts. The program is designed to provide federally assisted meals to children of school age. From the end of World War II to the early 1980s, funding for school food service expanded steadily. Today it helps to feed children in almost 100,000 schools across the United States. Its first function is to provide a nutritious lunch to all students; the second is to provide nutritious food at both breakfast and lunch to underprivileged children. If anything, the role of school food service as a replacement for what was once a family function has been expanded.

① The increase in the number of working women boosted the expansion of food service programs.

② The US government began to feed poor children during the Great Depression despite the food shortage.

③ The US school food service system presently helps to feed children of poor families.

④ The function of providing lunch has been shifted from the family to schools.

20 주어진 문장 다음에 이어질 글의 순서로 가장 적절한 것은?

> South Korea boasts of being the most wired nation on earth.

(A) This addiction has become a national issue in Korea in recent years, as users started dropping dead from exhaustion after playing online games for days on end. A growing number of students have skipped school to stay online, shockingly self-destructive behavior in this intensely competitive society.

(B) In fact, perhaps no other country has so fully embraced the Internet.

(C) But such ready access to the Web has come at a price as legions of obsessed users find that they cannot tear themselves away from their computer screens.

① (A) - (B) - (C)
② (A) - (C) - (B)
③ (B) - (A) - (C)
④ (B) - (C) - (A)

✅ 회독 CHECK 1 2 3

[01~02] 밑줄 친 부분에 들어갈 말로 가장 적절한 것을 고르시오.

01

A: Can I ask you for a favor?

B: Yes, what is it?

A: I need to get to the airport for my business trip, but my car won't start. Can you give me a lift?

B: Sure. When do you need to be there by?

A: I have to be there no later than 6:00.

B: It's 4:30 now. _____.
We'll have to leave right away.

① That's cutting it close

② I took my eye off the ball

③ All that glitters is not gold

④ It's water under the bridge

02

Fear of loss is a basic part of being human. To the brain, loss is a threat and we naturally take measures to avoid it. We cannot, however, avoid it indefinitely. One way to face loss is with the perspective of a stock trader. Traders accept the possibility of loss as part of the game, not the end of the game. What guides this thinking is a portfolio approach; wins and losses will both happen, but it's the overall portfolio of outcomes that matters most. When you embrace a portfolio approach, you will be _____
because you know that they are small parts of a much bigger picture.

① less inclined to dwell on individual losses

② less interested in your investments

③ more averse to the losses

④ more sensitive to fluctuations in the stock market

03 다음 글의 제목으로 가장 적절한 것은?

Over the last years of traveling, I've observed how much we humans live in the past. The past is around us constantly, considering that, the minute something is manifested, it is the past. Our surroundings, our homes, our environments, our architecture, our products are all past constructs. We should live with what is part of our time, part of our collective consciousness, those things that were produced during our lives. Of course, we do not have the choice or control to have everything around us relevant or conceived during our time, but what we do have control of should be a reflection of the time in which we exist and communicate the present. The present is all we have, and the more we are surrounded by it, the more we are aware of our own presence and participation.

① Travel: Tracing the Legacies of the Past
② Reflect on the Time That Surrounds You Now
③ Manifestation of a Hidden Life
④ Architecture of a Futuristic Life

04 밑줄 친 부분 중 어법상 옳지 않은 것은?

It would be difficult ① to imagine life without the beauty and richness of forests. But scientists warn we cannot take our forest for ② granted. By some estimates, deforestation ③ has been resulted in the loss of as much as eighty percent of the natural forests of the world. Currently, deforestation is a global problem, ④ affecting wilderness regions such as the temperate rainforests of the Pacific.

05 밑줄 친 부분의 의미와 가장 가까운 것은?

Robert J. Flaherty, a legendary documentary filmmaker, tried to show how indigenous people gathered food.

① native
② ravenous
③ impoverished
④ itinerant

06 밑줄 친 부분에 들어갈 말로 가장 적절한 것은?

Listening to music is _____ being a rock star. Anyone can listen to music, but it takes talent to become a musician.

① on a par with
② a far cry from
③ contingent upon
④ a prelude to

07 다음 글의 흐름상 가장 어색한 문장은?

Biologists have identified a gene that will allow rice plants to survive being submerged in water for up to two weeks—over a week longer than at present. Plants under water for longer than a week are deprived of oxygen and wither and perish. ① The scientists hope their discovery will prolong the harvests of crops in regions that are susceptible to flooding. ② Rice growers in these flood-prone areas of Asia lose an estimated one billion dollars annually to excessively waterlogged rice paddies. ③ They hope the new gene will lead to a hardier rice strain that will reduce the financial damage incurred in typhoon and monsoon seasons and lead to bumper harvests. ④ This is dreadful news for people in these vulnerable regions, who are victims of urbanization and have a shortage of crops. Rice yields must increase by 30 percent over the next 20 years to ensure a billion people can receive their staple diet.

08 밑줄 친 부분에 들어갈 말로 가장 적절한 것은?

A: Do you know how to drive?
B: Of course. I'm a great driver.
A: Could you teach me how to drive?
B: Do you have a learner's permit?
A: Yes, I got it just last week.
B: Have you been behind the steering wheel yet?
A: No, but I can't wait to _____.

① take a rain check
② get my feet wet
③ get an oil change
④ change a flat tire

09 다음 글의 내용과 일치하는 것은?

Sharks are covered in scales made from the same material as teeth. These flexible scales protect the shark and help it swim quickly in water. A shark can move the scales as it swims. This movement helps reduce the water's drag. Amy Lang, an aerospace engineer at the University of Alabama, studies the scales on the shortfin mako, a relative of the great white shark. Lang and her team discovered that the mako shark's scales differ in size and in flexibility in different parts of its body. For instance, the scales on the sides of the body are tapered—wide at one end and narrow at the other end. Because they are tapered, these scales move very easily. They can turn up or flatten to adjust to the flow of water around the shark and to reduce drag. Lang feels that shark scales can inspire designs for machines that experience drag, such as airplanes.

① A shark has scales that always remain immobile to protect itself as it swims.
② Lang revealed that the scales of a mako shark are utilized to lessen drag in water.
③ A mako shark has scales of identical size all over its body.
④ The scientific designs of airplanes were inspired by shark scales.

10 밑줄 친 부분 중 어법상 옳지 않은 것은?

Focus means ① getting stuff done. A lot of people have great ideas but don't act on them. For me, the definition of an entrepreneur, for instance, is someone who can combine innovation and ingenuity with the ability to execute that new idea. Some people think that the central dichotomy in life is whether you're positive or negative about the issues ② that interest or concern you. There's a lot of attention ③ paying to this question of whether it's better to have an optimistic or pessimistic lens. I think the better question to ask is whether you are going to do something about it or just ④ let life pass you by.

11 밑줄 친 부분 중 글의 흐름상 가장 어색한 것은?

Most people like to talk, but few people like to listen, yet listening well is a ① rare talent that everyone should treasure. Because they hear more, good listeners tend to know more and to be more sensitive to what is going on around them than most people. In addition, good listeners are inclined to accept or tolerate rather than to judge and criticize. Therefore, they have ② fewer enemies than most people. In fact, they are probably the most beloved of people. However, there are ③ exceptions to that generality. For example, John Steinbeck is said to have been an excellent listener, yet he was hated by some of the people he wrote about. No doubt his ability to listen contributed to his capacity to write. Nevertheless, the result of his listening didn't make him ④ unpopular.

12 다음 글의 주제로 가장 적절한 것은?

Worry is like a rocking horse. No matter how fast you go, you never move anywhere. Worry is a complete waste of time and creates so much clutter in your mind that you cannot think clearly about anything. The way to learn to stop worrying is by first understanding that you energize whatever you focus your attention on. Therefore, the more you allow yourself to worry, the more likely things are to go wrong! Worrying becomes such an ingrained habit that to avoid it you consciously have to train yourself to do otherwise. Whenever you catch yourself having a fit of worry, stop and change your thoughts. Focus your mind more productively on what you do want to happen and dwell on what's already wonderful in your life so more wonderful stuff will come your way.

① What effects does worry have on life?

② Where does worry originate from?

③ When should we worry?

④ How do we cope with worrying?

13 다음 글의 내용과 일치하지 <u>않는</u> 것은?

Students at Macaulay Honors College (MHC) don't stress about the high price of tuition. That's because theirs is free. At Macaulay and a handful of other service academies, work colleges, single-subject schools and conservatories, 100 percent of the student body receive a full tuition scholarship for all four years. Macaulay students also receive a laptop and $7,500 in "opportunities funds" to pursue research, service experiences, study abroad programs and internships. "The most important thing is not the free tuition, but the freedom of studying without the burden of debt on your back," says Ann Kirschner, university dean of Macaulay Honors College. The debt burden, she says, "really compromises decisions students make in college, and we are giving them the opportunity to be free of that." Schools that grant free tuition to all students are rare, but a greater number of institutions provide scholarships to enrollees with high grades. Institutions such as Indiana University Bloomington offer automatic awards to high-performing students with stellar GPAs and class ranks.

① MHC에서는 모든 학생이 4년간 수업료를 내지 않는다.
② MHC에서는 학생들에게 컴퓨터 구입 비용과 교외활동 비용을 합하여 $7,500를 지급한다.
③ 수업료로 인한 빚 부담이 있으면 학생들이 자유롭게 공부할 수 없다고 Kirschner 학장은 말한다.
④ MHC와 달리 학업 우수자에게만 장학금을 주는 대학도 있다.

[14~15] 밑줄 친 부분의 의미와 가장 가까운 것을 고르시오.

14

The police spent seven months working on the crime case but were never able to determine the identity of the <u>malefactor</u>.

① culprit
② dilettante
③ pariah
④ demagogue

15

While at first glance it seems that his friends are just leeches, they prove to be the ones he can depend on <u>through thick and thin</u>.

① in no time
② from time to time
③ in pleasant times
④ in good times and bad times

16 주어진 문장이 들어갈 위치로 가장 적절한 것은?

> Some remain intensely proud of their original accent and dialect words, phrases and gestures, while others accommodate rapidly to a new environment by changing their speech habits, so that they no longer "stand out in the crowd."

Our perceptions and production of speech change with time. (①) If we were to leave our native place for an extended period, our perception that the new accents around us were strange would only be temporary. (②) Gradually, we will lose the sense that others have an accent and we will begin to fit in—to accommodate our speech patterns to the new norm. (③) Not all people do this to the same degree. (④) Whether they do this consciously or not is open to debate and may differ from individual to individual, but like most processes that have to do with language, the change probably happens before we are aware of it and probably couldn't happen if we were.

17 다음 글의 내용과 일치하지 않는 것은?

Insomnia can be classified as transient, acute, or chronic. Transient insomnia lasts for less than a week. It can be caused by another disorder, by changes in the sleep environment, by the timing of sleep, severe depression, or by stress. Its consequences such as sleepiness and impaired psychomotor performance are similar to those of sleep deprivation. Acute insomnia is the inability to consistently sleep well for a period of less than a month. Acute insomnia is present when there is difficulty initiating or maintaining sleep or when the sleep that is obtained is not refreshing. These problems occur despite adequate opportunity and circumstances for sleep and they can impair daytime functioning. Acute insomnia is also known as short term insomnia or stress related insomnia. Chronic insomnia lasts for longer than a month. It can be caused by another disorder, or it can be a primary disorder. People with high levels of stress hormones or shifts in the levels of cytokines* are more likely than others to have chronic insomnia. Its effects can vary according to its causes. They might include muscular weariness, hallucinations, and/or mental fatigue. Chronic insomnia can also cause double vision.

*cytokines: groups of molecules released by certain cells of the immune system

① Insomnia can be classified according to its duration.

② Transient insomnia occurs solely due to an inadequate sleep environment.

③ Acute insomnia is generally known to be related to stress.

④ Chronic insomnia patients may suffer from hallucinations.

18 밑줄 친 부분에 들어갈 말로 가장 적절한 것은?

Kisha Padbhan, founder of Everonn Education, in Mumbai, looks at his business as nation-building. India's student-age population of 230 million (kindergarten to college) is one of the largest in the world. The government spends $83 billion on instruction, but there are serious gaps. "There aren't enough teachers and enough teacher-training institutes," says Kisha. "What children in remote parts of India lack is access to good teachers and exposure to good-quality content." Everonn's solution? The company uses a satellite network, with two-way video and audio _____. It reaches 1,800 colleges and 7,800 schools across 24 of India's 28 states. It offers everything from digitized school lessons to entrance exam prep for aspiring engineers and has training for job-seekers, too.

① to improve the quality of teacher training facilities

② to bridge the gap through virtual classrooms

③ to get students familiarized with digital technology

④ to locate qualified instructors across the nation

19 주어진 문장 다음에 이어질 글의 순서로 가장 적절한 것은?

A technique that enables an individual to gain some voluntary control over autonomic, or involuntary, body functions by observing electronic measurements of those functions is known as biofeedback.

(A) When such a variable moves in the desired direction (for example, blood pressure down), it triggers visual or audible displays—feedback on equipment such as television sets, gauges, or lights.

(B) Electronic sensors are attached to various parts of the body to measure such variables as heart rate, blood pressure, and skin temperature.

(C) Biofeedback training teaches one to produce a desired response by reproducing thought patterns or actions that triggered the displays.

① (A) - (B) - (C)   ② (B) - (C) - (A)

③ (B) - (A) - (C)   ④ (C) - (A) - (B)

20 우리말을 영어로 잘못 옮긴 것은?

① 그 연사는 자기 생각을 청중에게 전달하는 데 능숙하지 않았다.

   → The speaker was not good at getting his ideas across to the audience.

② 서울의 교통 체증은 세계 어느 도시보다 심각하다.

   → The traffic jams in Seoul are more serious than those in any other city in the world.

③ 네가 말하고 있는 사람과 시선을 마주치는 것은 서양 국가에서 중요하다.

   → Making eye contact with the person you are speaking to is important in western countries.

④ 그는 사람들이 생각했던 만큼 인색하지 않았다는 것이 드러났다.

   → It turns out that he was not so stingier as he was thought to be.

PART 2

지방직

꼭 읽어보세요!

2025년 영어 과목 출제기조 변화

　인사혁신처에서 출제하는 2025년 9급 공무원 시험부터는 문법(어법)이나 어휘 등 암기 영역의 문제가 줄어들고 이해력과 추론력을 평가하는 독해 문제의 비중이 커질 예정입니다. 또한, 실생활에서 많이 사용하는 어휘, 그리고 이메일이나 안내문 등으로 구성된 독해 지문이 많이 출제될 것으로 보입니다.

기출문제 학습 시 유의사항

　본서는 2025년 영어 과목 출제기조 변화에 따라 출제 유형에서 벗어나거나 달라지는 문항에 ×표시를 하였습니다. 이는 인사혁신처가 공개한 2025년 출제기조 전환 예시문제를 기준으로 한 것이며, 실제 출제 방향과 다를 수 있다는 점에 유의하시기 바랍니다. 또한, **인사혁신처에서 출제하는 국가직, 지방직 9급 기출문제에만** ×표시를 하였으니 이를 염두에 두고 학습에 임하시기 바랍니다.

　×표시를 한 문항은 출제되지 않는 영역이라는 의미가 아닌, 출제기조 변화에 따라 유형이 바뀔 수 있는 문항임을 표시한 것입니다. 어휘 영역은 문맥에 따라 밑줄에 들어갈 단어를 추론하는 유형으로 전환되며, 문법(어법) 영역은 밑줄이나 빈칸이 주어지고 문맥 속에서 묻는 부분이 무엇인지 명확하게 제시하는 방향으로 전환됩니다. 독해도 전자메일이나 안내문 등 업무현장에서 접할 수 있는 소재와 형식을 활용한 지문이 출제됩니다.

출제경향

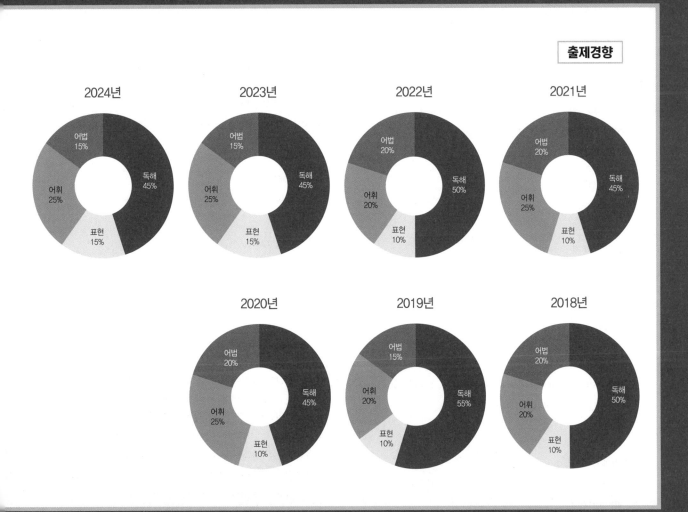

[01~04] 밑줄 친 부분의 의미와 가장 가까운 것을 고르시오.

01

While Shakespeare's comedies share many similarities, they also differ markedly from one another.

① softly
② obviously
③ marginally
④ indiscernibly

02

Jane poured out the strong, dark tea and diluted it with milk.

① washed
② weakened
③ connected
④ fermented

03

The Prime Minister is believed to have ruled out cuts in child benefit or pensions.

① excluded
② supported
③ submitted
④ authorized

04

If you let on that we are planning a surprise party, Dad will never stop asking you questions.

① reveal
② observe
③ believe
④ possess

05 밑줄 친 부분에 들어갈 말로 가장 적절한 것은?

Automatic doors in supermarkets _____ the entry and exit of customers with bags or shopping carts.

① ignore
② forgive
③ facilitate
④ exaggerate

06 밑줄 친 부분 중 어법상 옳지 않은 것은?

One of the many ① virtues of the book you are reading ② is that it provides an entry point into *Maps of Meaning*, ③ which is a highly complex work ④ because of the author was working out his approach to psychology as he wrote it.

07 밑줄 친 부분이 어법상 옳지 않은 것은?

① You must plan not to spend too much on the project.
② My dog disappeared last month and hasn't been seen since.
③ I'm sad that the people who daughter I look after are moving away.
④ I bought a book on my trip, and it was twice as expensive as it was at home.

08 우리말을 영어로 잘못 옮긴 것은?

① 그는 이곳에서 일하는 것이 흥미롭다는 것을 알았다.
→ He found it exciting to work here.
② 그녀는 나에게 일찍 떠날 것이라고 언급했다.
→ She mentioned me that she would be leaving early.
③ 나는 그가 오는 것을 원하지 않았다.
→ I didn't want him to come.
④ 좀 더 능숙하고 경험 많은 선생님이었다면 그를 달리 대했을 것이다.
→ A more skillful and experienced teacher would have treated him otherwise.

[09~11] 밑줄 친 부분에 들어갈 말로 가장 적절한 것을 고르시오.

09

A: Charles, I think we need more chairs for our upcoming event.
B: Really? I thought we already had enough chairs.
A: My manager told me that more than 350 people are coming.
B: _____
A: I agree. I am also a bit surprised.
B: Looks like I'll have to order more then. Thanks.

① I wonder if the manager is going to attend the event.
② I thought more than 350 people would be coming.
③ That's actually not a large number.
④ That's a lot more than I expected.

10

A: Can I get the document you referred to at the meeting yesterday?
B: Sure. What's the title of the document?
A: I can't remember its title, but it was about the community festival.
B: Oh, I know what you're talking about.
A: Great. Can you send it to me via email?
B: I don't have it with me. Mr. Park is in charge of the project, so he should have it.
A: _____
B: Good luck. Hope you get the document you want.

① Can you check if he is in the office?
② Mr. Park has sent the email to you again.
③ Are you coming to the community festival?
④ Thank you for letting me know. I'll contact him.

11

A: Hello, can I ask you a question about the presentation next Tuesday?

B: Do you mean the presentation about promoting the volunteer program?

A: Yes. Where is the presentation going to be?

B: Let me check. It is room 201.

A: I see. Can I use my laptop in the room?

B: Sure. We have a PC in the room, but you can use yours if you want.

A: _____

B: We can meet in the room two hours before the presentation. Would that work for you?

A: Yes. Thank you very much!

① A computer technician was here an hour ago.

② When can I have a rehearsal for my presentation?

③ Should we recruit more volunteers for our program?

④ I don't feel comfortable leaving my laptop in the room.

12 다음 이메일의 내용과 일치하지 않는 것은?

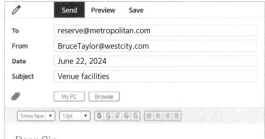

Dear Sir,

I am writing to ask for information about Metropolitan Conference Center.

We are looking for a venue for a three-day conference in September this year. We need to have enough room for over 200 delegates in your main conference room, and we would also like three small conference rooms for meetings. Each conference room needs wi-fi as well. We need to have coffee available mid-morning and mid-afternoon, and we would also like to book your restaurant for lunch on all three days.

In addition, could you please let me know if there are any local hotels with discount rates for Metropolitan clients or large groups? We will need accommodations for over 100 delegates each night.

I look forward to hearing from you.

Best regards,

Bruce Taylor, Event Manager

① 주 회의실은 200명 이상의 대표자를 수용할 수 있어야 한다.

② wi-fi가 있는 작은 회의실 3개가 필요하다.

③ 3일간의 저녁 식사를 위한 식당 예약이 필요하다.

④ 매일 밤 100명 이상의 대표자를 위한 숙박시설이 필요하다.

13 다음 글의 내용과 일치하지 않는 것은?

According to the historians, neckties date back to 1660. In that year, a group of soldiers from Croatia visited Paris. These soldiers were war heroes whom King Louis XIV admired very much. Impressed with the colored scarves that they wore around their necks, the king decided to honor the Croats by creating a military regiment called the Royal Cravattes. The word *cravat* comes from the word *Croat*. All the soldiers in this regiment wore colorful scarves or cravats around their necks. This new style of neckwear traveled to England. Soon all upper class men were wearing cravats. Some cravats were quite extreme. At times, they were so high that a man could not move his head without turning his whole body. The cravats were made of many different materials from plaid to lace, which made them suitable for any occasion.

① A group of Croatian soldiers visited Paris in 1660.

② The Royal Cravattes was created in honor of the Croatian soldiers wearing scarves.

③ Some cravats were too uncomfortable for a man to move his head freely.

④ The materials used to make the cravats were limited.

14 다음 글의 주제로 적절한 것은?

In recent years Latin America has made huge strides in exploiting its incredible wind, solar, geothermal and biofuel energy resources. Latin America's electricity sector has already begun to gradually decrease its dependence on oil. Latin America is expected to almost double its electricity output between 2015 and 2040. Practically none of Latin America's new large-scale power plants will be oil-fueled, which opens up the field for different technologies. Countries in Central America and the Caribbean, which traditionally imported oil, were the first to move away from oil-based power plants, after suffering a decade of high and volatile prices at the start of the century.

① booming oil industry in Latin America

② declining electricity business in Latin America

③ advancement of renewable energy in Latin America

④ aggressive exploitation of oil-based resources in Latin America

15 다음 글의 제목으로 적절한 것은?

Every organization has resources that it can use to perform its mission. How well your organization does its job is partly a function of how many of those resources you have, but mostly it is a function of how well you use the resources you have, such as people and money. You as the organization's leader can always make the use of those resources more efficient and effective, provided that you have control of the organization's personnel and agenda, a condition that does not occur automatically. By managing your people and your money carefully, by treating the most important things as the most important, by making good decisions, and by solving the problems that you encounter, you can get the most out of what you have available to you.

① Exchanging Resources in an Organization
② Leaders' Ability to Set up External Control
③ Making the Most of the Resources: A Leader's Way
④ Technical Capacity of an Organization: A Barrier to Its Success

16 다음 글의 흐름상 어색한 문장은?

Critical thinking sounds like an unemotional process but it can engage emotions and even passionate responses. In particular, we may not like evidence that contradicts our own opinions or beliefs. ① If the evidence points in a direction that is challenging, that can rouse unexpected feelings of anger, frustration or anxiety. ② The academic world traditionally likes to consider itself as logical and free of emotions, so if feelings do emerge, this can be especially difficult. ③ For example, looking at the same information from several points of view is not important. ④ Being able to manage your emotions under such circumstances is a useful skill. If you can remain calm, and present your reasons logically, you will be better able to argue your point of view in a convincing way.

17 주어진 글 다음에 이어질 글의 순서로 적절한 것은?

Computer assisted language learning(CALL) is both exciting and frustrating as a field of research and practice.

(A) Yet the technology changes so rapidly that CALL knowledge and skills must be constantly renewed to stay apace of the field.

(B) It is exciting because it is complex, dynamic and quickly changing—and it is frustrating for the same reasons.

(C) Technology adds dimensions to the domain of language learning, requiring new knowledge and skills for those who wish to apply it into their professional practice.

① (A) - (C) - (B)　　② (B) - (A) - (C)
③ (B) - (C) - (A)　　④ (C) - (B) - (A)

18 주어진 문장이 들어갈 위치로 적절한 것은?

> But she quickly popped her head out again.

The little mermaid swam right up to the small window of the cabin, and every time a wave lifted her up, she could see a crowd of well-dressed people through the clear glass. Among them was a young prince, the handsomest person there, with large dark eyes. (①) It was his birthday, and that's why there was so much excitement. (②) When the young prince came out on the deck, where the sailors were dancing, more than a hundred rockets went up into the sky and broke into a glitter, making the sky as bright as day. (③) The little mermaid was so startled that she dove down under the water. (④) And look! It was just as if all the stars up in heaven were falling down on her. Never had she seen such fireworks.

[19~20] 밑줄 친 부분에 들어갈 말로 적절한 것을 고르시오.

19

Javelin Research noticed that not all Millennials are currently in the same stage of life. While all Millennials were born around the turn of the century, some of them are still in early adulthood, wrestling with new careers and settling down. On the other hand, the older Millennials have a home and are building a family. You can imagine how having a child might change your interests and priorities, so for marketing purposes, it's useful to split this generation into Gen Y.1 and Gen Y.2. Not only are the two groups culturally different, but they're in vastly different phases of their financial life. The younger group is financial beginners, just starting to show their buying power. The latter group has a credit history, may have their first mortgage and is raising young children. The _____ in priorities and needs between Gen Y.1 and Gen Y.2 is vast.

① contrast
② reduction
③ repetition
④ ability

20

Cost pressures in liberalized markets have different effects on existing and future hydropower schemes. Because of the cost structure, existing hydropower plants will always be able to earn a profit. Because the planning and construction of future hydropower schemes is not a short-term process, it is not a popular investment, in spite of low electricity generation costs. Most private investors would prefer to finance _____, leading to the paradoxical situation that although an existing hydropower plant seems to be a cash cow, nobody wants to invest in a new one. Where public shareholders/owners (states, cities, municipalities) are involved, the situation looks very different because they can see the importance of the security of supply and also appreciate long-term investments.

① more short-term technologies
② all high technology industries
③ the promotion of the public interest
④ the enhancement of electricity supply

모바일 OMR

✅ 회독 CHECK 1 2 3

[01~04] 밑줄 친 부분의 의미와 가장 가까운 것을 고르시오.

01

Further explanations on our project will be given in subsequent presentations.

① required
② following
③ advanced
④ supplementary

02

Folkways are customs that members of a group are expected to follow to show courtesy to others. For example, saying "excuse me" when you sneeze is an American folkway.

① charity
② humility
③ boldness
④ politeness

03

These children have been brought up on a diet of healthy food.

① raised
② advised
③ observed
④ controlled

04

Slavery was not done away with until the nineteenth century in the U.S.

① abolished
② consented
③ criticized
④ justified

05 밑줄 친 부분에 들어갈 말로 가장 적절한 것은?

Voters demanded that there should be greater _____ in the election process so that they could see and understand it clearly.

① deception
② flexibility
③ competition
④ transparency

06 밑줄 친 부분 중 어법상 옳지 않은 것은?

One reason for upsets in sports—① in which the team ② predicted to win and supposedly superior to their opponents surprisingly loses the contest—is ③ what the superior team may not have perceived their opponents as ④ threatening to their continued success.

07 밑줄 친 부분이 어법상 옳지 않은 것은?

① I should have gone this morning, but I was feeling a bit ill.

② These days we do not save as much money as we used to.

③ The rescue squad was happy to discover an alive man.

④ The picture was looked at carefully by the art critic.

08 우리말을 영어로 잘못 옮긴 것은?

① 우리는 그의 연설에 감동하게 되었다.
→ We were made touching with his speech.

② 비용은 차치하고 그 계획은 훌륭한 것이었다.
→ Apart from its cost, the plan was a good one.

③ 그들은 뜨거운 차를 마시는 동안에 일몰을 보았다.
→ They watched the sunset while drinking hot tea.

④ 과거 경력 덕분에 그는 그 프로젝트에 적합하였다.
→ His past experience made him suited for the project.

[09~10] 밑줄 친 부분에 들어갈 말로 가장 적절한 것을 고르시오.

09

A: Pardon me, but could you give me a hand, please?

B: _____

A: I'm trying to find the Personnel Department. I have an appointment at 10.

B: It's on the third floor.

A: How can I get up there?

B: Take the elevator around the corner.

① We have no idea how to handle this situation.

② Would you mind telling us who is in charge?

③ Yes. I could use some help around here.

④ Sure. Can I help you with anything?

10

A: You were the last one who left the office, weren't you?

B: Yes. Is there any problem?

A: I found the office lights and air conditioners on this morning.

B: Really? Oh, no. Maybe I forgot to turn them off last night.

A: Probably they were on all night.

B: _____

① Don't worry. This machine is working fine.

② That's right. Everyone likes to work with you.

③ I'm sorry. I promise I'll be more careful from now on.

④ Too bad. You must be tired because you get off work too late.

11 두 사람의 대화 중 자연스럽지 않은 것은?

① A: How would you like your hair done?

B: I'm a little tired of my hair color. I'd like to dye it.

② A: What can we do to slow down global warming?

B: First of all, we can use more public transportation.

③ A: Anna, is that you? Long time no see! How long has it been?

B: It took me about an hour and a half by car.

④ A: I'm worried about Paul. He looks unhappy. What should I do?

B: If I were you, I'd wait until he talks about his troubles.

12 다음 글의 제목으로 가장 적절한 것은?

Well-known author Daniel Goleman has dedicated his life to the science of human relationships. In his book *Social Intelligence* he discusses results from neuro-sociology to explain how sociable our brains are. According to Goleman, we are drawn to other people's brains whenever we engage with another person. The human need for meaningful connectivity with others, in order to deepen our relationships, is what we all crave, and yet there are countless articles and studies suggesting that we are lonelier than we ever have been and loneliness is now a world health epidemic. Specifically, in Australia, according to a national Lifeline survey, more than 80% of those surveyed believe our society is becoming a lonelier place. Yet, our brains crave human interaction.

① Lonely People

② Sociable Brains

③ Need for Mental Health Survey

④ Dangers of Human Connectivity

13 다음 글의 주제로 가장 적절한 것은?

Certainly some people are born with advantages (e.g., physical size for jockeys, height for basketball players, an "ear" for music for musicians). Yet only dedication to mindful, deliberate practice over many years can turn those advantages into talents and those talents into successes. Through the same kind of dedicated practice, people who are not born with such advantages can develop talents that nature put a little farther from their reach. For example, even though you may feel that you weren't born with a talent for math, you can significantly increase your mathematical abilities through mindful, deliberate practice. Or, if you consider yourself "naturally" shy, putting in the time and effort to develop your social skills can enable you to interact with people at social occasions with energy, grace, and ease.

① advantages some people have over others

② importance of constant efforts to cultivate talents

③ difficulties shy people have in social interactions

④ need to understand one's own strengths and weaknesses

14 다음 글의 요지로 가장 적절한 것은?

Dr. Roossinck and her colleagues found by chance that a virus increased resistance to drought on a plant that is widely used in botanical experiments. Their further experiments with a related virus showed that was true of 15 other plant species, too. Dr. Roossinck is now doing experiments to study another type of virus that increases heat tolerance in a range of plants. She hopes to extend her research to have a deeper understanding of the advantages that different sorts of viruses give to their hosts. That would help to support a view which is held by an increasing number of biologists, that many creatures rely on symbiosis, rather than being self-sufficient.

① Viruses demonstrate self-sufficiency of biological beings.

② Biologists should do everything to keep plants virus-free.

③ The principle of symbiosis cannot be applied to infected plants.

④ Viruses sometimes do their hosts good, rather than harming them.

15 다음 글의 내용과 일치하지 않는 것은?

> The traditional way of making maple syrup is interesting. A sugar maple tree produces a watery sap each spring, when there is still lots of snow on the ground. To take the sap out of the sugar maple tree, a farmer makes a slit in the bark with a special knife, and puts a "tap" on the tree. Then the farmer hangs a bucket from the tap, and the sap drips into it. That sap is collected and boiled until a sweet syrup remains—forty gallons of sugar maple tree "water" make one gallon of syrup. That's a lot of buckets, a lot of steam, and a lot of work. Even so, most of maple syrup producers are family farmers who collect the buckets by hand and boil the sap into syrup themselves.

① 사탕단풍나무에서는 매년 봄에 수액이 생긴다.
② 사탕단풍나무의 수액을 얻기 위해 나무껍질에 틈새를 만든다.
③ 단풍나무시럽 1갤론을 만들려면 수액 40갤론이 필요하다.
④ 단풍나무시럽을 만들기 위해 기계로 수액 통을 수거한다.

16 다음 글의 흐름상 어색한 문장은?

> I once took a course in short-story writing and during that course a renowned editor of a leading magazine talked to our class. ① He said he could pick up any one of the dozens of stories that came to his desk every day and after reading a few paragraphs he could feel whether or not the author liked people. ② "If the author doesn't like people," he said, "people won't like his or her stories." ③ The editor kept stressing the importance of being interested in people during his talk on fiction writing. ④ Thurston, a great magician, said that every time he went on stage he said to himself, "I am grateful because I'm successful." At the end of the talk, he concluded, "Let me tell you again. You have to be interested in people if you want to be a successful writer of stories."

17 주어진 글 다음에 이어질 글의 순서로 가장 적절한 것은?

> Just a few years ago, every conversation about artificial intelligence (AI) seemed to end with an apocalyptic prediction.

> (A) More recently, however, things have begun to change. AI has gone from being a scary black box to something people can use for a variety of use cases.
>
> (B) In 2014, an expert in the field said that, with AI, we are summoning the demon, while a Nobel Prize winning physicist said that AI could spell the end of the human race.
>
> (C) This shift is because these technologies are finally being explored at scale in the industry, particularly for market opportunities.

① (A) - (B) - (C)

② (B) - (A) - (C)

③ (B) - (C) - (A)

④ (C) - (A) - (B)

18 주어진 문장이 들어갈 위치로 가장 적절한 것은?

> Yet, requests for such self-assessments are pervasive throughout one's career.

> The fiscal quarter just ended. Your boss comes by to ask you how well you performed in terms of sales this quarter. How do you describe your performance? As excellent? Good? Terrible? (①) Unlike when someone asks you about an objective performance metric (e.g., how many dollars in sales you brought in this quarter), how to subjectively describe your performance is often unclear. There is no right answer. (②) You are asked to subjectively describe your own performance in school applications, in job applications, in interviews, in performance reviews, in meetings—the list goes on. (③) How you describe your performance is what we call your level of self-promotion. (④) Since self-promotion is a pervasive part of work, people who do more self-promotion may have better chances of being hired, being promoted, and getting a raise or a bonus.

[19~20] 밑줄 친 부분에 들어갈 말로 가장 적절한 것을 고르시오.

19

We live in the age of anxiety. Because being anxious can be an uncomfortable and scary experience, we resort to conscious or unconscious strategies that help reduce anxiety in the moment—watching a movie or TV show, eating, video-game playing, and overworking. In addition, smartphones also provide a distraction any time of the day or night. Psychological research has shown that distractions serve as a common anxiety avoidance strategy. _____, however, these avoidance strategies make anxiety worse in the long run. Being anxious is like getting into quicksand-the more you fight it, the deeper you sink. Indeed, research strongly supports a well-known phrase that "What you resist, persists."

① Paradoxically

② Fortunately

③ Neutrally

④ Creatively

20

How many different ways do you get information? Some people might have six different kinds of communications to answer—text messages, voice mails, paper documents, regular mail, blog posts, messages on different online services. Each of these is a type of in-box, and each must be processed on a continuous basis. It's an endless process, but it doesn't have to be exhausting or stressful. Getting your information management down to a more manageable level and into a productive zone starts by _____. Every place you have to go to check your messages or to read your incoming information is an in-box, and the more you have, the harder it is to manage everything. Cut the number of in-boxes you have down to the smallest number possible for you still to function in the ways you need to.

① setting several goals at once

② immersing yourself in incoming information

③ minimizing the number of in-boxes you have

④ choosing information you are passionate about

영어 | 2022년 지방직 9급

✅ 회독 CHECK 1 2 3

[01~03] 밑줄 친 부분의 의미와 가장 가까운 것을 고르시오.

01

School teachers have to be <u>flexible</u> to cope with different ability levels of the students.

① strong   ② adaptable

③ honest   ④ passionate

02

Crop yields <u>vary</u>, improving in some areas and falling in others.

① change   ② decline

③ expand   ④ include

03

I don't feel inferior to anyone <u>with respect to</u> my education.

① in danger of   ② in spite of

③ in favor of   ④ in terms of

04 밑줄 친 부분에 들어갈 말로 가장 적절한 것은?

Sometimes we _____ money long before the next payday.

① turn into

② start over

③ put up with

④ run out of

[05~06] 어법상 옳지 않은 것을 고르시오.

05

① He asked me why I kept coming back day after day.

② Toys children wanted all year long has recently discarded.

③ She is someone who is always ready to lend a helping hand.

④ Insects are often attracted by scents that aren't obvious to us.

06

① You can write on both sides of the paper.

② My home offers me a feeling of security, warm, and love.

③ The number of car accidents is on the rise.

④ Had I realized what you were intending to do, I would have stopped you.

[07~08] 우리말을 영어로 잘못 옮긴 것을 고르시오.

07 ① 나는 단 한 푼의 돈도 낭비할 수 없다.
→ I can afford to waste even one cent.
② 그녀의 얼굴에서 미소가 곧 사라졌다.
→ The smile soon faded from her face.
③ 그녀는 사임하는 것 외에는 대안이 없었다.
→ She had no alternative but to resign.
④ 나는 5년 후에 내 사업을 시작할 작정이다.
→ I'm aiming to start my own business in five years.

08 ① 식사를 마치자마자 나는 다시 배고프기 시작했다.
→ No sooner I have finishing the meal than I started feeling hungry again.
② 그녀는 조만간 요금을 내야만 할 것이다.
→ She will have to pay the bill sooner or later.
③ 독서와 정신의 관계는 운동과 신체의 관계와 같다.
→ Reading is to the mind what exercise is to the body.
④ 그는 대학에서 의학을 공부했으나 결국 회계 회사에서 일하게 되었다.
→ He studied medicine at university but ended up working for an accounting firm.

09 두 사람의 대화 중 가장 어색한 것은?

① A: I like this newspaper because it's not opinionated.
B: That's why it has the largest circulation.
② A: Do you have a good reason for being all dressed up?
B: Yeah, I have an important job interview today.
③ A: I can hit the ball straight during the practice but not during the game.
B: That happens to me all the time, too.
④ A: Is there any particular subject you want to paint on canvas?
B: I didn't do good in history when I was in high school.

10 밑줄 친 부분에 들어갈 말로 가장 적절한 것은?

A: Hey! How did your geography test go?
B: Not bad, thanks. I'm just glad that it's over! How about you? How did your science exam go?
A: Oh, it went really well. _____.
I owe you a treat for that.
B: It's my pleasure. So, do you feel like preparing for the math exam scheduled for next week?
A: Sure. Let's study together.
B: It sounds good. See you later.

① There's no sense in beating yourself up over this
② I never thought I would see you here
③ Actually, we were very disappointed
④ I can't thank you enough for helping me with it

11 주어진 글 다음에 이어질 글의 순서로 가장 적절한 것은?

For people who are blind, everyday tasks such as sorting through the mail or doing a load of laundry present a challenge.

(A) That's the thinking behind Aira, a new service that enables its thousands of users to stream live video of their surroundings to an on-demand agent, using either a smartphone or Aira's proprietary glasses.

(B) But what if they could "borrow" the eyes of someone who could see?

(C) The Aira agents, who are available 24/7, can then answer questions, describe objects or guide users through a location.

① (A) - (B) - (C)
② (A) - (C) - (B)
③ (B) - (A) - (C)
④ (C) - (A) - (B)

12 주어진 문장이 들어갈 위치로 가장 적절한 곳은?

The comparison of the heart to a pump, however, is a genuine analogy.

An analogy is a figure of speech in which two things are asserted to be alike in many respects that are quite fundamental. Their structure, the relationships of their parts, or the essential purposes they serve are similar, although the two things are also greatly dissimilar. Roses and carnations are not analogous. (①) They both have stems and leaves and may both be red in color. (②) But they exhibit these qualities in the same way; they are of the same genus. (③) These are disparate things, but they share important qualities: mechanical apparatus, possession of valves, ability to increase and decrease pressures, and capacity to move fluids. (④) And the heart and the pump exhibit these qualities in different ways and in different contexts.

13 다음 글의 제목으로 가장 적절한 것은?

One of the areas where efficiency can be optimized is the work force, through increasing individual productivity—defined as the amount of work (products produced, customers served) an employee handles in a given time. In addition to making sure you have invested in the right equipment, environment, and training to ensure optimal performance, you can increase productivity by encouraging staffers to put an end to a modern-day energy drain: multitasking. Studies show it takes 25 to 40 percent longer to get a job done when you're simultaneously trying to work on other projects. To be more productive, says Andrew Deutscher, vice president of business development at consulting firm The Energy Project, "do one thing, uninterrupted, for a sustained period of time."

① How to Create More Options in Life
② How to Enhance Daily Physical Performance
③ Multitasking is the Answer for Better Efficiency
④ Do One Thing at a Time for Greater Efficiency

14 글의 흐름상 가장 어색한 문장은?

The skill to have a good argument is critical in life. But it's one that few parents teach to their children. ① We want to give kids a stable home, so we stop siblings from quarreling and we have our own arguments behind closed doors. ② Yet if kids never get exposed to disagreement, we may eventually limit their creativity. ③ Children are most creative when they are free to brainstorm with lots of praise and encouragement in a peaceful environment. ④ It turns out that highly creative people often grow up in families full of tension. They are not surrounded by fistfights or personal insults, but real disagreements. When adults in their early 30s were asked to write imaginative stories, the most creative ones came from those whose parents had the most conflict a quarter-century earlier.

[15~16] 다음 글의 내용과 일치하지 않는 것을 고르시오.

15

Christopher Nolan is an Irish writer of some renown in the English language. Brain damaged since birth, Nolan has had little control over the muscles of his body, even to the extent of having difficulty in swallowing food. He must be strapped to his wheelchair because he cannot sit up by himself. Nolan cannot utter recognizable speech sounds. Fortunately, though, his brain damage was such that Nolan's intelligence was undamaged and his hearing was normal; as a result, he learned to understand speech as a young child. It was only many years later, though, after he had reached 10 years, and after he had learned to read, that he was given a means to express his first words. He did this by using a stick which was attached to his head to point to letters. It was in this 'unicorn' manner, letter-by-letter, that he produced an entire book of poems and short stories, *Dam-Burst of Dreams*, while still a teenager.

① Christopher Nolan은 뇌 손상을 갖고 태어났다.
② Christopher Nolan은 음식을 삼키는 것도 어려웠다.
③ Christopher Nolan은 청각 장애로 인해 들을 수 없었다.
④ Christopher Nolan은 10대일 때 책을 썼다.

16

In many Catholic countries, children are often named after saints; in fact, some priests will not allow parents to name their children after soap opera stars or football players. Protestant countries tend to be more free about this; however, in Norway, certain names such as Adolf are banned completely. In countries where infant mortality is very high, such as in Africa, tribes only name their children when they reach five years old, the age in which their chances of survival begin to increase. Until that time, they are referred to by the number of years they are. Many nations in the Far East give their children a unique name which in some way describes the circumstances of the child's birth or the parents' expectations and hopes for the child. Some Australian aborigines can keep changing their name throughout their life as the result of some important experience which has in some way proved their wisdom, creativity or determination. For example, if one day, one of them dances extremely well, he or she may decide to re-name him/herself 'supreme dancer' or 'light feet'.

① Children are frequently named after saints in many Catholic countries.
② Some African children are not named until they turn five years old.
③ Changing one's name is totally unacceptable in the culture of Australian aborigines.
④ Various cultures name their children in different ways.

17 다음 글의 요지로 가장 적절한 것은?

In one study, done in the early 1970s when young people tended to dress in either "hippie" or "straight" fashion, experimenters donned hippie or straight attire and asked college students on campus for a dime to make a phone call. When the experimenter was dressed in the same way as the student, the request was granted in more than two-thirds of the instances; when the student and requester were dissimilarly dressed, the dime was provided less than half the time. Another experiment showed how automatic our positive response to similar others can be. Marchers in an antiwar demonstration were found to be more likely to sign the petition of a similarly dressed requester and to do so without bothering to read it first.

① People are more likely to help those who dress like themselves.

② Dressing up formally increases the chance of signing the petition.

③ Making a phone call is an efficient way to socialize with other students.

④ Some college students in the early 1970s were admired for their unique fashion.

18 (A)와 (B)에 들어갈 말로 가장 적절한 것은?

Duration shares an inverse relationship with frequency. If you see a friend frequently, then the duration of the encounter will be shorter. Conversely, if you don't see your friend very often, the duration of your visit will typically increase significantly.   (A) , if you see a friend every day, the duration of your visits can be low because you can keep up with what's going on as events unfold. If, however, you only see your friend twice a year, the duration of your visits will be greater. Think back to a time when you had dinner in a restaurant with a friend you hadn't seen for a long period of time. You probably spent several hours catching up on each other's lives. The duration of the same dinner would be considerably shorter if you saw the person on a regular basis.   (B) , in romantic relationships the frequency and duration are very high because couples, especially newly minted ones, want to spend as much time with each other as possible. The intensity of the relationship will also be very high.

	(A)	(B)
①	For example	Conversely
②	Nonetheless	Furthermore
③	Therefore	As a result
④	In the same way	Thus

[19~20] 밑줄 친 부분에 들어갈 말로 가장 적절한 것을 고르시오.

19

One of the most frequently used propaganda techniques is to convince the public that the propagandist's views reflect those of the common person and that he or she is working in their best interests. A politician speaking to a blue-collar audience may roll up his sleeves, undo his tie, and attempt to use the specific idioms of the crowd. He may even use language incorrectly on purpose to give the impression that he is "just one of the folks." This technique usually also employs the use of glittering generalities to give the impression that the politician's views are the same as those of the crowd being addressed. Labor leaders, businesspeople, ministers, educators, and advertisers have used this technique to win our confidence by appearing to be ＿＿＿＿＿ ＿＿＿＿＿.

① beyond glittering generalities

② just plain folks like ourselves

③ something different from others

④ better educated than the crowd

20

As a roller coaster climbs the first lift hill of its track, it is building potential energy—the higher it gets above the earth, the stronger the pull of gravity will be. When the coaster crests the lift hill and begins its descent, its potential energy becomes kinetic energy, or the energy of movement. A common misperception is that a coaster loses energy along the track. An important law of physics, however, called the law of conservation of energy, is that energy can never be created nor destroyed. It simply changes from one form to another. Whenever a track rises back uphill, the cars' momentum—their kinetic energy—will carry them upward, which builds potential energy, and roller coasters repeatedly convert potential energy to kinetic energy and back again. At the end of a ride, coaster cars are slowed down by brake mechanisms that create ＿＿＿＿＿ between two surfaces. This motion makes them hot, meaning kinetic energy is changed to heat energy during braking. Riders may mistakenly think coasters lose energy at the end of the track, but the energy just changes to and from different forms.

① gravity

② friction

③ vacuum

④ acceleration

01 밑줄 친 부분의 의미와 가장 가까운 것은?

> For many compulsive buyers, the act of purchasing, rather than what they buy, is what leads to gratification.

① liveliness

② confidence

③ tranquility

④ satisfaction

[02~04] 밑줄 친 부분에 들어갈 말로 가장 적절한 것을 고르시오.

02

> Globalization leads more countries to open their markets, allowing them to trade goods and services freely at a lower cost with greater _____ .

① extinction

② depression

③ efficiency

④ caution

03

> We're familiar with the costs of burnout: Energy, motivation, productivity, engagement, and commitment can all take a hit, at work and at home. And many of the _____ are fairly intuitive: Regularly unplug. Reduce unnecessary meetings. Exercise. Schedule small breaks during the day. Take vacations even if you think you can't afford to be away from work, because you can't afford not to be away now and then.

① fixes

② damages

③ prizes

④ complications

04

> The government is seeking ways to soothe salaried workers over their increased tax burdens arising from a new tax settlement system. During his meeting with the presidential aides last Monday, the President _____ those present to open up more communication channels with the public.

① fell on

② called for

③ picked up

④ turned down

05 밑줄 친 부분의 의미와 가장 가까운 것은?

> In studying Chinese calligraphy, one must learn something of the origins of Chinese language and of how they were originally written. However, except for those brought up in the artistic traditions of the country, its aesthetic significance seems to be very difficult to apprehend.

① encompass
② intrude
③ inspect
④ grasp

[06~07] 우리말을 영어로 잘못 옮긴 것을 고르시오.

06 ① 그의 소설들은 읽기가 어렵다.
  → His novels are hard to read.
② 학생들을 설득하려고 해 봐야 소용없다.
  → It is no use trying to persuade the students.
③ 나의 집은 5년마다 페인트칠 된다.
  → My house is painted every five years.
④ 내가 출근할 때 한 가족이 위층에 이사 오는 것을 보았다.
  → As I went out for work, I saw a family moved in upstairs.

07 ① 경찰 당국은 자신의 이웃을 공격했기 때문에 그 여성을 체포하도록 했다.
  → The police authorities had the woman arrested for attacking her neighbor.
② 네가 내는 소음 때문에 내 집중력을 잃게 하지 말아라.
  → Don't let me distracted by the noise you make.
③ 가능한 한 빨리 제가 결과를 알도록 해 주세요.
  → Please let me know the result as soon as possible.
④ 그는 학생들에게 모르는 사람들에게 전화를 걸어 성금을 기부할 것을 부탁하도록 시켰다.
  → He had the students phone strangers and ask them to donate money.

08 어법상 옳은 것은?

① My sweet-natured daughter suddenly became unpredictably.
② She attempted a new method, and needless to say had different results.
③ Upon arrived, he took full advantage of the new environment.
④ He felt enough comfortable to tell me about something he wanted to do.

09 다음 글의 제목으로 가장 적절한 것은?

The definition of 'turn' casts the digital turn as an analytical strategy which enables us to focus on the role of digitalization within social reality. As an analytical perspective, the digital turn makes it possible to analyze and discuss the societal meaning of digitalization. The term 'digital turn' thus signifies an analytical approach which centers on the role of digitalization within a society. If the linguistic turn is defined by the epistemological* assumption that reality is constructed through language, the digital turn is based on the assumption that social reality is increasingly defined by digitalization. Social media symbolize the digitalization of social relations. Individuals increasingly engage in identity management on social networking sites(SNS). SNS are polydirectional, meaning that users can connect to each other and share information.

*epistemological: 인식론의

① Remaking Identities on SNS
② Linguistic Turn Versus Digital Turn
③ How to Share Information in the Digital Age
④ Digitalization Within the Context of Social Reality

10 주어진 글 다음에 이어질 글의 순서로 가장 적절한 것은?

Growing concern about global climate change has motivated activists to organize not only campaigns against fossil fuel extraction consumption, but also campaigns to support renewable energy.

(A) This solar cooperative produces enough energy to power 1,400 homes, making it the first large-scale solar farm cooperative in the country and, in the words of its members, a visible reminder that solar power represents "a new era of sustainable and 'democratic' energy supply that enables ordinary people to produce clean power, not only on their rooftops, but also at utility scale."

(B) Similarly, renewable energy enthusiasts from the United States have founded the Clean Energy Collective, a company that has pioneered "the model of delivering clean power-generation through medium-scale facilities that are collectively owned by participating utility customers."

(C) Environmental activists frustrated with the UK government's inability to rapidly accelerate the growth of renewable energy industries have formed the Westmill Wind Farm Co-operative, a community-owned organization with more than 2,000 members who own an onshore wind farm estimated to produce as much electricity in a year as that used by 2,500 homes. The Westmill Wind Farm Co-operative has inspired local citizens to form the Westmill Solar Co-operative.

① (C) - (A) - (B)
② (A) - (C) - (B)
③ (B) - (C) - (A)
④ (C) - (B) - (A)

11 밑줄 친 부분에 들어갈 말로 가장 적절한 것은?

> A: Did you have a nice weekend?
> B: Yes, it was pretty good. We went to the movies.
> A: Oh! What did you see?
> B: *Interstellar*. It was really good.
> A: Really? _____
> B: The special effects. They were fantastic. I wouldn't mind seeing it again.

① What did you like the most about it?
② What's your favorite movie genre?
③ Was the film promoted internationally?
④ Was the movie very costly?

12 두 사람의 대화 중 가장 어색한 것은?

① A: I'm so nervous about this speech that I must give today.
　 B: The most important thing is to stay cool.

② A: You know what? Minsu and Yujin are tying the knot!
　 B: Good for them! When are they getting married?

③ A: A two-month vacation just passed like one week. A new semester is around the corner.
　 B: That's the word. Vacation has dragged on for weeks.

④ A: How do you say 'water' in French?
　 B: It is right on the tip of my tongue, but I can't remember it.

13 다음 글의 내용과 일치하지 않는 것은?

> Women are experts at gossiping, and they always talk about trivial things, or at least that's what men have always thought. However, some new research suggests that when women talk to women, their conversations are far from frivolous, and cover many more topics (up to 40 subjects) than when men talk to other men. Women's conversations range from health to their houses, from politics to fashion, from movies to family, from education to relationship problems, but sports are notably absent. Men tend to have a more limited range of subjects, the most popular being work, sports, jokes, cars, and women. According to Professor Petra Boynton, a psychologist who interviewed over 1,000 women, women also tend to move quickly from one subject to another in conversation, while men usually stick to one subject for longer periods of time. At work, this difference can be an advantage for men, as they can put other matters aside and concentrate fully on the topic being discussed. On the other hand, it also means that they sometimes find it hard to concentrate when several things have to be discussed at the same time in a meeting.

① 남성들은 여성들의 대화 주제가 항상 사소한 것들이라고 생각해 왔다.
② 여성들의 대화 주제는 건강에서 스포츠에 이르기까지 매우 다양하다.
③ 여성들은 대화하는 중에 주제의 변환을 빨리한다.
④ 남성들은 회의 중 여러 주제가 논의될 때 집중하기 어렵다.

14 다음 글의 흐름상 적절하지 않은 문장은?

There was no divide between science, philosophy, and magic in the 15th century. All three came under the general heading of 'natural philosophy'. ① Central to the development of natural philosophy was the recovery of classical authors, most importantly the work of Aristotle. ② Humanists quickly realized the power of the printing press for spreading their knowledge. ③ At the beginning of the 15th century Aristotle remained the basis for all scholastic speculation on philosophy and science. ④ Kept alive in the Arabic translations and commentaries of Averroes and Avicenna, Aristotle provided a systematic perspective on mankind's relationship with the natural world. Surviving texts like his *Physics*, *Metaphysics*, and *Meteorology* provided scholars with the logical tools to understand the forces that created the natural world.

15 어법상 옳지 않은 것은?

① Fire following an earthquake is of special interest to the insurance industry.

② Word processors were considered to be the ultimate tool for a typist in the past.

③ Elements of income in a cash forecast will be vary according to the company's circumstances.

④ The world's first digital camera was created by Steve Sasson at Eastman Kodak in 1975.

[16~17] 밑줄 친 부분에 들어갈 말로 가장 적절한 것을 고르시오.

16

The slowing of China's economy from historically high rates of growth has long been expected to _____ growth elsewhere. "The China that had been growing at 10 percent for 30 years was a powerful source of fuel for much of what drove the global economy forward", said Stephen Roach at Yale. The growth rate has slowed to an official figure of around 7 percent. "That's a concrete deceleration", Mr. Roach added.

① speed up
② weigh on
③ lead to
④ result in

17

As more and more leaders work remotely or with teams scattered around the nation or the globe, as well as with consultants and freelancers, you'll have to give them more _____. The more trust you bestow, the more others trust you. I am convinced that there is a direct correlation between job satisfaction and how empowered people are to fully execute their job without someone shadowing them every step of the way. Giving away responsibility to those you trust can not only make your organization run more smoothly but also free up more of your time so you can focus on larger issues.

① work
② rewards
③ restrictions
④ autonomy

18 다음 글의 요지로 가장 적절한 것은?

"In Judaism, we're largely defined by our actions," says Lisa Grushcow, the senior rabbi at Temple Emanu-El-Beth Sholom in Montreal. "You can't really be an armchair do-gooder." This concept relates to the Jewish notion of tikkun olam, which translates as "to repair the world." Our job as human beings, she says, "is to mend what's been broken. It's incumbent on us to not only take care of ourselves and each other but also to build a better world around us." This philosophy conceptualizes goodness as something based in service. Instead of asking "Am I a good person?" you may want to ask "What good do I do in the world?" Grushcow's temple puts these beliefs into action inside and outside their community. For instance, they sponsored two refugee families from Vietnam to come to Canada in the 1970s.

① We should work to heal the world.

② Community should function as a shelter.

③ We should conceptualize goodness as beliefs.

④ Temples should contribute to the community.

19 (A)와 (B)에 들어갈 말로 가장 적절한 것은?

Ancient philosophers and spiritual teachers understood the need to balance the positive with the negative, optimism with pessimism, a striving for success and security with an openness to failure and uncertainty. The Stoics recommended "the premeditation of evils," or deliberately visualizing the worst-case scenario. This tends to reduce anxiety about the future: when you soberly picture how badly things could go in reality, you usually conclude that you could cope.   (A)   , they noted, imagining that you might lose the relationships and possessions you currently enjoy increases your gratitude for having them now. Positive thinking,   (B)   , always leans into the future, ignoring present pleasures.

	(A)	(B)
①	Nevertheless	in addition
②	Furthermore	for example
③	Besides	by contrast
④	However	in conclusion

20 주어진 문장이 들어갈 위치로 가장 적절한 것은?

> And working offers more than financial security.

> Why do workaholics enjoy their jobs so much? Mostly because working offers some important advantages. (①) It provides people with paychecks—a way to earn a living. (②) It provides people with self-confidence; they have a feeling of satisfaction when they've produced a challenging piece of work and are able to say, "I made that". (③) Psychologists claim that work also gives people an identity; they work so that they can get a sense of self and individualism. (④) In addition, most jobs provide people with a socially acceptable way to meet others. It could be said that working is a positive addiction; maybe workaholics are compulsive about their work, but their addiction seems to be a safe—even an advantageous—one.

✅ 회독 CHECK 1 2 3

01 밑줄 친 부분에 들어갈 말로 가장 적절한 것은?

> The issue with plastic bottles is that they're not _____, so when the temperatures begin to rise, your water will also heat up.

① sanitary

② insulated

③ recyclable

④ waterproof

[02~04] 밑줄 친 부분의 의미와 가장 가까운 것을 고르시오.

02

> Strategies that a writer adopts during the writing process may alleviate the difficulty of attentional overload.

① complement

② accelerate

③ calculate

④ relieve

03

> The cruel sights touched off thoughts that otherwise wouldn't have entered her mind.

① looked after

② gave rise to

③ made up for

④ kept in contact with

04

> The school bully did not know what it was like to be shunned by the other students in the class.

① avoided

② warned

③ punished

④ imitated

05 어법상 옳은 것은?

① Of the billions of stars in the galaxy, how much are able to hatch life?

② The Christmas party was really excited and I totally lost track of time.

③ I must leave right now because I am starting work at noon today.

④ They used to loving books much more when they were younger.

06 밑줄 친 부분의 의미와 가장 가까운 것은?

> After Francesca made a case for staying at home during the summer holidays, an uncomfortable silence fell on the dinner table. Robert was not sure if it was the right time for him to tell her about his grandiose plan.

① objected to

② dreamed about

③ completely excluded

④ strongly suggested

07 밑줄 친 부분 중 어법상 옳지 않은 것은?

> Elizabeth Taylor had an eye for beautiful jewels and over the years amassed some amazing pieces, once ① declaring "a girl can always have more diamonds." In 2011, her finest jewels were sold by Christie's at an evening auction ② that brought in $115.9 million. Among her most prized possessions sold during the evening sale ③ were a 1961 bejeweled timepiece by Bulgari. Designed as a serpent to coil around the wrist, with its head and tail ④ covered with diamonds and having two hypnotic emerald eyes, a discreet mechanism opens its fierce jaws to reveal a tiny quartz watch.

08 우리말을 영어로 잘못 옮긴 것은?

① 보증이 만료되어서 수리는 무료가 아니었다.

→ Since the warranty had expired, the repairs were not free of charge.

② 설문지를 완성하는 누구에게나 선물카드가 주어질 예정이다.

→ A gift card will be given to whomever completes the questionnaire.

③ 지난달 내가 휴가를 요청했더라면 지금 하와이에 있을 텐데.

→ If I had asked for a vacation last month, I would be in Hawaii now.

④ 그의 아버지가 갑자기 작년에 돌아가셨고, 설상가상으로 그의 어머니도 병에 걸리셨다.

→ His father suddenly passed away last year, and, what was worse, his mother became sick.

09 밑줄 친 (A), (B)에 들어갈 말로 가장 적절한 것은?

Assertive behavior involves standing up for your rights and expressing your thoughts and feelings in a direct, appropriate way that does not violate the rights of others. It is a matter of getting the other person to understand your viewpoint. People who exhibit assertive behavior skills are able to handle conflict situations with ease and assurance while maintaining good interpersonal relations. ___(A)___, aggressive behavior involves expressing your thoughts and feelings and defending your rights in a way that openly violates the rights of others. Those exhibiting aggressive behavior seem to believe that the rights of others must be subservient to theirs. ___(B)___, they have a difficult time maintaining good interpersonal relations. They are likely to interrupt, talk fast, ignore others, and use sarcasm or other forms of verbal abuse to maintain control.

	(A)	(B)
①	In contrast	Thus
②	Similarly	Moreover
③	However	On one hand
④	Accordingly	On the other hand

10 다음 글의 주제로 가장 적절한 것은?

The e-book applications available on tablet computers employ touchscreen technology. Some touchscreens feature a glass panel covering two electronically-charged metallic surfaces lying face-to-face. When the screen is touched, the two metallic surfaces feel the pressure and make contact. This pressure sends an electrical signal to the computer, which translates the touch into a command. This version of the touchscreen is known as a resistive screen because the screen reacts to pressure from the finger. Other tablet computers feature a single electrified metallic layer under the glass panel. When the user touches the screen, some of the current passes through the glass into the user's finger. When the charge is transferred, the computer interprets the loss in power as a command and carries out the function the user desires. This type of screen is known as a capacitive screen.

① how users learn new technology
② how e-books work on tablet computers
③ how touchscreen technology works
④ how touchscreens have evolved

11 밑줄 친 부분에 들어갈 말로 가장 적절한 것은?

> A: Oh, another one! So many junk emails!
>
> B: I know. I receive more than ten junk emails a day.
>
> A: Can we stop them from coming in?
>
> B: I don't think it's possible to block them completely.
>
> A: _____?
>
> B: Well, you can set up a filter on the settings.
>
> A: A filter?
>
> B: Yeah. The filter can weed out some of the spam emails.

① Do you write emails often

② Isn't there anything we can do

③ How did you make this great filter

④ Can you help me set up an email account

12 우리말을 영어로 잘못 옮긴 것은?

① 나는 네 열쇠를 잃어버렸다고 네게 말한 것을 후회한다.

    → I regret to tell you that I lost your key.

② 그 병원에서의 그의 경험은 그녀의 경험보다 더 나빴다.

    → His experience at the hospital was worse than hers.

③ 그것은 내게 지난 24년의 기억을 상기시켜준다.

    → It reminds me of the memories of the past 24 years.

④ 나는 대화할 때 내 눈을 보는 사람들을 좋아한다.

    → I like people who look me in the eye when I have a conversation.

13 두 사람의 대화 중 가장 자연스러운 것은?

① A: Do you know what time it is?

   B: Sorry, I'm busy these days.

② A: Hey, where are you headed?

   B: We are off to the grocery store.

③ A: Can you give me a hand with this?

   B: OK. I'll clap for you.

④ A: Has anybody seen my purse?

   B: Long time no see.

14 다음 글의 제목으로 가장 적절한 것은?

> Louis XIV needed a palace worthy of his greatness, so he decided to build a huge new house at Versailles, where a tiny hunting lodge stood. After almost fifty years of labor, this tiny hunting lodge had been transformed into an enormous palace, a quarter of a mile long. Canals were dug to bring water from the river and to drain the marshland. Versailles was full of elaborate rooms like the famous Hall of Mirrors, where seventeen huge mirrors stood across from seventeen large windows, and the Salon of Apollo, where a solid silver throne stood. Hundreds of statues of Greek gods such as Apollo, Jupiter, and Neptune stood in the gardens; each god had Louis's face!

① True Face of Greek Gods

② The Hall of Mirrors vs. the Salon of Apollo

③ Did the Canal Bring More Than Just Water to Versailles?

④ Versailles: From a Humble Lodge to a Great Palace

15 글의 흐름상 가장 어색한 문장은?

Philosophers have not been as concerned with anthropology as anthropologists have with philosophy. ① Few influential contemporary philosophers take anthropological studies into account in their work. ② Those who specialize in philosophy of social science may consider or analyze examples from anthropological research, but do this mostly to illustrate conceptual points or epistemological distinctions or to criticize epistemological or ethical implications. ③ In fact, the great philosophers of our time often drew inspiration from other fields such as anthropology and psychology. ④ Philosophy students seldom study or show serious interest in anthropology. They may learn about experimental methods in science, but rarely about anthropological fieldwork.

16 밑줄 친 부분에 들어갈 말로 가장 적절한 것은?

All of us inherit something: in some cases, it may be money, property or some object—a family heirloom such as a grandmother's wedding dress or a father's set of tools. But beyond that, all of us inherit something else, something _____, something we may not even be fully aware of. It may be a way of doing a daily task, or the way we solve a particular problem or decide a moral issue for ourselves. It may be a special way of keeping a holiday or a tradition to have a picnic on a certain date. It may be something important or central to our thinking, or something minor that we have long accepted quite casually.

① quite unrelated to our everyday life
② against our moral standards
③ much less concrete and tangible
④ of great monetary value

17 다음 글의 요지로 가장 적절한 것은?

Evolutionarily, any species that hopes to stay alive has to manage its resources carefully. That means that first call on food and other goodies goes to the breeders and warriors and hunters and planters and builders and, certainly, the children, with not much left over for the seniors, who may be seen as consuming more than they're contributing. But even before modern medicine extended life expectancies, ordinary families were including grandparents and even great-grandparents. That's because what old folk consume materially, they give back behaviorally—providing a leveling, reasoning center to the tumult that often swirls around them.

① Seniors have been making contributions to the family.
② Modern medicine has brought focus to the role of old folk.
③ Allocating resources well in a family determines its prosperity.
④ The extended family comes at a cost of limited resources.

18 주어진 글 다음에 이어질 글의 순서로 가장 적절한 것은?

Nowadays the clock dominates our lives so much that it is hard to imagine life without it. Before industrialization, most societies used the sun or the moon to tell the time.

(A) For the growing network of railroads, the fact that there were no time standards was a disaster. Often, stations just some miles apart set their clocks at different times. There was a lot of confusion for travelers.

(B) When mechanical clocks first appeared, they were immediately popular. It was fashionable to have a clock or a watch. People invented the expression "of the clock" or "o'clock" to refer to this new way to tell the time.

(C) These clocks were decorative, but not always useful. This was because towns, provinces, and even neighboring villages had different ways to tell the time. Travelers had to reset their clocks repeatedly when they moved from one place to another. In the United States, there were about 70 different time zones in the 1860s.

① (A) - (B) - (C)

② (B) - (A) - (C)

③ (B) - (C) - (A)

④ (C) - (A) - (B)

19 주어진 문장이 들어갈 위치로 가장 적절한 것은?

But there is also clear evidence that millennials, born between 1981 and 1996, are saving more aggressively for retirement than Generation X did at the same ages, 22~37.

Millennials are often labeled the poorest, most financially burdened generation in modern times. Many of them graduated from college into one of the worst labor markets the United States has ever seen, with a staggering load of student debt to boot. (①) Not surprisingly, millennials have accumulated less wealth than Generation X did at a similar stage in life, primarily because fewer of them own homes. (②) But newly available data providing the most detailed picture to date about what Americans of different generations save complicates that assessment. (③) Yes, Gen Xers, those born between 1965 and 1980, have a higher net worth. (④) And that might put them in better financial shape than many assume.

20 다음 글의 내용과 일치하지 않는 것은?

> Carbonate sands, which accumulate over thousands of years from the breakdown of coral and other reef organisms, are the building material for the frameworks of coral reefs. But these sands are sensitive to the chemical make-up of sea water. As oceans absorb carbon dioxide, they acidify—and at a certain point, carbonate sands simply start to dissolve. The world's oceans have absorbed around one-third of human-emitted carbon dioxide. The rate at which the sands dissolve was strongly related to the acidity of the overlying seawater, and was ten times more sensitive than coral growth to ocean acidification. In other words, ocean acidification will impact the dissolution of coral reef sands more than the growth of corals. This probably reflects the corals' ability to modify their environment and partially adjust to ocean acidification, whereas the dissolution of sands is a geochemical process that cannot adapt.

① The frameworks of coral reefs are made of carbonate sands.

② Corals are capable of partially adjusting to ocean acidification.

③ Human-emitted carbon dioxide has contributed to the world's ocean acidification.

④ Ocean acidification affects the growth of corals more than the dissolution of coral reef sands.

[01~02] 밑줄 친 부분의 의미와 가장 가까운 것을 고르시오.

01

> I came to see these documents as relics of a sensibility now dead and buried, which needed to be excavated.

① exhumed

② packed

③ erased

④ celebrated

02

> Riding a roller coaster can be a joy ride of emotions: the nervous anticipation as you're strapped into your seat, the questioning and regret that comes as you go up, up, up, and the sheer adrenaline rush as the car takes that first dive.

① utter

② scary

③ occasional

④ manageable

03 두 사람의 대화 중 가장 어색한 것은?

① A: What time are we having lunch?

　B: It'll be ready before noon.

② A: I called you several times. Why didn't you answer?

　B: Oh, I think my cell phone was turned off.

③ A: Are you going to take a vacation this winter?

　B: I might. I haven't decided yet.

④ A: Hello. Sorry I missed your call.

　B: Would you like to leave a message?

04 밑줄 친 부분에 들어갈 말로 가장 적절한 것은?

> A: Hello. I need to exchange some money.
>
> B: Okay. What currency do you need?
>
> A: I need to convert dollars into pounds. What's the exchange rate?
>
> B: The exchange rate is 0.73 pounds for every dollar.
>
> A: Fine. Do you take a commission?
>
> B: Yes, we take a small commission of 4 dollars.
>
> A: ＿＿＿＿＿＿＿＿＿＿＿＿＿＿?
>
> B: We convert your currency back for free. Just bring your receipt with you.

① How much does this cost

② How should I pay for that

③ What's your buy-back policy

④ Do you take credit cards

05 밑줄 친 부분 중 어법상 옳지 않은 것은?

> Each year, more than 270,000 pedestrians ① lose their lives on the world's roads. Many leave their homes as they would on any given day never ② to return. Globally, pedestrians constitute 22% of all road traffic fatalities, and in some countries this proportion is ③ as high as two thirds of all road traffic deaths. Millions of pedestrians are non-fatally ④ injuring—some of whom are left with permanent disabilities. These incidents cause much suffering and grief as well as economic hardship.

06 어법상 옳은 것은?

① The paper charged her with use the company's money for her own purposes.

② The investigation had to be handled with the utmost care lest suspicion be aroused.

③ Another way to speed up the process would be made the shift to a new system.

④ Burning fossil fuels is one of the lead cause of climate change.

07 주어진 글 다음에 이어질 글의 순서로 가장 적절한 것은?

> There is a thought that can haunt us: since everything probably affects everything else, how can we ever make sense of the social world? If we are weighed down by that worry, though, we won't ever make progress.

> (A) Every discipline that I am familiar with draws caricatures of the world in order to make sense of it. The modern economist does this by building *models*, which are deliberately stripped down representations of the phenomena out there.
>
> (B) The economist John Maynard Keynes described our subject thus: "Economics is a science of thinking in terms of models joined to the art of choosing models which are relevant to the contemporary world."
>
> (C) When I say "stripped down," I really mean stripped down. It isn't uncommon among us economists to focus on one or two causal factors, exclude everything else, hoping that this will enable us to understand how just those aspects of reality work and interact.

① (A) - (B) - (C)

② (A) - (C) - (B)

③ (B) - (C) - (A)

④ (B) - (A) - (C)

08 다음 글의 내용과 일치하는 것은?

Prehistoric societies some half a million years ago did not distinguish sharply between mental and physical disorders. Abnormal behaviors, from simple headaches to convulsive* attacks, were attributed to evil spirits that inhabited or controlled the afflicted person's body. According to historians, these ancient peoples attributed many forms of illness to demonic possession, sorcery, or the behest* of an offended ancestral spirit. Within this system of belief, called *demonology*, the victim was usually held at least partly responsible for the misfortune. It has been suggested that Stone Age cave dwellers may have treated behavior disorders with a surgical method called *trephining*, in which part of the skull was chipped away to provide an opening through which the evil spirit could escape. People may have believed that when the evil spirit left, the person would return to his or her normal state. Surprisingly, trephined skulls have been found to have healed over, indicating that some patients survived this extremely crude operation.

*convulsive: 경련의
*behest: 명령

① Mental disorders were clearly differentiated from physical disorders.
② Abnormal behaviors were believed to result from evil spirits affecting a person.
③ An opening was made in the skull for an evil spirit to enter a person's body.
④ No cave dwellers survived trephining.

09 다음 글의 주제로 가장 적절한 것은?

As the digital revolution upends newsrooms across the country, here's my advice for all the reporters. I've been a reporter for more than 25 years, so I have lived through a half dozen technological life cycles. The most dramatic transformations have come in the last half dozen years. That means I am, with increasing frequency, making stuff up as I go along. Much of the time in the news business, we have no idea what we are doing. We show up in the morning and someone says, "Can you write a story about (pick one) tax policy/immigration/climate change?" When newspapers had once-a-day deadlines, we said a reporter would learn in the morning and teach at night—write a story that could inform tomorrow's readers on a topic the reporter knew nothing about 24 hours earlier. Now it is more like learning at the top of the hour and teaching at the bottom of the same hour. I'm also running a political podcast, for example, and during the presidential conventions, we should be able to use it to do real-time interviews anywhere. I am just increasingly working without a script.

① a reporter as a teacher
② a reporter and improvisation
③ technology in politics
④ fields of journalism and technology

10 글의 흐름상 가장 어색한 문장은?

Children's playgrounds throughout history were the wilderness, fields, streams, and hills of the country and the roads, streets, and vacant places of villages, towns, and cities. ① The term *playground* refers to all those places where children gather to play their free, spontaneous games. ② Only during the past few decades have children vacated these natural playgrounds for their growing love affair with video games, texting, and social networking. ③ Even in rural America few children are still roaming in a free-ranging manner, unaccompanied by adults. ④ When out of school, they are commonly found in neighborhoods digging in sand, building forts, playing traditional games, climbing, or playing ball games. They are rapidly disappearing from the natural terrain of creeks, hills, and fields, and like their urban counterparts, are turning to their indoor, sedentary cyber toys for entertainment.

[11~12] 밑줄 친 부분의 의미와 가장 가까운 것을 고르시오.

11

Time does seem to slow to a trickle during a boring afternoon lecture and race when the brain is engrossed in something highly entertaining.

① enhanced by
② apathetic to
③ stabilized by
④ preoccupied with

12

These daily updates were designed to help readers keep abreast of the markets as the government attempted to keep them under control.

① be acquainted with
② get inspired by
③ have faith in
④ keep away from

[13~14] 밑줄 친 (A), (B)에 들어갈 말로 가장 적절한 것을 고르시오.

13

In the 1840s, the island of Ireland suffered famine. Because Ireland could not produce enough food to feed its population, about a million people died of ___(A)___ ; they simply didn't have enough to eat to stay alive. The famine caused another 1.25 million people to ___(B)___ ; many left their island home for the United States; the rest went to Canada, Australia, Chile, and other countries. Before the famine, the population of Ireland was approximately 6 million. After the great food shortage, it was about 4 million.

	(A)	(B)
①	dehydration	be deported
②	trauma	immigrate
③	starvation	emigrate
④	fatigue	be detained

14

Today the technology to create the visual component of virtual-reality (VR) experiences is well on its way to becoming widely accessible and affordable. But to work powerfully, virtual reality needs to be about more than visuals. ___(A)___ what you are hearing convincingly matches the visuals, the virtual experience breaks apart. Take a basketball game. If the players, the coaches, the announcers, and the crowd all sound like they're sitting midcourt, you may as well watch the game on television—you'll get just as much of a sense that you are "there." ___(B)___, today's audio equipment and our widely used recording and reproduction formats are simply inadequate to the task of re-creating convincingly the sound of a battlefield on a distant planet, a basketball game at courtside, or a symphony as heard from the first row of a great concert hall.

	(A)	(B)
①	If	By contrast
②	Unless	Consequently
③	If	Similarly
④	Unless	Unfortunately

15 주어진 문장이 들어갈 위치로 가장 적절한 것은?

The same thinking can be applied to any number of goals, like improving performance at work.

The happy brain tends to focus on the short term. (①) That being the case, it's a good idea to consider what short-term goals we can accomplish that will eventually lead to accomplishing long-term goals. (②) For instance, if you want to lose thirty pounds in six months, what short-term goals can you associate with losing the smaller increments of weight that will get you there? (③) Maybe it's something as simple as rewarding yourself each week that you lose two pounds. (④) By breaking the overall goal into smaller, shorter-term parts, we can focus on incremental accomplishments instead of being overwhelmed by the enormity of the goal in our profession.

16 우리말을 영어로 잘못 옮긴 것은?

① 혹시 내게 전화하고 싶은 경우에 이게 내 번호야.
　→ This is my number just in case you would like to call me.
② 나는 유럽 여행을 준비하느라 바쁘다.
　→ I am busy preparing for a trip to Europe.
③ 그녀는 남편과 결혼한 지 20년 이상 되었다.
　→ She has married to her husband for more than two decades.
④ 나는 내 아들이 읽을 책을 한 권 사야 한다.
　→ I should buy a book for my son to read.

[17~18] 다음 글의 내용과 일치하지 않는 것을 고르시오.

17

In the nineteenth century, the most respected health and medical experts all insisted that diseases were caused by "miasma," a fancy term for bad air. Western society's system of health was based on this assumption: to prevent diseases, windows were kept open or closed, depending on whether there was more miasma inside or outside the room; it was believed that doctors could not pass along disease because gentlemen did not inhabit quarters with bad air. Then the idea of germs came along. One day, everyone believed that bad air makes you sick. Then, almost overnight, people started realizing there were invisible things called microbes and bacteria that were the real cause of diseases. This new view of disease brought sweeping changes to medicine, as surgeons adopted antiseptics and scientists invented vaccines and antibiotics. But, just as momentously, the idea of germs gave ordinary people the power to influence their own lives. Now, if you wanted to stay healthy, you could wash your hands, boil your water, cook your food thoroughly, and clean cuts and scrapes with iodine.

① In the nineteenth century, opening windows was irrelevant to the density of miasma.

② In the nineteenth century, it was believed that gentlemen did not live in places with bad air.

③ Vaccines were invented after people realized that microbes and bacteria were the real cause of diseases.

④ Cleaning cuts and scrapes could help people to stay healthy.

18

Followers are a critical part of the leadership equation, but their role has not always been appreciated. For a long time, in fact, "the common view of leadership was that leaders actively led and subordinates, later called followers, passively and obediently followed." Over time, especially in the last century, social change shaped people's views of followers, and leadership theories gradually recognized the active and important role that followers play in the leadership process. Today it seems natural to accept the important role followers play. One aspect of leadership is particularly worth noting in this regard: Leadership is a social influence process shared among all members of a group. Leadership is not restricted to the influence exerted by someone in a particular position or role; followers are part of the leadership process, too.

① For a length of time, it was understood that leaders actively led and followers passively followed.

② People's views of subordinates were influenced by social change.

③ The important role of followers is still denied today.

④ Both leaders and followers participate in the leadership process.

[19~20] 밑줄 친 부분에 들어갈 말로 가장 적절한 것을 고르시오.

19

Language proper is itself double-layered. Single noises are only occasionally meaningful: mostly, the various speech sounds convey coherent messages only when combined into an overlapping chain, like different colors of ice-cream melting into one another. In birdsong also, _____: the sequence is what matters. In both humans and birds, control of this specialized sound-system is exercised by one half of the brain, normally the left half, and the system is learned relatively early in life. And just as many human languages have dialects, so do some bird species: in California, the white-crowned sparrow has songs so different from area to area that Californians can supposedly tell where they are in the state by listening to these sparrows.

① individual notes are often of little value
② rhythmic sounds are important
③ dialects play a critical role
④ no sound-system exists

20

Nobel Prize-winning psychologist Daniel Kahneman changed the way the world thinks about economics, upending the notion that human beings are rational decision-makers. Along the way, his discipline-crossing influence has altered the way physicians make medical decisions and investors evaluate risk on Wall Street. In a paper, Kahneman and his colleagues outline a process for making big strategic decisions. Their suggested approach, labeled as "Mediating Assessments Protocol," or MAP, has a simple goal: To put off gut-based decision-making until a choice can be informed by a number of separate factors. "One of the essential purposes of MAP is basically to _____ intuition," Kahneman said in a recent interview with *The Post*. The structured process calls for analyzing a decision based on six to seven previously chosen attributes, discussing each of them separately and assigning them a relative percentile score, and finally, using those scores to make a holistic judgment.

① improve
② delay
③ possess
④ facilitate

영어 | 2018년 지방직 9급

모바일 OMR

✔ 회독 CHECK 1 2 3

[01~02] 밑줄 친 부분의 의미와 가장 가까운 것을 고르시오.

01

> The paramount duty of the physician is to do no harm. Everything else—even healing—must take second place.

① chief
② sworn
③ successful
④ mysterious

02

> It is not unusual that people get cold feet about taking a trip to the North Pole.

① become ambitious
② become afraid
③ feel exhausted
④ feel saddened

03 밑줄 친 부분 중 어법상 옳지 않은 것은?

> I am writing in response to your request for a reference for Mrs. Ferrer. She has worked as my secretary ① for the last three years and has been an excellent employee. I believe that she meets all the requirements ② mentioned in your job description and indeed exceeds them in many ways. I have never had reason ③ to doubt her complete integrity. I would, therefore, recommend Mrs. Ferrer for the post ④ what you advertise.

04 우리말을 영어로 잘못 옮긴 것은?

① 모든 정보는 거짓이었다.
   → All of the information was false.
② 토마스는 더 일찍 사과했어야 했다.
   → Thomas should have apologized earlier.
③ 우리가 도착했을 때 영화는 이미 시작했었다.
   → The movie had already started when we arrived.
④ 바깥 날씨가 추웠기 때문에 나는 차를 마시려 물을 끓였다.
   → Being cold outside, I boiled some water to have tea.

05 밑줄 친 부분의 의미와 가장 가까운 것은?

> The student who finds the state-of-the-art approach intimidating learns less than he or she might have learned by the old methods.

① humorous
② friendly
③ convenient
④ frightening

06 밑줄 친 부분에 들어갈 말로 가장 적절한 것은?

> Since the air-conditioners are being repaired now, the office workers have to _____ electric fans for the day.

① get rid of
② let go of
③ make do with
④ break up with

07 어법상 옳은 것은?

① Please contact to me at the email address I gave you last week.
② Were it not for water, all living creatures on earth would be extinct.
③ The laptop allows people who is away from their offices to continue to work.
④ The more they attempted to explain their mistakes, the worst their story sounded.

08 우리말을 영어로 옳게 옮긴 것은?

① 그는 며칠 전에 친구를 배웅하기 위해 역으로 갔다.
→ He went to the station a few days ago to see off his friend.
② 버릇없는 그 소년은 아버지가 부르는 것을 못 들은 체했다.
→ The spoiled boy made it believe he didn't hear his father calling.
③ 나는 버팔로에 가본 적이 없어서 그곳에 가기를 고대하고 있다.
→ I have never been to Buffalo, so I am looking forward to go there.
④ 나는 아직 오늘 신문을 못 읽었어. 뭐 재미있는 것 있니?
→ I have not read today's newspaper yet. Is there anything interested in it?

09 다음 글의 흐름상 가장 어색한 문장은?

> The Renaissance kitchen had a definite hierarchy of help who worked together to produce the elaborate banquets. ① At the top, as we have seen, was the *scalco*, or steward, who was in charge of not only the kitchen, but also the dining room. ② The dining room was supervised by the butler, who was in charge of the silverware and linen and also served the dishes that began and ended the banquet—the cold dishes, salads, cheeses, and fruit at the beginning and the sweets and confections at the end of the meal. ③ This elaborate decoration and serving was what in restaurants is called "the front of the house." ④ The kitchen was supervised by the head cook, who directed the undercooks, pastry cooks, and kitchen help.

10 다음 글의 요지로 가장 적절한 것은?

My students often believe that if they simply meet more important people, their work will improve. But it's remarkably hard to engage with those people unless you've already put something valuable out into the world. That's what piques the curiosity of advisers and sponsors. Achievements show you have something to give, not just something to take. In life, it certainly helps to know the right people. But how hard they go to bat for you, how far they stick their necks out for you, depends on what you have to offer. Building a powerful network doesn't require you to be an expert at networking. It just requires you to be an expert at something. If you make great connections, they might advance your career. If you do great work, those connections will be easier to make. Let your insights and your outputs—not your business cards—do the talking.

① Sponsorship is necessary for a successful career.
② Building a good network starts from your accomplishments.
③ A powerful network is a prerequisite for your achievement.
④ Your insights and outputs grow as you become an expert at networking.

11 밑줄 친 부분에 들어갈 말로 가장 적절한 것은?

A: My computer just shut down for no reason. I can't even turn it back on again.
B: Did you try charging it? It might just be out of battery.
A: Of course, I tried charging it.
B: _____
A: I should do that, but I'm so lazy.

① I don't know how to fix your computer.
② Try visiting the nearest service center then.
③ Well, stop thinking about your problems and go to sleep.
④ My brother will try to fix your computer because he's a technician.

12 다음 글에 나타난 화자의 심경으로 가장 적절한 것은?

My face turned white as a sheet. I looked at my watch. The tests would be almost over by now. I arrived at the testing center in an absolute panic. I tried to tell my story, but my sentences and descriptive gestures got so confused that I communicated nothing more than a very convincing version of a human tornado. In an effort to curb my distracting explanation, the proctor led me to an empty seat and put a test booklet in front of me. He looked doubtfully from me to the clock, and then he walked away. I tried desperately to make up for lost time, scrambling madly through analogies and sentence completions. "Fifteen minutes remain," the voice of doom declared from the front of the classroom. Algebraic equations, arithmetic calculations, geometric diagrams swam before my eyes. "Time! Pencils down, please."

① nervous and worried
② excited and cheerful
③ calm and determined
④ safe and relaxed

13 주어진 문장 다음에 이어질 글의 순서로 가장 적절한 것은?

> Devices that monitor and track your health are becoming more popular among all age populations.

> (A) For example, falls are a leading cause of death for adults 65 and older. Fall alerts are a popular gerotechnology* that has been around for many years but have now improved.
>
> (B) However, for seniors aging in place, especially those without a caretaker in the home, these technologies can be lifesaving.
>
> (C) This simple technology can automatically alert 911 or a close family member the moment a senior has fallen.
>
> *gerotechnology: 노인을 위한 양로 기술

① (B) - (C) - (A)
② (B) - (A) - (C)
③ (C) - (A) - (B)
④ (C) - (B) - (A)

[14~15] 밑줄 친 부분에 들어갈 말로 가장 적절한 것을 고르시오.

14

> A: Where do you want to go for our honeymoon?
> B: Let's go to a place that neither of us has been to.
> A: Then, why don't we go to Hawaii?
> B: _____

① I've always wanted to go there.
② Isn't Korea a great place to live?
③ Great! My last trip there was amazing!
④ Oh, you must've been to Hawaii already.

15

> The secret of successful people is usually that they are able to concentrate totally on one thing. Even if they have a lot in their head, they have found a method that the many commitments don't impede each other, but instead they are brought into a good inner order. And this order is quite simple: _____. In theory, it seems to be quite clear, but in everyday life it seems rather different. You might have tried to decide on priorities, but you have failed because of everyday trivial matters and all the unforeseen distractions. Separate off disturbances, for example, by escaping into another office, and not allowing any distractions to get in the way. When you concentrate on the one task of your priorities, you will find you have energy that you didn't even know you had.

① the sooner, the better
② better late than never
③ out of sight, out of mind
④ the most important thing first

16 다음 글의 제목으로 가장 적절한 것은?

With the help of the scientist, the commercial fishing industry has found out that its fishing must be done scientifically if it is to be continued. With no fishing pressure on a fish population, the number of fish will reach a predictable level of abundance and stay there. The only fluctuation would be due to natural environmental factors, such as availability of food, proper temperature, and the like. If a fishery is developed to take these fish, their population can be maintained if the fishing harvest is small. The mackerel of the North Sea is a good example. If we increase the fishery and take more fish each year, we must be careful not to reduce the population below the ideal point where it can replace all of the fish we take out each year. If we fish at this level, called the *maximum sustainable yield*, we can maintain the greatest possible yield, year after year. If we catch too many, the number of fish will decrease each year until we fish ourselves out of a job. Examples of severely overfished animals are the blue whale of the Antarctic and the halibut of the North Atlantic. Fishing just the correct amount to maintain a maximum annual yield is both a science and an art. Research is constantly being done to help us better understand the fish population and how to utilize it to the maximum without depleting the population.

① Say No to Commercial Fishing

② Sea Farming Seen As a Fishy Business

③ Why Does the Fishing Industry Need Science?

④ Overfished Animals: Cases of Illegal Fishing

17 밑줄 친 (A), (B)에 들어갈 말로 가장 적절한 것은?

Does terrorism ever work? 9/11 was an enormous tactical success for al Qaeda, partly because it involved attacks that took place in the media capital of the world and the actual capital of the United States, ___(A)___ ensuring the widest possible coverage of the event. If terrorism is a form of theater where you want a lot of people watching, no event in human history was likely ever seen by a larger global audience than the 9/11 attacks. At the time, there was much discussion about how 9/11 was like the attack on Pearl Harbor. They were indeed similar since they were both surprise attacks that drew America into significant wars. But they were also similar in another sense. Pearl Harbor was a great *tactical* success for Imperial Japan, but it led to a great *strategic* failure: Within four years of Pearl Harbor the Japanese empire lay in ruins, utterly defeated. ___(B)___, 9/11 was a great tactical success for al Qaeda, but it also turned out to be a great strategic failure for Osama bin Laden.

	(A)	(B)
①	thereby	Similarly
②	while	Therefore
③	while	Fortunately
④	thereby	On the contrary

18 다음 글의 내용과 일치하지 않는 것은?

We entered a new phase as a species when Chinese scientists altered a human embryo to remove a potentially fatal blood disorder—not only from the baby, but all of its descendants. Researchers call this process "germline modification." The media likes the phrase "designer babies." But we should call it what it is, "eugenics*." And we, the human race, need to decide whether or not we want to use it. Last month, in the United States, the scientific establishment weighed in. A National Academy of Sciences and National Academy of Medicine joint committee endorsed embryo editing aimed at genes that cause serious diseases when there is "no reasonable alternative." But it was more wary of editing for "enhancement," like making already-healthy children stronger or taller. It recommended a public discussion, and said that doctors should "not proceed at this time." The committee had good reason to urge caution. The history of eugenics is full of oppression and misery.

*eugenics: 우생학

① Doctors were recommended to immediately go ahead with embryo editing for enhancement.
② Recently, the scientific establishment in the U.S. joined a discussion on eugenics.
③ Chinese scientists modified a human embryo to prevent a serious blood disorder.
④ "Designer babies" is another term for the germline modification process.

19 주어진 문장이 들어갈 위치로 가장 적절한 것은?

If neither surrendered, the two exchanged blows until one was knocked out.

The ancient Olympics provided athletes an opportunity to prove their fitness and superiority, just like our modern games. (①) The ancient Olympic events were designed to eliminate the weak and glorify the strong. Winners were pushed to the brink. (②) Just as in modern times, people loved extreme sports. One of the favorite events was added in the 33rd Olympiad. This was the pankration, or an extreme mix of wrestling and boxing. The Greek word *pankration* means "total power." The men wore leather straps with metal studs, which could make a terrible mess of their opponents. (③) This dangerous form of wrestling had no time or weight limits. In this event, only two rules applied. First, wrestlers were not allowed to gouge eyes with their thumbs. Secondly, they could not bite. Anything else was considered fair play. The contest was decided in the same manner as a boxing match. Contenders continued until one of the two collapsed. (④) Only the strongest and most determined athletes attempted this event. Imagine wrestling "Mr. Fingertips," who earned his nickname by breaking his opponents' fingers!

20 밑줄 친 부분에 들어갈 말로 가장 적절한 것은?

In our time it is not only the law of the market which has its own life and rules over man, but also the development of science and technique. For a number of reasons, the problems and organization of science today are such that a scientist does not choose his problems; the problems force themselves upon the scientist. He solves one problem, and the result is not that he is more secure or certain, but that ten other new problems open up in place of the single solved one. They force him to solve them; he has to go ahead at an ever-quickening pace. The same holds true for industrial techniques. The pace of science forces the pace of technique. Theoretical physics forces atomic energy on us; the successful production of the fission bomb forces upon us the manufacture of the hydrogen bomb. We do not choose our problems, we do not choose our products; we are pushed, we are forced—by what? By a system which has no purpose and goal transcending it, and which _____.

① makes man its appendix

② creates a false sense of security

③ inspires man with creative challenges

④ empowers scientists to control the market laws

PART 3

서울시

출제경향

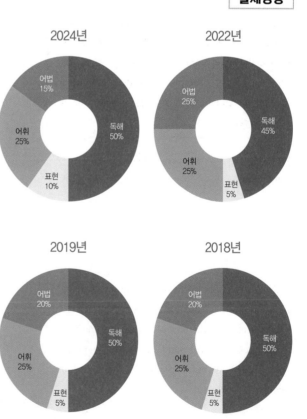

2024년

2022년

2019년

2018년

[01~03] 밑줄 친 부분의 의미와 가장 가까운 것은?

01

After receiving an attractive job offer from a renowned company, she finally chose to spurn it in order to pursue her dream of starting her own business.

① contemplate   ② postpone
③ decline   ④ denounce

02

Ever since the Red Sox traded Babe Ruth to the Yankees in 1918, Boston sports fans have learned to take the good with the bad. They have seen more basketball championships than any other city but haven't boasted a World Series title in over 75 years.

① waived   ② yielded
③ renounced   ④ bragged

03

Nell has a singular talent for getting into trouble; the other morning, she managed to break her leg, insult a woman at the post office, drop some eggs at the grocery store, paint her bedroom green, and cut down the big maple tree in the next-door neighbor's front yard.

① conventional   ② exceptional
③ martial   ④ plural

[04~05] 밑줄 친 부분에 들어갈 말로 가장 적절한 것은?

04

Instead of giving us an innovative idea on the matter in hand, the keynote speaker brought up a(n) _____ which was lengthy and made us feel tedium for quite a while.

① brainstorming   ② witticism
③ epigraph   ④ platitude

05

It has rained so little in California for the last six years that forest rangers need to be especially _____ in watching for forest fires.

① vigilant   ② relaxed
③ indifferent   ④ distracted

[06~07] 밑줄 친 부분에 들어갈 말로 가장 적절한 것은?

06

A: Sorry to keep you waiting, Ms. Krauss.

B: Well, I see that you've got a lot on your plate today. I won't keep you any longer.

A: Don't worry, Ms. Krauss. We'll get your order done on time.

B: Should I give you a call?

A: _____

① Well, you're a good customer. Let me see what I can do.

② No need for that. Come at 11:00 and I'll have your documents ready.

③ Tomorrow morning? No sweat. Can you get the documents to me before noon?

④ I'm afraid that might be difficult. I've got a lot of orders to complete this morning.

07

A: Did you see Emily's new haircut?

B: Yes, she chopped it all off _____!

A: I was so surprised. It's so different form before.

B: She said she needed a change.

A: Well, it definitely suits her.

B: Agreed, she looks fantastic!

① over the moon

② out of the blue

③ up in the air

④ under the weather

08 밑줄 친 부분 중 어법상 가장 옳은 것은?

① Despite the inconsistent and fairly sparse laboratory data regarding groupthink, the theory has been believed to have explanatory potential. ② Some of this continued confidence undoubtedly stems in part from a series of creative historical analysis that have been advanced to substantiate the model's various hypotheses. ③ Surely, we must be careful of such historical analysis for several reasons, as we cannot be certain that contradictory examples have not overlook. ④ Such case studies, however, do have the virtue of looking at cases which the antecedent conditions were strong enough to create the conditions deemed necessary by the model.

[09~10] 밑줄 친 부분 중 어법상 가장 옳지 않은 것은?

09

Research shows that tea drinkers can ① enjoy greater protection from heart disease, cancer, and stress, ② no matter how type of brew they choose. Experts say the antioxidants in tea leaves confer major health benefits. ③ That's why we admire how some creative cooks went beyond the cup to ④ find tasty ways to meld tea with their appetizers, meals, and desserts.

10

The rise of the modernist novel and poetry ① were accompanied between 1910 and 1930 by the rise of literary criticism ② as we know it. This is a kind of literary criticism ③ very different from the one that had existed in the nineteenth century, ④ not only in attitude but in vocation too, as criticism became increasingly academic and technical.

11 〈보기〉의 문장 다음에 이어질 글의 순서로 가장 적절한 것은?

─── 〈보 기〉 ───

During the first few times you choose to celebrate the achievements of members of the group, you may want to explain your thinking behind the small ceremony. By simply stating your intention to thank members of the group for their courage of hard work, people become aware of the meaning of the celebration and are less apt to dismiss it.

(A) It is quite possible as you begin this process that the member of the group being honored will feel self-conscious and awkward.

(B) Coupled with the fact that the event being celebrated is based on authentic achievement, it is likely that the members of the group will feel encouraged to participate in future celebrations.

(C) This is a natural response, especially in groups that do not know each other well or in organizations in which celebration is not a part of the culture.

① (B) - (A) - (C)   ② (B) - (C) - (A)

③ (C) - (A) - (B)   ④ (C) - (B) - (A)

12 글의 내용과 가장 일치하지 않는 것은?

The work of human body's immune system is carried out by the body's trillions of immune cells and specialized molecules. The first line of defense lies in the physical barriers of the skin and mucous membranes*, which block and trap invaders. A second, the innate system, is composed of cells including phagocytes*, whose basic job is to eat the invaders. In addition to these immune cells, many chemical compounds respond to infection and injury, move in to destroy pathogens*, and begin repairing tissue. The body's third line of defense is a final, more specific response. Its elite fighting units are trained on the job; that is, they are created in response to a pathogen that the body has not seen before. Once activated in one part of the body, the adaptive system functions throughout, and it memorizes the antigens* (a substance that provokes an immune system response). The next time they come along, the body hits back quicker and harder.

*mucous membranes: 점막

*phagocytes: 포식세포

*pathogens: 병원체

*antigens: 항원

① 면역체계의 첫 번째 방어선은 피부와 점막의 물리적 장벽에 있다.

② 면역체계의 두 번째 방어선의 기본 역할은 침입자를 소멸시키는 것이다.

③ 면역체계의 세 번째 방어선은 몸에 이전부터 지니고 있던 병원체에 반응한다.

④ 몸의 적응 시스템은 항원을 기억하여 차후 이 항원에 대해 더 빠르고 강하게 반격한다.

[13~14] 〈보기〉의 문장이 들어갈 위치로 가장 적절한 것은?

13

〈보 기〉

International management is applied by managers of enterprises that attain their goals and objectives across unique multicultural, multinational boundaries.

The term management is defined in many Western textbooks as the process of completing activities efficiently with and through other individuals. (①) The process consists of the functions or main activities engaged in by managers. These functions or activities are usually labeled planning, organizing, staffing, coordinating(leading and motivating), and controlling. (②) The management process is affected by the organization's home country environment, which includes the shareholders, creditors, customers, employees, government, and community, as well as technological, demographic, and geographic factors. (③) These business enterprises are generally referred to as international corporations, multinational corporations(MNCs), or global corporations. (④) This means that the process is affected by the environment where the organization is based, as well as by the unique culture, including views on ethics and social responsibility, existing in the country or countries where it conducts its business activities.

14

〈보 기〉

This kind of development makes us realize that removing safety hazards is far better than creating alarms to detect them.

Spinoff technology can help to make our homes and communities safer and more comfortable places to live. Most people are aware that carbon monoxide(CO) buildup in our homes can be very dangerous. This may come from a faulty furnace or fireplace. (①) Consequently, some people have carbon monoxide detectors in their homes, but these detectors only alert them if the level of carbon monoxide is unsafe. (②) However, using space technology, NASA developed an air-conditioning system that can not only detect dangerous amounts of carbon monoxide, but actually oxidizes the toxic gases into harmless carbon dioxide. (③) In addition to helping people to have clean air, having access to clean water is also of major importance for everyone. NASA engineers have been working with private companies to create better systems for clean, drinkable water for astronauts in space. (④) These systems, which have been developed for the astronauts, can quickly and affordably cleanse any available water. This is a major advantage to the people on Earth who live in remote or developing areas where water is scarce or polluted.

15 (A)와 (B)에 들어갈 말로 가장 적절한 것은?

Antibiotics are among the most commonly prescribed drugs for people. Antibiotics are effective against bacterial infections, such as strep throat, some types of pneumonia, eye infections, and ear infections. But these drugs don't work at all against viruses, such as those that cause colds or flu. Unfortunately, many antibiotics prescribed to people and to animals are unnecessary.　　(A)　　, the overuse and misuse of antibiotics help to create drug-resistant bacteria. Here's how that might happen. When used properly, antibiotics can help destroy disease-causing bacteria.　　(B)　　, if you take an antibiotic when you have a viral infection like the flu, the drug won't affect the viruses making you sick.

	(A)	(B)
①	However	Instead
②	Furthermore	Therefore
③	On the other hand	For example
④	Furthermore	However

[16~17] 글의 제목으로 가장 적절한 것은?

16

The assumption that politics and administration could be separated was ultimately disregarded as utopian. Wilson and Goodnow's idea of apolitical public administration proved unrealistic. A more realistic view—the so-called "politics school"—is that politics is very much a part of administration. The politics school maintains that in a pluralistic political system in which many diverse groups have a voice, public administrators with considerable knowledge play key roles. Legislation, for instance, is written by public administrators as much as by legislators. The public bureaucracy is as capable of engendering support for its interests as any other participant in the political process, and public administrators are as likely as any to be part of a policymaking partnership. Furthermore, laws are interpreted by public administrators in their execution, which includes many and often unforeseen scenarios.

① How to Cope with Unpredictable Situations in Politics

② Public Administrators' Surprising Influence in a Political System

③ Repetitive Attempts to Separate the Politics form Administration

④ Loopholes of the View that Politics and Administration are Inseparable

17

We are living in perhaps the most exciting times in all of human history. The technological advances we are witnessing today are giving birth to new industries that are producing devices, systems, and services that were once only reflected in the realm of science fiction and fantasy. Industries are being completely restructured to become better, faster, stronger, and safer. You no longer have to settle for something that is "close enough," because customization is reaching levels that provide you with exactly what you want or need. We are on the verge of releasing the potential of genetic enhancement, nanotechnology, and other technologies that will lead to curing many diseases and maybe even slowing the aging process itself. Such advances are due to discoveries in separate fields to produce these wonders. In the not so distant future, incredible visions of imagination such as robotic surgeons that keep us healthy, self-driving trucks that deliver our goods, and virtual worlds that entertain us after a long day will be commonplace. If ever there were a time that we were about to capture perfection, it is now—and the momentum is only increasing.

① The Era of Unprecedented Technological Advancements
② Struggles with Imperfect Solutions in Modern Industries
③ Historical Perspectives on Technological Progress
④ The Stagnant State of Contemporary Industries

[18~19] 밑줄 친 부분에 들어갈 말로 가장 적절한 것은?

18

Emotional strength isn't about maintaining a stiff upper lip, being stoic or never showing emotion—actually, it's the opposite. "Emotional strength is about having the skills you need to regulate your feelings," says psychotherapist Amy Morin. "You don't need to chase happiness all the time. Instead, you can develop the courage you need to work through uncomfortable feelings, like anxiety and sadness." Someone with emotional strength, for instance, will know when to shift their emotional state, says Morin. "If their anxiety isn't serving them well, they have strategies they can use to calm themselves. They also have the ability to tolerate difficult emotions, but they do so by _____ them, not suppressing them. They don't distract themselves from painful feelings, like loneliness.

① exaggerating   ② pursuing
③ embracing   ④ ignoring

19

Like many small organisms, fungi are often overlooked, but their planetary significance is outsize. Plants managed to leave water and grow on land only because of their collaboration with fungi, which acted as their root systems for millions of years. Even today, roughly 90 percent of plants and nearly all the world's trees depend on fungi, which supply crucial minerals by breaking down rock and other substances. They can also be a scourge, eradicating forests and killing humans. At times, they even seem to _____. When Japanese researchers released slime molds into mazes modeled on Tokyo's streets, the molds found the most efficient route between the city's urban hubs in a day, instinctively recreating a set of paths almost identical to the existing rail network. When put in a miniature floor map of Ikea, they quickly found the shortest route to the exit.

① gather   ② breed

③ enjoy   ④ think

20

Species (or higher taxa) may go extinct for two reasons. One is "real" extinction in the sense that the lineage has died out and left no descendants. For modern species, the meaning is unambiguous, but for fossils real extinction has to be distinguished from *pseudoextinction*. Pseudoextinction means that the taxon appears to go extinct, but only because of an error or artifact in the evidence, and not because the underlying lineage really ceased to exist. For instance, _____. As a lineage evolves, later forms may look sufficiently different from earlier ones that a taxonomist may classify them as different species, even though there is a continuous breeding lineage. This may be because the species are classified phenetically, or it may be because the taxonomist only has a few specimens, some from early in the lineage and some from late in the lineage such that the continuous lineage is undetectable.

① clues for extinction are found in many regions

② a lineage may disappear temporarily from the fossil record

③ a continuously evolving lineage may change its taxonomic name

④ some divergent lineages have been fully identified

영어 | 2022년 서울시 9급

✅ 회독 CHECK 1 2 3

[01~02] 밑줄 친 부분의 의미와 가장 가까운 것은?

01

> Norwegians led by Roald Amundsen arrived in Antarctica's Bay of Whales on January 14, 1911. With dog teams, they prepared to race the British to the South Pole. Amundsen's ship, *Fram*, loaned by <u>renowned</u> Arctic explorer Fridtjof Nansen, was the elite polar vessel of her time.

① famous
② intrepid
③ early
④ notorious

02

> In her presentation, she will give a <u>lucid</u> account of her future plan as a member of this organization.

① loquacious
② sluggish
③ placid
④ perspicuous

[03~05] 밑줄 친 부분에 들어갈 말로 가장 적절한 것은?

03

> People need to _____ skills in their jobs in order to be competitive and become successful.

① abolish
② accumulate
③ diminish
④ isolate

04

> Manhattan has been compelled to expand skyward because of the _____ of any other direction in which to grow. This, more than any other thing, is responsible for its physical majesty.

① absence
② decision
③ exposure
④ selection

05

> _____ is using someone else's exact words or ideas in your writing, and not naming the original writer or book, magazine, video, podcast, or website where you found them.

① citation
② presentation
③ modification
④ plagiarism

06 두 사람의 대화 중 가장 어색한 것은?

① A: I need to ask you to do me a favor.
  B: Sure thing, what is it?

② A: I'm afraid I have to close my account.
  B: OK, please fill out this form.

③ A: That was a beautiful wedding.
  B: I'll say. And the wedding couple looked so right for each other.

④ A: I bought this jacket last Monday and already the zipper was broken. I'd like a refund.
  B: OK, I will fix the zipper.

07 어법상 가장 옳은 것은?

① The poverty rate is the percentage of the population which family income falls below an absolute level.

② Not surprisingly, any college graduate would rather enter the labor force in a year of economic expansion than in a year of economic contraction.

③ It is hard that people pick up a newspaper without seeing some newly reported statistic about the economy.

④ Despite the growth is continued in average income, the poverty rate has not declined.

08 어법상 가장 옳지 않은 것은?

① With nothing left, she would have to cling to that which had robbed her.

② Send her word to have her place cleaning up.

③ Alive, she had been a tradition, a duty, and a care.

④ Will you accuse a lady to her face of smelling bad?

09 어법상 가장 옳지 않은 것은?

① An ugly, old, yellow tin bucket stood beside the stove.

② It is the most perfect copier ever invented.

③ John was very frightening her.

④ She thought that he was an utter fool.

[10~11] 밑줄 친 부분 중 어법상 가장 옳지 않은 것은?

10

People have opportunities to behave in sustainable ways every day when they get dressed, and fashion, when ① creating within a broad understanding of sustainability, can sustain people as well as the environment. People have a desire to make ② socially responsible choices regarding the fashions they purchase. As designers and product developers of fashion, we are challenged to provide responsible choices. We need to stretch the perception of fashion to remain ③ open to the many layers and complexities that exist. The people, processes, and environments ④ that embody fashion are also calling for new sustainable directions. What a fabulous opportunity awaits!

11

Newspapers, journals, magazines, TV and radio, and professional or trade publications ① provide further ② information that may help interpret the facts ③ given in the annual report or on developments since the report ④ published.

[12~13] 글의 흐름상 가장 어색한 문장은?

12

Tropical forests are incredibly rich ecosystems, which provide much of the world's biodiversity. ① However, even with increased understanding of the value of these areas, excessive destruction continues. There are a few promising signs, however. ② Deforestation in many regions is slowing as governments combat this practice with intensive tree planting. Asia, for example, has gained forest in the last decade, primarily due to China's large-scale planting initiatives. ③ One part of this challenge is to allow countries a more equitable share of the revenue from pharmaceutical products originating in the tropical forests. Moreover, the number of reserves designated for conservation of biodiversity is increasing worldwide with particularly strong gains in South America and Asia. ④ Unfortunately, despite these gains, the capacity for humans to destroy forests continues to appear greater than their ability to protect them.

13

In the early 1980s, a good friend of mine discovered that she was dying of multiple myeloma, an especially dangerous, painful form of cancer. I had lost elderly relatives and family friends to death before this, but I had never lost a personal friend. ① I had never watched a relatively young person die slowly and painfully of disease. It took my friend a year to die, and ② I got into the habit of visiting her every Saturday and taking along the latest chapter of the novel I was working on. This happened to be *Clay's Ark*. With its story of disease and death, it was thoroughly inappropriate for the situation. But my friend had always read my novels. ③ She insisted that she no longer wanted to read this one as well. I suspect that neither of us believed she would live to read it in its completed form—④ although, of course, we didn't talk about this.

14 글의 요지로 가장 적절한 것은?

From computers to compact-disc players, railway engines to robots, the origins of today's machines can be traced back to the elaborate mechanical toys that flourished in the eighteenth century. As the first complex machines produced by man, automata represented a proving ground for technology that would later be harnessed in the industrial revolution. But their original uses were rather less utilitarian. Automata were the playthings of royalty, both as a form of entertainment in palaces and courts across Europe and as gifts sent from one ruling family to another. As a source of amusement, the first automata were essentially scaled-down versions of the elaborate mechanical clocks that adorned cathedrals. These clocks provided the inspiration for smaller and increasingly elaborate automata. As these devices became more complicated, their time-keeping function became less important, and automata became first and foremost mechanical amusements in the form of mechanical theaters or moving scenes.

① The history of machine has less to do with a source of amusement.
② Modern machine has a non-utilitarian origin.
③ Royalty across Europe was interested in toy industry.
④ The decline of automata is closely associated with the industrial revolution.

15 글의 내용과 가장 일치하지 않는 것은?

When Ali graduated, he decided he didn't want to join the ranks of commuters struggling to work every day. He wanted to set up his own online gift-ordering business so that he could work from home. He knew it was a risk but felt he would have at least a fighting chance of success. Initially, he and a college friend planned to start the business together. Ali had the idea and Igor, his friend, had the money to invest in the company. But then just weeks before the launch, Igor dropped a bombshell: he said he no longer wanted to be part of Ali's plans. Despite Ali's attempts to persuade him to hang fire on his decision. Igor said he was no longer prepared to take the risk and was going to beat a retreat before it was too late. However, two weeks later Igor stole a march on Ali by launching his own online gift-ordering company. Ali was shell-shocked by this betrayal, but he soon came out fighting. He took Igor's behaviour as a call to arms and has persuaded a bank to lend him the money he needs. Ali's introduction to the business world has certainly been a baptism of fire, but I'm sure he will be really successful on his own.

① 본래 온라인 선물주문 사업은 Ali의 계획이었다.
② Igor가 먼저 그 사업에서 손을 떼겠다고 말했다.
③ Igor가 Ali보다 앞서서 자기 소유의 선물주문 회사를 차렸다.
④ Ali는 은행을 설득하여 Igor에게 돈을 빌려주게 했다.

[16~17] (A)와 (B)에 들어갈 말로 가장 적절한 것은?

16

Scientists are working on many other human organs and tissues. For example, they have successfully generated, or grown, a piece of liver. This is an exciting achievement since people cannot live without a liver. In other laboratories, scientists have created a human jawbone and a lung. While these scientific breakthroughs are very promising, they are also limited. Scientists cannot use cells for a new organ from a very diseased or damaged organ. ___(A)___, many researchers are working on a way to use stem cells to grow completely new organs. Stem cells are very simple cells in the body that can develop into any kind of complex cells, such as skin cells or blood cells and even heart and liver cells. ___(B)___, stem cells can grow into all different kinds of cells.

	(A)	(B)
①	Specifically	For example
②	Additionally	On the other hand
③	Consequently	In other words
④	Accordingly	In contrast

17

To speak of 'the aim' of scientific activity may perhaps sound a little ___(A)___ ; for clearly, different scientists have different aims, and science itself (whatever that may mean) has no aims. I admit all this. And yet it seems that when we speak of science we do feel, more or less clearly, that there is something characteristic of scientific activity; and since scientific activity looks pretty much like a rational activity, and since a rational activity must have some aim, the attempt to describe the aim of science may not be entirely ___(B)___ .

	(A)	(B)
①	naive	futile
②	reasonable	fruitful
③	chaotic	acceptable
④	consistent	discarded

18 〈보기〉의 문장 다음에 이어질 글의 순서로 가장 적절한 것은?

─────〈보 기〉─────

The child that is born today may possibly have the same faculties as if he had been born in the days of Noah; if it be otherwise, we possess no means of determining the difference.

(A) That development is entirely under the control of the influences exerted by the society in which the child may chance to live.

(B) If such society be altogether denied, the faculties perish, and the child grows up a beast and not a man; if the society be uneducated and coarse, the growth of the faculties is early so stunted as never afterwards to be capable of recovery; if the society be highly cultivated, the child will be cultivated also, and will show, more or less, through life the fruits of that cultivation.

(C) Hence each generation receives the benefit of the cultivation of that which preceded it.

(D) But the equality of the natural faculties at starting will not prevent a vast difference in their ultimate development.

① (A) - (B) - (D) - (C)
② (A) - (D) - (B) - (C)
③ (D) - (A) - (B) - (C)
④ (D) - (B) - (A) - (C)

[19~20] 밑줄 친 부분에 들어갈 말로 가장 적절한 것은?

19

It is quite clear that people's view of what English should do has been strongly influenced by what Latin does. For instance, there is (or used to be—it is very infrequently observed in natural speech today) a feeling that an infinitive in English should not be split. What this means is that you should not put anything between the *to* which marks an infinitive verb and the verb itself: you should say *to go boldly* and never *to boldly go*. This 'rule' is based on Latin, where the marker of the infinitive is an ending, and you can no more split it from the rest of the verb than you can split *-ing* from the rest of its verb and say *goboldlying* for *going boldly*. English speakers clearly do not feel that *to* and *go* belong together _____ *go* and *-ing*. They frequently put words between this kind of *to* and its verb.

① less closely than
② as closely as
③ more loosely than
④ as loosely as

20

A company may be allowed to revalue non-current assets. Where the fair value of non-current assets increases this may be reflected in an adjustment to the value of the assets shown in the statement of financial position. As far as possible, this should reflect the fair value of assets and liabilities. However, the increase in value of a non-current asset does not necessarily represent _____ for the company. A profit is made or realized only when the asset is sold and the resulting profit is taken through the income statement. Until this event occurs prudence—supported by common sense—requires that the increase in asset value is retained in the balance sheet. Shareholders have the right to any profit on the sale of company assets, so the shareholders' stake (equity) is increased by the same amount as the increase in asset valuation. A revaluation reserve is created and the balance sheet still balances.

① the fair value
② an actual cost
③ an immediate profit
④ the value of a transaction

영어 | 2019년 서울시 9급

모바일 OMR

✔ 회독 CHECK 1 2 3

[01~02] 밑줄 친 부분의 의미와 가장 가까운 것은?

01

> At least in high school she made one decision where she finally saw eye to eye with her parents.

① quarreled

② disputed

③ parted

④ agreed

02

> Justifications are accounts in which one accepts responsibility for the act in question, but denies the pejorative quality associated with it.

① derogatory

② extrovert

③ mandatory

④ redundant

[03~05] 밑줄 친 부분에 들어갈 말로 가장 적절한 것은?

03

> Tests ruled out dirt and poor sanitation as causes of yellow fever, and a mosquito was the _____ carrier.

① suspected

② uncivilized

③ cheerful

④ volunteered

04

> Generally speaking, people living in 2018 are pretty fortunate when you compare modern times to the full scale of human history. Life expectancy _____ at around 72 years, and diseases like smallpox and diphtheria, which were widespread and deadly only a century ago, are preventable, curable, or altogether eradicated.

① curtails

② hovers

③ initiates

④ aggravates

05

To imagine that there are concrete patterns to past events, which can provide _____ for our lives and decisions, is to project on to history a hope for a certainty which it cannot fulfill.

① hallucinations   ② templates

③ inquiries   ④ commotion

06 대화 중 가장 어색한 것은?

① A: What was the movie like on Saturday?

B: Great. I really enjoyed it.

② A: Hello. I'd like to have some shirts pressed.

B: Yes, how soon will you need them?

③ A: Would you like a single or a double room?

B: Oh, it's just for me, so a single is fine.

④ A: What time is the next flight to Boston?

B: It will take about 45 minutes to get to Boston.

[07~10] 밑줄 친 부분 중 어법상 가장 옳지 않은 것은?

07

Inventor Elias Howe attributed the discovery of the sewing machine ① for a dream ② in which he was captured by cannibals. He noticed as they danced around him ③ that there were holes at the tips of spears, and he realized this was the design feature he needed ④ to solve his problem.

08

By 1955 Nikita Khrushchev ① had been emerged as Stalin's successor in the USSR, and he ② embarked on a policy of "peaceful coexistence" ③ whereby East and West ④ were to continue their competition, but in a less confrontational manner.

09

Squid, octopuses, and cuttlefish are all ① types of cephalopods. ② Each of these animals has special cells under its skin that ③ contains pigment, a colored liquid. A cephalopod can move these cells toward or away from its skin. This allows it ④ to change the pattern and color of its appearance.

10

There is a more serious problem than ① maintaining the cities. As people become more comfortable working alone, they may become ② less social. It's ③ easier to stay home in comfortable exercise clothes or a bathrobe than ④ getting dressed for yet another business meeting!

11 글의 제목으로 가장 적절한 것은?

Economists say that production of an information good involves high fixed costs but low marginal costs. The cost of producing the first copy of an information good may be substantial, but the cost of producing(or reproducing) additional copies is negligible. This sort of cost structure has many important implications. For example, cost-based pricing just doesn't work: a 10 or 20 percent markup on unit cost makes no sense when unit cost is zero. You must price your information goods according to consumer value, not according to your production cost.

① Securing the Copyright
② Pricing the Information Goods
③ Information as Intellectual Property
④ The Cost of Technological Change

12 밑줄 친 부분이 지칭하는 대상이 다른 것은?

Dracula ants get their name for the way they sometimes drink the blood of their own young. But this week, ① the insects have earned a new claim to fame. Dracula ants of the species *Mystrium camillae* can snap their jaws together so fast, you could fit 5,000 strikes into the time it takes us to blink an eye. This means ② the blood-suckers wield the fastest known movement in nature, according to a study published this week in the journal *Royal Society Open Science*. Interestingly, the ants produce their record-breaking snaps simply by pressing their jaws together so hard that ③ they bend. This stores energy in one of the jaws, like a spring, until it slides past the other and lashes out with extraordinary speed and force—reaching a maximum velocity of over 200 miles per hour. It's kind of like what happens when you snap your fingers, only 1,000 times faster. Dracula ants are secretive predators as ④ they prefer to hunt under the leaf litter or in subterranean tunnels.

13 밑줄 친 부분에 들어갈 말로 가장 옳은 것은?

I am writing to you from a train in Germany, sitting on the floor. The train is crowded, and all the seats are taken. However, there is a special class of "comfort customers" who are allowed to make those already seated _____ their seats.

① give up
② take
③ giving up
④ taken

[14~16] 글의 흐름상 빈칸에 들어갈 말로 가장 적절한 것은?

14

A country's wealth plays a central role in education, so lack of funding and resources from a nation-state can weaken a system. Governments in sub-Saharan Africa spend only 2.4 percent of the world's public resources on education, yet 15 percent of the school-age population lives there. _____, the United States spends 28 percent of all the money spent in the world on education, yet it houses only 4 percent of the school-age population.

① Nevertheless

② Furthermore

③ Conversely

④ Similarly

15

"Highly conscientious employees do a series of things better than the rest of us," says University of Illinois psychologist Brent Roberts, who studies conscientiousness. Roberts owes their success to "hygiene" factors. Conscientious people have a tendency to organize their lives well. A disorganized, unconscientious person might lose 20 or 30 minutes rooting through their files to find the right document, an inefficient experience conscientious folks tend to avoid. Basically, by being conscientious, people _____ they'd otherwise create for themselves.

① deal with setbacks

② do thorough work

③ follow norms

④ sidestep stress

16

Climate change, deforestation, widespread pollution and the sixth mass extinction of biodiversity all define living in our world today—an era that has come to be known as "the Anthropocene". These crises are underpinned by production and consumption which greatly exceeds global ecological limits, but blame is far from evenly shared. The world's 42 wealthiest people own as much as the poorest 3.7 billion, and they generate far greater environmental impacts. Some have therefore proposed using the term "Capitalocene" to describe this era of ecological devastation and growing inequality, reflecting capitalism's logic of endless growth and _____.

① the better world that is still within our reach

② the accumulation of wealth in fewer pockets

③ an effective response to climate change

④ a burning desire for a more viable future

17 글의 흐름상 빈칸에 들어갈 말로 가장 적절한 것은?

Ever since the time of ancient Greek tragedy, Western culture has been haunted by the figure of the revenger. He or she stands on a whole series of borderlines: between civilization and barbarity, between _____ and the community's need for the rule of law, between the conflicting demands of justice and mercy. Do we have a right to exact revenge against those who have destroyed our loved ones? Or should we leave vengeance to the law or to the gods? And if we do take action into our own hands, are we not reducing ourselves to the same moral level as the original perpetrator of murderous deeds?

① redemption of the revenger from a depraved condition

② divine vengeance on human atrocities

③ moral depravity of the corrupt politicians

④ an individual's accountability to his or her own conscience

18 글의 흐름상 가장 적절하지 않은 문장은?

It seems to me possible to name four kinds of reading, each with a characteristic manner and purpose. The first is reading for information—reading to learn about a trade, or politics, or how to accomplish something. ① We read a newspaper this way, or most textbooks, or directions on how to assemble a bicycle. ② With most of this material, the reader can learn to scan the page quickly, coming up with what he needs and ignoring what is irrelevant to him, like the rhythm of the sentence, or the play of metaphor. ③ We also register a track of feeling through the metaphors and associations of words. ④ Courses in speed reading can help us read for this purpose, training the eye to jump quickly across the page.

19 〈보기〉의 문장이 들어갈 위치로 가장 적절한 것은?

─ 〈보 기〉 ─

In this situation, we would expect to find less movement of individuals from one job to another because of the individual's social obligations toward the work organization to which he or she belongs and to the people comprising that organization.

Cultural differences in the meaning of work can manifest themselves in other aspects as well. (①) For example, in American culture, it is easy to think of work simply as a means to accumulate money and make a living. (②) In other cultures, especially collectivistic ones, work may be seen more as fulfilling an obligation to a larger group. (③) In individualistic cultures, it is easier to consider leaving one job and going to another because it is easier to separate jobs from the self. (④) A different job will just as easily accomplish the same goals.

20 글을 문맥에 가장 어울리는 순서대로 배열한 것은?

㉠ To navigate in the dark, a microbat flies with its mouth open, emitting high-pitched squeaks that humans cannot hear. Some of these sounds echo off flying insects as well as tree branches and other obstacles that lie ahead. The bat listens to the echo and gets an instantaneous picture in its brain of the objects in front of it.

㉡ Microbats, the small, insect-eating bats found in North America, have tiny eyes that don't look like they'd be good for navigating in the dark and spotting prey.

㉢ From the use of echolocation, or sonar, as it is also called, a microbat can tell a great deal about a mosquito or any other potential meal. With extreme exactness, echolocation allows microbats to perceive motion, distance, speed, movement, and shape. Bats can also detect and avoid obstacles no thicker than a human hair.

㉣ But, actually, microbats can see as well as mice and other small mammals. The nocturnal habits of bats are aided by their powers of echolocation, a special ability that makes feeding and flying at night much easier than one might think.

① ㉠ - ㉢ - ㉡ - ㉣
② ㉡ - ㉣ - ㉠ - ㉢
③ ㉡ - ㉢ - ㉣ - ㉠
④ ㉠ - ㉣ - ㉢ - ㉡

◆ 회독 CHECK 1 2 3

[01~03] 밑줄 친 부분과 의미가 가장 가까운 것은?

01

Man has continued to be disobedient to authorities who tried to muzzle new thoughts and to the authority of long-established opinions which declared a change to be nonsense.

① express ② assert
③ suppress ④ spread

02

Don't be pompous. You don't want your writing to be too informal and colloquial, but you also don't want to sound like someone you're not—like your professor or boss, for instance, or the Rhodes scholar teaching assistant.

① presumptuous ② casual
③ formal ④ genuine

03

Surgeons were forced to call it a day because they couldn't find the right tools for the job.

① initiate ② finish
③ wait ④ cancel

04 대화 중 가장 어색한 것은?

① A: I'd like to make a reservation for tomorrow, please.
 B: Certainly. For what time?
② A: Are you ready to order?
 B: Yes, I'd like the soup, please.
③ A: How's your risotto?
 B: Yes, we have risotto with mushroom and cheese.
④ A: Would you like a dessert?
 B: Not for me, thanks.

05 밑줄 친 부분 중 어법상 가장 옳지 않은 것은?

His survival ① over the years since independence in 1961 does not alter the fact that the discussion of real policy choices in a public manner has hardly ② never occurred. In fact, there have always been ③ a number of important policy issues ④ which Nyerere has had to argue through the NEC.

06 밑줄 친 부분 중 어법상 가장 옳은 것은?

> More than 150 people ① have fell ill, mostly in
> Hong Kong and Vietnam, over the past three weeks.
> And experts ② are suspected that ③ another 300
> people in China's Guangdong province had the
> same disease ④ begin in mid-November.

07 글의 흐름상 빈칸에 들어갈 단어로 가장 옳은 것은?

> Social learning theorists offer a different
> explanation for the counter-aggression exhibited
> by children who experience aggression in the
> home. An extensive research on aggressive
> behavior and the coercive family concludes
> that an aversive consequence may also elicit
> an aggressive reaction and accelerate ongoing
> coercive behavior. These victims of aggressive acts
> eventually learn via modeling to _____
> aggressive interchanges. These events perpetuate
> the use of aggressive acts and train children how
> to behave as adults.

① stop

② attenuate

③ abhor

④ initiate

08 밑줄 친 인물(Marcel Mauss)에 대한 설명으로 가장 옳지 않은 것은?

> Marcel Mauss (1872-1950), French sociologist,
> was born in Épinal (Vosges) in Lorraine, where he
> grew up within a close-knit, pious, and orthodox
> Jewish family. Emile Durkheim was his uncle.
> By the age of 18 Mauss had reacted against the
> Jewish faith; he was never a religious man. He
> studied philosophy under Durkheim's supervision
> at Bordeaux; Durkheim took endless trouble in
> guiding his nephew's studies and even chose
> subjects for his own lectures that would be most
> useful to Mauss. Thus Mauss was initially a
> philosopher (like most of the early Durkheimians),
> and his conception of philosophy was influenced
> above all by Durkheim himself, for whom he
> always retained the utmost admiration.

① He had a Jewish background.

② He was supervised by his uncle.

③ He had a doctrinaire faith.

④ He was a sociologist with a philosophical background.

09 글의 문맥에 가장 어울리는 순서대로 배열한 것은?

ⓐ Today, however, trees are being cut down far more rapidly. Each year, about 2 million acres of forests are cut down. That is more than equal to the area of the whole of Great Britain.

ⓑ There is not enough wood in these countries to satisfy the demand. Wood companies, therefore, have begun taking wood from the forests of Asia, Africa, South America, and even Siberia.

ⓒ While there are important reasons for cutting down trees, there are also dangerous consequences for life on earth. A major cause of the present destruction is the worldwide demand for wood. In industrialized countries, people are using more and more wood for paper.

ⓓ There is nothing new about people cutting down trees. In ancient times, Greece, Italy, and Great Britain were covered with forests. Over the centuries those forests were gradually cut back. Until now almost nothing is left.

① ⓐ - ⓑ - ⓒ - ⓓ
② ⓓ - ⓐ - ⓑ - ⓒ
③ ⓑ - ⓐ - ⓒ - ⓓ
④ ⓓ - ⓐ - ⓒ - ⓑ

10 글의 흐름상 빈칸에 들어갈 표현으로 가장 옳은 것은?

Contemporary art has in fact become an integral part of today's middle class society. Even works of art which are fresh from the studio are met with enthusiasm. They receive recognition rather quickly—too quickly for the taste of the surlier culture critics. _____, not all works of them are bought immediately, but there is undoubtedly an increasing number of people who enjoy buying brand new works of art. Instead of fast and expensive cars, they buy the paintings, sculptures and photographic works of young artists. They know that contemporary art also adds to their social prestige. _____, since art is not exposed to the same wear and tear as automobiles, it is a far better investment.

① Of course - Furthermore
② Therefore - On the other hand
③ Therefore - For instance
④ Of course - For example

11 밑줄 친 부분과 의미가 가장 먼 것은?

As a prerequisite for fertilization, pollination is essential to the production of fruit and seed crops and plays an important part in programs designed to improve plants by breeding.

① crucial
② indispensable
③ requisite
④ omnipresent

12 글의 흐름상 빈칸에 들어갈 단어로 가장 옳은 것은?

> Mr. Johnson objected to the proposal because it was founded on a _____ principle and also was _____ at times.

① faulty - desirable

② imperative - reasonable

③ conforming - deplorable

④ wrong - inconvenient

[13~14] 밑줄 친 부분 중 어법상 가장 옳지 않은 것은?

13

> I'm ① pleased that I have enough clothes with me. American men are generally bigger than Japanese men so ② it's very difficult to find clothes in Chicago that ③ fits me. ④ What is a medium size in Japan is a small size here.

14

> Blue Planet Ⅱ, a nature documentary ① produced by the BBC, left viewers ② heartbroken after showing the extent ③ to which plastic ④ affects on the ocean.

15 글의 흐름상 빈칸에 들어갈 가장 적절한 문장은?

> What became clear by the 1980s, however, as preparations were made for the 'Quincentenary Jubilee', was that many Americans found it hard, if not impossible, to see the anniversary as a 'jubilee'. There was nothing to celebrate the legacy of Columbus. _____

① According to many of his critics, Columbus had been the harbinger not of progress and civilization, but of slavery and the reckless exploitation of the environment.

② The Chicago World's Fair of 1893 reinforced the narrative link between discovery and the power of progress of the United States.

③ This reversal of the nineteenth-century myth of Columbus is revealing.

④ Columbus thus became integrated into Manifest Destiny, the belief that America's progress was divinely ordained.

16 글의 흐름상 빈칸에 들어갈 단어로 가장 옳지 않은 것은?

Following his father's imprisonment, Charles Dickens was forced to leave school to work at a boot-blacking factory alongside the River Thames. At the run-down, rodent-ridden factory, Dickens earned six shillings a week labeling pots of "blacking," a substance used to clean fireplaces. It was the best he could do to help support his family. Looking back on the experience, Dickens saw it as the moment he said goodbye to his youthful innocence, stating that he wondered "how he could be so easily cast away at such a young age." He felt _____ by the adults who were supposed to take care of him.

① abandoned

② betrayed

③ buttressed

④ disregarded

17 글의 내용과 일치하는 것은?

A family hoping to adopt a child must first select an adoption agency. In the United States, there are two kinds of agencies that assist with adoption. Public agencies generally handle older children, children with mental or physical disabilities, or children who may have been abused or neglected. Prospective parents are not usually expected to pay fees when adopting a child from a public agency. Fostering, or a form of temporary adoption, is also possible through public agencies. Private agencies can be found on the Internet. They handle domestic and international adoption.

① Public adoption agencies are better than private ones.

② Parents pay huge fees to adopt a child from a foster home.

③ Children in need cannot be adopted through public agencies.

④ Private agencies can be contacted for international adoption.

18 글의 흐름상 빈칸에 들어갈 단어로 가장 옳은 것은?

Moths and butterflies both belong to the order Lepidoptera, but there are numerous physical and behavioral differences between the two insect types. On the behavioral side, moths are _____ and butterflies are diurnal(active during the day). While at rest, butterflies usually fold their wings back, while moths flatten their wings against their bodies or spread them out in a "jet plane" position.

① nocturnal

② rational

③ eternal

④ semi-circular

19 글의 흐름상 빈칸에 들어갈 표현으로 가장 옳은 것은?

The idea of clowns frightening people started gaining strength in the United States. In South Carolina, for example, people reported seeing individuals wearing clown costumes, often hiding in the woods or in cities at night. Some people said that the clowns were trying to lure children into empty homes or the woods. Soon, there were reports of threatening-looking clowns trying to frighten both children and adults. Although there were usually no reports of violence, and many of the reported sightings were later found to be false, this _____.

① benefited the circus industry

② promoted the use of clowns in ads

③ caused a nationwide panic

④ formed the perfect image of a happy clown

20 글의 내용과 가장 부합하는 속담은?

It is one thing to believe that our system of democracy is the best, and quite another to impose it on other countries. This is a blatant breach of the UN policy of non-intervention in the domestic affairs of independent nations. Just as Western citizens fought for their political institutions, we should trust the citizens of other nations to do likewise if they wish to. Democracy is also not an absolute term—Napoleon used elections and referenda to legitimize his hold on power, as do leaders today in West Africa and Southeast Asia. States with partial democracy are often more aggressive than totally unelected dictatorships which are too concerned with maintaining order at home. The differing types of democracy make it impossible to choose which standards to impose. The U.S. and European countries all differ in terms of restraints on government and the balance between consensus and confrontation.

① The grass is always greener on the other side of the fence.

② One man's food is another's poison.

③ There is no rule but has exceptions.

④ When in Rome, do as the Romans do.

PART 4

법원직

출제경향

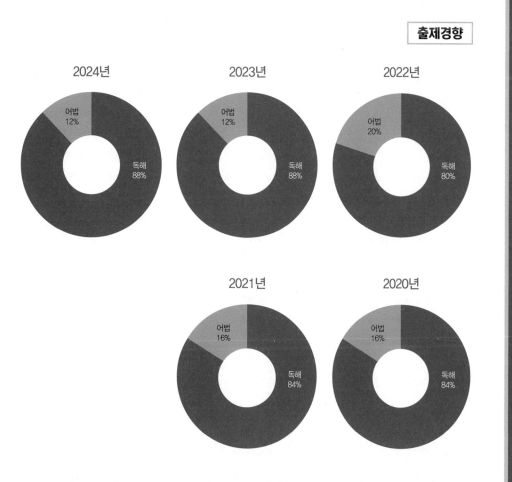

01 주어진 글 다음에 이어질 글의 순서로 가장 적절한 것은?

Now we stand at the edge of a turning point as we face the rise of a coming wave of technology that includes both advanced AI and biotechnology. Never before have we witnessed technologies with such transformative potential, promising to reshape our world in ways that are both awe-inspiring and daunting*.

(A) With AI, we could create systems that are beyond our control and find ourselves at the mercy of algorithms that we don't understand. With biotechnology, we could manipulate the very building blocks of life, potentially creating unintended consequences for both individuals and entire ecosystem.

(B) With biotechnology, we could engineer life to tackle diseases and transform agriculture, creating a world that is healthier and more sustainable. But on the other hand, the potential dangers of these technologies are equally vast and profound.

(C) On the one hand, the potential benefits of these technologies are vast and profound. With AI, we could unlock the secrets of the universe, cure diseases that have long eluded* us and create new forms of art and culture that stretch the bounds of imagination.

*daunt: 겁먹게(기죽게) 하다.

*elude: (사물이) ~에게 이해되지 않다.

① (B) - (A) - (C) ② (B) - (C) - (A)
③ (C) - (A) - (B) ④ (C) - (B) - (A)

02 다음 빈칸에 들어갈 말로 가장 적절한 것은?

Controversy over new art-making technologies is nothing new. Many painters recoiled at the invention of the camera, which they saw as a debasement of human artistry. Charles Baudelaire, the 19th-century French poet and art critic, called photography "art's most mortal enemy." In the 20th century, digital editing tools and computer-assisted design programs were similarly dismissed by purists for requiring too little skill of their human collaborators. What makes the new breed of A.I. image generating tools different is not just that they're capable of producing beautiful works of art with minimal effort. It's how they work. These tools are built by scraping millions of images from the open web, then teaching algorithms to recognize patterns and relationships in those images and generate new ones in the same style. That means that artists who upload their works to the internet may be unwittingly*

_____.

*unwittingly: 자신도 모르게, 부지불식간에

① helping to train their algorithmic competitors
② sparking a debate over the ethics of A.I.-generated art
③ embracing digital technology as part of the creative process
④ acquiring the skills of utilizing internet to craft original creations

03 Duke Kahanamoku에 대한 다음 글의 내용과 가장 일치하지 않는 것은?

Duke Kahanamoku, born August 26, 1890, near Waikiki, Hawaii, was a Hawaiian surfer and swimmer who won three Olympic gold medals for the United States and who for several years was considered the greatest freestyle swimmer in the world. He was perhaps most widely known for developing the flutter kick, which largely replaces the scissors kick. Kahanamoku set three universally recognized world records in the 100-yard freestyle between July 5, 1913, and September 5, 1917. In the 100-yard freestyle Kahanamoku was U.S. indoor champion in 1913, and outdoor titleholder in 1916-17 and 1920. At the Olympic Games in Stockholm in 1912, he won the 100-metre freestyle event, and he repeated that triumph at the 1920 Olympics in Antwerp, Belgium, where he also was a member of the victorious U.S. team in the 800-metre relay race. Kahanamoku also excelled at surfing, and he became viewed as one of the icons of the sport. Intermittently* from the mid-1920s, Kahanamoku was a motion-picture actor. From 1932 to 1961 he was sheriff* of the city and county of Honolulu. He served in the salaried office of official greeter of famous personages for the state of Hawaii from 1961 until his death.

*intermittently: 간헐적으로

*sheriff: 보안관

① 하와이 출신의 서퍼이자 수영 선수로 올림픽 금메달리스트이다.
② 그는 플러터 킥을 대체하는 시저스 킥을 개발한 것으로 널리 알려져 있다.
③ 벨기에 앤트워프 올림픽의 800미터 계주에서 우승한 미국팀의 일원이었다.
④ 그는 1920년대 중반부터 간헐적으로 영화배우로도 활동했다.

04 다음 빈칸에 들어갈 말로 가장 적절한 것은?

The understandings that children bring to the classroom can already be quite powerful in the early grades. For example, some children have been found to hold onto their preconception of a flat earth by imagining a round earth to be shaped like a pancake. This construction of a new understanding is guided by a model of the earth that helps the child explain how people can stand or walk on its surface. Many young children have trouble giving up the notion that one-eighth is greater than one-fourth, because 8 is more than 4. If children were blank slates, just telling them that the earth is round or that one-fourth is greater than one-eighth would be _____. But since they already have ideas about the earth and about numbers, those ideas must be directly addressed in order to transform or expand them.

① familiar
② adequate
③ improper
④ irrelevat

05 Urban farming에 관한 다음 글의 내용과 가장 일치하지 않는 것은?

> Urban farming, also known as urban agriculture, involves growing food within city environments, utilizing spaces like rooftops, abandoned buildings, and community gardens. This sustainable practice is gaining traction* in cities across the world, including New York, Chicago, San Francisco, London, Amsterdam, and Berlin, as well as in many African and Asian cities where it plays a crucial role in food supply and local economies. Urban farming not only helps reduce carbon footprints by minimizing transport emissions but also increases access to fresh, healthy food in urban areas. It bolsters* local economies by creating jobs and keeping profits within the community. Additionally, urban farms enhance cityscapes, improve air quality, conserve water, provide educational opportunities, promote biodiversity, connect people with nature, and improve food security by producing food locally, making cities more resilient to disruptions like natural disasters.
>
> *traction: 흡입력, 견인력
> *bolster: 강화시키다

① 옥상, 버려진 건물, 그리고 공동체 정원과 같은 공간을 활용하여 도시 환경 내에서 식량을 재배하는 것이다.

② 지속 가능한 관행으로 식량 공급과 지역 경제에서 중요한 역할을 하는 많은 아프리카와 아시아를 포함한 세계의 도시들에서 인기를 얻고 있다.

③ 운송 배출을 최소화하여 탄소 발자국을 줄이는 것을 도울 뿐만 아니라 도시 지역에서 신선하고 건강한 식량에 대한 접근성을 증가시킨다.

④ 생물 다양성을 촉진하고, 지역에서 식량을 생산함으로써 식량의 안정성을 향상시키나, 자연 재해와 같은 혼란에 대한 도시의 회복력은 약화시킨다.

06 밑줄 친 "unfinished animals."가 다음 글에서 의미하는 바로 가장 적절한 것은?

> Ideas or theories about human nature have a unique place in the sciences. We don't have to worry that the cosmos will be changed by our theories about the cosmos. The planets really don't care what we think or how we theorize about them. But we do have to worry that human nature will be changed by our theories of human nature. Forty years ago, the distinguished anthropologist said that human beings are "unfinished animals." What he meant is that it is human nature to have a human nature that is very much the product of the society that surrounds us. That human nature is more created than discovered. We "design" human nature, by designing the institutions within which people live. So we must ask ourselves just what kind of a human nature we want to help design.

① stuck in an incomplete stage of development

② shaped by society rather than fixed by biology

③ uniquely free from environmental context

④ born with both animalistic and spiritual aspect

07 다음 글의 내용을 한 문장으로 요약하고자 한다. 빈칸 (A), (B)에 들어갈 말로 가장 적절한 것은?

Passive House is a standard and an advanced method of designing buildings using the precision of building physics to ensure comfortable conditions and to deeply reduce energy costs. It removes all guesswork from the design process. It does what national building regulations have tried to do. Passive House methods don't affect "buildability", yet they close the gap between design and performance and deliver a much higher standard of comfort and efficiency than government regulations, with all their good intentions, have managed to achieve. When we use Passive House methods, we learn how to use insulation and freely available daylight, in the most sensible way and in the right amounts for both comfort and energy efficiency. This is, I believe, fundamental to good design, and is the next step we have to make in the evolution of our dwellings and places of work. The improvements that are within our grasp are potentially transformative for mankind and the planet.

⇩

Passive House utilizes precise building physics to ensure comfort and energy efficiency, ___(A)___ traditional regulations and offering transformative potential for ___(B)___ design.

	(A)	(B)
①	persisting	sustainable
②	persisting	unsustainable
③	surpassing	unsustainable
④	surpassing	sustainable

08 다음 글의 밑줄 친 부분 중 문맥상 낱말의 쓰임이 가장 적절하지 않은 것은?

Today, there is only one species of humans, Homo sapiens, left in the world. But that one species, despite the fact that it is over 99.9 percent genetically ① identical, has adapted itself to a wide array of disparate environments. And while some degree of human genetic variation results from each society's adaptation to its own unique environment, the cultural adaptations that each society makes in so adjusting itself will, in their turn, exact some further degree of ② variation on that society's genetic makeup. In other words, we are so entangled with our local ecologies that not only do we humans ③ transform the environment as we cull from it the various resources upon which we come to depend but also the environment, which we have so transformed, transforms us in its turn: at times exerting upon us profound biological pressures. In those regions of the world, for example, where our environmental exploitation has included the domestication of cattle-northern Europe, for instance, or East Africahuman populations have ④ reduced adult lactose* tolerance: the ability to digest milk past infancy.

*lactose: 유당, 젖당

09 주어진 글 다음에 이어질 글의 순서로 가장 적절한 것은?

> Briefly consider a metaphor that plays a significant role in how we live our daily lives: Time Is Money.

(A) We often speak of time as if it were money— for example, in everyday expressions such as "You're wasting my time," "This device will save you hours of work," "How will you spend your weekend?" and "I've invested a lot of time in this relationship."

(B) Every metaphor brokers what is made visible or invisible; this one highlights how time is like money and obscures* ways it is not. Time thus becomes something that we can waste or lose, and something that diminishes as we grow older. It is abstracted in a very linear, orderly fashion.

(C) This metaphor, however, fails to disclose important phenomenological aspects of time, such as how it may speed up or slow down, depending on our engagement with what we are doing. We may instead conceive of time as quite fluid—as a stream, for example— thought we lose sight of this to the extent that we have adopted the worldview of Time Is Money.

*obscure: 모호하게 하다

① (A) - (B) - (C)
② (A) - (C) - (B)
③ (B) - (A) - (C)
④ (C) - (B) - (A)

10 다음 글의 밑줄 친 부분 중, 어법상 틀린 것은?

His last thought were for his wife. "He is afraid she would ① hardly be able to bear it," he said to Burnet, the bishop* who was allowed to be with him the last few days. Tears came into his eyes when he spoke of her. The last day came, and Lady Russell brought the three little children to say good-bye for ever to their father. "Little Fubs" was only nine, her sister Catherine seven, and the baby three years old, too young to realize his loss. He kissed them all ② calmly, and sent them away. His wife stayed and they ate their last meal together. Then they kissed in silence, and silently she left him. When she had gone, Lord Russel broke down completely. "Oh, what a blessing she has been to me!" he cried. "It is a great comfort to me to leave my children in such a mother's care; she has promised me to take care of ③ her for their sake; she will do it," he added resolutely. Lady Russell returned heavy-hearted to the sad home ④ to which she would never welcome him again. On July 21st, 1683, she was a widow, and her children fatherless. They left their dreary London house, and went to an old abbey in the country.

*bishop: 주교(성직자)

11 The gig economy에 관한 다음 글의 내용과 가장 일치하지 않는 것은?

The gig economy, referring to the workforce of people engaged in freelance and side-hustle work*, is growing rapidly in the United States, with 36% of employed participants in a 2022 McKinsey survey identifying as independent workers, up from 27% in 2016. This workforce includes a wide range of jobs from highly-paid professionals like lawyers to lower-earning roles like delivery drivers. Despite the flexibility and autonomy it offers, most independent workers desire more stable employment; 62% prefer permanent positions due to concerns over job security and benefits. The challenges faced by gig workers include limited access to healthcare, housing, and other basic needs, with a significant reliance on government assistance. Technological advancements have facilitated the rise in independent work, making remote and freelance jobs more accessible and appealing. The trend reflects broader economic pressures such as inflation and job market dynamics, influencing individuals to choose gig work for survival, flexibility, or enjoyment.

*side-hustle work: 부업

① 조사에 참가한 사람들 중 독립 근로자의 비율이 2016년의 27%에서 36%까지 상승하였다.
② 대부분의 독립 근로자들은 안정적인 고용보다는 직업이 제공하는 유연성과 자율성을 선호하고 있다.
③ 근로자들이 직면한 어려움에는 의료, 주거 및 기타 기본 요구 사항에 대한 제한된 접근성이 포함된다.
④ 기술 발전은 독립 근로의 증가를 촉진하여 원격 및 프리랜서 일자리를 접근하기 쉽고 매력적인 것으로 만들고 있다.

12 주어진 글 다음에 이어질 글의 순서로 가장 적절한 것은?

We come to know and relate to the world by way of categories.

(A) The notion of an animal species, for instance, might in one setting best be thought of as described by folklore and myth, in another as a detailed legal construct, and in another as a system of scientific classification.

(B) Ordinary communication is the most immediate expression of this faculty. We refer to things through sounds and words, and we attach ideas to them that we call concepts.

(C) Some of our categories remain tacit*; others are explicitly governed by custom, law, politics, or science. The application of category systems for the same things varies by context and in use.

*tacit: 암묵적인, 무언의

① (B) - (A) - (C)
② (B) - (C) - (A)
③ (C) - (A) - (B)
④ (C) - (B) - (A)

13 다음 글에 나타난 화자의 심경으로 가장 적절한 것은?

It's three in the morning, and we are making our way from southern to northern Utah, when the weather changes from the dry chill of the desert to the freezing gales* of an alpine winter. Ice claims the road. Snowflakes flick against the windshield like tiny insects, a few at first, then so many the road disappears. We push forward into the heart of the storm. The van skids* and jerks*. The wind is furious, the view out the window pure white. Richard pulls over. He says we can't go any further. Dad takes the wheel, Richard moves to the passenger seat, and Mother lies next to me and Audrey on the mattress. Dad pulls onto the highway and accelerates, rapidly, as if to make a point, until he has doubled Richard's speed. "Shouldn't we drive slower?" Mother asks. Dad grins. "I'm not driving faster than our angels can fly." The van is still accelerating. To fifty, then to sixty. Richard sits tensely, his hand clutching the armrest, his knuckles bleaching each time the tires slip. Mother lies on her side, her face next to mine, taking small sips of air each time the van fishtails*, then holding her breath as Dad corrects and it snakes back into the lane. She is so rigid, I think she might shatter. My body tenses with hers; together we brace a hundred times for impact.

*gale: 강풍, 돌풍
*skid: 미끄러지다
*jerk: 홱 움직이다
*fishtail: (차량)뒷부분이 좌우로 미끄러지다

① excited and thrilled
② anxious and fearful
③ cautious but settled
④ comfortable and relaxed

14 글의 흐름으로 보아, 주어진 문장이 들어가기에 가장 적절한 곳은?

However, there are now a lot of issues with the current application of unmanned distribution.

The city lockdown policy during COVID-19 has facilitated the rapid growth of numerous takeaways, vegetable shopping, community group buying, and other businesses. (①) Last-mile delivery became an important livelihood support during the epidemic. (②) At the same time, as viruses can be transmitted through aerosols, the need for contactless delivery for last-mile delivery* has gradually increased, thus accelerating the use of unmanned logistics to some extent. (③) For example, the community space is not suitable for the operation of unmanned delivery facilities due to the lack of supporting logistics infrastructure. (④) In addition, the current technology is unable to complete the delivery process and requires the collaboration of relevant space as well as personnel to help dock unmanned delivery nodes.

*last-mile delivery: 최종 단계의 배송

15 주어진 글 다음에 이어질 글의 순서로 가장 적절한 것은?

> People are too seldom interested in having a genuine exchange of points of view where a desire to understand takes precedence over the desire to convince at any price.

(A) Yet conflict isn't just an unpopular source of pressure to act. There's also a lot of energy inherent to it, which can be harnessed to create positive change, or, in other words, improvements, with the help of a skillful approach. Basically, today's misery is the starting shot in the race towards a better future.

(B) A deviating opinion is quickly accompanied by devaluation, denigration*, insults, or even physical confrontations. If you look at the "discussions" taking place on social media networks, you don't even have to look to such hot potatoes as the refugee crisis or terrorism to see a clear degradation in the way people exchange opinions.

(C) You probably know this from your own experience, too, when you have succeeded in finding a constructive solution to a conflict and, at the end of an arduous* clarification process, realize that the successful outcome has been worth all the effort.

*denigration: 명예훼손
*arduous: 몹시 힘든 고된

① (B) - (A) - (C)
② (B) - (C) - (A)
③ (C) - (A) - (B)
④ (C) - (B) - (A)

16 다음 중 Belus Smawley에 대한 내용과 가장 일치하지 않는 것은?

> Belus Smawley grew up on a farm with his parents and six siblings. In his freshman years, he was tall and able to jump higher than any other boy, trying to improve his leaping ability by touching higher and higher limbs of the oak tree on their farm. This is where his first jump shot attempt is said to have taken place. When Belus Smawley started using his shot regularly, he became the leading scorer. At the age of 18, he got accepted for a position on an AAU18 basketball team. He finished high school afterwards and got an All-American athletic scholarship for Appalachian State University (majoring in history and physical education). He became player-coach until he went to the Navy. He started playing in their basketball team and refined his jump shot. He got married and either worked as a high school teacher and basketball coach or further pursued his NBA basketball career playing fulltime for several teams. Eventually he focused on family and his teaching career, becoming the principal of a junior high school.

① 부모님과 여섯 형제와 함께 농장에서 자랐다.
② 나무의 더 높은 가지를 만지면서 점프 연습을 하였다.
③ 애팔래치아 주립대학교에서 전미 체육 장학금을 받았다.
④ 결혼 후 NBA 농구 선수로서 한 팀에서 활동했다.

17 글의 흐름으로 보아, 주어진 문장이 들어가기에 가장 적절한 곳은?

> It might be understandable, then, for us to want to expect something similar from our machines: to know not only what they think they see but where, in particular, they are looking.

Humans, relative to most other species, have distinctly large and visible sclera*—the whites of our eyes—and as a result we are uniquely exposed in how we direct our attention, or at the very least, our gaze. (①) Evolutionary biologists have argued, via the "cooperative eye hypothesis," that this must be a feature, not a bug: that it must point to the fact that cooperation has been uncommonly important in our survival as a species, to the point that the benefits of shared attention outweigh* the loss of a certain degree of privacy or discretion*. (②) This idea in machine learning goes by the name of "saliency*": the idea is that if a system is looking at an image and assigning it to some category, then presumably some parts of the image were more important or more influential than others in making that determination. (③) If we could see a kind of "heat map" that highlighted these critical portions of the image, we might obtain some crucial diagnostic information that we could use as a kind of sanity check to make sure the system is behaving the way we think it should be. (④)

*sclera: (눈의)공막
*outweigh: 보다 더 크다
*discretion: 신중함
*saliency: 특징, 중요점

18 다음 (A), (B), (C) 중, 어법상 옳은 것끼리 고른 것은?

> The climate of the irrigated plains can be glimpsed in the murals. The summer sun beats down on the hard ground, and the king himself is shaded by a large umbrella. War, often present, is also carved in vivid detail. In or about 878 BC, three men are depicted (A) (fleeing / fled) from a city which has probably been captured. Dressed in long robes, they jump into the Euphrates River (B) (which / where) one is swimming while the others hug a lifebuoy to their chests. Like a long pillow, the lifebuoy consists of the skin of an animal, inflated with air. As the hands of the refugees (C) (is / are) clutching the inflated lifebuoy, and as much of their breath is expended in blowing air into it, they can only stay afloat by swimming with their legs. Whether they reached the opposite shore will never be known.

	(A)	(B)	(C)
①	fleeing	which	is
②	fleeing	where	are
③	fled	which	is
④	fled	where	are

19 다음 글의 내용과 가장 일치하지 않는 것은?

When the Dutch arrived in the 17th century in what's now New York City, their encounters with the indigenous peoples, known as the Lenape, were, at first, mostly amicable, according to historical records. They shared the land and traded guns, beads and wool for beaver furs. The Dutch even "purchased" Manahatta island from the Lenape in 1626. The transaction, enforced by the eventual building of wall around New Amsterdam, marked the very beginning of the Lenape's forced mass migration out of their homeland. The wall, which started showing up on maps in the 1660s, was built to keep out the Native Americans and the British. It eventually became Wall Street, and Manahatta became Manhattan, where part of the Lenape trade route, known as Wickquasgeck, became Brede weg, later Broadway. The Lenape helped shape the geography of modern-day New York City, but other traces of their legacy have all but vanished.

① 네덜란드인과 르나페 원주민들은 총과 동물의 털을 교환하는 무역을 했다.

② 이후에 월스트리트가 된 지역에 지어진 벽은 르나페 원주민이 영국인을 막기 위해 세웠다.

③ 르나페 원주민의 무역로의 일부가 나중에 브로드웨이가 되었다.

④ 르나페 원주민은 현대 뉴욕시의 지형을 형성하는 데 도움을 주었다.

20 다음 글의 밑줄 친 부분 중 어법상 가장 틀린 것은?

Today, we take for granted that the media and the celebrity culture it sustains have created new forms of publicness, ① through which we might have intimate relationships with people we have never met. Thanks to media technologies we ② are brought ever closer to the famous, allowing us to enjoyan illusion of intimacy with them. To a greater or lesser degree, we have internalized celebrities, unconsciously made them a part of our consciousness, just ③ as if they were, infact, friends. Celebrities take up permanent residence in our inner lives as well, ④ become central to our reveries* and fantasies, guides to action, to ambition. Now, indeed, celebrity culture can be permanently insinuated* into our sensibilities, as many of us carry them, their traits, and our relationships with them around as part of our mental luggage.

*reverie: 몽상

*insinuate: 암시하다, 일부가 되다

21 다음 글의 빈칸에 들어갈 말로 가장 적절한 것은?

> Festivals are significant cultural events that showcase tradition, heritage and community spirit globally. They serve as platforms to celebrate diversity, with each festival reflecting unique traditions like Brazil's Carnival or India's Diwali. Festivals also commemorate* historical moments, such as Independence Day in the US or Bastille Day in France. Additionally, they preserve customs and rituals that strengthen personal and cultural identity, while fostering strong community ties through shared activities. Festivals reflect societal values, promote local crafts and arts, enhance spirituality, and attract tourism, which facilitates cultural exchange and understanding. Seasonal festivals, like Holi in India, align with natural cycles, celebrating times of renewal. Ultimately, participating in festivals reinforces community and individual identity, contributing to a global narrative that _____.
>
> *commemorate: 기념하다

① makes the participants forget their daily concerns and pains

② values diversity and encourages mutual respect and understanding

③ allows people to break the link between personal life and social life

④ keeps the festivals from determining how people think about themselves

22 밑줄 친 you've been thrown a curve ball이 다음 글에서 의미하는 바로 가장 적절한 것은?

> Life is full of its ups and downs. One day, you may feel like you have it all figured out. Then, in a moment's notice, you've been thrown a curve ball. You're not alone in these feelings. Everyone has to face their own set of challenges. Learning how to overcome challenges will help you stay centered and remain calm under pressure. Everyone has their own preferences for how to face a challenge in life. However, there are a few good tips and tricks to follow when the going gets tough. There's no need to feel ashamed for asking for help. Whether you choose to rely on a loved one, a stranger, a mentor, or a friend, there are people who want to help you succeed. You have to be open and willing to accept support. People who come to your aid truly do care about you. Be open to receiving help when you need it.

① 어려운 상황에 직면하다.

② 흥미로운 상황을 맞이하게 되다.

③ 대안적인 방법을 적용하게 되다.

④ 정면 승부를 피하여 에둘러 가다.

23 다음 중 글에 설명된 사회적 지배력과 번식 성공 사이의 관계를 가장 잘 요약한 것은?

Social dominance* refers to situations in which an individual or a group controls or dictates others' behavior primarily in competitive situations. Generally, an individual or group is said to be dominant when "a prediction is being made about the course of future interactions or the outcome of competitive situations". Criteria for assessing and assigning dominance relationships can vary from one situation to another. It is difficult to summarize available data briefly, but generally it has been found that dominant individuals, when compared to subordinate individuals, often have more freedom of movement, have priority of access to food, gain higher-quality resting spots, enjoy favorable grooming relationships, occupy more protected parts of a group, obtain higher-quality mates, command and regulate the attention of other group members, and show greater resistance to stress and disease. Despite assertions that suggest otherwise, it really is not clear how powerful the relationship is between an individual's dominance status and its lifetime reproductive success.

*dominance: 지배, 우세

① 하위 개체에 비해 모든 지배적인 개체는 평생 동안 높은 번식 성공률을 보인다.
② 개체의 우세 상태와 평생 번식 성공 사이의 관계는 다면적이며 명확하게 정립되어 있다고 할 수는 없다.
③ 사회적 지배력을 갖춘 존재는 음식 및 짝과 같은 자원에 대한 접근을 통해 번식 성공에 영향을 미친다.
④ 하위 개체는 스트레스 수준이 높지 않기 때문에 평생 번식 성공률이 더 높은 경향이 있다.

24 다음 글의 주제로 가장 적절한 것은?

While mindfulness meditation is generally safe, concerns arise from its side effects like panic attacks and psychosis*, which are seldom reported and poorly understood in academic studies. Critics argue the rapid adoption of mindfulness by organizations and educational systems may inappropriately shift societal issues to individuals, suggesting that personal stress is due to a lack of meditation rather than addressing systemic causes like environmental pollution or workplace demands. Critics like Professor Ronald Purser suggest that mindfulness may make individuals more compliant* with adverse conditions instead of empowering them to seek change. Despite these concerns, the critique isn't against mindfulness itself but against its promotion as a universal solution by entities resistant to change. For a more thorough understanding of mindfulness' benefits and risks, long-term and rigorously controlled studies are essential.

*psychosis: 정신 질환
*compliant: 순응하는

① the criticism regarding the safety and societal implications of the widespread adoption of mindfulness meditation
② the social and national measures which are taken to relieve personal stress and prevent social and cultural confusion
③ the basic elements of mindfulness that must precede the resolution of social problems rather than individual problems
④ the disadvantages that individuals and societies face due to the meditation performed improperly and the lack of meditation

25 Mike Mansfield에 관한 다음 글의 내용과 가장 일치하지 않는 것은?

A man of few words and great modesty, Mike Mansfield often said he did not want to be remembered. Yet, his fascinating life story and enormous contributions are an inspiration for all who follow. Mike Mansfield was born in New York City on March 16, 1903. Following his mother's death when Mike was 7, his father sent him and his two sisters to Great Falls, Montana, to be raised by an aunt and uncle there. At 14, he lied about his age in order to enlist in the U.S. Navy for the duration of World War I. Later, he served in the Army and the Marines, which sent him to the Philippines and China, awakening a lifelong interest in Asia. Mike Mansfield's political career was launched in 1942 when he was elected to the U.S. House of Representatives*. He served five terms from Montana's 1st District. In 1952, he was elected to the U.S. Senate* and re-elected in 1958, 1964 and 1970. His selection as Democratic Assistant Majority Leader* was followed by election in 1961 as Senate Majority Leader. He served in that capacity until his retirement from the Senate in 1977, longer than any other Majority Leader in history.

*House of Representatives: 하원
*Senate: 상원
*Majority Leader: 다수당 원내대표

① 말수가 적고 겸손했으며 자신이 기억되지 않기를 원했었다.
② 모친이 사망한 이후 친인척의 보살핌을 받았다.
③ 군 복무 중 아시아 파병을 계기로 아시아에 대한 관심이 커졌다.
④ 상원의원에 5번 당선되었으며 가장 긴 다수당 원내대표를 역임했다.

✅ 회독 CHECK 1 2 3

01 Henry Molaison에 대한 다음 글의 내용과 가장 일치하지 않는 것은?

Henry Molaison, a 27-year-old man, suffered from debilitating seizures* for about a decade in the 1950s. On September 1, 1953, Molaison allowed surgeons to remove a section of tissue from each side of his brain to stop the seizures. The operation worked, but Molaison was left with permanent amnesia*, unable to form new memories. This tragic outcome led to one of the most significant discoveries in 20th century brain science: the discovery that complex functions like learning and memory are linked to specific regions of the brain. Molaison became known as "H.M." in research to protect his privacy. Scientists William Scoville studied Molaison and nine other patients who had similar surgeries, finding that only those who had parts of their medial temporal lobes* removed experienced memory problems, specifically with recent memory. He discovered that a specific structure in the brain was necessary for normal memory. Molaison's life was a series of firsts, as he couldn't remember anything he had done before. However, he was able to acquire new motor skills over time. Studies of Molaison allowed neuroscientists to further explore the brain networks involved in conscious and unconscious memories, even after his death in 2008.

*seizure: 발작

*amnesia: 기억 상실증

*medial temporal lobe: 내측 측두엽

① 외과의사들이 발작을 멈추기 위해 그의 뇌의 양쪽에서 조직의 한 부분을 제거하게 했다.
② 수술 결과는 학습과 기억과 같은 복잡한 기능들이 뇌의 특정 영역과 연결되어 있다는 발견으로 이어졌다.
③ 살아가면서 이전에 한 일을 조금씩 기억할 수 있었지만, 시간이 지나면서 운동 능력이 약화되었다.
④ 그에 대한 연구는 의식적 기억 및 무의식적 기억과 관련된 뇌의 연결 조직을 더 탐구할 수 있게 하였다.

02 다음 글의 밑줄 친 부분 중, 어법상 가장 틀린 것은?

Humans have an inborn affinity* for nature that goes beyond the tangible benefits we derive from the microbes, plants, and animals of the biomes* ① in which we live. The idea that nature in the form of landscapes, plants, and animals ② are good for our well-being is old and can be traced to Charles Darwin or earlier. This idea was called biophilia by psychologist Erich Fromm and was studied by Harvard ant biologist Edward O. Wilson and Stephen Kellert. In 1984, Wilson published *Biophilia*, which was followed by another book, The Biophilia Hypothesis, ③ edited by Kellert and Wilson, in 1995. Their biophilia hypothesis is ④ that humans have a universal desire to be in natural settings.

*affinity: 친밀감

*biome: 생물군계(生物群系)

03 다음 글의 내용과 가장 일치하지 않는 것은?

Life on Earth faced an extreme test of survivability during the Cryogenian Period*, which began 720 million years ago. The planet was frozen over most of the 85 million-year period. But life somehow survived during this time called "Snowball Earth". Scientists are trying to better understand the start of this period. They believe a greatly reduced amount of the sun's warmth reached the planet's surface as its radiation bounced off the white ice sheets. Also, they said the fossils found in black shale and identified as seaweed are a sign that livable water environments were more widespread at the time than they once believed. The findings of some research support the idea that the planet was more of a "Slushball Earth" with melting snow. This enabled the earliest forms of complex life to survive in areas once thought to have been frozen solid. The researchers said the most important finding was that ice-free, open water conditions existed in place during the last part of so-called "the Ice Age". The findings demonstrate that the world's oceans were not completely frozen. It means areas of habitable refuge existed where multicellular organisms could survive.

*Cryogenian Period: 크라이오제니아기

(600~850만 년 전 시기)

① 지구는 8천 5백만 년의 대부분의 기간 동안 얼어 있었지만 생명체는 살아남았다.
② 과학자들은 "눈덩이 지구" 기간 동안에도 지구의 표면에 다다른 태양의 온기가 크게 감소하지 않았다고 믿고 있다.
③ "슬러시볼 지구"의 기간 동안에 초기 형태의 복잡한 생명체가 생존하는 것은 가능했다.
④ 연구결과 "빙하 시대" 후반기의 세계의 바다가 완전히 얼지 않았다는 것이 입증되었다.

04 다음 빈칸에 들어갈 말로 가장 적절한 것은?

As global temperatures rise, so do sea levels, threatening coastal communities around the world. Surprisingly, even small organisms like oysters _____. Oysters are keystone species with ripple effects* on the health of their ecosystems and its inhabitants. Just one adult oyster can filter up to fifty gallons of water in a single day, making waterways cleaner. Healthy oyster reefs also provide a home for hundreds of other marine organisms, promoting biodiversity and ecosystem balance. As rising sea levels lead to pervasive flooding, oyster reefs act as walls to buffer storms and protect against further coastal erosion.

*ripple effect: 파급효과

① can come to our defense
② can be the food for emergency
③ may be contaminated by microplastics
④ can increase the income of local residents

05 다음 글의 내용을 한 문장으로 요약하고자 한다. 빈칸 (A), (B)에 들어갈 말로 가장 적절한 것은?

The myth of the taste map, which claims that different sections of the tongue are responsible for specific tastes, is incorrect, according to modern science. The taste map originated from the experiments of German scientist David Hänig in the early 1900s, which found that the tongue is most sensitive to tastes along the edges and not so much at the center. However, this has been misinterpreted over the years to claim that sweet is at the front of the tongue, bitter is at the back, and salty and sour are at the sides. In reality, different tastes are sensed by taste buds* all over the tongue. Taste buds work together to make us crave or dislike certain foods, based on our long-term learning and association. For example, our ancestors needed fruit for nutrients and easy calories, so we are naturally drawn to sweet tastes, while bitterness in some plants serves as a warning of toxicity. Of course, different species in the animal kingdom also have unique taste abilities: carnivores do not eat fruit and therefore do not crave sugar like humans do.

*taste bud: 미뢰

⇩

The claim that different parts of the tongue are responsible for specific tastes has been proven to be ___(A)___ by modern science, and the taste preferences are influenced by the ___(B)___ history.

	(A)	(B)
①	correct	evolutionary
②	false	evolutionary
③	false	psychological
④	correct	psychological

06 다음 글의 밑줄 친 부분 중 어법상 가장 틀린 것은?

Language is the primary means ① by which people communicate with one another. Although most creatures communicate, human speech is more complex, more creative, and ② used more extensively than the communication systems of other animals. Language is an essential part of what it means to be human and is a basic part of all cultures. Linguistic anthropology is concerned with understanding language and its relation to culture. Language is an amazing thing ③ what we take for granted. When we speak, we use our bodies—our lungs, vocal cords, mouth, tongue, and lips—to produce noises of varying tone and pitch. And, somehow, when we and others ④ do this together, we are able to communicate with one another, but only if we speak the same language. Linguistic anthropologists want to understand the variation among languages and how language is structured, learned, and used.

07 글의 흐름으로 보아, 주어진 문장이 들어가기에 가장 적절한 곳은?

> Healthcare chatbots have been purposed to solve this problem and ensure proper diagnosis and advice for people from the comfort of their homes.

> People have grown hesitant to approach hospitals or health centers due to the fear of contracting a disease or the heavy sum of consultation fees. (①) This leads them to self-diagnose themselves based upon unverified information sources on the Internet. (②) This often proves harmful effects on the person's mental and physical health if misdiagnosed and improper medicines are consumed. (③) Based upon the severity of the diagnosis, the chatbot prescribes over the counter treatment or escalates the diagnosis to a verified healthcare professional. (④) Interactive chatbots that have been trained on a large and wide variety of symptoms, risk factors, and treatment can handle user health queries with ease, especially in the case of COVID-19.

08 주어진 글 다음에 이어질 글의 순서로 가장 적절한 것은?

> Sports fan depression is a real phenomenon that affects many avid* sports fans, especially during times of disappointment or defeat.

> (A) Fans may experience a decrease in mood, appetite, and sleep quality, as well as an increase in stress levels and a heightened risk of developing anxiety or depression. There are many factors that can contribute to sports fan depression, including personal investment in a team's success, social pressures to support a particular team, and the intense media coverage and scrutiny that often accompanies high-profile sports events.
>
> (B) For many fans, their emotional investment in their favorite teams or athletes can be so intense that losing or failing to meet expectations can lead to feelings of sadness, frustration, and even depression. Research has shown that sports fan depression can have a range of negative effects on both mental and physical health.
>
> (C) To mitigate the negative effects of sports fan depression, it's important for fans to maintain a healthy perspective on sports and remember that they are ultimately just games. Engaging in self-care activities such as exercise, spending time with loved ones, and seeking support from a mental health professional can also be helpful.
>
> *avid: 열심인

① (A) - (C) - (B)
② (B) - (A) - (C)
③ (B) - (C) - (A)
④ (C) - (B) - (A)

09 Roald Dahl에 관한 다음 글의 내용과 가장 일치하지 않는 것은?

> Roald Dahl (1916-1990) was born in Wales of Norwegian parents. He spent his childhood in England and, at age eighteen, went to work for the Shell Oil Company in Africa. When World War II broke out, he joined the Royal Air Force and became a fighter pilot. At the age of twenty-six he moved to Washington, D.C., and it was there he began to write. His first short story, which recounted his adventures in the war, was bought by *The Saturday Evening Post*, and so began a long and illustrious career. After establishing himself as a writer for adults, Roald Dahl began writing children's stories in 1960 while living in England with his family. His first stories were written as entertainment for his own children, to whom many of his books are dedicated. Roald Dahl is now considered one of the most beloved storytellers of our time.

① 어린 시절을 영국에서 보냈고, 18세에 아프리카에서 일했다.

② 2차 세계대전이 발발했을 때는 공군에 입대하여 조종사가 되었다.

③ 전쟁에서 자신의 모험을 다룬 첫 번째 단편 소설을 썼다.

④ 성인을 위한 작가가 된 뒤 영국에서 가족과 떨어져 혼자 살면서 글을 썼다.

10 다음 글에서 전체 흐름과 가장 관계없는 문장은?

> One of the most interesting discoveries in the field of new sources of sustainable energy is bio-solar energy from jellyfish. Scientists have discovered that the fluorescent protein in this animal can be used to generate solar energy in a more sustainable way than current photovoltaic* energy. How is this energy generated? ① The process involves converting the jellyfish's fluorescent protein into a solar cell that is capable of generating energy and transferring it to small devices. ② There has been constant criticism that the natural environment is being damaged by reckless solar power generation. ③ The main advantage of using these living beings as a natural energy source is that they are a clean alternative that does not use fossil fuels or require the use of limited resources. ④ Although this project is still currently in the trial phase, the expectation is that this source of energy will be able to be expanded and become a green alternative for powering the type of small electronic devices that are becoming more and more common.
>
> *photovoltaic: 광전기성의

11 주어진 글 다음에 이어질 글의 순서로 가장 적절한 것은?

> On the human level, a cow seems simple. You feed it grass, and it pays you back with milk. It's a trick whose secret is limited to cows and a few other mammals (most can't digest grass).

> (A) A cow's complexity is even greater. In particular, a cow (plus a bull) can make a new generation of baby cows. This is a simple thing on a human level, but inexpressibly complex on a microscopic level.
>
> (B) Seen through a microscope, though, it all gets more complicated. And the closer you look, the more complicated it gets. Milk is not a single substance, but a mixture of many. Grass is so complex that we still don't fully understand it.
>
> (C) You don't need to understand the details to exploit the process: it's a straightforward transformation from grass into milk, more like chemistry—or alchemy*—than biology. It is, in its way, magic, but it's rational magic that works reliably. All you need is some grass, a cow and several generations of practical knowhow.
>
> *alchemy: 연금술

① (B) - (A) - (C)
② (B) - (C) - (A)
③ (C) - (A) - (B)
④ (C) - (B) - (A)

12 글의 흐름으로 보아, 주어진 문장이 들어가기에 가장 적절한 곳은?

> But here it's worth noting that more than half the workforce has little or no opportunity for remote work.

> COVID-19's spread flattened the cultural and technological barriers standing in the way of remote work. One analysis of the potential for remote work to persist showed that 20 to 25 percent of workforces in advanced economies could work from home in the range of three to five days a week. (①) This is four to five times more remote work than pre-COVID-19. (②) Moreover, not all work that can be done remotely should be; for example, negotiations, brainstorming, and providing sensitive feedback are activities that may be less effective when done remotely. (③) The outlook for remote work, then, depends on the work environment, job, and the tasks at hand, so hybrid* work setups, where some work happens on-site and some remotely, are likely to persist. (④) To unlock sustainable performance and well-being in a hybrid world, the leading driver of performance and productivity should be the sense of purpose work provides to employees, not compensation.
>
> *hybrid: 혼합체

13 Sigmund Freud에 관한 다음 글의 내용과 가장 일치하지 않는 것은?

Sigmund Freud was a doctor of psychology in Vienna, Austria at the end of the nineteenth century. He treated many patients with nervous problems through his "talk cure." For this type of treatment, Freud simply let his patients talk to him about anything that was bothering them. While treating his patients, he began to realize that although there were events in a patient's past that she or he might not remember consciously, these events could affect the person's actions in her or his present life. Freud called the place where past memories were hidden the unconscious mind. Images from the unconscious mind might show up in a person's dreams or through the person's actions. Freud wrote a book about his theories about the unconscious mind and dreaming in 1899. The title of the book was "The Interpretation of Dreams"

① 오스트리아의 정신과 의사였다.
② 신경 문제가 있는 환자들을 대화를 통해 치료했다.
③ 기억이 나지 않는 과거는 환자에게 영향을 미치지 못한다고 주장했다.
④ "꿈의 해석"이라는 책을 썼다.

14 다음 글의 요지로 가장 적절한 것은?

All emotions tell us something about ourselves and our situation. But sometimes we find it hard to accept what we feel. We might judge ourselves for feeling a certain way, like if we feel jealous, for example. But instead of thinking we should not feel that way, it's better to notice how we actually feel. Avoiding negative feelings or pretending we don't feel the way we do can backfire*. It's harder to move past difficult feelings and allow them to fade if we don't face them and try to understand why we feel that way. You don't have to dwell on your emotions or constantly talk about how you feel. Emotional awareness simply means recognizing, respecting, and accepting your feelings as they happen.

*backfire: 역효과를 내다

① 부정적인 감정은 잘 조절해서 표현해야 한다.
② 과거의 부정적 감정은 되도록 빨리 극복해야 한다.
③ 감정을 수용하기 어렵다면 전문가의 도움을 받아야 한다.
④ 우리의 감정을 인식하고 존중하며 그대로 받아들여야 한다.

15 주어진 글 다음에 이어질 글의 순서로 가장 적절한 것은?

> At the level of lawmaking, there is no reason why tech giants should have such an ironclad grip on technological resources and innovation.

> (A) As the Daily Wire's Matt Walsh has pointed out, for example, if you don't buy your kid a smartphone, he won't have one. There is no need to put in his hand a device that enables him to indulge his every impulse without supervision.

> (B) At the private and personal level, there's no reason why they should have control of your life, either. In policy, politics, and our personal lives, it should not be taken as "inevitable" that our data will be sold to the highest bidder, our children will be addicted to online games, and our lives will be lived in the metaverse.

> (C) As a free people, we are entitled to exert absolute control over which kinds of digital products we consume, and in what quantities. Most especially, parents should control what tech products go to their kids.

① (B) - (A) - (C)　　　② (B) - (C) - (A)
③ (C) - (A) - (B)　　　④ (C) - (B) - (A)

16 글의 흐름으로 보아, 주어진 문장이 들어가기에 가장 적절한 곳은?

> These may appear as challenges which may be impossible to address because of the uncertainty in our ability to predict future climate.

> Global warming is a reality man has to live with. (①) This is a very important issue to recognize, because, of all the parameters that affect human existence, on planet earth, it is the food security that is of paramount importance to life on earth and which is most threatened by global warming. (②) Future food security will be dependent on a combination of the stresses, both biotic and abiotic*, imposed by climate change, variability of weather within the growing season, development of cultivars* more suited to different ambient* conditions, and, the ability to develop effective adaptation strategies which allow these cultivars to express their genetic potential under the changing climate conditions. (③) However, these challenges also provide us the opportunities to enhance our understanding of soil-plant-atmosphere interaction and how one could utilize this knowledge to enable us achieve the ultimate goal of enhanced food security across all areas of the globe. (④)

*abiotic: 비생물적인
*cultivar: 품종
*ambient: 주변의

17 다음 글의 밑줄 친 부분 중, 어법상 가장 틀린 것은?

Anthropologist Paul Ekman proposed in the 1970s that humans experience six basic emotions: anger, fear, surprise, disgust, joy, and sadness. However, the exact number of emotions ① disputing, with some researchers suggesting there are only four, and others counting as many as 27. Additionally, scientists debate whether emotions are universal to all human cultures or whether we're born with them or learn them through experience. ② Despite these disagreements, emotions are clear products of activity in specific regions of the brain. The amygdala* and the insula or insular cortex* are two representative brain structures most ③ closely linked with emotions. The amygdala, a paired, almond-shaped structure deep within the brain, integrates emotions, emotional behavior, and motivation. It interprets fear, helps distinguish friends from foes, and identifies social rewards and how to attain ④ them. The insula is the source of disgust. The experience of disgust may protect you from ingesting poison or spoiled food.

*amygdala: 편도체
*insula cortex: 대뇌 피질

18 다음 글의 주제로 가장 적절한 것은?

Do you want to be a successful anchor? If so, keep this in mind. As an anchor, the individual will be called upon to communicate news and information to viewer during newscasts, special reports and other types of news programs. This will include interpreting news events, adlibbing, and communicating breaking news effectively when scripts are not available. Anchoring duties also involve gathering and writing stories. The anchor must be able to deliver scripts clearly and effectively. Strong writing skills, solid news judgement and a strong sense of visual storytelling are essential skills. This individual must be a self-starter who cultivates sources and finds new information as a regular part of job. Live reporting skills are important, as well as the ability to adlib and describe breaking news as it takes place.

① difficulties of producing live news
② qualifications to become a news anchor
③ the importance of the social role of journalists
④ the importance of forming the right public opinion

19 다음 글의 내용과 가장 일치하지 않는 것은?

Modern sculpture is generally considered to have begun with the work of French sculptor Auguste Rodin. Rodin, often considered a sculptural Impressionist, did not set out to rebel against artistic traditions, however, he incorporated novel ways of building his sculpture that defied classical categories and techniques. Specifically, Rodin modeled complex, turbulent, deeply pocketed surfaces into clay. While he never self-identified as an Impressionist, the vigorous, gestural modeling he employed in his works is often likened to the quick, gestural brush strokes* aiming to capture a fleeting moment that was typical of the Impressionists. Rodin's most original work departed from traditional themes of mythology and allegory*, in favor of modeling the human body with intense realism, and celebrating individual character and physicality.

*brush stroke: 붓놀림
*allegory: 우화, 풍자

① 현대 조각은 일반적으로 로댕의 작품에서 시작된 것으로 여겨진다.

② 로댕은 고전적인 기술을 거부하며 조각품을 만드는 새로운 방법을 통합했다.

③ 로댕은 자신을 인상파라고 밝히며 인상파의 전형적인 붓놀림을 보여주었다.

④ 로댕의 가장 독창적인 작품은 신화와 우화의 전통적인 주제에서 벗어나고자 했다.

20 다음 글의 주제로 가장 적절한 것은?

Cosmetics became so closely associated with portraiture that some photography handbooks included recipes for them. American photographers also, at times, used cosmetics to retouch negatives and prints, enlivening women's faces with traces of rouge. Some customers with dark skin requested photographs that would make them look lighter. A skin lightener advertisement that appeared in an African American newspaper in 1935 referenced this practice by promising that its product could achieve the same look produced by photographers: a lighter skin Cop free of blemishes*. By drawing attention to the face and encouraging cosmetics use, portrait photography heightened the aesthetic valuation of smooth and often light-colored skin.

*blemish: (피부 등의) 티

① side effects of excessive use of cosmetics

② overuse of cosmetics promoted by photographers

③ active use of cosmetics to make the face look better

④ decreased use of cosmetics due to advances in photography

21 다음 글의 밑줄 친 부분 중 문맥상 낱말의 쓰임이 가장 적절하지 않은 것은?

"Play is something done for its own sake." says psychiatrist Stuart Brown, author of "Play" He writes: "It's voluntary, it's pleasurable, it offers a sense of engagement, it takes you out of time. And the act itself is more important than the outcome." With this definition in mind, it's easy to recognize play's potential benefits. Play ① nurtures relationships with oneself and others. It ② relieves stress and increases happiness. It builds feelings of empathy, creativity, and collaboration. It supports the growth of sturdiness* and grit. When children are deprived of opportunities for play, their development can be significantly ③ enhanced. Play is so important that the United Nations High Commission on Human Rights declared it a ④ fundamental right of every child. Play is not frivolous*. It is not something to do after the "real work" is done. Play is the real work of childhood. Through it, children have their best chance for becoming whole, happy adults.

*sturdiness: 강건함

*frivolous: 경박한, 하찮은

22 다음 빈칸에 들어갈 말로 가장 적절한 것은?

Lewis Pugh is a British endurance swimmer, who is best known for his long-distance swims in cold and open waters. He swims in cold places as a way to draw attention to the urgent need to protect the world's oceans and waterways from the effects of climate change and pollution. In 2019, Pugh decided to swim in Lake Imja, which is located in the Khumbu region of Nepal, near Mount Everest. After a failed first attempt, Lewis had a debrief* to discuss the best way to swim at 5,300 meters above sea level. He is usually very aggressive when he swims because he wants to finish quickly and get out of the cold water. But this time he showed _____ and swam slowly.

*debrief: 평가회의

① grief   ② anger

③ humility   ④ confidence

23 다음 글에서 전체 흐름과 가장 관계없는 문장은?

Fast fashion is a method of producing inexpensive clothing at a rapid pace to respond to the latest fashion trends. With shopping evolving into a form of entertainment in the age of fast fashion, customers are contributing to what sustainability experts refer to as a throwaway culture. This means customers simply discard products once they are deemed useless rather than recycling or donating them. ① The consumers are generally satisfied with the quality of fast fashion brand clothing. ② As a result, these discarded items add a huge burden to the environment. ③ To resolve the throwaway culture and fast fashion crisis, the concept of sustainability in fashion is brought to the spotlight. ④ Sustainable fashion involves apparel, footwear, and accessories that are produced, distributed, and utilized as sustainably as possible while taking into account socio-economic and environmental concerns.

24 다음 글의 요지로 가장 적절한 것은?

Wrinkles are a sure sign of aging, and may also hint that bone health is on the decline. Researchers at Yale School of Medicine found that some women with deepening and worsening skin wrinkles also had lower bone density, independent of age and factors known to influence bone mass. Skin and bones share a common building-block protein, type 1 collagen, which is lost with age, says study author Dr. Lubna Pal. Wrinkles between the eyebrows—the vertical lines above the bridge of the nose—appear to be the strongest markers of brittle* bones, she says. Long-term studies are needed, but it appears the skin reflects what's happening at the level of the bone, says Pal.

*brittle: 잘 부러지는

① 나이가 들면서 주름이 생기는 것은 당연한 현상이다.
② 골밀도 감소와 주름 생성의 관계에 관해서는 연구가 더 필요하다.
③ 여성이 남성보다 주름이 더 많이 생기는 이유는 골밀도 차이 때문이다.
④ 주름은 단지 피부 노화와만 연관된 것이 아니라 뼈 건강 상태와도 연관이 있다.

25 다음 글의 내용과 가장 일치하지 않는 것은?

Meditation can improve your quality of life thanks to its many psychological and physical benefits. Mindfulness-based interventions, such as meditation, have been shown to improve mental health, specifically in the area of stress, according to a study in the Clinical Psychology Review. When faced with a difficult or stressful moment, our bodies create cortisol, the steroid hormone responsible for regulating stress and our natural fight-or-flight response, among many other functions. Chronic stress can cause sustained and elevated levels of cortisol, which can lead to other negative effects on your health, including cardiovascular* and immune systems and gut health. Meditation, which focuses on calming the mind and regulating emotion, can help to reduce chronic stress in the body and lower the risk of its side effects.

*cardiovascular: 심혈관계의

① Meditation benefits us both mentally and physically.

② Cortisol is released in a stressful situation.

③ Stress does not usually affect our cardiovascular systems.

④ Meditation can help lower chronic stress in the body.

✅ 회독 CHECK 1 2 3

01 (A), (B), (C)의 각 네모 안에서 어법에 맞는 표현으로 가장 적절한 것은?

The selection of the appropriate protective clothing for any job or task (A) is / are usually dictated by an analysis or assessment of the hazards presented. The expected activities of the wearer as well as the frequency and types of exposure, are typical variables that input into this determination. For example, a firefighter is exposed to a variety of burning materials. Specialized multilayer fabric systems are thus used (B) to meet / meeting the thermal* challenges presented. This results in protective gear that is usually fairly heavy and essentially provides the highest levels of protection against any fire situation. In contrast, an industrial worker who has to work in areas (C) where / which the possibility of a flash fire exists would have a very different set of hazards and requirements. In many cases, a flame-resistant coverall worn over cotton work clothes adequately addresses the hazard.

*thermal: 열의

	(A)	(B)	(C)
①	is	to meet	where
②	is	meeting	which
③	are	meeting	where
④	are	to meet	which

02 다음 글의 내용을 한 문장으로 요약하고자 한다. 빈칸 (A), (B)에 들어갈 말로 가장 적절한 것은?

In India, approximately 360 million people—one-third of the population—live in or very close to the forests. More than half of these people live below the official poverty line, and consequently they depend crucially on the resources they obtain from the forests. The Indian government now runs programs aimed at improving their lot by involving them in the commercial management of their forests, in this way allowing them to continue to obtain the food and materials they need, but at the same time to sell forest produce. If the programs succeed, forest dwellers will be more prosperous, but they will be able to preserve their traditional way of life and culture, and the forest will be managed sustainably, so the wildlife is not depleted.

⇩

The Indian government is trying to ____(A)____ the lives of the poor who live near forests without ____(B)____ the forests.

	(A)	(B)
①	improve	ruining
②	control	preserving
③	improve	limiting
④	control	enlarging

03 다음 글의 내용을 한 문장으로 요약하고자 한다. 빈칸 (A), (B)에 들어갈 말로 가장 적절한 것은?

In the absence of facial cues or touch during pandemic, there is a greater need to focus on other aspects of conversation, including more emphasis on tone and inflection, slowing the speed, and increasing loudness without sounding annoying. Many nuances* of the spoken word are easily missed without facial expression, so eye contact will assume an even greater importance. Some hospital workers have developed innovative ways to try to solve this problem. One of nurse specialists was deeply concerned that her chronically sick young patients could not see her face, so she printed off a variety of face stickers to get children to point towards. Some hospitals now also provide their patients with 'face—sheets' that permit easier identification of staff members, and it is always useful to reintroduce yourself and colleagues to patients when wearing masks.

*nuance: 미묘한 차이, 뉘앙스

⇩

Some hospitals and workers are looking for ___(A)___ ways to ___(B)___ conversation with patients during pandemic.

	(A)	(B)
①	alternative	complement
②	bothering	analyze
③	effective	hinder
④	disturbing	improve

04 주어진 글 다음에 이어질 글의 순서로 가장 적절한 것은?

Once they leave their mother, primates have to keep on making decisions about whether new foods they encounter are safe and worth collecting.

(A) By the same token, if the sampler feels fine, it will reenter the tree in a few days, eat a little more, then wait again, building up to a large dose slowly. Finally, if the monkey remains healthy, the other members figure this is OK, and they adopt the new food.

(B) If the plant harbors a particularly strong toxin, the sampler's system will try to break it down, usually making the monkey sick in the process. "I've seen this happen," says Glander. "The other members of the troop are watching with great interest—if the animal gets sick, no other animal will go into that tree. There's a cue being given—a social cue."

(C) Using themselves as experiment tools is one option, but social primates have found a better way. Kenneth Glander calls it "sampling." When howler monkeys move into a new habitat, one member of the troop will go to a tree, eat a few leaves, then wait a day.

① (A) - (B) - (C)
② (B) - (A) - (C)
③ (C) - (B) - (A)
④ (C) - (A) - (B)

05 다음 글의 Zainichi에 관한 내용으로 가장 일치하지 않는 것은?

Following Japan's defeat in World War II, the majority of ethnic Koreans (1-1.4 million) left Japan. By 1948, the population of ethnic Koreans settled around 600,000. These Koreans and their descendants are commonly referred to as Zainichi (literally "residing in Japan"), a term that appeared in the immediate postwar years. Ethnic Koreans who remained in Japan did so for diverse reasons. Koreans who had achieved successful careers in business, the imperial bureaucracy, and the military during the colonial period or who had taken advantage of economic opportunities that opened up immediately after the war—opted to maintain their relatively privileged status in Japanese society rather than risk returning to an impoverished and politically unstable post-liberation Korea. Some Koreans who repatriated* were so repulsed by the poor conditions they observed that they decided to return to Japan. Other Koreans living in Japan could not afford the train fare to one of the departure ports, and among them who had ethnic Japanese spouses and Japanese-born, Japanese-speaking children, it made more sense to stay in Japan rather than navigate the cultural and linguistic challenges of a new environment.

*repatriate: 본국으로 송환하다

① 주로 제2차 세계대전 이후에 일본에 남은 한국인들과 후손을 일컫는다.
② 전쟁 후에 경제적인 이득을 취한 사람들도 있었다.
③ 어떤 사람들은 한국에 갔다가 다시 일본으로 돌아왔다.
④ 한국으로 돌아갈 교통비를 마련하지 못한 사람들은 일본인과 결혼했다.

06 다음 빈칸에 들어갈 말로 가장 적절한 것은?

There are a few jobs where people have had to _____. We see referees and umpires using their arms and hands to signal directions to the players—as in cricket, where a single finger upwards means that the batsman is out and has to leave the wicket*. Orchestra conductors control the musicians through their movements. People working at a distance from each other have to invent special signals if they want to communicate. So do people working in a noisy environment, such as in a factory where the machines are very loud, or lifeguards around a swimming pool full of school children.

*wicket: (크리켓에서) 삼주문

① support their parents and children
② adapt to an entirely new work style
③ fight in court for basic human rights
④ develop their signing a bit more fully

07 다음 글의 내용과 가장 일치하지 않는 것은?

Opponents of the use of animals in research also oppose use of animals to test the safety of drugs or other compounds. Within the pharmaceutical industry, it was noted that out of 19 chemicals known to cause cancer in humans when taken, only seven caused cancer in mice and rats using standards set by the National Cancer Instituted(Barnard and Koufman, 1997). For example, and antidepressant, nomifensin, had minimal toxicity in rats, rabbits, dogs, and monkeys yet caused liver toxicity and anemia[*] in humans. In these and other cases, it has been shown that some compounds have serious adverse reactions in humans that were not predicted by animal testing resulting in conditions in the treated humans that could lead to disability, or even death. And researchers who are calling for an end to animal research state that they have better methods available such as human clinical trials, observation aided by laboratory of autopsy tests.

*anemia: 빈혈

① 한 기관의 실험 결과 동물과 달리 19개의 발암물질 중에 7개는 인간에게 영향을 미쳤다.
② 어떤 약물은 동물 실험 때와 달리 인간에게 간독성과 빈혈을 일으켰다.
③ 동물 실험에서 나타난 결과가 인간에게는 다르게 작용될 수 있다.
④ 동물 실험을 반대하는 연구자들은 대안적인 방법들을 제시하고 있다.

08 다음 중 문맥상 낱말의 쓰임이 가장 적절하지 않은 것은?

Cold showers are any showers with a water temperature below 70°F. They may have health benefits. For people with depression, cold showers can work as a kind of gentle electroshock therapy. The cold water sends many electrical impulses to your brain. They jolt* your system to ① increase alertness, clarity, and energy levels. Endorphins, which are sometimes called happiness hormones, are also released. This effect leads to feelings of well-being and ② optimism. For people that are obese, taking a cold shower 2 or 3 times per week may contribute to increased metabolism. It may help fight obesity over time. The research about how exactly cold showers help people lose weight is ③ clear. However, it does show that cold water can even out certain hormone levels and heal the gastrointestinal* system. These effects may add to the cold shower's ability to lead to weight loss. Furthermore, when taken regularly, cold showers can make our circulatory system more efficient. Some people also report that their skin looks better as a result of cold showers, probably because of better circulation. Athletes have known this benefit for years, even if we have only ④ recently seen data that supports cold water for healing after a sport injury.

*jolt: 갑자기 덜컥 움직이다
*gastrointestinal: 위장의

09 다음 글의 내용을 한 문장으로 요약하고자 한다. 빈칸 (A), (B)에 들어갈 말로 가장 적절한 것은?

> Researchers have been interested in the habitual ways a single individual copes with conflict when it occurs. They've called this approach conflict styles. There are several apparent conflict styles, and each has its pros and cons. The collaborating style tends to solve problems in ways that maximize the chances that the best result is provided for all involved. The pluses of a collaborating style include creating trust, maintaining positive relationship, and building commitment. However, it's time consuming and it takes a lot of energy to collaborate with another during conflict. The competing style may develop hostility in the person who doesn't achieve their goals. However, the competing style tends to resolve a conflict quickly.

⇩

> The collaborating style might be used for someone who put a great value in ___(A)___, while a person who prefers ___(B)___ may choose the competing style.

	(A)	(B)
①	financial ability	interaction
②	saving time	peacefulness
③	mutual understanding	time efficiency
④	effectiveness	consistency

10 주어진 글 다음에 이어질 글의 순서로 가장 적절한 것은?

> The historical evolution of Conflict Resolution gained momentum in the 1950s and 1960s, at the height of the Cold War, when the development of nuclear weapons and conflict between the superpowers seemed to threaten human survival.

> (A) The combination of analysis and practice implicit in the new ideas was not easy to reconcile with traditional scholarly institutions or the traditions of practitioners such as diplomats and politicians.
>
> (B) However, they were not taken seriously by some. The international relations profession had its own understanding of international conflict and did not see value in the new approaches as proposed.
>
> (C) A group of pioneers from different disciplines saw the value of studying conflict as a general phenomenon, with similar properties, whether it occurs in international relations, domestic politics, industrial relations, communities, or between individuals.

① (B) - (A) - (C)
② (B) - (C) - (A)
③ (C) - (A) - (B)
④ (C) - (B) - (A)

11 (A), (B), (C)의 각 네모 안에서 어법에 맞는 표현으로 가장 적절한 것은?

The key to understanding economics is accepting (A) [that / what] there are always unintended consequences. Actions people take for their own good reasons have results they don't envision or intend. The same is true with geopolitics*. It is doubtful that the village of Rome, when it started its expansion in the seventh century BC, (B) [had / have] a master plan for conquering the Mediterranean world five hundred years later. But the first action its inhabitants took against neighboring villages set in motion a process that was both constrained by reality and (C) [filled / filling] with unintended consequences. Rome wasn't planned, and neither did it just happen.

*geopolitics: 지정학

	(A)	(B)	(C)
①	that	had	filled
②	what	had	filling
③	what	have	filled
④	that	have	filling

12 다음 빈칸에 들어갈 말로 가장 적절한 것을 고르시오.

Water and civilization go hand-in-hand. The idea of a "hydraulic* civilization" argues that water is the unifying context and justification for many large-scale civilizations throughout history. For example, the various multi-century Chinese empires survived as long as they did in part by controlling floods along the Yellow River. One interpretation of the hydraulic theory is that the justification for gathering populations into large cities is to manage water. Another interpretation suggests that large water projects enable the rise of big cities. The Romans understood the connections between water and power, as the Roman Empire built a vast network of aqueducts* throughout land they controlled, many of which remain intact. For example, Pont du Gard in southern France stands today as a testament to humanity's investment in its water infrastructure. Roman governors built roads, bridges, and water systems as a way of _____.

*hydraulic: 수력학의

*aqueduct: 송수로

---

① focusing on educating young people

② prohibiting free trade in local markets

③ concentrating and strengthening their authority

④ giving up their properties to other countries

13 주어진 글 다음에 이어질 글의 순서로 가장 적절한 것은?

> Ambiguity is so uncomfortable that it can even turn good news into bad. You go to your doctor with a persistent stomachache. Your doctor can't figure out what the reason is, so she sends you to the lab for tests.

> (A) And what happens? Your immediate relief may be replaced by a weird sense of discomfort. You still don't know what the pain was! There's got to be an explanation somewhere.
>
> (B) A week later you're called back to hear the results. When you finally get into her office, your doctor smiles and tells you the tests were all negative.
>
> (C) Maybe it is cancer and they've just missed it. Maybe it's worse. Surely they should be able to find a cause. You feel frustrated by the lack of a definitive answer.

① (B) - (A) - (C)

② (B) - (C) - (A)

③ (C) - (A) - (B)

④ (C) - (B) - (A)

14 글의 흐름으로 보아, 주어진 문장이 들어가기에 가장 적절한 곳은?

> The effect, however, was just the reverse.

> How we dress for work has taken on a new element of choice, and with it, new anxieties. (①) The practice of having a "dress-down day" or "casual day," which began to emerge a decade or so ago, was intended to make life easier for employees, to enable them to save money and feel more relaxed at the office. (②) In addition to the normal workplace wardrobe, employees had to create a "workplace casual" wardrobe*. (③) It couldn't really be the sweats and T-shirts you wore around the house on the weekend. (④) It had to be a selection of clothing that sustained a certain image—relaxed, but also serious.
>
> *wardrobe: 옷, 의류

15 다음 글의 밑줄 친 부분 중 어법상 가장 틀린 것은?

> You should choose the research method ① that best suits the outcome you want. You may run a survey online that enables you to question large numbers of people and ② provides full analysis in report format, or you may think asking questions one to one is a better way to get the answers you need from a smaller test selection of people. ③ Whichever way you choose, you will need to compare like for like. Ask people the same questions and compare answers. Look for both similarities and differences. Look for patterns and trends. Deciding on a way of recording and analysing the data ④ are important. A simple self created spreadsheet may well be enough to record some basic research data.

16 다음 글의 요지로 가장 적절한 것은?

Some criminal offenders may engage in illegal behavior because they love the excitement and thrills that crime can provide. In his highly influential work *Seductions of Crime*, sociologist Jack Katz argues that there are immediate benefits to criminality that "seduce" people into a life of crime. For some people, shoplifting and vandalism* are attractive because getting away with crime is a thrilling demonstration of personal competence. The need for excitement may counter fear of apprehension and punishment. In fact, some offenders will deliberately seek out especially risky situations because of the added "thrill". The need for excitement is a significant predictor of criminal choice.

*vandalism: 기물 파손

① 범죄를 줄이기 위해서 재소자를 상대로 한 교육이 필요하다.
② 범죄 행위에서 생기는 흥분과 쾌감이 범죄를 유발할 수 있다.
③ 엄격한 형벌 제도와 법 집행을 통해 강력 범죄를 줄일 수 있다.
④ 세밀하고 꼼꼼한 제도를 만들어 범죄 피해자를 도울 필요가 있다.

17 다음 빈칸에 들어갈 말로 가장 적절한 것은?

In one classic study showing the importance of attachment, Wisconsin University psychologists Harry and Margaret Harlow investigated the responses of young monkeys. The infants were separated from their biological mothers, and two surrogate* mothers were introduced to their cages. One, the wire mother, consisted of a round wooden head, a mesh of cold metal wires, and a bottle of milk from which the baby monkey could drink. The second mother was a foam-rubber form wrapped in a heated terry-cloth blanket. The infant monkeys went to the wire mother for food, but they overwhelmingly preferred and spent significantly more time with the warm terry-cloth mother. The warm terry-cloth mother provided no food, but did provide _____.

*surrogate: 대리의

① jobs
② drugs
③ comfort
④ education

18 다음 글의 밑줄 친 부분 중 어법상 가장 틀린 것은?

I was released for adoption by my biological parents and ① spend the first decade of my life in orphanages. I spent many years thinking that something was wrong with me. If my own parents didn't want me, who could? I tried to figure out ② what I had done wrong and why so many people sent me away. I don't get close to anyone now because if I do they might leave me. I had to isolate ③ myself emotionally to survive when I was a child, and I still operate on the assumptions I had as a child. I am so fearful of being deserted ④ that I won't venture out and take even minimal risks. I am 40 years old now, but I still feel like a child.

19 다음 글의 밑줄 친 부분 중 어법상 가장 틀린 것은?

Music can have psychotherapeutic* effects that may transfer to everyday life. A number of scholars suggested people ① to use music as psychotherapeutic agent. Music therapy can be broadly defined as being 'the use of music as an adjunct to the treatment or rehabilitation of individuals to enhance their psychological, physical, cognitive or social ② functioning'. Positive emotional experiences from music may improve therapeutic process and thus ③ strengthen traditional cognitive/behavioral methods and their transfer to everyday goals. This may be partially because emotional experiences elicited by music and everyday behaviors ④ share overlapping neurological pathways responsible for positive emotions and motivations.

*psychotherapeutic: 심리 요법의

20 다음 빈칸에 들어갈 말로 가장 적절한 것은?

Cultural interpretations are usually made on the basis of _____ rather than measurable evidence. The arguments tend to be circular. People are poor because they are lazy. How do we "know" they are lazy? Because they are poor. Promoters of these interpretations rarely understand that low productivity results not from laziness and lack of effort but from lack of capital inputs to production. African farmers are not lazy, but they do lack soil nutrients, tractors, feeder roads, irrigated plots, storage facilities, and the like. Stereotypes that Africans work little and therefore are poor are put to rest immediately by spending a day in a village, where backbreaking labor by men and women is the norm.

① statistics
② prejudice
③ appearance
④ circumstances

21 글의 흐름으로 보아, 주어진 문장이 들어가기에 가장 적절한 곳은?

> But the demand for food isn't elastic*; people don't eat more just because food is cheap.
>
> *elastic: 탄력성 있는

The free market has never worked in agriculture and it never will. (①) The economics of a family farm are very different than a firm's: When prices fall, the firm can lay off people and idle factories. (②) Eventually the market finds a new balance between supply and demand. (③) And laying off farmers doesn't help to reduce supply. (④) You can fire me, but you can't fire my land, because some other farmer who needs more cash flow or thinks he's more efficient than I am will come in and farm it.

22 다음 글의 주제로 가장 적절한 것은?

Daily training creates special nutritional needs for an athlete, particularly the elite athlete whose training commitment is almost a fulltime job. But even recreational sport will create nutritional challenges. And whatever your level of involvement in sport, you must meet these challenges if you're to achieve the maximum return from training. Without sound eating, much of the purpose of your training might be lost. In the worst-case scenario, dietary problems and deficiencies may directly impair training performance. In other situations, you might improve, but at a rate that is below your potential or slower than your competitors. However, on the positive side, with the right everyday eating plan your commitment to training will be fully rewarded.

① how to improve body flexibility

② importance of eating well in exercise

③ health problems caused by excessive diet

④ improving skills through continuous training

23 다음 글의 주제로 가장 적절한 것은?

A very well-respected art historian called Ernst Gombrich wrote about something called "the beholder's share". It was Gombrich's belief that a viewer "completed" the artwork, that part of an artwork's meaning came from the person viewing it. So you see—there really are no wrong answers as it is you, as the viewer who is completing the artwork. If you're looking at art in a gallery, read the wall text at the side of the artwork. If staff are present, ask questions. Ask your fellow visitors what they think. Asking questions is the key to understanding more—and that goes for anything in life—not just art. But above all, have confidence in front of an artwork. If you are contemplating an artwork, then you are the intended viewer and what you think matters. You are the only critic that counts.

① 미술 작품의 가치는 일정 부분 정해져 있다.

② 미술 작품을 제작할 때 대중의 요구를 반영해야 한다.

③ 미술 작품은 감상하는 사람으로 인하여 비로소 완성된다.

④ 미술 감상의 출발은 작가의 숨겨진 의도를 파악하는 것이다.

24 Argentina에 관한 다음 글의 내용과 가장 일치하지 않는 것은?

Argentina is the world's eighth largest country, comprising almost the entire southern half of South America. Colonization by Spain began in the early 1500s, but in 1816 Jose de San Martin led the movement for Argentine independence. The culture of Argentina has been greatly influenced by the massive European migration in the late nineteenth and early twentieth centuries, primarily from Spain and Italy. The majority of people are at least nominally Catholic, and the country has the largest Jewish population (about 300,000) in South America. From 1880 to 1930, thanks to its agricultural development, Argentina was one of the world's top ten wealthiest nations.

① Jose de San Martin이 스페인으로부터의 독립운동을 이끌었다.

② 북미 출신 이주민들이 그 문화에 많은 영향을 끼쳤다.

③ 남미지역 중에서 가장 많은 유대인들이 살고 있는 곳이다.

④ 농업의 발전으로 한때 부유한 국가였다.

25 Sonja Henie에 관한 다음 글의 내용과 가장 일치하지 않는 것은?

> Sonja Henie is famous for her skill into a career as one of the world's most famous figure skaters— in the rink and on the screen. Henie, winner of three Olympic gold medals and a Norwegian and European champion, invented a thrillingly theatrical and athletic style of figure skating. She introduced short skirts, white skates, and attractive moves. Her spectacular spins and jumps raised the bar for all competitors. In 1936, Twentieth-Century Fox signed her to star in One in a Million, and she soon became one of Hollywood's leading actresses. In 1941, the movie 'Sun Valley Serenade' received three Academy Award nominations which she played as an actress. Although the rest of Henie's films were less acclaimed, she triggered a popular surge in ice skating. In 1938, she launched extravagant touring shows called Hollywood Ice Revues. Her many ventures made her a fortune, but her greatest legacy was inspiring little girls to skate.

① 피겨 스케이터와 영화배우로서의 업적으로 유명하다.

② 올림픽과 다른 대회들에서 좋은 성적을 거두었다.

③ 출연한 영화가 1941년에 영화제에서 3개 부문에 수상했다.

④ 어린 여자아이들에게 스케이트에 대한 영감을 주었다.

✅ 회독 CHECK 1 2 3

01 다음 글의 내용을 한 문장으로 요약하고자 한다. 빈칸 (A)와 (B)에 들어갈 말로 가장 적절한 것은?

Microorganisms are not calculating entities. They don't care what they do to you any more than you care what distress you cause when you slaughter them by the millions with a soapy shower. The only time a pathogen* cares about you is when it kills you too well. If they eliminate you before they can move on, then they may well die out themselves. This in fact sometimes happens. History, Jared Diamond notes, is full of diseases that "once caused terrifying epidemics and then disappeared as mysteriously as they had come." He cites the robust but mercifully transient English sweating sickness, which raged from 1485 to 1552, killing tens of thousands as it went, before burning itself out. Too much efficiency is not a good thing for any infectious organism.

*pathogen: 병원체

⇩

The more ___(A)___ pathogens are, the faster it is likely be to ___(B)___.

	(A)	(B)
①	weaker	disappear
②	weaker	spread
③	infectious	spread
④	infectious	disappear

02 밑줄 친 "drains the mind"가 위 글에서 의미하는 바로 가장 적절한 것은?

If the writing is solid and good, the mood and temper of the writer will eventually be revealed and not at the expense of the work. Therefore, to achieve style, begin by affecting none—that is, draw the reader's attention to the sense and substance of the writing. A careful and honest writer does not need to worry about style. As you become proficient in the use of language, your style will emerge, because you yourself will emerge, and when this happens you will find it increasingly easy to break through the barriers that separate you from other minds and at last, make you stand in the middle of the writing. Fortunately, the act of composition, or creation, disciplines the mind; writing is one way to go about thinking, and the practice and habit of writing drains the mind.

① to heal the mind
② to help to be sensitive
③ to satisfy his/her curiosity
④ to place oneself in the background

03 (A), (B), (C)의 각 네모 안에서 어법에 맞는 표현으로 가장 적절한 것은?

Some of our dissatisfactions with self and with our lot in life are based on real circumstances, and some are false and simply (A) perceive / perceived to be real. The perceived must be sorted out and discarded. The real will either fall into the changeable or the unchangeable classification. If it's in the latter, we must strive to accept it. If it's in the former, then we have the alternative to strive instead to remove, exchange, or modify it. All of us have a unique purpose in life; and all of us are gifted, just (B) different / differently gifted. It's not an argument about whether it's fair or unfair to have been given one, five, or ten talents; it's about what we have done with our talents. It's about how well we have invested (C) them / those we have been given. If one holds on to the outlook that their life is unfair, then that's really holding an offense against God.

	(A)	(B)	(C)
①	perceive	different	them
②	perceive	differently	those
③	perceived	different	them
④	perceived	differently	those

04 주어진 글 다음에 이어질 글의 순서로 가장 적절한 것은?

People assume that, by charging a low price or one lower than their competitors, they will get more customers. This is a common fallacy.

(A) It is, therefore, far better to have lower-volume, higher-margin products and services as you start; you can always negotiate to reduce your price if you are forced to, but it is rare that you will be able to negotiate an increase.

(B) It is because when you charge reduced prices compared to your competition, you attract the lower end of the customer market. These customers want more for less and often take up more time and overhead in your business. They may also be your most difficult customers to deal with and keep happy.

(C) You also, ironically, repel* the better customers because they will pay a higher price for a higher level of product or service. We have seen many competitors come into the market and charge day rates that aren't sustainable. They often struggle even to fill their quota, and soon enough they give up and move on to doing something else.

*repel: 쫓아 버리다

① (B) - (A) - (C)

② (B) - (C) - (A)

③ (C) - (A) - (B)

④ (C) - (B) - (A)

05 다음 글의 밑줄 친 부분 중 어법상 가장 틀린 것은?

Children who enjoy writing are often interested in seeing ① their work in print. One informal approach is to type, print, and post their poetry. Or you can create a photocopied anthology* of the poetry of many child writers. But for children who are truly dedicated and ambitious, ② submit a poem for publication is a worthy goal. And there are several web and print resources that print children's original poetry. Help child poets become familiar with the protocol* for submitting manuscripts (style, format, and so forth). Let them choose ③ which poems they are most proud of, keep copies of everything submitted, and get parent permission. Then celebrate with them when their work is accepted and appear in print. Congratulate them, ④ publicly showcase their accomplishment, and spread the word. Success inspires success. And, of course, if their work is rejected, offer support and encouragement.

*anthology: 문집, 선집
*protocol: 규약, 의례

06 글의 흐름으로 보아, 주어진 문장이 들어가기에 가장 적절한 곳은?

With love and strength from the tribe, the tiny seeds mature and grow tall and crops for the people.

In the Pueblo indian culture, corn is to the people the very symbol of life. (①) The Corn Maiden "grandmother of the sun and the light" brought this gift, bringing the power of life to the people. (②) As the corn is given life by the sun, the Corn Maiden brings the fire of the sun into the human bodies, giving man many representations of his love and power through nature. (③) Each Maiden brings one seed of corn that is nurtured with love like that given to a child and this one seed would sustain the entire tribe forever. (④) The spirit of the Corn Maidens is forever present with the tribal people.

07 다음 빈칸에 들어갈 말로 가장 적절한 것은?

Beeches, oaks, spruce and pines produce new growth all the time, and have to get rid of the old. The most obvious change happens every autumn. The leaves have served their purpose: they are now worn out and riddled with insect damage. Before the trees bid them adieu, they pump waste products into them. You could say they are taking this opportunity to relieve themselves. Then they grow a layer of weak tissue to separate each leaf from the twig it's growing on, and the leaves tumble to the ground in the next breeze. The rustling leaves that now blanket the ground—and make such a satisfying scrunching sound when you scuffle through them—are basically _____.

① tree toilet paper　　② the plant kitchen
③ lungs of the tree　　④ parents of insects

08 글의 흐름상 가장 어색한 문장은?

Fiction has many uses and one of them is to build empathy. When you watch TV or see a film, you are looking at things happening to other people. Prose fiction is something you build up from 26 letters and a handful of punctuation marks, and you, and you alone, using your imagination, create a world and live there and look out through other eyes. ① You get to feel things, and visit places and worlds you would never otherwise know. ② Fortunately, in the last decade, many of the world's most beautiful and unknown places have been put in the spotlight. ③ You learn that everyone else out there is a me, as well. ④ You're being someone else, and when you return to your own world, you're going to be slightly changed.

09 다음 빈칸에 들어갈 말로 가장 적절한 것은?

The seeds of willows and poplars are so minuscule* that you can just make out two tiny dark dots in the fluffy flight hairs. One of these seeds weighs a mere 0.0001 grams. With such a meagre energy reserve, a seedling can grow only 1-2 millimetres before it runs out of steam and has to rely on food it makes for itself using its young leaves. But that only works in places where there's no competition to threaten the tiny sprouts. Other plants casting shade on it would extinguish the new life immediately. And so, if a fluffy little seed package like this falls in a spruce or beech forest, the seed's life is over before it's even begun. That's why willows and poplars _____.

*minuscule: 아주 작은

① prefer settling in unoccupied territory
② have been chosen as food for herbivores
③ have evolved to avoid human intervention
④ wear their dead leaves far into the winter

10 다음 글의 밑줄 친 부분 중 문맥상 낱말의 쓰임이 가장 적절하지 않은 것은?

Good walking shoes are important. Most major athletic brands offer shoes especially designed for walking. Fit and comfort are more important than style; your shoes should feel ① supportive but not tight or constricting. The uppers should be light, breathable, and flexible, the insole moisture-resistant, and the sole ② shock-absorbent. The heel wedge should be ③ lowered, so the sole at the back of the shoe is two times thicker than at the front. Finally, the toe box should be ④ spacious, even when you're wearing athletic socks.

① supportive　　② shock-absorbent
③ lowered　　④ spacious

11 다음 글의 요지로 가장 알맞은 것은?

If your kids fight every time they play video games, make sure you're close enough to be able to hear them when they sit down to play. Listen for the particular words or tones of voice they are using that are aggressive, and try to intervene before it develops. Once tempers have settled, try to sit your kids down and discuss the problem without blaming or accusing. Give each kid a chance to talk, uninterrupted, and have them try to come up with solutions to the problem themselves. By the time kids are elementary-school age, they can evaluate which of those solutions are win-win solutions and which ones are most likely to work and satisfy each other over time. They should also learn to revisit problems when solutions are no longer working.

① Ask your kids to evaluate their test.
② Make your kids compete each other.
③ Help your kids learn to resolve conflict.
④ Teach your kids how to win an argument.

12 다음 글의 요지로 가장 적절한 것은?

There's a current trend to avoid germs at all cost. We disinfect our bathrooms, kitchens, and the air. We sanitize our hands and gargle with mouthwash to kill germs. Some folks avoid as much human contact as possible and won't even shake your hand for fear of getting germs. I think it's safe to say that some people would purify everything but their minds. Remember the story of "the Boy in the Bubble"? He was born without an immune system and had to live in a room that was completely germ free, with no human contact. Of course, everyone should take prudent measures to maintain reasonable standards of cleanliness and personal hygiene, but in many cases, aren't we going overboard? When we come in contact with most germs, our body destroys them, which in turn strengthens our immune system and its ability to further fight off disease. Thus, these "good germs" actually make us healthier. Even if it were possible to avoid all germs and to live in a sterile environment, wouldn't we then be like "the Boy in the Bubble"?

① 세균에 감염되지 않도록 개인의 위생 환경 조성이 필요하다.
② 면역 능력이 상실된 채로 태어난 유아에 대한 치료가 시급하다.
③ 지역사회의 방역 능력 강화를 위해 국가의 재정 지원이 시급하다.
④ 과도하게 세균을 제거하려고 하는 것이 오히려 면역 능력을 해친다.

13 다음 글의 밑줄 친 부분을 어법상 바르게 고친 것이 아닌 것은?

① Knowing as the Golden City, Jaisalmer, a former caravan center on the route to the Khyber Pass, rises from a sea of sand, its 30-foot-high walls and medieval sandstone fort ② shelters carved spires and palaces that soar into the sapphire sky. With its tiny winding lanes and hidden temples, Jaisalmer is straight out of The Arabian Nights, and so little has life altered here ③ which it's easy to imagine yourself back in the 13th century. It's the only fortress city in India still functioning, with one quarter of its population ④ lived within the walls, and it's just far enough off the beaten path to have been spared the worst ravages of tourism. The city's wealth originally came from the substantial tolls it placed on passing camel caravans.

① Knowing → Known
② shelters → sheltering
③ which → that
④ lived → lives

14 다음 글에서 필자가 주장하는 바로 가장 적절한 것은?

The learned are neither apathetic* nor indifferent regarding the world's problems. More books on these issues are being published than ever, though few capture the general public's attention. Likewise, new research discoveries are constantly being made at universities, and shared at conferences worldwide. Unfortunately, most of this activity is self-serving. With the exception of science—and here, too, only selectively—new insights are not trickling* down to the public in ways to help improve our lives. Yet, these discoveries aren't simply the property of the elite, and should not remain in the possession of a select few professionals. Each person must make his and her own life's decisions, and make those choices in light of our current understanding of who we are and what is good for us. For that matter, we must find a way to somehow make new discoveries accessible to every person.

*apathetic: 냉담한, 무관심한
*trickle: 흐르다

① 학자들은 연구 논문을 작성할 때 주관성을 배제해야 한다.
② 새로운 연구 결과에 모든 사람이 접근할 수 있게 해야 한다.
③ 소수 엘리트 학자들의 폐쇄성을 극복할 계기를 마련해야 한다.
④ 학자들이 연구 과정에서 겪는 어려움을 극복하도록 도와야 한다.

15 다음 글의 주제로 가장 알맞은 것은?

Language gives individual identity and a sense of belonging. When children proudly learn their language and are able to speak it at home and in their neighborhood, the children will have a high self-esteem. Moreover, children who know the true value of their mother tongue will not feel like they are achievers when they speak a foreign language. With improved self-identity and self-esteem, the classroom performance of a child also improves because such a child goes to school with less worries about linguistic marginalization*.

*linguistic marginalization: 언어적 소외감

① the importance of mother tongue in child development
② the effect on children's foreign language learning
③ the way to improve children's self-esteem
④ the efficiency of the linguistic analysis

16 다음 글의 주제로 가장 적절한 것은?

Many animals are not loners. They discovered, or perhaps nature discovered for them, that by living and working together, they could interact with the world more effectively. For example, if an animal hunts for food by itself, it can only catch, kill, and eat animals much smaller than itself—but if animals band together in a group, they can catch and kill animals bigger than they are. A pack of wolves can kill a horse, which can feed the group very well. Thus, more food is available to the same animals in the same forest if they work together than if they work alone. Cooperation has other benefits: The animals can alert each other to danger, can find more food (if they search separately and then follow the ones who succeed in finding food), and can even provide some care to those who are sick and injured. Mating and reproduction are also easier if the animals live in a group than if they live far apart.

① benefits of being social in animals
② drawbacks of cooperative behaviors
③ common traits of animals and humans
④ competitions in mating and reproduction

17 다음 글의 밑줄 친 부분 중 문맥상 낱말의 쓰임이 가장 적절하지 않은 것은?

My own curiosity had been encouraged by my studies in philosophy at university. The course listed the numerous philosophers that we were supposed to study and I thought at first that our task was to learn and absorb their work as a sort of secular Bible. But I was ① delighted to discover that my tutor was not interested in me reciting their theories but only in helping me to develop my own, using the philosophers of the past as stimulants not authorities. It was the key to my intellectual ② freedom. Now I had official permission to think for myself, to question anything and everything and only agree if I thought it right. A ③ good education would have given me that permission much earlier. Some, alas, never seem to have received it and go on reciting the rules of others as if they were sacrosanct*. As a result, they become the unwitting* ④ opponents of other people's worlds. Philosophy, I now think, is too important to be left to professional philosophers. We should all learn to think like philosophers, starting at primary school.

*sacrosanct: 신성불가침의

*unwitting: 자신도 모르는

18 (A), (B), (C)의 괄호 안에서 어법에 맞는 표현으로 가장 적절한 것은?

Looking back, scientists have uncovered a mountain of evidence (A) [that / what] Mayan leaders were aware for many centuries of their uncertain dependence on rainfall. Water shortages were not only understood but also recorded and planned for. The Mayans enforced conservation during low rainfall years, tightly regulating the types of crops grown, the use of public water, and food rationing*. During the first half of their three-thousand-year reign, the Mayans continued to build larger underground artificial lakes and containers (B) [stored / to store] rainwater for drought months. As impressive as their elaborately decorated temples (C) [did / were], their efficient systems for collecting and warehousing water were masterpieces in design and engineering.

*rationing: 배급

	(A)	(B)	(C)
①	that	to store	were
②	what	stored	did
③	that	to store	did
④	what	stored	were

19 주어진 글 다음에 이어질 글의 순서로 가장 적절한 것은?

> Religion can certainly bring out the best in a person, but it is not the only phenomenon with that property.

> (A) People who would otherwise be self-absorbed or shallow or crude or simply quitters are often ennobled by their religion, given a perspective on life that helps them make the hard decisions that we all would be proud to make.
>
> (B) Having a child often has a wonderfully maturing effect on a person. Wartime, famously, gives people an abundance of occasions to rise to, as do natural disasters like floods and hurricanes.
>
> (C) But for day-in, day-out lifelong bracing, there is probably nothing so effective as religion: it makes powerful and talented people more humble and patient, it makes average people rise above themselves, it provides sturdy support for many people who desperately need help staying away from drink or drugs or crime.

① (B) - (A) - (C)
② (B) - (C) - (A)
③ (C) - (A) - (B)
④ (C) - (B) - (A)

20 주어진 글 다음에 이어질 글의 순서로 가장 적절한 것은?

> More people require more resources, which means that as the population increases, the Earth's resources deplete* more rapidly.
>
> *deplete: 고갈시키다, 대폭 감소시키다

> (A) Population growth also results in increased greenhouse gases, mostly from CO_2 emissions. For visualization, during that same 20th century that saw fourfold population growth, CO_2 emissions increased twelvefold.
>
> (B) The result of this depletion is deforestation and loss of biodiversity as humans strip the Earth of resources to accommodate rising population numbers.
>
> (C) As greenhouse gases increase, so do climate patterns, ultimately resulting in the long-term pattern called climate change.

① (A) - (B) - (C)
② (B) - (A) - (C)
③ (B) - (C) - (A)
④ (C) - (A) - (B)

21 다음 글에서 전체 흐름과 관계없는 문장은?

Medical anthropologists with extensive training in human biology and physiology study disease transmission patterns and how particular groups adapt to the presence of diseases like malaria and sleeping sickness. ① Because the transmission of viruses and bacteria is strongly influenced by people's diets, sanitation, and other behaviors, many medical anthropologists work as a team with epidemiologists* to identify cultural practices that affect the spread of disease. ② Though it may be a commonly held belief that most students enter medicine for humanitarian reasons rather than for the financial rewards of a successful medical career, in developed nations the prospect of status and rewards is probably one incentive. ③ Different cultures have different ideas about the causes and symptoms of disease, how best to treat illnesses, the abilities of traditional healers and doctors, and the importance of community involvement in the healing process. ④ By studying how a human community perceives such things, medical anthropologists help hospitals and other agencies deliver health care services more effectively.

*epidemiologist: 유행[전염]병학자

22 주어진 글 다음에 이어질 글의 순서로 가장 적절한 것은?

Sequoya (1760?~1843) was born in eastern Tennessee, into a prestigious family that was highly regarded for its knowledge of Cherokee tribal traditions and religion.

(A) Recognizing the possibilities writing had for his people, Sequoya invented a Cherokee alphabet in 1821. With this system of writing, Sequoya was able to record ancient tribal customs.

(B) More important, his alphabet helped the Cherokee nation develop a publishing industry so that newspapers and books could be printed. School-age children were thus able to learn about Cherokee culture and traditions in their own language.

(C) As a child, Sequoya learned the Cherokee oral tradition; then, as an adult, he was introduced to Euro-American culture. In his letters, Sequoya mentions how he became fascinated with the writing methods European Americans used to communicate.

① (B) - (A) - (C)
② (B) - (C) - (A)
③ (C) - (A) - (B)
④ (C) - (B) - (A)

23 Peanut Butter Drive에 관한 다음 안내문의 내용과 가장 일치하지 않는 것은?

SPREAD THE LOVE

Fight Hunger During the Peanut Butter Drive

Make a contribution to our community by helping local families who need a little assistance. We are kicking off our 4th annual area-wide peanut butter drive to benefit children, families and seniors who face hunger in Northeast Louisiana.

Peanut butter is a much needed staple at Food Banks as it is a protein-packed food that kids and adults love. Please donate peanut butter in plastic jars or funds to the Monroe Food Bank by Friday, March 29th at 4:00 pm. Donations of peanut butter can be dropped off at the food bank's distribution center located at 4600 Central Avenue in Monroe on Monday through Friday, 8:00 am to 4:00 pm. Monetary donations can be made here or by calling 427-418-4581.

For other drop-off locations, visit our website at https://www.foodbanknela.org

---

① 배고픈 사람들에게 도움을 주려는 행사이다.
② 토요일과 일요일에도 땅콩버터를 기부할 수 있다.
③ 전화를 걸어 금전 기부를 할 수도 있다.
④ 땅콩버터를 기부하는 장소는 여러 곳이 있다.

24 다음 글에 나타난 화자의 심경으로 가장 적절한 것은?

Our whole tribe was poverty-stricken*. Every branch of the Garoghlanian family was living in the most amazing and comical poverty in the world. Nobody could understand where we ever got money enough to keep us with food in our bellies. Most important of all, though, we were famous for our honesty. We had been famous for honesty for something like eleven centuries, even when we had been the wealthiest family in what we liked to think was the world. We put pride first, honest next, and after that we believed in right and wrong. None of us would take advantage of anybody in the world.

*poverty-stricken: 가난에 시달리는

---

① peaceful and calm
② satisfied and proud
③ horrified and feared
④ amazed and astonished

25 다음 글의 내용과 가장 일치하지 않는 것은?

Despite the increasing popularity of consuming raw foods, you can still gain nutrients from cooked vegetables. For example, our body can absorb lycopene more effectively when tomatoes are cooked. (Keep in mind, however, that raw tomatoes are still a good source of lycopene.) Cooked tomatoes, however, have lower levels of vitamin C than raw tomatoes, so if you're looking to increase your levels, you might be better off sticking with the raw. Whether you decide to eat them cooked or raw, it's important not to dilute* the health benefits of tomatoes. If you're buying tomato sauce or paste, choose a variety with no salt or sugar added—or better yet, cook your own sauce at home. And if you're eating your tomatoes raw, salt them sparingly and choose salad dressings that are low in calories and saturated fat.

*dilute: 희석하다, 묽게 하다

① 토마토를 요리하여 먹었을 때, 우리의 몸은 리코펜을 더 효과적으로 흡수할 수 있다.

② 더 많은 비타민C를 섭취하고 싶다면 생토마토보다 조리된 토마토를 섭취하는 것이 낫다.

③ 토마토 소스를 구입하고자 한다면, 소금이나 설탕이 첨가되지 않은 것으로 골라야 한다.

④ 생토마토를 섭취 시 소금을 적게 넣거나, 칼로리가 적은 드레싱을 선택하도록 한다.

모바일 OMR

✅ 회독 CHECK 1 2 3

01 다음 밑줄 친 (A), (B), (C)의 각 괄호 안에서 문맥에 맞는 낱말로 가장 적절한 것은?

> It's tempting to identify knowledge with facts, but not every fact is an item of knowledge. Imagine shaking a sealed cardboard box containing a single coin. As you put the box down, the coin inside the box has landed either heads or tails: let's say that's a fact. But as long as no one looks into the box, this fact remains unknown; it is not yet within the realm of (A) [fact / knowledge]. Nor do facts become knowledge simply by being written down. If you write the sentence 'The coin has landed heads' on one slip of paper and 'The coin has landed tails' on another, then you will have written down a fact on one of the slips, but you still won't have gained knowledge of the outcome of the coin toss. Knowledge demands some kind of access to a fact on the part of some living subject. (B) [With / Without] a mind to access it, whatever is stored in libraries and databases won't be knowledge, but just ink marks and electronic traces. In any given case of knowledge, this access may or may not be unique to an individual: the same fact may be known by one person and not by others. Common knowledge might be shared by many people, but there is no knowledge that dangles (C) [attached / unattached] to any subject.

	(A)	(B)	(C)
①	fact	with	unattached
②	knowledge	without	unattached
③	knowledge	with	attached
④	fact	without	attached

02 다음 빈칸에 들어갈 말로 가장 적절한 것은?

> Impressionable youth are not the only ones subject to _____. Most of us have probably had an experience of being pressured by a salesman. Have you ever had a sales rep try to sell you some "office solution" by telling you that 70 percent of your competitors are using their service, so why aren't you? But what if 70 percent of your competitors are idiots? Or what if that 70 percent were given so much value added or offered such a low price that they couldn't resist the opportunity? The practice is designed to do one thing and one thing only—to pressure you to buy. To make you feel you might be missing out on something or that everyone else knows but you.

① peer pressure
② impulse buying
③ bullying tactics
④ keen competition

03 다음 밑줄 친 (A), (B), (C)의 각 괄호 안에서 문맥에 맞는 낱말로 가장 적절한 것은?

People with high self-esteem have confidence in their skills and competence and enjoy facing the challenges that life offers them. They (A) [willingly / unwillingly] work in teams because they are sure of themselves and enjoy taking the opportunity to contribute. However, those who have low self-esteem tend to feel awkward, shy, and unable to express themselves. Often they compound their problems by opting for avoidance strategies because they (B) [deny / hold] the belief that whatever they do will result in failure. Conversely, they may compensate for their lack of self-esteem by exhibiting boastful and arrogant behavior to cover up their sense of unworthiness. Furthermore, such individuals account for their successes by finding reasons that are outside of themselves, while those with high self-esteem (C) [attempt / attribute] their success to internal characteristics.

	(A)	(B)	(C)
①	willingly	deny	attempt
②	willingly	hold	attribute
③	unwillingly	hold	attempt
④	unwillingly	deny	attribute

04 다음 글의 제목으로 가장 적절한 것은?

To be sure, no other species can lay claim to our capacity to devise something new and original, from the sublime* to the sublimely ridiculous. Other animals do build things—birds assemble their intricate nests, beavers construct dams, and ants dig elaborate networks of tunnels. "But airplanes, strangely tilted skyscrapers and Chia Pets*, well, they're pretty impressive," Fuentes says, adding that from an evolutionary standpoint, "creativity is as much a part of our tool kit as walking on two legs, having a big brain and really good hands for manipulating things." For a physically unprepossessing primate, without great fangs or claws or wings or other obvious physical advantages, creativity has been the great equalizer—and more—ensuring, for now, at least, the survival of Homo sapiens.

*sublime: 황당한, (터무니없이) 극단적인
*Chia Pets: 잔디가 머리털처럼 자라나는 피규어

① Where Does Human Creativity Come From?
② What Are the Physical Characteristics of Primates?
③ Physical Advantages of Homo Sapiens over Other Species
④ Creativity: a Unique Trait Human Species Have For Survival

05 다음 글의 요지를 한 문장으로 요약하고자 한다. 빈칸 (A), (B)에 들어갈 말로 가장 적절한 것은?

"Most of bird identification is based on a sort of subjective impression—the way a bird moves and little instantaneous appearances at different angles and sequences of different appearances, and as it turns its head and as it flies and as it turns around, you see sequences of different shapes and angles," Sibley says, "All that combines to create a unique impression of a bird that can't really be taken apart and described in words. When it comes down to being in the fieldland looking at a bird, you don't take time to analyze it and say it shows this, this, and this; therefore it must be this species. It's more natural and instinctive. After a lot of practice, you look at the bird, and it triggers little switches in your brain. It looks right. You know what it is at a glance."

⇩

According to Sibley, bird identification is based on _____(A)_____ rather than _____(B)_____ .

	(A)	(B)
①	instinctive impression	discrete analysis
②	objective research	subjective judgements
③	physical appearances	behavioral traits
④	close observation	distant observation

06 주어진 글 다음에 이어질 글의 순서로 가장 적절한 것은?

As cars are becoming less dependent on people, the means and circumstances in which the product is used by consumers are also likely to undergo significant changes, with higher rates of participation in car sharing and short-term leasing programs.

(A) In the not-too-distant future, a driverless car could come to you when you need it, and when you are done with it, it could then drive away without any need for a parking space. Increases in car sharing and short-term leasing are also likely to be associated with a corresponding decrease in the importance of exterior car design.

(B) As a result, the symbolic meanings derived from cars and their relationship to consumer self-identity and status are likely to change in turn.

(C) Rather than serving as a medium for personalization and self-identity, car exteriors might increasingly come to represent a channel for advertising and other promotional activities, including brand ambassador programs, such as those offered by Free Car Media.

① (A) - (C) - (B)
② (B) - (C) - (A)
③ (C) - (A) - (B)
④ (C) - (B) - (A)

07 주어진 글 다음에 이어질 글의 순서로 가장 적절한 것은?

There is a wonderful story of a group of American car executives who went to Japan to see a Japanese assembly line. At the end of the line, the doors were put on the hinges, the same as in America.

(A) But something was missing. In the United States, a line worker would take a rubber mallet and tap the edges of the door to ensure that it fit perfectly. In Japan, that job didn't seem to exist.

(B) Confused, the American auto executives asked at what point they made sure the door fit perfectly. Their Japanese guide looked at them and smiled sheepishly. "We make sure it fits when we design it."

(C) In the Japanese auto plant, they didn't examine the problem and accumulate data to figure out the best solution—they engineered the outcome they wanted from the beginning. If they didn't achieve their desired outcome, they understood it was because of a decision they made at the start of the process.

① (A) - (B) - (C)
② (A) - (C) - (B)
③ (B) - (A) - (C)
④ (B) - (C) - (A)

08 다음 글의 빈칸 (A), (B)에 들어갈 말로 가장 적절한 것은?

There has been much research on nonverbal cues to deception dating back to the work of Ekman and his idea of leakage. It is well documented that people use others' nonverbal behaviors as a way to detect lies. My research and that of many others has strongly supported people's reliance on observations of others' nonverbal behaviors when assessing honesty. ___(A)___, social scientific research on the link between various nonverbal behaviors and the act of lying suggests that the link is typically not very strong or consistent. In my research, I have observed that the nonverbal signals that seem to give one liar away are different than those given by a second liar. ___(B)___, the scientific evidence linking nonverbal behaviors and deception has grown weaker over time. People infer honesty based on how others nonverbally present themselves, but that has very limited utility and validity.

	(A)	(B)
①	However	What's more
②	As a result	On the contrary
③	However	Nevertheless
④	As a result	For instance

09 다음 글의 밑줄 친 부분 중 어법상 틀린 것은?

As soon as the start-up is incorporated it will need a bank account, and the need for a payroll account will follow quickly. The banks are very competitive in services to do payroll and related tax bookkeeping, ① starting with even the smallest of businesses. These are areas ② where a business wants the best quality service and the most "free" accounting help it can get. The changing payroll tax legislation is a headache to keep up with, especially when a sales force will be operating in many of the fifty states. And the ③ requiring reports are a burden on a company's add administrative staff. Such services are often provided best by the banker. The banks' references in this area should be compared with the payroll service alternatives such as ADP, but the future and the long-term relationship should be kept in mind when a decision is ④ being made.

10 다음 글의 밑줄 친 부분 중 어법상 틀린 것은?

Many people refuse to visit animal shelters because they find it too sad or ① depressed. They shouldn't feel so bad because so many lucky animals are saved from a dangerous life on the streets, ② where they're at risk of traffic accidents, attack by other animals or humans, and subject to the elements. Many lost pets likewise ③ are found and reclaimed by distraught owners simply because they were brought into animal shelters. Most importantly, ④ adoptable pets find homes, and sick or dangerous animals are humanely relieved of their suffering.

11 다음 밑줄 친 (A), (B), (C)의 각 괄호 안에서 문맥에 맞는 낱말로 가장 적절한 것은?

EQ testing, when performed with reliable testing methods, can provide you with very useful information about yourself. I've found, having tested thousands of people, that many are a bit surprised by their results. For example, one person who believed she was very socially responsible and often concerned about others came out with an (A) [average / extraordinary] score in that area. She was quite disappointed in her score. It turned out that she had very high standards for social responsibility and therefore was extremely (B) [easy / hard] on herself when she performed her assessment. In reality, she was (C) [more / less] socially responsible than most people, but she believed that she could be much better than she was.

	(A)	(B)	(C)
①	average	easy	less
②	average	hard	more
③	extraordinary	hard	less
④	extraordinary	easy	more

12 다음 빈칸에 들어갈 말로 가장 적절한 것은?

A person may try to _____ by using evidence to his advantage. A mother asks her son, "How are you doing in English this term?" He responds cheerfully, "Oh, I just got a ninety-five on a quiz." The statement conceals the fact that he has failed every other quiz and that his actual average is 55. Yet, if she pursues the matter no further, the mother may be delighted that her son is doing so well. Linda asks Susan, "Have you read much Dickens?" Susan responds, "Oh, *Pickwick Papers* is one of my favorite novels." The statement may disguise the fact that *Pickwick Papers* is the only novel by Dickens that she has read, and it may give Linda the impression that Susan is a great Dickens enthusiast.

① earn extra money
② effect a certain belief
③ hide memory problems
④ make other people feel guilty

13 다음 글의 내용을 한 문장으로 요약하고자 한다. 빈칸 (A), (B)에 들어갈 말로 가장 적절한 것은?

Whether we are complimented for our appearance, our garden, a dinner we prepared, or an assignment at the office, it is always satisfying to receive recognition for a job well done. Certainly, reinforcement theory sees occasional praise as an aid to learning a new skill. However, some evidence cautions against making sweeping generalizations regarding the use of praise in improving performance. It seems that while praise improves performance on certain tasks, on others it can instead prove harmful. Imagine the situation in which the enthusiastic support of hometown fans expecting victory brings about the downfall of their team. In this situation, it seems that praise creates pressure on athletes, disrupting their performance.

⇩

Whether ____(A)____ helps or hurts a performance depends on ____(B)____ .

	(A)	(B)
①	praise	task types
②	competition	quality of teamwork
③	praise	quality of teamwork
④	competition	task types

14 다음 글의 밑줄 친 부분 중 어법상 틀린 것은?

As we consider media consumption in the context of anonymous social relations, we mean all of those occasions that involve the presence of strangers, such as viewing television in public places like bars, ① going to concerts or dance clubs, or reading a newspaper on a bus or subway. Typically, there are social rules that ② govern how we interact with those around us and with the media product. For instance, it is considered rude in our culture, or at least aggressive, ③ read over another person's shoulder or to get up and change TV channels in a public setting. Any music fan knows what is appropriate at a particular kind of concert. The presence of other people is often crucial to defining the setting and hence the activity of media consumption, ④ despite the fact that the relationships are totally impersonal.

15 다음 글의 밑줄 친 부분 중 어법상 틀린 것은?

Many of us believe that amnesia, or sudden memory loss, results in the inability to recall one's name and identity. This belief may reflect the way amnesia is usually ① portrayed in movies, television, and literature. For example, when we meet Matt Damon's character in the movie *The Bourne Identity*, we learn that he has no memory for who he is, why he has the skills he does, or where he is from. He spends much of the movie ② trying to answer these questions. However, the inability to remember your name and identity ③ are exceedingly rare in reality. Amnesia most often results from a brain injury that leaves the victim unable to form new memories, but with most memories of the past ④ intact. Some movies do accurately portray this more common syndrome; our favorite *Memento*.

16 다음 빈칸에 들어갈 말로 가장 적절한 것은?

Much is now known about natural hazards and the negative impacts they have on people and their property. It would seem obvious that any logical person would avoid such potential impacts or at least modify their behavior or their property to minimize such impacts. However, humans are not always rational. Until someone has a personal experience or knows someone who has such an experience, most people subconsciously believe "It won't happen here" or "It won't happen to me." Even knowledgeable scientists who are aware of the hazards, the odds of their occurrence, and the costs of an event _____.

① refuse to remain silent
② do not always act appropriately
③ put the genetic factor at the top end
④ have difficulty in defining natural hazards

17 다음 글의 주제로 가장 적절한 것은?

The rise of cities and kingdoms and the improvement in transport infrastructure brought about new opportunities for specialization. Densely populated cities provided full-time employment not just for professional shoemakers and doctors, but also for carpenters, priests, soldiers and lawyers. Villages that gained a reputation for producing really good wine, olive oil or ceramics discovered that it was worth their while to specialize nearly exclusively in that product and trade it with other settlements for all the other goods they needed. This made a lot of sense. Climates and soils differ, so why drink mediocre wine from your backyard if you can buy a smoother variety from a place whose soil and climate is much better suited to grape vines? If the clay in your backyard makes stronger and prettier pots, then you can make an exchange.

① how climates and soils influence the local products
② ways to gain a good reputation for local specialties
③ what made people engage in specialization and trade
④ the rise of cities and full-time employment for professionals

18 밑줄 친 the issue가 가리키는 내용으로 가장 적절한 것은?

Nine-year-old Ryan Kyote was eating breakfast at home in Napa, California, when he saw the news: an Indiana school had taken a 6-year-old's meal when her lunch account didn't have enough money. Kyote asked if that could happen to his friends. When his mom contacted the school district to find out, she learned that students at schools in their district had, all told, as much as $25,000 in lunch debt. Although the district says it never penalized students who owed, Kyote decided to use his saved allowance to pay off his grade's debt, about $74—becoming the face of a movement to end lunch-money debt. When California Governor Gavin Newsom signed a bill in October that banned "lunch shaming," or giving worse food to students with debt, he thanked Kyote for his "empathy and his courage" in raising awareness of the issue. "Heroes," Kyote points out, "come in all ages."

① The governor signed a bill to decline lunch items to students with lunch debt.
② Kyote's lunch was taken away because he ran out of money in his lunch account.
③ The school district with financial burden cut the budget failing to serve quality meals.
④ Many students in the district who could not afford lunch were burdened with lunch debt.

19 청고래에 관한 다음 글의 내용과 일치하지 않는 것은?

The biggest heart in the world is inside the blue whale. It weighs more than seven tons. It's as big as a room. When this creature is born it is 20 feet long and weighs four tons. It is way bigger than your car. It drinks a hundred gallons of milk from its mama every day and gains 200 pounds a day, and when it is seven or eight years old it endures an unimaginable puberty and then it essentially disappears from human ken, for next to nothing is known of the mating habits, travel patterns, diet, social life, language, social structure and diseases. There are perhaps 10,000 blue whales in the world, living in every ocean on earth, and of the largest animal who ever lived we know nearly nothing. But we know this: the animals with the largest hearts in the world generally travel in pairs, and their penetrating moaning cries, their piercing yearning tongue, can be heard underwater for miles and miles.

① 아기 청고래는 매일 100갤런의 모유를 마시고, 하루에 200파운드씩 체중이 증가한다.

② 청고래는 사춘기를 지나면서 인간의 시야에서 사라져서 청고래에 대해 알려진 것이 많지 않다.

③ 세계에서 가장 큰 심장을 지닌 동물이면서, 몸집이 가장 큰 동물이다.

④ 청고래는 일반적으로 혼자서 이동하고, 청고래의 소리는 물속을 관통하여 수 마일까지 전달될 수 있다.

20 다음 글의 주제로 가장 적절한 것은?

In addition to controlling temperatures when handling fresh produce, control of the atmosphere is important. Some moisture is needed in the air to prevent dehydration during storage, but too much moisture can encourage growth of molds. Some commercial storage units have controlled atmospheres, with the levels of both carbon dioxide and moisture being regulated carefully. Sometimes other gases, such as ethylene gas, may be introduced at controlled levels to help achieve optimal quality of bananas and other fresh produce. Related to the control of gases and moisture is the need for some circulation of air among the stored foods.

① The necessity of controlling harmful gases in atmosphere

② The best way to control levels of moisture in growing plants and fruits

③ The seriousness of increasing carbon footprints every year around the world

④ The importance of controlling certain levels of gases and moisture in storing foods

21 다음 글의 밑줄 친 부분 중 문맥상 낱말의 쓰임이 가장 적절하지 않은 것은?

Even if lying doesn't have any harmful effects in a particular case, it is still morally wrong because, if discovered, lying weakens the general practice of truth telling on which human communication relies. For instance, if I were to lie about my age on grounds of vanity, and my lying were discovered, even though no serious harm would have been done, I would have ① undermined your trust generally. In that case you would be far less likely to believe anything I might say in the future. Thus all lying, when discovered, has indirect ② harmful effects. However, very occasionally, these harmful effects might possibly be outweighed by the ③ benefits which arise from a lie. For example, if someone is seriously ill, lying to them about their life expectancy might probably give them a chance of living longer. On the other hand, telling them the truth could possibly ④ prevent a depression that would accelerate their physical decline.

22 글의 흐름으로 보아, 아래 문장이 들어가기에 가장 적절한 곳은?

Water is also the medium for most chemical reactions needed to sustain life.

Several common properties of seawater are crucial to the survival and well-being of the ocean's inhabitants. Water accounts for 80-90% of the volume of most marine organisms. (①) It provides buoyancy and body support for swimming and floating organisms and reduces the need for heavy skeletal structures. (②) The life processes of marine organisms in turn alter many fundamental physical and chemical properties of seawater, including its transparency and chemical makeup, making organisms an integral part of the total marine environment. (③) Understanding the interactions between organisms and their marine environment requires a brief examination of some of the more important physical and chemical attributes of seawater. (④) The characteristics of pure water and sea water differ in some respects, so we consider first the basic properties of pure water and then examine how those properties differ in seawater.

23 (A), (B), (C)의 각 네모 안에서 문맥에 맞는 낱말로 가장 적절한 것은?

> Here's the even more surprising part: The advent of AI didn't (A) ┃diminish / increase┃ the performance of purely human chess players. Quite the opposite. Cheap, supersmart chess programs (B) ┃discouraged / inspired┃ more people than ever to play chess, at more tournaments than ever, and the players got better than ever. There are more than twice as many grand masters now as there were when Deep Blue first beat Kasparov. The top-ranked human chess player today, Magnus Carlsen, trained with AIs and has been deemed the most computerlike of all human chess players. He also has the (C) ┃highest / lowest┃ human grand master rating of all time.

	(A)	(B)	(C)
①	diminish	discouraged	highest
②	increase	discouraged	lowest
③	diminish	inspired	highest
④	increase	inspired	lowest

24 다음 글의 내용을 요약할 때 빈칸에 들어갈 말로 가장 적절한 것은?

> Aesthetic value in fashion objects, like aesthetic value in fine art objects, is self-oriented. Consumers have the need to be attracted and to surround themselves with other people who are attractive. However, unlike aesthetic value in the fine arts, aesthetic value in fashion is also other-oriented. Attractiveness of appearance is a way of eliciting the reaction of others and facilitating social interaction.

⇩

> Aesthetic value in fashion objects is _____ _____.

① inherently only self-oriented

② just other-oriented unlike the other

③ both self-oriented and other-oriented

④ hard to define regardless of its nature

25 글의 흐름으로 보아, 아래 문장이 들어가기에 가장 적절한 곳은?

> The great news is that this is true whether or not we remember our dreams.

Some believe there is no value to dreams, but it is wrong to dismiss these nocturnal dramas as irrelevant. There is something to be gained in remembering. (①) We can feel more connected, more complete, and more on track. We can receive inspiration, information, and comfort. Albert Einstein stated that his theory of relativity was inspired by a dream. (②) In fact, he claimed that dreams were responsible for many of his discoveries. (③) Asking why we dream makes as much sense as questioning why we breathe. Dreaming is an integral part of a healthy life. (④) Many people report being inspired with a new approach for a problem upon awakening, even though they don't remember the specific dream.

PART 5
고난도 기출문제

출제경향

2024년 국회직 8급

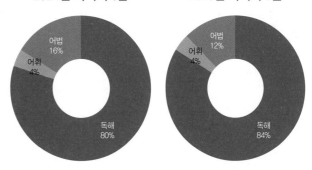

어법 16%
어휘 4%
독해 80%

2023년 국회직 8급

어법 12%
어휘 4%
독해 84%

2022년 국회직 8급

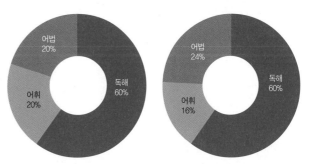

어법 20%
어휘 20%
독해 60%

2021년 국회직 8급

어법 24%
어휘 16%
독해 60%

01 Choose the one that is closest in meaning to the underlined word.

> Few people would think that the humble drinks can was anything special. But to a materials engineer, it is high technology. Look at the requirements. As far as possible we want to avoid seams. The can must not leak, should use as little metal as possible, and be recyclable. We have to choose a metal that is <u>ductile</u> to the point that it can be drawn into a single-piece can body from one small slug of metal. It must not corrode in beer or coke and, of course, it must be nontoxic. And it must be light and must cost almost nothing.

① brittle
② plausible
③ pliable
④ seductive
⑤ rigid

02 Which of the following best fits in the blank?

> If you do not know a language, the words (and sentences) of that language will be mainly incomprehensible, because the relationship between speech sounds and the meanings they represent is generally _____. When you are acquiring a language, you have to learn that the sounds represented by the letter *house* signify the concept "house"; if you know French, this same meaning is represented by *maison*; if you know Russian, by *dom*; if you know Spanish, by *casa*. The same sequence of sounds can represent different meanings in different languages. For example, the word *bolna* means "speak" in Hindi-Urdu and "aching" in Russian.

① iconic
② arbitrary
③ logical
④ systematic
⑤ predictable

03 Which of the following is NOT grammatically correct?

> Gender-variable differentiation is ① <u>reflected</u> in the relative frequency ② <u>with</u> which men and women use the same lexical items or ③ <u>other</u> linguistic features. If, as is often asserted, female English speakers use words such as *lovely* and *nice* more often than ④ <u>are</u> male speakers, we can claim that in this respect English speakers ⑤ <u>clearly</u> exhibit gender-variable differentiation.

04 Which of the following is NOT true according to the passage?

> Life in the big city has always had its drawbacks. Compared to small towns and rural communities, huge metropolitan areas like Los Angeles and New York are typically plagued by higher crime rates, more pollution, and high costs of living. But another major problem—traffic-choked highways—is quickly rising to the top of the list for many major cities. With drivers in some large cities now spending the equivalent of more than two workweeks per year stuck in traffic, gridlock is starting to stunt economic growth as businesses and young professionals choose not to move to metropolitan areas with chronically congested roads. To combat this problem, many political and business leaders are advocating the widening of existing highways into "superhighways" of nine or more lanes in each direction. Phoenix, Arizona, for example, plans to expand a 12-mile stretch of interstate 10 from 14 lanes to an average of 22 lanes. Atlanta, George, may widen a stretch of interstate 75 to 23 lanes. Both Houston, Texas, and Washington D.C., also hope to bring segments of their highways up to 18 lanes or more. Building bigger roads, they hope, will end bottlenecks, allowing the ever-growing number of vehicles to move freely and keeping the area economically competitive.

① Enormous metropolitan areas often suffer from more crime rates, greater pollution levels, and high costs of living.

② Traffic congestion is becoming a major issue in big cities.

③ The economic growth is being promoted by gridlock as businesses and young professionals opt against relocating to urban areas with persistently trafficated roads.

④ Numerous political and business leaders are promoting the expansion of current highways into "superhighways" with nine or more lanes in each direction.

⑤ Constructing larger roads is expected to help reduce traffic congestion.

05 Which of the following best fits in the blank?

> People in all countries and in all walks of life have gossiped for centuries. Psychologists have studied both the positive and negative impacts of this form of human communication. According to some researchers, gossip reinforces moral boundaries in a community. Gossip can also foster a sense of belonging to a certain group. However, gossip has many negative effects as well. Gossip can be used as a tool to isolate and ostracize people. When singled out and embarrassed by harmful rumors, individuals become depressed and lonely. Despite gossip's negative effect, it remains to be ubiquitous. Gossip exists in the workplace, in school, and in social groups. Seemingly, gossip will never go away. You must _____. You must refuse to participate in such damaging communication. Try to re-direct the conversation in a way that focuses on something positive.

① do your best to rise above it

② take a more proactive role in disseminating it

③ identify the sources and motives of the rumors

④ utterly disregard its presence

⑤ create rumors to offset the negative ones

06 Which of the following is NOT grammatically correct?

> AI may ① enable achieving educational priorities in better ways, at scale, and with lower costs. Addressing varied unfinished learning of students due to the pandemic is a policy priority, and AI may improve the adaptivity ② of learning resources to students' strengths and needs. Improving teaching jobs is a priority, and via ③ automated assistants or other tools, AI may provide teachers greater support. AI may also enable teachers to extend the support they ④ offer individual students when they run out of time. Developing resources that are responsive to the knowledge and experiences students bring to their learning is a priority, and AI may enable greater customizability of curricular resources to meet local needs. ⑤ As seen in voice assistants, mapping tools, shopping recommendations, essay-writing capabilities, and other familiar applications, AI may enhance educational services.

07 Which of the following is the most appropriate title of the passage?

> Artists themselves have no role in the interpretation of art, while scientists are the only consumers with sufficient observational skill to provide science's organized skepticism. The interpretation of art can be manifold and the artist's intention can be to provoke a multitude of interpretations— sometimes, the more interpretations the better. The scientist, on the other hand, must aspire to convey only one possible interpretation—the correct interpretation. What follows from this is that clarity is an imperative in science in a way that it is not in other cultural endeavors. Where multiple interpretations are encouraged, obscurity can be a virtue but where the aspiration is to produce only one interpretation, clarity is to be preferred. Obscurity is also privacy, and privacy is an obstacle to organized skepticism. It follows, from the fact that observation and skepticism are virtues in the pursuit of knowledge about the natural world, that clarity is also a virtue. There is an irony here, since science should seek maximum clarity and accessibility even while acknowledging that the only proper assessors of a scientific claim are small elites, while artists often seek obscurity or multiple interpretations even while accepting that the proper assessors are the public.

① How Scientists Analyze Art with Clear Perspectives

② Scientific Analysis of Artistic Ambiguity

③ How Scientists Create Artistic Interpretations

④ Importance of Precision in Art and Science

⑤ How Art and Science Interpret Clarity and Obscurity

08 Which of the following best fits in the blank?

> The US has one of the highest prisoner _____ rates in the world: over 70% of incarcerated people who are released from prison in the US will be rearrested within five years of their release date. That is not an accident. Our system of mass incarceration sets people up to fail as they leave the prison system and try to reintegrate into society.

① racism   ② recidivism
③ reincarnation   ④ jailbreak
⑤ release

09 Which of the following is the most logical sequence to complete the passage?

> All of the gasoline now pumped into automobile and airplane tanks began as crude oil formed millions of years ago beneath ocean floors.
>
> (A) This crude oil, lighter than both water and rock, drifted upward through microscopic spaces in the rock until it was stopped by a layer of dense, impermeable rock and forced to collect. Today, oil companies drill down into these reservoirs to extract this energy-rich petroleum: sent it to oil refineries, and convert it into fuel for vehicles.
>
> (B) In ancient seas, when tiny aquatic plants and animals died, they sank to the bottom. Sand and mud settled over them. This process was repeated over and over again, each time burying large quantities of organic material and pushing it deeper and deeper into the earth as new layers accumulated on top.
>
> (C) The heavy weight of the sediment created pressure and temperatures above 150° Fahrenheit, and the subterranean organic matter began to "cook." Over time, the heat transformed it into a liquid hydrogen and carbon substance.

① (A) - (B) - (C)
② (B) - (A) - (C)
③ (B) - (C) - (A)
④ (C) - (A) - (B)
⑤ (C) - (B) - (A)

10 Which of the following best fits in the blank?

> Suppose that we have an issue where the majority favors one policy, but the minority, which favors a different policy, cares much more strongly about it than the majority. Cases of this kind occur quite often. The fox-hunting debate may be a good example. Most people hold fairly negative views about fox-hunting, even if they do not hold strong moral views about the rights of animals. They see it as an archaic, snobbish, and generally distasteful spectacle; given the chance, they would vote to ban it. The fox-hunters themselves are a small minority, but they mostly feel very strongly that they should be allowed to continue hunting. It is an important social event in many rural communities, and people's livelihoods depend on it. A political judgement about fox-hunting ought to consider not only the number of preferences on either side, but also the strength of those preferences. It does not seem right that a lukewarm majority should in all cases _____ a passionate minority.

① deceive
② respect
③ follow
④ protect
⑤ override

11 Which of the following is NOT used appropriately in the context?

> Equality is recognizing that, as human beings, we all have the same value. This means we all have the same rights, we should all receive the same level of respect, and we have the same access to opportunities. Equity, however, is about everyone achieving equal ① outcomes. We all have the same value and deserve a good life, but we all start from a ② different place. We experience the world in our own unique way. It is because of these differences that we sometimes need to be treated ③ differently for us all to live equally. Equality, for example, would be giving everyone the ④ different type of ladder to pick mangoes at the top of a tree. ⑤ Equity would be realizing that not everyone can use the same type of ladder and providing another way for them to reach the mangoes at the top of the tree.

12 Which of the following best fits in the blank?

> Serious problems arise for utilitarianism when we remind ourselves that it enjoins us to bring about the best consequences. What does this mean? It doesn't mean the best consequences for me alone, or for my family or friends, or any other person taken individually. No, what we must do is, roughly, as follows: we must add up the separate satisfactions and frustrations of everyone likely to be affected by our choice, the satisfactions in one column, the frustrations in the other. We must total each column for each of the options before us. That is what it means to say the theory is _____. And then we must choose that option which is most likely to bring about the best balance of totaled satisfactions over totaled frustrations. Whatever act would lead to this outcome is the one we ought morally to perform—it is where our moral duty lies. And that act quite clearly might not be the same one that would bring about the best results for me personally, or for my family or friends, or for a lab animal.

① aggregative

② optimistic

③ ideal

④ individual specific

⑤ realistic

13 Which of the following is the most appropriate title of the passage?

More recently, some political philosophers have claimed that when we take part in elections, we agree to comply with the government that emerges and the laws it enacts. This looks more promising: we do at least have a free choice as to whether to vote or not, and there would be no point in holding elections unless people recognized the government that emerged as legitimate. But unfortunately there still seems to be a gap between voting and registering your consent. What if you deeply disagree with both parties, but vote because you think that one is slightly less bad than the other? Or what if you think that although you have in a sense consented to the overall package of policies that the winning party has announced in its manifesto, there are a few items that you find quite repugnant—and you had no chance to vote on these individually? Perhaps the voters' consent can help explain why governments have legitimate authority, but not why individual citizens have an obligation to obey the law.

① The Reason Why Elections Work
② Discordance between Voting and Voter Consent
③ Inaccuracies in Policies the Government Makes
④ The Perfect Alignment of Consent and Obligation
⑤ The Nexus of Policies and Government Legitimacy

14 Which of the following best fits in the blank?

Because adult stem cells can be obtained directly from the body of a willing donor, research with these cells has raised few ethical questions to date. This is not the case with embryonic stem cells, which are generally obtained from very early embryos. Most techniques for harvesting embryonic stem cells cause the destruction of an embryo. For this reason, individuals who regard the embryo as entitled to the rights and protections of any human being object to such work. This concern has made government funding of embryonic stem cell research an important political issue. Groups seeking to protect embryos oppose such research as unethical. Other groups support such research as essential for saving human lives and argue that it would be unethical to restrict research. It is possible, however, that in the not-too-distant future, both ethical concerns will be _____. Some recent experiments have suggested that there may be ways to extract a small number of stem cells from an early embryo without damaging the embryo itself. Other experiments have shown that it is possible to switch "on" a small number of genes that reprogram adult cells to look and function like pluripotent embryonic stem cells. Such a technique would do away with the need to involve embryos at all. It also might make it possible to tailor specific therapies to the needs of each individual patient. Approaches like these, if successful, might allow potentially lifesaving research to go forward while avoiding any destruction of embryonic life.

① repeated due to technology advancement
② solved with the advent of new stem cell regulations
③ clarified with more experiments
④ made more serious by new research skills
⑤ addressed with a technological solution

15 Which of the following is NOT used appropriately in the context?

We have developed our techniques for probabilistic reasoning in the context of static worlds, in which each random ① variable has a single fixed value. For example, when repairing a car, we assume that whatever is broken remains broken during the process of diagnosis; our job is to infer the state of the car from observed evidence, which also remains ② fixed. Now consider a slightly different problem: treating a diabetic patient. As in the case of car repair, we have evidence such as recent insulin doses, food intake, blood sugar measurements, and other ③ physical signs. The task is to assess the current state of the patient, including the actual blood sugar level and insulin level. Given this information, we can make a decision about the patient's food intake and insulin dose. Unlike the case of car repair, here the ④ static aspects of the problem are essential. Blood sugar levels and measurements thereof can ⑤ change rapidly over time, depending on recent food intake and insulin doses, metabolic activity, the time of day, and so on. To assess the current state from the history of evidence and to predict the outcomes of treatment actions, we must model these changes.

16 Which of the following best fits in the blank?

The way people think about problems varies greatly. Everyone is unique, but psychologists believe there are 5 different kinds of problem-solvers in the world: questioners, ideators, diggers, doers, and reasoners. As for reasoners, they are the people who like to keep things simple. When they deal with a complex problem, they prefer to focus on the most important elements. They don't want to worry about small details, which means they solve problems more quickly than other people. Also, for reasoners, the "best" solution is the solution that they came up with. Unfortunately, they also have a hard time listening to other people's ideas. As a result, people sometimes assume that they can be seen as _____.

① solicitous
② conceited
③ accommodative
④ sluggish
⑤ sanguine

17 Which of the following best fits in the blanks (A), (B), and (C)?

Many of features which characterize the turn-taking system of conversation are invested with meaning by their users. Even within a broadly defined community of speakers, there is often sufficient (A) _____ to cause misunderstanding. For example, some individuals expect that participation in a conversation will be very active, that speaking rate will be relatively fast, with almost no pausing between turns, and with some overlap or even completion of the other's turn. This is one conversational style. It has been called a high involvement style. It differs (B) _____ from another style in which speakers use a slower rate, expect longer pauses between turns, do not overlap, and avoid interruption or completion of the other's turn. This non-interrupting, non-imposing style has been called a high considerateness style. When a speaker who typically uses the first style gets into a conversation with a speaker who normally uses the second style, the talk tends to become one-sided. The active participation style will tend to overwhelm the other style. Neither speaker will necessarily recognize that it is the conversational styles that are slightly different. Instead, the more rapid-fire speaker may think the slower-paced speaker just does not have much to say, is shy, and perhaps boring or even stupid. In return he or she is likely to be viewed as noisy, pushy, domineering, selfish, and even tiresome. Features of conversational style will often be interpreted as (C) _____.

	(A)	(B)	(C)
①	inconsistency	minimally	individual characteristics
②	difficulty	fundamentally	emotional attributes
③	confusion	superficially	cultural properties
④	resemblance	basically	personal experiences
⑤	variation	substantially	personality traits

18 Which of the following is NOT grammatically correct?

The sun consists of a plasma—a material that is not a gas, a liquid, or a solid. Instead, a plasma is made up of charged particles, ① which make them a powerful conductor of electricity. In addition to these strong electronic fields, the sun ② is also packed with magnetic fields. Magnetic field lines wrap around the sun ③ like an enormous birdcage. The sun's magnetism powers a "solar wind" ④ that flings one million tons of plasma outward every second—plasma that travels at one million miles per hour. Sometimes this event can create powerful plasma explosions called solar flares, which release ⑤ the energy equivalent of hundreds of millions of megatons of dynamite. When this energy heads toward Earth, we feel the effects of a solar storm.

19 Which of the following is the most logical sequence to complete the passage?

At a young age, we begin to make decisions about how we look, who we hang out with, and how we spend our time. In making these choices, we may either be trying to fit in or to belong.

(A) Fitting in involves changing ourselves to match situations, such as wearing the right clothes, playing the most popular sport, or hanging out with the "best" social groups; however, it may cause feelings of anxiety or loneliness.

(B) In addition, young people who feel pressured to fit in in ways that aren't healthy to their overall identities may end up participating in unhealthy relationships or going along with the crowd.

(C) Belonging is something else. It is letting ourselves be seen and known as we really are—being our true or authentic selves. It is wearing clothing that makes us feel good or that allows us to show our uniqueness to people we can be our authentic selves with.

(D) It is easier in the sense that it doesn't require going against the norm. However, it is shame-based and implies to young people that they are not good enough. As we strive to conform to the expectations of others, we lose the sense of belonging to our real selves.

But it doesn't come easy. Being different can make us feel vulnerable—exposed to emotional uncertainty and risk. But it is this same vulnerability that becomes the foundation on which courage is built.

① (A) - (B) - (C) - (D)
② (A) - (D) - (B) - (C)
③ (B) - (A) - (D) - (C)
④ (C) - (A) - (D) - (B)
⑤ (C) - (D) - (B) - (A)

20 Which of the following is the most appropriate title of the passage?

People usually associate innovation with technology and products when, in fact, there are many significant process and service innovations that we experience every day. This mistaken belief takes its roots in the fact that the production processes are invisible to the end-users; similarly, services are intangible. As a result, less attention is drawn to them. Identifying how something can be produced more efficiently, in greater quantities or at a lesser cost, certainly involves considerable ingenuity and will undoubtably create genuine value. Also, since our economies are increasingly service-oriented, there are many opportunities to create value by imagining better ways of providing them. Thus, processes and services are important to keep in mind when looking for ways to innovate. In addition, with the advent of Software-as-a-Service (SaaS) and subscription-based computing models, functionalities that were previously provided as products are now moving into the realm of services.

① Ignoring Process and Service Innovations
② Focusing Solely on Technological Innovation
③ Beyond Products: Embracing Process and Service Innovations
④ Omitting Process and Service Innovation Significance
⑤ Innovation Limited to Technology and Product

21 Which of the following is NOT grammatically correct?

No matter ① what it looks like on television crime shows, posting bail after an arrest is no simple matter. When a suspect is arrested, he or she is first taken to a police station to be processed. The police officer in charge then records the suspect's personal information (name, address, birthday, appearance) along with information about the ② alleged crime. Next, the officer conducts a criminal background check, takes the suspect's fingerprints and mug shots, confiscates any personal property (to be returned later), and ③ places the suspect in a jail cell. For less serious crimes, suspects may be allowed to post bail immediately after ④ booking. For more serious crimes, suspects have to wait sometimes as long as two days, for a bail hearing, at which point a judge will determine if the accused is eligible for bail and at what cost. The amount of bail ⑤ depends on the severity of the crime.

22 Which of the following is the most appropriate main idea?

Bruce Friedman, who blogs regularly about the use of computers in medicine, also has described how the Internet has altered his mental habits, "I now have almost totally lost the ability to read and absorb a longish article on the web or in print," he wrote earlier this year. A pathologist who has long been on the faculty of the University of Michigan Medical School, Friedman elaborated on his comment in a telephone conversation with me. His thinking, he said, has taken on a "staccato" quality, reflecting the way he quickly scans short passages of text from many sources online. "I can't read *War and Peace* anymore," he admitted. "I've lost the ability to do that. Even a blog post of more than three or four paragraphs is too much to absorb. I skim it."

The anecdotes alone don't prove much. And we still await the long-term neurological and psychological experiments that will provide a definitive picture of how Internet use affects cognition. But a recently published study of online research habits, conducted by scholars from University College London, suggests that we may well be in the midst of a sea change in the way we read and think. As part of the five-year research program, the scholars examined computer logs documenting the behavior of visitors to two popular research sites, one operated by the British Library and one by a U.K. educational consortium, that provide access to journal articles, e-books, and other sources of written information. They found that people using the sites exhibited "a form of skimming activity," hopping from one source to another and rarely returning to any source they'd already visited. They typically read no more than one or two pages of an article or book before they would "bounce" out to another site. Sometimes they'd save a long article, but there's no evidence that they ever went back and actually read it.

① There is an increasing number of people who skim and quickly jump between sources without deeply engaging with the content.

② In-depth studies on the long-term effects of internet use on cognition will provide conclusive evidence on how it impacts only our thinking processes.

③ People tend to thoroughly scan through brief excerpts of text from various online sources.

④ Although individuals might bookmark or save lengthy articles, there is no evidence to suggest that they revisit and read them later.

⑤ People are experiencing a transformative change in the way they read and think due to their online research habits, skimming and quickly jumping between sources.

23 Where does the given sentence best fit in the passage?

> Morphology of plants also may be influenced by UV.

The most destructive effect of UV radiation on plants involves damage to DNA that results in mutations. Physiological effects also can occur, such as reductions in biomass production and non-stomatal aspects of photosynthesis. The damage to DNA and photosynthesis caused by UV radiation can be partially repaired by plants during both the day and the night. (A) Studies have been conducted with a specific cultivar of rice that is more UV-sensitive in that it exhibits greater growth inhibition and leaf browning than another cultivar of rice when subjected to UV-B radiation. (B) The UV-sensitive cultivar was deficient in both photo-repair during the day and excision repair of DNA during the night compared with the UV-tolerant cultivar. (C) Orange trees growing at very high altitudes in the Andes Mountains near Quito in Ecuador have a more branched appearance than the same scion growing at low elevations in a Mediterranean climatic zone at Riverside, California. (D) The effect was eliminated by installing UV-absorbing screens above the orange trees, indicating the excessive branching may be due to an effect of the high UV in the Andes on the meristems of the branches. (E) Protection against high UV may occur in plants by epidermal cells or leaf hairs that contain phenolic compounds.

① (A)

② (B)

③ (C)

④ (D)

⑤ (E)

24 Which of the following can be inferred from the passage?

Over the years, countless numbers of men and women have paid large sums of money for a treatment commonly known as *cell therapy*. Their reason was simple: They believed lamb-cell injections could help them maintain their youth. Such people apparently don't know that animal cells, when injected into the human body, are destroyed by the immune system. Others in a similar pursuit of youth have tried *chelation therapy*, which is supposed to pull heavy metals like lead and mercury from the body. Proponents claim that the treatments improve cell function, inhibit the aging process, and prevent heart disease, all by eliminating poison from the body, yet research shows no such effect. In fact, critics question the idea of there being poisons in the body to begin with, suggesting that the therapy has nothing to treat. Other seekers of the fountain of youth use Human Growth Hormone (HGH) tablets or sprays. These sprays and tablets can allegedly accomplish everything from eliminating wrinkles to improving memory and concentration. Yet such treatments have no research backing up these claims. There is, however, evidence that HGH in any form may produce side effects like an increased risk of cancer and cardiovascular disease.

① Therapies designed to keep people young are generally ineffective.

② It is better to rely on cell therapy more than chelation therapy.

③ HGH tablets are appealing to seekers of youth because of their fewer side effects.

④ Therapies for staying younger should be available for everyone, not just for those rich enough to afford them.

⑤ Treatments designed to help people maintain youth invariably do more harm than good.

25 Which of the following is true according to the passage?

> It's accepted wisdom that oil and water don't mix. The water and oil molecules have distinct chemical properties that don't interact well together. You may have seen this if you've attempted to make a salad dressing by shaking together oil and vinegar (which is mostly water), which gives a temporary suspension that quickly separates. There is a large energy cost to breaking apart and mixing the water and oil layers. The secret to blending them together is to add an extra ingredient known as a "surfactant" or emulsifier. The name surfactant is derived from "surface active." It highlights that these molecules work at the surface or interface to bridge the interactions between oil and water. This is similar to how detergents are able to remove grease from your dishes. Many vinaigrette recipes call for emulsifiers without specifically mentioning their crucial emulsifying role. Key examples are mustard and garlic, which contain "mucilage"—a mix of carbohydrates—that can act as emulsifiers. So if your vinegar/oil salad dressings are separating, make sure you're adding enough of these ingredients (which also contain wonderful flavor chemicals). Commercial salad dressings also contain naturally sourced emulsifying carbohydrates. These will often be listed on the ingredients as generic "vegetable gum" or similar, and you may need to read the label and delve a little deeper into the food additive number to find out the source. Researchers have raised questions about synthetic emulsifiers used in processed food, as studies in mice suggest they have health risks. It's too early to say exactly what this means for humans.

① Water and oil molecules have identical chemical properties.

② Shaking is an essential method for the formation of permanent mixing of oil and vinegar.

③ Mustard and garlic contain molecules that act as a bridge between oil and water.

④ Salad dressings on the market only contain artificial food additives.

⑤ The effects of chemical additives on the human body have been verified.

회독 CHECK 1 2 3

01 Choose the one that is closest in meaning to the underlined word.

> Efforts by European governments to shield households and businesses from higher energy costs have obvious benefits, not least mitigating inflationary pressures. But they carry much larger costs, which the European Commission should be highlighting, rather than ignoring.

① worsening
② increasing
③ alleviating
④ enhancing
⑤ aggravating

02 Which of the following best fits in the blank?

> A food desert is an area or neighborhood where people, for various reasons, have _____ to fresh, whole, and healthy foods. A lot of people tend to use the United States Department of Agriculture's (USDA) definition: "in urban food deserts, a significant percentage of the neighborhood's residents live more than one mile away from a fresh food provider such as a supermarket or farmers' market; in rural areas, a food desert must be at least ten miles away from a fresh food source."

① limited access
② uneasy moments
③ complicating emotions
④ limited distribution
⑤ uneasy preference

03 Which of the following is NOT grammatically correct?

> We should think of Cultural Intelligence as being something ① that we can continuously improve and ② develop over the duration of our lives. The difficulty is in acquiring it. We do this ③ through our experiences, but also with knowledge ④ impart by other people whom we trust—and who trust us ⑤ enough to give us their knowledge.

04 Which of the following can be inferred from the passage?

> Obesity represents the most serious health problem in the United States today. Almost 60 percent of adults in the US are either overweight or obese. This is not just a problem of appearance. Obesity often leads to serious health problems such as diabetes, heart attacks, high blood pressure, and even some forms of cancer.
>
> Medical professionals typically define obesity using the Body Mass Index (BMI). BMI can easily be calculated through dividing a person's weight in kilograms by the square of the person's height in meters. A normal or healthy BMI would be less than 25. A person with BMI between 25 and 29.9 would be considered overweight. A BMI of 30 to 34.9 is mildly obese, while 35 to 39.9 is substantially obese. People with BMI measures of 40 and over are considered extremely obese.

① More than half of Americans have a BMI over 30.

② Anyone with a BMI over 30 will develop cancer.

③ More than 60 percent of Americans do not know their BMI.

④ Few Americans have a BMI over 35.

⑤ A person is usually considered obese if his or her BMI is 30.

05 Which of the following is true according to the passage?

> Most people think cockroaches are disgusting. And if you've ever turned on a kitchen light, to find them skittering for dark corners, you probably agree. But of the thousands of species out there, only a few can be considered pests. There are well over 4,000 described species of cockroach around the world, with some experts estimating that there are another 5,000 species that have yet to be classified by taxonomists. Their classification is actually a point of contention—and I won't take a position on which suborder they're in, or how many families they consist of. An estimated 60 to 70 species can be found in the continental United States, but most people are likely to interact with no more than a dozen of them—depending on where they live.

① All cockroaches are harmful.

② There might be around 9,000 species of cockroach in the world according to some experts.

③ There is consensus about what sub-type 5,000 unclassified species of cockroach are in.

④ Most Americans can encounter about 24 different kinds of cockroach in their homes.

⑤ It is easy to figure out how many families cockroaches live in in the United States.

06 Which of the following is the most appropriate title of the passage?

> In some cases, a state may be externally sovereign in the sense of being independent and of not belonging to another state. However, its national tasks may be controlled from the outside, for example by a dominant neighboring state. International cooperation and integration between states make it increasingly difficult to argue that all public power in a state comes from the people or another internal source of sovereignty. International cooperation, and the creation of permanent international organizations that comprise several states, is increasingly necessary. Technological progress in the area of transportation and communication has made it more and more irrelevant where goods and services are produced, a trend captured by the term globalization. As people and economies become interconnected, decisions taken in one state may have an impact on the people in another state.

① A State and its National Tasks
② Public Power and Sovereignty
③ Global Technological Progress
④ International Relationship and Independence
⑤ Globalization and International Cooperation

07 Which of the following is true about Hendra according to the passage?

> In Sept. 1994, a violent disease began among a group of racehorses in a small town in Australia. The first victim was a female horse that was last seen eating grass beneath a fruit tree. Within hours, the horse's health declined rapidly. Three people worked to save the animal—the horse's trainer, an assistant, and a veterinarian. Nevertheless, the horse died two days later, leaving the cause of her death uncertain.
>
> Within two weeks, most of the other horses in the stable became ill as well. All had high fevers, difficulty breathing, facial swelling, and blood coming from their noses and mouths. Meanwhile, the trainer and his assistant also became ill, and within days, the trainer was dead, too. Laboratory analysis finally discovered the root of the problem: The horses and men had been infected by a virus, Hendra. This virus had originated in bats that lived in the tree where the first horse had been eating grass. The virus passed from the bats to the horse, then to other horses and to people—with disastrous results.

① Its symptoms in humans include high fevers, difficulty breathing, and facial swelling.
② It can be fatal to both humans and horses.
③ Horses got infected after eating the contaminated grass near the stable.
④ It can be transmitted from humans to animals.
⑤ Humans got infected directly from bats.

08 Which of the following is the most logical sequence to complete the passage?

We often worry about what others will think of us because of our clothes. But researchers are beginning to think that our clothing has an equally powerful effect on how we see ourselves. Researchers report that there is science behind our style.

(A) The scientists also believe that other kinds of symbolic clothes can influence the behavior of the people wearing them. A police officer's uniform or a judge's robe, for example, increases the wearer's feeling of power or confidence.

(B) In their research, researchers had some participants wear white lab coats similar to the ones scientists or doctors wear. Other participants wore their normal clothes. The participants took a test that measured their ability to pay attention.

(C) The people wearing the white coats performed better than the people in regular clothes. Researchers think that the white coats made the participants feel more confident and careful.

① (A) - (B) - (C)

② (A) - (C) - (B)

③ (B) - (A) - (C)

④ (B) - (C) - (A)

⑤ (C) - (A) - (B)

09 Which of the following best fits in the blank?

Nine judges, called Justices, work for the Supreme Court, and they all listen to every case presented to them. The President chooses the people that he wants to serve on the Court, and the Senate confirms or rejects each of the President's choices. He or she will remain on the Supreme Court for life. It is a great honor to be selected to serve on the Supreme Court, because it shows that the President and the Senate trust you to interpret the Constitution fairly. The Supreme Court has the power of _____. This means they have the power to determine if a law is constitutional. If the Justices decide the law does not line up with the Constitution, the law is invalid forever. It is a very difficult job, and often the Court is split 5-4 on tough decisions because everyone reads the Constitution differently.

① judicial review

② social discourse

③ legislative action

④ legal organization

⑤ extrajudicial opinion

10 Where does the given sentence best fit in the passage?

> This piece of evidence leads experts to believe that the underground city was built to protect the city's residents from enemies.

In 1963, a resident of the Cappadocia region of Turkey was doing some renovations on his house. When he knocked down one of his walls, he was surprised to find a hidden room carved into the stone. He explored the room, and found that it led to an underground city. (A) The underground city is over 60 meters deep—deep enough for 20-story building. (B) It contains massive stone doors that could only be opened or closed from the inside. (C) More than 20,000 people could hide inside it. Over 600 doors lead to the city, hidden under and around existing homes. The hidden city had its own religious centers, livestock stables, kitchens, and even schools. (D) However, experts are not sure exactly how old the underground city is, because any records of its construction and use have disappeared. (E)

① (A)
② (B)
③ (C)
④ (D)
⑤ (E)

11 Which of the following best fits in the blank?

> _____. The Portion Cap Ruling, commonly known as the soda ban, was to restrict the sale of sugary drinks larger than 16 ounces in restaurants, movie theaters, sports arenas and delis. The New York State Court of Appeals issued its final decision on the Portion Cap Ruling. The New York City Board of Health, in adopting the 'Sugary Drinks Portion Cap Rule', exceeded the scope of its regulatory authority. Without any legislative delegation or guidance, the Board engaged in law-making and thus violated the legislative jurisdiction of the City Council of New York.

① New York City lost its final appeal to limit the sale of sugary drinks larger than 16 ounces.
② Portion sizes have grown exponentially over the years and rates of obesity have skyrocketed.
③ We need to change our food environment if we want to reduce obesity rates.
④ The negative effects of sugary drink over-consumption on New Yorkers' health are evident.
⑤ We hope that we can all work together to promote a healthier food environment for our children to grow up in.

12 Which of the following is NOT grammatically correct?

> The Titanic was the most magnificent ship. It had luxuries and all comforts. It had electric light and heat, electric elevators, a swimming pool, a Turkish bath, libraries, etc. Most of the passengers were emigrants ① who were coming to America with hopes of a better life. The Titanic began to cross the Atlantic ocean on April 10. Nobody on the ship realized how much danger the ship was in. On April 14, at 11:40 p.m., an iceberg ② was spotted straight ahead. The captain tried to reverse the direction of his ship, but he couldn't because the Titanic was traveling too fast and it was too big. It hit the iceberg and started to sink. The Titanic originally had had 32 lifeboats, but 12 of them ③ had been removed to make the ship look better. While the ship was sinking, rich people ④ had put on the lifeboats. By the time the third-class were allowed to come up from their cabins, most of the lifeboats ⑤ had already left.

13 Which of the following is true according to the passage?

> Early movie star Anna May Wong, who broke into Hollywood during the silent film era, will become the first Asian American to appear on US currency, a century after she landed her first leading role. Wong's image, with her trademark blunt bangs and pencil-thin eyebrows, will feature on the back of new quarters from Monday. The design is the fifth to emerge from the American Women Quarters Program, which highlights pioneering women in their respective fields. The other four quarters, all put into production this year, feature poet and activist Maya Angelou; the first American woman in space, Sally Ride; Cherokee Nation leader Wilma Mankiller; and suffragist Nina Otero-Warren. The latter two were, along with Wong, selected with input from the public.

① Maya Angelou and Sally Ride were chosen by public supports.

② Wong's honor signifies a shift in the Hollywood's representation of women.

③ Anna May Wong was never recognized for her achievements during her lifetime.

④ Wong was the only woman considered for the American Women Quarters Program.

⑤ Five new quarters are produced to recognize pioneering women from various fields in the US.

14 Which of the following best fits in the blank?

> Have you ever been told not to say something? It is very common for families to have rules about what can or cannot be said at home, but governments do the very same thing. When a government passes a law restricting what people or organizations can say, it is called _____ .

① detention

② oppression

③ censorship

④ persecution

⑤ crackdown

15 Which of the following best fits in the blank?

> When most people think of the Civil Rights Movement and the people who led it, they think of Martin Luther King, Jr., Malcolm X, Medgar Evers, and other men. But in reality, women were very important participants in the movement. Though women at the time were expected to _____ , many women became leaders of organizations and protests. However, they are often forgotten in history. Rosa Parks is the most well-known woman in the Civil Rights Movement, but the way her story is told makes her seem like more of a symbol than the important leader that she really was.

① implement the rules

② activate their thoughts

③ rebel against society

④ participate more actively

⑤ play a background role

16 Which of the following is NOT grammatically correct?

> Marine debris which is known to cause entanglement ① includes derelict fishing gear such as nets and mono-filament line and also six-pack rings and fishing bait box strapping bands. This debris can cause death by drowning, suffocation, strangulation, starvation through reduced ② feeding efficiency, and injuries. Particularly affected ③ is seals and sea lions, probably due to their very inquisitive nature of investigating objects in their environment. Entanglement rates in these animals of up to 7.9% of a population ④ have been recorded. Furthermore, in some instances entanglement is a threat to the recovery of already ⑤ reduced population sizes. An estimated 58% of seal and sea lion species are known to have been affected by entanglement including the Hawaiian monk seal, Australian sea lions, New Zealand fur seals and species in the Southern Ocean.

17 Which of the following can be inferred from the passage?

> When it comes to making a cup of coffee, capsules have a reputation for being environmentally unfriendly, as they are often hard to recycle. While coffee is prepared in a variety of ways, coffee capsules have risen in popularity. Despite their popularity, capsules have long divided coffee drinkers who are conscious of the effect their caffeine habit has on the environment. The small plastic or aluminum pods have been criticized for being energy-intensive to produce and for causing unnecessary waste. But new research by the University of Quebec in Canada suggests that pods may not be as wasteful as preparing coffee using a traditional coffee maker, looking at the broader life cycle of a single cup from production to the amount of waste that ends up in a landfill.

① Capsules are wasteful and should be banned.

② New research suggests how to reduce the amount of waste from making coffee.

③ All coffee drinkers look for environmentally friendly products.

④ Capsules may not be as wasteful as other coffee-making methods.

⑤ Capsules are the most popular way of making coffee in the world.

18 Which of the following is NOT mentioned in the passage?

> When cases increase and transmission accelerates, it's more likely that new dangerous and more transmissible variants emerge, which can spread more easily or cause more severe illness. Based on what we know so far, vaccines are proving effective against existing variants, especially at preventing severe disease, hospitalization and death. However, some variants are having a slight impact on the ability of vaccines to guard against mild disease and infection. Vaccines are likely to stay effective against variants because of the broad immune response they cause. It means that virus changes or mutations are unlikely to make vaccines completely ineffective. WHO continues to constantly review the evidence and will update its guidance as we find out more.

① when variants show up

② the effectiveness of vaccines

③ how vaccines respond to variants

④ what makes vaccines always work

⑤ the role of WHO

19 Which of the following is the most appropriate title of the passage?

The James Webb Space Telescope can add another cosmic accomplishment to its list: The space observatory has been used to confirm the existence of an exoplanet for the first time. The celestial body is almost exactly the same size as the Earth. The rocky world is 41 light-years away in the Octans constellation. Previous data collected by NASA had suggested the planet might exist. A team of researchers, led by staff astronomers Kevin Stevenson and Jacob Lustig-Yaeger observed the target using Webb. "There is no question that the planet is there. Webb's pristine data validate it," Lustig-Yaeger said in a statement. The planet's discovery was announced Wednesday at the 241st meeting of the American Astronomical Society in Seattle.

① The Indispensable Role of NASA in Astronomy
② The James Webb Space Telescope's Discovery of a Planet
③ How to Use Space Exploration for Scientific Research
④ How Many Exoplanets the James Webb Space Telescope Has Found
⑤ The Controversy over the James Webb Space Telescope's Capability

20 Which of the following is true according to the passage?

Something was happening to books in 2020 that questions about human existence really were encouraging reading. Certainly, as the first reports came in of pandemic book sales, it did seem that people were at least buying more books. In the UK, physical book sales rose by 6 percent in the week prior to the first national lockdown, paperback fiction sales increased by 35 percent week on week, and Waterstones reported a 400 percent increase of online sales week on week. Physically closed, libraries reported significant growth in new digital users, with Hampshire County Council, for example, seeing an increase in loans of 770 percent. In Denmark, statistics showed that book sales increased by 5.6 percent in 2020 despite shops being closed. In addition, more people than ever subscribed to book streaming services in 2020.

① In 2020 people had less interest in questions about human existence.
② The pandemic created a moment for boosting sales of books.
③ More books were sold in Denmark than in the UK.
④ More people than ever visited libraries in 2020.
⑤ The pandemic has stimulated Denmark's economy.

21 Which of the following can be inferred from the passage?

> While relationships impact the bottom line in any organization, in the not-for-profit world relationships take on even greater importance. Whether you run the local soup kitchen or a membership organization for civil engineers, maintaining good relationships with your members, volunteers, and donors is critical to your success.
>
> In part, this comes from the fact that nonprofits are often seen as not really being businesses, even though many of them have multibillion dollar budgets. But the biggest reason that relationships matter to nonprofits is that the very nature of the operation relies on goodwill and volunteerism. Relationships are the foundation of the reputation and awareness that your public relationships and other marketing efforts have built. And without those relationships chances are no one would be donating or volunteering for anything. So if you don't have strong communal relationships with your constituencies, your organization will soon cease to survive. This is why it is critical to continuously measure the nature and efficacy of your relations.

① The success of a non-profit organization depends on the strength of its relationships with key stakeholders.

② The role of non-profit organizations is important for the survival and success of society.

③ People can make a lot of money based on the public relationships with major organizations.

④ Non-profit organizations do not necessarily focus on marketing for publicity.

⑤ People tend to donate and volunteer for the sake of enhancement of their own self-efficacy.

22 Which of the following is the most appropriate title of the passage?

> The majestic structures of ancient Rome have survived for millennia. But how did their construction materials help to keep giant buildings like the Pantheon and the Colosseum standing for more than 2,000 years? Roman concrete, in many cases, has proven to be longer-lasting than modern concrete, which can deteriorate within decades. Now, scientists behind a new study say they have uncovered the mystery ingredient that allowed the Romans to make their construction material so durable and build elaborate structures in challenging places such as docks, sewers and earthquake zones. A research team analyzed 2,000-year-old concrete samples from a city wall in central Italy. They found that white chunks in the concrete, gave the concrete the ability to heal cracks that formed over time. The white chunks previously had been overlooked as evidence of poor-quality raw material.

① The History of Roman Engineering

② The Durability of Ancient Roman Concrete

③ The Use of Concrete in Modern Construction

④ The Challenge of Building Structures in Earthquake Zones

⑤ The Discovery of a New Type of Concrete in Ancient Rome

23 Which of the following best fits in the blank?

> The term "herd behavior" comes from the behavior of animals in groups, particularly when they are in a dangerous situation such as escaping a predator. All of the animals band closely together in a group and, in panic mode, move together as a unit. It is very unusual for a member of the herd to stray from the movement of the unit. The term also applies to human behavior, and it usually describes large numbers of people acting the same way at the same time. It often has a(n) _____, as people's actions are driven by emotion rather than by thinking through a situation. Human herd behavior can be observed at large-scale demonstrations, riots, strikes, religious gatherings, sports events, and outbreaks of mob violence. When herd behavior sets in, an individual person's judgment and opinion-forming process shut down as he or she automatically follows the group's movement and behavior.

① rational reasoning

② difference with animals

③ feature of objects

④ demonstrative event

⑤ implication of irrationality

24 Which of the following is the most appropriate title of the passage?

> California has been struck by a final round of storms, bringing more rain and snow to a state. Rain and snow were expected Monday overnight and into early Tuesday morning in parts of the state. Although weather should improve this week, many areas are currently at risk of floods and landslides. Storms have battered California in recent weeks, flooding communities and forcing evacuations. The back-to-back deluges have eroded roads and felled trees, making each successive storm more liable to cause serious damage as soils weaken. One to three feet of snow fell in parts of California's Sierra Nevada range over the weekend. As of Monday, eight million people remain under flood watch on California's central coast, and more than 38,600 customers in the state remained without power on Monday.

① The Biggest Loser of Californian Weather

② How to Prepare for the Unpredictability of Rain and Storm

③ Devastated California after a Series of Storms

④ The Causes and Consequences of Floods in California

⑤ California's Self-Inflicted Disaster of Snow Storms

25 Which of the following is the most logical sequence to complete the passage?

> SHANGHAI, June 9—Tens of thousands of students and others held a protest rally and marched through the streets of this city today in a demonstration of continued defiance of the Communist leadership.
>
> (A) Estimates of the crowd by reporters and diplomats ranged from about 40,000 to more than 100,000. The rally, coming amid reports that security police were making arrests of participants in the democracy movement in Beijing, reflected a contrast between the two cities.
>
> (B) While the atmosphere in Beijing is solemn and fearful, the events of the day in Shanghai indicate a mood of continued anger and defiance in China's largest and economically most important city.
>
> (C) The demonstrators, led by students from Shanghai's many universities and technical institutes, marched to recorded funeral songs lamenting the thousands killed in Beijing when troops crushed the protest movement there.

① (A) - (C) - (B)

② (B) - (A) - (C)

③ (B) - (C) - (A)

④ (C) - (A) - (B)

⑤ (C) - (B) - (A)

01 Choose the one that is closest in meaning to the underlined word.

> People see themselves differently from how they see others. They are immersed in their own sensations, emotions, and cognitions at the same time that their experience of others is dominated by what can be observed externally. This distinction in the information that people possess when perceiving themselves versus others affects how people evaluate their own and others' behavior. People often view their own actions as caused by situational constraints, while viewing others' actions as caused by those others' internal dispositions. An example would be a person arriving late for a job interview and ascribing that lateness to bad traffic while his interviewer attributed it to personal irresponsibility.

① abhorrences
② indemnities
③ inducements
④ infatuations
⑤ temperaments

02 Choose the one that is closest in meaning to the underlined expression.

> The details of the latest deal were hammered out by the US Secretary of State and his Russian counterpart.

① settled   ② canceled
③ criticized   ④ renounced
⑤ argued about

03 Which of the following is NOT grammatically correct?

> Two partial solar eclipses—when the moon ① blocks part of the solar disc in the sky—will occur in 2022. The first will be visible in southern South America, parts of Antarctica, and over parts of the Pacific and the Southern Oceans. On April 30, the moon will pass between the Earth and the sun, with the maximum eclipse ② occurring at 20:41 UTC*, when up to 64 percent of the sun's disc will be covered by the moon. To see the greatest extent of the eclipse, viewers will have to ③ position in the Southern Ocean, west of the Antarctic Peninsula. However, eclipse chasers in the southernmost parts of Chile and Argentina will be able to see around 60 percent of the sun ④ blotted out by the moon. Protective eyewear is needed to safely view all phases of a partial solar eclipse. Even though the sun may not appear as ⑤ bright in the sky, staring at it directly can seriously injure your eyes.
>
> *UTC: Universal Time Coordinated

04 Which of the following best fits in the blanks (A) and (B)?

> "There! That's the life we lead. It's enough to make one cry. One works and does one's utmost; one wears oneself out, getting no sleep at night, and racks one's brain over what to do for the best. And then what happens? To begin with, the public is ignorant and (A) _____ . I give them the very best operetta, a dainty masque and first-rate music-hall artists. But do you suppose that's what they want? They don't appreciate anything of that sort. They want a clown; what they ask for is (B) _____ ."

	(A)	(B)
①	assiduous	popularity
②	sensible	sensation
③	boorish	vulgarity
④	peculiar	intelligence
⑤	bragging	improvisation

05 Which of the following is the most appropriate title of the passage?

> Fluid materials such as clay and finger paints are excellent media through which children can express anger as well as curiosity about body parts and functions. With clay, children can tear and pound harmlessly, and they can also create human figures that often have anatomically correct parts. With clay, sand, or blocks, they can be safely destructive and will learn that their own destructive impulses are not necessarily harmful and should not frighten them. Sometimes the pleasure of creating is enhanced by the anticipation of destroying what one has created. With dolls, children can create family scenes and explore family-related anxieties. If they are allowed to communicate freely when using hand puppets, children can reveal some of their innermost feelings, in actions or words, since it is not they but the puppets who are communicating. Adults need to exert control over the behavior of young children, so they must place restrictions on free expression with materials. For example, clay can be pounded, pulled apart, or squashed but should not be thrown at the wall or at other children. However, adults should try to remember that if they are overly restrictive, the play will lose some of its emotional value for children. They should also realize that even a young child can make a distinction between knocking over a block structure that he or she has created and knocking over the furniture in the classroom.

① Various Kinds of Fluid Materials

② Individual Differences in Play

③ The Influence of Culture on Play

④ Developing Expressivity through Play

⑤ Pros and Cons of Using Fluid Materials in Play

06 Which of the following is the most logical sequence to complete the passage?

> The "lessons-of-history" is indeed a familiar phrase, so much so that the lessons are sometimes learned too well. History never repeats itself exactly; no historical situation is the same as any other; even two like events differ in that the first has no precedent, while the second has. But even in this respect, history can teach a lesson—namely that nothing ever stays the same. The only unchanging thing in human affairs is the constancy of change itself. The process of history is unique, but nonetheless intelligible. Each situation and event is distinct, but each is connected to all the foregoing and succeeding ones by a complex web of cause and effect, probability and accident.

> (A) The unique present, just as each unique point in the past, is utterly unintelligible unless we understand the history of how it came to be. While history is a record of unique happenings, it is something more than chaos.
>
> (B) The present may be the consequence of accidents, or of irresistible forces, but in either case the present consequences of past events are real and irreversible.
>
> (C) To perceive the elements of order in the chaotic record of past events is the great task of the historian. Events, people, groups and institutions fall into certain classes that exhibit at least partial regularities.

① (A) - (C) - (B)

② (B) - (A) - (C)

③ (B) - (C) - (A)

④ (C) - (A) - (B)

⑤ (C) - (B) - (A)

07 According to the passage, which of the following would NOT be considered a transactive memory source?

> Search engines have changed the way we use the Internet, putting vast sources of information just a few clicks away. But a recent study shows that websites—and the Internet—are changing much more than technology itself. They are changing the way our memories function. Dr. Wegner's latest study, "Google Effects on Memory: Cognitive Consequences of Having Information at Our Fingertips," shows that when people have access to search engines, they remember fewer facts and less information because they know they can rely on "search" as a readily available shortcut. Wegner believes the new findings show that the Internet has become part of a transactive memory source, a method by which our brains compartmentalize information. First hypothesized by Wegner in 1985, transactive memory exists in many forms, as when a husband relies on his wife to remember a relative's birthday. "It is this whole network of memory where you don't have to remember everything in the world yourself," he says. "You just have to remember who knows it." Now computers and technology as well are becoming virtual extensions of our memory.

① Reminder apps that notify you of upcoming events

② A photo album of your childhood

③ GPS devices that help you find your way with saved routes

④ A written list of your passwords for different websites

⑤ Cell phones with your contact list

08 Which of the following is true according to the passage?

> It may happen that someone gets away, apparently unharmed, from the spot where he has suffered a shocking accident, for instance, a train collision. In the course of the following weeks, however, he develops a series of grave psychical and motor symptoms, which can be ascribed only to his shock or whatever else happened at the time of the accident. He has developed a "traumatic neurosis." This appears quite incomprehensible and is therefore a novel fact. The time that elapsed between the accident and the first appearance of the symptoms is called the "incubation period," a transparent allusion to the pathology of infectious disease. It is the feature one might term *latency*.

① The recurrence of suffering after a shocking accident is a well-known fact.

② A "traumatic neurosis" appears when one is infected by a virus.

③ The term *latency* does not have any relation to infectious disease.

④ A "traumatic neurosis" refers to the shock one feels right after an accident.

⑤ *Latency* refers to the period when the impact of the shocking events remains dormant.

09 Which of the following best fits in the blank?

> Being present to another person—a sustained, caring attention—can be seen as a basic form of compassion. Careful attention to another person also enhances empathy, letting us catch more of the fleeting facial expressions and other such cues that attune us to how that person actually feels in the moment. But if our attention "blinks," _____.

① we may be more attentive to the person

② our empathy will be enhanced

③ we are less attuned to the behavior of the person

④ we may miss those signals

⑤ we do feel apathy for the person

10 Which of the following is NOT grammatically correct?

> "Love yourself and recognize the common humanity in the experience," says researcher David Sbarra. This is called "self-compassion." People who express feelings of loving themselves ① <u>and who recognize they</u> are not alone and other people have felt what they feel have more resilience when dealing with a breakup. You know how ② <u>frustrating it is</u> when you're freaked out and someone tells you to "relax." That's part of the problem with learning self-compassion after a breakup. Anxiety will keep you away from breaking through to being kind and loving with yourself, but you can't force yourself away from the anxiety, and you certainly can't beat yourself up further. Personality plays a big part in how you react, and ③ <u>women tending to handle it</u> with more self-compassion than men. Be kinder to yourself after a breakup, keeping your experience in perspective. Many people experience a painful and difficult breakup, and you're not alone. A breakup is part of the human experience, and ④ <u>realizing you are</u> a part of a collective can help shift your perception to a healthier place. Dr. Sbarra also recommends ⑤ <u>remaining</u> mindful, and in the present. Notice when you feel anger or jealousy, and accept and release it—don't judge it, even if you struggle with releasing it.

11 Which of the following best fits in the blanks (A) and (B)?

> Yet the paradox is that scientific methodology is the product of human hands and thus cannot reach some permanent truth. We build scientific theories to organize and manipulate the world, to reduce phenomena into manageable units. Science is based on reproducibility and manufactured objectivity. As strong as that makes its ability to generate claims about matter and energy, it also makes scientific knowledge (A) _____ to the existential, visceral nature or human life, which is unique and subjective and unpredictable. Science may provide the most useful way to organize empirical, reproducible data, but its power to do so is predicated on its (B) _____ to grasp the most central aspects of human life: hope, fear, love, hate, beauty, envy, honor, weakness, striving, suffering, virtue, etc.

	(A)	(B)
①	inapplicable	inability
②	irrelevant	loathing
③	comparable	remnant
④	integral	mundanity
⑤	conform	merits

12 Which of the following is NOT grammatically correct?

> The capability ① <u>to form</u> memory is critical to the strategic adaptation of an organism ② <u>to changing</u> environmental demands. Observations ③ <u>indicating</u> that sleep benefits memory ④ <u>date back</u> to the beginning of experimental memory research, and since then ⑤ <u>has been fitted</u> with quite different concepts.

13 Which of the following is NOT used appropriately in the context?

For years, critics have argued about the ancient Greek play *Oedipus Rex*. Some have argued that Oedipus knows nothing of his guilt until the end of the play, when it is revealed that he murdered his own father. Others have insisted that Oedipus is aware all along of his ① guilt. According to this point of view, Oedipus, the brilliant solver of riddles, could not possibly have ② ignored the mounting evidence that he was the murderer of the king. Just how or why this debate has raged for so many years remains a mystery. The correct interpretation is so obvious. Oedipus knows from the beginning that he is ③ innocent. He just pretends to be ignorant of the truth. For example, when a servant tells the story of the king's murder, he uses the word 'bandits.' But when Oedipus repeats his story, he uses the ④ singular form 'bandit.' Sophocles provides clues like this one all the way through the play. Thus, it's hard to understand why anyone would think that Oedipus did not know the truth about his ⑤ crime.

14 Choose the one that is closest in meaning to the underlined word.

Is talent a bad thing? Are we all equally talented? No and no. The ability to quickly climb the learning curve of any skill is obviously a very good thing, and, like it or not, some of us are better at it than others. So why, then, is it such a bad thing to favor "naturals" over "strivers"? What's the downside of television shows like *America's Got Talent, The X Factor*, and *Child Genius*? Why shouldn't we separate children as young as seven or eight into two groups: those few children who are "gifted and talented" and the many, many more who aren't? What harm is there, really, in a talent show being named a "talent show"? In my view, the biggest reason a preoccupation with talent can be harmful is simple: By shining our spotlight on talent, we risk leaving everything else in the shadows. We inadvertently send the message that these other factors—including grit—don't matter as much as they really do.

① deliberately

② incoherently

③ concomitantly

④ surreptitiously

⑤ unintentionally

15 Which of the following is NOT grammatically correct?

> If AI is given more agency and takes over what humans used to do, ① how do we then attribute moral responsibility? Who is responsible for the harms and benefits of the technology when humans delegate agency and decisions to AI? The first problem is that an AI system can take actions and make decisions that have ethical consequences, but is not aware of what it does and not capable of moral thought and ② hence cannot hold morally responsible for what it does. Machines can be agents but not moral agents ③ since they lack consciousness, free will, emotions, the capability to form intentions, and the like. For example, on an Aristotelian view, only humans can perform voluntary actions and deliberate about their actions. If this is true, the only solution is to make humans responsible for what the machine does. ④ Humans then delegate agency to the machine, but retain the responsibility. However, this solution faces several problems. An AI system may make its decisions and actions very quickly, for example, in high-frequency trading or in a self-driving car, ⑤ which gives the human too little time to make the final decision or to intervene. How can humans take responsibility for such actions and decisions?

16 Which of the following best fits in the blank?

> People rely on _____ to be "normal"— amounts that are typical, expected, and not unusual. Normal rain and snow melt are necessary for consistent agriculture, to feed Earth's 7.3 billion humans. All plants and animals are adapted to a normal amount of moisture for their environment. However, "normal" does not always happen.

① circulation

② precipitation

③ sewage

④ drought

⑤ irrigation

17 What is the passage mainly about?

Trying new things requires a willingness to take risks. However, risk taking is not binary. I'd bet that you're comfortable taking some types of risk and find other types quite uncomfortable. You might not even see the risks that are comfortable for you to take, discounting their riskiness, but are likely to amplify the risk of things that make you more anxious. For example, you might love flying down a ski slope at lightning speed or jumping out of airplanes, and don't view these activities as risky. If so, you're blind to the fact that you're taking on significant physical risks. Others, like me who are not physical risk takers, would rather sip hot chocolate in the ski lodge or buckle themselves tightly into their airplane seats. Alternately, you might feel perfectly comfortable with social risks, such as giving a speech to a large crowd. This doesn't seem risky at all to me. But others, who might be perfectly happy jumping out of a plane, would never think to give a toast at a party.

① Taking both physical and social risks benefits us.

② We should separate risk into two categories: physical risk and social risk.

③ Taking physical risks poses a great challenge to the author.

④ Perception of riskiness differs from person to person.

⑤ The willingness to take risks is a prerequisite for success.

18 Which of the following best fits in the blanks (A), (B) and (C)?

All I could do was to offer you an opinion upon one minor point—a woman must have money and a room of her own if she is to write fiction. I am going to develop in your presence as fully and freely as I can the train of thought which led me to think so. Perhaps if I lay bare the ideas, the prejudices, that lie behind this statement, you will find that they have some (A) _____ upon women and some upon fiction. At any rate, when a subject is highly controversial—and any question about sex is that—one cannot hope to tell the truth. One can only show how one came to hold whatever opinion one does hold. One can only give one's audience the chance of (B) _____ their own conclusions as they observe the limitations, the prejudices and the idiosyncrasies of the speaker. Fiction here is likely to contain more truth than fact. Therefore, I propose, making use of all the liberties and (C) _____ of a novelist, to tell you the story of the two days that preceded my coming here.

	(A)	(B)	(C)
①	bearing	drawing	licenses
②	relieving	writing	imaginations
③	showing	drowning	creativities
④	relevance	throwing	obligations
⑤	giving	collecting	jobs

19 Which of the following is true according to the passage?

Have human beings permanently changed the planet? That seemingly simple question has sparked a new battle between geologists and environmental advocates over what to call the time period we live in. According to the International Union of Geological Sciences, we are officially in the Holocene epoch, which began 11,700 years ago after the last major ice age. But that label is outdated, some experts say. They argue for "Anthropocene"—from *anthropo*, for "man," and *cene*, for "new"—because humankind has caused mass extinctions of plant and animal species, polluted the oceans and altered the atmosphere, among other lasting impacts. However, many stratigraphers (scientists who study rock layers) criticize the idea, saying clear-cut evidence for a new epoch simply isn't there. According to them, when we start naming geologic-time terms, we need to define what exactly the boundary is, where it appears in the rock strata. Anthropocene is more about pop culture than hard science. The crucial question is specifying exactly when human beings began to leave their mark on the planet: The atomic era, for instance, has left traces of radiation in soils around the globe, while deeper down in the rock strata, agriculture's signature in Europe can be detected as far back as 900 A.D. The "Anthropocene," a stratigrapher says, "provides eye-catching jargon, but from the geologic side, I need the bare-bones facts that fit the code." Some Anthropocene proponents concede that difficulty. But don't get bogged down in the mud, they say, just stipulate a date and move on. Will Steffen, who heads Australia National University's Climate Change Institute, says that the new name sends a message: "It will be another strong reminder to the general public that we are now having undeniable impacts on the environment at the scale of the planet as a whole, so much so that a new geological epoch has begun."

① The geologists do not want the environmentalists to have an edge over them by favoring the action of renaming the time period.

② The stratigraphers need to consider the culture in renaming the time period of the Earth.

③ The environmental advocates believe that human beings will get aware of their rampant activities which cause destruction if the time period of the Earth is renamed.

④ The geologists believe that the changes caused by human beings have been going on for a short time.

⑤ Some Anthropocene proponents agree with stratigraphers that it is difficult to find samples in the mud.

20 Which of the following can be inferred from the passage?

Many people around the world work to consider consumer ethics and make ethical consumer choices in their everyday lives in response to the troubling conditions that plague global supply chains and the human-made climate crisis. In a system of consumer signs, those who make the ethical choice to purchase fair trade, organic, locally grown and sustainable goods are also often seen as morally superior to those who don't know, or don't care to make these kinds of purchases.

In the landscape of consumer goods, being an ethical consumer awards one with heightened cultural capital and a higher social status in relation to other consumers. For example, buying a hybrid vehicle signals to others that one is concerned about environmental issues, and neighbors passing by the car in the driveway might even view the car's owner more positively. However, someone who can't afford to replace their 20-year-old car may care about the environment just as much, but they would be unable to demonstrate this through their patterns of consumption. It is likely that those they encounter will assume them to be poor and undereducated. They may experience disrespect and disregard on a daily basis, despite how they behave toward others.

① Someone who does not replace his polluting diesel car with a hybrid model is not an ethical consumer.

② What we buy is often related to our cultural and educational capital, and consumption patterns can reinforce existing social hierarchies.

③ Increasing consumption of goods is a desirable goal of an ethical consumer.

④ Consumption is the means of practicing a truly ethical life.

⑤ People with more cultural capital are likely to be morally superior to those with low levels of cultural capital.

21 Which of the following best fits in the blank?

Inventing Eastern Europe was a project of philosophical and geographical synthesis carried out by the men and women of the Enlightenment. Obviously, the lands of Eastern Europe were not in themselves invented or fictitious; those lands and the people who lived in them were always quite real, and did indeed lie relatively to the east of other lands that lay relatively to the west. The project of invention was not merely a matter of endowing those real lands with invented or mythological attributes, though such endowment certainly flourished in the eighteenth century. The Enlightenment's accounts were not flatly false or fictitious; on the contrary, in an age of increasingly ambitious traveling and more critical observation, those lands were more frequently visited and thoroughly studied than ever before. The work of invention lay in the synthetic association of lands, which drew upon both fact and fiction, to produce the general rubric of Eastern Europe. That rubric represented an aggregation of general and associative observations over a diverse domain of lands and peoples. It is in that sense that Eastern Europe is a cultural construction, that is, _____ _____ of the Enlightenment.

① a fictitious idea

② an unconscious projection

③ a geographical mapping

④ an intellectual invention

⑤ a delirious dream

22 Where does the given sentence best fit in the passage?

> Humans have symbolic language, elaborate social and political institutions, codes of law, literature and art, ethics, and religion; humans build roads and cities, travel by motorcars, ships, and airplanes, and communicate by means of telephones, computers, and televisions.

> Chimpanzees are the closest relatives of Homo sapiens, our species. (A) There is a precise correspondence bone by bone between the skeletons of a chimpanzee and a human. Humans bear young like apes and other mammals. (B) Humans have organs and limbs similar to birds, reptiles, and amphibians; these similarities reflect the common evolutionary origin of vertebrates. (C) However, it does not take much reflection to notice the distinct uniqueness of our species. (D) Conspicuous anatomical differences between humans and apes include bipedal gait and an enlarged brain. Much more conspicuous than the anatomical differences are the distinct behaviors and institutions. (E)

① (A)   ② (B)

③ (C)   ④ (D)

⑤ (E)

23 Which of the following is NOT grammatically correct?

> If you're not into sport, you're probably planning to avoid university sports teams like the plague, ① determined to avoid reliving the horrible memories of sports classes in school ② etching in your memory. Don't rule out ③ playing sports at university at some level, though. Not only are there a vast array of possible sports to play at university, but there are also a wide range of ability levels, ④ catering for everyone from the very sporty to the complete novice. If you do find a sports club that suits you, here are some of the ways it will improve your university experience and not just by ⑤ helping you work off last night's pizza.

24 Which of the following is the most appropriate title of the passage?

> Identifying sleep patterns is difficult due to the lack of regular, high quality surveys. A 2004 study, however, found that average sleep duration is 7 hours, with two-thirds of the people surveyed sleeping 5.5-8.5 hours per night. About a third reported at least one episode of difficulty sleeping on a majority of nights. Whether sleep duration has decreased is hard to determine. According to one study (1983-2005), average adult sleep duration increased by 50 minutes, the prevalence of short sleep (less than 6 hours) decreased from 15% to 10%, and the prevalence of long sleep (greater than 9 hours) increased from 16% to 28%. Evidence on trends in children's sleep is inconclusive. However, a more recent study found that children's sleep increased by about 1 hour over the past century. Even if sleep has not worsened, experts emphasize that insufficient sleep duration is an important public health issue.

① Are We Really Sleep-Deprived?
② How are Sleep Disorders Diagnosed?
③ What are the Different Types of Sleep Disorders?
④ Why Do We Need Sufficient Sleep?
⑤ What are the Consequences of Sleep Deprivation?

25 Which of the following does NOT fit in the passage?

> Cartography is both a highly technical and a somewhat artistic pursuit, combining the tools of mathematics and engineering with those of graphic design. ① Maps should be accurate, portraying matter as it really exists rather than as distorted, improperly located, or mislabeled information. They should be visually easy to use, prominently displaying the material a user needs without clutter from unnecessary information. ② This is why road maps, for example, usually do not show mountains and hills except in the simplest ways. ③ Until the 1970s, most maps were being drawn with ink pens and rulers, but now they are composed on computers and printed by machine. To do so would add many extra lines to a map that is already filled with lines representing roads. ④ In converting geographic data from their original form on Earth's surface to a simplified form on a map, we must make many decisions about how this information should be represented. ⑤ No matter how we draw a map, we cannot possibly make it show the world exactly as it is in all its detail, nor would we want it to. Scale and projection are two fundamental properties of maps that determine how information is portrayed.

모바일 OMR

✅ 회독 CHECK 1 2 3

01 Which of the following best fits in the blank?

> Jack Nicklaus's success on the golf course, and the _____ increase in the size of his bank account, had made him the envy of all professional golfers.

① concomitant
② oscillating
③ festering
④ fledgling
⑤ vignette

02 Which of the following best fits in the blank?

> Draconian laws are the first written code of laws drawn up at Athens, believed to have been introduced in 621 or 620 B.C. by a statesman named Draco. Although their details are obscure, they apparently covered a number of offences. The modern adjective "Draconian," meaning excessively _____, reflects the fact that penalties laid down in the code were extremely severe: pilfering received the same punishment as murder—death. A 4th-century B.C. politician quipped that Draco wrote his laws not in ink, but in blood.

① benign
② vigilant
③ harsh
④ auspicious
⑤ propitious

03 Which of the following is NOT grammatically correct?

> A renaissance man is a person who ① is skilled in many fields and has a broad range of learning in many subjects. The term, renaissance man, ② originates from the artists and scholars of European Renaissance, ③ such as Leonardo Da Vinci or Michelangelo. In Renaissance period, educated men ④ aspired becoming a multi-talented man. They ⑤ were expected to speak several languages, to appreciate literature and art, and to be good sportsmen as well.

04 Which of the following is grammatically correct?

① The 3rd International Geography Conference will held in Seoul.
② I was so hurted when Susan left me.
③ If the weather had been better, I would have been sitting in the garden when he arrived.
④ It is very kind with him to invite me over for his 80th birthday party.
⑤ She has came up with some amazing scheme to double her income.

05 Choose the pair of words that are closest in meaning to the underlined words.

> "In one picture, I could read my non-existence in the clothes my mother had worn before I can remember her. There is a kind of (A) stupefaction in seeing a familiar being dressed differently," writes Roland Barthes in *Camera Lucida* as he searches through family photographs from before his birth. In that single picture, Barthes tells us, the young child rejoins the frail old woman he nursed through her last illness: "She had become my little girl, uniting for me with that essential child she was in her first photograph." There he finds his mother's assertive gentleness, her kindness. There he finds not only his mother but the qualities of their relationship, a (B) congruence between "my mother's being and my grief at her death."

	(A)	(B)
①	amazement	discrepancy
②	wonder	distinctiveness
③	happiness	harmony
④	astonishment	accordance
⑤	contentment	conformance

06 Where does the given sentence best fit in the passage?

> It eventually turned out that the signal was indeed a false alarm due to human error: a computer operator had by mistake inserted into the U.S. warning system computer a training tape simulating the launch of 200 Soviet ICBMs.

> Missile detection systems, like all complex technologies, are subject to malfunctions and to ambiguities of interpretation. (A) We know of at least three false alarms given by the American detection system. (B) For example, on November 9, 1979 the U.S. army general serving as watch officer for the U.S. system phoned then-Under-Secretary of Defense William Perry in the middle of the night to say, "My warning computer is showing 200 ICBMs in flight from the Soviet Union to the United States." (C) But the general concluded that the signal was probably a false alarm, Perry did not awaken President Carter, and Carter did not push the button and needlessly kill a hundred million Soviets. (D) We also know of at least one false alarm given by the Russian detection system: a single non-military rocket launched in 1995 from an island off Norway towards the North Pole was misidentified by the automatic tracking algorithm of Russian radar as a missile launched from an American submarine. (E) These incidents illustrate an important point: A warning signal is not unambiguous.

① (A)   ② (B)
③ (C)   ④ (D)
⑤ (E)

07 Which of the following is NOT grammatically correct?

> Job satisfaction is not universal in middle adulthood. ① <u>For some people, work becomes increasingly stressful as dissatisfaction with working conditions or with the nature of the job mount.</u> ② <u>In some cases, conditions become so bad that the result is burnout or a decision to change jobs.</u> Burnout occurs when workers experience dissatisfaction, disillusionment, frustration, and weariness from their jobs. It occurs most often in jobs that involve helping others, and ③ <u>it often strikes those who initially were the most idealistic and driven.</u> In some ways, such workers may be overcommitted to their jobs, and ④ <u>the realization that they can make only minor dents in huge societal problems such as poverty and medical care can be disappointing and demoralizing.</u> Thus, ⑤ <u>the idealism with which they may have entered a profession is replaced by pessimism</u> and the attitude that it is impossible to provide any kind of meaningful solution to a problem.

08 Which of the following is NOT true according to the passage?

> There is a mode of vital experience—experience of space and time, of the self and others, of life's possibilities and perils—that is shared by men and women all over the world today. I will call this body of experience "modernity." To be modern is to find ourselves in an environment that promises us adventure, power, joy, growth, transformation of ourselves and the world—and, at the same time, that threatens to destroy everything we have, everything we know, everything we are. Modern environments and experiences cut across all boundaries of geography and ethnicity, of class and nationality, of religion and ideology: in this sense, modernity can be said to unite all mankind. But it is a paradoxical unity, a unity of disunity: it pours us all into a maelstrom of perpetual disintegration and renewal, of struggle and contradiction, of ambiguity and anguish.

① Modernity refers to a mode of experience that is shared by people in the world.

② Modernity finds us in an environment that threatens to destroy everything we have.

③ Modernity separates mankind according to the different geographical locations.

④ Modernity is a mode of experience that encompasses life's possibilities and perils.

⑤ Modernity traverses boundaries of ethnicity, nationality, and ideology.

09 Which of the following best fits in the blank?

> The slogan "Global Britain" first gained currency in the months after the country's vote to leave the European Union in 2016. Theresa May deployed the phrase five times when she addressed the Conservative Party conference for the first time as prime minister. Days later it was the title of Boris Johnson's first policy speech as Mrs May's foreign secretary. What it meant in practice, beyond an attempt to reassure Britons that Brexit would not mean autarky, remained hazy. The idea is finally being fleshed out. On March 16th Mr Johnson's government published "Global Britain in a Competitive Age", a 114-page "integrated review" of the country's foreign, security, defence and aid policy, billed as the most radical such review since the end of the cold war. In many ways, _____. The text is free of the ebullient jingoism beloved of Mr Johnson and his cabinet. Many observers had anticipated a pivot away from Europe, where Britain is locked in diplomatic trench warfare with the EU, towards the rising powers of Asia.

① it defies expectations

② it gains popularity

③ it conforms to Brexit

④ this subscribes to the party's recommendations

⑤ this overlooks the country's economical situations

10 Which of the following is the most logical sequence of the four parts to complete the passage?

> According to the theories of physics, if we were to look at the Universe one second after the Big Bang, what we would see is a 10-billion degree sea of neutrons, protons, electrons, anti-electrons (positrons), photons, and neutrinos.

> (A) As it continued to cool, it would eventually reach the temperature where electrons combined with nuclei to form neutral atoms.
>
> (B) But when the free electrons were absorbed to form neutral atoms, the Universe suddenly became transparent.
>
> (C) Then, as time went on, we would see the Universe cool, the neutrons either decaying into protons and electrons or combining with protons to make deuterium (an isotope of hydrogen).
>
> (D) Before this "recombination" occurred, the Universe would have been opaque because the free electrons would have caused light (photons) to scatter the way sunlight scatters from the water droplets in clouds.

> Those same photons—the afterglow of the Big Bang known as cosmic background radiation—can be observed today.

① (A) - (B) - (C) - (D)

② (A) - (C) - (B) - (D)

③ (B) - (A) - (D) - (C)

④ (C) - (A) - (D) - (B)

⑤ (C) - (D) - (B) - (A)

11 Which of the following is the most appropriate title of the passage?

> Human population growth, rising incomes and preference shifts will considerably increase global demand for nutritious food in the coming decades. Malnutrition and hunger still plague many countries, and projections of population and income by 2050 suggest a future need for more than 500 megatonnes (Mt) of meat per year for human consumption. Scaling up the production of land-derived food crops is challenging, because of declining yield rates and competition for scarce land and water resources. Land-derived seafood (freshwater aquaculture and inland capture fisheries; we use seafood to denote any aquatic food resource, and food from the sea for marine resources specifically) has an important role in food security and global supply, but its expansion is also constrained. Similar to other land-based production, the expansion of land-based aquaculture has resulted in substantial environmental externalities that affect water, soil, biodiversity and climate, and which compromise the ability of the environment to produce food. Despite the importance of terrestrial aquaculture in seafood production, many countries—notably China, the largest inland-aquaculture producer— have restricted the use of land and public waters for this purpose, which constrains expansion. Although inland capture fisheries are important for food security, their contribution to total global seafood production is limited and expansion is hampered by ecosystem constraints. Thus, to meet future needs (and recognizing that land-based sources of fish and other foods are also part of the solution), we ask whether the sustainable production of food from the sea has an important role in future supply.

① The Rise of Global Food Demand
② The Future of Food from the Sea
③ Climate Change and Biodiversity Loss
④ Food-producing Sectors in the Ocean
⑤ Edible Food from the Sea and Marine Culture

12 Which of the following best fits in the blanks (A), (B) and (C)?

> Congress is considering a series of bills that, if passed into law, would (A) _____ changes to the Endangered Species Act that could shift control of conservation measures to state and local governments, accelerate decisions about whether species need protecting, and (B) _____ courts' power to overturn decisions to lift or loosen species protections, the Associated Press (AP) reports. Many Democrats and wildlife advocates argue that the proposed changes will put the world's biodiversity at risk. "The wildlife extinction package is an extreme and all-encompassing assault on the Endangered Species Act," Bob Dreher, senior vice president of conservation programs at the nonprofit conservation organization Defenders of Wildlife, says in a statement posted by YubaNet.com. "These bills discard science, increasing the likelihood of harm to species and habitat, create hurdles to protecting species, and (C) _____ citizen's ability to enforce the law in court, while delegating authority for species management to states—or even corporations and individuals— that are ill-equipped to assume it."

	(A)	(B)	(C)
①	initiate	hinder	rectify
②	bolster	indulge	remedy
③	nullify	expand	ruin
④	instruct	widen	block
⑤	institute	limit	undermine

13 Which of the following is NOT mentioned in the passage?

> In the first week of May 2000, unseasonably heavy rain drenched the rural town of Walkerton, Canada. As the rainstorms passed, Walkerton's residents began to fall ill in their hundreds. With ever more people developing gastroenteritis and bloody diarrhoea, the authorities tested the water supply. They discovered what the water company had been keeping quiet for days: the town's drinking water was contaminated with a deadly strain of E. coli. It transpired that bosses at the water company had known for weeks that the chlorination system on one of the town's wells was broken. During the rain, their negligence had meant that run-off from farmland had carried residues from manure straight into the water supply. A day after the contamination was revealed, three adults and a baby died from their illnesses. Over the next few weeks, three more people succumbed. In total, half of Walkerton's 5,000-strong population were infected in just a couple of weeks.

① when and where the incident happened
② main causes of the disease outbreak
③ compensation for damage by the water company
④ the number of deaths in the town
⑤ the population size of the town

14 Which of the following best fits in the blank?

> In most instances, it is illegal for representatives of two or more companies to secretly set similar prices for their products. This practice, known as price fixing, is generally held to be an anticompetitive act. Companies that _____ in this manner are generally trying to ensure higher prices for their products than would be generally available if markets are functioning freely.

① flout 　　　　　② scalp
③ endue 　　　　　④ collude
⑤ censure

15 Choose the one that is closest in meaning to the underlined expression.

> There is serious concern the poison may have been moved somewhere that we don't know about by other people who are at large and determined to carry out an attack.

① not disengaged
② not yet confined
③ disguised in group
④ vanished with people
⑤ secretly camouflaged

16 Which of the following is NOT grammatically correct?

> In Europe, rules on positive discrimination ① are being discussed in each country. The rules state that ② companies should give women ③ preference for non-executive posts where there is no better-qualified male candidate, until women reach a total of 40% in the boardroom. The draft law ④ made it possible to fine the companies which ignore the rules. ⑤ If endorsing, the rules will take seven years to come into force.

17 Which of the following is NOT grammatically correct?

> The distance to the stars can seem unfathomably immense. Physicist Freeman Dyson at Princeton suggests that, ① to reach them, we might learn something from the voyages of the Polynesians thousands of years ago. Instead of trying to make one extended journey across the Pacific, which ② would likely to have ended in disaster, they went island hopping, spreading across the ocean's landmasses one at a time. ③ Each time they reached an island, they would create a permanent settlement and then move on to the next island. He posits ④ that we might create intermediate colonies in deep space in the same way. The key to this strategy would be the comets, which, along with rogue planets that have somehow ⑤ been ejected from their solar systems, might litter the path to the stars.

18 Which of the following best fits in the blank?

> In the early years of Christianity, Easter was the main holiday; the birth of Jesus was not celebrated. In the fourth century, church officials decided to declare the birth of Jesus as a holiday. Unfortunately, the Bible does not mention date for his birth (a fact Puritans later pointed out in order to deny the legitimacy of the celebration). Although some evidence suggests that his birth _____ in the spring (why would shepherds be herding in the middle of winter?), Pope Julius I chose December 25. It is commonly believed that the church chose this date in an effort to adopt and absorb the traditions of the pagan Saturnalia festival.

① may have occurred

② might not occur

③ should occur

④ ought not occur

⑤ could not have occurred

19 Which of the following is true according to the passage?

> Power is something we are often uncomfortable naming and talking about explicitly. In our everyday talk, power has a negative moral vibe: "power-mad", "power-hungry", "power trip". But power is no more inherently good or evil than fire or physics. It just is. The only question is whether we will try to understand and harness it. In the culture and mythology of democracy, power is supposed to reside with the people. Here's my simple definition of power—it's the capacity to ensure that others do as you would want them to do. Civic power is that capacity exercised by citizens in public, whether in elections or government or in social and economic arenas. Power in civic life takes many forms: force, wealth, state action, ideas, social norms, numbers. And it flows through many conduits: institutions, organizations, networks, laws and rules, narratives and ideologies. Map these forms and conduits against each other, and you get what we think of as "the power structure." The problem today is that too many people aren't able to draw, read or follow such a map. Too many people are profoundly illiterate in power. As a result, it has become ever easier for those who do understand how power operates in civic life to wield a disproportionate influence and fill the void created by the ignorance of the majority.

① Power is the word that is widely welcomed and comfortably discussed.

② We citizens do not have the right to discuss and harness the logic of power.

③ Civic power is the capacity mainly exercised by officials in the government.

④ In everyday life, the majority of people tend to skillfully map the civic power.

⑤ Relations between the forms and conduits of power help identify its structure.

20 Which of the following is the most logical sequence of the three parts to complete the passage?

> In contrast to a growing number of scholars in other fields, economists have contributed relatively little to recent critiques of consumer society. With a few notable exceptions, contemporary economists have been hesitant to entertain questions about the relationship of consumption to quality of life.

> (A) Economists, moreover, are typically unwilling to engage in critical discussion of values and preferences. In the absence of such discussion, it is easily assumed that the existing configuration of consumer choice is optimal.
>
> (B) Otherwise, it would not be occurring. Actually the implications of the model are even stronger, as we shall see.
>
> (C) Their reluctance is not difficult to explain. Most economists subscribe to a model that holds that as long as standard assumptions are satisfied, consumption must be yielding welfare.

① (A) - (B) - (C)

② (B) - (A) - (C)

③ (B) - (C) - (A)

④ (C) - (A) - (B)

⑤ (C) - (B) - (A)

21 Which of the following best fits in the blank?

> Black Death, pandemic that ravaged Europe between 1347 and 1351, took a proportionately greater toll of life than any other known epidemic or war up to that time. The consequences of this violent catastrophe were many. A cessation of wars and a sudden slump in trade immediately followed but were only of short duration. A more lasting and serious consequence was the drastic reduction of the amount of land under cultivation, due to the deaths of so many labourers. This proved to be the ruin of many landowners. The shortage of labour compelled them to substitute wages or money rents in place of labour services in an effort to keep their tenants. There was also a general rise in wages for artisans and peasants. These changes brought a new _____ to the hitherto rigid stratification of society.

① fluidity

② violence

③ medicine

④ boundary

⑤ monarchy

22 Which of the following best fits in the blanks (A), (B) and (C)?

> Modern online disinformation exploits the attention-driven business model that powers most of the internet as we currently know it. Platforms like Google and Facebook make (A) _____ amounts of money grabbing and capturing our attention so they can show us paid advertisements. That attention is gamed using algorithms that measure what content we engage with and automatically show us more content like it. The problem, of course, emerges when these algorithms automatically recommend and (B) _____ our worst tendencies. As humans, we evolved to respond more strongly to negative stimuli than positive ones. These algorithms detect that and (C) _____ it, selecting content that sends us down increasingly negative rabbit holes.

	(A)	(B)	(C)
①	staggering	abridge	underestimate
②	astounding	compress	enunciate
③	staggering	amplify	reinforce
④	astounding	enlarge	revamp
⑤	awesome	compress	underpin

23 Which of the following does NOT fit in the passage?

① For at least 3,000 years, a fluctuating proportion of the world's population has believed that the end of the world is imminent. Scholars dispute its origins, but it seems likely that the distinctive construction of apocalyptic narratives that inflects much environmentalism today began around 1200 B.C., in the thought of the Iranian prophet Zoroaster, or Zarathustra. ② Notions of the world's gradual decline were widespread in ancient civilizations. ③ But Zoroaster bequeathed to Jewish, Christian and later secular models of history a sense of urgency about the demise of the world. From Zealots of Roman Judaea to the Branch Davidians, so many believers have fought and died in fear and hope of impending apocalypse, while some others including Nazis and communists have adopted apocalyptic rhetoric, again with catastrophic results as prophecies of crisis and conflict inexorably fulfil themselves. ④ Yet arguably similar rhetoric strategies have provided the green movement with some of its most striking successes. ⑤ Eurasians have not always believed that their world will end someday. With this in mind, it is crucial that we consider the past and future role of the apocalyptic narrative in environmental and radical ecological discourse.

24 Which of the following best fits in the blank?

Cells are considered the foundation of life, but viruses—with all their genetic diversity—may share in that role. Our planet's earliest viruses and cells likely evolved in an intertwined and often symbiotic relationship of predator and prey. Evidence even suggests that viruses may have started out as cells but _____ _____. This dependent relationship began a long history of coevolution. Viruses living in cells cause their hosts to adapt, and those changes then cause viruses to adapt in a never ending cycle of one-upmanship.

① injected many primitive characteristics into early cellular ancestors

② lost their autonomy as they evolved to thrive as parasites on other cells

③ transmitted to humans via saliva in a mosquito's bite and gotten independent from them

④ handed over through a cell's membrane by using receptors and continually modified

⑤ exposed to a weakened virus and recognized that specific invader

25 Which of the following is the most appropriate title of the passage?

Variation in a characteristic that is a result of genetic information from the parents is called inherited variation. Children usually look a little like their father, and a little like their mother, but they will not be identical to either of their parents. This is because they get half of their DNA and inherited features from each parent. Each egg cell and each sperm cell contains half of the genetic information needed for an individual. When these join at fertilization a new cell is formed with all the genetic information needed for an individual. Here are some examples of inherited variation in humans: eye colour, hair colour, skin colour, lobed or lobeless ears, ability to roll your tongue. Gender is inherited variation too, because whether you are male or female is a result of the genes you inherited from your parents.

① The Causes of Gender Difference
② Child and Parent Identification
③ Genetic Identification and DNA
④ Inherited Causes of Variation
⑤ Cause and Effect of Social Inheritance

시대에듀의
면접 도서 시리즈
라인업

지방직 공무원 면접
(교육행정직)

소방공무원 면접

국가직 공무원1 면접

국가직 공무원2 면접
(행정직)

국가직 공무원2 면접
(기술직)

※ 도서의 이미지 및 구성은 변경될 수 있습니다.

기출이 답이다

9급 공무원

영어

7개년 기출문제집

시대에듀

정가 **21,000원**(1·2권 포함)

발행일 2024년 10월 15일 | **발행인** 박영일 | **책임편집** 이해욱
편저 시대공무원시험연구소 | **발행처** (주)시대고시기획
등록번호 제10-1521호 | **대표전화** 1600-3600 | **팩스** (02)701-8823
주소 서울시 마포구 큰우물로 75 [도화동 538 성지B/D] 9F
학습문의 www.sdedu.co.kr

ISBN 979-11-383-7438-5

국가직 · 지방직 · 법원직 등 공무원 채용 대비

2025

안심도서
황균99.9%

기출이 답이다

편저 | 시대공무원시험연구소

여러분의 합격 9급

영어

7개년 기출문제집

해설편

시대에듀

영어

해설편

PART 1

국가직

한눈에 훑어보기

✔ 영역 분석

어휘   01   02   03   04   05
5문항, 25%

독해   12   13   14   15   16   17   18   19   20
9문항, 45%

어법   06   07   08
3문항, 15%

표현   09   10   11
3문항, 15%

✔ 빠른 정답

01	02	03	04	05	06	07	08	09	10
③	②	①	④	④	②	①	①	②	④
11	12	13	14	15	16	17	18	19	20
③	②	③	④	①	④	③	②	②	①

✔ 점수 체크

구분	1회독	2회독	3회독
맞힌 문항 수	/ 20	/ 20	/ 20
나의 점수	점	점	점

---

01   난도 ★☆☆   정답 ③

어휘 > 단어

정답의 이유

첫 번째 문장에서 언어 과목의 어떤 측면도 학습이나 교습에서 서로 분리되어 있지 않다고 했으므로 문맥상 밑줄에는 stands alone(분리되다)과 반대되는 뜻을 가진 단어가 와야 함을 유추할 수 있다. 따라서 밑줄 친 부분에 들어갈 말로 적절한 것은 ③ 'interrelated(서로 밀접하게 연관된)'이다.

오답의 이유

① 뚜렷한, 구별되는
② 왜곡된
④ 독자적인

본문해석

분명히, 언어 과목의 어떤 측면도 학습이나 교습에서 서로 분리되어 있지 않다. 듣기, 말하기, 읽기, 쓰기, 보기, 그리고 시각적 표현은 서로 밀접하게 연관되어 있다.

VOCA

• obviously   확실히[분명히]
• aspect   측면, 양상
• stand alone   독립하다, 분리되다, 혼자[따로] 떨어져 있다
• visually representing   시각적으로 나타내기

02   난도 ★☆☆   정답 ②

어휘 > 단어

정답의 이유

밑줄 친 concealed는 conceal(숨기다, 감추다)의 과거분사형으로 '숨겨진, 감춰진'이라는 뜻이다. 이와 의미가 가장 가까운 것은 ② 'hidden(숨겨진)'이다.

오답의 이유

① 사용된
③ 투자된
④ 배달된

본문해석

그 돈은 매우 교묘하게 숨겨져 있어서 우리는 그것에 대한 수색을 포기하도록 강요당했다.

VOCA

• be forced to   ~하도록 강요 당하다
• abandon   그만두다, 포기하다

03 난도 ★☆☆   정답 ①

어휘 > 단어

정답의 이유

밑줄 친 appease는 '달래다, 진정시키다'라는 뜻으로, 이와 의미가 가장 가까운 것은 ① 'soothe(진정시키다)'이다.

오답의 이유

② 반박하다, 대응하다
③ 교화하다
④ 동화되다[동화시키다]

본문해석

반대자들을 달래기 위해 그 무선사업자들은 출퇴근 시간대 라디오 방송에서 1,200만 달러의 공교육 캠페인을 시작했다.

VOCA

• critic 비평가, 반대자
• launch 시작[개시/착수]하다
• public-education campaign 공교육 캠페인
• drive-time 드라이브 타임(출퇴근 시간같이 하루 중 많은 사람들이 차를 운전하는 시간대)

04 난도 ★☆☆   정답 ④

어휘 > 어구

정답의 이유

밑줄 친 play down은 '경시하다'라는 뜻으로, 이와 의미가 가장 가까운 것은 ④ 'underestimate(과소평가하다)'이다.

오답의 이유

① 식별하다, 알아차리다
② 만족시키지 않다
③ 강조하다

본문해석

센터 관계자들은, 그것들이 전형적인 신생기업의 운영 방식이라고 말하면서, 그 문제들을 경시한다.

VOCA

• typical 전형적인, 대표적인
• start-up 신생기업

05 난도 ★☆☆   정답 ④

어휘 > 어구

정답의 이유

밑줄 친 had the guts는 '~할 용기가 있었다'라는 뜻으로, 이와 의미가 가장 가까운 것은 ④ 'was courageous(용감했다)'이다.

오답의 이유

① 걱정했다
② 운이 좋았다
③ 평판이 좋았다

본문해석

그녀는 부지런히 일했고 자신이 원하는 것을 시도할 용기가 있었다.

VOCA

• diligently 부지런히, 열심히
• go for ~을 시도하다, 찬성하다

06 난도 ★☆☆   정답 ②

어법 > 비문 찾기

정답의 이유

② those 앞에 be superior to(~보다 더 뛰어나다)가 있으므로 the quality of older houses(옛날 오래된 주택의 품질)와 those of modern houses(현대의 주택들의 품질)를 비교하고 있음을 알 수 있다. 여기서 those는 단수명사(quality)를 받고 있으므로 those → that이 되어야 한다.

오답의 이유

① 전치사 Despite 다음에 명사(구)인 the belief that the quality of older houses is superior to those of modern houses가 왔으므로 어법상 적절하게 사용되었다. the belief 다음의 that절 (that the quality of older houses is superior to those of modern houses)은 명사(the belief)를 가리키는 동격의 that절이다.

③ compared to의 비교 대상이 the foundations of most pre-20th-century houses와 today's이고, 문맥상 20세기 이전 주택의 기초는 오늘날의 주택 기초와 비교가 되는, 즉 수동의 의미이므로 과거분사(compared)가 적절하게 사용되었다.

④ their가 주절의 주어(the foundations ~ houses)를 받고 있으므로 어법상 대명사의 복수형으로 적절하게 사용되었다.

본문해석

예전의 오래된 주택의 품질이 현대 주택의 품질보다 우수하다는 믿음에도 불구하고, 대부분 20세기 이전 주택의 기초는 오늘날의 주택에 비해 기반이 극히 얕으며, 그것들의 목재 구조의 유연성이나 벽돌과 돌 사이의 석회 모르타르 덕분에 시간의 시험을 견뎌왔을 뿐이다.

VOCA

• be superior to ~보다 더 뛰어나다
• foundation (건물의) 토대[기초]
• dramatically 극적으로, 인상적으로
• shallow 얄팍한, 얕은
• stand 견디다
• flexibility 신축성, 유연성
• timber 목재
• framework (건물 등의) 뼈대[골조]
• lime mortar 석회 모르타르

양보 접속사 vs. 양보 전치사

- 양보 접속사

  though[although, even if, even though]+주어+동사: 비록 ～이지만, ～라 하더라도

  예 Sometimes, even though you may want to apologize, you just may not know how.

  (때로는, 사과하고 싶을지라도 단지 방법을 모를 수도 있다.)

  예 Though I loved reading about biology, I could not bring myself to dissect a frog in lab.

  (나는 생물학에 관해 읽는 것을 좋아했지만, 아무리 해도 실험실에서 개구리를 해부할 수 없었다.)

- 양보 전치사

  despite[in spite of]+명사[명사상당어구]: 비록 ～이지만, ～라 하더라도

  예 The US government began to feed poor children during the Great Depression despite the food shortage.

  (미국 정부는 식량 부족에도 불구하고 대공황 동안 가난한 아이들에게 급식을 시작했다.)

  예 Despite the common conceptions of deserts as hot, there are cold deserts as well.

  (사막은 덥다는 일반적 개념에도 불구하고, 추운 사막도 있다.)

07 난도 ★★☆   정답 ①

어법 > 비문 찾기

정답의 이유

① still more는 '하물며 ～은 말할 것도 없이'라는 의미의 비교급 관용구문으로, 긍정문에서는 still more를, 부정문에서는 still less를 쓴다. 제시된 문장은 부정문(are not interested in)이므로 still more → still less가 되어야 한다.

오답의 이유

② 밑줄 친 Once confirmed 다음에 목적어가 없으므로 주어와 동사가 생략된 분사구문이라는 것을 알 수 있다. 따라서 confirmed의 주어가 주절의 주어(the order)와 같고 수동의 의미이므로 어법상 과거분사(confirmed)가 적절하게 사용되었다.

③ 밑줄 친 provided (that)은 '～을 조건으로, ～한다면'이라는 뜻으로, 조건 부사절을 이끄는 분사형 접속사로 적절하게 사용되었다.

④ news는 셀 수 없는 명사이고, much가 수식하고 있으므로 어법상 적절하게 사용되었다.

① 그들은 시를 읽는 것에 관심이 없으며, 하물며 시를 쓰는 것은 더 아니다(관심이 없다).

② (주문이) 확인되면, 주문은 귀하의 주소로 발송될 것이다.

③ 페리가 정시에 출발한다면, 우리는 아침까지 항구에 도착해야 한다.

④ 외신 기자들은 단기간 수도에 체류하는 동안 가능한 한 많은 뉴스를 취재하기를 바란다.

- still less 하물며 ～은 아니다
- confirm 확인하다
- provided that ～라면
- ferry 연락선[(카)페리]
- cover 취재[방송/보도]하다

still[much] more vs. still[much] less

- still[much] more: 하물며 ～은 말할 것도 없이

  긍정의미 강화표현으로 긍정문 다음에 사용된다.

  예 Everyone has a right to enjoy his liberty, much more his life.

  (누구나 자유를 누릴 권리가 있으며, 자신의 삶은 말할 것도 없다.)

- still[much] less: 하물며 ～은 아니다

  부정의미 강화표현으로 부정문 다음에 사용된다.

  예 I doubt Clemson will even make the finals, much less win.

  (Clemson이 우승은 고사하고 하물며 결승까지 진출할지도 의심스럽다.)

  예 The students are not interested in reading poetry, still less in writing.

  (학생들은 시를 쓰는 것은 고사하고, 시를 읽는 것도 관심이 없다.)

08 난도 ★★☆   정답 ①

어법 > 영작하기

정답의 이유

① '감정 형용사(glad)+that ～'에서 that은 감정의 이유를 보충·설명하는 부사절을 이끄는 접속사이며, 주어(We)가 기쁜 이유(the number of applicants is increasing)를 설명하고 있으므로 어법상 적절하게 사용되었다. 또한, that절의 주어(the number of applicants)는 '～의 수'라는 뜻의 'the number of+복수명사+단수동사' 구문이므로 단수동사 is가 적절하게 사용되었다.

오답의 이유

② 과거 부사구(two years ago)가 있으므로 I've received → I received가 되어야 한다.

③ 관계대명사 which 다음에 불완전한 절이 와야 하는데, 1형식 완전자동사(sleep)가 왔으므로 어법상 적절하지 않다. 따라서 which → where(관계부사) 또는 on which(전치사+관계대명사)가 되어야 한다.

④ 'exchange A with B'는 'A를 B와 교환하다'라는 뜻으로, A(사람) 앞에는 전치사 with를 함께 써야 한다. 따라서 each other → with each other가 되어야 한다. each other는 '서로'라는 뜻의 대명사로, 부사처럼 단독으로 사용할 수 없다.

VOCA

• applicant 지원자
• increase 증가하다, 인상되다
• comfortable 편(안)한, 쾌적한
• exchange 교환하다[주고받다]

09 난도 ★☆☆　　　　　　　　　　정답 ②

표현 > 일반회화

정답의 이유

밑줄 앞에서 Ace Tour는 'Do you have any specific questions(혹시 구체적으로 궁금한 점이 있으신가요)?'라고 물었고, 뒤에서 'It'll take you to all the major points of interest in the city(도시의 흥미로운 주요 장소들을 모두 안내해 드릴 겁니다).'라고 대답했으므로 밑줄 친 부분에 들어갈 말로 적절한 것은 ② 'What does the city tour include(시티 투어에는 무엇이 포함되어 있나요)?'이다.

오답의 이유

① 투어 기간은 얼마나 됩니까?
③ 패키지여행 리스트가 있나요?
④ 좋은 여행 안내서를 추천해 주실 수 있나요?

본문해석

Brian: 안녕하세요, 시티 투어에 대한 정보를 얻을 수 있을까요?
Ace Tour: 문의주셔서 감사합니다. 혹시 구체적으로 궁금한 점이 있으신가요?
Brian: 시티 투어에는 무엇이 포함되어 있나요?
Ace Tour: 도시의 흥미로운 주요 장소들을 모두 안내해 드릴 겁니다.
Brian: 얼마인가요?
Ace Tour: 4시간 투어에 1인당 50달러입니다.
Brian: 알겠어요. 금요일 오후 티켓 4장을 예약할 수 있을까요?
Ace Tour: 물론입니다. 곧 결제정보를 보내드리겠습니다.

VOCA

• specific 구체적인
• of interest 흥미있는
• book 예약하다
• payment information 결제정보

10 난도 ★☆☆　　　　　　　　　　정답 ④

표현 > 일반회화

정답의 이유

밑줄 앞에서 A가 'Air freight costs will be added on the invoice(송장에 항공운임이 추가될 겁니다).'라고 한 다음 'I am afraid the free delivery service is no longer available(죄송하지만, 무료배송 서비스는 더 이상 제공되지 않습니다).'라고 했으므로 대화의 흐름상 밑줄 친 부분에 들어갈 말로 적절한 것은 ④ 'Wait a minute. I thought the delivery costs were at your expense(잠시만요. 배송비는 귀사에서 부담하는 줄 알았어요).'이다.

오답의 이유

① 알겠습니다. 송장은 언제 받게 될까요?
② 저희 부서가 2주 안에 결제하지 못할 수도 있어요.
③ 월요일에 저희가 귀사의 법인 계좌로 결제액을 송금해도 될까요?

본문해석

A: 감사합니다. 주문해주셔서 감사합니다.
B: 천만에요. 항공화물로 물품을 보내주실 수 있나요? 저희는 빨리 물건이 필요해요.
A: 네. 지금 바로 귀하의 부서로 보내겠습니다.
B: 알겠습니다. 다음 주 초에 물건을 받을 수 있으면 좋겠어요.
A: 모든 것이 일정대로 진행된다면 월요일까지 받을 수 있을 거예요.
B: 월요일 좋아요.
A: 2주 안에 결제 부탁드립니다. 송장에 항공운임이 추가될 겁니다.
B: 잠시만요. 배송비는 귀사에서 부담하는 줄 알았어요.
A: 죄송하지만, 무료배송 서비스는 더 이상 제공되지 않습니다.

VOCA

• appreciate 고마워하다
• goods 상품, 제품
• by air freight 항공편으로
• air freight cost 항공운임
• add 합하다[더하다]
• invoice 송장

11 난도 ★☆☆　　　　　　　　　　정답 ③

표현 > 일반회화

정답의 이유

밑줄 앞에서 A가 'Have you contacted the subway's lost and found office(지하철 분실물 센터에 연락해 봤어요)?'라고 물었고, 뒤에서 'If I were you, I would do that first(나라면 먼저 그렇게 하겠어요).'라고 했으므로 밑줄 친 부분에 들어갈 말로 적절한 것은 ③ 'I haven't done that yet, actually(사실, 아직 안 했어요)'이다.

오답의 이유

① 전화에 대해 문의하러 그곳에 갔어요
② 오늘 아침 사무실에 들렀어요
④ 모든 곳을 다 찾아봤어요

A: 휴대폰을 찾았나요?

B: 유감스럽게도, 못 찾았어요. 아직 찾고 있어요.

A: 지하철 분실물 센터에 연락해 봤어요?

B: 사실, 아직 안 했어요.

A: 나라면 먼저 그렇게 하겠어요.

B: 네, 맞는 말이에요. 새 휴대폰을 사기 전에 분실물 센터에 문의해 볼게요.

VOCA

• unfortunately 유감스럽게도

• lost and found 분실물 보관소

• check with ~에 문의[조회]하다

12 난도 ★☆☆   정답 ②

독해 > 세부 내용 찾기 > 내용 (불)일치

정답의 이유

두 번째 문장에서 'Entry to shows and lectures are first-come, first-served.'라고 했으므로 글의 내용과 일치하는 것은 ② '공연과 강연의 입장은 선착순이다.'이다.

오답의 이유

① 첫 번째 문장에서 'Kids 10 and under are free(10세 이하 어린이는 무료입니다.)'라고 했으므로 글의 내용과 일치하지 않는다.

③ 세 번째 문장에서 'All venues open rain or shine(모든 행사장은 날씨와 관계없이 운영합니다.)'이라고 했으므로 글의 내용과 일치하지 않는다.

④ 마지막 문장에서 'NEWE organizers may discontinue in-person ticket sales should any venue reach capacity (NEWE 주최 측은 행사장이 수용 인원에 도달하면 현장 입장권 판매를 중단할 수 있습니다.)'라고 했으므로 현장 판매도 한다는 것을 유추할 수 있다.

본문해석

북동부 야생동물 박람회(NEWE)

2024년 3월 30일 토요일 입장권

■ 가격: $40.00

■ 개장시간: 오전 10:00 – 오후 6:00

10세 이하 어린이는 무료입니다. 공연과 강연 입장은 선착순입니다. 모든 행사장은 날씨와 관계없이 운영합니다.

3월 20일은 2024 북동부 야생동물 박람회 입장권 온라인 구매 마지막 날입니다.

참고: NEWE 입장권을 사전에 구매하는 것이 모든 전시장 입장을 보장하는 최선의 방법입니다. NEWE 주최 측은 행사장이 수용 인원에 도달하면 현장 입장권 판매를 중단할 수 있습니다.

VOCA

• admission ticket 입장권

• entry 입장

• lecture 강의, 강연

• first-come, first-served 선착순

• rain or shine 날씨에 관계 없이

• guarantee 보장[약속]하다

• discontinue 중단하다

• reach ~에 이르다[도달하다]

• capacity 용량, 수용력

13 난도 ★★☆   정답 ③

독해 > 세부 내용 찾기 > 내용 (불)일치

정답의 이유

네 번째 문장에서 '~ they were written and produced several years apart and out of chronological order(그것들은 몇 년 간격으로 연대순을 벗어나 집필·제작되었다).'라고 했으므로 글의 내용과 일치하지 않는 것은 ③ 'The Theban plays were created in time order(테베의 희곡들은 시대순으로 창작되었다).'이다.

오답의 이유

① 소포클레스는 총 123편의 비극을 썼다. → 두 번째 문장에서 'Sadly, only seven of the 123 tragedies he wrote have survived(애석하게도, 그가 쓴 123편의 비극 중 단지 7편만 남아 있지만) ~'라고 했으므로 글의 내용과 일치한다.

② Antigone도 오이디푸스 왕에 관한 것이다. → 세 번째 문장에서 'The play was one of three written by Sophocles about Oedipus, the mythical king of Thebes (the others being *Antigone* and *Oedipus at Colonus*)[그 희곡은 테베의 신화적인 오이디푸스 왕에 대해 쓴 세 편 중 하나(나머지는 *Antigone*와 *Oedipus at Colonus*이다)인데] ~'라고 했으므로 글의 내용과 일치한다.

④ *Oedipus the King*은 고전적인 아테네 비극을 대표한다. → 마지막 문장에서 '*Oedipus the King* follows the established formal structure and it is regarded as the best example of classical Athenian tragedy(*Oedipus the King*은 정해진 형식적 구조를 따르며, 아테네 고전 비극의 가장 좋은 예로 여겨지고 있다).'라고 했으므로 글의 내용과 일치한다.

본문해석

그리스 극작가 소포클레스의 비극은 그리스 고전극의 절정으로 여겨지게 되었다. 애석하게도, 그가 쓴 123편의 비극 중 단지 7편만 남아 있지만, 이 중에서 가장 빼어난 작품은 *Oedipus the King*일 것이다. 그 희곡은 테베의 신화적인 오이디푸스 왕에 대해 쓴 세 편 중 하나(나머지는 *Antigone*와 *Oedipus at Colonus*이다)인데, 일괄적으로 테베의 희곡이라고 알려져 있다. 소포클레스는 이 희곡들을 각각 별개의 작품으로 구상했고, 그것들은 몇 년 간격으로 연대순을 벗어나 집필·제작되었다. *Oedipus the King*은 정해진 형식적 구조를 따르며, 아테네 고전 비극의 가장 좋은 예로 여겨지고 있다.

VOCA

- dramatist 극작가
- be regarded as ~로 여겨지다
- survive 살아남다, 생존[존속]하다
- mythical 신화적인, 신화[전설]상의
- collectively 전체적으로, 일괄하여
- conceive 생각해 내다, 착상하다
- separate 별개의
- entity 독립체
- chronological order 연대순

14 난도 ★★☆ 정답 ④

독해 > 대의 파악 > 제목, 주제

정답의 이유

제시문은 고고학자 Arthur Evans가 크노소스 궁전의 유적과 미노스 시대의 유물을 발굴해서 신화로만 여겨졌던 미노스 문명이 사실로 드러났다는 내용이다. 세 번째 문장에서 'But as Evans proved, this realm was no myth(그러나 Evans가 증명했듯이, 이 왕국은 신화가 아니었다).'라고 했고, 마지막 문장에서 'In a series of excavations in the early years of the 20th century, Evans found a trove of artifacts from the Minoan age(20세기 초 일련의 발굴에서, Evans는 미노스 시대의 유물들을 발견했는데) ~'라고 했으므로, 글의 주제로 적절한 것은 ④ 'Bringing the Minoan culture to the realm of reality(미노스 문명을 현실 영역으로 가져오기)'이다.

오답의 이유

① 미노스 왕의 성공적인 발굴
② 미노스 시대의 유물 감상하기
③ 크레타 섬 궁전의 웅장함

본문해석

한 사람이 전체 문명에 대한 우리의 눈을 뜨게 할 수 있다는 것은 믿기 힘든 것처럼 보이지만, 영국의 고고학자 Arthur Evans가 크레타섬에 있는 크노소스 궁전의 유적을 성공적으로 발굴하기 전까지 지중해의 위대한 미노스 문명은 사실보다는 전설에 가까웠다. 실제로 그곳의 가장 유명한 거주자는 신화에 나오는 생명체인 반인반우의 미노타우로스로, 전설적인 미노스 왕의 궁전 아래에서 살았다고 한다. 그러나 Evans가 증명했듯이, 이 왕국은 신화가 아니었다. 20세기 초 일련의 발굴에서, Evans는 기원전 1900년부터 1450년까지 최고로 번창했던 미노스 시대의 유물들을 발견했는데 보석, 조각품, 도자기, 황소 뿔 모양의 제단, 그리고 미노스 문명의 삶을 보여주는 벽화 등이었다.

VOCA

- be responsible for ~을 맡다, 담당하다
- archaeologist 고고학자
- excavate 발굴하다
- ruins 유적, 폐허
- Minoan culture 미노스 문명

- realm 왕국
- excavation 발굴
- trove 귀중한 발견물[수집품]
- reach its height 절정에 도달하다, 최고로 번창하다
- carving 조각품
- pottery 도자기
- altar 제단

15 난도 ★★☆ 정답 ①

독해 > 대의 파악 > 제목, 주제

정답의 이유

첫 번째 문장에서 '나쁜 버전의 화폐에 의한 좋은 화폐의 가치 저하는 귀금속 함량이 높은 동전이 더 낮은 가치의 금속과 희석되어 낮은 함량의 금 또는 은을 함유하여 재발행되는 방식으로 나타났다.'라고 한 다음, 뒷부분에서 왕이 좋은 화폐를 나쁜 화폐로 대체하는 방법을 설명하고 있으므로 글의 제목으로 적절한 것은 ① 'How Bad Money Replaces Good(나쁜 화폐가 좋은 화폐를 대체하는 법)'이다.

오답의 이유

② 좋은 동전의 요소
③ 동전을 녹이는 게 어때?
④ 나쁜 화폐는 무엇인가?

본문해석

나쁜 버전의 화폐에 의한 좋은 화폐의 가치 저하는 귀금속 함량이 높은 동전이 더 낮은 가치의 금속과 희석되어 금이나 은 함량이 더 낮은 동전으로 재발행되는 방식으로 나타났다. 이러한 변질은 나쁜 동전으로 좋은 동전을 몰아냈다. 아무도 좋은 동전을 사용하지 않았고, 보관했으므로, 좋은 동전은 유통되지 않았고 비축되기에 이르렀다. 한편, 이러한 조치의 배후에는 발행인(대부분 왕)이 있었는데, 왕은 끝없이 계속된 전쟁과 그 밖의 다른 방탕한 생활로 국고를 탕진한 상황이었다. 그들은 모을 수 있는 모든 좋은 옛날 동전을 모았으며, 그것들을 녹여서 더 낮은 순도로 재발행하고 그 잔액을 착복했다. 오래된 동전을 계속 가지고 있는 것은 종종 불법이었지만, 사람들은 그렇게 했고, 한편 왕은 최소한 잠깐 동안은 그의 국고를 보충했다.

VOCA

- currency 화폐, 통화
- debasement 저하, 하락
- occur 일어나다, 생기다
- reissue 재발행하다
- dilute 희석하다
- adulteration 불순물 섞기, 변질
- drive out 몰아내다, 쫓아내다
- circulation 유통, 순환
- hoard 비축, 축적, 저장
- interminable 끝없는
- warfare 전쟁

- dissolute 방탕한
- purity 순도
- pocket 착복하다, 횡령하다
- balance 차액, 차감, 잔액
- replenish 다시 채우다, 보충하다
- treasury 국고

- cite (이유·예를) 들다[끌어내다], 인용하다
- crucial to ~에 있어서 아주 중대한
- the Van Allen belt 밴 앨런 벨트(지구를 둘러싸고 있는 방사능을 가진 층)
- trap 가두다
- magnetic field 자기장

16 난도 ★★☆
정답 ④

독해 > 글의 일관성 > 무관한 어휘·문장

정답의 이유

제시문은 미국의 달 착륙이 미국 정부가 꾸며낸 음모론이라고 믿는 사람들의 주장에 관한 내용이다. 이런 음모론 옹호자들이 가장 결정적인 증거로 인용하는 것은 우주비행사들이 지구를 벗어나기 위해 밴 앨런 벨트를 통과하지 못했을 것이라는 주장이다. ③에서 'Crucial to their case is the claim that astronauts never could have safely passed through the Van Allen belt(그들의 논거에서 아주 중요한 것은 우주비행사들이 밴 앨런 벨트를 결코 안전하게 통과할 수 없었을 것이라는 주장이다) ~'라고 했고, 제시문의 마지막 문장에서 'If the astronauts had truly gone through the belt, say conspiracy theorists, they would have died(음모론자들은 말하기를, 만약 우주비행사들이 정말로 밴 앨런 벨트를 통과했다면 그들은 죽었을 것이라고 한다).'라고 했는데, ④에서는 우주선의 금속 덮개가 방사선을 차단하도록 설계되었다고 했으므로 글의 흐름상 어색한 문장은 ④이다.

본문해석

모든 반대되는 증거에도 불구하고, 나사의 아폴로 우주 프로그램이 실제로 사람들을 달에 착륙시킨 적이 없다고 진지하게 믿는 사람들이 있다. 이 사람들은 주장하기를 달 착륙은 러시아와의 필사적인 경쟁과 체면 깎이는 것을 염려한 미국 정부에 의해 영속된 거대한 음모에 불과했다고 했다. 이들 음모론자들의 주장은 미국이 우주 경쟁에서 러시아와 경쟁할 수 없다는 것을 알았고, 그래서 일련의 성공적인 달 착륙을 꾸며낼 수밖에 없었다는 것이다. 음모론 옹호자들은 자신들이 증거라고 생각하는 몇 가지를 인용한다. 그들의 논거에서 아주 중요한 것은 우주비행사들이 지구의 자기장인 밴 앨런 벨트(지구를 둘러싸고 있는 방사능을 가진 층)를 결코 안전하게 통과할 수 없었을 것이라는 주장이다. 그들은 또한 우주선의 금속 덮개가 방사선을 차단하도록 설계되었다는 사실을 지적한다. 음모론자들은 말하기를, 만약 우주비행사들이 정말로 밴 앨런 벨트를 통과했다면 그들은 죽었을 것이라고 한다.

VOCA

- claim (~이 사실이라고) 주장하다
- conspiracy 음모
- perpetuate 영속하게 하다, 불멸하게 하다
- in competition with ~와 경쟁하여
- lose face 체면을 잃다
- fake 위조[날조/조작]하다, 꾸며내다
- advocate 옹호자

17 난도 ★★☆
정답 ③

독해 > 글의 일관성 > 문장 삽입

정답의 이유

주어진 문장은 '부족의 구전 역사와 전해지는 증거에 따르면 1500년에서 1700년 사이의 어느 시기에 진흙 사태가 마을을 파괴했고 그 바람에 일부 전통 가옥 내부의 물건들이 봉인되었다'는 내용이다. ③ 앞 문장에서 'Ozette 마을은 수천 년 동안 그 지역에 기반을 둔 원주민인 Makah족이 살았던 다섯 개의 주요 마을 중 하나였다.'라고 했고, ③ 다음 문장에서 '그렇지 않았다면, 남아 있지 않았을 바구니, 의복, 요, 포경 도구를 포함한 수천 개의 유물들이 진흙 아래에 보존되어 있었다.'라고 했으므로 글의 흐름상 주어진 문장이 들어갈 위치로 적절한 것은 ③이다.

본문해석

워싱턴의 올림픽 반도 최서단에 위치한 Ozette 마을에서 Makah 부족민들이 고래를 사냥했다. 그들은 자신들의 어획물을 선반과 훈연실에서 훈제했으며, 주변의 Puget Sound와 인근의 Vancouver섬에서 온 이웃 부족들과 물물교환했다. Ozette 마을은 수천 년 동안 그 지역에 기반을 둔 원주민인 Makah족이 살았던 다섯 개의 주요 마을 중 하나였다. 부족의 구전 역사와 고고학적 증거는, 1500년에서 1700년 사이의 어느 시기에 진흙 사태가 마을 일부를 파괴했는데, 몇몇 전통 가옥들을 뒤덮고 그 내부에 있던 것들을 봉인했다고 시사한다. 그렇지 않았다면, 남아 있지 않았을 바구니, 의복, 요, 포경 도구를 포함한 수천 개의 유물들이 진흙 아래에 보존되어 있었다. 1970년, 폭풍이 해안침식을 일으켰으며, 이들 전통 가옥과 유물의 잔해가 드러났다.

VOCA

- westernmost 가장 서쪽의, 서단의
- smoke 훈제하다
- catch 잡은 것, 포획한 것
- rack 선반, 받침대, 시렁
- smokehouse 훈제실, 훈연장
- trade with ~와 무역[거래]하다
- neighboring 이웃의, 근체[인근]의
- inhabit 살다, 거주하다
- indigenous 토착의, 원산의
- archaeological 고고학의
- mudslide 진흙 사태
- longhouse (미국에서 일부 원주민들의) 전통 가옥
- seal 봉하다, 봉인하다
- preserve 보존하다
- coastal erosion 해안침식

18 난도 ★★☆
정답 ②

독해 > 글의 일관성 > 글의 순서

정답의 이유

주어진 글에서 유명 영화배우와 운동선수에 대한 관심은 그들의 영화와 경기장에서의 활약을 넘어선다고 하였다. 따라서 문맥상 주어진 글 다음에는 할리우드 영화배우들의 사생활을 취재하는 언론에 대한 내용인 (B)가 오는 것이 적절하며, 다음으로는 '마찬가지로 (similarly)' 숙련된 운동선수들의 평상시 행동도 대중의 관심을 받는다는 내용인 (A)로 이어지는 것이 자연스럽다. 마지막으로, 이들 '두 산업(Both industries)'이 '그런 관심(such attention)'을 활성화하는 것은 관객을 늘리고 수입을 증대하기 위한 것이지만, 기본적으로 영화배우와 운동선수들에게는 근본적인 차이가 있다고 마무리하는 (C)가 오는 것이 적절하다. 따라서 주어진 글 다음에 이어질 글의 순서로 적절한 것은 ② '(B) − (A) − (C)'이다.

본문해석

유명 영화배우와 운동선수에 대한 관심은 영화와 경기장에서의 그들의 활약을 넘어선다.
(B) 신문 칼럼, 전문적인 잡지, 텔레비전 프로그램, 웹사이트들은 때로 유명한 할리우드 배우들의 사생활을 정확하게 기록한다.
(A) 마찬가지로, 기량이 뛰어난 야구, 축구, 농구 선수들이 유니폼을 입지 않고 하는 평상시 행동도 대중의 관심을 끈다.
(C) 두 산업 모두 적극적으로 그러한 관심을 활성화하여, 관객을 늘리고 따라서 수입을 증가시킨다. 그러나 근본적인 차이가 그들을 구분한다. 유명 운동선수들이 생계를 위해 하는 일은 허구를 연기하는 영화배우들과는 다르게 진짜라는 것이다.

VOCA
• go beyond 넘어서다
• out of uniform 평복[사복]으로
• attract 불러일으키다[끌다]
• expand 확대[확장/팽창]시키다
• revenue 수입, 수익
• fundamental 근본적인, 기본적인
• authentic 진정성 있는, 진짜인

19 난도 ★★☆
정답 ②

독해 > 빈칸 완성 > 단어 · 구 · 절

정답의 이유

밑줄 다음에는 다양한 계층의 사람들이 자신들의 이익을 위해 여러 방법으로 설득하는 사례가 나열되어 있다. 정치인들은 대중을 설득하기 위해, 사업체와 이익 단체들은 정부를 설득하기 위해, 지역사회 활동가들은 시민들을 설득하기 위해, 직장에서 일반 관리자들은 동료를 설득하기 위해 노력한다고 했으므로 밑줄 친 부분에 들어갈 말로 적절한 것은 ② 'Persuasion shows up in almost every walk of life(설득은 삶의 거의 모든 분야에서 나타난다).'이다.

오답의 이유

① 사업가는 설득력이 있어야 한다

③ 수많은 광고판과 포스터를 만나게 될 것이다
④ 대중 미디어 캠페인은 정부에 유익하다

본문해석

설득은 삶의 거의 모든 분야에서 나타난다. 거의 모든 주요 정치인들이 대중에 어필하는 법을 조언하는 미디어 컨설턴트와 정치 전문가를 고용한다. 실질적으로 모든 주요 기업과 특수 이익 집단은 그 관심사를 의회 또는 주 정부와 지방정부에 전달하기 위해 로비스트를 고용해 왔다. 거의 모든 지역사회에서 활동가들은 중요한 정책 문제에 대해 동료 시민들을 설득하려고 노력한다. 직장도 역시 언제나 사무실 정치와 설득하기에 좋은 현장이었다. 한 연구는 추정하기를, 일반 관리자들이 그들의 시간 80% 이상을 언어적 의사소통에 소비하는데, 그 대부분이 동료 지원들을 설득하는 의도라고 한다. 복사기의 출현으로, 사무실에서의 설득을 위한 완전히 새로운 매체가 발명되었는데, 바로 복사된 메모다. 미국의 국방부에서만 1일 평균 35만 페이지를 복사하는데, 이것은 소설 1,000권에 해당하는 분량이다.

VOCA
• persuasion 설득
• show up 나타나다, 등장하다
• walk 영역, 부문, 분야, 사회[경제]적 지위, 직업
• appeal 호소하다, 관심을 끌다
• virtually 사실상, 실질적으로, 거의
• special−interest group 특수 이익 집단
• concern 관심사, 사건, 이해관계
• fertile 활동하기에 좋은, 비옥한
• with the intent of ∼할 의도를 가지고
• with the advent of ∼의 출현으로
• photocopy 복사하다
• the Pentagon 미국 국방부
• equivalent 상당하는 대등한

20 난도 ★★☆
정답 ①

독해 > 빈칸 완성 > 단어 · 구 · 절

정답의 이유

제시문은 사회적 상호작용에서 언어가 차지하는 비중이 성인과 어린아이가 서로 다르다는 내용이다. 성인의 경우 사회적 상호작용이 주로 언어를 통해서 발생하지만, 어린아이의 경우 사회적 상호작용에 언어가 그다지 필수적인 것이 아니라고 했다. 밑줄 앞 문장에서 어린아이들 사이에서 흔한 '평행 놀이'를 예로 들면서 아이들은 서로 별말 없이 혼자 놀면서 그냥 옆에 앉아만 있는 상태에도 만족할 수 있다고 했다. 또 밑줄 문장의 앞부분에서 'Adults rarely find themselves in situations where(성인들은 ∼ 상황에 처하는 경우가 거의 없다) ∼'라고 했으므로 밑줄에는 앞 문장의 평행 놀이 경우와는 상반되는 상황이 들어가야 함을 유추할 수 있다. 따라서 밑줄 친 부분에 들어갈 말로 적절한 것은 ① 'language does not play a crucial role in social interaction(언어가 사회적 상호작용에서 중요한 역할을 하지 않는)'이다.

② 그들의 의견이 동료들에 의해 선뜻 받아들여지는

③ 그들이 다른 언어를 사용하도록 요청받는

④ 의사소통 능력이 매우 요구되는

본문해석

성인의 경우 사회적 상호작용이 주로 언어 수단을 통해 이루어진다는 데 주목하는 것이 중요하다. 성인 원어민들이 그 언어를 사용하지 않는 누군가와의 상호작용에 시간을 할애하려는 경우는 거의 없으며, 그 결과 성인 외국인은 유의미하면서 폭넓은 언어 교환에 참여할 기회가 거의 없을 것이다. 반대로, 어린아이는 종종 다른 아이들에 의해, 심지어 성인들에 의해서도 선뜻 받아들여진다. 어린아이들의 경우 언어는 사회적 상호작용에 필수적인 것이 아니다. 예를 들어, 소위 '평행 놀이'는 어린아이들 사이에서 흔하다. 그들은 가끔 말하고 혼자 놀면서도 단지 서로 옆에 앉아 있는 것만으로도 만족할 수 있다. 성인들은 언어가 사회적 상호작용에서 중요한 역할을 하지 않는 상황에 처하는 경우가 거의 없다.

VOCA

- interaction 상호작용
- occur 일어나다, 발생하다
- devote to ~에 전념하다
- engage in 참여하다, 관련하다
- readily 선뜻, 기꺼이
- essential 필수적인, 극히 중요한
- parallel play 평행 놀이
- crucial 중대한, 결정적인

영어 | 2023년 국가직 9급

한눈에 훑어보기

✓ 영역 분석

어휘   01   02   03   04
5문항, 25%

독해   08   09   13   14   15   16   17   18   19   20
9문항, 45%

어법   05   06   07
4문항, 20%

표현   10   11   12
2문항, 10%

✓ 빠른 정답

01	02	03	04	05	06	07	08	09	10
②	②	④	①	③	④	②	④	④	①
11	**12**	**13**	**14**	**15**	**16**	**17**	**18**	**19**	**20**
②	③	③	①	②	②	③	③	③	①

✓ 점수 체크

구분	1회독	2회독	3회독
맞힌 문항 수	/ 20	/ 20	/ 20
나의 점수	점	점	점

01 난도 ★☆☆   정답 ②

어휘 > 단어

정답의 이유

밑줄 친 intimate는 '친한'의 뜻으로 이와 의미가 가장 가까운 것은 ② 'close(친한)'이다.

오답의 이유

① 참견하기 좋아하는

③ 외향적인

④ 사려 깊은

본문해석

Jane은 화려한 결혼식보다는 작은 결혼식을 하고 싶었다. 따라서 그녀는 가족과 그녀의 친한 친구 몇 명을 초대해 맛있는 음식을 먹고 즐거운 시간을 보내려고 계획했다.

VOCA

• fancy   화려한, 값비싼

• rather than   ~보다는

02 난도 ★☆☆   정답 ②

어휘 > 단어

정답의 이유

밑줄 친 incessant는 '끊임없는'의 뜻으로 이와 의미가 가장 가까운 것은 ② 'constant(끊임없는)'이다.

오답의 이유

① 빠른

③ 중요한

④ 간헐적인

본문해석

더 적은 비용으로 얻는 건강상 이점으로 인한 끊임없는 대중의 호기심과 소비자 수요가 기능성 식품에 대한 관심을 증가시켰다.

VOCA

• public   일반인[대중]의

• consumer demand   소비자 수요

• due to   ~에 기인하는, ~때문에

• benefit   혜택, 이득

• functional food   기능성[건강 보조] 식품

03 난도 ★☆☆　　　정답 ④

어휘 > 어구

[정답의 이유]

밑줄 친 hold off는 '미루다'의 뜻으로 이와 의미가 가장 가까운 것은 ④ 'suspend(연기하다)'이다.

[오답의 이유]

① 정교하게 만들다
② 풀어 주다, 석방[해방]하다
③ 수정하다

본문해석

전국적인 유행병 때문에 그 회사는 직원들에게 다양한 연수 프로그램을 제공하려는 계획을 미뤄야 했다.

VOCA

- pandemic 전국[전 세계]적인 유행병
- provide A with B A에게 B를 제공하다

04 난도 ★☆☆　　　정답 ①

어휘 > 어구

[정답의 이유]

밑줄 친 abide by는 '준수하다, 지키다'의 뜻으로 이와 의미가 가장 가까운 것은 ① 'accept(받아들이다, 수용하다)'이다.

[오답의 이유]

② 보고하다
③ 미루다
④ 발표하다

본문해석

신임 지방 주지사는 그 죄수를 석방하라는 고등법원의 결정을 준수할 것이라고 말했다.

VOCA

- Regional Governor 지방 주지사
- the High Court 고등법원
- release 풀어주다, 석방하다

05 난도 ★★★　　　정답 ③

어법 > 비문 찾기

[정답의 이유]

③ 밑줄 친 conceal의 주어는 단수명사(the biomedical view)이므로 3인칭 단수동사로 수일치해야 한다. 따라서 conceal → conceals가 되어야 한다.

[오답의 이유]

① 'make+it(가목적어)+목적격 보어+to부정사(진목적어)'는 'to부정사하는 것을 목적격 보어하게 만들다'라는 뜻이다. 이때 it은 가목적어로 진목적어(to extend the life of individuals with end-stage organ disease)를 대신하고 있으므로 올바르게 사용되었다.

② 'it(가주어)+is argued+that(진주어)' 구문에서 가주어(it)와 진주어(that 이하)가 올바르게 사용되었으며, 명사절 접속사 that 다음에 완전한 문장이 왔으므로 어법상 적절하다.

④ accurately는 동사(represents)를 수식하는 부사로 올바르게 사용되었다.

본문해석

이식 기술의 발전은 말기 장기(臟器) 질환 환자의 생명 연장을 가능하게 만들었지만, 장기이식을 일단 심장이나 신장을 성공적으로 교체하면 끝나는 한계성 사건으로 보는 생물 의학적인 견해는 장기이식 경험을 더 정확하게 보여주는 복잡하고 역동적인 과정을 숨기고 있다고 주장되고 있다.

VOCA

- advance 진전, 발전
- transplant 이식, 이식하다
- extend 연장하다
- end-stage 말기의
- biochemical 생물 의학적인
- organ transplantation 장기이식
- bounded 경계[한계]가 있는
- kidney 신장, 콩팥
- replace 바꾸다[교체하다]
- conceal 숨기다, 감추다
- accurately 정확하게
- represent 나타내다, 보여주다

06 난도 ★★☆　　　정답 ④

어법 > 비문 찾기

[정답의 이유]

④ '사역동사(have)+목적어+목적격 보어'는 '목적어를 ~하도록 하다'의 뜻으로 목적어와 목적격 보어의 관계가 능동이면 원형부정사를, 수동이면 과거분사를 목적격 보어로 취한다. had it remove에서 목적어 it이 가리키는 것은 the tip of a pencil인데, 문맥상 연필 끝은 머리에서 제거되는 수동의 관계에 있으므로 remove → removed가 되어야 한다.

[오답의 이유]

① 'be expected to+동사원형'은 '~할 것으로 기대된다'의 뜻이다. 과제(assignments)는 제출되는 수동의 대상이므로, 어법상 to be turned in이 올바르게 사용되었다.

② 'Hardly+had+주어+과거분사 ~ when+주어+과거동사'는 '~하자마자 …했다'의 뜻으로, 어법상 올바르게 사용되었다.

③ '주장·요구·명령·제안·조언·권고 동사+that절'에서 that절의 동사는 '(should)+동사원형'을 쓰므로 recommended that 다음에 should가 생략되어, 동사원형 형태인 buy가 올바르게 사용되었다.

① 모든 과제는 제시간에 제출될 것으로 예상된다.
② 나는 눈을 감자마자 그녀를 생각하기 시작했다.
③ 그 중개인은 그녀에게 즉시 주식을 사라고 권했다.
④ 머리에 연필심이 박힌 여자가 마침내 그것을 제거받았다.

VOCA

- assignment 과제, 임무
- turn in 제출하다
- broker 중개인
- stock (주로 복수로) 주식
- stick 찌르다(stick-stuck-stuck)

더 알아보기

사역동사+목적어+목적격 보어: '목적어를 ~하도록[당하도록] 하다'

'사역동사(have, make, let 등)+목적어+목적격 보어'에서 목적어와 목적격 보어가 능동 관계이면 목적격 보어로 원형부정사가 오고, 수동 관계이면 목적격 보어로 과거분사가 온다.

make	목적어를 ~하도록[당하도록] 만들다	• make/have/let + 목적어 + 목적격 보어(원형부정사): 능동
have	목적어를 ~하도록[당하도록] 하다	
let	목적어를 ~하도록[당하도록] 허락하다	• make/have/let + 목적어 + 목적격 보어(과거분사): 수동

예 He made his secretary fill orders and handle meetings with clients.
(그는 비서가 주문을 이행하고 고객들과의 회의를 진행하도록 했다.)

예 She refused to let her question ignored by the upper management.
(그녀는 고위 경영진들에 의해 그녀의 질문이 무시되는 것을 거부했다.)

---

07 난도 ★★☆　　　　　　　　　　　　정답 ②

어법 > 영작하기

정답의 이유

② 전치사 by는 동작의 완료를, until은 동작의 지속을 나타내는 동사와 함께 사용된다. finish는 '~을 마치다'의 뜻으로 동작의 완료를 나타내는 동사이므로, until → by가 되어야 한다.

오답의 이유

① '배수사+as+형용사/부사+as'의 배수사 비교 구문은 '~배만큼 …한[하게]'라는 뜻이다. '내 고양이'와 '그의 고양이'를 비교하고 있으므로, as 다음에 his cat이 소유대명사 his(그의 것=그의 고양이)가 올바르게 사용되었다.
③ 습관은 현재시제로 쓰므로 washes가 올바르게 사용되었다.
④ 'had better+동사원형'은 '~하는 편이 낫다'의 뜻으로 동사원형 take가 올바르게 사용되었다. in case는 '~에 대비하여'의 뜻으

로 조건 부사절을 이끄는 접속사구이다. 시간·조건 부사절에서 현재시제가 미래시제를 대신하므로, 어법상 현재시제 rains가 올바르게 사용되었다.

VOCA

- every other day 이틀에 한 번, 격일로
- in case ~에 대비하여
- had better ~하는 편이 낫다

더 알아보기

현재시제의 쓰임

- 현재의 사실, 동작, 상태를 나타낸다.
  예 She looks very happy.
  (그녀는 매우 행복해 보인다.)
- 현재의 습관, 반복적 동작을 나타낸다.
  예 She washes her hair every other day.
  (그녀는 이틀에 한 번 머리를 감는다.)
- 객관적인 진리, 사실, 격언, 사회적인 통념을 나타낸다.
  예 The early birds catch the worm.
  (일찍 일어나는 새가 벌레를 잡는다.)
- 왕래발착(go, come, arrive, leave, begin, start 등) 동사는 미래 부사구와 함께 쓰여 미래를 나타낸다.
  예 The flight to Seoul arrives ten o'clock tomorrow evening.
  (서울행 비행기는 내일 저녁 10시에 도착할 거야.)
- 시간·조건 부사절에서 현재시제가 미래시제를 대신한다.
  예 Employees are entitled to use sick leave if an illness prevents them from performing their duties.
  (직원들은 질병으로 인해 직무를 수행하지 못할 경우 병가를 사용할 권리가 있다.)
  예 The bus will depart after everyone fastens their safety belts.
  (버스는 모든 사람이 안전벨트를 맨 후에 출발할 것이다.)

---

08 난도 ★☆☆　　　　　　　　　　　　정답 ④

독해 > 세부 내용 찾기 > 내용 (불)일치

정답의 이유

마지막 문장에서 'Taylor Wallace, who worked on a recent analysis of choline intake in the United States, says, "There isn't enough awareness about choline even among health-care professionals because our government hasn't reviewed the data or set policies around choline since the late '90s."(최근 미국의 콜린 섭취량에 대한 분석을 시행한 Taylor Wallace는 "우리 정부가 90년대 후반 이후로 콜린에 관한 데이터를 검토하거나 정책을 수립하지 않았기 때문에 보건 전문가들 사이에서조차 그것에 대해 잘 모른다"라고 말한다).'라고 했으므로, 글의 내용과 일치하지 않는 것은 ④ 'The importance of choline has been stressed since the late '90s in the U.S(미국에서 90년대 후반부터 콜린의 중요성이 강조되었다)'.이다.

① 대다수 미국인들은 콜린을 충분히 섭취하고 있지 않다. → 네 번째 문장에서 'A shocking 90 percent of Americans aren't getting enough choline, according to a recent study(최근 연구에 따르면, 충격적이게도 미국인의 90%가 콜린을 충분히 섭취하고 있지 않다고 한다).'라고 했으므로 글의 내용과 일치한다.

② 콜린은 두뇌 발달에 필요한 필수 영양소이다. → 다섯 번째 문장에서 'Choline ~ is especially critical for brain development(콜린은 ~ 특히 두뇌 발달에 매우 중요하다).'라고 했으므로 글의 내용과 일치한다.

③ 간과 리마콩과 같은 음식은 콜린의 좋은 공급원이다. → 여덟 번째 문장에서 'Plus, the foods that are rich in choline aren't the most popular: think liver, egg yolks and lima beans(게다가 콜린이 풍부한 음식은 그다지 인기가 없다. 간, 달걀노른자, 리마콩을 생각해 보라).'라고 했으므로 글의 내용과 일치한다.

본문해석

당신은 콜린을 충분히 섭취하고 있는가? 아마 이 영양소는 심지어 당신의 레이더에 없을(알지도 못할) 것이다. 이제 콜린이 관심을 받을 만한 때이다. 최근 연구에 따르면, 충격적이게도 미국인의 90%가 콜린을 충분히 섭취하고 있지 않다고 한다. 콜린은 모든 연령과 (발달) 단계에서 건강에 필수적이며, 특히 두뇌 발달에 매우 중요하다. 왜 우리는 (콜린을) 충분히 섭취하고 있지 않을까? 콜린은 다양한 음식에서 발견되지만, 극소량이다. 게다가 콜린이 풍부한 음식은 그다지 인기가 없다. 간, 달걀노른자, 리마콩을 생각해 보라. 최근 미국의 콜린 섭취량에 대한 분석을 시행한 Taylor Wallace는 "우리 정부가 90년대 후반 이후로 콜린에 관한 데이터를 검토하거나 정책을 수립하지 않았기 때문에 보건 전문가들 사이에서조차 그것에 대해 잘 모른다."라고 말한다.

VOCA

- choline 콜린(비타민 B 복합체의 하나)
- chances are 아마 ~할 것이다
- nutrient 영양소, 영양분
- radar 레이더
- deserve ~을 받을 만하다, 마땅히 ~할 만하다
- essential 필수적인
- critical for ~에 매우 중요한
- lima bean 리마콩(연녹색의 둥글납작한 콩)
- intake 섭취(량)
- awareness 의식[관심]
- set policy 정책을 설정하다

독해 > 세부 내용 찾기 > 내용 (불)일치

정답의 이유

마지막 문장에서 '~ where a man chatted with his tablemates whether he knew them or not(그곳에서 아는 사람이든 모르는 사람이든 같은 테이블에 앉은 사람들과 대화를 나눴다).'이라고 했으므로 글의 내용과 일치하는 것은 ④ 'One could converse even with unknown tablemates in a coffeehouse(커피 하우스에서 같은 테이블에 앉은 사람들은 심지어 모르는 사람과도 대화할 수 있었다).'이다.

오답의 이유

① 커피 하우스의 수는 다른 어느 사업체 수보다도 적었다. → 첫 번째 문장에서 '~ occupying more premises and paying more rent than any other trade(다른 어느 업종보다도 더 많은 부지를 점유하고 더 많은 임차료를 내고 있었다고 한다).'라고 했으므로 글의 내용과 일치하지 않는다.

② 고객들은 커피 하우스에 한 시간 이상 머무를 수 없었다. → 두 번째 문장에서 '~ because for that price one could purchase a cup of coffee and sit for hours listening to extraordinary conversations(누구나 그 가격(1페니)에 커피 한 잔을 사면 몇 시간이고 앉아 특별한 대화들을 들을 수 있었기 때문이었다).'라고 했으므로 글의 내용과 일치하지 않는다.

③ 종교인들은 잡담하기 위해 커피 하우스에 모이지 않았다. → 마지막에서 두 번째 문장에서 'Others served Protestants, Puritans, Catholics, Jews, ~ actors, lawyers, or clergy(다른 곳들은 개신교도들, 청교도들, 천주교도들, 유대인들, ~ 배우들, 변호사들, 성직자들을 대접했다).'라고 했으므로 글의 내용과 일치하지 않는다.

본문해석

일설에 의하면, 1700년경 런던에 2,000개가 넘는 커피 하우스가 있었으며, 다른 어느 업종보다도 더 많은 부지를 점유하고 더 많은 임차료를 내고 있었다고 한다. 그것들은 'penny universities'로 알려지게 되었는데, 누구나 그 가격(1페니)에 커피 한 잔을 사면 몇 시간이고 앉아 특별한 대화들을 들을 수 있었기 때문이었다. 각각의 커피 하우스는 각기 다른 유형의 고객층을 전문으로 했다. 한 곳에서는 의사들이 상담받을 수 있었다. 다른 곳들은 개신교도들, 청교도들, 천주교도들, 유대인들, 문인들, 상인들, 무역 상인들, 휘그당원들, 토리당원들, 육군 장교들, 배우들, 변호사들, 성직자들을 대접했다. 커피 하우스는 영국 최초로 평등주의적 만남의 장소를 제공했고, 그곳에서 아는 사람이든 모르는 사람이든 같은 테이블에 앉은 사람들과 대화를 나눴다.

VOCA

- by some accounts 일설에 의하면[따르면]
- occupy 차지하다
- premises 부지[지역], 구내
- specialized 전문적인, 전문화된
- clientele 모든 고객들

- clergy 성직자들
- egalitarian 평등주의(자)의
- tablemate 함께 식사하는 사람

10 난도 ★★☆ 정답 ①

표현 > 일반회화

정답의 이유

A가 어제 새로 산 스킨 크림의 효능을 말하는 대화로 A가 빈칸 앞에서 'It is supposed to remove all wrinkles and make your skin look much younger(이것은 모든 주름을 없애주고 피부를 훨씬 어려 보이게 해줄 거야).'라고 말하고, 빈칸 다음에서 'Why don't you believe it(왜 안 믿는 거니)?'라고 했으므로 대화의 흐름상 B가 빈칸에서 크림의 효과를 믿지 않는다고 말했음을 유추할 수 있다. 따라서 빈칸에 들어갈 말로 알맞은 것은 ① 'I don't buy it(난 안 믿어).'이다.

오답의 이유

② 너무 비싸.

③ 난 널 도와줄 수 없어.

④ 믿거나 말거나 사실이야.

본문해석

A: 어제 약국에서 이 새 스킨 크림을 샀어. 이것은 모든 주름을 없애주고 피부를 훨씬 어려 보이게 해줄 거야.

B: 난 안 믿어.

A: 왜 안 믿는 거니? 난 블로그들에서 이 크림이 정말 효과 있다는 글도 읽었어.

B: 그 크림이 피부에는 좋겠지만, 크림 하나 쓴다고 주름이 없어지거나 마법처럼 더 어려 보이게 하는 게 가능하다고 생각하지 않아.

A: 넌 너무 비관적이야.

B: 아니야. 난 그냥 현실적인 거야. 난 네가 잘 속아 넘어가는 것 같아.

VOCA

- be supposed to ~하기로 되어 있다
- wrinkle 주름
- work 효과가 나다[있다]
- assume 추정[상정]하다
- get rid of 제거하다, 끝내다
- pessimistic 비관적인
- gullible 잘 속아 넘어가는
- pricey 돈[비용]이 드는, 비싼

11 난도 ★☆☆ 정답 ②

표현 > 일반회화

정답의 이유

대화에서 시내 관광을 원하는 A가 빈칸 앞에서 'What else should I check out(또 어떤 것을 봐야 하나요)?'이라고 물었고, 빈칸 다음에서 그럴 시간이 없다고 했으므로 빈칸에는 B가 추천한 관광 장소와 그 소요 시간에 관한 내용이 와야 함을 유추할 수 있다. 따라서

빈칸에 들어갈 말로 알맞은 것은 ② 'A guided tour to the river park. It takes all afternoon(강 공원으로 가는 가이드 투어요. 오후 내내 걸려요).'이다.

오답의 이유

① 이게 당신의 고객에게 필요한 지도예요. 여기 있어요.

③ 가능한 한 빨리 그걸 봐야 해요.

④ 체크아웃 시간은 3시입니다.

본문해석

A: 시내 관광을 하고 싶어요. 제가 어디로 가야 한다고 생각해요?

B: 국립 미술관을 방문하는 것을 강력히 추천해요.

A: 아, 좋은 생각이네요. 또 어떤 것을 봐야 하나요?

B: 강 공원으로 가는 가이드 투어요. 오후 내내 걸려요.

A: 그럴 시간이 없어요. 3시에 고객을 만나야 하거든요.

B: 아, 그렇군요. 그러면 국립 공원을 방문해보는 건 어때요?

A: 좋네요. 감사합니다!

VOCA

- go sightseeing 구경을 다니다
- check out (흥미로운 것을) 살펴보다[보다]

12 난도 ★★☆ 정답 ③

표현 > 일반회화

정답의 이유

A가 아이들이 생일 파티에 갈 거라고 하자 B가 'So, it was a piece of cake(그래서 그건 식은 죽 먹기였어).'라고 대답한 ③의 대화가 자연스럽지 않다.

본문해석

① A: 그가 마침내 흥행작에 출연했어!

　　B: 그래, 그는 성공했구나.

② A: 나 이제 좀 피곤해.

　　B: 오늘은 여기까지 하자.

③ A: 아이들이 생일 파티에 갈 거야.

　　B: 그래서 그건 식은 죽 먹기였어.

④ A: 어제 그가 왜 집에 일찍 갔는지 궁금해.

　　B: 내 생각엔 그가 몸이 안 좋았던 거 같아.

VOCA

- get it made 잘 풀리다, (부러울 정도로) 잘되다
- call it a day ~을 그만하기로 하다
- wonder 궁금해하다
- under the weather 몸이 안 좋은

13 난도 ★★☆　　　　　　　　　　　　정답 ③

독해 > 대의 파악 > 제목, 주제

주어진 글은 비언어적 신호의 중요성에 관한 내용이다. 두 번째 문장에서 'Nonverbal cues—rather than spoken words—make us feel that the person we are with is interested in, understands, and values us(비언어적인 신호는 말보다, 우리가 함께 있는 사람이 우리에게 관심을 갖고 이해하고 우리를 소중하게 여긴다는 것을 느끼게 한다).'라고 했으므로, 글의 제목으로 알맞은 것은 ③ 'Nonverbal Communication Speaks Louder than Words(비언어적 소통이 말보다 더 크게 말한다[중요하다])'이다.

① 야생동물들은 어떻게 생각하고 느낄까?
② 효과적으로 의사소통하는 것이 성공의 비결이다.
④ 언어적 신호: 감정을 표현하는 주요 도구

본문해석

사랑받는다는 느낌과 그것이 자극하는 생물학적 반응은 목소리의 톤, 얼굴 표정 혹은 딱 맞는 느낌의 손길 같은 비언어적인 신호에 의해 촉발된다. 비언어적인 신호는 말보다, 우리가 함께 있는 사람이 우리에게 관심을 갖고 이해하고 우리를 소중하게 여긴다는 것을 느끼게 한다. 우리는 그것들과 함께할 때, 안전하다고 느낀다. 우리는 심지어 야생에서도 비언어적인 신호의 힘을 본다. 포식자들의 추적을 피한 후에, 동물들은 종종 스트레스 해소의 수단으로 서로 코를 비빈다. 이러한 신체적 접촉은 안전에 대한 확신을 제공하고 스트레스를 덜어준다.

VOCA

- biological 생물체의
- stimulate 자극[격려]하다
- trigger 촉발시키다
- nonverbal 비언어적인
- cue 신호
- value 소중하게[가치 있게] 생각하다[여기다]
- evade 피하다[모면하다]
- chase 추적, 추격
- predator 포식자, 포식 동물
- nuzzle 코[입]를 비비다
- as a means of ~의 수단으로서
- bodily 신체의
- reassurance 안심시키는 말[행동]
- relieve 없애[덜어] 주다

14 난도 ★★☆　　　　　　　　　　　　정답 ①

독해 > 대의 파악 > 제목, 주제

제시문은 자녀에게 물건에 대한 '건강한 비의존성(healthy nondependency)'을 가르치는 방법을 설명하고 있다. 두 번째 문장에서 'You can use these times to teach a healthy nondependency on things(당신은 이 시기를 물건에 대한 건강한 비의존성을 가르치기 위해 이용할 수 있다).'라고 하면서 당신의 자녀를 장난감들로 둘러싸지 말고 그것들을 바구니에 정돈하고 한 번에 바구니 하나씩 꺼내놓으라고 했다. 또한 당신이 소유물을 잃어버리거나 망가뜨린 경우, 자녀가 물건에 집착하지 않는 태도를 기를 수 있도록 "난 그것을 가지고 있는 동안 감사했어!"라는 좋은 태도를 모범으로 보이려고 노력하라고 했으므로, 글의 주제로 알맞은 것은 ① 'building a healthy attitude toward possessions (소유물에 대한 건강한 태도를 형성하기)'이다.

② 다른 사람들과 장난감을 공유하는 것의 가치를 배우기
③ 장난감을 질서정연하게 정리하는 방법을 가르치기
④ 바람직하지 않은 방식으로 행동하는 것에 대한 책임을 받아들이기

본문해석

명절과 생일처럼 아이의 삶에 장난감과 선물이 쌓이는 시기가 있다. 당신은 이 시기를 물건에 대한 건강한 비의존성을 가르치기 위해 이용할 수 있다. 당신의 자녀를 장난감들로 둘러싸지 마라. 대신 그것들을 바구니들에 정리해 한 번에 바구니 하나씩 꺼내놓고 가끔 바구니들을 교체해라. 소중한 물건이 잠시 치워지면, 그것을 꺼내오는 것은 즐거운 기억과 관점의 신선함을 만들어 낸다. 가령 당신의 자녀가 한동안 치워둔 장난감을 요구한다고 가정해 보자. 당신은 이미 주위(환경)에 있는 물건이나 경험으로 관심을 이끌 수 있다. 당신이 소유물을 잃어버리거나 망가뜨린 경우, 당신의 자녀가 물건에 집착하지 않는 태도를 기를 수 있도록 "난 그것을 가지고 있는 동안 감사했어!"라는 좋은 자세를 모범으로 보이려고 노력하라. 아이의 장난감이 망가지거나 분실된 경우, 아이가 "재미있게 가지고 놀았어."라고 말하도록 도와줘라.

VOCA

- accumulate 모으다, 축적하다
- nondependency 비의존성
- surround 둘러싸다, 에워싸다
- arrange 정리하다, 배열하다
- rotate 회전하다[시키다]
- occasionally 가끔
- cherish 소중히 여기다, 아끼다
- put away 넣다[치우다]
- bring out ~을 꺼내다
- delightful 정말 기분 좋은[마음에 드는]
- outlook 관점, 세계관, 인생관
- suppose 가령[만약] ~이라고 하다
- direct 안내하다, 지휘하다, 총괄하다
- possession 소유물, 소지, 보유

독해 > 대의 파악 > 요지, 주장

정답의 이유

제시문은 부모가 자녀를 칭찬하는 방식이 아이들의 발달에 미치는 영향에 대한 내용이다. 네 번째 문장에서 노력보다 지능으로 칭찬받은 아이들은 결과에 지나치게 집착하게 된다는 사실을 발견했다고 했으며, 마지막 문장에서는 아이들의 지능을 칭찬하는 것은 그들로 하여금 어려움을 두려워하게 만드는데, 그것은 그들이 실패를 어리석음과 동일시하기 때문이라고 했다. 따라서 글의 요지로 알맞은 것은 ② 'Compliments on intelligence bring about negative effect(지능에 대한 칭찬은 부정적인 영향을 초래한다).'이다.

오답의 이유

① 잦은 칭찬이 아이들의 자존감을 증가시킨다.

③ 아이는 성공을 통해 실패에 대한 두려움을 극복해야 한다.

④ 부모들은 과정보다 결과에 집중해야 한다.

본문해석

많은 부모들이 '자존감 운동'에 의해 잘못 인도되었는데, 그 운동은 자녀들의 자존감을 개발하는 방식이 자녀들이 얼마나 어떤 일을 잘하는지 말하는 것이라고 알려준다. 안타깝게도, 당신의 자녀들에게 그들의 능력을 확신시키는 것은 실패할 가능성이 큰데, 그것은 인생이 아이들에게 성공과 실패를 통해 실제로 그들이 얼마나 유능하거나 무능한지를 명백히 알려주기 때문이다. 연구는 당신이 자녀를 칭찬하는 방식이 그들의 발달에 강력한 영향을 미친다는 것을 보여주었다. 일부 연구자들은 노력에 비해 지능에 대해 칭찬받은 아이들이 결과에 지나치게 집착하게 된다는 사실을 발견했다. 실패 후, 이 아이들은 끈기를 덜 보였고, 덜 즐거워했으며, 실패를 그들의 능력 부족 탓으로 돌리며, 향후 성취를 위한 노력에서 저조한 성과를 보였다. 아이들의 지능을 칭찬하는 것은 그들로 하여금 어려움을 두려워하게 만드는데, 그것은 그들이 실패를 어리석음과 동일시하기 때문이다.

VOCA

- misguide 잘못 이끌다
- build 만들어 내다, 창조[개발]하다
- self-esteem 자부심
- convince 납득시키다, 확신시키다
- competence 능숙함, 능숙도
- unequivocally 명백히
- capable ~을 할 수 있는
- as compared to ~과 비교하여
- overly 너무, 몹시
- persist 집요하게 계속하다
- attribute ~ to ~을 …의 탓으로 돌리다
- equate 동일시하다
- stupidity 어리석음, 우둔

독해 > 빈칸 완성 > 단어 · 구 · 절

정답의 이유

제시문은 소비자들의 온라인 활동이 활발해짐에 따라 글로벌 브랜드의 광고 표준화에 대한 필요성이 대두되고 있다는 내용이다. 세 번째 문장에서는 온라인상에서 연결된 소비자들이 인터넷과 소셜 미디어를 통해 국경을 넘나들어서 광고주들이 통제되고, 질서정연한 방식으로 캠페인을 펼치기 어렵다고 했다. 빈칸 앞 문장에서는 대부분 글로벌 브랜드들이 자신들의 디지털 사이트들을 국제적으로 대등하게 조정한다고 했고, 빈칸 다음 문장에서 친숙한 코카콜라의 붉은색과 상징적인 병 모양, 음악, 주제 등을 특징으로 한다고 했다. 따라서 빈칸에 들어갈 말로 알맞은 것은 ② 'uniform(획일적인)'이다.

오답의 이유

① 실험적인

③ 국지적인

④ 다양한

본문해석

최근 온라인 마케팅과 소셜 미디어 공유의 인기가 증가하면서 글로벌 브랜드의 광고 표준화에 대한 필요성이 커졌다. 대부분의 대형 마케팅 및 광고 캠페인은 대규모 온라인상에서의 영향력을 포함한다. (온라인상에서) 연결된 소비자들은 인터넷과 소셜 미디어를 통해 국경을 쉽게 넘나들 수 있게 되었는데, 이것은 광고주들로 하여금 통제되고 질서정연한 방식으로 맞춤화된 캠페인을 전개하는 것을 어렵게 한다. 그 결과, 대부분의 글로벌 소비자 브랜드들은 전 세계적으로 그들의 디지털 사이트를 대등하게 조정한다. 예를 들어, 코카콜라의 웹사이트와 소셜 미디어 사이트들은 호주와 아르헨티나에서부터 프랑스, 루마니아, 러시아에 이르기까지 놀랄 만큼 전 세계적으로 획일적이다. 모든 것이 친숙한 코카콜라의 붉은색, 코카콜라의 상징적인 병 모양, 코카콜라의 음악, "Taste the Feeling"이라는 주제 등을 특징으로 한다.

VOCA

- boost 신장시키다, 북돋우다
- advertising 광고
- standardization 표준화
- online presence 온라인상에서의 존재감, 영향력
- zip 쌩[획] 하고 가다[나아가게 하다]
- via 경유하여[거쳐]
- roll out 출시하다, 시작하다
- orderly 정돈된, 정연한
- coordinate ~을 대등하게 조정하다, 통합[일원화]하다
- feature 특징을 이루다

국가직 9급

영어

독해 > 글의 일관성 > 무관한 어휘 · 문장

정답의 이유

제시문은 하이브리드 근무 방식, 즉 사무실 출근과 재택근무를 병행하는 근무 형태가 점점 늘어나서 사무실에서 근무하는 일수가 줄어들었지만, 사무실 공간은 별로 줄지 않고 사무실 공간의 밀집도가 크게 낮아졌다는 내용이다. ③ 앞 문장에서 사무실에서의 고밀집도는 불편하고 많은 근로자들이 그들의 책상 주변이 붐비는 것을 싫어한다고 했고, ③ 다음 문장에서 밀집도로 인한 불편함은 로비, 주방, 엘리베이터까지 연장된다고 했다. 따라서 글의 흐름상 어색한 문장은 ③ 'Most employees want to work from home on Mondays and Fridays(대부분의 직원이 월요일과 금요일에 재택근무하기를 원한다).'이다.

본문해석

미국의 근로자 5,000명과 미국의 고용주 500명을 대상으로 매월 실시하는 우리의 설문조사에 따르면, 사무직 및 지식근로자 사이에서 하이브리드 근무로의 대규모 전환이 매우 뚜렷하게 보인다. 새롭게 나타난 표준은 1주일 중 3일은 사무실에서, 2일은 집에서 근무하는 것으로 현장근무일수가 30% 이상 줄었다. 당신은 이러한 단축으로 인해 사무실 공간 수요가 크게 감소될 것이라고 생각할 수도 있다. 그러나 우리의 설문조사 데이터는 사무실 공간은 평균 1~2%의 축소를 보여주는데, 이는 공간이 아닌 밀집도의 큰 감소를 시사한다. 우리는 그 이유를 이해할 수 있다. 사무실에서의 고밀집도는 불편하며 많은 근로자가 그들의 책상 주변이 붐비는 것을 싫어한다. 대부분의 직원이 월요일과 금요일에 재택근무하기를 원한다. 밀집도로 인한 불편함은 로비, 주방, 특히 엘리베이터까지 연장된다. 밀집도를 낮출 수 있는 유일하고 확실한 방법은 (사무실의) 평방 피트를 줄이지 않고 현장근무일을 줄이는 것이다. 우리의 조사 증거에 따르면, 밀집도에 대한 불편함은 앞으로도 계속될 것이다.

VOCA

- huge shift 엄청난 입장변화/전환
- hybrid 혼성체, 혼합물
- abundantly 풍부하게
- emerging 최근 생겨난
- norm 규범, 규준
- cutback 삭감, 감축
- imply 암시[시사]하다
- reduction 축소, 삭감
- density 밀도(빽빽한 정도)
- extend 연장하다
- sure-fire 확실한, 틀림없는
- reduce 줄이다[축소하다]
- square footage 평방 피트
- be here to stay 우리 생활의 일부이다

독해 > 글의 일관성 > 문장 삽입

정답의 이유

주어진 문장에서 '그들은 불법적인 국경 횡단 장소로 알려진 곳에 비디오카메라를 설치했고 실시간 비디오 자료를 웹사이트에 올렸다.'라고 했으므로 주어진 문장의 앞에는 They가 가리키는 대상이, 주어진 문장 다음에는 실시간 비디오 자료를 웹사이트에 올린 결과가 나와야 한다. They는 ③ 앞 문장의 불법 이민자들을 단속하는 Texas sheriffs를 가리키며, 새로운 인터넷 활용법(a novel use of the Internet)은 카메라를 설치하고 불법 국경 횡단자들이 찍힌 비디오 자료를 실시간으로 웹사이트에 올리는 것을 의미한다. ③ 다음 문장에서 국경 감시를 돕고자 하는 시민들은 온라인에 접속해 가상 보안관 역할을 할 수 있다고 했으므로 이것이 실시간 비디오 자료를 웹사이트에 올린 결과가 된다. 따라서 주어진 문장이 들어갈 위치로 알맞은 것은 ③이다.

본문해석

이민 개혁은 정치적 지뢰밭이다. 광범위한 정치적 지지를 받는 이민 정책의 거의 유일한 측면은 불법 이민자들의 흐름을 제한하기 위해 멕시코와 미국 사이 국경을 안전하게 지키겠다는 결의이다. 텍사스 보안관들은 최근에 그들의 국경 감시를 돕기 위해 새로운 인터넷 활용법을 개발했다. 그들은 불법적인 국경 횡단 장소로 알려진 곳에 비디오 카메라를 설치했고, 카메라의 실시간 비디오 자료를 웹사이트에 올렸다. 국경 감시를 돕고자 하는 시민들은 온라인에 접속해 '가상 텍사스 보안관' 역할을 할 수 있다. 국경을 넘으려는 사람을 발견하면 그들은 보안관 사무실에 보고서를 보내고, 이것은 때로 미국 국경 순찰대의 도움으로 추가 조사된다.

VOCA

- immigration 이민
- reform 개혁[개선]
- minefield 지뢰밭
- command (받아야 할 것을) 받다, 요구하다, 강요하다
- resolve 결심[결의]
- secure 획득[확보]하다
- illegal immigrant 불법 입국[체류]자
- sheriff 보안관
- novel 새로운, 신기한
- install 설치[설비]하다
- illegal 불법적인
- video feed 비디오 자료
- virtual 가상의
- follow up (방금 들은 내용에 대해) 더 알아보다

19 난도 ★★☆   정답 ③

독해 > 글의 일관성 > 글의 순서

정답의 이유

주어진 글은 모든 문명(civilization)이 정부 행정에 의존하고, 고대 로마의 문명이 가장 대표적 예시라는 내용이므로, 주어진 글에서 언급된 civilization이 라틴어의 *civis*에서 유래했다는 (B)로 이어지는 것이 자연스럽다. (B) 다음으로는 라틴어가 고대 로마의 언어였으며 로마의 영토에 대해 부연 설명하고 있는 (C)가 와야 한다. 마지막으로, 로마의 방대한 영토(an area that large)를 통치하기 위한 '효과적인 정부 행정 시스템(an effective system of government administration)'의 필요성을 말한 (A)로 마무리하는 것이 자연스럽다. 따라서 글의 순서로 알맞은 것은 ③ '(B) – (C) – (A)'이다.

본문해석

모든 문명은 정부 행정에 의존한다. 아마 고대 로마보다 이것을 대표적인 예시로 더 잘 보여주는 문명은 없을 것이다.

(B) 사실, '문명'이라는 단어 자체는 '시민'을 의미하는 라틴어 *civis* 에서 유래했다.

(C) 라틴어는 고대 로마의 언어였으며, 로마의 영토는 지중해 유역부터 북쪽의 영국 일부와 동쪽의 흑해까지 뻗어 있었다.

(A) 그렇게 넓은 영토를 통치하기 위해, 현재의 이탈리아 중부에 기반을 두고 있었던 로마인들은 효과적인 정부 행정 시스템이 필요했다.

VOCA

- rely on 의존하다
- administration 관리[행정]
- exemplify 전형적인 예가 되다
- come from ~에서 나오다
- territory 지역, 영토
- stretch 뻗어 있다
- basin 유역
- rule 통치하다, 다스리다
- based in ~에 기반을 둔

20 난도 ★★★   정답 ①

독해 > 빈칸 완성 > 단어 · 구 · 절

정답의 이유

제시문은 심리학의 하위분야들에 대한 통합의 필요성과 이 과정에서 심리 과학이 통합의 중추 역할을 할 것이라는 내용으로, 글의 세 번째 문장에서 'Science advances when distinct topics become theoretically and empirically integrated under simplifying theoretical frameworks(과학은 서로 다른 별개의 주제들이 단순화된 이론적 틀 아래에서 이론적, 경험적으로 통합될 때 발전한다).'라고 했다. 또한 빈칸 앞 문장에서 이러한 방식으로 심리 과학은 그 분야 내 모든 주요 분과/분파를 '하나의 학문하에(under one discipline)' 통합함으로써 심리학 전체에 대한 본보기 역할을 할 수 있을 것이라고 했으므로 빈칸 문장 앞부분의 'how to combine resources and study science(자료를 결합하고 과학을 연구하는

방법)'를 수식하는 빈칸에 들어갈 말로 알맞은 것은 ① 'from a unified perspective(통합된 관점에서)'임을 유추할 수 있다.

오답의 이유

② 역동적인 측면에서
③ 역사를 통틀어
④ 정확한 증거를 가지고

본문해석

지난 50년 동안 심리학의 모든 주요 하위분야는 교육이 점점 전문화되고 그 초점이 좁아짐에 따라 서로 점점 더 고립되어 왔다. 일부 심리학자들이 오랫동안 주장해 온 것처럼, 심리학 분야가 과학적으로 성숙해지고 발전하려면 그것의 이질적인 부분들 [예를 들어, 신경과학, 발달 (심리학), 인지 (심리학), 성격 (심리학), 사회 (심리학)]이 다시 하나가 되고 통합되어야 한다. 과학은 서로 다른 별개의 주제들이 단순화된 이론적 틀 아래에서 이론적, 경험적으로 통합될 때 발전한다. 심리 과학은 여러 하위영역의 심리학자들 간의 협업을 장려하여 이 분야가 지속적인 분열보다는 일관성을 성취하도록 도울 것이다. 이러한 방식으로 심리 과학은 그 분야 내 모든 주요 분과/분파를 하나의 학문하에 통합함으로써 심리학 전체에 대한 본보기 역할을 할 수 있을 것이다. 심리 과학이 통합된 관점에서 자료를 결합하고 과학을 연구하는 방법에 대한 모 학문의 모범이 될 수 있다면, 이는 결코 작은 업적이 아니며 그 중요도 또한 작지 않을 것이다.

VOCA

- subdiscipline 학문분야의 하위 구분
- isolated from ~에서 고립된
- in focus 초점[핀트]이 맞아
- mature (충분히) 발달하다
- advance 증진되다[진전을 보다]
- disparate 이질적인
- neuroscience 신경 과학
- developmental 발달[개발]상의
- cognitive 인식[인지]의
- integrate 통합시키다[되다]
- theoretically 이론상
- empirically 실증적으로
- simplify 간소화[단순화]하다
- framework 체제, 체계
- encourage 권장[장려]하다
- achieve 달성하다, 성취하다
- coherence 일관성
- fragmentation 균열, 분절
- act as ~으로서의 역할을 하다[맡다]
- template 견본, 본보기
- fraction 부분, 일부
- faction 파벌, 파당
- model 모범, 귀감
- feat 위업, 개가

영어 | 2022년 국가직 9급

한눈에 훑어보기

✓ 영역 분석

어휘   01 02 03 04 05
5문항, 25%

독해   07 09 10 15 16 17 18 19 20
9문항, 45%

어법   06 08 13 14
4문항, 20%

표현   11 12
2문항, 10%

✓ 빠른 정답

01	02	03	04	05	06	07	08	09	10
①	②	④	②	①	①	④	②	①	③
11	12	13	14	15	16	17	18	19	20
④	③	②	④	②	④	③	④	①	③

✓ 점수 체크

구분	1회독	2회독	3회독
맞힌 문항 수	/ 20	/ 20	/ 20
나의 점수	점	점	점

01 난도 ★☆☆   정답 ①

어휘 > 단어

정답의 이유

밑줄 친 unravel은 '(미스터리 등을) 풀다'의 뜻으로 이와 의미가 가장 가까운 것은 ① 'solve(풀다)'이다.

오답의 이유

② 창조하다
③ 모방하다
④ 알리다, 광고[홍보]하다

본문해석

수년 동안, 형사들은 쌍둥이 형제의 갑작스러운 실종에 대한 미스터리를 풀기 위해 애썼다.

VOCA

• detective 형사, 수사관
• mystery 수수께끼, 미스터리
• sudden 갑작스러운, 급작스러운
• disappearance 실종, 잠적

02 난도 ★☆☆   정답 ②

어휘 > 단어

정답의 이유

밑줄 친 opulent는 '호화로운'의 뜻으로 이와 의미가 가장 가까운 것은 ② 'luxurious(호화로운)'이다.

오답의 이유

① 숨겨진
③ 비어 있는
④ 단단한

본문해석

부부가 부모가 되기 전에는 침실 4개짜리 집이 불필요하게 호화로운 것 같았다.

VOCA

• parenthood 부모임
• seem ~인 것 같다[듯하다]
• unnecessarily 불필요하게

03 난도 ★☆☆ 정답 ④

어휘 > 어구

정답의 이유

밑줄 친 hit the roof는 '몹시 화가 나다'의 뜻으로 이와 의미가 가장 가까운 것은 ④ 'became extremely angry(매우 화가 났다)'이다.

오답의 이유

① 매우 만족했다

② 매우 놀랐다

③ 매우 침착해졌다

본문해석

사장은 우리가 그렇게 짧은 기간에 전체 예산을 이미 다 써버린 것을 보고 몹시 화를 냈다.

VOCA

• boss 사장, 상사

• entire 전체의, 온

• budget 예산, (지출 예상) 비용

• period of time 기간

04 난도 ★★☆ 정답 ②

어휘 > 단어

정답의 이유

카우치 포테이토는 텔레비전만 보며 많은 시간을 보내는 사람을 뜻하는 말이다. 마우스 포테이토는 텔레비전의 카우치 포테이토에 상응하는 표현이므로 빈칸에 들어갈 말로 가장 적절한 것은 ② 'equivalent(상응하는 것)'이다.

오답의 이유

① 기술자

③ 망

④ 모의실험

본문해석

마우스 포테이토는 컴퓨터에서 텔레비전의 카우치 포테이토에 상응하는 것이다. 즉, 카우치 포테이토가 텔레비전 앞에서 하는 것과 같은 방식으로 컴퓨터 앞에서 많은 여가 시간을 보내는 경향이 있는 사람이다.

VOCA

• mouse potato (일 · 오락을 위해) 컴퓨터 앞에서 시간을 많이 보내는 사람

• couch potato 오랫동안 가만히 앉아 텔레비전만 보는 사람

• tend to (~하는) 경향이 있다

• leisure 여가

05 난도 ★☆☆ 정답 ①

어휘 > 어구

정답의 이유

빈칸 다음에서 Spanish(스페인어)를 목적어로 취하고, 'before going to South America(남아메리카로 가기 전에)'라고 했으므로 빈칸에는 Mary가 남아메리카에 가기 전에 해야 할 행동에 관한 동사가 들어가야 함을 유추할 수 있다. 따라서 빈칸에 들어갈 말로 가장 적절한 것은 ① 'brush up on(~을 복습하다)'이다.

오답의 이유

② 끝까지 듣다

③ ~을 변호하다, 옹호하다

④ 그만하다, 해고하다

본문해석

Mary는 남아메리카로 가기 전에 스페인어를 복습하기로 결심했다.

06 난도 ★★☆ 정답 ①

어법 > 정문 찾기

정답의 이유

① 문장의 주어가 '말(A horse)'이고 feed는 '먹이를 주다'라는 뜻의 타동사이므로 수동태(should be fed)로 올바르게 쓰였으며, 주어(A horse)와 대명사(its)의 수일치도 적절하다.

오답의 이유

② 분사구문의 주어는 주절의 주어와 동일한 경우에만 생략할 수 있다. 여기서 주절의 주어는 '나의 모자(My hat)'이고, 부사절(while walking down a narrow street)의 주어는 '나(I)'이므로 부사절의 주어와 be동사를 생략할 수 없다. 따라서 while walking → while I walked[was walking]이 되어야 한다.

③ 주어(She)가 정치 만화가(political cartoonist)로 '알려진' 것이므로 수동태로 쓰는 것이 적절하다. 따라서 She has known → She has been known이 되어야 한다.

④ good은 형용사로 '좋은'이라는 의미이고, well은 부사로 '잘'이라는 의미이다. 여기서는 과거분사인 done을 수식하므로 good(형용사) → well(부사)이 되어야 한다.

본문해석

① 말은 개별적인 필요와 일의 성질에 따라 먹이를 공급받아야 한다.

② 내가 좁은 길을 걷는 동안, 바람에 의해 모자가 날아갔다.

③ 그녀는 경력 내내 정치 만화가로 주로 알려져 왔다.

④ 어린아이들조차도 잘된 일에 대해서는 칭찬받기를 좋아한다.

VOCA

• feed 먹이를 주다

• individual 각각[개개]의

• nature 천성, 본성, 종류, 유형

• blow off (바람 입김에) 날리다; (바람 입김에) 날려 보내다

• primarily 주로

• compliment 칭찬하다

독해 > 세부 내용 찾기 > 내용 (불)일치

정답의 이유

마지막 문장에서 'He died at his Milanese home of pancreatic cancer, from which he had been suffering for two years(그는 2년간 앓았던 췌장암으로 밀라노의 자택에서 사망했다) ~'라고 했으므로 글의 내용과 일치하지 않는 것은 ④ 'Eco died in a hospital of cancer(Eco는 암으로 병원에서 죽었다).'이다.

오답의 이유

① *The Name of the Rose*는 역사소설이다. → 두 번째 문장에서 *The Name of the Rose*는 역사 미스터리 소설이라고 했으므로 내용과 일치한다.

② Eco는 책을 이탈리아어로 번역했다. → 네 번째 문장에서 Eco는 Raymond Queneau의 책 *Exercices de style*을 이탈리아어로 번역했다고 했으므로 글의 내용과 일치한다.

③ Eco는 대학 학부를 설립했다. → 다섯 번째 문장에서 Eco는 산 마리노 공화국 대학교의 미디어학과 설립자였다고 했으므로 글의 내용과 일치한다.

본문해석

Umberto Eco는 이탈리아의 소설가, 문화 평론가, 철학자였다. 그는 1980년 소설 *The Name of the Rose*로 널리 알려졌는데, 그것은 역사 미스터리로, 소설 속에서 기호학과 성서 분석, 중세 연구, 문학 이론을 결합한 작품이다. 그는 후에 *Foucault's Pendulum*과 *The Island of the Day Before*를 포함한 다른 소설들을 썼다. 번역가이기도 했던 Eco는 Raymond Queneau의 책 *Exercices de style*을 이탈리아어로 번역했다. 그는 산 마리노 공화국 대학교 미디어학과의 설립자였다. 그는 2016년 2월 19일 밤에 2년간 앓았던 췌장암으로 밀라노의 자택에서 사망했다.

VOCA

• novelist 소설가
• cultural critic 문화 평론가
• be widely known for ~로 널리 알려져 있다
• combine with ~와 결합되다
• semiotics 기호학
• biblical analysis 성서 분석
• translator 번역가, 통역사
• founder 창립자, 설립자
• pancreatic cancer 췌장암
• suffer from ~로 고통받다

어법 > 비문 찾기

정답의 이유

② that절의 주어가 a combination of silver, copper, and zinc로 단수명사이므로 were → was로 고쳐야 한다.

오답의 이유

① which의 선행사는 때를 나타내는 the year 1800이므로 during which가 올바르게 쓰였다. '전치사+관계대명사(during which)'는 관계부사 when으로 대체할 수 있다.

③ 주어인 The enhanced design이 수식받는 대상이므로 과거분사(called)가 올바르게 쓰였다.

④ 원인과 결과를 나타내는 'so[such] ~ that' 구문에서 형용사나 부사를 수식할 때는 so를, 명사를 수식할 때는 such를 쓴다. 지문에서 talk는 '세평, 소문'이라는 뜻의 불가산명사이므로 such가 올바르게 쓰였다.

본문해석

좋은 출발점을 찾기 위해서는 최초의 현대식 전기 배터리가 개발된 1800년으로 돌아가야 한다. 이탈리아인 Alessandro Volta는 은과 구리, 아연의 조합이 전류 생성에 이상적이라는 것을 발견했다. 볼타의 전지라고 불리는 그 향상된 디자인은 바닷물에 적신 판지 디스크 사이에 이러한 금속 디스크들을 쌓아 올림으로써 만들어졌다. Volta의 연구에 대한 소문이 자자해 그는 Napoleon 황제 앞에서 직접 시연하라는 요청을 받았다.

VOCA

• starting point 출발점[기점]
• electric battery 전지
• combination 조합[결합](물)
• copper 구리, 동
• zinc 아연
• electrical current 전류
• enhanced 향상된
• stack 쌓다[포개다]; 쌓이다, 포개지다
• soaked 흠뻑 젖은
• talk 소문[이야기]
• conduct 수행하다
• demonstration 시연

더 알아보기

전치사＋관계대명사＝관계부사

- 관계부사(where, when, how, why)는 선행사를 수식하는 형용사절을 이끌면서, 그 절에서 선행사를 대신하는 부사 역할을 한다.
- 관계부사는 '부사＋접속사'의 역할을 하며, '전치사＋관계대명사(which)'로 바꿀 수 있다.
- 관계부사의 종류

선행사	관계부사	전치사＋which
시간(the time)	when	at which, on which, in which 등
장소(the place)	where	at which, on which, in which, to which 등
방법(the way)	how	in which 등
이유 (the reason)	why	for which 등

예 I don't know *the exact time*.＋The TV show will finish at *the exact time*.

= I don't know the exact time which the TV show will finish at. → 관계대명사

= I don't know the exact time at which the TV show will finish. → 전치사＋관계대명사

= I don't know the exact time when the TV show will finish. → 관계부사 – 시간

(나는 그 TV 쇼가 끝나는 정확한 시간을 모른다.)

09 난도 ★★☆   정답 ①

독해 > 대의 파악 > 제목, 주제

정답의 이유

첫 번째 문장에서 'Lasers are possible because of the way light interacts with electrons(레이저는 빛이 전자와 상호작용하는 방식 때문에 발생 가능하다).'라고 레이저의 발생 원리를 제시한 후에, 구체적으로 전자의 특징과 전자가 빛에 반응하여 특정 파장을 방출하는 방식을 설명하고 있으므로 글의 제목으로 가장 적절한 것은 ① 'How Is Laser Produced(레이저는 어떻게 생성되는가)?'이다.

오답의 이유

② 레이저는 언제 발명되었는가?

③ 레이저는 어떤 전자들을 방출하는가?

④ 전자들은 왜 빛을 반사하는가?

본문해석

레이저는 빛이 전자와 상호작용하는 방식 때문에 (발생이) 가능하다. 전자는 특정 원자 또는 분자의 특정한 에너지 준위 혹은 상태로 존재한다. 에너지 준위는 고리 또는 핵 주위의 궤도로 상상될 수 있다. 외부 고리의 전자는 내부 고리의 전자보다 에너지 준위가 더 높다. 전자는, 예를 들어, 섬광과 같은 에너지 주입에 의해 더 높은 에너지 준위로 상승할 수 있다. 전자가 외부에서 내부 에너지 준위로 떨어지면, '잉여' 에너지가 빛으로 발산된다. 발산된 빛의 파장 또는 색은 방출되는 에너지의 양과 정확하게 관련이 있다. 사용되는 특정 레이저 재료에 따라 (전자에 동력을 제공하거나 자극하기 위해) 특정 파장의 빛이 흡수되고, (전자가 초기 준위로 떨어질 때) 특정 파장이 방출된다.

VOCA

- interact with ~와 상호작용을 하다
- electron 전자
- energy level [물리] 에너지 준위, 맹렬히 활동하는 힘
- state 상태
- characteristic of ~에 특유한
- atom 원자
- molecule 분자
- ring 고리, 고리 모양의 것
- orbit 궤도
- nucleus 핵
- bump up 올리다, 인상하다
- injection 주입, 투여
- a flash of light 섬광
- drop from ~에서 떨어지다[떨어뜨리다]
- give off 발산하다, 방출하다, 뿜다
- wavelength 파장
- emit 발산하다, 방출하다, 내뿜다
- absorb 흡수하다
- energize 동력을 제공하다, 작동시키다
- excite 자극하다
- fall back to ~까지 후퇴하다
- initial 초기의, 처음의

10 난도 ★★☆   정답 ③

독해 > 글의 일관성 > 무관한 어휘·문장

정답의 이유

제시문은 수리권(water rights) 시장의 현황과 수리권의 중요성에 관한 내용인데, ③은 증류수의 효과에 대한 설명이므로 글의 흐름상 어색한 문장은 ③ 'Drinking distilled water can be beneficial, ~ by another source(증류수를 마시는 것은 유익할 수 있지만, ~ 최선의 선택은 아닐 수 있다).'이다.

인구 증가가 (물) 부족으로 이어지고 기후 변화가 가뭄과 기근을 초래함에 따라 수리권 시장은 변화할 것으로 보인다. 그러나 그것은 지역적이고 윤리적인 무역 관행을 기초로 할 것이며, 대부분의 상품 거래와는 다를 것이다. 반대자들은 물 거래가 비윤리적이고 심지어 인권 침해라고 주장하지만, 이미 수리권은 오만에서 호주까지 세계의 건조 지역에서 매매된다. 증류수를 마시는 것은 유익할 수 있지만, 특히 미네랄이 다른 공급원에 의해 보충되지 않는다면, 모두에게 최선의 선택이 아닐 수 있다. Ziad Abdelnour는 말하기를 "우리는 물이 향후 10년 동안과 그 이후에 사실상 새로운 금으로 바뀔 것이라고 굳게 믿습니다."라고 했다. "스마트 머니가 공격적으로 이 방향으로 움직이는 게 놀라운 일이 아닙니다."

VOCA

• water rights 수리권(수자원을 독점적으로 사용할 수 있는 권리)
• evolve 변하다, 진화하다
• lead to ~로 이어지다
• drought 가뭄
• famine 기근
• ethical 윤리적인, 도덕적인
• trading practices 무역 관행
• the bulk of ~의 대부분
• commodity 상품
• detractor 비방가, 반대자
• breach 침해
• arid 건조한
• distilled water 증류수
• beneficial 이로운
• supplement 보충하다
• smart money 스마트 머니(전문적인 지식을 갖고 투자·투기한 돈)
• aggressively 공격적으로

11 난도 ★☆☆   정답 ④

표현 > 일반회화

정답의 이유

대학교의 구내식당 메뉴 변경과 새로운 음식 공급업체를 구한 것에 대해 이야기하고 있는 상황이다. 빈칸 다음에서 B가 디저트 메뉴 선택지가 많아졌고, 일부 샌드위치 메뉴가 없어졌다고 말하고 있으므로 빈칸에 들어갈 말로 가장 적절한 것은 ④ 'What's the difference from the last menu(예전 메뉴와 다른 점이 무엇인가요)'이다.

오답의 이유

① 가장 좋아하는 디저트는 무엇인가요
② 그들의 사무실이 어디 있는지 아시나요
③ 메뉴에 관해 내 도움이 필요한가요

A: 대학교 구내식당 메뉴가 바뀌었다고 들었어요.
B: 맞아요, 내가 방금 확인했어요.
A: 그리고 새로운 공급업체를 구했대요.
B: 맞아요, Sam's Catering이에요.
A: 예전 메뉴와 다른 점이 무엇인가요?
B: 디저트 메뉴 선택지가 많아졌어요. 그리고 일부 샌드위치 메뉴는 없어졌어요.

VOCA

• cafeteria 구내식당, 카페테리아
• caterer 음식 공급자

12 난도 ★☆☆   정답 ③

표현 > 일반회화

정답의 이유

빈칸 앞에서 A가 스웨터 가격이 120달러라고 하고, 빈칸 다음에서 A가 다른 스웨터를 권하면서 50달러로 세일 중이라고 했으므로 문맥상 B가 처음 제안받은 스웨터의 가격이 비싸다고 말했음을 유추할 수 있다. 따라서 빈칸에 들어갈 말로 가장 적절한 것은 ③ 'It's a little out of my price range(제가 생각한 가격대를 좀 넘네요)'이다.

오답의 이유

① 그것과 어울리는 바지도 한 벌 필요해요
② 그 재킷은 저를 위한 완벽한 선물이에요
④ 토요일엔 오후 7시까지 영업합니다

A: 안녕하세요. 도와드릴까요?
B: 네, 스웨터를 찾고 있어요.
A: 음, 이게 가을 컬렉션으로 나온 최신 스타일입니다. 어떠세요?
B: 멋지네요. 얼마예요?
A: 가격 확인해드릴게요. 120달러예요.
B: 제가 생각한 가격대를 좀 넘네요.
A: 그럼 이 스웨터는 어떠세요? 지난 시즌에 나온 건데, 50달러로 세일 중이에요.
B: 완벽해요! 입어볼게요.

VOCA

• gorgeous (아주) 멋진
• try on 입어보다
• go with 어울리다
• price range 가격대, 가격폭

13 난도 ★☆☆ 정답 ②

어법 > 영작하기

정답의 이유

② 비교급을 사용해 최상급의 뜻을 나타내는 표현으로, as 앞에 비교급 more precious가 쓰였으므로 as → than으로 고쳐야 한다.

오답의 이유

① 난이형용사(easy, difficult 등)가 'It is easy[difficult 등]+to부정사' 구문으로 적절하게 쓰였으며, for us는 to부정사(to learn)의 의미상의 주어이다. 부사구 'by no means(결코 ~이 아닌)'가 삽입되었다.

③ cannot ~ too는 '아무리 ~해도 지나치지 않다'라는 뜻의 조동사 관용표현으로 적절하게 사용되었다. 주절의 주어와 부사절의 주어가 children으로 일치하므로 부사절의 주어를 생략하고 'when+현재분사(when crossing)'로 적절하게 쓰였다.

④ 관계대명사 what은 선행사를 포함하며, 동사 believes의 목적어로 명사절을 이끌고 있다.

VOCA

• by no means 결코 ~이 아닌
• precious 소중한
• cross (가로질러) 건너다; 가로지르다, 횡단하다

더 알아보기

원급과 비교급으로 최상급 표현하기

최상급	주어+동사+the 최상급
원급	부정 주어(No one/Nothing, No other one/thing)+동사+as 원급 as+주어로 썼던 명사
비교급	• 부정 주어(No one/Nothing, No other one/thing)+동사+비교급 than+주어로 썼던 명사 • 주어로 썼던 명사+동사+비교급 than+any other+단수명사

예 Time is the most precious in our life.
(시간은 우리 삶에서 가장 중요하다.)
= *Nothing* is more precious than time in our life.
= Time is more precious than *anything else* in our life.
= *Nothing* is as precious as time in our life.

예 This is the most expensive watch in the world.
(이것은 세상에서 가장 비싼 시계이다.)
= This is more expensive than *any other watch* in the world.
= *No other watch* in the world is as expensive as this.

14 난도 ★★☆ 정답 ④

어법 > 영작하기

정답의 이유

④ '~한 채로'의 동시 상황을 나타내는 'with+목적어+분사' 구문에서 목적어와 분사의 관계가 능동이면 현재분사, 수동이면 과거분사를 사용한다. 다리가 '꼬여지는' 것이므로 crossing → crossed가 되어야 한다.

오답의 이유

① 그녀가 커피 세 잔을 마신 시점이 잠을 이룰 수 없던 시점보다 이전이므로 완료형 분사구문(Having drunk)이 올바르게 사용되었다.

② As she is a kind person이라는 부사절의 분사구문(Being a kind person)으로 이때 Being은 생략할 수도 있다.

③ 주절의 주어(she)와 부사절의 주어(all things)가 다를 때 분사구문의 주어를 표시해 주는 독립분사구문으로, 부사절의 주어인 All things는 고려되는 대상이므로 수동형인 과거분사(considered)가 적절하게 쓰였다. 이때 All things (being) considered에서 being이 생략되었다.

VOCA

• fall asleep 잠들다
• best-qualified 가장 적임인
• position 직위, 지위
• raise 올리다[인상하다/높이다]
• blood pressure 혈압

15 난도 ★★☆ 정답 ②

독해 > 빈칸 완성 > 연결어

정답의 이유

다양한 애도 문화에 관한 글이다. 빈칸 (A) 앞 문장에서 'Yet among the Hopi Indians of Arizona, the deceased are forgotten as quickly as possible and life goes on as usual(하지만 애리조나의 Hopi 인디언들 사이에서는 고인이 가능한 한 빨리 잊히고 삶은 평소처럼 계속된다).'이라고 한 다음에, 빈칸 (A) 뒤에서 'the Hopi funeral ritual concludes with a break-off between mortals and spirits(Hopi의 장례 의식은 인간과 영혼 사이의 단절로 끝난다).'라고 했으므로 문맥상 빈칸 (A)에는 In fact 또는 Therefore가 들어가는 것이 적절하다. 빈칸 (B) 앞에서 유족들이 슬픔에 깊이 몰입하기를 권장하는 이집트에 관해서 서술하고, 빈칸 (B) 다음에 'in Bali, bereaved Muslims are encouraged to laugh and be joyful rather than be sad(발리에서는 이슬람교 유족들이 슬퍼하기보다는 웃고 기뻐하도록 권장된다).'라고 하면서 죽음을 애도하는 이집트와 발리의 대조적인 방식을 서술하고 있으므로 문맥상 빈칸 (B)에는 By contrast가 들어가는 것이 적절하다. 따라서 (A), (B)에 들어갈 말로 가장 적절한 것은 ②이다.

망자와의 관계 유지에 대한 믿음은 문화마다 다르다. 예를 들면, 일본의 종교의식에서는 고인과의 유대를 유지하는 것이 받아들여지고 지속된다. 하지만 애리조나의 Hopi 인디언들 사이에서는 고인이 가능한 한 빨리 잊히고 삶은 평소처럼 계속된다. (A) 실제로, Hopi의 장례 의식은 인간과 영혼 사이의 단절로 마무리된다. 애도의 다양성이 두 이슬람교 사회, 즉 이집트와 발리에서보다 더 극명한 곳은 없다. 이집트의 이슬람교도 사이에서 유족들은 비극적인 이야기에 유사하게 공감하고, 그들의 슬픔을 표현하는 다른 사람들에게 둘러싸여 슬픔에 오래 잠겨있도록 권장된다. (B) 반대로, 발리에서는 이슬람교 유족들이 슬퍼하기보다는 웃고 기뻐하도록 권장된다.

VOCA

- tie (강한) 유대(관계)
- vary 다르다
- the deceased 고인
- sustain 계속하다, 지속하다
- ritual 의식
- funeral 장례
- conclude with ~로 마무리짓다
- break-off 단절, 분리
- mortal (특히 아무 힘없는 일반 보통) 사람[인간]
- diversity 다양성
- grieve 비통해하다, 애도하다
- the bereaved 유족
- dwell on ~을 곱씹다, 숙고하다
- at length 오래
- grief 슬픔
- relate to ~에 공감하다
- tragic 비극적인
- account (있었던 일에 대한) 설명[이야기/말]

16 난도 ★★☆ 　　　　　정답 ④

독해 > 빈칸 완성 > 단어·구·절

정답의 이유

세 번째 문장에서 'Warm ocean water moving underneath the vast glaciers is causing them to melt even more quickly(거대한 빙하 아래에서 움직이는 따뜻한 바닷물이 빙하를 훨씬 더 빨리 녹게 하고 있다).'라고 했으며, 뒷부분에서 이와 관련된 구체적인 연구 결과에 관해 제시하고 있으므로 빈칸에 가장 적절한 것은 빙하가 더 빨리 녹는 과정에 대한 표현인 ④ 'accelerating(가속화하는)'이다.

오답의 이유

① 분리시키는
② 지연시키는
③ 방지하는

본문해석

과학자들은 더 높아진 대기 온도로 인해 그린란드 빙하의 표면이 녹고 있다는 것을 오래 전부터 알고 있었다. 하지만 새로운 연구는 아래로부터 빙하를 공격하기 시작한 또 다른 위협을 발견했는데, 거대한 빙하 아래에서 움직이는 따뜻한 바닷물이 빙하를 훨씬 더 빨리 녹게 하고 있다는 사실이다. 이 연구 결과는 그린란드 북동부에 위치한 빙하 79N(Nioghalvfjerdsfjorden Glacier)의 많은 'ice tongue' 중 하나를 연구한 연구자들에 의해 *Nature Geoscience*지에 실렸다. ice tongue은 육지의 빙하와 분리되지 않은 채로 물 위를 떠다니는 좁고 긴 얼음 조각이다. 이 과학자들이 연구한 그 거대한 ice tongue은 길이가 거의 50마일이다. 이 조사는 대서양에서 나온 따뜻한 물이 폭 1마일 이상의 수중 해류를 이루어 빙하로 직접 흘러갈 수 있으며, 많은 양의 열을 얼음과 접촉시켜 빙하가 녹는 것을 가속화하는 것을 밝혀냈다.

VOCA

- contribute to ~의 원인이 되다, ~에 기여하다
- ice sheet 대륙빙하
- glacier 빙하
- finding (조사·연구 등의) 결과, 결론
- strip 가느다랗고 긴 조각, 좁고 기다란 육지[바다]
- massive 거대한
- reveal 밝히다, 드러내다
- current 흐름, 해류, 기류

17 난도 ★★☆
정답 ③

독해 > 대의 파악 > 제목, 주제

정답의 이유

첫 문장에서 'Do people from different cultures view the world differently(다른 문화권의 사람들은 세상을 다르게 볼까)?'라고 질문하고, 이에 대한 답변으로 한 심리학자의 실험 결과를 제시하고 있다. 일본과 미국 학생들에게 동일한 수중 물체의 애니메이션 장면을 보여주었을 때 서로 다른 것에 초점을 두었다는 예시를 들어서로 다른 문화권의 사람들이 세상을 어떻게 다르게 보는지 설명하고 있으므로 글의 제목으로 적절한 것은 ③ 'Cultural Differences in Perception(인지에 있어서의 문화적 차이)'이다.

오답의 이유

① 일본인과 미국인 사이의 언어 장벽
② 뇌 안에서의 사물과 배경의 관련성
④ 꼼꼼한 사람들의 우수성

본문해석

다른 문화권의 사람들은 세상을 다르게 볼까? 한 심리학자가 일본과 미국 학생들에게 물고기와 다른 수중 물체의 사실적인 애니메이션 장면을 보여주며 그들이 본 것을 보고하도록 요구했다. 미국인들과 일본인들은 초점 물고기 수에 대해서는 거의 동일한 수를 언급했지만, 일본인들은 물, 바위, 거품, 그리고 비활동적인 동식물을 포함한 배경 요소들에 대해 60% 이상 더 많이 언급했다. 게다가, 일본과 미국의 참가자들은 활동적인 동물을 포함한 움직임에 대해서는 거의 동일한 수를 언급했지만, 일본의 참가자들은 비활동적인 배경 물체와 관련된 관계에 대해 거의 두 배 가까이 더 많이 언급했다. 아마도 가장 강력하게, 일본인 참가자들의 첫 문장은 환경을 나타내는 문장일 가능성이 높았던 반면, 미국인 참가자들의 첫 문장은 초점 물고기를 가리키는 문장이었을 가능성이 3배 더 많았다.

VOCA

• reference 언급
• focal 중심의, 초점의
• inert 비활성의, 비활동적인
• tellingly 강력하게
• language barrier 언어 장벽
• association 연상, 유대, 제휴

18 난도 ★★★
정답 ④

독해 > 글의 일관성 > 문장 삽입

정답의 이유

주어진 문장이 Thus(따라서)로 시작하므로 주어진 문장은 이전 문장의 결과를 설명하고 있음을 알 수 있다. 따라서, 주어진 문장 앞에는 '혈액이 뇌로 더 잘 순환될 수 있는 상황'이 제시되어야 한다. ④ 앞에서 앉거나 서 있는 대신 신체를 수평으로 하거나 누울 때 가해지는 중력은 혈액이 다리가 아닌 등에 울혈하기 때문에 사람들이 더 잘 견딜 수 있다고 했으므로 문맥상 주어진 문장이 들어갈 위치로 가장 적절한 곳은 ④이다.

본문해석

사람들은 다양한 방식으로 중력(g-force)에 노출될 수 있다. 그것은 등을 두드릴 때처럼 신체의 한 부위에만 영향을 미치는 국부적인 것일 수 있다. 그것은 또한 자동차 충돌사고 시 겪는 강한 힘처럼 순간적일 수도 있다. 중력의 세 번째 유형은 최소 몇 초 동안 이어지는 지속적인 것이다. 전신에 걸친 지속적인 중력이 사람들에게 가장 위험하다. 신체는 보통 지속적인 중력보다 국소적이거나 순간적인 중력을 더 잘 견디는데, 지속적인 중력은 혈액이 다리로 몰려 신체 나머지 부분에서 산소를 빼앗기 때문에 치명적일 수 있다. 앉거나 서 있는 대신 신체를 수평으로 하거나 누울 때 가해지는 지속적인 중력은 혈액이 다리가 아닌 등에 울혈하기 때문에 사람들이 더 잘 견딜 수 있는 경향이 있다. 따라서 심장이 혈액과 생명을 주는 산소를 뇌로 순환시키기 더 쉽다. 우주 비행사와 전투기 조종사 같은 일부 사람들은 중력에 대한 신체 저항을 증가시키기 위해 특별한 훈련 연습을 받는다.

VOCA

• circulate 순환시키다, 보내다
• gravitational force 중력, 인력
• localize 국한시키다[국부적이 되게 하다]
• momentary 순간적인
• endure 견디다
• sustain 지속[계속]시키다
• withstand 견디다, 참다
• deadly 치명적인
• deprive 빼앗다, 부족하게 하다
• horizontal 가로의, 수평의
• tend to ~하는 경향이 있다
• tolerable 참을 수 있는, 견딜 수 있는
• pool (피가) 울혈하다
• astronaut 우주비행사
• undergo 받다, 겪다
• resistance 저항

19 난도 ★★☆ 　　　　　　　　　정답 ①

독해 > 대의 파악 > 요지, 주장

[정답의 이유]

첫 문장 후반부에서 '~ you're usually better off proposing all your changes at once.'라며, 제안에 대한 협상을 한꺼번에 제시할 것을 조언하고 있다. 이어서 원하는 것을 한 가지씩 차례로 요구했을 경우 그로 인해 부정적인 결과가 야기될 수 있음을 암시하고 있다. 따라서 글의 요지로 가장 적절한 것은 ① 'Negotiate multiple issues simultaneously, not serially(여러 문제를 연속적이 아니라 동시에 협상해라).'이다.

[오답의 이유]

② 성공적인 협상을 위해 민감한 주제를 피하라.

③ 여러분의 협상을 위해 알맞은 시간을 선택하라.

④ 임금 협상을 할 때 너무 직설적으로 하지 마라.

본문해석

만약 누군가 여러분에게 제안하고 여러분이 그 일부에 대해 정당하게 걱정된다면, 보통 여러분의 모든 변경 요청을 한꺼번에 제안하는 것이 더 낫다. "월급이 좀 적어요. 어떻게 좀 해주시겠어요?"라고 말하고 나서 그녀가 작업을 마치면 "고맙습니다. 이제 제가 원하는 다른 두 가지가 있는데…"라고 말하지 마라. 처음에 한 가지만 요구한다면, 그녀는 그 한 가지가 해결된다면 여러분이 그 제안을 받아들일 준비가 되어 있다고 (적어도 결정을 내릴 준비가 되어 있다고) 생각할지 모른다. 만약 여러분이 계속해서 "그리고 한 가지 더…"라고 말한다면, 그녀는 관대하거나 이해심 많은 기분으로 계속 있지 않을 가능성이 높다. 게다가, 만약 여러분의 요구사항이 한 가지 이상이라면, 그 모든 것들을 A, B, C, D라고 단순히 언급하지 말고, 그것들 각각이 여러분에게 갖는 상대적 중요성에 대한 신호를 보내라. 그러지 않으면, 그녀는 여러분에게 제공하기 상당히 쉽다는 이유로 여러분이 가장 덜 중요하게 여기는 두 가지를 고르고, 여러분과 타협했다고 느낄지도 모른다.

VOCA

· legitimately 정당하게, 합법적으로

· be concerned about ~에 관심을 가지다, 걱정하다

· better off ~하는 것이 더 나은

· at once 동시에, 한번에

· initially 초기에, 처음에

· assume 추정하다, 가정하다

· relative 상대적인

· otherwise 그렇지 않으면

· meet ~ halfway ~와 타협[절충]하다

· negotiate 협상하다

· simultaneously 동시에, 일제히

· serially 연속으로

20 난도 ★★★ 　　　　　　　　　정답 ③

독해 > 글의 일관성 > 글의 순서

[정답의 이유]

주어진 글에서 두 번째 문장의 certain characteristics는 (B)의 첫 문장에서 these characteristics로 이어지고, (B)의 this idea에 관한 예시를 (C)에서 For example로 설명하고 있다. 마지막으로 획득형질 유전을 위해서는 DNA 변형이 필요하다는 (C)의 내용을 (A)에서 this로 받아 이것이 일어난다는 증거는 없지만 Lamarck의 가설이 Darwin의 장을 마련하는 데 도움이 되는 중요한 의미가 있다고 마무리 짓는 것이 자연스럽다. 따라서 글의 순서로 가장 적절한 것은 ③ '(B) - (C) - (A)'이다.

본문해석

오늘날, Lamarck는 적응이 어떻게 진화하는지에 대한 잘못된 설명으로 대부분 부당하게 기억된다. 그는 특정 신체 부위를 사용하거나 사용하지 않음으로써 유기체가 특정 형질을 발달시킨다고 제안했다.

(B) Lamarck는 이러한 형질이 자손에게 전해질 것이라고 생각했다. Lamarck는 이 발상을 '획득형질 유전'이라고 불렀다.

(C) 예를 들어, Lamarck는 캥거루의 강력한 뒷다리는 그 조상들이 점프로 그들의 다리를 강화시키고, 그 획득된 다리 힘을 자손에게 전한 결과라고 설명할 수 있다. 그러나 획득된 형질이 유전되려면 특정 유전자의 DNA를 어떻게든 변형시켜야 할 것이다.

(A) 이것이 일어난다는 증거는 없다. 그럼에도 불구하고, 유기체가 자신의 환경에 적응할 때 진화가 일어난다고 한 Lamarck의 제안에 주목하는 것은 중요하다. 이 발상은 Darwin을 위한 장을 마련하는 데 도움이 되었다.

VOCA

· unfairly 부당하게, 불공평하게

· adaptation 적응, 순응

· organism 유기체, 생물

· adapt to ~에 적응하다

· set the stage for ~을 위한 장을 마련하다

· pass on 넘겨주다, 물려주다, 전달하다

· offspring 자식, 자손, 새끼

· inheritance 유전

· acquire 획득하다, 얻다

· ancestor 조상

· somehow 어떻게든

· modify 변형하다, 수정하다

· gene 유전자

영어 | 2021년 국가직 9급

한눈에 훑어보기

✓ 영역 분석

어휘 01 02 03 04
4문항, 20%

독해 05 07 09 10 13 16 17 18 19 20
10문항, 50%

어법 06 08 14 15
4문항, 20%

표현 11 12
2문항, 10%

✓ 빠른 정답

01	02	03	04	05	06	07	08	09	10
①	②	②	④	④	②	③	③	④	④
11	**12**	**13**	**14**	**15**	**16**	**17**	**18**	**19**	**20**
①	②	④	④	②	①	②	③	④	①

✓ 점수 체크

구분	1회독	2회독	3회독
맞힌 문항 수	/ 20	/ 20	/ 20
나의 점수	점	점	점

---

01 난도 ★★☆   정답 ①

어휘 > 어구

[정답의 이유]

밑줄 친 in conjunction with는 '~와 함께'의 뜻으로 이와 의미가 가장 가까운 것은 ① 'in combination with(~와 결합하여)'이다.

[오답의 이유]

② ~에 비해서
③ ~ 대신에
④ ~의 경우

본문해석

사회적 관행으로서의 사생활은 다른 사회적 관행과 함께 개인의 행위를 형성하므로 사회생활의 중심이 된다.

VOCA

• shape 형성하다, 형태를 주다
• privacy 사생활
• practice 관행
• be central to ~의 중심이 되다

02 난도 ★☆☆   정답 ②

어휘 > 단어

[정답의 이유]

밑줄 친 pervasive는 '만연하는, 널리 퍼지는'의 뜻으로 이와 의미가 가장 가까운 것은 ② 'ubiquitous(어디에나 있는, 아주 흔한)'이다.

[오답의 이유]

① 기만적인, 현혹하는
③ 설득력 있는
④ 처참한

본문해석

재즈의 영향은 너무 만연해서 대부분의 대중음악은 재즈에 그 양식의 뿌리를 두고 있다.

VOCA

• owe A to B A는 B 덕분이다, A를 B에게 빚지다
• stylistic 양식의

03 난도 ★★☆   정답 ②

어휘 > 단어

[정답의 이유]

밑줄 친 vexed는 '짜증 난, 화난'의 뜻으로 이와 의미가 가장 가까운 것은 ② 'annoyed(짜증 난, 약이 오른)'이다.

[오답의 이유]

① 냉담한, 무정한

③ 평판이 좋은

④ 자신감 있는

[본문해석]

이 소설은 사업을 시작하기 위해 학교를 그만 둔 다루기 힘든 한 10대 청소년의 짜증 난 부모에 관한 것이다.

[VOCA]

- vexed 화가 난, 짜증 난, 골치 아픈
- unruly 제멋대로 구는, 다루기 힘든
- quit 그만두다

04 난도 ★★☆   정답 ④

어휘 > 어구

[정답의 이유]

밑줄 친 부분 다음의 the police station으로 미루어 문맥상 시위자들의 행위로 가장 적절한 표현은 ④ 'break into(침입하다, 난입하다)'이다.

[오답의 이유]

① 줄을 서다

② ~을 나눠 주다

③ 계속하다[가다]

[본문해석]

한 무리의 젊은 시위자들이 경찰서에 난입하려고 시도했다.

[VOCA]

- demonstrator 시위 참가자, 논쟁자
- attempt 시도하다

05 난도 ★★☆   정답 ④

독해 > 세부 내용 찾기 > 내용 (불)일치

[정답의 이유]

마지막 문장에서 '~ and slavery was also an institution in many African nations(또한 노예제도는 다수의 아프리카 국가들에서는 하나의 관행이었다)'라고 했으므로 글의 내용과 일치하는 것은 ④ 'Slavery existed even in African countries(노예제도는 심지어 아프리카 국가들에도 존재했다).'이다.

[오답의 이유]

① 아프리카 노동자들이 자발적으로 아메리카 대륙으로 이주했다. → 첫 번째 문장에서 'The most notorious case of imported labor is of course the Atlantic slave trade(수입 노동의 가장 악명 높은 사례는 당연히 대서양 노예매매인데) ~'라고 했으므로 글의 내용과 일치하지 않는다.

② 유럽인들은 노예 노동을 이용한 최초의 사람들이었다. → 두 번째 문장에서 '~ earlier, the ancient Egyptians used slave labor to build their pyramids, early Arab explorers were often also slave traders(일찍이 고대 이집트인들은 그들의 피라미드 건설에 노예 노동을 이용했고, 초기 아랍의 탐험가들은 종종 노예 상인이었으며) ~'라고 했으므로 글의 내용과 일치하지 않는다.

③ 아랍의 노예제도는 더 이상 어떠한 형태로도 존재하지 않는다. → 두 번째 문장의 마지막 부분에서 '~ and Arabic slavery continued into the twentieth century and indeed still continues in a few places(아랍의 노예제도는 20세기까지 계속되었고, 실제로 몇몇 지역에서는 여전히 지속되고 있다).'라고 했으므로 글의 내용과 일치하지 않는다.

[본문해석]

수입 노동의 가장 악명 높은 사례는 당연히 대서양 노예매매인데, 이것은 대규모 농장을 운영하기 위해 천만 명에 달하는 아프리카인 노예들을 아메리카 대륙으로 이주시켰다. 그러나 유럽인들이 노예제도를 가장 대규모로 실행하기는 했지만, 그들이 노예를 자신들의 지역사회로 데려온 유일한 사람들이 결코 아니었다. 일찍이 고대 이집트인들은 그들의 피라미드 건설에 노예 노동을 이용했고, 초기 아랍의 탐험가들은 종종 노예 상인이었으며, 아랍의 노예제도는 20세기까지 계속되었고, 실제로 몇몇 지역에서는 여전히 지속되고 있다. 아메리카 대륙에서 일부 원주민 부족들은 다른 부족의 원주민들을 노예로 삼았으며, 또한 노예제도는 특히 식민지 시대 이전에 다수의 아프리카 국가들에서는 하나의 관습이었다.

[VOCA]

- notorious 악명 높은
- enslave 노예로 만들다
- plantation 대규모 농장
- slavery 노예제도
- by no means 결코 ~이 아닌
- tribe 부족
- institution 관습, 제도
- colonial 식민지의
- voluntarily 자발적으로

06 난도 ★★☆　　정답 ②

어법 > 정문 찾기

정답의 이유

② since는 '~ 이래로'의 뜻으로 since가 포함된 전명구 또는 시간 부사절의 시제는 과거이며, 주절의 시제는 '기간'을 나타내는 현재완료 또는 현재완료진행이 사용된다. 따라서 have lived의 현재완료시제와 since I started의 과거시제가 모두 바르게 사용되었다.

오답의 이유

① 간접의문문의 어순은 '의문사＋주어＋동사'가 되어야 하므로 where should you visit → where you should visit가 되어야 한다.

③ 감정유발동사(excite)는 주어가 감정의 원인일 경우 현재분사(-ing)를 쓰고, 주어가 감정을 느끼는 경우 과거분사(-ed)를 쓴다. 소설이 흥미진진한 감정을 일으키는 것이므로 excited → exciting이 되어야 한다.

④ 부가의문문에서 주절이 부정문일 때 긍정부가의문문을 사용하고, 긍정문일 때 부정부가의문문을 사용한다. 동사가 be동사의 부정(is not)이므로 doesn't it → is it이 되어야 한다.

본문해석

① 이 안내책자는 여러분이 홍콩에서 어디를 방문해야 하는지를 알려준다.

② 나는 대만에서 태어났지만, 일을 시작한 이래로 나는 한국에서 살고 있다.

③ 그 소설은 너무 재미있어서 나는 시간 가는 줄 몰랐고 버스를 놓쳤다.

④ 서점들이 더 이상 신문을 취급하지 않는 것은 놀랍지 않다. 그렇지요?

VOCA

• lose track of time　시간 가는 줄 모르다
• carry　(가게에서 품목을) 취급하다

07 난도 ★★☆　　정답 ③

독해 > 대의 파악 > 제목, 주제

정답의 이유

제시문은 기후 변화와 물고기의 크기 감소에 관한 내용으로, 주제문은 따뜻한 수온과 바닷물 속의 산소 감소가 물고기의 크기를 줄어들게 할 것이라는 연구 결과를 언급하고 있는 첫 번째 문장이다. 그 이후에 구체적인 연구 내용에 대해 제시하고 있으므로 글의 제목으로 가장 적절한 것은 글의 중심 소재인 climate change, shrink, fish가 모두 포함된 ③ 'Climate Change May Shrink the World's Fish(기후 변화가 세계의 물고기 크기를 줄어들게 할 수 있다)'이다.

오답의 이유

① 현재 어류는 이전보다 더 빨리 성장한다
② 해양 온도에 미치는 산소의 영향
④ 해양생물이 낮은 신진대사로 생존하는 법

본문해석

따뜻해지는 기온과 바닷물 속 산소의 감소는 참치와 그루퍼부터 연어, 진환도상어, 해덕, 대구에 이르기까지 수백 종의 어종을 이전에 생각했던 것보다 더 많이 줄어들게 할 것이라고 새로운 연구는 결론이었다. 더 따뜻해진 바다는 신진대사를 활성화하기 때문에, 물고기와 오징어, 다른 수중 호흡 생물들은 바다에서 더 많은 산소를 흡수해야 할 것이다. 동시에, 온도가 상승하는 바다는 이미 해양의 많은 곳에서 산소 이용 가능성을 감소시키고 있다. University of British Columbia의 과학자 두 명은 주장하기를, 물고기의 몸통이 그들의 아가미보다 더 빠르게 자라기 때문에, 이 동물들은 결국 정상적으로 성장을 지속할 수 있을 만큼의 충분한 산소를 얻지 못하게 될 것이라고 한다. 저자 William Cheung은 말하기를, "우리가 발견한 것은 수온이 1도 상승할 때마다 물고기의 크기가 20~30퍼센트 줄어든다는 것이다."라고 한다.

VOCA

• shrink　줄어들게[오그라지게] 하다
• grouper　그루퍼(농엇과(科)의 식용어)
• thresher shark　진환도상어
• haddock　해덕(대구와 비슷하나 그보다 작은 바다 고기)
• cod　대구
• metabolism　신진대사
• draw　(연기나 공기를) 들이마시다[빨아들이다]
• argue　주장하다
• gill　아가미

08 난도 ★★☆　　정답 ③

어법 > 비문 찾기

정답의 이유

③ which 앞에 선행사가 없고, which 다음 문장이 목적어가 없는 불완전한 문장이다. Contrary to(전치사) 다음에는 명사 또는 명사구[절]가 와야 하므로, which → what이 되어야 한다. 이때 what은 동사(believe)의 목적어 역할을 하며, 명사절을 이끈다.

오답의 이유

① 타동사 realize의 뒤에 목적어가 없고, 주어 its potential은 '인식되는' 대상이므로 to부정사의 수동 형태(to be realized)가 올바르게 사용되었다.

② involve는 동명사를 목적어로 취하는 완전타동사로, creating은 타동사 involve의 목적어로 쓰였으므로 동명사 creating이 올바르게 사용되었다.

④ made 앞에 is가 생략된 수동태이다. 단수 주어(Valuable vacant land)에 맞춰 be동사가 is로 수일치되어 (is) made가 되었으며, 목적격 보어로 형용사 productive가 올바르게 사용되었다.

도시 농업(UA)은 오랫동안 도시에서는 마땅한 장소가 없는 비주류 활동이라고 무시되어 왔다. 그러나, 그것의 잠재력이 인식되기 시작하고 있다. 사실, 도시 농업(UA)은 식량 자립에 관한 것이다. 그것은 일자리 창출을 포함하며, 특히 가난한 사람들을 위한 식량 불안정에 대한 반응이다. 많은 사람들이 믿는 것과는 반대로, 도시 농업(UA)은 모든 도시에서 발견되는데, 그곳에서 이것은 때로 숨겨져 있거나, 때로는 확연히 보인다. 주의 깊게 살펴보면, 대도시에서는 사용되지 않는 공간이 거의 없다. 귀중한 공터는 방치된 곳이 거의 없고, 공식적으로든 비공식적으로든 종종 점유되어 있으며, 생산적이다.

VOCA

- dismiss 묵살하다, 일축하다, 치부하다
- fringe 비주류, 주변, 변두리
- self-reliance 자립, 자기 의존
- insecurity 불안정
- obvious 명백한, 분명한
- vacant 빈
- idle 사용되지 않고 있는, 노는
- take over 차지하다, 인수하다

더 알아보기

관계대명사 vs. what

- 선행사가 있으면 관계대명사가, 선행사가 없으면 what이 온다.

선행사	접속사	관계절 형태
있다	관계대명사 (that/ which / who/ whom)	주어+동사 동사+목적어
없다	what	불완전한 절(주어 또는 목적어가 없음)

- 관계대명사절은 선행사를 수식하는 형용사절이며, 불완전 문장이 이어진다.
- what절은 선행사가 없고 명사절(주어, 목적어, 보어 역할)이며, 불완전한 문장이 이어진다.

  예 I don't want to remember what they did to me.
  → what they did to me=to remember의 목적어
  (난 그들이 내게 한 짓을 기억하고 싶지 않다.)

  예 What is a medium size in Japan is a small size in here.
  → What is a medium size in Japan=문장의 주어
  (일본에서 중 사이즈는 여기서 소 사이즈이다.)

  예 That is what I mean.
  → what I mean=문장의 보어
  (그것이 내가 의미하는 것이다.)

- what=선행사+관계대명사

  예 She didn't understand what I said.
  =She didn't understand the fact that I said.
  (그녀는 내가 한 말을 이해하지 못했다.)

---

09 난도 ★★☆ 정답 ④

독해 > 글의 일관성 > 문장 삽입

정답의 이유

For example(예를 들어)로 시작하는 주어진 문장에서 '다수의 자료를 보관하고 있는 뉴저지주의 기록보관소'의 예시를 구체적으로 제시하고 있으므로 주어진 문장 이전에는 '기록보관소의 다양한 자료 보관'에 대한 일반적인 내용이 제시되어야 한다. ④ 앞의 문장에서 'Many state and local archives ~ an amazing, diverse resource(대다수 주 정부 기록보관소와 지역 기록보관소는 ~ 놀랍도록 다양한 자료들이다).'라고 한 다음에, 'For example, the state archives of New Jersey(예를 들어, 뉴저지의 주 기록보관소는 ~)'로 이어지는 것이 자연스럽다. 따라서 주어진 문장이 들어갈 위치로 가장 적절한 곳은 ④이다.

본문해석

기록보관소는 오디오에서 비디오, 신문, 잡지, 인쇄물들까지 자료들의 귀중한 발굴물이다. 이것이 그것들을 어떠한 역사 탐지 조사에서도 필수적으로 만든다. 도서관과 기록보관소가 동일하게 보일 수 있지만, 그 차이는 중요하다. 기록보관소의 수집품들은 거의 항상 1차 자료들로 구성되어 있지만, 도서관은 2차 자료들을 보유한다. 한국 전쟁에 대해 좀 더 배우기 위해, 여러분은 역사책을 보러 도서관에 갈 것이다. 정부 문서나 한국 전쟁 당시 군인들이 쓴 편지를 읽고 싶다면, 여러분은 기록보관소로 갈 것이다. 만약 정보를 찾고 있다면, 여러분을 위한 기록보관소에 있을 가능성이 있다. 대다수 주 정부 기록보관소와 지역 기록보관소는 공적인 기록을 저장하는데, 그것들은 놀랍도록 다양한 자료들이다. 예를 들어, 뉴저지의 주 기록보관소는 30,000입방 피트 이상의 문서와 25,000릴 이상의 마이크로 필름을 보유하고 있다. 주 정부 기록물을 온라인으로 검색하면, 입법부의 회의록보다 훨씬 더 많은 내용이 포함되어 있음을 즉시 보여줄 것이다. 정부 무상 불하지에 대한 자세한 정보가 발견될 수 있으며, 옛 마을지도, 범죄 기록 그리고 행상인 면허 신청서같이 특이한 것들도 발견된다.

VOCA

- archive 기록[공문서]보관소
- cubic feet 입방 피트
- reel (실 · 밧줄 · 녹음테이프 · 호스 등을 감는) 릴, 감는 틀
- treasure trove 보고, 매장물, 귀중한 발견
- indispensable 불가결의, 필수적인
- investigation 조사, 연구
- be made up of ~로 구성되다
- primary source (연구 · 조사 등의) 1차 자료
- secondary source 2차 자료(집필자가 원저작물이 아닌 다른 저작물을 통해 정보를 얻은 자료)
- chances are 아마 ~일 것이다, ~할 가능성이 충분하다
- diverse 다양한
- minutes 회의록
- legislature 입법부, 입법 기관
- land grant (대학 · 철도의 부지로서) 정부가 주는 땅, 무상 불하지

- oddity 괴짜, 괴상한 사람, 이상한 물건
- peddler 행상인

10 난도 ★★☆ 　　　　　　　　　　　정답 ④

독해 > 글의 일관성 > 무관한 어휘·문장

정답의 이유

제시문은 번아웃의 개념을 설명하는 글로, 번아웃이라는 용어의 개념을 감정의 소진, 개인적 성취감의 결여, 비인격화라는 세 가지 측면으로 나누어 설명하고 있다. ④는 번아웃과 반대되는 동기부여에 관한 내용이므로 글의 흐름상 가장 어색한 문장이다.

본문해석

번아웃(burnout)이라는 용어는 업무 압박으로부터 '소진되는[지치는]' 것을 의미한다. 번아웃은 일상의 업무 스트레스 요인이 직원들에게 피해를 준 결과 생기는 만성적인 질환이다. 가장 널리 채택된 번아웃에 대한 개념화는 사회복지 노동자들에 대한 연구에서 Maslach와 그녀의 동료들에 의해 개발되었다. Maslach는 번아웃이 세 가지 상호 관련된 측면으로 구성되어 있다고 보았다. 첫 번째 측면인 '감정의 소진'은 사실상 번아웃 현상의 핵심이다. 근로자들은 피곤하고, 좌절하고, 기진맥진하거나 직장에서 더 이상 일할 수 없다고 느낄 때 '감정의 소진'을 겪는다. 번아웃의 두 번째 측면은 개인적 성취감의 결여이다. 이러한 번아웃 현상의 측면은 자신을 실패자로 보면서 효과적으로 직무요건을 달성할 수 없다고 여기는 근로자들을 가리킨다. 감정 노동자들은 신체적으로 지쳤지만 매우 의욕적으로 그들의 일을 시작한다. 번아웃의 세 번째 측면은 비인격화이다. 이러한 측면은 일의 일부로 타인들(예를 들면, 고객, 환자, 학생들)과 대면하여 의사소통해야 하는 근로자들만 해당된다.

VOCA

- burnout 극도의 피로
- wear out 지치다
- chronic condition 만성질환
- take a[its] toll on ～에 큰 피해[타격]를 주다
- dimension 규모, 차원, 관점
- used up 몹시 지친
- depersonalization 몰개인화, 비인격화
- relevant 관련 있는, 적절한

11 난도 ★☆☆ 　　　　　　　　　　　정답 ①

표현 > 일반회화

정답의 이유

부엌의 위생 상태를 지적한 A가 빈칸 앞에서 'You know how important a clean kitchen is(깨끗한 주방이 얼마나 중요한지 알잖아요).'라고 했고, B가 빈칸 앞에서 'I'm sorry(죄송합니다).'라고 했으므로 빈칸에 들어갈 B의 답변으로 가장 적절한 것은 ① 'I won't let it happen again(다시는 이런 일이 일어나지 않게 할게요).'이다.

오답의 이유

② 계산서를 지금 드릴까요?
③ 그게 제가 어제 그것을 잊어버린 이유예요.
④ 주문한 음식이 제대로 나오도록 할게요.

본문해석

A: 어젯밤에 여기 있었나요?
B: 네. 마감 교대조로 일했어요. 왜 그러세요?
A: 오늘 아침에 주방이 엉망인 상태였어요. 스토브에 음식이 튀어 있었고, 제빙그릇은 냉장고에 있지 않았어요.
B: 제가 청소 체크리스트 점검을 잊어버린 것 같아요.
A: 깨끗한 주방이 얼마나 중요한지 알잖아요.
B: 죄송합니다. 다시는 이런 일이 일어나지 않게 할게요.

VOCA

- shift 교대 조
- mess 엉망인 상태
- spatter 튀기다
- ice tray 제빙그릇
- freezer 냉동고
- go over ～을 점검하다

12 난도 ★☆☆ 　　　　　　　　　　　정답 ②

표현 > 일반회화

정답의 이유

A가 감기에 걸린 B에게 비강 스프레이를 추천하는 상황의 대화문이다. 빈칸 앞에서 A가 비강 스프레이를 써봤는지 물었고, 대화의 마지막에 B가 'I don't like to put anything in my nose, so I've never used it(나는 코에 무엇이든 넣는 걸 싫어해서 사용해 본 적이 없어).'이라고 했으므로 B는 비강 스프레이 종류를 좋아하지 않아서 사용하지 않았다는 것을 알 수 있다. 따라서 빈칸에 적절한 것은 ② 'No, I don't like nose spray(아니, 난 비강 스프레이를 싫어해).'이다.

오답의 이유

① 응, 근데 도움이 되지 않았어.
③ 아니, 약국이 닫았어.
④ 응, 얼마나 써야 해?

본문해석

A : 감기를 낫게 하기 위해 무엇을 좀 먹었니?

B : 아니, 나는 그냥 코를 많이 풀어.

A : 비강 스프레이 써봤어?

B : 아니, 난 비강 스프레이를 싫어해.

A : 그거 효과가 좋아.

B : 아니, 괜찮아. 나는 코에 무엇이든 넣는 걸 싫어해서 사용해 본 적이 없어.

VOCA

- pharmacy 약국
- take (약을) 먹다
- blow one's nose 코를 풀다
- nose spray 비강 스프레이

13 난도 ★☆☆　　　　　　　　　　　　　　　　　정답 ④

독해 > 세부 내용 찾기 > 내용 (불)일치

정답의 이유

열 번째 문장에서 'The driest deserts, such as Chile's Atacama Desert, have parts(칠레의 Atacama 사막 같은 가장 건조한 사막에는 ~ 지역들이 있다) ~'라고 했으므로 글의 내용과 일치하지 않는 것은 ④ 'The Atacama Desert is one of the rainiest deserts (Atacama 사막은 비가 가장 많이 내리는 사막 중 하나이다).'이다. Atacama 사막은 연간 강수량이 2mm 미만인 가장 건조한 사막 중 하나이다.

오답의 이유

① 각 대륙에 적어도 하나의 사막이 있다. → 첫 번째 문장에서 '~ they are found on every continent(그것들은 모든 대륙에서 발견된다).'라고 했으므로 글의 내용과 일치한다.

② Sahara는 세계에서 가장 큰 더운 사막이다. → 여섯 번째 문장에서 'The largest hot desert in the world, northern Africa's Sahara, reaches temperatures of up to 50 degree Celsius(세계에서 가장 큰 더운 사막인 북아프리카의 Sahara는 최대 섭씨 50도의 온도에 도달한다) ~'라고 했으므로 글의 내용과 일치한다.

③ Gobi 사막은 추운 사막으로 분류된다. → 일곱 번째 문장에서 'But some deserts are always cold, like the Gobi Desert in Asia(하지만 아시아의 Gobi 사막 같은 일부 사막은 항상 춥다) ~'라고 했으므로 글의 내용과 일치한다.

본문해석

사막은 지구 육지의 1/5 이상을 덮고 있으며, 모든 대륙에서 발견된다. 일 년에 25센티미터(10인치) 미만의 비가 오는 장소는 사막으로 여겨진다. 사막은 건조 지역이라고 불리는 광범위한 지역의 일부이다. 이러한 지역들은 '수분 부족'인 상태인데, 그것은 이 지역들이 연간 강수량보다 증발을 통해서 수분을 더 많이 잃을 수 있다는 것을 의미한다. 사막은 덥다는 일반적 개념에도 불구하고, 추운 사막도 있다. 세계에서 가장 큰 더운 사막인 북아프리카의 Sahara 사막

은 낮 동안 최대 섭씨 50도(화씨 122도)의 온도에 도달한다. 하지만 아시아의 Gobi 사막과 세계에서 가장 큰 남극과 북극의 극지방 사막 같은 일부 사막은 항상 춥다. 다른 사막들에는 산이 많다. 오직 20퍼센트의 사막들만이 모래로 뒤덮여 있다. 칠레의 Atacama 사막 같은 가장 건조한 사막에는 1년에 강수량이 2mm(0.08인치) 미만인 지역들이 있다. 그러한 환경은 너무 황량하고 비현실적이어서 심지어 과학자들은 화성의 생명체에 대한 단서를 찾기 위해 그것들을 연구해 왔다. 반면에, 몇 년마다. 유난히 비가 많이 오는 시기는 'super blooms'를 만들어낼 수 있는데, 심지어 Atacama 사막조차도 야생화들로 뒤덮이게 된다.

VOCA

- continent 대륙
- moisture deficit 수분 부족
- evaporation 증발
- precipitation 강수, 강수량
- conception 이해, 개념
- antarctic 남극
- arctic 북극
- mountainous 산이 많은, 산지의
- harsh 혹독한
- otherworldly 비현실적인, 초자연적인
- super bloom 슈퍼 블룸(사막에 일시적으로 들꽃이 많이 피는 현상)

14 난도 ★☆☆　　　　　　　　　　　　　　　　　정답 ④

어법 > 영작하기

정답의 이유

④ '~도 역시 그렇다'는 표현은 긍정문의 경우는 so를 사용하며, so 다음에서 주어와 동사가 도치된다. 이때 동사가 일반 동사이면 do를 대신 써서 도치해야 하는데, 주어가 her son이고 동사가 일반 동사의 과거형인 loved이므로 did를 사용하여 'so did her son'이 올바르게 쓰였다.

오답의 이유

① 'look forward to -ing'는 '~하기를 고대하다'의 뜻으로 이때 to는 전치사이다. 따라서 목적어로 동명사가 와야 하므로 to receive → to receiving이 되어야 한다.

② rise는 자동사로 목적어를 가질 수 없는데, rise 다음에 목적어 (my salary)가 있으므로 rise → raise가 되어야 한다.

③ '~할 만한 가치가 있다'는 'be worth -ing'를 써야 하므로 worth considered → worth considering이 되어야 한다.

'역시 그렇다' *vs.* '역시 그렇지 않다'

• so+조동사[be동사]+주어: '주어도 역시 그렇다'

　예 Jane went to the movies, and so *did her sister*.

　　(Jane은 영화를 보러 갔고, 그녀의 여동생도 그랬다.)

　예 The answers people have come up with have changed a lot. So *has science* itself.

　　(사람들이 생각해낸 해답은 많이 달라졌다. 과학 그 자체도 그렇다.)

• neither[nor]+조동사[be동사]+주어: '주어도 역시 그렇지 않다'

　예 They didn't believe his story, and neither *did I*.

　　(그들은 그의 이야기를 믿지 않았고, 나도 믿지 않았다.)

　예 Not all companies seek to accomplish the same goals, nor *do they* operate with identical cultures.

　　(모든 회사가 동일한 목표를 달성하고자 하는 것은 아니며, 동일한 문화로 운영되는 것도 아니다.)

15　난도 ★☆☆　　　　　　　정답 ②

어법 > 영작하기

[정답의 이유]

② '너무 ~해서 …하다'라는 표현은 'so[such] ~ that'의 부사절 접속사 구문으로 쓴다. 'such ~ that' 표현의 경우 such 다음에 관사가 바로 오는 어순에 주의해야 한다. 'such+a[an]+형용사+명사'의 어순으로 바르게 사용되었다.

[오답의 이유]

① 'as if'는 '마치 ~인 것처럼'이라는 뜻의 접속사이므로 우리말 해석과 일치하지 않는다. '~일지라도'라는 양보의 의미가 되려면 '형용사[명사]+as+주어+동사'의 어순이 되어야 하므로 as if → as가 되어야 한다.

③ 'keep A −ing'는 'A가 계속 ~하게 하다'라는 의미이므로 우리말과 일치하지 않는 문장이다. 'A가 B 하는 것을 방해하다'라는 표현은 'keep A from B(−ing)'로 해야 한다. 따라서 kept her advancing → kept her from advancing으로 고쳐야 한다.

④ if는 바로 다음에 or not과 함께 쓸 수 없으므로 if가 whether로 바뀌거나 or not을 문장 끝으로 이동시켜야 한다.

VOCA

• sincere　진실한

• advance　전진하다, 나아가다, 진보[향상]하다

• meteor　유성

• abolish　폐지하다

16　난도 ★☆☆　　　　　　　정답 ①

독해 > 빈칸 완성 > 단어 · 구 · 절

[정답의 이유]

제시문은 영국인들의 온라인 쇼핑을 통한 소비 행태를 설명하는 내용으로, 두 번째 문장에서 소비자들은 온라인 쇼핑으로 고민 없이 옷을 사고 주요 의류 브랜드들이 저가의 옷들을 공급하기 때문에 소비자들은 그것들을 사서 두세 번 입고 버리는 일회용품 취급한다는 온라인 쇼핑의 문제점을 설명하고 있다. 빈칸 앞에서 '~ they're using it to buy things(그들은 ~한 물건을 사기 위해서도 돈을 쓰고 있다) ~'라고 했고, 빈칸 다음 문장에서 영국은 1년에 30만 톤의 의류를 버리는데, 그것의 대부분이 쓰레기 매립지로 간다고 했으므로 문맥상 빈칸에는 ① 'they don't need(그들이 필요하지 않은)' 물건을 구입하는 데 돈을 쓰고 있다는 내용이 들어가는 것이 적절하다.

[오답의 이유]

② 생활필수품인

③ 곧 재활용될

④ 그들이 다른 사람들에게 물려줄 수 있는

본문해석

소셜 미디어, 잡지 그리고 상점 진열장은 사람들에게 사야 할 것을 매일 쏟아내고, 영국 소비자들은 과거 어느 때보다 더 많은 옷과 신발을 구매하고 있다. 온라인 쇼핑은 소비자들이 고민하지 않고 쉽게 구매할 수 있으며 동시에 주요 브랜드들이 그러한 저가의 옷들을 공급하고 있기 때문에, 그 옷들은 두세 번 정도 입고 버려지는 일회용품처럼 취급될 수도 있다는 것을 의미한다. 영국에서, 일반 사람들은 매년 1,000파운드 이상을 새로운 의류 구입에 할애하며, 이는 그들의 수입 중 약 4%에 해당한다. 그것은 많은 것처럼 들리지 않을지도 모르지만, 그 수치에는 사회와 환경에 대한 두 가지 훨씬 더 우려되는 추세(경향)가 숨어 있다. 첫째, 소비자 지출의 많은 부분이 신용카드를 통해 이루어진다. 영국인들은 현재 신용카드 회사에 성인 1인당 거의 670파운드의 빚을 지고 있다. 이것은 평균 의류구입비 예산의 66%이다. 또한, 사람들은 가지고 있지 않은 돈을 소비할 뿐만 아니라, 필요하지 않은 물건을 사기 위해서도 돈을 쓰고 있다. 영국은 1년에 30만 톤의 의류를 버리는데, 그것의 대부분이 쓰레기 매립지로 간다.

VOCA

• bombard　퍼붓다[쏟아붓다]

• disposable　일회용의, 처분할 수 있는, 마음대로 쓸 수 있는

• income　소득, 수입

• figure　수치

• via　(특정한 사람 · 시스템 등을) 통하여

• approximately　거의, 대략, 대체로

• wardrobe　옷장, 옷

• budget　예산

• landfill　쓰레기 매립지

• necessity(necessities)　필요(성), 필수품, 불가피한 일

• recycle　재활용하다

• hand down to　~로 전하다, 물려주다

17 난도 ★☆☆   정답 ②

독해 > 빈칸 완성 > 단어 · 구 · 절

[정답의 이유]

빈칸 앞부분의 'Thus, only moderate savings are possible through improved efficiency, ~'에서 향상된 효율성을 통해서는 단지 중간 정도의 비용 절감만 가능하다고 했고, 그것은 가격 상승을 ~하게 만든다고 했으므로 서비스의 향상(세심한 개인적 서비스)을 위해서 가격 상승이 불가피한 것을 유추할 수 있다. 빈칸 다음에서 'Thus, the clientele of the fine-dining restaurant expects, ~'라고 탁월함을 위해 지불할 준비가 되어 있다고 언급하고 있으므로 밑줄 친 부분에 들어갈 말로 가장 적절한 것은 ② 'inevitable(불가피한)'이다.

[오답의 이유]

① 터무니없는

③ 엉뚱한

④ 상상도 할 수 없는

본문해석

탁월함은 고급 레스토랑에서는 절대적인 전제 조건인데, 그 이유는 청구되는 가격이 필연적으로 높기 때문이다. 운영자는 식당을 효율적으로 만들기 위해 가능한 할 수 있는 모든 것을 하겠지만, 손님들은 여전히 세심한 개인적 서비스, 즉 고도로 숙련된 주방장에 의해 (손님들의) 주문대로 음식이 준비되고 숙련된 서버가 서빙하는 것을 기대한다. 이 서비스는, 말 그대로, 육체노동이기 때문에, 오직 미미한 생산성 향상만이 가능하다. 예를 들어, 요리사, 서버 또는 바텐더는 인간 수행의 한계에 도달하기까지 단지 조금만 더 빨리 움직일 수 있다. 따라서 향상된 효율성을 통해 약간의 절약만이 가능하여 가격 상승이 불가피하다. (가격 상승에 따라 소비자들이 더 안목 있게 된다는 것은 경제학의 자명한 이치이다.) 따라서 고급 레스토랑의 고객은 탁월함을 기대하고, 요구하며, 기꺼이 탁월함에 대한 비용을 지불한다.

VOCA

• excellence 뛰어남, 탁월함

• absolute 절대적인

• prerequisite 전제 조건

• skilled 숙련된

• manual labor 수공일, 육체노동

• marginal 미미한

• only so much 제한된, 고작 이 정도까지인, 한계가 있는

• moderate 적절한, 적당한

• escalation 상승

• axiom 자명한 이치, 공리, 격언

• discriminating 안목 있는

• clientele (어떤 기관 · 상점 등의) 모든 의뢰인들[고객들]

18 난도 ★★☆   정답 ③

독해 > 글의 일관성 > 글의 순서

[정답의 이유]

주어진 글은 인간의 언어가 다른 동물들의 의사소통 체계와 비교하여 정교하다고 설명하고 있으므로 (C)의 영장류들조차도 기초적인 의사소통 체계 이상을 갖지 못한다는 내용으로 연결될 수 있다. 이어서 (A)에서 That said와 nevertheless를 사용해서 인간 외의 다른 많은 종들도 자연 환경에서 복잡한 의사소통을 한다는 내용으로 이어지는 게 자연스럽다. 결론적으로 (A)의 many species를 (B)에서 they로 받고, (A)의 '자연적 환경(natural settings)'과 대치되는 표현으로 (B)의 '인위적인 상황(artificial contexts)'을 제시하고 있다. 따라서 주어진 글 다음에 이어지는 글의 순서로 적절한 것은 ③ '(C) - (A) - (B)'이다.

본문해석

분명히, 인간의 언어는 원숭이나 영장류들의 명백히 제한된 발성보다 뛰어나다. 게다가 그것은 다른 형태 동물의 의사소통을 훨씬 능가하는 정교함을 보여준다.

(C) 심지어 우리와 가장 가까운 영장류 사촌들조차 수년 동안 집중적인 훈련을 거친 이후에도 기초적인 의사소통 체계 이상의 것은 습득하지 못하는 것처럼 보인다. 언어라는 복잡성은 확실히 한 종에만 국한된 고유한 특성이다.

(A) 그렇긴 해도, 인간의 언어에는 훨씬 못 미치지만, 그럼에도 불구하고 많은 종들이 자연환경에서 인상적으로 복잡한 의사소통 체계를 보인다.

(B) 그리고 그것들은 인간과 함께 키워질 때처럼, 인위적인 환경에서 훨씬 더 복잡한 체계를 배울 수 있다.

VOCA

• decidedly 확실히, 분명히, 단호히

• vocalization 발성(된 단어 · 소리), 발성(하기)

• ape 유인원

• sophistication 교양, 세련

• exhibit 드러내다, 보여주다

• artificial 인위적인, 인공적인

• context 상황, 환경

• primate 영장류

• incapable of ~할 수 없는

• rudimentary 가장 기본[기초]적인

• communicative 의사 전달의

• complexity 복잡성, 복잡함

• species-specific 한 종에만 국한된

• trait 특성

독해 > 대의 파악 > 제목, 주제

정답의 이유

제시문은 세계 자본주의의 영향과 반응에 관한 내용의 글이다. 세계화가 좋은 결과를 가지고 오긴 했지만, 저임금 노동자들을 착취하고 독점적 형태의 자본주의가 되었다고 비판하고, 이로 인해 자발적으로 민간단체 등에 가입하거나, 국제적 연합 세력 등이 생겨나는 등 여러 사회적 반응들이 나타났다고 기술하고 있으므로 글의 주제로 가장 적절한 것은 ④ 'The exploitative characteristics of global capitalism and diverse social reactions against it(세계 자본주의의 착취적인 성격과 그에 대한 다양한 사회적 반응들)'이다.

오답의 이유

① 과거 개발도상국에서 세계화에 대한 긍정적인 현상들
② 20세기의 사회주의의 쇠퇴와 자본주의의 출현
③ 세계 자본 시장과 좌익 정치 조직 간의 갈등

본문해석

20세기 후반에 사회주의는 서양과 개발도상국의 넓은 지역에서 후퇴하고 있었다. 시장 자본주의의 발전이라는 새로운 국면 동안, 세계의 무역 거래 형태는 점점 상호 연결되었고, 정보 기술의 발달은 규제가 해제된 금융 시장이 순식간에 국가 경계를 초월하여 거대한 자본의 흐름을 바꿀 수 있었다는 것을 의미했다. '세계화'는 무역을 활성화하고, 생산성 향상을 고취하고, 가격을 낮췄지만, 비평가들은 그것이 저임금 노동자들을 착취했고 환경 문제에 무관심하며, 제3세계 자본주의라는 독점적인 형태의 지배를 받게 했다고 주장했다. 이러한 과정에 대해 항의하고 싶었던 서양 사회의 많은 급진주의자들은 소외된 좌파 정당보다는 자발적인 단체, 자선 단체 그리고 다른 비정부 단체들에 가입했다. 환경 운동 자체는 세계가 서로 연결되어 있다는 인식에서 성장했으며, 만약 확산된다면 분노한 국제 이익 연합세력들이 출현했다.

VOCA

• retreat　후퇴, 철수
• interlink　연결하다
• deregulate　규제를 철폐하다
• boundary　경계
• allege　주장하다
• indifferent　무관심한
• subject A to B　A를 B에 복종[종속]시키다
• monopolistic　독점적인
• marginalize　(특히 사회의 진보에서) 처지다, 사회에서 소외되다
• interconnect　연결하다
• diffuse　분산되다, 확산되다
• coalition　연합(체)
• exploitative　착취적인

독해 > 대의 파악 > 분위기, 어조, 심경

정답의 이유

제시문은 우연히 특이한 돌을 발견한 어린 광부 Johnbull이 그것을 다른 광부에게 보여준 다음에 그 광부가 보인 반응을 보고 마음속으로 그 돌이 정말 보석일 수도 있다고 기대한다는 내용이다. 마지막 문장 'Could it be(과연 그럴까)?'로 미루어 그 돌이 진짜 다이아몬드일지도 모른다는 기대감을 지니고 있음을 유추할 수 있으므로 Johnbull의 심경으로 가장 적절한 것은 ① 'thrilled and excited (신나고 흥분한)'이다.

오답의 이유

② 고통스럽고 낙담한
③ 거만하고 확신에 찬
④ 무심하고 무관심한

본문해석

이글거리는 한낮의 태양 아래, 최근에 캐낸 자갈 더미에서 노란 달걀 모양의 돌멩이가 눈에 띄었다. 16살의 광부 Komba Johnbull은 호기심에 그것을 집어 들고 피라미드 모양의 납작한 면을 만지작거렸다. Johnbull은 다이아몬드를 본 적이 없었지만, 아무리 큰 발견물이라고 해도 그의 엄지손톱보다 크지 않을 거라는 사실 정도는 충분히 알고 있었다. 그럼에도 불구하고, 그 돌멩이는 다른 사람의 의견을 들어볼 만큼 충분히 특이했다. 그는 조심스럽게 정글 깊숙한 곳에서 진흙투성이 틈을 작업하고 있는 더 경험이 많은 광부들 중한 명에게 그것을 가지고 갔다. 현장 감독은 그 돌을 보고 눈이 휘둥그레졌다. "그것을 주머니에 넣어라." 그가 속삭였다. "계속해서 캐라." 그 나이 많은 광부는 누군가가 그들이 뭔가 대단한 것을 발견했다고 생각한다면 위험해질 수 있다고 그에게 경고했다. 그래서 Johnbull은 해질 때까지 계속해서 삽질하면서, 가끔 멈추어 그의 주먹에 있는 그 무거운 돌을 움켜잡았다. 과연 그럴까?

VOCA

• blazing　불타는 듯한
• stand out　눈에 띄다, 두드러지다
• unearth　파다
• gravel　자갈
• merit　받을 만하다[자격/가치가 있다]
• second opinion　다른 사람의 의견
• sheepishly　소심하게
• gash　(바위 등의) 갈라진 금[틈]
• pit boss　(광산의) 현장 감독
• dig　파다
• shovel　삽, 부삽, 삽으로 푸다

영어 | 2020년 국가직 9급

한눈에 훑어보기

✓ 영역 분석

어휘   01   02   03   04
4문항, 20%

독해   08   09   10   13   14   15   16   17   18   19   20
11문항, 55%

어법   05   06   07
3문항, 15%

표현   11   12
2문항, 10%

✓ 빠른 정답

01	02	03	04	05	06	07	08	09	10
①	④	③	①	④	②	③	②	①	④
11	12	13	14	15	16	17	18	19	20
④	③	②	③	③	④	④	③	①	②

✓ 점수 체크

구분	1회독	2회독	3회독
맞힌 문항 수	/ 20	/ 20	/ 20
나의 점수	점	점	점

---

01   난도 ★☆☆   정답 ①

어휘 > 단어

[정답의 이유]
밑줄 친 candid는 '솔직한, 정직한'의 뜻으로 이와 의미가 가장 가까운 것은 ① 'frank(솔직한)'이다.

[오답의 이유]
② 논리적인
③ 암시된
④ 열정적인

본문해석

전자레인지 모델과 스타일에 대한 광범위한 목록은 솔직한 고객 리뷰 및 가격대와 함께 가전제품 비교 웹사이트에서 이용할 수 있다.

VOCA

- extensive   (다루는 정보가) 광범위한, 폭넓은
- microwave oven   전자레인지
- price range   가격대
- appliance   (가정용) 기기, 전기 제품[기구]

02   난도 ★★☆   정답 ④

어휘 > 단어

[정답의 이유]
밑줄 친 conspicuous는 '눈에 잘 띄는, 뚜렷한'의 뜻으로 이와 의미가 가장 가까운 것은 ④ 'noticeable(뚜렷한, 현저한)'이다.

[오답의 이유]
① 수동적인
② 수증기가 가득한
③ 위험한

본문해석

Yellowstone이 사실상 화산 작용에 의해 만들어졌다는 것은 오랫동안 알려져 있었으며, 화산의 한 가지 특징은 일반적으로 눈에 잘 띈다는 것이다.

VOCA

- for a long time   오랫동안, 장기간
- volcanic   화산 작용에 의해 만들어진, 화산의
- in nature   사실상, 현실적으로

03 난도 ★☆☆　　　　　　　　　　　　　　정답 ③

어휘 > 어구

[정답의 이유]

밑줄 친 inside out은 '(안팎을) 뒤집어'라는 뜻으로, know ~ inside out은 '~을 (자기 손바닥 들여다보듯이) 환하게 알다'의 의미이다. 따라서 문맥상 그가 도시를 '속속들이 훤하게' 알고 있기 때문에 길을 안내할 적임자라는 것이므로 정답은 ③ 'thoroughly(완전히, 철저히)'이다.

[오답의 이유]

① 결국, 종내
② 문화적으로
④ 시험적으로, 망설이며

본문해석

그는 그 도시에 대해 속속들이 알고 있기 때문에, 당신에게 그곳에 어떻게 가는지 알려줄 적임자이다.

04 난도 ★★☆　　　　　　　　　　　　　　정답 ①

어휘 > 어구

[정답의 이유]

밑줄 친 pay tribute to는 '~에게 경의를 표하다'의 뜻으로 이와 의미가 가장 가까운 것은 ① 'honor(존경하다, 경의를 표하다)'이다.

[오답의 이유]

② 구성하다
③ 공표하다
④ 참여하다

본문해석

판지에, 눈에, 공작용 판지에 새겨진 메시지를 포함하여 그 팀에게 경의를 표하려는 수천 개의 소박한 시도들이 길을 따라 있었다.

VOCA

- homespun 소박한
- tribute 헌사[찬사], 공물
- etch 아로새기다
- cardboard 판지
- construction paper 공작용 판지

05 난도 ★★☆　　　　　　　　　　　　　　정답 ④

어법 > 정문 찾기

[정답의 이유]

④ be related to는 '~와 관계가 있다'의 뜻으로 전치사(to)의 목적어로 간접의문문이 왔다. 간접의문문의 어순은 '의문사＋형용사＋명사＋주어＋동사'이므로 'how much gray the color contains'로 올바르게 사용되었다.

[오답의 이유]

① 대명사(those)가 받는 대상이 단수명사(the traffic)이므로 those → that이 되어야 한다.
② 시간・조건 부사절에서 현재시제가 미래시제를 대신하므로 when절의 I'll be lying → I am lying이 되어야 한다.
③ '~하는 사람들'은 'the＋형용사'이므로 the wealth → the wealthy가 되어야 한다.

본문해석

① 대도시의 교통은 소도시의 그것보다 더 혼잡하다.
② 다음 주에 해변에 누워 있을 때, 나는 너를 생각할 거야.
③ 건포도는 한때 값비싼 음식이어서 부유한 사람들만 그것을 먹었다.
④ 색의 명도는 그 색이 얼마나 회색을 포함하고 있는지와 관련되어 있다.

VOCA

- raisin 건포도
- intensity 강도, 명도
- contain ~이 들어 있다

더 알아보기

간접의문문의 어순

- 의문사가 이끄는 명사절이 문장의 일부가 되는 것을 간접의문문이라고 한다.
- 간접의문문의 어순은 '의문사＋주어＋동사'이다.

　예 How much she pays for her clothes or where she buys them does not interest her husband.
　　(그녀가 옷값을 얼마나 내는지 혹은 어디서 구입하는지는 남편의 관심을 끌지 못한다.)

　예 I don't know how old this building is.
　　(나는 이 건물이 몇 년 된 건물인지 모른다.)

- 의문대명사와 의문부사

의문대명사	who, what, which＋불완전한 절
의문부사	when, where, why, how＋완전한 절

　예 I don't know what the password is.
　　(비밀번호가 뭔지 모르겠어요.)

　예 Could you tell me how I can get there?
　　(제가 거기에 어떻게 갈 수 있는지 말씀해 주시겠어요?)

어법 > 영작하기

정답의 이유

② '주장, 요구, 명령, 제안'을 나타내는 동사 다음에 that절이 오는 경우 that절의 동사는 '(should)+동사원형'이 되어야 하므로 동사원형(cease)이 적절하게 사용되었다. cease는 자동사 · 타동사 둘 다 가능한데, 제시된 문장에서는 자동사로 쓰였다.

오답의 이유

① raise는 '발생시키다'라는 의미의 타동사로 목적어가 필요하다. have raised 다음에 목적어가 없으므로 수동태인 have been raised 또는 '(사건 등이) 발생하다'는 의미의 자동사인 arise를 써서 have arisen으로 고쳐야 한다.

③ 주절의 시제는 과거(had to fight)인데 종속절의 시제가 미래(will blow)이므로 비문이다. 주절의 시제가 과거일 경우 종속절의 시제는 과거 또는 과거완료가 되어야 하므로 will blow → blew로 고쳐야 한다.

④ survive는 자동사로 '살아남다', 타동사로 '~보다 더 오래 살다'라는 뜻으로, 주어진 우리말에서 '살아남는다'라고 제시되었으므로 자동사로 사용되어야 한다. 따라서 are survived by → survive로 고쳐야 한다.

VOCA

• command 명령하다, 지시하다
• cease 중지하다, 그만두다
• harsh 혹독한, 가혹한

어법 > 영작하기

정답의 이유

③ promote는 타동사로 '승진시키다'의 뜻인데 promote의 목적어가 없고, 의미상 목적어인 him이 승진되는 것이므로 promoting → being promoted가 되어야 한다. 한편 prohibit은 완전타동사로서 'prohibit+목적어+from -ing'는 '목적어가 ~하는 것을 금지하다'의 뜻으로 적절하게 사용되었다.

오답의 이유

① 주어(Human beings)와 동사(adapt)의 수일치가 적절하며, 재귀대명사인 themselves 역시 올바르게 사용되었다.

② 'have no choice but to부정사' 구문은 '~하지 않을 수 없다'의 뜻으로 but 다음에 to부정사가 올바르게 사용되었다. cannot help but 동사원형, cannot help -ing로도 쓸 수 있다.

④ 가주어-진주어 구문으로 가주어(It), 진주어(to assemble and take apart the toy car)가 올바르게 사용되었다. 일반적으로 가주어-진주어 구문에는 난이형용사(easy, difficult 등)가 사용된다.

VOCA

• adapt (상황에) 적응하다
• assemble 조립하다; 모으다
• take apart 분해하다

독해 > 대의 파악 > 요지, 주장

정답의 이유

제시문은 대화에서의 듣기와 말하기의 조화가 중요하다는 내용으로, 대화에서의 듣기의 역할을 언급하고 경청 없이 말하는 것은 존중받지 못할 것이라고 설명하고 있다. 따라서 글의 요지로 적절한 것은 원만한 의사소통을 위해 상대방의 말을 잘 듣고, 동시에 자신의 의견을 목소리를 내어 주장해야 한다는 두 가지를 다 포함하는 ② 'We need to listen and speak up in order to communicate well(우리는 의사소통을 잘하기 위해서 경청하고 의견을 거리낌 없이 말할 필요가 있다).'이다.

오답의 이유

① 우리는 다른 사람들을 설득하기 위해 더 단호해야 한다.

③ 우리는 우리가 보는 세상에 대한 믿음을 바꾸기를 주저한다.

④ 우리는 오직 우리가 선택한 것만 듣고 다른 의견들을 무시하려고 한다.

본문해석

다른 사람의 생각을 듣는다는 것은 여러분 자신과 세상 안에서의 여러분의 위치뿐만 아니라, 여러분이 세상에 대해 믿는 이야기가 온전한지 알 수 있는 한 가지 방법이다. 우리는 모두 우리의 신념을 살펴보고, 그것들을 환기하고 그것들이 숨쉬게 할 필요가 있다. 다른 사람들이, 특히 우리가 기본적이라고 여기는 개념에 대해 말해야 하는 것을 듣는 것은 우리 정신과 마음에서 창문을 여는 것과 같다. 의견을 내는 것은 중요하다. 하지만 듣지 않고 의견을 내는 것은 냄비와 팬을 동시에 세게 치는 것과 같다. 비록 그것이 관심을 끌지라도, 존중받지는 못할 것이다. 대화가 의미를 갖기 위해서는 세 가지 전제 조건이 있다. 1. 여러분이 무엇에 대해 말하고 있는지 알아야 한다. 이는 여러분이 독창적인 요점을 가지고 있으며 진부하고 물려받은 또는 미리 만들어낸 주장을 그대로 따라 하지 않는다는 것을 의미한다. 2. 여러분과 이야기하고 있는 사람들을 존중하고, 비록 그들의 입장에 동의하지 않더라도 기꺼이 그들을 정중하게 대해야 한다. 3. 여러분은 계속해서 좋은 유머와 안목을 가지고 주제에 대한 자신의 관점을 다루면서 상대방이 말하는 것을 경청할 만큼 충분히 영리하고 정보를 잘 알아야 한다.

VOCA

• intact 온전한
• air out 환기하다
• foundational 기본의, 기초적인
• prerequisite 전제 조건
• worn-out 진부한, 흔해 빠진; 낡은
• hand-me-down 물려받은
• argument 주장, 논쟁
• authentically 진정으로, 확실하게
• courteously 예의바르게, 공손하게
• informed (특정 주제 · 상황에 대해) 잘 아는
• opposition (사업 · 경기 등에서의) 상대측
• perspective 관점, 시각

- uninterrupted 중단되지 않는, 연속된
- discernment 안목

- anonymity 익명(성)
- desirable 바람직한
- authenticity 진짜임, 진실성, 진정성
- collective 집단의, 공동의

09 난도 ★★☆   정답 ①

독해 > 대의 파악 > 제목, 주제

정답의 이유

첫 번째 문장과 두 번째 문장에서 '미래'와 '변화'라는 핵심 소재를 제시하였으며, 이후에 미래는 불확실한 것이고 변화하는 미래에 예술이 어떤 기능을 하고, 변화에 반응하는 예술의 모습은 어떨지 구체적인 예시를 들면서 설명하고 있다. 따라서 글의 제목으로 가장 적절한 것은 ① 'What will art look like in the future(미래에 예술은 어떤 모습일 것인가)?'이다.

오답의 이유

② 지구온난화는 우리의 삶에 어떻게 영향을 미칠 것인가?
③ 인공지능은 환경에 어떻게 영향을 미칠 것인가?
④ 정치 운동으로 인해 어떤 변화가 생길 것인가?

본문해석

미래는 불확실할지도 모르지만 기후 변화, 인구통계의 변화, 지정학 같은 어떤 것들은 부인할 수 없는 명백한 사실이다. 단 한 가지 확실한 것은 변화가 있으리라는 점인데, 그 변화는 좋을 수도 있고 끔찍할 수도 있다. 예술이 현재와 미래에 어떤 목적을 제공할지 뿐만 아니라, 이러한 변화에 예술가들이 어떻게 대응할지 고려할 가치가 있다. 보고서는 시사하기를 2040년까지 인간이 초래한 기후 변화의 영향은 피할 수 없을 것이며, 이는 20년 후 예술과 삶의 중심에서 큰 쟁점이 될 것이라고 한다. 미래의 예술가들은 포스트 휴먼과 포스트 인류세의 가능성, 즉 인공지능, 외계의 인간 식민지, 잠재적 파멸과 씨름할 것이다. #미투(MeToo)와 Black Lives Matter 운동을 중심으로 예술에서 보이는 정체성 정치는 환경주의, 국경 정치, 이주가 더욱 확실하게 뚜렷해지면서 성장할 것이다. 예술은 더욱 다양해질 것이고 우리가 기대하는 것만큼 '예술처럼 보이지' 않을 수도 있다. 미래에, 우리는 모두가 볼 수 있는 온라인에서 보여지는 우리의 삶에 지치고 우리의 사생활이 거의 없어지면, 익명성이 명성보다 더 바람직할 수도 있다. 수천, 수백만의 '좋아요'와 팔로워들 대신, 우리는 진실성과 관계를 갈망하게 될 것이다. 결과적으로, 예술은 개인적이기보다는 더 집단적이고 경험적인 것이 될 수 있다.

VOCA

- demographics 인구 통계 (자료)
- geopolitics 지정학
- guarantee 굳은 약속, 확약
- inescapable 피할 수 없는
- wrestle with ~을 해결하려고 애쓰다
- post-human 포스트 휴먼
- Anthropocene 인류세
- identity politics 정체성 정치학
- Black Lives Matter BLM 운동(아프리카계 미국인에 대한 경찰의 잔인함에 대항하는 비폭력 시민불복종 옹호 운동)
- come into focus (상황 따위가) 뚜렷해지다

10 난도 ★★☆   정답 ④

독해 > 세부 내용 찾기 > 내용 (불)일치

정답의 이유

제시문의 마지막 문장에서 미국의 총기 관련 범죄들이 1990년 최고치 이후로 감소해 왔다고 총기 소유권 지지자들이 언급한다고 했으므로 글의 내용과 일치하지 않는 것은 ④ 'Gun crimes in the U.S. have steadily increased over the last three decades(미국에서 총기 관련 범죄는 지난 30년간 꾸준히 증가해 왔다).'이다.

오답의 이유

① 2008년에 미국 대법원은 권총을 금지하는 워싱턴 DC 법안을 번복했다. → 세 번째 문장에서 법원이 권총을 금지하는 워싱턴 DC 법안을 폐지했다고 언급하고 있으므로 글의 내용과 일치한다.
② 대다수 총기 지지자들은 총기 소지가 생득권이라고 주장한다. → 네 번째 문장에서 언급하고 있으므로 글의 내용과 일치한다.
③ 선진국 중에서 미국은 총기에 의한 살인율이 가장 높다. → 일곱 번째 문장에서 언급하고 있으므로 글의 내용과 일치한다.

본문해석

미국 헌법 수정조항 제2조는, '잘 통제된 민병대는 자유주(남북 전쟁 전에 노예를 사용하지 않던 주)의 안보에 필수적이므로 무기를 소지하고 휴대할 국민의 권리는 침해될 수 없다.'라고 명시하고 있다. 대법원 판결들은 이 조항을 인용하면서 총기 규제에 대한 주의 권리를 유지해 왔다. 하지만 2008년 개인의 무기 소지와 휴대권에 대한 확인 판결에서, 법원은 개인의 총기소지 금지와 가정 내 권총을 잠가 두거나 분해할 것을 요구하는 워싱턴 DC 법안을 폐지했다. 많은 총기 지지자들은 총기 소유권을 생득권이자 국가 유산의 필수적인 부분으로 간주한다. 스위스에 본부를 두고 있는 Small Arms Survey의 2007년 보고서에 따르면, 전 세계 인구의 5%보다 적은 미국은 세계 민간 소유 총기의 약 35~50%를 차지하고 있다. 미국은 1인당 총기 소지에서 1위를 차지한다. 미국은 또한 선진국 중에서 총기에 의한 살인율이 가장 높다. 그러나 많은 총기 소유권 지지자들은 이 통계수치가 인과관계를 나타내지 못한다고 말하며, 미국의 총기 살인과 다른 총기 관련 범죄율은 1990년대 초 최고치 이후 떨어졌다고 언급한다.

VOCA

- Second Amendment 미국 헌법 수정조항 제2조
- constitution 헌법
- well-regulated 규칙이 잘 선
- militia 민병대, 의용군
- security 안보, 방위; 보장
- uphold (법·원칙 등을) 유지시키다[옹호하다]
- regulate 규제[통제/단속]하다
- firearm (소지가 가능한 권총 등의) 화기

- strike down (법정에서) 법률의 폐기를 결정하다
- birthright 생득권
- civilian-owned 민간 소유의
- per capita 1인당
- homicide 살인
- proponent (어떤 사상 · 행동 방침의) 지지자

11 난도 ★☆☆   정답 ④

표현 > 일반회화

정답의 이유

④ 요리 대회에서 입상했다는 A의 말에 대한 응답으로 마치 자신이 상을 탄 것처럼 얘기하는 B의 대답은 대화의 흐름상 어색하다.

본문해석

① A: 납부 기한이 언제입니까?
   B: 다음 주까지 내셔야 합니다.
② A: 이 짐을 부쳐야 할까요?
   B: 아니요, 기내에 갖고 탈 만큼 충분히 작네요.
③ A: 우리 언제 어디서 만날까?
   B: 8시 30분에 네 사무실로 태우러 갈게.
④ A: 요리 대회에서 상 탔어요.
   B: 당신이 없었다면 전 그것을 못했을 거예요.

VOCA

- payment 지급, 납입
- due (돈을) 지불해야 하는
- check ~ in (비행기 등을 탈 때) ~을 부치다
- pick ~ up ~을 (차에) 태우러 가다, 태우다

12 난도 ★☆☆   정답 ③

표현 > 일반회화

정답의 이유

빈칸 앞에서 A가 디럭스룸과 스위트룸 두 가지 객실을 제시하고, 빈칸 다음에서 A가 스위트룸의 특징을 설명하고 있으므로 빈칸에는 두 객실의 차이점을 묻는 ③ 'What's the difference between them(그것들의 차이점은 무엇이죠)'이 적절하다.

오답의 이유

① 또 필요한 게 있으신가요
② 객실 번호를 알 수 있을까요
④ 객실에 반려동물이 허용되나요

본문해석

A: Royal Point 호텔 예약 부서에 전화 주셔서 감사합니다. 제 이름은 Sam입니다. 무엇을 도와드릴까요?
B: 안녕하세요, 객실을 예약하고 싶어요.
A: 저희는 디럭스룸과 럭셔리 스위트룸 두 가지 타입을 제공하고 있습니다.

B: 그것들의 차이점은 무엇이죠?
A: 우선, 스위트룸은 매우 넓습니다. 침실 이외에도 주방, 거실, 식당이 있습니다.
B: 비쌀 것 같네요.
A: 네, 1박에 200달러 이상입니다.
B: 그러면, 저는 디럭스룸으로 할게요.

VOCA

- suite (호텔의) 스위트룸(연결된 몇 개의 방으로 이루어진 공간)
- in addition to ~에 더하여, 게다가
- in that case 그런 경우에는[그렇다면]

13 난도 ★☆☆   정답 ②

독해 > 빈칸 완성 > 연결어

정답의 이유

② 제시문은 홈스쿨링에 대한 찬반 입장을 서술하는 글이다. (A) 앞에서 홈스쿨링의 장점을 언급하였고, (A) 다음에는 홈스쿨링 반대자들의 의견을 제시하고 있으므로 (A)에는 대조의 연결사 In contrast(그에 반해서)가 적절하다. (B) 바로 앞 문장에서 홈스쿨링으로 학습한 아이들의 발달에 문제가 없다는 연구 결과를 제시하고, (B) 다음에서는 비평가들이 홈스쿨링을 하는 부모의 능력에 대한 우려를 제기한다고 하였으므로 (B)에는 양보의 연결사인 In spite of this(그럼에도 불구하고)가 적절하다.

오답의 이유

① 그러므로 - 그럼에도 불구하고
③ 그러므로 - 그와는 반대로
④ 그에 반해서 - 더욱이

본문해석

홈스쿨링을 지지하는 사람들은 아이들이 안정감 있고 애정 어린 환경에 있을 때 더 잘 배운다고 믿는다. 많은 심리학자들은 집을 가장 자연스러운 학습 환경으로 보고 있으며, 원래 집은 학교가 설립되기 훨씬 전에 교실이었다. 홈스쿨링을 하는 부모들은 자녀의 교육을 관찰할 수 있고 전통적인 학교 환경에서의 부족한 관심을 줄 수 있다고 주장한다. 학생들은 또한 무엇을 공부할지, 언제 공부할지 선택할 수 있어서 그들 자신의 속도로 학습할 수 있게 한다. (A) 그에 반해서, 홈스쿨링을 비판하는 사람들은 교실에 있지 않은 아이들은 또래와의 상호작용이 거의 없기 때문에 중요한 사회적 기능을 배우는 것을 놓친다고 말한다. 그렇지만 여러 연구들은 가정에서 교육받은 아이들이 그들의 행복에 신경을 쓰는 부모의 지도로 편안하고 안정적인 가정에서 더 많은 시간을 보내면서, 사회적이고 감정적인 발달에 있어 다른 학생들만큼 잘하는 것처럼 보인다는 것을 제시했다. (B) 그럼에도 불구하고, 많은 홈스쿨링 비판자들은 아이들을 효과적으로 가르칠 수 있는 부모의 능력에 대한 우려를 제기해 왔다.

VOCA

- advocate 옹호자, 지지자; 옹호하다
- pick and choose 까다롭게 고르다

- at one's own pace 자신만의 속도로
- critic (무엇의 나쁜 점을 특히 공적으로) 비판하는 사람; 비평가
- miss out on ~을 놓치다
- in terms of ~면에서

연결사의 종류

구분	연결사	의미
예시	for example, for instance	예를 들면
결과	thus, therefore, as a result	그러므로, 그 결과
결론	in conclusion, accordingly	결과적으로
열거	likewise, first of all, to begin with, finally, at last	마찬가지로, 우선, 마지막으로
부연	also, in addition, additionally, moreover, furthermore, besides	게다가
유사	similarly, likewise, in the same way	유사하게, 마찬가지로
요약	in brief[short], in summary, to sum up, to summarize	간단히 말하자면
반복	in other words, that is (to say), namely	다시 말하면, 즉
강조	in fact, indeed, above all, needless to say	사실은, 무엇보다도, 말할 필요도 없이
역접	but, however, still, though, nevertheless, nonetheless, despite, after all	그러나, 그럼에도 불구하고, ~에도 불구하고, 결국에는
비교 · 대조	on the other hand, in[by] contrast, on the contrary, while, contrary to, instead, rather	반면에, 대조적으로, 정반대로, ~와는 반대로, 대신에, 오히려

14 난도 ★★☆   정답 ③

독해 > 대의 파악 > 제목, 주제

정답의 이유

제시문은 과거에는 강박적으로 일에 몰두했지만 최근에는 여가와 업무의 유연성을 중요하게 생각한다는 내용으로, 세 번째 문장에서 'But increasingly, younger workers are pushing back(하지만 점점 젊은 근로자들이 반발하고 있다).'라고 한 다음에 근무 유연성에 대한 예로 원격 근무, 유급 출산 휴가, 넉넉한 휴가 기간, 출퇴근 시간의 유연성, 여가 확보 등을 제시하고 있으므로 글의 주제로 적절한 것은 ③ 'increasing call for flexibility at work(직장에서의 유연성에 대한 요구의 증가)'이다.

오답의 이유

① 급여를 인상시키는 방법
② 불평등을 감소시키려는 강박
④ 긴 휴가가 있는 생활의 장점

본문해석

많은 사람들에게 일은 강박이 되었다. 사람들이 급여를 위해 하는 일 외에 아이들, 열정적으로 하는 취미 활동, 반려동물, 혹은 어떤 종류의 생활을 위해서든 시간을 내려고 애쓰면서, 강박은 극도의 피로, 불행, 성 불평등을 초래했다. 하지만 점점 젊은 근로자들이 반발하고 있다. 그들 중 더 많은 이들이 유연성을 기대하고 요구하는데, 예를 들어 원격 근무, 늦은 출근이나 이른 퇴근 혹은 운동이나 명상을 위해 시간을 내는 것 같은 일상적인 것과 더불어 신생아를 위한 유급 휴가와 넉넉한 휴가 기간 등이다. 그들 생활의 나머지 부분이 특정한 장소나 시간에 얽매이지 않고 전화기상에서 일어나는데, 일이라고 달라야 할 이유가 있는가?

VOCA

- obsession 강박 관념
- burnout 극도의 피로
- inequity 불공평
- paycheck 급료
- push back 반발하다; 미루다
- remotely 원격으로, 멀리서
- tied to ~에 얽매이다

15 난도 ★☆☆   정답 ③

독해 > 글의 일관성 > 글의 순서

정답의 이유

주어진 글은 빈번한 심리적 스트레스 경험이 심혈관계 질병의 주요 원인이 될 수 있다는 내용이므로 가장 흔한 스트레스 원인 중 하나인 운전을 언급하는 (C)와 연결되는 것이 자연스럽다. (A)에서 this로 받아서 운전과 심장 질병과의 관계와 스트레스를 줄일 방안에 대해 묻는다. (B)에서 그에 대한 대답으로 '있다(there is)'라고 이어지며, 운전 중 음악 청취라는 방법을 소개한다. 따라서 주어진 글 다음에 이어질 글의 순서로 가장 적절한 것은 ③ '(C) - (A) - (B)'이다.

본문해석

과거의 연구는 빈번한 심리적 스트레스를 경험하는 것이 미국의 20세 이상 성인 중 거의 절반에게 영향을 주는 질환인 심혈관계 질병의 주요 위험 요인이 될 수 있다는 것을 보여주었다.

(C) 빈번한 스트레스의 한 가지 원인은 운전인데, 그것은 교통체증과 연관된 스트레스 요인 때문이거나 초보 운전자들에게 흔히 동반되는 불안 때문이다.

(A) 그렇지만, 이것이 매일 운전하는 사람들은 심장 질병에 걸리도록 예정되어 있다는 의미일까? 그게 아니면 운전 스트레스를 덜어줄 간단한 방법이 있을까?

(B) 새로운 연구에 따르면, (그 방법이) 있다. 연구원들은 운전하면서 음악을 듣는 것이 심장 건강에 영향을 미치는 스트레스를 완화시키는 데 도움이 된다고 언급했다.

16 난도 ★★☆ 정답 ④

독해 > 글의 일관성 > 무관한 어휘·문장

정답의 이유

제시문은 뇌가 위험을 인지한 상황에서 여러 신체 기관과 호르몬들이 어떻게 작용하는지 설명하는 글이다. ①~③은 위험 상황에서 부신이 아드레날린을 분비하여 동공을 넓히고, 혈액과 여분의 호르몬이 계속 흘러가도록 심장을 더 빠르게 펌프질하고, 골격근을 긴장시켜 위험에 반격하거나 달아날 준비를 시키는 등의 신체 반응이 일어난다고 했다. 하지만 '인간이 의식적으로 분비샘을 조절한다'는 ④는 다음 문장이 '호르몬은 설득되지 않는다'는 내용과도 논리적으로 이어지지 않으므로 흐름상 어색한 문장이다.

본문해석

뇌가 인접한 환경에서 위험을 감지하면, 뇌는 신체에서 복잡한 일련의 일을 시작한다. 뇌는 화학적 호르몬을 혈류로 내보내는 기관인 여러 분비샘에 전기 메시지를 보낸다. 혈액은 다양한 활동을 하도록 촉진되는 다른 기관들로 이러한 호르몬을 빠르게 운반한다. 예를 들어, 신장 위에 있는 부신은 신체의 스트레스 호르몬인 아드레날린을 만들어낸다. 아드레날린은 위험 신호를 살피기 위해 동공을 확장시키고, 혈액과 여분의 호르몬이 계속 흘러가도록 심장을 더 빠르게 펌프질하고, 골격근을 긴장시켜 위험에 반격하거나 위험으로부터 도망칠 준비를 하는 것 같은 일을 하면서 온몸을 돌아다닌다. 이 전체 과정은 투쟁-도피 반응이라고 불리는데, 그것은 신체가 살기 위해 싸우거나 도망치도록 준비시키기 때문이다. <u>인간은 다양한 호르몬의 분비를 조절하기 위해 분비샘을 의식적으로 통제한다.</u> 일단 이 반응이 시작되면 그것을 무시하는 것은 불가능한데, 호르몬들은 설득될 수 없기 때문이다.

VOCA

- perceive 인지하다, 감지하다
- initiate 시작하다
- a string of 여러 개의, 일련의
- gland (분비)샘
- adrenal glands 부신
- pump out (많은 양의) ～을 쏟아 내다[만들어 내다]
- be on the lookout for 세심히 살피다
- tense (사람·근육·신경 등을) 긴장시키다, 팽팽하게 하다
- skeletal muscle 골격근
- lash out at (～을) 마구 몰아세우다; 공격하다
- fight-or-flight response 투쟁-도피 반응(긴박한 위험 앞에서 자동적으로 나타나는 생리적 각성 상태)

17 난도 ★★☆ 정답 ④

독해 > 글의 일관성 > 문장 삽입

정답의 이유

제시문은 우연히 유리 플라스크를 깨뜨린 실수 때문에 안전유리를 발명하게 된 화학자에 대한 내용으로 시간 순서대로 전개되었다. 주어진 문장의 마지막 부분에서 '～ he imagined that a special coating might be applied to a glass windshield to keep it from shattering(그는 유리창이 산산조각 나는 것을 막기 위해서 앞 유리창에 특수 코팅이 적용될 수 있을 것이라고 상상했다).'이라고 했으므로 주어진 문장은 'Not long thereafter, he succeeded in producing the world's first sheet of safety glass(그 후 얼마 지나지 않아, 그는 세계 최초로 안전유리를 생산하는 데 성공했다).'라는 마지막 문장 앞인 ④에 들어가는 것이 적절하다.

본문해석

1903년 프랑스 화학자 Edouard Benedictus는 어느 날 단단한 바닥에 유리 플라스크를 떨어뜨려 깨트렸다. 그러나 놀랍게도 플라스크는 산산조각 나지 않았으며, 여전히 원래 형태를 대부분 유지하고 있었다. 그가 플라스크를 살폈을 때 (플라스크) 안쪽에 필름 코팅이 있는 것을 발견했는데, 잔여물이 플라스크에 담아두었던 콜로디온 용액에 남아 있었다. 그는 이 특이한 현상을 기록해두었으나, 몇 주 뒤 자동차 사고로 날아온 앞유리 파편에 의해 중상을 입은 사람들에 관한 기사를 읽고 나서야 그것에 관해 생각하게 되었다. <u>바로 그 때 그는 유리 플라스크에 관한 자신의 경험을 떠올렸고, 그는 재빨리 유리창이 산산조각 나는 것을 막기 위해서 앞 유리창에 특수 코팅이 적용될 수 있을 것이라고 상상했다.</u> 그 후 얼마 지나지 않아, 그는 세계 최초의 안전유리를 생산하는 데 성공했다.

VOCA

- flask (화학실험용) 플라스크
- apply to ～에 적용되다
- windshield (자동차의) 앞유리
- astonishment 깜짝 놀람
- shatter 산산이 부서지다, 산산조각 나다
- retain 계속 유지하다
- contain ～이 들어 있다
- collodion [화학] 콜로디온
- phenomenon 현상
- thereafter 그 후에
- succeed in ～에 성공하다

정답의 이유

네 번째 문장에서 Dubrovnik 시는 크루즈 관광을 억제하는 데 주도적이었다고 했으므로 글의 내용과 일치하지 않는 것은 ③ 'Dubrovnik 시는 크루즈 여행을 확대하려고 노력해 왔다.'이다.

오답의 이유

① 두 번째 문장에서 도시의 주요 관광명소가 80피트 중세 시대 벽으로 둘러싸인 해안가의 Old Town이라고 했으므로 글의 내용과 일치한다.

② 세 번째 문장에서 크루즈 배가 정박하면 Old Town은 탱크톱을 입은 관광객들이 거리를 확보한다고 했으므로 글의 내용과 일치한다.

④ 다섯 번째 문장에서 여분의 돈을 벌 수 있다는 유혹은 Old Town의 많은 집주인들이 자신들의 집을 Airbnb(숙박업소)로 바꾸도록 자극해서, 마을의 성벽 부분을 거대한 하나의 호텔이 되게 했다고 했으므로 글의 내용과 일치한다.

본문해석

크로아티아의 Dubrovnik는 엉망인 상태이다. 이 곳의 주요 관광명소가 80피트의 중세 시대 벽으로 둘러싸인 해안가의 Old Town이기 때문에 이 달마티안식 해안 마을은 방문객들을 잘 받아들이지 못한다. 그리고 크루즈 배가 이곳에 정박하면, 탱크톱을 입은 관광객 무리가 석회암으로 덮인 거리를 확보하면서 Old Town의 분위기를 불쾌하게 만든다. 그렇다. Dubrovnik 시는 크루즈 관광을 억제하려고 적극적으로 대책을 강구했지만, 어떤 것도 끊임없이 몰려드는 관광객 무리로부터 Old Town을 구할 수는 없을 것이다. 설상가상으로, 여분의 돈을 벌 수 있다는 유혹은 Old Town의 많은 집주인들을 자극해서 자신들의 집을 Airbnb(숙박업소)로 만들어, 마을의 성벽 부분을 거대한 하나의 호텔이 되게 했다. Old Town 시가지에서 지역 주민처럼 '진짜' Dubrovnik를 경험하기 원하는가? 여러분은 이 곳에서 그것을 발견하지 못할 것이다. 영원히.

VOCA

- medieval 중세의
- legion (특정한 유형의) 많은 사람들; 군단, 부대
- miasma (지저분한·불쾌한) 공기[기운]
- clad ~(옷)을 입은
- limestone 석회암
- blanketed ~로 덮인
- proactive 사전 대책을 강구하는
- curb 억제하다, 제한하다
- perpetual 끊임없이 계속되는, 영원한
- swarm (사람·동물의) 무리, 떼
- lure 유혹
- turn over (권리·책임 등을) 넘기다
- authentic 진정한, 진짜의

정답의 이유

(A)의 앞 문장에서 탄소-14가 질소로 붕괴된다고 하였으므로 (A)에는 시간이 지남에 따라 탄소-14의 양은 '감소한다(decreases)'는 내용이 와야 한다. (B)의 앞 문장에서 'Over time, less and less radiation from carbon-14 is produced(시간이 흐르면서 탄소-14에서 나오는 방사선의 양이 점점 줄어든다).'라고 했으므로 생물이 '죽은(dead)' 지 오래될수록 탄소-14 방사선의 양이 점점 더 줄어든다는 것을 유추할 수 있다. 따라서 (A), (B)에 들어갈 말로 가장 적절한 것은 ① (A) 'decreases(감소하다)' – (B) 'dead(죽은)'이다.

오답의 이유

② 증가하다 – 살아있는

③ 감소하다 – 생산적인

④ 증가하다 – 활발하지 않은

본문해석

유기체가 살아있을 때, 그것은 주변의 공기로부터 이산화탄소를 흡수한다. 이산화탄소의 대부분은 탄소-12로 이루어져 있지만, 아주 소량은 탄소-14로 구성된다. 그래서 살아있는 유기체는 언제나 매우 적은 양의 방사성 탄소인 탄소-14를 포함하고 있다. 살아있는 유기체 옆의 측정기는 유기체에서 탄소-14에 의해 방출된 방사선을 기록한다. 유기체가 죽으면 그 유기체는 더 이상 이산화탄소를 흡수하지 않는다. 새로운 탄소-14가 더해지지 않으며, 오래된 탄소-14는 서서히 질소로 자연 붕괴한다. 탄소-14의 양은 시간이 지남에 따라 서서히 (A) 감소한다. 시간이 흐르면서 탄소-14에서 나오는 방사선의 양이 점점 줄어든다. 따라서 유기체에서 감지된 탄소-14 방사선의 양은 유기체가 (B) 죽은 지 얼마나 되었는지를 측정하는 척도이다. 유기체의 나이를 결정짓는 이러한 방법을 방사성 탄소-14 연대측정법이라고 한다. 탄소-14의 붕괴는 고고학자들이 이전에 살았던 물질의 연대를 알아낼 수 있게 해준다. 남아있는 방사선의 양을 측정하면 대략적인 연대를 알 수 있다.

VOCA

- organism 유기체, (극도로 작은) 생물체
- take in 흡수하다, 섭취하다
- radioactive 방사성[능]의
- detector 탐지기, 측정기
- give off (냄새·열·빛 등을) 내다[발하다]
- decay (방사성 물질이) 자연 붕괴하다; 부패하다
- nitrogen 질소
- as time goes on 시간이 지남에 따라, 갈수록
- measure (판단·측정의) 척도[기준]
- archaeologist 고고학자
- indicate (사실임·존재함을) 나타내다, 보여주다
- approximate 거의 정확한, 근사한, 대략의

독해 > 빈칸 완성 > 단어·구·절

정답의 이유

제시문은 수많은 종들이 과거에 사라졌고, 앞으로 멸종할 것이지만 이를 대체하기 위해 새로운 종들이 계속해서 등장하고 있다는 내용이다. 빈칸 앞 문장에서 소수의 단순한 유기체로부터 대단히 많은 복잡한 다세포적 형태들이 오랜 기간에 걸쳐 진화했다고 하였고, 빈칸 다음 문장에서 '~ the actual number is possibly closer to 10 million(실제 숫자는 아마 1천만에 가까울 것이다).'이라고 했으므로 빈칸에 가장 적절한 것은 ② 'diversity of living creatures(생명체의 다양성)'이다.

오답의 이유

① 생물학자들의 기술
③ 멸종 유기체의 목록
④ 멸종 위기 종 모음

본문해석

과거와 현재의 모든 생물들은 이미 사라졌거나 앞으로 멸종할 것이다. 그러나 과거 38억 년 지구 생명체 역사에 걸쳐 각 종들이 사라지면 새로운 종들이 필연적으로 등장해서 이들을 대신하거나 새로 생겨난 자원을 소비했다. 아주 단순한 소수의 유기체로부터 대단히 많은 복잡한 다세포적 형태들이 이 어마어마한 기간 동안 진화했다. 19세기 영국의 박물학자인 Charles Darwin이 한때 '불가사의 중의 불가사의'라고 언급했던 새로운 종의 기원은 인간이 지구를 공유하고 있는 이 놀라운 생명체의 다양성을 발생시키는 자연스러운 종 형성의 과정이다. 분류학자들이 현재 150만의 생물 종을 인지하고 있지만, 실제 숫자는 아마 1천만에 가까울 것이다. 이러한 다수의 생물학적 상태를 인식하는 것은 무엇이 하나의 종을 이루는지에 대한 명확한 이해가 필요한데, 이것은 진화생물학자들이 보편적으로 수용 가능한 하나의 정의에 대해 아직 합의하지 못했음을 감안하면 쉬운 일이 아니다.

VOCA

• extinct 멸종된
• vanish 사라지다, 없어지다
• inevitably 필연적으로, 불가피하게
• exploit 이용하다, 착취하다
• multicellular 다세포의
• evolve 진화하다, 발달하다
• refer to A as B A를 B라고 언급하다
• speciation 종 형성, 종 분화
• taxonomist 분류학자
• constitute ～을 구성하다[이루다]
• have yet to+동사원형 아직 ～하지 않았다

한눈에 훑어보기

✓ 영역 분석

어휘   01 02 14 15
4문항, 20%

독해   09 10 11 12 13 16 17 18 19 20
10문항, 50%

어법   05 06 07 08
4문항, 20%

표현   03 04
2문항, 10%

✓ 빠른 정답

01	02	03	04	05	06	07	08	09	10
①	②	④	②	②	①	②	④	④	③
11	12	13	14	15	16	17	18	19	20
④	②	③	③	①	①	④	③	②	④

✓ 점수 체크

구분	1회독	2회독	3회독
맞힌 문항 수	/ 20	/ 20	/ 20
나의 점수	점	점	점

01 난도 ★☆☆   정답 ①

어휘 > 단어

정답의 이유

밑줄 친 discern은 '구별하다'의 뜻으로 이와 의미가 가장 가까운 것은 ① 'distinguish(구별하다)'이다.

오답의 이유

② 강화하다

③ 약화시키다

④ 버리다, 포기하다

본문해석

Natural Gas World 구독자들은 그 산업에서 무엇이 일어나고 있는지에 대하여 정확하고 신뢰할 만한 중요한 사실과 수치를 받게 되므로 그들은 무엇이 그들의 사업과 관계되는지 충분히 구별할 수 있다.

VOCA

• subscriber 구독자

• reliable 신뢰할 만한

• concern ~에 관계하다, 관여하다

02 난도 ★☆☆   정답 ②

어휘 > 어구

정답의 이유

밑줄 친 stand out은 '눈에 띄다, 두드러지다'의 뜻으로 이와 의미가 가장 가까운 것은 ② 'was impressive(돋보였다)'이다.

오답의 이유

① 압도되었다

③ 우울했다

④ 긍정적이었다

본문해석

여자 1,500미터 경기 은메달리스트인 Ms. West는 경기 내내 돋보였다.

03 난도 ★★☆   정답 ④

표현 > 일반회화

정답의 이유

④ 'Do you mind ~?'로 질문할 경우 긍정은 'No(네, 좋아요)', 부정은 'Yes(아니요, 싫어요)'이다. B가 처음에 'Never mind(신경 쓰지 마세요).'라고 했으므로 이어지는 대답은 'Go ahead(계속 하세요).'가 되어야 한다.

본문해석

① A: 해외여행을 갈 예정이야. 하지만 난 다른 나라에서 머무는 게 익숙하지 않아.
  B: 걱정하지 마. 곧 익숙해질 거야.
② A: 나는 사진 대회에서 상 받고 싶어.
  B: 받을 거라고 확신해. 행운을 빌게!
③ A: 가장 친한 친구가 세종시로 이사 갔어. 그녀가 너무 보고 싶어.
  B: 그래. 네 기분이 어떨지 알 것 같아.
④ A: 잠시 이야기해도 괜찮을까요?
  B: 신경 쓰지 마세요. 저는 지금 매우 바빠요.

VOCA

• get accustomed to ~에 익숙해지다
• in no time 곧, 당장에
• keep one's fingers crossed 행운을 빌다

04 난도 ★☆☆   정답 ②

표현 > 일반회화

정답의 이유

빈칸 다음에서 A가 'You pick one up with your chopsticks like this and dip it into the sauce(이렇게 젓가락으로 하나를 집어서 소스에 찍으면 돼요).'라고 먹는 방법을 설명하고 있으므로 빈칸에는 먹는 방법을 물어보는 ② 'how do I eat them(제가 그것들을 어떻게 먹어야 하죠)'이 적절하다.

오답의 이유

① 그것들은 얼마인가요
③ 그것들은 얼마나 매운가요
④ 그것들을 어떻게 요리하나요

본문해석

A: 딤섬 좀 드시겠어요?
B: 네, 감사합니다. 맛있어 보이네요. 안에 뭐가 들었죠?
A: 이것들은 돼지고기와 다진 채소가 들어 있고, 저것들은 새우가 들어 있어요.
B: 그리고, 음, 제가 그것들을 어떻게 먹어야 하죠?
A: 이렇게 젓가락으로 하나를 집어서 소스에 찍으면 돼요. 쉬워요.
B: 알겠어요. 한번 해볼게요.

05 난도 ★★☆   정답 ②

어법 > 영작하기

정답의 이유

② shy of는 '모자라는, 부족한'의 뜻으로 전치사 before 또는 ago 처럼 쓰인다. 우리말에서 '5분이 지난 후'라고 했으므로 five minutes shy of midnight → five minutes past midnight로 고쳐야 한다.

오답의 이유

① The new teacher가 선행사이며, 전치사 about의 목적어 역할을 하는 목적격 관계대명사(whom)가 생략되어 바르게 영작되었다.
③ 선행사를 포함한 관계대명사 what은 '~하는 것'의 뜻으로 명사절(What appeared to be a shark)이 문장의 주어이며, what절은 단수동사로 수일치하므로 was가 올바르게 쓰였다.
④ reach는 자동사로 혼동하기 쉬운 타동사로 전치사구가 아닌 목적어 the mountain summit를 올바르게 사용했다. '숫자+단위'의 명사가 뒤의 명사를 수식하는 형용사의 기능을 할 때는 단수로 표현하므로 16-year-old가 올바르게 쓰였다.

06 난도 ★★☆   정답 ①

어법 > 영작하기

정답의 이유

① per person은 '개인당'의 뜻이므로 '개인용 컴퓨터'는 computers per person → personal computers로 고쳐야 한다.

오답의 이유

② 명사절 What happened to my lovely grandson last summer는 문장의 주어로 what은 선행사를 포함하고 있는 관계대명사이다. what절은 단수동사로 수일치하므로 was가 올바르게 사용되었다.
③ 긍정문에 대한 동의를 나타낼 때 'So+do[does/did]+주어' 또는 'So+be동사+주어'의 어순이므로 올바르게 사용되었다.
④ since는 '~ 이후로'의 뜻으로 주절은 현재완료진행(have been doing), 부사절은 과거시제(retired)로 올바르게 사용되었다.

07 난도 ★★☆   정답 ②

어법 > 비문 찾기

정답의 이유

② 분사구문의 의미상 주어가 주절의 주어(animals)와 같고, 이 주어(animals)가 다른 기술과 함께 이용된다는 '수동'의 의미이므로 Utilizing(현재분사) → Utilized(과거분사)가 되어야 한다.

오답의 이유

① 명사(machines)를 수식하는 형용사가 전치사와 함께 사용하는 형용사구일 때는 명사 뒤에서 수식한다.
③ '명사+to부정사'의 형용사적 용법으로 '~할 명사'의 뜻이다. carry는 타동사로 목적어(burdens)를 취한다.
④ 'of+추상명사'는 형용사로 쓰이므로 'of great benefit'이 beneficial의 뜻으로 올바르게 사용되었다.

가축화된 동물은 인간이 이용할 수 있는 최초의 가장 효과적인 '기계'이다. 그들은 인간의 등과 팔의 부담을 덜어준다. 다른 기술들과 함께 이용될 때, 가축들은 (고기와 우유의 단백질 같은) 보충 식량으로서, 짐을 옮기고, 물을 들어 올리고, 곡물을 빻는 기계로서 인간 삶의 기준을 매우 향상시킬 수 있다. 그것들은 분명히 큰 이득이 되기 때문에, 우리는 수 세기에 걸쳐 인간이 그들이 기르고 있는 동물들의 수와 질을 증가시킨다는 것을 발견하기를 예상할지도 모른다. 놀랍게도, 이것은 대체로 그렇지는 않았다.

VOCA

- domesticated 가축화된
- strain 부담, 압박; 혹사하다
- considerably 상당히, 많이
- supplementary 보충의, 추가의
- foodstuff 식품, 식량

더 알아보기

분사구문

- 분사 vs. 분사구문

분사	형용사적 성격: 명사를 수식하여 명사구를 만든다. 예 energy stored in muscle (근육에 저장된 에너지) 예 A drowning man will catch a straw. (물에 빠진 사람은 지푸라기라도 잡는다.) 예 Do you know the man mowing the lawn? (잔디를 깎고 있는 남자를 알고 있니?)
분사 구문	부사적 성격: 부사절이 변형된 표현으로, 분사(현재분사와 과거분사)를 포함한다. 예 It being cold outside, I boiled some water to have tea. (바깥 날씨가 추워서, 나는 차를 마시기 위해 물을 끓였다.) 예 Covered with confusion, he left the conference room. (그가 혼란에 빠진 채로 회의실을 떠났다.)

- 분사구문의 형태
  - 능동태: 주절의 주어가 분사구문의 동작을 행하는 경우
    - 예 Walking on the street, I witnessed a car accident.
      (거리를 걷다가 나는 교통사고를 목격했다.)
  - 수동태: 주절의 주어가 분사구문의 동작을 당하는 경우
    - 예 Seen from the universe, the earth is blue.
      (우주에서 보면 지구는 푸른색이다.)

08 난도 ★★☆　　　　　　　　정답 ④

어법 > 비문 찾기

정답의 이유

④ refer to A as B는 'A를 B로 언급하다'의 뜻으로, 의미상으로 볼 때 the Old and New Testaments가 '언급되는' 것이므로 refer to as → be referred to as가 되어야 한다.

오답의 이유

① help는 to부정사와 동사원형(원형부정사)을 모두 취할 수 있다.
② try는 to부정사와 동명사를 취하며, 'try+to부정사'는 '~하려고 노력하다', 'try+동명사'는 '~를 시도해 보다'의 뜻이다. 문맥상 '이해하려고 노력하는'의 뜻이므로 try to make가 올바르게 사용되었다.
③ that은 선행사(stories)를 수식하는 관계대명사로 관계대명사절의 주어 역할을 하는 주격 관계대명사에 해당한다.

신화는 한 문화의 종교적, 철학적, 도덕적, 정치적 가치를 구현하고, 어떤 경우에는 설명을 도와주는 서사이다. 신들과 초자연적인 존재의 이야기를 통해서, 신화는 자연 세계 내 현상들을 이해하려고 노력한다. 대중의 어법과는 반대로, 신화는 '거짓말'을 의미하지는 않는다. 가장 넓은 의미에서, 신화는 거짓일 뿐만 아니라 진실일 수도 있고, 부분적으로 진실일 수도 있는 이야기들, 보통은 이야기들의 전체적인 모음이다. 하지만 정확성의 정도와는 상관없이 신화는 주로 한 문화의 가장 깊은 믿음을 표현한다. 이 정의에 따르면, 일리아드와 오딧세이, 코란, 구약성서와 신약성서는 모두 신화로 언급될 수 있다.

VOCA

- supernatural 초자연적인
- make sense 의미가 통하다, 이해가 되다
- occurrence 발생하는 것, 발생, 나타남
- contrary to ~에 반해서
- falsehood 거짓임, 거짓말
- regardless of ~에 상관없이

09 난도 ★★★　　　　　　　　정답 ④

독해 > 대의 파악 > 제목, 주제

정답의 이유

지도 제작이 전통적인 개념을 벗어나 다양한 분야에서 활용되고 있음을 설명하는 글로 첫 번째 문장에서 'Mapping technologies are being used in many new applications(지도 제작술은 많은 새로운 응용 분야에서 사용되고 있다).'라고 했으므로 글의 제목으로 가장 적절한 것은 ④ 'Mapping New Frontiers(새로운 분야의 지도 제작)'이다.

오답의 이유

① 컴퓨터화된 지도 vs. 전통적인 지도
② 지도 제작은 어디에서 시작되는가?
③ DNA 비밀에 대한 방식 찾기

지도 제작술은 많은 새로운 응용 분야에서 사용되고 있다. 생물학을 연구하는 사람들은 DNA의 분자 구조를 분석(게놈의 지도화)하고 있으며, 지구 물리학자들은 지구 중심핵의 구조를 지도화하고, 해양학자들은 해저를 지도화하고 있다. 컴퓨터 게임에는 다양한 가상의 '땅' 또는 단계가 있어 규칙, 위험, 보상이 변한다. 컴퓨터화는 이제 특별한 상황을 자극하는 인공의 환경인 '가상 현실'로 현실에 도전하는데, 그것은 훈련과 오락에 유용할지도 모른다. 지도 제작 기술들은 아이디어 영역에서도 사용되고 있다. 예를 들어, 아이디어 간의 관계는 개념도라 불리는 것을 사용하여 나타낼 수 있다. 일반적이거나 '중심적인' 생각에서 시작하여 관련된 아이디어들은 주요 개념을 중심으로 망을 구축하면서 연결될 수 있다. 이것은 어떠한 전통적인 정의에 의한 지도는 아니지만, 지도 제작술의 도구와 기법이 그것을 생산하기 위해 이용되었으며, 어떤 면에서 그것은 지도와 닮았다.

- application 적용, 응용
- molecular 분자의
- geophysicist 지구 물리학자
- oceanographer 해양학자
- imaginary 가상의
- realm 영역, 범위; 왕국
- cartography 지도 제작(법)

10 난도 ★★☆   정답 ③

독해 > 대의 파악 > 요지, 주장

정답의 이유

제시문은 상대방에게 피드백을 줄 때는 상대방을 고려해야 한다는 내용으로 첫 번째 문장이 글의 요지이며, 고성과자, 적절한 성과가 있는 사람, 성과가 좋지 않은 사람마다 피드백이 달라야 한다는 구체적인 예시를 들어 설명하고 있다. 따라서 글의 요지로 적절한 것은 ③ 'Tailor feedback to the person(피드백을 사람들에게 맞춰라).'이다.

오답의 이유

① 피드백 시기를 잘 조절하라.
② 부정적인 피드백을 사람들에게 맞춰서 하라.
④ 목표 지향적인 피드백을 피해라.

본문해석

성과에 대한 피드백을 줄 때, 여러분은 피드백을 받는 사람의 과거 성과와 빈도, 양, 내용 설계에 있어 그[그녀]의 장래 잠재력에 대한 여러분의 추정치를 고려해야 한다. 성장 가능성이 있는 고성과자에게는 그들이 수정 조치를 취하도록 자극할 만큼 피드백을 자주 주어야 하지만, 그것이 통제로 경험되거나 그들의 자주성을 약화게 할 정도로 너무 빈번하게 해서는 안 된다. 자신들의 업무에 정착하여 승진 가능성이 제한적인 적절한 성과자들에게는 피드백은 거의 필요하지 않는데, 왜냐하면 그들은 과거에 믿음직스럽고 안정된 행동

을 보였으며 자신들의 업무를 알고 있고 무엇을 해야 하는지도 인식하고 있기 때문이다. 저성과자, 즉 성과가 향상되지 않으면 직장에서 퇴출되어야 할 사람들에게 있어 피드백은 자주, 매우 구체적이어야 하며 피드백에 따른 행동과 일시 해고 또는 해고 같은 부정적인 제재 간의 연관성을 명시해야 한다.

- prod ~ into ~에게 …하도록 자극하다
- sap 약화시키다
- initiative 계획; 결단력, 자주성
- settle into 윤곽이 잡히다; 정리되다, 자리 잡다
- sanction 처벌, 벌칙
- explicit 분명한

11 난도 ★★☆   정답 ④

독해 > 세부 내용 찾기 > 내용 (불)일치

정답의 이유

마지막 문장에서 '~ Hughes attacked racial prejudice in a way that was natural and witty(Hughes는 자연스럽고 재치 있는 방식으로 인종 편견을 공격했다).'라고 했으므로 글의 내용과 일치하지 않는 것은 ④ 'Hughes는 인종 편견을 엄숙한 문체로 공격하였다.'이다.

오답의 이유

① 첫 번째 문장에서 '~ in which many African-American students have pursued their academic disciplines(그곳에서 많은 아프리카계 미국 학생들이 자신들의 학문을 추구하였다).'라고 했으므로 글의 내용과 일치한다.
② 세 번째 문장에서 'Hughes incorporated authentic dialect in his work(Hughes는 그의 작품에 실제 방언을 포함했고) ~'라고 했으므로 글의 내용과 일치한다.
③ 세 번째 문장에서 '~ and created characters and themes that reflected elements of lower-class black culture(하층 계급 흑인의 문화 요소들을 반영하는 인물과 주제를 창조했다).'라고 했으므로 글의 내용과 일치한다.

본문해석

Langston Hughes는 미주리주의 조플린에서 태어났으며 Lincoln 대학교를 졸업했는데, 그곳에서 많은 아프리카계 미국 학생들이 자신들의 학문을 추구하였다. 18세에, Hughes는 그의 가장 널리 알려진 시 중 한 편인 "Negro Speaks of Rivers."를 출간했다. 창의적이고 실험적인 Hughes는 그의 작품에 실제 방언을 포함했고, 블루스와 재즈의 리듬과 분위기를 아우르기 위해 전통적인 시의 형태들을 각색했으며 하층 계급 흑인의 문화 요소들을 반영하는 인물과 주제를 창조했다. 심각한 내용과 유머러스한 스타일을 결합시키는 그의 능력으로 Hughes는 자연스럽고 재치 있는 방식으로 인종 편견을 공격했다.

VOCA

- pursue 추구하다, 계속하다, 뒤쫓다
- discipline 학문
- incorporate (일부로) 포함하다
- authentic 진짜의, 정확한
- dialect 방언, 사투리
- cadence 억양, (시의) 운율, 리듬
- embrace 수용하다
- adapt 각색하다, 번안하다
- fuse A with B A와 B를 융합하다
- prejudice 편견

12 난도 ★★☆   정답 ②

독해 > 글의 일관성 > 무관한 어휘 · 문장

정답의 이유

제시문은 2007년 월스트리트 은행들의 위험한 투자로 인해 경제 위기가 초래되었으나, 그 이후 거대 기관의 정기적인 스트레스 테스트가 이루어지고 있다는 것이 중심 내용이므로 글의 흐름상 어색한 문장은 가상화폐에 대해 설명하는 ②이다.

본문해석

2007년 우리의 가장 큰 걱정거리는 '파산하기에는 너무 크다'는 것이었다. 월스트리트의 은행들은 너무도 믿기 어려운 크기로 성장했고, 금융 시스템의 건전성이 매우 중요해졌기 때문에 어떤 분별력 있는 정부라도 결코 그들을 무너지게 내버려 둘 수 없었다. 은행은 보호받는 그들의 지위를 인식하여, 주택 시장에 지나치게 위험한 배팅을 했고 심지어 훨씬 더 복잡한 금융 파생상품을 고안해 냈다. 비트코인과 이더리움 같은 새로운 가상화폐는 돈이 어떻게 작용할 수 있고 작용해야 하는지에 대한 우리의 이해를 급격하게 변화시켰다. 그 결과는 1929년 경제 붕괴 이후의 가장 최악의 금융 위기였다. 2007년 이후로 몇 년 동안, 우리는 '파산하기에는 너무나 큰' 딜레마를 다루는 데 대단한 진전을 이루었다. 우리의 은행들은 그 전보다 더 자본화되었다. 우리의 규제 담당자들은 거대 기관의 정기적인 스트레스 테스트를 실시한다.

VOCA

- staggering (너무 엄청나서) 충격적인, 믿기 어려운
- rational 합리적인, 이성적인
- status 지위, 신분
- excessively 지나치게, 심히
- derivative 파생물
- virtual currency 가상통화, 가상화폐
- radically 철저히, 근본적으로
- breakdown 실패, 붕괴

13 난도 ★★☆   정답 ③

독해 > 대의 파악 > 제목, 주제

정답의 이유

제시문은 단순한 이름을 가진 사람과 복잡한 이름을 가진 사람을 예로 들면서 단순한 이름을 가진 사람들이 사회생활에서 얻는 이점을 설명하고 있다. 마지막 문장에서 'So simplicity is one key feature in names that determines various outcomes(그러므로 단순성은 다양한 결과들을 결정하는 이름에서 하나의 핵심적 특징이다).'라고 했으므로 글의 주제로 가장 적절한 것은 ③ 'the benefit of simple names(단순한 이름의 장점)'이다.

오답의 이유

① 법적 이름의 발전
② 매력적인 이름의 개념
④ 외국 이름의 기원

본문해석

두 사람이 같은 날 로펌에서 근무를 시작했다고 상상해 보라. 한 사람은 아주 단순한 이름을 가지고 있다. 다른 한 사람은 아주 복잡한 이름을 가지고 있다. 우리는 그들이 이후 16년 이상의 경력 과정 동안 더 단순한 이름을 가진 사람이 더 빠르게 법조계의 고위층에 오를 것이라는 꽤 타당한 근거를 가지고 있다. 그들은 경력 중간에 더 빠르게 파트너십을 이룰 것이다. 그리고 로스쿨을 졸업한 지 8년 내지 9년차 쯤까지 더 단순한 이름을 가진 사람들이 파트너가 될 가능성이 약 7~10% 더 높은데, 이는 놀라운 결과이다. 우리는 다른 대안이 되는 모든 종류의 설명을 없애려고 시도한다. 예를 들어, 우리는 그것이 외래성에 관한 것은 아니라는 것을 보여주려고 하는데, 왜냐하면 외국 이름이 발음하기에 더 어려운 경향이 있기 때문이다. 그러나 정말로 진정한 내집단에 속하는 영미식 이름을 가진 백인 남성들을 보더라도, 영국계 이름을 가진 그 백인 남성들 사이에서 만약 그들의 이름이 더 단순하다면, 그들이 더 올라갈 가능성이 높다는 것을 알게 된다. 그러므로 단순성은 다양한 결과들을 결정하는 이름에서 하나의 핵심적 특징이다.

VOCA

- over the course of ~ 동안
- hierarchy (사회나 조직 내의) 계급[계층], 지배층[고위층]
- partnership 공동 경영, 동반자 관계, 동업
- attain 이루다
- be likely to ~할 것 같다
- striking 눈에 띄는, 현저한
- eliminate 없애다, 제거하다
- alternative 대안이 되는, 대체 가능한
- in-group 내집단(조직 · 사회 내부의 배타적인 소규모 집단)

14 난도 ★★☆   정답 ③

어휘 > 단어

정답의 이유

밑줄 친 compulsory는 '의무적인, 필수의'의 뜻으로 이와 의미가 가장 가까운 것은 ③ 'mandatory(의무적인)'이다.

오답의 이유

① 상호 보완적인

② 체계적인

④ 혁신적인

본문해석

학교 교육은 미국의 모든 어린이들에게 의무적이지만, 학교 출석이 요구되는 연령대는 주(州)마다 다르다.

VOCA

• schooling 학교 교육

• age range 연령대

• school attendance 학교 출석

• vary from A to B A에서 B까지 다양하다

15 난도 ★★☆   정답 ①

어휘 > 단어

정답의 이유

밑줄 친 disclose는 '밝히다, 폭로하다'의 뜻으로 이와 의미가 가장 가까운 것은 ① 'let on(누설하다)'이다.

오답의 이유

② 발사하다, 면하게 해주다

③ 누그러지다

④ 실망시키다

본문해석

비록 그 여배우가 그녀의 경력에서 많은 혼란을 겪었지만, 그녀는 결코 누구에게도 그녀가 행복하지 않다는 것을 밝히지 않았다.

VOCA

• turmoil 혼란, 소란

16 난도 ★★★   정답 ①

독해 > 빈칸 완성 > 연결어

정답의 이유

① 빈칸 (A) 앞에서 선지자들은 무언가를 처음으로 발견하는 사람들이며, 그 장점은 아무도 그것을 발견하지 못했을 때 존재한다고 했다. (A) 다음에서 그들은 충분히 테스트된[이미 발견된] 상품을 구매하지 않는다고 했으므로 (A)에는 인과를 나타내는 'therefore(그러므로)'가 적절하다. 빈칸 (B) 다음에서 선지자들이 발견한 내용을 바탕으로 물건을 사는 실용주의자들에 대해 설명하고 있으므로 (B)에는 대조를 나타내는 'on the other hand(반면에)'가 적절하다.

오답의 이유

② 그러나 – 게다가

③ 그렇기는 하지만 – 동시에

④ 더욱이 – 끝으로

본문해석

선지자들은 그들의 업종 부문에서 새로운 기술의 잠재력을 알아보는 최초의 사람들이다. 기본적으로, 그들은 경쟁사에 있는 그들과 대등한 지위의 사람들보다 자신들이 더 똑똑하다고 생각하는데, 꽤 자주, 정말 그렇다. 실제로 경쟁우위로 이용하기 원하는 것을 가장 먼저 보는 것이 그들의 능력이다. 이 장점은 오직 아무도 그것을 발견하지 못했을 때만 일어난다. (A) 그러므로 그들은 광범위한 업계의 참고목록을 통해서 충분히 테스트된 제품을 구매하는 것을 기대하지 않는다. 정말로 만약 이와 같은 참고자료의 근거가 존재한다면, 그것은 사실상 그들을 흥미 잃게 만들지도 모르는데, 이는 어쨌든 그들이 그 기술에 대해 이미 너무 늦었다는 것을 나타내기 때문이다. (B) 반면에, 실용주의자들은 다른 회사에 있는 동료의 경험을 높이 평가한다. 그들은 구매할 때, 광범위한 참고자료를 기대하고 그들 자신의 업종 부문 내 기업들로부터 더 많은 참고자료가 나오기를 원한다.

VOCA

• visionary 선지자, 선견지명 있는, 환영의

• segment 분야, 부문

• leverage into ∼을 이용하다

• come about 생기다, 일어나다

• turn off 신경을 끊다, 생각하지 않다

• indicate 나타내다, 보여주다

• pragmatist 실용주의자

17 난도 ★★☆　　　　　　정답 ④

독해 > 글의 일관성 > 문장 삽입

정답의 이유

주어진 문장의 'Some of these ailments are short-lived; others may be long-lasting(이러한 질병들 중 일부는 단기적이지만, 다른 경우에는 오래 지속될 수 있다).'은 ④ 앞 문장의 'physiological and psychological problems(생리적, 심리적 문제)'와 연결된다. 또한 ④ 다음에서 우주비행사들 중 3분의 2 이상이 무중력 환경을 여행하는 도중 멀미와 메스꺼움으로 고통받는다고 했으므로 주어진 문장이 들어갈 위치로 가장 적절한 것은 ④이다.

본문해석

수 세기 동안, 인간은 하늘을 올려다보고 지구의 영역 너머에 무엇이 존재하는지 궁금해했다. 고대의 천문학자들은 우주에 관하여 더 많은 것을 알기를 원하며 밤하늘을 조사했다. 최근 들어서, 어떤 영화들은 우주 공간에서 인간의 삶을 유지할 수 있는 가능성을 탐구했고, 반면 다른 영화들은 외계 생명체가 우리 행성을 방문했을 수도 있는지에 대한 의문을 제기했다. 우주비행사 Yuri Gagarin이 1961년에 우주를 여행한 최초의 인간이 된 이후, 과학자들은 지구 대기권 너머의 환경이 어떤지와 우주여행이 인체에 어떤 영향을 주는지를 연구했다. 비록 대부분 우주비행사들이 우주에서 몇 개월 이상을 보내지는 않지만, 많은 이들이 지구로 돌아왔을 때 생리적, 심리적 문제를 경험한다. 이러한 질병들 중 일부는 단기적이지만, 다른 것들은 오래 지속될 수 있다. 모든 우주비행사들 중 3분의 2 이상이 우주를 여행하는 동안 멀미로 고통받는다. 무중력 환경에서, 신체는 위아래를 구별할 수 없다. 체내 균형체계는 뇌에 혼란스러운 신호들을 보내는데, 이것은 며칠 동안 메스꺼움을 유발할 수 있다.

VOCA

- extraterrestrial　지구 밖 생명체의, 외계의
- physiological　생리적인, 생리학의
- ailment　질병
- suffer from　~으로 고통받다
- motion sickness　멀미
- differentiate　구별하다
- nausea　메스꺼움

18 난도 ★★★　　　　　　정답 ③

독해 > 빈칸 완성 > 단어 · 구 · 절

정답의 이유

빈칸 다음에서 문학 수업에서 유전자에 대해 배우지 않고, 물리학 수업에서 진화를 배우지 않는다고 했고, 'So you get a partial view of the world(따라서 여러분은 세계에 대한 부분적인 시각을 갖게 된다).'라고 했으므로 빈칸에 들어갈 가장 적절한 것은 ③ 'Today, we teach and learn about our world in fragments(오늘날, 우리는 우리의 세계에 대해 단편적으로 가르치고 배운다)'이다.

오답의 이유

① 과거에, 역사 연구는 과학으로부터 각성을 요구했다
② 최근에, 과학은 우리에게 많은 기발한 비결들과 의의를 주었다
④ 최근, 역사는 몇 가지 분야로 나누어졌다

본문해석

왜 모든 것의 역사를 신경 쓰는가? 오늘날, 우리는 우리의 세계에 대해 단편적으로 가르치고 배운다. 문학 수업에서 여러분은 유전자에 대해 배우지 않고, 물리학 수업에서 인류의 진화에 대해 배우지 않는다. 따라서 여러분은 세계에 대한 부분적인 시각을 갖게 된다. 이것이 교육의 '의미'를 찾기 어렵게 만든다. 프랑스의 사회학자 Emile Durkheim은 이러한 방향 감각 상실과 무의미함을 anomie(사회적 무질서)라고 부르고, 이것이 절망과 심지어 자살로 이어질 수 있다고 주장했다. 독일의 사회학자 Max Weber는 세상의 "환멸"에 관해 이야기했다. 과거에, 사람들은 자신들의 세상에 대한 통합된 시각, 즉 그 시각은 대체로 그들의 종교적 전통의 기원 설화에 의해 제공되는 시각이 있었다. 그 통합된 시각은 목적과 의미, 심지어 세상과 삶에 대한 황홀감을 주었다. 하지만 오늘날, 많은 작가들은 무의미함이 과학과 합리성의 세계에서 불가피하다고 주장했다. 현대성이란 무의미함을 의미하는 것처럼 보인다.

VOCA

- disorientation　방향 감각 상실, 혼미
- meaninglessness　무의미함, 목표가 없음
- anomie　사회적[도덕적] 무질서, 아노미
- disenchantment　환멸
- enchantment　황홀감, 환희
- inevitable　불가피한, 필연적인
- rationality　합리성

19 난도 ★★☆ 정답 ②

독해 > 세부 내용 찾기 > 내용 (불)일치

정답의 이유

두 번째 문장에서 대공황 때 잉여 농산물 활용의 필요성과 빈곤층 아동들에게 음식을 제공하려는 관심이 합쳐졌다고 했으므로 글의 내용과 일치하지 않는 것은 ② 'The US government began to feed poor children during the Great Depression despite the food shortage(미국 정부는 식량 부족에도 불구하고 대공황 동안 가난한 아이들에게 급식을 하는 것을 시작했다).'이다.

오답의 이유

① 일하는 여성의 증가가 급식 프로그램의 확장을 신장시켰다. → 세 번째 문장에서 '~ the explosion in the number of working women fueled the need for a broader program(일하는 여성의 수가 폭발적으로 증가하면서 더 광범위한 프로그램의 필요성을 부채질했다).'이라고 했으므로 글의 내용과 일치한다.

③ 미국 학교 급식 시스템은 현재 빈곤 가정 어린이들에게 음식을 제공하는 것을 돕는다. → 아홉 번째 문장에서 '~ the second is to provide nutritious food at both breakfast and lunch to underprivileged children(두 번째는 소외계층 아동들에게 아침과 점심 둘 다 영양가 높은 음식을 제공하는 것이다).'이라고 했으므로 글의 내용과 일치한다.

④ 점심 제공 기능은 가정에서 학교로 옮겨지고 있다. → 네 번째 문장에서 'What was once a function of the family—providing lunch—was shifted to the school food service system(한때 가정의 기능이었던 점심 제공이 학교 급식으로 이동했다).'이라고 했으므로 글의 내용과 일치한다.

본문해석

최초의 정부 급식 서비스 프로그램은 1900년대경 유럽에서 시작했다. 미국의 프로그램은 대공황으로부터 시작되었는데, 당시 잉여 농산물의 활용 필요성과 빈곤 가정 어린이들에 대한 급식 제공 관심이 맞물린 상황이었다. 제2차 세계대전과 그 이후, 일하는 여성의 수가 폭발적으로 증가하면서 더 광범위한 프로그램의 필요성을 부채질했다. 한때 가정의 기능이었던 점심 제공이 학교 급식으로 이동했다. National School Lunch Program은 이러한 노력의 결과이다. 이 프로그램은 연방정부의 지원을 받는 식사를 학령 아동들에게 제공하도록 고안되었다. 제2차 세계대전 말부터 1980년대 초까지 학교 급식을 위한 재정 지원이 꾸준하게 확대되었다. 오늘날 이것은 미국 전역 거의 10만 개의 학교에서 아이들에게 급식을 제공하는 것을 돕는다. 이것의 첫 번째 기능은 모든 학생들에게 영양가 높은 점심을 제공하는 것이다. 두 번째는 소외계층 아동들에게 아침과 점심 둘 다 영양가 높은 음식을 제공하는 것이다. 이전에는 가정의 기능이었던 것의 대체물로서 오히려 학교 급식의 역할이 확대되었다.

VOCA

• date from ~로부터 시작되다
• surplus 과잉
• commodity 상품, 물품
• fuel 부채질하다, 자극하다
• federally 연방정부의
• nutritious 영양가 높은
• underprivileged 불우한
• if anything 오히려

20 난도 ★★☆ 정답 ④

독해 > 글의 일관성 > 글의 순서

정답의 이유

주어진 문장에서 대한민국의 높은 인터넷 보급률을 제시하고, In fact로 시작하는 (B)에서 어떤 나라도 인터넷을 그렇게 전적으로 받아들인 나라는 없을 것이라고 재진술하는 것이 자연스럽다. (A)의 This addiction은 (C)의 'ready access to the Web has come at a price as legions of obsessed users'를 받고 있으므로 주어진 문장 다음에 이어질 글의 순서로 적절한 것은 ④ '(B) - (C) - (A)'이다.

본문해석

대한민국은 지구상에서 인터넷 연결이 가장 잘 되어 있는 국가임을 자랑한다.

(B) 사실상, 아마 어떤 나라도 인터넷을 그렇게 전적으로 받아들인 나라는 없을 것이다.

(C) 하지만 이러한 빠른 인터넷 접속은 다수의 중독된 사용자들이 자신들을 컴퓨터 화면에서 떼어낼 수 없다는 것을 알게 되면서 상당한 대가를 치르고 있다.

(A) 이러한 중독은 사용자들이 며칠간 계속 온라인 게임을 하고 난 뒤 탈진으로 급사하기 시작하면서, 최근 한국에서 국가적 문제가 되었다. 점점 더 많은 학생들이 온라인 상태를 유지하기 위해서 학교를 결석했는데, 이는 극도로 경쟁적인 이러한 사회에서 충격적일 정도의 자멸적인 행동이다.

VOCA

• addiction 중독
• drop dead 급사하다
• skip 거르다[빼먹다]
• self-destructive 자멸적인
• embrace 받아들이다
• legion 많은 사람들, 군단
• tear away (~에서) 억지로 떼어내다

영어 | 2018년 국가직 9급

한눈에 훑어보기

✓ 영역 분석

어휘　　05　06　14　15
4문항, 20%

독해　　02　03　07　09　11　12　13　16　17　18　19
11문항, 55%

어법　　04　10　20
3문항, 15%

표현　　01　08
2문항, 10%

✓ 빠른 정답

01	02	03	04	05	06	07	08	09	10
①	①	②	③	①	②	④	②	②	③

11	12	13	14	15	16	17	18	19	20
④	④	②	①	④	④	②	②	③	④

✓ 점수 체크

구분	1회독	2회독	3회독
맞힌 문항 수	/ 20	/ 20	/ 20
나의 점수	점	점	점

---

01 난도 ★☆☆　　　　　정답 ①

표현 > 일반회화

[정답의 이유]

밑줄 친 부분 앞에서 현재 시각을 말하고, 다음에서 바로 떠나야 한다고 말하고 있으므로 밑줄 친 부분에는 ① 'That's cutting it close(시간이 촉박해요)'가 적절하다.

[오답의 이유]

② 한눈 팔았어요(주의를 기울이지 않았어요)

③ 반짝이는 것이 모두 금은 아니에요

④ 이미 지나간 일이에요

[본문해석]

A: 부탁 하나 해도 될까요?

B: 네, 무엇인가요?

A: 출장 때문에 공항에 가야 하는데, 제 차가 시동이 안 걸리네요. 저 좀 태워줄 수 있으세요?

B: 물론이에요. 언제까지 거기에 도착해야 하죠?

A: 6시까지는 가야 해요.

B: 지금 4시 30분이네요. 시간이 촉박해요. 우리 지금 바로 떠나야 겠어요.

[VOCA]

• start (기계가) 시동이 걸리다, 작동되기 시작하다

• give (somebody) a lift ~을 태워주다

02 난도 ★★☆　　　　　정답 ①

독해 > 빈칸 완성 > 단어 · 구 · 절

[정답의 이유]

빈칸 앞 문장에서 포트폴리오 접근법에서는 당장의 손실보다 전체적인 포트폴리오를 더 중요하게 여긴다고 했고, 빈칸 다음에서 그것들이 훨씬 더 큰 그림의 작은 일부에 지나지 않는 것을 알고 있기 때문이라고 했으므로 빈칸에 들어갈 말로 가장 적절한 것은 ① 'less inclined to dwell on individual losses(개별적인 손실을 깊이 생각하려는 경향이 적다)'이다.

[오답의 이유]

② 당신의 투자에 흥미를 덜 갖는다

③ 손실을 더 싫어한다

④ 주식 시장의 변화에 더 민감하다

손실에 대한 두려움은 인간의 기본적인 부분이다. 뇌에 있어서, 손실은 위협이고 우리는 자연스럽게 그것을 피하기 위한 조치를 취한다. 하지만 우리는 그것을 영원히 피할 수 없다. 손실에 직면하는 하나의 방법은 주식 중개인의 관점을 가지는 것이다. 중개인들은 손실 가능성을 게임의 결과가 아닌 게임의 일부로 받아들인다. 이러한 사고를 이끄는 것은 포트폴리오 접근법이다. 이익과 손실은 모두 발생할 것이지만, 결과들의 전체적인 포트폴리오가 가장 중요하다는 것이다. 여러분이 포트폴리오 접근법을 받아들일 때, 개별적인 손실을 깊이 생각하려는 경향이 적어질 것인데 그것들이 훨씬 더 큰 그림의 작은 일부에 지나지 않는다는 것을 알기 때문이다.

- fear 두려움
- naturally 자연스럽게, 당연히, 선천적으로
- take measure 조치를 취하다
- indefinitely 무기한으로, 모호하게
- face 직면하다
- perspective 관점
- stock trader 주식 중개인
- end 결과, 끝
- approach 접근법
- matter 중요하다, 문제되다
- embrace 껴안다, 수락하다
- dwell on ～을 깊이 생각하다, 심사숙고하다

03 난도 ★★☆   정답 ②

독해 > 대의 파악 > 제목, 주제

정답의 이유

끝에서 두 번째 문장에서 '～ but what we do have control of should be a reflection of the time in which we exist and communicate the present.'라고 하고, 마지막 문장에서 '현재는 우리가 가진 모든 것이며, 우리가 그것에 더 많이 둘러싸여 있을수록, 우리는 우리 자신의 존재와 참여에 대해 더 많이 인지하게 된다.'라고 했으므로 글의 제목으로 적절한 것은 ② 'Reflect on the Time That Surrounds You Now(현재 여러분을 둘러싸고 있는 시간을 되돌아보라)'이다.

오답의 이유

① 여행: 과거의 유산 추적하기
③ 숨겨진 삶의 징후
④ 미래 생활의 건축

지난 몇 년 동안 여행하면서, 나는 우리 인간들이 얼마나 많이 과거에 살고 있는지 관찰해 왔다. 어떤 것이 나타나는 순간, 그것이 곧 과거가 되어버린다는 것을 고려하면, 과거는 끊임없이 우리 주변에 있다. 우리의 주변과 가정, 환경, 건축물, 제품들은 모두 과거의 산물들이다. 우리는 우리 시대의 일부분과 집단의식의 부분들, 우리의 삶에서 만들어진 것들과 함께 살아야 한다. 물론, 우리 시대 동안에, 관련되거나 마음속으로 생각한 주변의 모든 것에 대한 선택권이나 통제권을 갖고 있지는 않지만, 우리가 통제권을 소유하고 있는 것은 우리가 지금 존재하고 소통하는 현재라는 시대의 반영이어야 한다. 현재는 우리가 가진 모든 것이며, 우리가 그것에 더 많이 둘러싸여 있을수록, 우리는 우리 자신의 존재와 참여에 대해 더 많이 인지하게 된다.

- observe 관찰하다, 보다, 지키다, 준수하다
- the minute ～하자마자
- manifest 나타나다, 드러나다, 명백한
- construct 건설하다, 구성하다
- collective 집단의, 단체의
- consciousness 자각, 의식
- conceive (마음에) 품다, 상상하다, 임신하다
- reflection 상, 반영, 사상, 생각, 성찰
- be aware of ～을 인지하다

04 난도 ★☆☆   정답 ③

어법 > 비문 찾기

정답의 이유

③ result가 자동사로 쓰일 때 'result in＋결과/result from＋원인' 등과 같이 result 다음에 '전치사＋명사' 형태가 온다. 자동사는 수동태로 사용할 수 없으므로 has been resulted → has resulted가 되어야 한다.

오답의 이유

① 가주어-진주어 구문으로, 가주어(it)가 진주어(to imagine)를 대신하고 있으므로 to imagine은 올바른 표현이다.
② take ～ for granted는 '～을 당연하게 여기다'라는 관용표현이다.
④ 분사구문(affecting wilderness regions ～)으로, affecting 다음에 목적어(wilderness regions)가 있고 주절의 주어(deforestation)와 분사구문이 '삼림 벌채가 야생 지역에 영향을 미친다'로 능동 관계이다. 따라서 현재분사(affecting)가 올바르게 사용되었다.

본문해석

숲의 아름다움과 풍요로움이 없는 삶을 상상하는 것은 어려울 것이다. 하지만 과학자들은 우리가 우리의 숲을 당연하게 여겨서는 안 된다고 경고한다. 어떤 추정치에 따르면, 삼림 벌채는 전 세계 자연 숲의 80%에 달하는 손실을 초래해 왔다. 현재 삼림 벌채는 전 세계적인 문제이며, 태평양의 온대강우림 같은 야생 지역들에 영향을 끼치고 있다.

VOCA

- take A for granted A를 당연하게 여기다
- estimate 추정치, 견적, 평가
- deforestation 산림 벌채, 산림 개간, 삼림 파괴
- wilderness 황야, 야생
- temperate rainforest 온대강우림

05 난도 ★★☆   정답 ①

어휘 > 단어

정답의 이유

밑줄 친 indigenous는 '토착의'의 뜻으로 이와 의미가 가장 가까운 것은 ① 'native(토착의, 원시의)'이다.

오답의 이유

② 몹시 시장한
③ 빈곤한, 결핍된
④ 떠돌아다니는, 유랑의

본문해석

전설적인 다큐멘터리 영화감독인 Robert J. Flaherty는 원주민들이 어떻게 식량을 모았는지를 보여주려고 노력했다.

VOCA

- legendary 전설적인

06 난도 ★★☆   정답 ②

어휘 > 어구

정답의 이유

빈칸 다음 문장에서 누구나 음악을 감상할 수 있지만, 음악가가 되려면 재능이 필요하다는 상반된 서술이 나오므로 밑줄 친 부분에는 ② 'a far cry from(~와는 거리가 먼, 전혀 다른)'이 적절하다.

오답의 이유

① ~와 동등하게
③ ~여하에 달린
④ ~의 서막

본문해석

음악 감상과 록스타가 되는 것은 전혀 다른 것이다. 누구나 음악을 감상할 수 있지만, 음악가가 되는 것은 재능이 필요하다.

07 난도 ★☆☆   정답 ④

독해 > 글의 일관성 > 무관한 어휘·문장

정답의 이유

제시문은 벼의 수중 생존 능력을 높여서 홍수 위험 지역의 농민들이 이로 인한 재정적 손해를 줄일 수 있다는 내용이다. 이는 희소식이므로 글의 흐름상 가장 어색한 문장은 ④ 'This is dreadful news for people in these vulnerable regions, who are victims of urbanization and have a shortage of crops(이것은 이러한 취약한 지역에 사는 사람들에게는 끔찍한 소식인데, 그들은 도시화의 피해자들이며 작물이 부족하다).'이다.

본문해석

생물학자들은 벼가 지금보다 일주일 이상 더 긴 2주 동안까지 물에 잠긴 상태로 생존할 수 있게 하는 유전자를 알아냈다. 일주일 이상 물에 잠긴 식물은 산소를 빼앗기고 시들어 죽는다. 과학자들은 자신들의 발견이 홍수에 영향받기 쉬운 지역들의 작물 수확 시기를 연장시키기를 희망한다. 범람하기 쉬운 이러한 아시아 지역에서 벼 재배자들은 심하게 침수된 논에서 매년 10억 달러로 추정되는 돈을 잃는다. 그들은, 이 새로운 유전자가 태풍과 장마철에 발생하는 재정적 피해를 줄이고 풍작으로 이어질 수 있는 더 강한 벼 품종으로 이어지기를 바라고 있다. 이것은 이러한 취약한 지역에 사는 사람들에게는 끔찍한 소식인데, 그들은 도시화의 피해자들이며 작물이 부족하다. 쌀 생산량은 10억 명의 사람들이 주식으로 먹을 수 있도록 보장하기 위해 다음 20년에 걸쳐 30퍼센트 증가해야 한다.

VOCA

- identify 밝혀내다, 알아내다
- submerge 잠수하다, 물속에 잠기다
- up to ~까지
- deprive 빼앗다, 박탈하다
- wither 시들다
- perish 죽다, 죽이다
- prolong 연장하다
- be susceptible to ~에 영향을 받기 쉽다
- flood-prone 범람하기 쉬운
- annually 매년
- waterlogged 물에 잠긴
- paddy 논
- strain 종류, 품종
- incur 초래하다, 발생하다
- monsoon season 우기, 장마철
- bumper harvest 풍작
- dreadful 끔찍한, 무시무시한
- vulnerable 취약한
- urbanization 도시화
- yield 산출량
- staple diet 주식

08 난도 ★☆☆

정답 ②

표현 > 일반회화

정답의 이유

A는 B에게 운전하는 방법을 알려달라고 요청하고 있다. 빈칸 앞에서 운전 경험이 없지만 '~을 더는 기다릴 수 없다'고 말하고 있으므로 빈칸에 들어갈 말로 가장 적절한 것은 ② 'get one's feet wet(시작하다)'이다.

오답의 이유

① 다음을 기약하다
③ 엔진오일을 교체하다
④ 펑크 난 타이어를 교체하다

본문해석

A: 너 운전할 줄 알아?
B: 물론이지. 나 운전 잘 해.
A: 나에게 운전하는 법 좀 가르쳐 줄 수 있어?
B: 너 임시 운전면허증 가지고 있니?
A: 응, 바로 지난주에 받았어.
B: 자동차를 운전해 본 적은 있어?
A: 아니, 하지만 난 시작하는 것을 기다릴 수가 없어.

VOCA

• learner's permit 임시 운전면허증
• be behind the steering wheel 운전하다(운전대 앞에 앉다)

09 난도 ★☆☆

정답 ②

독해 > 세부 내용 찾기 > 내용 (불)일치

정답의 이유

제시문의 아홉 번째 문장에서 'They can turn up or flatten to adjust to the flow of water around the shark and to reduce drag(그것들은 상어 주변의 해류에 적응하고 항력을 줄이기 위해 위로 젖히거나 납작해진다).'라고 했으므로 글의 내용과 일치하는 것은 ② 'Lang revealed that the scales of a mako shark are utilized to lessen drag in water(Lang은 청상아리의 비늘이 물의 항력을 줄이기 위해 이용된다는 것을 밝혀냈다).'이다.

오답의 이유

① 상어는 헤엄칠 때 자신을 보호하기 위해서 언제나 움직이지 않는 비늘을 지니고 있다. → 세 번째 문장에서 'A shark can move the scales as it swims(상어는 수영하면서 비늘을 움직일 수 있다).'라고 했으므로 글의 내용과 일치하지 않는다.
③ 청상아리는 몸 전체에 똑같은 크기의 비늘을 가지고 있다. → 여섯 번째 문장에서 '~ the mako shark's scales differ in size and in flexibility in different parts of its body.'라고 했으므로 글의 내용과 일치하지 않는다.
④ 비행기의 과학적인 디자인은 상어 비늘에서 영감을 받았다. → 마지막 문장에서 그와 같은 내용이 나오지만, 그것은 Lang이 그렇게 생각한다(Lang feels that ~)는 것이지 실제 그렇다는 것이 아니다.

본문해석

상어는 치아와 동일한 물질로 구성된 비늘로 덮여 있다. 이 신축성 있는 비늘은 상어를 보호하고 물에서 빠르게 수영할 수 있게 돕는다. 상어는 수영하면서 비늘을 움직일 수 있다. 이러한 움직임은 물의 항력을 줄이는 것을 돕는다. 앨라배마 대학의 항공 우주 공학자 Amy Lang은 대백상어의 동족인 청상아리의 비늘을 연구한다. Lang과 그녀의 팀은 청상아리의 비늘이 그것의 몸의 다른 부분들에서 크기와 유연성에 차이가 있다는 것을 알아냈다. 예를 들어, 몸의 측면에 있는 비늘은 점점 가늘어져, 한쪽 끝은 넓고 다른 쪽 끝은 좁다. 비늘들이 점점 가늘어지기 때문에, 이러한 비늘들은 아주 쉽게 움직인다. 그것들은 상어 주변의 해류에 적응하고 항력을 줄이기 위해 위로 젖히거나 납작해진다. Lang은 상어의 비늘이 비행기처럼 항력을 경험하는 기계들을 디자인하는 데에 영감을 줄 수 있다고 생각한다.

VOCA

• scale 비늘, 저울, 눈금, 규모
• flexible 유연한
• drag 끌어당기는 힘, 방해, 항력, 장애물
• aerospace 항공 우주
• relative 친척, 동족
• great white shark 대백상어
• shortfin mako 청상아리
• taper 가늘어지다, 점점 줄다
• turn up 나타나다, (위로) 일어서다
• flatten 납작해지다

10 난도 ★★☆

정답 ③

어법 > 비문 찾기

정답의 이유

③ paying은 attention을 수식하는 분사로 관심이 '주어지는' 것이므로 paying to this question → paid to this question이 되어야 한다.

오답의 이유

① 타동사 mean의 목적어로 getting(동명사)이 올바르게 사용되었으며, 준사역동사 get의 목적어인 stuff와 목적격 보어의 관계가 수동이므로 과거분사 done이 올바르게 사용되었다.
② 선행사 the issues를 수식하는 주격 관계대명사 that이 올바르게 사용되었으며, 주어가 복수이므로 동사 interest, concern의 수일치도 적절하다.
④ 사역동사 let의 목적어 life와 목적격 보어인 pass가 능동 관계이므로 원형부정사가 올바르게 사용되었다.

집중은 일을 끝내는 것을 의미한다. 많은 사람들이 훌륭한 생각을 갖고 있지만 그것들에 따라 행동하지는 않는다. 예를 들어, 나에게 기업가의 정의는 새로운 아이디어를 실행하는 능력을 가지고 혁신과 창의성을 결합할 수 있는 사람이다. 어떤 사람들은 삶의 주요 이분법이 여러분의 흥미를 끌거나 영향을 미치는 이슈들에 대해 낙관적인지 아니면 비관적인지에 관한 것이라고 생각한다. 긍정적인 관점을 갖는 것이 더 나은지, 아니면 부정적 관점을 갖는 것이 더 나은지에 대한 이 질문에 관심이 집중되어 있다. 내 생각에 더 적절한 질문은 여러분이 그것에 대해 뭔가를 할 것인지, 아니면 인생이 그저 지나쳐 가도록 내버려 둘 것인지 묻는 것이다.

VOCA

- stuff 물건, 어떤 것, 일
- act on ~에 따라 행동하다, 실천하다
- entrepreneur 사업가
- combine A with B A와 B를 결합하다
- ingenuity 독창성
- execute 실행하다
- dichotomy 이분법
- optimistic 낙관적인
- pessimistic 비관적인
- pass ~ by (아무런 영향을 주지 않고) ~을 스쳐 지나가다

더 알아보기

5형식 동사+목적어+목적격 보어

- 5형식(불완전타동사+목적어+목적격 보어) 구문에서 목적어와 목적격 보어가 수동관계이면 목적격 보어로 과거분사가 온다.
  - 사역동사(have, make, get, help 등)+과거분사: '~되도록 시키다/~당하다'로 해석한다.
    예 I had the roof repaired before the rainy season.
    (나는 장마가 오기 전에 지붕이 수리되도록 시켰다.)
  - 지각동사(see, hear, watch, feel 등)+과거분사: '~되는 것을 보다/듣다/느끼다'로 해석한다.
    예 I heard my name called on the school broadcast.
    (나는 학교 방송에서 내 이름이 불리는 것을 들었다.)
- get+목적어+목적격 보어

get+목적어+ to부정사	I'll get him to carry my luggage to the hotel. (목적어가 ~하도록 하다)
get+목적어+ 과거분사(p.p.)	I'll never get all this work finished. (목적어가 ~되도록 하다/시키다)
get+목적어+ 현재분사(-ing)	Get her talking, figure out if she's lying. (목적어가 ~하도록 시작하게 만들다)

11 난도 ★☆☆ 정답 ④

독해 > 글의 일관성 > 무관한 어휘 · 문장

정답의 이유

제시문은 듣는 것을 좋아하는 사람은 거의 없지만, 잘 듣는 사람은 사람들로부터 인기가 있다는 내용인데, 여섯 번째 문장에서 'However, there are exceptions to that generality(그러나 그 일반화에는 예외가 있다).'라고 한 다음에 일반적으로 경청하는 사람들은 사랑받는 사람들이지만 John Steinbeck은 이에 대한 예외라고 했다. 마지막에서 두 번째 문장에서 그의 듣는 능력이 쓰는 능력에 도움을 주었다고 했고, 마지막 문장의 nevertheless(그럼에도 불구하고)와 부정어(didn't)로 미루어 문맥상 ④ 'unpopular → popular'가 되어야 한다.

대부분의 사람은 말하기를 좋아하지만, 듣는 것을 좋아하는 사람은 거의 없다. 하지만 경청은 모두가 소중히 여겨야 하는 희귀한 재능이다. 좋은 청자는 더 많이 듣기 때문에 대부분의 사람들보다 그들 주변에서 일어나는 일들을 더 많이 알고 더 세심한 경향이 있다. 게다가, 좋은 청자는 판단하고 비판하기보다는 받아들이고 관대하게 대하는 경향이 있다. 그러므로 그들은 대부분 사람들보다 적이 더 적다. 사실, 그들은 아마도 가장 사랑받는 사람들일 것이다. 그러나 그 일반화에는 예외가 있다. 예를 들어서, John Steinbeck은 훌륭한 청자였지만, 그는 그의 글에 썼던 몇몇 사람들에게는 미움을 받았다고 한다. 의심할 여지 없이, 그의 경청 능력은 그의 글쓰기 능력에 기여했다. 그럼에도 불구하고, 그의 경청 결과가 그를 인기 없게 (→ 인기 있게) 만들지는 못했다.

VOCA

- treasure 간직하다, 소중히 여기다, 보물
- sensitive 민감한, 세심한
- be inclined to ~하는 경향이 있다
- tolerate 참다, 허용하다, 너그럽게 봐주다, 견디다
- beloved 사랑받는
- generality 일반화
- contribute to ~에 공헌하다, ~에 기여하다
- capacity (수용) 능력

12 난도 ★★☆ 정답 ④

독해 > 대의 파악 > 제목, 주제

정답의 이유

제시문은 걱정이 우리 삶에 끼치는 부정적 영향을 서술한 후, 그에 대한 해결책을 제시하고 있다. 특히 제시문의 마지막 부분에서 '일어나길 원하는 일에 집중하고 이미 가지고 있는 멋진 것들에 대해 생각하라'고 걱정에 대처하는 방법을 제시하고 있으므로 글의 주제로 적절한 것은 ④ 'How do we cope with worrying(우리는 어떻게 걱정에 대처하는가)?'이다.

오답의 이유

① 걱정은 인생에 어떠한 영향을 끼치는가?

② 걱정은 어디서부터 시작되는가?

③ 우리는 언제 걱정해야 하는가?

본문해석

걱정은 흔들목마와 같다. 아무리 빨리 간다고 해도 여러분은 절대로 어느 곳으로도 갈 수 없다. 걱정은 완벽한 시간 낭비이며, 여러분의 마음을 너무나 어수선하게 만들어서 그 어떤 것도 명확하게 생각할 수 없다. 걱정을 멈추는 것을 배우는 법은 무엇이든 먼저 여러분이 집중하고 있는 것에 에너지를 소모하고 있다는 것을 이해하는 것이다. 그러므로 여러분이 자신을 걱정하도록 내버려 둘수록, 일은 점점 더 잘못된다! 걱정은 너무나 몸에 밴 습관이 되기 때문에 그것을 피하기 위해서는 그렇게 하지 않도록 의식적으로 자신을 훈련시켜야 한다. 여러분이 걱정거리에 사로잡힐 때마다, 멈추고 생각을 바꾸어라. 여러분에게 일어나길 바라는 무언가에 좀 더 건설적으로 집중하고 이미 여러분의 삶에서 일어난 멋진 일들을 깊이 생각하라. 그러면 더 멋진 일들이 여러분 앞에 펼쳐질 것이다.

VOCA

• rocking horse 흔들목마

• clutter 잡동사니, 어수선함

• ingrained 뿌리 깊은, 깊이 몸에 밴

• fit (감정 · 행동의) 격발

• productively 생산적으로, 건설적으로

• dwell on ~을 깊이 생각하다, 심사숙고하다

13 난도 ★★★   정답 ②

독해 > 세부 내용 찾기 > 내용 (불)일치

정답의 이유

네 번째 문장에서 학생들이 노트북 1대와 7,500달러를 받는다고 했으므로 글의 내용과 일치하지 않는 것은 ② 'MHC에서는 학생들에게 컴퓨터 구입 비용과 교외활동 비용을 합하여 $7,500를 지급한다.'이다.

오답의 이유

① 두 번째, 세 번째 문장에서 모든 학생이 4년 동안 전액 장학금을 받는다고 했으므로 글의 내용과 일치한다.

③ 여섯 번째 문장에서 언급한 Kirschner 학장의 의견이 올바르게 서술되어 있다.

④ 마지막 문장에서 우수 학생들에게만 장학금을 주는 학교가 서술되어 있으므로 글의 내용과 일치한다.

본문해석

Macaulay Honors College(MHC) 학생들은 고액의 등록금에 대한 스트레스를 받지 않는다. 등록금이 무료이기 때문이다. Macaulay와 몇몇 군 사관학교, 직업 대학, 단과 대학, 음악 대학에서는 학생 전원이 전액 장학금을 4년 내내 받는다. Macaulay 학생들은 또한 노트북 한 대와 7,500달러의 '기회 자금'을 받는데 그것은 연구, 업무 경험, 유학 프로그램과 인턴십 등을 수행하기 위한 것이다. "가장 중요한 것은 무료 등록금이 아니라, 빚을 짊어지지 않고 공부할 자유입니다."라고 Macaulay Honors 대학의 학장 Ann Kirschner는 말

한다. 그녀는 또 말하기를, 빚 부담은 "학생들이 대학에서 하는 선택들과 타협하게 하며, 우리는 그들에게 그것으로부터 자유로울 기회를 주고 있습니다."라고 했다. 모든 학생에게 무료 등록금을 제공하는 학교들은 드물다. 하지만 더 많은 교육기관들이 높은 성적을 받은 등록자들에게 장학금을 제공한다. Indiana 대학교 Bloomington 캠퍼스 같은 기관들은 평점과 수업에서의 석차가 특출한 높은 성취도를 나타내는 학생들에게 자동적으로 장학금을 제공한다.

VOCA

• tuition 등록금

• a handful of 소수의, 한 줌의, 몇몇의

• service academy 군 사관학교

• conservatory 음악 학교

• pursue 추구하다, 밀고 나가다, 수행하다

• on one's back ~의 등에 지고 있는

• dean 학장, 원장

• burden 부담, 짐

• compromise 절충하다, 타협하다

• enrollee 등록자, 가입자

• stellar 특출한

14 난도 ★★☆   정답 ①

어휘 > 단어

정답의 이유

밑줄 친 malefactor는 '범죄자, 악인'의 뜻으로 이와 의미가 가장 가까운 것은 ① 'culprit(범인)'이다.

오답의 이유

② 호사가

③ 버림받은 사람, 천민

④ 선동 정치가

본문해석

경찰은 7개월을 그 범죄 사건에 소비했지만 범인의 신원을 결코 밝혀낼 수 없었다.

VOCA

• crime case 범죄 사건

• identity 신원

15 난도 ★☆☆   정답 ④

어휘 > 어구

정답의 이유

밑줄 친 through thick and thin은 '좋을 때나 안 좋을 때나'의 뜻으로 이와 의미가 가장 가까운 것은 ④ 'in good times and bad times(좋을 때나 나쁠 때나)'이다.

오답의 이유

① 당장에

② 가끔

③ 기쁠 때에

언뜻 보기에는 그의 친구들이 단지 거머리에 지나지 않는 것처럼 보이지만, 그들은 좋을 때나 나쁠 때나 그가 의지할 수 있는 사람들이라는 것이 증명되었다.

VOCA

• leech 거머리, 기생충

16 난도 ★★★ 정답 ④

독해 > 글의 일관성 > 문장 삽입

정답의 이유

주어진 문장은 어떤 사람들은 자신들의 출생지의 말투를 자랑스러워하는 반면, 다른 사람들은 자신들의 언어 습관을 바꿈으로써 재빨리 새로운 환경에 적응한다는 내용이다. ④ 앞 문장에서 'Not all people do this to the same degree.'라고 했으므로, 다음에 'Some ~ , while others ~'로 대조적인 두 종류의 사람들을 설명하는 내용이 이어지는 것이 자연스럽다. 따라서 주어진 문장이 들어갈 위치로 적절한 것은 ④이다.

본문해석

말에 대한 우리의 인식과 생산은 시간에 따라 변한다. 우리가 고향을 오랫동안 떠나 있다면, 우리 주변의 새로운 억양이 이상하다고 인지하는 것은 일시적일 뿐이다. 점차, 우리는 사람들의 억양이 다르다는 것을 인식하지 못할 것이고, 우리의 발화 패턴을 맞추기 시작할 것인데, 즉 새로운 규범에 적응하기 시작할 것이다. 모든 사람들이 이것을 같은 정도로 하는 것은 아니다. 어떤 이들은 자신들의 출생지의 억양과 사투리, 관용구, 제스처를 매우 자랑스러워하는 반면, 다른 이들은 자신들의 언어 습관들을 고침으로써 빠르게 새로운 환경에 적응해서 그들은 더 이상 '군중 속에서 눈에 띄지' 않는다. 그들이 이것을 의식적으로 하는지 아닌지는 논쟁의 여지가 있으며 아마도 개인마다 다를 테지만, 언어와 관련된 대부분 과정과 마찬가지로, 변화는 아마도 우리가 그것을 인지하기 전에 발생하며, 만일 우리가 알았다면 일어날 수 없었을 것이다.

VOCA

• intensely 강하게, 열심히
• dialect 사투리, 방언
• accommodate to ~에 적응하다, 수용하다
• stand out 눈에 띄다
• perception 인식, 지각
• extended 확장된, 연장한, 늘어난, 긴
• gradually 점차
• fit in 맞추다, 적응하다
• norm 표준, 기준
• degree 정도
• open to debate 논쟁의 여지가 있는
• have to do with ~와 관련이 있다

17 난도 ★★☆ 정답 ②

독해 > 세부 내용 찾기 > 내용 (불)일치

정답의 이유

세 번째 문장에서 일시적 불면증은 부적절한 수면 환경 외에도 수면 시간, 심각한 우울증 혹은 스트레스에 의해 생길 수 있다고 했으므로 글의 내용과 일치하지 않는 것은 ② 'Transient insomnia occurs solely due to an inadequate sleep environment(일시적 불면증은 오직 부적절한 수면 환경에 의해서만 발생한다).'이다.

오답의 이유

① 불면증은 그 기간에 의해서 분류될 수 있다. → 제시문에서 'Transient insomnia lasts for less than a week(일시적인 불면증은 일주일 이내로 지속된다).'라고 했고, 한 달 이내로 지속되는 급성 불면증과 한 달 이상 지속되는 만성 불면증으로 분류할 수 있다고 했다.

③ 급성 불면증은 일반적으로 스트레스와 관련되어 있다고 알려져 있다. → 여덟 번째 문장에서 급성 불면증은 스트레스와 관련된 질병으로 알려져 있다고 언급하고 있다.

④ 만성 불면증 환자들은 환각으로 고통받을지도 모른다. → 끝에서 두 번째 문장에서 만성 불면증의 영향으로 근육 약화, 환각, 정신적 피로를 제시했다.

본문해석

불면증은 일시적인, 급성인, 혹은 만성적인 것으로 분류될 수 있다. 일시적인 불면증은 일주일 이내로 지속된다. 그것은 다른 질병, 수면 환경의 변화, 수면 시간, 심각한 우울증 혹은 스트레스에 의해서 생길 수 있다. 졸음, 정신 운동 기능 장애 같은 결과들은 수면 결핍의 결과와 비슷하다. 급성 불면증은 한 달 이내의 기간 동안 지속적으로 숙면을 취할 수 없는 것이다. 급성 불면증은 잠드는 데 또는 지속적인 수면에 문제가 있을 때, 혹은 잠자고 나도 상쾌하지 않을 때 발생한다. 이러한 문제들은 수면을 위한 충분한 기회와 환경에도 불구하고 발생하며 주간 활동에 손상을 줄 수도 있다. 급성 불면증은 또한 단기 불면증이나 스트레스 관련 불면증으로도 알려져 있다. 만성 불면증은 한 달 이상 지속된다. 그것은 다른 질병에 의해서 생기거나, 그 자체가 일차 질병이 되기도 한다. 스트레스 호르몬 수치가 높거나 사이토카인* 수치에 변화가 있는 사람들은 다른 사람들보다 만성 불면증에 걸리기 쉽다. 그 영향은 원인에 따라서 다양할 수 있다. 만성 불면증의 영향은 근육 약화, 환각 그리고/혹은 정신적 피로를 포함할 수 있다. 만성 불면증은 또한 복시를 일으킬 수도 있다.

*사이토카인: 면역 체계의 특정 세포에 의해 방출되는 분자 그룹

VOCA

• insomnia 불면증
• classify 분류하다
• transient 일시적인
• acute 급성의
• chronic 만성의
• disorder 장애, 무질서, 질환
• depression 우울증, 불경기

- impaired 손상된, 제 기능을 못하는
- psychomotor 정신 운동의
- deprivation 결핍, 결여
- circumstance 상황
- weariness 피로, 권태
- hallucination 환각
- fatigue 피로감

18 난도 ★★☆ 정답 ②

독해 > 빈칸 완성 > 단어·구·절

정답의 이유

빈칸 앞 문장에서 인도 교육의 문제를 외딴 지역의 학생들이 좋은 교사와 콘텐츠에 대한 접근성이 떨어지는 데에 있다고 지적하고 있으며, 빈칸 앞부분의 'The company uses a satellite network, with two-way video and audio'로 미루어 빈칸에 가장 적절한 것은 ② 'to bridge the gap through virtual classrooms(가상 수업을 통해 그 격차를 메우기 위해)'이다.

오답의 이유

① 교사 훈련 기관의 질을 향상하기 위해
③ 학생들이 디지털 기술에 익숙하게 하기 위해
④ 자격 있는 교육자들을 전국 각지에 배치하기 위해

본문해석

뭄바이에 있는 Everonn Education의 창립자인 Kisha Padbhan은 자신의 사업을 국가 건설로 본다. 인도의 2억 3천만에 달하는 (유치원부터 대학까지) 학령 인구는 세계에서 가장 큰 규모 중의 하나이다. 정부는 830억 달러를 교육에 지출하지만, 심각한 격차가 있다. "교사와 교사 훈련 기관이 충분하지 않아요."라고 Kisha는 말한다. "인도의 외딴 지역에 사는 어린이들에게 부족한 것은 좋은 교사에 대한 접근 기회와 양질의 콘텐츠에 대한 노출이에요." Everonn의 해결책은? 그 회사는 가상 수업을 통해 그 격차를 메우기 위해 양방향 영상과 음향을 갖춘 위성 네트워크를 사용한다. 네트워크는 인도에 있는 28개 주 중에서 24개 주를 걸쳐 1,800개 대학교와 7,800개 학교에 도달한다. 디지털화된 학교 수업부터 미래의 엔지니어들을 위한 입학시험 준비까지 모든 것을 제공하며, 구직자들을 위한 훈련 과정도 있다.

VOCA

- nation-building 국가 건설
- institute 기관, 연구소
- exposure to ~에 대한 노출
- satellite network 위성 네트워크
- two-way 양방향의
- digitized 디지털화된
- prep 예습, 사전준비
- aspiring 장차 ~가 되려는
- job-seeker 구직자

19 난도 ★★☆ 정답 ③

독해 > 글의 일관성 > 글의 순서

정답의 이유

주어진 글에서 생체자기제어 기술을 제시하고 있는데, (B)에서 전자 센서들을 신체의 다양한 부분에 부착하여 심박수, 혈압, 피부 온도 같은 변수들을 측정하는 구체적인 방법을 설명하고 있으므로 주어진 글 다음에 (B)가 와야 한다. (A)의 such a variable은 (B)에서 언급된 변수들(variables)을 다시 언급하는 표현이므로 variables가 나열된 (B) 다음에 (A)가 와야 한다. (A)의 visual or audible displays가 (C)의 the displays로 연결되어 최종적으로 biofeedback을 통해 개인들이 어떻게 신체에 대한 자발적 통제를 하도록 훈련받을 수 있는지 설명하고 있다. 따라서 주어진 문장 다음에 이어질 글의 순서로 적절한 것은 ③ '(B) - (A) - (C)'이다.

본문해석

개인이 자율적이거나 무의식적인 신체 기능에 대한 전자적 수치를 관찰함으로써 어떤 자발적인 제어력을 얻을 수 있게 하는 기술은 생체자기제어로 알려져 있다.
(B) 심박수, 혈압, 피부 온도 같은 변수들을 측정하기 위해 전자 센서들을 신체의 다양한 부분에 부착한다.
(A) 그러한 변수(예를 들어, 혈압 저하)가 원하는 방향으로 이동하면, 그것은 시각적 혹은 청각적인 표시, 즉 TV 수신기, 측정기 혹은 전등과 같은 장치에서 나타나는 반응을 촉발시킨다.
(C) 생체자기제어 훈련은 이러한 표시를 촉발시킨 사고 패턴 또는 행동을 재생산함으로써 원하는 반응을 일으키도록 지도한다.

VOCA

- involuntary 자기도 모르게 하는, 무의식적인
- biofeedback 생체자기제어(심장 박동처럼 보통 의식적인 제어가 안되는 체내 활동을 전자 장치로 측정하고 그 결과를 이용하여 의식적인 제어를 훈련하는 방법)
- variable 변수
- trigger 촉발하다, 일으키다
- equipment 기계, 장비, 부품
- gauge 계측 장치
- attach 부착하다, 첨부하다, 애착을 느끼게 하다
- reproduce 번식하다, 복제하다, 재현하다

20 난도 ★☆☆ 정답 ④

어법 > 영작하기

정답의 이유

④ 원급 비교의 부정인 'not so[as]+형용사[부사]+as'(~만큼 ~하지 않다) 구문이 사용되었는데, 'not so[as] ~ as' 사이에는 원급이 와야 하므로 stingier → stingy가 되어야 한다.

오답의 이유

① be good at은 '~에 능숙하다'라는 표현으로, 전치사(at) 다음에 동명사 getting이 올바르게 사용되었다. get across도 '~을 (~에게) 전달하다, 이해시키다'의 의미로 적절하게 쓰였다.

② 복수 주어(traffic jams)이므로 동사(are)의 수일치가 올바르다. 'more ~ than any other＋단수명사' 구문은 올바른 최상급 표현이며, 비교 대상인 traffic jams와 those의 수일치도 올바르다.

③ 동명사 주어(making eye contact ~ speaking to)와 동사(is)의 수일치가 올바르다. the person 다음에 목적격 관계대명사 whom이 생략되었다.

VOCA
- turn out ～이 드러나다
- stingy 인색한

더 알아보기

원급 비교와 비교급 비교
- 원급 비교는 비교 대상의 동등함을 나타내며, 'as＋형용사[부사]＋as＋비교 대상'으로 나타낸다.

동등 비교	as＋형용사[부사]의 원급＋as＋비교 대상	～만큼 형용사[부사]하다
열등 비교	not so[as]＋형용사[부사]의 원급＋as＋비교 대상	～만큼 형용사[부사]하지 않다

예 She felt that she was as *good a swimmer* as he was, if not better. → 동등 비교
(그녀는 비록 그보다 더 낫지는 않지만, 자신이 그만큼 훌륭한 수영선수라고 느꼈다.)

예 He is not so *young* as he looks. → 열등 비교
(그는 보이는 것처럼 그렇게 어리지는 않다.)

- 비교급 비교는 둘 이상의 대상의 우열을 비교할 때 사용하며, '비교급 형용사[부사]＋than＋비교 대상'으로 나타낸다.

우등 비교	원급＋-er[more 원급]＋than＋비교 대상	A가 B보다 더 ～하다
열등 비교	less＋원급＋than＋비교 대상	A가 B보다 덜 ～하다

예 Gold is *heavier* than copper. → 우등 비교
(금은 구리보다 무겁다.)

예 Few living things are linked together more *intimately* than bees and flowers. → 우등 비교
(벌과 꽃들만큼 친밀하게 함께 연관되어 있는 생물은 거의 없다.)

예 People are less *tolerant* of smokers in public places.
→ 열등 비교
(사람들은 공공장소에서의 흡연자들을 덜 용인하고 있다.)

무언가를 시작하는 방법은 말하는 것을 멈추고 행동을 하는 것이다.

\- 월트 디즈니 \-

PART 2

지방직

한눈에 훑어보기

✓ 영역 분석

어휘 01 02 03 04 05
5문항, 25%

독해 12 13 14 15 16 17 18 19 20
9문항, 45%

어법 06 07 08
3문항, 15%

표현 09 10 11
3문항, 15%

✓ 빠른 정답

01	02	03	04	05	06	07	08	09	10
②	②	①	①	③	④	③	②	④	④
11	12	13	14	15	16	17	18	19	20
②	③	④	③	③	③	③	④	①	①

✓ 점수 체크

구분	1회독	2회독	3회독
맞힌 문항 수	/ 20	/ 20	/ 20
나의 점수	점	점	점

---

01 난도 ★☆☆ 　　　　　　　　　　　　정답 ②

어휘 > 단어

[정답의 이유]
밑줄 친 markedly는 '현저하게'라는 뜻으로, 이와 의미가 가까운 것은 ② 'obviously(분명하게)'이다.

[오답의 이유]
① 부드럽게
③ 조금만, 가까스로
④ 분별할 수 없게

본문해석
셰익스피어의 희극들은 많은 유사점을 갖고 있지만, 그것들은 또한 서로 현저하게 다르다.

VOCA
• similarity 유사성, 닮음
• differ from ~와 다르다

02 난도 ★☆☆ 　　　　　　　　　　　　정답 ②

어휘 > 단어

[정답의 이유]
밑줄 친 diluted는 'dilute(희석하다)'의 과거형으로, 이와 의미가 가장 가까운 것은 ② 'weakened(약화시켰다)'이다.

[오답의 이유]
① 세척했다
③ 연결했다
④ 발효시켰다

본문해석
Jane은 진한 흑차를 따르고 그것을 우유로 희석했다.

03 난도 ★☆☆ 　　　　　　　　　　　　정답 ①

어휘 > 어구

[정답의 이유]
밑줄 친 ruled out은 'rule out(제외하다)'의 과거형으로, 이와 의미가 가장 가까운 것은 ① 'excluded(제외했다)'이다.

② 지지했다

③ 제출했다

④ 재가했다

본문해석

수상은 육아 수당 또는 연금 삭감을 제외했던 것으로 여겨진다.

VOCA

- Prime Minister 수상
- be believed to ~로 여겨지다
- cuts 삭감, 감축, 인하
- child benefit (정부가 지급하는) 육아 수당
- pension 연금, 생활 보조금

04 난도 ★☆☆   정답 ①

어휘 > 어구

정답의 이유

밑줄 친 let on은 '(비밀을) 말하다, 털어놓다'라는 뜻으로, 이와 의미가 가장 가까운 것은 ① 'reveal(밝히다, 폭로하다)'이다.

오답의 이유

② 관찰[관측]하다

③ 믿다

④ 소유하다

본문해석

우리가 깜짝 파티를 계획하고 있다고 네가 털어놓으면, 아빠는 네게 질문을 멈추지 않을 거야.

05 난도 ★☆☆   정답 ③

어휘 > 단어

정답의 이유

빈칸 앞에 '슈퍼마켓의 자동문'이 있고, 빈칸 다음에 'the entry and exit of customers with bags or shopping carts(가방이나 쇼핑 카트를 지닌 고객의 출입)'라고 했으므로 문맥상 빈칸에는 슈퍼마켓 자동문의 역할을 나타내는 말이 와야 한다. 따라서 빈칸에 들어갈 말로 적절한 것은 ③ 'facilitate(용이하게 하다)'이다.

오답의 이유

① 무시하다, 묵살하다

② 용서하다

④ 과장하다

본문해석

슈퍼마켓의 자동문은 가방이나 장바구니를 든 고객의 출입을 용이하게 한다.

06 난도 ★☆☆   정답 ④

어법 > 비문 찾기

정답의 이유

④ 전치사구인 because of 다음에는 명사(구)가 와야 하는데, 여기서는 절(the author was working out his approach to psychology as he wrote it)이 왔으므로 because of → because로 고쳐야 한다.

오답의 이유

① one of 다음에 복수명사(virtues)가 어법상 바르게 사용되었으며, virtues를 수식하는 수 형용사인 many가 적절하게 사용되었다.

② 문장의 주어가 One이므로 단수동사(is)가 수일치되어 어법상 바르게 사용되었다.

③ 밑줄 친 which 앞의 Maps of Meaning과 which 다음에 오는 동사(is)가 있고 불완전한 문장이 왔으므로, which는 주격 관계대명사가 계속적 용법으로 올바르게 사용되었다.

본문해석

여러분이 읽고 있는 책의 여러 덕목 중 하나는 *Maps of Meaning*에 대한 진입점을 제공한다는 것이며, *Maps of Meaning*은 상당히 복잡한 작품인데, 작가가 그것을 집필할 때 심리에 대한 자신의 접근법을 끌어냈기 때문이다.

VOCA

- virtue 미덕, 덕목
- entry point 입구, 진입 지점
- work out 이끌어내다, ~을 계획해[생각해] 내다
- psychology 심리, 심리학

07 난도 ★★☆   정답 ③

어법 > 비문 찾기

정답의 이유

③ 관계대명사 who 다음에 daughter가 있고, 이어지는 절(I look after)이 목적어가 없는 불완전한 절이므로, 주격 관계대명사가 아닌 소유격 관계대명사가 와야 한다. 따라서 who → whose가 되어야 한다. that절에서 주어는 the people(관계대명사의 선행사), 동사는 are moving away이다.

오답의 이유

① plan은 to부정사를 목적어로 취하는 동사로, to부정사의 부정은 'not+to부정사'이므로 not to spend가 어법상 올바르게 사용되었다.

② disappear는 '사라지다, 없어지다'라는 뜻의 자동사이다. 따라서 수동태로 쓸 수 없으며, 뒤에 last month라는 과거 시점 부사구가 있으므로 과거동사(disappeared)가 올바르게 사용되었다.

④ '~배만큼 ~한[하게]'이란 의미를 지닌 배수사 비교 구문은 '배수사+as+형용사/부사+as'이며, 2형식 동사 was의 주격 보어는 형용사이므로 twice as expensive as가 올바르게 사용되었다.

① 프로젝트에 너무 많은 돈을 쓰지 않도록 계획해야 한다.

② 내 개가 지난달에 사라졌고 그 이후로 보이지 않았다.

③ 내가 돌봐주는 딸의 부모들이 이사 가게 되어 유감이다.

④ 나는 여행 중에 책을 한 권 샀는데, 그것은 본국에서보다 두 배나 더 비쌌다.

VOCA

• look after 돌봐주다, 보살피다

• move away 이사[이전]하다

• at home 본국에서

더 알아보기

수동태로 쓸 수 없는 동사

• 목적어를 갖지 않는 자동사는 수동태로 쓸 수 없다.

> appear, disappear, occur, happen, remain, come, arrive 등

예 My dog disappeared last month and hasn't been seen since.
(내 개가 지난달에 사라졌고 그 이후로 보이지 않았다.)

예 I'll be there whatever happens.
(나는 무슨 일이 있어도 거기 갈 것이다.)

예 All passengers should arrive at the railway station on time. (O)
All passengers should be arrived at the railway station on time. (×)
(모든 승객은 제시간에 기차역에 도착해야 한다.)

• 대상의 성질 또는 상태를 나타내는 상태동사는 수동태로 쓸 수 없다.

> have, resemble, cost, weigh, equal, lack 등

예 Tom resembles his father. (O)
His father is resembled by Tom. (×)
(Tom은 그의 아버지를 닮았다.)

예 This area lacks enough rain for rice farming.
(이 지역은 벼농사를 짓기에는 비가 부족하다.)

08 난도 ★★☆　　　　　　　　　　　　정답 ②

어법 > 영작하기

정답의 이유

② mention은 3형식 동사이기 때문에 수여동사로 쓸 수 없으므로 간접목적어(me) 앞에 전치사 to를 써야 한다. 따라서 mentioned me that → mentioned to me that이 되어야 한다. leave(떠나다)는 진행형으로 가까운 미래를 나타낼 수 있는 왕래발착동사로 would be leaving이 올바르게 사용되었다.

오답의 이유

① find가 to부정사를 목적어로 취하는 경우 'find+가목적어(it)+목적격 보어+to부정사'의 구조로 'to부정사가 목적격 보어한 것을 알다[생각하다]'라는 뜻을 갖는다. 그런데 목적어인 'to work

here(이곳에서 일하는 것)'가 '흥미를 느끼게 된' 것이 아니라 '흥미를 유발하는 것'이므로, 목적격 보어로 능동의 현재분사인 exciting이 올바르게 사용되었다.

③ 'want+목적어+to부정사'는 '목적어가 to부정사 하기를 원하다'의 뜻이므로, 목적격 보어로 to come이 올바르게 사용되었다.

④ 형용사 skillful과 experienced가 등위접속사 and로 병렬되어 뒤의 명사 teacher를 수식하고 있다. 또한 '좀 더 능숙하고 경험 많은 선생님이었다면 그를 달리 대했을 것'이라며 과거 사실의 반대를 가정하고 있으므로, 가정법 과거완료로 '조동사 과거형+have p.p.'가 올바르게 사용되었다.

더 알아보기

4형식으로 쓸 수 없는 완전타동사

다음 동사는 수여동사로 사용할 수 없는 완전타동사이다.

believe, explain, describe, announce, introduce, say, mention, prove, suggest, confess, propose 등	+(to+사람)+that절[의문사절]

예 Police believe (that) the man may be armed.
(경찰은 그 남자가 무기를 갖고 있을지도 모른다고 생각한다.)

예 She explained to them what to do in an emergency. (O)
She explained them what to do in an emergency. (×)
(그녀는 비상시에는 어떻게 해야 하는지를 그들에게 설명했다.)

cf. that절 또는 의문사절을 직접목적어로 취하는 4형식 동사

tell, convince, inform, notify, remind 등	+간접목적어(사람)+that절[의문사절]

예 They've told us (that) they're not coming.
(그들은 오지 않을 거라고 우리에게 말했다.)

예 Will you tell me what I should do next?
(이제 내가 다음에 뭘 해야 하는지 알려 줄래?)

예 The doctor advised to me(→ me) that I should stop smoking.
(의사는 나에게 내가 금연해야 한다고 충고했다.)

09 난도 ★☆☆　　　　　　　　　　　　정답 ④

표현 > 일반회화

정답의 이유

A와 B는 행사에 사용할 의자를 더 주문해야 하는지에 대해 대화를 나누고 있다. 빈칸 뒤에서 A가 'I agree. I am also a bit surprised(맞아요. 저도 조금 놀랐어요).'라고 하자 B가 'Looks like I'll have to order more then(그럼 더 주문해야 할 것 같네요).'이라고 했으므로, 빈칸에는 예상한 것보다 참석자가 많아서 놀랐다는 내용이 들어가야 한다. 따라서 빈칸에 들어갈 말로 가장 적절한 것은 ④ 'That's a lot more than I expected(내가 예상했던 것보다 훨씬 더 많네요).'이다.

오답의 이유

① 그 매니저가 행사에 참석할지 궁금해요.

② 나는 350명 이상 참석할 것으로 생각했어요.

③ 그다지 많은 수는 아니에요.

10 난도 ★☆☆ 정답 ④

표현 > 일반회화

정답의 이유

대화는 어제 회의에서 언급했던 문서를 이메일로 요청하는 상황으로, B가 빈칸 앞에서 'I don't have it with me. Mr. Park is in charge of the project, so he should have it(내가 그것을 가지고 있지 않아요. Mr. Park이 프로젝트 담당자이니까 가지고 있을 겁니다).'라고 했고, 빈칸 다음에서 'Hope you get the document you want(원하는 문서를 받으시길 바랍니다).'라고 했으므로, 대화의 흐름상 빈칸에 들어갈 말로 적절한 것은 ④ 'Thank you for letting me know. I'll contact him(알려주셔서 감사합니다. 그에게 연락해 볼게요).'이다.

오답의 이유

① 그가 사무실에 있는지 확인해 주시겠습니까?

② Mr. Park이 당신에게 다시 이메일을 보냈어요.

③ 지역 축제에 오시나요?

본문해석

A: 어제 회의에서 언급했던 문서를 받을 수 있을까요?

B: 네, 문서 제목이 뭐지요?

A: 제목은 기억이 나지 않는데, 지역 축제에 관한 것이었어요.

B: 네, 무엇을 얘기하고 계신지 알아요.

A: 좋아요. 그것을 내게 이메일로 보내주실 수 있나요?

B: 내가 그것을 가지고 있지 않아요. Mr. Park이 프로젝트 담당자이니까 갖고 있을 겁니다.

A: 알려주셔서 감사합니다. 그에게 연락해 볼게요.

B: 행운을 빌어요. 원하는 문서를 받으시길 바랍니다.

VOCA

• refer to 언급[지칭]하다

• community 주민, 지역 사회

• via (특정한 사람·시스템 등을) 통하여

• in charge of ~을 맡아서, 담당해서

11 난도 ★☆☆ 정답 ②

표현 > 일반회화

정답의 이유

대화는 다음 주 화요일에 있을 프레젠테이션에 관해 A가 B에게 질문하는 상황으로, 빈칸 다음에서 B가 프레젠테이션 2시간 전에 강의실에서 만날 수 있다고 하였으므로, 대화의 흐름상 빈칸에는 프레젠테이션 전에 미리 만나야 하는 이유와 관련된 내용이 들어가야 함을 유추할 수 있다. 따라서 빈칸에 들어갈 말로 가장 적절한 것은 ② 'When can I have a rehearsal for my presentation(프레젠테이션 리허설은 언제 할 수 있나요?)'이다.

오답의 이유

① 컴퓨터 기술자가 한 시간 전에 여기에 왔어요.

③ 우리 프로그램을 위해 더 많은 자원봉사자를 모집해야 할까요?

④ 회의실에 내 노트북을 두고 가는 게 불편해요.

본문해석

A: 안녕하세요, 다음 주 화요일에 있을 프레젠테이션에 대해 질문을 해도 될까요?

B: 자원봉사 프로그램 홍보에 대한 프레젠테이션 말인가요?

A: 네. 프레젠테이션 장소는 어디인가요?

B: 확인해 보겠습니다. 201호입니다.

A: 그렇군요. 회의실에서 노트북을 사용할 수 있나요?

B: 물론입니다. 회의실에 PC가 있긴 한데 원하시면 본인 것을 사용하실 수 있어요.

A: 프레젠테이션 리허설은 언제 할 수 있나요?

B: 프레젠테이션 2시간 전에는 회의실에서 만날 수 있어요. 괜찮으신가요?

A: 네. 정말 감사합니다!

VOCA

• promote 홍보하다

• laptop 휴대용[노트북] 컴퓨터

• rehearsal 리허설, 예행연습

• Would that work for you? 괜찮으세요?

• technician 기술자, 기사

• recruit 모집하다[뽑다]

12 난도 ★☆☆ 정답 ③

독해 > 세부 내용 찾기 > 내용 (불)일치

정답의 이유

이메일에서 'we would also like to book your restaurant for lunch on all three days(3일 내내 귀사의 레스토랑에 점심식사를 예약하고 싶습니다).'라고 했으므로 이메일의 내용과 일치하지 않는 것은 ③ '3일간의 저녁 식사를 위한 식당 예약이 필요하다.'이다.

① 'We need to have enough room for over 200 delegates in your main conference room(귀사의 주 회의실에 200명 이상의 대표자를 수용할 수 있는 충분한 공간이 필요하며) ~'이라고 했으므로 내용과 일치한다.

② '~ we would also like three small conference rooms for meetings. Each conference room needs wi-fi as well(회의를 위한 소회의실도 3곳이 필요합니다. 각 회의실에는 와이파이도 필요합니다.)'이라고 했으므로 내용과 일치한다.

④ 'We will need accommodations for over 100 delegates each night(매일 밤 100명 이상의 대표단 숙소가 필요합니다.)'라고 했으므로 내용과 일치한다.

본문해석

담당자님께,

Metropolitan Conference Center에 대한 정보를 요청하고자 메일 드립니다.

저희는 올해 9월에 3일 동안 컨퍼런스를 위한 장소를 찾고 있습니다. 귀사의 주 회의실에 200명 이상의 대표자를 수용할 수 있는 충분한 공간이 필요하며, 회의를 위한 소회의실도 3곳이 필요합니다. 각 회의실에는 와이파이도 필요합니다. 오전과 오후 중간에 커피를 마실 수 있어야 하고, 3일 내내 귀사의 레스토랑에 점심식사를 예약하고 싶습니다.

더불어, 메트로폴리탄 고객이나 대규모 단체를 위한 할인이 적용되는 현지 호텔이 있는지 알려주시겠습니까? 매일 밤 100명 이상의 대표단 숙소가 필요합니다.

회신 기다리겠습니다.

안부를 전하며,

Bruce Taylor, 행사 매니저 드림

VOCA

- venue (콘서트 · 스포츠 경기 · 회담 등의) 장소
- delegate 대표(자)
- available 구할[이용할] 수 있는
- book 예약하다
- discount rate 할인율
- accommodation 숙박 시설

13 난도 ★☆☆　　　　　　　　　　　　정답 ④

독해 > 세부 내용 찾기 > 내용 (불)일치

정답의 이유

마지막 문장에서 'The cravats were made of many different materials from plaid to lace(cravat는 격자무늬부터 레이스까지 많은 다른 재료들로 제작되어) ~'라고 했으므로 글의 내용과 일치하지 않는 것은 ④ 'The materials used to make the cravats were limited(cravat를 만드는 데 사용된 재료는 제한적이었다.)'이다.

① 1660년 한 무리의 크로아티아 군인이 파리를 방문했다. → 첫 번째, 두 번째 문장에서 'According to the historians, neckties date back to 1660. In that year, a group of soldiers from Croatia visited Paris(역사학자들에 따르면, 넥타이는 1660년까지 거슬러 올라간다. 그 해에, 크로아티아에서 온 한 무리의 군인들이 파리를 방문했다).'라고 했으므로 글의 내용과 일치한다.

② Royal Cravattes는 스카프를 두른 크로아티아 군인들을 기리기 위해 만들어졌다. → 네 번째 문장에서 '~ the king decided to honor the Croats by creating a military regiment called the Royal Cravattes(왕은 Royal Cravattes라고 불리는 군사 연대를 만들어 크로아티아인들을 기리기로 결정했다).'라고 했으므로 글의 내용과 일치한다.

③ 일부 cravat는 남자가 머리를 자유자재로 움직이기에는 너무 불편했다. → 열 번째 문장에서 'At times, they were so high that a man could not move his head without turning his whole body(때로, 그것들이 너무 높아서 남자가 온몸을 돌리지 않고는 자신의 머리를 움직일 수 없었다).'라고 했으므로 글의 내용과 일치한다.

본문해석

역사학자들에 따르면, 넥타이는 1660년까지 거슬러 올라간다. 그 해에, 크로아티아에서 온 한 무리의 군인들이 파리를 방문했다. 이 군인들은 루이 14세가 매우 존경했던 전쟁 영웅들이었다. 그들이 목에 걸었던 색깔이 있는 스카프에 감명받은 왕은 Royal Cravattes라고 불리는 군사 연대를 만들어 크로아티아인들을 기리기로 결정했다. cravat라는 단어는 크로아티어 단어로부터 생겼다. 이 연대의 모든 군인들은 다양한 색깔의 스카프 또는 cravat를 목에 걸었다. 이 새로운 스타일의 목에 두르는 물건은 영국으로 이동했다. 곧 모든 상류층 남자들이 cravat를 착용하고 있었다. 일부 cravat는 꽤 극단적이었다. 때로, 그것들이 너무 높아서 남자가 온몸을 돌리지 않고는 자신의 머리를 움직일 수 없었다. cravat는 격자무늬부터 레이스까지 많은 다른 재료들로 제작되어, 어떤 행사에도 어울렸다.

VOCA

- historian 사학자
- date back ~까지 거슬러 올라가다
- admire 존경하다, 칭찬하다
- impressed with ~에 감동하다, 깊은 감명을 받다
- honor ~에게 영광을 베풀다
- military regiment 군대 연대
- come from ~에서 생겨나다
- cravat 크라바트(넥타이처럼 매는 남성용 스카프)
- plaid 격자[타탄(tartan)무늬 천
- suitable for ~에 알맞은[어울리는]
- occasion 행사[의식/축하]

14 난도 ★☆☆   정답 ③

독해 > 대의 파악 > 제목, 주제

[정답의 이유]

도입부에서 최근 라틴 아메리카는 풍력, 태양열, 지열 및 바이오 연료 에너지 자원을 활용하는 데 큰 진전을 이루어서 전력 부문의 석유 의존도를 낮추기 시작했다고 했고, 마지막 문장에서 'Countries in Central America and the Caribbean, ~ were the first to move away from oil-based power plants(중앙 아메리카와 카리브해 국가들은 ~ 석유 기반 발전소로부터 가장 먼저 벗어났다) ~'라고 했으므로 글의 주제로 적절한 것은 ③ 'advancement of renewable energy in Latin America(라틴 아메리카의 재생 에너지 발전)'이다.

[오답의 이유]

① 호황을 누리고 있는 라틴 아메리카의 석유 산업
② 감소하는 라틴 아메리카의 전기 사업
④ 라틴 아메리카의 공격적인 석유 기반 자원 개발

[본문해석]

최근 몇 년 동안 라틴 아메리카는 엄청난 풍력, 태양열, 지열 및 바이오 연료 에너지 자원을 활용하는 데 막대한 진전을 이루었다. 라틴 아메리카의 전력 부문은 이미 석유에 대한 의존도를 점차 낮추기 시작했다. 라틴 아메리카는 2015년에서 2040년 사이에 전력 생산량을 거의 두 배로 늘릴 것으로 예상된다. 사실상 라틴 아메리카의 새로운 대규모 발전소 중 석유를 연료로 사용하는 발전소가 거의 없을 것이고, 이는 다른 기술을 위한 장을 열어줄 것이다. 중앙 아메리카와 카리브해 국가들은 전통적으로 석유를 수입했는데, 금세기 초 10년 동안 높고 불안정한 (석유) 가격으로 고통받은 후에 석유 기반 발전소로부터 가장 먼저 벗어났다.

[VOCA]

- stride 진전
- exploit 이용하다
- geothermal 지열의
- biofuel 바이오 연료
- energy resource 동력 자원
- electricity sector 전기 부분
- gradually 서서히
- decrease 줄다[감소하다]
- dependence 의존, 의지
- output 생산량, 산출량
- practically 사실상, 거의
- power plant 발전소
- oil-fueled 기름을 연료로 쓰는
- open up ~을[이] 가능하게 하다[가능해지다]
- volatile 변덕스러운, 불안한
- boom 호황을 맞다, 번창[성공]하다
- advancement 발전, 진보
- renewable energy 재생 에너지
- aggressive 공격적인[대단히 적극적인]

15 난도 ★★☆   정답 ③

독해 > 대의 파악 > 제목, 주제

[정답의 이유]

두 번째 문장에서 조직의 직무 수행은 자원을 얼마나 갖고 있느냐의 역할이라기보다는 보유 자원을 얼마나 잘 활용하느냐의 역할이라고 했고, 세 번째 문장에서 'You as the organization's leader can always make the use of those resources more efficient and effective(여러분은 조직의 리더로서 항상 이러한 자원을 더 능률적이고 효과적으로 사용할 수 있는데) ~'라고 했다. 마지막 문장에서 조직의 리더로서 주어진 자원을 효율적으로 이용할 수 있는 구체적인 방법을 제시하고 있으므로 글의 제목으로 적절한 것은 ③ 'Making the Most of the Resources: A Leader's Way(자원을 최대한 활용하기: 리더의 길)'이다.

[오답의 이유]

① 조직 내 자원 교환하기
② 외부 통제를 설정하는 리더의 능력
④ 조직의 기술적 역량: 성공을 가로막는 장벽

[본문해석]

모든 조직은 임무를 수행하기 위해 사용할 수 있는 자원을 가지고 있다. 조직이 얼마나 직무를 잘 수행하느냐는 부분적으로 이러한 자원을 얼마나 많이 가지고 있느냐에 달려있지만, 대부분 인력과 자금 같은 보유 자원을 얼마나 잘 활용하느냐에 달려있다. 조직의 인사와 정책에 대한 통제권을 가지고 있다는 조건하에, 여러분은 조직의 리더로서 항상 이러한 자원을 더 능률적이고 효과적으로 사용할 수 있는데, 이는 자동적으로 발생하는 조건이 아니다. 인력과 자금을 신중하게 관리하고, 가장 중요한 일을 가장 중요하게 취급하고, 좋은 결정을 내리고, 직면한 문제를 해결함으로써 여러분은 여러분이 이용 가능한 것들을 최대한 활용할 수 있다.

[VOCA]

- resource 자원, 재원
- mission 임무
- function 기능, 역할
- make use of ~을 이용하다, 활용하다
- efficient 능률적인, 유능한
- effective 효과적인
- personnel 인원[직원들]
- agenda 의제[안건] (목록)
- occur 일어나다, 발생하다
- automatically 자동적으로
- treat 대하다[다루다/취급하다/대우하다]
- encounter 접하다[마주치다]
- set up 설립[수립]하다
- external 외부의[외부적인]
- capacity 용량, 수용력
- barrier 장애물[장벽]

독해 > 글의 일관성 > 무관한 어휘 · 문장

정답의 이유

제시문은 비판적 사고 과정에서 드러나는 감정을 잘 관리하여 자신의 의견을 설득력 있게 주장해야 한다는 내용이다. ③ 앞 문장에서 '학계는 전통적으로 스스로 논리적이고 감정이 없는 것으로 여기는 것을 좋아하기 때문에, 감정을 드러낼 경우, 이는 특히 어려울 수 있다.'라고 했고, ③ 다음 문장에서 감정을 관리하는 것은 유용한 기술이라고 했다. ③은 '예를 들어, 동일한 정보를 여러 관점에서 보는 것이 중요하지 않다.'라는 내용이므로 글의 흐름상 어색한 문장이다.

본문해석

비판적 사고는 감정적이지 않은 과정처럼 들리지만, 감정과 심지어 격렬한 반응을 끌어들일 수 있다. 특히, 우리는 우리 자신의 의견이나 신념에 반하는 증거를 좋아하지 않을 수도 있다. 만약 그 증거가 도전적인 방향을 향하면, 그것은 예상치 못한 분노, 좌절감 또는 불안감을 불러일으킬 수 있다. 학계는 전통적으로 스스로 논리적이고 감정이 없다고 여기는 것을 좋아하기 때문에, 감정을 드러낼 경우, 이는 특히 어려울 수 있다. 예를 들어, 동일한 정보를 여러 관점에서 보는 것은 중요하지 않다. 그런 상황에서 여러분의 감정을 관리할 수 있는 것은 유용한 기술이다. 만약 여러분이 침착함을 유지하고 논리적으로 자신의 이유를 제시할 수 있다면, 여러분은 자신의 관점을 설득력 있는 방법으로 더 잘 주장할 수 있을 것이다.

VOCA

- unemotional 감정을 드러내지 않는, 침착한
- engage (주의 · 관심을) 사로잡다[끌다]
- passionate 열정적인, 열렬한
- evidence 증거, 흔적
- contradict 부정[부인]하다, 반박하다
- point (특정 방향으로) 향하다[향하게 되다]
- challenging 도전적인, 도전 의식을 북돋우는
- rouse (어떤 감정을) 불러일으키다[자아내다]
- unexpected 예기치 않은, 예상 밖의, 뜻밖의
- emerge 드러나다, 알려지다
- circumstance 환경, 상황, 정황
- remain (없어지지 않고) 남다
- present 보여 주다[나타내다/묘사하다]
- argue 주장하다, 논증하다
- convincing 설득력 있는, (승리 등이) 확실한

독해 > 글의 일관성 > 글의 순서

정답의 이유

주어진 글에서 컴퓨터 보조언어학습(CALL)이 흥미와 좌절감을 동시에 준다고 했으므로, 문맥상 그 두 가지 감정을 주는 이유를 설명하는 (B)가 오는 것이 자연스럽다. (C)에서 '기술(Technology)'이 언어학습 영역에서 새로운 차원을 더해 주어 실무에 적용하려는 사람들에게 새로운 지식과 기술을 요구한다고 했고, (A)에서 '그러나 (Yet)' 그 기술(the technology)이 너무 빨리 변해서 따라잡으려면 컴퓨터 보조언어학습의 지식과 기술도 끊임없이 갱신되어야 한다고 했으므로, 흐름상 (C)가 오고 다음에 (A)가 와야 한다. 따라서 주어진 글 다음에 이어질 순서로 적절한 것은 ③ '(B) – (C) – (A)'이다.

본문해석

컴퓨터 보조언어학습(CALL)은 연구 및 실습 분야로서 흥미로우면서 좌절감을 주기도 한다.
(B) 그것은 복잡하고 역동적이면서 빠르게 변하기 때문에 흥미로운데, 같은 이유로 인해 좌절감을 주기도 한다.
(C) 기술은 언어학습 영역에 차원을 더하여 전문적인 실습에 적용하려는 사람들에게 새로운 지식과 기술을 요구한다.
(A) 하지만 그 기술은 너무 빠르게 변해서 CALL 지식과 기술이 그 분야에서 발맞추기 위해서는 끊임없이 갱신되어야 한다.

VOCA

- assist 돕다, 도움이 되다
- frustrating 좌절감을 주는
- dynamic 역동적인
- dimension 차원, 관점
- domain 영역[분야], (책임의) 범위
- apply 꼭 들어맞다, 적용되다,
- constantly 끊임없이, 계속
- renewed 새롭게 한, 회복된, 갱신된
- apace 발맞추어, 빨리

독해 > 글의 일관성 > 문장 삽입

정답의 이유

주어진 문장에서 '그러나 인어공주(she)가 재빨리 다시 머리를 내밀었다.'라고 했으므로 주어진 문장은 물속으로 들어가는 내용 다음에 위치해야 한다. ④ 앞 문장의 후반부에서 '~ she dove down under the water(그녀는 물속으로 들어갔다).'라고 했으므로 주어진 문장이 들어갈 위치로 적절한 것은 ④이다.

본문해석

인어공주는 선실의 작은 창문까지 헤엄쳐 올라갔고, 파도가 그녀를 들어올릴 때마다, 그녀는 투명한 유리를 통해 옷을 잘 차려입은 사람들의 무리를 볼 수 있었다. 그중에 커다란 검은 눈을 가진 젊은 왕자가 있었는데, 그곳에서 가장 잘생긴 사람이었다. 그날은 왕자의 생일이었고, 그것이 바로 그토록 신나는 이유였다. 젊은 왕자가 선원들이 춤추고 있는 갑판으로 나왔을 때, 100개가 넘는 폭죽이 하늘로 올라갔다가 반짝이면서 부서져서 하늘을 낮처럼 밝게 만들었다. 인어공주는 너무 놀라서 물속으로 들어갔다. 그러나 그녀는 재빨리 다시 머리를 내밀었다. 이것 봐! 마치 하늘에 있는 모든 별들이 그녀에게로 떨어지는 것 같았다. 그녀는 그런 불꽃놀이를 본 적이 없었다.

VOCA

• pop 잠깐[불쑥] 내놓다

• mermaid 인어

• lift 들어올리다[올리다]

• rocket 폭죽

• glitter 반짝반짝 빛나다

• startled ~에 놀란

• dive 잠수하다

• firework 불꽃놀이

독해 > 빈칸 완성 > 단어 · 구 · 절

정답의 이유

제시문은 모든 밀레니얼 세대가 현재 같은 삶의 단계에 있는 것이 아니라고 하면서, 나이에 따라 Y.1세대와 Y.2세대로 구분하여 설명하고 있다. 다섯 번째 문장에서 'Not only are the two groups culturally different, but they're in vastly different phases of their financial life(두 집단은 문화적으로 다를 뿐만 아니라, 재정적으로도 크게 다른 단계에 있다).'라고 했고, 이후에서 더 어린 집단(The younger group)과 후자의 집단(The latter group)의 차이를 서술하고 있다. 따라서 빈칸에 들어갈 말로 적절한 것은 ① 'contrast(차이)'이다.

오답의 이유

② 축소, 삭감

③ 반복, 재현

④ 능력, 역량

본문해석

Javelin Research는 모든 밀레니얼 세대가 현재 같은 삶의 단계에 있는 것은 아니라는 것을 주목했다. 모든 밀레니얼 세대는 세기의 전환기에 출생했지만, 그들 중 일부는 아직 성인 초기 단계에 있어서, 새로운 직업과 씨름하면서 정착하고 있다. 반면에, 더 나이가 많은 밀레니얼 세대는 집이 있고 가족을 형성하고 있다. 여러분은 아이를 갖는 것이 여러분의 관심사와 우선순위를 어떻게 바꿀 수 있는지 상상해볼 수 있을 것이다. 따라서 마케팅적인 목적을 위해 이 세대를 Y.1세대와 Y.2세대로 나누는 것이 유용하다. 두 집단은 문화적으로 다를 뿐만 아니라, 재정적으로도 크게 다른 단계에 있다. 나이가 더 어린 집단은 재정적으로 초보자로, 이제 막 그들의 구매력을 보여주기 시작한다. 후자의 집단은 신용 기록이 있고, 그들의 첫 번째 대출을 받았을 수도 있고 어린아이들을 키우고 있다. Y.1세대와 Y.2세대 사이의 우선순위와 필요의 차이는 방대하다.

VOCA

• notice 주목하다, 관심을 기울이다

• Millennials 밀레니얼 세대(1980년대에서 2000년대 사이에 태어난 세대)

• currently 현재는, 지금은

• adulthood 성인(임), 성년

• wrestle with ~을 해결하려고 애쓰다

• settle down 정착하다

• priority 우선순위

• split 분열되다, 의견이 갈리다; 분열시키다

• vastly 대단히, 엄청나게

• phase 단계[시기/국면]

• financial 금융[재정]의

• mortgage (담보) 대출(금), 융자(금)

• vast 어마어마한[방대한/막대한]

20 난도 ★★☆   정답 ①

독해 > 빈칸 완성 > 단어 · 구 · 절

[정답의 이유]

제시문은 자유화된 시장에서 비용 압박이 기존 수력 발전 계획과 미래의 수력 발전 계획에 미치는 서로 다른 영향에 대한 내용이다. 두 번째 문장에서 'Because of the cost structure, existing hydropower plants will always be able to earn a profit(비용 구조 때문에 기존 수력 발전소는 항상 이익을 얻을 수 있을 것이다).'라고 한 다음에, 세 번째 문장에서 미래의 수력 발전 계획과 건설은 단기적인 과정이 아니기 때문에, 낮은 발전 비용에도 불구하고 대중적인 투자가 아니라고 했다. 빈칸 앞에서 '대부분의 민간 투자자들은 ~에 자금을 조달하는 것을 선호할 것'이라고 했고, 빈칸 다음에서 '기존 수력 발전소가 고수익 사업처럼 보이지만 아무도 새로운 곳에 투자하기를 원하지 않는 역설적인 상황으로 이어진다.'라고 했으므로 빈칸에는 '단기적인 투자'와 관련된 내용이 와야 함을 알 수 있다. 따라서 빈칸에 들어갈 말로 적절한 것은 ① 'more short-term technologies(더 단기적인 기술)'이다.

[오답의 이유]

② 모든 첨단 기술 산업

③ 공익의 증진

④ 전력 공급의 향상

본문해석

자유화된 시장에서 비용 압력은 기존의 그리고 미래의 수력 발전 계획에 다른 영향을 미친다. 비용 구조 때문에 기존 수력 발전소는 항상 이익을 얻을 수 있을 것이다. 미래의 수력 발전 계획과 건설은 단기간의 프로세스가 아니기 때문에, 낮은 발전 비용에도 불구하고 대중적인 투자가 아니다. 대부분 민간 투자자들은 더 단기적인 기술에 자금을 조달하는 것을 선호할 것이고, 이는 기존 수력 발전소가 고수익 사업처럼 보이지만 누구도 새로운 곳(수력 발전소)에 투자하기를 원하지 않는 역설적인 상황으로 이어진다. 공공 주주들/소유자들(주, 시, 지방자치단체)이 관련된 경우, 상황은 매우 다르게 보이는데, 그들이 공급 안정성의 중요성을 이해할 수 있고 장기적인 투자를 높이 평가하기 때문이다.

VOCA

- cost pressure 비용 압박
- have effects on ~에 영향을 미치다
- existing 기존의, 현재 사용되는
- hydropower 수력 전기(력)
- scheme 계획, 제도, 책략
- cost structure 원가구조
- short-term process 단기간의 프로세스
- investment 투자
- electricity generation costs 발전(전기 생산) 비용
- prefer to ~보다 선호하다
- finance 자금[재원]을 대다
- paradoxical 역설적인
- cash cow 고수익[효자] 상품[사업]

- shareholder 출자자, 주주
- municipality 지방자치제, 지방자치제 당국
- security 안전, 무사(safety), 안전 확보
- appreciate (가치를) 정당하게 평가하다, 높이 평가하다
- public interest 공익, 일반 대중의 관심
- enhancement 고양, 증진, 증대, 강화
- electricity supply 전력 공급

76 시대에듀 | 국가직 · 지방직 · 법원직 공무원

영어 | 2023년 지방직 9급

한눈에 훑어보기

✓ 영역 분석

어휘 01 02 03 04 05
5문항, 25%

독해 12 13 14 15 16 17 18 19 20
9문항, 45%

어법 06 07 08
3문항, 15%

표현 09 10 11
3문항, 15%

✓ 빠른 정답

01	02	03	04	05	06	07	08	09	10
②	④	①	①	④	③	③	①	④	③
11	12	13	14	15	16	17	18	19	20
③	②	②	④	④	④	②	②	①	③

✓ 점수 체크

구분	1회독	2회독	3회독
맞힌 문항 수	/ 20	/ 20	/ 20
나의 점수	점	점	점

01 난도 ★☆☆　　　　　　　　정답 ②

어휘 > 단어

[정답의 이유]

밑줄 친 subsequent는 '차후의, 그 다음의'의 뜻으로, 의미가 가장 가까운 것은 ② 'following(그 다음에 나오는)'이다.

[오답의 이유]

① 필수의

③ 선진의

④ 보충의, 추가의

본문해석

우리의 프로젝트에 대한 추가적인 설명은 <u>차후의</u> 프레젠테이션에서 제공될 것이다.

VOCA

• further　그 이상의

• explanation　설명

02 난도 ★☆☆　　　　　　　　정답 ④

어휘 > 단어

[정답의 이유]

밑줄 친 courtesy는 '공손함, 정중함'이라는 뜻으로, 의미가 가장 가까운 것은 ④ 'politeness(공손함, 예의바름)'이다.

[오답의 이유]

① 자선, 자비

② 겸손, 겸양

③ 대담, 배짱

본문해석

사회적 관행은 한 집단의 구성원들이 다른 사람들에게 공손함을 보이기 위해 따라야 하는 관습이다. 예를 들어, 재채기를 할 때 "실례합니다."라고 말하는 것은 미국의 사회적 관행이다.

VOCA

• folkway　민속, 사회적 관행

• custom　관습, 풍습, 관행

• be expected to　~하도록 기대된다, 예상된다

• follow　따르다[따라 하다]

• sneeze　재채기하다

03 난도 ★☆☆ 정답 ①

어휘 > 어구

[정답의 이유]

bring up은 '~을 기르다[양육하다]'라는 뜻인데, 주어진 문장에서는 수동의 뜻인 '양육되어지다'로 사용되었으므로, 의미가 가장 가까운 것은 ① 'raised(길러진)'이다.

[오답의 이유]

② 조언받은

③ 관찰된

④ 관리[운영/통제]된

본문해석

이 아이들은 건강에 좋은 음식을 주식으로 먹고 양육되었다.

VOCA

• on a diet of ~을 주식[먹이]으로

• healthy food 건강에 좋은 음식

04 난도 ★★☆ 정답 ①

어휘 > 어구

[정답의 이유]

do away with는 '~을 폐지하다'라는 뜻인데, 주어진 문장에서는 수동의 의미로 쓰였으므로, 의미가 가장 가까운 것은 ① 'abolished(폐지된)'이다.

[오답의 이유]

② 합의된

③ 비판된

④ 정당화된

본문해석

노예제는 19세기까지 미국에서 폐지되지 않았다.

VOCA

• slavery 노예, 노예제도

05 난도 ★☆☆ 정답 ④

어휘 > 단어

[정답의 이유]

주어진 문장의 뒷부분에서 'so that they could see and understand it clearly(그들이 그것을 명확하게 보고 이해할 수 있도록)'이라고 했고, 앞부분에서 '유권자들은 선거 과정에서 더 많은 ~이 있어야 한다고 요구했다.'라고 했으므로, 밑줄 친 부분에 들어갈 말로 가장 적절한 것은 ④ 'transparency(투명성)'이다.

[오답의 이유]

① 속임, 속임수

② 융통성, 유연성

③ 경쟁, 경쟁 상대

본문해석

유권자들은 선거 절차를 명확히 보고 이해할 수 있도록 선거 과정에서 더 많은 투명성이 있어야 한다고 요구했다.

VOCA

• voter 투표자, 유권자

• demand 요구하다

• election process 선거 과정

• so that can ~할 수 있도록

06 난도 ★★☆ 정답 ③

어법 > 비문 찾기

[정답의 이유]

③ what은 선행사를 포함하는 관계대명사로 다음에 불완전한 절이 와야 하는데, what 다음에 'the superior team may not have perceived their opponents ~ their continued success'인 완전한 절이 왔다. 따라서 동사(is) 다음에 명사절 접속사 that이 와야 하므로, what → that이 되어야 한다.

[오답의 이유]

① in which(전치사+관계대명사) 다음에 완전한 절인 'the team ~ surprisingly loses the contest'가 왔으므로, 적절하게 사용되었다.

② predicted는 바로 앞의 명사(the team)를 수식하는 분사로, the team은 승리할 것이라고 '예측되는' 대상이므로 과거분사인 predicted가 적절하게 사용되었다. 이때 predicted 앞에는 'which was'가 생략된 것이다. 문맥상 관계사절(in which the team predicted to win ~ loses the contest)의 동사는 loses 이다.

④ 'perceive A as B'는 'A를 B라고 여기다'의 뜻으로, their opponents가 '위협하는' 것이므로, 능동의 현재분사 threatening이 적절하게 사용되었다.

본문해석

스포츠에서 우승할 것으로 예상되고 상대 팀보다 우세할 것으로 추정되는 팀이 놀랍게도 경기에서 지는 뜻밖의 패배의 한 가지 이유는 우세한 팀이 상대 팀을 자신의 지속적인 성공에 위협적이라고 여기지 않았을 수도 있기 때문이다.

VOCA

• upset 뜻밖의 패배

• predict 예측[예견]하다

• supposedly 추정상, 아마

• superior to ~보다 뛰어난

• opponent (시합·논쟁 등의) 상대

• surprisingly 놀랍게도

• threatening 위협적인

• continued 지속적인

관계대명사 what

• 선행사를 포함하는 관계대명사 what은 '~하는 것'의 뜻으로, the thing which[that]로 쓸 수 있다. 관계대명사 what은 명사절을 이끌며 문장에서 주어, 목적어, 보어 역할을 한다.

예 They are fully able to discern what concerns their business. (to discern의 목적어)

(그들은 자신들의 사업과 관련된 것을 완전히 분별할 수 있다.)

• what＝선행사＋관계대명사

예 She didn't understand what I said. = She didn't understand the fact that I said.

(그녀는 내가 한 말을 이해하지 못했다.)

• 관계대명사 what vs. 접속사 that

관계대명사 what과 접속사 that은 둘 다 명사절을 이끌고 what 다음에는 불완전한 절이, 접속사 that 다음에는 완전한 절이 온다.

예 I believe what he told me.

(나는 그가 내게 말한 것을 믿는다.)

→ what이 believe의 목적어가 되는 명사절을 이끌며, what 이하는 불완전한 문장이다.

예 I can't believe that he's only 17.

(나는 그가 겨우 17세라는 것을 믿을 수 없다.)

→ that이 believe의 목적어가 되는 명사절을 이끌며, that 이하는 완전한 문장이다.

07 난도 ★★☆   정답 ③

어법 > 비문 찾기

정답의 이유

③ alive는 '살아 있는'의 뜻으로 서술적 용법으로만 쓰이는 형용사이므로, an alive man → a living man이 되어야 한다. 그 밖에 서술적 용법으로만 사용되는 형용사로는 alive, asleep, afloat 등이 있다.

오답의 이유

① 'should have p.p.'는 '~했어야 했는데 (안 했다)'의 뜻으로, 'but I was feeling a bit ill'에 하지 않은 이유가 나오고 있으므로 어법상 적절하게 사용되었다.

② 'as ~ as' 원급 비교 구문에서 두 번째 as 다음에 'we used to'가 왔으므로, as가 접속사로 적절하게 사용되었다. 'used to 동사원형'은 '(~하곤) 했다'라는 뜻으로 과거의 습관을 나타내는 표현으로 to 다음에 save money가 생략되었다.

④ '자동사＋전치사'인 look at은 '~을 보다'의 뜻으로, 수동태로 전환할 때 전치사를 생략할 수 없으므로, was looked at이 적절하게 사용되었다. 이 문장을 능동태로 바꾸면 'The art critic looked at the picture carefully.'가 된다.

① 나는 오늘 아침에 갔어야 했는데, 몸이 좀 안 좋았다(그래서 못 갔다).

② 요즘 우리는 예전에 그랬던 것만큼 많은 돈을 저축하지 않는다.

③ 구조대는 살아있는 남자를 발견해서 기뻤다.

④ 그 그림은 미술 평론가에 의해 주의 깊게 관찰되었다.

• a bit 조금, 약간

• save 모으다, 저축하다

• rescue squad 구조대

• discover 발견하다, 찾다

• art critic 미술 비평가

형용사가 서술적 용법으로 사용되는 경우

• afraid, alone, ashamed, alive, asleep, alike, awake, aware 등 'a-' 형용사는 서술적 용법(주격 보어, 목적격 보어)으로만 사용되며 한정적 용법으로는 쓰일 수 없다.

예 He caught a living tiger. (○)

He caught an alive tiger. (×)

(그는 살아있는 호랑이를 잡았다.)

예 He caught a tiger alive. (○)

(그는 호랑이 한 마리를 산 채로 잡았다.)

• alert, aloof 등은 한정적 용법, 서술적 용법 모두 사용된다.

예 An alert guard stopped the robbers.

(기민한 경비원이 강도들을 막았다.)

예 Being aware of this, you will be alert and attentive to meaning.

(이것을 알게 되면, 여러분은 방심하지 않고 의미에 주의를 기울일 것이다.)

• 형용사 다음에 to부정사, 전치사구, that절이 연결되면 서술적 용법으로 사용된다. –able, likely, famous, sure 등은 한정적 용법과 서술적 용법 둘 다 가능한데, to부정사, 전치사구, that절과 함께 나올 때 서술적 용법으로 사용된다.

예 the most likely cause of the problem

(그 문제의 가장 유력한 원인)

예 Children who live in the country's rural areas are very likely to be poor.

(시골 지역에 사는 어린이들은 가난할 가능성이 매우 높다.)

• well, unwell, ill, poorly, faint 등 건강 상태를 나타내는 형용사는 서술적 용법으로만 사용된다.

예 I have been well. (나는 그동안 건강하게 지냈다.)

예 Jane felt unwell and went home.

(Jane은 몸이 좋지 않아서 집에 갔다.)

08 난도 ★☆☆   정답 ①

어법 > 영작하기

[정답의 이유]

① 'He made us touched with his speech.'의 수동태 문장으로, 목적어인 us는 '감동을 주는' 것이 아니라 '감동을 받는' 것이므로 touching → touched가 되어야 한다.

[오답의 이유]

② apart from은 '~은 차치하고, ~은 제외하고'라는 뜻의 전치사구로, 뒤에 명사(its cost)가 온 것 역시 적절하다. 부정대명사 one은 the plan 대신 사용되었다.

③ 'while drinking hot tea'는 분사구문으로, 주절과 부사절의 주어가 they로 같기 때문에 부사절에서 they were를 생략하였다. 또한 they는 차를 '마시는' 능동적인 대상이므로 능동의 의미인 현재분사 drinking은 적절하게 사용되었다.

④ '사역동사(make)+목적어+목적격 보어'에서 목적어 him 다음에 '어울리는, 적당한'이라는 뜻의 형용사 suited가 목적격 보어로 적절하게 사용되었다.

09 난도 ★☆☆   정답 ④

표현 > 일반회화

[정답의 이유]

대화에서 A가 빈칸 앞에서 도움을 요청하고 빈칸 다음에서 인사과를 찾는다고 말했으므로, 대화의 흐름상 빈칸에는 B가 도와주겠다고 말하는 내용이 들어가야 함을 유추할 수 있다. 따라서 빈칸에 들어갈 말로 가장 적절한 것은 ④ 'Sure. Can I help you with anything(물론이죠. 무엇을 도와드릴까요)?'이다.

[오답의 이유]

① 우리는 이 상황을 어떻게 처리해야 할지 모르겠어요.

② 담당자가 누구인지 말씀해 주시겠어요?

③ 네. 여기 도움이 필요해요.

본문해석

A: 죄송하지만, 좀 도와주실 수 있나요?

B: 물론이죠. 무엇을 도와드릴까요?

A: 인사과를 찾으려 하고 있어요. 10시에 약속이 있어요.

B: 3층에 있어요.

A: 어떻게 올라가죠?

B: 모퉁이를 돌아서 엘리베이터를 타세요.

VOCA

• give a hand 도와주다

• Personnel Department 인사과

• have no idea 전혀 모르다

• in charge of ~을 맡은, 담당인

• could use some help 도움이 필요하다

10 난도 ★☆☆   정답 ③

표현 > 일반회화

[정답의 이유]

대화는 A가 B에게 사무실 전등과 에어컨을 끄지 않고 퇴근한 것에 대해 주의를 주는 상황으로, 빈칸 앞에서 A가 'Probably they were on all night.'이라고 했으므로, 빈칸에 들어갈 말로 가장 적절한 것은 ③ 'I'm sorry. I promise I'll be more careful from now on(죄송합니다. 앞으로 더 조심하겠습니다).'이다.

[오답의 이유]

① 걱정하지 마세요. 이 기계는 잘 작동하고 있어요.

② 맞아요. 모든 사람들이 당신과 함께 일하는 것을 좋아해요.

④ 안됐군요. 너무 늦게 퇴근해서 피곤하시겠어요.

본문해석

A: 마지막으로 퇴근하셨죠, 그렇죠?

B: 네. 무슨 문제라도 있나요?

A: 오늘 아침에 사무실 전등과 에어컨이 켜져 있는 것을 발견했어요.

B: 정말요? 아, 이런. 아마 어젯밤에 그것들을 끄는 것을 깜빡 잊었나 봐요.

A: 아마 밤새 켜져 있었을 거예요.

B: 죄송합니다. 앞으로 더 조심하겠습니다.

VOCA

• turn off (전기 · 가스 · 수도 등을) 끄다

• from now on 이제부터, 향후

11 난도 ★☆☆   정답 ③

표현 > 일반회화

[정답의 이유]

A가 오랜만에 만나서 얼마 만에 보는 건지 물었는데, 차로 한 시간 반 정도 걸렸다는 B의 대답은 어색하다. 따라서 대화 중 자연스럽지 않은 것은 ③이다.

본문해석

① A: 머리는 어떻게 해 드릴까요?

   B: 머리 색깔이 좀 싫증나서요. 염색하고 싶어요.

② A: 지구 온난화를 늦추기 위해 우리가 할 수 있는 일은 무엇일까요?

   B: 우선, 대중교통을 더 많이 이용할 수 있어요.

③ A: Anna, 당신이에요? 오랜만이에요! 이게 얼마 만이죠?

   B: 차로 한 시간 반 정도 걸렸어요.

④ A: Paul이 걱정돼요. 불행해 보여요. 어떻게 해야 하죠?

   B: 내가 당신이라면, 그가 자기 문제에 대해 말할 때까지 기다릴 거예요.

VOCA

• be tired of ~에 질리다

• dye 염색하다

• slow down 속도를 늦추다

- global warming 지구 온난화
- public transportation 대중교통
- be worried about ~에 대해 걱정하다

12 난도 ★★★   정답 ②

독해 > 대의 파악 > 제목, 주제

정답의 이유

주어진 글은 인간 관계학의 유명한 작가 Daniel Goleman의 주장을 바탕으로 인간의 뇌가 얼마나 사교적인지를 주장하는 내용이다. 세 번째 문장에서 'we are drawn to other people's brains whenever we engage with another person.'이라고 했고, 마지막 문장에서 'Yet, our brains crave human interaction.'이라고 했으므로, 글의 제목으로 가장 적절한 것은 ② 'Sociable Brains(사교적인 두뇌)'이다.

오답의 이유

① 외로운 사람들
③ 정신 건강 조사의 필요성
④ 인간 연결성의 위험

본문해석

저명한 작가 Daniel Goleman은 인간관계 과학에 평생을 바쳐 왔다. 그의 저서 'Social Intelligence'에서 그는 인간의 뇌가 얼마나 사교적인지 설명하기 위해 신경사회학의 결과를 논한다. Goleman에 따르면, 우리는 다른 사람과 관계를 맺을 때마다 다른 사람의 뇌에 마음이 끌린다고 한다. 우리의 관계를 깊이 있게 하기 위해 다른 사람들과의 의미 있는 연결에 대한 인간의 욕구는 우리 모두가 갈망하는 것이지만, 우리는 그 어느 때보다 더 외로우며 이제 외로움은 세계적인 유행병이 되었음을 시사하는 수많은 기사와 연구들이 있다. 특히 호주에서 전국적인 Lifeline 설문조사에 따르면, 조사 대상자의 80% 이상이 우리 사회가 더 외로운 곳이 되어가고 있다고 생각한다. 하지만 우리의 뇌는 인간 간의 상호 작용을 갈망한다.

VOCA

- well-known 유명한, 잘 알려진
- dedicate 전념하다
- sociable 사교적인, 붙임성 있는
- be drawn to (마음이) 끌리다
- engage with ~와 관계를 맺다
- connectivity 연결(성)
- deepen 깊어지다[깊게 하다]
- crave 갈망[열망]하다
- epidemic (유행성) 전염병
- interaction 상호 작용

13 난도 ★☆☆   정답 ②

독해 > 대의 파악 > 제목, 주제

정답의 이유

주어진 글은 어떤 사람들은 선천적으로 특별한 재능을 가지고 태어나지만, 그렇지 않은 사람이라도 오랜 기간 꾸준한 연습을 통해서 재능을 발달시키고 성공할 수 있다고 주장하는 글이다. 두 번째 문장에서 'Yet only dedication to mindful, deliberate practice over many years ~ advantages into talents and those talents into successes.'라고 했고, 세 번째 문장에서 동일한 종류의 헌신적인 연습을 통해 그러한 장점을 갖고 태어나지 않은 사람들도 재능을 개발할 수 있다고 했으므로, 글의 주제로 가장 적절한 것은 ② 'importance of constant efforts to cultivate talents(재능을 키우기 위한 지속적인 노력의 중요성)'이다.

오답의 이유

① 일부 사람들이 다른 사람들에 비해 가지고 있는 장점들
③ 수줍음 많은 사람들이 사회적 상호 작용에서 겪는 어려움들
④ 자신의 강점과 약점에 대한 이해의 필요성

본문해석

확실히 어떤 사람들은 장점을 가지고 태어난다(예를 들어, 기수들의 신체적 크기, 농구선수들의 키, 음악가들의 음악에 대한 '귀'). 하지만 오랜 기간에 걸쳐 의도적이고 계획적으로 연습에 전념해야만 이러한 장점을 재능으로, 그리고 그 재능을 성공으로 바꿀 수 있다. 동일한 종류의 헌신적인 연습을 통해 그러한 장점을 가지고 태어나지 않은 사람들도 자연이 그들이 닿을 수 있는 곳보다 좀 더 멀리 놓아둔(타고나지 않은) 재능을 개발할 수 있다. 예를 들어, 여러분이 수학적인 재능을 타고나지 않았다고 느낄지라도, 의식적이고, 계획적인 연습을 통해 여러분의 수학적 능력을 크게 개발할 수 있다. 혹은 여러분이 스스로 '천성적으로' 수줍음이 많다고 생각한다면 사교적 능력을 개발하기 위해 시간과 노력을 들이는 것은 여러분이 사교적인 행사에서 사람들과 활기차게, 우아하게, 편안하게 교류할 수 있도록 만든다.

VOCA

- certainly 틀림없이, 분명히
- be born with 타고나다
- advantage 유리한 점, 장점
- jockey 기수
- height 키[신장]
- dedication 전념, 헌신
- mindful ~을 염두에 두는[의식하는]
- deliberate 신중한, 의도[계획]적인
- nature 천성, 본성
- significantly 상당히[크게]
- enable ~을 할 수 있게 하다
- interact with ~와 상호 작용을 하다
- occasion (특별한) 행사, 의식, 축하
- with energy 힘차게

14 난도 ★★☆　　　　　　　　　　　　　정답 ④

독해 > 대의 파악 > 요지, 주장

정답의 이유

주어진 글은 Dr. Roossinck가 우연히 발견한 사실, 즉 바이러스가 식물에 미치는 이로운 영향에 대한 내용이다. 첫 문장에서 'a virus increased resistance to drought on a plant(바이러스가 식물의 가뭄에 대한 저항력을 증가시킨다)'고 했고, 세 번째 문장에서 다른 종류의 바이러스가 식물의 내열성을 증가시키는 실험을 하고 있다고 했다. 마지막에서 두 번째 문장에서 다른 종류의 바이러스가 그들의 숙주들에게 주는 이점을 더 깊이 있게 이해하기 위해 연구를 확장하기를 희망한다고 했으므로, 글의 요지로 가장 적절한 것은 ④ 'Viruses sometimes do their hosts good, rather than harming them(바이러스는 때로 숙주에게 해가 되기보다는 도움이 된다).'이다.

오답의 이유

① 바이러스는 생물학적 존재들의 자급자족을 증명한다.

② 생물학자들은 식물에 바이러스가 없는 상태로 유지하기 위해 모든 것을 해야 한다.

③ 공생의 원리는 감염된 식물에는 적용될 수 없다.

본문해석

Roossinck 박사와 그녀의 동료들은 바이러스가 식물학 실험에서 널리 사용되는 식물의 가뭄에 대한 저항력을 증가시킨다는 사실을 우연히 발견했다. 관련 바이러스를 이용한 추가실험은 그 사실이 15종의 다른 식물 종에서도 사실이라는 것을 보여주었다. Roossinck 박사는 현재 다양한 식물의 내열성을 증가시키는 또 다른 유형의 바이러스 연구를 위한 실험을 수행하고 있다. 그녀는 다양한 종류의 바이러스가 그들의 숙주들에게 주는 이점을 더 깊이 있게 이해하기 위해 그녀의 연구를 확장하기를 희망한다. 이는 많은 생물들이 자급자족보다는 공생에 의존한다는 점점 더 많은 생물학자들이 주장하는 견해를 뒷받침하는 데 도움이 될 것이다.

VOCA

- colleague 동료
- by chance 우연히, 뜻밖에
- resistance 저항[반대]
- drought 가뭄
- botanical 식물(학)의
- experiment 실험
- related 동족[동류]의
- species 종
- heat tolerance 내열성
- a range of 다양한
- extend 연장하다
- host (기생 생물의) 숙주
- support 지지[옹호/재청]하다
- biologist 생물학자
- creature 생물
- rely on ~에 의지[의존]하다

- symbiosis 공생
- self-sufficient 자급자족할 수 있는

15 난도 ★★☆　　　　　　　　　　　　　정답 ④

독해 > 세부 내용 찾기 > 내용 (불)일치

정답의 이유

주어진 글은 사탕단풍나무 수액을 채취해서 시럽을 만드는 과정을 설명하는 내용이다. 마지막 문장에서 '대부분의 단풍나무시럽 생산자들은 손으로 통을 수거하고, 직접 수액을 끓여 시럽으로 만든다.'고 했으므로, 글의 내용과 일치하지 않는 것은 ④ '단풍나무시럽을 만들기 위해 기계로 수액 통을 수거한다.'이다.

오답의 이유

① 두 번째 문장에서 'A sugar maple tree produces a watery sap each spring, ~'이라고 했으므로, 글의 내용과 일치한다.

② 세 번째 문장에서 'To take the sap out of the sugar maple tree, a farmer makes a slit in the bark with a special knife, ~'라고 했으므로, 글의 내용과 일치한다.

③ 다섯 번째 문장 후반부에서 '~ forty gallons of sugar maple tree "water" make one gallon of syrup.'이라고 했으므로, 글의 내용과 일치한다.

본문해석

단풍나무시럽을 만드는 전통적인 방법은 흥미롭다. 매년 봄, 사탕단풍나무는 땅에 여전히 많은 눈이 있을 때 물기가 많은 수액을 생산한다. 사탕단풍나무에서 수액을 채취하기 위해 농부는 특수한 칼로 나무껍질에 틈을 만들고 나무에 '수도꼭지'를 단다. 그리고 나서 농부가 꼭지에 통을 걸면, 수액이 그 안으로 떨어진다. 채취된 수액은 달콤한 시럽이 남을 때까지 끓여지는데, 사탕단풍나무 '물' 40갤론이 시럽 1갤론을 만든다. 이는 수많은 통, 수많은 증기, 수많은 노동을 의미한다. 그렇기는 하지만, 대부분의 단풍나무시럽 생산자들은 손으로 통을 수거하고, 직접 수액을 끓여 시럽으로 만드는 가족 단위의 농부들이다.

VOCA

- sugar maple tree 사탕단풍나무
- watery 물기가 많은
- sap 수액
- slit 구멍[틈]
- bark 나무껍질
- tap 수도꼭지
- hang 걸다, 매달다
- drip 방울방울[뚝뚝] 흘리다[떨어뜨리다]
- collect 모으다, 수집하다
- boil 끓다[끓이다]

독해 > 글의 일관성 > 무관한 어휘 · 문장

정답의 이유

주어진 글은 단편소설 쓰기 수업에서 필자가 들었던 경험에 대한 내용이다. 수업 중에 한 유명한 편집자가 작가는 사람들에게 관심을 갖는 것이 중요하다고 강조한 것을 제시했는데, ④는 마술사가 무대에 오를 때마다 스스로에게 말했던 내용이므로, 글의 흐름상 어색한 문장이다.

본문해석

나는 언젠가 단편소설 쓰기 강좌를 들은 적이 있는데, 그 강좌 중에 선두적인 잡지의 한 유명한 편집자가 우리 수업에서 강연했다. 그는 매일 자신의 책상에 오는 수십 편의 이야기들 중에서 어느 것이든 하나를 골라 몇 단락만 읽어도 그 작가가 사람들을 좋아하는지 아닌지를 느낄 수 있다고 말했다. "작가가 사람들을 좋아하지 않는다면, 사람들도 그 또는 그녀의 이야기를 좋아하지 않을 것"이라고 그는 말했다. 그 편집자는 소설 쓰기 강연에서 사람들에게 관심을 갖는 것의 중요성을 계속해서 강조했다. <u>위대한 마술사 Thurston은 그가 무대에 오를 때마다 스스로에게 "나는 성공했으니 감사한다."라고 말했다고 했다.</u> 강연 끝부분에서, 그는 "다시 한 번 말씀드리겠습니다. 성공적인 이야기 작가가 되고 싶다면 사람들에게 관심을 가져야 합니다."라며 끝맺었다.

VOCA

• renowned   유명한, 명성 있는
• leading   선두적인
• dozens of   수십의, 많은
• stress   강조하다
• conclude   결론[판단]을 내리다

독해 > 글의 일관성 > 글의 순서

정답의 이유

주어진 문장에서 몇 년 전만 해도 인공지능(AI)에 대한 종말론적인 예측으로 끝나는 것 같다고 했으므로, 주어진 문장 다음에는 'In 2014'로 시작하는 (B)에서 AI에 대한 부정적인 의견들을 서술하는 것이 자연스럽다. 그런 다음에 however로 시작하는 (A)에서 AI에 대한 과거의 부정적인 의견이 최근 긍정적인 것으로 바뀌었다고 서술하는 내용으로 이어지는 것이 적절하며, 마지막으로 (A)에서 설명한 변화를 This shift로 받는 (C)로 이어져야 한다. 따라서 글의 순서로 가장 적절한 것은 ② '(B) - (A) - (C)'이다.

본문해석

몇 년 전만 해도, 인공지능(AI)에 대한 모든 대화는 종말론적인 예측으로 끝나는 것 같았다.

(B) 2014년에 이 분야의 한 전문가는 말하기를, 우리가 AI로 악마를 소환하고 있다고 했으며, 한 노벨상을 수상한 물리학자는 AI가 인류의 종말을 불러올 수 있다고 말했다.

(A) 하지만 최근에는 상황이 달라지기 시작했다. AI는 무서운 블랙박스에서 사람들이 다양한 활용 사례에 이용할 수 있는 것으로 변했다.

(C) 이러한 변화는 이 기술들이 마침내 업계에서 특히 시장 기회를 위해 대규모로 탐색되고 있기 때문이다.

VOCA

• apocalyptic   종말론적
• prediction   예측, 예견
• summon   호출하다, (오라고) 부르다
• demon   악령, 악마
• spell   (보통 나쁜 결과를) 가져오다[의미하다]
• shift   (위치 · 입장 · 방향의) 변화
• at scale   대규모로

독해 > 글의 일관성 > 문장 삽입

정답의 이유

'그렇지만(Yet)'으로 시작하는 주어진 문장의 앞에는 상반되는 내용이 나와야 한다. ② 앞 문장에서 '정답은 없다.'라고 했는데, 주어진 문장에서 '그러한 자기 평가에 대한 요청은 한 사람의 경력 전반에 걸쳐 만연하다.'라고 했으므로, 주어진 문장이 들어갈 위치로 적절한 것은 ②이다. 또한 ② 다음 문장의 입학, 입사, 면접, 성과 검토, 회의 등이 주어진 문장의 'pervasive throughout one's career'를 부연 설명하고 있으며, 주어진 문장의 such self-assessments는 앞부분의 'how to subjectively describe your performance(주관적으로 여러분의 성과를 설명하는 법)'을 받는다.

본문해석

회계 분기가 막 끝났다. 여러분의 상사가 여러분에게 이번 분기의 매출에서 여러분이 얼마나 좋은 성과를 보였는지 물어보기 위해 잠시 들른다. 여러분은 어떻게 자신의 성과를 설명할 것인가? 매우 뛰어남? 훌륭함? 나쁨? 누군가가 여러분에게 객관적인 성과 지표(예를 들어, 이번 분기에 몇 달러의 매출을 가져왔는지)에 대해 물어볼 때와는 다르게, 주관적으로 여러분의 성과를 설명하는 법은 종종 불분명하다. 정답은 없다. 그렇지만, 그러한 자기 평가에 대한 요청은 한 사람의 경력 전반에 걸쳐 만연하다. 여러분은 입학지원서, 입사지원서, 면접, 성과 검토, 회의 등에서 여러분의 성과를 주관적으로 설명할 것을 요구받고, 이런 목록은 계속 이어진다. 여러분이 자신의 성과를 설명하는 법이 소위 말하는 자기 홍보의 수준이다. 자기 홍보는 업무의 일부로 만연되었기 때문에 자기 홍보를 더 많이 하는 사람들이 채용되고, 승진되고, (연봉) 인상 또는 상여금을 받을 기회가 더 많을 수 있다.

VOCA

• self-assessment 자기 평가
• pervasive 만연한, 널리 퍼진
• fiscal 회계의, 재정의
• in terms of ~에 있어서
• objective 객관적인
• metric 측정기준
• subjectively 주관적으로
• what we call 소위, 이른바
• self-promotion 자기 홍보
• get a raise 급여를 인상받다

독해 > 빈칸 완성 > 단어·구·절

정답의 이유

제시문은 우리는 불안의 시대에 살고 있으며, 우리의 불안 회피 전략은 오히려 불안을 가중시킨다는 내용이다. 빈칸 문장에 역접의 접속사인 'however'가 있으므로 앞에 상반되는 내용이 나와야 하는데, 빈칸 앞 문장에서 스마트폰처럼 밤낮으로 주의를 산만하게 하는 것들이 불안 회피 전략 역할을 한다고 했고, 빈칸 다음에서 이러한 회피 전략은 결국에는 불안을 더욱 가중시킨다는 모순을 지적하고 있으므로, 빈칸에 들어갈 말로 가장 적절한 것은 ① 'Paradoxically(역설적으로)'이다.

오답의 이유

② 다행스럽게도
③ 중립적으로
④ 독창적으로

본문해석

우리는 불안의 시대에 살고 있다. 불안해하는 것은 불편하고 무서운 경험이 될 수 있으므로, 우리는 영화나 TV쇼 시청하기, 먹기, 비디오게임 하기, 과로하기 등 순간의 불안을 줄이는 데 도움이 되는 의식적 또는 무의식적 전략들에 의지한다. 또한, 스마트폰은 낮이든 밤이든 언제든지 주의를 산만하게 만들기도 한다. 심리학 연구는 주의를 산만하게 하는 것들이 일반적인 불안 회피 전략의 역할을 한다는 것을 보여주었다. 그러나 역설적으로, 이러한 회피 전략은 결국에는 불안을 더욱 가중시킨다. 불안해하는 것은 들어가면 헤어나오지 못하는 모래 속에 빠지는 것과 같아서 여러분이 그것에 맞서 싸울수록 더 깊이 가라앉는다. 실제로, 연구는 "여러분이 저항하는 것은 지속된다."라는 잘 알려진 문구를 강력하게 지지한다.

VOCA

• anxiety 불안(감), 염려
• resort to ~에 의지하다
• conscious 의식하는, 자각하는
• reduce 줄이다[축소하다]
• overworking 과로, 혹사
• distraction 정신을 산만하게 만드는 것
• serve as ~의 역할을 하다
• avoidance 회피, 방지
• in the long run 결국에는
• get into 처하다[처하게 만들다]
• quicksand 유사, 헤어나기 힘든[위험한] 상황
• fight 싸우다[전투하다]
• sink 가라앉다[빠지다]
• resist 저항[반대]하다
• persist 집요하게[고집스럽게/끈질기게] 계속하다

독해 > 빈칸 완성 > 단어 · 구 · 절

정답의 이유

주어진 글은 정보를 효율적인 방식으로 얻기 위해서 메일 수신함을 간소화할 필요성과 관리 방법을 서술하는 내용이다. 빈칸 다음 문장의 후반부에서 메일 수신함이 많을수록 관리하기 어려워진다고 했고, 마지막 문장에서 'Cut the number of in-boxes you have down to the smallest number possible for you ~'라고 했으므로, 빈칸에 들어갈 말로 가장 적절한 것은 ③ 'minimizing the number of in-boxes you have(여러분이 가진 메일 수신함의 수를 최소화하는 것)'이다.

오답의 이유

① 한 번에 여러 목표를 설정하는 것
② 들어오는 정보에 몰두하는 것
④ 여러분이 열중해 있는 정보를 선택하는 것

본문해석

여러분은 얼마나 다양한 방법으로 정보를 얻는가? 어떤 사람들은 문자 메시지, 음성 메일, 종이 문서, 일반우편, 블로그 게시물, 다양한 온라인 서비스의 메시지라는 6가지 서로 다른 종류의 통신 수단에 응답해야 할지도 모른다. 이것들은 각각 일종의 메일 수신함으로, 지속적으로 처리되어야 한다. 그것은 끝없는 과정이지만, 기진맥진하거나 스트레스 받을 필요는 없다. 정보 관리를 더 관리하기 쉬운 수준으로 낮추고 생산적인 영역으로 전환하는 것은 <u>여러분이 가진 메일 수신함의 수를 최소화하는 것</u>으로 시작한다. 여러분이 메시지를 확인하거나 수신 정보를 읽으러 가야 하는 모든 장소는 메일 수신함이며, 메일 수신함이 많을수록 모든 것을 관리하기가 더 어려워진다. 여러분이 해야 하는 방식으로 여전히 기능하기 위해서 메일 수신함의 수를 가능한 한 최소한으로 줄여라.

VOCA

· in-box 메일 수신함[미결 서류함]
· process 처리하다
· on a continuous basis 지속적으로
· exhausting 기진맥진하게 만드는
· stressful 스트레스가 많은
· manageable 관리[감당/처리]할 수 있는
· productive 생산적인
· zone 구역
· minimize 최소화하다
· incoming 도착하는, 들어오는
· function 기능하다[작용하다]

영어 | 2022년 지방직 9급

한눈에 훑어보기

✓ 영역 분석

어휘 01 02 03 04
4문항, 20%

독해 11 12 13 14 15 16 17 18 19 20
10문항, 50%

어법 05 06 07 08
4문항, 20%

표현 09 10
2문항, 10%

✓ 빠른 정답

01	02	03	04	05	06	07	08	09	10
②	①	④	④	②	②	①	①	④	④
11	12	13	14	15	16	17	18	19	20
③	③	④	③	③	③	①	①	②	②

✓ 점수 체크

구분	1회독	2회독	3회독
맞힌 문항 수	/ 20	/ 20	/ 20
나의 점수	점	점	점

01 난도 ★☆☆ 정답 ②

어휘 > 단어

[정답의 이유]

밑줄 친 flexible은 '융통성 있는'의 뜻으로 이와 의미가 가장 가까운 것은 ② 'adaptable(적응할 수 있는)'이다.

[오답의 이유]

① 강한

③ 정직한

④ 열정적인

본문해석

학교 교사들은 학생들의 다양한 능력 수준에 대처하기 위해 융통성이 있어야 한다.

VOCA

• cope with ~에 대처하다

02 난도 ★☆☆ 정답 ①

어휘 > 단어

[정답의 이유]

밑줄 친 vary는 '달라지다[다르다]'의 뜻으로 이와 의미가 가장 가까운 것은 ① 'change(변하다, 달라지다)'이다.

[오답의 이유]

② 줄어들다

③ 확장되다

④ 포함하다

본문해석

곡물 수확량은 달라지는데, 일부 지역에서는 개선되고 다른 지역에서는 하락한다.

VOCA

• crop yields 곡물 수확량

• improving 개량[개선]하는

• falling 하락하는; 감퇴하는

03 난도 ★☆☆ 　　　　　　　　　　　정답 ④

어휘 > 어구

정답의 이유

밑줄 친 with respect to는 '~에 관하여'의 뜻으로 이와 의미가 가장 가까운 것은 ④ 'in terms of(~에 관하여)'이다.

오답의 이유

① ~의 위기에 처한

② ~에도 불구하고

③ ~에 찬성하여

본문해석

나의 교육에 관하여 나는 누구에게도 열등하다고 느끼지 않는다.

VOCA

• inferior to ~보다 열등한

04 난도 ★☆☆ 　　　　　　　　　　　정답 ④

어휘 > 어구

정답의 이유

빈칸 다음의 목적어(money)와 부사구(long before the next payday)로 미루어 문맥상 빈칸에는 급여일 전에 돈과 관련된 표현이 들어감을 유추할 수 있으므로 빈칸에 들어갈 말로 가장 적절한 것은 ④ 'run out of(~을 다 써버리다)'이다.

오답의 이유

① ~으로 변하다

② 다시 시작하다

③ ~을 참다

본문해석

때때로 우리는 다음 급여일 훨씬 이전에 돈을 다 써버린다.

VOCA

• payday 급여[임금] 지급일

05 난도 ★★☆ 　　　　　　　　　　　정답 ②

어법 > 비문 찾기

정답의 이유

② 문장의 주어(Toys children wanted all year long)가 복수명사(Toys)이므로 동사가 복수형이어야 한다. 이때 children wanted all year long은 toys를 수식하는 관계대명사절로 목적격 관계대명사(that)가 생략되었다. 또한 장난감이 '버려지는' 것이므로 능동태가 아닌 수동태를 써야 한다. 따라서 has recently discarded → have recently been discarded가 되어야 한다.

오답의 이유

① ask의 직접목적어인 간접의문문의 어순이 '의문사(why)+주어+동사'로 올바르게 사용되었다. keep은 동명사를 목적어로 취하는 동사로 '계속 ~하다'의 뜻으로 kept coming이 올바르게 사용되었다.

③ 주격 관계대명사 who의 선행사가 단수명사(someone)이므로 관계사절의 동사(is)의 수일치가 올바르게 사용되었다. 'be ready to+동사원형'은 '~할 준비가 되어 있다'의 뜻이며, 'lend[give] a (helping) hand'는 '도움을 주다'의 뜻이다.

④ 주어(insects)가 냄새에 '이끌리는' 것이므로 수동태(are often attracted by scents)로 올바르게 사용되었으며 빈도부사(often)는 be동사 다음에 위치한다. 또한 관계대명사 that의 선행사가 scents이므로 관계사절의 동사 aren't의 수일치도 올바르게 사용되었다.

본문해석

① 그는 내게 왜 매일 계속 돌아왔는지 물었다.

② 아이들이 일 년 내내 원했던 장난감들이 최근 버려졌다.

③ 그녀는 언제나 도움을 줄 준비가 되어 있는 사람이다.

④ 곤충들은 종종 우리에게는 분명하지 않은 냄새에 이끌린다.

VOCA

• discard (불필요한 것을) 버리다, 폐기하다

• be attracted by ~에 마음을 빼앗기다, 매혹되다

• scent 냄새

• obvious 분명한[명백한]

06 난도 ★★☆ 　　　　　　　　　　　정답 ②

어법 > 비문 찾기

정답의 이유

② a feeling of 다음에 명사 A, B, and C가 병렬 구조로 이어지는데, warm은 형용사이므로 warm → warmth가 되어야 한다.

오답의 이유

① 'both+복수명사'이므로 sides가 올바르게 사용되었다. write는 '(글자·숫자를) 쓰다'라는 뜻의 자동사로 쓰였다.

③ The number of(~의 수)는 단수 취급하므로 단수동사(is)가 올바르게 사용되었다.

④ 가정법 과거완료에서 if가 생략되면, 주어와 동사가 도치되어 'Had+주어+p.p.'가 되므로 'Had I realized ~'로 올바르게 사용되었다. 또한 what you were intending to do는 realized의 목적어가 되는 간접의문문이므로 '의문사(what)+주어+동사'의 어순이 올바르게 사용되었다.

본문해석

① 너는 종이의 양면에 글을 쓸 수 있다.

② 나의 집은 내게 안정감, 따뜻함 그리고 사랑의 느낌을 준다.

③ 자동차 사고의 수가 증가하고 있다.

④ 네가 무엇을 하려고 했는지 알았더라면, 내가 너를 말렸을 텐데.

VOCA

• offer 내놓다[제공하다]

• be on the rise 증가하고 있다

• intend to ~할 작정이다, ~하려고 생각하다

자동사로도 쓰이는 타동사

• 타동사와 자동사 둘 다 쓰이는 동사

동사	자동사/타동사	동사	자동사/타동사
sell	팔리다/팔다	photograph	사진이 잘 나오다/ ~의 사진을 찍다
read	(~하게) 읽히다/ ~을 읽다	write	써지다/~을 쓰다
peel	벗겨지다/ ~을 벗기다	wash	씻기다/~을 씻다
eat	식사하다/~을 먹다	open	열리다/~을 열다

예 The door opened. → 자동사: 열리다

(그 문이 열렸다.)

예 She opened the door. → 타동사: ~을 열다

(그녀는 그 문을 열었다.)

예 This pen won't write. → 자동사: 써지다

(이 펜은 [글씨가] 잘 안 써진다.)

예 Ellen hopes to write a book about her experiences one day. → 타동사: ~을 쓰다

(Ellen은 언젠가는 자신의 경험에 대한 책을 쓰고 싶어 한다.)

• 동사의 상태를 설명하는 양태부사와 함께 쓸 경우 '주어+자동사 +양태부사'로 쓰며, 수동의 의미로 해석한다.

예 The book sold well and was reprinted many times.

→ 자동사: 팔리다

(그 책은 잘 팔려서 여러 번 재인쇄되었다.)

예 Most supermarkets sell a range of organic products.

→ 타동사: 팔다

(대부분 슈퍼마켓이 다양한 유기농 제품들을 판다.)

예 We have to eat well to be healthy. → 자동사: 식사하다

(우리는 건강해지기 위해 잘 먹어야 한다.)

예 I don't eat meat. → 타동사: ~을 먹다

(나는 고기[육류]를 안 먹는다.)

예 Sally just doesn't photograph well. → 자동사: 사진이 잘 나오다

(Sally는 그냥 사진이 잘 안 받는다.)

예 He has photographed some of the world's most beautiful scenes. → 타동사: ~의 사진을 찍다

(그는 세계에서 가장 아름다운 장면들 중 일부의 사진을 찍었다.)

---

07 난도 ★☆☆ 　　　　　　　　　　 정답 ①

어법 > 영작하기

정답의 이유

① afford to는 '~할 여유가 있다'의 뜻으로 주어진 우리말이 단 한 푼의 돈도 낭비할 수 '없다'이므로 can → cannot이 되어야 한다.

오답의 이유

② fade from은 '~에서 사라지다'의 뜻이며, fade는 자동사로 올바르게 사용되었다.

③ have no alternative but to는 '~하는 것 외에는 대안이 없다 [~할 수밖에 없다]'라는 뜻의 관용표현으로, to 다음에 동사원형 (resign)이 올바르게 사용되었다. have no choice but to와 같은 뜻이다.

④ aim은 to부정사를 목적어로 취하는 동사이므로 to start가 올바르게 사용되었으며, 현재진행시제(I'm aiming)가 '~할 작정이 다'의 뜻으로 미래시제를 대신해서 올바르게 사용되었다. in five years는 '5년 후에'의 뜻으로 사용되었다.

VOCA

• resign 사임하다

• aim 목표하다, 작정이다

더 알아보기

자주 출제되는 준동사 관용표현

cannot help –ing/cannot but+동사원형/have no choice [alternative] but to 동사원형: '~하지 않을 수 없다, ~하는 수밖에 없다, ~하는 것 외에 대안이 없다'

예 We couldn't but cry over the war victims.

(우리는 전쟁 희생자들을 보고 울지 않을 수 없었다.)

예 I can't help thinking he knows more than he has told us.

(나는 그가 우리에게 말한 것보다 더 많은 것을 알고 있다고 생각할 수밖에 없다.)

예 She had no choice but to give up her goal because of the accident.

(그녀는 그 사고 때문에 그녀의 목표를 포기할 수밖에 없었다.)

예 We have no alternative but to withdraw.

(우리는 철수하는 수밖에 없다.)

08 난도 ★★☆　　　　　　　　　정답 ①

어법 > 영작하기

정답의 이유

① 부정어가 문두에 오면 주어와 동사가 도치된다. '~하자마자 ~
했다'는 'No sooner+had+주어+p.p.+than+주어+과거동
사'이므로 I have finishing → had I finished가 되어야 한다.

오답의 이유

② 주어진 우리말이 '~해야만 할 것이다'이므로 'will have to+동
사원형(will have to pay)'이 올바르게 사용되었다. sooner or
later는 '조만간'이라는 뜻이다.

③ 관계대명사 what의 관용표현으로 'A is to B what C is to D'는
'A와 B의 관계는 C와 D의 관계와 같다'의 뜻이다.

④ end up −ing는 '결국 ~하게 되다'라는 의미의 표현으로 올바르
게 사용되었다.

더 알아보기

관계대명사 what의 관용표현

what we[they, you] call = what is called = what one calls	소위, 이른바, 말하자면
what one is[was, used to be] what one has what one does	현재[과거]의 인격, 인물, 본성 소유물 행동
A is to B what C is to D = A is to B as C is to D = What C is to D, A is to B = As C is to D, (so) A is to B	A와 B에 대한 관계는 C와 D에 대한 관계와 같다

예 They experience what is called jet lag.
　　(그들은 소위 시차를 경험한다.)

예 Reading is to the mind what food is to the body.
　　= Reading is to the mind as food is to the body.
　　= What food is to the body, reading is to the mind.
　　= As food is to the body, (so) reading is to the mind.
　　(독서와 정신에 대한 관계는 음식과 몸에 대한 관계와 같다.)

예 Words are to language what notes are to music.
　　(단어와 언어의 관계는 음표와 음악의 관계와 같다.)

09 난도 ★☆☆　　　　　　　　　정답 ④

표현 > 일반회화

정답의 이유

④ A가 캔버스에 그리고 싶은 '대상(subject)'이 있는지 물었는데,
B가 고등학교 때 역사 과목(subject)을 잘하지 못했다고 대답했
으므로 적절한 응답이 아니다.

본문해석

① A: 나는 이 신문이 편견이 없어서 좋아.
　　B: 그 점이 그 신문이 판매 부수가 가장 많은 이유야.

② A: 잘 차려입은 이유라도 있는 거니?
　　B: 응, 오늘 중요한 면접이 있어.

③ A: 나는 연습 때는 공을 똑바로 칠 수 있지만, 경기 중에는 칠 수
　　　없어.
　　B: 나도 항상 그래.

④ A: 캔버스에 그리고 싶은 특별한 대상이 있니?
　　B: 나는 고등학교 때 역사 과목을 잘하지 못했어.

VOCA

• opinionated　자기 의견을 고집하는, 독선적인

• circulation　(신문·잡지의) 판매 부수

• dress up　옷을 갖춰[격식을 차려] 입다

• subject　(그림·사진 등의) 대상[소재], 과목

10 난도 ★☆☆　　　　　　　　　정답 ④

표현 > 일반회화

정답의 이유

시험 결과에 대한 대화로 빈칸 앞에서 B가 과학 시험에 대해 묻자
A가 시험을 잘 봤다고 말하고, 빈칸 다음에서 'I owe you a treat
for that.'라고 했으므로 B가 시험과 관련하여 A에게 도움을 줬다
는 것을 유추할 수 있다. 따라서 빈칸에 들어갈 말로 가장 적절한
것은 ④ 'I can't thank you enough for helping me with it(도와
줘서 정말 고마워)'이다.

오답의 이유

① 이 일로 자책해도 소용없어

② 여기서 너를 만날 줄은 몰랐어

③ 사실, 우리는 매우 실망했어

본문해석

A: 이봐! 지리학 시험은 어땠어?
B: 나쁘지 않아, 고마워. 난 그저 끝나서 기뻐! 넌 어때? 과학 시험
　은 어땠어?
A: 오, 정말 잘 봤어. 도와줘서 정말 고마워. 내가 한턱낼게.
B: 천만에. 그러면, 다음 주에 예정된 수학 시험을 준비하고 싶니?
A: 물론이야. 같이 공부하자.
B: 좋은 생각이야. 나중에 봐.

VOCA

• geography　지리학

• go　(일의 진행이 어떻게) 되다[되어 가다]

• owe　빚지다, 신세지다

• treat　대접, 한턱

• beat oneself up　(~을 두고) 몹시 자책하다

11 난도 ★★☆   정답 ③

독해 > 글의 일관성 > 글의 순서

정답의 이유

주어진 글은 시각장애인들에게는 일상적인 모든 일들이 어렵다는 내용으로, 주어진 문장의 'people who are blind'는 (B)의 they로 연결된다. (B)의 다른 사람의 눈을 '빌리다(borrow)'라는 개념은 'That's the thinking ~'으로 구체적으로 설명하는 (A)로 이어지는 것이 자연스럽다. 마지막으로 직원과 연결되어 실시간 영상으로 송출하는 (A) 이후의 상황을 'can then answer questions, ~'라고 부연 설명하는 (C)로 연결하는 것이 자연스럽다. 따라서 글의 순서로 가장 적절한 것은 ③ '(B) − (A) − (C)'이다.

본문해석

시각 장애인들에게 우편물 분류나 한 무더기의 빨래 세탁과 같은 일상적인 일은 힘겨운 일이다.

(B) 하지만 만약 그들이 볼 수 있는 누군가의 눈을 '빌릴' 수 있다면 어떨까?

(A) 그것은 수천 명의 사용자들이 스마트폰이나 Aira 전매특허의 안경을 사용하여 그들 주변 환경의 실시간 영상을 상시 대기 직원에게 스트리밍할 수 있게 해주는 새로운 서비스인 Aira를 지지하는 생각이다.

(C) 연중무휴 이용 가능한 Aira 직원들은, 그러면, 질문에 답하고 사물을 설명하거나, 사용자에게 위치를 안내할 수 있다.

VOCA

- sort 분류하다
- a load of 많은, 한 짐의
- laundry 세탁물
- present (문제 등을) 야기하다[겪게 하다]
- challenge 도전, 문제, 과제
- behind 뒤에서 (지지[후원]하는)
- stream 스트림 처리하다(데이터 전송을 연속적으로 이어서 하다)
- on–demand 요구만 있으면 (언제든지)
- what if ~면 어쩌지[~라면 어떻게 될까]?
- available 24/7 연중무휴로 이용 가능한
- guide 안내하여 데려가다[보여주다]

12 난도 ★★★   정답 ③

독해 > 글의 일관성 > 문장 삽입

정답의 이유

주어진 문장의 역접 접속사(however)로 미루어 앞의 내용과 대조되는 내용임을 유추할 수 있다. 주어진 문장에서 심장과 펌프를 비교하는 것은 진정한 비유라고 했으므로 그 이전에는 비유가 될 수 없는 것에 대한 내용이 제시되었을 것을 유추할 수 있다. ③ 이전 문장에서 장미와 카네이션이 비유가 될 수 없는 이유로 같은 속에 속하는 장미와 카네이션이 같은 방식으로 특성들을 보여주고 있기 때문이라고 했는데, ③ 바로 다음 문장에서 'These are disparate things, but they share important qualities(그것들은 서로 전혀 다른 것들이지만, 중요한 특성들을 공유한다) ~'라고 했으므로 글의 흐름이 앞서 서술한 장미와 카네이션의 경우와는 대조적인 방향으로 나감을 알 수 있다. 따라서 주어진 문장이 들어갈 위치로 적절한 곳은 ③이다.

본문해석

비유는 두 사물이 아주 근본적인 여러 면에서 비슷하다고 주장되는 수사적 표현이다. 비록 그 두 사물이 전혀 다름에도 불구하고, 그것들의 구조, 부분과의 관계, 또는 그것들이 기여하는 본질적인 목적이 유사하다. 장미와 카네이션은 유사하지 않다. 그것들은 둘 다 줄기와 잎을 가지고 있으며 둘 다 빨간색이다. 그러나 그것들은 같은 속이기 때문에, 같은 방식으로 이러한 특성들을 드러낸다. 하지만 심장을 펌프에 비교하는 것은 진정한 비유이다. 그것들은 서로 전혀 다른 것들이지만, 중요한 특성들, 즉 역학적인 장치(기관), 밸브(판막)의 보유, 압력 증감 능력, 액체를 흐르게 하는 능력 등을 공유한다. 그리고 심장과 펌프는 이러한 특성들을 다른 상황에서 다른 방식으로 보여준다.

VOCA

- genuine 진짜의, 진품의
- analogy 비유, 유사점
- figure of speech 비유적 표현
- assert ~을 단언하다, 주장하다
- fundamental 근본[본질]적인
- serve 도움이 되다, 기여하다
- dissimilar 같지 않은, 다른
- analogous 유사한, 비슷한, 닮은
- stem (식물의) 줄기
- exhibit (감정 · 특질 등을) 보이다[드러내다]
- genus (생물 분류상의) 속(屬)
- disparate 다른, 공통점이 없는
- mechanical 기계(상)의, 역학적인
- apparatus 기구, 장치, 기관
- fluid 유체(流體), 유동체
- context 맥락, 전후 사정, 상황

독해 > 대의 파악 > 제목, 주제

정답의 이유

제시문은 생산성 향상을 통한 효율성 최적화에 관한 글로, 개인의 생산성 향상 방법을 제시하고 있다. 마지막 문장에서 'do one thing, uninterrupted, for a sustained period of time.'이라고 했으므로 글의 제목으로 가장 적절한 것은 ④ 'Do One Thing at a Time for Greater Efficiency(효율성을 더 높이려면 한 번에 한 가지 일을 하라)'이다.

오답의 이유

① 인생에서 더 많은 선택지를 만드는 방법
② 일상적 신체 능력 향상법
③ 멀티태스킹은 더 나은 효율성을 위한 답이다

본문해석

효율성이 최적화될 수 있는 분야 중 하나는 노동력인데, 직원 한 명이 주어진 시간 안에 처리하는 작업량(제품 생산량, 고객 서비스량)으로 정의되는 개인 생산성 향상을 통해 가능하다. 최적의 성과를 내기 위해 적절한 장비와 환경 및 교육에 대한 투자 외에도, 직원들이 현대의 에너지 소모인 '멀티태스킹'을 하지 않도록 함으로써 생산성을 높일 수 있다. 연구에 따르면, 동시에 다른 프로젝트들을 수행하려 할 때 한 가지 작업을 완료하는 데 25~40% 더 오래 걸린다고 한다. 컨설팅 회사 The Energy Project의 사업 개발 부사장인 Andrew Deutscher는 생산성을 더 높이기 위해서 "한 가지 일을, 중단 없이, 지속적인 기간 동안 하세요."라고 말한다.

VOCA

• efficiency　효율성
• optimize　최적화하다, 가장 효과적으로 하다
• work force　노동자, 노동력
• define　정의하다
• invest　투자하다
• equipment　설비
• optimal　최고의, 최적의
• staffer　직원
• drain　(많은 시간·돈 등을) 고갈시키는[잡아먹는] 것
• multitasking　멀티태스킹, 동시에 몇 가지의 일을 하는 것
• put an end to　~을 끝내다, 그만두게 하다
• simultaneously　동시에, 일제히
• uninterrupted　중단되지 않은, 연속되는

독해 > 글의 일관성 > 무관한 어휘·문장

정답의 이유

제시문은 논쟁의 기술이 인생에서 매우 중요하다는 내용으로 갈등 상황에서 창의력을 더욱 키울 수 있다는 것이 글의 요지이다. ②번 문장에서 아이들이 의견 충돌에 노출되지 않는다면, 우리는 결국 그들의 창의력을 제한하는 것일지도 모른다고 했고, ④번 문장에서 '~ highly creative people often grow up in families full of tension(창의력이 뛰어난 사람들은 종종 갈등이 많은 가정에서 성장한다).'이라고 했다. 따라서 글의 흐름상 가장 어색한 문장은 ③ 'Children are most creative when they are free to brainstorm with lots of praise and encouragement in a peaceful environment(어린이들은 평화로운 환경에서 많은 칭찬과 격려로 자유롭게 브레인스토밍을 할 때 가장 창의적이다).'이다.

본문해석

좋은 논쟁을 하는 기술은 인생에서 매우 중요하다. 하지만 이것은 부모들이 자녀들에게 거의 가르치지 않는 기술이다. 우리는 아이들에게 안정적인 가정을 주기 원해서 형제자매가 서로 싸우지 못하게 하고 우리들만 비밀리에 논쟁한다. 하지만 아이들이 의견 충돌에 노출되지 않는다면, 우리는 결국 그들의 창의력을 제한하는 것일지도 모른다. 아이들은 평화로운 환경에서 칭찬과 격려를 많이 받으며 자유롭게 브레인스토밍을 할 때 가장 창의적이다. 창의력이 뛰어난 사람들은 종종 갈등이 많은 가정에서 성장한 것으로 밝혀진다. 그들은 주먹다짐이나 인신공격이 아니라, 실제적인 의견 충돌에 둘러싸여 있다. 30대 초반의 성인들이 상상의 이야기를 써달라고 요청받았을 때, 가장 창의적인 이야기들은 25년 전 가장 심한 갈등을 겪은 부모를 둔 이들로부터 나왔다.

VOCA

• critical　중요한
• stable　안정적인
• sibling　형제자매
• quarrel　다투다, 언쟁하다
• behind closed doors　비밀리에, 밀실에서
• expose　노출시키다
• disagreement　의견 차이, 의견 충돌
• fistfight　주먹다짐
• insult　모욕
• imaginative　상상의
• conflict　갈등

지방직 9급

영어

독해 > 세부 내용 찾기 > 내용 (불)일치

[정답의 이유]

다섯 번째 문장에서 '청력은 정상적이었다(his hearing was normal)' 라고 했으므로 글의 내용과 일치하지 않는 것은 ③ 'Christopher Nolan은 청각 장애로 인해 들을 수 없었다.'이다.

[오답의 이유]

① Christopher Nolan은 뇌 손상을 갖고 태어났다. → 두 번째 문장에서 'Brain damaged since birth, ~'라고 했으므로 글의 내용과 일치한다.

② Christopher Nolan은 음식을 삼키는 것도 어려웠다. → 두 번째 문장에서 'even to the extent of having difficulty in swallowing food.'라고 했으므로 글의 내용과 일치한다.

④ Christopher Nolan은 10대일 때 책을 썼다. → 마지막 문장에서 'he produced an entire book of poems and short stories, *Dam−Burst of Dreams*, while still a teenager.'라고 했으므로 글의 내용과 일치한다.

본문해석

Christopher Nolan은 영어권에서 꽤 유명한 아일랜드의 작가이다. Nolan은 선천적으로 뇌 손상을 갖고 태어났기 때문에 신체의 근육을 거의 통제할 수 없었는데, 심지어 음식을 삼키는 것조차 힘들었다. 그는 혼자 똑바로 앉을 수 없기 때문에 휠체어에 묶여 있어야 했다. Nolan은 알아들을 수 있는 말소리를 낼 수 없었다. 그러나 다행히도, 그의 뇌 손상이 지능이 손상되지 않고 청력은 정상인 정도였기 때문에. 그 결과, 그는 어렸을 때 말을 이해하는 것을 배웠다. 그러나 그가 10세가 된 후에 그리고 읽기를 배운 지 여러 해가 지나고 나서야 비로소 그는 자신의 첫 단어를 표현할 수 있는 수단을 갖게 되었다. 그는 글자를 가리키도록 머리에 붙어 있는 막대기를 사용함으로써 그것을 했다. 그가 아직 10대일 때 시와 단편으로 이루어진 *Dam−Burst of Dreams*라는 책 한 권을 만들어 냈는데, 바로 한 글자씩 하는 이런 '유니콘'의 방식을 통한 것이었다.

VOCA

• renown 명성, 유명
• have control over ～을 관리하다[～을 제어하다]
• to the extent of ～할[일] 정도까지
• swallow 삼키다
• strap (끈으로) 묶다
• utter 말하다
• recognizable 인식 가능한
• attach 붙이다

독해 > 세부 내용 찾기 > 내용 (불)일치

[정답의 이유]

마지막에서 두 번째 문장에서 'Some Australian aborigines can keep changing their name throughout their life(호주의 어떤 원주민들은 그들의 이름을 일생 동안 계속해서 바꿀 수 있는데) ~'라고 했으므로 글의 내용과 일치하지 않는 것은 ③ 'Changing one's name is totally unacceptable in the culture of Australian aborigines(이름을 바꾸는 것은 호주 원주민들의 문화에서 전혀 용납될 수 없다).'이다.

[오답의 이유]

① 많은 가톨릭 국가에서 아이들은 종종 성인의 이름을 따서 이름 지어진다. → 첫 번째 문장에서 'In many Catholic countries, children are often named after saints ~'라고 했으므로 글의 내용과 일치한다.

② 일부 아프리카 아이들은 5살이 될 때까지 이름이 지어지지 않는다. → 세 번째 문장에서 'In countries ~ such as in Africa, tribes only name their children when they reach five years old, ~'라고 했으므로 글의 내용과 일치한다.

④ 여러 문화권에서 다른 방식으로 자녀의 이름을 짓는다. → 제시문 전체를 통해 알 수 있다.

본문해석

많은 가톨릭 국가에서, 아이들은 종종 성인의 이름을 따서 이름지어진다. 실제로, 일부 성직자들은 부모들이 아이들의 이름을 드라마 스타나 축구 선수의 이름을 따서 짓는 것을 허락하지 않을 것이다. 개신교 국가들은 이것에 대해 더 자유로운 경향이 있다. 그러나. 노르웨이에서는 Adolf 같은 특정 이름들은 완전히 금지된다. 아프리카에서와 같이 영아 사망률이 매우 높은 나라들에서는 부족들은 아이들이 다섯 살이 되어서야 이름을 짓는데, 이때가 아이들의 생존 가능성이 높아지기 시작하는 나이이다. 그때까지, 아이들은 자신들의 연령으로 불린다. 극동의 많은 나라들은 아이들에게 출생 상황이나 아이에 대한 부모의 기대와 희망을 어떤 식으로든 묘사하는 특별한 이름을 지어준다. 호주의 어떤 원주민들은 그들의 이름을 일생 동안 계속해서 바꿀 수 있는데, 이는 지혜와 창의성 또는 결단력을 어떤 식으로든 증명하는 몇몇 중요한 경험의 결과이다. 예를 들어, 어느 날 그들 중 한 명이 춤을 아주 잘 춘다면, 그 또는 그녀는 자신의 이름을 '최고의 무용수' 또는 '빛나는 발'로 바꾸기로 결정할 수도 있다.

VOCA

• saint 성인
• soap opera (텔레비전 · 라디오) 연속극[드라마]
• protestant 개신교
• ban 금지하다
• infant 유아, 젖먹이, 아기
• mortality 사망률
• be referred to ～로 언급되다, 불리다
• circumstance 상황, 환경
• aborigine 원주민; (보통 Aborigine) 오스트레일리아 원주민

- determination 결심, 투지
- unacceptable 받아들일 수 없는

17 난도 ★★☆

독해 > 대의 파악 > 요지, 주장

정답 ①

정답의 이유

제시문은 실험을 통해 사람들이 자신과 비슷한 복장을 한 사람들에게 더 긍정적으로 반응한다는 것이 밝혀졌다는 내용이므로 글의 요지로 가장 적절한 것은 ① 'People are more likely to help those who dress like themselves(사람들은 자신들처럼 옷 입은 사람들을 도와줄 가능성이 더 크다).'이다.

오답의 이유

② 격식을 갖춘 옷차림은 탄원서 서명의 가능성을 높인다.
③ 전화를 거는 것은 다른 학생들과 어울리는 효율적인 방법이다.
④ 1970년대 초반 일부 대학생들은 자신들만의 독특한 패션으로 동경 받았다.

본문해석

젊은이들이 'hippie(히피)' 또는 'straight(단정한)' 패션으로 입는 경향이 있던 1970년대 초 시행된 한 연구에서, 히피 또는 단정한 복장을 한 실험자들이 캠퍼스에서 학생들에게 전화를 걸기 위해 10센트 동전을 빌려달라고 요청했다. 실험자가 학생과 같은 방식으로 옷을 입었을 때, 그 요청은 3분의 2 이상이 받아들여졌고, 학생과 요청자가 서로 다른 방식으로 옷 입었을 때, 동전은 절반보다 적게 제공되었다. 또 다른 실험은 우리의 긍정적인 반응이 비슷한 복장을 한 다른 사람들에게 얼마나 자동적일 수 있는지를 보여주었다. 반전 시위 참가자들은 비슷하게 옷을 입은 요청자들의 탄원서에 서명하는데, 먼저 그것을 읽지도 않고 그렇게 할 가능성이 더 큰 것으로 밝혀졌다.

VOCA

- don ~을 입다, 쓰다, 신다
- attire 의복
- dime 다임(미국 · 캐나다의 10센트짜리 동전)
- experimenter 실험자
- grant 승인하다
- instance 사례, 경우
- dissimilarly 닮지 않게, 다르게
- antiwar demonstration 반전 시위
- petition 탄원서
- formally 형식상, 정식으로
- socialize with ~와 어울리다, 교제하다
- admire 숭배하다, 동경하다

18 난도 ★★★

독해 > 빈칸 완성 > 연결어

정답 ①

정답의 이유

① 빈칸 (A) 앞부분에서 지속 시간과 빈도는 반비례 관계로, 친구를 자주 만나면 지속 시간이 줄어들고 자주 만나지 않으면 지속 시간이 늘어난다고 했고, 빈칸 (A) 다음에서 그에 대한 구체적인 예시를 제시하고 있으므로 빈칸 (A)에 들어갈 말로 가장 적절한 것은 'For example(예를 들어)'이다.

빈칸 (B) 앞부분에서 정기적으로 만나는 사람과의 식사 시간은 짧다고 했는데, 빈칸 (B) 다음에서 연인 관계에서는 지속 시간과 빈도가 둘 다 매우 길다고 했으므로 빈칸 (B) 앞 · 뒤의 상황이 대조적이다. 따라서 빈칸 (B)에 들어갈 말로 가장 적절한 것은 'Conversely(반대로)'이다.

오답의 이유

② 그럼에도 불구하고 – 게다가
③ 그러므로 – 결과적으로
④ 같은 방법으로 – 따라서

본문해석

지속 시간은 빈도와 반비례한다. 만약 여러분이 친구를 자주 만난다면, 만남의 시간은 더 짧아질 것이다. 반대로 친구를 그다지 자주 보지 않으면, 방문 지속 시간은 일반적으로 상당히 늘어날 것이다. (A) 예를 들어, 만약 여러분이 친구를 매일 본다면, 여러분은 사건이 전개되면서 일어나는 일들에 대해 알 수 있기 때문에 여러분의 방문 지속 시간이 짧을 수 있다. 하지만, 만약 여러분이 친구를 일 년에 두 번만 본다면, 여러분의 방문 지속 시간은 더 길어질 것이다. 오랫동안 보지 못했던 친구와 식당에서 저녁 식사를 했던 때를 생각해 봐라. 여러분은 아마도 서로의 삶을 따라잡는 데 몇 시간을 보냈을 것이다. 만약 여러분이 그 사람을 정기적으로 본다면, 같은 저녁 식사 시간은 상당히 짧을 것이다. (B) 반대로, 연인 관계에서는 빈도와 지속 시간이 모두 매우 높은데, 커플들, 특히 최근에 사귄 커플들은 서로 가능한 한 많은 시간을 보내고 싶어 하기 때문이다. 관계의 강도 또한 매우 높을 것이다.

VOCA

- duration 지속 시간
- inverse relationship 반비례
- keep up with 시류[유행]를 따르다; ~에 밝다, 정통하다
- unfold 전개하다, 일어나다, 진행되다
- think back (~을) 돌이켜 생각하다[보다]
- catch up on (밀린 일을) 보충하다[따라잡다]
- on a regular basis 정기적으로
- minted 최근에 생겨난[생산된, 발명된]
- intensity 격렬함, 강렬함, 강도

19 난도 ★★★　　　　　　　　　　　　　　정답 ②

독해 > 빈칸 완성 > 단어 · 구 · 절

정답의 이유

제시문은 지도자들이 자신들이 대변하는 일반 대중들과 같아 보이려고 사용하는 보편적인 선전 기술에 대한 내용이다. 빈칸 앞부분에서 '~ have used this technique to win our confidence by appearing(~처럼 보임으로써 우리의 신뢰를 얻기 위해 이 기술을 사용해 왔다) ~'라고 했으므로 문맥상 빈칸에 들어갈 말로 적절한 것은 ② 'just plain folks like ourselves(우리들 같이 평범한 사람들인 것처럼)'이다.

오답의 이유

① 화려한 추상어를 넘어선
③ 남들과는 다른 무언가
④ 군중보다 교육을 더 잘 받은

본문해석

가장 자주 사용되는 선전 기술 중 하나는 선전자의 견해가 보통 사람의 견해를 반영하고 있으며 그 또는 그녀가 그들의 최선의 이익을 위해 일하고 있다고 대중을 설득하는 것이다. 블루칼라(육체노동자) 청중에게 말하는 정치인은 소매를 걷어붙이고 넥타이를 풀고 군중들이 사용하는 특정 관용구를 사용하려고 시도할 수 있다. 그는 심지어 자신이 '그들 중 한 명일 뿐'이라는 인상을 주려고 일부러 (맞춤법이) 부정확한 언어를 사용할 수도 있다. 이 기술은 또한 정치가의 견해가 연설을 듣는 대중의 견해와 같다는 인상을 주기 위해 화려한 추상어를 사용한다. 노동 지도자들, 사업가들, 성직자들, 교육자들, 그리고 광고주들은 우리들 같이 평범한 사람들인 것처럼 보임으로써 우리의 신뢰를 얻기 위해 이 기술을 사용해 왔다.

VOCA

- propaganda 선전
- convince 설득하다
- blue-collar 블루칼라[육체노동자]의
- roll up (소매, 바지 등을) 걷다
- undo 풀다[열다/끄르다]
- attempt 시도하다, 애써 해보다
- employ 쓰다[이용하다]
- glittering generality 화려한 추상어, 미사여구(어떤 인물, 제품 또는 주장을 돋보이도록 하기 위해 호의적인 반응을 얻어낼 수 있는 단어들을 사용하는 선전 기술)
- address 연설하다
- advertiser 광고주
- appear ~처럼 보이다

20 난도 ★★☆　　　　　　　　　　　　　　정답 ②

독해 > 빈칸 완성 > 단어 · 구 · 절

정답의 이유

제시문은 롤러코스터가 작동하면서 발생하는 에너지에 관한 내용이다. 빈칸 앞 문장에서 '~ roller coasters repeatedly convert potential energy to kinetic energy and back again.'이라고 했고, 빈칸 다음 문장에서 '~ makes them hot, meaning kinetic energy is changed to heat energy during braking.'이라고 했다. 또한 빈칸 다음의 'between two surfaces(두 표면 사이에서)'로 미루어 보아, 빈칸에 들어갈 말로 가장 적절한 것은 ② 'friction(마찰 저항)'임을 유추할 수 있다.

오답의 이유

① 중력
③ 진공
④ 가속

본문해석

롤러코스터는 트랙의 첫 번째 오르막 언덕을 오를 때, 위치에너지를 만들고 있다. 더 위로 올라갈수록, 끌어당기는 중력이 더 강해질 것이다. 롤러코스터가 오르막 언덕을 넘어 하강하기 시작할 때, 그것의 위치에너지는 운동에너지, 즉 이동에너지가 된다. 일반적인 오해는 롤러코스터가 트랙을 따라 에너지를 잃는다는 것이다. 그러나, 에너지 보존의 법칙이라고 불리는 물리학의 중요한 법칙은 에너지가 결코 생성되거나 파괴될 수 없다는 것이다. 그것은 단지 한 형태에서 다른 형태로 바뀔 뿐이다. 트랙이 오르막으로 되돌아올 때마다, 롤러코스터의 운동량—운동에너지—가 그것들을 위로 운반하여 위치에너지를 만들고 롤러코스터는 반복적으로 위치에너지를 운동에너지로 변환하고 다시 되돌린다. 탑승 마지막 구간에서, 롤러코스터 차체는 두 표면 사이에서 마찰 저항을 일으키는 브레이크 장치에 의해 속도를 늦춘다. 이 움직임은 그것들을 뜨겁게 만드는데, 이는 속도를 줄이는 동안 운동에너지가 열에너지로 바뀐다는 것을 의미한다. 탑승객들은 롤러코스터가 트랙의 끝에서 에너지를 잃는다고 잘못 생각할 수도 있지만, 에너지는 단지 다른 형태로 바뀔 뿐이다.

VOCA

- potential energy 위치에너지
- pull 인력
- gravity 중력
- crest (산 따위의) 꼭대기에 이르다
- descent 하강, 강하
- kinetic energy 운동에너지
- misperception 오인, 오해
- the law of conservation of energy 에너지 보존의 법칙
- momentum 운동량
- convert 전환시키다[개조하다]
- slow down [속도 · 진행]을 늦추다
- mistakenly 잘못하여, 실수로

영어 | 2021년 지방직 9급

한눈에 훑어보기

✔ 영역 분석

어휘 01 02 03 04 05
5문항, 25%

독해 09 10 13 14 16 17 18 19 20
9문항, 45%

어법 06 07 08 15
4문항, 20%

표현 11 12
2문항, 10%

✔ 빠른 정답

01	02	03	04	05	06	07	08	09	10
④	③	①	②	④	④	②	②	④	①
11	12	13	14	15	16	17	18	19	20
①	③	②	②	③	②	④	①	③	②

✔ 점수 체크

구분	1회독	2회독	3회독
맞힌 문항 수	/ 20	/ 20	/ 20
나의 점수	점	점	점

01 난도 ★☆☆   정답 ④

어휘 > 단어

정답의 이유

밑줄 친 gratification은 '만족감, 큰 기쁨'의 뜻으로 이와 의미가 가장 가까운 것은 ④ 'satisfaction(만족)'이다.

오답의 이유

① 원기, 활기
② 신뢰, 자신감
③ 평온, 고요

본문해석

많은 충동 구매자들에게 그들이 무엇을 구매하는지보다 구매를 하는 행위가 만족으로 이어지는 것이다.

VOCA

• compulsive 강제적인, 충동적인
• purchase 구매하다, 사다
• lead to ~을 야기하다, ~로 이어지다
• gratification 만족감

02 난도 ★☆☆   정답 ③

어휘 > 단어

정답의 이유

빈칸 앞에서 더 낮은 비용으로 상품과 서비스를 자유롭게 거래할 수 있게 해준다고 했으므로 문맥상 빈칸에는 긍정적인 표현이 와야 한다. 따라서 빈칸에 들어갈 말로 가장 적절한 것은 ③ 'efficiency(효율)'이다.

오답의 이유

① 멸종
② 불경기, 우울증
④ 조심, 경고

본문해석

세계화는 더 많은 나라들이 그들의 시장을 개방하도록 이끌어서, 그들이 더 낮은 가격에 더 높은 효율로 상품과 서비스를 자유롭게 거래할 수 있게 한다.

03 난도 ★★☆   정답 ①

어휘 > 단어

정답의 이유

빈칸 앞부분에서는 번아웃의 대가에 대해 언급하고 있고, 빈칸 다음에 번아웃에서 벗어날 수 있는 방법들(Regularly unplug. Reduce unnecessary meetings. Exercise. Schedule small breaks during the day. Take vacations ~)이 열거되고 있으므로 문맥상 빈칸에 가장 적절한 것은 ① 'fixes(해결책들)'이다.

오답의 이유

② 손해들
③ 상들
④ (복잡한) 문제들

본문해석

우리는 번아웃(극도의 피로)의 대가에 대해 잘 알고 있다. 즉, 에너지, 동기부여, 생산성, 참여와 헌신이 직장에서나 가정에서나 모두 타격을 입을 수 있다. 그리고 해결책들의 대다수가 상당히 직관적이다. 정기적으로 코드를 뽑아라. 불필요한 회의를 줄여라. 운동을 하라. 낮에 잠깐 동안의 휴식을 일정에 넣어라. 여러분이 직장을 벗어날 수 없다고 생각할지라도 휴가를 내라. 왜냐하면 때로 여러분은 떠나지 못하는 것을 감당할 수 없기 때문이다.

VOCA

- engagement 약속, 업무, 참여
- commitment 약속, 헌신
- take a hit 타격을 입다
- intuitive 직감에 의한, 직감하는
- afford ~할 여유가 있다, ~할 수 있다
- now and then 때때로, 가끔

04 난도 ★★☆   정답 ②

어휘 > 어구

정답의 이유

제시문은 정부가 증가된 세금 부담을 완화시키기 위해 해결책을 모색하고 있다는 내용으로 빈칸 다음에서 '~ those present to open up more communication channels with the public(참석자들에게 대중들과 더 많은 소통 채널을 열 것을)'이라고 했으므로 문맥상 빈칸에 들어갈 말로 가장 적절한 것은 ② 'called for(요청했다)'이다. 'call for A to부정사'는 'A에게 ~할 것을 요청하다'이다.

오답의 이유

① ~ 위에 떨어졌다
③ ~을 (차에) 태웠다
④ ~을 거절했다

본문해석

정부는 새로운 세금 정산 제도로 인해 늘어난 세금 부담에 대해 급여 노동자들을 달래기 위한 방안을 모색하고 있다. 지난 월요일 대통령 보좌관들과의 회의 동안, 대통령은 참석자들에게 대중과의 더 많은 소통 채널을 열 것을 요청했다.

VOCA

- soothe 달래다
- salaried 봉급을 받는
- tax settlement 세금 정산
- presidential aides 대통령 보좌관
- present 참석한

05 난도 ★★☆   정답 ④

어휘 > 어구

정답의 이유

밑줄 친 apprehend는 '이해하다, 파악하다'의 뜻으로 이와 의미가 가장 가까운 것은 ④ 'grasp(파악하다)'이다.

오답의 이유

① 포함하다
② 침입하다
③ 검사하다

본문해석

중국의 서예를 공부할 때, 중국어의 기원과 그것이 원래 어떻게 쓰였는지 배워야 한다. 하지만, 그 나라의 예술적 전통에서 자란 사람들을 제외하고는, 그것의 미적인 의미를 파악하기는 매우 어려운 것처럼 보인다.

VOCA

- calligraphy 서예, 달필
- bring up 기르다, 양육하다
- aesthetic 미적인
- significance 중요성, 의미

06 난도 ★★☆   정답 ④

어법 > 영작하기

정답의 이유
④ '지각동사＋목적어＋원형부정사[-ing/p.p.]'인데, 목적어(a
family)가 위층에 '이사 오는' 능동 관계이므로 moved → moving
이 되어야 한다.

오답의 이유
① '수일치'와 '형용사＋to부정사'에 대한 문제이다. 주어(His
novels)는 복수명사이므로 복수동사(are)가 올바르게 쓰였으며,
to부정사(to read)가 난이형용사(hard, easy, difficult 등)를 수
식하여 '~하기 …하다'로 올바르게 사용되었다.
② 'It is no use -ing(~해도 소용없다)'는 동명사의 관용표현이므
로 'It is no use trying ~'이 올바르게 사용되었다.
③ 주어(My house)가 페인트 칠해지는 것이므로 수동태(is
painted)가 올바르게 쓰였다. '매 ~마다'는 'every＋기수＋복수
명사(every five years)'로 올바르게 사용되었다.

VOCA
• persuade 설득하다
• move in 이사 오다

더 알아보기
지각동사＋목적어＋원형부정사/현재분사(-ing)/과거분사(p.p.): '목
적어가 ~하는 것을 …하다'

see, watch, observe	보다	＋목적어＋원형부정사/현재분사(-ing) → 능동
notice	알아채다	
hear, listen to	듣다	＋목적어＋과거분사(p.p.) → 수동
feel	느끼다	

예 We noticed them *coming* in. → 능동
(우리는 그들이 들어오는 것을 알아챘다.)
예 Even dogs yawn in response to seeing their owners or even
strangers *yawn*. → 능동
(심지어 개들도 그들의 주인이나 심지어 낯선 사람들이 하품하는
것을 보고 반응하여 하품을 한다.)
예 I heard the door *shut* by itself. → 수동
(나는 문이 저절로 닫히는 소리를 들었다.)

07 난도 ★★★   정답 ②

어법 > 영작하기

정답의 이유
② '사역동사＋목적어＋원형부정사[p.p.]' 문제이다. 사역동사 let은
과거분사를 목적격 보어로 취할 수 없으므로 목적어와 목적격
보어가 수동 관계일 경우 'let＋목적어＋be＋p.p.'로 나타낸다.
따라서 distracted → be distracted가 되어야 한다.

오답의 이유
① 사역동사(had) 다음에 목적어(the woman)가 '수동(체포되는)
관계'이므로 목적격 보어에 과거분사(arrested)가 올바르게 사용
되었다.
③ 사역동사(let) 다음에 목적어(me)가 '능동(아는) 관계'이므로 동
사원형(know)이 올바르게 사용되었다.
④ 사역동사(had) 다음에 목적어(the students)가 '능동(전화를 걸
다, 요청하다) 관계'이므로 동사원형(phone, ask)이 올바르게
사용되었으며, phone과 ask가 접속사(and)로 연결되었다.
'ask＋목적어＋to부정사'는 '목적어에게 ~할 것을 부탁하다'의
뜻으로 올바르게 사용되었다.

VOCA
• distract 집중이 안 되게 하다
• police authorities 경찰 당국
• donate 기부하다

더 알아보기
사역동사＋목적어＋원형부정사/과거분사(p.p.): '목적어를 ~하도
록(당하도록) 하다'

make	~하게 만들다	＋목적어＋원형부정사 → 능동
have	~하게 하다	＋목적어＋p.p. → 수동
let	~하도록 허락하다	＋목적어＋원형부정사 → 능동
		＋목적어＋be p.p. → 수동

예 The mother made her daughter *clean* the room. → 능동
(어머니는 딸에게 방청소를 시켰다.)
예 He had his political enemies *imprisoned*. → 수동
(그는 그의 정적들을 투옥시켰다.)
예 I will let you *know* if I can accompany you on your walk.
→ 능동
(내가 산책에 동행할 수 있는지 네게 알려 줄게.)

08 난도 ★★☆   정답 ②

어법 > 정문 찾기

정답의 이유
② 병렬 구조와 needless to say에 대한 문제이다. 접속사(and)로
연결된 과거시제 동사(attempted와 had)가 병렬 구조를 이루어
올바르게 쓰였다. needless to say는 '~는 말할 것도 없이'라는
뜻의 관용표현이다.

오답의 이유
① 2형식 동사(become)는 주격 보어를 취하는 동사로 주격 보어에
는 명사나 형용사가 와야 하므로 unpredictably → unpredictable
이 되어야 한다.
③ upon -ing는 '~하자마자'의 뜻으로, 전치사(upon) 다음에 명사
상당어구가 와야 하므로 Upon arrived → Upon arriving
[arrival]이 되어야 한다.
④ enough는 형용사 혹은 부사 다음에서 후치 수식하므로 enough
comfortable → comfortable enough가 되어야 한다.

09 난도 ★★☆　　　　　　　　　　정답 ④

독해 > 대의 파악 > 제목, 주제

정답의 이유

제시문은 '디지털 전환(digital turn)'의 정의와 사회적 현실에서의 역할, 개인에게 미치는 영향에 대해 서술하고 있으므로 글의 제목으로 가장 적절한 것은 ④ 'Digitalization Within the Context of Social Reality(사회적 현실의 맥락 안에서의 디지털화)'이다.

오답의 이유

① SNS에서 정체성 다시 만들기

② 언어적 전환 대 디지털 전환

③ 디지털 시대의 정보 공유 방법

본문해석

'전환'의 정의는 우리가 사회적 현실에서 디지털화의 역할에 집중할 수 있도록 하는 분석 전략으로써 디지털 전환을 묘사한다. 분석적 관점으로 보면, 디지털 전환은 디지털화의 사회적 의미를 분석하고 토론하는 것을 가능하게 한다. 따라서 '디지털 전환'이라는 용어는 한 사회 내에서 디지털화의 역할에 초점을 맞춘 분석적 접근 방식을 의미한다. 만약 언어적 전환이 언어를 통해 현실이 구성된다는 인식론적 가정에 의해 정의된다면, 디지털 전환은 사회적 현실이 점점 디지털화에 의해 정의된다는 가정에 기반을 둔다. 소셜 미디어는 사회적 관계의 디지털화를 상징한다. 개인들은 더욱더 소셜 네트워킹 사이트(SNS)상에서의 정체성 관리에 관여한다. SNS는 다방향적인데, 이는 사용자가 서로 연결되고 정보를 공유할 수 있다는 것을 의미한다.

VOCA

• definition 정의

• cast 던지다, 제시하다

• perspective 관점

• signify 의미하다

• center on 초점을 맞추다

• linguistic 언어적인

• assumption 가정

• engage in 관여하다

• polydirectional 다방향의

10 난도 ★★★　　　　　　　　　　정답 ①

독해 > 글의 일관성 > 글의 순서

정답의 이유

주어진 글의 마지막 부분에 재생에너지(renewable energy) 캠페인이 조직되었다는 내용이 나오는데, (C)의 첫 문장에서 '~ the UK government's inability to rapidly accelerate the growth of renewable energy industries ~'라고 했으므로 문맥상 (C)로 이어지는 것이 적절하다. (C)의 마지막 문장에 언급된 'the Westmill Solar Co-operative'를 (A)의 'This solar cooperative'로 받는다. (B)에서 'Similarly'로 시작하면서 미국에서도 재생에너지를 지지하는 Clean Energy Collective가 설립되었다고 마무리하고 있으므로 주어진 글 다음에 이어질 글의 순서로 가장 적절한 것은 ① '(C) – (A) – (B)'이다.

본문해석

세계 기후 변화에 대하여 증가하는 우려는 활동가들이 화석 연료 추출 소비에 대한 반대 캠페인뿐만 아니라 재생에너지 지원 캠페인도 조직하도록 동기를 부여해 왔다.

(C) 재생에너지 산업 성장을 신속하게 가속화하는 데 대한 영국 정부의 무능력함에 좌절한 환경 운동가들은 Westmill Wind Farm Co-operative를 결성했는데, 이는 2,000명 이상 회원이 있는 지역사회 소유 단체이며, 연간 2,500가구의 소비량만큼의 전력을 생산하는 것으로 추정되는 육상 풍력 발전단지를 소유하고 있다. Westmill Wind Farm Co-operative는 지역 시민들에게 Westmill Solar Co-operative를 만들도록 고무시켰다.

(A) 이 태양열 협동조합은 1,400가구에 전력을 공급하기에 충분한 에너지를 생산하여, 국내 최초의 대규모 태양열 농장 협동조합이 되었으며, 회원들에 따르면, 이 태양열 발전은 "일반인들이 자신의 옥상에서뿐만 아니라 공익사업 규모로도 청정 전력을 생산할 수 있는 지속 가능하고 '민주적인' 에너지 공급의 새로운 시대"를 대표한다는 가시적인 신호이다.

(B) 유사하게, 미국의 재생에너지 지지자들은 Clean Energy Collective를 설립했는데, 이 기업은 '참여하는 공공 설비 소비자들에 의해 공동으로 소유된 중간 규모의 설비를 통해 청정 전력 발전을 가져올 모델'을 개척해 왔다.

VOCA

• extraction 추출

• reminder 상기시키는 것

• sustainable 지속 가능한

• utility (수도 전기 가스 같은) 공익사업, 공공 설비

• enthusiast 열렬한 지지자

• pioneer 개척하다

• collectively 집합적으로, 총괄하여

• frustrate 좌절감을 주다, 불만스럽게 만들다

• inability 무능, 불능

• accelerate 가속화되다, 가속화하다

• onshore 육지의

• inspire 고무하다

11 난도 ★☆☆　　　　　　　　　　　　　　　　정답 ①

표현 > 일반회화

정답의 이유

B가 빈칸 앞에서 'It was really good.'이라고 했고, 빈칸 다음에서 그 영화의 특수효과가 환상적이었다고 했으므로 문맥상 빈칸에는 A가 B에게 영화에서 좋았던 점을 구체적으로 물어보는 표현이 와야 함을 유추할 수 있다. 따라서 빈칸에는 ① 'What did you like the most about it(어떤 점이 가장 좋았어)?'이 가장 적절하다.

오답의 이유

② 네가 가장 좋아하는 영화 장르가 뭐야?

③ 그 영화는 국제적으로 홍보되었니?

④ 그 영화는 매우 비쌌니?

본문해석

A: 주말 잘 보냈어?

B: 응, 꽤 괜찮았어. 우리는 영화 보러 갔었어.

A: 오! 뭘 봤는데?

B: *Interstellar*. 정말 좋았어.

A: 정말? 어떤 점이 가장 좋았어?

B: 특수효과야. 정말 환상적이었어. 다시 봐도 좋을 것 같아.

VOCA

• special effect 특수효과

• mind 꺼리다

12 난도 ★☆☆　　　　　　　　　　　　　　　　정답 ③

표현 > 일반회화

정답의 이유

A가 두 달 방학이 일주일처럼 지나갔다고 하면서 시간의 빠름을 말하고 있는데, B가 '내 말이 그 말이야. 방학이 몇 주 동안 느릿느릿 지나갔어.'라고 했으므로 앞뒤가 맞지 않는 어색한 대화는 ③이다.

본문해석

① A: 오늘 내가 해야 하는 이 연설 때문에 너무 떨려.

　 B: 가장 중요한 건 침착함을 유지하는 거야.

② A: 그거 알아? 민수와 유진이가 결혼한대!

　 B: 잘됐다! 그들은 언제 결혼하니?

③ A: 두 달 방학이 마치 일주일처럼 지나갔어. 새 학기가 코앞이야.

　 B: 내 말이 그 말이야. 방학이 몇 주 동안 느릿느릿 지나갔어.

④ A: '물'을 프랑스어로 어떻게 말해?

　 B: 기억이 날 듯 말 듯한데, 그게 기억이 안 나.

VOCA

• tie the knot 결혼하다

• be around the corner 목전에 닥치다, 임박하다

• drag on 질질 끌다, 계속되다

• on the tip of one's tongue 혀끝에서 맴도는, 기억이 날 듯 안 나는

13 난도 ★★☆　　　　　　　　　　　　　　　　정답 ②

독해 > 세부 내용 찾기 > 내용 (불)일치

정답의 이유

제시문은 여성과 남성의 대화 방식의 차이에 관한 글이다. 세 번째 문장에서 'Women's conversations range from health to their houses, from politics to fashion, ~ but sports are notably absent.'라고 하면서 여성들은 대화의 주제 범위가 다양하지만 스포츠에 대한 대화는 없다고 했으므로 글의 내용과 일치하지 않는 것은 ② '여성들의 대화 주제는 건강에서 스포츠에 이르기까지 매우 다양하다.'이다.

오답의 이유

① 첫 번째 문장에서 '~ and they always talk about trivial things, or at least that's what men have always thought.'라고 했으므로 글의 내용과 일치한다.

③ 다섯 번째 문장에서 '~ women also tend to move quickly from one subject to another in conversation, ~'라고 했으므로 글의 내용과 일치한다.

④ 마지막 문장에서 '~ they sometimes find it hard to concentrate when several things have to be discussed at the same time in a meeting.'이라고 했으므로 글의 내용과 일치한다.

본문해석

여성들은 수다에 능숙하고, 그들은 항상 시소한 것들에 대해 이야기한다. 혹은 적어도 남성들은 항상 그렇게 생각해 왔다. 하지만 몇몇 새로운 연구는 여성들이 여성들과 대화할 때, 그들의 대화는 하찮음과는 거리가 멀고, 남성들이 다른 남성들과 대화할 때보다 더 많은 주제(최대 40개의 주제)를 다루고 있다는 것을 시사한다. 여성들의 대화는 건강부터 집에 관한 것까지, 정치부터 패션까지, 영화에서 가족까지, 교육에서 관계 문제까지를 총망라하지만, 스포츠는 눈에 띄게 없다. 남성들은 더 제한된 범위의 주제를 가지는 경향이 있는데, 가장 인기 있는 것은 일, 스포츠, 농담, 자동차, 여성들이다. 1,000명이 넘는 여성들을 인터뷰했던 심리학자인 Petra Boynton 교수에 의하면 여성들은 또한 대화 중에 한 주제에서 다른 주제로 빠르게 이동하는 경향이 있는 반면, 남성들은 대체로 더 오랫동안 한 주제를 고수한다. 직장에서, 이러한 차이점은 남성들에게 장점으로 작용할 수 있는데, 그들은 다른 문제들을 제쳐두고 토의하는 주제에 온전하게 집중할 수 있기 때문이다. 다시 말하면, 이것은 또한 때로 회의에서 여러 가지 일을 동시에 논의해야 할 때 남성들이 그것들에 집중하기 힘들다는 것을 의미한다.

VOCA

• be an expert at ~에 능숙하다

• frivolous 시시한, 하찮은

• notably 특히, 현저히

• psychologist 심리학자

• stick to ~을 고수하다

14 난도 ★★☆

정답 ②

독해 > 글의 일관성 > 무관한 어휘 · 문장

정답의 이유

제시문은 15세기 과학, 철학, 미술의 구분이 없었을 때 아리스토텔레스의 철학이 학자들에게 어떤 영향을 주었는지에 관한 글이므로 글의 흐름상 적절하지 않은 문장은 ② 'Humanists quickly realized the power of the printing press for spreading their knowledge(인문주의자들은 자신들의 지식을 전파하는 인쇄기의 위력을 빠르게 깨달았다).'이다.

본문해석

15세기에는 과학, 철학, 미술 사이에 구분이 없었다. 세 분야 모두 '자연 철학'의 일반적인 주제에 포함되어 있었다. 자연 철학 발전의 중심이 되는 것은 고전적인 작가들의 회복이었는데, 가장 중요한 것이 아리스토텔레스의 작품이었다. 인문주의자들은 자신들의 지식을 전파하는 인쇄기의 위력을 빠르게 깨달았다. 15세기 초에 아리스토텔레스는 철학과 과학에서 모든 학문적 성찰의 기초가 되었다. Averroes와 Avicenna의 아랍어 번역본과 주석 속에서 생생하게 살아 있는 아리스토텔레스는 자연계와 인류의 관계에 대한 체계적인 관점을 제공했다. Physics, Metaphysics, Meteorology 같은 현존하는 그의 저서들은 학자들에게 자연 세계를 창조한 힘을 이해할 수 있는 논리적인 도구들을 제공했다.

VOCA

- heading 제목, 주제
- central to ~에 중심이 되는
- humanist 인문주의자
- printing press 인쇄기
- scholastic 학자의, 학문적인
- speculation 사색, 성찰; 추론, 추측
- perspective 관점, 시각
- Metaphysics 형이상학
- Meteorology 기상학

15 난도 ★★☆

정답 ③

어법 > 비문 찾기

정답의 이유

③ vary는 '다르다'라는 뜻의 자동사이므로 will be vary → will vary가 되어야 한다.

오답의 이유

① 'of+추상명사'는 형용사 역할을 하며 '~한'으로 해석하므로 be 동사 다음에 of special interest는 보어로 어법에 맞게 쓰였다.

② 과거 시간 부사(in the past)가 있으므로 과거시제(were)가 올바르게 쓰였다. consider는 'consider+목적어+(to be)+형/명'으로 쓰이는 5형식 동사로 수동태가 되면 'be considered+(to be)+형/명'이 되므로 were considered to be the ultimate tool for a typist로 올바르게 사용되었다.

④ 과거 시간 부사(in 1975)가 있으므로 과거시제(was)가 올바르게 쓰였다. 주어(The world's first digital camera)가 '만들어지는' 수동 관계이므로 수동태(was created)가 올바르게 쓰였다.

본문해석

① 지진 후에 뒤따르는 화재는 보험 업계에서 특히 관심이 있다.

② 워드 프로세서는 과거에 타자수에게 최고의 도구로 여겨졌다.

③ 현금 예측에서 소득의 요소들은 회사 상황에 따라 달라질 것이다.

④ 세계 최초의 디지털 카메라는 1975년 Eastman Kodak에서 Steve Sasson에 의해서 만들어졌다.

VOCA

- insurance industry 보험 업계
- ultimate 최고의, 궁극적인
- element 요소
- circumstance 상황, 환경

16 난도 ★★☆

정답 ②

독해 > 빈칸 완성 > 단어 · 구 · 절

정답의 이유

빈칸 다음의 'growth elsewhere'와 이후 문장에서 30년 동안 10% 성장을 지속해 왔던 중국이 세계 경제를 앞으로 나아가게 한 강력한 동력원이었는데, 성장률이 공식적으로 약 7%로 둔화되었다고 했으므로 문맥상 빈칸에는 중국 경제의 둔화가 다른 나라들의 성장에 어떤 영향을 미치는지에 대한 내용이 와야 함을 유추할 수 있다. 따라서 빈칸에 들어갈 말로 가장 적절한 것은 ② 'weigh on(압박하다)'이다.

오답의 이유

① 속도를 더 내다

③ 이어지다

④ 결과적으로 ~이 되다

본문해석

역사적으로 높은 성장률로부터 중국 경제의 둔화는 다른 곳의 성장을 압박할 것으로 오랫동안 예상되어 왔다. "30년 동안 10% 성장해 왔던 중국은 세계 경제를 앞으로 나아가게 한 많은 것들에 대한 강력한 동력원이었습니다."라고 Yale대의 Stephen Roach는 말했다. 성장률이 공식적인 수치로는 약 7%대로 둔화되었다. "그것은 명확한 감속입니다."라고 Roach가 덧붙였다.

VOCA

- rate 비율, 속도, 등급, 평가하다
- weigh on 압박하다, 무거운 짐이 되다
- source 근원, 원천
- figure 수치
- concrete 실제의, 명확한, 구체적인
- deceleration 감속

17 난도 ★★☆ 정답 ④

독해 > 빈칸 완성 > 단어 · 구 · 절

정답의 이유

빈칸 다음 문장에서 'The more trust you bestow, the more others trust you.'라고 했고, 직무 만족도와 완전한 직무 수행을 위해 얼마나 권한을 부여받았는지의 사이에는 직접적인 상관관계가 있다고 했으므로 빈칸에 들어갈 말로 가장 적절한 것은 ④ 'autonomy(자율성)'이다.

오답의 이유

① 일
② 보상
③ 제한

본문해석

점점 더 많은 리더들이 원격으로 일하거나, 컨설턴트와 프리랜서뿐만 아니라 전국이나 전 세계에 흩어져 있는 팀과 함께 일하게 됨에 따라 여러분은 그들에게 더 많은 자율성을 주어야 할 것이다. 여러분이 더 많은 신뢰를 줄수록, 다른 사람들은 여러분을 더욱더 신뢰한다. 나는 직무 만족도와 업무 매 단계마다 그들을 그림자처럼 따라다니는 사람 없이 완벽하게 자신들의 업무를 수행하기 위해 권한을 얼마나 부여받았는지의 사이에는 직접적인 상관관계가 있다는 것을 확신한다. 신뢰하는 사람들에게 책임을 나누어 주는 것은 조직을 원활하게 돌아갈 수 있게 할 뿐만 아니라, 여러분의 시간을 더 자유롭게 해서 여러분이 더 큰 문제에 집중할 수 있도록 할 수 있다.

VOCA

• remotely 멀리서, 원격으로
• scattered 흩어져 있는
• bestow 수여[부여]하다
• correlation 연관성, 상관관계
• empower 권한을 주다
• execute 수행하다
• shadow 그림자처럼 따라다니다, 미행하다
• give away 거저 주다, 나누어 주다
• free up ~을 해방하다, 풀어주다; 해소하다

18 난도 ★★☆ 정답 ①

독해 > 대의 파악 > 요지, 주장

정답의 이유

제시문은 유대교의 교리에 기초하여 우리가 행할 의무를 설명하는 글로, 중반에서 인간으로서의 '우리의 일은 우리 자신과 서로를 돌보는 것뿐만 아니라 우리 주변에 더 나은 세상을 만드는 것이 우리에게 주어진 의무이다.'라는 Lisa Grushcow의 주장을 보여주고 있다. 따라서 이 글의 요지로 가장 적절한 것은 ① 'We should work to heal the world(우리는 세상을 고치기 위해 노력해야 한다).'이다.

오답의 이유

② 공동체는 피난처로서 기능을 해야 한다.
③ 우리는 선을 믿음으로 개념화해야 한다.
④ 사원들은 지역사회에 기여해야 한다.

본문해석

"유대교에서, 우리는 대체로 우리의 행동에 의해 정의됩니다."라고 Montreal의 Emanu-El-Beth Sholom 사원의 수석 랍비인 Lisa Grushcow가 말한다. "당신은 실제로 탁상공론적인 공상적 사회 개혁론자가 될 수 없어요." 이 개념은 tikkun olam이라는 유대교 관념과 관련 있는데, '세상을 고치기 위해서'로 번역된다. 그녀는, 인간으로서의 "우리의 일은 망가진 것을 고치는 것입니다. 우리 자신과 서로를 돌보는 것뿐만 아니라 우리 주변에 더 나은 세상을 만드는 것이 우리에게 주어진 의무입니다."라고 말한다. 이러한 철학은 선을 봉사에 기반을 둔 무언가로 개념화한다. "내가 좋은 사람인가?"라고 묻는 대신에, 여러분은 "내가 세상에서 어떤 이로운 일을 할 수 있을까?"라고 물어보고 싶을지도 모른다. Grushcow의 사원은 이러한 믿음을 그들의 공동체 안팎에서 행동으로 옮긴다. 예를 들어, 그들은 1970년대에 베트남 출신의 두 난민 가족이 캐나다로 오도록 후원했다.

VOCA

• Judaism 유대교
• define 규정하다, 정의하다
• rabbi [유대인 목사 · 학자 · 교사에 대한 존칭으로] 선생
• armchair 탁상공론의
• do-gooder 공상적 사회 개혁론자
• Jewish 유대인[유대교]의
• mend 고치다, 수리하다
• incumbent on ~에게 의무로 지워지는
• conceptualize 개념화하다
• sponsor 후원하다
• refugee 난민

독해 > 빈칸 완성 > 연결어

정답의 이유

③ 제시문은 균형의 중요성에 대한 내용으로, 이에 대한 예시로 스토아 학파의 사상을 들어 설명하고 있다. 스토아 학자들은 최악의 상황을 의도적으로 시각화할 것을 권고했으며, (A) 앞 문장에서 'This tends to reduce anxiety about the future(이것이 미래에 대한 걱정을 줄여주는 경향이 있다).'라고 했고, 빈칸 (A) 다음에서 'increases your gratitude for having them now(현재 소유하고 있는 것에 대한 감사를 증가시킨다)'라고 했으므로 (A)에는 부연 설명하는 'Besides(게다가)' 혹은 'Furthermore (더군다나)'가 적절하다.

빈칸 (B) 앞 문장에서 부정적 사고(imagining that you might lose the relationships and possessions you currently enjoy ~)에 대해 말하고 있는데, (B) 문장에서 'Positive thinking ~ always leans into the future, ignoring present pleasures.'라고 했으므로, (B)에는 대조를 뜻하는 'by contrast(반면에)'가 적절하다.

오답의 이유

① 그럼에도 불구하고 - 게다가
② 뿐만 아니라 - 예를 들어
④ 그러나 - 결론적으로

본문해석

고대 철학자들과 영적 스승들은 긍정적인 것과 부정적인 것, 낙관주의와 비관주의, 성공과 보장을 위한 노력과 실패와 불확실성에 대한 열린 마음에 대하여 균형을 유지하는 것의 필요성을 이해했다. 스토아 학자들은 '악을 미리 생각하기', 즉 최악의 상황을 의도적으로 시각화할 것을 권고했다. 이것은 미래에 대한 걱정을 줄여주는 경향이 있다. 여러분이 현실에서 상황이 얼마나 악화될 수 있는지를 냉정하게 그려낼 때, 여러분은 보통 대처할 수 있다고 결론 내린다. (A) 게다가, 그들은 지적하기를, 여러분이 현재 누리고 있는 관계와 소유물을 잃게 될 수도 있다고 상상하는 것은 현재 그것들을 소유하고 있는 것에 대한 감사를 증가시킨다고 했다. (B) 반면에, 긍정적인 사고는 항상 미래에 의지하고, 현재의 즐거움을 무시한다.

VOCA

• spiritual 영적인, 정신의
• optimism 낙관주의
• pessimism 비관주의
• strive 분투하다
• Stoics 스토아 학파
• premeditation 미리 생각함, 미리 계획함
• deliberately 고의로, 의도적으로
• visualize 마음속에 그려보다, 상상하다
• soberly 냉정하게
• cope 대처하다
• gratitude 감사
• lean ~에 기울어지다; ~에 기대다

독해 > 글의 일관성 > 문장 삽입

정답의 이유

주어진 문장은 일이 재정적 보장 이상을 제공한다는 내용이다. ② 앞에 생계유지 수단인 봉급 지급 내용이 있으므로 주어진 문장이 들어갈 위치로 가장 적절한 것은 ②이다.

본문해석

왜 일 중독자들은 그들의 업무를 그렇게 즐길까? 그 이유는 주로 일이 몇 가지 중요한 이점들을 제공하기 때문이다. 그것은 사람들에게 생계유지 수단인 봉급을 제공한다. 그리고 일은 재정적인 보장 이상을 제공한다. 그것은 사람들에게 자신감을 주는데, 그들은 도전적인 작업을 생산하고 "내가 해냈어."라고 말할 수 있을 때 만족감을 느낀다. 심리학자들은 일이 또한 사람들에게 정체성을 준다고 주장한다. 그들은 자아와 개성을 느낄 수 있도록 일한다. 게다가, 대부분의 일은 사람들에게 다른 사람을 만나기 위한 사회적으로 용인된 방법을 제공한다. 일은 긍정적인 중독이라고 말할 수 있다. 아마도 일 중독자들은 그들의 일에 대해 강박적일 수 있지만, 그들의 중독은 안전하고 심지어 이로운 것처럼 보인다.

VOCA

• financial 재정적인
• advantage 이점, 이익
• provide A with B A에게 B를 제공하다
• paycheck 급료, 봉급
• earn a living 생계를 유지하다
• challenging 도전적인, 힘든
• individualism 개성
• acceptable 용인되는
• compulsive 강박적인
• advantageous 이로운

영어 | 2020년 지방직 9급

한눈에 훑어보기

✓ 영역 분석

어휘   01   02   03   04   06
5문항, 25%

독해   09   10   14   15   16   17   18   19   20
9문항, 45%

어법   05   07   08   12
4문항, 20%

표현   11   13
2문항, 10%

✓ 빠른 정답

01	02	03	04	05	06	07	08	09	10
②	④	②	①	③	④	③	②	①	③
11	12	13	14	15	16	17	18	19	20
②	①	②	④	③	③	①	③	④	④

✓ 점수 체크

구분	1회독	2회독	3회독
맞힌 문항 수	/ 20	/ 20	/ 20
나의 점수	점	점	점

01 난도 ★★☆   정답 ②

어휘 > 단어

[정답의 이유]
빈칸 다음에서 'so when the temperatures begin to rise, your water will also heat up.'이라고 했으므로 문맥상 빈칸에는 온도와 관련된 문제점을 언급하고 있음을 알 수 있다. 따라서 플라스틱병이 단열 처리가 되지 않아 기온이 올라가면 병 안의 물 온도 역시 올라가는 게 자연스러우므로 빈칸에는 ② 'insulated(단열 처리가 된)'가 적절하다.

[오답의 이유]
① 위생적인
③ 재활용할 수 있는
④ 방수의

본문해석
플라스틱병에 관련된 문제는 그것이 단열 처리가 되지 않아서, 온도가 상승하기 시작하면, 당신의 물도 뜨거워질 것이라는 것이다.

02 난도 ★☆☆   정답 ④

어휘 > 단어

[정답의 이유]
밑줄 친 alleviate는 '완화하다'의 뜻으로 이와 의미가 가장 가까운 것은 ④ 'relieve(덜어주다, 완화하다)'이다.

[오답의 이유]
① 보완하다
② 가속화하다
③ 계산하다

본문해석
작가가 글을 쓰는 과정에서 취하는 전략은 주의력 과부하의 어려움을 완화할 수도 있다.

VOCA
• strategy (특정 목표를 위한) 전략[계획]
• adopt (특정한 방식이나 자세를) 쓰다, 취하다
• attentional 주의력의
• overload 과부하

03 난도 ★★☆ 정답 ②

어휘 > 어구

정답의 이유

밑줄 친 touched off는 '촉발했다, 발단이 되었다'의 뜻으로 이와 의미가 가장 가까운 것은 ② 'gave rise to(일으켰다, 유발했다)'이다.

오답의 이유

① ~을 보살펴 주었다
③ (손실 따위를) 보상했다
④ ~와 접촉[연락]을 유지했다

본문해석

그 잔인한 광경은 그렇지 않다면(보지 않았다면) 그녀의 마음속에 떠오르지 않았을 생각을 불러일으켰다.

VOCA

• enter one's mind 생각이 떠오르다, 마음에 떠오르다

04 난도 ★☆☆ 정답 ①

어휘 > 단어

정답의 이유

밑줄 친 shunned는 '피해지는, 소외당하는'의 뜻으로 이와 의미가 가장 가까운 것은 ① 'avoided(피해지는)'이다. 학교에서 남을 괴롭히는 학생과 나머지 학생들의 관계를 생각해 보면 단어의 뜻을 몰라도 그 의미를 추론할 수 있다.

오답의 이유

② 경고받는
③ 처벌받는
④ 모방되는

본문해석

학교 불량배는 반에서 다른 학생들에 의해 피해지는 게 어떤 것인지 알지 못했다.

VOCA

• school bully 학교에서 남을 괴롭히는 학생

05 난도 ★★☆ 정답 ③

어법 > 정문 찾기

정답의 이유

③ 왕래발착 동사(start)는 예정된 미래(at noon today)를 나타낼 때 현재시제나 현재진행시제를 사용하므로 현재진행시제(am starting)를 쓴 것은 어법상 적절하다.

오답의 이유

① 가산명사(stars)는 much로 받을 수 없으므로 How much → How many가 되어야 한다.
② 감정유발동사(~한 감정을 일으키다)는 현재분사인 경우 '~한 감정을 일으키는'의 의미이며, 과거분사인 경우 '~한 감정을 가진'을 뜻한다. excite는 감정유발동사로 크리스마스 파티가 신이 나는 감정을 유발하는 것이므로 excited → exciting이 되어야 한다.
④ 과거의 규칙적인 습관이지만 지금은 하지 않을 때 'used to+동사원형(~하곤 했다)'을 사용하므로 loving → love가 되어야 한다.

본문해석

① 은하계에 있는 수십억 개의 별들 중에서 생명체를 부화할 수 있는 것은 얼마나 될까?
② 크리스마스 파티가 너무 신나서 나는 시간 가는 줄 몰랐다.
③ 나는 오늘 정오에 업무를 시작할 예정이기 때문에 지금 당장 떠나야만 한다.
④ 그들은 더 어렸을 때 책을 훨씬 더 좋아하곤 했다.

VOCA

• hatch 부화시키다
• lose track of time 시간 가는 줄 모르다

06 난도 ★★☆ 정답 ④

어휘 > 어구

정답의 이유

밑줄 친 made a case for는 '~에 대해 (긍정적인) 의견을 주장했다'의 뜻으로 이와 의미가 가장 가까운 것은 ④ 'strongly suggested (강력하게 제안했다)'이다.

오답의 이유

① ~에 반대했다
② ~을 꿈꾸었다
③ 전적으로 배제했다

본문해석

Francesca가 여름 휴가 동안 집에서 머물 것을 주장한 후에, 불편한 침묵이 저녁 식탁을 엄습했다. Robert는 지금이 그녀에게 그의 거창한 계획에 대해 말할 적기인지 확신하지 못했다.

VOCA

• fall on ~을 엄습하다; ~에 떨어지다
• grandiose (너무) 거창한

07 난도 ★★☆   정답 ③

어법 > 비문 찾기

정답의 이유

③ 부사구(Among her most prized possessions sold during the evening sale)를 강조하기 위해 문두로 이동시킬 경우 주어와 동사가 도치된다. 주어(a 1961 bejeweled timepiece)가 단수이므로 동사는 were → was가 되어야 한다.

오답의 이유

① 분사구문의 의미상 주어인 Elizabeth Taylor가 선언한 것이므로 능동을 의미하는 현재분사(declaring)가 올바르게 쓰였다.

② 관계대명사 that의 선행사는 an evening auction이며, that절에 주어가 없으므로 주격 관계대명사로 적절하게 쓰였다.

④ 'with 분사구문(with+목적어+목적격 보어)'에서 목적어(its head and tail)가 다이아몬드로 '덮였다'는 수동 의미이므로 과거분사(covered)가 올바르게 사용되었다.

본문해석

Elizabeth Taylor는 아름다운 보석들을 보는 안목이 있었고, 수년에 걸쳐 놀라운 보석 몇 점을 수집하였으며, 한 번은 "여자라면 언제나 더 많은 다이아몬드를 가질 수 있다."라고 단언했다. 2011년 그녀의 가장 최상품의 보석들이 Christie(경매회사)의 어느 저녁 경매에서 1억 1,590만 달러에 팔렸다. 그날 저녁 경매에서 팔린 그녀의 가장 소중한 소유물 중에는 1961년 불가리가 만든 보석으로 장식된 시계 한 점이 있었다. 손목을 휘감아 도는 뱀 형상으로 디자인되었으며, 머리와 꼬리는 다이아몬드로 덮여 있고, 최면을 거는 듯한 두 개의 에메랄드 눈을 가진 이 정교한 기계장치는 작은 수정 시계를 드러내기 위해 무시무시한 턱을 벌린다.

VOCA

- have an eye for ~을 보는 안목이 있다
- amass 모으다, 축적하다
- declare 선언하다, 단언하다
- bring in (이익·이자를) 가져오다
- prized 소중한
- bejeweled 보석으로 장식한, 보석을 두른
- timepiece 시계
- serpent (특히 큰) 뱀
- coil (고리 모양으로) 감다, 휘감다
- hypnotic 최면을 거는 듯한
- discreet 신중한, 조심스러운
- fierce 사나운, 맹렬한
- quartz watch 수정(발진식) 시계

더 알아보기

with 분사구문: with+-ing[p.p.] '목적어가 ~한 채로'

- with[without]+목적어+-ing[p.p.]의 형태로 '목적어가 ~한[하지 않은] 채로'의 뜻이다.
- 목적어와 목적격 보어[-ing/p.p.]의 관계가 능동이면 현재분사[-ing], 수동이면 과거분사[p.p.]를 사용한다.

  예 With sunshine *streaming* through the window Hugh found it impossible to sleep. → 능동

  (햇빛이 창을 통해서 계속 비치고 있어서, Hugh는 자는 게 불가능하다는 걸 알았다.)

  예 Amy was listening to music with her eyes *closed*. → 수동

  (Amy는 눈을 감고서 음악을 감상하고 있었다.)

- with+신체의 일부+-ing/p.p. 주요 표현
  - with one's eyes closed: 눈을 감은 채로
  - with one's legs crossed: 다리를 꼰 채로
  - with one's heart beating: 심장이 두근대면서
  - with one's eyes blinking: 두 눈을 깜박이면서
  - with one's arms folded: 팔짱을 낀 채로
  - with tears rolling down one's face: 눈물을 흘리며

08 난도 ★★☆   정답 ②

어법 > 영작하기

정답의 이유

② 복합관계대명사는 명사절이나 부사절을 이끌며 동시에 절 내에서 주어, 목적어, 보어의 역할을 한다. whomever(anyone whom)는 목적격으로 쓰이는데, 주어 자리에 있으므로 주격 복합관계대명사 whoever로 고쳐야 한다. 참고로, whoever가 이끄는 명사절이 전치사 to의 목적어이다.

오답의 이유

① 보증이 만료된 시점이 더 이전의 일이므로 과거완료(had p.p.)를 사용한 것은 적절하며, '무료로'라는 표현인 free of charge 역시 올바르게 쓰였다. 또한 expire는 자동사이므로 능동태(had expired)로 올바르게 사용되었다.

③ if절과 주절의 시제가 다르므로 혼합가정법임을 알 수 있다. if절에는 가정법 과거완료시제(had asked)가, 주절에는 가정법 과거시제(would be)가 모두 올바르게 쓰였다.

④ 과거 부사구인 last year가 있으므로 과거시제(passed)가 올바르게 사용되었으며, '설상가상으로(what was worse)' 역시 과거시제에 맞게 올바르게 사용되었다.

더 알아보기

복합관계대명사

- 복합관계대명사(관계사+ever)는 명사절 또는 부사절(양보) 역할을 한다.

복합관계대명사	명사절	부사절
whoever [whomever/ whosever]	any one who [whom/whose] (~하는 사람이면 누구나)	no matter who (~하는 사람이면 누구든지 간에)
whichever	anything that (~하는 것이면 어느 것이든)	no matter which (~하는 것이면 어느 것이든지 간에)
whatever	anything that (~하는 것이면 무엇이든)	no matter what (~하는 것이면 무엇이든지 간에)

- 예 Whoever made this cake is a real artist. → 명사절
  (누구든 이 케이크를 만든 사람은 진짜 예술가이다.)
- 예 I'll be there whatever happens. → 부사절
  (나는 무슨 일이 있어도 거기 갈 것이다.)
- whoever vs. whomever: 주격(whoever)과 목적격(whomever)을 선택하는 문제가 주로 출제된다.
  - 예 Whoever says that is a liar. → 주격
    (누구든 그 말을 하는 사람은 거짓말쟁이이다.)
  - 예 He was free to marry whomever he chose. → 목적격
    (그는 누구든지 자기가 선택하는 사람과 자유롭게 결혼할 수 있었다.)

독해 > 빈칸 완성 > 연결어

정답의 이유

① (A) 앞부분에서 확신에 찬 행동에 대한 설명이 나오고, (A) 다음에는 이와는 대조적으로 공격적 행동에 대한 설명이 등장하므로 (A)에는 대조의 연결어인 'In contrast(그에 반해서)'가 적절하다. (B) 앞 문장에서 공격적인 행동을 보이는 사람들은 타인의 권리가 자신의 권리보다 중요하지 않다고 여기는 것 같다고 하였고, (B) 다음에서 그들은 원만한 대인관계를 유지하기 힘들다는 결과가 나오므로 (B)에는 인과의 연결어인 'Thus(따라서)'가 적절하다.

오답의 이유

② 마찬가지로 – 게다가
③ 그러나 – 한편으로는
④ 그런 이유로 – 다른 한편으로는

본문해석

확신에 찬 행동은 타인의 권리를 침해하지 않는 직접적이고 적절한 방식으로 여러분의 권리를 옹호하고, 여러분의 생각과 감정을 표현하는 것을 포함한다. 그것은 다른 사람이 여러분의 관점을 이해하도록 하는 것의 문제이다. 확신에 찬 행동 기술을 보이는 사람들은 원만한 대인관계를 유지하면서 갈등 상황을 쉽고 자심감 있게 처리할 수 있다. (A) 그에 반해서, 공격적인 행동은 공공연하게 타인의 권리를 침해하는 방식으로 여러분의 생각과 감정을 표현하고 여러분의 권리를 옹호하는 것을 포함한다. 공격적인 행동을 보이는 사람들은 다른 사람들의 권리가 그들의 권리보다 덜 중요해야만 한다고 믿는 것 같다. (B) 따라서 그들은 원만한 대인관계를 유지하는 데 어려움을 겪는다. 그들은 통제력을 유지하기 위해 말을 중단시키고, 빠르게 말하고, 타인을 무시하며, 비꼬거나 언어폭력의 다른 형태를 사용할 가능성이 있다.

10 난도 ★☆☆　　　　　　　　　　정답 ③

독해 > 대의 파악 > 제목, 주제

정답의 이유

제시문의 핵심 소재는 터치스크린 기술로, 저항식 스크린과 정전식 스크린의 두 가지 작동 방식을 설명하고 있으므로 글의 주제로 적절한 것은 ③ 'how touchscreen technology works(터치스크린 기술이 작동하는 방식)'이다.

오답의 이유

① 사용자들이 새로운 기술을 배우는 방식

② 전자책이 태블릿 컴퓨터에서 작동하는 방식

④ 터치스크린이 진화한 방식

본문해석

태블릿 컴퓨터에서 이용 가능한 전자책 애플리케이션은 터치스크린 기술을 이용한다. 일부 터치스크린은 전자식으로 충전된 마주 놓여 있는 두 개의 금속판을 덮고 있는 유리 패널을 포함한다. 화면을 터치하면 두 금속판은 압력을 감지하고 전류를 연결한다. 이 압력은 컴퓨터에 전기 신호를 보내는데, 이것이 터치를 명령어로 전환한다. 이 버전의 터치스크린은 화면이 손가락의 압력에 반응하기 때문에 저항식 (터치) 스크린으로 알려져 있다. 다른 태블릿 컴퓨터는 유리 패널 아래에 전기가 통하는 한 개의 금속층을 특징으로 한다. 사용자가 화면을 터치하면 전류 일부가 유리를 통과해 사용자의 손가락으로 전해진다. 전하가 이동하면 컴퓨터는 에너지의 손실을 명령어로 해석하고 사용자가 원하는 기능을 수행한다. 이러한 유형의 스크린은 정전식 (터치) 스크린이라고 알려져 있다.

VOCA

• employ (기술·방법을) 이용하다[쓰다]

• feature 특별히 포함하다, 특징으로 삼다

• face-to-face 마주 보는

• make contact (전류를) 연결하다

• command 명령, 명령어, 명령하다

• resistive 저항성의, 저항력이 있는

• react to ~에 반응하다

• electrify 전기를 통하게 하다

• current 전류

• charge 전하(電荷)

• interpret (특정한 뜻으로) 해석[이해]하다

• capacitive 전기 용량의

11 난도 ★☆☆　　　　　　　　　　정답 ②

표현 > 일반회화

정답의 이유

빈칸 앞에서 B가 정크 메일을 완전히 막을 수는 없다고 했고, 빈칸 다음에서 B가 'you can set up a filter on the settings.'라고 했으므로 대화의 흐름상 빈칸에 적절한 것은 대처 방안을 묻는 ② 'Isn't there anything we can do(우리가 할 수 있는 게 없을까)'이다.

오답의 이유

① 이메일 자주 쓰니

③ 이 훌륭한 차단 프로그램을 어떻게 만들었니

④ 이메일 계정 만드는 것 좀 도와줄래

본문해석

A: 저런, 또 왔어! 정크 메일이 너무 많이 왜!

B: 맞아. 난 하루에도 열 통 이상씩 받아.

A: 정크 메일이 들어오는 걸 막을 수 있을까?

B: 완전히 차단하기는 힘들 것 같아.

A: 우리가 할 수 있는 게 없을까?

B: 글쎄. 설정에서 차단 프로그램을 설치할 수 있어.

A: 차단 프로그램?

B: 그래. 차단 프로그램이 스팸 메일 일부를 거를 수 있거든.

VOCA

• block 막다, 차단하다

• weed out 거르다, 추려내다

12 난도 ★☆☆　　　　　　　　　　정답 ①

어법 > 영작하기

정답의 이유

① regret은 목적어로 to부정사와 동명사를 모두 취할 수 있지만, 그 의미가 다르다. 'regret+to부정사'는 '(미래에) ~하게 되어 유감이다'이며, 'regret+동명사'는 '(과거의 일을) 후회하다'이다. 주어진 우리말에서는 '(과거에) 네 열쇠를 잃어버렸다고 말한 것'을 후회한다고 했으므로 to tell → telling이 되어야 한다.

오답의 이유

② 소유대명사(hers)가 올바르게 쓰였는지 묻는 문제로 비교 대상이 his experience이므로 her experience를 의미하는 소유대명사 hers가 올바르게 사용되었다.

③ 통보·고지·환기류의 동사에는 advise(조언하다), inform(알리다), remind(상기시키다), convince(확신시키다) 등이 있는데 이러한 '알리다'의 의미를 가지는 동사들은 '~에게'에 해당하는 사람이나 대상이 목적어로 나온 후에 전하는 내용은 주로 'of 전치사구' 또는 that절 형태로 온다. remind도 이러한 유형의 동사이므로 목적어인 me 다음에 전하는 내용이 'of 전치사구'로 올바르게 표현되었다.

④ look A in the eye는 'A의 눈을 똑바로 쳐다보다'의 뜻이므로 look me in the eye가 올바르게 사용되었다. 또한 선행사 people이 사람이고 관계절에서 주어 역할을 하므로 주격 관계대명사 who가 올바르게 사용되었다.

13 난도 ★☆☆

정답 ②

표현 > 일반회화

정답의 이유

A가 어디로 가는지 묻고, B가 식료품점으로 향한다고 대답했으므로 대화 중 가장 자연스러운 것은 ②이다.

본문해석

① A: 지금 몇 시인지 아니?

　　B: 미안, 내가 요즘 바빠.

② A: 이봐, 어디로 가는 길이야?

　　B: 우리는 식료품점으로 가.

③ A: 이것 좀 도와줄래?

　　B: 그래. 너를 위해 박수 칠게.

④ A: 내 지갑 본 사람 있니?

　　B: 오랜만이야.

VOCA

- head　(특정 방향으로) 가다[향하다]
- be off to　~로 떠나다

14 난도 ★☆☆

정답 ④

독해 > 대의 파악 > 제목, 주제

정답의 이유

제시문은 오두막 한 채만 있었으나 50년에 걸친 공사 끝에 화려한 방들로 가득한 거대한 궁전으로 변모했다는 내용이다. 따라서 글의 제목으로 가장 적절한 것은 오두막에서 궁전으로 변하는 과정을 표현한 ④ 'Versailles: From a Humble Lodge to a Great Palace(베르사유: 초라한 오두막에서 거대한 궁전으로)'이다.

오답의 이유

① 그리스 신들의 진짜 얼굴

② 거울의 방 vs. 아폴로의 방

③ 운하가 베르사유에 단지 물 이상의 것을 가져왔는가?

본문해석

루이 14세는 자신의 위대함에 걸맞은 궁전이 필요해서 베르사유에 거대한 새 집을 짓기로 결정했는데, 그곳에는 아주 작은 사냥꾼 오두막 한 채가 있었다. 거의 50년에 걸친 노동 후에 이 작은 사냥꾼 오두막은 4분의 1마일 길이의 웅장한 궁전으로 탈바꿈했다. 강에서 물을 끌어오고 습지대에서 물을 빼내기 위해 운하가 파내졌다. 베르사유는 거울의 방과 아폴로의 방처럼 공들여 장식한 방들로 가득했다. 유명한 '거울의 방'에는 17개의 거대한 거울이 17개의 커다란 창문 맞은편에 배열되어 있으며, '아폴로의 방'에는 순은으로 만들어진 왕좌가 놓여 있었다. 아폴로, 주피터, 넵튠 같은 그리스 신들의 조각상 수백여 점이 정원에 있었는데, 각각의 신은 루이의 얼굴을 하고 있었다!

VOCA

- lodge　오두막
- transform into　~로 변형시키다
- canal　운하, 수로
- drain　배수관, 물을 빼내다
- marshland　습지대
- elaborate　정성을 들인, 정교한
- solid　순-, 순수한(다른 물질이 섞이지 않은)
- throne　왕좌, 왕위
- statue　조각상
- humble　변변찮은, 작은; 겸손한

15 난도 ★★☆

정답 ③

독해 > 글의 일관성 > 무관한 어휘 · 문장

정답의 이유

첫 번째 문장에서 철학자들은 인류학에 별다른 관심을 가지지 않았다고 언급하며, 이를 뒷받침하는 근거들을 제시하여 자신의 주장을 전개시키고 있다. 하지만 ③은 철학자들이 인류학이나 심리학 같은 다른 분야에서 영감을 얻는다는 내용이므로 글의 흐름과 맞지 않는다.

본문해석

철학자들은 인류학자들이 철학에 관심을 가진 것만큼 인류학에 관심을 가진 적이 없다. 그들의 연구에서 인류학 연구들을 고려하는 영향력 있는 현대 철학자들은 거의 없다. 사회과학의 철학을 전공한 사람들은 인류학 연구의 사례를 고려하거나 분석할 수도 있지만, 대부분 개념적 요점이나 인식론적 차이를 설명하거나 인식론적 또는 윤리적 함의를 비판하기 위해 이것을 한다. 실제로, 우리 시대의 위대한 철학자들은 종종 인류학이나 심리학 같은 다른 분야에서 영감을 얻었다. 철학을 공부하는 학생들은 좀처럼 인류학을 공부하거나 진지한 관심을 거의 보이지 않는다. 그들은 과학에서 실험 방법에 대해 배울지도 모르지만, 인류학적 현장 연구에 대해서는 거의 배우지 않는다.

VOCA

- anthropology　인류학
- influential　영향력 있는, 영향력이 큰
- contemporary　현대의, 당대의; 동시대의
- take into account　~을 고려하다
- specialize in　~을 전문으로 하다
- illustrate　설명하다, 예증하다
- conceptual　개념의
- epistemological　인식론의
- distinction　차이, 대조
- ethical　윤리적인, 도덕적으로 옳은
- implication　함축, 함의
- fieldwork　현장 연구

16 난도 ★★☆　　　　　　　　　　　　　정답 ③

독해 > 빈칸 완성 > 단어 · 구 · 절

정답의 이유

첫 번째 문장에서 우리는 '유형의 유산(돈, 재산, 가보 등)'을 물려받는다고 했다. 두 번째 다음 문장에서 하지만 우리는 '무형의 유산'도 물려받는데, 그것은 '심지어 우리가 완전히 인식하지 못하는 어떤 것(something we may not even be fully aware of)'이라고 했고, 다음 문장에서 일상생활 방식, 문제 해결 방식, 전통을 지키는 방식 등의 추상적인 것들을 예로 들었다. 따라서 빈칸에 들어갈 말로 적절한 것은 ③ 'much less concrete and tangible(훨씬 덜 구체적이고 덜 유형적인)'이다.

오답의 이유

① 우리 일상생활과는 아주 관련 없는
② 우리의 도덕적 기준에 반하는
④ 엄청난 금전적 가치를 가진

본문해석

우리는 모두 무언가를 물려받는다. 어떤 경우, 그것은 돈이나 재산이 될 수도 있고, 할머니의 웨딩드레스나 아버지의 공구세트 같이 집안의 가보인 어떤 물건일 수도 있다. 하지만 그것 이상으로 우리는 모두 다른 어떤 것, 즉 훨씬 덜 구체적이고 덜 유형적인 어떤 것, 심지어 우리가 완전히 인식할 수 없는 것도 물려받는다. 그것은 일상 업무를 하는 방식일 수도 있고, 특정 문제를 해결하거나 도덕적 문제를 스스로 결정하는 방식일 수도 있다. 그것은 휴일을 지키는 특별한 방식일 수도 있고 특정한 날에 소풍을 가는 전통일 수도 있다. 그것은 우리 사고에 중요하거나 중심이 되는 것이거나, 또는 우리가 오랫동안 아주 무심코 받아들여 온 사소한 것일 수도 있다.

VOCA

• inherit 상속받다, 물려받다
• property 재산, 소유물; 부동산
• heirloom (집안의) 가보
• casually 무심코, 문득, 우연히, 아무 생각 없이
• unrelated 관련[관계] 없는
• tangible 유형의, 분명히 실제하는, 만질 수 있는
• of value 가치 있는
• monetary 금전상의

17 난도 ★★☆　　　　　　　　　　　　　정답 ①

독해 > 대의 파악 > 요지, 주장

정답의 이유

제시문의 도입부에서 진화론적 입장에 따라 소비하는 양에 비해 기여하는 게 없어 보이는 노인들에게 자원이 적게 분배되는 것이 합리적이라는 내용이 전개되지만, 세 번째 문장의 But 이하에서 노인들의 정신적 지주로서의 역할을 설명하기 위해 어조가 전환된다. 네 번째 문장에서 '노인들이 물질적으로 소비한 것을 행동으로 돌려주기 때문'이라고 했으므로 글의 요지로 적절한 것은 ① 'Seniors have been making contributions to the family(노인들은 가족에 기여해 왔다).'이다.

오답의 이유

② 현대 의학은 노인들의 역할에 초점을 맞추고 있다.
③ 가족 내에서 자원을 잘 분배하는 것이 가족의 번영을 결정한다.
④ 대가족은 제한된 자원이라는 대가를 치른다.

본문해석

진화론적으로, 생존을 희망하는 종이라면 그것의 자원을 신중하게 관리해야 한다. 그것은 식량과 먹기 좋은 것들은 분명히 우선적으로 양육자들과 전사들, 사냥꾼들, 농부들, 건설자들 그리고 아이들에게 돌아가고, 노인들에게는 그다지 남아있는 게 없다는 것을 뜻하는데, 노인들은 기여하는 것보다는 소비하는 게 더 많아 보일지도 모른다. 그러나 현대 의학이 기대 수명을 연장하기 전에도 보통의 가정에는 조부모와 심지어 증조부모까지 있었다. 그것은 노인들이 물질적으로 소비한 것을 행동으로 돌려주는데, 그들이 종종 가족 주변에 휘몰아치는 소동에서 균형 잡히고 합리적인 중심을 제공하기 때문이다.

VOCA

• evolutionarily 진화론적으로, 진화로
• call ~에 대한 요구
• goody 먹기 좋은 것, 매력적인 것
• breeder 사육자
• life expectancy 기대 수명, 평균 수명
• leveling 평등화, 균일화
• tumult 소란, 소동
• swirl 소용돌이치다, 빙빙 돌다
• allocate 할당하다
• prosperity 번영, 번성
• extended family 대가족
• come at a cost 대가가 따르다

독해 > 글의 일관성 > 글의 순서

정답의 이유

주어진 글은 '오늘날(Nowadays)' 시계에 대한 일반론적인 관점을 서술하는 문장으로 시작하며 두 번째 문장에서 '산업화 시대 이전 (Before industrialization)'에는 시간을 알기 위해 해나 달을 이용했다고 했으므로, 주어진 글 다음에는 기계식 시계의 첫 등장을 서술한 (B)가 적절하다. (C)의 These clocks는 (B)의 mechanical clocks와 연결되고, (C)에서 표준시가 없었기 때문에 발생하는 문제점에 대해 소개한 것은 몇 마일 떨어진 철도역의 사례를 들어 좀 더 구체적인 예시를 들어 설명한 (A)로 이어지므로 글의 순서는 ③ '(B) − (C) − (A)'가 적절하다.

본문해석

오늘날 시계는 우리의 삶을 너무 많이 지배해서 시계가 없는 삶은 상상하기가 어렵다. 산업화 이전에 대부분의 사회는 시간을 보기 위해 해나 달을 이용했다.

(B) 기계식 시계가 처음 등장했을 때, 그것들은 즉시 인기가 있었다. 시계나 손목시계를 갖는 것이 유행이었다. 사람들은 시간을 보는 이 새로운 방식을 나타내기 위해 'of the clock', 즉 'o'clock' 이라는 표현을 만들어냈다.

(C) 이러한 시계들은 장식용이었지만 항상 유용한 것은 아니었다. 마을과 지방, 심지어 이웃 동네마다 시간을 표시하는 방식이 달랐기 때문이었다. 여행자들은 한 장소에서 다른 곳으로 이동할 때마다 반복해서 시계를 다시 맞춰야 했다. 1860년대에 미국에는 약 70개의 서로 다른 표준시간대가 있었다.

(A) 철도망이 증가하면서 표준시가 없다는 사실은 재앙과 같았다. 종종, 몇 마일 떨어져 있는 역들이 그들의 시계를 서로 다른 시간대에 맞췄다. 여행객들에게는 어마어마한 혼란이 있었다.

VOCA

• dominate 지배하다

• industrialization 산업화

• tell the time 시계를 보다[볼 줄 알다]

• decorative 장식이 된, 장식용의

• time zone 표준시간대

독해 > 글의 일관성 > 문장 삽입

정답의 이유

주어진 문장이 역접의 접속사 But으로 시작하므로 앞 문장에는 이와 반대되는 내용이 와야 한다는 것을 알 수 있다. 주어진 문장은 밀레니얼 세대는 X세대가 같은 나이대에 했던 것보다 저축을 더 공격적으로 하고 있다는 내용으로, 주어진 문장 앞에는 밀레니얼 세대가 X세대보다 경제적으로 궁핍하다는 내용이 오게 될 것임을 추론할 수 있으므로 주어진 문장이 들어갈 위치는 ④가 적절하다. ④ 다음 문장의 them은 주어진 문장의 millennials를 받으며, 공격적으로 저축함으로써 재정 형편이 더 나아진다는 내용으로 자연스럽게 연결된다.

본문해석

밀레니얼 세대는 현대에 들어서 가장 가난하고 가장 재정적으로 부담을 지고 있는 세대라는 꼬리표가 종종 붙는다. 그들 중 대다수가 대학을 졸업해서 그것도 학자금 대출이라는 엄청난 빚을 진 채로 미국이 여태까지 본 최악의 노동시장 중 하나로 진입했다. 놀랄 것도 없이 밀레니얼 세대는 X세대가 비슷한 나이대에 했던 것보다 부를 덜 축적했는데, 그 이유는 그들 중 극소수만이 집을 소유하고 있기 때문이다. 그러나 서로 다른 세대의 미국인들이 저축한 것에 대해 현재까지 가장 상세한 설명을 제공하는 새롭게 이용 가능한 자료가 그러한 평가를 복잡하게 만든다. 그렇다, 1965년에서 1980년 사이에 태어난 X세대는 순자산이 더 많다. 그러나 1981년에서 1996년 사이에 태어난 밀레니얼 세대는 X세대가 같은 연령대인 22~37세에 했던 것보다 은퇴를 위해 더 공격적으로 저축하고 있다는 명백한 근거도 있다. 그리고 그것이 많은 사람들이 예측하는 것보다 그들을 더 나은 재정 상태에 놓이게 할지도 모른다.

VOCA

• millennials 밀레니얼 세대(1981~1996년 사이에 태어난 세대로 IT에 능통하고 대학교육을 받은 사람이 많지만 경기 불황으로 취직에 어려움을 겪어 평균 소득이 다른 세대보다 낮음)

• aggressively 공격적으로

• label 꼬리표를 붙이다

• staggering 충격적인, 엄청난

• to boot 그것도(앞서 한 말에 대해 다른 말을 덧붙일 때)

• accumulate 모으다, 축적하다

• to date 지금까지, 오늘에 이르기까지

• net worth 순자산

• assume 추정하다

독해 > 세부 내용 찾기 > 내용 (불)일치

[정답의 이유]

여섯 번째 문장에서 해양 산성화는 산호의 성장보다 산호초 모래의 용해에 더 영향을 줄 것이라고 했으므로 글의 내용과 일치하지 않는 것은 ④ 'Ocean acidification affects the growth of corals more than the dissolution of coral reef sands(해양 산성화는 산호초 모래의 용해보다 산호의 성장에 더 영향을 끼친다).'이다.

[오답의 이유]

① 산호초의 뼈대는 탄산염 모래로 만들어진다. → 첫 번째 문장에서 'Carbonate sands, ~ are the building material for the frameworks of coral reefs.'라고 했으므로 글의 내용과 일치한다.

② 산호는 부분적으로 해양 산성화에 적응할 수 있다. → 마지막 문장에서 'This probably reflects the corals' ability to modify their environment and partially adjust to ocean acidification, ~'라고 했으므로 글의 내용과 일치한다.

③ 인간이 배출한 이산화탄소는 전 세계 해양 산성화에 기여했다. → 세 번째 문장과 네 번째 문장에서 설명하고 있으므로 글의 내용과 일치한다.

본문해석

탄산염 모래는 산호와 다른 암초 유기체들의 분해로부터 수천 년에 걸쳐 축적되었으며, 산호초 뼈대를 만드는 재료이다. 하지만 이 모래는 바닷물의 화학적 구성 요소에 민감하다. 해양이 이산화탄소를 흡수하면서 특정 시점에 산성화되자, 탄산염 모래는 그저 용해되기 시작한다. 전 세계 해양은 인간이 배출한 이산화탄소의 약 3분의 1을 흡수해 왔다. 모래가 용해되는 속도는 상층 해수의 산성도와 크게 관련이 있었고, 해양 산성화에 산호의 성장보다 열 배나 더 민감했다. 다시 말해서, 해양 산성화는 산호의 성장보다 산호초 모래의 용해에 더욱 영향을 줄 것이다. 이것은 아마도 자신의 환경을 바꾸고 해양 산성화에 부분적으로 적응하는 산호초의 능력을 반영하는 반면, 모래의 용해는 적응할 수 없는 지구 화학적 과정이다.

VOCA

• carbonate sand 탄산염 모래
• breakdown 분해
• organism 유기체
• make-up 구성 (요소)
• acidify 산성화되다
• dissolve 용해되다
• overlie ~위에 가로놓이다
• modify (더 알맞도록) 변경하다, 바꾸다
• adjust 적응하다, 조정[조절]하다
• geochemical 지구 화학적
• adapt (새로운 용도·상황에) 맞추다[조정하다]

한눈에 훑어보기

✔ 영역 분석

어휘   01   02   11   12
4문항, 20%

독해   07   08   09   10   13   14   15   17   18   19   20
11문항, 55%

어법   05   06   16
3문항, 15%

표현   03   04
2문항, 10%

✔ 빠른 정답

01	02	03	04	05	06	07	08	09	10
①	①	④	③	④	②	②	②	②	④
11	12	13	14	15	16	17	18	19	20
④	①	③	④	④	③	①	③	①	②

✔ 점수 체크

구분	1회독	2회독	3회독
맞힌 문항 수	/ 20	/ 20	/ 20
나의 점수	점	점	점

---

01 난도 ★★☆   정답 ①

어휘 > 단어

정답의 이유

밑줄 친 excavated는 '발굴되어진'의 뜻으로 이와 의미가 가장 가까운 것은 ① 'exhumed(발굴되어진)'이다.

오답의 이유

② 포장된

③ 지워진

④ 기념된

본문해석

나는 이 문서들을 이제는 죽어서 묻혀 있는 감성의 유물로서 보게 되었는데, 그것들은 발굴되어야 했다.

VOCA

• relic   유물, 유적

• sensibility   감성[감수성]

• excavate   발굴하다; 출토하다

02 난도 ★★☆   정답 ①

어휘 > 단어

정답의 이유

밑줄 친 sheer는 '순전한, 순수한'의 뜻으로 이와 의미가 가장 가까운 것은 ① 'utter(완전한)'이다.

오답의 이유

② 무서운, 겁나는

③ 가끔의

④ 관리[처리]할 수 있는

본문해석

롤러코스터를 타는 것은 감정의 폭주일 수 있다. 여러분이 좌석 안전벨트에 매어질 때의 긴장된 기대감. 위로 계속 올라갈 때 오는 의구심과 후회 그리고 (롤러코스터의) 차량이 첫 번째로 급강하할 때 완전한 아드레날린의 분출이다.

VOCA

• joy ride   폭주, 난폭 운전

• anticipation   예상, 예측, 기대

• strap   끈[줄/띠]으로 묶다

03 난도 ★☆☆
정답 ④

표현 > 일반회화

정답의 이유

'전화를 못 받아서 미안하다'는 A의 말에 '메시지를 남기시겠습니까?'라는 B의 대답은 적절하지 않으므로 두 사람의 대화 중 가장 어색한 것은 ④이다.

본문해석

① A: 우리 몇 시에 점심 먹을 건가요?

　 B: 정오 전에 준비될 거예요.

② A: 당신에게 여러 번 전화했어요. 왜 받지 않았어요?

　 B: 이런, 제 휴대전화의 전원이 꺼졌던 것 같아요.

③ A: 이번 겨울에 휴가를 가시나요?

　 B: 갈지도 몰라요. 아직은 결정 못 했어요.

④ A: 여보세요. 전화 못 받아서 죄송합니다.

　 B: 메시지를 남기겠습니까?

04 난도 ★☆☆
정답 ③

표현 > 일반회화

정답의 이유

빈칸에 들어갈 A의 질문에 B가 다시 환전할 때는 비용이 없으며 영수증만 가져오라고 설명하므로 밑줄 친 부분에 들어갈 말로 가장 적절한 것은 통화를 되파는 것과 관련된 ③ 'What's your buy-back policy(환매 정책은 어떻게 되죠)'이다.

오답의 이유

① 이거 얼마예요

② 어떻게 지불하면 되나요

④ 신용카드로 되나요

본문해석

A: 안녕하세요. 돈을 조금 환전해야 해요.

B: 예, 어떤 통화가 필요하신가요?

A: 달러를 파운드로 바꿔야 합니다. 환율이 어떻게 되나요?

B: 1달러당 0.73파운드입니다.

A: 좋아요. 수수료를 떼시나요?

B: 예. 4달러의 소액의 수수료를 받습니다.

A: 환매 정책은 어떻게 되죠?

B: 저희는 무료로 매입합니다. 영수증만 챙겨 오시면 됩니다.

VOCA

• currency 통화(각국의 나라에서 사용하는 돈)

• convert A into B A를 B로 바꾸다

• exchange rate 외환 시세; 환율

• commission 수수료

• buy-back 환매(외국 통화를 다시 자국 통화로 바꿔주는 것)

05 난도 ★★☆
정답 ④

어법 > 비문 찾기

정답의 이유

④ injure는 타동사로 '부상을 입다'의 뜻인데, 다음에 목적어가 없고 주어(Millions of pedestrians)가 '부상을 당하는' 수동의 의미이므로 injuring → injured가 되어야 한다.

오답의 이유

① 주어가 27만 명 이상의 보행자들이므로 복수동사 lose가 올바르게 쓰였다.

② 'never to부정사'는 '결국 ~하지 않게 되다'의 뜻으로, 결과를 나타내는 to부정사의 부사적 용법이므로 to return이 올바르게 사용되었다.

③ 원급 비교구문인 'as+원급+as' 사이에는 형용사나 부사가 들어가므로 형용사 high가 올바르게 사용되었다. 또한 be동사의 보어 자리이므로 형용사가 와야 한다.

본문해석

매년, 27만 명 이상의 보행자들이 세계의 도로 위에서 목숨을 잃는다. 많은 사람들은 여느 때처럼 집을 나서고 결국 다시 돌아오지 못한다. 전 세계적으로 보행자는 전체 도로 교통 사망자의 22%를 차지하고, 일부 국가에서는 이 비율이 전체 도로 교통 사망자의 3분의 2를 차지할 만큼 높다. 수백만 명의 보행자들이 치명적이지 않은 상해를 입으며, 일부는 영구적인 장애를 갖게 된다. 이러한 사고들은 경제적 어려움뿐만 아니라 많은 고통과 비통함을 야기한다.

VOCA

• pedestrian 보행자

• constitute ~이 되다, ~을 구성하다[이루다]

• fatality 사망자, 치사율

• proportion 비율, 부분

더 알아보기

to부정사의 부사적 용법(결과)

• 부사적 용법: to부정사가 목적, 이유, 결과, 감정의 원인, 정도 등을 나타내는 부사 역할을 한다.

• 결과의 의미로 사용하는 'only[never] to부정사'에 유의한다.

예 They had tasted freedom *only to lose* it again.

　 (그들은 자유를 맛보았으나, 결국 다시 잃게 되었다.)

예 He left *never to return*.

　 (그는 떠나간 후 다시는 돌아오지 않았다.)

• 부사적 용법의 종류

목적 (~하기 위해서)	예 He came to Seoul to look for work. (그는 일자리를 찾기 위해 서울에 왔다.)
결과 (결국 ~하게 되다)	예 Time is flying never to return. (시간은 쏜살처럼 흘러서 다시는 돌아오지 않는다.)

감정의 원인 (~해서, ~하니)	예 He was deeply saddened to hear of his son's death. (그는 아들의 사망 소식을 듣고 몹시 슬퍼했다.)
정도 (…하기에는 너무 ~하다/ …할 만큼 충분히 ~하다)	예 Harlem is too *dangerous* to travel alone after sunset. (할렘은 해가 진 후에 혼자 여행하기에는 너무 위험하다.) 예 It's *warm* enough to eat outside. (밖에서 식사해도 될 정도로 날이 따뜻하다.)
판단의 근거 (~하다니)	예 She must be very upset to speak like that. (그녀가 그렇게 말하다니 매우 화가 났음에 틀림없다.)

06 난도 ★★☆   정답 ②

어법 > 정문 찾기

정답의 이유

② 부사절 접속사 'lest+(should)+동사원형'은 '~하지 않도록'이라는 부정의 뜻이며 should는 생략할 수 있으므로 동사원형인 be가 올바르게 사용되었다.

오답의 이유

① charge A with B는 'A를 B라는 이유로 고소하다, 비난하다'의 의미로 전치사 with의 목적어로 동명사가 와야 하므로 use → using이 되어야 한다.

③ make는 타동사로 목적어(the shift)가 있으므로 능동태가 되어야 하며, '~하는 것이다'의 뜻이 되려면 be동사의 보어가 될 수 있는 to부정사 또는 동명사가 와야 하므로 made → to make[making]이 되어야 한다.

④ 수량을 나타내는 'one of the' 뒤에는 복수명사가 와야 하므로 cause → causes가 되어야 하고, lead는 cause of climate change를 수식하는 형용사가 되어야 하므로 lead → leading이 되어야 한다.

본문해석

① 그 신문은 그녀가 회삿돈을 그녀 자신의 목적을 위해 사용했다고 고소했다.

② 수사는 의혹이 발생하지 않도록 극도로 조심스럽게 다뤄져야만 했다.

③ 이 과정을 가속화하는 또 다른 방법은 새로운 시스템으로 전환하는 것이다.

④ 화석연료를 태우는 것은 기후 변화의 주된 원인 중 하나이다.

VOCA

• suspicion 혐의[의혹]

• speed up 속도를 더 내다[높이다]

• fossil fuels 화석연료

07 난도 ★★★   정답 ②

독해 > 글의 일관성 > 글의 순서

정답의 이유

주어진 글에서 '사회적 세계를 이해하는 방법(how can we ever make sense of the social world?)'을 묻는 질문을 (A)에서 'in order to make sense of it'으로 받아 설명하고 있으므로 주어진 글 다음에 (A)가 이어지는 것이 적절하다. 그런 다음 (A)에서 언급된 stripped down에 대해 when I say "stripped down"이라고 구체적으로 설명하는 (C)가 뒤따라야 하며, 결론을 내는 연결사 thus를 통해 경제학자의 말을 인용하여 이런 현상에 대해 마무리 짓는 (B)가 이어지는 것이 적절하다. 따라서 주어진 글 다음에 이어질 글의 순서로 가장 적절한 것은 ② '(A) – (C) – (B)'이다.

본문해석

우리의 뇌를 떠나지 않고 괴롭히는 생각이 하나 있다. 모든 것이 아마도 다른 모든 것에 영향을 주기 때문에, 우리가 어떻게 사회적 세계를 이해할 수 있을까 하는 것이다. 하지만, 만약 우리가 그런 걱정에 짓눌린다면, 우리는 결코 전진할 수 없을 것이다.

(A) 내가 익숙한 모든 분야들은 그것을 이해하기 위해서 세상의 캐리커처를 그린다. 현대 경제학자들은 '모형'을 구축함으로써 이것을 하는데, 이 모형들은 바깥 현상에 대한 설명들이 모두 의도적으로 제거되어 있다.

(C) 내가 '제거된'이라고 말할 때, 나는 실제로 불필요한 것을 모두 뺀 것을 의미한다. 우리 경제학자들 사이에서는 현실의 단지 이런 양상들이 어떻게 작동하고 상호작용하는지 이해할 수 있게 되기를 바라면서 한두 개의 인과적 요소에만 초점을 맞추고, 그 밖의 모든 것들을 배제하는 것은 드문 일이 아니다.

(B) 따라서 경제학자 John Maynard Keynes는 우리의 주제를 다음과 같이 묘사했다. "경제학은 현대 세계와 관련된 모형을 선택하는 기술과 결합된 모형의 관점에서 사고의 과학이다."

VOCA

• haunt 계속 문제가 되다[괴롭히다], 뇌리에서 떠나지 않다

• make sense 이해가 되다

• be weighed down 짓눌리다

• make progress 나아가다, 진전하다

• deliberately 의도적으로

• stripped down 불필요한 것을 모두 뺀, 가장 기본적인[꼭 필요한] 것만 남긴

• phenomena 현상들 (phenomenon의 복수)

• in terms of ~의 면에서는

• relevant to ~에 관련된

• exclude 제외[배제]하다

08 난도 ★★☆   정답 ②

독해 > 세부 내용 찾기 > 내용 (불)일치

정답의 이유

두 번째 문장에서 이상 행동들은 고통받는 사람들의 신체에 살거나 통제하는 악령에 기인한다고 여겨졌다고 했으므로 글의 내용과 일치하는 것은 ② 'Abnormal behaviors were believed to result from evil spirits affecting a person(이상 행동들은 악령이 사람에게 영향을 미친 결과라고 믿어졌다).'이다.

오답의 이유

① 정신장애는 신체장애와 분명하게 구별되었다. → 첫 문장을 통해 정신장애와 신체장애가 구별되지 않았음을 알 수 있다.

③ 악령이 사람의 신체로 들어가기 위해서 두개골 안에 구멍이 만들어졌다. → 다섯 번째 문장을 통해 악령이 들어가는 것이 아니라 나올 수 있도록 두개골 천공 수술을 했다는 것을 알 수 있다.

④ 동굴 거주자들은 두개골 천공 수술에서 살아남지 못했다. → 마지막 문장을 통해 상처가 아문 채로 발견된 생존자가 있었음을 알 수 있다.

본문해석

약 50만 년 전 선사시대의 사회는 정신장애와 신체장애를 뚜렷하게 구별하지 않았다. 단순한 두통부터 경련의 공격까지, 이상행동들은 고통받는 사람들의 신체에 살거나 통제하는 악령에 기인한다고 여겨졌다. 역사학자들에 따르면, 이와 같은 고대 사람들은 많은 병의 형태를 악령의 빙의, 주술 또는 기분 상한 선대 영혼의 명령 탓으로 여겼다. '귀신학'이라 불리는 이런 신념 체계 내에서, 대개 희생자는 적어도 부분적으로 불행에 대한 책임이 있었다. 석기시대 동굴 거주자들은 악령이 빠져나갈 수 있는 구멍을 제공하기 위해 두개골의 일부를 잘라내는 '두개골 천공'이라고 불리는 외과적 수술 방법으로 행동장애를 치료했을지도 모른다고 제기되었다. 사람들은 악령이 떠나면 그 사람이 자신의 정상 상태로 돌아올 것이라고 믿었을지도 모른다. 놀랍게도, 두개골 천공 수술을 받은 두개골들은 상처가 아문 상태로 발견되었는데, 이는 일부 환자들이 이와 같은 극도로 조잡한 수술에서 살아남았다는 사실을 시사한다.

VOCA

- prehistoric 선사시대의
- sharply 뚜렷하게, 선명하게
- disorder 장애
- abnormal 비정상적인
- be attributed to ~을 탓으로 하다, ~의 책임으로 하다
- inhabit 살다
- afflicted 괴로워하는, 고민하는
- demonic possession 악령 빙의
- sorcery 마법, 마술
- offend 기분 상하게 하다
- demonology 귀신학
- be held responsible for ~에 책임이 있다
- chip away 잘라내다, 벗겨지다

09 난도 ★★☆   정답 ②

독해 > 대의 파악 > 제목, 주제

정답의 이유

제시문은 기자 생활을 오래 한 화자가 언론계에서 기술적 발전이 가져온 변화에 관해 자신의 경험을 서술하고 있다. 하루에 한 번 마감이 있어 하루 동안 기사를 준비할 수 있었던 과거와는 달리, 기술의 발전으로 인해 현재는 실시간으로 소식을 전한다는 것, 각본 없이 일하고 있다는 것 등을 강조하고 있으므로 글의 주제로 가장 적절한 것은 ② 'a reporter and improvisation(기자와 즉흥성)'이다.

오답의 이유

① 교사로서의 기자

③ 정치학에서의 기술

④ 언론과 기술의 분야들

본문해석

디지털 혁명이 전국의 뉴스룸을 뒤집어놓고 있기 때문에, 여기 모든 기자들을 위한 나의 조언이 있다. 나는 25년이 넘는 동안 기자로 지내왔으며 여섯 번의 기술적 수명 주기를 경험했다. 가장 극적인 변화는 마지막 6년에 왔다. 그것은 내가 점점 더 빈번하게 일을 진행하면서 이야기를 만들어내고 있다는 것을 의미한다. 뉴스 업계에서 많은 시간 동안, 우리는 우리가 무엇을 하는지 모른다. 아침에 출근하면 누군가 말하기를, "세금 정책, 이민, 기후 변화에 대한 기사를 써줄 수 있나요?"라고 한다. 신문이 하루에 한 번 마감하던 시절, 우리는 말하기를, '기자는 아침에 배워서 밤에 가르치는 거야. 24시간 전에 기자 자신도 알지 못했던 주제에 대해 내일의 독자에게 알려줄 이야기를 쓰는 거야.'라고 하곤 했다. 지금은 더 나아가서 매 정시에 배운 것을 매 시 30분에 독자에게 가르치는 데 가깝다. 예를 들면, 나 역시 정치 관련 팟캐스트를 운영하고 있으며, 대통령 후보 전당대회 동안 어디에서나 실시간 인터뷰를 진행하기 위해 그 팟캐스트를 사용해야만 한다. 나는 점점 더 대본 없이 일하고 있다.

VOCA

- upend 뒤집다, 반전시키다
- live through ~을 겪다
- with increasing frequency 빈번하게, 비일비재하게
- make up 지어내다, 만들다
- at the top of the hour 매 정시에
- at the bottom of the hour 매 시 30분에
- convention (정당 등의 대규모) 대회
- improvisation 즉석에서 하기

10 난도 ★★☆   정답 ④

독해 > 글의 일관성 > 무관한 어휘 · 문장

정답의 이유

제시문은 아이들의 놀이 공간이 실외인 자연 공간에서 실내로 바뀌어 가고 있음을 설명하고 있는데, ④에서는 여전히 아이들이 밖에서 각종 놀이를 하는 모습을 관찰할 수 있다고 했으므로 ④는 주제와 상반된 내용으로 흐름상 어색하다.

본문해석

역사를 통틀어 아이들의 놀이터는 황무지, 들판, 개울과 시골 언덕, 도로, 거리, 마을과 소도시, 도시의 공터였다. '놀이터'라는 용어는 아이들이 자유롭게 즉흥적인 놀이를 위해서 모이는 이런 모든 장소를 가리킨다. 불과 지난 몇십 년 동안 아이들은 비디오 게임, 문자 메시지, SNS에 대해 늘어나는 열광적인 관심으로 인해 이런 자연의 놀이터를 떠나고 있다. 심지어 미국 시골에서도 어른들 없이 자유롭게 돌아다니는 아이들은 거의 없다. 방과 후에, 그들이 근처에서 모래를 파고, 모래성을 짓고, 전통 게임을 하고, 산을 오르거나 공놀이를 하는 모습이 흔히 발견되었다. 그들은 개울, 언덕, 들판과 같은 자연 공간에서 빠르게 사라져가고 있으며, 도시에 있는 그들의 동년배들과 마찬가지로 앉아서 할 수 있는 실내 사이버 오락거리들로 눈을 돌리고 있다.

VOCA

• vacant 비어 있는
• spontaneous 자발적인, 즉흥적인
• vacate 비우다, 떠나다
• love affair 연애, 열광
• social networking 사회 연결망
• roam 방랑하다, 돌아다니다
• free-ranging 자유로운 범위의
• unaccompanied by ～을 동반하지 않은
• fort 요새, 진지
• terrain 지형, 지역
• creek 작은 만, 개울, 시내
• counterpart 상대, 대응 관계에 있는 것
• sedentary 주로 앉아서 하는, 앉아서 지내는

11 난도 ★★☆   정답 ④

어휘 > 어구

정답의 이유

밑줄 친 engrossed in은 '～에 몰두한'의 뜻으로 이와 의미가 가장 가까운 것은 ④ 'preoccupied with(～에 사로잡힌)'이다.

오답의 이유

① ～에 의해 향상된
② ～에 대해 냉담한
③ ～에 의해 안정된

본문해석

시간은 지루한 오후 수업 시간 동안에는 눈곱만큼 줄어드는 것 같고, 뇌가 매우 재미있는 무언가에 몰두할 때는 경주하는[빠르게 흘러가는] 것 같다.

VOCA

• slow to a trickle 눈곱만큼으로 줄어들다
• race 경주하다
• entertaining 재미있는, 즐거움을 주는

12 난도 ★★☆   정답 ①

어휘 > 어구

정답의 이유

밑줄 친 keep abreast of는 '최근 정황을 잘 챙겨 알아두다'의 뜻으로 이와 의미가 가장 가까운 것은 ① 'be acquainted with(～을 알다)'이다.

오답의 이유

② ～에 의해 영감을 받다
③ ～을 믿고 있다
④ ～을 멀리하다

본문해석

이러한 일일 업데이트는, 시장을 통제하려는 정부의 계속되는 시도에 따라, 독자들이 시장의 최근 정황을 알도록 돕기 위해 고안되었다.

VOCA

• attempt 시도하다
• under control 통제되는

13 난도 ★☆☆
정답 ③

독해 > 빈칸 완성 > 단어 · 구 · 절

③ 세미콜론(;)은 앞 문장에 대해 부연할 때 사용된다. 빈칸 (A) 다음에서 'they simply didn't have enough to eat to stay alive.'라고 했으므로 (A)에 가장 적절한 말은 식량과 관련된 'starvation(기아, 굶주림)'이다. 빈칸 (B) 다음에서 많은 사람들이 고향을 떠나 미국으로 갔다고 했으므로 (B)에 가장 적절한 말은 'emigrate(이주하다)'이다.

① 탈수 − 추방당하다

② 정신적 외상 − 이주해 오다

④ 피곤 − 구금되다

본문해석

1840년대에, 아일랜드는 기근에 시달렸다. 아일랜드가 주민을 먹일 충분한 음식을 생산할 수 없었기 때문에, 약 100만 명의 사람들이 (A) 굶주림으로 사망했다. 즉, 그들은 그야말로 생존하기 위해 먹을 충분한 양을 가지고 있지 않았다. 기근은 다른 125만 명의 사람들이 (B) 이주하는 원인이 되었다. 많은 사람들이 그들의 고향인 섬을 떠나 미국으로 갔고, 나머지는 캐나다, 호주, 칠레 그리고 다른 나라들로 갔다. 기근 전에 아일랜드의 인구는 약 6백만 명이었다. 엄청난 식량 부족 이후에, 인구는 대략 4백만 명이었다.

VOCA

• suffer 시달리다, 고통받다

• famine 기근

• feed 먹이다, 먹이를 주다

• die of ~로 죽다

• approximately 거의

14 난도 ★★☆
정답 ④

독해 > 빈칸 완성 > 연결어

④ 빈칸 (A) 다음의 주절에서 가상 경험이 분리된다고 했으므로 빈칸 (A)가 있는 조건절에서 듣는 것과 시각적인 것이 일치하지 않는 것에 대해 가정하고 있음을 유추할 수 있다. 즉, '소리가 시각적 장면과 일치하지 않으면 가상 경험이 분리된다'라는 의미가 되려면 (A)에는 'Unless(그렇지 않으면)'가 적절하다. 빈칸 (B) 앞 문장에서 농구 경기를 예로 들어서 농구 경기장에 정말 와 있는 듯한 소리가 구현된다면 텔레비전으로 경기를 보아도 '그곳'에 있는 것처럼 느낄 것이라고 했는데, 빈칸 (B) 다음에서 오늘날의 청각적 장비와 녹음, 재생 포맷 등은 현장에 있는 것 같은 설득력 있는 소리를 구현하기에 적절하지 않다고 했으므로, (B)에는 부정적인 의미의 'Unfortunately(불행하게도)'가 적절하다.

① 만약 ~라면 − 대조적으로

② 만약 ~하지 않다면 − 결과적으로

③ 만약 ~라면 − 마찬가지로

본문해석

오늘날 가상현실(VR) 경험의 시각적 요소를 만드는 기술은 폭넓게 접근 가능해지고 가격이 저렴해지고 있다. 하지만 강력하게 작동하기 위해, 가상현실은 시각적인 것 이상이 되어야 한다. 여러분이 듣고 있는 것이 보이는 것과 확실하게 일치하지 (A) 않는다면, 가상 경험은 분리된다. 농구 경기를 예로 들어보자. 만일 선수들, 코치들, 아나운서들과 관중들 모두가 미드코트에 앉아 있는 것처럼 들린다면 여러분은 텔레비전으로 경기를 보는 것이 낫다. 여러분은 그냥 '그곳'에 있는 것처럼 느낄 것이다. (B) 불행하게도, 오늘날의 오디오 장비와 널리 사용되는 녹음 및 재생 형식은 멀리 떨어진 행성에서의 전투, 경기장 가운데서의 농구 경기 또는 거대한 콘서트홀의 첫 번째 열에서 듣는 교향곡의 소리를 설득력 있게 재현하는 일에 결코 적합하지 않다.

VOCA

• be well on the way to ~을 거의 다 해가다, 진척되어 가다

• accessible 접근 가능한, 이해하기 쉬운

• affordable 알맞은, 줄 수 있는

• convincingly 설득력 있게, 확실하게

• break apart 산산조각이 나다, 분리되다

• simply 아주, (부정어 앞에서) 결코

• inadequate 불충분한

15 난도 ★★★
정답 ④

독해 > 글의 일관성 > 문장 삽입

주어진 문장의 the same thinking은 문맥상 'to consider what short-term goals ~ accomplishing long-term goals'를 의미하는데, 그 생각이 직장에서(at work)도 적용된다고 언급했고, ④ 다음 문장의 'the goal in our profession(우리 직업의 목표)'에서 그것을 적용하는 방식을 설명하고 있으므로 주어진 문장이 들어갈 위치로 적절한 것은 ④이다.

본문해석

행복한 뇌는 단기적인 것에 집중하는 경향이 있다. 사실이 그렇다면, 결국 장기적인 목표를 성취할 수 있게끔 하는. 우리가 성취할 수 있는 단기적 목표들을 고려하는 것은 좋은 생각이다. 예를 들어, 만일 여러분이 6개월에 30파운드를 감량하고 싶다면, 그 목표에 이르게 하는 더 적은 무게를 빼는 것과 연관시킬 수 있는 단기적 목표는 무엇이겠는가? 그것은 여러분이 매주 2파운드를 감량할 때마다 여러분 자신에게 상을 주는 것과 같은 간단한 어떤 것일 수 있다. 동일한 사고방식이 직장에서 업무 성과 향상 같은 많은 목표에 적용될 수 있다. 전체 목표를 더 세분화하고 더 단기적인 부분들로 쪼갬으로써, 우리는 업무에서 목표의 거대함에 압도되는 대신 서서히 증가하는 성취에 집중할 수 있다.

- any number of 많은, 얼마든지
- that being the case 그것이 사실인 이상, 사실이 그렇다면
- associate 연관짓다
- increment 증가
- get there 달성하다
- overwhelm 압도하다
- enormity 엄청남[막대함], 심각함
- profession 직업, 업무, 전문직

16 난도 ★★☆   정답 ③

어법 > 영작하기

정답의 이유

③ marry가 '~와 결혼한 상태이다'의 뜻으로 쓰일 때는 'be married to+목적어'를 써야 하며, 결혼한 지 20년이 되었다고 하였으므로 완료시제를 써야 한다. 따라서 has married to → has been married to가 되어야 한다.

오답의 이유

① in case는 '만일의 경우를 대비하여'의 뜻으로 사용하는 접속사이며, would like to 다음에 동사원형을 올바르게 사용했다.

② '~하느라 바쁘다'는 be busy -ing이므로 올바르게 사용하였다.

④ to read는 a book을 수식하는 형용사적 용법으로 쓰였으며 for my son이 to부정사의 의미상 주어로 올바르게 사용되었다.

17 난도 ★★☆   정답 ①

독해 > 세부 내용 찾기 > 내용 (불)일치

정답의 이유

두 번째 문장에서 독기가 방의 안팎 어느 쪽에 더 많은지에 따라 (depending on whether there was more miasma inside or outside the room) 창문을 열거나 닫았다고 했으므로 글의 내용과 일치하지 않는 것은 ① 'In the nineteenth century, opening windows was irrelevant to the density of miasma(19세기에 창문을 여는 것은 독기의 밀도와 관련이 없었다).'이다.

오답의 이유

② 19세기에 신사들은 나쁜 공기가 있는 곳에 살지 않는다고 믿어졌다. → 두 번째 문장의 끝부분인 'it was believed that ~ because gentlemen did not inhabit quarters with bad air.'를 통해 알 수 있다.

③ 백신은 사람들이 미생물과 박테리아가 질병의 실제 원인이라는 것을 깨닫고 난 뒤 개발되었다. → 여섯 번째 문장의 'This new view of disease ~ as surgeons adopted antiseptics and scientists invented vaccines and antibiotics.'를 통해 알 수 있다.

④ 상처와 찰과상을 깨끗하게 하는 것은 사람들이 건강을 유지하는 데 도움을 줄 수 있다. → 마지막 문장 'Now, if you wanted to stay healthy ~'를 통해 알 수 있다.

19세기에 가장 존경받는 보건 의학 전문가들은 모두 질병이 나쁜 공기를 뜻하는 고급 용어인 '독기'에서 야기되는 것이라고 주장했다. 서양 사회의 보건 체계는 이러한 가정을 기초로 한 것으로, 즉 질병 예방을 위해 독기가 방 안팎 어느 쪽에 더 많은지에 따라 창문을 열거나 닫아 두었다. 신사들은 나쁜 공기가 있는 지역에 살지 않으므로, 의사들은 질병을 옮길 수 없다고 믿었다. 그 이후로 세균에 대한 개념이 생겨났다. 어느 날 모든 사람들이 나쁜 공기가 사람들을 아프게 한다고 믿었다. 그러다 거의 하룻밤 사이에 사람들은 질병의 실제 원인인 미생물과 박테리아라고 불리는 보이지 않는 것들이 있다는 것을 깨닫기 시작했다. 질병에 대한 이 새로운 관점은 의학에 전면적인 변화를 가져와서, 의사들은 소독제를 쓰고 과학자들은 백신과 항생제를 발명했다. 그러나 똑같이 중대하게 세균에 대한 생각은 평범한 사람들에게 그들 자신의 삶에 영향을 끼칠 수 있는 힘을 주었다. 오늘날, 여러분이 건강을 유지하기를 원한다면, 손을 씻고, 물을 끓이고, 음식을 완전히 익히고 베인 상처와 찰과상을 요오드로 소독할 수 있다.

- miasma (지저분한 · 불쾌한) 공기[기운/냄새]
- assumption 가정, 추정
- pass along 전달하다
- quarter 구역
- come along 생기다, 나타나다
- microbe 미생물
- sweeping 전면적인, 포괄적인
- antiseptic 소독약
- antibiotic 항생제, 항생물질
- momentously 중요하게, 중대하게
- thoroughly 완전히, 철저하게
- scrape 찰과상, 긁힌 자국
- iodine 요오드

정답의 이유

네 번째 문장에서 오늘날에는 부하직원들의 역할이 중요하다고 받아들이는 것이 자연스럽다고 언급했으므로 글의 내용과 일치하지 않는 것은 ③ 'The important role of followers is still denied today(부하직원들의 중요한 역할은 오늘날에도 여전히 부인된다).' 이다.

오답의 이유

① 오랜 기간 동안, 리더들은 적극적으로 이끌고 부하직원들은 수동적으로 따라야 한다고 생각되었다. → 두 번째 문장을 통해 알 수 있다.

② 하급자들에 대한 사람들의 관점이 사회 변화에 의해 영향을 받았다. → 세 번째 문장을 통해 알 수 있다.

④ 리더와 부하직원들 모두가 리더십 과정에 참여한다. → 마지막 문장을 통해 알 수 있다.

본문해석

부하직원들은 리더십 상황에서 중요한 부분이지만, 그들의 역할이 언제나 인정받았던 것은 아니다. 오랫동안, 사실상 '리더십에 대한 일반적인 견해는 리더가 적극적으로 리드하고, 후에 부하직원이라고 불리는 하급자들이 수동적으로 그리고 순순히 따라간다는 것이었다.' 시간이 흐르고, 특히 지난 세기의 사회적 변화는 부하직원에 대한 사람들의 견해를 형성했고, 리더십 이론은 점차 리더십 과정에서 부하직원들이 행하는 적극적이고 중요한 역할을 인정했다. 오늘날에는 부하직원들의 역할이 중요하다는 것을 받아들이는 것이 자연스러워 보인다. 리더십의 한 측면은 특히 이러한 점에서 주목할 가치가 있다. 리더십은 그룹 내의 모든 구성원들이 공유하는 사회적 영향의 과정이다. 리더십은 특정 지위나 역할에 있는 어느 누군가가 행사하는 영향에 제한되지 않으며, 부하직원들도 그 리더십 과정의 일부이다.

VOCA

- follower 추종자, 부하직원
- equation 상황, 문제, 방정식
- appreciate 인정하다, 고마워하다
- subordinate 부하, 하급자
- obediently 순순히, 공손하게
- shape 형성하다
- in this regard 이러한 점에서
- exert (권력이나 영향력을) 가하다, 행사하다

정답의 이유

제시문은 인간의 언어와 새의 노랫소리를 비교 · 설명하고 있다. 빈칸 앞에서 '추가'의 의미를 가지는 전환어 also를 통해 빈칸은 앞 내용과 논조가 같다는 점을 유추할 수 있다. 빈칸 앞 문장에서 사람의 음성은 하나의 중첩된 고리로 결합될 때(only when combined into an overlapping chain)만 일관된 메시지를 전달한다고 하였으므로 이와 연결된 내용으로 빈칸에 들어갈 적절한 것은 ① 'individual notes are often of little value(각각의 음은 보통 거의 가치가 없다)'이다.

오답의 이유

② 리듬감 있는 소리가 중요하다

③ 방언이 중요한 역할을 한다

④ 소리 체계가 존재하지 않는다

본문해석

언어는 특유한 그 자체의 이중층이 있다. 단일한 잡음들은 가끔씩만 의미를 가진다. 즉, 대부분 다양한 음성들은 오직 다른 색깔의 아이스크림이 녹아 서로 섞이는 것처럼, 하나의 중첩된 고리로 결합될 때에만 일관된 메시지를 전달한다. 새소리에서도 마찬가지로, 각각의 음은 보통 거의 가치가 없다. 그 순서가 중요한 것이다. 인간과 새 모두에게, 이 특별한 소리 체계의 통제는 보통 좌뇌인 뇌의 반쪽에 의해 행해지며, 그 체계는 상대적으로 생의 초기에 학습된다. 그리고 많은 인간의 언어들이 방언을 가지고 있는 것처럼, 일부 새의 종들도 그러하다. 캘리포니아에서 노랑턱멧새는 지역마다 그 노랫소리가 너무 달라서 아마 캘리포니아 사람들은 이들 멧새의 소리를 듣고 그들이 캘리포니아주 내 어디에서 서식하는지 추정할 수 있다.

VOCA

- proper 엄밀한 의미의 적절한, 제대로 된
- occasionally 가끔, 이따금
- convey 전달하다, 운반하다
- coherent 일관성 있는, 논리 정연한
- white−crowned sparrow 노랑턱멧새
- supposedly 아마, 추정상
- note (음악) 음, 음표

20 난도 ★★☆　　　　　　　　　　　　　　　정답 ②

정답의 이유

빈칸 앞 문장에서 'MAP의 목적은 많은 개별적 요인들을 통해 선택이 분명해질 때까지 직관에 따른 의사 결정을 미루는 것(To put off gut-based decision-making)'이라고 했으므로 빈칸에 들어갈 적절한 것은 ② 'delay(연기하다)'이다.

오답의 이유

① 개선하다

③ 소유하다

④ 용이하게 하다

본문해석

노벨상을 수상한 심리학자 Daniel Kahneman은, 인간이 이성적인 의사결정자라는 개념을 뒤집으면서, 세계가 경제에 대해 생각하는 방식을 바꾸었다. 그 과정에서, 학문을 넘나드는 그의 영향력은 의사가 의학적 결정을 내리는 방법이나 월스트리트에서 투자자가 리스크를 평가하는 방식을 바꾸었다. 한 논문에서, Kahneman과 그의 동료들은 큰 전략적 결정을 내리는 과정을 개략적으로 설명했다. '조정을 통한 평가 프로토콜' 즉 MAP이라고 불리는 그들의 권장 접근법은 단순한 목표가 있다. 많은 개별적 요인들을 통해 선택이 알려질 때까지 직감에 따른 의사 결정을 미루는 것이다. "MAP의 본질적인 목적들 중 하나는 기본적으로 직관을 연기하는 것입니다."라고 Kahneman이 *The Post*와의 최근 인터뷰에서 말했다. 구조화된 과정은 이전에 선택된 6~7개의 특성들에 기반한 결정을 분석하고, 그것들 각각을 개별적으로 논의하여, 그것들에 상대적인 백분위 점수를 부여하여, 마지막으로 그 점수들을 이용해 통합적인 판단을 내리는 것을 요구한다.

VOCA

- upend 뒤집다, 거꾸로 하다
- along the way 그 과정에서
- alter 바꾸다
- physician 의사; 내과 의사
- outline 개요를 서술하다, 나타내다, 윤곽을 보여주다
- gut 직감, 배짱
- intuition 직감, 직관
- call for ~을 필요로 하다
- attribute 속성, 자질
- assign 배정하다, 부과하다, 맡기다, 파견하다
- relative 상대적인, 비교상의
- percentile 백분위의
- holistic 전체론의

영어 | 2018년 지방직 9급

한눈에 훑어보기

✔ 영역 분석

어휘   01   02   05   06
4문항, 20%

독해   09   10   12   13   15   16   17   18   19   20
10문항, 50%

어법   03   04   07   08
4문항, 20%

표현   11   14
2문항, 10%

✔ 빠른 정답

01	02	03	04	05	06	07	08	09	10
①	②	④	④	④	③	②	①	③	②
11	12	13	14	15	16	17	18	19	20
②	①	②	①	④	③	①	①	④	①

✔ 점수 체크

구분	1회독	2회독	3회독
맞힌 문항 수	/ 20	/ 20	/ 20
나의 점수	점	점	점

01   난도 ★★☆   정답 ①

어휘 > 단어

정답의 이유

밑줄 친 paramount는 '매우(가장) 중요한'의 뜻으로 이와 의미가 가장 가까운 것은 ① 'chief(주된)'이다.

오답의 이유

② 맹세한

③ 성공한

④ 신비한

본문해석

의사의 가장 중요한 의무는 해를 끼치지 않는 것이다. 나머지 모든 것들은, 심지어 치료조차도 다음 순위가 되어야 한다.

VOCA

• physician   의사

• do harm   해를 끼치다

02   난도 ★★☆   정답 ②

어휘 > 어구

정답의 이유

밑줄 친 get cold feet은 '겁이 나다'의 뜻으로 이와 의미가 가장 가까운 것은 ② 'become afraid(두려워지다)'이다.

오답의 이유

① 야망을 가지다

③ 지치다

④ 슬퍼하다

본문해석

사람들이 북극으로 여행가는 것에 대해 겁이 나는 것은 드문 일이 아니다.

어법 > 비문 찾기

정답의 이유

④ 관계대명사 what은 선행사를 포함하므로 선행사(the post)와 같이 쓸 수 없다. 관계대명사절이 목적어가 생략된 불완전한 문장이므로 목적격 관계대명사이면서 선행사(the post)를 수식하는 which 또는 that으로 바꿔야 한다.

오답의 이유

① 전치사 for는 기간을 나타내는 시간 표현으로 주로 완료시제에 사용된다. '지난 3년 동안'의 기간을 나타내므로 for the last three years와 현재완료시제(has worked)가 올바르게 사용되었다.

② 분사(mentioned)가 명사(all the requirements)를 수식하며, 직무기술서에 '언급되는'의 뜻으로 수동 관계이므로 과거분사가 올바르게 사용되었다.

③ to부정사의 형용사적 용법(명사+to부정사)으로 to doubt가 명사(reason)를 수식하며, to doubt의 목적어(integrity)가 있으므로 to부정사의 능동형이 올바르게 사용되었다.

본문해석

나는 Mrs. Ferrer에 대한 귀사의 추천서 요청에 답변하고자 씁니다. 그녀는 지난 3년 동안 내 비서로서 일했으며 훌륭한 직원이었습니다. 나는 그녀가 귀사의 직무기술서에 언급된 모든 요건을 충족하며, 실제로 여러 방면에서 그것들(자격 요건)을 능가한다고 믿습니다. 그녀의 완벽한 성실성을 의심할 이유가 결코 없었습니다. 그러므로 나는 귀사가 광고하는 그 직책에 Mrs. Ferrer를 추천합니다.

VOCA

- reference 추천서, 추천인
- requirement 필요한 것, 요건, 자격
- meet 충족시키다, 만나다
- job description 직무기술서
- in many ways 여러모로
- integrity 성실, 정직, 완전한 상태

어법 > 영작하기

정답의 이유

④ 분사구문의 주어(it)와 주절의 주어(I)가 다르므로 분사구문의 주어(it)를 생략할 수 없다. 따라서 Being cold outside → It being cold outside가 되어야 한다.

오답의 이유

① all of+명사(All of the information)의 경우, 명사와 동사가 수일치해야 하는데, information이 불가산명사이므로 단수 주어로 취급하여 단수동사(was)가 올바르게 사용되었다.

② should[ought to] have p.p.는 '~해야 했는데(하지 못했다)'라는 의미로 과거의 일에 대한 유감이나 후회를 나타내므로 올바르게 사용되었다.

③ 우리가 도착하기(arrived) 전에 이미 영화가 시작했으므로 영화가 시작된 시점은 한 시제 더 앞서는 과거완료시제(had started)가 올바르게 사용되었다.

더 알아보기

독립분사구문

- 분사구문의 의미상 주어가 주절의 주어와 다를 경우, 분사구문의 의미상 주어를 생략할 수 없다.
  - 예 I'll come tomorrow, weather *permitting*. → I≠weather
    (내일 날씨가 괜찮으면 제가 오겠어요.)
  - 예 The sun *having set*, we gave up looking for them. → The sun≠we
    (해가 졌기 때문에 우리는 그들을 찾는 걸 포기했다.)
- 분사구문의 의미상 주어가 일반인(we, you, they, one 등)인 경우, 분사구문의 의미상 주어를 생략할 수 있다.

Generally[Frankly, Strictly] speaking	일반적으로[솔직하게, 엄격하게] 말해서
Granting[Granted] that ~	비록 ~이라 할지라도
Judging from[by]	~로 판단하건대
Considering ~	~을 고려하면
Regarding+명사	~에 관하여

어휘 > 단어

정답의 이유

밑줄 친 intimidating은 '위협적인'의 뜻으로 이와 의미가 가장 가까운 것은 ④ 'frightening(무서운)'이다.

오답의 이유

① 유머러스한

② 친절한

③ 편리한

본문해석

최신의 접근법이 위협적이라고 생각하는 학생은 그 또는 그녀가 예전 방식으로 배웠을지도 모르는 것보다 덜 배운다.

VOCA

- state-of-the-art 최신의

06 난도 ★★☆
정답 ③

어휘 > 어구

정답의 이유

빈칸 앞 부분에서 'Since the air-conditioners are being repaired now'라고 했고, 빈칸 다음에 'electric fans for the day'로 미루어 빈칸에는 선풍기로 '임시방편하다'라는 의미가 온다는 것을 유추할 수 있으므로 빈칸에 들어갈 말로 적절한 것은 ③ 'make do with(~으로 임시변통하다)'이다.

오답의 이유

① ~을 처리하다[없애다]

② ~에서 손을 놓다

④ ~와 결별하다

본문해석

에어컨들이 현재 수리 중이기 때문에, 근무자들은 그날은 선풍기로 임시변통해야 한다.

VOCA

• repair 수리하다, 상황을 바로잡다; 수리, 보수

• electric fan 선풍기

07 난도 ★★☆
정답 ②

어법 > 정문 찾기

정답의 이유

② 가정법 과거에서 if가 생략되어 주어와 동사가 도치되었으므로 Were it not for water로 올바르게 사용되었다. 가정법 과거에서 if절의 be동사는 were를 사용하며, 주절의 동사는 '조동사 과거(would/could/should/might)+동사원형'이다.

오답의 이유

① contact는 완전타동사로 전치사를 동반할 수 없으므로 contact to me → contact me가 되어야 한다.

③ 관계사절의 동사는 선행사(people)에 수일치시켜야 하므로 who is away → who are away가 되어야 한다. allow는 to부정사를 목적격 보어로 취하는 5형식 동사로 to continue가 올바르게 사용되었다.

④ 'The 비교급+주어+동사, the 비교급+주어+동사'는 '~하면 할수록 더욱 …하다'의 뜻으로 the 다음에 비교급이 와야 하므로 the worst → the worse가 되어야 한다.

본문해석

① 제가 지난주에 드렸던 이메일 주소로 연락해 주세요.

② 물이 없다면, 지구상의 모든 생명체는 멸종되었을 것이다.

③ 노트북 컴퓨터는 사무실에서 떨어져 있는 사람들이 업무를 계속 하도록 한다.

④ 그들이 그들의 실수를 설명하려고 더 시도하면 할수록, 그들의 이야기는 더 나쁘게 들렸다.

VOCA

• creature 생명이 있는 존재, 생물

• extinct (동 · 식물 등의 종류가) 멸종된

더 알아보기

The 비교급, the 비교급

• The 비교급+주어+동사, the 비교급+주어+동사: '~하면 할수록 더 …하다'

　예 The older you grow, the more difficult it becomes to learn a foreign language.

　　(나이가 들어갈수록, 그만큼 더 외국어 공부하기가 어려워진다.)

• the가 비교급 양쪽에 모두 있어야 하며, the 다음에는 반드시 비교급이 와야 한다.

　예 The higher prices rose, the more money the workers asked for.

　　(물가가 오를수록, 노동자들은 더 많은 돈을 요구했다.)

• be동사인 경우에는 도치, 생략이 가능하다.

　예 The more expensive a hotel *is*, the better its service *is*.

　　= The more expensive *is* a hotel, the better *is* its service.

　　= The more expensive a hotel, the better its service.

　　(더 비싼 호텔일수록, 서비스도 더 좋다.)

08 난도 ★★☆
정답 ①

어법 > 영작하기

정답의 이유

① '시간 표현+ago'는 과거시제와 자주 쓰이는 시간표현이므로 a few days ago와 과거시제(went)가 올바르게 사용되었다. to see off는 to부정사의 부사적 용법(목적: ~하기 위해서)으로 올바르게 사용되었다.

오답의 이유

② make가 5형식에서 사용될 경우 'make+목적어+동사원형'이지만 선지의 make believe는 '~인 체(척)하다'라는 관용표현으로 쓰였으므로 made it believe → made believe가 되어야 한다.

③ '~을 학수고대하다, 간절히 기다리다'는 look forward to -ing이므로 looking forward to go → looking forward to going이 되어야 한다.

④ 감정유발동사(interest)의 경우 수식 받는 명사(anything)가 감정의 원인이면 현재분사를, 감정을 느끼는 주체이면 과거분사를 써야 한다. 수식받는 명사(anything)가 감정의 원인이므로 anything interested → anything interesting이 되어야 한다.

독해 > 글의 일관성 > 무관한 어휘 · 문장

정답의 이유

제시문은 르네상스 시대 주방의 명확한 위계질서를 설명하는 글로 ①에서 집사장(steward), ②에서는 집사(butler), ④에서는 수석 주방장(head cook)의 역할에 관해 각각 설명하고 있는데, ③에서는 식당의 영업 부문, 즉 '접객, 고객 응대'를 언급했으므로 글의 흐름상 어색한 문장은 ③이다.

본문해석

르네상스의 주방에는 정교한 연회를 만들기 위해 함께 일하는 조력자들의 명확한 위계질서가 있었다. 최상위에는 우리가 보아왔던 것처럼 *scalco*(집사), 즉 steward(집사장)가 있는데, 이 사람은 주방뿐만 아니라 식당도 담당했다. 식당은 butler(집사)에 의해서 감독되었는데, 그는 은 식기류와 리넨 식탁보를 담당했고, 연회의 처음부터 마지막까지 요리들, 즉 냉요리, 샐러드, 치즈, 과일 등의 전채요리부터 사탕류와 당과 등의 후식까지 요리를 차려냈다. <u>이러한 정교한 장식과 응대는 식당에서 영업 부문, 즉 '접객, 응대'라고 불리는 것이었다.</u> 주방은 head cook(수석 주방장)에 의해 감독되었는데, 그는 요리사의 조수들과 페이스트리 전문 요리사들, 주방 보조들을 감독했다.

VOCA

• definite　명확한
• hierarchy　(특히 사회나 조직 내의) 계급, 계층
• elaborate　정교한, 정성을 들인
• banquet　(공식) 연회, 만찬
• dining room　식당(방), 다이닝 룸
• silverware　은(銀) 식기류(특히 나이프, 포크, 접시 등)
• confection　당과 제품, 설탕 절임
• front of the house　영업 부문(호텔 등에서 고객을 직접 대면하고 서비스를 제공하는 영역)
• undercook　요리사의 조수

독해 > 대의 파악 > 요지, 주장

정답의 이유

글의 중반부에서 스스로가 중요한 사람이 되어야 중요한 사람들에게서 도움을 받을 수 있다고 했고, 마지막에서 두 번째 문장에서 'If you do great work, those connections will be easier to make.'라고 하였다. 즉, 좋은 네트워크를 형성하기 위해서는 먼저 본인이 성과를 내야 한다는 것이므로 글의 요지로 적절한 것은 ② 'Building a good network starts from your accomplishments(좋은 네트워크 형성은 여러분의 성과로부터 시작한다).'이다.

오답의 이유

① 후원은 성공적인 경력을 위해서 필수적이다.
③ 강력한 네트워크는 여러분의 성공을 위한 전제조건이다.
④ 여러분의 통찰력과 결과물은 여러분이 네트워크 형성 전문가가 되면서 성장한다.

본문해석

나의 학생들은 종종 그들이 단순히 매우 중요한 사람을 만나기만 한다면, 그들의 작업이 향상될 것이라고 믿는다. 그러나 여러분이 이미 이 세상에 중요한 무언가를 내어놓지 않는 한, 그러한 사람들과 관계를 맺는 것은 상당히 어렵다. 그것이 바로 자문가와 후원자의 호기심을 자극하는 것이다. 성취는 단지 받기만 하는 것이 아니라 여러분에게도 무언가 주어야 할 것이 있다는 것을 보여준다. 인생에서 올바른 사람을 아는 것은 확실히 도움이 된다. 하지만 그들이 여러분을 얼마나 열심히 도와줄지와 여러분을 위해 얼마나 위험을 감수할지는 여러분이 그들에게 무엇을 제공하는가에 달려 있다. 강력한 인적 네트워크 구축은 여러분에게 인적 네트워크 형성 전문가가 되는 것을 요구하지 않는다. 그것은 단지 여러분에게 무언가의 전문가가 될 것을 요구한다. 만약 여러분이 좋은 인맥을 쌓으면, 그들은 아마 여러분의 경력을 발전시켜 줄지도 모른다. 만약 여러분이 좋은 성과를 낸다면, 그러한 인맥을 쌓기 훨씬 더 쉬울 것이다. 명함이 아닌, 여러분의 통찰력과 결과물이 대변하도록 하라.

VOCA

• remarkably　매우, 몹시
• engage　관계를 맺다
• pique　불쾌하게 하다, 자극하다
• go to bat for　～을 도와주다
• stick one's neck out for　～을 위해 위험을 무릅쓰다
• network　(긴밀한 사람, 기업체 등의) 망, 관계, 네트워크
• connection　(주로 복수로) 연줄이 닿는[있는] 사람[기관]
• career　직업, 직장 생활

11 난도 ★☆☆　　　　　　　　　　정답 ②

표현 > 일반회화

[정답의 이유]

A의 컴퓨터가 고장난 상황의 대화문으로 빈칸 다음에서 A가 '그래야 하는데'라고 대답했으므로 B가 빈칸에서 해결책을 조언했을 것이다. 컴퓨터 고장에 대한 해결책으로 ②와 ④가 제시될 수 있는데, A가 대답 후반부에 '나는 게으르다'고 했으므로 B는 A가 직접 행동을 해야 하는 해결책을 제시했다고 유추할 수 있다. 따라서 빈칸에 들어갈 말로 적절한 것은 ② 'Try visiting the nearest service center then(그러면 가까운 서비스 센터에 방문해 봐).'이다.

[오답의 이유]

① 나는 네 컴퓨터를 고치는 법을 몰라.

③ 음, 네 문제에 대한 생각은 그만하고 자러 가.

④ 내 남동생이 컴퓨터 기술자여서 네 컴퓨터를 고쳐주려고 할 거야.

본문해석

A: 내 컴퓨터가 아무 이유 없이 그냥 꺼졌어. 난 그것을 다시 켤 수도 없어.

B: 충전은 해 봤니? 단순히 배터리가 다 돼서 그럴 수도 있어.

A: 물론, 나는 그것을 충전하는 것을 시도해 봤어.

B: 그러면 가장 가까운 서비스 센터에 방문해 봐.

A: 그래야 하는데, 난 너무 게을러.

VOCA

• shut down　(기계가) 멈추다[정지하다], 문을 닫다

• turn back　돌려놓다

• charge　충전하다

• be out of battery　배터리가 다 되다

12 난도 ★☆☆　　　　　　　　　　정답 ①

독해 > 대의 파악 > 분위기, 어조, 심경

[정답의 이유]

제시문의 화자는 시험에 지각해서 급하게 문제를 풀지만 곧 시험이 끝나버리는 상황에서 허둥대며 시험을 치르는 긴박한 상황을 묘사하고 있으므로 화자의 심경으로 가장 적절한 것은 ① 'nervous and worried(초조하고 걱정되는)'이다.

[오답의 이유]

② 신나고 활기찬

③ 침착하고 단호한

④ 안전하고 느긋한

본문해석

내 얼굴은 백지장처럼 하얗게 되었다. 나는 나의 시계를 보았다. 시험은 지금쯤 이미 거의 끝났을 것이다. 나는 완전히 공황 상태에 빠져 시험장에 도착했다. 나는 나의 사정을 이야기하려고 했지만, 나의 문장과 설명하는 몸짓은 너무 혼란스러워서 나는 인간 토네이도의 매우 확실한 버전에 불과한 의사소통을 했다(정리되지 않은 말들을 토네이도처럼 쏟아냈다). 정신없는 내 설명을 제지하려고, 시험 감독관은 빈자리로 나를 안내했고, 내 앞에 시험지를 두었다. 그는 미심쩍은 눈으로 나에게서 시계로 시선을 돌리고는 걸어 나갔다. 나는 필사적으로 놓친 시간을 만회하려 노력했고, 미친듯이 허둥지둥 유추 문제와 문장 완성 문제를 간신히 끝냈다. "15분 남았습니다."라는 슬픈 운명의 목소리가 교실 앞쪽에서 흘러나왔다. 대수 방정식과 산술 계산, 기하학 도형이 눈앞에서 헤엄쳐 다녔다. "시간 다 됐습니다! 연필 내려 놓으세요."

VOCA

• descriptive　묘사하는

• nothing more than　~에 불과한

• convincing　설득력 있는, 그럴듯한, 이해가 가는

• tornado　토네이도, (감정·활동의) 격발, 폭발

• in an effort to　~해 보려는 노력으로

• curb　억제[제한]하다

• distracting　산만한, 정신없는

• proctor　시험 감독관

• desperately　필사적으로, 절망적으로, 자포자기하여

• make up for　만회하다, 보상하다

• scramble through　급히 서둘러 일을 해치우다, 간신히 끝내다

• analogy　유추

• doom　죽음, (나쁜) 운명

• declare　선언하다, 분명히 말하다

• algebraic　대수의

• equation　방정식

• arithmetic　산수, 연산

• geometric　기하학의

• diagram　도표, 도해

독해 > 글의 일관성 > 글의 순서

정답의 이유

주어진 글은 건강을 관찰·추적하는 장치(devices)가 모든 연령대에 인기가 있다는 내용이다. 주어진 문장의 Devices를 (B)의 these technologies로 받으며, 심지어 노인층의 생명을 구할 수도 있는 장치의 장점에 대한 설명으로 이어지는 것이 자연스럽다. (A)에서 낙상 경보를 예로 소개하고, (C)의 This simple technology는 (A)에서 언급된 낙상 경보 기술(Fall alerts)을 받아서 구체적으로 설명하고 있다. 따라서 주어진 글에 이어질 글의 순서로 적절한 것은 ② '(B) – (A) – (C)'이다.

본문해석

여러분의 건강을 관찰하고 추적하는 장치는 모든 연령대에서 점점 더 인기를 얻고 있다.

(B) 그러나 특히 집에 보호자가 없이 재가 생활을 하는 노인들에게, 이러한 기술들은 생명을 구할 수도 있다.

(A) 예를 들어, 낙상은 65세 이상 성인들에게 사망의 주요한 원인이다. 낙상 경보(fall alerts)는 오랫동안 노인을 위한 양로 기술이었는데, 현재 개선되었다.

(C) 이 간단한 기술은 노인이 넘어지는 순간 자동으로 911이나 가까운 가족에게 위험을 알릴 수 있다.

VOCA

- device 장치
- fall 낙상
- alert 경계경보, 위험을 알리다
- aging in place 재가 복지(살던 집에서 노후 보내기)
- caretaker 보호자

표현 > 일반회화

정답의 이유

빈칸 앞에서 신혼여행으로 하와이에 가는 것이 어떠냐고 묻는 A의 질문에 대한 답변으로 ①, ③, ④가 가능하지만, 앞서 두 사람이 가보지 않은 곳으로 여행을 가자는 B의 제안을 고려하면 빈칸에 들어갈 말로 가장 적절한 것은 ① 'I've always wanted to go there(나는 항상 그곳에 가고 싶었어).'이다.

오답의 이유

② 한국은 살기 좋은 곳이 아니니?

③ 좋아! 그곳에서의 나의 지난 여행은 굉장했어!

④ 오, 너는 이미 하와이에 다녀왔음이 틀림없구나.

본문해석

A: 우리 신혼여행지로 너는 어디를 가고 싶어?

B: 우리 둘 다 가본 적이 없는 곳으로 가자.

A: 그럼, 하와이로 가는 건 어때?

B: 나는 항상 그곳에 가고 싶었어.

독해 > 빈칸 완성 > 단어·구·절

정답의 이유

첫 문장에서 성공한 사람들의 비결은 '온전히 한 가지에 집중하는 것(concentrate totally on one thing)'이라고 제시했다. 빈칸 앞의 'this order is simple'과 마지막 문장의 '우선순위에 따라 한 가지 일에 집중할 때(When you concentrate on the one task of your priorities)'로 미루어 빈칸에는 '우선순위(priorities)'와 관련된 것이 적절하다는 것을 유추할 수 있다. 따라서 빈칸에 들어갈 말로 가장 적절한 것은 ④ 'the most important thing first(가장 중요한 일은 제일 먼저)'이다.

오답의 이유

① 빠르면 빠를수록 좋다

② 늦더라도 하지 않는 것보다 낫다

③ 눈에서 멀어지면 마음에서도 멀어진다

본문해석

성공한 사람들의 비결은 일반적으로 그들이 한 가지 일에 온전히 집중할 수 있다는 것이다. 그들은 머릿속에 많은 것이 있어도, 그 많은 일이 서로 방해하게 하지 않고, 오히려 그 일들을 적절한 내적 순서로 자리 잡게 하는 방법을 알고 있다. 그리고 이 순서는 꽤 간단하다. 가장 중요한 일을 첫 번째로 하는 것이다. 이론상으로는 꽤 분명해 보이지만, 일상생활에서는 오히려 다르게 보인다. 여러분은 아마 우선순위를 정하려고 노력했을지도 모르지만, 일상의 사소한 문제들과 예상하지 못한 모든 방해 요소들 때문에 실패했다. 예를 들어, 다른 사무실로 피해서 어떤 방해물도 끼어들지 못하게 함으로써 집중을 방해하는 것들을 분리하라. 여러분의 우선순위에 있는 한 가지 과업에 집중할 때, 여러분은 심지어 가지고 있는지도 알지 못했던 에너지가 있다는 것을 알게 될 것이다.

VOCA

- commitment 일, 책무, 이행, 전념
- impede (운동·진행 등을) 방해하다, 훼방 놓다
- bring into ~로 이동시키다, 운반하다
- unforeseen 예측하지 못한, 뜻밖의
- distraction 집중을 방해하는 것
- separate 가르다, 분리하다
- disturbance 방해, 장애
- get in the way 방해가 되다

16 난도 ★★☆　　　　　　　　　　　　　정답 ③

독해 > 대의 파악 > 제목, 주제

정답의 이유

첫 번째 문장에서 '~ its fishing must be done scientifically if it is to be continued.'라고 한 후에, 어업이 과학의 도움을 받을 수 있는 방식에 대한 설명으로 이어진다. 마지막 문장에서 '물고기 개체 수와 그 개체 수를 감소시키지 않고 최대한 활용할 수 있는 방법을 더 잘 이해하도록 연구가 끊임없이 이루어지고 있다'고 했으므로 글의 제목으로 적절한 것은 ③ 'Why Does the Fishing Industry Need Science(왜 어업에 과학이 필요할까)?'이다.

오답의 이유

① 상업적인 어업 활동을 거부하라
② 어업 사업으로 간주되는 바다 양식업
④ 남획된 어류: 불법조업 사례

본문해석

과학자들의 도움으로, 상업적 수산업은 활동이 계속되려면 어업이 반드시 과학적으로 행해져야 한다는 사실을 알게 되었다. 물고기 개체 수에 대한 어획 압박이 없다면, 물고기 개체 수는 예상 가능한 풍부함의 수준에 도달하고 그 상태를 유지하게 될 것이다. 유일한 변동은, 예를 들어, 먹이 확보 가능성과 적당한 수온 같은 자연 환경적인 요소들뿐일 것이다. 만약 어업이 이러한 물고기들을 포획하기 위해 개발된다면, 어획량이 적다면 그들의 개체 수는 유지될 수 있다. 북해의 고등어가 좋은 예이다. 만약 우리가 어업 활동을 늘리고 매년 더 많은 물고기를 잡아들인다면, 우리는 해마다 잡아들이는 모든 물고기를 대체할 수 있는 이상적인 지점 이하로 개체 수를 감소시키지 않도록 주의해야 한다. 만약 우리가 '지속 가능한 최대 생산량'이라 불리는 이 지점까지 어업 활동을 한다면, 우리는 매년 가능한 최대치의 생산량을 유지할 수 있다. 만약 우리가 너무 많이 포획한다면 우리들이 어업 활동을 할 수 없을 때까지 매년 물고기 개체 수가 감소할 것이다. 심각하게 남획된 동물의 예로는 남극의 흰긴수염고래와 북대서양의 큰 넙치가 있다. 매년 최대 어획량을 유지하기 위해 정확한 양만 포획하는 것은 과학이자 예술이다. 우리가 어류 개체 수를 더 잘 이해하여 그 개체 수를 고갈시키지 않고 최대한 이를 활용하는 방법을 돕기 위한 연구가 지속적으로 행해지고 있다.

VOCA

• commercial 상업용의, 상업적인; 광고
• abundance 풍부, 대량
• fluctuation 변동, 동요, 파동
• fishery 어업, 수산업, 어장
• mackerel 고등어
• sustainable 지속 가능한, 고갈되지 않는, 견딜 수 있는
• yield 수확량
• blue whale 흰긴수염고래
• halibut 큰 넙치
• utilize 활용하다, 이용하다, 유지하다
• deplete 고갈시키다, 다 써버리다, 비우다

17 난도 ★★☆　　　　　　　　　　　　　정답 ①

독해 > 빈칸 완성 > 연결어

정답의 이유

① (A) 앞부분은 al Qaeda가 미국의 중심지를 공격했다는 내용이고, (A) 다음에는 그 사건이 엄청난 언론의 관심을 받았다는 내용이 나오므로 인과관계가 성립하기 위해서 빈칸 (A)에는 'thereby(그렇게 함으로써)'가 적절하다. (B) 앞에서 진주만 공격이 전술적인 성공(tactical success)이었지만 전략적 실패(strategic failure)로 이어졌다고 했고, (B) 다음에서 9/11 테러도 al Qaeda에게는 전술적 성공이었지만 Osama bin Laden에게는 전략적으로는 실패라는 점에서 두 사건의 유사성을 설명하고 있으므로 빈칸 (B)에는 'Similarly(유사하게도)'가 적절하다.

오답의 이유

② ~동안에 – 그러므로
③ ~동안에 – 다행히
④ 그렇게 함으로써 – 반면에

본문해석

테러리즘이 과연 효과가 있을까? 9/11 테러는 al Qaeda에게는 엄청난 전술적 성공이었는데, 부분적으로 그것은 세계 언론의 중심지이자 미국의 실질적인 중심지에서 발생한 공격을 포함했고, (A) 그렇게 함으로써 사건의 가능한 가장 광범위한 언론 보도 영역을 확보했기 때문이다. 만약 테러리즘이 많은 사람이 보기를 원하는 연극의 형태라면, 인류 역사상 9/11 테러보다 더 많은 세계의 관람객이 관람한 사건은 없었을 것이다. 당시에 9/11 테러와 진주만 공격이 얼마나 유사했는지에 대한 많은 토론이 있었다. 둘 다 미국을 중요한 전쟁으로 끌어들인 갑작스러운 공격이었기 때문에, 그 둘은 실제로 유사했다. 그러나 그들은 또한 다른 의미에서도 유사했다. 진주만은 일본제국의 엄청난 '전술적' 성공이었지만, 중대한 '전략적' 실패로 이어졌다. 진주만 공격 이후 4년 만에 일본제국은 황폐해졌고, 완전히 패배했다. (B) 유사하게도, 9/11 테러는 al Qaeda의 지대한 전술적 성공이었지만, 그것은 또한 Osama bin Laden에게는 큰 전략적 실패로 드러났다.

VOCA

• tactical 작전의, 전략적인, 전술적인
• ensure 반드시 ~하게 하다, 보장하다
• coverage (신문 · 텔레비전 등) 보도, 범위
• draw into ~에 끌어들이다
• utterly 완전히, 아주, 전혀
• strategic 전략상 중요한, 전략적인
• defeat 패배시키다
• turn out 모습을 드러내다, (일 · 결과가 특정 방식으로) 되다

18 난도 ★★☆ 정답 ①

독해 > 세부 내용 찾기 > 내용 (불)일치

정답의 이유

아홉 번째 문장에서 의사들은 현재 시점에서는 배아 변형을 더 진행해서는 안 된다(should not proceed at this time)고 권고하고 있으므로 글의 내용과 일치하지 않는 것은 ① 'Doctors were recommended to immediately go ahead with embryo editing for enhancement(의사들은 향상을 위한 배아 수정을 즉시 추진할 것을 권고받았다).'이다.

오답의 이유

② 최근에, 미국의 과학기구가 우생학 관련 토론에 참여했다. → 여섯 번째 문장에서 미국의 과학기구가 개입했다고 했으므로 글의 내용과 일치한다.

③ 중국 과학자들은 심각한 혈액 질환을 예방하고자 인간의 배아를 변형했다. → 첫 번째 문장에서 중국 과학자들이 잠재적인 혈액 질환을 제거하기 위해서 배아를 변형했다고 언급하고 있으므로 글의 내용과 일치한다.

④ '맞춤 아기'는 생식세포 변형 과정의 또 다른 용어이다. → 두 번째, 세 번째 문장에서 '생식세포 변형(germline modification)'을 언론매체는 '맞춤 아기(designer babies)'라고 표현하는 것을 좋아한다고 했으므로 글의 내용과 일치한다.

본문해석

중국 과학자들이 아기뿐만 아니라 그 아기의 모든 후손들로부터 잠재적으로 치명적인 혈액 질환을 제거하기 위해 인간 배아를 변형했을 때 우리는 한 종으로서 새로운 국면을 맞이하게 되었다. 연구자들은 이 과정을 '생식세포 변형(germline modification)'이라고 부른다. 언론 매체는 '맞춤 아기(designer babies)'라고 표현하는 것을 좋아한다. 그러나 우리는 그것을 있는 그대로 '우생학'이라고 불러야 한다. 그리고 우리 인류는 우리가 그것을 이용하길 원하는지 원하지 않는지를 결정해야 한다. 지난달 미국에서 과학기구가 개입했다. National Academy of Sciences와 National Academy of Medicine의 합동 위원회는 '합리적인 대안이 없는 경우' 심각한 질병을 야기하는 유전자를 겨냥한 배아 변형을 지지했다. 하지만 이미 건강한 아이를 더욱 강하거나 키를 크게 만드는 경우와 같은 '향상'을 위한 변형은 훨씬 경계했다. 위원회는 공개적 토론을 권고했고, 의사들은 '현 시점에서 진행해서는 안 된다.'라고 말했다. 위원회가 신중함을 촉구하는 데는 그럴만한 이유가 있다. 우생학의 역사는 심한 차별과 비참함으로 가득하다.

VOCA

- phrase 단계
- human embryo 인간 배아
- fatal 치명적인
- blood disorder 혈액 질환
- germline 생식세포
- modification 수정
- weigh in (논의 · 언쟁 · 활동 등에) 끼어들다, 관여하다, 거들다
- endorse 지지하다, 승인하다

- alternative 대안, 선택 가능한 것; 대안적인, 대체의
- wary of ~을 경계하는, 조심하는
- enhancement 향상
- urge 재촉하다, 격려하다
- oppression 억압, 압박, 억제, 학대, 심한 차별
- misery 고통, 빈곤, 비참함

19 난도 ★★★ 정답 ④

독해 > 글의 일관성 > 문장 삽입

정답의 이유

주어진 문장은 둘 중 누구도 항복하지 않는 특정 상황을 가정하고 이 경우에 경기가 종료되는 방법을 제시하고 있으므로 주어진 문장의 앞부분에서 경기가 종료되기 위한 조건이 언급되어야 글의 흐름이 논리적이다. ④의 바로 앞 문장에서 'Contenders continued until one of two collapsed(경쟁자들은 둘 중 하나가 쓰러질 때까지 계속했다.)'라고 경기 종료 조건이 나오므로 주어진 문장이 들어갈 위치로 가장 적절한 것은 ④이다.

본문해석

고대 올림픽은 마치 오늘날의 경기들처럼 운동선수들에게 그들의 건강함과 우월함을 입증할 기회를 제공하였다. 고대 올림픽 경기는 약자를 탈락시키고 강자를 찬미하기 위해 고안되었다. 승자들은 벼랑 끝까지 내몰렸다. 마치 현대와 같이 사람들은 익스트림 스포츠를 즐겼다. 인기 있는 경기 중 하나가 33번째 올림픽에 추가되었다. 이것은 판크라티온, 다시 말하면 레슬링과 권투의 극한 조합이다. 그리스어로 pankration은 '온전한 힘'을 의미한다. 선수는 금속 징이 박힌 가죽끈을 착용했는데, 이것은 상대 선수에게 끔찍한 상황을 만들어낼 수 있었다. 이 위험한 형태의 레슬링은 시간이나 무게 제한이 없었다. 이 경기에서 오직 두 가지 규칙만 적용되었다. 첫째, 선수들이 엄지손가락으로 눈을 찌르는 것은 허용되지 않았다. 둘째, 깨물면 안 되었다. 그 외의 것들은 정정당당한 방법이라고 여겨졌다. 경기는 권투경기와 동일한 방식으로 결정되었다. 경쟁자들은 둘 중 하나가 쓰러질 때까지 계속했다. 만약 둘 중 누구도 항복하지 않는다면, 두 사람은 누군가 하나가 녹아웃될 때까지 치고 받았다. 가장 강한 자와 가장 확신에 찬 선수들만이 이 경기에 참가했다. 상대방의 손가락을 부러뜨림으로써 그의 별명을 얻은 'Mr. Fingertips'와 레슬링하는 것을 상상해 보라!

VOCA

- surrender 항복하다, 투항하다
- blow 세게 때림, 강타, 충격
- knock out 녹아웃[KO]시키다, 때려눕히다
- fitness 신체 단련, 건강
- superiority 우월성, 우세
- glorify 미화하다, 영웅을 찬양하다
- brink (위험하거나 흥미로운 상황이 발생하기) 직전
- stud 못[징], 작은 금속 단추
- mess 엉망[진창]인 상태, 엉망인 상황
- opponent 상대, 반대자

- gouge 찌르다
- contender 도전자[경쟁자]
- collapse 쓰러지다, 주저앉다, 실패하다, 붕괴하다

20 난도 ★★★ 정답 ①

독해 > 빈칸 완성 > 단어 · 구 · 절

정답의 이유

제시문은 오늘날 과학의 문제점으로 인간이 문제들을 선택하는 것이 아니라, 문제들이 인간에게 강요하는 현상을 지적하고 있다. 일례로 원자 폭탄이 발명된 이후에 수소 폭탄의 발명을 강요하는 것을 들었다. 빈칸은 바로 앞의 단어인 시스템(a system)을 수식하고 있으므로 빈칸에 들어갈 말로 적절한 것은 '인간들이 문제들에 떠밀리는' 형태와 가장 유사한 ① 'makes man its appendix(인류를 그것의 부속물로 만들다)'이다.

오답의 이유

② 안전에 대한 잘못된 인식을 만들다
③ 인류에게 창의적인 도전에 대한 영감을 주다
④ 과학자들에게 시장의 법칙을 지배할 권한을 주다

본문해석

우리 시대에 그 자체의 생명을 가지고 인간을 지배하는 것은 시장의 법칙뿐만 아니라, 과학과 기술의 발전도 그러하다. 수많은 이유로, 오늘날 과학의 문제점들과 구조는 과학자가 그의 문제를 선택하지 않는다는 그런 것이다. 문제들이 스스로 과학자에게 자신들을 강요한다. 그가 한 가지 문제를 해결하면, 그 결과는 그가 더 안심하거나 확신하는 게 아니라, 해결된 한 가지 문제 자리에 10가지의 다른 새로운 문제들이 모습을 드러낸다는 것이다. 그것들은 그에게 그것들을 해결하도록 강요한다. 그는 매우 빠른 속도로 문제를 해결해야 한다. 동일한 내용이 산업 기술에도 적용된다. 과학의 속도는 기술의 속도를 강제한다. 이론 물리학은 우리에게 원자력 에너지를 강요한다. 원자 폭탄의 성공적인 생산은 우리에게 수소 폭탄 제조를 강요한다. 우리는 우리의 문제를 선택하지 못하고, 우리의 생산물을 선택하지 못하고, 우리는 등 떠밀리고, 강요당한다. 무엇에 의해서? 그것을 초월하는 목표와 목적이 없는, <u>인류를 그것의 부속물로 만들어버리는</u> 시스템에 의해서이다.

VOCA

- force (～을 하도록) ～을 강요하다
- secure 안심하는, 안전한, 신뢰할 수 있는
- in place of ～을 대신해서
- theoretical 이론의, 이론상으로 (가능한)
- fission bomb 핵분열 폭탄, 원자 폭탄
- hydrogen bomb 수소 폭탄
- transcend 초월하다
- appendix 부록
- empower 권한을 주다

당신이 저지를 수 있는 가장 큰 실수는, 실수를 할까 두려워하는 것이다.

– 앨버트 하버드 –

PART 3

서울시

영어 | 2024년 서울시 9급

한눈에 훑어보기

✔ 영역 분석

어휘   01   02   03   04   05
5문항, 25%

독해   11   12   13   14   15   16   17   18   19   20
10문항, 50%

어법   08   09   10
3문항, 15%

표현   06   07
2문항, 10%

✔ 빠른 정답

01	02	03	04	05	06	07	08	09	10
③	④	②	④	①	②	②	①	②	①
11	12	13	14	15	16	17	18	19	20
①	③	③	③	④	②	①	③	④	③

✔ 점수 체크

구분	1회독	2회독	3회독
맞힌 문항 수	/ 20	/ 20	/ 20
나의 점수	점	점	점

01 난도 ★☆☆   정답 ③

어휘 > 단어

정답의 이유

밑줄 친 spurn은 '퇴짜 놓다, 거절하다'의 뜻으로, 이와 의미가 가장 가까운 것은 ③ 'decline(거절하다, 사양하다)'이다.

오답의 이유

① 생각하다[예상하다]
② 연기하다, 미루다
④ 비난하다, 매도하다

본문해석

그녀는 유명한 회사로부터 매력적인 일자리 제안을 받은 후에, 창업의 꿈을 추구하기 위해 결국 그것을 거절하기로 결정했다.

VOCA

- attractive 마음을 끄는, 매력적인
- renowned 유명한
- choose ~하기를 원하다[결정하다]
- pursue 추구하다

02 난도 ★☆☆   정답 ④

어휘 > 단어

정답의 이유

밑줄 친 boasted는 '뽐내다, 자랑하다'의 뜻인 boast의 과거(분사)형으로, 이와 의미가 가장 가까운 것은 ④ 'bragged(자랑했다)'이다.

오답의 이유

① 포기했다
② 항복[굴복]했다
③ 포기했다

본문해석

1918년 Red Sox가 Babe Ruth를 Yankees로 트레이드한 이후로, 보스턴 스포츠 팬들은 좋은 점뿐만 아니라 나쁜 점도 받아들이는 법을 알게 되었다. 그들은 다른 어떤 도시보다 더 많은 농구 선수권 대회를 보았지만, 75년 이상 동안 월드 시리즈 타이틀을 자랑하지 못했다.

VOCA

- trade (스포츠에서 선수를) 트레이드하다
- take the good with the bad 좋은 점뿐만 아니라 나쁜 점도 받아들이다

03 난도 ★☆☆ 　　　　　　　　　　정답 ②

어휘 > 단어

정답의 이유

밑줄 친 singular는 '뛰어난, 두드러진'의 뜻으로, 이와 의미가 가장 가까운 것은 ② 'exceptional(이례적일 정도로 우수한, 특출한)'이다.

오답의 이유

① 극히 평범한[인습적인]
③ 전쟁의
④ 복수형의

본문해석

Nell은 문제를 일으키는 데 두드러진 재능이 있다. 다른 날 아침, 그녀는 자신의 다리를 부러뜨리고, 우체국에서 여성을 모욕하고, 식료품점에서 계란을 떨어뜨리고, 침실을 녹색으로 칠하고, 이웃집 앞마당에 있는 큰 단풍나무를 베어 쓰러뜨렸다.

VOCA

• get into trouble　말썽이 나다, 문제를 일으키다
• insult　모욕하다
• cut down　베어 쓰러뜨리다
• maple tree　단풍나무
• front yard　앞뜰, 앞마당

04 난도 ★☆☆ 　　　　　　　　　　정답 ④

어휘 > 단어

정답의 이유

빈칸이 있는 문장에서 '~ which was lengthy and made us feel tedium for quite a while.'이라고 했으므로 빈칸에는 장황하고 (lengthy) 지루한(tedium) 것과 관련된 단어가 들어가야 함을 유추할 수 있다. 따라서 빈칸에 들어갈 말로 적절한 것은 ④ 'platitude (진부한 이야기)'이다.

오답의 이유

① 브레인스토밍
② 경구, 명언
③ 비문[비명]

본문해석

기조연설자는 우리에게 당면한 문제에 대해 혁신적인 아이디어를 제시하는 대신, 진부한 이야기를 장황하게 늘어놓아서 우리가 꽤 오랫동안 지루함을 느끼게 만들었다.

VOCA

• innovative　획기적인
• matter in hand　당면한 문제
• keynote speaker　기조연설자
• bring up　(화제를) 꺼내다
• lengthy　너무 긴, 장황한
• tedium　지루함

05 난도 ★☆☆ 　　　　　　　　　　정답 ①

어휘 > 단어

정답의 이유

빈칸 앞부분에서 'It has rained so little in California for the last six years that forest rangers need to be especially(지난 6년간 캘리포니아에 비가 너무 적게 내려서 산림 경비원들은 특히 ~해야 한다.)'라고 했고, 빈칸 뒷부분에서 'in watching for forest fires(산불을 조심하는 데)'라고 했으므로, 문맥상 빈칸에는 '경계하는'을 의미하는 단어가 들어가야 함을 유추할 수 있다. 따라서 빈칸에 들어갈 말로 적절한 것은 ① 'vigilant(바짝 경계하는, 조금도 방심하지 않는)'이다.

오답의 이유

② 느긋한, 여유 있는
③ 무관심한
④ 산만[산란]해진

본문해석

지난 6년간 캘리포니아에 비가 너무 적게 내려서 산림 경비원들은 산불을 조심하는 데 특히 주의를 기울여야 한다.

VOCA

• forest ranger　산림 감시[경비]원

06 난도 ★☆☆ 　　　　　　　　　　정답 ②

표현 > 일반회화

정답의 이유

A가 'We'll get your order done on time(주문하신 시간에 맞춰 드리겠습니다.)'이라고 하자 B가 'Should I give you a call(제가 전화해야 하나요?)'이라고 물었으므로 빈칸에 들어갈 말로 적절한 것은 ② 'No need for that. Come at 11:00 and I'll have your documents ready(그럴 필요 없어요. 11시에 오시면 서류를 준비해 드릴게요.)'이다.

오답의 이유

① 좋은 고객이시군요. 제가 무엇을 할 수 있는지 알아보겠습니다.
③ 내일 아침이요? 걱정하지 마세요. 정오 전에 서류를 내게 가져다주실 수 있나요?
④ 그건 어려울 것 같아요. 오늘 아침에 완료해야 할 주문이 많아요.

본문해석

A: 기다리게 해서 죄송해요, Ms. Krauss.
B: 음, 오늘은 일이 많으시네요. 더 이상은 붙잡지 않겠어요.
A: 걱정하지 마세요, Ms. Krauss. 주문하신 시간에 맞춰 드리겠습니다.
B: 제가 전화해야 하나요?
A: 그럴 필요 없어요. 11시에 오시면 서류를 준비해 드릴게요.

VOCA

• get a lot on your plate　할 일이 엄청 많다
• No sweat　(감탄사적으로) 걱정마라

07 난도 ★☆☆　　　　　　　　　　정답 ②

표현 > 일반회화

정답의 이유

A가 'Did you see Emily's new haircut(Emily의 새로운 헤어스타일 봤니)?'이라고 물었고, 빈칸 다음에 A가 'I was so surprised. It's so different form before(정말 깜짝 놀랐어. 이전과 너무 다른 모습이야).'이라고 했으므로 빈칸에는 A가 놀란 것과 관련 있는 표현이 들어가야 함을 유추할 수 있다. 따라서 빈칸에 들어갈 말로 적절한 것은 ② 'out of the blue(갑자기, 난데없이)'이다.

오답의 이유

① 하늘을 둥둥 떠다니는 듯한[너무나도 황홀한]
③ 아직 미정인
④ 몸이 좀 안 좋은

본문해석

A: Emily의 새로운 헤어스타일 봤니?
B: 응, 갑자기 머리를 다 잘라버렸어!
A: 정말 깜짝 놀랐어. 이전과 너무 다른 모습이야.
B: 변화가 필요했다고 그녀가 말했어.
A: 음, 확실히 잘 어울려.
B: 맞아, 정말 멋있어 보여!

VOCA

• chop ~ off ~을 (~에서) 잘라내다
• suit 어울리다

08 난도 ★★★　　　　　　　　　　정답 ①

어법 > 정문 찾기

정답의 이유

① '~함에도 불구하고'라는 뜻의 전치사 despite 다음에는 명사 또는 명사상당어구가 와야 하므로, 명사(laboratory data)가 어법상 적절하게 사용되었다. 또한, '~로 여겨지다'의 뜻인 be believed to가 현재완료시제(has been believed to)로 올바르게 사용되었다.

오답의 이유

② 'some of+단수명사'는 단수동사로, 'some of+복수명사'는 복수동사로 수일치해야 하므로 Some of this continued confidence 다음에 단수동사(stems)가 올바르게 사용되었다. 'historical analysis that have been ~'에서 that은 analysis를 수식하는 주격 관계대명사로 analysis가 단수명사이므로 that 다음에 동사 have been → has been이 되어야 한다.
③ 'cannot be certain that ~'은 '~을 확신할 수 없다'의 뜻으로, 이 문장에서 that절은 명사절로 사용되었다. that절의 overlook 다음에 목적어가 없어 수동태가 되어야 하므로 have not overlook → have not been overlooked가 되어야 한다.
④ which 다음에 완전한 문장이 왔으므로 which는 cases를 수식하는 관계대명사가 아니라 관계부사의 역할임을 알 수 있다. 따라서 which → in which가 되어야 한다.

본문해석

집단 사고에 관한 일관성 없고 상당히 희박한 실험실 데이터에도 불구하고, 그 이론은 설명이 가능한 것으로 여겨져 왔다. 이 지속적인 신뢰 중 일부는 의심할 여지 없이 모델의 다양한 가설을 입증하기 위해 발전되어 온 일련의 창의적인 역사적 분석에서 유래한다. 물론, 우리는 몇 가지 이유로 그러한 역사적 분석에 주의해야 하는데, 모순된 사례들이 간과되지 않았다고 확신할 수 없기 때문이다. 그러나 그러한 사례 연구는 선행 조건들이 그 모델에 의해 필요하다고 여겨지는 조건을 생성할 만큼 충분히 강력했던 사례들을 보는 미덕이 있다.

VOCA

• inconsistent 일관성 없는, 내용이 다른[모순되는]
• sparse 드문, (밀도가) 희박한
• explanatory 이유를 밝히는, 설명하기 위한
• potential 가능성이 있는, 잠재적인
• stem 비롯되다, 생기다
• analysis 분석 연구
• substantiate 입증하다
• contradictory 모순되는
• virtue 미덕, 덕목
• antecedent 선행 사건
• deem (~로) 여기다[생각하다]

더 알아보기

관계대명사 vs. 관계부사

• 관계대명사는 문장 속에서 주어, 보어 또는 목적어 역할, 즉 명사를 대신하므로 관계대명사절은 불완전한 문장이다.

예 She never listened to the advice which I gave it to her.
　 (그녀는 내가 그녀에게 했던 조언을 결코 듣지 않았다.)
　 → which는 선행사 advice를 수식하는 목적격 관계대명사로 관계절에서 목적어 역할을 하며, 관계절은 목적어(it)가 없는 불완전한 절이다.

예 I met a student yesterday in the cafeteria who said she knew you.
　 (나는 어제 너를 알고 있다고 말한 한 여학생을 식당에서 만났다.)
　 → who는 선행사 a student를 수식하는 주격 관계대명사로 관계절에서 주어 역할을 하며, 관계절은 주어(a student)가 없는 불완전한 절이다.

• 관계부사는 부사를 대신하므로 관계부사절은 부사가 없어도 가능한 완전한 문장이다.

예 Trees must be fitted for the places where they live.
　 (나무들은 그들이 살고 있는 장소에 맞아야 한다.)
　 → where는 선행사 the places를 수식하는 관계부사로 관계절에서 부사의 역할을 하며, 관계절은 완전한 문장이다. 이때 관계부사 where는 전치사+관계대명사(in which)로 바꿔쓸 수 있다.

어법 > 비문 찾기

정답의 이유

② no matter how 다음에는 형용사/부사가 오고, no matter what 다음에는 명사가 오는데, how 다음에 명사(type)가 왔으므로 no matter how → no matter what이 되어야 한다.

오답의 이유

① 조동사(can) 다음에 동사원형(enjoy)으로 올바르게 사용되었다.

③ That's why는 '그래서 ~하다'의 뜻으로, 'That's why+주어+동사'의 형태로 사용되므로, 어법상 올바르게 사용되었다.

④ 밑줄 친 find는 '목적(~하기 위해서)'을 나타내는 부정사의 부사적 용법으로 올바르게 사용되었다.

본문해석

연구에 따르면 차를 마시는 사람들은 어떤 종류의 차를 선택하든지 심장병, 암, 그리고 스트레스로부터 더 큰 보호를 누릴 수 있다고 한다. 전문가들은 찻잎에 들어있는 산화 방지제가 주요한 건강상의 이점을 준다고 말한다. 그래서 우리는 몇몇 창의적인 요리사들이 전채 요리, 식사, 그리고 디저트와 차를 혼합해서 차 한 잔 이상으로 맛있는 방법을 찾아낸 것에 감탄하고 있다.

VOCA

• enjoy 누리다
• brew (커피·차를) 끓이다[만들다]
• antioxidant 산화[노화] 방지제
• confer 수여[부여]하다
• go beyond ~을 초과하다
• meld 섞다, 혼합하다

더 알아보기

no matter+의문사[how/what]: '아무리 ~ 하든지 간에, ~ 할지라도'

• no matter how+형용사/부사+주어+동사(완전한 문장): no matter how는 however로 바꿔쓸 수 있다.
  예 No matter how *fast* you go, you never move anywhere.
  = However *fast* you go, you never move anywhere.
  (아무리 빨리 간다고 해도 당신은 절대 어느 곳으로도 갈 수 없다.)
  예 No matter how we draw a map, we cannot possibly make it show the world exactly as it is in all its detail, nor would we want it to.
  (우리가 지도를 어떻게 그리든지 간에, 우리는 세상의 모든 상세한 부분을 있는 그대로 정확하게 보여줄 수 없으며 또 그것을 원하지도 않을 것이다.)
• no matter what(의문대명사)+주어+동사(불완전한 문장): what은 의문대명사로, what절의 주어, 목적어, 보어가 될 수 있다.
  예 No matter what you heard, it's not the truth. → what은 heard의 목적어
  (네가 무엇을 들었든지 상관없이, 그것은 진실이 아니다.)

• no matter what(의문형용사)+명사+주어+동사(불완전한 문장): 'what+명사'는 명사구로 what절의 주어, 목적어, 보어가 될 수 있다.
  예 Research shows that tea drinkers can enjoy greater protection from heart disease, cancer, and stress, no matter what type of brew they choose. → what type of brew는 choose의 목적어
  (연구에 따르면 차를 마시는 사람들은 어떤 종류의 차를 선택하든지 간에, 심장병, 암, 그리고 스트레스로부터 더 큰 보호를 누릴 수 있다고 한다.)
  예 One can only show how one came to hold no matter what opinion one does hold. → what opinion은 hold의 목적어
  (어떤 의견을 가지고 있든지 간에, 자신이 어떻게 그런 의견을 갖게 되었는지 단지 보여줄 수 있을 뿐이다.)

어법 > 비문 찾기

정답의 이유

① 밑줄 친 were accompanied는 주어(The rise of the modernist novel and poetry)가 단수이므로 were accompanied → was accompanied가 되어야 한다.

오답의 이유

② 밑줄 친 as we know it은 '우리가 그것을 알고 있는 대로'라는 뜻으로, as가 접속사로 올바르게 사용되었다. 이때 it은 앞에 나오는 literary criticism을 가리킨다.

③ 'very different from the one ~'은 명사(criticism)를 수식하는 형용사절로 앞에 which is가 생략되었고, the one은 criticism을 받으며 전치사(from)의 목적어로 사용되었다.

④ not only A but (also) B는 'A뿐만 아니라 B도'의 뜻으로 A와 B 모두 강조할 때 사용하는 표현이다. 이때 A와 B는 병렬구조로 같은 구조를 가져야 하는데, 밑줄 친 부분에서 in attitude, in vocation으로 올바르게 사용되었다.

본문해석

모더니즘 소설과 시의 등장은 1910년과 1930년 사이에 우리가 현재 알고 있는 대로의 문학비평의 발생에 의해 동반되었다. 이는 19세기에 있었던 문학비평과는 매우 다른 종류의 문학비평이며, 비평이 점차 학문적이고 전문적으로 발전하면서 태도뿐만 아니라 직업적인 면에서도 그러했다.

VOCA

• attitude 태도[자세], 사고방식
• vocation 천직, 소명
• academic 학리적인, 학문의
• technical 전문적인

11 난도 ★★☆

정답 ①

독해 > 글의 일관성 > 글의 순서

정답의 이유

주어진 글에서 '기념행사에서 구성원들의 업적을 축하하고 노고에 대해 말함으로써 사람들에게 기념행사의 의미를 인식하게 한다'고 하였으므로, 문맥상 '기념행사가 진정한 성취를 기반으로 하고, 이와 결부되어 구성원들이 향후 기념행사에 참여하도록 장려받는다'고 말한 (B)가 오는 것이 자연스럽다. 다음으로는 (B) 마지막 문장의 '향후 기념행사(future celebrations)'를 '이 과정(this process)'으로 받는 (A)가 오는 것이 적절하며, (A)의 마지막에서 '~ the member of the group being honored will feel self-conscious and awkward(기념 대상이 된 구성원은 남의 시선을 의식해서 어색해할 수도 있다).'라고 하였으므로, 문맥상 'This is a natural response(이것은 자연스러운 반응인데) ~'로 시작하는 (C)로 이어지는 것이 자연스럽다. 따라서 〈보기〉의 문장 다음에 이어질 글의 순서로 적절한 것은 ① '(B) - (A) - (C)'이다.

본문해석

여러분이 그룹 구성원들의 업적을 축하하기 위해 선택한 처음 몇 번 동안, 그 작은 행사 뒤에 숨겨진 여러분의 생각을 설명하고 싶지도 모른다. 그저 그룹 구성원들의 노고에 대한 용기에 감사하는 여러분의 의도를 말함으로써, 사람들은 그 기념행사의 의미를 인식하게 되고 그것을 덜 무시하게 된다.

(B) 그 기념행사가 진정한 성취를 기반으로 한다는 사실과 결부되어, 그룹 구성원들은 향후 기념행사 참여를 장려받게 될 것이다.

(A) 이 과정을 시작하면 그 단체에서 기념 대상이 된 구성원은 남의 시선을 의식해서 어색해할 수도 있다.

(C) 이것은 자연스러운 반응인데, 특히 서로 간에 잘 모르는 단체, 기념행사 문화가 없는 조직에서 그러하다.

VOCA

- state (정식으로) 말하다[쓰다]
- apt to ~하는 경향이 있다
- dismiss 묵살[일축]하다
- self-conscious 남의 시선을 의식하는
- awkward 어색한
- coupled with ~와 결부된
- authentic 진짜인, 정확한
- encouraged 격려받은, 고무된
- participate 참가하다, 관여하다

12 난도 ★★☆

정답 ③

독해 > 세부 내용 찾기 > 내용 (불)일치

정답의 이유

③ 여섯 번째 문장에서 '~ they are created in response to a pathogen that the body has not seen before(그것들은 인체가 이전에는 보지 못했던 병원균에 대한 대응으로 생성된다는 것이다).'라고 했으므로 글의 내용과 일치하지 않는다.

오답의 이유

① 두 번째 문장에서 'The first line of defense lies in the physical barriers of the skin and mucous membranes, which block and trap invaders(첫 번째 방어선은 침입자를 막고 가두는 피부와 점막의 물리적 장벽에 놓여 있다).'라고 했으므로 글의 내용과 일치한다.

② 세 번째 문장에서 'A second, the innate system, is composed of cells including phagocytes, whose basic job is to eat the invaders(두 번째로, 선천적인 (면역)체계는 포식세포를 포함한 세포들로 구성되어 있는데, 그것들의 기본적인 임무는 침입자를 잡아먹는 것이다).'라고 했으므로 글의 내용과 일치한다.

④ 제시문의 마지막 부분에서 '~ it memorizes the antigens ~ The next time they come along, the body hits back quicker and harder(적응 체계는 항원을 기억한다 ~ 다음에 그것들이 오면, 인체는 더욱더 신속하고 강력하게 반격한다).'라고 했으므로 글의 내용과 일치한다.

본문해석

인체 면역체계의 임무는 수조 개의 면역세포와 전문화된 분자들에 의해 수행된다. 첫 번째 방어선은 침입자를 막고 가두는 피부와 점막의 물리적 장벽에 놓여 있다. 두 번째로, 선천적인 (면역)체계는 포식세포를 포함한 세포들로 구성되어 있는데, 그것들의 기본적인 임무는 침입자를 잡아먹는 것이다. 이러한 면역세포들 외에도, 많은 화합물들이 감염과 부상에 반응하여 병원균을 파괴하고 세포조직을 복구하기 시작한다. 인체의 세 번째 방어선은 최종적이고 보다 구체적인 대응이다. (병원균에 맞서 싸우는) 인체의 정예 전투부대는 임무에 대해 훈련받는데, 다시 말하면, 그것들은 인체가 이전에는 보지 못했던 병원균에 대한 대응으로 생성된다는 것이다. 일단 인체의 한 부분에서 활성화되면, 적응 체계는 전체적으로 기능하며, 항원(면역체계 반응을 일으키는 물질)을 기억한다. 다음에 그것들이 오면, 인체는 더욱더 신속하고, 강력하게 반격한다.

VOCA

- immune system 면역체계
- carry out 수행하다
- trillion 1조
- immune cell 면역세포
- specialized 전문적인, 전문화된
- molecule 분자
- physical barrier 물리적 장벽
- innate 선천적인, 타고난
- chemical compound 화합물
- infection 감염, 전염병
- tissue (세포들로 이뤄진) 조직
- activated 활성화된
- memorize 기억하다, 암기하다
- provoke (특정한 반응을) 유발하다
- come along 함께 가다[오다]
- hit back 응수하다[되받아치다]

13 난도 ★★☆　　　　　　　　　　정답 ③

독해 > 글의 일관성 > 문장 삽입

정답의 이유

제시문의 처음부터 ③ 이전까지는 경영의 정의와 경영 과정에 영향을 주는 요인에 대한 내용이고, ③ 다음부터 끝까지는 국제 기업에 영향을 주는 환경적 요인에 대한 내용이다. ③ 다음 문장의 'These business enterprises(이들 비즈니스 기업)'은 〈보기〉의 '~ enterprises that attain their goals and objectives across unique multicultural, multinational boundaries(고유한 다문화, 다국적 경계를 넘어 그들의 목표와 목적을 달성하는 기업).'으로 받아 이러한 기업이 국제 기업, 다국적 기업(MNC) 또는 글로벌 기업이라 불린다고 설명하고 있으므로 〈보기〉의 문장이 들어갈 위치로 적절한 것은 ③이다.

본문해석

경영이라는 용어는 다수의 서양 교과서에서 다른 개인들과 함께, 그리고 다른 개인들을 통해 효율적으로 활동을 완료하는 과정으로 정의된다. 그 과정은 경영자들이 참여하는 기능이나 주요 활동으로 이루어진다. 이러한 기능이나 활동은 보통 계획, 조직, 인력 배치, 조정(주도적이고 동기부여를 하는), 통제라는 라벨을 붙여 분류된다. 그 경영 과정은 기술적, 인구통계학적, 지리적 요인뿐만 아니라 주주, 채권자, 고객, 직원, 정부, 지역사회를 포함하는 조직이 속한 자국의 환경에 의해 영향을 받는다. 국제 경영은 고유한 다문화, 다국적 경계를 넘어 그들의 목표와 목적을 달성하는 기업의 경영자들에 의해 적용된다. 이러한 비즈니스 기업은 일반적으로 국제 기업, 다국적 기업(MNC) 또는 글로벌 기업이라고 불린다. 이것이 의미하는 바는 그 과정이 조직이 기반을 두고 있는 환경에 의해 영향을 받을 뿐만 아니라, 조직이 사업 활동을 수행하는 국가 또는 복수 국가 내 존재하는 윤리와 사회적 책임에 대한 견해를 포함한 고유한 문화에 의해서도 영향을 받는다는 것이다.

VOCA

- label 라벨을 붙여 분류[명시]하다
- staffing 직원 채용
- shareholder 주주
- creditor 채권자
- demographic 인구 통계(학)의
- enterprise 기업, 회사
- attain 달성하다, 얻다
- conduct 실시하다, 수행하다

14 난도 ★★☆　　　　　　　　　　정답 ③

독해 > 글의 일관성 > 문장 삽입

정답의 이유

〈보기〉 문장이 'This kind of development(이러한 종류의 개발)'로 시작하고 있으므로 새로운 개발을 소개하는 내용 다음에 온다는 것을 유추할 수 있다. ③ 앞 문장에서 NASA가 우주기술을 사용해서 위험한 양의 일산화탄소를 감지할 수 있을 뿐만 아니라, 실제로 그 유독가스를 인체에 무해한 이산화탄소로 산화시킬 수 있는 에어컨 시스템을 개발했다고 했고, ③ 다음 문장에서 'In addition to helping people to have clean air, ~'라며 공기를 정화하는 것 이외에 깨끗한 물을 이용하게 쉽게 만들어 주는 것 또한 중요하다고 하였으므로 〈보기〉의 문장이 들어갈 위치는 ③이 적절하다.

본문해석

스핀오프(spinoff) 기술은 우리의 집과 지역사회를 살기에 더 안전하고 편안한 장소로 만드는 데 도움을 줄 수 있다. 대다수 사람들은 우리들의 집에 일산화탄소가 축적되면 매우 위험할 수 있다는 사실을 알고 있다. 이것은 결함이 있는 용광로나 벽난로에서 나올 수 있다. 그 결과, 일부 사람들은 자신들의 집에 일산화탄소 감지기를 가지고 있지만, 이러한 감지기는 일산화탄소 수준이 안전하지 않을 때만 경보를 발한다. 그러나 우주기술을 사용하여, NASA는 위험한 양의 일산화탄소를 감지할 수 있을 뿐만 아니라, 실제로 그 유독가스를 인체에 무해한 이산화탄소로 산화시킬 수 있는 에어컨 시스템을 개발했다. 이러한 종류의 개발은 우리에게 안전 위험 요소를 제거하는 것이 그것을 감지하는 경보를 만드는 것보다 훨씬 더 낫다는 것을 깨닫게 한다. 사람들이 깨끗한 공기를 갖게 도와주는 것 외에, 깨끗한 물을 이용하기 쉽게 하는 것도 모든 사람에게 매우 중요하다. NASA 공학자들은 우주에서 우주 비행사들이 마실 수 있는 깨끗한 물을 위한 더 나은 시스템을 만들기 위해 민간 회사들과 협력해 오고 있다. 우주 비행사들을 위해 개발된 이 시스템은 사용 가능한 물을 신속하고 감당 가능한 비용으로 정화할 수 있다. 이것은 지구상에서 외딴 지역 또는 물이 부족하거나 오염된 개발지역에서 살고 있는 사람들에게 중요한 혜택이다.

VOCA

- carbon monoxide(CO) 일산화탄소
- buildup 강화, 증강
- faulty 결점이 있는, 불완전한
- furnace 아궁이, 난로, 용광로
- alert 알리다, 경보를 발하다
- oxidize 산화시키다, 녹슬게 하다
- toxic gas 유독가스
- hazard 위험 (요소)
- affordably 알맞게, 감당할 수 있게
- cleanse 세척하다
- scarce 부족한, 드문
- polluted 오염된, 더럽혀진

15 난도 ★★☆　　　　　　　　　　　　정답 ④

독해 > 빈칸 완성 > 연결어

정답의 이유

(A) 앞 문장에서 'Unfortunately, many antibiotics prescribed to people and to animals are unnecessary(불행하게도, 사람들과 동물들에게 처방되는 많은 항생제는 불필요하다).'라고 했고, (A) 다음에서 항생제 남용과 오용은 약제내성균의 생성을 돕는다고 했으므로 빈칸 (A)에는 첨가의 의미인 Furthermore가 적절하다.

(B) 앞 문장에서 'When used properly, antibiotics can help destroy disease-causing bacteria(적절하게 사용될 경우, 항생제는 질병을 일으키는 박테리아를 파괴하는 데 도움이 될 수 있다).'라고 했고, (B) 다음에서 독감과 같은 바이러스 감염에 걸렸을 경우 항생제를 복용하면, 그 약은 여러분을 아프게 만드는 바이러스에 영향을 끼치지 않을 것이라고 했으므로 빈칸 (B)에는 서로 반대되는 내용을 연결하는 접속사 However가 적절하다.

본문해석

항생제는 사람들에게 가장 흔하게 처방되는 약품 중 하나다. 항생제는 패혈성 인후염, 일부 유형의 폐렴, 눈 감염, 귀 감염과 같은 박테리아 감염에 효과적이다. 하지만 이 약들은 감기나 독감의 원인이 되는 바이러스에는 전혀 효과가 없다. 불행하게도, 사람들과 동물들에게 처방되는 많은 항생제는 불필요하다. (A) 게다가, 항생제 남용과 오용은 약제내성균의 생성을 돕는다. 어떻게 그런 일이 일어나는지는 다음과 같다. 적절하게 사용될 경우, 항생제는 질병을 일으키는 박테리아를 파괴하는 데 도움이 될 수 있다. (B) 하지만, 독감과 같은 바이러스 감염에 걸렸을 때 항생제를 복용하면, 그 약은 여러분을 아프게 만드는 바이러스에 영향을 주지 않을 것이다.

VOCA

• antibiotic　항생제
• prescribe　처방하다
• bacterial infection　박테리아 감염
• strep throat　패혈성 인후염
• pneumonia　폐렴
• work　(약이 사람에게) 잘 듣다, 효과가 있다
• overuse　남용
• misuse　오용, 악용
• drug-resistant bacteria　약제내성균

16 난도 ★★☆　　　　　　　　　　　　정답 ②

독해 > 대의 파악 > 제목, 주제

정답의 이유

제시문은 정치가 행정의 많은 부분을 차지한다는 내용으로, 입법 과정에서 상당한 지식을 가진 행정관들이 중요한 역할을 하고 있으며, 정책 입안에서 동반자 관계가 될 가능성이 높다고 했다. 또한, 다섯 번째 문장에서 'Legislation, for instance, is written by public administrators as much as by legislators(예를 들어, 법률 제정은 입법자들만큼 행정관들에 의해서도 작성된다).'라고 했고, 마지막 문장에서 'Furthermore, laws are interpreted by public administrators in their execution(게다가 법률은 법률 집행에서 행정관들에 의해 해석되는데) ~'이라고 했으므로 글의 제목으로 적절한 것은 ② 'Public Administrators' Surprising Influence in a Political System(정치 체제에서 행정관들의 놀라운 영향력)'이다.

오답의 이유

① 정치에서 예측 불가능한 상황에 대처하는 방법
③ 행정으로부터 정치를 분리하려는 반복적 시도
④ 정치와 행정이 분리할 수 없다는 관점의 허점

본문해석

정치와 행정이 분리될 수 있다는 가정은 결국 이상주의적(비현실적)이라고 무시되었다. Wilson과 Goodnow의 정치와 무관한 공공 행정에 대한 개념은 비현실적인 것으로 판명되었다. 더 현실적인 관점인 이른바 '정치학파'는 정치가 행정의 많은 부분을 차지한다는 것이다. 정치학파는 다양한 집단이 목소리를 내는 다원적인 정치 체제에서 행정관들이 상당한 지식을 사용하여 핵심 역할을 하고 있다고 주장한다. 예를 들어, 법률 제정은 입법자들만큼 행정관들에 의해서도 작성된다. 정부 관료제는 정치 과정에서 다른 참여자들과 마찬가지로 자신의 이익을 위한 지지를 이끌어낼 수 있으며, 행정관들도 정책 입안에 대한 동반자 관계의 일부가 될 가능성이 높다. 게다가 법률은 법률 집행에서 행정관들에 의해 해석되는데, 이것은 많은 경우 예측하지 못한 뜻밖의 시나리오를 포함한다.

VOCA

• assumption　가정, 추정
• disregard　~을 묵살[무시]하다, ~에 주의하지 않다
• utopian　이상향의, 이상적이지만 비현실적인
• apolitical　정치에 무관심한, 어떤 정파[정당]에 관련되지 않은
• public administration　공공 행정
• unrealistic　비현실적인, 비현실주의의
• pluralistic　여러 직업을 겸한
• diverse　가지각색의, 다양한
• legislation　법률의 제정, 입법 행위
• legislator　입법자, 국회[의회]의원
• public bureaucracy　정부 관료제
• engender　(어떤 감정 · 상황을) 낳다[불러일으키다]
• policymaking　정책 입안
• partnership　동반자 관계
• unforeseen　예측하지 못한, 뜻밖의

17 난도 ★★☆　　　　　　　　　　　　　　정답 ①

독해 > 대의 파악 > 제목, 주제

정답의 이유

첫 번째 문장에서 'We are living in perhaps the most exciting times in all of human history(우리는 아마 인류 역사상 가장 흥미로운 시기에 살고 있을 것이다).'라고 한 다음에, 세 번째 문장에서 'Industries are being completely restructured to become better, faster, stronger, and safer(산업은 더 좋고, 더 빠르고, 더 강하고, 더 안전하도록 완전히 재구성되고 있다).'라고 했다. 그리고 마지막 부분에서 가까운 미래에 우리를 건강하게 해주는 로봇 외과의사, 우리의 상품을 배달하는 자율주행 트럭, 그리고 긴 하루를 마친 후 우리를 즐겁게 해주는 가상 세계와 같은 상상 속 놀라운 일들이 일상화될 것이라고 했으므로 글의 제목으로 적절한 것은 ① 'The Era of Unprecedented Technological Advancements(유례없는 기술 발전의 시대)'이다.

오답의 이유

② 현대산업의 불완전한 해결책과의 고투
③ 기술의 발전에 대한 역사적 관점
④ 동시대 산업의 침체 상태

본문해석

우리는 아마 인류 역사상 가장 흥미로운 시기에 살고 있을 것이다. 오늘날 우리가 목격하고 있는 기술의 발전은 한때 과학 소설과 판타지 영역에서만 나타났던 장치, 시스템 및 서비스를 생산하는 새로운 산업을 일으키고 있다. 산업은 더 좋고, 더 빠르고, 더 강하고, 더 안전하도록 완전히 재구성되고 있다. 당신은 더 이상 '충분히 가까운' 무언가에 만족할 필요가 없는데, 맞춤화가 여러분이 원하고 필요로 하는 것을 정확하게 제공하는 수준에 도달하고 있기 때문이다. 우리는 유전학 발전의 가능성, 나노 기술, 많은 질병을 치료하고 심지어 노화 과정 자체를 늦출 수 있는 다른 기술을 공개하려는 시점에 있다. 그러한 발전은 이런 놀라운 것들을 생산하는 별개의 분야에서의 발견 덕분이다. 그리 머지않은 미래에, 우리를 건강하게 해주는 로봇 외과의사, 우리의 상품을 배달하는 자율주행 트럭, 그리고 긴 하루를 마친 후 우리를 즐겁게 해주는 가상 세계와 같은 상상 속 놀라운 일들이 일상화될 것이다. 우리가 완벽함을 포착하려는 시기가 있다면, 그것은 지금이고 그 가속도가 붙었을 뿐이다.

VOCA

- advance　진전, 발전
- witness　목격하다
- give birth to　～을 일으키다, ～의 원인이 되다
- realm　영역[범위]
- restructure　구조를 조정하다[개혁하다]
- settle for　～으로 만족하다, ～을 (불만스럽지만) 받아들이다
- customization　주문에 따라 만듦
- be on the verge of　～하기 직전에
- genetic　유전의, 유전학의
- enhancement　고양, 증진
- nanotechnology　나노 기술

- surgeon　외과의사
- commonplace　보통인, 흔해 빠진
- momentum　탄력[가속도]

18 난도 ★★☆　　　　　　　　　　　　　　정답 ③

독해 > 빈칸 완성 > 단어·구·절

정답의 이유

제시문은 감정적인 힘은 감정을 보이지 않고 억누르는 것이 아니라 감정을 조절하는 기술을 갖는 것이라는 내용을 담고 있다. 네 번째 문장에서 '~ you can develop the courage you need to work through uncomfortable feelings, like anxiety and sadness(여러분은 불안과 슬픔 같은 불편한 감정을 극복하는 용기를 키울 수 있습니다).'라고 한 다음에 다섯 번째 문장에서 감정적인 힘을 가진 사람은 언제 그들의 감정 상태를 전환해야 하는지를 알 것이라고 했다. 빈칸이 있는 문장의 앞부분에서 그들은 '힘든 감정을 견디는 능력(the ability to tolerate difficult emotions)'을 갖고 있는데, 그들은 '그것들을 억누르지 않는다(not suppressing them)'고 했으므로, 문맥상 빈칸에는 not suppressing them과 동일한 의미를 가진 단어가 들어가야 함을 추론할 수 있다. 따라서 빈칸에 들어갈 말로 적절한 것은 ③ 'embracing(포용하는)'이다.

오답의 이유

① 과장하는
② 추구하는
④ 무시하는

본문해석

감정적인 힘은 불굴의 정신을 유지하는 것, 금욕적인 것, 또는 감정을 전혀 드러내지 않는 것이 아니라, 그 반대이다. "감정적인 힘은 감정조절에 필요한 기술을 갖는 것에 대한 것입니다."라고 심리치료사 Amy Morin이 말한다. "여러분은 항상 행복을 추구할 필요는 없습니다. 대신, 여러분은 불안과 슬픔 같은 불편한 감정을 극복하는 용기를 키울 수 있습니다." 예를 들어, 감정적인 힘이 있는 사람은 언제 그들의 감정 상태를 전환해야 하는지 알 것이라고 Morin은 말한다. "만약 불안한 감정이 그들에게 쓸모가 없다면, 그들은 자신들을 진정시키기 위해 사용할 수 있는 전략을 갖고 있습니다. 그들은 또한 힘든 감정을 견디는 능력이 있지만, 그 감정들을 억누르지 않고 그것들을 <u>포용함</u>으로써 그렇게 합니다. 그들은 외로움과 같은 고통스러운 감정에서 주의를 딴 데로 돌리지 않습니다."

VOCA

- stiff upper lip　불굴의 정신
- stoic　금욕주의자, 극기심이 강한 사람
- regulate　조절[조정]하다
- psychotherapist　심리치료사
- shift　이동하다[되다], 자세를 바꾸다
- calm　진정시키다
- tolerate　참다, 견디다
- suppress　(감정·감정 표현을) 참다[억누르다]
- distract from　～에서 (주의를) 딴 데로 돌리다

독해 > 빈칸 완성 > 단어 · 구 · 절

정답의 이유

제시문은 유기체로서의 곰팡이가 지구상에서 식물과 인간에게 끼치는 영향력을 설명하는 내용으로, 전반부에서는 곰팡이가 식물의 성장에 매우 중요한 역할을 하고 있다고 했다. 빈칸 다음 문장에서 일본 도쿄의 거리를 모형으로 한 미로에 곰팡이를 방출하자 하루 만에 도시 중심부 사이에서 가장 효율적인 경로를 찾았으며, 본능적으로 기존 철도 네트워크와 거의 동일한 경로를 재현했다고 했으므로, 빈칸에 들어갈 적절한 말은 ④ 'think(생각하다)'이다.

오답의 이유

① 모으다

② 사육하다[재배하다]

③ 즐기다

본문해석

다수의 작은 유기체들처럼, 곰팡이는 종종 간과되지만, 지구상에서 그들의 중요성은 지대하다. 식물들이 물을 떠나 육지에서 성장할 수 있었던 것은 오직 수백만 년 동안 식물의 뿌리 시스템으로 역할을 다했던 곰팡이와 협력했기 때문이다. 심지어 오늘날에도, 식물의 약 90%와 전 세계적으로 거의 모든 수목이 곰팡이에 의존해서 사는데, 곰팡이는 바위와 다른 물질들을 분해함으로써 중요한 미네랄을 공급한다. 그것들은 또한 숲을 박멸하고 인류를 죽이는 재앙이 될 수도 있다. 때때로, 그것들은 심지어 <u>생각하는</u> 것처럼 보인다. 일본의 연구원들이 도쿄의 거리를 모형으로 만든 미로에 점액 곰팡이를 방출하자, 그 곰팡이들은 하루 만에 도시의 중심부들 사이에서 가장 효율적인 경로를 찾았으며, 기존 철도망과 거의 동일한 일련의 경로를 본능적으로 재현했다. 이케아의 소형 바닥 지도에 넣었을 때도, 그것들은 출구로 가는 최단 경로를 재빨리 찾았다.

VOCA

• organism 유기체

• fungi fungus(균류, 곰팡이류)의 복수

• overlook 간과하다

• planetary 행성의, 지구(상)의

• significance 중요성, 중대성

• outsize 대형의

• collaboration 공동작업[연구]

• act as ~으로서의 역할을 하다[맡다]

• supply 공급하다

• crucial 중대한, 결정적인

• mineral 무기물, 미네랄

• break down 고장나다, 실패하다, 아주 나빠지다

• substance 물질, 실체, 본질

• scourge 재앙, 골칫거리

• eradicate 근절하다, 뿌리뽑다

• slime 끈적끈적한 물질, 점액

• mold 곰팡이

• maze 미로

• model on ~을 본떠서 만들다

• identical 동일한, 똑같은

독해 > 빈칸 완성 > 단어 · 구 · 절

정답의 이유

제시문에서 종의 멸종에는 두 가지 이유가 있는데, 그중 하나는 '실제 멸종(real extinction)'이라고 했다. 세 번째 문장에서 화석의 경우 실제 멸종은 '유사 별종(pseudoextinction)'과 구별되어야 한다고 했고, 네 번째 문장에서 '~ but only because of an error or artifact in the evidence, and not because the underlying lineage really ceased to exist(유사 별종은 단지 그 흔적에서의 오류 또는 인공물 때문일 뿐이고, 근원적인 혈통이 실제 소멸했기 때문이 아니라고)'라고 유사 별종을 정의했다. 빈칸 앞의 'For instance(예를 들면)'로 미루어 빈칸에는 유사 별종의 예시가 들어감을 유추할 수 있다. 따라서 빈칸에 들어갈 적절한 말은 ③ 'a continuously evolving lineage may change its taxonomic name(계속 진화하는 혈통은 그것의 분류학적 명칭을 바꿀 수도 있다)'이다.

오답의 이유

① 다수의 지역에서 멸종의 단서가 발견되고 있다

② 어떤 혈통은 화석 기록에서 일시적으로 사라질 수도 있다

④ 일부 서로 다른 혈통들이 완전히 파악되었다

본문해석

종(또는 더 높은 분류군)은 두 가지 이유로 멸종할 수 있다. 하나는 혈통이 사라지고 후손이 없다는 점에서 '실제' 멸종이다. 현대의 종에게 그 의미는 명백하지만, 화석에 있어서는 실제 멸종과 '유사 멸종'이 구별되어야 한다. 유사 멸종은 그 분류군이 멸종한 것처럼 보이지만, 그것은 단지 흔적에서의 오류 또는 인공물 때문일 뿐이고, 근원적인 혈통이 실제 소멸했기 때문이 아니라는 것을 의미한다. 예를 들어, <u>계속적으로 진화하는 혈통은 그것의 분류학적 명칭을 바꿀 수도 있다</u>. 혈통이 진화함에 따라 이후의 형태는 이전의 형태와 충분히 다르게 보일 수 있어서, 연속적인 번식 혈통이 있을지라도, 분류학자는 그것을 다른 종으로 분류할 수 있다. 이것은 종이 표형적으로 분류되었기 때문이거나 분류학자가 단지 소수의 표본만 가지고 있는데, 일부는 혈통 초기의 것이고, 일부는 혈통 후기의 것이어서, 연속적인 혈통을 발견할 수 없기 때문일지도 모른다.

VOCA

• species 종

• taxa taxon(분류군)의 복수

• in the sense that ~라는 점에서

• unambiguous 모호하지 않은[분명한/확실한]

• pseudoextinction 유사[의사] 멸종(한 종(種)이 전혀 다른 종으로 발전하는 것)

• artifact 인공물

• underlying 기초를 이루는, 근원적인

• taxonomic 분류법의, 분류학의

- evolve 진화하다
- taxonomist 분류학자
- phenetic system 표형적 분류. 다수의 형질이 총체적으로 가지는 유사성의 정도를 기본으로 하여 생물집단의 종류의 구성을 분류하는 방법
- classify 분류[구분]하다
- specimen 표본, 시료
- undetectable 발견[탐지, 검출]될 수 없는

영어 | 2022년 서울시 9급

한눈에 훑어보기

✔ 영역 분석

어휘   01 02 03 04 05
5문항, 25%

독해   12 13 14 15 16 17 18 19 20
9문항, 45%

어법   07 08 09 10 11
5문항, 25%

표현   06
1문항, 5%

✔ 빠른 정답

01	02	03	04	05	06	07	08	09	10
①	④	②	①	④	④	②	②	③	①

11	12	13	14	15	16	17	18	19	20
④	③	③	②	④	③	①	③	②	③

✔ 점수 체크

구분	1회독	2회독	3회독
맞힌 문항 수	/ 20	/ 20	/ 20
나의 점수	점	점	점

01 난도 ★☆☆   정답 ①

어휘 > 단어

정답의 이유

밑줄 친 renowned는 '유명한'이라는 뜻으로, 이와 의미가 가장 가까운 것은 ① 'famous(유명한)'이다.

오답의 이유

② 용감무쌍한
③ 초기의
④ 악명 높은

본문해석

Roald Amundsen이 이끄는 노르웨이인들이 1911년 1월 14일 남극의 Whales 만에 도착했다. 개 무리와 함께, 그들은 영국인들을 남극까지 경주하게 할 준비를 했다. 유명한 북극 탐험가 Fridtjof Nansen이 대여한 Amundsen의 배 *Fram*은 당시 정예의 극지방 선박이었다.

VOCA

- arrive in ～에 도착하다
- race (동물·자동차를) 경주하게 하다
- loan 빌려주다, 대여하다
- Arctic 북극의, 북극 지방의
- explorer 답사[탐사]자, 탐험가
- polar 북극[남극]의, 극지의
- vessel (대형) 선박[배]

02 난도 ★☆☆   정답 ④

어휘 > 단어

정답의 이유

밑줄 친 lucid는 '명쾌한, 명료한'이라는 뜻으로, 이와 의미가 가장 가까운 것은 ④ 'perspicuous(명쾌한)'이다.

오답의 이유

① 말이 많은
② 느릿느릿 움직이는, 부진한
③ 차분한[얌전한]

본문해석

그녀는 발표에서 이 조직의 일원으로서 자신의 미래 계획에 대해 명쾌한 설명을 할 것이다.

VOCA

- presentation 발표[설명], 프레젠테이션
- account 기술, 설명, 해석
- organization 조직(체), 단체, 기구

03 난도 ★☆☆　　　　　　　　　　　정답 ②

어휘 > 단어

정답의 이유

빈칸 다음에 명사(skills)가 있으므로, 빈칸에는 '기술(skills)'을 목적어로 취하는 동사가 와야 하는데, 끝부분의 부사구(in order to be competitive and become successful)로 미루어 문맥상 빈칸에는 사람들이 경쟁력을 갖추고 성공하기 위해 직장에서 해야 할 필요가 있는 의미의 동사가 들어가야 함을 유추할 수 있다. 따라서 빈칸에 들어갈 말로 가장 적절한 것은 ② 'accumulate(축적하다)'이다.

오답의 이유

① 폐지하다

③ 줄이다, 약화시키다

④ 격려하다, 고립시키다

본문해석

사람들은 직장에서 경쟁력을 갖추고 성공하기 위해 기술을 축적할 필요가 있다.

VOCA

- need to ~을 할 필요가 있다
- competitive 경쟁력 있는, 뒤지지 않는
- successful 성공한, 성공적인

04 난도 ★★★　　　　　　　　　　　정답 ①

어휘 > 단어

정답의 이유

빈칸 앞에 because of가 있으므로, 빈칸에는 Manhattan이 어쩔 수 없이 하늘로 확장되어야 했던 '이유'와 관련된 단어가 들어가야 함을 짐작할 수 있다. 빈칸 다음에 'any other direction in which to grow'가 있으므로, 문맥상 성장할 다른 방향이 '없음(absence)'이 자연스럽다. 따라서 빈칸에 들어갈 말로 가장 적절한 것은 ① 'absence(없음)'이다.

오답의 이유

② 결정

③ 노출

④ 선발, 선택

본문해석

Manhattan은 성장할 다른 방향이 없기 때문에 어쩔 수 없이 하늘로 확장될 수밖에 없었다. 이것은 다른 무엇보다도 그것의 물리적인 장엄함에 책임이 있다.

VOCA

- be compelled to 하는 수 없이 ~하다
- expand 확대[확장/팽창]되다
- skyward 하늘 쪽으로, 위로
- be responsible for ~에 책임이 있다
- physical 물질의, 물질[물리]적인
- majesty 장엄함, 위풍당당함

05 난도 ★☆☆　　　　　　　　　　　정답 ④

어휘 > 단어

정답의 이유

빈칸 다음에서 'using someone else's exact words or ideas(다른 사람의 단어나 아이디어를 출처를 밝히지 않고 그대로 사용하는 것)'이라고 했으므로, 빈칸에 들어갈 말로 가장 적절한 것은 ④ 'plagiarism(표절)'이다.

오답의 이유

① 인용

② 발표

③ 수정

본문해석

표절은 다른 사람의 단어나 아이디어를 여러분의 글에 그대로 사용하고, 원작자나 여러분이 그것을 발견한 책, 잡지, 비디오, 팟캐스트, 웹사이트를 밝히지 않는 것이다.

VOCA

- exact 정확한, 정밀한
- name 이름을 대다[밝히다/확인하다]
- podcast 팟캐스트, 인터넷망을 통해 다양한 콘텐츠를 제공하는 서비스

06 난도 ★☆☆　　　　　　　　　　　정답 ④

표현 > 일반회화

정답의 이유

대화에서 A가 지난 월요일에 산 재킷의 지퍼가 고장 나서 환불을 원한다고 했는데, 지퍼를 고쳐주겠다고 한 B의 대답은 흐름상 어색하다. 따라서 대화 중 가장 어색한 것은 ④이다.

본문해석

① A: 부탁이 있어요.

　　B: 물론이죠. 무엇인가요?

② A: 제 계좌를 해지해야 할 것 같아요.

　　B: 네, 이 양식을 작성해 주세요.

③ A: 아름다운 결혼식이었어요.

　　B: 동감이에요. 그리고 결혼한 그 커플이 서로 너무 잘 맞아보였어요.

④ A: 지난 월요일 이 재킷을 샀는데 벌써 지퍼가 고장 났어요. 환불하고 싶어요.

　　B: 알겠습니다. 지퍼를 고쳐드릴게요.

07 난도 ★★★ 정답 ②

어법 > 정문 찾기

정답의 이유

② would rather A than B는 'B하기보다는 차라리 A하겠다'라는 뜻으로, would rather와 than 다음에 동사원형이 나와야 한다. would rather 다음에 동사원형(enter)이 왔고, than 다음에 enter the labor force가 생략되었으므로 어법상 적절하게 사용되었다.

오답의 이유

① 관계대명사 which 다음에 완전한 문장이 왔고, 문맥상 '그 인구의 가족소득'이라는 뜻이어야 한다. 따라서 소유격 관계대명사가 들어가야 하므로 which → whose가 되어야 한다.

③ 난이형용사(hard)는 'It+be+난이형용사+의미상 주어(for+목적격)+to부정사' 구조로 사용해야 하므로, that people pick up → for people to pick up이 되어야 한다.

④ 전치사 Despite 다음에는 절이 올 수 없으므로, Despite → Although[Though]가 되어야 한다.

본문해석

① 빈곤율은 가족소득이 절대수준 이하로 떨어지는 인구 비율이다.

② 당연히, 대졸자들은 경기가 축소되는 해보다 경기가 확장되는 해에 노동력에 진입할 것이다.

③ 사람들은 경제에 관한 새로 보고된 통계를 보지 않고는 신문을 집어 들기 어렵다.

④ 평균 소득 성장이 지속되고 있음에도 불구하고, 빈곤율은 감소하지 않았다.

더 알아보기

난이형용사 구문

- 난이형용사의 종류

난이도	easy, simple, hard, tough, difficult, impossible 등
고락	joy, painful, pleasant, amusing, interesting, delightful, entertaining, comfortable 등
우량도	super, wonderful, fantastic, great, miserable, terrible, awful 등
안전도	safe, dangerous, unhealthy 등

- 난이형용사 구문 유형

It(가주어)+be+난이형용사+to부정사+목적어 (○)
= 일반주어+be+난이형용사+to부정사 (목적어가 주어 자리로 이동)

예 We were easy to find *the house*. (×)
→ *The house* was easy to find. (○)
= It was for us easy to find *the house*. (○)
(그 집을 찾는 것은 쉬웠다.)

- to부정사의 의미상의 주어가 문장의 주어가 될 수 없다.

It(가주어)+be+난이형용사+to부정사+전치사
= 일반주어+be+난이형용사+to부정사+전치사(전치사 생략 불가)

예 *Jane's plan* was hard for me to object. (×)
→ It was hard for me to object to *Jane's plan*. (○)
= *Jane's plan* was hard for me to object to. (○)
(나는 Jane의 계획에 반대하기 어려웠다.)

- that절을 가져올 수 없다(to부정사만 가능).

예 It is hard that we please him. (×)
→ It is hard for us to please him. (○)
(우리가 그를 기쁘게 해주기는 어렵다.)

- 수동형은 to부정사로 쓸 수 없다.

예 The problem is easy to be solved. (×)
→ The problem is easy to solve. (○)
(그 문제는 풀기에 쉬웠다.)

08 난도 ★★☆ 정답 ②

어법 > 비문 찾기

정답의 이유

② have가 사역동사로 쓰일 경우, 목적어와 목적격 보어의 관계가 능동이면 원형부정사를, 수동이면 과거분사(p.p.)를 사용한다. 여기서 그녀의 장소는 '청소되는' 것이므로, cleaning → cleaned가 되어야 한다.

오답의 이유

① 'with+목적어+현재분사[과거분사]' 분사구문으로 부대상황을 나타내고 있으며, '남은' 것이 아무것도 없는 수동의 의미이므로 과거분사(left)가 적절하게 사용되었다. 'she would have to cling to that which ~'에서 that은 대명사이자 관계대명사

which의 선행사이며, 관계사절(which had robbed her.)의 시제가 그것에 매달려야 했던 시점인 과거시제보다 이전이므로 과거완료(had robbed) 시제가 적절하게 사용되었다.

③ 부사절(While she was alive)의 분사구문에서 While she being이 생략되어 Alive만 남은 구조이다.

④ 'accuse A of B'는 'A를 B의 이유로 비난[기소]하다'라는 뜻으로, 전치사 of가 적절하게 쓰였다.

본문해석

① 아무것도 남지 않은 상태에서, 그녀는 그녀를 강탈했던 그것에 매달려야만 했을 것이다.

② 그녀에게 집을 청소하라고 전해주세요.

③ 살아 있는 동안, 그녀는 전통이자 의무이자 보살핌이었다.

④ 여자에게 악취가 난다고 면전에서 비난할 것인가?

VOCA

• cling to ～에 매달리다, ～을 고수하다
• rob (사람·장소를[에서]) 털다[도둑질하다]
• clean up (～을) 치우다[청소하다]
• alive 살아 있는
• tradition 전통
• duty 직무, 임무

더 알아보기

with 분사구문: with+목적어+-ing[p.p.] '목적어가 ～한 채로'

• with 분사구문은 'with+목적어+현재분사[과거분사]'로 '목적어가 ～한 채, ～하고서'라는 뜻이다. 부대상황을 강조하기 위해 사용하며, 연속동작(and)이나 동시동작(while)으로 해석한다.

• with 분사구문의 유형

with+명사+현재분사(-ing)	부사절의 주어와 동사가 능동 관계일 때
with+명사+과거분사(p.p.)	부사절의 주어와 동사가 수동 관계일 때
with+명사+(being)+형용사, 부사(구), 전치사(구)	being은 주로 생략됨

예 I can't do my homework while all this noise was going on.
→ I can't do my homework with all this noise going on.
(이 모든 소음이 계속되는 상황에서 나는 숙제를 할 수 없다.)

예 Amy was listening to music and her eyes were closed.
→ Amy was listening to music with her eyes closed.
(Amy는 눈을 감고서 음악을 감상하고 있었다.)

예 We lay in bed with the window open. (형용사 open)
(우리는 창문을 열어놓은 채 침대에 누웠다.)

예 She was knitting, with the television on. (부사 on)
(그녀는 텔레비전을 켜놓은 채 뜨개질을 하고 있었다.)

예 Helen was waiting for her mother with her back against the wall. (전치사 against)
(Helen은 벽에 등을 기대고 그녀의 어머니를 기다리고 있었다.)

09 난도 ★★★ 정답 ③

어법 > 비문 찾기

정답의 이유

③ 부사 very는 동사를 수식할 수 없으므로, very를 생략하거나 'John was very frightening to her.'로 쓸 수 있다.

오답의 이유

① 자동사 stood 다음에 전치사 beside가 '～옆에'라는 뜻으로 적절하게 사용되었다. 참고로 부사 besides는 '게다가, 덧붙여'라는 뜻이다. 또한 명사 앞에서 형용사가 2개 이상 쓰이는 경우 '대·소+모양+성질·상태+신·구+색깔+재료+명사'의 순서로 사용되므로, ugly(모양)+old(신·구)+yellow(색깔)+tin(재료)+bucket(명사)의 어순으로 적절하게 사용되었다.

② ever invented는 '지금까지 발명된'의 뜻으로, 최상급인 the most perfect가 적절하게 사용되었다.

④ 형용사 utter(완전한, 순전한)가 명사 fool(바보)을 수식하고 있으므로, 어법상 적절하게 사용되었다.

본문해석

① 못생기고 낡은 노란색 양철 양동이가 난로 옆에 서 있었다.

② 그것은 지금까지 발명된 복사기 중 가장 완벽한 복사기다.

③ John은 그녀를 겁주고 있었다.

④ 그녀는 그가 완전한 바보라고 생각했다.

VOCA

• tin bucket 양철통
• stand (특정한 곳에) 세[위치해] 있다
• beside 옆에
• perfect 완벽한[완전한/온전한]
• invent 발명하다
• frighten 겁먹게[놀라게] 만들다

10 난도 ★★☆ 정답 ①

어법 > 비문 찾기

정답의 이유

① 'when creating within a broad understanding of sustainability'에서 creating 다음에 목적어가 없으므로, 문맥상 creating의 의미상의 주어 fashion이 '창조되는'의 의미가 되어야 한다. 따라서 creating → created가 되어야 한다.

오답의 이유

② 부사 socially가 형용사인 responsible을 적절하게 수식하고 있다.

③ 2형식 동사인 remain 다음에 형용사 open이 적절하게 쓰였다.

④ that이 The people, processes, and environments를 선행사로 받는 주격 관계대명사로 적절하게 쓰였다.

본문해석

사람들은 매일 옷을 입을 때 지속 가능한 방식으로 행동할 기회를 갖고 있으며, 패션이 지속 가능성에 대한 폭넓은 이해 안에서 만들어질 때 환경뿐만 아니라 사람들도 살아가게 할 수 있다. 사람들은 그들이 구매하는 패션에 관하여 사회적으로 책임감 있는 선택을 하려는 욕구가 있다. 우리는 패션 디자이너와 제품 개발자로서, 책임감 있는 선택권을 제공해야 한다. 우리는 패션에 대한 인식을 확장하여 존재하는 많은 층과 복잡성에 대한 개방성을 유지할 필요가 있다. 패션을 구현하는 사람과 과정, 환경 또한 지속 가능한 새로운 방향을 요청하고 있다. 정말 멋진 기회가 기다리고 있다!

VOCA

- behave 처신[행동]하다
- sustainable 지속 가능한
- get dressed 옷을 입다
- sustain (필요한 것을 제공하여) 살아가게[존재하게/지탱하게] 하다
- regarding ~에 관하여[대하여]
- purchase 구입[구매/매입]하다
- be challenged to 도전을 받다
- stretch 늘이다, 늘어지다
- perception 인식
- layer 막[층/겹/켜]
- complexity 복잡성, 복잡함
- embody 상징[구현]하다
- call for ~을 필요로 하다, (공식적으로) 요구하다
- fabulous 엄청난, 굉장한
- await (어떤 일이 사람 앞에) 기다리다

11 난도 ★★☆   정답 ④

어법 > 비문 찾기

정답의 이유

④ publish는 '출판하다'라는 뜻의 타동사인데, published 다음에 목적어가 없고 문맥상 주어(the report)가 '출판되는' 것이어야 하므로 published → was published가 되어야 한다.

오답의 이유

① 문장의 주어가 'Newspapers, journals, magazines, TV and radio, and professional or trade publications'로 복수명사이므로, 동사(provide)의 수일치가 적절하다.

② information은 불가산명사이므로 무관사명사로 적절하게 사용되었다.

③ the facts는 연례 보고서에서 '주어진' 것이므로 과거분사(given)가 적절하게 사용되었다.

본문해석

신문, 저널, 잡지와 TV, 라디오, 그리고 전문적인 출판물 혹은 무역 간행물은 연례 보고서에 제시된 사실 또는 보고서가 출판된 이후의 발전에 관한 사실을 설명하는 데 도움이 될 수 있는 추가 정보를 제공한다.

VOCA

- journal 저널, 학술지
- professional 전문적인
- provide 제공하다
- interpret 설명[해석]하다
- annual report 연례 보고서

12 난도 ★★☆   정답 ③

독해 > 글의 일관성 > 무관한 어휘·문장

정답의 이유

주어진 글은 많은 지역에서 나무심기를 통해 산림 파괴와 싸우고 보호구역을 지정해서 산림 보호를 위해 노력하지만, 숲을 보호하는 능력보다 숲을 파괴하는 능력이 더 크다는 내용이다. ③ 앞 문장에서 지난 10년 동안 '중국의 대규모 식재 계획(China's large-scale planting initiatives)'의 결과로 아시아에서 산림 파괴 속도가 느려지고 있다는 것을 예로 들었으며, ③ 다음 문장에서 '게다가, 생물 다양성 보존을 위해 지정된 보호구역의 수는 전 세계적으로 남아메리카와 아시아에서 특히 강력한 이익과 함께 전 세계적으로 증가하고 있다.'라고 했는데, ③은 열대우림에서 유래한 약학적 생산물의 수익을 국가들에게 더 공평하게 분배하도록 허용한다는 내용이므로, 글의 흐름상 가장 어색한 문장은 ③이다.

본문해석

열대우림은 믿을 수 없을 정도로 풍부한 생태계이며, 세계의 생물 다양성의 많은 부분을 제공한다. 그러나 이들 지역(열대우림)의 가치에 대한 이해가 높아졌음에도 불구하고, 과도한 파괴가 계속되고 있다. 하지만 몇 가지 희망적인 징후들이 있다. 정부가 집중적인 나무 심기로 이 관행과 싸우면서, 많은 지역의 산림 파괴[벌채]가 느려지고 있다. 예를 들어, 아시아는 주로 중국의 대규모 식재 계획으로 인해 지난 10년 동안 숲을 얻었다. 이 도전의 한 부분은 열대우림에서 유래한 약학적 생산물의 수익을 국가들에게 더 공평하게 분배하도록 허용하는 것이다. 게다가 생물 다양성 보존을 위해 지정된 보호구역의 수는 특히 남아메리카와 아시아에서 강력한 이익과 함께 전 세계적으로 증가하고 있다. 불행하게도, 이러한 이득에도 불구하고, 인간이 숲을 보호하는 능력보다 숲을 파괴하는 능력이 지속적으로 더 큰 것으로 보인다.

VOCA

- tropical forest 열대우림
- incredibly 믿을 수 없을 정도로, 엄청나게
- ecosystem 생태계
- biodiversity 생물 다양성
- increased 증가한
- excessive 지나친, 과도한
- destruction 파괴, 파멸
- promising 유망한, 촉망되는
- deforestation 삼림 벌채[파괴]
- region 지방, 지역

독해 > 글의 일관성 > 무관한 어휘 · 문장

정답의 이유

주어진 글은 화자의 친구가 다발성 골수종으로 투병 중에 화자가 그녀를 방문할 때마다 들고 간 질병과 죽음에 관한 소설을 친구가 항상 읽었다는 내용이다. ③ 바로 앞 문장에서 'But my friend had always read my novels.'라고 했는데, ③에서 '그녀는 더 이상 이 책을 읽고 싶지 않다고 주장했다.'라고 했으므로, 글의 흐름상 가장 어색한 문장은 ③이다.

본문해석

1980년대 초, 나의 좋은 친구는 자신이 특히 위험하고 고통스러운 암인 다발성 골수종으로 죽어가고 있다는 것을 알았다. 나는 이 전에 나이 든 친척들과 가족의 친구들을 죽음으로 잃은 적이 있지만, 개인적인 친구를 잃은 적은 없었다. 나는 비교적 젊은 사람이 병으로 서서히 고통스럽게 죽는 것을 본 적이 없었다. 내 친구가 죽는 데 1년이 걸렸고, 나는 매주 토요일마다 그녀를 찾아가고 내가 작업하고 있는 소설의 가장 최근 챕터를 가지고 가는 습관이 생겼다. 이것은 우연히도 'Clay's Ark'였다. 그것은 질병과 죽음에 대한 이야기였으므로, 그 상황에는 완전히 부적절했다. 하지만 내 친구는 항상 나의 소설을 읽었다. 그녀는 더 이상 이 책을 읽고 싶지 않다고 주장했다. 물론, 우리가 이것에 대해 얘기하지는 않았지만, 나는 우리 둘 다 그녀가 살아서 그 책을 완성된 형태로 읽을 것이라고 믿지 않았을 것을 어렴풋이 알아챘다.

VOCA

• discover 발견하다, 찾다[알아내다]

• die of ~로 죽다

• multiple myeloma 다발성 골수종

• cancer 암

• elderly 연세가 드신

• relative 친척

• relatively 비교적

• disease 질병, 병, 질환

• get into (특정한 습관을) 들이다

• habit of ~하는 버릇[습관]

• take along 가지고[데리고] 가다

• happen 우연히[마침] ~하다[이다]

• inappropriate for ~에 대해 부적절한, ~에 어울리지 않는

• situation 상황, 처지, 환경

• insist 고집하다[주장하다/우기다]

• suspect ~이 아닌가 의심하다. (위험 · 음모 따위를) 어렴풋이 느끼다[알아채다]

독해 > 대의 파악 > 요지, 주장

정답의 이유

② 주어진 글은 오늘날 기계의 기원이었던, 18세기 최초의 복잡한 기계인 '오토마타(automata)'에 대한 내용이다. 세 번째 문장에서 'But their original uses were rather less utilitarian(하지만 그들의 원래 용도는 덜 실용적이었다).'라고 했고, 네 번째 문장에서 '오토마타는 왕족의 장난감들로, 유럽 전역의 궁전과 궁정 안에서 오락의 한 형태이자 한 지배 가문이 다른 가문에게 보내는 선물'이라고 했으므로, 글의 요지로 가장 적절한 것은 ② 'Modern machine has a non-utilitarian origin(현대 기계는 비실용적인 기원을 가지고 있다).'이다.

오답의 이유

① 기계의 역사는 오락의 근원과는 관련이 적다.

③ 유럽 전역의 왕족들은 장난감 산업에 관심이 있었다.

④ 오토마타의 쇠퇴는 산업혁명과 밀접한 관련이 있다.

본문해석

컴퓨터부터 CD 플레이어, 철도기관차부터 로봇에 이르기까지 오늘날 기계의 기원은 18세기에 번성했던 정교한 기계식 장난감으로 거슬러 올라갈 수 있다. '오토마타(automata)'는 인간이 생산한 최초의 복잡한 기계로서 후에 산업혁명에 사용될 기술에 대한 검증의 장을 대표했다. 하지만 그것들의 원래 용도는 오히려 덜 실용적이었다. 오토마타는 왕족의 장난감이었으며, 유럽 전역의 궁전과 궁정에서 일종의 오락 형태이자, 한 지배 가문이 다른 가문에게 보내는 선물이었다. 오락의 원천으로서, 최초의 오토마타는 본질적으로 대성당을 장식하는 정교한 기계식 시계들의 축소판이었다. 이 시계들은 더 작아지고 더 정교해진 오토마타에 영감을 주었다. 이러한 장치들이 더 복잡해지면서, 그들의 시간 기록 기능은 덜 중요해졌으며, 오토마타는 기계식 극장이나 움직이는 장면 형태에서, 최초의 가장 중요한 기계식 오락물이 되었다.

VOCA

• be traced back ~로부터 시작되다

• elaborate 정교한

• mechanical toy 기계 장치가 달린 장난감

• flourish 번창하다

• automata automaton(자동 기계 장치)의 복수형

• represent 대표[대신]하다

• prove 입증[증명]하다

• harness 이용[활용]하다

• industrial revolution 산업혁명

• utilitarian 실용적인

• plaything 노리개(장난감처럼 가지고 노는 사람 · 물건)

• royalty 왕족(들)

• amusement 오락, 놀이

• time-keeping 시간[근무 시간]을 엄수하는

• foremost 가장 중요한[유명한], 맨 앞에 위치한

독해 > 세부 내용 찾기 > 내용 (불)일치

정답의 이유

마지막에서 두 번째 문장에서, 'He ~ has persuaded a bank to lend him the money he needs.'에서 Ali는 은행을 설득하여 자신이 필요한 돈을 빌려주게 했다고 했으므로, 글의 내용과 일치하지 않는 것은 ④ 'Ali는 은행을 설득하여 Igor에게 돈을 빌려주게 했다.'이다.

오답의 이유

① 두 번째 문장에서, 'He wanted to set up his own online gift-ordering business so that he could work from home(그는 집에서 일할 수 있도록 온라인 선물 주문 사업을 시작하기를 원했다).'라고 했으므로, 글의 내용과 일치한다.

② 여섯 번째 문장에서 '~ he said he no longer wanted to be part of Ali's plans(그는 더 이상 Ali의 계획에 참여하고 싶지 않다고 말했다).'라고 했으므로, 글의 내용과 일치한다.

③ 아홉 번째 문장에서 '~Igor stole a march on Ali by launching his own online gift-ordering company(Igor는 그의 온라인 선물 주문 회사를 설립함으로써 Ali의 사업을 가로챘다).'라고 했으므로, 글의 내용과 일치한다.

본문해석

Ali가 졸업했을 때, 그는 매일 일하기 위해 고군분투하는 통근자들의 대열에 합류하고 싶지 않다고 결심했다. 그는 집에서 일할 수 있도록 온라인 선물 주문 사업을 시작하고 싶었다. 그는 그것이 위험하다는 것을 알았지만 적어도 성공할 가능성은 있다고 느꼈다. 처음에, 그는 대학 친구와 함께 사업을 시작하기로 계획했다. Ali는 아이디어를 가지고 있었고 그의 친구인 Igor는 회사에 투자할 자금이 있었다. 그러나 출시 몇 주 전에 Igor는 폭탄선언을 했다. 그는 더 이상 Ali의 계획에 참여하고 싶지 않다고 말했다. Ali가 그(Igor)에게 결정을 연기하도록 설득했음에도 불구하고, Igor가 말하기를 자신은 더 이상 위험을 감수할 준비가 되지 않았으며 너무 늦기 전에 철수할 것이라고 했다. 하지만, 2주 뒤에 Igor는 그의 온라인 선물 주문 회사를 설립함으로써 Ali의 사업을 가로챘다. Ali는 이 배신에 충격을 받았지만, 곧 맞서 싸웠다. 그는 Igor의 행동을 적절한 조치가 필요한 사태로 간주했으며, 은행을 설득하여 자신이 필요한 돈을 빌렸다. Ali가 사업에 입문한 것은 분명 힘든 시작이었지만, 나는 그가 스스로 정말 성공할 것이라고 확신한다.

VOCA

• rank (사람들 · 사물들의) 줄[열]
• commuter 통근자
• struggling 발버둥 치는, 기를 쓰는, 분투하는
• set up 설립[수립]하다, 준비하다
• online gift-ordering business 온라인 선물 판매 사업
• risk 위험 요소[요인]
• invest 투자[출자]하다
• launch (상품을) 출시[출간]하다
• drop a bombshell 폭탄선언[발언]을 하다

• attempt 시도
• persuade 설득하다, 설득하여 ~하게 하다
• hang fire 결단을 못 내리다, 꾸물대다
• beat a retreat 서둘러 가 버리다[돌아가다]
• steal a march on 선수를 쓰다, ~을 앞지르다
• shell-shocked (곤경에 처해) 어쩔 줄 모르는
• betrayal 배신, 배반
• come out fighting (무언가에) 강하게 반응하다
• baptism of fire (새 직장 · 활동의) 힘든 시작[첫 경험]

독해 > 빈칸 완성 > 연결사

정답의 이유

③ 주어진 글은 병들거나 손상된 장기의 세포를 새로운 장기에 사용할 수 없으므로, 많은 연구자들이 복잡한 세포로 발전할 수 있는 줄기세포를 사용하는 방법을 연구하고 있다는 내용이다. 빈칸 (A) 앞 문장에서 과학자들은 병들거나 손상된 장기의 세포를 새로운 장기에 사용할 수 없다고 했고, (A) 다음 문장에서 과학자들이 새로운 장기를 성장시키기 위해 줄기세포 연구를 하고 있다고 했으므로, 빈칸 (A)에는 원인과 결과를 나타내는 Consequently(결과적으로) 또는 Accordingly(그런 이유로)가 적절하다. 빈칸 (B) 앞 문장에서 줄기세포는 피부 세포나 혈액세포, 심지어 심장과 간 세포와 같은 어떤 종류의 복잡한 세포로도 발전할 수 있는 신체의 매우 단순한 세포라고 하면서 줄기세포의 특징을 설명했는데, (B) 다음 문장에서 'stem cells can grow into all different kinds of cells(줄기세포는 모든 다른 종류의 세포로 자랄 수 있다).'라고 (B) 앞 문장에서 언급된 줄기세포의 특징을 간략하게 다시 말하고 있으므로, 빈칸 (B)에는 앞부분을 부연설명하는 In other words(다시 말해서)가 적절하다.

본문해석

과학자들은 많은 다른 인간의 장기와 조직에 대해 연구하고 있다. 예를 들어, 그들은 성공적으로 간 조각을 생성하거나 성장시켰다. 이것은 흥미로운 성과인데, 사람은 간 없이는 살 수 없기 때문이다. 다른 실험실에서 과학자들은 인간의 턱뼈와 폐를 만들었다. 이러한 과학적 발전은 매우 유망하지만, 그 역시 제한적이다. 과학자들은 매우 병들거나 손상된 장기의 세포를 새로운 장기에 사용할 수 없다. (A) 그 결과, 많은 연구자들은 완전히 새로운 장기를 성장시키기 위해 줄기세포를 사용하는 방법을 연구하고 있다. 줄기세포는 신체의 매우 단순한 세포인데, 피부세포나 혈액세포, 심지어 심장과 간 세포와 같이 매우 복잡한 세포로 발달할 수 있다. (B) 다시 말하면, 줄기세포는 모든 다른 종류의 세포로 자랄 수 있다.

VOCA

• human organs 인간 장기
• tissue (세포들로 이뤄진) 조직
• generate 발생시키다, 만들어 내다
• liver 간
• achievement 업적, 성취한 것

- jawbone (아래)턱뼈
- lung 폐, 허파
- breakthrough 돌파구
- promising 유망한, 촉망되는
- stem cell 줄기세포
- grow into ～로 성장하다

17 난도 ★★☆   정답 ①

독해 > 빈칸 완성 > 단어

정답의 이유

① 빈칸 (A) 다음 문장에서 과학자들은 서로 다른 목표를 갖고 있고 과학 자체에는 목표가 없다는 내용으로 미루어 문맥상 과학적 활동의 목표를 말하는 것은 의미가 없다는 내용이 와야 함을 유추할 수 있으므로, 빈칸 (A)에는 'naive(순진한)'가 적절하다. 빈칸 (B) 앞부분에서 과학적 활동은 이성적 활동인 것처럼 보이고, 이성적 활동에는 어떤 목표가 있어야만 하기 때문에 '과학적 목표를 설명하려는 시도가 완전히 ～하지는 않을 수도 있다'라고 했으므로, 문맥상 빈칸 (B)에는 'futile(헛된, 쓸데없는)'이 적절하다.

본문해석

과학적 활동의 '목표'에 대해 말하는 것은 어쩌면 약간 (A) 순진하게 들릴지도 모른다. 그것은 분명하게, 다른 과학자들이 다른 목표를 갖고 있으며, 과학 그 자체는 (그것이 무엇을 의미하든 간에) 목표가 없기 때문이다. 나는 이 모든 것을 인정한다. 그렇지만 과학에 대해 말할 때, 우리는 과학적 활동의 특징적인 무언가가 있다는 것을 다소 명확하게 느끼는 것처럼 보인다. 그리고 과학적 활동은 거의 이성적인 활동인 것처럼 보이고 이성적인 활동은 어떤 목표가 있어야만 하기 때문에, 과학의 목표를 설명하려는 시도가 완전히 (B) 헛된 것은 아닐 수도 있다.

VOCA

- speak of ～에 대해 말하다
- aim 목표
- admit 인정[시인]하다
- more or less 거의, 약[대략]

18 난도 ★★☆   정답 ③

독해 > 글의 일관성 > 글의 순서

정답의 이유

주어진 문장은 오늘날에 태어나는 아이가 노아의 시대에 태어난 아이와 동일한 능력을 갖고 태어난다는 것을 전제로 하고 만약 그렇지 않다고 해도 그 차이를 알 수 없다는 내용이므로, 주어진 문장 다음에는 역접의 접속사 But으로 시작하여 선천적인 능력은 동일해도 궁극적인 발달에선 큰 차이가 있다는 내용의 (D)가 와야 자연스럽다. (D)의 마지막에 언급된 'a vast difference in their ultimate development(궁극적인 능력 발달에서의 엄청난 차이)'를 (A)에서 That development로 받아 '그 발달은 전적으로 아이가 살

지도 모르는 사회에 의해 행사되는 영향력의 통제 아래 있다.'라는 내용으로 이어지는 것이 자연스럽다. (A) 후반부의 'by the society in which the child may chance to live'를 (B)의 'If such society be altogether denied,'로 받고, (B)에서 교양 없는 사회와 교양 있는 사회에서 자라는 예시를 다양하게 들고 난 후에 'Hence(이런 이유로)'로 시작하는 (C)에서 '각 세대는 이전 세대의 함양의 혜택을 받는다.'라는 내용으로 마무리하는 것이 적절하다. 따라서 글의 순서로 가장 적절한 것은 ③ '(D) – (A) – (B) – (C)'이다.

본문해석

아마 오늘날 태어나는 아이는 노아 시대에 태어난 아이와 동일한 능력을 갖고 있을 수 있다. 그렇지 않다고 해도 우리는 그 차이를 판단할 방법이 없다.

(D) 그러나 시작할 때의 선천적인 능력의 동등함이 궁극적인 능력 발달에서의 엄청난 차이를 막지는 못할 것이다.

(A) 그 발달은 전적으로 아이가 살 기회가 있는 사회에 의해 행사되는 영향력의 통제 아래 있다.

(B) 만약 그러한 사회가 완전히 부정된다면, 그 능력은 소멸되고 아이는 인간이 아닌 짐승으로 성장한다. 만약 사회가 교양 없고 고상하지 않다면, 능력의 성장은 그 후에 절대 회복할 수 없을 정도로 일찍부터 저해당할 것이다. 만약 사회가 고도로 교양 있다면, 아이도 역시 함양될 것이고 그 함양의 결실을 일생을 통해 다소나마 보여줄 것이다.

(C) 이런 이유로, 각 세대는 이전 세대의 함양의 혜택을 받는다.

VOCA

- possibly 아마
- faculty (사람이 타고나는 신체적 · 정신적) 능력[기능]
- possess (자질 · 특징을) 지니다[갖추고 있다]
- determine 알아내다, 밝히다
- exert (권력 · 영향력을) 가하다[행사하다]
- perish 소멸되다
- uneducated 교육을 못 받은, 배운 데 없는, 무지한
- coarse 거친
- stunted 성장[발달]을 저해당한
- recovery 회복
- cultivated 세련된, 교양 있는
- cultivation 경작, 재배, 함양
- hence 이런 이유로
- precede ～에 앞서다[선행하다]
- ultimate 궁극[최종]적인, 최후의

독해 > 빈칸 완성 > 단어 · 구 · 절

정답의 이유

주어진 글은 영어에서 부정사와 −ing의 규칙에 관한 내용이다. 글의 전반부에서 영어에서 부정사를 나타내는 to와 동사 사이에는 아무것도 들어가서는 안 된다고 했고, 그것은 부정사의 표기가 마침이 되어야 하는 라틴어에서 유래했다고 했는데, 그것은 '−ing'의 경우에도 마찬가지라고 했다. 빈칸 문장에서 '영어 사용자들은 분명히 'to'와 'go'가, 'go'와 '−ing'만큼 ~하게 세트로 묶여있다고 느끼지는 않는다.'라고 했는데, 빈칸 다음 문장에서 '그들은 자주 이런 종류의 'to'와 동사 사이에 단어들을 넣는다.'라고 했으므로, 문맥상 'to'와 'go'가 'go'와 '−ing'만큼 한 세트로 밀접하게 묶여있을 필요는 없음을 유추할 수 있다. 빈칸이 포함된 that절 앞에 not이 있는 것에 유의했을 때, 빈칸에 들어갈 말로 가장 적절한 것은 ② 'as closely as(~만큼 밀접하게)'이다.

오답의 이유

① ~보다 덜 밀접하게
③ ~보다 더 느슨하게
④ ~만큼 느슨하게

본문해석

영어가 무엇을 해야 하는지에 대한 사람들의 관점이 라틴어가 무엇을 하는지에 의해 크게 영향을 받아왔다는 것은 꽤 분명하다. 예를 들어, 영어에서 부정사는 분리되어서는 안 된다는 느낌이 있다. (혹은 있었는데, 그것은 오늘날 자연스러운 구어에서는 매우 드물게 관찰된다.) 이것이 의미하는 바는 부정사를 표시하는 'to'와 동사 사이에 아무것도 넣으면 안 된다는 것인데, 즉 'to go boldly'라고 말해야지 'to boldly go'라고 말해서는 안 된다는 것이다. 이 '규칙'은 라틴어를 바탕으로 한 것으로, 라틴어에서 부정사의 표기는 마침이 되어야 하며 그것을 동사의 나머지 부분으로부터 분리할 수 없는 것은 '−ing'를 동사의 나머지 부분으로부터 분리하여 'going boldly'를 'goboldlying'라고 말할 수 없는 것과 같다. 영어 사용자들은 분명히 'to'와 'go'가, 'go'와 '−ing'만큼 밀접하게 세트로 묶여있다고 느끼지는 않는다. 그들은 자주 이런 종류의 'to'와 동사 사이에 단어들을 넣는다.

VOCA

• influence 영향을 주다[미치다]
• infrequently 드물게
• observe 관찰[관측/주시]하다
• infinitive 동사원형, 부정사
• split (작은 부분들로) 나뉘다[나누다]
• marker 표시[표지]
• belong together (물건이) 세트로 되어 있다

독해 > 빈칸 완성 > 단어 · 구 · 절

정답의 이유

두 번째 문장에서 '비유동자산의 적정가치가 증가하는 경우, 이것이 재무상태표에 표시된 자산가치의 조정에 반영될 수 있다.'라고 했는데, 빈칸 다음 문장에서 'A profit is made or realized only when the asset is sold and the resulting profit is taken through the income statement(이익은, 자산이 매각되고 그 결과에 따른 이익이 손익계산서로 받아들여져야만 발생하거나 실현된다).'라고 했으므로, 비유동자산의 가치 증가가 곧 기업의 '현재' 이익을 나타내진 않는다는 것을 유추할 수 있다. 따라서 빈칸에 들어갈 말로 가장 적절한 것은 ③ 'an immediate profit(즉각적인 이익)'이다.

오답의 이유

① 적정가치
② 실제 원가
④ 거래 가치

본문해석

기업은 비유동자산을 재평가하는 것이 허용될 수 있다. 비유동자산의 적정가치가 증가하는 경우, 이것이 재무상태표에 표시된 자산가치의 조정에 반영될 수 있다. 가능한 한, 이것은 자산과 부채의 적정가치를 반영해야 한다. 그러나 비유동자산의 가치 증가가 반드시 기업의 즉각적인 이익을 의미하지는 않는다. 이익은, 자산이 매각되고 그 결과에 따른 이익이 손익계산서로 받아들여져야만 발생하거나 실현된다. 이러한 일이 일어날 때까지 (상식으로 뒷받침되는) 신중함은 자산가치의 증가를 대차대조표에 유지할 것을 요구한다. 주주는 기업 자산의 매각에 따른 어떠한 이익도 얻을 권리가 있으므로, 주주들의 지분은 자산평가의 증가액과 동일한 금액만큼 증가한다. 재평가적립금이 생성되고 대차대조표는 여전히 잔액이 맞아떨어진다.

VOCA

• revalue 재평가하다, (통화를) 평가 절상하다
• non−current assets 비유동자산
• fair value (판매 · 과세 등의 기준으로서의) 적정가치
• adjustment 수정[조정]
• financial position 재무상태
• liabilities 부채
• income statement 손익계산서
• occur 일어나다, 발생하다
• prudence 사려 분별, 조심, 빈틈없음
• support 지지[옹호/재청]하다
• common sense 상식, 양식
• asset value 자산가치
• retain 유지[보유]하다
• balance sheet 대차대조표, 재정증명서
• shareholder 주주
• stake 지분
• asset valuation 자산평가
• revaluation reserve 재평가적립금
• balance (계산 · 장부 잔액이) 맞아떨어지다

영어 | 2019년 서울시 9급

한눈에 훑어보기

✓ 영역 분석

어휘   01 02 03 04 05
5문항, 25%

독해   11 12 13 14 15 16 17 18 19 20
10문항, 50%

어법   07 08 09 10
4문항, 20%

표현   06
1문항, 5%

✓ 빠른 정답

01	02	03	04	05	06	07	08	09	10
④	①	①	②	②	④	①	①	③	④
11	12	13	14	15	16	17	18	19	20
②	③	①	③	④	②	④	③	③	②

✓ 점수 체크

구분	1회독	2회독	3회독
맞힌 문항 수	/ 20	/ 20	/ 20
나의 점수	점	점	점

---

01 난도 ★★☆   정답 ④

어휘 > 어구

[정답의 이유]
밑줄 친 saw eye to eye는 '의견을 같이했다'의 뜻으로 이와 의미가 가장 가까운 것은 ④ 'agreed(동의했다)'이다.

[오답의 이유]
① 다퉜다
② 반박했다
③ 헤어졌다

본문해석
적어도 고등학교에서 그녀는 마침내 부모님과 의견을 같이했던 한 가지 결정을 내렸다.

VOCA
• at least 적어도
• decision 결정

02 난도 ★★☆   정답 ①

어휘 > 단어

[정답의 이유]
밑줄 친 pejorative는 '경멸적인'의 뜻으로 이와 의미가 가장 가까운 것은 ① 'derogatory(경멸하는, 비판적인)'이다.

[오답의 이유]
② 외향적인
③ 의무적인
④ 불필요한, 쓸모없는

본문해석
정당화란 문제의 행동에 대한 책임을 인정하면서도, 그에 관련된 경멸적인 특성을 부정하는 설명이다.

VOCA
• justification 타당한 이유, 정당성
• account 설명

03 난도 ★☆☆   정답 ①

어휘 > 단어

정답의 이유

빈칸 앞부분에서 황열병의 원인으로 먼지와 열악한 위생을 배제한다고 했으므로 문맥상 모기가 '의심되는' 매개체(carrier)라고 유추할 수 있다. 따라서 빈칸에 적절한 것은 ① 'suspected(의심되는)'이다.

오답의 이유

② 문명화되지 않은

③ 유쾌한

④ 자원한

본문해석

검사들은 먼지와 불결한 위생을 황열병의 원인에서 배제했고, 모기가 의심되는 매개체였다.

VOCA

• rule out 제외시키다, 배제하다

• sanitation 위생

• yellow fever 황열병

• carrier 보균자, 매개체

04 난도 ★★☆   정답 ②

어휘 > 단어

정답의 이유

기대 수명에 대한 서술어를 고르는 문제이다. 빈칸 다음에서 '불과 1세기 전에 만연했고 치명적이었던 질병들은 예방, 치료가 가능하거나 혹은 완전히 퇴치되었다.'라고 했으므로 빈칸에는 기대 수명에 대한 긍정적인 표현이 와야 한다. 따라서 빈칸에 적절한 것은 ② 'hovers(머물다, 맴돌다)'이다.

오답의 이유

① 축소시키다

③ 시작하다

④ 악화시키다

본문해석

일반적으로 말해서, 2018년에 살고 있는 사람들은 현대를 인류 역사 전체에 비교해 봤을 때 꽤 운이 좋다. 기대 수명은 약 72세에 머물고, 불과 1세기 전에 만연했던 천연두와 디프테리아 같은 치명적이었던 질병들은 예방, 치료가 가능하거나 완전히 퇴치되었다.

VOCA

• generally speaking 일반적으로 말해서

• life expectancy 기대 수명

• smallpox 천연두

• diphtheria 디프테리아

• deadly 치명적인

• eradicate 근절하다, 퇴치하다

05 난도 ★★☆   정답 ②

어휘 > 단어

정답의 이유

빈칸 앞에서 '~을 제공할 수 있는 과거의 사건들에 구체적인 패턴이 있다고 상상하는 것(To imagine that there are concrete patterns to past events, which can provide ~)'이라고 했고, 빈칸 다음 마지막 부분에서 '그것이 수행할 수 없는 확실성에 대한 희망을 역사에 투사하는 것'이라고 했으므로, 문맥상 빈칸에 들어갈 적절한 것은 ② 'templates(본보기)'이다.

오답의 이유

① 환각들

③ 질문들

④ 소동

본문해석

우리의 삶과 결정을 위한 본보기를 제공할 수 있는 과거의 사건들에 구체적인 패턴이 있다고 상상하는 것은 그것이 수행할 수 없는 확실성에 대한 희망을 역사에 투사하는 것이다.

VOCA

• concrete 구체적인

• project 투사하다, 투영하다

• certainty 확실성

• fulfill 이행하다, 수행하다

06 난도 ★☆☆   정답 ④

표현 > 일반회화

정답의 이유

④ 출발 시간을 묻는 'What time ~?'에 대한 대답으로 소요되는 시간을 설명하고 있으므로 적절한 응답이 아니다.

본문해석

① A: 토요일에 봤던 영화 어땠어?

　　B: 좋았어. 정말 즐거웠어.

② A: 안녕하세요. 셔츠 몇 장을 다림질하고 싶은데요.

　　B: 네, 언제까지 그것들이 필요하신가요?

③ A: 싱글 룸으로 하시겠습니까? 더블 룸으로 하시겠습니까?

　　B: 음, 저 혼자라 싱글 룸이 좋아요.

④ A: Boston으로 가는 다음 비행기는 몇 시인가요?

　　B: Boston까지는 45분 정도 걸릴 겁니다.

VOCA

• press 다리다, 다림질하다

07 난도 ★★☆   정답 ①

어법 > 비문 찾기

정답의 이유

① attribute A to B는 'A를 B 덕분으로 여기다'의 뜻으로 문맥상
재봉틀을 발견한 것이 꿈 덕분임을 알 수 있으므로 for → to가
되어야 한다.

오답의 이유

② a dream이 선행사로 he was captured by cannibals in a
dream이 '전치사+관계대명사(in which he was captured by
cannibals)'로 올바르게 사용되었다.

③ 동사(noticed)의 목적어로 명사절을 이끄는 접속사 that이 올바
르게 사용되었다. noticed와 that 사이에 삽입된 'as they
danced around him'은 부사절이다.

④ need는 to부정사를 목적어로 취하는 동사이므로 to solve가 올
바르게 사용되었다.

본문해석

발명가 Elias Howe는 재봉틀의 발견이 식인종에게 포로로 잡힌 꿈
덕분이라고 했다. 그는 식인종들이 그를 둘러싸고 춤출 때 창끝에
구멍이 있다는 것을 알아차렸고, 이것이 그의 문제를 해결하는 데
필요한 디자인의 특성이라는 것을 깨달았다.

VOCA

- attribute A to B A를 B 덕분으로 여기다
- cannibal 식인종
- tip 끝
- spear 창

08 난도 ★★☆   정답 ①

어법 > 비문 찾기

정답의 이유

① emerge는 완전자동사로 수동태로 쓸 수 없으므로 had been
emerged as → had emerged as로 고쳐야 한다.

오답의 이유

② embark on은 '~에 착수하다'라는 뜻의 타동사구이다.

③ whereby는 '~에 의하여'의 뜻을 가진 관계부사로 쓰였으며, 뒤
에 완전한 문장이 왔으므로 올바르게 사용되었다.

④ 주어(East and West)와 동사(were)의 수일치가 올바르게 사용
되었으며, were to는 'be+to용법'으로 '예정'을 뜻한다.

본문해석

1955년까지 Nikita Khrushchev는 소련에서 Stalin의 후계자로 부
상하였으며 그는 '평화 공존' 정책에 착수했는데, 그 정책에 의하면
동서양은 계속 경쟁하면서도 덜 대립적인 태도를 취할 예정이었다.

VOCA

- successor 후계자
- coexistence 공존
- confrontational 대립을 일삼는

더 알아보기

be+to용법

'be+to용법'은 to부정사의 형용사적 용법으로, be동사 다음에서
'be+to부정사' 형식으로 쓰여 보어 역할을 하며, 예정, 의무, 의도,
가능, 운명의 의미를 나타낸다.

예정 (~할 예정이다)	예 They *are* to get married next week. (그들은 다음 주에 결혼할 예정이다.)
의무 (~해야 한다)	예 You *are* to fasten your seatbelt on the highway. (고속도로에서는 안전벨트를 매야 한다.)
가능 (~할 수 있다)	예 Not a sound *was* to be heard in the dark forest. (어두운 숲에서는 어떤 소리도 들을 수 없었다.)
운명 (~할 운명이다)	예 He *was* ultimately to die in the war. (그는 결국 전쟁에서 죽을 운명이었다.)
의도(~하려면): 주로 if절 안에서	예 If you *are* to participate in the workshop, you should fill out this form. (워크숍에 참여하려면 이 양식을 작성해야 한다.)

09 난도 ★★☆   정답 ③

어법 > 비문 찾기

정답의 이유

③ 관계대명사 that의 선행사는 skin이 아니라 special cells이므로
contains → contain이 되어야 한다.

오답의 이유

① all은 복수형의 가산명사와 함께 쓰므로 types가 올바르게 사용
되었다.

② Each of these animals는 '이 각각의 동물들'을 의미하며, each
는 단수 취급하므로 has가 올바르게 사용되었다.

④ allow는 to부정사를 목적격 보어로 취하는 5형식 동사로 'allow
+목적어+to부정사'는 '목적어가 ~하게 허용하다'의 뜻이므로
to change가 올바르게 사용되었다.

본문해석

오징어, 문어, 갑오징어는 모두 두족류의 유형이다. 이 각각의 동물
들은 피부 아래에 색소, 즉 유색 액체가 들어 있는 특별한 세포를
갖고 있다. 두족류는 이 세포들을 피부 쪽으로 향하게 하거나 피부
로부터 멀어지게 할 수 있다. 이것은 두족류가 자신의 외양의 패턴
과 색을 바꿀 수 있게 한다.

VOCA

- cephalopod 두족류 동물(문어 · 오징어 등)
- contain ~이 들어 있다
- pigment 색소
- appearance 외양, 외모

every vs. each

- every는 '모든'의 뜻으로 항상 단수명사 앞에 쓰며 단수 취급한다.
- each는 '각각(의)'의 뜻으로 다음에 오는 명사와 관계없이 항상 단수 취급한다.

구분	every	each
부정대명사	대명사로 쓸 수 없음	• each+단수동사 • each+of+복수명사+단수동사
부정형용사	every+단수명사+단수동사	each+단수명사+단수동사

예 Every person at the meeting *is* fond of the idea.
(그 회의에 참석한 모든 사람은 그 아이디어를 좋아한다.)

예 Each *was* given a pen and a piece of paper.
(각각에게 펜과 종이 한 장이 주어졌다.)

예 Each of the staffs *is* our great asset.
(직원 한 명 한 명이 우리의 큰 자산이다.)

- every A and B도 단수 취급한다.

예 Every boy and girl *is* to join the school club.
(모든 소년과 소녀는 교내 동아리에 가입해야 한다.)

---

10 난도 ★★☆   정답 ④

어법 > 비문 찾기

정답의 이유

④ 비교구문 'It's easier to stay home ~ than getting ~'에서 비교 대상은 품사나 구조가 동일해야 한다. easier 다음에 to부정사구 'to stay home ~'가 나왔으므로, than 다음에도 to부정사구가 나와야 한다. 따라서 getting → (to) get이 되어야 한다. 이때 to get의 to는 생략할 수 있다.

오답의 이유

① than 앞에 명사(more serious problem)가 왔으므로 than 다음에도 같은 구조인 명사 역할의 동명사(maintaining the cities)가 올바르게 쓰였다.
② 형용사(social)의 열등비교의 경우, 'less+형용사 원급'이므로 less social이 올바르게 사용되었다.
③ 형용사(easy)의 비교급으로 than과 함께 easier가 올바르게 사용되었다.

본문해석

도시를 유지하는 것보다 더 심각한 문제가 있다. 사람들이 혼자 일하는 것을 더 편안해할수록, 덜 사회적이게 될 수도 있다. 편안한 운동복이나 목욕가운을 입고 집에 머무는 것이 연달아 이어지는 업무상 미팅을 위해 옷을 차려입는 것보다 더 쉽다!

VOCA

- bathrobe 목욕가운
- get dressed 옷을 입다
- yet another 꼬리를 물고, 잇따라

---

11 난도 ★☆☆   정답 ②

독해 > 대의 파악 > 제목, 주제

정답의 이유

첫 문장에서 '~ production of an information good involves high fixed costs but low marginal costs(정보재의 생산이 높은 고정비용과 낮은 한계비용을 수반한다).'라고 했고, 마지막 문장에서 '~ must price your information goods according to consumer value(소비자 가치에 따라 정보재의 가격을 책정해야 한다) ~'라고 했으므로 글의 제목으로 적절한 것은 ② 'Pricing the Information Goods(정보재의 가격 책정)'이다.

오답의 이유

① 저작권 보호
③ 지적 재산으로서의 정보
④ 기술적 변화의 비용

본문해석

경제학자들은 정보재의 생산이 높은 고정비용과 낮은 한계비용을 수반한다고 말한다. 정보재의 초본을 만드는 비용은 상당할 수 있지만, 추가 사본을 제작(혹은 복제)하는 비용은 크지 않다. 이러한 종류의 비용 구조는 많은 중요한 의미를 가진다. 예를 들어, 비용 기반의 가격 책정은 효과가 없다. 단가가 0인 경우에는 단가에 대한 10~20% 가격 인상은 의미가 없다. 생산비용이 아닌 소비자 가치에 따라 정보재의 가격을 책정해야 한다.

VOCA

- information good 정보재
- fixed cost 고정비용(생산량의 변동 여하에 관계없이 불변적으로 지출되는 비용)
- marginal cost 한계비용(생산을 한 단위 추가로 생산할 때 필요한 총비용의 증가분)
- substantial 상당한, 많은
- negligible 무시해도 될 정도의, 보잘 것 없는
- implication 영향, 결과, 함축, 의미
- markup 가격 인상
- unit cost 단가

12 난도 ★★☆　　　　　　　　　정답 ③

독해 > 세부 내용 찾기 > 지칭 추론

정답의 이유

①, ②, ④는 모두 드라큘라 개미를 가리키지만 ③의 they는 드라큘라 개미의 턱을 가리킨다.

본문해석

드라큘라 개미는 때때로 자기 새끼의 피를 마시는 방법 때문에 그러한 이름이 붙는다. 하지만 이번 주에, 그 곤충은 새로운 유명한 이유를 얻게 되었다. *Mystrium camillae* 종의 드라큘라 개미는 그들의 턱을 아주 빠르게 맞부딪칠 수 있어서, 우리가 눈을 깜빡이는 데 걸리는 시간에 5,000번의 맞물림이 일어날 수 있다. 이번 주에 출판된 *Royal Society Open Science* 저널에 게재된 연구에 따르면, 이것은 그 흡혈 곤충이 자연에서 가장 빠르다고 알려진 움직임을 행한다는 것을 의미한다. 흥미롭게도, 이 개미들은 단지 턱을 아주 세게 눌러서 그것들(드라큘라 개미의 턱)이 구부러지게 하는 것만으로도, 기록을 깨는 스냅을 만들어낸다. 그것이 시속 200마일 이상의 최대 속도에 도달하면서 다른 쪽 턱을 지나쳐 엄청난 속도와 힘으로 강타할 때까지, 이것은 한쪽 턱에 마치 용수철처럼 에너지를 저장한다. 이것은 여러분이 손가락으로 딱 소리를 낼 때 일어나는 일과 비슷하지만, 단지 1,000배 더 빠를 뿐이다. 드라큘라 개미는 비밀스러운 포식자들이어서 그들은 낙엽 밑이나 지하 터널에서 사냥하는 것을 선호한다.

VOCA

- claim to fame　(~가) 유명한[흥미로운] 이유
- blink　깜빡이다
- wield　행사하다, 휘두르다
- slide past　지나치다
- lash out　강타하다
- secretive　비밀스러운
- leaf litter　낙엽

13 난도 ★★☆　　　　　　　　　정답 ①

독해 > 빈칸 완성 > 단어 · 구 · 절

정답의 이유

'사역동사(make)+목적어+목적격 보어'는 '목적어가 ~하도록 만들다'의 뜻으로 문맥상 '편안한 고객'이라는 특별한 등급은 이미 앉아 있는 사람들이 자리를 take가 아니라, give up하도록 만드는 것이 자연스럽다. 이때 목적어(those already seated)와 목적격 보어(give up)의 관계가 능동이므로 빈칸에 들어갈 말로 적절한 것은 ① 'give up(포기하도록)'이다.

본문해석

나는 독일의 한 기차 바닥에 앉아 너에게 이 편지를 쓰고 있다. 기차는 북적대고, 좌석은 모두 찼다. 하지만 이미 앉아 있는 사람들이 자신의 좌석을 <u>포기하도록</u> 허락된 '편안한 고객'이라는 특별한 등급이 있다.

14 난도 ★★☆　　　　　　　　　정답 ③

독해 > 빈칸 완성 > 연결어

정답의 이유

제시문은 아프리카 지역과 미국의 교육 예산을 비교하는 내용이다. 빈칸 앞 문장에서 학령 인구에 비해 교육비 지출이 적은 아프리카 일부 지역에 대해 서술하고 있고, 빈칸 다음에서 미국은 학령 인구 대비 교육비 지출이 크다는 상반된 내용을 서술하고 있다. 따라서 빈칸에 들어갈 적절한 것은 상반되는 두 가지 사실을 연결할 때 쓰는 ③ 'Conversely(반면에)'이다.

오답의 이유

① 그럼에도 불구하고
② 게다가
④ 비슷하게

본문해석

한 국가의 부는 교육에서 중심적인 역할을 수행하므로 국가의 자금과 자원 부족은 시스템을 약화시킬 수 있다. 사하라 사막 이남의 아프리카 정부들은 세계 공공자원의 2.4%만을 교육에 지출하지만, 학령 인구 중 15%가 그곳에 거주한다. 반면에, 미국은 전 세계에서 소비하는 모든 돈의 28%를 교육에 소비하지만, 그것은 학령 인구의 4%만을 수용한다.

VOCA

- lack　부족, 결핍, 결여
- funding　자금, 자금 제공[재정 지원]
- resources　자원
- sub-Saharan　사하라 사막 이남의
- school-age population　학령 인구
- house　수용하다

독해 > 빈칸 완성 > 단어 · 구 · 절

[정답의 이유]

빈칸 앞 문장에서 성실한 사람들은 불성실한 사람들이 겪는 비효율적인 경험을 피하려고 하는 경향이 있다고 했고, 빈칸 다음에서 'they'd otherwise create for themselves'라고 했으므로 문맥상 빈칸에 들어갈 말로 적절한 것은 ④ 'sidestep stress(스트레스를 피하다)'이다.

[오답의 이유]

① 차질을 해결하다

② 철저하게 일하다

③ 규범을 따르다

[본문해석]

"매우 성실한 직원들은 우리보다 일련의 일을 더 잘합니다."라고 성실성을 연구하는 Illinois 대학교의 심리학자 Brent Roberts는 말한다. Roberts는 그들의 성공이 '위생' 요인 덕분이라고 여긴다. 성실한 사람들은 자신의 삶을 잘 정리하는 경향이 있다. 체계적이지 못하고 불성실한 사람들은 파일을 뒤져 올바른 문서를 찾는 데 20~30분을 소비할 수도 있는데, 성실한 사람들은 이런 비효율적인 경험을 피하려는 경향이 있다. 기본적으로, 사람들은 성실함으로써 그들이 그렇지 않을 경우 스스로 만들 수 있는 <u>스트레스를 피한다</u>.

[VOCA]

- conscientious 성실한, 양심적인
- conscientiouness 성실성
- disorganized 체계적이지 못한
- root (무엇을) 찾기 위해 파헤치다[뒤지다]
- folk (일반적인) 사람들

독해 > 빈칸 완성 > 단어 · 구 · 절

[정답의 이유]

제시문은 지구의 생태학적 위기에 대한 책임이 균일하게 분배되지 않고 있다는 내용이다. 가장 부유한 42명이 가난한 37억 명의 재산을 합한 만큼 소유하고, 이들은 훨씬 더 환경에 영향을 미치고 있다고 했으므로 빈칸에 들어갈 적절한 것은 ② 'the accumulation of wealth in fewer pockets(더 적은 주머니 속 부의 축적)'이다.

[오답의 이유]

① 여전히 우리의 도달 범위 안에 있는 더 나은 세상

③ 기후 변화에 대한 효과적인 대응

④ 더 실행 가능한 미래에 대한 불타는 욕망

[본문해석]

기후 변화, 삼림 벌채, 광범위한 공해, 생물 다양성에 있어 여섯 번째 대량 멸종은 모두 오늘날 우리 세계, 즉 '인류세'로 알려진 시대에 살고 있다는 것을 정의한다. 이러한 위기는 지구의 생태학적 한계를 훨씬 넘어서는 생산과 소비에 의한 것이라고 뒷받침되고 있지만, 책임은 공평하게 공유되지 않는다. 세계에서 가장 부유한 42명은 가장 빈곤한 37억 명의 재산만큼 소유하고 있으며, 그들은 훨씬 더 큰 환경적 영향을 초래한다. 그리하여 일부는 끝없는 성장과 <u>더 적은 주머니 속 부의 축적</u>에 대한 자본주의의 논리를 반영하여 이러한 생태계 황폐화와 증가하는 불평등 시대를 묘사하기 위해 '자본세'라는 용어 사용을 제안했다.

[VOCA]

- deforestration 삼림 벌채
- biodiversity 생물 다양성
- underpin 뒷받침하다, 근거를 대다
- exceed 초과하다
- blame 책임, 탓
- devastation 황폐(상태), 폐허

17 난도 ★★★ 정답 ④

독해 > 빈칸 완성 > 단어 · 구 · 절

[정답의 이유]

제시문은 개인적 복수의 정당성에 대한 내용으로 우리는 사회적 · 개인적 입장의 경계선에 서 있다고 했다. 빈칸 앞의 'between civilization and barbarity'로 미루어, 문맥상 빈칸에는 'the community's need for the rule of law(법규범에 대한 공동체의 필요)'와 상반되는 내용이 들어감을 유추할 수 있다. 따라서 빈칸에 들어갈 적절한 것은 ④ 'an individual's accountability to his or her own conscience(그 또는 그녀 자신의 양심에 대한 개인의 책임)'이다.

[오답의 이유]

① 타락한 상황으로부터의 복수자의 구원
② 인간의 잔학한 행위에 대한 성스러운 복수
③ 부패한 정치가들의 도덕적 타락

본문해석

고대 그리스 비극 시대 이후 줄곧, 서양 문화는 복수자의 형상에 시달려 왔다. 그 혹은 그녀는 문명과 야만 사이에서, 그 또는 그녀 자신의 양심에 대한 개인의 책임과 법규범에 대한 공동체의 필요 사이에서, 정의와 자비라는 상반되는 요구 사이에서 완전한 일련의 경계선에 서 있다. 우리가 사랑하는 사람을 파괴한 사람에 대하여 복수할 권리가 우리에게 있을까? 아니면 복수를 법이나 신의 처분에 맡겨야 할까? 그리고 만일 우리가 직접 행동을 취한다면, 우리는 스스로를 살인을 저질렀던 원래의 가해자와 똑같은 도덕 수준으로 전락시키는 것은 아닌가?

VOCA

- haunt 뇌리에서 떠나지 않다, 계속 떠오르다
- borderline 경계선
- barbarity 야만적 행위
- exact (남에게 나쁜 일을) 가하다
- vengeance 복수, 앙갚음
- moral level 도덕적 수준
- perpetrator 가해자, 범인
- murderous 사람을 죽이려 드는
- deed 행위

18 난도 ★★☆ 정답 ③

독해 > 글의 일관성 > 무관한 어휘 · 문장

[정답의 이유]

제시문은 정보를 얻기 위한 독서 방식에 대한 내용이다. ③ 앞 문장에서 '자신이 필요한 것을 찾아내고, 문장 음운이나 은유의 유희 같은 관련 없는 것들은 무시한다'고 했는데, ③은 단어의 은유와 연관성을 통해 감정의 궤적을 나타낸다고 했으므로 전체 글의 흐름상 적절하지 않은 문장이다.

본문해석

내가 보기에는 독서를 4가지로 명명하는 게 가능해 보이며, 각각 특유의 방식과 목적이 있다. 첫 번째는 정보를 위한 독서로, 무역이나 정치, 혹은 무언가 이루는 방법에 대해 배우기 위해서 읽는 것이다. 우리는, 이러한 방식으로, 신문이나 대부분 교과서들 또는 자전거 조립법 설명서 같은 것들을 읽는다. 이런 자료의 대부분을 가지고 독자는 빠르게 페이지를 훑어 읽는 방식을 배울 수 있는데, 필요한 것을 찾아내고, 문장 음운이나 은유의 유희 같은 관련 없는 것들은 무시한다. 우리는 또한 단어의 은유와 연관성을 통해서 감정의 궤적을 나타낸다. 속독 강좌는 눈으로 페이지를 빠르게 건너뛰어 읽도록 훈련함으로, 이 목적을 위한 우리의 독서에 도움을 줄 수 있다.

VOCA

- assemble 조립하다
- material 자료
- come up with ~을 생각해 내다, ~을 찾아내다
- irrelevant 무관한, 관련 없는
- metaphor 은유
- register (감정을) 나타내다[표하다]
- association 연관; 연관성

19 난도 ★★☆   정답 ③

독해 > 글의 일관성 > 문장 삽입

정답의 이유

③의 앞 문장에서 '특히 집단주의 문화권에서는, 일이 더 큰 집단에 대한 의무 이행의 의미로 보이는 경우가 더 많을 수 있다'라고 했고, 보기 문장에서 '이런 상황에서는(In this situation)' 사회적 의무 때문에 개인의 이직률이 낮을 것이라고 부연 설명하고 있으므로 〈보기〉의 문장이 들어갈 위치로 적절한 것은 ③이다.

본문해석

일의 의미에서의 문화적인 차이는 다른 측면에서도 확실히 드러날 수 있다. 예를 들어, 미국 문화에서는 일을 단순히 돈을 모으고 생계를 유지하는 수단이라고 생각하기 쉽다. 다른 문화권, 특히 집단주의 문화권에서는, 일이 더 큰 집단에 대한 의무 이행의 의미로 보이는 경우가 더 많을 수 있다. 이런 상황에서는, 우리는 그 또는 그녀가 속한 업무 조직과 그 조직을 구성하는 사람들에 대한 개인의 사회적 의무로 인하여 한 직장에서 다른 직장으로의 개인의 이동이 더 적을 것이라고 예상한다. 개인주의 문화권에서는, 한 직장을 떠나 다른 직장으로 이동하는 것이 더 쉽게 여겨지는데, 이는 개인과 일을 분리하기가 더 쉽기 때문이다. 다른 직장에서도 같은 목표를 쉽게 달성할 것이다.

VOCA

• obligation 의무
• comprise 구성하다, 차지하다
• manifest 나타나다, 드러내 보이다
• aspect 측면, 양상
• accumulate 모으다, 축적하다
• make a living 생계를 꾸리다
• collectivistic 집산주의의, 집산주의적인
• individualistic 개인주의적인
• separate 분리하다

20 난도 ★★★   정답 ②

독해 > 글의 일관성 > 글의 순서

정답의 이유

② 먼저 마이크로박쥐가 무엇인지 설명하는 ⓒ으로 시작하는데, '마이크로박쥐의 작은 눈 때문에 어둠 속에서 먹이를 찾는 데 어려움이 있을 것 같다'는 내용 다음에 But으로 시작하는 ⓔ에서 '사실 마이크로박쥐는 잘 볼 수 있다'고 하는 내용으로 연결되는 것이 자연스럽다. ⓔ에 소개된 반향 위치 측정(echolocation)의 원리에 대하여 부연 설명하는 ⓐ이 그 뒤에 이어진다. 마지막으로 ⓒ에서 반향 위치 측정(echolocation)이 먹이를 찾는 데 도움이 된다고 설명한다.

본문해석

ⓒ 마이크로박쥐는 곤충을 잡아먹는, 북아메리카에서 발견되는 박쥐로 어둠 속에서 길을 찾고 먹이를 찾아내는 데 도움이 될 것 같지 않은 아주 작은 눈을 가지고 있다.

ⓔ 하지만, 실제로 마이크로박쥐는 쥐나 다른 작은 포유동물들만큼 잘 볼 수 있다. 박쥐의 야행성 습성은 반향 위치 측정의 힘에 의해 도움을 받는데, 그 특별한 능력은 밤에 먹이를 먹고 비행하는 것을 우리가 생각하는 것보다 훨씬 더 쉽게 만들어준다.

ⓐ 어둠 속에서 길을 찾기 위해서, 마이크로박쥐는 입을 벌린 상태로 사람이 들을 수 없는 높은 음조의 끽끽거리는 소리를 내며 비행한다. 이러한 소리들 중 일부는 나뭇가지 또는 앞에 서 있는 다른 장애물들뿐만 아니라 날아다니는 곤충으로부터도 반향된다. 박쥐는 이 메아리를 듣고 그 앞에 있는 물체들의 이미지를 즉각적으로 머릿속에 그려낸다.

ⓒ 반향 위치 측정, 즉 sonar라고 불리는 것의 사용으로, 마이크로박쥐는 모기나 다른 가능한 먹잇감들에 대해 많은 것을 알아낼 수 있다. 반향 위치 측정은, 극도로 정확하게, 마이크로박쥐가 움직임, 거리, 속도, 행동. 모양을 감지할 수 있게 해준다. 박쥐들은 또한 인간의 머리카락보다 두껍지 않은 장애물도 감지해서 피할 수 있다.

VOCA

• navigate 길을 찾다
• emit 내다[내뿜다]
• high-pitched 아주 높은
• squeak 끼익[깩/찍]하는 소리
• echo off 메아리로 튕겨내다
• obstacle 장애물
• instantaneous 즉각적인
• spot 발견하다, 찾다
• echolocation 반향 위치 측정; 반향정위
• perceive 감지[인지]하다
• nocturnal 야행성의

영어 | 2018년 서울시 9급

한눈에 훑어보기

✔ 영역 분석

어휘 01 02 03 11 12
5문항, 25%

독해 07 08 09 10 15 16 17 18 19 20
10문항, 50%

어법 05 06 13 14
4문항, 20%

표현 04
1문항, 5%

✔ 빠른 정답

01	02	03	04	05	06	07	08	09	10
③	①	②	③	②	③	④	③	④	①
11	12	13	14	15	16	17	18	19	20
④	④	③	④	①	③	④	①	③	②

✔ 점수 체크

구분	1회독	2회독	3회독
맞힌 문항 수	/ 20	/ 20	/ 20
나의 점수	점	점	점

01 난도 ★★☆   정답 ③

어휘 > 단어

정답의 이유

밑줄 친 muzzle은 '재갈을 물리다, 입을 틀어막다'의 뜻으로 이와 의미가 가장 가까운 것은 ③ 'suppress(억압하다, 진압하다)'이다.

오답의 이유

① 표현하다

② 주장하다

④ 펼치다[펴다]

본문해석

인류는 새로운 사고에 재갈을 물리려는 권력자들과 변화를 허튼 소리라고 선언한 오랜 기간 확립된 견해들의 권위에 계속 반항해 왔다.

VOCA

• disobedient 반항하는, 거역하는

• authority 당국, 권위, 권위자, 권력자

• declare 선언하다, 분명히 말하다

• nonsense 터무니없는 생각, 허튼 소리

02 난도 ★★☆   정답 ①

어휘 > 단어

정답의 이유

밑줄 친 pompous는 '거만한'의 뜻으로 이와 의미가 가장 가까운 것은 ① 'presumptuous(주제넘은)'이다.

오답의 이유

② 평상시의

③ 공식적인

④ 진실된, 진짜의

본문해석

거만하지 마십시오. 여러분은 여러분의 글이 너무 격식 없고 구어적인 것을 원하지 않지만, 또한, 여러분이 아닌 누군가, 예를 들어, 교수나 상사, 로즈 장학금을 받는 조교처럼 들리는 것도 원하지 않는다.

VOCA

• informal (언어가) 일상적인, 격식에 얽매이지 않은

• colloquial 구어체의, 구어의, 일상 회화의

• sound like ～일 것 같다, ～처럼 들리다

• for instance 예를 들어

• assistant 보조, 조수, 비서

03 난도 ★☆☆

정답 ②

어휘 > 어구

정답의 이유

밑줄 친 call it a day는 '~을 그만하기로 하다'의 뜻으로 이와 의미가 가장 가까운 것은 ② 'finish(마치다)'이다.

오답의 이유

① 개시하다

③ 기다리다

④ 취소하다

본문해석

외과의사들은 그 업무에 적합한 도구를 찾지 못했기 때문에 (일을) 그만하도록 강요받았다.

VOCA

• surgeon 외과의사

• be forced to ~하도록 강요받다

• right 적합한

04 난도 ★☆☆

정답 ③

표현 > 일반회화

정답의 이유

A가 리소토가 어떤지 묻는데, B가 버섯과 치즈가 들어 있는 리소토가 있다고 메뉴를 소개하고 있으므로 가장 어색한 대화는 ③이다. A의 질문에 대한 응답으로는 리소토의 맛에 대한 평가가 적절하다.

본문해석

① A: 내일 날짜에 예약하려고 해요.

　 B: 알겠습니다. 몇 시에 해드릴까요?

② A: 주문하시겠습니까?

　 B: 네, 저 수프로 주세요.

③ A: 리소토는 어떤가요?

　 B: 네, 우리는 버섯과 치즈가 들어 있는 리소토가 있습니다.

④ A: 디저트 좀 드실래요?

　 B: 저는 됐어요. 감사합니다.

VOCA

• make a reservation 예약하다

• certainly 분명히, 확실히, 정말로, (대답) 알았습니다, 물론입니다

• be ready to ~할 준비가 되어 있다

• risotto 리소토(이탈리아식 볶음밥)

• mushroom 버섯

05 난도 ★★☆

정답 ②

어법 > 비문 찾기

정답의 이유

② 부정어 never는 이미 부정의 의미를 포함하고 있는 hardly(거의 ~하지 않는)와 함께 쓸 수 없으므로 never → ever로 고쳐야 한다.

오답의 이유

① 전치사 over는 기간을 나타내는 표현과 함께 '~동안, ~에 걸쳐서'의 뜻으로 over the years는 '수년에 걸쳐, 수년 동안'의 의미이다.

③ a number of는 '많은'의 뜻으로 many, several이 동의어이다. 'a number of+복수명사+복수동사'이고, 'the number of+복수명사+단수동사'이다.

④ 선행사(policy issues)가 관계사절의 동사(has had to argue)의 목적어 역할을 하므로 목적격 관계대명사 which가 올바르게 사용되었다.

본문해석

1961년 독립 이후 수년 동안의 그의 생존이 실제 정책안에 대한 공적 토론이 거의 일어나지 않았다는 사실을 바꾸지 않는다. 사실 Nyerere가 NEC를 통해 논의했어야 하는 수많은 중요한 정책 사안들은 항상 존재해 왔다.

VOCA

• independence 독립

• alter 바꾸다, 변경하다

• manner 방식, 태도

• occur 발생하다, 일어나다

더 알아보기

a number of vs. the number of

• a number of: '많은'의 뜻으로, 'a number of+복수명사'는 복수동사를 쓴다. many, a lot of와 같은 뜻이다.

　예 A number of the monuments *are* of considerable antiquity.

　　(많은 유물들은 상당히 오래된 것이다.)

• the number of: '~의 수'의 뜻으로, 'the number of+복수명사'는 단수동사를 쓴다.

　예 The number of visitors to Seoul *is decreasing*.

　　(서울의 방문객 수가 감소하고 있다.)

• 'many+복수명사'는 복수동사를 쓰고, 'many a+단수명사'는 단수동사를 쓴다.

　예 Many people *feel* that the law should be changed.

　　(많은 사람들은 법이 바뀌어야 한다고 생각한다.)

　예 'Many a true word *is* spoken in jest,' thought Rosie.

　　(Rosie는 '농담 속에 많은 진실이 담겨 있는 법'이라고 생각했다.)

어법 > 정문 찾기

정답의 이유

③ another는 주로 'another+단수명사'로 쓰지만 'another+기수+복수명사'로도 쓸 수 있으므로 another 300 people(또 다른 300명의 사람들)로 올바르게 사용되었다.

오답의 이유

① fall의 3단 변화는 fall-fell-fallen이므로 have fell ill → have fallen ill이 되어야 한다.

② that절 이하가 타동사 suspect의 목적어인 명사절이므로 are suspected → suspected가 되어야 한다.

④ that절에 주어(another 300 people), 동사(had), 목적어(the same disease)가 있으므로 begin은 명사(disease)를 수식하는 분사가 된다. 따라서 begin in → beginning in이 되어야 한다.

본문해석

지난 3주 동안 주로 홍콩과 베트남에서 150명이 넘는 사람들이 병에 걸렸다. 그리고 전문가들은, 중국 광동성에 있는 또 다른 300명의 사람들이 11월 중순에 시작한 동일한 질병에 걸린 것으로 의심했다.

VOCA

• fall ill 병이 나다
• suspect 의심하다
• province (수도 외의) 지방

더 알아보기

another, other, others

another+단수명사	예 One man's meat is another *man's poison*. (갑의 약은 을의 독)
another+기수 +복수명사	예 We've still got another *forty miles* to go. (우리는 아직 40마일을 더 가야 한다.)
other+복수명사	예 Are there any other *questions*? (무슨 다른 질문 있으세요?)
others(다른 사람들)	예 Others have met similar problems. (다른 사람들도 비슷한 문제를 겪어 왔다.)

cf. A is one thing and B is another: A와 B는 별개의 문제이다
　예 *Knowing* is one thing and *teaching* is quite another.
　　(아는 것과 가르치는 것은 별개이다.)

독해 > 빈칸 완성 > 단어 · 구 · 절

정답의 이유

빈칸 앞의 'learn via modeling(모델링을 통해 학습하다)'으로 인해 빈칸 뒤의 'aggressive interchanges(공격적 교환)'라는 결과가 나온 것이므로 글의 흐름상 빈칸에 들어갈 단어로 가장 옳은 것은 ④ 'initiate(시작하다)'이다.

오답의 이유

① 중단하다
② 약화시키다
③ 혐오하다

본문해석

사회 학습 이론가들은 가정에서 공격성을 경험한 아이들이 보여주는 대항 공격[반격]에 대한 다른 설명을 제시한다. 공격적인 행동과 강압적인 가족에 관한 광범위한 연구는 혐오스러운 결과가 또한 공격적인 반응을 이끌어내고 계속되는 강압적인 행동을 촉진할 수도 있다고 결론 내린다. 이러한 공격적 행동의 희생자들은 결국 모델링을 통해 공격적 (행동의) 교환을 시작하는 것을 학습한다. 이러한 사건들이 공격적 행동의 사용을 영구화하고, 아이들에게 어른처럼 행동하는 법을 훈련한다.

VOCA

• social learning theorist 사회 학습 이론가
• counter-aggression (공격에 대한) 반격
• coercive 강압[강제]적인
• aversive 피하려고 하는, 회피적인, 혐오의
• consequence (발생한 일의) 결과
• elicit 이끌어내다
• interchange (생각 · 정보의) 교환
• perpetuate 영구화하다, 영속시키다

독해 > 세부 내용 찾기 > 내용 (불)일치

정답의 이유

'교조적(doctrinaire)'이란 '어떠한 상황에서도 절대로 변하지 않는 진리인 듯 믿고 따르는 또는 그런 것'을 의미한다. 세 번째 문장에서 'By the age of 18 Mauss had reacted against the Jewish faith'라고 했으므로 그가 종교적 교리를 맹목적으로 믿었다고 볼 수 없다. 따라서 Marcel Mauss에 대한 설명으로 가장 옳지 않은 것은 ③ 'He had a doctrinaire faith(그는 교조적인 믿음을 가지고 있었다).'이다.

오답의 이유

① 그는 유대인 배경을 가지고 있었다. → 첫 번째 문장에서 'where he grew up within a close-knit, pious, and orthodox Jewish family.'라고 했으므로 글의 내용과 일치한다.

② 그는 그의 삼촌의 감독하에 있었다. → 네 번째 문장에서 'He studied philosophy under Durkheim's supervision at Bordeaux'라고 했으므로 글의 내용과 일치한다.

④ 그는 철학적 배경을 가진 사회학자였다. → 첫 번째 문장에서 Marcel Mauss는 프랑스의 사회학자라고 했고, 다섯 번째 문장에서 'Mauss was initially a philosopher ~'라고 했으므로 글의 내용과 일치한다.

본문해석

Marcel Mauss(1872~1950)는 프랑스 사회학자로 Lorraine 지방의 Vosges 주 Épinal에서 태어났고, 그곳에서 집단 구성원들이 유대가 긴밀하며, 독실한 정통파 유대교인 가정에서 성장했다. Emile Durkheim이 그의 삼촌이었다. Mauss는 18살까지 유대교 신앙에 반발했다. 그는 결코 종교적인 사람이 아니었다. 그는 Bordeaux에서 Durkheim의 감독하에 철학을 공부했다. Durkheim은 조카의 공부를 지도하는 데 끊임없이 노력했고, 심지어 Mauss에게 가장 유용할 과목들을 자신의 강의 과목으로 선택하기도 했다. 따라서 Mauss는 (대부분 초기 뒤르켐주의자들과 마찬가지로) 처음에는 철학자였고, 그의 철학 개념은 특히 Durkheim의 영향을 받았으며, 그는 언제나 Durkheim에 대한 최고의 존경심을 간직하고 있었다.

VOCA

• close-knit 집단 구성원들이 긴밀히 맺어진, 단결된
• pious 경건한, 독실한
• orthodox (특히 신앙 · 행동이) 정통의, 전통적인
• Jewish 유대인[유대교]의, 유대교인인
• faith 믿음, 신뢰, 신앙
• religious 독실한, 신앙심이 깊은, 종교적인
• supervision 감독, 관리, 지휘, 감시, 통제
• take trouble in 힘을 들이다, 애쓰다
• initially 처음의, 초기의
• be influenced by ~에 영향을 받다
• retain (계속) 유지[보유]하다
• utmost 최고의, 극도의
• admiration 감탄, 존경

독해 > 글의 일관성 > 글의 순서

정답의 이유

④ 우선 however가 제시된 ⓐ와 these countries가 제시된 ⓑ는 첫 문장이 될 수 없으므로, 가장 일반적인 내용이면서 주제인 벌목을 제시하는 ⓓ가 처음에 오는 것이 적절하다. 이후 고대(In ancient times)의 국가들의 경우를 언급하고, 이와 대조적으로 매년 200만 에이커가 벌목되는 현대의 벌목 현황을 설명하는 ⓐ가 온다. ⓒ에서 현대 삼림 파괴의 원인과 결과에 따른 영향을 언급하는데, ⓒ의 마지막 문장의 'In industrialized countries'는 ⓑ의 'in these countries'로 연결된다.

본문해석

ⓓ 사람들에게 벌목은 더 이상 새로운 것이 아니다. 고대에 그리스, 이탈리아, 영국은 숲으로 뒤덮여 있었다. 수 세기 동안 그 숲들은 서서히 줄어들었다. 지금까지 남아 있는 것은 거의 없다.

ⓐ 그러나, 오늘날 나무들은 훨씬 빠른 속도로 잘려나가고 있다. 매년 약 200만 에이커의 숲이 베어진다. 그것은 거의 영국 전체 면적 이상의 넓이다.

ⓒ 나무를 베는 데는 중요한 이유가 있지만, 또한 지구 생명체에 위험한 결과도 있다. 현재 파괴의 주요 원인은 전 세계적인 목재 수요이다. 산업화된 국가들에서, 사람들은 종이를 만들기 위해 점점 더 많은 나무를 사용하고 있다.

ⓑ 이 국가들에는 수요를 충족시킬 만큼 목재가 충분하지 않다. 따라서 목재 회사들은 아시아, 아프리카, 남아메리카, 심지어 시베리아의 숲에서 목재를 가져오기 시작했다.

VOCA

• rapidly 급속히, 신속히
• satisfy 만족시키다
• consequence 결과
• destruction 파괴, 파멸, 말살
• be covered with ~으로 뒤덮인
• gradually 서서히
• cut back 축소하다, 삭감하다

10 난도 ★★☆　　　　　　　　　　　정답 ①

독해 > 빈칸 완성 > 연결어

정답의 이유

① 첫 번째 빈칸 다음에서 'not all works of them ~ but there is undoubtedly an increasing(그 모든 작품이 즉시 팔리는 것은 아니지만, 새로운 예술품 구매를 즐기는 사람들이 증가하고 있다) ~'라고 했으므로 첫 번째 빈칸에 적절한 것은 동의와 반론을 동시에 제기하는 'Of course(물론)'이다. 두 번째 빈칸의 앞 문장에서 'They know that contemporary art also adds to their social prestige.'라고 했고, 빈칸 다음에서 예술작품은 자동차처럼 마모에 노출되는 게 아니기 때문에 투자 가치가 있다고 했으므로 두 번째 빈칸에 적절한 것은 첨가의 의미인 'Furthermore(게다가)'이다.

오답의 이유

② 그러므로 – 반면에

③ 그러므로 – 예를 들어

④ 물론 – 예를 들어

본문해석

사실상 현대 미술은 오늘날 중산층의 필수적인 부분이 되었다. 심지어 화실에서 갓 나온 예술작품들도 열광을 받는다. 그것들은 다소 빨리 인정받는다. 더 불친절한 문화 비평가들의 취향에는 너무 빠르다. 물론 그 모든 작품이 다 즉시 팔리는 것은 아니지만, 새로운 예술품 구매를 즐기는 사람들이 증가하고 있다는 것은 의심할 여지가 없다. 빠르고 비싼 자동차 대신에 그들은 젊은 예술가들의 그림, 조각, 사진 작품을 구매한다. 그들은 현대 미술품이 또한 자신들의 사회적 명성을 더해준다는 사실을 알고 있다. 게다가 예술 작품은 자동차처럼 마모에 노출되지 않기 때문에 그것은 훨씬 더 투자 가치가 있다.

VOCA

• contemporary 동시대의, 현대의, 당대의

• integral (전체를 구성하는 일부로서) 필수적인, 필요불가결한

• enthusiasm 열광, 열정, 열의, 열광하는 대상

• recognition 인식, 인정

• surly 무례한, 성질 못된

• critic 비평가

• undoubtedly 의심할 여지 없이, 확실히

• prestige 위신, 명망

• wear and tear (일상적인 사용에 의한) 마모

11 난도 ★★★　　　　　　　　　　　정답 ④

어휘 > 단어

정답의 이유

밑줄 친 essential은 '필수적인, 가장 중요한'의 뜻으로 이와 의미가 가장 먼 단어는 ④ 'omnipresent(편재하는, 어디에나 있는)'이다.

오답의 이유

① 중대한, 결정적인

② 필수적인, 없어서는 안 될

③ (어떤 목적에) 필요한, 필수 조건

본문해석

수정의 전제조건으로서, 수분은 과일과 씨앗 작물의 생산에 필수적이며, 품종 개량을 통한 식물을 개선하기 위해 고안된 프로그램에서 중요한 역할을 한다.

VOCA

• prerequisite 전제조건

• fertilization (생물) 수정, 다산화, 비옥화

• pollination (식물) 수분

12 난도 ★★☆　　　　　　　　　　　정답 ④

어휘 > 단어

정답의 이유

빈칸에는 제안을 반대하는 이유가 와야 하므로 모두 부정적인 단어가 적절하다. 따라서 글의 흐름상 빈칸에 들어갈 단어로 적절한 것은 ④ 'wrong(잘못된) – inconvenient(불편한)'이다.

오답의 이유

① 흠이 있는 – 바람직한

② 반드시 해야 하는 – 합리적인

③ 순응하는 – 개탄스러운

본문해석

Mr. Johnson은 그 제안에 반대했는데, 왜냐하면 그것이 잘못된 원칙에 기반했고 또한 때때로 불편했기 때문이다.

VOCA

• object to ~에 반대하다

• proposal 제안, 제의

• principle (개인의 도덕·신념과 관련된) 원칙

13 난도 ★★☆   정답 ③

어법 > 비문 찾기

정답의 이유

③ 관계대명사 that의 선행사(clothes)가 복수명사이므로 fits →
　fit이 되어야 한다.

오답의 이유

① 감정유발동사(please)의 경우, 주어가 감정의 원인이면 현재분
　사를 쓰고, 감정을 느끼는 주체이면 과거분사를 쓴다. 문맥상 내
　가 감정을 '느끼는' 것이므로 과거분사(pleased)가 올바르게 사
　용되었다.

② 부정사구(to find clothes in Chicago)가 문장의 주어인 경우,
　진주어(to find clothes in Chicago) 자리에 가주어(it)가 대신
　쓰이므로 it's가 올바르게 사용되었다.

④ 'What is a medium size in Japan'에서 What은 명사절 접속사
　로, 문장의 주어 역할을 하므로 what 다음에는 주어가 없는 불
　완전한 절(is a medium size in Japan)이 온다. what절이 주어
　일 때는 단수 취급하므로 동사(is)의 수일치가 올바르게 사용되
　었다.

본문해석

나는 내가 입을 충분한 옷이 있어서 기쁘다. 미국 남자들은 일반적
으로 일본 남자들보다 크기 때문에 시카고에서 나에게 맞는 옷을
찾는 것은 매우 어려운 일이다. 일본에서 중간 사이즈인 것은 이곳
에서는 작은 사이즈이다.

14 난도 ★★☆   정답 ④

어법 > 비문 찾기

정답의 이유

④ affect는 '~에 영향을 미치다'라는 뜻의 타동사로, 전치사 없이
　목적어를 취하므로 affects on → affects가 되어야 한다.

오답의 이유

① documentary가 BBC에 의해 제작된 것이므로 과거분사
　(produced)가 올바르게 사용되었다.

② '불완전타동사(leave)+목적어+목적격 보어'는 '목적어가 ~하
　게 그대로 두다'의 뜻으로, 목적어(viewers)와 목적격 보어가 수
　동 관계이므로 과거분사(heartbroken)가 올바르게 사용되었다.

③ which의 선행사(the extent)는 전치사 to와 함께 쓰이므로, '전
　치사+관계대명사(to which)'로 올바르게 사용되었다.

본문해석

BBC에 의해 제작된 자연 다큐멘터리 *Blue Planet II*는 플라스틱이
대양에 영향을 미치는 정도를 보여준 이후 시청자들을 비통하게 했다.

VOCA

• documentary 다큐멘터리, 기록물
• heartbroken 비통해하는

15 난도 ★★★   정답 ①

독해 > 빈칸 완성 > 단어 · 구 · 절

정답의 이유

빈칸의 앞 문장에서 Columbus의 업적을 기념할 것이 아무것도 없
었다고 했으므로 빈칸에 들어갈 적절한 문장은 앞 문장을 구체적으
로 설명한 ① '그의 많은 비평가들에 따르면, Columbus는 진보와
문명의 선구자가 아니라 노예제도와 무분별한 자연 환경 개발의 선
구자였다.'이다.

오답의 이유

② 1893년 시카고 세계 박람회는 미국의 발견과 진보의 힘 사이의
　서술적 연결 고리를 강화했다.

③ 19세기 Columbus 신화에 대한 이 반전이 흥미로운 사실을 밝
　힌다.

④ 따라서 Columbus는 결국 명백한 사명설, 즉 미국의 진보는 신
　의 힘으로 정해졌다는 믿음으로 통합되었다.

본문해석

그러나 1980년대에 이르러 명확해진 것은 Quincentenary Jubilee
를 위한 준비가 갖춰지면서, 많은 미국인들이 불가능하지는 않을지
라도, 그 기념일을 '기념(축제)'으로 보기는 어렵다는 사실을 알았다
는 것이다. Columbus의 업적을 기념할 만한 것은 하나도 없었다.
<u>그의 많은 비평가들에 따르면, Columbus는 진보와 문명의 선구자
가 아니라 노예제도와 무분별한 자연 환경 개발의 선구자였다.</u>

VOCA

• preparation 준비[대비]
• be made for ~을 위해 만들어지다
• quincentenary 500주년
• jubilee (특히 25주년이나 50주년) 기념일
• legacy 유산
• harbinger 선구자, 조짐[전조]
• progress 진전, 진보
• reckless 무모한, 신중하지 못한, 난폭한
• exploitation 개발, 착취
• reinforce 강화하다
• narrative 서술, 서술의
• reversal 전환, 반전, 역전
• integrate 통합시키다
• Manifest Destiny 명백한 사명설(미국이 북아메리카 전체를 지배할
　운명을 갖고 있다는 주장)

16 난도 ★★☆

독해 > 빈칸 완성 > 단어·구·절

정답의 이유

빈칸 앞 문장에서 '~ he wondered "how he could be so easily cast away at such a young age."'라고 하면서 양육의 책임이 있는 어른들로부터 보호받지 못하고 일을 해야 했던 어린 시절을 회상하고 있으므로 문맥상 빈칸에는 부정적인 의미의 단어가 들어가야 함을 유추할 수 있다. 따라서 글의 흐름상 빈칸에 들어갈 단어로 가장 옳지 않은 것은 긍정적인 의미인 ③ 'buttressed(지지받은)'이다.

오답의 이유

① 버려진

② 배신당한

④ 외면당한

본문해석

그의 아버지가 수감된 이후, Charles Dickens는 Thames 강 옆에 있는 구두약 공장에서 일하기 위해서 학교를 떠나도록 강요받았다. 쥐가 득실대는 황폐한 공장에서 Dickens는 벽난로 청소에 사용되는 재료인 '흑색 도료' 통에 상표를 붙이면서 일주일에 6실링을 벌었다. 그것은 그가 가족을 부양하기 위해 할 수 있는 최선이었다. 자신의 경험을 되돌아보면서, Dickens는 그때를 자신의 젊은 날의 순수함에 작별을 고한 순간으로 생각했으며, "어떻게 그렇게 어린 나이에 그토록 쉽게 그가 버림받을 수 있었는지 의아했다."라고 말했다. 그는 그를 돌보아야 할 의무가 있는 어른들로부터 <u>버림받은/배신당한/외면당한</u> 느낌을 받았다.

VOCA

• imprisonment 투옥, 구금

• alongside 옆에, 나란히

• run-down 황폐한

• rodent-ridden 설치류가 들끓는

• substance 물질, (토대의) 재료

• look back (과거를) 되돌아보다

• youthful (성인이 되기 이전의) 어린 시절

• innocence 결백, 무죄; 천진난만

• wonder 궁금해하다, 궁금하다, ~할까 생각하다

17 난도 ★★☆

독해 > 세부 내용 찾기 > 내용 (불)일치

정답의 이유

④ 마지막 문장에서 'They handle domestic and international adoption(그들은 국내 입양과 해외 입양을 다룬다).'이라고 했으므로 글의 내용과 일치하는 것은 ④ 'Private agencies can be contacted for international adoption(사설기관은 해외 입양을 위해 연락될 수 있다).'이다.

오답의 이유

① 공공 입양기관은 사설 입양기관보다 낫다. → 공공 입양기관과 사설 입양기관 중 어디가 더 나은지에 대해서는 언급되지 않았다.

② 부모들은 위탁가정에서 아동을 입양하기 위해서 많은 비용을 지불한다. → 입양 가정에서의 입양을 위해 많은 돈을 내야 한다고는 언급되지 않았다.

③ 도움이 필요한 아동들은 공공기관을 통해 입양될 수 없다. → 세 번째 문장에서 공공기관에서는 나이가 많은 아동, 정신적 혹은 신체적으로 장애가 있는 아동들, 학대받거나 버림받은 아동들까지 모두 입양할 수 있도록 다룬다고 했으므로 글의 내용과 일치하지 않는다.

본문해석

아동 입양을 원하는 가정은 우선 입양기관을 선택해야 한다. 미국에서는 입양을 돕는 두 가지 종류의 기관이 있다. 공공기관은 일반적으로 나이가 많은 아동, 정신적 혹은 신체적 장애가 있는 아동들 혹은 학대받거나 방치되었을 아동들을 다룬다. 예비 부모는 대개 공공기관에서 아동을 입양할 때 비용을 지불하지 않을 것으로 예상된다. 위탁 양육, 즉 일시적인 입양의 형태도 공공기관을 통해 가능하다. 사설기관은 인터넷에서 찾을 수 있다. 그들은 국내 입양과 해외 입양을 다룬다.

VOCA

• adopt 입양하다

• adoption agency 입양기관

• assist with ~을 돕다

• handle 다루다

• mental disability 정신적 장애

• physical disability 신체적 장애

• abused 학대받은

• neglected 방치된, 도외시된

• prospective 장래의, 예정의

• fostering 위탁 양육

• temporary 일시적인

18 난도 ★★☆

독해 > 빈칸 완성 > 단어·구·절

정답의 이유

제시문은 분류학상 같은 목에 속한 나방과 나비의 차이점을 설명하는 내용이다. 빈칸 앞 문장의 후반부에서 이 두 종류의 곤충 사이에는 많은 신체적·행동적 차이가 있다고 했고, 빈칸 다음에서 'butterflies are diurnal(active during the day).'이라고 했으므로 빈칸에 들어갈 적절한 것은 'diurnal(주행성의)'의 반대 의미인 ① 'nocturnal(야행성의)'이다.

오답의 이유

② 합리적인, 이성적인

③ 영원한, 끊임없는

④ (원예학) 반원형, 반원형의

나방과 나비는 모두 인시목에 속하지만, 이 두 종류의 곤충 사이에는 많은 신체적·행동적 차이가 있다. 행동적 측면에서, 나방은 야행성이고, 나비는 주행성(낮 동안에 활동하는)이다. 움직이지 않을 때는 나비는 날개를 주로 뒤로 접지만, 나방은 날개를 자신들의 몸에 딱 붙여서 납작하게 하거나 '제트기' 자세로 날개를 펼쳐 놓는다.

- lepidoptera (곤충) 인시목(나비나 나방류를 포함하는 곤충강의 한 목)
- numerous 많은
- behavioral 행동의, 행동에 관한
- at rest 움직이지 않는
- fold 접다, 접어 포개다
- flatten 납작[반반]해지다, 납작하게[반반하게] 만들다
- spread out 몸을 뻗다, 활짝 펼치다

19 난도 ★★☆   정답 ③

독해 > 빈칸 완성 > 단어·구·절

빈칸 문장의 앞부분에서 '비록(although) 대체로 폭력에 관한 신고는 없었고, 신고된 목격담 대부분이 이후 거짓으로 밝혀졌지만,'으로 미루어 빈칸에는 앞의 내용과 반대되는 상황, 즉 이것이 부정적인 결과를 초래했음을 유추할 수 있다. 따라서 글의 흐름상 빈칸에 들어갈 표현으로 옳은 것은 ③ 'caused a nationwide panic(전국적인 공황 상태를 야기했다)'이다.

① 서커스 산업에 이익이 되었다.
② 광고에서 광대의 사용이 촉진되었다.
④ 행복한 광대의 완벽한 이미지를 형성했다.

사람들을 깜짝 놀라게 하는 광대에 대한 생각은 미국 내에서 힘을 얻기 시작했다. 예를 들어, South Carolina에서 사람들은 야간에 광대 복장을 한 사람들이 종종 숲이나 도심에 숨어 있는 것을 보았다고 신고했다. 몇몇 사람들은 광대들이 어린이들을 빈집이나 숲으로 유인하려 했다고 말했다. 곧 이어서, 위협적인 외모의 광대가 어린이들과 성인들 모두를 놀라게 하려고 했다는 신고도 있었다. 비록 대체로 폭력에 관한 신고는 없었고, 신고된 목격담 대부분이 이후 거짓으로 밝혀졌지만, 이것은 전국적인 공황 상태를 야기했다.

- clown 광대
- frightening 무서운, 깜짝 놀라게 하는
- lure 꾀다, 유혹하다
- violence 폭행, 폭력, 맹렬함
- sighting 목격
- nationwide 전국적인

20 난도 ★★★   정답 ②

독해 > 대의 파악 > 요지, 주장

첫 문장에서 'It is one thing to believe that our system of democracy is the best, and quite another to impose it on other countries.'라고 했으므로 민주주의가 최고라고 믿는 것과 다른 나라에 이를 강요하는 것은 별개의 문제, 즉 같은 민주주의 시스템도 서로 다른 사회환경에서는 다른 결과를 가져올 수 있다는 민주주의의 상대성을 말하고 있다. 따라서 글의 내용과 가장 부합하는 속담은 ② 'One man's food is another's poison(한 사람에게는 음식인 것이 다른 사람에게는 독이다).'이다.

① 남의 떡이 커 보인다.
③ 예외 없는 법칙은 없다.
④ 로마에 가면 로마법을 따르라.

우리의 민주주의 체제가 최고라고 믿는 것과 다른 나라에 이를 강요하는 것은 별개의 문제이다. 이것은 독립 국가의 국내적 사안에 개입하지 않겠다는 UN 정책에 대한 노골적인 위반이다. 서양의 시민들이 그들의 정치 제도를 위해 투쟁했듯이, 우리는 다른 국가의 시민들이 그와 같은 것을 하기를 원한다면 그렇게 할 수 있을 것이라고 신뢰해야 한다. 민주주의는 또한 절대적인 용어가 아니다. Napoleon은 선거와 국민 투표를 이용해서 그의 권력 유지를 합법화했고, 마찬가지로 오늘날 서아프리카나 동남아시아의 지도자들도 그렇게 하고 있다. 부분적 민주주의를 실시하는 국가들은 종종 자국의 국내 질서 유지에 지나치게 신경 쓰는 비선출 독재 정권보다 훨씬 더 공격적이다. 서로 다른 민주주의 유형은 어떤 기준을 적용할지 선택하는 것을 불가능하게 만든다. 미국과 유럽 국가들은 정부에 대한 규제와 합의와 대립 사이의 균형 면에서 모두 다르다.

- impose 강요하다, 부과하다
- blatant 행동이 뻔한, 노골적인
- breach 위반
- political institution 정치 제도
- referenda 국민 투표, 총선거
- legitimize 정당화하다, 합법화하다
- aggressive 공격적인
- dictatorship 독재 정부

PART 4
법원직

한눈에 훑어보기

✓ 빠른 정답

01	02	03	04	05	06	07	08	09	10
④	①	②	②	④	②	④	④	①	③

11	12	13	14	15	16	17	18	19	20
②	②	②	③	①	④	②	②	②	④

21	22	23	24	25
②	①	②	①	④

✓ 점수 체크

구분	1회독	2회독	3회독
맞힌 문항 수	/ 25	/ 25	/ 25
나의 점수	점	점	점

---

01 난도 ★★★ 정답 ④

독해 > 글의 일관성 > 글의 순서

[정답의 이유]

주어진 글에서 지금 우리는 인공지능과 생명공학을 모두 포함하는 첨단기술의 물결 상승에 직면하여 전환점의 가장자리에 있으며, 우리는 이런 변형 기술을 이전에 결코 목격하지 못했다고 하였다. 글의 흐름상 (C) 첫 번째 문장의 these technologies는 주어진 글에서 말한 '변형 기술'을 의미하므로 주어진 글 다음에는 (C)가 오는 것이 적절하다. 또한, (C)에서 변형 기술 중 하나인 인공지능의 이점에 대해 설명하고 있으므로, (C) 다음에는 또 다른 변형 기술 중 하나인 생명공학의 이점에 대해 설명하는 (B)가 오는 것이 자연스럽다. (B)의 마지막 문장에서 '하지만 다른 한편으로(But on the other hand)' 이들 기술의 잠재적인 위험 역시 방대하고 심오하다고 했으므로, 인공지능과 생명공학의 위험성에 대해서 설명하는 (A)가 와야 한다. 따라서 주어진 글 다음에 이어질 글의 순서로 적절한 것은 ④ '(C) − (B) − (A)'이다.

[본문해석]

이제 우리는 인공지능과 생명공학을 모두 포함하는 앞으로 다가올 첨단기술의 물결 상승에 직면하면서 전환점의 가장자리에 서 있다. 우리는 경외심을 불러일으키는 동시에 우리를 기죽게 하는 방식으로 우리 세계의 구조를 다시 만드는 혁신적인 잠재력을 가진 그러한 변형 기술을 이전에 결코 목격한 적이 없다.

(C) 한편으로는, 이 기술들의 잠재적인 이점들은 방대하고 심오하다. 인공지능을 통해, 우리는 우주의 비밀을 풀 수 있고, 오랫동안 우리에게 이해되지 않았던 질병들을 치료할 수 있고, 상상의 경계를 넓히는 새로운 형태의 예술과 문화를 창조할 수 있다.

(B) 생명공학 기술로, 우리는 생명을 조작하여 질병과 싸우고 농업을 변화시켜 더 건강하고 지속 가능한 세상을 만들 수 있다. 그러나 다른 한편으로, 이러한 기술들의 잠재적인 위험은 똑같이 방대하고 심오하다.

(A) 인공지능을 사용하면, 우리가 통제할 수 없는 시스템을 만들고 이해할 수 없는 알고리즘의 영향을 받을 수 있다. 생명공학을 사용하면 생명의 구성 요소를 조작하여 잠재적으로 개인과 생태계 전체에 의도하지 않은 결과를 초래할 수 있다.

VOCA

- biotechnology 생명공학
- witness (사건 · 사고를) 목격하다
- transformative 변화시키는, [언어] 변형의
- potential 가능성이 있는, 잠재적인

- promising 유망한, 촉망되는
- reshape 모양[구조]을 고치다
- awe-inspiring 경외심을 불러일으키는, 장엄한
- on the one hand 한편으로는
- stretch 늘이다, 뻗어 있다[펼쳐지다/이어지다], 이어지다[계속되다]
- engineer (일을) 꾀하다[획책하다]
- tackle (힘든 문제 · 상황과) 씨름하다
- sustainable 지속 가능한
- at the mercy of ~의 처분(마음)대로
- algorithm 알고리즘
- manipulate 다루다[조작하다/처리하다]
- unintended 의도하지 않은
- ecosystem 생태계

02 난도 ★★☆　　　　　　　　　　　　　　정답 ①

독해 > 빈칸 완성 > 단어 · 구 · 절

정답의 이유

다섯 번째, 여섯 번째 문장에서 새로운 인공지능 이미지 생성 도구의 품종을 다르게 만드는 것은 최소한의 노력으로 아름다운 예술 작품을 생산할 수 있기 때문이 아니라 그것들이 작동하는 방식이라고 했다. 그리고 일곱 번째 문장에서 'These tools are built by scraping millions of images from the open web, then teaching algorithms to recognize patterns and relationships in those images and generate new ones in the same style(이 도구들은 오픈 웹으로부터 수백만 개의 이미지를 긁어낸 다음, 알고리즘에게 해당 이미지의 패턴과 관계를 인식하고 동일한 스타일로 새로운 이미지를 생성하도록 교육하여 만들어진다).'이라고 했고 빈칸 문장의 앞부분에서 그것을 다시 설명하고 있으므로, 빈칸에 들어갈 말로 가장 적절한 것은 ① 'helping to train their algorithmic competitors (그들의 알고리즘 경쟁자들을 훈련시키는 것을 돕고 있을)'이다.

오답의 이유

② 인공지능으로부터 발생한 예술의 윤리성에 대한 논쟁을 유발하고 있을
③ 창조적 과정의 부분으로 디지털 기술을 수용하고 있을
④ 독창적인 창작물을 만들기 위해 인터넷 활용 기술을 습득하고 있을

본문해석

새로운 예술 제작 기술에 대한 논란은 새로운 것이 아니다. 많은 화가들이 카메라의 발명에 흠칫 놀랐는데, 그들이 그것을 인간의 예술성을 저하시키는 것으로 보았기 때문이다. 19세기 프랑스 시인이자 예술 비평가인 Charles Baudelaire는 사진을 '예술의 가장 치명적인 적'이라고 불렀다. 20세기에, 디지털 편집 도구와 컴퓨터 지원 디자인 프로그램이 순수주의자들에 의해 유사하게 묵살되었는데, 인간 (협력자)들의 기술을 너무 적게 요구한다는 이유 때문이었다. 새로운 인공지능 이미지 생성 도구의 품종을 다르게 만드는 것은 단지 그것들이 최소한의 노력으로 아름다운 예술 작품을 생산할 수 있다는 것이 아니다. 그것은 바로 그것들이 작동하는 방식이다. 이

도구들은 오픈 웹으로부터 수백만 개의 이미지를 긁어낸 다음, 알고리즘에게 해당 이미지의 패턴과 관계를 인식하고 동일한 스타일로 새로운 이미지를 생성하도록 교육하여 만들어진다. 그것은 인터넷에 자신들의 작품을 올리는 예술가들이 자신들도 모르게 그들의 알고리즘 경쟁자들을 훈련시키는 것을 돕고 있을 수도 있다는 것을 의미한다.

VOCA

- controversy 논란
- art-making 작품 활동
- recoil 움찔하다[흠칫 놀라다]
- debasement (품위 · 품질의) 저하
- artistry 예술가적 기교
- mortal 치명적인, 대단히 심각한
- dismiss 묵살[일축]하다
- purist 순수주의자
- collaborator 공동 연구자[저자], 합작자
- breed 품종
- minimal 아주 적은, 최소의
- scrape (무엇을 떼어 내기 위해) 긁다, 긁어내다
- algorithmic 알고리즘의
- competitor 경쟁자[경쟁 상대]
- spark 촉발시키다, 유발하다
- a debate over ~에 대한 토론
- embrace 받아들이다[수용하다]
- acquire 습득하다[얻다]
- utilize 활용[이용]하다
- craft 공들여 만들다

03 난도 ★☆☆　　　　　　　　　　　　　　정답 ②

독해 > 세부 내용 찾기 > 내용 (불)일치

정답의 이유

② 두 번째 문장에서 'He was perhaps most widely known for developing the flutter kick, which largely replaces the scissors kick(그는 아마 플러터 킥을 개발한 것으로 가장 널리 알려졌는데, 그것은 주로 시저스 킥을 대체하는 영법이다).'이라고 했으므로, 글의 내용과 일치하지 않는다.

오답의 이유

① 첫 번째 문장에서 'Duke Kahanamoku ~ was a Hawaiian surfer and swimmer who won three Olympic gold medals ~'라고 했으므로 글의 내용과 일치한다.
③ 다섯 번째 문장에서 '~ at the 1920 Olympics in Antwerp, Belgium, where he also was a member of the victorious U.S. team in the 800-metre relay race.'라고 했으므로 글의 내용과 일치한다.
④ 일곱 번째 문장에서 'Intermittently from the mid-1920s, Kahanamoku was a motion-picture actor.'라고 했으므로 글의 내용과 일치한다.

1890년 8월 26일 하와이 와이키키 근처에서 태어난 Duke Kahanamoku는 하와이의 서퍼이자 수영선수로 미국을 위해 3개의 올림픽 금메달을 땄고 몇 년 동안 세계에서 가장 위대한 자유형 수영선수로 여겨졌다. 그는 아마 플러터 킥(flutter kick)을 개발한 것으로 가장 널리 알려졌는데, 그것은 주로 시저스 킥(scissors kick)을 대체하는 영법이다. Kahanamoku는 1913년 7월 5일과 1917년 9월 5일 사이에 1000야드 자유형에서 세 개의 세계 기록을 세웠다. Kahanamoku는 1000야드 자유형에서 1913년 미국 실내 챔피언이었고 1916~17년, 1920년에는 실외 타이틀 보유자였다. 1912년 스톡홀름 올림픽에서 그는 100미터 자유형 경기에서 우승했고, 1920년 벨기에 앤트워프 올림픽에서 그 승리를 반복했는데, 그곳에서 800미터 계주에서 승리한 미국 팀의 일원으로도 활약했다. Kahanamoku는 또한 서핑에 뛰어났으며, 그 스포츠의 아이콘 중 하나로 여겨지게 되었다. 1920년대 중반부터 Kahanamoku는 간헐적으로 영화배우로 활동했다. 1932년부터 1961년까지 그는 호놀룰루시와 카운티의 보안관이었다. 그는 1961년부터 사망할 때까지 하와이주에서 유명인사들을 맞이하는 공식 접객원으로 유급 관리직으로 근무했다.

VOCA

- surfer 서퍼
- freestyle 자유형(수영)
- be most widely known for ~로 가장 널리 알려져 있다
- replace 대신[대체]하다
- indoor 실내의, 실내용의
- outdoor 옥외[야외]의
- titleholder 선수권 보유자(champion)
- triumph 업적[승리], 대성공
- victorious 승리한, 승리를 거둔; 승리로 끝나는
- excel at ~에 뛰어나다
- view as ~으로 간주하다
- icon 우상[아이콘]
- official 공식적인[공적인]
- greeter (식당·상점 등에서) 손님을 맞이하는 사람
- personage 저명인사, 명사

04 난도 ★★★   정답 ②

독해 > 빈칸 완성 > 단어·구·절

정답의 이유

제시문은 아이들은 이미 저학년 때부터 자신들 고유의 이해[생각]을 갖고 있다는 내용이다. 빈칸 앞 문장에서 'Many young children have trouble giving up the notion that one-eighth is greater than one-fourth, because 8 is more than 4(많은 어린 아이들이 8이 4보다 크기 때문에 8분의 1이 4분의 1보다 크다는 개념을 포기하는 데 어려움을 겪는다).'라고 했고, 빈칸 문장의 앞부분의 'If children were blank slates, just telling them that the earth is round or that one-fourth is greater than one-

eighth would be(만약 아이들이 백지상태라면, 지구가 둥글다거나 4분의 1이 8분의 1보다 크다고 말하는 것만으로도 ~ 것이다) ~.'로 미루어 빈칸에는 blank slates(백지상태)에 적합한 단어가 들어가야 함을 유추할 수 있다. 따라서 빈칸에 들어갈 말로 적절한 것은 ② 'adequae(충분한)'이다.

오답의 이유

① 친밀한
③ 부적당한
④ 무관한

아이들이 교실로 가져오는 이해는 이미 저학년에 꽤 강력할 수 있다. 예를 들어, 일부 아이들은 둥근 지구를 팬케이크처럼 생겼다고 상상함으로써 평평한 지구에 대한 선입견을 고수하는 것으로 밝혀졌다. 이러한 새로운 이해의 구성은 아이들이 어떻게 사람들이 지구의 표면에서 서 있거나 걸을 수 있는지를 설명하도록 도와주는 지구 모형에 의해 인도된다. 많은 어린 아이들이 8이 4보다 크기 때문에 8분의 1이 4분의 1보다 크다는 개념을 포기하는 데 어려움을 겪는다. 만약 아이들이 백지상태라면, 지구가 둥글다거나 4분의 1이 8분의 1보다 크다고 말하는 것만으로도 충분할 것이다. 하지만 아이들은 이미 지구와 숫자에 대한 개념을 가지고 있기 때문에, 그것들을 변형하거나 확장하기 위해서는 그러한 개념들이 직접적으로 다루어져야 한다.

VOCA

- bring to ~로 가지고 오다
- preconception 선입견
- have trouble ~하는 데 어려움을 겪다
- notion 관념, 생각
- blank slates 백지상태
- address 고심하다[다루다]
- transform 변형시키다
- expand 확장되다[시키다]

05 난도 ★★☆   정답 ④

독해 > 세부 내용 찾기 > 내용 (불)일치

정답의 이유

④ 마지막 문장에서 'Additionally, urban farms ~ making cities more resilient to disruptions like natural disasters(게다가, 도시 농장은 ~ 자연재해와 같은 파괴에 대하여 도시를 더 회복력이 있도록 만든다).'라고 했으므로 글의 내용과 일치하지 않는다.

오답의 이유

① 첫 번째 문장에서 'Urban farming ~ involves growing food within city environments, utilizing spaces like rooftops, abandoned buildings, and community gardens.'라고 했으므로 글의 내용과 일치한다.

② 두 번째 문장에서 'This sustainable practice is gaining traction in cities across the world ~ as well as in many African and Asian cities where it plays a crucial role in food supply and local economies.'라고 했으므로 글의 내용과 일치한다.

③ 세 번째 문장에서 'Urban farming not only helps reduce carbon footprints by minimizing transport emissions but also increases access to fresh, healthy food in urban areas.'라고 했으므로 글의 내용과 일치한다.

본문해석

도시 농업이라고도 알려진 도시 농사는 옥상, 버려진 빌딩, 커뮤니티 가든 같은 공간을 활용하여 도시 환경 내에서 식량을 재배하는 것을 포함한다. 이 지속 가능한 관행은 식량 공급과 지역 경제에서 중요한 역할을 하는 다수의 아프리카와 아시아 도시뿐만 아니라 뉴욕, 시카고, 샌프란시스코, 런던, 암스테르담, 베를린을 포함한 전 세계의 도시에서 견인력을 얻고 있다. 도시 농업은 운송 배출을 최소화함으로써 탄소 발자국을 줄이는 것을 도울 뿐만 아니라 도시 지역에서 신선하고 건강한 식량에 대한 접근성을 높인다. 그것은 일자리를 창출하고 지역사회 내에서 이익을 유지함으로써 지역 경제를 강화시킨다. 게다가, 도시 농장은 도시 경관을 높이고, 대기질을 개선하고, 물을 보존하고, 교육 기회를 제공하고, 생물 다양성을 촉진하고, 사람들과 자연을 연결하고, 지역에서 식량을 생산함으로써 식량 안전 보장을 향상시켜서, 자연재해와 같은 파괴에 대하여 도시를 더 회복력이 있도록 만든다.

VOCA

- urban farming 도시 농업
- involve 수반[포함]하다
- reduce 줄이다[축소하다]
- carbon footprint 탄소 발자국
- minimize 최소화하다
- transport 수송하다
- emission 배출물, 배기가스
- access 접근하다, 들어가다, 이용하다
- profit 이익, 수익, 이윤
- enhance 높이다[향상시키다]
- cityscape 도시 경관, 도시 사진
- promote 촉진[고취]하다
- biodiversity 생물의 다양성
- resilient 회복력 있는
- disruption 파괴, 분열, 붕괴

06 난도 ★☆☆ 정답 ②

독해 > 세부 내용 찾기 > 지칭 추론

정답의 이유

밑줄 친 'unfinished animals' 다음 문장에서 'What he meant is that it is human nature to have a human nature that is very much the product of the society that surrounds us(그가 의미한 것은 인간 본성이 우리를 둘러싸고 있는 사회의 산물이라는 것이다).'라고 했고 다음 문장에서 '인간 본성은 발견된 것보다는 창조된 것에 가깝다.'라고 했으므로, 밑줄 친 'unfinished animals'가 의미하는 바로 적절한 것은 ② 'shaped by society rather than fixed by biology(생물학에 의해 고정된 것이기보다는 오히려 사회에 의해 형성된)'이다.

오답의 이유

① 불완전한 발달단계에 갇혀있는
③ 환경적 맥락에서 독특하게 자유로운
④ 동물적인 면과 정신적인 면을 겸비하여 태어난

본문해석

인간 본성에 대한 생각이나 이론은 과학에서 독특한 위치를 차지한다. 우리는 우주에 대한 우리의 이론에 의해 우주가 바뀔 것이라고 걱정할 필요가 없다. 그 행성들은 우리가 그것들에 대해 무엇을 생각하거나 어떻게 이론을 세우든 상관하지 않는다. 하지만 우리는 인간 본성에 대한 우리의 이론에 의해 인간 본성이 바뀔 것이라는 사실을 걱정해야 한다. 40년 전, 저명한 인류학자는 인간은 '미완성된 동물'이라고 말했다. 그가 의미한 바는 인간 본성이 우리를 둘러싸고 있는 사회의 산물이라는 것이다. 인간 본성은 발견된 것보다는 창조된 것에 가깝다. 우리는 사람들이 살고 있는 시설을 디자인함으로써 인간 본성을 '디자인'한다. 그래서 우리는 우리가 디자인하는 것을 돕고자 하는 인간 본성이 어떤 종류의 것인지 우리 스스로에게 물어야 한다.

VOCA

- unique 유일무이한, 독특한
- have a place 위치를 차지하다, 존재하다
- cosmos 우주
- planet 행성
- theorize 이론을 제시하다[세우다]
- distinguished 유명한, 성공한
- anthropologist 인류학자
- unfinished 완료되지[끝나지] 않은
- surround 둘러싸다, 에워싸다
- design 설계하다
- institution 시설, 제도[관습]
- stuck 움직일 수 없는[꼼짝 못하는]
- incomplete 불완전한, 미완성의
- fixed 고정된
- environmental context 환경적 맥락
- animalistic 동물성의

독해 > 빈칸 완성 > 단어 · 구 · 절

정답의 이유

(A) 네 번째 문장에서 'Passive House methods don't affect "buildability", yet they close the gap between design and performance and deliver a much higher standard of comfort and efficiency than government regulations(패시브 하우스 방식은 '시공성'에 영향을 미치지 않지만, 디자인과 성능 사이의 차이를 줄이고 모든 좋은 의도를 가지고 정부 규제가 달성한 것보다 훨씬 높은 수준의 편안함과 효율성을 제공한다) ~.'라고 했으므로, 빈칸 (A)에 들어갈 말로 적절한 것은 'surpassing(능가하는)'이다.

(B) 마지막에서 두 번째 문장에서 'This is, I believe, fundamental to good design, and is the next step we have to make in the evolution of our dwellings and places of work(나는 이것이 좋은 디자인의 기본이며, 우리가 거주지와 작업 장소의 진화에서 해야 할 다음 단계라고 믿는다).'라고 한 다음에 마지막 문장에서 'The improvements that are within our grasp are potentially transformative for mankind and the planet(우리가 파악할 수 있는 개선 사항은 잠재적으로 인류와 지구를 변화시키는 힘이 있다).'이라고 했으므로, 빈칸 (B)에 들어갈 말로 적절한 것은 'sustainable(지속 가능한)'이다.

오답의 이유

① 고집하는 - 지속 가능한
② 고집하는 - 지속 불가능한
③ 능가하는 - 지속 불가능한

본문해석

패시브 하우스는 쾌적한 조건을 보장하고 에너지 비용을 깊이 절감하기 위해 건물 물리학의 정밀도를 사용하여 건물을 설계하는 표준적이고 진보적인 방식이다. 그것은 설계 과정에서 모든 추측을 제거한다. 그것은 국가의 건축 규제가 하려고 노력했던 것을 수행한다. 패시브 하우스 방식은 '시공성'에 영향을 미치지 않지만, 디자인과 성능 사이의 차이를 줄이고 모든 좋은 의도를 가지고 정부 규제가 달성한 것보다 훨씬 높은 수준의 편안함과 효율성을 제공한다. 패시브 하우스 방식을 사용할 때, 단열재와 자유롭게 이용할 수 있는 일광에 대한 사용법을 가장 합리적인 방법으로, 쾌적함과 에너지 효율성 모두를 위한 적합한 양으로 사용하는 방법으로 배운다. 나는 이것이 좋은 디자인의 기본이며, 우리가 거주지와 작업 장소의 진화에서 해야 할 다음 단계라고 믿는다. 우리가 파악할 수 있는 개선 사항은 잠재적으로 인류와 지구를 변화시키는 힘이 있다.

↓

Passive House는 편안함과 에너지 효율성을 보장하기 위해 정밀한 건물 물리학을 활용하여 전통적인 규제를 (A) <u>능가하며</u> (B) <u>지속 가능한</u> 디자인을 위한 변형 잠재력을 제공한다.

VOCA

- Passive House   패시브 하우스(단열재 등을 이용해 내부 열이 밖으로 새어 나가는 것을 막음으로써 에너지 사용량을 절감하는 집. 외부 에너지원을 적극적으로 활용하지 않고 내부의 에너지를 보존한다는 의미에서 붙은 이름)
- precision   정확(성), 정밀(성), 신중함
- ensure   반드시 ~하게[이게] 하다, 보장하다
- guesswork   짐작, 추측
- regulation   규칙, 법령, 기본통달
- buildability   시공성
- performance   실적, 성과
- deliver   내놓다[산출하다]
- efficiency   효율(성), 능률
- achieve   달성하다, 성취하다
- insulation   절연[단열/방음] 처리[처리용 자재]
- daylight   햇빛, 일광
- sensible   분별[양식] 있는, 합리적인
- fundamental   근본[본질]적인
- evolution   진화
- dwelling   주거(지), 주택
- within one's grasp   이해할 수 있는
- utilize   활용[이용]하다

독해 > 글의 일관성 > 무관한 어휘 · 문장

정답의 이유

제시문의 네 번째 문장에서 '우리는 우리의 지역 생태계와 너무 얽혀 있어서, ~ 환경을 변형시킬 뿐만 아니라 그렇게 변형시킨 환경도, 우리를 결국 변형시킨다.'라고 했다. ④ 문장의 앞부분의 '소의 가축화를 포함한 환경적 착취가 있는 세계의 지역들인 북유럽과 동아프리카의 인간 개체군'과 ④ 다음의 'adult lactose tolerance: the ability to digest milk past infancy(유아기를 지나 우유를 소화하는 능력인 성인 유당 내성)'로 미루어 환경의 변형(소의 가축화로 인한 우유 소비량 증가)이 인간 유전자의 변형(성인 유당 내성 증가)을 가져왔다는 의미가 되어야 하므로 reduced(감소시켰다) → increased(증가시켰다)가 되어야 한다.

오늘날 인류는 호모 사피엔스라는 한 종밖에 남아 있지 않다. 하지만 그 한 종은, 유전적으로 99.9%가 넘는 유전적 동일성이 있음에도 불구하고, 다양한 이질적인 환경에 적응했다. 그리고 인간의 유전적 변이는 각 사회가 자신의 고유한 환경에 적응함으로써 발생하지만, 각 사회가 그 자체를 조정함으로써 이루어지는 문화적 적응은, 결국, 그 사회의 유전적 구성에 어느 정도 더 변이를 강요하게 될 것이다. 다시 말해서, 우리는 우리의 지역 생태계와 너무 얽혀 있어서, 우리가 의존하게 된 다양한 자원을 인간이 환경으로부터 도태시키면서 환경을 변형시킬 뿐만 아니라 그렇게 변형시킨 환경도, 우리를 결국 변형시킨다. 때로는 우리에게 심오한 생물학적 압력을 가한다. 예를 들어, 소의 가축화를 포함한 우리의 환경적 착취가 있는 세계의 지역들에서, 이를 테면, 북유럽이나 동아프리카 인간 개체군은 유아기를 지나 우유를 소화하는 능력인 성인 유당 내성을 감소(→ 증가)시켰다.

- species 종(생물 분류의 기초 단위)
- genetically 유전적으로 결정되는/전해지는
- identical 동일한, 똑같은
- array (인상적인) 집합체[모음/무리]
- disparate 서로 전혀 다른, 이질적인
- genetic variation 유전 변이
- result from 기인하다
- adaptation 각색, 적응
- exact 강요하다, 부득이 ~하게 하다
- makeup 조립, 구성
- be entangled with ~에 걸려들다, 말려들다; ~에 관련되다
- local ecology 지역 생태계
- cull (특정 동물을 그 수를 제한하기 위해) 도태시키다
- exert 가하다[행사하다]
- domestication 가축화
- digest (음식을) 소화하다
- past 지난, 최근의
- infancy (발달의) 초창기[초기]

09 난도 ★★☆   정답 ①

독해 > 글의 일관성 > 글의 순서

[정답의 이유]

주어진 글에서 우리가 일상생활에서 중요하게 생각하는 '시간은 돈이다.'라는 비유를 간단히 생각해 보라고 했으므로 주어진 글 다음에는 '시간은 돈이다.'라는 비유를 우리가 일상생활에서 사용하는 경우를 부연·설명하는 (A)로 이어지는 것이 자연스럽다. (C)에서 'This metaphor, however, fails to disclose important phenomenological aspects of time(그러나 이 비유는 시간의 중요한 현상학적 측면을 밝히지 못한다) ~'이라고 했으므로, (C)는 글의 흐름상 'Every metaphor brokers what is made visible or invisible(모든 비유는 눈에 보이거나 보이지 않게 되는 것을 중개

한다)'이라고 비유의 일반적인 점을 설명하는 (B) 다음에 와야 한다. 따라서 주어진 글 다음에 이어질 글의 순서로 적절한 것은 ① '(A) - (B) - (C)'이다.

우리가 일상생활을 하는 데 중요한 역할을 하는 비유를 간단히 생각해 보라. 시간은 돈이다.

(A) 우리는 종종 시간이 돈인 것처럼 이야기한다. 예를 들어, 다음과 같은 일상적인 표현에서 그렇다. "넌 내 시간을 낭비하고 있어." "이 장치는 여러분이 일하는 시간을 절약할 것이다." "당신은 주말을 어떻게 보낼 것입니까?" "나는 이 관계에 많은 시간을 투자했어요."

(B) 모든 비유는 눈에 보이거나 보이지 않게 되는 것을 중개한다. 이것은 시간이 얼마나 돈과 같은지를 강조하고, 얼마나 그렇지 않은지를 모호하게 한다. 따라서 시간은 우리가 낭비하거나 잃을 수 있는 것이 되고, 나이가 들면서 줄어들 수 있는 것이 된다. 그것은 매우 선형적이고 질서정연한 방식으로 추출된다.

(C) 그러나 이 비유는 시간의 중요한 현상학적 측면, 예를 들어 우리가 하는 일에 대한 우리의 참여에 따라 시간이 얼마나 빨라지거나 느려지는지 밝히지 못한다. 대신에 우리는 시간을 흐르는 시냇물처럼 꽤 유동적이라고 생각할 수도 있는데, 예를 들어, 우리가 시간은 돈이라는 세계관을 채택했을 정도로 우리는 이것을 보지 못한다.

- briefly 간단히, 일시적으로
- metaphor 비유, 은유
- broker 중개하다
- visible 가시적인, 뚜렷한
- invisible 보이지 않는, 볼 수 없는
- highlight 강조하다
- diminish 깎아내리다, 폄하하다
- abstract 추출하다, 끌어내다
- linear 선의, 선으로 된
- orderly 정돈된, 정연한
- fashion 방법, 방식, 풍(風)
- fail 실패하다, ~하지 못하다
- disclose 밝히다[폭로하다]
- phenomenological 현상학적인, 현상론의
- speed up 속도를 더 내다[높이다]
- slow down [속도·진행]을 늦추다
- engagement 관계함, 참여
- conceive 마음속으로 하다[품다], 상상하다
- fluid 유동[가변]적인
- lose sight of ~을 잃다, 안보이다
- to the extent ~ 어느 정도로
- worldview 세계관

10 난도 ★★☆   정답 ③

어법 > 비문 찾기

정답의 이유

③ 밑줄 친 her 앞의 'she has promised me to take care of'와 her 다음의 'for their sake(그들을 위해)'로 미루어 보아 문맥상 her는 문장의 주어인 she와 동일 대상임을 유추할 수 있으므로, her → herself가 되어야 한다.

본문해석

그의 마지막 생각은 그의 아내를 위한 것이었다. "그는 그녀가 그것을 견디지 못할까 봐 염려합니다."라고 그가 지난 며칠 동안 자신과 함께 있도록 허락받은 버넷 주교에게 말했다. 그가 그녀에 대해 말했을 때 그의 눈에는 눈물이 고였다. 마지막 날이 왔고, Lady Russel은 세 명의 아이들을 데리고 그들의 아버지에게 영원한 작별을 고했다. '리틀 펍스'는 겨우 아홉 살이었고, 그녀의 여동생 캐서린은 일곱 살이었고, 아기는 세 살이었기에 그의 상실을 인지하기에는 너무 어렸다. 그는 침착하게 그들에게 입맞추었고, 그들을 보냈다. 그의 아내는 머물렀고 그들은 함께 마지막 식사를 했다. 그러고 나서 그들은 침묵 속에서 키스했고, 그녀는 조용히 그를 떠났다. 그녀가 떠나자, Lord Russel은 완전히 무너졌다. "오, 그녀는 나에게 얼마나 큰 축복인가요!"라고 그는 울부짖었다. "아이들을 그런 어머니의 보살핌 속에 내버려 둔다는 것은 나에게 큰 위안입니다. 그녀는 그들을 위해 그녀 자신을 돌보겠다고 약속했고, 그녀는 그렇게 할 거예요."라고 그는 단호하게 덧붙였다. Lady Russel은 무거운 마음으로 그녀가 다시는 그를 맞이할 수 없는 슬픈 집으로 돌아갔다. 1683년 7월 21일, 그녀는 과부였고, 그녀의 아이들은 아버지가 없었다. 그들은 음산한 런던 집을 떠나 시골의 오래된 수도원으로 갔다.

VOCA

- allow 허락하다, 용납하다
- silence 고요, 적막
- break down 감정을 주체하지 못하다[허물어지다]
- blessing 다행스러운 것, 좋은 점
- promise 약속하다
- resolutely 단호히, 결연히
- dreary 음울한, 지루한
- abbey 대수도원

11 난도 ★☆☆   정답 ②

독해 > 세부 내용 찾기 > 내용 (불)일치

정답의 이유

② 세 번째 문장에서 'Despite the flexibility and autonomy it offers, most independent workers desire more stable employment(대부분의 독립 근로자는 유연성과 자율성에도 불구하고 보다 안정적인 고용을 원한다) ~.'라고 했으므로 글의 내용과 일치하지 않는다.

오답의 이유

① 첫 번째 문장에서 '~ is growing rapidly in the United States, with 36% of employed participants in a 2022 McKinsey survey identifying as independent workers, up from 27% in 2016.'라고 했으므로 글의 내용과 일치한다.

③ 네 번째 문장에서 'The challenges faced by gig workers include limited access to healthcare, housing, and other basic needs, ~'라고 했으므로 글의 내용과 일치한다.

④ 다섯 번째 문장에서 'Technological advancements have facilitated the rise in independent work, making remote and freelance jobs more accessible and appealing.'이라고 했으므로 글의 내용과 일치한다.

본문해석

프리랜서 및 부업에 종사하는 사람들의 노동력을 지칭하는 긱 이코노미(gig economy)가 미국에서 빠르게 성장하고 있으며, 2022년 McKinsey survey에서 고용된 참가자 중 36%가 독립 근로자로 확인되었는데, 이는 2016년 27%에서 증가한 수치이다. 이 노동력에는 변호사와 같은 고임금 전문가부터 배달 기사와 같은 저소득자까지 다양한 직업이 포함된다. 대부분의 독립 근로자는 유연성과 자율성에도 불구하고 보다 안정적인 고용을 원하며, 62%는 고용 안정성과 혜택에 대한 우려로 인해 정규직을 선호한다. 긱 경제 근로자(gig worker)가 직면한 어려움에는 의료, 주택 및 기타 기본 요구 사항에 대한 제한된 접근성과 정부 지원에 크게 의존하는 것이 포함된다. 기술 발전은 독립 근로의 증가를 촉진하여 원격 및 프리랜서 일자리를 접근하기 쉽고 매력적인 것으로 만들고 있다. 이러한 추세는 인플레이션 및 고용 시장 역동성 같은 광범위한 경제적 압력을 반영하여 개인이 생존, 유연성 또는 즐거움을 위해 긱 경제 근무를 선택하는 데 영향을 미친다.

VOCA

- gig economy 긱 이코노미, 임시직 선호 경제(일자리에 계약직이나 프리랜서 등을 주로 채용하는 현상)
- workforce (모든) 노동자[직원]
- identify as ~라고 밝히다
- a wide range of 광범위한, 다양한
- flexibility 유연성, 융통성
- autonomy 자율[자주](성)
- stable employment 안정된 고용
- challenge 도전
- face 직면하다
- gig worker 긱 경제 근로자(계약직이나 임시직으로 일하는 프리랜서처럼 소속된 곳이 없는 근로자)
- reliance 의존, 의지
- facilitate 가능하게[용이하게] 하다
- appealing 매력적인, 흥미로운
- dynamic 원동력, 역동적인
- gig work 긱 경제 근무(정규직보다는 임시직, 계약직을 선호하는 사회에서의 업무나 일)

독해 > 글의 일관성 > 글의 순서

정답의 이유

주어진 글에서 우리는 '범주의 방식에 의해(by way of categories)' 세상을 알고 관계를 맺게 된다고 했으므로, 주어진 글 다음에는 주어진 문장의 범주의 방식을 'this faculty(이러한 능력)'로 지칭하며, 통상적인 의사소통의 범주화 과정을 설명하는 (B)가 오는 것이 자연스럽다. (C)에서 암묵적으로 유지되는 범주와 명시적으로 지배되는 범주를 비교한 다음에 마지막 문장에서 'The application of category systems for the same things varies by context and in use(동일한 사물에 대한 범주 시스템의 적용은 맥락과 용도에 따라 다르다).'라고 했으므로, (C) 다음에는 예를 들어 동물 종은 민속과 신화에 의해 묘사되는 것처럼 다른 환경에서는 법적 구성물로, 또 다른 환경에서는 과학적 분류체계로 간주될 수 있다고 설명한 (A)가 와야 한다. 따라서 주어진 글 다음에 이어질 글의 순서로 적절한 것은 ② '(B) – (C) – (A)'이다.

본문해석

우리는 범주의 방식에 의해 세상을 알고 관계를 맺게 된다.
(B) 통상적인 의사소통이 이 능력의 가장 즉각적인 표현이다. 우리는 소리와 말을 통해 사물을 언급하고, 우리가 개념이라고 부르는 아이디어를 그 안에 붙인다.
(C) 우리의 범주 중 일부는 암묵적으로 유지된다. 다른 범주는 관습, 법, 정치 또는 과학에 의해 명시적으로 지배된다. 동일한 사물에 대한 범주 시스템의 적용은 맥락과 용도에 따라 다르다.
(A) 예를 들어, 동물 종의 개념은 어떤 환경에서는 민속과 신화에 의해 묘사되는 것처럼, 다른 환경에서는 세부적인 법적 구성물로, 또 다른 환경에서는 과학적 분류 체계로 가장 잘 간주될 수 있다.

VOCA

• relate to ~와 관계가 있다
• category 범주
• ordinary 보통의, 일상적인
• communication 의사소통, 연락
• immediate 즉각적인
• faculty 능력[기능]
• attach 붙이다, 첨부하다
• concept 개념
• explicitly 명쾌하게
• govern 통치하다[다스리다]
• application 적용, 응용
• category system 범주 체계
• notion 개념, 관념, 생각
• detailed 상세한
• legal construct 법적 구조(구조물)
• scientific classification 과학적 분류

독해 > 대의 파악 > 분위기, 어조, 심경

정답의 이유

마지막 문장에서 'My body tenses with hers; together we brace a hundred times for impact(내 몸은 엄마와 함께 긴장하고, 우리는 함께 충격에 대해 백 번을 대비한다).'라고 했으므로, 글에 나타난 화자의 심경으로 적절한 것은 ② 'anxious and fearful(불안하고 두려운)'이다.

오답의 이유

① 흥분하고 오싹한
③ 조심스럽지만 안정된
④ 편안하고 긴장을 푼

본문해석

지금은 새벽 3시이고, 우리는 남부에서 북부 유타 주로 가고 있는데, 날씨가 사막의 메마른 추위에서 고산 지역의 겨울 매서운 강풍으로 바뀌고 있다. 얼음이 도로를 차지한다. 눈송이가 작은 곤충들처럼 자동차 앞유리에 가볍게 튕기고, 처음에는 몇 개, 그리고 나서 아주 많은 도로가 사라진다. 우리는 폭풍의 중심부를 향해서 앞으로 나아간다. 밴이 미끄러지고 홱 움직인다. 바람은 맹렬하고, 창밖의 풍경은 순백이다. Richard가 차를 한 쪽에 댄다. 우리는 더 이상 갈 수 없다고 그가 말한다. 아빠가 핸들을 잡고, Richard는 조수석으로 이동하고, 엄마는 나와 Audrey 옆에 매트리스 위에 눕는다. 아빠는 고속도로에 들어가서 마치 주장을 입증하는 것처럼, Richard의 속도의 두 배가 될 때까지 빠르게 속도를 더했다. "우리 더 천천히 운전해야 하지 않을까요?"라고 엄마가 묻는다. 아빠는 씨익 웃는다. "나는 천사들이 날 수 있는 것보다 더 빨리 운전하지 않아." 밴은 여전히 속도를 내고 있다. 50에서 60으로, Richard는 긴장된 상태로 앉아 손으로 팔걸이를 잡고 있는데, 타이어가 미끄러질 때마다 손가락 마디가 하얗게 된다. 엄마는 내 옆자리에 얼굴을 내 옆으로 하고 누워서 밴의 뒷부분이 좌우로 미끄러질 때마다 조금씩 공기를 들이마시고는. 아빠가 바로잡고 차로로 돌아가자 숨을 죽인다. 엄마는 너무 경직되어 있어서, 내 생각에, 엄마가 산산조각이 날지도 모르겠다. 내 몸은 엄마와 함께 긴장하고, 우리는 함께 충격에 대해 백 번을 대비한다.

VOCA

• make one's way 나아가다, 가다
• freezing 꽁꽁 얼게[너무나] 추운
• alpine 고산의, 알프스의
• claim 얻다, 차지하다
• snowflake 눈송이
• flick 가볍게 치다, 홱 튀기다
• windshield (자동차 앞부분의) 방풍 유리
• furious 맹렬한, 사나운
• pull over 차[보트]를 한쪽에 대다
• take the wheel 핸들[타륜]을 잡다, 운전하다
• passenger seat (자동차의) 조수석
• make a point 주장을 입증하다

- tensely 긴장하여, 긴박하여
- clutch ~ 꽉 쥐다
- armrest (의자 등의) 팔걸이
- knuckle 손가락 관절, 손가락 마디
- lane 차선, 차로
- shatter 산산이 부수다, 박살내다
- tense with ~으로 긴장한
- brace 재빨리 대비하다
- impact 영향, 충격

14 난도 ★★☆　　　　　　　　　　　　　　정답 ③

독해 > 글의 일관성 > 문장 삽입

정답의 이유

주어진 문장은 현재 무인 유통의 적용에는 많은 문제가 있다는 내용이다. ③ 앞 문장에서 바이러스가 에어로졸을 통해 바이러스를 전염시킬 수 있기 때문에 최종 단계의 배송을 위한 비접촉식 배송의 필요성이 점차 증가하여 무인 물류 사용이 어느 정도 가속화되었다고 했고, 'For example(예를 들어)'로 시작하는 ③ 다음 문장에서 무인 물류 유통의 문제점을 구체적으로 예를 들어서 설명하고 있으므로 주어진 문장이 들어가기에 적절한 곳은 ③이다.

본문해석

COVID-19 기간의 도시 봉쇄 정책은 수많은 테이크아웃, 야채 쇼핑, 커뮤니티 단체 구매 및 기타 비즈니스의 급속한 성장을 촉진했다. 최종 단계의 배송은 전염병 기간 동안 중요한 생계 지원이 되었다. 동시에 에어로졸을 통해 바이러스를 전염시킬 수 있기 때문에 최종 단계의 배송을 위한 비접촉식 배송의 필요성이 점차 증가하여 무인 물류 사용이 어느 정도 가속화되었다. <u>그러나 현재 무인 유통의 적용에는 많은 문제가 있다.</u> 예를 들어 커뮤니티 공간은 지원 물류 인프라의 부족으로 인해 무인 배송 시설 운영에 적합하지 않다. 게다가, 현재 기술은 배송 과정을 완료할 수 없으며 무인 배송 노드의 도킹을 돕기 위해 관련 공간뿐만 아니라 인력의 협업이 필요하다.

VOCA

- lockdown 봉쇄
- facilitate 가능하게[용이하게] 하다
- livelihood support 생계 지원
- epidemic 유행병, 유행성 (전염병)
- transmit 전염시키다
- contactless 비접촉식의
- accelerate 가속화되다, 가속화하다
- unmanned (기계 · 차량 등이) 무인의
- logistics 물류, 화물, 택배
- distribution (상품의) 유통(기구), 판매망
- suitable 적합한, 알맞은
- logistics infrastructure 물류 인프라
- collaboration 협력, 공동, 협업
- relevant 관계가 있는, (~에 있어서) 적절한
- personnel 전 직원, 인원

15 난도 ★★☆　　　　　　　　　　　　　　정답 ①

독해 > 글의 일관성 > 글의 순서

정답의 이유

주어진 글은 사람들은 이해하려는 욕구가 설득하려는 욕구보다 우선하는 경우에는 관점의 교환에는 거의 관심이 없다고 했으므로, 예상을 벗어난 일탈적인 의견은 순식간에 평가절하, 명예훼손, 모욕, 심지어 물리적인 대립을 동반한다는 내용의 (B)로 이어져야 한다. (B)의 마지막에서 '논쟁'이 벌어지는 경우 사람들의 의견 교환 방식이 확실히 저하된다고 했으므로, '그러나 갈등은 단지 행동하기 위한 인기 없는 압력의 원천이 아니다.'라는 문장으로 시작하는 (A)가 와야 한다. (A)의 마지막 문장인 'Basically, today's misery is the starting shot in the race towards a better future.'를 (C)의 첫 문장에서 'You probably know this from your own experience, too ~'라며 'this'로 받아서 마무리짓고 있다. 따라서 주어진 글 다음에 이어질 글의 순서로 적절한 것은 ① '(B) - (A) - (C)'이다.

본문해석

사람들은 이해하려는 욕구가 어떤 대가를 치르더라도 설득하려는 욕구보다 우선하는 경우의 진정한 관점을 교환하는 것에는 거의 관심이 없다.

(B) 예상을 벗어난 일탈적인 의견은 순식간에 평가절하, 명예훼손, 모욕, 심지어 물리적인 대립이 동반된다. 소셜 미디어 네트워크에서 벌어지고 있는 '논쟁'을 보면, 난민 사태나 테러 같은 뜨거운 감자를 볼 필요도 없이 사람들의 의견 교환방식이 확실히 저하된다.

(A) 그러나 갈등은 단지 행동하기 위한 인기 없는 압력의 원천이 아니다. 또한 갈등에는 많은 에너지가 내재되어 있으며, 이는 능숙한 접근법의 도움으로 긍정적인 변화, 다시 말해, 개선을 창출하는 데 활용될 수 있다. 기본적으로 오늘의 고통은 더 나은 미래를 향한 경주의 출발점이다.

(C) 갈등에 대한 건설적인 해결책을 찾는 데 성공하고, 고된 해명 과정의 끝에서 성공적인 결과가 모든 노력의 가치가 있음을 깨달았을 때, 여러분은 아마 여러분 자신의 경험을 통해서도 이 사실을 알고 있을 것이다.

VOCA

- genuine 진짜의, 진품의
- take precedence over ~보다 우위에 서다, 우선하다
- convince 납득시키다, 확신시키다
- at any price 어떤 대가를 치르더라도
- deviate (일상 · 예상 등을) 벗어나다
- devaluation 평가 절하
- hot potato 뜨거운 감자, 난감한 문제[상황 등]
- degradation 저하, 악화
- inherent 내재하는
- harness (동력원 등으로) 이용[활용]하다
- approach 접근법, 처리 방법
- misery 고통, 빈곤

- clarification 설명, 해명
- outcome 결과, 성과, 소산

16 난도 ★☆☆　　　　　　　　　　　　　정답 ④

독해 > 세부 내용 찾기 > 내용 (불)일치

정답의 이유

④ 마지막에서 두 번째 문장에서 'He got married and ~ pursued his NBA basketball career playing fulltime for several teams(그는 결혼했고 ~ 여러 팀에서 풀타임 선수로 활약하면서 NBA 농구 경력을 계속 이어갔다).'라고 했으므로 글의 내용과 일치하지 않는다.

오답의 이유

① 첫 번째 문장에서 'Belus Smawley grew up on a farm with his parents and six siblings.'라고 했으므로 글의 내용과 일치한다.

② 두 번째 문장의 후반부에서 '~ trying to improve his leaping ability by touching higher and higher limbs of the oak tree on their farm.'이라고 했으므로 글의 내용과 일치한다.

③ 여섯 번째 문장에서 'He ~ and got an All-American athletic scholarship for Appalachian State University ~'라고 했으므로 글의 내용과 일치한다.

본문해석

Belus Smawley는 부모님과 여섯 형제와 함께 농장에서 자랐다. 1학년 때, 그는 키가 컸고 다른 어떤 소년보다 더 높이 뛸 수 있었고, 그들의 농장에 있는 참나무의 더 높은 나뭇가지를 만지면서 자신의 점프력을 향상시키려고 노력했다. 이곳이 그의 첫 번째 점프슛 시도가 있었던 곳이라고 한다. Belus Smawley가 자신의 슛을 규칙적으로 사용하기 시작했을 때, 그는 최고 득점자가 되었다. 18세에, 그는 AAU18 농구팀에 합격했다. 그는 고등학교를 마치고 나서 Appalachian 주립대학교(역사와 체육 전공)에서 전미 체육 장학금을 받았다. 그는 해군에 가기 전까지 선수 겸 코치가 되었다. 그는 그들의 농구팀에서 뛰기 시작했고 점프슛 기량을 갈고 닦았다. 그는 결혼했고 고등학교 교사이자 농구 코치로 근무하거나 여러 팀에서 풀타임 선수로 활약하면서 NBA 농구 경력을 계속 이어갔다. 마침내, 그는 가족과 교사 경력에 집중하여 중학교 교장이 되었다.

VOCA

- sibling 형제자매[동기]
- limb 나뭇가지
- oak tree 오크나무
- scorer (스포츠의) 득점자
- All-American 미국을 대표하는
- athletic 운동선수의, 체육의
- scholarship 장학금
- refine 갈고 닦다
- pursue 추구하다, 추진하다

17 난도 ★★★　　　　　　　　　　　　　정답 ②

독해 > 글의 일관성 > 문장 삽입

정답의 이유

주어진 문장에서 '그러면, 우리가 기계로부터 무언가 비슷한 것을 기대하는 것을 이해할 수 있을 것이다.'로 미루어 주어진 문장의 앞에는 '무언가 비슷한 것(something similar)'과 관련된 내용이 나와야 함을 유추할 수 있다. ② 앞 문장에서 관심을 공유함으로써 얻는 이익이 어느 정도 사생활 또는 행동의 자유의 상실보다 크다는 점에서, 협력이 한 종으로서 우리의 생존에 있어 현저하게 중요했다는 사실을 지적해야 한다고 했으므로, 그 내용을 주어진 문장에서 'something similar'로 받고 있다. 또 ② 다음 문장에서 'This idea in machine learning goes by the name of "saliency"(기계 학습에서 이러한 생각은 '중요점'이라는 이름에 의거해서 판단한다).'라고 했으므로, 글의 흐름상 주어진 문장이 들어가기에 적절한 곳은 ②이다.

본문해석

인간은 대부분의 다른 종에 비해 뚜렷하게 크고 눈에 보이는 공막(눈의 흰자)을 가지고 있으며, 그 결과 우리는 특이하게도 주의를 기울이는 방식, 다시 말해 시선이 드러난다. 진화 생물학자들은 '협력적 눈 가설'을 통해 이것은 결함이 아니라 특징임에 틀림없다고 주장했다. 즉, 관심을 공유함으로써 얻는 이익이 어느 정도 사생활 또는 행동의 자유의 상실보다 크다는 점에서, 협력이 한 종으로서 우리의 생존에 있어 현저하게 중요했다는 사실을 지적해야 한다는 것이다. 그러면, 우리가 기계로부터 무언가 비슷한 것을 기대하는 것을 이해할 수 있을 것이다. 즉, 그것들(기계들)이 무엇을 본다고 생각하는지 뿐만 아니라, 특히 어디를 보고 있는지를 아는 것이다. 기계 학습에서 이러한 생각은 '중요점'이라는 이름에 의거해서 판단한다. 시스템이 이미지를 보고 어떤 범주에 할당한다면, 아마도 이미지의 일부분이 그러한 결정을 내리는 데 다른 부분보다 더 중요하거나 더 영향력이 있었을 것이라는 것이다. 이미지의 이러한 중요한 부분을 강조하는 일종의 '적외선 열지도'를 볼 수 있다면, 시스템이 우리가 생각하는 방식으로 작동하는지 확인하기 위한 일종의 정상성 점검으로 사용할 수 있는 중요한 진단 정보를 얻을 수 있을 것이다.

VOCA

- relative to ~에 관하여
- gaze 응시하다[바라보다]
- evolutionary biologist 진화 생물학자
- via 경유하여[거쳐], 통하여
- hypothesis 가설
- bug 결함, 불량한 곳
- uncommonly 두드러지게, 현저하게
- survival 생존, 유물
- assign 맡기다[배정하다/부과하다]
- presumably 아마, 짐작건대
- determination 투지, 결정
- heat map 적외선 열지도
- portion 부분[일부]

- obtain 얻다[구하다/입수하다]
- crucial 중대한, 결정적인
- diagnostic 진단의
- sanity 온전한 정신 (상태)

18 난도 ★☆☆ 정답 ②

어법 > 정문 찾기

정답의 이유

(A) 앞부분의 'three men are depicted'와 (A) 다음의 'from a city'로 미루어 세 명의 남자가 도시로부터 '달아나는'의 능동의 뜻이므로, 빈칸 (A)에는 현재분사인 fleeing이 적절하다.

(B) 앞에 장소 명사인 'the Euphrates River'가 있고 (B) 다음 문장이 'one is swimming ~'으로 완전한 문장이므로 빈칸 (B)에는 관계부사 where가 적절하다.

(C) 문장의 주어가 'the hands of the refugees'로 복수명사이다. 따라서 빈칸 (C)에는 복수동사인 are가 적절하다.

본문해석

벽화에서 관개된 평원의 기후를 어렴풋이 감지할 수 있다. 여름 태양이 단단한 지면에 쨍쨍 내리쬐고, 왕이 커다란 우산에 의해 그늘이 드리워져 있다. 종종 있는 전쟁 모습도 생생하고 세밀하게 조각되어 있다. 대략 기원전 878년에 세 명의 남자들이 포로로 사로잡힌 것으로 추정되는 도시에서 달아나고 있는 모습이 묘사되어 있다. 긴 옷을 입은 그들은 유프라테스 강으로 뛰어들었는데, 그곳에서 한 사람은 헤엄치고 있고 두 사람은 구명정을 가슴에 껴안고 있다. 긴 베개처럼 생긴 구명정은 동물의 피부로 되어 있으며, 공기를 넣어 부풀렸다. 난민들은 손으로 구명정을 움켜쥐고 있고, 구명정에 공기를 불어넣는 데 숨이 많이 들어가는 만큼 다리로 헤엄쳐야만 물 위에 떠 있을 수 있다. 그들이 반대편 해안에 도달했는지 아닌지는 결코 알 수 없다.

VOCA

- irrigated 관개된
- glimpse 잠깐[언뜻] 보다, 깨닫다, 이해하다
- mural 벽화
- beat down (햇볕이) 쨍쨍 내리쬐다
- vivid 생생한
- in detail 상세하게
- depict 묘사하다[그리다]
- fleeing 도망치는
- capture 포로로 잡다, 억류하다
- lifebuoy 구명용품
- pillow 베개
- inflate (공기나 가스로) 부풀리다[부풀다]
- refugee 난민, 망명자
- clutch (꽉) 움켜잡다
- afloat (물에) 뜬

더 알아보기

관계부사

- 관계부사의 종류

관계부사	선행사
when	시간(the time, the day, the year 등)을 나타내는 명사
where	장소(the place, the house, the station 등)를 나타내는 명사
why	이유(the reason)를 나타내는 명사
how	방법(the way)을 나타내는 명사 * 관계부사 how는 선행사(the way)와 관계부사(how)를 함께 쓸 수 없다.

예 Celebrities often compete in *television competitions* where they raise awareness of charities. → (장소 television competitions = where)
(유명인사들은 자선단체에 대한 인식을 높이는 텔레비전 대회에서 종종 경쟁한다.)

예 It's hard to know ~~the way how~~ a magician performs his tricks. (×)
It's hard to know the way[how] a magician performs his tricks. (○)
(마술사가 트릭을 쓰는 방법을 알기 어렵다.)

- 관계부사 vs. 관계대명사

구분	선행사	관계절
관계 부사	있음	• 관계부사 다음에는 완전한 문장이 온다. • 관계부사는 '전치사+관계대명사'로 바꾸어 쓸 수 있다.
관계 대명사		• 관계대명사 다음에는 불완전한 문장이 온다. • 관계대명사는 관계절 안에서 주어, 목적어 역할을 한다.

예 He proposed creating a space where musicians would be able to practice for free. → 관계부사(where = in which)
(그는 음악가들이 무료로 연습할 수 있는 공간을 만들자고 제안했다.)

예 She wants to rent the apartment which she saw last Sunday. → 관계대명사(which)
(그녀는 지난 일요일에 보았던 아파트를 빌리고 싶어한다.)

19 난도 ★☆☆ 정답 ②

독해 > 세부 내용 찾기 > 내용 (불)일치

정답의 이유

② 다섯 번째, 여섯 번째 문장에서 'The wall ~ was built to keep out the Native Americans and the British. It eventually became Wall Street(그 장벽은 ~ 북미 원주민과 영국인들의 출입을 금지하기 위해 세워졌다. 그것은 결국 월스트리트가 되었으며) ~'라고 했으므로 글의 내용과 일치하지 않는다.

① 두 번째 문장에서 'They shared the land and traded guns, beads and wool for beaver furs.'라고 했으므로 글의 내용과 일치한다.

③ 마지막에서 두 번째 문장의 후반부에서 '~ where part of the Lenape trade route, known as Wickquasgeck, became Brede weg, later Broadway.'라고 했으므로 글의 내용과 일치한다.

④ 마지막 문장에서 'The Lenape helped shape the geography of modern-day New York City, ~'라고 했으므로 글의 내용과 일치한다.

본문해석

네덜란드인들이 17세기에 현재의 뉴욕시에 도착했을 때, 역사적 기록에 따르면 Lenape로 알려진 원주민들과의 만남은 처음에는 대부분 우호적이었다. 그들은 땅을 공유했고 총, 구슬, 양모를 비버의 모피와 교역했다. 네덜란드인들은 심지어 1626년에 Lenape로부터 Manahatta 섬을 '구매'했다. 결국 뉴 암스테르담 주변에 장벽을 건설함으로써 시행된 그 거래는 Lenape가 그들의 고향을 떠나도록 하는 강제적인 대량 이주의 시작을 알렸다. 그 장벽은 1660년대에 지도에 나타나기 시작했는데, 북미 원주민과 영국인들의 출입을 금지하기 위해 세워졌다. 그것은 결국 월스트리트가 되었으며, Manahatta는 맨해튼이 되었고, 그곳에서 Wickquasgeck로 알려진 Lenape 통상로의 일부는 Brede weg가 되었는데, 후에 브로드웨이가 되었다. Lenape는 현대 뉴욕시의 지리학적 형태를 형성하는 데 도움을 주었지만, 그들의 유산의 다른 흔적들은 거의 사라졌다.

VOCA

- encounter 만남[접촉/조우]
- indigenous 원산의[토착의]
- amicable 우호적인, 원만한
- trade 거래[교역/무역]하다
- bead 구슬, 염주, 묵주
- transaction 거래, 매매
- enforce 집행[시행/실시]하다
- eventual 궁극[최종]적인
- forced 강제적인, 강요된
- mass migration 집단 이주
- keep out (~에) 들어가지 않다
- trace 추적하다, (추적하여) 찾아내다
- legacy 유산
- vanish 사라지다

20 난도 ★★☆

정답 ④

어법 > 비문 찾기

④ become 앞의 문장이 Celebrities(주어) take up(동사) permanent residence(목적어) in our inner lives as well(전명구)로 완전한 문장이고 콤마(,) 앞에 접속사가 없으므로 become → becoming이 되어야 한다.

본문해석

오늘날, 우리는 미디어와 그것이 유지하는 유명인 문화가 우리가 만난 적이 없는 사람들과 친밀한 관계를 가질 수 있는 새로운 형태의 공공성을 만들어 냈다는 것을 당연한 것으로 여긴다. 미디어 기술 덕분에 우리는 유명인들과 더욱 가까워지고, 그들과 친밀한 관계를 갖는 환상을 즐기게 한다. 어느 정도 우리는 유명인들을 내면화하고, 마치 그들이 실제로 친구인 것처럼 무의식적으로 우리 의식의 일부로 만들었다. 유명인들은 우리 내면의 삶에서도 영구적인 거주지를 차지하고, 우리의 몽상과 환상, 행동 지침, 야망의 중심이 된다. 많은 사람들이 유명인들의 특성과 그들과의 관계를 우리의 정신적 수하물의 일부로 소지하고 다니기 때문에, 사실, 유명인 문화는 영구적으로 우리 감성의 일부가 될 수 있다.

VOCA

- take for granted 당연한 것으로 여기다, ~을 당연한 것이라고 생각하다
- celebrity culture 유명인 문화(유명인, 연예인 등이 사람들 사이에 과도하게 언급되고 그들의 사생활까지 관심의 대상이 되는 현상)
- sustain 살아가게[존재하게/지탱하게] 하다
- publicness 공공화된 것[상태]
- intimate 친(밀)한
- illusion 오해[착각]
- intimacy 친밀함
- to a greater or lesser degree 어느 정도
- internalized 내면화된
- take up 차지하다[쓰다]
- permanent 영구적인
- residence 주택, 거주지
- sensibility 감성[감수성]
- trait 특성

가정법

• as if / as though 가정법

과거	주어+동사+as if[as though]+주어+과거 동사	마치 ~인 것처럼
과거완료	주어+동사+as if[as though]+주어+had p.p.	마치 ~이었던 것처럼

예 Two to eight months of not exercising at all will reduce your fitness level to as if you never *exercised* before.
(2~8개월 동안 전혀 운동을 하지 않는 것은 여러분의 건강 척도를 마치 이전에 전혀 운동을 한 적이 없는 것처럼 만든다.)

예 He looked at me as if I *were* mad.
(그는 마치 나를 미친 사람인 것처럼 쳐다봤다.)

예 He looks as if he *had seen* a ghost.
(그는 마치 귀신이라도 본 것처럼 보인다.)

• 기타 가정법

기타 가정법	의미
I wish 가정법	~라면 좋을[좋았을] 텐데
without 가정법	~이 없다면
It is high time 가정법 과거	~할 시간이다(그러나 하지 않았다)

예 It's high time we *pulled* together and *got* the job done right.
(우리가 마음을 다잡고 일을 제대로 할 때이다.)

예 Sometimes I wish I *had* never *been* born.
(가끔은 태어나지 않았으면 좋았을 때도 있다.)

• 자주 쓰이는 가정법 관련 표현

표현	의미
What if	~하면 어쩌지
as it were(= so to speak)	말하자면
if not all	전부는 아니지만
if anything	사실은
if any	만약에 있다면, 만일 있다 해도
if at all	기왕에 ~할 거면

21 난도 ★★☆   정답 ②

독해 > 빈칸 완성 > 단어·구·절

[정답의 이유]

첫 번째 문장에서 '축제는 전 세계적으로 전통, 유산, 공동체 정신을 소개하는 의미 있는 문화 행사이다.'라고 했고, 두 번째 문장에서 'They serve as platforms to celebrate diversity, with each festival reflecting unique traditions(축제는 다양성을 기념하는 플랫폼 역할을 하는데, 각각의 축제들은 독특한 전통을 반영한다)~'라고 했다. 다섯 번째 문장에서 'Festivals reflect societal values, promote local crafts and arts, enhance spirituality, and attract tourism, which facilitates cultural exchange and understanding(축제는 사회적 가치를 반영하고 지역 공예와 예술을 장려하며 영성을 강화하고 관광을 유치하여 문화 교류와 이해를 촉진한다).'이라고 했고, 빈칸 문장의 앞부분에서 '궁극적으로 축제에 참여하면 공동체와 개인의 정체성을 강화하며 ~ 글로벌 서사에 기여한다.'라고 했으므로, 빈칸에 들어갈 말로 적절한 것은 ② 'values diversity and encourages mutual respect and understanding(다양성을 중시하고 상호 존중과 이해를 장려하는)'이다.

[오답의 이유]

① 참가자들이 그들의 일상적인 걱정과 고통을 잊게 만드는

③ 사람들이 개인적인 삶과 사회적인 삶 사이의 연결고리를 끊게 해주는

④ 축제가 사람들이 그들 자신에 대해 어떻게 생각하는지 결정하지 못하게 하는

[본문해석]

축제는 전 세계적으로 전통, 유산, 공동체 정신을 소개하는 의미 있는 문화 행사이다. 그것들은 다양성을 기념하는 플랫폼 역할을 하는데, 브라질의 카니발이나 인도의 등명제(Diwali) 같은 각각의 축제들은 독특한 전통을 반영한다. 축제는 또한 미국의 독립기념일이나 프랑스의 혁명기념일 같은 역사적인 순간을 기념한다. 또한 그것들은 개인적, 문화적 정체성을 강화하는 관습과 의식을 보존하고 공유 활동을 통해 강한 공동체 유대감을 형성한다. 축제는 사회적 가치를 반영하고 지역 공예와 예술을 장려하며 영성을 강화하고 관광을 유치하여 문화 교류와 이해를 촉진한다. 인도의 홀리(Holi) 같은 계절적인 축제는 자연 주기와 일치하여 소생의 시간을 기념한다. 궁극적으로 축제에 참여하면 공동체와 개인의 정체성을 강화하며 다양성을 중시하고 상호 존중과 이해를 장려하는 글로벌 서사에 기여한다.

VOCA

• showcase 진열[전시]하다, 소개하다
• community spirit 공동체 의식
• globally 전세계적[전체적]으로
• celebrate 기념하다, 축하하다
• diversity 상이(점), 다양(성)
• Bastille Day 프랑스의 혁명기념일
• preserve 보존하다, 유지하다
• ritual 의식 절차
• strengthen ~을 강화하다, 증강시키다
• cultural identity 문화정체감
• foster 조성하다, 발전시키다
• societal value 사회적 가치
• promote 촉진[고취]하다
• enhance 높이다[향상시키다]
• spirituality 정신성, 영성
• align with ~에 맞추어 조정하다
• natural cycle 자연적 주기
• reinforce 강화하다, 보강하다

- diversity 다양성, 포괄성
- encourage 권장[장려]하다
- mutual 상호간의, 서로의
- allow 허락하다, 용납하다

22 난도 ★☆☆ 　　　　　　　　　　　　정답 ①

독해 > 세부 내용 찾기 > 지칭 추론

정답의 이유

제시문의 첫 번째 문장에서 'Life is full of its ups and downs(인생은 굴곡으로 가득 차 있다).'라고 했고, 다섯 번째 문장에서 'Everyone has to face their own set of challenges(모든 사람은 그들만의 어려운 상황에 직면해야 한다).'라고 했으므로, 밑줄 친 you've been thrown a curve ball이 의미하는 바로 적절한 것은 ① '어려운 상황에 직면하다.'이다.

본문해석

인생은 굴곡으로 가득 차 있다. 어느 날, 여러분은 모든 것을 완벽하게 알아냈다고 느낄지도 모른다. 그러고 나서, 당장 여러분은 어려운 상황에 직면한다. 이러한 감정 속에 여러분만 있는 것이 아니다. 모든 사람은 그들만의 어려운 상황에 직면해야 한다. 어려움을 극복하는 방법을 배우는 것은 여러분이 중심을 잡고 압박감 속에서 침착할 수 있도록 도와줄 것이다. 누구나 인생에서 어려움에 직면하는 방법에 대해 그들 자신의 선호가 있다. 그러나 상황이 힘들어지면 따라야 할 몇 가지 좋은 조언과 요령이 있다. 도움을 요청하는 것을 부끄러워할 필요가 없다. 여러분이 사랑하는 사람, 낯선 사람, 멘토, 또는 친구 중 누구에게 의지하기를 선택하든 간에, 여러분이 성공하는 것을 돕고 싶은 사람들이 있다. 여러분은 개방적이어야 하고 기꺼이 지원을 수락해야 한다. 여러분을 돕기 위해 오는 사람들은 진심으로 여러분을 아끼고 있다. 도움이 필요할 때 순순히 도움을 받으십시오.

VOCA

- ups and downs 성쇠, 부침
- a moment's notice 당장, 즉석에서
- a curve ball 예기치 못한 문제, 사건, 일, 예상하지 못한 상황
- throw a curve ball 커브로 던지다, 속이다, 유쾌하지 못한 방법으로 놀라게 하다
- set of challenges 일련의 어려움들
- overcome 극복하다
- stay centered 중심을 잡다
- under pressure 압력을 받다
- preference 좋아하기, (~에 대한) 애호
- tip 조언, 경고, 암시, 힌트
- trick 비결, 요령, 교묘한 방법[수법]
- be open to ~을 순순히 받아들이다

23 난도 ★☆☆ 　　　　　　　　　　　　정답 ②

독해 > 대의 파악 > 요지, 주장

정답의 이유

마지막 문장에서 'Despite assertions that suggest otherwise, it really is not clear how powerful the relationship is between an individual's dominance status and its lifetime reproductive success(그렇지 않다는 주장에도 불구하고, 개체의 지배적 지위와 평생의 번식 성공 사이의 관계가 얼마나 강력한지는 명확하지 않다).'라고 했으므로 사회적 지배력과 번식 성공 사이의 관계를 가장 잘 요약한 것은 ② '개체의 우세 상태와 평생 번식 성공 사이의 관계는 다면적이며 명확하게 정립되어 있다고 할 수는 없다.'이다.

본문해석

사회적 지배는 개인이나 집단이 주로 경쟁 상황에서 다른 사람의 행동을 통제하거나 지시하는 상황을 말한다. 일반적으로 개인이나 집단이 '미래의 상호 작용 과정이나 경쟁 상황의 결과에 대해 예측이 이루어지고 있을 때' 지배적이라고 한다. 지배적 관계를 평가하고 할당하는 기준은 상황마다 다를 수 있다. 이용 가능한 데이터를 간략하게 요약하는 것은 어렵지만 일반적으로 지배적인 개인은 종속된 개인과 비교할 때 종종 더 많은 이동의 자유를 가지며, 음식에 대한 접근의 우선순위를 가지고, 더 높은 품질의 휴식 공간을 얻고, 유리한 몸단장 관계를 즐기고, 집단의 더 보호된 부분을 차지하고, 더 높은 품질의 짝을 얻고, 다른 집단 구성원의 관심을 지시하고 규정하며, 스트레스와 질병에 더 큰 저항력을 보이는 것으로 밝혀졌다. 그렇지 않다는 주장에도 불구하고, 개체의 지배적 지위와 평생의 번식 성공 사이의 관계가 얼마나 강력한지는 명확하지 않다.

VOCA

- refer to 언급[지칭]하다
- dictate 구술하다
- prediction 예측, 예견
- interaction 상호 작용
- competitive 경쟁을 하는
- criterion (판단이나 결정을 위한) 기준(복수형 criteria)
- assess 재다[가늠하다]
- assign 맡기다[배정하다/부과하다]
- vary from ~ to ~에서 …까지 다양하다
- summarize 요약하다
- dominant 우세한, 지배적인
- compared to ~와 비교하여
- subordinate 종속된
- higher-quality 높은 품질
- grooming 차림새, 몸단장
- occupy 차지하다, 사용하다[거주하다]
- resistance 저항, 내성
- assertion 주장, 행사
- status 신분[자격], 지위
- lifetime 일생, 평생, 생애
- reproductive 재생[재현]하는, 복사하는

24 난도 ★★☆

정답 ①

독해 > 대의 파악 > 제목, 주제

정답의 이유

첫 번째 문장에서 '마음 챙김 명상은 일반적으로 안전하지만, 공황 발작과 정신 질환 같은 부작용 발생의 우려가 있는데, 학계 연구에서 드물게 보고되고, 알려져 있지 않다.'라고 했고, 마지막 문장에서 'For a more thorough understanding of mindfulness' benefits and risks(마음 챙김의 유익성과 위해성에 대한 보다 철저한 이해를 위해서) ~.'라고 했다. 따라서 글의 주제로 적절한 것은 ① 'the criticism regarding the safety and societal implications of the widespread adoption of mindfulness meditation(마음 챙김 명상에 대한 안정성과 광범위한 채택의 사회적 영향에 관한 비판)' 이다.

오답의 이유

② 개인적인 스트레스를 해소하고 사회적 · 문화적 혼란을 방지하기 위해 취해지는 사회적 · 국가적 조치

③ 개인의 문제보다는 사회적 문제의 해결에 선행되어야 하는 마음 챙김의 기본적인 요소들

④ 부적절하게 수행된 명상과 명상의 부족으로 인해 개인과 사회가 직면하는 불이익

본문해석

마음 챙김 명상은 일반적으로 안전하지만, 공황 발작과 정신 질환 같은 부작용 발생의 우려가 있는데, 학계 연구에서 드물게 보고되고, 알려져 있지 않다. 비평가들은 조직과 교육 시스템에 의한 마음 챙김에 대한 신속한 채택이 부적절하게 사회 문제를 개인에게 옮길 수 있다고 주장하는데, 이는 개인적인 스트레스는 환경 오염이나 직장 요구 같은 전체에 영향을 주는 원인을 고심하기보다 차라리 명상 부족에서 기인한 것이라는 사실을 시사한다. Ronald Purser 교수 같은 비평가들은 마음 챙김이 개인에게 변화를 추구하도록 권한을 부여하는 대신 불리한 조건에 더 순응하도록 만들 수 있다고 제의했다. 이러한 우려에도 불구하고, 그 비판은 마음 챙김 그 자체에 반대하는 것이 아니라 변화에 저항하는 주체들에 의한 보편적인 해결책으로서의 그것의 추진에 반대하는 것이다. 마음 챙김의 유익성과 위해성에 대한 보다 철저한 이해를 위해서, 장기적이면서 엄격하게 통제된 연구가 필수적이다.

VOCA

- mindfulness meditation 마음 챙김 명상
- arise from ~에서 발생하다[일어나다]
- side effect 부작용
- panic 극심한 공포, 공황
- attack 공격하다, 덤벼들다
- argue 주장하다, 논증하다
- adoption 채택
- inappropriately 부적합하게, 온당치 않게
- shift 옮기다, 이동하다
- societal 사회의
- address 고심하다[다루다]

- systemic 전체[전신]에 영향을 주는
- cause 원인, 이유
- workplace 직장, 업무 현장
- demand 요구 (사항), 일[부담]
- adverse 부정적인, 불리한
- empower 권한을 주다, 자율권을 주다
- critique 평론
- entity 독립체
- resistant to ~에 대해 저항하는
- rigorously 엄격히, 엄밀히
- controlled 세심히 관리[통제/조정]된
- implication 영향[결과], 함축, 암시
- relieve 없애[덜어] 주다, 완화하다
- confusion 혼란, 혼동
- precede ~에 앞서다[선행하다]
- resolution 결의안, 해결
- disadvantage 불리한 점, 약점, 난점
- improperly 적절하지 않게

25 난도 ★☆☆

정답 ④

독해 > 세부 내용 찾기 > 내용 (불)일치

정답의 이유

④ 마지막에서 세 번째 문장에서 'In 1952, he was elected to the U.S. Senate and re-elected in 1958, 1964 and 1970(1952년에, 그는 미국 상원의원으로 선출되었고 1958년, 1964년, 1970년에 재선되었다).'라고 4번의 연도가 나오므로, 글의 내용과 일치하지 않는다.

오답의 이유

① 첫 번째 문장에서 'A man of few words and great modesty, Mike Mansfield often said he did not want to be remembered.'라고 했으므로 글의 내용과 일치한다.

② 네 번째 문장에서 'Following his mother's death ~ his father sent him and his two sisters to Great Falls, Montana, to be raised by an aunt and uncle there.'라고 했으므로 글의 내용과 일치한다.

③ 여섯 번째 문장에서 'Later, he served in the Army and the Marines, which sent him to the Philippines and China, awakening a lifelong interest in Asia.'라고 했으므로 글의 내용과 일치한다.

말수가 적고 겸손한 사람인 Mike Mansfield는 종종 기억되고 싶지 않다고 말했다. 하지만, 그의 매혹적인 인생 이야기와 엄청난 기여는 그를 따르는 모든 사람들에게 영감을 준다. Mike Mansfield는 1903년 3월 16일 뉴욕에서 태어났다. Mike가 일곱 살 때 어머니가 사망한 후, 그의 아버지는 Mike와 두 여동생을 Montana주 Great Fall로 보냈으며, 그곳에서 이모와 삼촌 밑에서 양육되었다. 열네 살에, 그는 세계 1차 대전 동안 미 해군에 입대하기 위해 자신의 나이에 대해 거짓말을 했다. 나중에, 그는 육군과 해병대에서 복무했는데, 필리핀과 중국에 파병되어, 아시아에 대한 평생의 관심이 눈뜨게 되었다. Mike Mansfield의 정치 경력은 1942년 그가 미국 하원의원으로 선출되던 해에 시작되었다. 그는 Montana주 제1구역에서 5번의 임기를 봉사했다. 1952년에, 그는 미국 상원의원으로 선출되었고 1958년, 1964년, 1970년에 재선되었다. 그가 민주당 다수당 원내부대표로 선출된 후에 1961년에 상원의 다수당 원내대표로 선출되었다. 그는 1977년에 상원에서 은퇴할 때까지 그 직무를 수행했는데, 이는 역사상 다른 다수당 원내대표보다 더 길었다.

VOCA

- modesty 겸손
- fascinating 대단히 흥미로운, 매력적인
- contribution 기여, 공헌
- inspiration 영감
- follow (~의 뒤를) 따라가다[오다]
- enlist 요청하(여 얻)다
- duration 지속, (지속되는) 기간
- awakening 사람을 깨닫게[놀라게] 하는
- launch 개시[출시/진수/발사](하는 행사)
- re-elect (어떤 사람을) 다시 선출하다

영어 | 2023년 법원직 9급

01 난도 ★☆☆ 정답 ③

독해 > 세부 내용 찾기 > 내용 (불)일치

[정답의 이유]

여덟 번째 문장에서 'Molaison's life was a series of firsts, as he couldn't remember anything he had done before.'라고 했고, 그 다음 문장에서 '하지만, 그는 시간이 지나면서 새로운 운동 기능을 습득할 수 있었다.'라고 했으므로, 글의 내용과 일치하지 않는 것은 ③ '살아가면서 이전에 한 일을 조금씩 기억할 수 있었지만, 시간이 지나면서 운동 능력이 약화되었다.'이다.

[오답의 이유]

① 두 번째 문장에서 '~ Molaison allowed surgeons to remove a section of tissue from each side of his brain to stop the seizures.'라고 했으므로, 글의 내용과 일치한다.

② 네 번째 문장 후반부에서 '~ the discovery that complex functions like learning and memory are linked to specific regions of the brain.'이라고 했으므로, 글의 내용과 일치한다.

④ 마지막 문장에서 'Studies of Molaison allowed neuroscientists to further explore the brain networks involved in conscious and unconscious memories, ~'라고 했으므로, 글의 내용과 일치한다.

본문해석

27세 남성 Henry Molaison은 1950년대에 약 10년 동안 심신을 약화시키는 발작을 겪었다. 1953년 9월 1일, Molaison은 발작을 멈추기 위해 외과의사들에게 그의 뇌의 양쪽으로부터 조직의 한 부분을 제거하기로 했다. 수술은 효과가 있었지만, Molaison은 새로운 기억을 형성할 수 없는 영구적인 기억상실증 상태로 남았다. 이 비극적인 결과는 20세기 뇌 과학에서 가장 중요한 발견들 중 하나로 이어졌는데, 학습과 기억과 같은 복잡한 기능들은 뇌의 특정한 영역과 연결되어 있다는 발견이다. Molaison은 연구에서 그의 사생활을 보호하기 위해서 'H.M.'으로 알려지게 되었다. 과학자 William Scoville은 Molaison과 비슷한 수술을 받은 9명의 환자들을 연구했는데, 그들의 내측 측두엽의 일부를 제거한 사람들만이 기억력 문제, 특히 최근 기억의 문제를 경험했다는 것을 발견했다. 그는 뇌의 특정한 구조가 정상적인 기억을 위해 필요하다는 것을 발견했다. Molaison의 삶은 그가 전에 한 일을 기억할 수 없었기 때문에 첫 번째의 연속이었다. 하지만, 그는 시간이 지나면서 새로운 운동 기능을 습득할 수 있었다. Molaison에 대한 연구는 신경과학자들에게 심지어 2008년 그의 죽음 이후에도 의식적인 기억 및 무의식적인 기억과 관련된 뇌의 연결 조직을 더 탐구할 수 있게 했다.

02 난도 ★☆☆ 정답 ②

어법 > 비문 찾기

정답의 이유

② that nature in the form of landscapes, plants, and animals 는 선행사 idea를 수식하는 관계대명사절로 are는 관계사절의 주어인 nature를 받는 동사이므로, are → is가 되어야 한다.

오답의 이유

① in which we live는 선행사 biome(생물군계)을 수식하는 관계 사절로 '전치사＋관계대명사(in which)'는 where로 대체할 수 있으며, 전치사 in을 뒤로 보내 which we live in으로도 쓸 수 있다.

③ edited 다음에 목적어가 없고 by Kellert and Wilson이 있으므로, 수동인 '편집된'의 뜻으로 과거분사가 적절하게 사용되었다. 명사(The Biophilia Hypothesis)를 수식하며, '관계대명사＋be 동사(which was)'가 생략되었다.

④ that은 동사 is의 보어가 되는 명사절(that humans have a universal desire to be in natural settings)을 이끄는 접속사로 사용되었다.

본문해석

인간은 우리가 살고 있는 생물군계의 미생물, 식물, 동물로부터 유래한 분명히 보이는 혜택을 초월하는 자연에 대한 선천적인 친밀감을 가지고 있다. 풍경, 식물, 동물 형태인 자연이 우리의 행복에 좋다는 생각은 오래되었으며, Charles Darwin이나 그 이전으로 거슬러 올라갈 수 있다. 이러한 생각은 심리학자 Erich Fromm에 의해 생명애라고 불렸으며, 하버드의 개미 생물학자 Edward O. Wilson과 Stephen Kellert에 의해 연구되었다. 1984년, Wilson은 *Biophilia*를 출판했는데 그것은 1995년 Kellert와 Wilson이 편집한 또 다른 책인 *Biophilia Hypothesis*의 출판으로 이어졌다. 그들의 생명애 가설(biophilia hypothesis)은 인간이 자연적인 환경에 있고 싶은 보편적인 욕망을 가지고 있다는 것이다.

더 알아보기

명사절을 이끄는 접속사 that

- 문장 앞에 붙은 의미가 없는 that은 명사절을 이끄는 접속사로, that절은 '～라는 것'으로 해석하며 문장의 주어, 목적어, 보어 역할을 한다.

  예 The reason for my happiness is that I focus on the positive. (보어)

  (내 행복의 이유는 내가 긍정적인 측면에 초점을 맞추는 데에 있다.)

- know, think, guess, believe, hope 등의 동사는 that이 이끄는 절을 목적어로 가지며, that은 아무 뜻이 없고 생략 가능하다.

  예 I believe that imagination is stronger than knowledge. (목적어)

  = I believe imagination is stronger than knowledge.

  (나는 상상력이 지식보다 강력하다는 것을 믿는다.)

- that은 접속사의 역할만 하므로 뒤에는 완벽한 절의 형태를 갖추어야 한다.

  예 It has turned out that she didn't go to school yesterday.

  (그녀가 어제 학교를 가지 않았다는 것이 밝혀졌다.)

- 앞에 나온 명사의 내용과 일치할 때 that절은 동격의 that절이다.

  예 The fact that he is your brother-in-law should not affect your decision. (the fact와 동격)

  (그가 네 처남이라는 사실이 네 결정에 영향을 주어서는 안 된다.)

- 전치사의 목적어로는 사용할 수 없다.

  예 She is aware of that he will not come back. (×)

- what vs. that: what＋불완전한 절 vs. that＋완전한 절

  예 I can't believe what he told me. (what절이 목적어가 없는 불완전한 문장)

  (나는 그가 나에게 한 말을 믿을 수 없다.)

  예 What we are worried about is his too much work. (what절이 목적어가 없는 불완전한 문장)

  (우리가 걱정하는 것은 그의 과도하게 많은 일이다.)

  예 I can't believe that he got married to her. (that절이 완전한 문장)

  (나는 그가 그녀와 결혼을 했다는 사실을 믿을 수 없다.)

03 난도 ★☆☆　　　　　　　　　　　　　　　　정답 ②

독해 > 세부 내용 찾기 > 내용 (불)일치

정답의 이유

② 다섯 번째 문장에서 'They believe a greatly reduced amount of the sun's warmth reached the planet's surface ~'라고 했으므로, 주어진 글의 내용과 일치하는 않는 것은 ② '학자들은 "눈덩이 지구" 기간 동안에도 지구의 표면에 다다른 태양의 온기가 크게 감소하지 않았다고 믿고 있다.'이다.

오답의 이유

① 세 번째 문장에서 'But life somehow 'survived(살아남았다)' during this time called "Snowball Earth."'라고 했으므로, 글의 내용과 일치한다.

③ 여덟 번째 문장에서 'This enabled the earliest forms of complex life to survive in areas ~'라고 했으므로, 글의 내용과 일치한다.

④ 마지막에서 세 번째와 두 번째 문장에서 '~ that ice-free, open water conditions existed in place during the last part of so-called "the Ice Age" ~ the world's oceans were not completely frozen.'이라고 했으므로, 글의 내용과 일치한다.

본문해석

지구상의 생명체들은 7억 2천만 년 전에 시작된 크라이오제니아기 동안 생존 가능성에 대한 극단적인 시험에 직면했다. 그 행성은 8천 5백만 년의 대부분 기간 동안 얼어 있었다. 하지만 생명체는 '눈덩이 지구'라고 불리는 이 시기에 어떻게든 살아남았다. 과학자들은 이 시기의 시작을 더 잘 이해하려고 노력하고 있다. 그들은 태양의 복사열이 하얀 빙상에 반사되자 크게 감소한 태양의 온기가 행성 표면에 도달했다고 믿고 있다. 또한 그들이 말하기를 흑색의 혈암에서 발견되어 해초로 판명된 화석들은 살기에 적합한 물 환경이 그들이 한때 믿었던 것보다 더 널리 퍼져 있었다는 신호라고 했다. 일부 연구의 결과는 눈이 녹자 그 행성이 '슬러시볼 지구'에 더 가까웠다는 생각을 뒷받침한다. 이것은 한때 꽁꽁 얼어붙은 지역으로 여겨졌던 곳에서 가장 초기 형태의 복잡한 생명체의 생존을 가능하게 했다. 연구원들에 따르면, 가장 중요한 발견은 소위 '빙하 시대'의 마지막 시기 동안 얼음이 없는 개방된 물의 조건이 존재했다는 것이다. 그 연구 결과는 세계의 바다가 완전히 얼어 있었던 것은 아니라는 것을 입증한다. 그것은 거주 가능한 피난처 구역이 있어서 그곳에서 다세포 유기체가 살아남을 수 있었다는 것을 의미한다.

VOCA

- face　(상황에[이]) 직면하다[닥쳐오다]
- extreme　극도의, 극심한
- survivability　살아 남을 수 있는 힘, 생존 가능성
- frozen　얼어붙은, 결빙된
- somehow　어떻게든
- radiation　(열·에너지 등의) 복사
- fossil　화석
- shale　혈암, 이판암
- seaweed　해초
- livable　살기에 적합한[좋은]
- ice-free　얼지 않는, 결빙(結氷)하지 않는
- demonstrate　증거[실례]를 들어가며 보여주다, 입증[실증]하다
- habitable　(장소가 사람이) 주거할 수 있는
- refuge　피신(처), 도피(처)
- multicellular organism　다세포 유기체

04 난도 ★★☆　　　　　　　　　　　　　　　　정답 ①

독해 > 빈칸 완성 > 단어·구·절

정답의 이유

첫 번째 문장에서 '지구의 온도가 상승함에 따라 해수면도 상승하여 전 세계 해안 지역 공동체를 위협하고 있다.'라고 문제를 제시했으므로, 빈칸 문장에는 문제에 대한 'solution(해결책)'을 제시하는 내용이 와야 함을 유추할 수 있다. 빈칸 앞부분에서 '놀랍게도, 심지어 굴과 같은 작은 유기체까지도 ~이다.'라고 했고, 빈칸 다음 문장에서 'Oysters are keystone species with ripple effects on the health of their ecosystems and its inhabitants.'라고 했으므로, 빈칸에 들어갈 말로 가장 적절한 것은 ① 'can come to our defense(우리의 방어 수단이 될 수 있다)'이다.

오답의 이유

② 비상식량이 될 수 있다
③ 미세 플라스틱에 의해 오염될 수 있다
④ 지역 주민들의 수입을 증가시킬 수 있다

본문해석

지구의 온도가 상승함에 따라 해수면도 상승하여 전 세계 해안 지역 공동체를 위협하고 있다. 놀랍게도, 심지어 굴과 같은 작은 유기체까지도 우리의 방어 수단이 될 수 있다. 굴은 그들의 생태계와 거주민들의 건강에 파급효과가 있는 핵심 종이다. 성체 굴 한 마리는 하루에 최대 50갤런의 물을 여과할 수 있으며, 수로를 더 깨끗하게 만든다. 건강한 굴 암초는 또한 수백의 다른 해양 생물들에게 집을 제공하고, 생물 다양성과 생태계 균형을 촉진한다. 해수면 상승이 광범위한 홍수로 이어짐에 따라, 굴 암초는 폭풍의 충격을 완충하고 추가적인 해안 침식으로부터 보호하는 방벽 역할을 한다.

- threaten 위태롭게 하다, 위협하다
- coastal community 연안 지역 공동체
- organism 유기적 조직체, 유기체
- oyster 굴
- keystone species 핵심 종
- ecosystem (특정 지역의) 생태계
- inhabitant 주민[서식 동물]
- filter 여과하다, 거르다
- oyster reef 굴 암초
- promote 촉진[고취]하다
- biodiversity 생물 다양성
- ecosystem balance 생태계 균형
- pervasive 만연하는, (구석구석) 스며[배어]드는
- flooding 침수
- buffer (충격을) 완화하다
- coastal erosion 해안 침식

05 난도 ★★☆   정답 ②

독해 > 빈칸 완성 > 단어 · 구 · 절

정답의 이유

(A) 빈칸 앞부분에서 '혀의 다른 부분들이 특정한 맛을 담당하고 있
다는 주장은 현대 과학에 의해 ~라고 입증되었고'라고 했는데,
주어진 글의 첫 번째 문장에서 '~ claims that different
sections of the tongue are responsible for specific tastes,
is incorrect, according to modern science.'라고 했으므로,
빈칸 (A)에 들어갈 말은 'false(사실이 아닌)'가 적절하다.

(B) 빈칸 앞부분에서 '맛 선호는 ~ 역사에 의해 영향을 받는다.'라
고 했는데, 주어진 글의 여섯 번째 문장에서 '우리의 조상들
(our ancestors)'이 영양소와 쉽게 칼로리를 얻기 위해 과일이
필요했으므로, 우리는 자연스럽게 단맛에 끌리게 되었다고 했
으므로, 빈칸 (B)에 들어갈 말은 'evolutionary(진화의)'가 적절
하다.

오답의 이유

① 정확한 - 진화의
③ 사실이 아닌 - 정신의
④ 정확한 - 정신의

현대 과학에 따르면 미각 지도에 대한 통념, 즉 혀의 다른 부분들이
특정한 맛을 담당한다는 주장은 사실이 아니다. 미각 지도는 1900
년대 초 독일 과학자 David Hänig의 실험에서 비롯되었는데, 그것
은 혀가 중심부가 아닌 가장자리 부분을 따라서 맛에 가장 민감하
다는 사실을 발견했다. 하지만 이것은 단맛이 혀의 앞쪽에 있고, 쓴
맛이 뒤쪽에 있으며, 짠맛과 신맛이 옆에 있다고 주장하는 것으로
수년간 잘못 해석되어 왔다. 실제로, 혀 전체에 있는 미뢰를 통해 다
양한 맛이 감지된다. 미뢰는 우리의 장기적인 학습과 연관성에 근거
하여, 우리가 어떤 음식을 갈망하거나 싫어하게 만들도록 함께 작용
한다. 예를 들어, 우리 조상들이 영양소와 칼로리를 손쉽게 얻기 위
해 과일을 필요로 했으므로 우리가 자연스럽게 단맛에 끌리는 반면,
몇몇 식물들의 쓴맛은 독성에 대한 경고 역할을 한다. 물론, 동물계
의 다른 종들도 독특한 미각 능력을 가지고 있지만, 육식동물들은
과일을 먹지 않기 때문에 사람들처럼 설탕을 갈망하지 않는다.

⇩

혀의 다른 부분들이 특정한 맛을 담당하고 있다는 주장은 현대 과학
에 의해 (A) 사실이 아닌 것으로 입증되었고, 맛 선호는 (B) 진화의
역사에 의해 영향을 받는다.

- taste map 미각 지도
- claim 주장하다
- originate from ~에서 비롯되다
- sensitive 예민한[민감한]
- misinterpret 잘못 해석[이해]하다
- taste bud 미뢰[맛봉오리]
- crave 갈망[열망]하다
- long-term 장기적인
- ancestor 조상, 선조
- nutrient 영양소, 영양분
- serve as ~의 역할을 하다
- warning 경고, 계고
- toxicity 유독성
- carnivores 육식동물
- evolutionary history 진화의 역사

어법 > 비문 찾기

정답의 이유

③ 관계대명사 what은 선행사를 포함하며, the thing which로 바꿔 쓸 수 있는데, what 앞에 amazing thing이 있으므로 어법상 what → which가 되어야 한다. 이때 관계대명사 what 다음에는 불완전한 문장이 와야 하는데, we take for granted에서 take 뒤에 목적어가 없다는 것에 유의한다.

오답의 이유

① by which는 선행사 means를 수식하는 '전치사+관계대명사'로 어법상 적절하게 사용되었다.

② used는 동사(is)에 연결되어 '사용된'의 뜻의 과거분사가 형용사 역할을 하는 것으로 적절하게 사용되었다.

④ 부사절(when we and others do this together)의 주어 we and others가 복수명사이므로, 어법상 동사 do가 적절하게 사용되었다.

본문해석

언어는 사람들이 서로 의사소통하는 주요한 수단이다. 대부분의 생물들이 의사소통을 하지만, 인간의 말은 다른 동물들의 의사소통 시스템보다 더 복잡하고, 더 창의적이고, 더 광범위하게 사용된다. 언어는 인간이 되는 것을 뜻하는 것의 필수적인 부분이고 모든 문화의 기본적인 부분이다. 언어인류학은 언어와 문화의 관계를 이해하는 것과 관련있다. 언어는 우리가 당연시하는 놀라운 것이다. 우리가 말할 때, 다양한 음색과 음높이를 가진 소리를 내기 위해 우리의 신체인 폐, 성대, 입, 혀, 입술을 사용한다. 그리고 어쨌든, 우리와 다른 사람들이 함께 이것을 할 때, 우리는 서로 의사소통을 할 수 있지만, 우리가 같은 언어를 사용할 때만 가능하다. 언어인류학자들은 언어들 사이의 변형과 언어가 구조화되고, 학습되고, 사용되는 방법을 이해하기를 원한다.

VOCA

• primary 주된, 주요한, 기본적인
• means 수단, 방법, 방도
• communicate with ~와 연락하다
• creative 창조적인, 창의적인
• extensively 광범위하게
• linguistic anthropology 언어인류학
• be concerned with ~에 관계가 있다, ~에 관심이 있다
• understanding 이해
• amazing 놀라운
• take A for granted A를 당연한 일로[의문의 여지가 없다고] 생각하다
• lung 폐, 허파
• vocal cord 성대(聲帶), 목청
• tone 어조, 말투
• pitch 음의 높이
• anthropologist 인류학자
• variation 변화

독해 > 글의 일관성 > 문장 삽입

정답의 이유

주어진 글은 의료서비스 챗봇은 이 문제를 해결하고 가정에서 사람들이 편안하게 적절한 진단과 조언을 받는 것을 보장한다는 내용이므로, 주어진 글 앞에는 '이 문제(this problem)'에 대한 내용이 나와야 한다. ③ 앞 문장에서 'This often proves harmful effects on the person's mental and physical health if misdiagnosed and improper medicines are consumed.'에서 문제에 대한 내용이 나오고, ③ 다음 문장에서 '~ the chatbot prescribes over the counter treatment ~'라고 문제에 대한 해결책을 설명하고 있으므로 글의 흐름상 주어진 문장이 들어가기에 적절한 곳은 ③이다.

본문해석

질병에 걸린다는 두려움 혹은 과도한 진료비 때문에 병원이나 보건소에 가는 것을 망설이는 사람들이 많아졌다. 이것은 그들로 하여금 인터넷에서 검증되지 않은 정보를 근거로 스스로 자가 진단하게 한다. 만약 오진되고 부적절한 약품을 섭취한다면 이것은 종종 사람의 정신적, 신체적 건강에 해로운 영향을 미친다는 것을 증명한다. 의료서비스 챗봇은 이 문제를 해결하고 가정에서 편안하게 사용할 수 있는 사람들을 위한 적절한 진단과 조언을 보장하는 것을 목적으로 한다. 진단의 심각성을 기초로 하여, 챗봇은 처방전이 필요 없는 일반의약품을 처방하거나 검증된 의료 전문가에게 진단을 확대한다. 광범위한 다양한 증상과 위험 요인 및 치료법에 대해 훈련받은 상호 작용 챗봇은 특히 COVID-19의 경우, 사용자의 건강 문의를 쉽게 처리할 수 있다.

VOCA

• hesitant 주저하는, 망설이는
• contract (병에) 걸리다
• consultation fee 진료비
• self-diagnose 자가 진단하다
• unverified 증명[입증]되지 않은, 미증명의
• misdiagnose (질병·문제를) 오진하다
• severity 심각성
• prescribe 처방을 내리다, 처방하다
• treatment 치료, 처치
• escalate 확대[증가/악화]되다[시키다]
• diagnosis 진단
• verify 입증하다
• interactive 상호적인, 상호 작용을 하는
• symptom 증상
• risk factor 위험 요인
• handle 다루다[다스리다/처리하다]
• query 문의, 의문

08 난도 ★★★   정답 ②

독해 > 글의 일관성 > 글의 순서

정답의 이유

주어진 글에서 스포츠팬 우울증은 특히 실망하거나 패배할 때 '다수의 열성적인 스포츠팬들(many avid sports fans)'에게 영향을 미치는 실제 현상이라고 했는데, (B)에서 '많은 팬들에게(For many fans)' 선호하는 팀이나 선수들에 대한 감정의 투자가 너무나 강렬해서 기대가 충족되지 못하면 우울증으로 이어질 수 있다고 부연·설명하고 있다. (B)의 마지막에서 스포츠팬들의 우울증이 정신적, 신체적 건강에 '부정적인 영향(negative effects)'을 끼칠 수 있다고 했으므로, 문맥상 부정적인 영향을 구체적으로 설명하는 (A)로 이어져야 한다. (A)의 마지막 부분에서 'There are many factors that can contribute to sports fan depression, ~'이라고 스포츠팬 우울증의 원인이 되는 요소들을 나열했으므로, 스포츠팬 우울증의 부정적인 영향을 '완화하기(mitigate)' 위한 방안을 제시하는 (C)로 이어지는 것이 자연스럽다. 따라서 주어진 글 다음에 이어질 글의 순서로 적절한 것은 ② '(B) - (A) - (C)'이다.

본문해석

스포츠팬 우울증은 특히 실망하거나 패배할 때 많은 열성적인 스포츠팬들에게 영향을 미치는 실제 현상이다.

(B) 많은 팬들에게 선호하는 팀이나 운동선수들에 대한 그들의 감정의 투자는 너무나 강렬해서 패배하거나 기대를 충족시키지 못하면 슬픔, 좌절, 그리고 심지어 우울증으로 이어질 수 있다. 연구는 스포츠팬들의 우울증이 정신 건강과 신체 건강에 모두 여러 가지 부정적인 영향을 미칠 수 있다는 것을 보여주었다.

(A) 팬들은 스트레스 수준 상승과 불안 또는 우울감 발달의 위험이 증가할 뿐만 아니라 기분, 식욕, 수면의 질이 떨어지는 것을 경험할 수 있다. 스포츠팬 우울증의 원인이 될 수 있는 많은 요소들은 팀의 성공에 대한 개인적인 투자, 특정 팀을 지원하는 사회적인 압력, 종종 세간의 이목을 끄는 유명한 스포츠 행사에 동반되는 언론의 과열된 보도와 감시를 포함한다.

(C) 스포츠팬 우울증에 대한 부정적인 영향을 완화하기 위해서는 팬들이 스포츠에 대한 건강한 시각을 유지하고 결국 그것들은 단지 게임에 불과하다는 것을 기억하는 것이 중요하다. 운동을 하고, 사랑하는 사람들과 시간을 보내고, 정신 건강 전문가로부터 지원을 구하는 것처럼 자기 스스로를 돌보는 활동에 참여하는 것도 도움이 될 수 있다.

VOCA

• depression 우울함, 암울함

• affect 영향을 미치다

• frustration 불만, 좌절감

• appetite 식욕

• sleep quality 수면의 질

• heightened 고조된

• contribute to ~에 기여하다

• intense media coverage 언론의 과열된 취재

• high-profile 세간의 이목을 끄는

09 난도 ★☆☆   정답 ④

독해 > 세부 내용 찾기 > 내용 (불)일치

정답의 이유

여섯 번째 문장에서 'After establishing himself as a writer for adults, Roald Dahl began writing children's stories in 1960 while living in England with his family.'라고 했으므로, Roald Dahl에 관한 글의 내용과 가장 일치하지 않는 것은 ④ '성인을 위한 작가가 된 뒤 영국에서 가족과 떨어져 혼자 살면서 글을 썼다.'이다.

오답의 이유

① 두 번째 문장에서 'He spent his childhood in England and, at age eighteen, went to work for the Shell Oil Company in Africa.'라고 했으므로, 글의 내용과 일치한다.

② 세 번째 문장에서 'When World War II broke out, he joined the Royal Air Force and became a fighter pilot.'이라고 했으므로, 글의 내용과 일치한다.

③ 다섯 번째 문장에서 'His first short story, which recounted his adventures in the war ~'라고 했으므로, 글의 내용과 일치한다.

본문해석

Roald Dahl(1916~1990)은 노르웨이인 부모님 사이에서 Wales에서 태어났다. 그는 영국에서 어린 시절을 보냈으며, 18세에 아프리카에 있는 Shell Oil 회사에서 일하기 위해 갔다. 2차 세계대전이 발발했을 때, 그는 영국 공군에 입대했고 전투기 조종사가 되었다. 26세에 워싱턴 D.C.로 이사했는데, 그가 글을 쓰기 시작한 곳은 바로 그곳이었다. 그의 전쟁에서의 모험에 대해 이야기한 첫 번째 단편 소설이 The Saturday Evening Post에 팔려서 장기간의 유명한 경력을 시작했다. 어른을 위한 작가로서의 입지를 굳힌 후, Roald Dahl은 1960년 가족과 함께 영국에서 사는 동안에 어린이들의 이야기를 쓰기 시작했다. 그의 첫 번째 이야기는 그의 많은 책들이 헌정된 그의 자녀들을 위한 오락으로 쓰였다. Roald Dahl은 이제 우리 시대의 가장 사랑받는 작가들 중 한 명으로 여겨진다.

VOCA

• fighter pilot 전투기 조종사

• recount (특히 자기가 경험한 것에 대해) 이야기하다[말하다]

• illustrious 저명한, 걸출한

• career 직업, 직장 생활, 경력

• establish 설립[설정]하다

• entertainment 오락(물), 여흥

• dedicate (책·음악·작품·공연을) 헌정하다[바치다]

• beloved 사랑받는

10 난도 ★★☆　　　　　　　　　　　　정답 ②

독해 > 글의 일관성 > 무관한 어휘·문장

정답의 이유

주어진 글은 지속 가능한 새로운 에너지원으로 부각되고 있는 해파리의 형광 단백질을 이용한 에너지 발생에 대한 내용이다. ② 앞 문장에서 해파리의 형광 단백질을 태양광 전지로 전환하여 에너지를 발생시키는 과정을 설명했고, ② 다음 문장에서 그것의 주요한 이점이 '화석 연료와 제한된 에너지원을 사용하지 않는 깨끗한 대안'이라고 했다. 따라서 문맥상 글의 전체 흐름과 관계없는 문장은 ② 'There has been constant criticism that the natural environment is being damaged by reckless solar power generation(무분별한 태양광 발전으로 자연환경이 훼손되고 있다는 계속적인 비판이 있다).'이다.

본문해석

지속 가능한 에너지의 새로운 자원 분야에서 가장 흥미로운 발견 중 하나는 해파리의 바이오 태양 에너지이다. 과학자들은 이 동물의 형광 단백질이 현재의 광전기성 에너지보다 더 지속 가능한 방법으로 태양 에너지를 발생시키는 데 사용될 수 있다는 것을 발견했다. 이 에너지는 어떻게 생성되는가? 그 과정은 해파리의 형광 단백질을 태양광 전지로 전환시키는 것을 포함하는데, 태양광 전지는 에너지를 생성해서 그것을 작은 장치로 이동시키는 것이 가능하다. 무분별한 태양광 발전으로 자연환경이 훼손되고 있다는 계속적인 비판이 있다. 이 생명체들을 천연 에너지원으로 사용하는 것의 주요한 이점은 화석 연료를 사용하지 않거나 제한된 자원을 사용할 필요가 없는 깨끗한 대안이라는 것이다. 비록 이 프로젝트가 아직 시험 단계에 있지만, 이 에너지원이 발전하여 점점 더 보편화되고 있는 소형 전기 장치 유형에 전력을 공급하기 위한 환경 친화적인 대안이 될 수 있을 것으로 기대된다.

VOCA

- sustainable energy　지속 가능한 에너지
- jellyfish　해파리
- fluorescent　형광성의, 야광의
- protein　단백질
- generate　발생시키다, 만들어 내다
- convert　전환시키다[개조하다]
- transfer　옮기다, 이동[이송/이전]하다
- reckless　무모한, 신중하지 못한
- solar power　태양 에너지
- generation　(특히 전기·열 등의) 발생
- fossil fuel　화석 연료
- limited resources　제한된 자원
- trial　시험[실험]
- phase　단계[시기/국면]
- green　환경 보호의[친화적인], 녹색의

11 난도 ★★★　　　　　　　　　　　　정답 ④

독해 > 글의 일관성 > 글의 순서

정답의 이유

주어진 글의 첫 번째 문장에서 '인간의 수준에서, 소는 단순해 (simple) 보인다.'라고 했으므로, 문맥상 소가 풀을 먹고 우유를 생산하는 과정을 화학적인 또는 연금술처럼 '단순한(straightforward)' 변화로 설명한 (C)가 오는 것이 자연스럽다. (C)의 후반부에서 'All you need is some grass, a cow and several generations of practical knowhow.'라는 문장은 'though'로 시작한 (B)에서 '현미경으로 보면, 모든 것이 더 복잡해진다.'라는 문장과 연결된다. (B)의 후반부에서 우유는 하나의 물질이 아니라 많은 물질의 혼합물이며, 풀 또한 우리가 완전히 이해할 수 없을 정도로 복잡하다고 했으므로 'A cow's complexity is even greater.'라고 시작하는 (A)로 이어지는 것이 자연스럽다. 따라서 주어진 글 다음에 이어질 글의 순서로 적절한 것은 ④ '(C) - (B) - (A)'이다.

본문해석

인간의 수준에서, 소는 단순해 보인다. 여러분이 소에게 풀을 먹이면, 소는 우유를 여러분에게 돌려준다. 그것은 그 비밀이 소와 몇몇 다른 포유동물(대부분은 풀을 소화할 수 없음)에 국한된 마술이다.

(C) 그 과정을 이용하기 위해 세부적인 것들을 이해할 필요는 없다. 그것은 풀에서 우유로의 간단한 변화이며, 생물학보다는 화학 혹은 연금술에 더 가깝다. 그것은 그 나름대로는 마술이지만 확실하게 작동하는 합리적인 마술이다. 필요한 것은 약간의 풀과 소 한 마리, 그리고 몇 세대에 걸친 실용적인 노하우가 전부이다.

(B) 하지만 현미경으로 보면, 모든 것이 더 복잡해진다. 자세히 들여다보면 볼수록 더 복잡해진다. 우유는 하나의 물질이 아니라 많은 물질의 혼합물이다. 풀은 너무 복잡해서 우리는 아직도 풀을 완전히 이해하지 못한다.

(A) 소의 복잡성은 훨씬 더 거대하다. 특히, 소는 (황소를 더하여) 새로운 세대의 어린 소를 만들 수 있다. 이것은 인간의 수준에서는 단순한 것이지만, 미시적인 차원에서는 표현할 수 없을 정도로 복잡하다.

VOCA

- pay back　갚다[돌려주다]
- mammal　포유동물
- digest　소화하다[소화시키다]
- exploit　활용하다
- straightforward　간단한, 쉬운
- transformation　변화[탈바꿈], 변신
- alchemy　연금술
- reliably　믿을 수 있게, 확실히
- microscope　현미경
- complicated　복잡한
- substance　물질
- mixture　혼합물[혼합체]
- inexpressibly　표현하기 어려울 정도로, 대단히
- microscopic　미세한, 현미경으로 봐야만 보이는

12 난도 ★★☆ 정답 ②

독해 > 글의 일관성 > 문장 삽입

정답의 이유

'But'으로 시작하는 주어진 문장에서 '여기서 주목할 점은 절반 이상의 인력이 원격 근무를 할 기회가 거의 없거나 전혀 없다는 것이다.'라고 했으므로, 앞뒤에 상반되는 내용이 있는 곳에 들어가야 한다는 것을 유추할 수 있다. ② 앞 문장에서 '이것은 COVID-19 이전보다 4~5배 더 많은 원격 근무'라고 했고, ② 다음 문장에서 'Moreover, not all work that can be done remotely should be ~'라고 한 다음에, '예를 들어, 협상, 브레인스토밍, 그리고 민감한 피드백을 제공하는 것들은 원격으로 수행할 때 덜 효과적일 수 있는 활동이다.'라고 했으므로, 글의 흐름으로 보아, 주어진 문장이 들어가기에 가장 적절한 곳은 ②이다.

본문해석

COVID-19의 확산은 원격 근무를 방해하는 문화적, 기술적 장벽을 넘어뜨렸다. 원격 근무를 이어갈 잠재력에 대한 분석에 따르면 선진 경제 근로자의 20~25%가 1주일에 3~5일의 범위에서 재택근무를 할 수 있다는 것을 보여주었다. 이것은 COVID-19 이전보다 4~5배 더 많은 원격 근무이다. 그러나 여기서 주목할 점은 절반 이상의 인력이 원격 근무를 할 기회가 거의 없거나 전혀 없다는 것이다. 게다가 원격으로 수행될 수 있다고 해서 모든 작업이 그래야만 하는 것은 아니다. 예를 들어, 협상, 브레인스토밍, 그리고 민감한 피드백을 제공하는 것들은 원격으로 수행될 때 덜 효과적일 수 있는 활동이다. 그리고 원격 근무에 대한 전망은 근무 환경, 직업 및 당면한 임무에 따라 달라지므로 일부 작업은 현장에서 수행되고 일부 작업은 원격으로 수행되는 혼합 방식의 근무 설정이 이어질 가능성이 높다. 혼합체 세계에서 지속 가능한 성과와 웰빙을 열기 위해서는 성과와 생산성에 대한 선도적인 추진 원동력은 직원들에게 제공하는 것이 보상이 아닌 목적 의식이어야 한다.

VOCA

- It's worth noting that ~하다는 것은 주목할 가치가 있다
- spread 확산, 전파
- flatten 깨부수다[넘어뜨리다]
- barrier 장애물[장벽]
- stand in the way of ~을 훼방 놓다
- remote work 원격 근무
- potential 가능성이 있는, 잠재적인
- persist 집요하게[고집스럽게/끈질기게] 계속하다
- workforce 노동 인구[노동력]
- negotiation 협상, 교섭
- brainstorming 창조적 집단 사고, 브레인스토밍
- hybrid 혼합체
- on-site 현장의, 현지의
- unlock 열다, (비밀 등을) 드러내다
- productivity 생산성
- sense of purpose 목적 의식

13 난도 ★☆☆ 정답 ③

독해 > 세부 내용 찾기 > 내용 (불)일치

정답의 이유

네 번째 문장에서 '~ he began to realize that although there were events in a patient's past that she or he might not remember consciously, these events could affect the person's actions in her or his present life.'라고 했으므로, 글의 내용과 일치하지 않는 것은 ③ '기억이 나지 않는 과거는 환자에게 영향을 미치지 못한다고 주장했다.'이다.

오답의 이유

① 첫 번째 문장에서 'Sigmund Freud was a doctor of psychology in Vienna, Austria ~'라고 했으므로, 글의 내용과 일치한다.
② 두 번째 문장에서 'He treated many patients with nervous problems through his "talk cure."'라고 했으므로, 글의 내용과 일치한다.
④ 마지막 부분에서 'Freud wrote a book ~ The title of the book was "The Interpretation of Dreams."'라고 했으므로, 글의 내용과 일치한다.

본문해석

Sigmund Freud는 19세기 말 오스트리아 빈의 정신과 의사였다. 그는 자신의 'talk cure'를 통해 신경 문제가 있는 많은 환자들을 치료했다. 이런 종류의 치료를 위해 Freud는 환자들에게 그들을 괴롭히고 있는 것은 무엇이든지 그에게 말하도록 했다. 환자들을 치료하면서 그는 환자의 과거에서 그녀 또는 그가 의식적으로 기억하지 못하는 사건들이 있을 수도 있지만, 이 사건들이 현재의 삶에서 그 사람의 행동에 영향을 미칠 수 있다는 것을 깨닫기 시작했다. Freud는 과거의 기억이 숨겨져 있던 곳을 무의식이라고 불렀다. 무의식으로부터의 이미지는 사람의 꿈이나 행동을 통해 나타날 수 있다. Freud는 1899년에 무의식과 꿈에 대한 자신의 이론에 대한 책을 썼다. 그 책의 제목은 'The Interpretation of Dreams'였다.

VOCA

- treat 치료하다, 처치하다
- nervous 신경이 과민한, 신경의
- bother 신경 쓰이게 하다, 괴롭히다
- consciously 의식적으로
- affect 영향을 미치다
- unconscious mind 잠재의식, 무의식
- show up 나타나다

14 난도 ★☆☆　　　　　　　　　　　　　　　정답 ④

독해 > 세부 내용 찾기 > 요지, 주장

정답의 이유

네 번째 문장 후반부에서 '우리가 실제로 어떻게 느끼는지 알아차리는 것(to notice how we actually feel)'이 더 낫다고 한 다음에, 마지막 문장에서 감정적 인식이 단순히 '여러분의 감정을 일어나는 대로 인식하고, 존중하고, 받아들이는 것(recognizing, respecting, and accepting your feelings as they happen)'을 의미한다고 했으므로 글의 요지로 적절한 것은 ④ '우리의 감정을 인식하고 존중하며 그대로 받아들여야 한다.'이다.

본문해석

모든 감정은 우리들에게 우리 자신과 상황에 대해 무언가 말해준다. 하지만 때때로 우리는 우리가 느끼는 것을 받아들이기 어렵다. 예를 들면, 마치 우리가 질투심을 느끼는 것처럼 특정한 방식으로 우리 자신을 판단할 수도 있다. 하지만 우리가 그렇게 느껴서는 안 된다고 생각하는 대신에, 차라리 우리가 실제로 어떻게 느끼는지 알아차리는 것이 더 낫다. 부정적인 감정을 피하거나 우리가 그 방식을 느끼지 않는 척하는 것은 역효과를 가져올 수 있다. 우리가 그것들을 마주하지 않고 우리가 왜 그렇게 느끼는지 이해하려고 노력하지 않는다면, 어려운 감정들을 지나치고 그것들이 사라지도록 내버려두는 것이 더 어렵다. 여러분의 감정에 대해 깊이 생각하거나 여러분이 어떻게 느끼는지 계속 말할 필요는 없다. 감정적 인식은 단순히 여러분의 감정을 일어나는 대로 인식하고, 존중하고, 받아들이는 것을 의미한다.

VOCA

- accept 받아들이다[인정하다]
- jealous 질투하는
- notice ~을 의식하다[(보거나 듣고) 알다]
- avoid (회)피하다
- pretend ~인 척하다[것처럼 굴다]
- backfire 역효과를 낳다
- fade 서서히 사라지다, 점점 희미해지다
- dwell on ~을 깊이 생각하다, 숙고하다
- awareness 의식[관심]

15 난도 ★★★　　　　　　　　　　　　　　　정답 ②

독해 > 글의 일관성 > 글의 순서

정답의 이유

'At the level of lawmaking(입법 수준에서)'으로 시작하는 주어진 글은 거대 기술기업들이 기술적 자원과 혁신에 대해 변경할 수 없는 통제력을 가져야 할 이유가 없다는 내용이므로, 글의 흐름상 주어진 글 다음에는 'At the private and personal level(사적이고 개인적인 수준에서)'로 시작한 (B)에서 'control of your life(여러분의 삶을 통제)'해야 할 이유도 역시 없다는 내용이 오는 것이 자연스럽다. (B)의 후반부에서 정책과 정치, 우리의 개인적인 생활에서 우리들의 데이터가 팔리고 아이들이 게임에 중독되고, 우리들이 사이버 공간에서 살게 될 것을 '불가피한(inevitable)' 사실로 받아들여서는 안 된다고 했으므로 문맥상 'As a free people(자연인으로서)'로 시작하는 (C)에서 우리는 우리가 소비하는 디지털 제품의 종류와 양에 대해 '절대적인 통제(absolute control)'를 행사할 권리가 있다는 내용이 와야 한다. (C) 후반부의 'parents should control what tech products go to their kids.'를 받아 (A)에서 '아이에게 스마트폰을 사주지 않으면 아이는 스마트폰을 가질 수 없다.'라고 한 Daily Wire사의 Matt Walsh의 말로 이어지는 것이 자연스럽다. 따라서 주어진 글 다음에 이어질 글의 순서로 적절한 것은 ② '(B) – (C) – (A)'이다.

본문해석

입법 수준에서, 거대 기술기업들이 기술적인 자원과 혁신에 대해 이의를 제기할 수 없는 통제력을 가져야 할 이유가 없다.

(B) 사적이고 개인적인 수준에서도 그들이 여러분의 삶을 통제해야 할 이유도 역시 없다. 정책, 정치, 그리고 우리의 개인적인 생활에서 우리의 데이터가 최고 입찰자에게 팔릴 것이며 우리의 아이들이 온라인 게임에 중독될 것이고, 우리들이 사이버 공간에서 살게 될 것을 '불가피한' 것으로 받아들여서는 안 된다.

(C) 자유인으로서 우리는 우리가 소비하는 디지털 제품의 종류와 양에 대해 절대적인 통제를 행사할 권리가 있다. 특히, 부모들은 어떤 기술 제품이 아이들에게 전달되는지 통제해야 한다.

(A) Daily Wire사의 Matt Walsh가 지적했듯이, 예를 들어, 아이에게 스마트폰을 사주지 않으면 아이는 스마트폰을 가질 수 없다. 감시 없이 모든 충동을 만족시킬 수 있는 장치를 아이의 손에 쥐여 줄 필요는 없다.

VOCA

- lawmaking 입법(의)
- tech giant 거대 기술기업
- ironclad 이의를 제기할 수 없는, 변경할 수 없는
- grip 통제, 지배
- innovation 혁신, 쇄신
- inevitable 불가피한, 필연적인
- highest bidder 최고 입찰인
- be addicted to ~에 빠지다[중독되다]
- metaverse 사이버 공간, 가상공간
- be entitled to ~에 대한 권리가/자격이 주어지다, ~가 주어지다
- exert (권력·영향력을) 가하다[행사하다]
- absolute control 절대적인 통제
- digital products 디지털 제품
- consume 소모하다
- point out 가리키다, 지적하다
- indulge 마음껏 하다
- impulse 충동
- supervision 감독[지도]

16 난도 ★★★

독해 > 글의 일관성 > 문장 삽입

정답의 이유

주어진 글이 'These may appear as challenges ~'로 시작하므로 주어진 글 앞에는 These에 해당하는 것들이 나와야 하며, 주어진 글 다음에는 'challenges'를 받는 내용이 와야 한다. ③ 앞 문장에서 미래의 식량 안보가 의지할 것들(a combination of the stresses ~, variability of weather ~, development of cultivars ~, the ability to develop effective adaptation strategies ~)을 나열하고 있는데, 주어진 문장에서 'These'로 받았으며, 주어진 문장의 challenges를 ③ 다음 문장에서 'these challenges also provide us ~'로 받고 있으므로, 글의 흐름으로 보아, 주어진 문장이 들어가기에 가장 적절한 곳은 ③이다.

본문해석

지구 온난화는 인간이 감수해야 하는 현실이다. 이것은 인식해야 할 매우 중요한 사안인데, 그것은 지구상의 인간 존재에 영향을 미치는 모든 매개 변수들 중에서 지구상의 생명체에게 가장 중요하고 지구 온난화에 의해 가장 위협받는 것은 바로 식량 안보이기 때문이다. 미래의 식량 안보는 기후 변화에 의해 부과되는 생물학적 및 비생물학적 스트레스, 식물 성장 시기 내 기후의 가변성, 서로 다른 주변 조건에 더 적합한 품종의 개발, 그리고 이러한 품종들이 변화하는 기후 조건 하에서 자신들의 유전적 잠재력을 표현할 수 있도록 하는 효과적인 적응 전략을 개발하는 능력에 의존할 것이다. 이것들은 미래의 기후를 예측하는 우리 능력의 불확실성 때문에 다루기 불가능한 도전으로 보일 수도 있다. 그러나 이러한 도전들은 또한 우리에게 토양식물대기 상호 작용에 대한 우리의 이해를 증진시킬 수 있는 기회를 제공하고, 우리가 이 지식을 활용하여 전 세계의 모든 지역에 걸쳐 향상된 식량 안보라는 궁극적인 목표를 달성할 수 있도록 할 수 있는 방법을 제공한다.

VOCA

- address (문제·상황 등에 대해) 고심하다[다루다]
- global warming 지구 온난화
- issue 주제[안건], 쟁점, 사안
- parameter (일정하게 정한) 한도; 매개 변수
- food security 식량 안보
- paramount 중요한, 최고의
- threatened 멸종할 위기에 직면한
- biotic 생물의, 생물에 관련된
- variability 가변성, 변동성
- genetic 유전의, 유전학의
- potential 가능성이 있는, 잠재적인
- enhance 높이다[향상시키다]
- soil-plant-atmosphere 토양식물대기
- interaction 상호 작용
- achieve 달성하다, 성취하다

17 난도 ★☆☆

정답 ①

어법 > 비문 찾기

정답의 이유

① 밑줄 친 disputing은 '이의를 제기하다'라는 뜻의 타동사 dispute의 현재분사형인데, disputing 다음에 목적어가 없고, 주어가 '정확한 감정의 수(the exact number of emotions)'이므로 수동의 의미이다. 따라서 disputing → disputed가 되어야 한다. 'with some researchers suggesting ~'은 'with+명사+분사구문'의 부대상황을 나타내는 부사구이다.

오답의 이유

② Despite는 '~에도 불구하고'라는 뜻의 전치사로, despite 다음에 명사(these disagreements)가 왔으므로, 어법상 적절하게 사용되었다.
③ closely는 '밀접하게'라는 뜻의 부사로, 형용사 linked(연계된)를 수식하고 있으므로 어법상 적절하게 사용되었다.
④ them은 to attain의 목적어로 social rewards를 받고 있으므로, 어법상 적절하게 사용되었다.

본문해석

인류학자 Paul Ekman은 1970년대에 인간이 6가지 기본적인 감정들, 즉 분노, 두려움, 놀라움, 혐오, 기쁨, 슬픔을 경험한다고 제안했다. 하지만 감정의 수에 대해서는 논란의 여지가 있는데, 어떤 연구자들은 단지 4개에 불과하다고 제안하고, 다른 사람들은 그 수를 27개까지로 보고 있다. 게다가 과학자들은 감정이 모든 인간 문화에 보편적인지 아닌지 혹은 우리가 감정을 가지고 태어났는지 아니면 경험을 통해 그것을 배우는지에 대해 논쟁한다. 이러한 의견의 불일치에도 불구하고, 감정은 뇌의 특정 영역에서의 활동의 분명한 산물이다. 편도체와 (뇌·췌장의) 섬, 즉 대뇌 피질은 감정과 가장 밀접하게 관련된 두 가지 대표적인 뇌 구조이다. 편도체는 뇌 깊숙한 곳에 있는 한 쌍의 아몬드 모양의 구조로 감정, 감정적 행동, 그리고 자극을 통합한다. 그것은 두려움을 해석하고, 친구와 적을 구별하는 것을 돕고, 사회적 보상과 그것들을 얻는 방법을 알아낸다. (뇌·췌장의) 섬은 혐오의 근원이다. 혐오에 대한 경험은 독이나 상한 음식을 섭취하는 것으로부터 여러분을 보호할 수도 있다.

VOCA

- anthropologist 인류학자
- additionally 게다가
- debate 논의[토의/논쟁]하다
- disagreement 의견 충돌[차이], 다툼, 불일치
- insula (뇌·췌장의) 섬
- almond-shaped 아몬드형의, (한쪽 또는 양쪽의) 끝이 뾰족한 타원형의
- integrate 통합시키다[되다]
- distinguish from ~와 구별하다
- attain 이루다[획득하다]
- source of disgust 혐오의 근원
- ingest 삼키다[먹다]
- spoiled food 상한 음식

PART 4 | 2023년 법원직 9급 **193**

18 난도 ★☆☆   정답 ②

독해 > 대의 파악 > 제목, 주제

정답의 이유

글의 첫 부분에서 'Do you want to be a successful anchor? If so, keep this in mind.'라고 한 다음에 뉴스 앵커로서 필요한 자질을 말하고 있으므로, 글의 주제로 적절한 것은 ② 'qualifications to become a news anchor(뉴스 앵커가 되기 위한 자격)'이다.

오답의 이유

① 생방송 뉴스 제작의 어려움
③ 언론인의 사회적 역할의 중요성
④ 올바른 여론 형성의 중요성

본문해석

성공적인 앵커가 되기를 원하는가? 그렇다면, 이 점을 명심하라. 앵커로서 개인은 뉴스 방송, 특별 보도 및 기타 유형의 뉴스 프로그램 동안 시청자에게 뉴스와 정보를 전달하도록 요청될 것이다. 이것은 뉴스 사건의 해석과 애드리브, 스크립트를 사용할 수 없을 때 뉴스 속보를 효과적으로 전달하는 것이 포함된다. 뉴스를 진행하는 앵커의 업무는 또한 이야기를 수집하고 쓰는 것을 포함한다. 앵커는 스크립트를 명확하고 효과적으로 전달할 수 있어야 한다. 견고한 글쓰기 능력, 믿을 수 있는 뉴스 판단력, 그리고 시각적 스토리텔링에 대한 강한 감각이 필수적인 기술이다. 이 사람은 본업으로 정보원을 양성하고 새로운 정보를 발견하는 자발적으로 행동하는 사람이어야 한다. 뉴스 속보를 발생하면 애드리브하고 설명하는 능력뿐만 아니라 생방송 보도기술이 중요하다.

VOCA

• anchor 앵커맨, (뉴스를) 진행하다, 앵커를 하다
• call upon ~을 청하다, 요구하다
• viewer (텔레비전) 시청자
• newscast 뉴스 프로그램
• adlib (연설·연기 등을) 즉흥적으로 하다, 애드리브로 하다
• communicate (정보 등을) 전달하다
• breaking news 뉴스 속보
• solid 확실한, 믿을 수 있는
• news judgement 뉴스 판단력
• self-starter 자발적으로 행동하는 사람
• cultivate 기르다[함양하다]

19 난도 ★☆☆   정답 ③

독해 > 세부 내용 찾기 > 내용 (불)일치

정답의 이유

네 번째 문장에서 'While he never self-identified as an Impressionist, ~ to the quick, gestural brush strokes aiming to capture a fleeting moment that was typical of the Impressionists.'라고 했으므로, 글의 내용과 일치하지 않는 것은 ③ '로댕은 자신을 인상파라고 밝히며 인상파의 전형적인 붓놀림을 보여주었다.'이다.

오답의 이유

① 첫 번째 문장에서 'Modern sculpture is generally considered to have begun with the work of French sculptor Auguste Rodin.'이라고 했으므로, 글의 내용과 일치한다.
② 두 번째 문장의 후반부에서 '~ he incorporated novel ways of building his sculpture that defied classical categories and techniques.'라고 했으므로, 글의 내용과 일치한다.
④ 마지막 문장에서 'Rodin's most original work departed from traditional themes of mythology and allegory, ~'라고 했으므로, 글의 내용과 일치한다.

본문해석

현대 조각은 일반적으로 프랑스의 조각가 Auguste Rodin의 작품에서 시작되었다고 여겨진다. 종종 조각의 인상주의자로 여겨지는 Rodin은 예술적 전통에 반항하는 것을 시작하지 않았지만, 고전적인 기술을 거부하며 자신의 조각을 만드는 새로운 방식을 통합했다. 구체적으로, Rodin은 복잡하고 격동적이며 깊게 팬 표면을 점토로 형태화했다. 그는 결코 인상파라고 자칭하지는 않았지만, 그가 작품에 사용한 격렬한 몸짓을 표현하는 모델링은 종종 인상파 화가들의 전형이었던 찰나의 순간을 포착하기 위한 재빠른 손짓의 붓놀림에 비유된다. Rodin의 가장 독창적인 작품은 신화와 우화의 전통적인 주제에서 벗어나 강력한 사실주의로 인체를 모델링하고 개인의 기질과 신체적 특질을 찬양하는 것을 선호한다.

VOCA

• sculptor 조각가
• set out 착수하다[나서다]
• rebel against ~에 대항[저항]하다
• incorporate 통합하다
• defy 반항[저항/거역]하다
• turbulent 격동의, 격변의
• self-identify as ~로 자칭하다
• impressionist 인상파 화가
• vigorous 활발한, 격렬한
• gestural 몸짓의, 손짓의
• modeling 양감의 표현, (조각의) 살 붙임
• employ (기술·방법 등을) 쓰다[이용하다]
• liken (~에) 비유하다, 비기다
• brush stroke 붓놀림
• fleeting 순식간의, 잠깐 동안의
• depart from ~에서 벗어나다
• allegory 우화, 풍자
• in favor of ~에 찬성[지지]하여
• celebrate 찬양하다, 기리다
• physicality 신체적 특징, 육체적 적응 (능력)

20 난도 ★☆☆   정답 ③

독해 > 대의 파악 > 제목, 주제

정답의 이유

마지막 문장에서 'By drawing attention to the face and encouraging cosmetics use, portrait photography heightened the aesthetic valuation of smooth and often light-colored skin.'이라고 했으므로, 글의 주제로 적절한 것은 ③ 'active use of cosmetics to make the face look better(얼굴을 더 좋게 만들기 위한 화장품의 적극적인 사용)'이다.

오답의 이유

① 화장품 과다 사용의 부작용
② 사진작가들에 의해 조장된 화장품 남용
④ 사진술의 발달로 인해 줄어든 화장품 사용

본문해석

화장품은 인물사진 기법과 매우 밀접하게 연관되어 있어서 일부 사진 핸드북은 화장품 만드는 법을 포함했다. 미국의 사진작가들은 또한 네거티브와 프린트를 수정하기 위해 가끔 화장품을 사용하기도 했으며, 조금의 볼연지로 여성의 얼굴을 생동감 있게 만들었다. 어두운 피부를 가진 일부 고객들은 더 밝아 보이는 사진을 요청했다. 1935년 아프리카계 미국인 신문에 실린 피부 미백제 광고는 이 제품이 사진작가들에 의해 만들어진 것과 동일한 외모, 즉 잡티 하나 없는 더 밝은 피부를 얻을 수 있다고 약속함으로써 이 관행을 언급했다. 얼굴에 관심을 끌고 화장품 사용을 장려함으로써, 인물사진은 매끄러운 피부와 종종 밝은 색 피부에 대한 심미적 가치를 고조시켰다.

VOCA

• cosmetics 화장품
• portraiture 초상화법, 인물사진 기법
• retouch (그림·사진을) 수정[가필]하다
• enliven 더 재미있게[생동감 있게] 만들다
• skin lightener 피부 미백제
• achieve 달성하다, 성취하다
• blemish (피부 등의) 티
• draw attention to ~에 이목을 끌다
• portrait photography 인물사진
• heighten (감정·효과가[를]) 고조되다[고조시키다]
• aesthetic 심미적, 미학적
• valuation 판단, (판단된) 중요성
• light-colored 옅은[밝은] 색의

21 난도 ★★☆   정답 ③

독해 > 글의 일관성 > 무관한 어휘·문장

정답의 이유

주어진 글은 '놀이'의 중요성에 대한 내용으로, 다섯 번째 문장부터 '놀이'의 이점에 대해 나열하고 있다. 다섯 번째 문장에서 놀이는 자신과 다른 사람들과의 관계를 '양성한다(nurtures)'라고 한 다음에, 연이어서 놀이는 스트레스를 '해소하고(relieves)' 행복감을 증가시키며 공감, 창의성, 그리고 협력의 감정을 형성하고, 강건함과 근성의 성장을 지원한다고 했다. 밑줄 친 ③ 앞부분에서 'When children are deprived of opportunities for play(아이들이 놀 기회를 박탈당하면)'라고 했으므로, 문맥상 뒷부분에는 부정적인 의미가 와야 함을 유추할 수 있다. 따라서 ③ 'enhanced(향상된) → impaired(손상된) 등'이 되어야 한다.

본문해석

"놀이는 그 자체를 위해 행해지는 것이다."라고 '놀이'의 저자인 정신과 의사 Stuart Brown은 말한다. 그는 그의 저서에서 쓰기를, "그것은 자발적이고, 즐겁고, 몰입감을 제공하고, 시간을 빼앗는다. 그리고 결과보다 행동 자체가 더 중요하다."라고 했다. 이 정의를 염두에 두면 놀이의 잠재적 이점을 쉽게 인식할 수 있다. 놀이는 자신과 다른 사람들과의 관계를 양성한다. 그것은 스트레스를 해소하고 행복감을 증가시킨다. 그것은 공감, 창의성, 그리고 협력의 감정을 형성한다. 강건함과 근성의 성장을 지원한다. 아이들이 놀 기회를 박탈당하면, 그들의 발달 기회는 크게 향상될(→ 저해될) 수 있다. 놀이는 너무나 중요해서 유엔고등인권위원회는 그것을 모든 어린이의 기본적인 권리라고 선언했다. 놀이는 하찮은 것이 아니다. 그것은 '진짜 일'이 끝난 후에 하는 무언가가 아니다. 놀이는 어린 시절의 진짜 일이다. 그것을 통해, 아이들은 온전하고 행복한 어른이 될 수 있는 최고의 기회를 갖게 된다.

VOCA

• for its own sake 그 자체의 목적으로
• psychiatrist 정신과 의사
• voluntary 자발적인, 임의적인, 자진한
• pleasurable 즐거운
• definition 정의
• nurture 육성[양성]하다
• relieve (불쾌감·고통 등을) 없애[덜어] 주다
• empathy 감정이입, 공감
• sturdiness 강건함
• grit 투지, 기개
• be deprived of ~을 빼앗기다
• enhance 높이다[향상시키다]
• declare 선언[선포/공표]하다
• fundamental 근본[본질]적인
• frivolous 경박한, 하찮은
• whole 온전한

22 난도 ★★☆ 정답 ③

독해 > 빈칸 완성 > 단어 · 구 · 절

정답의 이유

네 번째 문장에서 '첫 번째 시도가 실패한 후, Lewis는 해발 5,300미터에서 수영하는 가장 좋은 방법에 대해 논의하기 위한 평가회의를 가졌다.'라고 했으므로, 다음 부분에 평가회의의 결과에 대한 내용이 나와야 한다. 빈칸 앞 문장에서 'He is usually very aggressive when he swims because he wants to finish quickly and get out of the cold water.'라고 했고, 빈칸 문장이 But으로 시작하고 있으므로 빈칸에 들어갈 말로 적절한 것은 aggressive와 반대되는 ③ '겸손함(humility)'임을 유추할 수 있다.

오답의 이유

① 슬픔
② 분노
④ 자신감

본문해석

Lewis Pugh는 영국의 지구력 수영 선수로, 차가운 개방 구역에서 장거리 수영을 하는 것으로 가장 잘 알려져 있다. 그는 기후 변화와 공해의 영향으로부터 세계의 바다와 수로를 보호해야 하는 긴급한 필요성에 대한 관심을 끄는 방법의 하나로 추운 곳에서 수영한다. 2019년에 Pugh는 Everest산 근처 네팔의 Khumbu지역에 위치한 Imja호에서 수영하기로 결정했다. 첫 번째 시도가 실패한 후, Lewis는 해발 5,300미터에서 수영하는 가장 좋은 방법에 대해 논의하기 위해 평가회의를 했다. 그는 보통 수영을 할 때 매우 공격적인데, 빨리 끝내고 차가운 물에서 벗어나고 싶기 때문이다. 하지만 이번에 그는 겸손함을 보여주었고 천천히 수영했다.

VOCA

- endurance 인내(력), 참을성
- long-distance 장거리의
- open water 개빙(開氷) 구역(부빙(浮氷)이 수면의 10분의 1 이하)
- failed 실패한
- attempt 시도
- aggressive 공격적인

23 난도 ★★☆ 정답 ①

독해 > 글의 일관성 > 무관한 어휘 · 문장

정답의 이유

주어진 글은 패스트 패션의 일회용 소비 문화로 인하여 버려진 물건들이 환경에 큰 부담을 더하고 있으며, 이것을 해결하기 위해 패션의 지속 가능성 개념에 주목하고 있다는 내용이다. ①의 앞 문장에서 'This means customers simply discard products ~'라고 했고, ②에서 '그 결과, 이러한 버려진 물건들은 환경에 큰 부담을 더한다.'라고 했으므로, 글의 전체 흐름과 관계없는 문장은 ① 'The consumers are generally satisfied with the quality of fast fashion brand clothing(소비자들은 일반적으로 패스트 패션 브랜드 의류의 품질에 만족한다).'이다.

본문해석

패스트 패션은 최신 패션 트렌드에 대응하기 위해 빠른 속도로 저렴한 의류를 생산하는 방식이다. 패스트 패션 시대에 쇼핑이 오락의 한 형태로 진화하면서, 고객들은 지속 가능성 전문가들이 말하는 일회용 소비문화에 기여하고 있다. 이것은 물건들이 쓸모없다고 판단되면 고객들은 재활용하거나 기부하기보다 그 물건들을 그냥 버린다는 것을 의미한다. 소비자들은 일반적으로 패스트 패션 브랜드 의류의 품질에 만족한다. 그 결과, 이러한 버려진 물건들은 환경에 큰 부담을 더한다. 일회용 소비문화와 패스트 패션의 위기를 해결하기 위해 패션의 지속 가능성 개념이 주목받고 있다. 지속 가능한 패션은 사회 경제적, 환경적 관심사를 고려하여 가능한 한 지속 가능하게 생산되고, 유통되고, 활용되는 의류, 신발류, 액세서리류를 포함한다.

VOCA

- respond 대응[반응/부응]하다
- entertainment 오락(물), 여흥
- sustainability 지속[유지] 가능성
- refer to 언급[지칭]하다
- throwaway (값싸게 만들어져) 그냥 쓰고 버리는
- discard 버리다, 폐기하다
- deem (~로) 여기다[생각하다]
- recycle 재활용[재생]하다
- donate 기부[기증]하다
- burden 부담, 짐
- resolve 해결하다
- bring to ~로 이끌다
- spotlight 스포트라이트, 환한 조명
- apparel (매장에서 판매되는) 의류
- footwear 신발(류)
- distribute (상품을) 유통시키다
- utilize 활용[이용]하다
- take into account ~을 고려하다
- socio-economic 사회 경제적
- environmental 환경의[환경과 관련된]
- concern 우려[걱정]

24 난도 ★★☆
정답 ④

독해 > 대의 파악 > 요지, 주장

정답의 이유

두 번째 문장에서 '~ some women with deepening and worsening skin wrinkles also had lower bone density, independent of age and factors known to influence bone mass.'라고 했으므로, 글의 요지로 적절한 것은 ④ '주름은 단지 피부 노화와만 연관된 것이 아니라 뼈 건강 상태와도 연관이 있다.'이다.

본문해석

주름은 노화의 확실한 신호이며, 뼈 건강이 감소하고 있다는 것을 암시할 수도 있다. 예일 의과 대학의 연구원들은 피부 주름이 깊어지고 악화되는 일부 여성들은 나이와 골부피에 영향을 주는 것으로 알려진 요소들과는 별개로 더 낮은 골밀도를 가지고 있다는 것을 발견했다. 피부와 뼈는 나이가 들면서 소실되는 1형 콜라겐이라는 공통된 구성 요소 단백질을 공유한다고 연구 저자인 Lubna Pal 박사는 말한다. 그녀는 말하기를, 눈썹 사이의 주름, 즉 콧대 위의 수직선은 잘 부러지는 뼈의 가장 강력한 표시인 것처럼 보인다고 한다. 장기적인 연구가 필요하지만, 피부가 뼈 수준에서 일어나고 있는 것을 반영하는 것처럼 보인다고 Pal은 말한다.

VOCA

- wrinkle (특히 얼굴의) 주름
- sure sign 확실한 신호
- hint 넌지시 알려주다, 암시[힌트]를 주다
- bone health 뼈 건강
- on the decline 기울어져, 쇠퇴하여
- deepen 깊어지다, 악화되다, 악화시키다
- worsen 악화되다, 악화시키다
- bone density 골밀도
- bone mass 골부피
- share 함께 쓰다, 공유하다
- vertical line 수직선, 연직선
- the bridge of the nose 콧대
- reflect 나타내다[반영하다]

25 난도 ★☆☆
정답 ③

독해 > 세부 내용 찾기 > 내용 (불)일치

정답의 이유

네 번째 문장에서 'Chronic stress can cause ~ which can lead to other negative effects on your health, including cardiovascular and immune systems and gut health.'라고 했으므로, 글의 내용과 일치하지 않는 것은 ③ 'Stress does not usually affect our cardiovascular systems(스트레스는 보통 우리의 심혈관계에 영향을 주지 않는다).'이다.

오답의 이유

① 명상은 우리에게 정신적으로나 육체적으로 모두 이롭다. → 첫 번째 문장에서 'Meditation can improve your quality of life thanks to its many psychological and physical benefits.'라고 했으므로, 글의 내용과 일치한다.

② 코르티솔은 스트레스가 많은 상황에서 방출된다. → 세 번째 문장에서 'When faced with a difficult or stressful moment, our bodies create cortisol, ~'이라고 했으므로, 글의 내용과 일치한다.

④ 명상은 신체에서 만성적인 스트레스를 낮추는 데 도움을 줄 수 있다. → 마지막 문장에서 'Meditation, ~ can help to reduce chronic stress in the body and lower the risk of its side effects.'라고 했으므로, 글의 내용과 일치한다.

본문해석

명상은 많은 심리적, 육체적 이점 덕분에 삶의 질을 향상시킬 수 있다. Clinical Psychology Review의 연구에 따르면, 명상과 같이 마음 챙김에 기초한 개입들은 특히 스트레스 영역에서 정신 건강을 향상시키는 것으로 나타났다. 곤란하거나 스트레스가 많은 순간에 직면했을 때, 우리의 신체는 스트레스 조절 기능을 담당하는 스테로이드 호르몬인 코르티솔과 다른 많은 기능들 가운데 우리의 선천적인 투쟁 혹은 도피 반응을 만들어낸다. 만성적인 스트레스는 지속적이고 높은 수준의 코르티솔을 유발할 수 있는데, 그것은 심혈관계와 면역체계, 내장 건강을 포함한 여러분의 건강에 다른 부정적인 영향으로 이어질 수 있다. 마음을 진정시키고 감정을 조절하는 데 초점을 맞춘 명상은 신체의 만성적인 스트레스를 줄이고 부작용의 위험을 낮추는 데 도움을 줄 수 있다.

VOCA

- meditation 명상, 묵상
- mindfulness-based 마음 챙김에 기초한
- intervention 개입
- face with ~을 가지고 직면하다
- create 일으키다, 만들어내다
- cortisol 코르티솔(부신 피질에서 생기는 스테로이드 호르몬의 일종)
- responsible for ~에 책임이 있는, 원인이 있는
- regulate 조절[조정]하다
- fight-or-flight response 투쟁 혹은 도피 반응, 싸움 혹은 도주 반응
- chronic stress 만성적 스트레스
- cause ~을 야기하다[초래하다]
- sustained 지속된, 한결같은, 일관된
- elevated 높은
- cardiovascular 심혈관계의
- immune system 면역체계
- gut 소화관, 내장
- calm 진정시키다
- side effect 부작용

한눈에 훑어보기

✅ 영역 분석

독해　02 03 04 05 06 07 08 09 10 12 13 14
16 17 20 21 22 23 24 25
20문항, 80%

어법　01 11 15 18 19
5문항, 20%

✅ 빠른 정답

01	02	03	04	05	06	07	08	09	10
①	①	①	③	④	④	①	③	③	④
11	**12**	**13**	**14**	**15**	**16**	**17**	**18**	**19**	**20**
①	③	①	②	④	②	③	①	①	②
21	**22**	**23**	**24**	**25**					
③	②	③	②	③					

✅ 점수 체크

구분	1회독	2회독	3회독
맞힌 문항 수	/ 25	/ 25	/ 25
나의 점수	점	점	점

01 난도 ★☆☆　　　　　　　　　　　　정답 ①

어법 > 정문 찾기

정답의 이유

(A) 주어진 문장의 주어는 The selection으로 단수이므로 be동사
역시 단수명사와 함께 쓰이는 is가 옳다.

(B) '~에 사용되다'에 해당하는 숙어는 'be used to 동사원형'이므
로 to meet가 옳다.

(C) 선행사 areas를 수식하는 관계사를 찾는 문제이다. 관계사 뒤
에 이어지는 문장은 문장의 구성요소를 모두 갖춘 완전한 문장
(관계절 내의 동사 'exist'는 자동사이므로 목적어를 필요로 하
지 않는다)이므로 관계부사 where가 옳다.

본문해석

어떤 직업 또는 작업을 위한 적절한 보호복 선택은 주로 보여지는
위험에 대한 분석 또는 평가에 의해 좌우된다. 착용자의 노출 빈도
와 유형뿐 아니라 예상되는 활동은 이러한 결정에 입력되는 일반적
인 변수이다. 예를 들면, 소방관은 다양한 연소 물질들에 노출된다.
따라서 전문화된 다층 직물 구조가 주어진 열 문제들을 대처하는
데 사용된다. 그 결과 일반적으로 상당히 무거우며 근본적으로 어떠
한 화재 상황에서도 최고 수준의 보호를 제공하는 보호 장비가 된
다. 반대로, 돌발적인 화재의 가능성이 있는 지역에서 일하는 산업
노동자는 매우 다른 일련의 위험 요소와 필요조건들을 가지고 있을
것이다. 많은 경우에, 면 작업복 위에 입는 방염 작업복이 이 위험을
적절하게 해결해 준다.

VOCA

• appropriate　적절한
• protective　보호하는
• dictate　~을 좌우하다
• analysis　분석
• assessment　평가
• determination　결정
• variable　변하는[변하기 쉬운] 것[성질], 변수
• requirement　필요조건
• adequately　적절하게, 충분히

관계대명사 vs. 관계부사

- 관계대명사는 문장 속에서 주어, 보어 또는 목적어 역할, 즉 명사를 대신하므로 관계대명사절은 불완전한 문장이다.

  예 She never listened to the advice which I gave it to her.

  (그녀는 내가 그녀에게 했던 조언을 결코 듣지 않았다.)

  → which는 선행사 advice를 수식하는 목적격 관계대명사로 관계절에서 목적어 역할을 하며, 관계절은 목적어(it)가 없는 불완전한 절이다.

  예 I met a student yesterday in the cafeteria who said she knew you.

  (나는 어제 너를 알고 있다고 말한 한 여학생을 식당에서 만났다.)

  → who는 선행사 a student를 수식하는 주격 관계대명사로 관계절에서 주어 역할을 하며, 관계절은 주어(a student)가 없는 불완전한 절이다.

- 관계부사는 부사를 대신하므로 관계부사절은 부사가 없어도 가능한 완전한 문장이다.

  예 Trees must be fitted for the places where they live.

  (나무들은 그들이 살고 있는 장소에 맞아야 한다.)

  → where는 선행사 the places를 수식하는 관계부사로 관계절에서 부사의 역할을 하며, 관계절은 완전한 문장이다. 이때 관계부사 where는 전치사+관계대명사(in which)로 바꿔쓸 수 있다.

02 난도 ★★☆   정답 ①

독해 > 빈칸 완성 > 단어 · 구 · 절

정답의 이유

① 세 번째 문장에서 'The Indian government now runs programs aimed at improving their lot(인도 정부는 숲 근처에 사는 사람들의 지역을 향상시키는 것을 목표로 하는 프로그램을 운영하는데) ~'이라고 했으므로 (A)에는 'improve(향상시키다)'가 적절하다. 마지막 문장에서 그 프로그램이 성공한다면 숲은 지속 가능하게 관리될 것이라고 했으므로 (B)에는 'ruining(파괴하는)'이 적절하다.

오답의 이유

② 통제하다 – 보존하는

③ 향상시키다 – 제한하는

④ 통제하다 – 확대하는

본문해석

인도에서는 대략 3억 6천만 명, 즉 인구의 3분의 1이 숲속에 또는 숲과 아주 가까운 곳에 산다. 이 사람들의 절반 이상은 공식적인 빈곤선 아래에 살고 있으며, 그 결과 그들은 숲으로부터 얻는 자원에 결정적으로 의존한다. 인도 정부는 현재 숲의 상업적인 관리에 그들을 참여시킴으로써 그들의 지역을 개선하는 것을 목표로 프로그램을 운영하는데, 이러한 방식으로 그들이 필요로 하는 식량과 재료를 계속해서 얻을 수 있게도 하지만, 동시에 숲에서 나오는 수확물을

판매하게 하기도 한다. 만약 프로그램이 성공하면, 숲 거주자들은 더 번영할 것이지만 그들은 자신들의 전통적인 생활 방식과 문화를 보존할 수 있을 것이고, 그래서 숲은 지속 가능하게 관리될 것이며 야생동물들이 고갈되지 않는다.

⇩

인도 정부는 숲을 (B) 파괴하지 않고 숲 근처에 사는 사람들의 삶을 (A) 향상시키기 위해 노력하고 있다.

VOCA

- depend   의존하다
- crucially   결정적으로
- obtain   얻다
- dweller   거주자
- prosperous   번영하는
- sustainably   지속 가능하게
- deplete   고갈시키다

03 난도 ★☆☆   정답 ①

독해 > 빈칸 완성 > 단어 · 구 · 절

정답의 이유

① 병원 직원들이 마스크 때문에 환자와의 소통이 어려워지자 마스크를 끼고도 상대방의 표정과 마음을 읽을 수 있는 방법을 개발하는 내용이다. 세 번째 문장에서 'Some hospital workers have developed innovative ways to try to solve this problem(이 문제를 해결하기 위해 혁신적인 방법을 고안했다).'이라고 했으므로, 문맥상 빈칸 (A)에는 'alternative(대안적인)', 빈칸 (B)에는 'complement(보완하다)'가 적절하다.

오답의 이유

② 성가신 – 분석하다

③ 효과적인 – 방해하다

④ 충격적인 – 향상시키다

본문해석

얼굴의 신호나 접촉이 없는 팬데믹 기간 동안에는, 어조와 억양에 대한 더 많은 강조, 속도를 늦추고 성가신 소리 없이 음량을 높이는 것을 포함하여 대화의 다른 측면에 더 집중할 필요가 있다. 얼굴 표정 없이는 말의 많은 뉘앙스를 쉽게 놓칠 수 있기 때문에, 눈 맞춤이 훨씬 더 큰 중요성을 가질 것이다. 일부 병원 직원들은 이 문제를 해결하기 위해 혁신적인 방법을 고안했다. 한 전문 간호사는 만성적으로 아픈 어린 환자들이 그녀의 얼굴을 볼 수 없다는 것을 몹시 걱정해서 아이들이 가리킬 수 있는 다양한 얼굴 스티커를 인쇄했다. 또한 일부 병원들은 현재 직원들을 쉽게 식별할 수 있는 '얼굴—시트'를 환자들에게 제공하고 있다. 그리고 이것은 마스크를 착용한 채로 동료와 환자들에게 자기 자신을 다시 소개하는 데 항상 유용하다.

⇩

일부 병원들과 직원들은 팬데믹 기간 동안 환자들과의 대화를 (B) 보완할 (A) 대안적인 방법을 찾고 있다.

VOCA

- in the absence of ~이 없을 때에, ~이 없어서
- pandemic 팬데믹, 전 세계적인(전국적인) 유행병
- emphasis 강조
- assume ~을 취하다, ~을 띠다, 가지다
- innovative 혁신적인
- chronically 만성적으로
- identification 식별
- colleague 동료

04 난도 ★★☆　　　　　　　　　　　　　　　정답 ③

독해 > 글의 일관성 > 글의 순서

정답의 이유

영장류가 새로운 음식을 검사하고 익숙해지는 과정에 대한 내용이다. 실험자 Kenneth Glander가 이 방법을 먼저 소개한 뒤, 그 방법의 구체적인 예시가 이어지는 두괄식의 글이다. 따라서 정답은 주제 – 예시에 맞는 ③ '(C) – (B) – (A)'이다.

본문해석

일단 어미를 떠나면, 영장류는 그들이 마주친 새로운 음식이 안전하고 수집할 가치가 있는지에 대해 계속 결정해야 한다.

(C) 자기 스스로를 실험 도구로 사용하는 것은 하나의 옵션이지만, 사회적 영장류는 더 나은 방법을 찾아냈다. Kenneth Glander는 이것을 '견본추출'이라고 부른다. 짖는 원숭이들이 새로운 서식지로 이동하면, 무리 중 하나가 나무로 가서 나뭇잎 몇 개를 먹고 하루를 기다릴 것이다.

(B) 만약 식물에 특히 강력한 독소가 들어있다면, 그 시식자의 몸이 그것을 분해하려 할 것이며, 이 과정에서 대개 원숭이들을 아프게 할 것이다. Glander는 "이런 것을 본 적이 있어요.'라고 말했다. "무리의 다른 원숭이들이 큰 관심을 가지고 지켜보고 있습니다. 만약 그 동물이 아프면, 다른 동물들도 그 나무에 다가가지 않을 것입니다. 이것은 주어지는 신호, 즉 사회적 신호입니다."

(A) 마찬가지로 그 시식자가 괜찮다고 느껴지면, 며칠 안에 다시 나무 속에 들어가서 조금 더 먹고 다시 기다리며 천천히 많은 양을 모을 것이다. 마지막으로 그 원숭이가 건강하면 다른 원숭이들도 이것이 괜찮다는 것을 알고 새로운 음식을 택한다.

VOCA

- primates 영장류
- encounter 마주하다
- by the same token 같은 이유로[마찬가지로]
- adopt 채택하다
- experiment 실험
- habitat 서식지
- troop 무리, 떼

05 난도 ★★☆　　　　　　　　　　　　　　　정답 ④

독해 > 세부 내용 찾기 > 내용 (불)일치

정답의 이유

④ 마지막 문장 'Other Koreans living in Japan could not afford the train fare ~ and among them who had ethnic Japanese spouses and Japanese-born, Japanese-speaking children, ~'에서 교통비가 없는 한국인들 중에서 이미 일본인과 결혼해서 일본에서 태어나 일본어를 말하는 자녀들이 있는 한국인들이 일본에 남았다고 했으므로 글의 내용과 일치하지 않는다.

오답의 이유

① 세 번째 문장에서 일본에 남은 한국인들과 그들의 후손들을 Zainichi라 하다고 했으므로 글의 내용과 일치한다.

② 다섯 번째 문장에서 전쟁 직후 경제적 기회를 누렸던 한국인들이 일본에 머무르는 것을 선택했다고 했으므로 글의 내용과 일치한다.

③ 여섯 번째 문장에서 한국의 열악한 환경에 싫증을 느껴 일본에 돌아가기로 했다고 했으므로 글의 내용과 일치한다.

본문해석

일본이 제2차 세계대전에서 패전한 후, 많은 한국인들이 (100~140만 명) 일본을 떠났다. 1948년까지 일본에 자리잡은 한국인의 인구는 약 60만 명이었다. 이 한국인들과 그들의 후손은 보통 Zainichi(문자 그대로 '일본에 거주하는')라고 불리며, 이 용어는 종전 직후 몇 년 동안 등장했다. 일본에 남은 한국인들은 다양한 이유로 그렇게 했다. 식민지 시대 동안 사업, 제국의 관료 사회, 군대에서 성공적인 커리어를 쌓았거나, 전쟁 직후에 열린 경제적 기회를 누렸던 한국인들은 빈곤하고 정치적으로 불안정했던 해방 직후의 한국으로 돌아오는 위험을 무릅쓰기보다는 일본 사회에서의 상대적으로 특권을 가진 지위를 유지하기로 했다. 본국으로 송환된 일부 한국인들은 그들이 본 열악한 환경에 싫증을 느껴 일본으로 돌아가기로 하기도 했다. 일본에 사는 다른 한국인들은 출발 항구까지 가는 기차비를 감당할 수 없었고, 그들 중 일본인 배우자와 일본어를 사용하는 자녀가 있는 사람들에게는 새로운 환경의 문화적이고 언어적인 도전을 처리하는 것보다 일본에 머무르는 것이 더 합리적이었다.

VOCA

- ethnic 민족의
- bureaucracy 관료
- colonial period 식민지 시대
- privileged status 특권을 가진 지위
- impoverished 빈곤한
- repulse 구역질나게 하다, 혐오감을 주다
- navigate (힘든 상황을) 다루다, 처리하다

독해 > 빈칸 완성 > 단어 · 구 · 절

정답의 이유

빈칸 다음에서 심판, 오케스트라 지휘자가 손과 팔, 몸의 움직임을 통해서 의사를 전달한다고 했고, 네 번째 문장에서 'People working at a distance from each other have to invent special signals if they want to communicate.'라고 한 다음에 공장이나 수영장 같은 시끄러운 환경에서 일하는 사람들도 자신들만의 신호가 필요하다고 했다. 따라서 빈칸에 들어갈 말로 가장 적절한 것은 ④ 'develop their signing a bit more fully(더 확실하게 그들의 신호를 발전시키다)'이다.

오답의 이유

① 부모와 자녀를 지원하다
② 완전히 새로운 업무 스타일을 도입하다
③ 기본적인 인권을 위해 법정에서 싸우다

본문해석

사람들이 좀 더 확실하게 그들의 신호를 발전시켜야 했던 직업이 있다. 우리는 심판들이 그들의 팔과 손을 사용해서 선수들에게 신호로 지시를 내리는 것을 본다.—크리켓에서 한 손가락이 위쪽을 향하는 것은 타자가 아웃되고 삼주문을 떠나야 한다는 것을 의미한다. 오케스트라 지휘자들은 그들의 움직임을 통해 연주자들을 통제한다. 서로 멀리 떨어져서 일하는 사람들은 의사소통을 원한다면 특별한 신호를 만들어야 한다. 기계들이 몹시 시끄러운 소리를 내는 공장에서와 같은 소란한 환경에서 일하는 사람들이나 학교 아이들로 가득찬 수영장 주변의 구조원들도 마찬가지이다.

VOCA

• refree (축구, 권투, 농구 등의) 심판
• umpire (야구, 크리켓, 테니스 등의) 심판
• conductor 지휘자
• invent 발명하다

독해 > 세부 내용 찾기 > 내용 (불)일치

정답의 이유

두 번째 문장에서 인간에게 암을 유발하는 19가지의 화학물질 중 7가지가 생쥐와 쥐에게 암을 유발한다고 했으므로 글의 내용과 일치하지 않는 것은 그와 반대되는 내용의 ①이다.

오답의 이유

② 세 번째 문장에서 항우울제인 노미펜신이 쥐, 토끼 등에게 극소의 독성을 가지고 있지만 인간에게는 간독성과 빈혈을 유발했다고 했으므로 글의 내용과 일치한다.
③ 네 번째 문장에서 동물 실험에서는 예측되지 않았던 심각한 부작용을 사람에게는 일으켜서 장애 또는 심지어 사망을 초래할 수도 있다는 것이 밝혀졌다고 했으므로 글의 내용과 일치한다.
④ 마지막 문장에서 동물 연구 중단을 요구하는 연구원들은 인간 임상 실험, 부검 실험실의 도움을 받은 관찰 같은 더 나은 방법이 있다고 했으므로 글의 내용과 일치한다.

본문해석

연구에 동물 사용을 반대하는 사람들은 약물 또는 기타 화합물들의 안전성 테스트에 동물을 사용하는 것 또한 반대한다. 제약업계에서는, 국립암연구소가 정한 기준에 의하면 복용 시 인간에게 암을 유발하는 것으로 알려진 19개 화학물질 중에서 생쥐와 쥐에게 암을 유발하는 것은 7개에 불과하다는 사실에 주목했다(Barnard and Koufman, 1997). 예를 들면 항우울제인 노미펜신은 쥐, 토끼, 개, 원숭이에게 극소의 독성을 가지고 있지만, 인간에게는 간독성과 빈혈을 유발했다. 이것과 다른 경우에서, 일부 화합물들이 동물 실험에서는 예측되지 않았던 심각한 부작용을 사람에게 일으켜서 치료받는 사람들에게 장애 또는 심지어 사망으로 이어질 수도 있는 상태를 초래한다는 것이 밝혀졌다. 그리고 동물 연구 중단을 요구하는 연구원들은 인간 임상 실험, 부검 실험실의 도움을 받는 관찰 같은 더 나은 방법이 있다고 명시한다.

VOCA

• compound 화합물
• pharmaceutical 제약의
• antidepressant 항우울제
• toxicity 유독성
• disability 장애
• autopsy 부검

독해 > 글의 일관성 > 무관한 어휘·문장

정답의 이유

'clear(확실한)' 다음에 오는 However로 시작하는 문장에서 찬물 샤워의 긍정적인 영향에 대해 서술하고 있으므로 이전 문장에서는 찬물 샤워가 체중 감량에 도움이 되는지에 대한 연구는 확실하지 않다는 내용이 서술되어야 한다. 찬물 샤워의 효과가 확실하지는 않더라도 많은 사람들의 경험과 증언을 통해 그 효과를 입증할 수 있다고 전개되어야 하므로 문맥상 낱말의 쓰임이 적절하지 않은 것은 ③ 'clear(확실한)'이다.

본문해석

찬물 샤워는 수온이 70℉ 미만인 모든 샤워이다. 이것은 건강상 이점이 있을 수 있다. 우울증이 있는 사람에게는 찬물 샤워가 일종의 가벼운 전기충격 요법으로 작용할 수 있다. 찬물은 많은 전기적 자극을 뇌에 보내준다. 찬물은 주의력, 명료함, 에너지 레벨을 높이기 위해 당신의 체계를 덜컥 움직이게 한다. 때때로 행복 호르몬이라고도 일컫는 엔돌핀 또한 분비된다. 이 효과는 웰빙과 낙관주의로 이어진다. 비만인 사람의 경우, 일주일에 2~3번 찬물 샤워를 하는 것이 신진대사 증가에 기여할 수도 있다. 이것은 장기적으로 비만을 이겨내는 데 도움이 될 수도 있다. 찬물 샤워가 사람들의 체중 감량에 정확히 어떻게 도움이 되는지에 대한 연구는 <u>확실하다(→ 확실하지 않다)</u>. 하지만 찬물이 특정 호르몬 수치를 균일하게 만들고 위장 계통을 치료할 수 있음을 보여준다. 이런 효과들은 체중 감량으로 이어지는 찬물 샤워의 능력에 추가된다. 또한 규칙적으로 하면 찬물 샤워는 순환 계통을 더 효율적으로 만들 수 있다. 일부 사람들은 또한 찬물 샤워의 결과로 피부가 더 좋아보인다고 보고했는데, 아마도 순환이 더 잘되기 때문일 것이다. 우리는 부상 후 치료를 위한 찬물을 지지하는 데이터를 최근에 봤음에도 운동선수들은 이러한 이점을 수년간 알고 있었다.

VOCA

- depression 우울, 우울증
- impulse 자극
- alertness 기민성
- obese 비만인
- metabolism 신진대사
- circulatory system 순환계
- efficient 효율적인

독해 > 빈칸 완성 > 단어·구·절

정답의 이유

③ 네 번째 문장에서 협력 스타일은 모든 사람에게 이로운 방향으로 문제를 해결하려 한다고 했으므로 (A)에는 '상호 이해'가 적절하다. 반면 마지막 문장에서 경쟁 스타일은 문제를 빠르게 해결하는 경향이 있다고 했으므로 (B)에는 '시간 효율성'이 적절하다.

오답의 이유

① 재정적 능력 - 상호작용
② 시간 절약 - 평화로움
④ 유효성 - 일관성

본문해석

연구원들은 갈등이 발생했을 때 한 개인이 대처하는 습관적인 방법에 대해 관심을 가져왔다. 그들은 이 접근 방식을 갈등 스타일이라고 불렀다. 여러 가지 분명한 갈등 스타일이 있으며 각각은 장점과 단점을 가지고 있다. 협력 스타일은 모든 사람들에게 최상의 결과가 제공될 가능성을 극대화하는 방식으로 문제를 해결하는 경향이 있다. 협력 스타일의 장점은 신뢰 형성, 긍정적인 관계 유지, 그리고 헌신 구축을 포함한다. 그러나, 그것은 시간이 걸리고 갈등 중에 다른 사람과 협력하려면 많은 에너지가 필요하다. 경쟁 스타일은 목표에 도달하지 못하는 사람에게 적대감을 키울 수 있다. 하지만, 경쟁 스타일은 갈등을 빠르게 해결하는 경향이 있다.

⇩

협력 스타일은 (A) <u>상호 이해</u>에 큰 가치를 두는 사람에게 사용될 수 있는 반면, (B) <u>시간 효율성</u>을 선호하는 사람은 경쟁 스타일을 선택할 수도 있다.

VOCA

- habitual 습관적인
- apparent 분명한
- pros and cons 장단점, 찬반 양론
- maximize 극대화하다
- commitment 헌신
- hostility 적의

10 난도 ★★★ 정답 ④

독해 > 글의 일관성 > 글의 순서

정답의 이유

갈등 해결의 역사적 진화는 1950년대와 1960년대에 추진력을 얻었다는 주어진 글 다음에 다양한 학문 연구에서 온 한 개척자 그룹 (A group of pioneers)이 일반적인 현상으로서 갈등 연구의 가치를 알았다는 내용의 (C)로 이어지는 것이 자연스럽다. 역접 연결사 'However(그러나)'로 시작하는 (B)에서 개척자 그룹을 그들(they)로 받으며 일부 사람들에게는 진지하게 받아들여지지 않았다고 하면서 국제 관계 종사자들의 예를 들고, 마지막으로 (A)에서 새로운 사상 속에 내재하는 분석과 실천의 결합이 실무자들의 전통과 조화를 이루기가 쉽지 않았다는 것으로 마무리하는 것이 적절하다. 따라서 글의 순서로 가장 적절한 것은 ④ '(C) - (B) - (A)'이다.

본문해석

갈등 해결의 역사적 진화는 핵무기 개발과 초강대국들 사이의 갈등이 인류 생존을 위협하는 것으로 보였던 냉전이 한창이던 1950년대와 1960년대에 추진력을 얻었다.

(C) 다양한 학문 연구에서 온 한 개척자 그룹은 갈등이 국제적인 관계, 국내 정치, 산업 관계, 지역사회 또는 개인 사이에서 발생하든 간에 관계없이, 유사한 특성을 가진 일반적인 현상으로서 갈등을 연구하는 것의 가치를 보았다.

(B) 하지만, 그들은 일부 사람들에게는 그리 진지하게 받아들여지지 않았다. 국제 관계 전문가들은 국제 갈등에 대한 자신만의 이해를 가지고 있었으며 제안된 새로운 접근 방식에서 가치를 보지 못했다.

(A) 새로운 사상 속에 내재하는 분석과 실천의 결합은 전통적인 학술 기관 또는 외교관이나 정치인 같은 실무자들의 전통과 조화를 이루는 것이 쉽지 않았다.

VOCA

- momentum 추진력, 탄력
- at the height of ~의 최고조에
- superpower 초강대국
- implicit 내재된
- reconcile 조화를 이루다
- disciplines 학문

11 난도 ★★☆ 정답 ①

어법 > 정문 찾기

정답의 이유

(A) 타동사(is accepting) 뒤에는 목적어가 와야 한다. 이어지는 문장 'there are always unintended consequences'는 존재구문으로 주어와 술어, 보어를 모두 갖춘 완전한 문장이므로, 완전한 문장을 끌어올 수 있는 명사절 접속사인 that이 옳다.

(B) 로마의 역사를 과거 시점에서 표현하고 있으므로 과거동사 had가 사용되어야 한다.

(C) 선행사 a process를 수식하는 관계대명사절이 등위접속사 and로 연결되어 that was both constrained by reality와 병렬 구조를 이루어야 하고, 의미상 process는 '채우는'이 아니라 '채워지는'이라는 수동태 표현이 더 적절하므로 filled with가 되어야 한다.

오답의 이유

②·③ 관계대명사 what은 주어, 보어 또는 목적어를 대신하고 있으므로 그 뒤에 나오는 문장은 불완전해야 한다.

③·④ 역사적 사실을 이야기하는 문장이므로 현재시제 have는 옳지 않다.

②·④ filling with가 능동 형태로 쓰이려면 목적어가 함께 와야 하는데 현 문장에는 목적어가 없으므로 옳지 않다.

본문해석

경제학을 이해하는 열쇠는 언제나 의도되지 않은 결과가 있다는 것을 받아들이는 것이다. 사람들이 나름대로 합당한 이유로 하는 행동들은 그들이 예상하거나 의도하지 않았던 결과를 불러오기도 한다. 지정학에서도 마찬가지이다. 로마의 마을이 기원전 7세기에 확장을 시작했을 때에, 500년 후에 지중해 세계를 정복하기 위한 종합 계획을 가지고 있었는지 의심스럽다. 하지만 주민들이 이웃 마을을 상대로 취한 첫 번째 행동은 현실에 제약받으면서도 의도되지 않은 결과로 가득 찬 과정의 도화선에 불을 당긴 것이었다. 로마는 계획된 것은 아니지만, 그냥 일어난 일도 아니었다.

VOCA

- unintended 의도되지 않은
- consequences 결과
- envision 상상하다
- expansion 확장
- set in motion ~의 도화선에 불을 당기다
- constrained 제약된

12 난도 ★★☆   정답 ③

독해 > 빈칸 완성 > 단어 · 구 · 절

정답의 이유

여섯 번째 문장에서 로마가 물이 곧 권력이라는 것을 이해하고 제국의 번성을 위해 수로를 건설했다는 내용이 언급되어 있으므로 빈칸에 들어갈 말로 가장 적절한 것은 ③ 'concentrating and strengthening their authority(그들의 권력을 집중하고 강화하는)'이다.

오답의 이유

① 청년들을 교육하는 것에 집중하는
② 지역 시장에서 자유로운 무역을 금지하는
④ 그들의 재산을 다른 나라에 넘겨주는

본문해석

물과 문명은 밀접한 관련이 있다. '수력 문명'이라는 개념은 물이 역사를 통틀어 많은 대규모의 문명을 위한 통일적인 맥락이자 타당한 이유라고 주장한다. 예를 들면, 여러 세기에 걸친 중국 제국은 부분적으로 황하를 따라 홍수를 통제하는 한 살아남았다. 수력학적 이론에 대한 한가지 해석은 대도시로 인구를 모으는 타당한 이유는 물을 관리하기 위함이라는 것이다. 또 다른 해석은 대규모 물 프로젝트가 대도시의 번성을 가능하게 한다고 제안한다. 로마 제국은 그들이 통제했던 땅 전체에 방대한 송수로 망을 건설했기 때문에, 로마는 물과 권력 사이의 관계를 이해했는데, 그중 상당 부분이 손상되지 않은 채로 남아 있다. 예를 들어, 프랑스 남부의 Pont de Gard가 물 공공 기반 시설에 대한 인류의 투자에 대한 증거로 오늘날 존재하고 있다. 로마 총독들은 그들의 권력을 집중하고 강화하는 방식으로 도로, 다리, 수로 시스템을 건설했다.

VOCA

• unifying 통일[통합]하는, 통일적인
• interpretation 해석
• intact 손상되지 않은 채로
• testament 증거
• infrastructure 사회[공공] 기반 시설
• governor 총독, 주지사
• authority 권한

13 난도 ★★☆   정답 ①

독해 > 글의 일관성 > 글의 순서

정답의 이유

주어진 글의 첫 번째 문장 'Ambiguity is so uncomfortable that it can even turn good news into bad.'에서 모호함의 불편함을 언급하고 그 예로 병원에서 검사받는 상황을 들고 있으므로 검사 결과를 듣는 상황인 (B)로 이어지는 것이 자연스럽다. 검사 결과 음성이라는 (B) 다음에는 통증의 원인에 대한 설명이 필요하다는 (A)가 이어진다. 마지막으로 (C)에서 모호한 결과는 또 다른 불안감을 가져오게 될 것이고 좌절감을 느끼게 할 것이라고 마무리 짓고 있다. 따라서 주어진 글 다음에 이어질 글의 순서로 적절한 것은 ① '(B) – (A) – (C)'이다.

본문해석

모호함은 너무 불편해서 좋은 소식을 나쁜 소식으로 바꿀 수도 있다. 당신은 지속적인 복통으로 의사를 찾는다. 의사는 복통의 이유를 찾을 수 없어 검사를 위해 당신을 검사실로 보낸다.

(B) 일주일 후 결과를 듣기 위해 당신은 전화를 받는다. 당신이 마침내 그녀의 사무실에 도착하면, 당신의 의사는 웃으며 검사 결과는 모두 음성이었다고 말한다.

(A) 그리고 무슨 일이 생길까? 당신의 즉각적인 안도감은 기이한 불편감으로 바뀔 수도 있다. 당신은 여전히 그 통증이 무엇이었는지 모른다. 어딘가에는 설명이 있어야 한다.

(C) 아마도 암일 수도 있고 그들이 그것을 놓쳤을 수도 있다. 어쩌면 그것은 악화되었을지도 모른다. 분명히 그들은 원인을 찾아낼 수 있어야 할 것이다. 확실한 답이 없기 때문에 당신은 좌절감을 느낀다.

VOCA

• ambiguity 모호함
• uncomfortable 불편한
• persistent 지속적인
• negative 음성
• immediate 즉각적인
• relief 안도감
• definitive 확실한

14 난도 ★★☆ 정답 ②

독해 > 글의 일관성 > 문장 삽입

정답의 이유

주어진 문장은 however가 사용되었으므로 상반되는 내용의 중간에 들어가야 한다. ②의 앞 문장에서 '평상복 출근날' 실행의 긍정적인 의도를 서술하고, ② 다음 문장에서 '~ employees had to create a "workplace casual wardrobe"(직원들은 '직장용 평상복' 의류를 마련해야 했다).'라고 평상복 출근의 역효과를 말하고 있으므로 주어진 문장이 들어가기에 적절한 위치는 ②이다.

본문해석

출근할 때 옷 입는 방식은 새로운 선택의 요소가 되었으며, 그것과 함께 새로운 걱정거리가 되었다. 약 10년 전에 등장한 '자유 복장의 날' 또는 '평상복 출근날' 실행은 직원들의 삶을 더 편하게 만들고, 그들이 돈을 절약하고 사무실에서 더 편안함을 느낄 수 있게 하기 위해 의도되었다. 하지만 효과는 정반대였다. 일반적인 직장 출근복 외에 직원들은 '직장용 평상복' 의류를 마련해야 했다. 이 평상복은 사실 주말 동안 집에서 입고 다니던 스웨트 셔츠나 티셔츠가 될 수는 없었다. 이 평상복은 편안하면서도 진중한 어떤 특정한 이미지를 유지하는 의상이어야 했다.

VOCA

- anxiety 걱정거리
- dress-down day 약식[자유] 복장으로 근무하는 날
- reverse (정)반대
- sustain 유지하다, 지속하다

15 난도 ★★☆ 정답 ④

어법 > 비문 찾기

정답의 이유

④ 동명사구(Deciding on ~)가 주어의 역할을 하고 있는 문장으로, 동명사는 단수 취급하므로 동사는 are → is가 되어야 한다.

오답의 이유

① 주격 관계대명사 that이 선행사 method를 수식하고 있다.

② 선행사 survey online을 수식하는 관계사 that절 속에 있는 동사 enables와 provides가 등위접속사 and로 연결되어 병렬을 이루고 있다. 선행사가 단수이므로 3인칭 단수동사 provides가 올바르게 사용되었다.

③ Whichever는 복합관계대명사이다. Whichever way가 하나의 명사로 목적어의 역할을 하고 있다. 주어 you, 동사 choose와 함께 사용되어 '어떤 방법을 선택하더라도'라는 의미의 부사절로 사용되었다.

본문해석

당신은 당신이 원하는 결과에 가장 적합한 연구 방법을 선택해야 한다. 당신은 수많은 사람들에게 질문하고 리포트 형식으로 전체 분석을 제공할 수 있는 온라인 설문 조사를 실행할 수 있다. 또는 일대일 질문을 하는 것이 더 소수의 실험 대상으로 선택된 사람들로부터 여러분이 필요한 답변을 얻는 더 나은 방법이라고 생각할 수도 있다. 어떤 방법을 선택하든, 비슷한 것들끼리 비교할 필요가 있을 것이다. 사람들에게 같은 질문을 하고 답변을 비교해 보아라. 유사점과 차이점을 둘 다 찾아보아라. 패턴과 트렌드를 찾아보아라. 데이터를 기록하고 분석하는 방법을 결정하는 것은 중요하다. 간단한 자체 생성 스프레드시트는 일부 기본적인 연구 데이터를 기록하기에 충분할 것이다.

VOCA

- suit ~에 잘 맞다, 적합하다
- outcome 결과
- format 형식
- spreadsheet 스프레드시트

16 난도 ★☆☆ 정답 ②

독해 > 대의 파악 > 요지, 주장

정답의 이유

제시문은 범죄자가 범죄를 저지르는 이유를 설명하는 글로, 첫 번째 문장에서 'Some criminal offenders may engage in illegal behavior because they love the excitement and thrills that crime can provide.'라고 하면서 '범죄가 제공하는 흥분과 전율'을 범죄 이유로 제시하고 있다. 마지막 문장 'The need for excitement is a significant predictor of criminal choice.'에서 범죄에서 흥분 욕구가 범죄 선택의 주요 예측 변수라고 했으므로 글의 요지로 가장 적절한 것은 ② '범죄 행위에서 생기는 흥분과 쾌감이 범죄를 유발할 수 있다.'이다.

본문해석

일부 범죄자들은 범죄가 제공하는 흥분과 전율을 사랑하기 때문에 불법행위에 가담할 수 있다. 사회학자 Jack Katz는 매우 영향력 있는 그의 저서 *Seductions of Crime*에서 범죄 행위에는 사람들을 범죄 생활로 '유혹'하는 즉각적인 이점이 있다고 주장한다. 어떤 사람들에게는 좀도둑질과 기물파손이 매력적인데, 범죄를 잘 해내는 것이 개인의 능력을 증명하는 스릴 넘치는 일이기 때문이다. 흥분욕구는 체포와 처벌에 대한 두려움과 맞설 수 있다. 사실, 일부 범죄자들은 이 추가된 '전율' 때문에 특히 위험한 상황을 의도적으로 찾는다. 흥분욕구는 범죄 선택의 중요한 예측 변수이다.

VOCA

- offender 범죄자
- engage in ~에 관여하다
- seduction 유혹
- shoplifting 절도
- get away with ~을 잘 해내다, ~을 벌 받지 않고 (무난히) 해내다

- demonstration 증명
- apprehension 체포
- predictor 예측 변수

17 난도 ★☆☆   정답 ③

독해 > 빈칸 완성 > 단어 · 구 · 절

정답의 이유

제시문은 새끼 원숭이의 대리모 실험에 관한 내용이다. 빈칸 앞 문장에서 '~ they overwhelmingly preferred and spent significantly more time with the warm terry-cloth mother'라고 했으므로 대리모가 따뜻한 천으로 새끼 원숭이에게 심리적 편안함을 주었다고 유추할 수 있다. 따라서 빈칸에 들어갈 말로 가장 적절한 것은 ③ 'comfort(편안함)'이다.

오답의 이유

① 직업
② 약물
④ 교육

본문해석

애착의 중요성을 보여주는 한 고전적인 연구에서, Wisconsin 대학의 심리학자인 Harry와 Margaret Harlow는 어린 원숭이들의 반응을 조사했다. 새끼 원숭이들은 생물학적 어미로부터 분리되었고, 두 대리모가 우리 안으로 들여보내졌다. 하나는 철사 어미로 동그란 나무 머리, 차가운 금속 철사 그물망 그리고 새끼 원숭이가 우유를 마실 수 있는 우유병으로 구성되어 있었다. 두 번째 어미는 따뜻한 테리 직물 담요로 감싸져 있는 스펀지 고무 형태였다. 새끼 원숭이들은 음식을 위해 철사 어미에게 다가갔지만 그들은 압도적으로 따뜻한 테리 직물 어미를 선호하며 상당히 더 많은 시간을 보냈다. 따뜻한 테리 직물 어미는 음식을 제공하지 않았지만 편안함을 제공했다.

VOCA

- attachment 애착
- investigate 조사하다
- terry-cloth 테리 직물
- overwhelmingly 압도적으로

18 난도 ★☆☆   정답 ①

어법 > 비문 찾기

정답의 이유

① 등위접속사 and로 연결된 문장으로, and 앞이 과거(was released)이므로 and 다음에도 과거동사가 사용되어야 한다. 따라서 spend → spent가 되어야 한다.

오답의 이유

② what 명사절이 figure out의 목적어로 사용되었다. 명사절 속에서 what은 동사 had done의 목적어 역할을 한다.
③ 주어 I의 재귀대명사 myself가 isolate의 목적어로 사용되었다.
④ so+형용사[부사]+that ~ 구문은 '너무 ~해서 …하다'라고 해석된다. 이때 that은 문장을 이끄는 접속사이므로 that 다음에는 완전한 문장이 온다.

본문해석

나는 친부모에 의해 입양 보내졌고, 내 인생의 첫 10년을 고아원에서 보냈다. 나는 몇 년 동안 내게 무슨 문제가 있을까 고민하며 보냈다. 만약 내 부모님이 나를 원하지 않았다면, 누가 원할 수 있을까? 나는 내가 무엇을 잘못했고 왜 많은 사람들이 나를 쫓아 보냈는지 알아내려 노력했다. 나는 현재 누구에게도 가까이 다가가지 않는데 만약 내가 그것을 하면 사람들이 나를 떠날 수도 있기 때문이다. 어렸을 때 나는 살아남기 위해 감정적으로 나 스스로를 고립시켜야만 했고, 여전히 어렸을 때 가졌던 가정들을 바탕으로 움직인다. 나는 버림받는 것이 너무도 두렵기에 위험을 무릅쓰고 나아가지 않을 것이고 최소한의 모험도 하지 않을 것이다. 나는 지금 마흔 살이지만 여전히 어린아이 같은 기분이 든다.

VOCA

- release 방출하다
- adoption 입양
- orphanage 고아원
- assumption 가정, 추측
- deserted 버림받은
- venture 과감히 가다, 위험을 무릅쓰고 나아가다
- take a risk 모험을 하다

19 난도 ★★☆

정답 ①

어법 > 비문 찾기

정답의 이유

① suggest는 5형식 동사가 아닌 3형식 동사로 that절이 목적어로 사용되었으며 that이 생략되었으므로 suggested people to use → suggested people (should) use가 되어야 한다.

오답의 이유

② 명사 functioning이 동사 enhance의 목적어로 사용되었다.

③ 주어 positive emotional experiences from music을 받는 본 동사는 (may) improve와 (may) strengthen이며, 이 두 동사는 and로 연결되어 병렬 구조를 이루고 있다.

④ because 부사절 속에서 주어는 emotional experiences와 everyday behaviors이고, 동사는 share이다. 주어가 복수이므로 복수형 동사인 share가 사용된 것이 옳다.

본문해석

음악은 일상 생활로 옮겨갈 수 있는 심리 요법 효과를 가질 수 있다. 많은 학자들은 사람들에게 음악을 심리 요법 매개체로 사용할 것을 제안했다. 음악치료는 '그들의 심리적, 신체적, 인지적 또는 사회적 기능을 향상시키기 위한 개인의 치료 또는 재활의 부속물로써 음악을 사용'하는 것으로 광범위하게 정의될 수 있다. 음악으로부터 받은 긍정적인 감정의 경험은 치료과정을 개선할 수 있으므로 전통적인 인지적/행동적 방법과 일상적인 목표로의 전환을 강화시킬 수 있다. 이것은 아마도 부분적으로 음악과 일상적인 행동들에 의해 유발된 감정적 경험이 긍정적인 감정과 자극을 담당하는 중복된 신경학적 경로를 공유하기 때문일지도 모른다.

VOCA

• music therapy 음악치료
• adjunct 부속물
• rehabilitation 재활
• cognitive 인지의
• elicited 유발된
• neurological 신경학의

20 난도 ★☆☆

정답 ②

독해 > 빈칸 완성 > 단어 · 구 · 절

정답의 이유

첫 번째 문장에서 '문화적 해석은 보통 측정할 수 있는 증거보다는 ~ 에 근거하여 만들어진다.'라고 했으므로 빈칸에는 '측정할 수 있는 증거'와 대조되는 표현이 들어가는 것을 유추할 수 있다. 빈칸 이후에서 전반적으로 '가난한 사람은 게으르다.'라는 편파적인 명제가 잘못되었다고 서술하고 있고, 마지막 문장에서 '아프리카 사람들이 일을 적게 해서 가난하다는 고정관념은 남녀의 고된 노동이 일상인 마을에서 하루만 시간을 보내면 그 즉시 잠재워진다.'라고 했으므로 첫 번째 문장의 측정할 수 있는 증거와 대조되는 개념은 고정관념과 유사한 개념이라는 것을 알 수 있다. 따라서 빈칸에 들어갈 말로 적절한 것은 ② 'prejudice(편견)'이다.

오답의 이유

① 통계
③ 외모
④ 상황

본문해석

문화적 해석은 주로 측정할 수 있는 증거보다는 편견에 근거하여 만들어진다. 이 논쟁은 순환하는 경향이 있다. 사람들은 게으르기 때문에 가난하다. 그들이 게으르다는 것을 어떻게 알까? 그들이 가난하기 때문이다. 이러한 해석을 옹호하는 사람들은 낮은 생산성은 게으름이나 노력 부족의 결과가 아니라 생산에 투입되는 자금 부족의 결과라는 것을 거의 이해하지 못한다. 아프리카 농부들은 게으르지 않지만 토양 영양분, 트랙터, 지선 도로, 관개된 대지, 저장 시설 등이 부족한 것이다. 아프리카 사람들이 일을 거의 하지 않아서 가난하다는 고정관념은 남녀의 고된 노동이 일상인 마을에서 하루만 시간을 보내면 그 즉시 잠재워진다.

VOCA

• measurable 눈에 띄는, 측정할 수 있는
• productivity 생산성
• nutrient 영양분
• feeder road 지선 도로
• irrigated plot 관개된 대지
• stereotype 고정관념

21 난도 ★★★ 정답 ③

독해 > 글의 일관성 > 문장 삽입

정답의 이유

주어진 문장은 But으로 시작하므로 역접 관계의 문장 사이에 들어가야 한다. 두 번째, 세 번째 문장에서 가격이 떨어지면 회사가 사람들을 해고함으로써 공급과 수요의 균형을 맞춘다고 하였는데, ③ 다음 문장에서는 농부를 해고하는 것이 공급을 줄이는 데 도움이 되지 않는다는 반대의 내용이 나왔으므로 주어진 문장이 들어가기에 적절한 곳은 ③이다.

본문해석

자유 시장은 농업에서 작동한 적은 없으며 앞으로도 없을 것이다. 가족 농장의 경제는 회사의 경제와 매우 다르다. 가격이 떨어지면, 회사는 사람들을 해고하고 공장을 멈출 수 있다. 결국 시장은 공급과 수요의 새로운 균형을 찾게 된다. 그러나 식량에 대한 수요는 탄력적이지 않다. 사람들은 음식이 저렴하다고 더 많이 먹지 않는다. 그리고 농부들을 해고하는 것이 공급을 줄이는 데 도움이 되지 않는다. 당신은 나를 해고할 수는 있지만 나의 토지를 해고할 수는 없다. 왜냐하면 현금 흐름이 더 필요하거나 나보다 더 효율적이라고 생각하는 다른 농부가 와서 경작할 것이기 때문이다.

VOCA

• agriculture 농업
• idle 놀리다, 쉬게 하다
• cash flow 현금 유동성

22 난도 ★★☆ 정답 ②

독해 > 대의 파악 > 제목, 주제

정답의 이유

본문에서는 운동과 훈련에 건강한 식사가 없이는 훈련의 성과가 소실될 수 있으며, 규칙적인 식사 계획을 통해서 훈련이 보상을 받을 수 있다고 했다. 따라서 글의 주제는 ② 'importance of eating well in exercise(운동에서 잘 먹는 것의 중요성)'이다.

오답의 이유

① 몸의 유연성을 향상시키는 방법
③ 과도한 다이어트에 의해 유발되는 건강 문제들
④ 꾸준한 훈련을 통해 기술 향상시키기

본문해석

매일의 훈련은 운동선수, 특히 훈련에 전념하는 것이 정규 직업인 엘리트 운동선수에게는 특별한 영양분의 필요성을 만들어낸다. 하지만 레크리에이션 스포츠조차도 영양적인 어려움을 만들어 낼 것이다. 그리고 당신이 스포츠에 얼마나 참여하는지 그 정도에 상관없이, 만약 훈련으로부터 최대한의 결과치를 달성하기 위해서라면 당신은 이러한 어려움에 대처해야만 한다. 건강한 식사 없이는 당신의 훈련의 목적의 많은 부분이 소실될 수 있다. 최악의 시나리오에서는, 식습관의 문제와 결함은 훈련 성과를 직접적으로 손상시킬 수 있다. 다른 상황에서는, 당신이 향상될지라도 그 정도가 당신의 잠

재력보다 낮거나 당신의 경쟁자보다 더 느릴 수도 있다. 하지만 긍정적인 측면에서는, 올바른 매일의 식사 계획을 통해서 훈련에 대한 당신의 헌신이 충분히 보상받을 것이다.

VOCA

• nutritional 영양의
• commitment 헌신, 약속, 전념
• sound 건강한
• dietary 식습관의
• deficiency 결핍, 결함
• impair 손상시키다

23 난도 ★★☆ 정답 ③

독해 > 대의 파악 > 제목, 주제

정답의 이유

본문은 '보는 사람이 작품을 완성시킨다'는 예술 역사가의 말로 시작하며 작품을 보는 사람들의 생각과 질문이 그 작품을 완성하는 데 얼마나 중요한지 설명하고 있다. 따라서 정답은 ③ '미술 작품은 감상하는 사람으로 인하여 비로소 완성된다.'이다.

본문해석

매우 존경받는 예술 역사가 Ernst Gombrich는 '보는 사람의 몫'이라 불리는 것에 대해 글을 썼다. Gombrich의 신념은 보는 사람이 작품을 '완성시키고' 작품의 의미의 일부가 그것을 보는 사람에게서 나온다는 것이었다. 따라서 보다시피—작품을 완성시키는 보는 사람은 바로 당신이기에 틀린 답이란 없다. 만약 당신이 갤러리에서 작품을 바라보고 있다면, 작품 옆에 있는 설명을 읽어라. 만약 직원이 있다면, 질문을 해라. 당신의 동료 방문자에게 어떻게 생각하는지 물어봐라. 질문을 하는 것은 더 많이 이해하는 것의 열쇠이고 그것은 예술뿐 아니라 삶의 모든 것에 적용된다. 하지만 무엇보다도, 작품 앞에서 자신감을 가져라. 만약 당신이 작품에 대해 고심한다면, 당신은 의도된 보는 사람이며 당신이 생각하는 것은 중요하다. 당신이 중요하고 유일한 비평가이다.

VOCA

• well-respected 존경을 받는
• beholder 보는 사람
• complete 완성시키다
• confidence 자신감
• contemplate 심사숙고하다

24 난도 ★☆☆ 정답 ②

독해 > 세부 내용 찾기 > 내용 (불)일치

정답의 이유

세 번째 문장에서 아르헨티나의 문화는 스페인과 이탈리아에서 온 유럽인들의 이주에 의해 큰 영향을 받았다고 했으므로 글의 내용과 일치하지 않는 것은 ② '북미 출신 이주민들이 그 문화에 많은 영향을 끼쳤다.'이다.

오답의 이유

① 두 번째 문장에서 Jose de San Martin이 아르헨티나의 독립운동을 이끌었다고 하였으므로 글의 내용과 일치한다.
③ 네 번째 문장에서 아르헨티나에는 남아메리카에서 가장 많은 유대인들이 있다고 했으므로 글의 내용과 일치한다.
④ 마지막 문장에서 1880년에서 1930년 사이 농업의 발전으로 세계 10대 부유한 국가 중 하나였다고 했으므로 글의 내용과 일치한다.

본문해석

아르헨티나는 남아메리카의 거의 남쪽 절반을 차지하는, 세계에서 8번째로 큰 나라이다. 1500년대 초에 스페인에 의한 식민지화가 시작되었지만 1816년 Jose de San Martin이 아르헨티나의 독립운동을 이끌었다. 아르헨티나의 문화는 19세기 후반과 20세기 초반, 주로 스페인과 이탈리아에서 온 대규모의 유럽인들의 이주에 의해 큰 영향을 받았다. 대다수의 사람들은 최소한 명목상으로는 가톨릭교이고, 그 나라에는 남아메리카에서 가장 많은 유대인들(약 30만 명)이 있다. 1880년에서 1930년 사이, 농업의 발전 덕분에, 아르헨티나는 세계 10대 부유한 국가들 중 하나였다.

VOCA

- comprising 포함하는
- colonization 식민지화
- massive 거대한
- primarily 주로
- nominally 명목상으로

25 난도 ★★☆ 정답 ③

독해 > 세부 내용 찾기 > 내용 (불)일치

정답의 이유

여섯 번째 문장에서 1941년, 그녀가 여배우로 출연한 영화는 아카데미 시상식 3개 부문의 후보(nominations)에 올랐다고 했으므로 ③ '출연한 영화가 1941년에 영화제에서 3개 부문에 수상했다.'는 글의 내용과 일치하지 않는다.

오답의 이유

① 첫 번째 문장에서 스케이트장과 스크린을 누빈 세계에서 가장 유명한 피겨스케이팅 선수 중 한 명으로, 자신의 기술을 직업이 되게 한 것으로 유명하다고 했으므로 글의 내용과 일치한다.
② 두 번째 문장에서 Henie가 올림픽에서 3개의 금메달을 딴 메달리스트이자 노르웨이와 유럽 챔피언이라고 했으므로 글의 내용과 일치한다.
④ 마지막 문장에서 그녀의 가장 큰 유산은 어린 소녀들이 스케이트를 타도록 영감을 준 것이라고 했으므로 글의 내용과 일치한다.

본문해석

Sonja Henie는 스케이트장과 스크린을 누빈 세계에서 가장 유명한 피겨스케이팅 선수 중 한 명으로 자신의 기술을 직업이 되게 한 것으로 유명하다. 올림픽에서 3개의 금메달을 딴 메달리스트이자 노르웨이와 유럽 챔피언인 Henie는 스릴 넘치게 연극적이고 활발한 피겨스케이팅 스타일을 고안했다. 그녀는 짧은 스커트, 흰색 스케이트와 매력적인 움직임을 도입했다. 그녀의 화려한 회전과 점프는 모든 경쟁자들의 기준을 높였다. 1936년, 20세기 폭스사는 그녀가 영화 'One in a Million'의 주연으로 출연하도록 계약했고, 그녀는 머지않아 할리우드의 주요한 여배우들 중 한 명이 되었다. 1941년, 그녀가 여배우로 출연한 영화 'Sun Valley Serenade'는 아카데미상 3개 부문의 후보에 올랐다. Henie의 다른 영화들은 찬사를 덜 받았지만, 그녀는 아이스 스케이팅의 인기를 촉발시켰다. 1938년, 그녀는 Hollywood Ice Revues라고 하는 호화로운 순회공연을 시작했다. 그녀의 많은 모험은 그녀에게 부를 만들어 주었지만, 그녀의 가장 큰 유산은 어린 소녀들로 하여금 스케이트를 타도록 영감을 준 것이었다.

VOCA

- thrillingly 스릴 넘치게
- theatrical 연극적인
- spectacular 화려한
- raise the bar 기대치를 높이다
- nomination 후보
- acclaim 칭송하다, 찬사
- surge 급증
- extravagant 호화로운, 사치스러운
- fortune 많은 돈, 행운
- inspire 영감을 주다, 고무하다

한눈에 훑어보기

✔ 빠른 정답

01	02	03	04	05	06	07	08	09	10
④	④	④	②	②	④	①	②	①	③
11	**12**	**13**	**14**	**15**	**16**	**17**	**18**	**19**	**20**
③	④	④	②	①	①	④	①	②	②
21	**22**	**23**	**24**	**25**					
②	③	②	②	②					

✔ 점수 체크

구분	1회독	2회독	3회독
맞힌 문항 수	/ 25	/ 25	/ 25
나의 점수	점	점	점

01 난도 ★★☆   정답 ④

독해 > 빈칸 완성 > 단어 · 구 · 절

[정답의 이유]

제시문의 중반부에서 Jared Diamond가 'once caused terrifying epidemics and then disappeared as mysteriously as they had come.'이라고 한 다음, 이어서 그 예로 수만 명을 죽음으로 내몬 후 사그라진 영국의 속립열을 인용했다. 마지막 문장에서 '지나친 효율성은 어떤 전염성 유기체에도 좋은 것은 아니다.'라고 했으므로 빈칸에 들어갈 말로 가장 적절한 것은 ④ '(A) infectious(전염성이 있는) − (B) disappear(사라지다)'이다.

[오답의 이유]

① 더 약한 − 사라지다

② 더 약한 − 퍼지다

③ 전염성이 있는 − 퍼지다

[본문해석]

미생물은 계산적인 존재가 아니다. 비누 거품 샤워로 수백만에 달하는 그것들을 학살할 때 여러분이 그것들에게 어떤 고통을 주는지 신경 쓰지 않는 것처럼 그것들도 자신들이 여러분에게 무엇을 하는지 상관하지 않는다. 병원균이 유일하게 신경 쓰는 때는 여러분을 매우 잘 죽일 때뿐이다. 만일 그것들이 이동하기 전에 여러분을 제거한다면, 그것들은 아마도 스스로 멸종할 것이다. 사실 이러한 일은 때때로 일어난다. Jared Diamond는 언급하기를, 역사는 '한때 무서운 전염병을 일으켰다가 그것들이 왔던 것처럼 신기하게 사라진' 질병으로 가득하다고 한다. 그는 그 기세가 맹렬했지만 다행히 일시적이었던 영국의 속립열을 인용하는데, 그 유행병은 1485년부터 1552년까지 맹위를 떨치며 수만 명을 죽음으로 내몬 후 스스로 사그라졌다. 지나친 효율성은 어떤 전염성 유기체에도 좋은 것은 아니다.

⇩

병원체들이 (A) 전염성이 강할수록, 그것은 더 빨리 (B) 사라질 가능성이 높다.

VOCA

• microorganism 미생물
• entity 독립체, 존재(물)
• distress 고통
• slaughter 학살하다
• pathogen 병원균, 병원체
• epidemic (병의) 유행, 유행병, 전염병
• cite 인용하다

- robust 강한
- mercifully 다행히도
- transient 일시적인, 순간적인
- sweating sickness 속립열
- rage (질병·화재 등이) 급속히 번지다, 맹위를 떨치다
- infectious 전염성의, 병을 옮길 수 있는

02 난도 ★★★   정답 ④

독해 > 대의 파악 > 지칭 추론

정답의 이유

밑줄 친 'drains the mind'는 '마음을 비우다'의 뜻으로 바로 앞 문장의 '~ at last, make you stand in the middle of the writing (마침내 여러분을 글 한가운데 서게 하다)'과 의미가 비슷하다. 따라서 'drains the mind'가 뜻하는 바로 가장 적절한 것은 ④ 'to place oneself in the background(배경에 자신을 두다)'이다.

오답의 이유

① 마음을 치유하다
② 감성적이 되도록 돕다
③ 그/그녀의 호기심을 만족시키다

본문해석

만약 글이 탄탄하고 좋으면, 작가의 분위기와 기질은 그 작품을 훼손시키지 않으면서 결국 드러날 것이다. 그러므로 스타일[문체]을 얻으려면, 어떤 것에도 영향을 주지 않는 것부터 시작하라. 즉, 글의 느낌과 본질로 독자의 관심을 이끌어 내라는 것이다. 신중하고 정직한 작가는 문체에 대해 걱정할 필요가 없다. 언어 사용에 능숙해지면, 여러분의 문체가 드러날 것이며, 여러분 자신이 나타날 것이기 때문에, 이런 일이 일어나면, 여러분을 다른 마음들로부터 분리하는 장벽을 깨고, 마침내 여러분을 글 한가운데 서게 만드는 것이 점점 더 쉽다는 것을 알게 될 것이다. 다행스럽게도, 글쓰기, 즉 창작 행위는 마음을 단련시킨다. 글쓰기는 사고를 시작하는 한 가지 방식이며, 글쓰기의 연습과 습관은 마음을 비운다.

VOCA

- solid 단단한, 확실한, 훌륭한
- temper 기질, 성질
- at the expense[cost] of ~을 희생하면서
- composition 작문, 작곡
- discipline 훈련하다
- drain 배수하다, 빼내 가다[소모시키다]

03 난도 ★★☆   정답 ④

어법 > 정문 찾기

정답의 이유

(A) 'A and B'의 병렬 구조로, and 앞에 형용사(false)가 있으므로 (과거분사형) 형용사(perceived)가 적절하다.

(B) 형용사(gifted)를 수식하므로 부사(differently)가 적절하다.

(C) 앞 문장의 복수명사 talents를 대신하면서 관계절(we have been given)의 수식을 받고 있으므로 지시대명사 those가 적절하다. those는 '~ 하는 것들[사람들]'을 뜻하며 수식어[전치사구, 관계절, 분사]의 수식을 받는다. those 다음에는 관계대명사 which[that]가 생략되었다.

오답의 이유

① 인식하다 – 다른 – 그들을
② 인식하다 – 다르게 – ~ 하는 것들
③ 인식된 – 다른 – 그들을

본문해석

자신 그리고 인생에서 우리의 운명에 대한 불만 중 일부는 실제 상황을 근거로 하고 있으며, 일부는 거짓이고 단순히 현실로 인식된 것이다. 인식된 것은 정리되고 버려져야 한다. 진짜는 변경할 수 있거나 변경할 수 없는 것으로 분류될 것이다. 만약 그것이 후자에 속한다면, 우리는 그것을 받아들이기 위해 노력해야 한다. 만약 그것이 전자에 속한다면, 그런 경우 우리는 대신 그것을 제거, 교환, 수정하기 위해 노력할 수 있는 대안이 있다. 우리는 모두 인생에서 특별한 목적이 있고, 모두 재능이 있는데, 단지 다르게 타고난 재능이 있는 것일 뿐이다. 그것은 1, 5, 10개의 재능을 부여받은 것이 공평한지 불공평한지에 대한 논쟁이 아니다. 그것은 우리가 우리의 재능을 가지고 무엇을 했는가에 대한 것이다. 그것은 우리에게 주어진 것들(재능)을 얼마나 잘 투자했는가에 대한 것이다. 만약 누군가가 그들의 삶이 불공평하다는 견해를 고수한다면, 그것은 정말로 신에 대한 모욕이다.

VOCA

- lot 운명, 운
- sort out 선별하다, 분류하다; 문제를 해결하다
- discard 버리다, 폐기하다
- fall into ~로 나뉘다
- strive 분투하다
- alternative 대안, 대체, 대신의, 다른
- modify 수정[변경]하다, 바꾸다
- gifted 재능이 있는

독해 > 글의 일관성 > 글의 순서

정답의 이유

주어진 글의 마지막 문장 'This is a common fallacy(이것은 일반적인 오류이다).'에 대한 이유를 (B)에서 'It is because ~'로 설명하고 있으므로, 주어진 글 다음에는 (B)로 이어지는 것이 자연스럽다. (B) 마지막의 'most difficult customers'와 대비되는 'the better customers'로 이어서 설명하는 (C)가 오는 것이 자연스럽다. 마지막으로 'therefore'로 시작하는 (A)에서 '시작할 때 더 적은 양으로 더 높은 이윤의 제품과 서비스를 갖는 것이 훨씬 더 낫다.'라고 마무리 짓는 내용이 오는 것이 자연스럽다. 따라서 주어진 글 다음에 이어질 글의 순서로 적절한 것은 ② '(B) – (C) – (A)'이다.

본문해석

사람들은 낮은 가격을 청구하거나 경쟁사보다 낮은 가격을 책정함으로써, 더 많은 고객을 얻을 것이라고 추측한다. 이것은 일반적인 오류이다.

(B) 그것은 경쟁사에 비해서 인하된 가격을 부과하면, 고객 시장의 하위층을 끌어들이기 때문이다. 이 고객들은 더 적은 것으로 더 많은 것을 원하며, 종종 여러분의 사업에서 더 많은 시간과 간접비를 차지한다. 그들은 또한 여러분이 가장 다루기 어렵고 행복하게 하기 어려운 고객일 수도 있다.

(C) 또한 역설적으로 더 좋은 고객들을 쫓아버리는데, 그것은 그들이 더 높은 품질의 제품 또는 서비스를 위하여 더 비싼 가격을 지불할 것이기 때문이다. 우리는 많은 경쟁사들이 시장에 나와 지속 가능하지 않은 일일 요금을 부과하는 것을 보아왔다. 그들은 종종 심지어 그들의 할당량을 채우기 위해 고군분투하다가, 곧 포기하고 다른 일을 하는 것으로 옮기기도 한다.

(A) 그러므로, 시작할 때 더 적은 양으로 더 높은 이윤의 제품과 서비스를 갖는 것이 훨씬 더 낫다. 어쩔 수 없이 가격을 낮추기 위해 언제든지 협상할 수 있지만, 인상을 협상할 수 있는 경우는 거의 없기 때문이다.

VOCA

- charge (요금을) 청구하다
- fallacy 틀린 생각, (인식상의) 오류
- end 끝, 선단, 말단
- take up (시간 · 장소를) 차지하다
- overhead 간접비(의)
- repel 쫓아버리다
- sustainable 지속 가능한, 지탱할 수 있는
- quota 쿼터, 할당

어법 > 비문 찾기

정답의 이유

② '출판을 위해 시를 제출하는 것(submit a poem for publication)'이 문장의 주어이므로 submit → submitting(동명사)이 되어야 한다.

오답의 이유

① 'their work in print'에서 their는 children의 소유격으로 올바르게 사용되었다.

③ 'which poems they are most proud of'는 '그들이 가장 자랑스러워하는 어떤 시'의 뜻으로, which는 의문형용사로 어법상 올바르게 사용되었다.

④ 'publicly showcase their accomplishment'에서 publicly는 동사(showcase)를 수식하는 부사로 올바르게 사용되었다.

본문해석

글쓰기를 즐기는 아이들은 종종 자신들의 작품을 인쇄물로 보는 것에 흥미를 느낀다. 한 가지 비공식적인 접근은 그들의 시를 타자로 쳐서 인쇄해서 게시하는 것이다. 또는 많은 어린이 작가들의 시를 복사한 문집을 만들 수도 있다. 하지만 진정으로 헌신적이고 야심적인 아이들에게 있어서, 출판을 위해 시를 제출하는 것은 가치 있는 목표이다. 그리고 아이들의 독창적인 시를 인쇄하는 몇 가지 웹과 인쇄 자료들이 있다. 어린이 시인들이 원고(양식, 형식 등)의 제출 프로토콜에 익숙해지도록 도움을 주어라. 그들이 가장 자랑스러워하는 시를 고르도록 하고, 제출된 모든 것의 복사본을 보관하고, 부모님의 허락을 받도록 하라. 그리고 나서 그들의 작품이 채택되어 인쇄되어 나올 때 함께 축하하라. 그들을 축하하고, 그들의 성취를 공개적으로 전시하며, 널리 알려라. 성공은 성공을 고무한다. 그리고 물론, 만약 그들의 작품이 거절당한다면, 지원과 격려를 해 주어라.

VOCA

- post 게시[공고]하다
- photocopy 복사하다
- anthology 명시 선집, 선집, 명문집
- dedicated 헌신적인, 전용의, 몰두하고 있는
- ambitious 야심 있는
- worthy 가치 있는, 훌륭한
- protocol 의례, 프로토콜, 원안
- manuscript 원고
- showcase 전시하다, 소개하다
- accomplishment 성취, 업적, 재주, 기량
- spread 퍼뜨리다
- inspire 고무[격려]하다

더 알아보기

동명사

- 동명사는 문장 내에서 주어, 목적어, 보어, 전치사의 목적어 역할을 한다.

  예 Smoking cigarettes may kill you. → 주어

  (담배를 피우면 죽을 수도 있다.)

  예 My favorite activity is reading thrillers. → 보어

  (내가 가장 좋아하는 활동은 스릴러물을 읽는 것이다.)

  예 I enjoy finding a bargain when I go shopping.

  → 타동사의 목적어

  (나는 쇼핑갈 때 싼 물건을 찾는 것을 즐긴다.)

  예 We sit on the couch and ponder the idea of taking a walk.

  → 전치사의 목적어

  (우리는 소파에 앉아서 산책하는 것에 대해 골똘히 생각한다.)

- 동명사와 명사의 차이

동명사	명사
• 명사의 역할: 주어, 목적어, 보어로 쓰임 • 동사의 역할: 목적어를 취함	• 명사의 역할: 주어, 목적어, 보어로 쓰임 • 동사가 아니므로 목적어를 취할 수 없음

  예 The paper charged her with use(→ using) the company's money for her own purpose.

  (그 신문은 그녀가 자신의 목적을 위해 회삿돈을 사용했다고 비난했다.)

06 난도 ★★☆   정답 ④

독해 > 글의 일관성 > 문장 삽입

정답의 이유

주어진 문장의 '~ from the tribe, the tiny seeds ~'로 미루어 앞에 부족과 작은 씨앗에 대한 설명이 나와야 함을 유추할 수 있다. ④ 앞 문장에서 'one seed', 'this one seed', 'entire tribe'가 처음으로 언급되었으므로 주어진 문장이 들어가기에 적절한 곳은 ④이다.

본문해석

Pueblo 인디언 문화에서 옥수수는 사람들에게 곧 생명의 상징이다. '태양과 빛의 할머니'인 Corn Maiden이 이 선물을 가져와 사람들에게 삶의 힘을 주었다. 옥수수가 태양에 의해 생명을 부여받으면서, Corn Maiden은 태양의 불을 인간의 몸으로 가져와, 자연을 통해 인간에게 그의 사랑과 힘의 많은 표상들을 준다. 각각의 Maiden은 아이에게 주는 것처럼 사랑으로 길러지는 옥수수 씨앗을 하나씩 가져오는데, 이 하나의 씨앗이 부족 전체를 영원히 지탱할 것이다. 부족의 사랑과 힘으로 그 작은 씨앗들은 성숙하고 크게 자라서, 사람들을 위한 작물로 재배된다. Corn Maidens의 영혼은 부족 사람들과 영원히 함께 있다.

VOCA

- tribe 부족
- bring 가져오다, 데려오다
- representation 묘사[표현]
- nurture (잘 자라도록) 양육하다, 보살피다
- sustain 살아가게 하다, 지속시키다
- entire 전체의, 온

07 난도 ★★☆   정답 ①

독해 > 빈칸 완성 > 단어 · 구 · 절

정답의 이유

제시문의 네 번째 문장의 '~ they pump waste products into them(그것들은 폐기물을 그것들에 퍼붓는다)'와 다섯 번째 문장의 '~ they are taking this opportunity to relieve themselves(그것들이 용변을 보기 위해 이 기회를 이용하고 있다)'로 미루어 빈칸에 들어갈 말로 적절한 것은 ① 'tree toilet paper(나무 화장지)'이다.

오답의 이유

② 그 식물 주방

③ 나무의 폐

④ 곤충의 부모

본문해석

너도밤나무, 참나무, 가문비나무, 그리고 소나무는 항상 새롭게 생장하며, 오래된 것을 없애야 한다. 가장 분명한 변화는 매년 가을에 일어난다. 나뭇잎들은 제 역할을 했다. 즉, 그것들은 이제 낡았고 충해로 인해 구멍이 숭숭 뚫렸다. 그것들에 작별을 고하기 전에, 나무들은 폐기물을 그것들에 퍼붓는다. 여러분은 그것들이 용변을 보기 위해 이 기회를 이용하고 있다고 말할 수 있다. 그리고 나서, 그것들은 연약한 조직층을 성장시켜서 각각의 나뭇잎을 그것이 나 있는 나뭇가지로부터 떼어내고, 그 잎들은 다음번 산들바람에 땅으로 굴러떨어진다. 이제 지면을 덮은 채 여러분이 그것들을 밟고 지나다닐 때 매우 만족스러운 저르륵저르륵 소리를 내는 바스락거리는 나뭇잎들은 기본적으로 나무 화장지이다.

VOCA

- beech 너도밤나무
- oak 참나무
- spruce 가문비나무
- riddle 수수께끼, 구멍을 숭숭 뚫다, 벌집같이 만들다
- bid (고어 · 시에서) 고하다, 명하다
- adieu 작별
- relieve oneself 용변을 보다, 배변하다
- breeze 산들바람
- rustling 바스락[사각, 와작] 소리나는, 바스락거리는 소리
- scrunch 저르륵저르륵[뽀드득뽀드득] 소리를 내다
- scuffle 휙[슉] 움직이다

독해 > 글의 일관성 > 무관한 어휘·문장

정답의 이유

제시문은 소설의 쓰임새 중 하나가 공감을 쌓는 것이라고 주장하고 나서 소설을 통해 공감을 쌓는 과정을 그리고 있다. ②는 그러한 과정과 상관없는 내용이므로 논점에서 어긋나는 문장이다. 따라서 글의 흐름상 어색한 문장은 ②이다.

본문해석

소설은 많은 쓰임새가 있는데, 그것들 중 한 가지는 공감을 쌓는 것이다. TV나 영화를 볼 때, 여러분은 다른 사람들에게 일어나는 일들을 보고 있다. 산문 소설은 26개의 글자[알파벳]와 몇 개의 구두점으로 만들어 낸 것으로 여러분은 여러분만의 상상력을 발휘하여 세상을 만들고, 그곳에서 살면서 다른 눈으로 바깥을 바라본다. 여러분은 사물을 느끼고, 그렇지 않았다면 결코 알지 못했을 장소와 세계를 방문하게 된다. 다행스럽게도, 지난 10년 동안, 세계에서 가장 아름답고 알려지지 않은 많은 장소들이 주목받았다. 저 바깥에 있는 다른 사람들도 모두 또 하나의 '나'라는 것을 알게 된다. 여러분은 다른 누군가가 되고 있고, 여러분 자신의 세계로 돌아오면, 여러분은 약간 변화될 것이다.

VOCA

• empathy　공감, 감정이입
• prose　산문, 산문의
• a handful of　소수의
• punctuation mark　구두점
• put in the spotlight　주목[관심]을 받다

독해 > 빈칸 완성 > 단어·구·절

정답의 이유

빈칸 앞부분에서 '그것에 그늘을 드리우는 다른 식물들은 새로운 생명을 즉시 소멸시킬(Other plants casting shade on it would extinguish the new life immediately) 것'이며, '만약 이런 솜털 같은 작은 씨앗 꾸러미가 가문비나무나 너도밤나무 숲에 떨어진다면, 씨앗의 생은 시작도 하기 전에 끝난다.'라고 했으므로 문맥상 빈칸에는 작은 씨앗 꾸러미가 가문비나무나 너도밤나무 숲에 떨어지는 것보다 ① 'prefer settling in unoccupied territory(비어 있는 지역에 정착하기를 선호한다)'가 적절하다.

오답의 이유

② 초식동물의 먹이로 선택되었다
③ 인간의 개입을 피하려고 진화했다
④ 먼 겨울까지 죽은 잎을 달고 있다

본문해석

버드나무와 포플러의 씨앗은 너무 작아서 여러분은 솜털로 뒤덮여 날아다니는 털에서 작고 어두운 두 개의 점으로만 알아볼 수 있다. 이 씨앗들 중 하나는 무게가 0.0001그램밖에 나가지 않는다. 이렇게 약한 에너지를 비축해서, 묘목은 수증기가 다 떨어지기 전에 겨우 1~2밀리미터만 자랄 수 있고 어린잎을 이용해 스스로 만든 양분에 의존해야 한다. 하지만 그것은 작은 새싹을 위협하는 경쟁이 없는 곳에서만 효과가 있다. 그것에 그늘을 드리우는 다른 식물들은 새로운 생명을 즉시 소멸시킬 것이다. 그래서 만약 이런 솜털 같은 작은 씨앗 꾸러미가 가문비나무나 너도밤나무 숲에 떨어진다면, 씨앗의 생은 시작도 하기 전에 끝난다. 그래서 버드나무와 포플러는 비어 있는 지역에 정착하기를 선호한다.

VOCA

• willow　버드나무
• minuscule　아주 작은
• make out　~을 알아보다
• fluffy　솜털 같은, 솜털로 덮인
• weigh　무게[체중]가 ~이다
• meagre[＝meager]　빈약한, 메마른, 결핍한
• reserve　비축[예비](물)
• seedling　묘목, 어린 나무
• run out of　~을 다 써버리다, ~이 없어지다
• steam　수증기, (작은) 물방울
• rely on　기대다, 의존하다
• threaten　위태롭게 하다, 위협하다
• sprout　싹이 트다, 새싹
• cast　(그림자를) 드리우다
• shade　그늘
• extinguish　소멸시키다

독해 > 글의 일관성 > 무관한 어휘·문장

정답의 이유

제시문은 좋은 워킹화에 관해 설명하는 글이다. ③ lowered 다음에서 '~ the sole at the back of the shoe is ~ thicker(신발 뒷부분의 밑창이 ~ 더 두껍다) ~'라고 했으므로 문맥상 낱말의 쓰임이 적절하지 않은 것은 ③ 'lowered(낮아진)'이다. lowered → heightened(높여진) 또는 raised(올려진)가 되어야 한다.

오답의 이유

① 지지하는
② 충격 흡수 능력을 가진
④ 넓찍한

본문해석

좋은 워킹화는 중요하다. 대부분 주요 운동 브랜드들은 특히 걷기를 위해 고안된 신발을 제공한다. 스타일보다는 착용감과 편안함이 더 중요한데, 신발은 끼거나 조이지 않고, 지지감이 느껴져야 한다. 상부는 가벼우면서 통기성이 뛰어나고 유연해야 하며, 안창은 방습성이 있어야 하고, 밑창은 충격을 흡수해야 한다. 신발 뒤꿈치 굽의 쐐기가 낮아야(→ 높아야) 하므로 신발 뒷부분의 밑창이 앞부분보다 두 배 더 두껍다. 마지막으로, 운동용 양말을 신을 때도 앞심이 넓어야 한다(공간이 있어야 한다).

VOCA

- constricting 수축되는, 조이는
- insole 구두의 안창
- absorbent (특히 액체를) 잘 빨아들이는, 흡수력 있는
- heel (신발의) 굽
- wedge 쐐기
- toe box (구두 끝의 안쪽에 넣는) 앞심

11 난도 ★★☆ 정답 ③

독해 > 대의 파악 > 요지, 주장

정답의 이유

첫 문장의 'If your kids fight every time ~ make sure you're close enough to be able to hear them(여러분의 자녀들이 ~ 할 때마다 싸운다면, ~ 여러분이 그들의 소리를 들을 수 있을 만큼 반드시 충분히 가까이 있도록 하라) ~'와 마지막 문장의 'They should also learn to revisit problems(그들은 또한 ~ 문제를 다시 논의하는 법을 배워야 한다) ~'로 미루어 글의 요지로 가장 알맞은 것은 ③ 'Help your kids learn to resolve conflict(여러분의 아이들이 갈등을 해결하는 법을 배우도록 도와라).'임을 유추할 수 있다.

오답의 이유

① 여러분의 아이들에게 그들의 시험을 평가해 달라고 요청하라.
② 여러분의 아이들이 서로 경쟁하도록 하라.
④ 여러분의 아이들에게 논쟁에서 이기는 법을 가르쳐라.

본문해석

여러분의 자녀들이 비디오 게임을 할 때마다 싸운다면, 아이들이 게임을 하기 위해 앉을 때 여러분이 그들의 소리를 들을 수 있을 만큼 반드시 충분히 가까이 있도록 하라. 그들이 사용하는 공격적인 특정한 단어나 목소리 톤을 듣고, 그것이 더 격해지기 전에 개입하려고 노력하라. 일단 화가 진정되면, 아이들을 앉히고 탓하거나 비난하지 말고 앉아서 그 문제에 대해 의논해 보라. 아이들 각자에게 방해받지 않고 말할 기회를 주고, 그들 스스로 그 문제에 대한 해결책을 제시하도록 노력하게 하라. 아이들이 초등학생이 될 때쯤이면, 그들은 어떤 것들이 서로에게 유리한 해결책이고, 어떤 것들이 시간이 지나면서 가장 효과가 있고 서로를 만족시킬 가능성이 있는지 평가할 수 있게 된다. 그들은 또한 해결책이 더 이상 효과가 없을 때 문제를 다시 논의하는 법을 배워야 한다.

VOCA

- aggressive 공격적인, 적극적인, 활동적인
- intervene 개입하다, 끼어들다
- temper 성격, 기질, 화
- settle 진정되다
- accuse 비난하다
- uninterrupted 방해받지 않는
- come up with 제시하다
- revisit 다시 논의하다
- resolve 해결하다

12 난도 ★★☆ 정답 ④

독해 > 대의 파악 > 요지, 주장

정답의 이유

제시문은 세균의 이점을 설명하는 내용으로, '우리가 대부분의 세균과 접촉할 때, 우리 몸은 그것들을 파괴하고, 그 결과 우리의 면역 체계와 질병과 싸워 이기는 그것의 능력을 강화한다.'라고 한 다음, 결론적으로 'these "good germs" actually make us healthier(이러한 유익균은 실제로 우리를 더 건강하게 만든다).'라고 했으므로 글의 요지로 적절한 것은 ④ '과도하게 세균을 제거하려고 하는 것이 오히려 면역 능력을 해친다.'이다.

본문해석

어떤 희생을 치르더라도 세균을 피하는 게 요즘 추세이다. 우리는 욕실과 부엌, 공기를 소독한다. 우리는 세균을 죽이기 위해 손을 소독하고 구강청결제로 입안을 헹군다. 일부 사람들은 되도록 사람들과 접촉하는 것을 피하고, 세균 감염에 대한 두려움 때문에 심지어 악수도 하지 않으려 한다. 내 생각에는 어떤 사람들은 마음을 제외한 모든 것을 정화할 것이라고 해도 무방할 것 같다. 'the Boy in the Bubble' 이야기를 기억하는가? 그는 면역 체계 없이 태어났고, 사람들과의 접촉을 차단당한 채 완전히 무균 상태인 방에서 살아야 했다. 물론, 모든 사람들은 합리적인 수준의 청결함과 개인위생 상태를 유지하기 위해 신중한 조치를 취해야 하지만, 많은 경우, 우리가 너무 지나친 것은 아닐까? 우리가 대부분의 세균과 접촉할 때, 우리 몸은 그것들을 파괴하고, 그 결과 우리의 면역 체계와 더 나아가 질병과 싸워 이기는 그것의 능력을 강화한다. 따라서 이러한 '유익균'은 실제로 우리를 더 건강하게 만든다. 모든 세균을 피하고 무균 환경에서 사는 게 가능하다고 해도, 그러면 우리는 'the Boy in the Bubble'처럼 되지 않을까?

VOCA

- germ 세균, 미생물, 병원체
- disinfect 소독[살균]하다, (컴퓨터의) 바이러스를 제거하다
- sanitize 위생 처리하다, 살균하다
- for fear of ~하는 것을 두려워하여, ~할까 봐
- safe to say ~이라고 말해도 무방하다
- purify 정화하다
- take a measure 조치를 취하다
- prudent 신중한

- come in contact with ～와 접촉하다
- fight off 물리치다
- sterile 무균의

13 난도 ★★☆ 정답 ④

어법 > 비문 찾기

정답의 이유

④ 부대상황 분사구문으로, 'with＋목적어＋현재분사[과거분사]'의 형식인데, 목적어와 관계가 능동이면 현재분사, 수동이면 과거분사를 사용한다. '～ with one quarter of its population lived within the walls, ～'에서 'population'과 'lived'의 관계가 능동이므로 lived → living이 되어야 한다.

오답의 이유

① 'Knowing as the Golden City, ～'는 분사구문으로, 주절의 주어(Jaisalmer)와 분사구문의 주어가 일치하여 생략한 경우이다. 문맥상 주어(Jaisalmer)가 Golden City로 '알려진' 수동 관계이므로 Knowing → Known으로 올바르게 고쳤다.

② 문장의 동사(rises)가 나와 있으므로 shelters는 'its 30-foot-high walls and medieval sandstone fort'를 수식하는 분사인데, 문맥상 성벽과 요새가 '보호하는' 능동 관계이므로 shelters → sheltering으로 올바르게 고쳤다.

③ '부정어구 도치(so little has life)' 문장으로, 'so little has life altered here'로 미루어 'so ～ that' 구문 문장임을 유추할 수 있으므로 which → that으로 올바르게 고쳤다.

본문해석

Golden City로 알려진 Jaisalmer는 Khyber Pass로 가는 길목에 있는 예전의 카라반 중심지였으며, 모래바다로부터 우뚝 솟아있고, 30피트 높이 성벽과 중세 사암 요새가 사파이어 빛 하늘로 치솟은 조각 첨탑과 궁전을 보호하고 있다. 꼬불꼬불한 작은 길과 숨겨진 사원으로 인해 Jaisalmer는 아라비안나이트에서 바로 나온 것 같이 생겼고, 이곳의 삶이 거의 변하지 않아서 여러분 자신이 13세기로 되돌아간 것으로 상상하기 쉽다. 이곳은 아직도 기능을 하는 인도의 유일한 요새 도시로, 인구의 4분의 1이 성벽 안에 살고 있으며 자주 다니는 길목에서 충분히 먼 거리에 있어서 관광업으로 인한 최악의 피해를 면했다. 그 도시의 부는 원래 그곳을 지나가는 낙타 카라반들에게 부과되었던 상당한 통행료에서 나왔다.

VOCA

- medieval 중세의, 중고의
- fort 요새
- shelter 보호하다
- spire 뾰족탑
- soar 우뚝 솟다
- winding 꼬불꼬불한
- alter 변하다, 바뀌다
- ravage 파괴
- substantial 실질적인, 상당한
- toll 통행료

14 난도 ★★☆ 정답 ②

독해 > 대의 파악 > 요지, 주장

정답의 이유

제시문의 마지막 문장에서 '우리는 어떻게든 모든 사람들이 새로운 발견에 접근 가능한 방법을 찾아야 한다'라고 했으므로 필자가 주장하는 바는 ② '새로운 연구 결과에 모든 사람이 접근할 수 있게 해야 한다.'이다.

본문해석

학자들은 세계의 문제에 대해 냉담하지도 무관심하지도 않다. 일반 대중들의 관심을 끄는 책은 거의 없지만, 이러한 문제에 관한 책들이 그 어느 때보다 많이 출판되고 있다. 마찬가지로, 새로운 연구 발견은 대학에서 지속적으로 이루어지고 있으며, 전 세계 컨퍼런스에서 공유되고 있다. 불행히도, 이 활동의 대부분은 자기 잇속만 차리는 활동이다. 이것 또한 오직 선택적으로, 과학을 제외하고, 새로운 식견은 우리의 삶을 개선하는 데 도움이 되는 방법으로 대중에게 흘러내려 가지 않고 있다. 그러나 이러한 발견은 단순히 엘리트들의 소유물이 아니며, 선택된 소수 전문가들의 소유로 남아서도 안 된다. 각자는 그 또는 그녀의 삶의 결정을 내려야 하며, 우리가 누구인지, 무엇이 우리에게 좋은지에 대한 현재의 이해를 고려하여 그러한 선택을 해야 한다. 그 점에 있어서, 우리는 어떻게든 모든 사람들이 새로운 발견에 접근 가능한 방법을 찾아야 한다.

VOCA

- apathetic 무관심한, 냉담한
- indifferent 무관심한
- capture (흥미를) 사로잡다
- self-serving 이기적인, 자기 잇속만 차리는
- selectively 선택적으로
- property 소유물
- possession 소유
- in light of ～을 고려하여
- accessible 접근 가능한

15 난도 ★★☆ 정답 ①

독해 > 대의 파악 > 제목, 주제

정답의 이유

첫 문장에서 '언어는 개인에게 정체성과 소속감을 준다.'라고 했고, 마지막 문장에서 향상된 자아 정체성과 자존감 덕분에 아이의 수업 성적 또한 향상된다고 했으므로 글의 주제로 적절한 것은 ① 'the importance of mother tongue in child development(아동 발달에서 모국어의 중요성)'이다.

오답의 이유

② 아이들의 외국어 학습에 대한 영향

③ 아이들의 자존감을 향상시키는 방안

④ 언어학적 분석의 효율성

언어는 개인에게 정체성과 소속감을 준다. 아이들이 자랑스럽게 그들의 언어를 배우고 가정과 이웃에서 그것을 말할 수 있을 때, 아이들은 높은 자존감을 갖게 될 것이다. 게다가, 모국어의 진정한 가치를 아는 아이들은 외국어로 말할 때 자신을 성공한 사람이 된 것처럼 느끼지 않을 것이다. 향상된 자아 정체성과 자존감 덕분에, 아이의 수업 성적 또한 향상되는데, 그것은 이러한 아이는 언어적 소외감에 대한 걱정을 덜 가지고 등교하기 때문이다.

- identity   정체성, 자신, 신원, 신분; 독자성, 동질감
- sense of belonging   소속감
- self-esteem   자부심, 자존감, 자긍심
- mother tongue   모국어
- linguistic marginalization   언어적 소외감

16 난도 ★☆☆   정답 ①

독해 > 대의 파악 > 제목, 주제

정답의 이유

여섯 번째 문장에서 'Cooperation has other benefits(협력에는 다른 이점이 있다).'라고 했고, 이후 부분에서 서로 위험을 경고하고, 더 많은 먹이를 찾고, 병들거나 다친 것들을 보살피는 등 함께 생활하는 것의 이점을 나열하고 있다. 따라서 글의 주제로 적절한 것은 ① 'benefits of being social in animals(동물들이 사회적인 것의 장점)'이다.

오답의 이유

② 협동 행동의 단점
③ 동물과 인간의 공통적 특성
④ 짝짓기와 번식에서의 경쟁

많은 동물들이 홀로 지내지 않는다. 그들은 함께 생활하고 일함으로써 더 효과적으로 세계와 상호작용할 수 있다는 사실을 발견했는데, 어쩌면 자연이 그들을 위해 발견해 준 것일 수도 있다. 예를 들어, 만약 동물이 홀로 먹이를 사냥한다면, 자신보다 훨씬 더 작은 동물들만 잡고 죽이고 먹을 수 있지만, 만약 동물들이 한 무리로 뭉친다면, 그들은 자신보다 더 큰 동물들을 잡고 죽일 수 있다. 한 무리의 늑대는 말 한 마리를 죽일 수 있고, 무리는 매우 잘 먹을 수 있다. 그러므로 동물들은 혼자 일하는[사냥하는] 것보다 함께 일한다면, 같은 숲에 있는 동종의 동물들이 더 많은 먹이를 얻을 수 있다. 협력에는 다른 이점이 있다. 즉, 동물들은 서로에게 위험을 경고할 수 있고, (만약 각자 탐색한 다음, 먹이를 찾는 데 성공한 동물을 따라간다면) 더 많은 먹이를 찾을 수 있으며, 심지어 병들거나 다친 것들을 어느 정도는 보살필 수 있다. 동물들이 멀리 떨어져 사는 것보다 무리를 지어 살면 짝짓기와 번식에도 더 용이하다.

- loner   외톨이
- interact   상호작용하다

- band together   함께 뭉치다, 무리를 이루다
- pack   무리, 떼
- alert   알리다, 주의를 환기시키다
- mating   짝짓기
- reproduction   번식
- drawback   결점
- trait   특징

17 난도 ★★☆   정답 ④

독해 > 글의 일관성 > 무관한 어휘·문장

정답의 이유

제시문은 철학은 스스로 생각할 수 있게 해주므로 초등학교 때부터 철학자처럼 생각하는 법을 배워야 한다는 취지의 글이다. ④ 앞의 문장에서 'go on reciting the rules of others as if they were sacrosanct(다른 사람들의 법칙을 마치 신성불가침이라도 되는 것처럼 계속 암송한다).'라고 했으므로 문맥상 ④에서 결과적으로 그들은 자신도 모르게 다른 사람들의 세계의 proponents(지지자들)가 된다고 하는 것이 적절하다. 따라서 문맥상 낱말의 쓰임이 적절하지 않은 것은 ④ 'opponents(반대자들)'이다.

내 자신의 호기심은 대학에서의 철학 공부에 의해 고무되었다. 그 과정에는 우리가 공부하기로 되어 있는 수많은 철학자들이 목록에 있었고, 나는 처음에는 우리의 과제가 일종의 세속적인 성서로서 그들의 작품을 배우고 받아들이는 것이라고 생각했다. 하지만 내가 기뻤던 것은, 지도교수의 관심이 내가 그들의 이론을 암송하는 게 아니라, 과거 철학자들을 권위자가 아닌 자극제로 사용하여 내 자신의 이론을 발전시키는 데 도움을 주는 것이라는 걸 알게 된 것이었다. 그것이 내 지적 자유의 비결이었다. 이제 나는 스스로 생각하고, 무엇이든 모든 것에 의문을 제기하고, 내가 옳다고 생각하는 경우에만 동의할 공식적인 허락을 받았다. 좋은 교육을 받았더라면, 훨씬 더 일찍 그 허락을 받았을 것이다. 아아, 어떤 사람들은, 그것을 받은 적이 없는 것 같아 보이고, 다른 사람들의 법칙을 마치 신성불가침이라도 되는 것처럼 계속 암송한다. 결과적으로, 그들은 자신도 모르게 다른 사람들의 세계의 반대자들(→ 지지자들)이 된다. 이제, 나는 철학이 전문 철학자들에게만 맡겨지기에는 너무 중요하다고 생각한다. 우리는 모두 초등학교 때부터 철학자처럼 생각하는 법을 배워야 한다.

- absorb   받아들이다
- secular   세속의, 속인의, 세속적인
- delighted   기뻐하는
- recite   암송하다
- stimulant   각성제, 자극이 되는 것, 자극성의
- authority   당국, 권한, 권위, 권위자
- intellectual   지적인
- alas   아아, 슬프도다
- unwitting   모르는, 의식하지 않은

어법 > 정문 찾기

정답의 이유

(A) 명사(evidence) 다음에 완전한 문장[주어(Mayan leaders)+동사(were aware of)+목적어(their uncertain dependence)]이 나오므로 명사(evidence)를 보충·설명하는 동격 명사절을 이끄는 'that'이 적절하다. 동격의 that은 일반적으로, '명사(fact, news, evidence, belief, idea)+that'의 형식으로 쓰인다.

(B) 문맥상 '저장하기 위해'라는 의미가 되어야 하므로 (B)에는 to부정사의 부사적 용법으로 쓰인 'to store'가 적절하다.

(C) 'as+보어+as+주어+동사'에서 as가 양보 부사절 접속사로 쓰였으므로 (C)에는 주격 보어(impressive)를 취하는 be동사 'were'가 적절하다.

본문해석

과거를 되돌아보면, 과학자들은 마야의 지도자들이 강우에 대한 자신들의 불안정한 의존에 대해 여러 세기 동안 알고 있었다는 산더미 같은 증거를 발견했다. (그들은) 물 부족에 대해 알고 있었을 뿐만 아니라 기록도 하고 계획도 세웠다. 마야인들은 강우량이 적은 해에는 재배할 작물의 종류, 공공 용수의 사용, 식량 배급을 엄격하게 통제하면서 (물) 보존을 시행했다. 3천 년 통치 기간의 처음 절반 동안 마야인들은 가뭄기에 대비해 빗물을 저장하기 위해 더 큰 규모의 지하 인공 호수와 수조를 계속 만들었다. 공들여 꾸민 그들의 신전들도 인상적이었지만, 물을 모으고 저장하기 위한 그들의 효율적인 체계는 설계와 공법에 있어서 걸작이었다.

VOCA

• look back 되돌아보다
• uncover 발견하다
• a mountain of 많은, 산더미 같은
• uncertain 불안정한, 불확실한
• dependence 의존성
• enforce 시행하다, 강요하다
• conservation 보존, 보호
• regulate 통제하다
• reign 통치, 통치 기간
• artificial 인공의
• drought 가뭄
• elaborately 공들여, 정교하게
• masterpiece 걸작

독해 > 글의 일관성 > 글의 순서

정답의 이유

② 주어진 글은 종교가 사람에게서 가장 좋은 것을 끌어내는 유일한 현상은 아니라고 했으므로 문맥상 아이를 갖는 것과 전쟁, 자연재해도 인간을 성숙하게 하는 효과가 있다고 한 (B)로 이어지는 것이 자연스럽다. 이어서 (C)에서 '하지만(But) 종교만큼 효과적인 것도 없다'라고 이야기하고 나서 (A)에서 종교가 없었다면(otherwise) 자아도취하거나 천박할 사람들도 종교에 의해 종종 고상해지고 어려운 결정을 내리는 데 도움을 주는 인생에 대한 관점(a perspective on life)을 얻게 된다고 마무리하는 것이 자연스럽다. 따라서 주어진 글 다음에 이어질 글의 순서로 적절한 것은 ② '(B) - (C) - (A)'이다.

본문해석

종교는 확실히 한 사람에게서 가장 좋은 것을 끌어낼 수 있지만, 그것이 그 속성만이 가진 유일한 현상은 아니다.

(B) 아이를 갖는 것은 종종 한 사람을 놀랄 만큼 성숙하게 하는 효과가 있다. 유명한 말이지만, 전시는 홍수나 허리케인 같은 자연재해가 그러한 것처럼, 사람들에게 능력을 발휘할 많은 기회를 제공한다.

(C) 그러나 하루하루 빠짐없이 평생을 대비하기 위해서는 아마도 종교만큼 효과적인 것은 없을 것이다. 즉, 그것은 강력하고 재능 있는 사람들을 더 겸손하고 인내심 있게 만들고, 보통 사람들이 자기 자신을 넘어설 수 있게 만들며, 음주나 마약 또는 범죄로부터 벗어나기 위해 필사적으로 도움을 필요로 하는 많은 사람들에게 견고한 지원을 제공한다.

(A) 그렇지 않았다면 자기 일만 생각하거나, 천박하거나, 조잡하거나, 그저 쉽게 단념해버렸을 사람들도, 종종 종교에 의해 고상해지고, 모두가 자랑스러워할 어려운 결정을 내리는 데 도움을 주는 인생에 대한 관점이 주어진다.

VOCA

• bring out ～을 꺼내다, ～을 끌어내다
• property 속성
• phenomenon 현상
• self-absorbed 자기도취의, 자기 일에 몰두한
• shallow 얕은, 천박한
• crude 가공하지 않은, 미숙한
• quitter 쉽게 체념해 버리는 사람, 겁쟁이, 비겁자
• ennoble 고상하게 하다
• an abundance of 많은, 풍부한
• occasion (～을 위한/～할) 시기; 기회, 호기
• rise to 능력을 발휘하다
• day in, day out (오랫동안) 해가 뜨나 해가 지나[하루도 빠짐없이]
• brace 버티다, 대응 태세를 갖추다
• sturdy 튼튼한, 견고한, 불굴의, 단단한
• desperately 절실하게, 필사적으로, 절망적으로
• stay away from ～을 가까이하지 않다

20 난도 ★★☆   정답 ②

독해 > 글의 일관성 > 글의 순서

정답의 이유

주어진 글 끝부분의 'deplete more rapidly(더 빠르게 고갈되다)'는 (B)의 'The result of this depletion(이러한 고갈의 결과는)'으로 이어지고, (B) 끝부분의 'rising population numbers(증가하는 인구수)'는 (A)의 'Population growth(인구 증가)'로 이어진다. 그런 다음 (A)의 'increased greenhouse gases, mostly from CO2 emissions(주로 이산화탄소 배출로 인해 온실가스가 증가하는)'는 (C)의 'As greenhouse gases increase(온실가스가 증가함에 따라)'로 마무리된다. 따라서 주어진 글 다음에 이어질 글의 순서는 ② '(B) - (A) - (C)'이다.

본문해석

더 많은 사람들이 더 많은 자원을 필요로 하는데, 이는 인구가 증가함에 따라 지구의 자원이 더 빠르게 고갈된다는 것을 의미한다.
(B) 이러한 고갈의 결과는 인간이 증가하는 인구수를 수용하기 위해 지구에서 자원을 제거함으로써 발생하는 삼림 벌채와 생물 다양성의 손실이다.
(A) 인구 증가는 또한 온실가스 증가를 초래하는데, 이는 주로 이산화탄소 배출로 인한 것이다. 가시화해 보면, 20세기 동안, 인구는 4배로 증가했는데, 이산화탄소 배출량은 12배 증가했다.
(C) 온실가스가 증가함에 따라 기후 패턴도 그러한데[늘어나는데], 이것은 결국 기후 변화라고 불리는 장기적인 패턴을 야기한다.

VOCA

- deplete 고갈시키다, 다 써버리다, 비우다
- emission (빛·열·가스 등의) 배출, 배출물, 배기가스
- visualization 눈에 보이게 함[하는 힘], 시각화
- fourfold 4중(四重)의[으로], 4배의[로], 4배, 4중, 네 겹
- deforestation 삼림 파괴
- strip 없애다
- accommodate 편의를 도모하다, 수용하다
- ultimately 결국, 궁극적으로

21 난도 ★★☆   정답 ②

독해 > 글의 일관성 > 무관한 어휘·문장

정답의 이유

제시문은 의학 인류학자와 전염병 학자가 협업하여, 질병의 확산에 영향을 미치는 요인과 질병의 원인과 증상, 어떻게 질병을 잘 치료할 수 있는지 등을 연구하여 효과적인 보건 의료 서비스를 제공하는 것에 대한 내용이다. 따라서 전체 흐름과 관계없는 문장은 '의사가 되고자 하는 동기(incentive)'에 대해 설명한 ②이다.

본문해석

인간 생물학 및 생리학의 광범위한 훈련을 받은 의학 인류학자들은 질병 전염 패턴과 특정 집단들이 말라리아와 수면병 같은 질병의 존재에 어떻게 적응하는지를 연구한다. 바이러스와 박테리아의 전염은 사람들의 식생활, 위생, 기타 행동의 영향을 많이 받기 때문에 많은 의학 인류학자들은 전염병 학자와 팀을 이루어 질병의 확산에 영향을 미치는 문화적 관행을 파악한다. 대부분의 학생들이 성공적인 의학 경력에 주어지는 금전적 보상보다는 인도주의적 이유로 의사가 된다는 것이 일반적인 믿음일지도 모르지만, 선진국에서는 지위와 보상에 대한 전망도 아마 하나의 동기일 것이다. 서로 다른 문화들은 질병의 원인과 증상, 질병을 가장 잘 치료하는 방법, 전통 치료사와 의사의 능력 그리고 치유 과정에서의 지역사회 참여의 중요성에 대해 저마다 생각이 다르다. 의학 인류학자들은 인류 공동체가 이러한 것들을 어떻게 인식하는지 연구함으로써, 병원 및 다른 기관이 보다 효과적으로 보건 의료 서비스를 제공할 수 있도록 지원한다.

VOCA

- anthropologist 인류학자
- physiology 생리학
- transmission 전염, 전파
- adapt 적응하다
- presence 존재
- sanitation 공중위생
- epidemiologist 유행[전염]병 학자
- identify 확인하다
- enter medicine 의사가 되다
- humanitarian 인도주의적인, 인도주의의
- prospect 전망
- deliver 전달하다, 전하다

22 난도 ★★☆   정답 ③

독해 > 글의 일관성 > 글의 순서

정답의 이유

주어진 글에서 Sequoya의 출생에 대해 소개하고, (C)에서 'As a child(어린 시절) ~'로 이어지는 것이 자연스럽다. 그 다음으로 (A) 와 (B) 중에서 (B)의 'More important(더 중요한 것은) ~'로 미루어, (B) 앞에 다른 '중요한 것'이 나와 있을 것으로 유추할 수 있으므로 (A) 다음에 (B)가 이어진다는 것을 유추할 수 있다. 따라서 주어진 글 다음에 이어질 글의 순서로 적절한 것은 ③ '(C) – (A) – (B)' 이다.

본문해석

Sequoya(1760?~1843)는 Tennessee 주 동부에서 Cherokee 부족의 전통과 종교에 대한 지식으로 높이 존경받는 한 명문가에서 태어났다.

(C) 어린 시절, Sequoya는 Cherokee 구전을 배웠고, 그 이후 성인이 되어 유로 아메리카 문화를 소개받았다. 그의 편지에서, Sequoya는 의사소통에 사용되는 유럽계 미국인들의 글쓰기 방법에 어떻게 매료되었는지를 언급한다.

(A) 글쓰기가 그의 민족에게 갖는 가능성을 인식한 Sequoya는 1821년에 체로키 알파벳을 발명했다. 이 글자 체계로, Sequoya는 고대 부족의 관습을 기록할 수 있었다.

(B) 더 중요한 것은 그의 알파벳이 Cherokee 국가의 출판 산업 발전을 도와서 신문과 책이 발행될 수 있었다는 점이다. 따라서 학령기 아이들은 그들 자신의 언어로 Cherokee 문화와 전통에 대해 배울 수 있었다.

VOCA

- be born into[to] ~의 가정에 태어나다
- be highly regarded for ~에 대해 높이 존경받다
- prestigious 명망 있는[높은], 일류의
- recognize 인식하다, 알다
- oral tradition 구전
- fascinated 매료된

23 난도 ★☆☆   정답 ②

독해 > 세부 내용 찾기 > 내용 (불)일치

정답의 이유

두 번째 문단의 세 번째 문장에서 'Donations of peanut butter can be dropped off ~ on Monday through Friday, 8:00 am to 4:00 pm(월요일부터 금요일까지 매일 오전 8시부터 오후 4시까지 ~ 땅콩버터를 기부하실 수 있습니다.)'이라고 했으므로 안내문의 내용과 일치하지 않는 것은 ② '토요일과 일요일에도 땅콩버터를 기부할 수 있다.'이다.

오답의 이유

① 첫 번째 문단의 두 번째 문장에서 'to benefit children, families and seniors who face hunger in Northeast Louisiana'라고 했으므로 안내문의 내용과 일치한다.

③ 두 번째 문단의 마지막 문장에서 'Monetary donations can be made here or by calling 427-418-4581.'이라고 했으므로 안내문의 내용과 일치한다.

④ 안내문의 마지막 문장에서 'For other drop-off locations, visit our website ~'라고 했으므로 안내문의 내용과 일치한다.

본문해석

사랑을 나누세요
땅콩버터 운동 동안에 배고픔과 싸우기

작은 도움이 필요한 지역 가족들을 도움으로써 우리 지역 사회에 기여하세요. Louisiana주 북동부의 굶주림에 직면한 아이들과 가족들, 노인들에게 도움이 되기 위해 올해로 제4회를 맞이한 전 지역 땅콩버터 기부 운동을 시작합니다.

땅콩버터는 어린이들과 어른들이 좋아하는 고단백 식품이기 때문에, 푸드 뱅크에서 많이 필요한 주요 식품입니다. 3월 29일 금요일 오후 4시까지 플라스틱 단지에 담긴 땅콩버터나 기금을 Monroe 푸드 뱅크에 기부해 주세요. 월요일부터 금요일까지 매일 오전 8시부터 오후 4시까지 Monroe Central Avenue 4600번지에 위치한 푸드 뱅크의 배급 센터에 땅콩버터를 기부하실 수 있습니다. 금전 기부는 이곳 또는 427-418-4581로 전화해서 하실 수 있습니다.

다른 기부처를 원하시면 저희 웹사이트인 https://www.foodbanknela.org를 방문해 주세요.

VOCA

- make a contribution 공헌하다, 기부하다
- assistance 도움
- kick off 시작하다
- benefit 도움이 되다
- staple 주요한, 주요 산물, 기본 식품
- packed ~이 가득 찬, 꽉 찬
- drop off at ~에 갖다 놓다[내려주다]
- distribution 배급, 유통
- monetary 금전적인

독해 > 대의 파악 > 분위기, 어조, 심경

[정답의 이유]

화자가 네 번째 문장에서 자신의 부족이 가난했지만, 정직함으로 유명했다(we were famous for our honesty)고 한 것과, 여섯 번째 문장의 'We put pride first, honest next, and after that we believed in right and wrong.'으로 미루어 자신의 부족에 대한 화자의 자부심을 짐작할 수 있다. 따라서 화자의 심경으로 적절한 것은 ② 'satisfied and proud(만족스럽고 자랑스러운)'이다.

[오답의 이유]

① 평화롭고 고요한
③ 겁에 질리고 무서워하는
④ 놀라고 경악한

본문해석

우리 부족 전체가 가난에 시달렸다. Garoghlanian 가문의 모든 지파가 세상에서 가장 놀랍고 우스꽝스러운 가난 속에 살고 있었다. 우리가 우리 뱃속을 계속해서 채울 수 있을 만한 돈을 도대체 어디서 구했는지 아무도 이해할 수 없었다. 하지만 가장 중요한 것은, 우리가 정직하기로 유명했다는 것이다. 우리는 대략 11세기 동안 정직함으로 유명했는데, 심지어 우리가 바로 세상이라고 생각하고 싶었던 곳에서 가장 부유한 일족이었을 때도 그랬다. 우리는 자부심을 최우선에 두었고, 다음으로는 정직을, 그다음으로 옳고 그름을 믿었다. 우리 중 누구도 이 세상 어느 누구도 이용하지 못했을 것이다.

VOCA

• branch 일가, 가족
• comical 우스꽝스러운
• belly 배, 부풀다
• something like 거의, 약(about)
• put A first A를 가장 중시하다
• take advantage of ~을 이용하다
• horrified 겁에 질린
• astonished 깜짝 놀란

독해 > 세부 내용 찾기 > 내용 (불)일치

[정답의 이유]

네 번째 문장에서 'Cooked tomatoes, however, have lower levels of vitamin C than raw tomatoes, so if you're looking to increase your levels, you might be better off sticking with the raw(하지만 조리된 토마토는 생토마토보다 비타민C의 수치가 낮으므로 만약 수치를 늘리고 싶다면, 계속해서 생토마토로 먹는 편이 더 나을 것이다).'라고 했으므로 글의 내용과 일치하지 않는 것은 ② '더 많은 비타민C를 섭취하고 싶다면 생토마토보다 조리된 토마토를 섭취하는 것이 낫다.'이다.

[오답의 이유]

① 두 번째 문장에서 '~ our body can absorb lycopene more effectively when tomatoes are cooked'라고 했으므로 글의 내용과 일치한다.
③ 여섯 번째 문장에서 'If you're buying tomato sauce or paste, choose a variety with no salt or sugar added ~'라고 했으므로 글의 내용과 일치한다.
④ 마지막 문장에서 '~ if you're eating your tomatoes raw, salt them sparingly and choose salad dressings that are low in calories ~'라고 했으므로 글의 내용과 일치한다.

본문해석

음식을 날로 먹는 것에 대한 인기가 점점 늘어남에도 불구하고, 여전히 조리된 야채로부터 영양분을 얻을 수 있다. 예를 들어, 우리 몸은 토마토가 익었을 때 리코펜을 더 효과적으로 흡수할 수 있다. (그러나 생토마토는 여전히 리코펜의 좋은 공급원이라는 것을 잊지 마라.) 하지만 조리된 토마토는 생토마토보다 비타민C의 수치가 낮으므로 만약 수치를 늘리고 싶다면, 계속해서 생토마토로 먹는 편이 더 나을 것이다. 익혀서 먹든 생으로 먹든, 토마토가 가진 건강상의 이점을 희석시키지 않는 것이 중요하다. 토마토 소스나 토마토 페이스트를 산다면, 소금이나 설탕이 첨가되지 않은 종류를 고르라. 아니면 그보다 좋은 것은, 집에서 자신의 소스를 만들어라. 그리고 만약 토마토를 날것으로 먹는다면, 소금을 약간만 뿌리고 칼로리와 포화 지방이 낮은 샐러드 드레싱을 선택하라.

VOCA

• nutrient 영양, 영양소, 영양분
• lycopene 리코펜(토마토 따위의 붉은 색소)
• stick with ~을 고수하다
• variety (같은 종류의 것에서 다른) 종류
• sparingly 조금만
• saturated fat 포화 지방

법원직 9급   영어

한눈에 훑어보기

✓ 영역 분석

독해   01   02   03   04   05   06   07   08   11   12   13   16
          17   18   19   20   21   22   23   24   25
21문항, 84%

어법   09   10   14   15
4문항, 16%

✓ 빠른 정답

01	02	03	04	05	06	07	08	09	10
②	①	②	④	①	①	①	①	③	①
11	**12**	**13**	**14**	**15**	**16**	**17**	**18**	**19**	**20**
②	②	①	③	③	②	③	④	④	④
21	**22**	**23**	**24**	**25**					
④	②	③	③	④					

✓ 점수 체크

구분	1회독	2회독	3회독
맞힌 문항 수	/ 25	/ 25	/ 25
나의 점수	점	점	점

01   난도 ★☆☆   정답 ②

독해 > 빈칸 완성 > 단어·구·절

[정답의 이유]

(A) 첫 번째 문장에서 '~ not every fact is an item of knowledge (모든 사실이 지식에 속하는 것은 아니다).'라고 하였고, 네 번째 문장에서 'But as long as no one looks into the box, this fact remains unknown(하지만 아무도 그 상자 안을 들여다보지 않는 한, 이 사실은 아직 알려지지 않은 채로 남아있다) ~'라고 하였으므로 문맥에 맞는 (A)에 적절한 낱말은 'knowledge (지식)'이다.

(B) 괄호 앞 문장에서 'Knowledge demands some kind of access to a fact on the part of some living subject.'라고 했고, (B)가 있는 문장 뒷부분에 '~ whatever is stored in libraries and databases won't be knowledge, ~'라고 했으므로, 문맥에 맞는 (B)에 적절한 낱말은 'Without(~ 없이)'이다.

(C) 일곱 번째 문장에 'Knowledge demands some kind of access to a fact on the part of some living subject(지식은 현재 존재하는 어떤 대상에 관한 사실에 모종의 접근을 요구한다).'라고 되어 있으므로 이와 일관성이 있으려면, 지식은 어떠한 대상에 소속되지 않고는 존재할 수 없다는 의미의 문장이 되어야 한다. 따라서 문맥에 맞는 낱말로 적절한 것은 'unattached(소속되지 않은)'이다.

[오답의 이유]

① 사실 − ~를 가지고 − 소속되지 않은
③ 지식 − ~를 가지고 − 소속된
④ 사실 − ~없이 − 소속된

본문해석

지식을 사실과 동일시하는 것은 꽤 구미가 당기는 일이지만, 모든 사실이 지식의 한 항목인 것은 아니다. 동전 하나가 들어 있는 밀봉된 판지 상자를 흔든다고 상상해 보자. 상자를 내려놓을 때, 그 상자 안의 동전은 앞면 또는 뒷면 중 한 면으로 떨어졌다. 예를 들어 그것이 사실이라고 가정해 보자. 하지만 아무도 그 상자 안을 들여다보지 않는 한, 이 사실은 알려지지 않은 채로 남아 있다. 그것은 아직 (A) 지식의 영역에 속하지 않는다. 단순히 글로 적히는 것에 의해 사실이 지식이 되지는 않는다. 만일 여러분이 종이쪽지 하나에는 '동전이 앞면이 나왔다'라고 쓰고, 또 다른 종이쪽지에는 '동전이 뒷면이 나왔다'라는 문장을 쓴다면, 둘 중 어느 하나의 종이쪽지에는 사실을 적은 것이겠지만, 여전히 여러분은 동전 던지기의 결과에 대한 지식을 획득하지 못할 것이다. 지식은 현재 존재하는 어떤 대상에 대한 사실에 모종의 접근을 요구한다. 그것에 접근할 마음이 (B) 없다면, 도서관과 데이터베이스에 저장된 것이 무엇이든지 간에, 그것은 지식이 아니라 단지 잉크 자국과 전자적인 흔적일 뿐이다. 어떤 주어진 지식의 경우에, 이러한 접근은 한 개인에게 고유할 수도 있고 그렇지 않을 수도 있다. 동일한 사실이 한 사람에 의해 알려질 수 있고, 다른 사람에 의해 알려지지 않을 수도 있다. 누구나 알고 있는 상식은 많은 사람에 의해 공유될 수 있지만, 어떤 대상에도 (C) 소속되지 않고 매달리는 지식은 없다.

VOCA

- tempting 솔깃한, 구미가 당기는
- identify ~ with … ~을 …와 동일시하다
- heads and tails 동전의 앞면과 뒷면
- realm 영역, 범위
- slip (작은 종이 조각, 쪽지
- on the part of ~에 관해서는, ~ 편에서는
- dangle (달랑) 매달리다, 달랑거리다
- unattached 소속[연관]되지 않은

02 난도 ★★★   정답 ①

독해 > 빈칸 완성 > 단어 · 구 · 절

정답의 이유

제시문의 핵심 소재는 '영업사원의 구매 전략'이며, 주제는 '여기서 여러분만 소외되었다고 압력을 가함으로써 구매를 꾀한다.'이다. 마지막 두 문장에서 강조하는 것처럼, 다른 모든 사람들이 이미 구매한 물건을 여러분'도' 구매해야 한다고 압력을 가하는 것이므로 빈칸에는 ① 'peer pressure(또래 집단 압력)'가 적절하다.

오답의 이유

② 충동구매
③ 괴롭히기 작전
④ 치열한 경쟁

본문해석

쉽게 외부의 영향을 받는 젊은이들만이 또래 집단 압력을 경험하는 것은 아니다. 우리들 대부분은 아마 영업사원으로부터 압력을 받은 경험이 있을 것이다. 영업사원이 여러분에게 '당신의 경쟁사 중 70퍼센트가 그들의 서비스를 이용하는데 왜 이용하지 않느냐'라고 하면서, '사무용 솔루션'을 판매하려고 했던 적이 있는가? 하지만 그 70퍼센트의 경쟁사들이 바보라면? 혹은 그 70퍼센트의 경쟁사들이 추가로 값어치 있는 것을 꽤 많이 제공받았거나 도저히 거부할 수 없는 기회인 낮은 가격을 제시받았다면? 그 관행은 오직 한 가지 일을 하기 위해 고안된 것으로, 여러분이 구매하게끔 압력을 가하기 위한 것이다. 여러분이 뭔가 놓치고 있다고 느끼게 하기 위해서 혹은 다른 사람들은 다 알고 있는 것을 여러분만 모르고 있다고 느끼게 하기 위해서이다.

VOCA

- impressionable 쉽게 외부의 영향을 받는

- be subject(ed) to ~을 경험하다, ~의 대상이 되다
- sales rep 외판원, 영업사원
- idiot 바보, 멍청이
- value 가치, 값
- miss out on ~을 놓치다

03 난도 ★☆☆   정답 ②

독해 > 빈칸 완성 > 단어 · 구 · 절

정답의 이유

이러한 유형의 문제는 글의 흐름을 잘 따라가면 된다. 정확하게 그 단어의 뜻이 문맥과 어울리는지보다 맥락상 부정적인 단어가 들어갈 것인지, 긍정적인 단어가 들어갈 것인지를 판단하는 것이 도움이 된다.

(A) because로 연결된 인과관계의 종속절에서 그들은 자신감에 차 있고 기여할 기회를 즐긴다고 하였으므로 문맥상 'willingly(기꺼이)'가 적절하다.

(B) because로 연결된 인과관계가 성립하기 위해서는 그들이 문제를 악화시키는 이유로 실패한다는 믿음을 가지고 있어야 하므로 문맥상 'hold(가지다)'가 적절하다.

(C) 문맥상 자존감이 높은 사람들은 그들의 성공을 자신들의 내부적인 특성의 결과로 본다는 의미의 'attribute(~ 때문이라고 여기다)'가 적절하다.

오답의 이유

① 기꺼이 - 부인하다 - 시도하다
③ 마지못해 - 가지다 - 시도하다
④ 마지못해 - 부인하다 - ~때문이라고 여기다

본문해석

자존감이 높은 사람들은 자신의 기술과 능력에 대한 자신감이 있으며 삶이 그들에게 주는 고난에 맞서는 것을 즐긴다. 그들은 (A) 기꺼이 팀을 이뤄 일하는데, 왜냐하면 그들은 자신감에 차 있고 (팀에) 기여할 기회를 즐기기 때문이다. 그러나 자존감이 낮은 사람들은 어색함과 수줍음을 느끼며 자기 자신을 표현하지 못하는 경향이 있다. 종종 그들은 회피 전략을 선택함으로써 문제를 악화시키는데, 왜냐하면 그들은 자신이 어떤 일을 하더라도 실패한다는 믿음을 (B) 가지고 있기 때문이다. 반대로, 그들은 자신들이 하찮다는 느낌을 숨기기 위해 허풍을 떨고 거만한 행동을 보여줌으로써 자존감 부족을 보충할지도 모른다. 게다가 그러한 개인들은 자신의 성공 요인을 외부에서 찾음으로써 설명하는 반면, 자존감이 높은 사람들은 그들의 성공을 내부적 특성 (C) 때문이라고 여긴다.

VOCA

- self-esteem 자존감
- confidence 자신감, 확신
- competence 능력
- sure of oneself 확신에 찬
- compound 악화시키다
- opt for ~을 선택하다
- compensate for 보상하다, 보충하다

- boastful 뽐내는, 허풍을 떠는
- arrogant 거만한, 오만한
- cover up 숨기다[은폐하다]
- unworthiness 가치 없음, 하찮음
- account for 설명하다, 처리하다
- attribute A to B A(결과)가 B(원인) 때문이라고 여기다

04 난도 ★★☆ 정답 ④

독해 > 대의 파악 > 제목, 주제

[정답의 이유]

제시문은 주제가 글의 시작과 끝에 등장하는 양괄식 구조의 글이다. 첫 번째 문장에서 핵심 소재로 '고안해 낼 수 있는 능력'을, 주제로 '인간이 가진 능력은 창조성이다'를 파악할 수 있으며, 마지막 문장에서 이 주제를 다시 언급하여 '인간이 가진 창조성'을 강조하고 있다. 핵심 소재와 주제를 모두 포함하는 제목으로는 ④ 'Creativity: a Unique Trait Human Species Have For Survival(창의력: 인간이 생존을 위해 가지고 있는 독특한 특성)'이 적절하다.

[오답의 이유]

① 인간의 창조성은 어디에서 오는가?
② 영장류의 신체적인 특징은 무엇인가?
③ 다른 종들보다 뛰어난 호모 사피엔스의 신체적 장점들

본문해석

확실히, 다른 어떤 종도 황당한 것부터 심하게 터무니없는 것에 이르기까지 새롭고 독창적인 것을 고안해 낼 수 있는 우리의 능력에 대한 권리를 주장할 수 없다. 다른 동물들도 무언가를 만든다. 새들은 복잡한 동지를 조립하고, 비버는 댐을 만들고, 개미는 정교한 터널망을 판다. Fuentes는 말하기를, "그러나 비행기, 기이하게 기울어진 고층빌딩과 치아 펫은 정말 인상적이에요."라고 한다. 그는 진화적인 관점에서 덧붙이기를, "창조성이란 두 다리로 걷는 것, 큰 두뇌와 사물을 조작하는 데 참 좋은 손을 가진 것과 마찬가지로 우리의 도구 세트의 일부분이죠."라고 한다. 큰 송곳니나 발톱, 날개나 다른 명백한 신체적 이점이 없는, 육체적으로 볼품없는 영장류에게 있어서, 창조성은 위대한 보완책이었으며, 더 나아가서, 적어도 현재의 호모 사피엔스의 생존을 보장하는 것이다.

VOCA

- lay claim to ~에 대한 권리를 주장하다
- devise 고안하다
- sublimely 완전히
- ridiculous 웃기는, 말도 안 되는, 터무니없는
- assemble 조립하다
- intricate 복잡한
- elaborate 정교한
- tilt 기울다
- skyscraper 고층빌딩
- standpoint 관점, 견지
- unprepossessing 매력 없는, 호감을 주지 못하는
- primate 영장류

- fang 송곳니
- equalizer 동등하게 하는 것, 동점골

05 난도 ★☆☆ 정답 ①

독해 > 빈칸 완성 > 단어 · 구 · 절

[정답의 이유]

첫 번째 문장에서 핵심 소재 'bird identification(조류 식별)'과 주제 'Most of bird identification is based on a sort of subjective impression(대부분의 조류 식별은 ~ 일종의 주관적인 느낌에 기초한다) ~'을 제시하였다. 또한 글의 중반부에서 'All that combines to create a unique impression of a bird that can't really be taken apart(이 모든 것이 합쳐져서 새의 독특한 인상을 만들어 내는데, 그것은 실제로 분해될 수도 ~ 없다) ~'라고 하였으므로 글의 요지를 한 문장으로 요약하면 각 빈칸에 들어갈 말로 적절한 것은 ① '(A) instinctive impression(직관적인 느낌) – (B) discrete analysis(개별적인 분석)'이다.

[오답의 이유]

② 객관적 연구 – 주관적 판단
③ 신체적 외모 – 행동적 특성
④ 밀착 관찰 – 원격 관찰

본문해석

"대부분의 조류 식별은 새가 움직이는 방식과 다른 각도에서 보이는 아주 순간적인 외양 그리고 연속적으로 나타나는 서로 다른 모습과 같이 일종의 주관적인 느낌에 기초하며, 그것이 고개를 돌릴 때와 날아갈 때 그리고 방향을 바꿀 때 연속적인 다른 모양과 각도를 볼 수 있습니다."라며 Sibley는 말한다. "이 모든 것이 합쳐져서 새의 독특한 인상을 만들어 내는데, 그것은 실제로 분해될 수도, 말로 표현될 수도 없지요. 들판에서 새를 보게 되면, 당신은 그것을 분석하고 그것이 이렇게, 이렇게, 그리고 이렇게 보이는 것으로 보아 그것은 분명히 이런 종이라고 말하는 데 시간이 걸리지 않을 것입니다. 그것이 더 자연스럽고 직관적이죠. 많은 연습 후에, 새를 보면 그것이 당신의 뇌에 작은 스위치를 켭니다. 그것이 맞습니다. 당신은 한눈에 그게 무엇인지 알 것입니다."

⇩

Sibley의 말에 따르면, 조류 식별은 (B) 개별적인 분석보다는 (A) 직관적인 느낌에 기초한다.

VOCA

- identification 동일시하는[되는] 것, 식별
- subjective 주관적인
- instantaneous 즉각적인
- sequence 연속성, 연속적인 장면, 하나의 순서로 이루어진 움직임/장면들
- take apart 분해하다
- when it comes down to ~ing ~할 기회가 되면
- instinctive 직관적인, 본능적인
- trigger [총을] 쏘다, [방아쇠를] 당기다
- at a glance 첫눈에, 한눈에

독해 > 글의 일관성 > 글의 순서

정답의 이유

주어진 글에서 '~ are also likely to undergo significant changes (엄청난 변화를 겪을 가능성이 있다) ~'라고 했는데, 'In the not-too-distant future(머지 않은 미래에)'로 시작하는 (A)에서 필요할 때 운전자가 필요 없는 자동차를 이용할 수도 있다는 내용으로 이어지는 것이 자연스럽다. (A)의 마지막에서 카셰어링과 단기 임대의 증가로 자동차 외관 디자인의 중요성이 감소될 가능성이 있다고 했는데, (C)에서 자동차 외관이 점차 광고 및 홍보 활동을 위한 수단으로서의 채널을 대표하게 될 수 있다는 내용으로 이어진다. 마지막으로 이러한 변화를 (B)에서 As a result로 정리해주고 있으므로 주어진 글 다음에 이어질 글의 순서로 적절한 것은 ① '(A) – (C) – (B)'이다.

본문해석

자동차가 사람을 덜 의존하게 됨에 따라, 카셰어링과 단기 임대 프로그램의 사용이 높아짐과 동시에 상품이 소비자에 의해 사용되는 방식이나 상황 또한 엄청난 변화를 겪을 가능성이 있다.

(A) 머지않은 미래에, 운전자가 필요 없는 자동차가 당신이 필요할 때 당신에게 올 수도 있고, 당신이 이용을 끝내면 그것이 주차 공간을 찾을 필요도 없이 떠날 수도 있다. 카셰어링과 단기 임대의 증가는 또한 그에 상응하는 자동차 외관 디자인의 중요성의 감소와 연관될 가능성이 있다.

(C) 자동차의 외관은 개인화와 자기 동일성을 위한 수단의 역할을 하기보다는, 점차 Free Car Media에 의해 제공되는 브랜드 홍보대사 프로그램 같은 것들을 포함한 광고와 다른 홍보 활동을 위한 채널을 대표하게 될 수 있다.

(B) 결과적으로, 자동차에서 파생되는 상징적인 의미와 소비자의 자기 동일성 및 지위의 관계가 차례로 바뀔 가능성이 있다.

VOCA

- undergo 겪다
- significant 중대한, 심각한
- not-too-distant 머지않은
- corresponding 해당하는, 상응하는, 부합하는
- personalization 개인화; 인격화
- derive from ~에서 나오다, 유래하다, 파생하다
- channel 경로, 수단
- medium 매체, 도구, 수단
- brand ambassador 홍보 대사
- in turn 차례로, 교대로

독해 > 글의 일관성 > 글의 순서

정답의 이유

주어진 글의 끝부분에 '~ the doors were put on the hinges, the same as in America(자동차 문이 경첩에 달리는데, 이것은 미국에서도 똑같다).'가 있으므로 주어진 글 다음에는 그러한 작업의 연결선상에 있으면서 역접의 의미를 가지는 But이 등장하는 (A)가 와야 한다. (A)의 마지막 문장에 'In Japan, that job didn't seem to exist(일본에서는, 그러한 작업이 없는 것 같았다).'라고 나와 있으므로 이에 대한 미국 자동차 회사 임원들의 반응(당황함)과 질문을 서술한 (B)가 (A) 다음에 와야 한다. (B)에 제시된 일본 안내원의 설명을 자세하게 풀어쓴 것이 (General → Specific 두괄식) (C)이므로 주어진 글 다음에 이어질 글의 순서로 적절한 것은 ① '(A) – (B) – (C)'이다.

본문해석

일본의 조립 라인을 보기 위해 일본을 방문한 미국 자동차 회사 임원단의 놀랄 만한 이야기가 있다. 조립 라인 마지막 부분에, 자동차 문이 경첩에 달리는데, 이것은 미국에서도 똑같았다.

(A) 하지만 뭔가 빠져 있었다. 미국에서는, 조립 라인의 한 노동자가 차문이 완벽하게 끼워졌는지 확인하기 위해 고무망치를 가지고 차문의 가장자리를 두드려 본다. 일본에서는, 그러한 작업이 없는 것 같았다.

(B) 당황한 미국 자동차 회사 임원들은 어느 시점에 자동차 문이 완벽하게 들어맞는지 확인하는지를 물었다. 일본인 안내원이 그들을 쳐다보고 겸연쩍게 웃었다. "우리는 그것을 설계할 때 꼭 맞게 만듭니다."

(C) 일본 자동차 공장에서, 그들은 최적의 해결책을 찾기 위해 문제를 조사하고 데이터를 축적하지 않았다. 그들은 시작 단계에서부터 자신들이 원하는 결과가 나오도록 설계했다. 그들이 원하는 결과를 얻지 못했다면, 그것은 전체 과정을 시작할 때 내린 결정 때문이라고 그들은 이해했다.

VOCA

- assembly line 조립 라인
- hinge 경첩
- mallet 나무망치
- sheepishly 겸연쩍게, 멋쩍게, 소심하게
- engineer 수작을 부리다, 교묘하게 만들다; (설계해서) 제작하다
- outcome 결과

08 난도 ★☆☆　　　　　　　　　　　　　정답 ①

독해 > 빈칸 완성 > 연결어

[정답의 이유]

① 접속부사를 선택하는 문제로, 앞뒤 문장의 논리 관계를 판단해야 한다(접속부사는 해당 문장과 앞 문장의 관계를 설명한다). (A)의 앞 문장에는 '~ has strongly supported(강력하게 뒷받침했다)'라는 긍정적인 견해가 나와 있는 데 반해 (A)가 있는 문장에는 '~ not very strong or consistent(매우 강하지 않거나 혹은 일관적이지 않다)'라는 부정적인 견해가 나와 있으므로 이 두 내용은 역접의 접속부사로 연결해야 한다. 따라서 (A)에는 'However(하지만)'가 들어가야 한다. (B)의 앞 문장에는 '~ I have observed ~ different than(나는 ~ 다르다는 것을 발견해냈다) ~'이라는 말이 나와 있고 (B)가 있는 문장에는 '~ has grown weaker over time(더욱 설득력이 없어지고 있다).'이라는 말이 나와 있으므로 둘 다 부정적인 견해를 드러냈다. 이와 같이 둘은 같은 논조를 유지하고 있으므로 (B)에는 역접이 아닌 첨가의 접속부사 'what's more(게다가)'가 들어가야 한다.

[오답의 이유]

② 그 결과 − 대조적으로
③ 하지만 − 그럼에도 불구하고
④ 그 결과 − 예를 들어

본문해석

속임수를 알 수 있는 비언어적 단서에 대한 많은 연구들이 있었는데, 이는 Ekman의 연구와 그의 (기밀) 누출에 대한 아이디어로 거슬러 올라간다. 사람들이 다른 이들의 비언어적 행동을 거짓말을 감지하는 한 가지 방법으로 사용한다는 사실은 충분히 입증되었다. 나의 연구와 또 다른 많은 이들의 연구는 사람들이 정직성을 평가할 때 타인의 비언어적 행동 관찰에 의존한다는 것을 강력하게 뒷받침했다. (A) 하지만, 다양한 비언어적 행동과 거짓말을 하는 행동 사이의 연관성에 대한 사회 과학적 연구는 그 연관성이 일반적으로 매우 강하지 않거나 혹은 일관적이지 않다는 것을 보여준다. 내 연구에서, 나는 한 명의 거짓말쟁이가 누설하는 것처럼 보이는 비언어적 신호들이 두 번째 거짓말쟁이에 의해 주어지는 그것들(신호들)과 다르다는 것을 발견해냈다. (B) 게다가, 비언어적 행동들과 기만행위를 연관 짓는 과학적 증거들은 시간이 지남에 따라 더욱 설득력이 없어지고 있다. 사람들은 타인이 비언어적으로 자신을 나타내는 방식을 근거로 정직성을 추론하지만, 그것은 유용성과 타당성이 매우 제한적이다.

VOCA

- nonverbal　말로 할 수 없는, 말을 쓰지 않는
- deception　속임, 사기, 기만
- leakage　누출, 새어나감
- document　서류로 입증하다, 뒷받침하다
- well documented　(문서로 된) 관련 증거가 많은, 문서에 의해 충분히 입증된
- detect　발견하다, 알아내다, 감지하다
- give away　[정체를] 폭로하다; [비밀·진의 등을] 누설하다

- utility　유용성
- validity　타당성
- assess　~의 가치[성질, 능력]를 판단[평가]하다

09 난도 ★☆☆　　　　　　　　　　　　　정답 ③

어법 > 비문 찾기

[정답의 이유]

③ '요구하는(requiring) 보고서'가 아닌 '요구되는(required) 보고서'의 뜻으로, 수동의 의미를 갖는 과거분사가 와야 하므로 requiring → required가 되어야 한다.

[오답의 이유]

① 분사구문을 사용한 문장으로, 원래 문장 'as the banks start ~'를 보면 '주어−동사' 관계가 능동이므로 능동 의미인 현재분사(starting)가 올바르게 사용되었다.
② 관계부사(where)는 선행사가 존재하고 종속절에 완전한 문장이 따라오며, 해석상 'in[at]+which'를 집어넣어 올바른 의미인지 확인해야 한다. 선행사 areas 다음에 그 영역 '안에서' 일어나는 일을 완전한 문장으로 표현하였으므로 어법상 옳다.
④ is being made의 주어는 a decision으로, 문맥상 수동 관계이므로 진행형(be+−ing)과 수동태(be+p.p.)가 함께 올바르게 쓰였다.

본문해석

신생 기업은 법인 조직이 되자마자 은행 계좌가 필요할 것이며, 급여 계좌의 필요성도 빠르게 뒤따를 것이다. 은행들은 급여를 지급하고 관련 세무 부기를 처리하는 서비스에 있어서 매우 경쟁적인데, 심지어 가장 소규모 사업이라고 할지라도 그러하다. 이것들은 하나의 사업체가 최고 품질의 서비스와 대부분 '무료'인 회계 업무를 지원받기 원하는 분야이다. 변동이 있는 지급 급여 세법은 따라잡기가 골칫거리인데, 특히 50개 주나 되는 많은 지역에서 판매 인력이 활동하려고 할 때 그렇다. 그리고 요구하는(→ 요구되는) 보고서는 회사의 관리 직원에게 부담을 더한다. 그러한 서비스는 종종 은행원에 의해서 가장 잘 제공된다. 이 분야에서의 은행의 참고자료는 ADP와 같은 급여 지급 대체 서비스와 비교되어야 하지만, 결정을 내릴 때는 미래의 장기적인 관계를 염두에 두어야 한다.

VOCA

- start-up　신생 기업, 신규 업체(특히 인터넷 기업)
- incorporated　유한 책임의, 법인 조직의
- payroll　급여
- bookkeeping　부기
- sales force　판매 인력
- legislation　법안, 법제
- administrative　일반 관리, 행정

관계부사 where

• 관계부사의 기능

접속사＋부사	선행사를 수식하는 형용사절을 이끌면서 그 절에서 '접속사＋부사'의 역할을 한다.
전치사＋관계대명사	선행사를 수식하는 형용사절을 이끌며, '전치사＋관계대명사'로 바꿔 쓸 수 있다.

예 A mutual aid group is *a place* where an individual brings a problem and asks for assistance.

(상조모임은 개인이 문제를 가져와 도움을 요청하는 곳이다.)

예 Trees must be fitted for *the places* where they live.

→ where＝in which

(나무들은 그들이 살고 있는 장소에 맞아야 한다.)

• 관계부사와 관계대명사의 차이

구분	선행사	관계절 형태
관계부사	있음	관계부사 다음에는 완전한 문장이 온다.
관계대명사		관계대명사 다음에는 불완전한 문장이 온다(관계절의 주어, 목적어 역할).

예 He proposed creating *a space* where musicians would be able to practice for free. → 관계부사

(그는 음악가들이 무료로 연습할 수 있는 공간을 만들자고 제안했다.)

예 She wants to rent *the apartment* which she saw last Sunday. → 관계대명사

(그녀는 지난 일요일에 보았던 아파트를 빌리고 싶어 한다.)

10 난도 ★★☆　　정답 ①

어문 > 비문 찾기

정답의 이유

① 감정동사(depress, surprise, amaze 등)는 주어가 감정의 원인이면 현재분사(-ing)를, 주어가 감정을 느끼는 대상이면 과거분사(p.p.)를 써야 한다. 문맥상 find의 목적어 it(=to visit animal shelters)이 감정의 원인이므로 depressed → depressing이 되어야 한다.

오답의 이유

② 관계부사(where)는 선행사가 있고, 종속절에 완전한 문장이 온다. 선행사(streets) 다음에 완전한 절(they're ~ the elements)이 왔으므로 관계부사 where가 어법상 올바르게 쓰였다.

③ 문맥상 '주인들에 의해 발견되고 되찾아지다'라는 뜻으로, 동사(are found) 다음에 목적어가 없으므로 수동태가 올바르게 쓰였다.

④ 형용사(adoptable)가 명사(pets)를 수식하므로 어법상 올바르게 사용되었다.

많은 사람들이 동물보호소를 방문하는 게 너무 슬프거나 우울하다고 느끼기 때문에 그곳에 방문하기를 거부한다. 그들이 그렇게 안 좋게 느끼지 않아야 하는 이유는 아주 많은 유종은 동물들이 교통사고의 위험, 다른 동물이나 인간의 공격을 받을 위험과 비바람을 맞기 쉬운 길거리의 위험한 삶에서 구조되기 때문이다. 또한 많은 길잃은 애완동물들이 단지 동물보호소로 이송되었다는 이유만으로 마음이 심란한 주인들에 의해 발견되고 되찾아진다. 가장 중요한 것은, 입양할 수 있는 동물들이 집을 찾고, 아프거나 위험에 처한 동물들은 인도적으로 고통을 덜게 된다는 것이다.

VOCA

• animal shelter 동물보호소
• depressing 우울한, 우울한 감정을 만드는
• be subject to ~을 당하기(입기) 쉬운, 걸리기 쉬운
• elements 비바람, 악천후
• likewise 또한, 마찬가지로
• reclaim 되찾다, 되돌려 달라고 하다
• distraught 심란한, (흥분해서) 완전히 제정신이 아닌
• adoptable 양자로 삼을 수 있는, 입양할 수 있는
• relieve ~ of … ~의 …을 덜어주다

11 난도 ★★☆　　정답 ②

독해 > 빈칸 완성 > 단어 · 구 · 절

정답의 이유

(A) 자신을 매우 사회적으로 책임감 있다고 믿었던 여성의 검사 결과에 대한 내용으로, (A) 다음 문장에서 자신의 점수에 매우 실망했다고 하였으므로 그녀의 기대와 다르게 '평균적인(average)' 결과가 나왔음을 추론할 수 있다.

(B) 인과관계를 설명하는 접속부사 therefore의 앞부분에서 그녀는 사회적 책임에 매우 높은 기준을 가지고 있었다고 했으므로 평가할 때 자기 자신에게 '엄격했음(hard)'을 추론할 수 있다.

(C) 앞 문장에서 자기 자신에게 엄격했다는 내용과 연결해야 한다. 자신의 높은 기준으로 보았을 때 자신에게 실망한 것이므로 실제로는(In reality) 책임감이 없어서 실망한 것이 아니라 책임감이 '더 많은(more)' 편이었지만 그조차도 만족하지 못했다는 설명이 논리상 적절하다.

오답의 이유

① 평균적인 – 관대한 – 더 적게
③ 보기 드문 – 엄격한 – 더 적게
④ 보기 드문 – 관대한 – 더 많이

본문해석

EQ 검사는 신뢰할 수 있는 테스트 방식으로 진행될 때 여러분들에게 여러분 자신에 대한 매우 유용한 정보를 제공할 수 있다. 나는 몇천 명의 사람들을 검사해 보았고, 많은 사람들이 그들의 결과에 다소 놀라워한다는 사실을 발견했다. 예를 들어, 자신이 매우 사회적으로 책임감이 있고 타인에 대해 신경 쓴다고 믿고 있었던 한 여성은 그 부분에서 (A) 평균적인 점수를 보였다. 그녀는 자신의 점수에 매우 실망했다. 그녀는 사회적 책임감에 매우 높은 기준을 가지고 있었으므로, 자기 자신을 평가할 때 극도로 (B) 엄격했던 것으로 드러났다. 사실, 그녀는 대다수 사람보다 사회적 책임감이 (C) 더 많았지만, 그녀 자신은 그보다 더 잘할 수 있다고 믿었던 것이다.

VOCA

- reliable 신뢰할 만한, 믿음직한
- come out with ~을 하다; ~을 보여주다, 공표하다
- extraordinary 특출한, 뛰어난
- assessment 평가
- in reality 사실은[실제로는]

12 난도 ★★☆ 정답 ②

독해 > 빈칸 완성 > 단어·구·절

[정답의 이유]

주제가 앞부분에 등장하는 두괄식 구성의 글로, 나머지 내용을 전부 이해한 후 전체 내용을 요약할 수 있는 문장을 완성하면 된다. 두 가지 사례 모두 질문에 대해 사실의 특정 부분만 떼어 대답함으로써 '잘못된 사실을 믿게 만든다'는 내용이므로 빈칸에 들어갈 말로 가장 적절한 것은 ② 'effect a certain belief(특정한 믿음을 초래하다)'이다.

[오답의 이유]

① 추가 금액을 벌다
③ 기억 문제를 숨기다
④ 다른 이들이 죄책감이 들도록 하다

본문해석

사람은 자신에게 유리한 증거를 사용해 특정한 믿음을 초래하려고 노력할지도 모른다. 한 어머니가 아들에게 묻는다. "이번 학기에 영어는 잘하고 있니?" 아들은 명랑하게 대답한다. "아, 저 이번 쪽지 시험에서 95점을 받았어요." 이 말은 그가 다른 모든 쪽지 시험을 망쳤고, 그의 실제 평균은 55점이라는 사실을 감추고 있다. 하지만, 만일 이 문제를 더 추궁하지 않는다면, 어머니는 아들이 잘하고 있음을 기뻐할지도 모른다. Linda가 Susan에게 묻는다. "Dickens 소설 많이 읽어봤어?" Susan이 대답하기를, "아, *Pickwick Papers*가 내가 가장 좋아하는 소설 중 하나지."라고 한다. 이 진술은 *Pickwick Papers*가 그녀가 읽은 유일한 Dickens의 소설이라는 사실을 숨기고, 이는 아마 Linda에게 Susan이 엄청난 Dickens의 광팬이라는 인상을 줄지도 모른다.

VOCA

- effect (어떤 결과를) 가져오다, 초래하다

- evidence 증거, 흔적
- advantage 유리한 점, 이점, 장점
- statement 성명, 진술, 서술
- conceal 감추다, 숨기다
- pursue 쫓다
- delighted 아주 기뻐[즐거워]하는
- disguise 변장하다, 위장하다
- enthusiast 열광적인 지지자

13 난도 ★☆☆ 정답 ①

독해 > 빈칸 완성 > 단어·구·절

[정답의 이유]

① 첫 번째 문장에서 핵심 소재로 '칭찬'을 제시하고 있으며, 두 번째 문장과 However로 시작하는 세 번째 문장에서 칭찬이 도움이 되기도 하지만 포괄적인 일반화를 하지는 말자는 화자의 논조를 파악할 수 있다. (A)에는 핵심 소재인 'praise(칭찬)'가 들어가야 한다. 칭찬이 긍정적·부정적일 수 있는 기준으로 네 번째 문장에서 'on certain tasks, on others(=other tasks)'를 통해 과업의 유형에 따라 다를 수 있다는 견해를 제시하므로 (B)에는 quality of teamwork(협동작업의 질)이 아닌 'task types(과업의 유형)'가 들어가야 한다.

[오답의 이유]

② 경쟁 – 협동작업의 질
③ 칭찬 – 협동작업의 질
④ 경쟁 – 과업의 종류

본문해석

우리의 외모, 정원, 우리가 준비한 저녁 식사 혹은 회사 업무에 대해 칭찬을 받든지 간에, 잘한 일로 인정받는 것은 언제나 만족감을 준다. 확실히, 강화 이론은 가끔의 칭찬을 새로운 기술 학습에 도움이 되는 것으로 본다. 하지만, 일부 증거는 수행을 향상시키기 위해 칭찬을 하는 것과 관련하여 포괄적인 일반화를 하지 않아야 한다고 경고한다. 어떤 과업에서는 칭찬이 수행을 향상시키지만, 또 다른 과업에서는 오히려 해로운 것으로 판명되는 것 같다. 승리를 기대하는 홈팬들의 열광적인 응원이 그 팀의 몰락을 가져오는 상황을 상상해 보아라. 이러한 상황에서, 칭찬은 운동선수들에게 압박을 주며, 그들의 경기력에 지장을 주는 것으로 보인다.

⇩

(A) 칭찬이 수행에 도움이 되느냐 해가 되느냐는 (B) 과업의 유형에 달려 있다.

VOCA

- assignment 과제, 임무
- caution ~하지 말라고 주의를 주다, 경고를 주다
- sweeping 전면적인, 광범위한, 포괄적인
- task 과업
- enthusiastic 열광적인
- downfall 몰락
- disrupt 방해하다, 지장을 주다

어법 > 비문 찾기

정답의 이유

③ 문맥상 read는 앞에 나온 가주어 it의 원래 주어인 진주어임을 알 수 있다. It(가주어) ~ 진주어 구문에서 진주어는 to부정사나 that절 형태가 되어야 하므로 read → to read로 수정해야 한다.

오답의 이유

① 등위접속사 or는 병렬 구조로 연결되므로 동명사 viewing, going, reading을 올바르게 연결했다.

② 관계대명사절 동사의 수, 시제 일치를 묻는 문제이다. 관계대명사 that은 선행사 social rules를 수식하며, 3인칭 복수명사를 서술하는 동사로 현재형 govern을 올바르게 사용했다.

④ despite(~에도 불구하고)는 전치사로 다음에 명사[명사 상당 어구]가 와야 하는데, despite 다음에 '명사(the fact)+동격의 명사절(that the relationships are totally impersonal)'이 왔으므로 올바르게 쓰였다.

본문해석

익명의 사회적 관계라는 맥락에서 미디어 소비를 고려할 때 술집과 같은 공공장소에서 텔레비전을 보는 것, 콘서트나 댄스 클럽에 가는 것, 혹은 버스나 지하철에서 신문을 읽는 것과 같이 낯선 사람들의 존재를 포함하는 모든 경우를 의미한다. 일반적으로, 우리가 주변 사람들과, 그리고 미디어 제품과 상호작용을 하는 방식을 통제하는 사회적인 규칙이 존재한다. 예를 들어, 다른 사람의 어깨 너머로 (그가 읽는 것을) 읽는다거나 혹은 공공장소에서 일어나 TV 채널을 바꾸는 것은 우리 문화에서 무례한 것으로, 혹은 적어도 과격한 것으로 여겨진다. 음악 팬이라면 특정한 콘서트 형태에서 무엇이 적절한 행동인지를 알고 있다. 다른 사람들의 존재는, 그 관계가 전적으로 개인적인 정을 나누지 않는다는 사실에도 불구하고, 종종 그 환경을 규정하고 그에 따라 미디어 소비 활동을 규정하는 데에 결정적이다.

VOCA

· anonymous 익명의, 특색 없는

· occasion 때, 경우

· aggressive 공격적인

· appropriate 적절한

· setting (주변) 환경, 배경

· impersonal 특정 개인과 상관없는, 개인적인 정을 나누지 않는

어법 > 비문 찾기

정답의 이유

③ 주어는 name and identity가 아닌 inability이며 3인칭 불가산 명사이므로 단수 취급하여 be동사를 are → is로 써야 한다.

오답의 이유

① the way를 수식하는 관계부사절의 주어 amnesia는 해석상 '묘사하는' 것이 아니라 '묘사되는' 것이므로 과거분사(portrayed)가 올바르게 사용되었다.

② spend는 돈이나 시간을 '쓰다'라는 의미이며 'spend+(돈, 시간)+(on)+-ing' 형태로 쓰이므로 trying이 올바르게 사용되었다. 같은 뜻으로 take를 쓸 때에는 'take+(돈, 시간)+to부정사' 형태로 쓰인다.

④ 부대상황을 나타내는 'with+명사+형용사' 분사구문으로 형용사 intact가 올바르게 쓰였다.

본문해석

우리 중 다수는 기억상실증, 즉 갑작스런 기억의 상실이 자신의 이름이나 정체성을 기억하지 못하는 결과로 이어진다고 믿는다. 이러한 믿음은 보통 영화, TV, 그리고 문학 작품에서 기억상실증이 묘사된 방식을 반영하는 것일지도 모른다. 예를 들어, 우리가 영화 *The Bourne Identity*(본 아이덴티티)에서 Matt Damon이 연기한 인물을 볼 때, 그는 자기 자신이 누구인지, 자신이 왜 그런 기술들을 가지고 있는지, 혹은 그가 어디에서 왔는지 전혀 기억하지 못한다. 그는 영화의 상당 부분을 이 질문들에 답하기 위해 노력하는 데 할애한다. 하지만, 당신의 이름과 정체성을 기억해내지 못하는 것은 현실에서는 대단히 드물다. 기억상실은 뇌 손상에 의한 것이 가장 흔한데, 이는 환자가 새로운 기억을 형성하지 못하게 할 뿐, 과거의 대부분의 기억은 온전하다. 어떤 영화들은 더 흔한 이 증상을 정확하게 묘사하는데, 우리가 좋아하는 *Memento*이다.

VOCA

· amnesia 기억상실증

· portray (풍경 따위)를 묘사하다; ~을 극적으로 표현하다

· exceedingly 대단히

· victim 희생자

· intact 온전한, 전혀 다치지 않은

· accurately 정확히, 정밀하게

· syndrome 증후군, 증상

16 난도 ★★☆　　　　　　　　　　정답 ②

독해 > 빈칸 완성 > 단어 · 구 · 절

정답의 이유

첫 번째 문장에서 핵심 소재로 'natural hazards(자연재해)'를 제시하였으며, However가 포함된 세 번째 문장에서 'humans are not always rational(사람이 언제나 이성적인 것은 아니다).'이라는 주제를 제시하였으므로 맨 마지막 문장의 빈칸에는 그 주제문에 부합하는 내용이 들어가야 한다. 따라서 빈칸에 들어갈 말로 적절한 것은 ② 'do not always act appropriately(언제나 적절하게 행동하는 것은 아니다)'이다.

오답의 이유

① 침묵하기를 거부한다
③ 유전적 요인을 가장 꼭대기에 둔다
④ 자연재해를 정의하는 데에는 어려움이 있다

본문해석

자연재해와 그것이 사람들과 그들의 재산에 미치는 부정적인 영향에 대해서는 현재 많은 것이 알려져 있다. 논리적인 사람이라면 그러한 잠재적인 영향을 피하거나, 혹은 그러한 영향을 최소화하기 위해 적어도 그들의 행동이나 그들의 재산을 변경하리라는 것은 명백해 보인다. 하지만, 사람이 언제나 이성적인 것은 아니다. 개인적인 경험을 하거나 혹은 그러한 경험을 한 사람을 알게 될 때까지, 대부분의 사람들은 무의식적으로 '여기서는 일어나지 않을 거야.' 또는 '나에게 일어나지는 않을 거야.'라고 믿는다. 심지어 위험 요소, 사건의 발생 가능성과 사건의 손실을 알고 있는 박식한 과학자들조차도 언제나 적절하게 행동하는 것은 아니다.

VOCA

• natural hazard (지리학) 자연재해
• property 소유물, 건물, 재산
• modify (모양 · 성질 · 계획 · 의견 따위)를 변경하다, 수정하다
• subconsciously 무의식적으로
• knowledgeable 아는 것이 많은, 많이 아는
• odds 공산, 가능성
• occurrence 발생

17 난도 ★☆☆　　　　　　　　　　정답 ③

독해 > 대의 파악 > 제목, 주제

정답의 이유

첫 번째 문장에서 핵심 소재로 'specialization(전문화)'을 제시하고 있으며, 이 핵심 소재가 들어가 있는 선지는 ③뿐이다. 이후에는 전문화된 직업의 나열, 전문화에 따른 교역의 발달을 설명하고 있다. 따라서 이 글의 주제로 적절한 것은 ③ 'what made people engage in specialization and trade(사람들을 전문화와 교역에 참여하게 만든 것)'이다.

오답의 이유

① 기후와 토양이 지역 상품에 얼마나 영향을 미치는가
② 지역 특산물을 위해 좋은 평판을 얻는 방법
④ 도시의 번영과 전문직들의 상근직 고용

본문해석

도시와 왕국의 번영과 교통 인프라의 발전은 전문화를 위한 새로운 기회를 가져왔다. 인구 밀도가 높은 도시들은 전문적인 제화공들과 의사들뿐만 아니라 목수, 성직자, 군인, 그리고 변호사들에게도 상근직 고용을 제공했다. 정말 훌륭한 와인, 올리브 오일 또는 도자기를 만든다는 명성을 얻은 마을들은 그 상품을 거의 독점적으로 전문화하고 그들이 필요했던 다른 모든 제품을 위해 다른 촌락들과 그것을 교역할 가치가 있음을 발견했다. 이것은 타당했다. 기후와 토양은 다르므로 토양과 기후가 포도 덩굴에 훨씬 더 적합한 곳에서 난 더 부드러운 품종을 구입할 수 있는데 왜 당신의 뒤뜰에서 난 그저 그런 와인을 마시겠는가? 만일 당신 뒤뜰의 점토가 더 단단하고 더 예쁜 도자기를 만들어낼 수 있다면, 당신은 교환할 수 있다.

VOCA

• full-time employment 상근, 매일 일정한 시간에 근무함
• be worth one's while ～할 가치가 있다
• mediocre 썩 좋지는 않은
• smoother smooth(부드러운)의 비교급
• variety 품종

독해 > 세부 내용 찾기 > 지칭 추론

정답의 이유

밑줄 친 'the issue'가 있는 문장, '~ signed a bill ~ banned "lunch shaming," or giving worse food to students with debt ~'와 제시문의 전체 내용을 통해 'the issue'가 가리키는 것이 '급식비 미납 학생과 관련된 문제'임을 알 수 있다. 따라서 밑줄 친 the issue가 가리키는 내용은 ④ 'Many students in the district who could not afford lunch were burdened with lunch debt(그 지역에서 급식비를 낼 수 없는 많은 학생들이 급식비 미납의 부담을 짊어졌다).'이다.

오답의 이유

① 주지사는 급식비 미납 학생들의 급식 품목을 축소하는 법안에 서명했다.

② Kyote는 급식비 계좌에 돈이 떨어져 급식을 빼앗겼다.

③ 재정 부담을 겪는 학구는 예산을 삭감하여 양질의 급식을 제공하지 못했다.

본문해석

아홉 살인 Ryan Kyote는 캘리포니아주 Napa에 있는 집에서 아침을 먹고 있을 때, 인디애나주의 한 학교가 6살 아이의 급식비 계좌에 충분한 돈이 없어서 그녀의 식사를 빼앗았다는 뉴스를 보았다. Kyote는 그의 친구들에게도 그런 일이 일어날 수 있는지를 물었다. 그의 엄마가 알아보기 위해 지역 교육청에 연락했을 때, 그들 지역에 있는 학교의 학생들이 통틀어 25,000달러의 급식비를 내지 못하고 있다는 것을 알게 되었다. 그 지역은 미납 학생들에게 절대로 불이익을 준 적이 없다고 말하지만, Kyote는 자신이 저축해 둔 용돈을 그와 같은 학년 학생의 미납금을 위해 사용하기로 결심했고, 그것은 약 74달러였다. 이것은 급식비 미납금 청산을 위한 운동의 국면이 되었다. 10월에 캘리포니아 주지사 Gavin Newsom은 '대체 급식으로 망신 주는 것', 즉 급식비 미납 학생들에게 더 질 나쁜 음식을 제공하는 것을 금지하는 법안에 서명했으며, 그는 이 문제에 대한 의식을 높이는 데 있어서 Kyote의 '공감과 용기'에 감사를 표했다. Kyote는 "영웅들은 예나 지금이나 나옵니다."라고 지적한다.

VOCA

- district 지역, 구역, 지역구
- all told 모두 합쳐서, 통틀어
- bill 법안
- penalize 벌칙을 가하다, 처벌하다
- ban 금하다
- raise awareness 의식을 높이다
- point out 가리키다, 지적하다

독해 > 세부 내용 찾기 > 내용 (불)일치

정답의 이유

마지막 문장에 'generally travel in pairs(일반적으로 짝을 지어 이동하며)'라고 되어 있으므로 글의 내용과 일치하지 않는 것은 ④이다.

오답의 이유

① · ② 여섯 번째 문장에서 직접 언급하였다.

③ 첫 번째 문장의 'The biggest heart in the world ~'에서 심장이 가장 크다고 하였고, 일곱 번째 문장의 'the largest animal who ever lived ~'에서 가장 큰 동물이라고 언급하였다.

본문해석

세상에서 가장 큰 심장은 청고래[흰긴수염고래] 안에 있다. 그것은 무게가 7톤이 넘는다. 그것은 방 하나만큼 크다. 이 생명체는 태어날 때 길이가 20피트에 무게가 4톤이나 나간다. 그것은 당신의 자동차보다 훨씬 더 크다. 그것은 매일 어미로부터 100갤런의 우유를 마시고 하루에 200파운드씩 몸집이 커지는데, 7세나 8세가 되면 상상할 수 없는 사춘기를 견뎌내고 그런 다음 기본적으로 인간의 시야에서 사라지며 짝짓기 습성, 이동 패턴, 식성, 사회적 관계, 언어, 사회 구조와 질병에 대해 거의 알려진 것이 없다. 아마도 전 세계에 약 10,000마리의 청고래가 지구의 모든 바다에 살고 있을 것인데, 지금까지 살았던 가장 큰 동물에 관해 인간이 알아낸 것은 거의 없다. 하지만 우리는 다음과 같은 것을 알고 있다. 세계에서 가장 큰 심장을 가진 이 동물들은 일반적으로 짝을 지어 이동하며, 그들의 날카로운 울음소리, 귀청을 찢는 사랑의 언어는 몇 마일이나 멀리 떨어진 물속에서도 들릴 수 있다.

VOCA

- way 큰 차이로, 훨씬
- unimaginable 상상할 수도 없는
- puberty 사춘기, 성장기
- ken 알다, 시야, 안계; 지식의 범위, 이해의 범위 (beyond one's ken: ~의 이해력 밖의)
- essentially 본질적으로; 본래(는); 반드시
- next to nothing 거의 제로에 가까운, 없는 것이나 다름없는
- penetrating 귀를 찢는 듯한, 날카로운
- moan 신음하다
- piercing 날카로운
- yearning 동경, 사모

독해 > 대의 파악 > 제목, 주제

정답의 이유

첫 번째 문장에서 핵심 소재로 'produce(농산물)'를, 주제로 'when handling fresh produce, control of the atmosphere is important(농산물 취급 시 공기 조절은 중요하다)'를 파악할 수 있으며, 마지막 문장에서 이 주제를 다시 언급하여 'Related to the control of gases and moisture is the need for some circulation of air among the stored foods(공기와 수분 조절과 관련하여 저장된 음식에 어느 정도의 공기 순환이 필요하다는 것이다).'라고 했다. 핵심 소재와 주제를 모두 포함하는 선택지는 ④ 'The importance of controlling certain levels of gases and moisture in storing foods(식품 저장 시 공기와 수분 조절의 중요성)'이다.

오답의 이유

① 대기 중 유해 기체 관리의 필요성
② 식물과 과일 재배 시 최적의 수분 조절법
③ 매년 전 세계적으로 증가하는 탄소발자국의 심각성

본문해석

신선한 농산물을 취급할 때 온도를 조절하는 것 외에도, 공기의 조절은 중요하다. 보관 중 건조를 막기 위해서 공기 중에 약간의 수분이 필요하지만, 너무 많은 수분은 곰팡이의 성장을 촉진할 수 있다. 일부 상업용 창고는 공기를 조절하는데, 신중하게 이산화탄소와 습도의 수준을 조절한다. 가끔은 에틸렌 가스 같은 다른 기체를 세심하게 농도를 조절해 투입할 수도 있는데, 이는 바나나와 다른 신선한 농산물을 최적의 품질로 만드는 데 도움을 주기 위해서다. 공기와 수분 조절과 관련하여 저장된 음식에 어느 정도의 공기 순환이 필요하다는 것이다.

VOCA

• atmosphere 대기, 공기; 분위기
• dehydration 건조, 탈수
• mold 곰팡이
• optimal 최선의, 최상의, 최적의

독해 > 글의 일관성 > 무관한 어휘·문장

정답의 이유

④의 앞 문장에서 병자에게 거짓말을 하면 긍정적인 결과가 나올 수 있다고 했으며, On the other hand로 시작하는 문장은 그 반대 경우를 묘사하는 문장이다. 반대되는 경우는 병자에게 진실을 말했을 때 부정적인 결과가 나와야 하고, 여기서는 우울증을 막는 것이 아니라 유발할 수 있으므로 ④에는 cause, trigger, encourage, induce(유발하다) 등이 들어가야 한다.

오답의 이유

① 앞 문장에서 거짓말의 부정적인 결과에 대해 언급하고, For instance를 통해 부연설명을 해주는 문장이다. 거짓말을 한 상황이므로 신뢰를 얻는 것이 아니라 잃는 것이 거짓말의 부정적인 결과이므로 'undermined'는 적절하게 사용되었다.
② 앞에서 거짓말의 부정적 결과를 묘사했으며, Thus를 통해 그 논조를 이어가고 있다. 긍정적인 영향이 아닌 부정적인 영향을 끼치는 것이 논리상 올바르다.
③ outweigh, surpass 등은 의미상 비교급 표현인 동사들이다. 비교의 대상은 언제나 동등한 대상 둘의 반대되는 특성이므로 주어(harmful effects)와 반대되는 것으로 benefits는 적절하다.

본문해석

거짓말이 어떤 상황에서는 아무런 해를 끼치지 않는다고 할지라도, 만일 알려진다면 거짓말은 인간의 의사소통이 따르는 진실을 말하는 일반적 관행을 약화시키기 때문에 여전히 도덕적으로 옳지 않다. 예를 들어, 만일 내가 허영을 부리기 위해 내 나이를 속이고, 내 거짓말이 들통난다면, 아무런 심각한 피해가 발생하지 않았다고 할지라도 나는 전반적으로 당신의 신뢰를 서서히 약화시켰을 것이다. 그러한 경우에 당신은 내가 이후에 말하는 모든 것을 믿을 가능성이 매우 적을 것이다. 그러므로 모든 거짓말은, 알려질 때, 간접적인 해로운 영향을 끼친다. 그러나 아주 가끔은, 거짓말로 생기는 이로움에 의해 아마도 이러한 해로운 영향의 결점을 메우기에 충분할지도 모른다. 예를 들어, 만일 누군가가 심각하게 아프다면, 그들의 기대 수명에 대해 거짓말하는 것은 그들에게 더 오래 살 기회를 주는 것이 될지도 모른다. 반면에, 그들에게 사실을 말해주는 것은 신체적 쇠약을 가속화시킬 우울증을 막을(→ 유발할) 가능성이 있다.

VOCA

• on grounds of ~을 이유[근거]로
• vanity 자만, 허영; 자만심, 허영심; 헛됨, 무의미
• undermine 약화시키다
• outweigh ~보다 더 크다, 대단하다, ~의 결점을 메우기에 충분하다
• life expectancy 기대 수명
• accelerate 가속화되다, 가속화하다

독해 > 글의 일관성 > 문장 삽입

정답의 이유

주어진 문장의 'also(또한)'는 앞 문장과 같은 논조를 펼치며 새로운 소재를 소개할 때 쓰이므로 주어진 문장은 '물은 생명을 유지하기 위해 필요하다'라는 논조를 가진 문장 뒷부분에 들어가야 함을 알 수 있다. 물이 해양 생명체에 도움이 된다는 내용은 ②의 앞 문장이므로 주어진 문장은 ②에 들어가야 한다.

본문해석

해수의 일반적인 몇 가지 특성들은 해양 서식동물들의 생존과 복지에 필수적이다. 물은 대부분의 해양 생물들 부피의 80~90퍼센트를 차지한다. 이것은 수영하고 떠다니는 생명체들에게 부력을 제공하고 몸을 지탱해주며 무거운 골격계의 필요성을 줄인다. 물은 또한 생명 유지에 필요한 대부분의 화학 반응을 위한 매개물이다. 해양 생명체들의 삶의 과정은 결국 그 투명성과 화학적 구성을 포함한 해수의 기본적인 물리적, 화학적 성질을 많이 변화시켜서 생명체를 전체 해양 환경의 필수 불가결한 부분으로 만든다. 생물들과 그들의 해양 환경 사이의 상호 작용을 이해하기 위해 필요한 것은 해수의 물리적, 화학적 특성 중 보다 중요한 몇 가지를 간단히 검사해 보는 것이다. 담수와 해수의 특성은 많은 부분에서 다르므로 우리는 먼저 담수의 기본적인 특성을 고려한 뒤 그 특성들이 해수에서는 어떻게 다른지 조사한다.

VOCA

• property 특성, 고유성, 속성
• inhabitant (특정 지역의) 주민[서식 동물]
• account for 해명하다; (부분, 비율을) 차지하다
• buoyancy 부력
• medium 수단, 매체, 매개물
• integral 필수적인
• transparency 투명도
• attribute 자질, 속성

독해 > 빈칸 완성 > 단어 · 구 · 절

정답의 이유

이러한 유형의 문제는 글의 흐름을 잘 따라가면 된다. 정확하게 그 단어의 뜻이 문맥과 어울리는지보다, 맥락상 부정적인 단어가 들어갈 것인지, 긍정적인 단어가 들어갈 것인지를 판단하는 것이 도움이 된다.

(A) 글의 전체 논조에 대한 가장 큰 힌트는 세 번째 문장의 and 다음 부분에서 찾을 수 있다. 'the players got better than ever'라는 표현을 통해 AI에 대해 비판적인 시각보다는 우호적인 시각임을 알아낼 수 있으므로 (A)에는 인간의 경기력을 'diminish(약화시키지)' 않았다가 논리적으로 옳다.

(B) 체스 프로그램에 대한 우호적인 관점을 표현하는 것은 'inspired(고무하였다)'이다.

(C) AI가 도움이 되었다는 전체 논조에 따라 AI로 훈련한 이 선수는 'highest(가장 높은)' 순위를 보유한다고 보는 것이 논리적으로 옳다.

오답의 이유

① 약화시키다 – 의욕을 꺾었다 – 가장 높은
② 증가시키다 – 의욕을 꺾었다 – 가장 낮은
④ 증가시키다 – 고무하였다 – 가장 낮은

본문해석

여기에 다음과 같이 훨씬 더 놀라운 점이 있다. AI의 등장은 순수하게 인간 체스 선수들의 경기력을 (A) 약화시키지 않았다. 오히려 반대다. 값싸고 매우 똑똑한 체스 프로그램들은 그 어느 때보다 더 많은 사람들이 그 어느 때보다 많은 체스경기에서 체스를 두게끔 (B) 고무하였으며 체스 선수들은 그 어느 때보다 더 잘 하고 있다. 현재는 Deep Blue가 Kasparov를 처음 이겼을 때보다 2배 이상의 그랜드 마스터(최고 수준의 체스 선수)들이 있다. 현재 체스 랭킹 1위인 인간 체스 선수는 Magnus Carlsen인데, 그는 AI들을 이용해 훈련하였으며 모든 인간 체스 선수 중에 가장 컴퓨터 같다고 여겨진다. 그는 또한 역사상 (C) 가장 높은 인간 그랜드 마스터 순위를 보유하고 있다.

VOCA

• advent 등장, 시작, 도입
• diminish 약화시키다, 줄이다, 낮아지다
• top-ranked 최상위의
• ranking 순위, 평가
• deem 간주하다, 생각하다, 여기다

독해 > 빈칸 완성 > 단어 · 구 · 절

정답의 이유

첫 번째 문장에서 핵심 소재로 'fashion objects(패션 제품)'을 제시하였고, 'self-oriented(자기 지향적)'라는 주제가 등장한다. However로 시작하는 세 번째 문장에서 'is also other-oriented(또한 타자 지향적이기도 하다)'라고 했으므로 글의 내용을 요약할 때 빈칸에 들어갈 말로 가장 적절한 것은 ③ 'both self-oriented and other-oriented(자기 지향적인 동시에 타자 지향적)'이다.

오답의 이유

① 본질적으로 오직 자기 지향적
② 다른 것들과는 다르게 오직 타자 지향적
④ 그 본질과 관계없이 정의하기 어려운

본문해석

패션 제품들의 미적 가치는 순수 미술 작품들의 미적 가치와 마찬가지로 자기 지향적이다. 소비자들은 (그 제품들에) 매력을 느끼려 하고 매력적인 사람들로 둘러싸이고자 하는 욕구를 가진다. 하지만, 순수 예술의 미적 가치와는 다르게, 패션의 미적 가치는 또한 타자 지향적이기도 하다. 외모의 매력은 타인의 반응을 끌어내고 사회적 상호작용을 촉발시키는 방식이다.

⇩

패션 제품들의 미적 가치는 자기 지향적인 동시에 타자 지향적이다.

VOCA

- aesthetic 미적인, 미적
- fine art 순수 예술
- self-oriented 자기 지향적인, 자기 자신에 집중한
- other-oriented 타자 지향적인
- elicit 끌어내다
- facilitate (행동 · 조치 등을) 촉진[조성]하다
- inherently 본질적으로; 타고나서

독해 > 글의 일관성 > 문장 삽입

정답의 이유

주어진 문장에는 대명사 'this'가 있으며, 이것이 어떤 것을 가리키고 있는지 찾아 그다음 부분에 위치시키면 된다. 또 하나의 중요한 힌트는 주어진 문장 내에서, '꿈을 기억하든 기억하지 못하든 간에'라는 조건이 등장했다는 점이다. 따라서 꿈을 기억할 때의 장점만을 서술한 ①의 앞 문장을 기준으로 이 기억할 때의 장점에 관련된 이야기가 언제 끝나는지, 기억과 상관없는 꿈의 장점이 어디에서 시작하는지를 체크해야 한다. 기억과 상관없이 꿈이 도움이 된다는 이야기는 유일하게 ④의 다음 문장에 등장하므로 정답은 ④이다. 대명사 'this'가 뜻하는 것은 ④의 앞 문장인 '꿈꾸는 것은 건강한 삶의 필수적인 부분인 것'이다.

본문해석

어떤 이들은 꿈에 아무런 가치가 없다고 믿지만, 이 밤에 일어나는 이러한 드라마를 무의미한 것으로 일축하는 것은 잘못이다. 꿈을 기억하면 얻어지는 것들이 있다. 우리는 더 연결되어 있고, 더 완전하고, 더 잘 해내고 있다고 느낄 수 있다. 우리는 영감, 정보, 그리고 위안을 받을 수 있다. 알베르트 아인슈타인은 자신의 상대성 이론은 꿈에서 영감을 받은 것이라고 말했다. 사실, 그는 그의 발견 중 많은 것들이 꿈에 의한 것이었다고 주장했다. 우리가 꿈을 꾸는 이유를 묻는 것은 우리가 숨을 쉬는 이유를 묻는 것만큼이나 타당하다. 꿈꾸는 것은 건강한 삶의 필수적인 부분이다. 좋은 소식은 우리가 꿈을 기억하든 기억하지 못하든 간에 이것이 사실이라는 것이다. 많은 사람들은 비록 그들이 구체적인 꿈을 기억하지 못해도 깨어나자마자 문제에 대한 새로운 해결책을 떠올리게 되었다고 말한다.

VOCA

- dismiss 일축하다
- nocturnal 야행성의, 밤에 일어나는
- irrelevant 관계가 없는, 무의미한
- on track (원하는 결과를 향해) 착착 나아가는[진행 중인]
- integral 필수적인

PART 5

고난도 기출문제

영어 | 2024년 국회직 8급

한눈에 훑어보기

✔ 영역 분석

어휘 01
1문항, 4%

독해 02 04 05 07 08 09 10 11 12 13 14 15
16 17 19 20 22 23 24 25
20문항, 80%

어법 03 06 18 21
4문항, 16%

✔ 빠른 정답

01	02	03	04	05	06	07	08	09	10
③	②	④	③	①	④	⑤	②	③	⑤
11	**12**	**13**	**14**	**15**	**16**	**17**	**18**	**19**	**20**
④	①	②	⑤	④	②	⑤	①	②	③
21	**22**	**23**	**24**	**25**					
④	⑤	③	①	③					

✔ 점수 체크

구분	1회독	2회독	3회독
맞힌 문항 수	/ 25	/ 25	/ 25
나의 점수	점	점	점

01 난도 ★☆☆ 정답 ③

어휘 > 단어

정답의 이유

밑줄 친 ductile은 '연성인, 잡아 늘일 수 있는'의 뜻이므로 밑줄 친 단어와 그 의미가 가장 가까운 것은 ③ 'pliable(유연한, 잘 휘어지는)'이다.

오답의 이유

① 깨지기 쉬운
② 그럴듯한
④ 고혹적인
⑤ 엄격한

본문해석

보잘것없는 음료수 캔이 특별한 것이라고 생각하는 사람은 거의 없을 것이다. 하지만 재료 공학자에게 그것은 첨단 기술이다. 필요조건을 보라. 가능한 한 우리는 이음매를 피하기를 원한다. 캔은 새지 않아야 하고, 가능한 한 금속을 조금 사용해야 하며, 재활용할 수 있어야 한다. 우리는 작은 하나의 금속 조각으로부터 일체형 캔 본체로 끌어들일 수 있을 정도로 연성이 있는 금속을 선택해야 한다. 맥주나 콜라에 부식되지 않아야 하며, 물론 무독성이어야 한다. 그리고 그것은 가볍고, 비용이 거의 들지 않아야 한다.

VOCA

• humble 보잘것없는
• drinks can 음료수 캔
• materials engineer 물질 엔지니어, 재료 공학자
• requirement 필요조건, 요건
• seam 솔기, 이음매
• leak 새다
• metal 금속
• recyclable 재활용 가능한
• draw into ~에 끌어들이다
• corrode 부식하다
• nontoxic 무독성의

02 난도 ★★☆

정답 ②

독해 > 빈칸 완성 > 단어 · 구 · 절

정답의 이유

빈칸이 있는 문장에서, 언어를 모르면 그 언어의 단어와 문장을 이해하기 어렵다고 하며 단어의 소리와 의미의 관계에 대해 설명하고 있다. 또한, 빈칸 다음 문장에서 한 언어를 습득할 때는 글자에 의해 표현되는 소리가 의미하는 개념을 배워야 한다고 했고 그 예로 영어에서 '집'을 뜻하는 house는 프랑스어에서는 maison, 러시아어에서는 dom, 스페인어에서는 casa로 각각 다르다고 하였다. 이는 '언어를 구성하는 형태와 내용이 본질적으로 관련이 없고 자의적으로 형성되었다'는 언어의 자의성에 대한 설명으로 문맥상 빈칸에 들어갈 알맞은 말은 ② 'arbitrary(임의적인)'이다.

오답의 이유

① ~의 상징[아이콘]이 되는
③ 논리적인
④ 체계적인
⑤ 예측[예견]할 수 있는

본문해석

만약 여러분이 한 언어를 모른다면, 그 언어의 단어들(과 문장들)을 주로 이해할 수 없을 것인데, 일반적으로 말소리와 그것들이 나타내는 의미 사이의 관계가 임의적이기 때문이다. 한 언어를 습득할 때, 여러분은 글자 house로 표현되는 소리가 '집'이라는 개념을 의미한다는 것을 배워야 한다. 만약 여러분이 프랑스어를 안다면, 이 동일한 의미는 'maison'으로, 러시아어를 안다면 'dom'으로, 스페인어를 안다면 'casa'로 표현된다. 동일한 일련의 연속적인 소리는 다른 언어들에서 다른 의미를 나타낼 수 있다. 예를 들어, 'bolna'라는 단어는 힌디어-우르두어로는 '말하다'를, 러시아어로는 '아프다'를 의미한다.

VOCA

- incomprehensible 이해할 수 없는
- represent 말로 표현하다
- acquire 습득하다[얻다]
- signify 의미하다, 뜻하다
- sequence (연속적으로 일어나는) 순서, 차례

03 난도 ★★☆

정답 ④

어법 > 비문 찾기

정답의 이유

④ are는 바로 앞의 than 이전의 'female English speakers use words such as lovely and nice more often'에서 동사인 use를 받는 대동사가 되어야 하므로, are → do가 되어야 한다. than 다음에 주어(male speakers)와 동사(do)가 도치되었다.

본문해석

성별 변수의 차별성은 남성과 여성이 동일한 어휘 항목 또는 다른 언어학적 특징을 사용하는 상대적 빈도에서 반영된다. 흔히 주장하듯이, 영어권의 여성 화자들이 남성 화자들보다 'lovely(사랑스러운)'라는 말과 'nice(멋진)'라는 단어를 더 자주 쓴다면, 우리는 이 점에서 영어권의 여성 화자가 명확하게 성별 변수의 차별성을 나타낸다고 할 수 있다.

VOCA

- differentiation 차이, 구별
- reflect 나타내다[반영하다]
- relative 비교상의, 상대적인
- frequency 빈도
- lexical item 어휘 항목(어휘 목록(lexicon)을 이루는 단위, 단어에 해당)
- linguistic 언어(학)의
- feature 특색, 특징
- assert 주장하다
- claim 주장하다
- exhibit (감정 · 특질 등을) 보이다[드러내다]

더 알아보기

대동사 do

- 대동사는 이미 앞에 언급된 술어부분(동사+문장성분+수식어) 전체를 대신 받는 동사이다.
  - 앞에 일반동사가 있으면 do가, be동사가 있으면 be동사가 대동사가 된다.
  - 의문문에서 대답할 때 질문의 동사를 대신한다.
  - 예 Does he like ice cream? Yes, he does.
    (그는 아이스크림을 좋아하니? 응, 좋아해.)
  - 예 He said he wouldn't see her again, but he did.
    (그는 그녀를 다시는 보지 못할 거라고 말했지만, 그는 그녀를 보았다.)
  - 예 My friends were at the concert yesterday, but I was not.
    (어제 친구들은 콘서트에 참석했지만, 나는 가지 않았다.)
  - 예 Internet has changed our lives much faster than it did one hundred years ago.
    (인터넷은 100년 전에 그랬던 것보다 우리들의 삶을 더 빠르게 바꾸었다.)
- do는 도치구문에서 본동사를 대신해서 사용된다.
  - 예 You need that money more than do I.
    → than 다음에 주어 동사가 도치됨
    (너는 나보다 그 돈이 더 필요하다.)
  - 예 As the demand rises, so do prices.
    → so 다음에 주어 동사가 도치됨
    (수요가 증가하면 가격도 오른다.)

04 난도 ★★☆   정답 ③

독해 > 세부 내용 찾기 > 내용 (불)일치

정답의 이유

③ 기업과 젊은 전문가들이 지속적으로 교통이 혼잡한 도시 지역으로 이전하는 것을 반대함에 따라 경제 성장이 교통 정체에 의해 촉진되고 있다. → 네 번째 문장에서 '~ gridlock is starting to stunt economic growth as businesses and young professionals choose not to move to metropolitan areas with chronically congested roads(기업들과 젊은 전문가들이 만성적으로 혼잡한 도로가 있는 대도시 지역으로 이동하지 않기로 선택함에 따라 교통 체증이 경제 성장을 저해하기 시작했다).'라고 했으므로 글의 내용과 일치하지 않는다.

오답의 이유

① 거대한 대도시 지역은 종종 더 많은 범죄율, 더 큰 오염 수준 및 높은 생활비로 고통받는다. → 첫 번째 문장에서 '~ huge metropolitan areas like Los Angeles and New York are typically plagued by higher crime rates, more pollution, and high costs of living(로스앤젤레스와 뉴욕 같은 거대한 대도시 지역들은 전형적으로 더 높은 범죄율, 더 많은 공해, 그리고 높은 생활비로 골머리를 앓고 있다).'라고 했으므로 글의 내용과 일치한다.

② 교통 체증은 대도시에서 주요 이슈가 되고 있다. → 세 번째 문장에서 'But another major problem—traffic-choked highways—is quickly rising to the top of the list for many major cities(그러나 또 다른 주요 문제—교통 체증이 심한 고속도로—는 많은 주요 도시들에서 빠르게 그 순위가 상승하고 있다).'라고 했으므로 글의 내용과 일치한다.

④ 수많은 정·재계 지도자들이 현재의 고속도로를 각 방향으로 9차선 이상의 '슈퍼하이웨이'로 확장하는 방안을 추진하고 있다. → 다섯 번째 문장에서 '~ many political and business leaders are advocating the widening of existing highways into "superhighways" of nine or more lanes in each direction(많은 정·재계 지도자들이 기존 고속도로를 각 방향으로 9차선 또는 그 이상의 '슈퍼하이웨이'로 확장하는 것을 옹호하고 있다).'이라고 했으므로 글의 내용과 일치한다.

⑤ 더 큰 도로를 건설하는 것은 교통 체증을 줄이는 데 도움이 될 것으로 예상된다. → 마지막 문장에서 'Building bigger roads, ~ will end bottlenecks, allowing the ever-growing number of vehicles to move freely(더 큰 도로를 건설하는 것은 병목 현상을 종식시켜 계속 늘어나는 차량이 자유롭게 이동하고) ~'라고 했으므로, 글의 내용과 일치한다.

대도시에서의 생활은 항상 단점을 가지고 있다. 작은 마을과 시골 지역사회와 비교할 때, 로스앤젤레스와 뉴욕 같은 거대한 대도시 지역들은 전형적으로 더 높은 범죄율, 더 많은 공해, 그리고 높은 생활비로 골머리를 앓고 있다. 그러나 또 다른 주요 문제—교통 체증이 심한 고속도로—는 많은 주요 도시들에서 빠르게 그 순위가 상승하고 있다. 현재 일부 대도시의 운전자들이 연간 2주 이상의 기간을 교통 체증에 갇혀 허비하고 있으며, 기업들과 젊은 전문가들이 만성적으로 혼잡한 도로가 있는 대도시 지역으로 이동하지 않기로 선택함에 따라 교통 체증이 경제 성장을 저해하기 시작했다. 이 문제를 해결하기 위해, 많은 정·재계 지도자들이 기존 고속도로를 각 방향으로 9차선 또는 그 이상의 '슈퍼하이웨이(superhighway)'로 확장하는 것을 옹호하고 있다. 예를 들어, 아리조나주 피닉스는 10번 주간 고속도로의 12마일 차로를 14차선에서 평균 22차선으로 확장할 계획이다. 조지아주 애틀랜타는 75번 주간 고속도로를 23차선으로 확장할 것이다. 텍사스주 휴스턴과 워싱턴 D.C.도 역시 고속도로의 일부 구간을 18차선 또는 그 이상으로 확장하기를 희망하고 있다. 더 큰 도로를 건설하는 것은 병목 현상을 종식시켜 계속 늘어나는 차량이 자유롭게 이동하고 그 지역을 경제적으로 경쟁력 있게 유지할 수 있을 것이라고 기대하고 있다.

VOCA
- drawback 결점, 문제점
- compared to ~와 비교하여
- metropolitan 대도시[수도]의
- plague 괴롭히다, 성가시게 하다
- choked 막힌
- equivalent 해당하는, 맞먹는, 동등한
- stuck in ~에 갇힌
- gridlock 교통 정체
- stunt 방해하다
- chronically 만성적으로
- congested 밀집한
- combat ~와 싸우다, ~을 상대로 항쟁하다
- advocate 지지하다, 옹호하다
- widening 넓히는 것, 확대
- interstate 주(州) 사이의
- segment 부분, 구획
- bottleneck 교통 체증이 생기는 지점
- ever-growing 점점 커지는, 계속 늘어나는
- competitive 경쟁의, 경쟁적인

독해 > 빈칸 완성 > 단어·구·절

정답의 이유

제시문은 가십(gossip)의 긍정적인 영향과 부정적인 영향을 설명하는 내용으로, 빈칸 앞 문장에서 가십은 직장, 학교, 사회적인 그룹 등 어디에나 있으며 결코 없어지지 않을 것처럼 보인다고 했다. 빈칸 다음 문장에서 'You must refuse to participate in such damaging communication.'이라고 했으므로, 빈칸에는 해로운 의사소통에 참여하는 것을 거부하는 것과 관련된 내용이 와야 함을 유추할 수 있다. 따라서 빈칸에 들어갈 말로 적절한 것은 ① 'do your best to rise above it(그것에 초연하려고 최선을 다하다)'이다.

오답의 이유

② 그것을 퍼뜨리는 데 보다 주도적인 역할을 하다
③ 소문의 출처와 동기를 밝혀내다
④ 그것의 존재를 완전히 무시하다
⑤ 부정적인 영향을 상쇄하기 위해 소문을 만들다

본문해석

사람들은 모든 나라와 모든 계층에서 수 세기 동안 남 얘기(gossip)를 해왔다. 심리학자들은 이러한 형태의 인간 의사소통의 긍정적인 영향과 부정적인 영향을 모두 연구해 왔다. 일부 연구자들에 따르면, 가십(gossip)은 공동체에서 도덕적인 경계를 강화한다. 가십은 또한 특정 집단에 소속감을 조성할 수 있다. 그러나, 가십은 많은 부정적인 영향도 가지고 있다. 가십은 사람들을 고립시키고 따돌리는 도구로 사용될 수 있다. 해로운 소문들에 의해 선정되어 당황하면, 개인들은 의기소침해지고 외로워진다. 가십의 부정적인 영향에도 불구하고, 그것은 아주 흔한 일이다. 가십은 직장, 학교, 그리고 사회적인 집단에 존재한다. 겉으로 보기에, 가십은 절대 사라지지 않을 것이다. 당신은 그것에 초연하려고 최선을 다해야 한다. 당신은 그러한 해로운 의사소통에 참여하는 것을 거부해야 한다. 무언가 긍정적인 것에 초점을 맞추는 방식으로 그 대화를 전환하려고 노력해라.

VOCA

• walk of life　직업, 신분, 계급
• gossip　소문, 험담, 험담[남 얘기]을 하다
• impact　영향, 충격
• reinforce　강화하다
• foster　조성하다, 발전시키다, 아이를 맡아 기르다[위탁·양육하다]
• isolate　격리하다, 고립시키다
• ostracize　외면하다[배척하다]
• single out　선발하다, 선정하다
• ubiquitous　어디에나 있는, 아주 흔한
• seemingly　외견상으로, 겉보기에는
• rise above　~에 초연하다
• take a role　역할을 맡다
• disseminate　퍼뜨리다[전파하다]
• identify　확인하다[알아보다]
• disregard　무시[묵살]하다
• offset　상쇄[벌충]하다

어법 > 비문 찾기

정답의 이유

offer A to B는 'B에게 A를 제공하다'의 뜻이므로, ④ offer individual students → offer to individual students가 되어야 한다. offer의 직접목적어는 support로 관계대명사 that의 선행사이다.

본문해석

AI는 더 나은 방식, 규모, 더 낮은 비용으로 교육 우선 사항을 달성하게 할 수 있다. 팬데믹으로 인한 학생들의 다양한 미완성 학습을 해결하는 것이 정책적 우선 사항이며, AI는 학생들의 강점과 필요에 따라 학습 자원의 적응력을 향상시킬 수 있다. 교사의 직무 개선이 우선 사항이며, 자동화된 보조원 또는 기타 도구를 통해서 AI는 교사에게 더 큰 지원을 제공할 수 있다. AI는 또한 교사가 시간이 부족할 때 개별 학생에게 교사가 제공하는 지원을 확장할 수 있도록 할 수 있다. 학생들이 학습에 가져온 지식과 경험에 반응하는 자원을 개발하는 것이 우선 사항이며, AI는 지역의 요구를 충족시키기 위해 교육과정 자원을 더 맞춤화할 수 있다. 음성 보조원, 매핑 도구, 쇼핑 추천, 에세이 작성 기능 및 기타 친숙한 애플리케이션에서 보이는 것처럼, AI는 교육적인 서비스를 향상시킬 수 있다.

VOCA

• priority　우선 사항, 우선권
• address　(문제를) 역점을 두어 다루다
• varied　가지가지의, 가지각색의
• adaptivity　적응성, 순응성
• automated　자동화된, 자동의
• assistant　조수, 보조원
• extend　확장하다, 확대하다
• responsive　대답하는, 응하는
• customizability　맞춤화
• curricular　교육과정의
• enhance　높이다[향상시키다]

더 알아보기

수여동사의 3형식 전환

• 수여동사는 '~에게 …하다'의 뜻을 가진 동사로, 목적어를 2개[직접목적어(D.O.), 간접목적어(I.O.)] 취한다.
• 수여동사는 4형식 문장에서 사용되며, S+V+I.O.+D.O.의 문장 구조를 가진다.
• 수여동사는 '~에게'에 해당하는 간접목적어 앞에 전치사를 붙여 3형식으로 전환할 수 있다.
　- 4형식: S+V+I.O.+D.O.
　- 3형식: S+V+D.O.+전치사구(전치사+I.O.)
　예 Mom *made* me an apple pie. (4형식)
　　→ Mom *made* an apple pie for me. (3형식)

• 수여동사의 3형식 전환 시 전치사

to+I.O.	give, offer, pass, write, lend, send, show, bring, hand
for+I.O.	get, buy, make, secure, choose, leave, cook, prepare
of+I.O.	ask, inquire, require, request, demand, beg

예 He poured some wine into a glass and *gave* it to her.
(그는 와인을 잔에 조금 부었고, 그것을 그녀에게 주었다.)

예 When I got home, Stephano was busy *preparing* lunch for me.
(집에 도착했을 때, Stephano는 내게 점심을 차려 주느라 바빴다.)

예 The teacher *asked* a question of the students.
(선생님은 학생들에게 질문을 하나 했다.)

07 난도 ★★☆   정답 ⑤

독해 > 세부 내용 찾기 > 제목, 주제

[정답의 이유]

제시문은 예술과 과학의 해석에 대한 접근과 차이를 설명하는 내용으로, 첫 번째 문장에서 과학자들은 과학의 조직화된 회의론을 제공하는 충분한 관찰 기술을 가진 유일한 소비자인 반면 예술가들은 자신들의 예술을 해석하는 데 아무런 역할을 하지 않는다고 했다. 또한, 다섯 번째 문장에서 'Where multiple interpretations are encouraged, obscurity can be a virtue but where the aspiration is to produce only one interpretation, clarity is to be preferred(다양한 해석이 장려되는 분야에서는 모호함이 미덕이 될 수 있지만, 단 하나의 해석을 생산하는 것이 목표인 분야에서는 명료함이 선호된다).'라고 했고, 마지막 문장에서 '~ since science should seek maximum clarity and accessibility even while acknowledging that the only proper assessors of a scientific claim are small elites, while artists often seek obscurity or multiple interpretations even while accepting that the proper assessors are the public(과학은 과학적 주장에 대한 유일한 적절한 평가자가 소수의 엘리트라는 사실을 인정하면서도 최대의 명료함과 접근 가능성을 추구해야 하는 반면, 예술가들은 적절한 평가자가 대중이라는 것을 인정하면서도 종종 모호함이나 다양한 해석을 추구하기 때문이다).'라고 하였으므로 글의 제목으로 적절한 것은 ⑤ 'How Art and Science Interpret Clarity and Obscurity(예술과 과학이 명료함과 모호함을 해석하는 방법)'이다.

[오답의 이유]

① 과학자들이 명확한 시각으로 예술을 분석하는 법
② 예술적 모호성에 대한 과학적 분석
③ 과학자들이 예술적 해석을 만드는 방법
④ 예술과 과학에서 정밀함의 중요성

과학자들은 과학의 조직된 회의론을 제공하기에 충분한 관찰 기술을 가진 유일한 소비자인 반면, 예술가들은 그들 스스로 예술을 해석하는 데 아무런 역할을 하지 않는다. 예술에 대한 해석은 다양할 수 있고 예술가의 의도는 다양한 해석을 유발하는 것일 수 있다—때로는 해석이 많을수록 더 좋다. 반면에, 과학자는 단 하나의 가능한 해석—정확한 해석을 전달하는 것을 열망해야 한다. 이것으로부터 이어지는 것은, 과학에서는 명확성이 다른 문화적 노력과는 달리 필수적이라는 것이다. 다양한 해석이 장려되는 분야에서는 모호함이 미덕이 될 수 있지만, 단 하나의 해석을 생산하는 것이 목표인 분야에서는 명료함이 선호된다. 모호함은 또한 사적인 것이고, 사적인 것은 조직화된 회의적인 태도에 대한 장애물이다. 관찰과 회의가 자연계의 지식을 추구하는 데 있어 미덕이라는 사실로부터, 명료함 또한 미덕이라는 결론이 나온다. 여기에 모순이 있는데, 과학은 과학적 주장에 대한 유일한 적절한 평가자가 소수의 엘리트라는 사실을 인정하면서도 최대의 명료함과 접근 가능성을 추구해야 하는 반면, 예술가들은 적절한 평가자가 대중이라는 것을 인정하면서도 종종 모호함이나 다양한 해석을 추구하기 때문이다.

• interpretation 해석, 이해, 설명
• sufficient 충분한, 족한
• observational 관찰[관측]의, 감시의
• organized 조직화된, 조직적인
• skepticism 회의론[설], 무신론
• manifold (수가) 많은, 여러 가지의
• provoke 유발하다
• a multitude of 다수의
• aspire 열망[염원]하다
• convey 전달하다[전하다]
• imperative 반드시 해야 하는, 긴요한
• obscurity 모호함, 모호한 것
• obstacle 장애, 장애물
• in the pursuit of ~을 추구하여
• accessibility 접근 (가능성), 접근하기 쉬움
• acknowledge 인정하다
• assessor 평가자

08 난도 ★★☆

독해 > 빈칸 완성 > 단어·구·절

[정답의 이유]

빈칸 뒷부분에서 'over 70% of incarcerated people who are released from prison in the US will be rearrested within five years of their release date(미국에서 출소한 수감자의 70% 이상이 출소일로부터 5년 이내에 재검거될 것이다).'라고 하였고, 마지막 문장에서 미국의 집단 수감 시스템이 사람들이 감옥을 떠나 다시 사회에 통합하려는 것을 실패하게 만든다고 하였으므로 빈칸에 들어갈 말로 적절한 것은 ② 'recidivism(재범)'이다.

[오답의 이유]

① 인종 차별

③ 환생

④ 탈옥

⑤ 출소

본문해석

미국은 세계에서 재소자 재범률이 높은 나라 중 하나인데, 미국에서 출소한 수감자의 70% 이상이 출소일로부터 5년 이내에 재검거될 것이다. 그것은 우연이 아니다. 우리의 집단 수감 시스템은 사람들이 감옥 시스템을 떠나 사회에 재통합하려고 할 때 실패하게 만든다.

VOCA

- recidivism 재범
- incarcerate 감금[투옥]하다
- release 풀어 주다, 석방[해방]하다
- rearrest 재검거하다
- release date 출소일
- mass 대량의, 대규모의, 대중적인
- incarceration 투옥, 감금, 유폐
- reintegrate 재통합하다

09 난도 ★★★

독해 > 글의 일관성 > 글의 순서

[정답의 이유]

주어진 문장 후반부의 millions of years ago beneath ocean floors(수백만 년 전 해저)는 In ancient seas(고대의 바다에서)로 시작하는 (B)로 이어지는 것이 자연스럽다. (B) 마지막의 as new layers accumulated on top(그 위에 새로운 층이 쌓이면서)은 (C)의 'sediment(퇴적물)'로 이어진다. (C) 마지막 문장의 'a liquid hydrogen and carbon substance(액체 수소와 탄소 물질)'는 (A)의 'crude oil(원유)'로 이어진다. 따라서 주어진 글의 다음에 이어질 글의 순서로 적절한 것은 ③ '(B) - (C) - (A)'이다.

본문해석

오늘날 자동차와 비행기 탱크에 주입되는 모든 휘발유는 수백만 년 전 해저에서 원유가 형성되면서 시작되었다.

(B) 고대의 바다에서는 작은 수생식물과 동물들이 죽으면 그것들은 바닥으로 가라앉았다. 그 위에 모래와 진흙이 떨어져 자리 잡았다. 이런 과정이 계속 반복되었고, 그때마다 많은 양의 유기물을 묻고, 그 위에 새로운 층이 쌓이면서 점점 더 깊숙이 바닥으로 밀려 들어갔다.

(C) 퇴적물의 무거운 무게로 인해 압력과 화씨 150도 이상의 온도가 발생했고, 지하의 유기물이 '조리'되기 시작했다. 시간이 지나면서, 그 열기가 그것을 액체 수소와 탄소 물질로 변환시켰다.

(A) 물과 바위보다 가벼운 이 원유는 바위의 미세한 공간을 통해 위로 떠다니다가 고밀도의 불침투성 바위층에 의해 멈춰져 강제로 모이게 되었다. 오늘날 석유 회사들은 에너지가 풍부한 이 석유를 추출하기 위해 이 저류층을 시추하여 정유공장으로 보내 차량 연료로 전환한다.

VOCA

- pump into ~에 쏟아 붓다[주입하다]
- crude oil 원유
- ocean floor 대양저
- aquatic plant 수생식물
- settle (한동안) 머물다[남아 있다]
- bury 묻다[매장하다]
- quantity 양, 수량, 분량
- accumulated 축적된, 누적된
- sediment 침전물, 퇴적물
- pressure 압박, 압력
- subterranean 지하의
- organic matter 유기물
- transform 변형시키다
- liquid hydrogen 액체 수소
- carbon 탄소
- substance 물질
- drift 떠가다, 표류[부유]하다
- microscopic 미세한, 현미경으로 봐야만 보이는
- dense 빽빽한, 밀집한
- impermeable 통과시키지 않는, 불침투성의
- extract 추출하다
- energy-rich 고에너지의
- petroleum 석유
- oil refinery 정유공장
- convert into ~으로 바꾸다[전환하다]

10 난도 ★★☆ 　　　　　　　　　정답 ⑤

독해 > 빈칸 완성 > 단어 · 구 · 절

정답의 이유

제시문은 어떤 이슈에 대해 미온적인 다수가 찬성하는 정책과 열정적인 소수가 찬성하는 정책 사이에서 결정할 때는 선호하는 사람들의 수뿐만 아니라 그 선호도의 강도를 고려해야 한다는 내용이다. 빈칸 문장의 앞부분 'It does not seem right that a lukewarm majority should in all cases'와 빈칸 다음의 'a passionate minority'로 미루어 빈칸에 들어갈 말로 적절한 것은 ⑤ 'override (우선하다)'이다.

오답의 이유

① 속이다
② 경의를 표하다
③ 따르다
④ 보호하다

본문해석

다수가 한 정책을 찬성하지만, 다른 정책을 찬성하는 소수가 그것에 대해 훨씬 더 강하게 관심을 갖고 있는 문제가 있다고 가정해 보자. 이런 경우는 꽤 자주 발생한다. 여우 사냥 논쟁이 좋은 예가 될 수 있다. 대부분 사람들은 동물의 권리에 대해 강한 도덕적 견해를 가지고 있지 않더라도 여우 사냥에 대해 상당히 부정적인 견해를 가지고 있다. 그들은 그것을 구식이고, 속물적이며, 일반적으로 혐오스러운 행사로 본다. 기회가 주어진다면, 그들은 그것을 금지하는 데 표를 던질 것이다. 여우 사냥꾼들은 소수이지만, 대부분 그들이 사냥을 계속하도록 허용되어야 한다고 매우 강하게 생각한다. 그것은 많은 농촌 사회에서 중요한 사회적 행사이며, 사람들의 생계가 그것에 달려 있다. 여우 사냥에 대한 정치적 판단은 둘 중 하나를 선호하는 사람들의 수뿐만 아니라 그 선호도의 강도도 고려해야 한다. 미온적인 다수가 모든 경우에서 열정적인 소수보다 <u>우선해야</u> 한다는 것은 정당한 것 같지 않다.

VOCA

- favor 찬성하다
- occur 일어나다, 발생하다
- fox-hunting 여우 사냥
- debate 토론[토의/논의]
- archaic 낡은, 폐물이 된
- snobbish 속물적인, 고상한 체하는
- distasteful 불쾌한, 혐오스러운
- spectacle 구경거리[행사]
- ban 금(지)하다
- preference 선호(도), 애호
- lukewarm 미적지근한, 미온적인
- passionate 열정적인, 열렬한

11 난도 ★★☆ 　　　　　　　　　정답 ④

독해 > 글의 일관성 > 무관한 어휘 · 문장

정답의 이유

제시문은 평등(equality)과 공평(equity)의 차이를 설명한 내용으로, 평등은 우리가 모두 동일한 가치와 권리를 지니고 태어났으며 동일한 존엄을 받고 기회에 대한 동일한 접근성을 지닌 것을 뜻한다고 했다. 공평은 모든 사람들이 동일한 결과를 얻는 것으로, 사람마다 자신만의 독특한 방식으로 세계를 경험한다고 했다. 여섯 번째 문장에서 'It is because of these differences that we sometimes need to be treated differently for us all to live equally(이러한 차이들 때문에 모두가 동등하게 삶을 영위하려면 때로 다르게 대우받아야 한다).'라고 했고, 마지막 문장에서 공평은 모든 사람이 동일한 종류의 사다리를 사용할 수 없다는 것을 깨닫고 나무 꼭대기에 있는 망고에 도달할 수 있는 또 다른 방법을 제공하는 것이라고 했으므로 글의 문맥상 ④ different → same이 되어야 한다.

본문해석

평등은, 인간으로서, 우리가 모두 동일한 가치를 지니고 있다는 사실을 인식하는 것이다. 이것은 우리가 모두 동일한 권리를 가지고 있고, 동일한 수준으로 존중받아야 하며, 기회에 대한 동일한 접근성을 가지고 있어야 한다는 것을 의미한다. 그러나 공평은 모든 사람이 동등한 결과물을 달성하는 것이다. 우리는 모두 동일한 가치를 가지고 있고 좋은 삶을 살 자격이 있지만, 모두 다른 장소에서 출발한다. 우리는 자신만의 독특한 방식으로 세상을 경험한다. 이러한 차이들 때문에 모두가 동등하게 삶을 영위하려면 때로 다르게 대우받아야 한다. 예를 들어, 평등은 모든 사람에게 나무 꼭대기에서 망고를 딸 수 있는 <u>다른 → 동일한</u> 종류의 사다리를 제공하는 것이다. 공평은 모든 사람이 동일한 종류의 사다리를 사용할 수 없다는 것을 깨닫고 나무 꼭대기에 있는 망고에 도달할 수 있는 또 다른 방법을 제공하는 것이다.

VOCA

- equality 평등, 균등
- access 접근
- opportunity 기회
- equity 공평, 공정
- achieve 달성하다, 성취하다
- outcome 결과
- deserve ~을 받을 만하다[누릴 자격이 있다]
- unique 유일무이한, 독특한
- treat 대하다[다루다/취급하다]

242 **시대에듀** | 국가직 · 지방직 · 법원직 공무원

12 난도 ★★☆   정답 ①

독해 > 빈칸 완성 > 단어 · 구 · 절

정답의 이유

네 번째 문장의 후반부에서 'we must add up the separate satisfactions and frustrations of everyone likely to be affected by our choice(우리는 우리의 선택에 의해 영향을 받을 가능성이 있는 모든 사람들의 개별적인 만족과 좌절을 합산해야 하는데) ~'라고 했고, 빈칸 앞 문장에서 우리는 우리 앞에 놓인 각각의 선택지에 대해 각 열의 합계를 내야 한다고 했다. 또 빈칸 다음 문장에서 '좌절의 총합보다 만족의 총합에 대한 최선의 균형(the best balance of totaled satisfactions over totaled frustrations)'을 유발할 가능성이 가장 높은 선택지를 선택해야 한다고 했으므로 빈칸에 들어갈 적절한 것은 ① 'aggregative(집합적인)'이다.

오답의 이유

② 낙관적인

③ 이상적인

④ 개인 특유의

⑤ 현실적인

본문해석

공리주의가 우리에게 최선의 결과를 가져오도록 요구한다는 것을 우리 자신에게 상기시킬 때 공리주의에 심각한 문제가 발생한다. 이것은 무엇을 의미하는가? 이것은 나 혼자만을 위한 것이거나 내 가족 또는 친구들, 개인적으로 취해진 다른 어떤 사람들을 위한 최선의 결과를 의미하지 않는다. 아니, 우리가 해야 할 일은 대략 다음과 같다. 우리는 우리의 선택에 의해 영향을 받을 가능성이 있는 모든 사람들의 개별적인 만족과 좌절을 합산해야 하는데, 만족을 한 쪽 열에, 좌절을 다른 열에 두어야 한다. 우리는 우리 앞에 놓인 각각의 선택지에 대해 각 열의 합계를 내야 한다. 그것이 바로 그 이론이 집합적이라고 말하는 것의 의미이다. 그리고 나서 좌절의 총합보다 만족의 총합에 대한 최선의 균형을 유발할 가능성이 가장 높은 그 선택지를 선택해야 한다. 이러한 결과를 초래할 수 있는 행동이 무엇이든지 간에 우리가 도덕적으로 수행해야 할 행동이다—바로 여기에 우리의 도덕적 의무가 있다. 그리고 그 행동은 개인적으로 나, 또는 가족이나 친구들, 실험동물을 위한 최선의 결과를 가져다줄 동일한 행동이 아닐 수도 있다.

VOCA

• arise 생기다, 발생하다

• utilitarianism 공리주의

• remind 상기시키다

• enjoin 명하다, 요구하다

• bring about ~을 유발[초래]하다

• add up (조금씩) 늘어나다, 합산하다

• satisfaction 만족(감), 흡족

• frustration 불만, 좌절감

• total 합계[총] ~이 되다

• perform 행하다[수행하다/실시하다]

• lab animal 실험동물

---

13 난도 ★★☆   정답 ②

독해 > 세부 내용 찾기 > 제목, 주제

정답의 이유

세 번째 문장에서 'But unfortunately there still seems to be a gap between voting and registering your consent(그러나 불행하게도 투표를 하는 것과 여러분의 동의를 등록하는 것 사이에는 여전히 격차가 있는 것 같다).'라고 한 다음에 양쪽 당 모두 동의하지 않지만, 그중에서 덜 나쁜 쪽에 투표한 경우와 여러분이 투표한 정당의 정책에 대부분 동의하지만, 그중 일부 정책을 매우 싫어해도 개별 정책에 대해 따로 투표할 수 없는 경우를 예로 들었다. 그리고 마지막 문장에서 'Perhaps the voters' consent can help explain why governments have legitimate authority, but not why individual citizens have an obligation to obey the law(아마도 유권자들의 동의는 정부가 합법적인 권한이 있는 이유를 설명하는 데는 도움이 되겠지만, 개별 시민들이 법을 준수해야 할 의무가 있는 이유를 설명하는 데는 도움이 되지 못할 것이다).'라고 했으므로, 글의 제목으로 적절한 것은 ② 'Discordance between Voting and Voter Consent(투표와 유권자 동의의 불일치)'이다.

오답의 이유

① 선거가 작동하는 이유

③ 정부 정책의 부정확성

④ 동의와 의무의 완벽한 일치

⑤ 정책과 정부의 합법성에 대한 연계

본문해석

최근 몇몇 정치철학자들은 우리가 선거에 참여하면 우리는 새로 등장하는 정부와 그 정부가 제정하는 법을 준수하는 데 동의하는 것이라고 주장했다. 이것은 더 유망한 것처럼 보인다. 우리는 적어도 투표 여부에 대해 자유로운 선택을 할 수 있고, 사람들이 등장한 정부를 합법적인 정부로 인정하지 않는 한 선거를 실시하는 것은 의미가 없기 때문이다. 그러나 불행하게도 투표를 하는 것과 여러분의 동의를 등록하는 것 사이에는 여전히 격차가 있는 것 같다. 만약 여러분이 두 당에 모두 매우 동의할 수 없지만, 한 쪽이 다른 쪽보다 약간 덜 나쁘다고 생각하기 때문에 투표한다면 어떨까? 또는 승리한 정당이 선언문에서 발표한 종합적인 정책에 어떤 의미에서는 동의했다고 생각하지만, 여러분이 상당히 혐오스럽다고 생각하는 몇 가지 항목이 있고, 이것들에 대해 개별적으로 투표할 기회가 없다면 어떨까? 아마도 유권자들의 동의는 정부가 합법적인 권한이 있는 이유를 설명하는 데는 도움이 되겠지만, 개별 시민이 법을 준수해야 할 의무가 있는 이유를 설명하는 데는 도움이 되지 못할 것이다.

VOCA

• claim 승인을 요구하다, 주장하다

• comply with 순응하다, 지키다, 준수하다

• emerge 나오다[모습을 드러내다]

• enact 제정하다

• promising 유망한, 촉망되는

• legitimate 정당한, 타당한, 적당한

• register 등록[기재]하다, 신고하다

- consent 동의[허락], 동의[허락]하다
- slightly 약간, 조금
- manifesto 성명서[선언문]
- repugnant 불쾌한[혐오스러운]
- obligation 의무

14 난도 ★★☆   정답 ⑤

독해 > 빈칸 완성 > 단어·구·절

정답의 이유

세 번째 문장에서 'Most techniques for harvesting embryonic stem cells cause the destruction of an embryo(배아 줄기세포를 수확하는 대부분 기술은 배아의 파괴를 야기한다).'라고 했고, 배아를 생명체로 보는 측에서는 배아 줄기세포 채취를 비윤리적이라고 반대하지만, 다른 측에서는 줄기세포 연구가 인간의 생명을 구하는 필수적인 연구라는 면에서 지지한다고 했다. 또한 빈칸 다음 문장에서 일부 최근의 실험들은 배아 자체를 손상시키지 않고 초기 배아로부터 소수의 줄기세포를 추출할 수 있는 방법이 있을 수 있다는 사실을 시사했다고 했으므로, 문맥상 빈칸에 들어갈 적절한 것은 ⑤ 'addressed with a technological solution(기술적인 해법으로 처리되는)'이다.

오답의 이유

① 기술 발전으로 반복되는
② 새로운 줄기세포 규제의 출현으로 해결된
③ 더 많은 실험으로 명확해진
④ 새로운 연구 기술에 의해 더 심각해진

본문해석

성체 줄기세포는 자발적인 기증자의 신체에서 직접 얻을 수 있기 때문에, 이 세포들을 이용한 연구는 지금까지 거의 윤리적인 의문을 일으키지 않았다. 이것은 일반적으로 매우 초기의 배아로부터 얻어지는 배아 줄기세포의 경우에는 해당되지 않는다. 배아 줄기세포를 수확하는 대부분 기술은 배아의 파괴를 야기한다. 이런 이유로, 배아를 인간의 권리와 보호를 받을 권리가 있다고 여기는 개인들은 이러한 작업을 반대한다. 이러한 우려는 배아 줄기세포 연구에 대한 정부의 자금 지원을 중요한 정치적 이슈로 만들었다. 배아를 보호하려는 단체들은 이러한 연구가 비윤리적이라고 반대한다. 다른 단체들은 그러한 연구를 인간의 생명을 구하는 필수적인 것으로 지지하고 연구를 제한하는 것이 비윤리적이라고 주장한다. 그러나 머지않은 미래에 두 가지 윤리적인 우려는 기술적인 해법으로 처리될 수 있을 것이다. 일부 최근의 실험들은 배아 자체를 손상시키지 않고 초기 배아로부터 소수의 줄기세포를 추출할 수 있는 방법이 있을 수 있다는 사실을 시사했다. 다른 실험들은 성체 세포가 다능성 배아 줄기세포처럼 보이고 기능하도록 재프로그래밍하는 소수의 유전자 스위치를 '켜는' 것이 가능하다는 것을 보여주었다. 이러한 기술은 배아를 모두 배양할 필요성을 없앨 것이다. 또한 개별 환자의 필요에 따라 특정 치료법을 맞춤화하는 것이 가능할 수도 있다. 이 접근법이 성공한다면, 배아 생명의 파괴를 피하면서 잠재적으로 생명을 구하는 연구를 진행할 수 있을 것이다.

15 난도 ★★☆   정답 ④

독해 > 글의 일관성 > 무관한 어휘·문장

정답의 이유

제시문에서 자동차를 수리할 때는 관찰된 증거로부터 자동차의 상태를 추론하지만, 당뇨병 환자를 치료할 때는 환자의 실제 혈당 수치와 인슐린 수치를 바탕으로 환자의 음식 섭취량과 인슐린 투여량을 결정하되, 혈당 수치와 측정값은 시간이 지남에 따라 빠르게 변하는 것을 고려해야 한다고 하였다. 따라서 정적인 증거에 의해 결정되는 자동차 수리와는 달리 당뇨병 환자 치료는 동적인 증거에 의해 결정됨을 파악할 수 있으므로 글의 흐름상 ④ 'static(정적인) → dynamic(동적인)'이 되어야 한다.

본문해석

우리는 각각의 확률 변수가 하나의 고정된 값을 갖는 정적 세계의 맥락에서 확률적 추론 기술을 개발했다. 예를 들어, 자동차를 수리할 때, 우리는 고장 난 부분이 진단 과정에서 고장 난 상태로 남아 있다고 가정하고, 관찰된 증거로부터 자동차의 상태를 추론하는 것이 우리의 일이며, 이 역시 고정된 상태로 남아 있다. 이제 약간 다른 문제인 당뇨병 환자를 치료하는 것을 고려해 보라. 자동차 수리의 경우와 마찬가지로, 최근 인슐린 투여량, 음식 섭취량, 혈당 측정 및 기타 신체적 징후와 같은 증거가 있다. 이 작업은 실제 혈당 수치와 인슐린 수치를 포함한 환자의 현재 상태를 평가하는 것이다. 이러한 정보를 바탕으로, 환자의 음식 섭취량과 인슐린 투여량을 결정할 수 있다. 자동차 수리의 경우와 달리, 여기서는 문제의 정적인 → 동적인 측면이 필수적이다. 혈당 수치와 측정값은 시간이 지남에 따라 최근 음식 섭취량과 인슐린 투여량, 대사 활동, 하루 중 시간대 등에 따라 빠르게 변할 수 있다. 증거 이력으로부터 현재 상태를 평가하고 치료 조치의 결과를 예측하기 위해 우리는 이러한 변화를 모형화해야 한다.

VOCA

- probabilistic reasoning 확률 추론
- in the context of ~의 맥락에서
- static 고정된[고정적인]
- random variable 확률 변수
- fixed value 고정된 형태
- assume 당연한 것으로 여기다, 당연하다고 생각하다
- diagnosis 진단
- infer 추론하다
- observed evidence 관찰된 증거
- diabetic 당뇨병 환자(용)의
- insulin dose 인슐린 투여량
- food intake 식품 섭취
- blood sugar measurement 혈당 측정
- assess 재다[가늠하다]
- blood sugar level 혈당치
- make a decision 결정하다
- thereof 그것의
- metabolic activity 대사 활동

16 난도 ★★☆   정답 ②

독해 > 빈칸 완성 > 단어 · 구 · 절

정답의 이유

빈칸 앞 문장에서 추론가들은 자신들이 제시한 해결책이 최선이라고 여기며 다른 사람들의 아이디어를 듣는 데 어려움을 겪는다고 하였으므로 문맥상 빈칸에 들어갈 적절한 말은 ② 'conceited(자만심이 강한, 젠체하는)'이다.

오답의 이유

① 전념하는
③ 적응[순응]적인
④ 지지부진한
⑤ 낙천적인

본문해석

사람들이 문제에 대해 생각하는 방식은 매우 다양하다. 모든 사람들이 독특하지만, 심리학자들은 세상에는 5가지 다른 유형의 문제 해결자인 질문자, 발상가, 문제를 파고드는 사람, 행동가, 추론가가 있다고 믿는다. 추론가에 관해서 말하면, 그들은 일을 단순하게 유지하는 것을 좋아하는 사람들이다. 복잡한 문제를 다룰 때, 그들은 가장 중요한 요소들에 집중하는 것을 선호한다. 그들은 작은 세부 사항에 대해 걱정하는 것을 원하지 않는데, 이것은 그들이 다른 사람들보다 더 빨리 문제를 해결한다는 것을 의미한다. 또한, 추론가들에게 있어서 '최선'의 해결책은 자신들이 제시한 해결책이다. 불행하게도, 그들은 또한 다른 사람들의 아이디어를 듣는 데 어려움을 겪는다. 그 결과, 사람들은 때때로 그들이 자만심이 강한 것으로 보일 수 있다고 가정한다.

VOCA

- problem-solver 문제 해결자
- questioner 질문자
- ideator 발상가
- reasoner 추론가
- prefer 선호하다
- come up with 제시[제안]하다
- assume 생각하다, 가정하다, 추측하다

17 난도 ★★☆   정답 ⑤

독해 > 빈칸 완성 > 단어 · 구 · 절

정답의 이유

⑤ 빈칸 (A) 앞에서 'Even within a broadly defined community of speakers, there is often sufficient'라고 했고, (A) 다음의 'to cause misunderstanding'으로 미루어 빈칸 (A)에는 '오해를 일으킬 만큼' 충분히 다르다는 의미의 단어가 들어가야 함을 유추할 수 있다. 따라서 빈칸 (A)에 들어갈 적절한 말은 'variation(차이)'이다. 빈칸 (B) 앞부분에서 언급한 참여도가 높은 대화 스타일의 특징과 빈칸 (B) 다음에 언급된 'from another style in which speakers use a slower rate, ~ and avoid interruption or completion of the other's turn.'으로 미루어 빈칸 (B)에는 두 대화 스타일이 매우 다르다는 것을 나타내는 단어가 들어가야 함을 유추할 수 있다. 따라서 빈칸 (B)에 들어갈 적절한 말은 'substantially(상당히)'이다. 빈칸 (C) 앞 문장에서 빨리 말하는 화자는 더 느리게 말하는 화자를 그저 수줍음 많고, 지루하고 멍청한 사람으로, 더 느리게 말하는 화자는 빨리 말하는 화자를 시끄럽고, 거만하고, 이기적이고, 지겨운 사람이라고 생각할 수 있다고 했고, 빈칸 (C) 앞에서 'Features of conversational style will often be interpreted as'라고 했으므로, 빈칸 (C)에 들어갈 적절한 말은 'personality traits(성격 특성)'이다.

오답의 이유

① 불일치 – 최소한의 – 개인적 특성
② 어려움 – 근본적으로 – 감정적 속성
③ 혼란 – 표면적으로 – 문화재
④ 유사성 – 기본적으로 – 개인적인 경험

고난도 기출

영어

교대로 말을 주고받는 대화 시스템을 특징짓는 많은 기능들은 사용자들에 의해 의미를 띠게 된다. 심지어 광범위하게 정의된 화자들의 집단 내에서도, 오해를 일으킬 수 있는 (A) 차이가 종종 있다. 예를 들어, 어떤 사람들은 대화 참여가 매우 활발하고 말하는 속도가 비교적 빠르며, 대화 사이에 일시 정지가 거의 없으며, 상대방의 차례와 겹치거나 심지어 상대방이 말을 끝내는 것을 기대한다. 이것이 하나의 대화 스타일이다. 이것은 참여도가 높은 스타일이라고 불린다. 이것은 화자가 더 느린 속도로 말하고, 차례 중간에 더 오래 멈추고 겹치지 않으며, 상대방의 차례가 끝나거나 중단되는 것을 피하는 또 다른 스타일과는 (B) 상당히 다르다. 방해받지 않고, 강요하지 않는 이런 스타일은 배려심이 높은 스타일이라고 불린다. 일반적으로 첫 번째 스타일의 화자가 두 번째 스타일의 화자와 대화를 나눌 때, 대화가 일방적으로 진행되는 경향이 있다. 참여도가 높은 적극적인 스타일의 화자가 다른 스타일 화자를 압도하는 경향이 있다. 두 화자가 모두 서로 대화 스타일이 약간 다르다는 것을 반드시 인식하는 것은 아니다. 대신, 속사포 쏘아대듯 빠르게 말하는 화자는 더 느리게 말하는 화자를 그저 할 말이 별로 없고, 수줍음이 많으며, 아마 지루하거나 심지어 멍청한 사람이라고 생각할 수 있다. 반대로, 그 또는 그녀는 시끄럽고, 억지스럽고, 거만하고, 이기적이고, 심지어 지겨운 사람이라고 여겨질 가능성이 높다. 대화 스타일의 특징은 종종 (C) 성격 특성으로 해석된다.

VOCA

- characterize ~의 특색을 이루다, 특징짓다
- turn-taking 돌아가면서 (교대로) 하는 것
- invest with (특정한 자질·특징 등을) 띠게 하다
- misunderstanding 오해, 잘못 생각함
- participation 참가, 참여
- speaking rate 발화 속도
- interruption (말을) 가로막음[방해함]
- considerateness 사려 깊음, 배려심 있음
- rapid-fire 잇따라 쏘아 대는, 속사포 같은
- pushy 억지가 센, 밀어붙이는
- domineering 오만한, 거만한
- tiresome 피곤한, 지겨운

18 난도 ★★☆   정답 ①

어법 > 비문 찾기

[정답의 이유]

관계대명사 which의 선행사가 복수명사(charged particles)로 관계사절의 동사(make)가 복수형 동사로 적절하게 사용되었다. 이때 목적어(them)는 단수명사인 a plasma를 가리키고 있으므로, ① 'which make them → which make it'이 되어야 한다.

태양은 기체, 액체, 고체가 아닌 물질인 플라즈마로 구성되어 있다. 대신, 플라즈마는 전하를 띤 입자들로 구성되어 있는데, 그것들은 플라즈마를 강력한 전기 전도체로 만든다. 이러한 강력한 전자기장뿐만 아니라, 태양은 자기장으로 가득 차 있다. 자기장 선들이 거대한 새장처럼 태양을 둘러싸고 있다. 태양의 자력은 매초 백만 톤의 플라즈마를 바깥쪽으로 날리는 '태양풍'을 일으키는데, 플라즈마는 시속 100만 마일로 이동한다. 때때로 이 사건은 수억 메가톤의 다이너마이트에 해당하는 에너지를 방출하는 태양 표면의 폭발(solar flare)이라고 불리는 강력한 플라즈마 폭발을 일으킬 수 있다. 이 에너지가 지구를 향하면, 우리는 태양 폭풍의 영향을 느낀다.

VOCA

- consist of ~로 구성되다
- plasma 플라즈마
- particle 미립자
- conductor (열·전기·소리 등의) (전)도체
- electricity 전기
- be packed with ~으로 가득 차다
- magnetic field 자기장, 자장
- wrap 싸다[둘러싸다]
- magnetism 자성(磁性), 자력
- solar wind 태양풍(風)
- fling 던지다[내밀다]
- outward 밖으로 향하는
- explosion 폭발, 폭파
- solar flare 태양 표면의 폭발
- release 놓아 주다[날려 보내다/방출하다]
- equivalent 동등한[맞먹는]
- megaton 메가톤(폭발력 측정 단위. TNT 100만 톤 상당)
- solar storm 태양 폭풍

19 난도 ★★★   정답 ②

독해 > 글의 일관성 > 글의 순서

[정답의 이유]

두 번째 문장의 '~ we may either be trying to fit in or to belong.' 다음에는 문맥상 'Fitting in involves changing ourselves to match situations, ~'라고 환경에 우리 자신을 맞추는 방식을 설명하는 (A)가 와야 한다. 또한 (A) 마지막의 'feelings of anxiety or loneliness'를 (D)에서 'It is easier in the sense that it doesn't require going against the norm.'이라고 부연 설명하고 있으므로 (A) 뒤에는 (D)가 오는 것이 자연스럽다. (D) 마지막 부분을 보면, 다른 사람의 기대에 맞추려고 애쓰면 우리의 진정한 자아에 대한 소속감을 상실한다고 했는데, (B)에서 '게다가(In addition)' 다른 사람에게 맞추려는 압박감에 건강하지 못한 관계에 참여하거나 대중에 편승하게 된다고 하면서 환경에 자신을 맞추는 방식의 또 다른 단점을 언급하고 있으므로 (D) 다음에 (B)가 오는 것이 적절하다. 마지막으로 (C)에서 소속한다는 것은 있는 그대로의 우리의 진

정한 또는 진짜 자신으로 알려지도록 하는 것이라고 설명한 다음에, '다르다는 것은 우리에게 감정적인 불확실성과 위험에 노출된 취약성'을 느끼게 만들 수 있지만, '~ this same vulnerability that becomes the foundation on which courage is built.'라고 결론을 맺고 있다. 따라서 글의 순서로 가장 적절한 것은 ② '(A) – (D) – (B) – (C)'이다.

본문해석

어린 나이에, 우리는 우리가 어떻게 보이는지, 누구와 어울릴지, 시간을 어떻게 보낼지 결정하기 시작한다. 이런 선택을 하면서, 우리는 맞추려고 하거나 소속감을 느끼려고 노력할 것이다.
(A) 맞춘다는 것은 상황에 맞게 우리 자신을 변화하는 것으로, 예를 들어 적절한 옷을 입고, 가장 인기 있는 스포츠를 하거나, '최고'의 사교적인 단체들과 함께 어울리는 것 등을 포함하지만, 그것은 불안감이나 외로움을 유발할 수 있다.
(D) 그것은 규범을 반대할 필요가 없다는 점에서 더 쉽다. 하지만, 그것은 수치심을 기반으로 하며 젊은이들에게 자신들이 충분하지 않다는 것을 암시한다. 타인의 기대에 순응하려고 애쓰다 보면, 진정한 자아에 대한 소속감을 상실한다.
(B) 게다가, 전반적으로 자신들의 정체성에 건전하지 않은 방식으로 맞춰야 한다는 압박감을 느낀 젊은이들은 결국 건강하지 못한 관계에 참여하거나 대중에 편승하게 될 수 있다.
(C) 소속한다는 것은 다른 것이다. 그것은 우리 자신을 보이는 것이고, 있는 그대로의 우리의 진정한 또는 진짜 자신으로 알려지도록 하는 것이다. 그것은 우리를 기분 좋게 하거나 우리가 진정한 자신이 될 수 있는 사람들에게 우리의 독특함을 보여줄 수 있도록 해주는 옷을 입는 것이다.
하지만 그것은 쉽지 않다. 남들과 다르다는 것은 우리에게 감정적인 불확실성과 위험에 노출된 취약성을 느끼게 만들 수 있다. 하지만 용기를 만드는 기반이 되는 것은 바로 이러한 취약성이다.

VOCA

- hang out with ~와 시간을 보내다
- fit in 맞추다, 정하다
- require 필요하다, 요구하다
- norm 규범, 기준
- shame-based 수치심에 사로잡힌
- strive 분투하다
- conform 따르다[순응하다]
- feel pressured to 반드시 ~해야 한다고 생각하다
- end up 결국 (어떤 처지에) 처하게 되다
- authentic 진본[진품]인
- uniqueness 독특성, 고유성
- vulnerable 취약한, 연약한
- exposed to ~에 드러내다
- uncertainty 불확실성, 반신반의
- vulnerability 취약성

20 난도 ★★☆ 정답 ③

독해 > 세부 내용 찾기 > 제목, 주제

정답의 이유

여섯 번째 문장에서 'Thus, processes and services are important to keep in mind when looking for ways to innovate(따라서 혁신 방법을 찾을 때 프로세스와 서비스를 염두에 두는 것이 중요하다).'라고 한 다음에, 마지막에서 서비스형 소프트웨어(SaaS)와 구독 기반 컴퓨팅 모델의 출현으로 이전에 제품으로 제공되던 기능이 이제 서비스의 영역으로 이동하고 있다고 했으므로 글의 제목으로 적절한 것은 ③ 'Beyond Products: Embracing Process and Service Innovations(제품을 넘어서: 프로세스 및 서비스 혁신에 대한 수용)'이다.

오답의 이유

① 프로세스 및 서비스 혁신에 대한 무시
② 기술적인 혁신에만 집중
④ 프로세스 및 서비스 혁신의 중요성 간과
⑤ 기술 및 제품에 한정된 혁신

본문해석

실제로 우리가 매일 경험하는 중요한 프로세스 및 서비스 혁신이 많은 경우에, 사람들은 일반적으로 혁신을 기술 및 제품과 연관시킨다. 이러한 잘못된 믿음은 생산 프로세스가 최종 사용자에게 보이지 않고, 마찬가지로 서비스도 무형적이라는 사실에 그 뿌리를 두고 있다. 그 결과, 더 적은 관심이 그것들에 간다. 어떤 것을 더 효율적으로, 더 많은 양 또는 더 적은 비용으로 생산할 수 있는 방법을 발견하는 것은 확실하게 상당한 독창성을 수반하며, 의심할 여지 없이 진정한 가치를 창출할 것이다. 또한, 우리 경제가 점점 더 서비스 지향적으로 되고 있기 때문에, 더 나은 서비스 제공 방법을 상상함으로써 가치를 창출할 수 있는 기회도 많다. 따라서 혁신 방법을 찾을 때 프로세스와 서비스를 염두에 두는 것이 중요하다. 게다가, 서비스형 소프트웨어(SaaS)와 구독 기반 컴퓨팅 모델의 출현으로 이전에 제품으로 제공되던 기능이 이제 서비스의 영역으로 이동하고 있다.

VOCA

- associate 관련시키다
- mistaken 잘못된, (생각이) 틀린
- take roots in ~에 뿌리를 박다
- invisible 눈에 보이지 않는, 감추어진
- end-user 최종 사용자
- intangible 만질 수 없는, 무형의
- identify 찾다, 발견하다
- ingenuity 기발한 재주, 재간, 독창성
- genuine 진짜의, 진품의
- service-oriented 서비스 지향적인, 봉사 위주의
- with the advent of ~의 도래(출현)으로(에 따라)
- Software-as-a-Service 서비스형 소프트웨어
- subscription-based 구독 기반의
- functionality 기능성, (컴퓨터·전자 장치의) 기능
- realm 영역[범위]

21 난도 ★★☆　　　　　　　　　　　정답 ④

정답의 이유

book은 타동사로 '(피의자에 대해) 기록하다'의 뜻인데, booking 다음에 목적어가 없고 용의자가 '기록되는' 수동의 의미이므로 수동태가 되어야 한다. 이때, 전치사(after) 다음에는 명사 상당어구가 와야 하므로, ④ 'booking → being booked'가 되어야 한다.

본문해석

텔레비전 범죄 쇼에서 어떻게 보여지든, 체포 후 보석금을 내는 것은 간단한 문제가 아니다. 용의자가 체포되면, 우선 그 또는 그녀는 절차를 진행하기 위해 경찰서로 이송된다. 그러고 나서 담당 경찰관이 용의자의 신상 정보(이름, 주소, 생일, 용모)를 범죄 혐의 정보와 함께 기록한다. 다음에, 경찰관은 범죄경력조회를 수행하고 용의자의 지문과 범인 식별용 사진인 머그샷을 찍고 (추후 반환될) 모든 개인 재산을 압수하고 용의자를 구치소에 수감한다. 덜 심각한 범죄의 경우, 용의자는 경찰 기록부에 기록된 후에 바로 보석이 허용될 수 있다. 좀 더 심각한 범죄의 경우, 용의자는 때때로 보석 심리를 위해 2일 정도 기다려야 하는데, 그때 판사가 피고인의 보석 가능 여부와 보석금을 결정한다. 보석금 액수는 범죄의 심각성에 달려 있다.

VOCA

- post　(보석금을) 내다
- bail　보석
- arrest　체포하다
- suspect　혐의자, 용의자
- alleged　가정의, 추정의
- criminal background check　범죄경력조회
- mug shot　범인 식별용 얼굴 사진
- confiscate　몰수[압수]하다
- book　[피의자를] 경찰 기록부에 기록하다
- bail hearing　보석 심리
- determine　(공식적으로) 확정[결정]하다
- accused　피의자[피고(인)]
- be eligible for　~할 자격이 있다
- severity　심각성

22 난도 ★★☆　　　　　　　　　　　정답 ⑤

독해 > 대의 파악 > 요지, 주장

정답의 이유

두 번째 단락에서 인터넷 검색 습관이 개인의 사고와 읽기에 미치는 영향에 대한 실험 결과를 설명하는데, 두 번째 문장의 후반부에서 실험 결과에 대해 '~ suggests that we may well be in the midst of a sea change in the way we read and think.'라고 했다. 마지막에서 세 번째 문장에서 사이트를 사용하는 사람들이 여러 사이트를 빠르게 점프하듯이 이동하는 '훑어보기 활동(skimming activity)'을 한다는 것을 발견했다고 했으므로, 글의 요지로 적절한 것은 ⑤ 'People are experiencing a transformative change in the way they read and think due to their online research habits, skimming and quickly jumping between sources(사람들은 출처 사이를 훑어보고 재빨리 점프하듯이 이동하는 자신들의 온라인 검색 습관으로 인해 읽고 생각하는 방식에서 변혁적인 변화를 겪고 있다).'이다.

오답의 이유

① 콘텐츠에 깊이 관여하지 않고 출처를 대충 훑어보고 빠르게 다른 것으로 이동하는 사람들이 늘어나고 있다.

② 인터넷 사용이 인지에 미치는 장기적인 영향의 심층 연구는 인터넷이 우리의 사고 과정에만 영향을 미치는지에 대한 결정적인 증거를 제공할 것이다.

③ 사람들은 다양한 온라인 소스의 간략한 발췌 텍스트를 철저하게 스캔하는 경향이 있다.

④ 개인이 긴 기사를 북마크하거나 저장할 수는 있지만, 후에 재방문해서 그것들을 읽었다고 볼 수 있는 증거는 없다.

본문해석

의학 분야에서의 컴퓨터 사용에 대해 정기적으로 블로그에 기록하는 Bruce Friedman은 인터넷이 그의 정신적 습관을 어떻게 바꾸어 놓았는지 설명했다. "나는 이제 웹이나 인쇄물에 있는 긴 기사를 읽고 흡수하는 능력을 거의 완전히 상실했어요."라고 그는 연초에 썼다. 미시간 대학교 의과대학 교수로 오랫동안 재직해 온 병리학자인 Friedman은 나와의 전화 통화에서 자신의 의견을 자세히 설명했다. 그의 말에 따르면, 그의 사고는 '스타카토'의 특성을 띠는데, 다수의 온라인 자료로부터 짧은 텍스트를 빠르게 스캔하는 그의 방식을 반영한다고 했다. "나는 더 이상 '전쟁과 평화'를 읽을 수 없어요."라고 그는 시인했다. "나는 그렇게 할 수 있는 능력을 상실했어요. 심지어 서너 단락 이상의 블로그 게시물도 파악하기에 너무 많아요. 나는 그것을 대충 훑어보지요."

일화들만으로는 많은 것을 증명할 수 없다. 그리고 우리는 여전히 인터넷 사용이 인지에 어떻게 영향을 미치는지에 대한 확실한 그림을 제공할 장기적이고 신경학적 그리고 심리학적 실험들을 기다린다. 하지만 University College London의 학자들에 의해 실시된 온라인 탐색 습관에 대한 최근 발표된 연구는 우리가 읽고 생각하는 방식에 있어 변화의 바다 한복판에 있을 수도 있음을 시사한다. 5년간 연구 프로그램의 일환으로, 학자들은 저널 기사, 전자책, 그리고 다른 출처의 문서 정보에 접근할 수 있는 영국 도서관과 영국의 교육 컨소시엄에 의해 운영되는 두 개의 인기 있는 연구 사이트 방문자들의 행동을 기록하는 컴퓨터 로그를 조사했다. 그들은 그 사이트를 사용하는 사람들이 한 출처에서 다른 출처로 점프하여 이동하는데, 그들이 이미 방문했던 출처로는 거의 돌아가지 않는 일종의 '훑어보기 활동'을 보인다는 것을 발견했다. 그들은 다른 사이트로 '이동'하기 전에, 일반적으로 한두 페이지 이하의 기사나 책을 읽는다. 때로 그들은 긴 기사를 저장하기는 했지만, 그들이 되돌아가서 실제로 그것을 읽었다는 증거는 없다.

VOCA

- blog　블로그를 기록하다
- absorb　(정보를) 받아들이다

- longish 꽤[약간] 긴
- pathologist 병리학자
- elaborate 자세히 말[설명]하다
- take on (성질·기운 등을) 띠다
- skim 훑어보다
- anecdote 일화
- await 기다리다
- neurological 신경의, 신경학의
- cognition 인식, 인지
- in the midst of ~의 한가운데에
- consortium 컨소시엄, 협력단

23 난도 ★★☆   정답 ③

독해 > 글의 일관성 > 문장 삽입

정답의 이유

주어진 문장에서 '식물의 형태학도 자외선에 의해 영향을 받을 수 있다.'라고 했는데, (C) 다음에서 에콰도르 키토 근처 안데스 산맥의 매우 높은 고도에서 자라는 오렌지 나무는 캘리포니아 리버사이드의 지중해 기후대의 낮은 고도에서 자라는 동일한 어린 가지보다 더 가지가 갈라진 외형을 가지고 있다고 했으므로, 문맥상 주어진 문장이 들어갈 위치로 적절한 곳은 (C)이다.

본문해석

식물에 대한 자외선의 가장 파괴적인 영향은 돌연변이를 일으키는 DNA의 손상과 관련 있다. 생물량 생산의 감소와 광합성의 비기공적인 측면과 같은 생리학적인 영향이 발생할 수 있다. 식물은 낮과 밤 동안에 자외선에 의한 DNA 손상과 광합성 손상을 부분적으로 복구할 수 있다. 중파장 자외선(UV-B)의 복사에너지를 쬐었을 때 다른 벼 품종보다 더 큰 성장 억제와 잎 갈변 현상을 나타낸다는 점에서, 자외선에 더 민감한 특정 벼 품종을 대상으로 연구가 진행되었다. 자외선에 민감한 품종은 자외선에 내성이 있는 품종에 비해 주간의 광복구(photo-repair)와 야간의 DNA 절제수복(excision repair of DNA)이 모두 부족했다. 식물 형태학도 자외선에 의해 영향을 받을 수 있다. 에콰도르 키토 근처 안데스 산맥의 매우 높은 고도에서 자라는 오렌지 나무는 캘리포니아 리버사이드의 지중해 기후대의 낮은 고도에서 자라는 동일한 어린 가지보다 더 가지가 갈라진 외형을 가지고 있다. 그 효과는 오렌지 나무 위에 자외선을 흡수하는 스크린을 설치함으로써 제거되었는데, 이는 과도하게 갈라진 가지 모양은 안데스 산맥의 높은 자외선이 가지의 분열에 미치는 영향 때문일 수 있음을 나타낸다. 높은 자외선에 대한 보호 작용이 식물에서 페놀 화합물을 포함한 표피 세포나 잎 털에 의해 발생할 수 있다.

VOCA

- UV radiation 자외선 복사
- mutation 돌연변이 (과정)
- biomass 생물량(어떤 지역 내의 단위 면적[체적]당 수치로 표시된 생물의 현존량)
- non-stomatal 비기문, 비기공

- aspect 측면, 양상
- photosynthesis 광합성
- cultivar 품종
- UV-sensitive 자외선에 민감한
- inhibition 억제, 금지
- browning [식물] 갈변
- deficient 부족한[결핍된]
- UV-tolerant 자외선 저항력이 있는
- morphology 형태학
- branched 가지가 있는, 가지가 갈라진
- scion 어린 가지, 접가지
- elevation 고도, 높이
- climatic zone 기후대
- install 정착하게[자리잡게] 하다
- UV-absorbing 자외선을 흡수하는
- meristem (식물)분열 조직
- epidermal cell 표피세포
- phenolic compound 페놀성 화합물

24 난도 ★★☆   정답 ①

독해 > 대의 파악 > 추론

정답의 이유

세 번째 문장에서 cell therapy의 효과에 대해서 '~ animal cells, when injected into the human body, are destroyed by the immune system(동물 세포가 인체에 주사되었을 때 면역 체계에 의해 파괴된다).'이라고 했고, 다섯 번째 문장의 후반부에서 chelation therapy의 효과에 대해서 '~ yet research shows no such effect(그러한 효과를 보여주는 연구가 없다).'라고 했다. 마지막 문장에서 HGH tablets or spray의 효과에 대해서 'There is, however, evidence that HGH in any form may produce side effects like an increased risk of cancer and cardiovascular disease(그러나 어떤 형태로든 HGH가 암과 심혈관 질환의 위험 증가 같은 부작용을 일으킬 수 있다는 증거가 있다).'라고 했으므로, 주어진 글에서 추론할 수 있는 것은 ① 'Therapies designed to keep people young are generally ineffective(사람들의 젊음을 유지하기 위해 고안된 치료법은 일반적으로 효과가 없다).'이다.

오답의 이유

② 중금속 제거 요법보다는 세포 (주입) 요법에 더 의존하는 것이 더 낫다.

③ HGH 정제는 부작용이 더 적기 때문에 젊음을 추구하는 사람들에게 매력적이다.

④ 젊음을 더 유지하려는 치료법들은 단지 그 비용을 충분히 감당할 수 있는 부유한 사람들만을 위한 것이 아니라 모든 사람들이 이용할 수 있어야 한다.

⑤ 사람들이 젊음을 유지하도록 돕기 위해 고안된 치료법은 언제나 항상 좋은 점보다는 해로운 점이 더 많다.

수년에 걸쳐 수많은 남성들과 여성들이 세포 주입 요법으로 알려진 치료법에 거액을 지불했다. 그 이유는 단순했다. 어린 양의 세포 주사가 젊음을 유지하는 데 도움을 줄 수 있다고 믿었기 때문이다. 그런 사람들은 동물 세포가 인체에 주사되었을 때 면역 체계에 의해 파괴된다는 것을 알지 못하는 듯하다. 비슷한 방식으로 젊음을 추구하는 다른 사람들은 중금속 제거 요법을 시도했는데, 그것은 인체로부터 납, 수은 같은 중금속을 끌어내는 것이다. 지지자들은, 그 요법이 인체에서 독을 제거함으로써 세포 기능을 개선하고, 노화 과정을 억제하며, 심장병을 예방한다고 주장하지만, 그러한 효과를 보여주는 연구가 없다. 사실, 비평가들은 인체에 독이 있다는 생각부터 의문을 제기하며, 그 치료법으로 치료할 수 있는 것이 없다는 것을 암시한다. 젊음의 샘을 찾는 다른 사람들은 인간 성장 호르몬(HGH) 정제나 스프레이를 사용한다. 이 스프레이와 알약은 주름 제거부터 기억력과 집중력 향상까지 모든 것을 해낼 수 있다고 추정된다. 그러나 그러한 치료법들은 이런 주장을 뒷받침하는 연구가 없다. 그러나 어떤 형태로든 HGH가 암과 심혈관 질환의 위험 증가 같은 부작용을 일으킬 수 있다는 증거가 있다.

- treatment 치료, 처치
- cell therapy 세포 (주입) 요법[양(羊)의 태아의 세포를 주입하는 회춘법(回春法)]
- maintain 유지하다[지키다]
- apparently 보기에 (…인 듯하다), 외관상으로는
- immune system 면역 체계
- pursuit 추구, (원하는 것을) 좇음[찾음]
- chelation therapy 중금속 제거 요법
- heavy metal 중금속
- proponent 옹호자, 지지자
- question 의문을 갖다, 이의를 제기하다
- allegedly 전해지는 바에 의하면
- accomplish 이루어 내다, 성취하다
- wrinkle 주름
- back up ~을 뒷받침하다[도와주다], 지지하다
- side effect 부작용
- cardiovascular disease 심장혈관계 질병

25 난도 ★★☆ 정답 ③

독해 > 세부 내용 찾기 > 내용 (불)일치

정답의 이유

열 번째 문장에서 'Key examples are mustard and garlic, which contain "mucilage"—a mix of carbohydrates—that can act as emulsifiers(주요한 사례는 유화제 역할을 할 수 있는 탄수화물의 혼합물이 끈적끈적한 '점액'을 포함하고 있는 겨자와 마늘이다).'라고 했으므로 글의 내용과 일치하는 것은 ③ 'Mustard and garlic contain molecules that act as a bridge between oil and water(겨자와 마늘에는 기름과 물의 가교 역할을 하는 분자가 들어 있다).'이다.

오답의 이유

① 물과 기름의 분자는 동일한 화학적 성질을 갖고 있다. → 두 번째 문장에서 'The water and oil molecules have distinct chemical properties that don't interact well together(물과 기름의 분자는 서로 잘 상호작용하지 않는 뚜렷한 화학적 성질을 가지고 있다).'라고 했으므로 글의 내용과 일치하지 않는다.

② 흔드는 것은 오일과 식초의 영구적인 혼합 형성을 위한 필수적인 방법이다. → 다섯 번째 문장에서 'The secret to blending them together is to add an extra ingredient known as a "surfactant" or emulsifier(그것들을 함께 혼합하는 비결은 '계면활성제' 또는 유화제라고 알려진 여분의 성분을 추가하는 것이다).'라고 했으므로 글의 내용과 일치하지 않는다.

④ 시판되는 샐러드 드레싱에는 인공 식품 첨가물만 함유되어 있다. → 마지막에서 네 번째 문장에서 'Commercial salad dressings also contain naturally sourced emulsifying carbohydrates(상업용 샐러드 드레싱에도 자연적으로 공급되는 유화 탄수화물이 포함되어 있다).'라고 했으므로 글의 내용과 일치하지 않는다.

⑤ 화학첨가제가 인체에 미치는 영향이 검증되었다. → 마지막 문장에서 'It's too early to say exactly what this means for humans(이것이 인간에게 무엇을 의미하는지를 정확하게 말하기는 시기적으로 너무 이르다).'라고 했으므로 글의 내용과 일치하지 않는다.

기름과 물이 섞이지 않는 것은 일반적인 상식이다. 물과 기름의 분자는 서로 잘 상호작용하지 않는 뚜렷한 화학적 성질을 가지고 있다. 기름과 식초(대부분 물)를 함께 흔들어 샐러드 드레싱을 만들려고 하면, 일시적으로 현탁액이 생겨 금방 분리되는 것을 본 적이 있을 것이다. 물과 기름층을 분해하고 섞는 데는 큰 에너지 비용이 든다. 그것들을 함께 혼합하는 비결은 '계면활성제' 또는 유화제라고 알려진 여분의 성분을 추가하는 것이다. 계면활성제라는 이름은 '표면 활성'에서 유래되었다. 이는 표면 또는 계면에서 작용하여 기름과 물 사이의 상호작용을 연결한다는 것을 강조한다. 이것은 세제가 접시에서 기름기를 제거하는 방법과 유사하다. 많은 비네그레트 레시피가 유화제의 결정적인 유화 역할에 대해 특별히 언급하지 않고 유화제를 요청한다. 주요한 사례는 유화제 역할을 할 수 있는 탄수화물의 혼합물인 끈적끈적한 '점액(mucilage)'을 포함하고 있는 겨

자와 마늘이다. 따라서 식초/식용유 샐러드 드레싱이 분리되고 있다면, (멋진 향의 화학 물질도 포함되어 있는) 이러한 성분을 충분히 첨가하고 있는지 확인해라. 상업용 샐러드 드레싱에도 자연적으로 공급되는 유화 탄수화물이 포함되어 있다. 이것들은 종종 '식물성 껌' 또는 이와 유사한 일반적인 명칭으로 표시되는 경우가 많으므로, 출처를 알아내려면 라벨을 읽고 식품 첨가물 번호를 좀 더 깊이 파고들어 철저히 조사할 필요가 있다. 연구원들은 가공식품에 사용되는 합성 유화제에 대해 의문을 제기하고 있는데, 생쥐 대상 연구에서 그것들이 건강상 위험성을 갖고 있다는 사실이 알려졌기 때문이다. 이것이 인간에게 무엇을 의미하는지를 정확하게 말하기는 시기적으로 너무 이르다.

VOCA

- molecule 분자
- distinct 뚜렷한, 분명한
- chemical property 화학적 성질
- interact 상호작용을 하다
- vinegar 식초
- suspension 현탁액, 부유액
- separate 분리되다, 나뉘다
- break apart 분리되다, 분해되다
- blend 섞다, 혼합하다
- ingredient 재료[성분]
- surfactant 계면[표면]활성제
- emulsifier 유화제
- interface 접속하다[되다]
- bridge 다리를 놓다, ~에게 중개 역할을 하다
- interaction 상호 작용[영향]
- detergent 세제
- carbohydrate 탄수화물
- generic 포괄적인, 총칭[통칭]의
- delve 깊이 파고들다, 철저히 조사하다
- additive 첨가물, 첨가제
- synthetic 합성한, 인조의

영어 | 2023년 국회직 8급

한눈에 훑어보기

✅ 영역 분석

어휘 01
1문항, 4%

독해 02 04 05 06 07 08 09 10 11 13 14 15
17 18 19 20 21 22 23 24 25
21문항, 84%

어법 03 12 16
3문항, 12%

✅ 빠른 정답

01	02	03	04	05	06	07	08	09	10
③	①	④	⑤	②	⑤	②	④	①	③
11	12	13	14	15	16	17	18	19	20
①	④	⑤	③	⑤	③	④	④	②	②
21	22	23	24	25					
①	②	⑤	③	④					

✅ 점수 체크

구분	1회독	2회독	3회독
맞힌 문항 수	/ 25	/ 25	/ 25
나의 점수	점	점	점

01 난도 ★☆☆ 정답 ③

어휘 > 단어

[정답의 이유]

밑줄 친 mitigating은 '완화하다, 경감시키다'라는 뜻의 mitigate의 분사형으로 명사 benefits를 수식하고 있다. 따라서 밑줄 친 단어와 그 의미가 가장 가까운 것은 ③ 'alleviating(완화하는)'이다.

[오답의 이유]

① 악화시키는
② 증대하는
④ 향상시키는
⑤ 악화시키는

[본문해석]

높은 에너지 비용으로부터 가정과 기업을 보호하기 위한 유럽 정부의 노력은 명백한 이점들, 특히 인플레이션 압력을 완화하는 이점들을 갖고 있다. 하지만 그것들은 훨씬 더 큰 비용을 수반하는데, 유럽연합 집행기관은 이를 무시하기보다는 강조해야 한다.

[VOCA]

- shield 보호하다, 가리다
- household 가정
- not least 특히
- mitigate 완화[경감]시키다
- European Commission 유럽연합 집행기관
- highlight 강조하다

02 난도 ★★☆ 정답 ①

독해 > 빈칸 완성 > 단어 · 구 · 절

[정답의 이유]

주어진 글은 식품 사막의 정의가 도시와 시골에 따라 다르다는 내용이다. 빈칸 문장에서 '식품 사막은 신선하고, 흠 없는 건강한 음식으로의 ~을 가지고 있는 지역이나 주민이다.'라고 한 다음에 빈칸 다음 문장에서 도시의 식품 사막에서는 상당 비율의 지역주민들이 신선한 음식 제공자로부터 1마일 이상 떨어져 살고 있으며, 시골 지역에서는 신선한 음식 공급원으로부터 적어도 10마일은 떨어져 있어야 한다고 했으므로, 문맥상 빈칸에 들어갈 알맞은 말은 ① 'limited access(제한된 접근)'이다.

[오답의 이유]

② 불안한 순간들
③ 복잡한 감정들

④ 한정된 배급

⑤ 불안한 선호

식품 사막은 여러 이유 때문에 사람들이 신선하고, 흠이 없고, 건강한 음식으로의 제한된 접근을 가지고 있는 지역이나 주민이다. 많은 사람들이 미국 농무부(USDA)의 정의를 사용하는 경향이 있다. "도시의 식품 사막에서는 지역 주민의 상당 비율이 슈퍼마켓이나 농부들의 직거래 시장과 같은 신선한 음식 제공자로부터 1마일 이상 떨어져 살고 있다. 시골 지역에서는 식품 사막은 신선한 음식 공급원으로부터 적어도 10마일은 떨어져 있다."

VOCA

- food desert 식품 사막(신선한 음식을 구매하기 어렵거나 그런 음식이 너무 비싼 지역)
- whole 흠 없는, 온전한, 순수한
- tend (~하는) 경향이 있다
- urban 도시의, 도회지의
- significant 특별한 의미가 있는, 중요한
- farmers' market (농부들이 경작한 상품을 직접 내다 파는) 직거래 시장
- resident 거주자[주민]
- rural area 시골 지역

03 난도 ★★☆ 　　　　　　　　　　　　정답 ④

어법 > 비문 찾기

정답의 이유

④ 앞의 전치사구인 with knowledge 다음에 by other people이 있으므로 impart는 명사 knowledge를 수식하는 과거분사가 되어야 한다. 즉, 문맥상 knowledge와 impart의 관계가 수동인 '전달받는' 것이므로, impart → imparted가 되어야 한다.

오답의 이유

① that은 선행사 something을 수식하는 목적격 관계대명사로 어법상 적절하게 사용되었다.

② develop은 관계사절의 동사로 can이 있으므로, improve와 함께 동사원형으로 적절하게 사용되었다.

③ 전치사 through는 '~을 통해'라는 뜻이며, 다음에 명사(our experiences)가 왔으므로 어법상 적절하게 사용되었다.

⑤ 'enough+to부정사'는 '충분히 ~만큼 …하다'의 뜻이므로, 어법상 적절하게 사용되었다.

우리는 문화지능(Cultural Intelligence)을 우리가 생애 동안 지속적으로 개선하고 발전할 수 있는 무언가로 생각해야 한다. 그것을 얻는 데는 어려움이 있다. 우리는 우리의 경험을 통해서 이것을 하지만, 우리가 신뢰하고 우리에게 그들의 지식을 나눠줄 만큼 충분히 우리를 신뢰하는 다른 사람들에 의해 전달받은 지식으로도 이것을 한다.

VOCA

- Cultural Intelligence 문화지능
- think of A as B A를 B로 생각하다
- continuously 연달아
- duration of our lives 우리의 수명
- acquire 습득하다[얻다]

더 알아보기

관계대명사 that

- 관계대명사 that은 선행사가 사람, 사물, 동물에 상관없이 모두 사용할 수 있으므로 관계대명사(who, whom, which)를 대신할 수 있다. 다만, 관계대명사의 소유격(whose, of which)을 대신할 수는 없다.

  예 Movies that[which] are popular have a few characteristics in common.
  (인기 있는 영화들은 공통적인 몇몇 특징이 있다.)

  예 She is the greatest novelist that[who] has ever lived.
  (그녀는 생존했던 소설가 중에 가장 위대한 소설가이다.)

- 다음 경우에는 관계대명사 that을 쓴다.

선행사	관계대명사
사람+사물 의문사(who/what) the only[very/same]+명사 최상급/서수 all[little/much/any/some/nothing/ something/anything]	+관계대명사 that

  예 *Who* that has a family to support would waste so much money?
  (부양해야 할 가족을 가진 사람으로서 누가 그렇게 많은 돈을 낭비할까?)

  예 Man is *the only animal* that can speak.
  (사람은 말할 수 있는 유일한 동물이다.)

  예 You are *the very person* that I'd like to employ.
  (당신은 내가 채용하고픈 바로 그 사람이다.)

  예 *All* that glitters is not gold. (반짝이는 모든 것이 금은 아니다.)

  예 Timmy fixed almost *everything* that needed repairing.
  (Timmy는 수리가 필요한 거의 모든 것을 고쳤다.)

- 관계대명사 that은 계속적 용법(, that)과 전치사+that이 불가능하다.

  예 I said nothing, that made him angry. (×)

  → I said nothing, which made him angry. (○)
  (나는 아무 말도 안 했고, 그것이 그를 화나게 만들었다.)

04 난도 ★★☆

정답 ⑤

독해 > 대의 파악 > 추론

정답의 이유

마지막에서 두 번째 문장에서 'A BMI of 30 to 34.9 is mildly obese, while 35 to 39.9 is substantially obese(BMI가 30에서 34.9는 약간 비만인 반면, 35에서 39.9는 상당히 비만이다).'라고 했으므로, BMI 30부터 비만으로 간주한다는 것을 추론할 수 있다. 따라서 주어진 글에서 추론할 수 있는 것은 ⑤ 'A person is usually considered obese if his or her BMI is 30(BMI가 30인 사람은 보통 비만으로 간주된다).'이다.

오답의 이유

① 미국인의 절반 이상이 BMI 30 이상이다.
② BMI 30 이상인 사람은 누구나 암에 걸릴 것이다.
③ 60퍼센트 이상의 미국인들은 그들의 BMI를 알지 못한다.
④ BMI가 35 이상인 미국인은 거의 없다.

본문해석

비만은 오늘날 미국에서 가장 심각한 건강 문제에 해당한다. 미국 성인의 거의 60%가 과체중이거나 비만이다. 이것은 단지 외모의 문제가 아니다. 비만은 종종 당뇨병, 심장마비, 고혈압, 그리고 심지어 몇몇 형태의 암과 같은 심각한 건강 문제로 이어진다. 의료 전문가들은 일반적으로 체질량지수(BMI)를 사용하여 비만을 정의한다. BMI는 개인의 체중(킬로그램 단위)을 키(미터 단위)의 제곱으로 나누어 쉽게 계산할 수 있다. 정상적이거나 건강한 BMI는 25보다 작을 것이다. 체질량지수가 25에서 29.9 사이인 사람은 과체중으로 간주된다. BMI가 30에서 34.9는 약간 비만이지만, 35에서 39.9는 상당히 비만이다. 체질량지수가 40 이상인 사람들은 고도 비만으로 여겨진다.

VOCA

- obesity 비만
- represent (~에) 해당[상당]하다
- overweight 과체중의, 비만의
- obese 비만인
- lead to ~로 이어지다
- diabetes 당뇨병
- heart attacks 심근경색, 심장마비
- high blood pressure 고혈압
- Body Mass Index (BMI) 체질량지수
- substantially 상당히, 많이

05 난도 ★★☆

정답 ②

독해 > 세부 내용 찾기 > 내용 (불)일치

정답의 이유

주어진 글은 바퀴벌레는 많은 사람들이 싫어하지만, 실제 사람들에게 영향을 끼치는 종은 많지 않다는 내용이다. 네 번째 문장에서 'There are well over 4,000 described species of cockroach around the world, with some experts estimating that there are another 5,000 species that have yet to be classified by taxonomists.'라고 했으므로, 윗글의 내용과 일치하는 것은 ② 'There might be around 9,000 species of cockroach in the world according to some experts(일부 전문가들에 따르면, 세계에는 약 9,000종의 바퀴벌레가 있을 수 있다고 한다).'이다.

오답의 이유

① 모든 바퀴벌레는 해롭다. → 세 번째 문장에서 'But of the thousands of species out there, only a few can be considered pests.'라고 했으므로, 글의 내용과 일치하지 않는다.
③ 분류되지 않은 5천 종의 바퀴벌레가 어떤 하위 유형에 속하는지에 대해서는 의견이 일치한다. → 다섯 번째 문장에서 'Their classification is actually a point of contention ~'라고 했으므로, 글의 내용과 일치하지 않는다.
④ 대부분 미국인들은 그들의 집에서 약 24종의 다른 바퀴벌레를 만날 수 있다. → 마지막 문장에서 '~ but most people are likely to interact with no more than a dozen of them ~'라고 했으므로, 글의 내용과 일치하지 않는다.
⑤ 미국에 얼마나 많은 바퀴벌레의 과(科)가 사는지 아는 것은 쉽다. → 다섯 번째 문장의 후반부에서 '그것들이 어느 아목에 속하는지, 혹은 그것들이 얼마나 많은 과(科)로 구성되어 있는지'는 논쟁거리라고 했으므로 글의 내용과 일치하지 않는다.

본문해석

대부분의 사람들은 바퀴벌레가 역겹다고 생각한다. 그리고 만약 부엌의 불을 켰는데, 어두운 구석으로 재빨리 미끄러지듯이 사라지는 그것들을 발견한다면, 여러분은 아마도 동의할 것이다. 하지만 수천 종의 생물들 중 불과 몇몇 종만이 해충으로 간주될 수 있다. 전 세계적으로 4,000종 이상의 바퀴벌레가 기술되어 있으며, 일부 전문가들은 추측하기를 분류학자들에 의해 아직 분류되지 않은 또 다른 5,000종의 바퀴벌레가 있다고 한다. 그것들의 분류는 실제로 논쟁거리이며, 나는 그것들이 어느 아목에 속하는지 혹은 그것들이 얼마나 많은 과(科)로 구성되어 있는지에 대하여 입장을 취하지 않을 것이다. 대략 60~70여 종이 미국 대륙에서 발견될 수 있지만, 대부분 사람들은 그들이 사는 곳에 따라 그것들 중 단지 12종 정도의 바퀴벌레들만 영향을 끼칠 가능성이 높다.

VOCA

- cockroach 바퀴벌레
- disgusting 구역질나는, 정말 싫은
- skitter (잽싸게) 나아가다[달리다, 미끄러지다]
- pest 해충, 독충, 해를 끼치는 짐승, 유해물
- classify 분류[유별]하다, 등급으로 나누다
- taxonomist 분류학자
- classification 분류(법), 유별, 종별
- contention 말다툼, 논쟁, 논전
- take a position 태도[입장]를 취하다
- suborder 아목(亞目)
- interact with 상호 작용하다, 서로 영향을 끼치다
- no more than 단지 ~에 지나지 않다, ~일 뿐(only)

06 난도 ★★☆　　　　　　　　　　　　정답 ⑤

독해 > 대의 파악 > 제목, 주제

[정답의 이유]

주어진 글은 국가의 주권이 교통·통신 분야 기술의 발전으로 국가 간에 사람들과 경제가 서로 연결되면서 영향을 끼친다는 내용이다. 네 번째 문장에서 'International cooperation, ~ is increasingly necessary.'라고 했고, 다음 문장에서 'Technological progress ~ a trend captured by the term globalization.'이라고 했으므로 글의 흐름상 글의 제목으로 적절한 것은 ⑤ 'Globalization and International Cooperation(세계화와 국제협력)'이다.

[오답의 이유]

① 국가와 국가적인 과제
② 공권력과 주권
③ 세계적인 기술의 발전
④ 국제 관계와 독립

본문해석

어떤 경우에, 독립적이고 다른 국가에 속하지 않는다는 점에서 한 국가는 외부적으로 자주적일 수 있다. 그러나 국가적 과제는 외부로부터 예를 들어, 지배적인 이웃 국가에 의해 통제될 수 있다. 국가 간의 국제적인 협력과 통합은 국가의 모든 공권력이 국민이나 다른 내부적인 주권의 원천에서 나온다고 주장하는 것을 점점 더 어렵게 만든다. 국제적인 협력과 여러 국가로 구성된 상설 국제기구의 창설이 점점 더 필요해진다. 교통과 통신 분야의 기술적인 발전은 제품과 서비스가 생산되는 곳을 점점 더 상관없게 만드는데, 이는 세계화라는 용어에 의해 관심을 끌고 있는 추세이다. 사람들과 경제가 서로 연결되면서, 한 국가에서 내린 결정은 다른 국가의 사람들에게 영향을 미칠 수 있다.

VOCA

- externally　외부적으로
- sovereign　자주적인, 독립된
- dominant　우세한, 지배적인
- neighboring　근처[인근]의, 인접한
- integration　통합
- sovereignty　통치권, 자주권
- comprise　포함하다, 의미하다, 이루어지다, 구성되다
- irrelevant　부적절한, 무관한, 상관없는
- have an impact on　~에 영향을 주다

07 난도 ★★☆　　　　　　　　　　　　정답 ②

독해 > 세부 내용 찾기 > 내용 (불)일치

[정답의 이유]

주어진 글은 사람과 말에게 모두 전염되는 Hendra 바이러스에 대한 내용이다. 두 번째 문단의 후반부에서 질병의 원인은 박쥐에게서 나온 Hendra 바이러스라고 했고, 마지막 문장에서 'The virus passed from the bats to the horse, then to other horses and to people—with disastrous results.'라고 했으므로 Hendra 바이러스에 대한 내용과 일치하는 것은 ② 'It can be fatal to both humans and horses(그것은 인간과 말 모두에게 치명적일 수 있다).'이다.

[오답의 이유]

① 사람에게 나타나는 증상은 고열, 호흡곤란, 얼굴이 붓는 것을 포함한다. → 두 번째 문단의 두 번째 문장에서 'All had high fevers, difficulty breathing, facial swelling, and blood coming from their noses and mouths.'라고 했는데, 여기서 All은 바로 앞문장의 most of the other horses를 가리키고 있으므로, 글의 내용과 일치하지 않는다.

③ 말들은 마구간 근처의 오염된 풀을 먹은 후에 감염되었다. → 마지막에서 두 번째 문장에서 'This virus had originated in bats that lived in the tree where the first horse had been eating grass.'라고 했으므로, 글의 내용과 일치하지 않는다.

④ 그것은 인간으로부터 동물로 전염될 수 있다. → 마지막 문장에서 'The virus passed from the bats to the horse, then to other horses and to people ~'이라고 했으므로, 글의 내용과 일치하지 않는다.

⑤ 인간은 박쥐로부터 직접 감염되었다. → 마지막 문장에서 'The virus passed from the bats to the horse, then to other horses and to people ~'이라고 했으므로, 글의 내용과 일치하지 않는다.

본문해석

1994년 9월, 호주의 작은 마을에서 한 무리의 경주마들 사이에서 끔찍한 질병이 시작되었다. 첫 번째 희생자는 과일나무 아래에서 풀을 먹는 것이 마지막으로 목격된 암말이었다. 몇 시간 안에, 그 말의 건강은 급속도로 악화되었다. 세 명의 사람들, 즉 말 조련사와 조수, 수의사가 이 동물을 구하기 위해 힘썼다. 그럼에도 불구하고 그 말은 이틀 후에 죽었는데, 죽음의 원인은 불확실했다.

2주 내에 마구간에 있는 대부분의 다른 말들도 역시 병에 걸렸다. 모두가 고열, 호흡곤란 증상이 있었으며, 얼굴이 붓고, 코와 입에서 피가 나왔다. 한편, 조련사와 그의 조수도 병에 걸렸는데, 며칠 만에 조련사도 죽었다. 실험실 분석을 통해 마침내 문제의 근원을 발견했다. 말과 사람들은 Hendra 바이러스에 감염되었던 것이다. 이 바이러스는 첫 번째 말이 풀을 먹은 나무에 살던 박쥐들에게서 시작되었다. 그 바이러스는 박쥐에게서 말에게로, 그런 다음 다른 말들과 사람들에게 옮겨졌으며 그것은 재앙적인 결과를 낳았다.

VOCA

- racehorse　경주마(racer)
- veterinarian　수의사
- stable　마구간, (때로) 외양간
- facial　얼굴의, 안면의
- swell　부풀게 하다, 붓게 하다
- infect　전염시키다, 감염시키다
- pass from　~에서 옮겨지다
- disastrous　재해[재난]를 일으키는

독해 > 글의 일관성 > 글의 순서

정답의 이유

주어진 글의 마지막 문장에서 'Researchers report that there is science behind our style.'이라고 했으므로, 주어진 글 다음에는 'In their research(그들의 연구에서)'로 시작하는 (B)가 오는 것이 자연스럽다. (B)의 마지막 문장에서 참가자들이 집중하는 능력을 측정하는 시험을 했다고 했으므로, 문맥상 실험 결과를 설명하는 (C)에서 흰 가운을 입은 참가자가 평상복을 입은 참가자보다 수행 능력이 낫다고 한 내용으로 이어져야 한다. (C)의 마지막 문장에서 '연구원들은 흰 가운이 참가자들을 더 자신감 있고 조심스럽게 느끼도록 만들었다고 생각한다.'라고 하였으므로, (C) 다음에는 상징적인 의복이 사람들의 행동에 영향을 미치며 그 예로 경찰관의 제복과 판사의 법복을 설명하는 (A)가 와야 한다. 따라서 주어진 글에 이어질 글의 순서로 논리적인 것은 ④ '(B) − (C) − (A)'이다.

본문해석

우리는 종종 우리의 옷 때문에 다른 사람들이 우리를 어떻게 생각할지 걱정한다. 하지만 연구원들은 우리의 옷이 우리가 우리 자신을 보는 방법에 똑같이 강력한 영향을 미친다고 생각하기 시작했다. 연구원들은 우리의 스타일의 이면에는 과학이 있다고 보고한다.
(B) 그들의 연구에서, 연구원들은 일부 참가자들에게 과학자나 의사들이 입는 것과 유사한 흰색 실험실 가운을 입도록 했다. 다른 참가자들은 평범한 옷을 입었다. 참가자들은 집중하는 능력을 측정하는 시험을 치렀다.
(C) 흰 가운을 입은 사람들이 평상복을 입은 사람들보다 더 잘 수행했다. 연구원들은 흰 가운이 참가자들에게 더 자신감 있고 조심스럽게 느끼게 만들었다고 생각한다.
(A) 과학자들은 또한 다른 종류의 상징적인 의복이 그것을 입는 사람들의 행동에 영향을 미칠 수 있다고 믿는다. 예를 들면, 경찰관의 제복이나 판사의 법복은 입은 사람에게 권력이나 확신을 증가시킨다.

VOCA

• participant 참가자, 참여자
• lab coat 실험실 가운
• measure 측정하다, 치수를 재다
• confident 확신하고 (있는)
• judge 판사
• robe 예복, 관복, 법복

독해 > 빈칸 완성 > 단어 · 구 · 절

정답의 이유

주어진 글은 대법관 임명 과정과 대법관의 권한에 대한 내용이다. 빈칸 문장에서 '대법원은 ~하는 권한을 갖고 있다.'라고 했고, 빈칸 다음 문장에서 'This means they have the power to determine if a law is constitutional.'이라고 하면서 법이 합헌인지 아닌지에 대한 결정권을 가지고 있다는 것을 부연설명하고 있다. 따라서 빈칸에 들어갈 말로 적절한 것은 ① 'judicial review(위헌법률심사권)'이다.

오답의 이유

② 사회적 담론
③ 입법 행위
④ 법률 조직
⑤ 불요(不要)의 의견

본문해석

대법관이라고 불리는 9명의 판사들은 대법원에서 일하며, 그들은 모두 그들에게 제출된 모든 사건을 경청한다. 대통령이 대법원에서 근무하기를 원하는 사람들을 선택하면 상원은 대통령의 선택을 각각 확정하거나 거부한다. 그 혹은 그녀는 평생 대법원에 남을 것이다. 대법원에서 근무하도록 선택된다는 것은 대단한 명예인데, 그것은 대통령과 상원이 여러분이 헌법을 공정하게 해석할 것을 신뢰한다는 것을 보여주는 것이기 때문이다. 대법원은 위헌법률심사권을 가지고 있다. 이것은 그들이 법이 합헌인지 아닌지에 대한 결정권을 가지고 있다는 것을 의미한다. 만약 판사들이 그 법이 헌법과 일치하지 않다고 결정한다면, 그 법은 영원히 무효이다. 그것은 매우 어려운 일이며, 법원은 종종 어려운 결정을 내릴 때 5대 4로 의견이 갈리는데 그것은 모든 사람들이 헌법을 다르게 이해하기 때문이다.

VOCA

• Justice 판사, 재판관
• Supreme Court 대법원
• Senate 상원
• confirm (지위 · 합의 등을) 확정하다[공식화하다]
• reject 거부[거절]하다
• judicial review 위헌법률심사권(미국에서 연방 대법원의 위헌여부 판단권)
• constitutional 합헌적인, 헌법에 따르는
• line up with ~과 함께 일렬로 세우다
• invalid 효력 없는[무효한]
• tough decision 어려운 결정
• extrajudicial opinion 불요(不要)의 의견(당해 사건의 판결에 필요 불가결하지 않은 사항 또는 논점 외의 사항에 관하여 진술된 법원의 의견)

10 난도 ★★★   정답 ③

독해 > 글의 일관성 > 문장 삽입

정답의 이유

주어진 문장은 '이 증거는 전문가들에게 그 지하 도시가 적들로부터 도시의 주민들을 보호하기 위해 지어졌다는 사실을 믿게 한다.'라는 내용이다. (C) 이전 부분은 집을 수리하다가 우연히 발견한 벽 뒤에 숨겨진 방이 거대한 지하 도시로 연결되었다는 것을 발견했다는 내용이다. (C) 앞 문장에서 '그것은 안쪽에서만 열거나 닫을 수 있는 거대한 돌문을 포함하고 있다.'라고 했으므로, 주어진 문장의 'This piece of evidence(이 증거)'를 가리키고 있다는 것을 유추할 수 있다. (C) 다음 문장에서는 2만 명 이상의 사람들이 그 안에 숨을 수 있으며 600개가 넘는 문들이 기존의 집들 아래와 주변에 숨겨져 있는 도시로 이어진다고 했으므로 문맥상 주어진 문장이 들어가기에 적절한 곳은 ③ (C)이다.

본문해석

1963년, 튀르키예의 Cappadocia 지역의 한 거주자가 그의 집을 개조하고 있었다. 그의 벽들 중 하나를 철거하자, 그는 돌에 새겨서 만들어진 숨겨진 방을 발견하고 놀랐다. 그는 그 방을 탐험했고, 그것이 지하 도시로 이어진다는 것을 발견했다. 그 지하 도시는 깊이가 60미터가 넘었는데, 20층 건물을 짓기에 충분한 깊이였다. 그것은 안쪽에서만 열거나 닫을 수 있는 거대한 돌문을 포함하고 있다. 이 증거는 전문가들에게 그 지하 도시가 적들로부터 도시의 주민들을 보호하기 위해 지어졌다는 사실을 믿게 한다. 2만 명 이상의 사람들이 그 안에 숨을 수 있었다. 600개가 넘는 문들이 기존의 집들 아래와 주변에 숨겨져 있는 도시로 이어진다. 그 숨겨진 도시는 그들만의 종교 센터, 가축 마구간, 부엌, 그리고 심지어 학교까지 가지고 있었다. 하지만 전문가들은 그 지하 도시가 정확하게 얼마나 오래되었는지 정확하게 알지 못하는데, 그 지하 도시의 건설과 사용에 대한 기록이 사라졌기 때문이다.

VOCA

- renovation 수리, 수선
- knock down (건물을) 때려 부수다[철거하다]
- carve into 새겨서 ~을 만들다
- massive 거대한
- existing 기존의, 현재 사용되는
- livestock 가축
- stable 마구간

11 난도 ★★☆   정답 ①

독해 > 빈칸 완성 > 단어 · 구 · 절

정답의 이유

빈칸 다음 문장에서 'The Portion Cap Ruling, commonly known as the soda ban, was to restrict the sale of sugary drinks larger than 16 ounces in restaurants, movie theaters, sports arenas and delis.'라고 The Portion Cap Ruling을 부연설명하고 있고, 마지막 문장에서 '뉴욕시 보건국은 어떠한 입법적 위임이나 지침도 없이 입법에 참여했으며, 그리하여 뉴욕 시의회의 입법 관할권을 위반했다.'라고 패소한 이유를 말했다. 따라서 빈칸에 들어갈 알맞은 것은 ① 'New York City lost its final appeal to limit the sale of sugary drinks larger than 16 ounces(뉴욕시는 16온스 이상의 설탕이 든 음료의 판매를 제한하는 최종 항소에서 패소했다).'이다.

오답의 이유

② 1회 제공량은 몇 년 동안 기하급수적으로 증가했고 비만율은 치솟았다.

③ 비만율을 줄이고 싶다면, 우리는 음식 환경을 바꿔야 한다.

④ 설탕이 든 음료의 과소비가 뉴욕 시민들의 건강에 미치는 부정적 영향은 명백하다.

⑤ 우리는 우리 아이들이 성장하는 더 건강한 음식 환경을 만들기 위해 모두가 함께 일할 수 있기를 바란다.

본문해석

뉴욕시는 16온스 이상의 설탕이 든 음료의 판매를 제한하는 최종 항소에서 패소했다. 일반적으로 탄산음료 금지로 알려진 Portion Cap Ruling은 식당, 영화관, 스포츠 경기장, 델리에서 16온스 이상의 설탕이 든 음료의 판매를 제한했다. 뉴욕주 항소법원은 Portion Cap Ruling에 대한 최종 판결을 내렸다. 뉴욕시 보건국은 'Sugary Drinks Portion Cap Rule'을 채택하는 데 있어서 규제 기관의 범위를 넘어섰다. 뉴욕시 보건국은 어떠한 입법적 위임이나 지침도 없이 입법에 참여했으며, 그리하여 뉴욕 시의회의 입법 관할권을 위반했다.

VOCA

- final appeal 최종 항소, 상고
- limit 한정[제한]하다
- sugary drink 설탕이 든 음료
- restrict 제한[한정]하다
- New York State Court of Appeals 뉴욕주 항소법원
- issue 발표[공표]하다
- New York City Board of Health 뉴욕시 보건국
- exceed 넘다, 상회하다
- scope (주제 · 조직 · 활동 등이 다루는) 범위
- regulatory authority 규제 기관
- legislative 입법의, 입법부의
- delegation 위임
- guidance 지침, 유도, 지표
- engage in ~에 관여[참여]하다
- legislative jurisdiction 입법 관할권

어법 > 비문 찾기

정답의 이유

④ 'While the ship was sinking, rich people had put on a lifeboat.'는 문맥상 '배가 가라앉는 동안, 부자들이 구명보트에 올라탔다.'로 '동시 동작(주절과 부사절 시제가 동일)'이므로, had put → put[got]이 되어야 한다. get on은 '~에 타다'의 뜻이다.

오답의 이유

① who were coming은 선행사 emigrants를 수식하는 주격 관계대명사절로 어법상 적절하게 사용되었다.

② spot는 '발견하다, 알아채다'라는 뜻의 타동사인데, 주어가 an iceberg이고 목적어가 없으므로 수동태(was spotted)로 어법상 적절하게 사용되었다.

③ remove는 '~을 없애다[제거하다]'라는 뜻의 타동사인데, 주어가 12 of them이고 목적어가 없으므로 과거완료 수동(had been removed)으로 어법상 적절하게 사용되었다. to make the ship look better(배를 더 좋게 보이게 하기 위해)는 '~하기 위해서'라는 뜻을 나타내며 목적을 나타내는 to부정사의 부사적 용법으로 쓰였다.

⑤ 부사절(By the time the third-class were allowed to come up from their cabins)의 시제가 과거(were allowed)인데, 주절의 시제는 그보다 먼저 일어난 일이므로, 과거완료인 had already left가 적절하게 사용되었다.

본문해석

타이타닉호는 가장 웅장한 배였다. 그 배는 사치품과 모든 편의시설을 가지고 있었다. 그 배에는 전등과 열, 전기 엘리베이터, 수영장, 튀르키예식 목욕탕, 도서관 등이 있었다. 대부분의 승객들은 더 나은 삶에 대한 희망을 가지고 미국으로 오는 이민자들이었다. 타이타닉호는 4월 10일 대서양을 횡단하기 시작했다. 그 배에 탄 어느 누구도 그 배가 얼마나 위험에 처해 있는지 몰랐다. 4월 14일 오후 11시 40분에 빙산이 바로 앞에서 발견되었다. 선장은 배의 방향을 바꾸려고 노력했지만, 타이타닉호는 너무 빨리 가고 있었고 너무 컸기 때문에 그럴 수 없었다. 그 배는 빙산에 부딪혔고 가라앉기 시작했다. 타이타닉호는 원래 32척의 구명보트를 가지고 있었지만, 그 중에서 12척은 배를 더 좋게 보이기 위해 제거되었다. 배가 가라앉는 동안, 부자들이 구명보트에 올라탔다. 3등석이 선실에서 올라오는 것이 허락되었을 때, 대부분 구명보트는 이미 떠났다.

VOCA

- magnificent 거대한, 장대한
- comforts 편의 시설[도구]
- emigrant 이민자[이주민]
- iceberg 빙산
- spot 발견하다, 찾다, 알아채다
- reverse 후진하다, (차를) 후진시키다
- sink 가라앉다[빠지다]
- lifeboat 구명보트

- be allowed to ~하도록 허용되다
- cabin (배의) 객실, 선실

독해 > 세부 내용 찾기 > 내용 (불)일치

정답의 이유

세 번째 문장에서 'The design is the fifth to emerge from the American Women Quarters Program, which highlights pioneering women in their respective fields.'라고 했고, 다음 문장에서 'The other four quarters, all put into production this year, ~'라고 했으므로 5개의 새로운 쿼터(25센트 동전)가 생산된다는 것을 유추할 수 있다. 따라서 글의 내용과 일치하는 것은 ⑤ 'Five new quarters are produced to recognize pioneering women from various fields in the US(미국의 다양한 분야의 선구적인 여성들을 인정하기 위해 5개의 새로운 25센트 동전이 생산된다).'이다.

오답의 이유

① Maya Angelou와 Sally Ride는 대중의 지지를 받아 선택되었다. → 마지막 문장에서 'The latter two were, along with Wong, selected with input from the public.'이라고 했으므로, 글의 내용과 일치하지 않는다. 여기서 the latter two는 바로 앞 문장의 Wilma Mankiller와 Nina Otero-Warren을 말한다.

② Wong의 명예는 할리우드 여성의 대표성에서 변화를 의미한다. → 첫 번째 문장에서 'Anna May Wong, ~ will become the first Asian American to appear on US currency, ~'라고 했으므로, 글의 내용과 일치하지 않는다.

③ Anna May Wong은 그녀의 일생 동안 그녀의 업적에 대해 결코 인정받지 못했다. → 첫 번째 문장에서 'Early movie star Anna May Wong, who broke into Hollywood during the silent film era, ~'라고 했으므로, 글의 내용과 일치하지 않는다.

④ Wong은 American Women Quarters Program에 고려된 유일한 여성이었다. → 세 번째 문장에서 'The design is the fifth to emerge from the American Women Quarters Program, ~'라고 했으므로, 글의 내용과 일치하지 않는다.

본문해석

초기 영화배우 Anna May Wong은 무성 영화 시대에 할리우드에 진출했으며, 처음 주연을 맡은 지 100년 만에 미국 화폐에 등장하는 최초의 아시아계 미국인이 될 것이다. 트레이드마크인 뭉툭한 앞머리와 연필처럼 얇은 눈썹을 가진 Wong의 모습이 월요일부터 새로운 25센트 동전의 뒷면에 등장할 예정이다. 이 디자인은 American Women Quarters Program에서 다섯 번째로 등장했으며, 각각의 분야에서 선구적인 여성들을 강조한다. 나머지 4개의 25센트 동전들은 모두 올해 제작에 들어갔으며, 각각 시인이자 활동가인 Maya Angelou, 우주에 간 최초의 미국 여성 Sally Ride, 체로키 민족 지도자인 Wilma Mankiller, 여성 참정권론자인 Nina Otero-Warren 등을 특별히 포함한다. 후자인 두 사람은 Wong과 함께 대중의 의견을 받아 선정되었다.

VOCA

- break into (갑자기) ~하기 시작하다
- silent film era 무성영화 시대
- appear 나타나다
- land 차지[획득]하다
- trademark 트레이드마크(어떤 사람의 특징이 되는 행위 · 복장 등)
- blunt 무딘, 뭉툭한
- bangs (단발머리의) 앞머리
- feature (~의) 특징을 이루다
- quarter (미국 · 캐나다의) 25센트짜리 동전
- pioneering 개척[선구]적인
- in their respective fields 각각의 분야에서
- suffragist 여성 참정권론자

14 난도 ★★☆   정답 ③

독해 > 빈칸 완성 > 단어 · 구 · 절

[정답의 이유]

첫 문장에서 '어떤 말을 하지 말라는 말을 들은 적이 있나요?'라고 했으며, 빈칸 앞부분의 '정부가 사람들이나 조직이 말할 수 있는 것을 제한하는 법을 통과시킬 때 ~'로 미루어 빈칸에 들어갈 말로 적절한 것은 ③ 'censorship(검열)'임을 알 수 있다.

[오답의 이유]

① 구금[구류]
② 탄압
④ 박해
⑤ 강력 단속

본문해석

어떤 말을 하지 말라는 말을 들은 적이 있는가? 가정에서는 가정에서 말할 수 있는 것과 말할 수 없는 것에 대한 규칙을 갖는 것이 매우 일반적이지만, 정부도 마찬가지이다. 정부가 사람들이나 조직이 말할 수 있는 것을 제한하는 법을 통과시킬 때, 그것은 검열이라고 불린다.

VOCA

- pass a law 법을 통과시키다
- restrict 제한[한정]하다

15 난도 ★☆☆   정답 ⑤

독해 > 빈칸 완성 > 단어 · 구 · 절

[정답의 이유]

빈칸 문장의 부사절이 양보를 나타내는 'Though'로 시작하여 '당시 여성들은 ~ 할 것으로 기대되었지만'이라고 했고, 빈칸 다음에서 'many women became leaders of organizations and protests.'라고 했으므로 빈칸에는 'leaders'와 반대되는 뜻의 말이 들어가야 함을 유추할 수 있다. 따라서 빈칸에 들어갈 말로 적절한 것은 ⑤ 'play a background role(배경 역할을 하다)'이다.

[오답의 이유]

① 규칙을 시행하다
② 그들의 생각을 활성화시키다
③ 사회에 반항하다
④ 더 적극적으로 참여하다

본문해석

대부분의 사람들이 인권 운동과 그것을 주도한 사람들을 생각할 때, 그들은 Martin Luther King, Jr.와 Malcolm X, Medgar Evers, 그리고 다른 남성들을 생각한다. 하지만 실제로, 여성들은 그 운동에서 매우 중요한 참가자들이었다. 당시 여성들은 배경 역할을 할 것으로 기대되었지만, 많은 여성들은 단체와 시위의 지도자가 되었다. 하지만 그들은 종종 역사에서 잊혀진다. Rosa Parks는 인권 운동에서 가장 잘 알려진 여성이지만, 그녀의 이야기가 전해지는 방식은 그녀를 실제로 중요한 지도자라기보다는 하나의 상징처럼 보이게 한다.

VOCA

- Civil Rights Movement 인권 운동
- play a role 역할을 맡다, 한 몫을 하다

16 난도 ★★★   정답 ③

어법 > 비문 찾기

[정답의 이유]

③ 2형식 문장에서 보어(Particularly affected)가 도치된 구문으로, 복수 주어(seals and sea lions)이므로, 동사가 is → are가 되어야 한다.

[오답의 이유]

① 'which is known to cause entanglement'는 주어(Marine debris)를 수식하는 주격 관계대명사절이며, includes는 Marine debirs의 동사이므로 3인칭 단수형으로 적절하게 사용되었다.
② 전치사구인 'through reduced feeding efficiency, and injuries'에서 feeding은 '급식, 섭취'의 뜻으로, 전치사 through 다음에 명사로 적절하게 사용되었다.
④ 동사(have been recorded)를 받는 주어(Entanglement rates)가 복수명사 형태이며, recorded 다음에 목적어가 없고 '기록되는'이라는 수동의 의미를 표현한 현재완료 수동형태인 have been recorded가 어법상 적절하게 사용되었다.
⑤ of already reduced population size는 명사 recovery를 수식하는 형용사구이며, '줄어든'의 의미이므로 과거분사 reduced가 어법상 적절하게 사용되었다.

빠져나갈 수 없는 얽힘을 초래하는 것으로 알려진 해양 폐기물은 그물과 모노필라멘트 라인 같은 버려진 어구와 식스팩 고리, 미끼 상자 끈을 포함한다. 이 폐기물은 익사, 질식, 목 졸림, 섭취 효율 저하로 인한 굶주림과 부상 등에 의한 사망을 초래할 수 있다. 바다표범과 바다사자가 특히 영향을 받는데, 아마도 자신들의 환경에서 사물을 탐구하는 호기심 많은 그들의 습성 때문일 것이다. 이 동물들 개체수의 최대 7.9%에서 얽힘 현상이 기록되었다. 게다가, 어떤 경우에는 얽힘 현상은 이미 줄어든 개체군 크기의 회복에 위협이 된다. 대략 58%의 바다표범과 바다사자 종은 얽힘 현상에 의해 영향을 받는 것으로 알려졌는데, 그것들에는 하와이안 몽크 바다표범, 호주 바다사자, 뉴질랜드 물범, 그리고 남대양의 종들이 포함된다.

- marine debris 해양 폐기물
- cause ~을 야기하다[초래하다]
- entanglement (빠져나갈 수 없는 것에) 얽혀 듦[걸려듦]
- derelict 버려진, 유기된
- fishing gear 낚시장비
- fishing bait box 낚시미끼상자
- strap 끈[줄/띠]으로 묶다
- drowning 익사
- suffocation 질식
- strangulation 교살, 교살당함
- starvation 기아, 굶주림
- inquisitive 꼬치꼬치 캐묻는
- threat 위협(받는 상황), 위험
- Hawaiian monk seal 하와이안 몽크 바다표범
- Australian sea lion 호주 바다사자
- New Zealand fur seal 뉴질랜드 물범

17 난도 ★☆☆   정답 ④

독해 > 대의 파악 > 추론

정답의 이유

마지막 문장에서 캐나다 퀘벡 대학의 연구에 의하면 '~ pods may not be as wasteful as preparing coffee using a traditional coffee maker ~'라고 했으므로, 주어진 글에서 추론할 수 있는 것은 ④ 'Capsules may not be as wasteful as other coffee-making methods(캡슐은 커피를 만드는 다른 방식들만큼 낭비되지 않을 수도 있다).'이다.

오답의 이유

① 캡슐은 낭비이고 금지되어야 한다.
② 새로운 연구는 커피 만들 때 나오는 쓰레기의 양 줄이는 방법을 제안한다.
③ 커피를 마시는 모든 사람들은 환경 친화적인 제품을 찾는다.
⑤ 캡슐은 세계에서 커피를 만드는 가장 인기 있는 방법이다.

커피 한 잔을 만드는 것에 관하여 캡슐은 환경 친화적이지 않다는 평판을 가지고 있는데, 그것들은 종종 재활용하기 어렵기 때문이다. 다양한 방식으로 커피가 준비되는 동안, 커피 캡슐은 인기가 많아졌다. 그 인기에도 불구하고, 캡슐은 자신들의 카페인 습관이 환경에 미치는 영향을 의식하는 커피를 마시는 사람들을 오랫동안 갈라놓았다. 소형 플라스틱 또는 알루미늄 용기는 생산하는 데 많은 에너지를 소비하고 불필요한 폐기물을 유발한다는 비판을 받아왔다. 그러나 캐나다 퀘벡 대학의 새로운 연구에 따르면, 생산에서 쓰레기 매립지에 버려지는 양에 이르기까지 커피 한 잔의 더 넓은 수명주기를 고려할 때, 전통적인 커피 제조기를 사용하여 커피를 준비하는 것만큼 낭비가 아닐 수도 있다는 사실을 시사한다.

- when it comes to ~에 관하여
- reputation 평판, 명성
- environmentally 환경적으로
- be conscious of ~을 자각하다, 알고 있다
- energy-intensive 많은 에너지를 소비하는, 에너지 집약적인
- end up 결국 (어떤 처지에) 처하게 되다
- landfill 매립지

18 난도 ★★☆   정답 ④

독해 > 세부 내용 찾기 > 내용 (불)일치

정답의 이유

세 번째 문장에서 '~ some variants are having a slight impact on the ability of vaccines to guard against mild disease and infection(일부 변종들은 가벼운 질병과 감염이 생기지 않도록 하는 백신의 능력에 약간의 영향을 미치고 있다).'라는 내용은 있지만, 백신을 항상 작용하게 만드는 것에 대한 내용은 나오지 않았다. 따라서 주어진 글에 언급되어 있지 않은 것은 ④ 'what makes vaccines always work(백신을 항상 작용하게 만드는 것)'이다.

오답의 이유

① 변형이 등장하는 때 → 첫 번째 문장에서 'When cases increase and transmission accelerates, it's more likely that new dangerous and more transmissible variants emerge, ~'라고 했으므로, 주어진 글에 언급된 내용이다.
② 백신의 효과 → 두 번째 문장에서 '~ vaccines are proving effective against existing variants, especially at preventing severe disease, hospitalization and death.'라고 했으므로, 주어진 글에 언급된 내용이다.
③ 백신이 변종에 반응하는 법 → 네 번째 문장에서 'Vaccines are likely to stay effective against variants because of the broad immune response they cause.'라고 했으므로, 주어진 글에 언급된 내용이다.
⑤ WHO의 역할 → 마지막 문장에서 'WHO continues to constantly review the evidence and will update its guidance as we find out more.'라고 했으므로, 주어진 글에 언급된 내용이다.

환자가 증가하고 전염이 가속화되면 위험하고 전염성이 높은 새로운 변종이 나타날 가능성이 더 높은데, 그것은 더 쉽게 확산되거나 더 심각한 질병을 유발할 수 있다. 우리가 지금까지 알고 있는 것을 바탕으로 한 백신은 기존의 변종, 특히 심각한 질병과 입원 및 사망을 예방하는 데 효과적이라고 입증되고 있다. 하지만 일부 변종들은 가벼운 질병과 감염이 생기지 않도록 하는 백신의 능력에 약간의 영향을 미치고 있다. 백신은 그들이 일으키는 광범위한 면역 반응 때문에 변종에 대해 효과적으로 유지될 가능성이 높다. 그것은 바이러스의 변화나 돌연변이가 백신을 완전히 효력 없는 것으로 만들 가능성은 낮다는 것을 뜻한다. WHO는 지속적으로 그 증거를 검토하고 있으며 더 많은 것을 알게 되면 지침을 업데이트할 것이다.

VOCA

- case (질병 · 부상) 사례[환자]
- transmission 전염, 전파, 전달
- accelerate 가속화되다, 가속화하다
- transmissible 보낼[전할, 전도할] 수 있는, 전염하는
- variant 변종, 이형
- emerge 나오다[모습을 드러내다]
- spread 퍼지다[확산되다]
- severe 극심한, 심각한
- illness 병[질환]
- based on ~에 근거하여
- so far 지금까지[이 시점까지]
- vaccine (예방) 백신
- hospitalization 입원
- have an impact on ~에 영향을 미치다
- guard against ~이 생기지 않도록 조심[경계]하다
- immune response 면역 반응
- mutation 돌연변이, 변화[변형]
- ineffective 효과[효력] 없는, 효과적이지 못한

19 난도 ★★☆   정답 ②

독해 > 대의 파악 > 제목, 주제

정답의 이유

첫 번째 문장에서 'The James Webb Space Telescope can add another cosmic accomplishment to its list'라고 한 다음에, 'The space observatory has been used to confirm the existence of an exoplanet for the first time(그 우주망원경은 외계 행성의 존재를 처음으로 확인하는 데 사용되었다).'이라고 하였다. 따라서 글의 제목으로 가장 적절한 것은 ② 'The James Webb Space Telescope's Discovery of a Planet(James Webb 우주망원경의 행성 발견)'이다.

오답의 이유

① 천문학에서 NASA의 필수적인 역할
③ 과학적 연구를 위한 우주탐사 사용법
④ James Webb 우주망원경이 발견한 외계 행성의 수
⑤ James Webb 우주망원경의 성능에 대한 논란

James Webb 우주망원경은 목록에 또 다른 우주 업적을 추가할 수 있다. 그 우주망원경은 외계 행성의 존재를 처음으로 확인하는 데 사용되었다. 그 천체는 지구와 거의 정확하게 동일한 크기이다. 그 바위투성이의 세계는 팔분의자리 성좌에서 41광년 떨어져 있다. NASA에 의해 수집된 이전의 데이터는 그 행성이 존재할 수도 있다는 것을 암시했다. 천문학자인 Kevin Stevenson과 Jacob Lustig-Yaeger가 이끄는 연구팀은 Webb 망원경을 사용하여 그 표적을 관찰했다. "그 행성이 그곳에 있다는 것은 의심의 여지가 없습니다. Webb의 원시 데이터가 이를 입증합니다."라고 Lustig-Yaeger가 성명서에서 말했다. 그 행성의 발견은 수요일 시애틀에서 열린 미국 천문학회 제241차 회의에서 발표되었다.

VOCA

- Space Telescope 우주망원경
- cosmic 우주의, 장대한, 어마어마한
- accomplishment 업적, 공적
- space observatory 우주망원경
- confirm 사실임을 보여주다[확인해 주다]
- exoplanet 태양계외 행성
- celestial body 천체
- rocky 바위[암석]로 된, 바위[돌]투성이의
- Octans 팔분의(八分儀)자리
- constellation 별자리, 성좌
- astronomer 천문학자
- pristine 자연[원래] 그대로의, 오염되지 않은
- validate 입증하다

20 난도 ★★☆   정답 ②

독해 > 세부 내용 찾기 > 내용 (불)일치

정답의 이유

두 번째 문장에서 'Certainly, as the first reports came in of pandemic book sales, it did seem that people were at least buying more books.'라고 했고, 다음 문장에서 영국에서는 첫 번째 국가 봉쇄가 내려지기 전주에 도서 판매가 6% 증가했다고 했으므로 글의 내용과 일치하는 것은 ② 'The pandemic created a moment for boosting sales of books(전염병이 도서 판매를 증가시키는 계기를 만들었다).'이다.

오답의 이유

① 2020년에 사람들은 인간 존재에 대한 질문에 관심을 덜 보였다. → 첫 번째 문장의 '~ in 2020 that questions about human existence really were encouraging reading.'으로 미루어 2020년에 사람들이 인간 존재에 대한 질문에 관심을 더 보였다고 유추할 수 있으므로 글의 내용과 일치하지 않는다.
③ 영국보다 덴마크에서 더 많은 책이 팔렸다. → 세 번째 문장에서 영국에서 봉쇄 전주에 도서 판매량이 6% 증가했다고 했고, 다섯 번째 문장에서 덴마크에서 2020년 도서 판매량이 5.6% 증가했다고 했으므로 글의 내용과 일치하지 않는다.

④ 2020년에는 그 어느 때보다 많은 사람들이 도서관을 방문했다.
→ 네 번째 문장에서 'Physically closed, libraries reported significant growth in new digital users(도서관이 물리적으로 폐쇄되어 새로운 디지털 사용자가 크게 증가했다고 보고했으며),'라고 했으므로, 글의 내용과 일치하지 않는다.

⑤ 팬데믹이 덴마크의 경제를 자극했다. → 다섯 번째 문장에서 2020년에 덴마크에서 도서 판매량이 5.6% 증가했지만, 후반부의 '~ in 2020 despite shops being closed'로 미루어 팬데믹이 덴마크의 경제를 자극했다고는 할 수 없으므로 글의 내용과 일치하지 않는다.

본문해석

2020년에 책에서 어떤 일이 일어나고 있었는데, 그것은 인간 존재에 대한 질문들이 실제로 독서를 장려하고 있었다는 것이다. 확실히 팬데믹 도서 판매량에 대한 첫 번째 보고서가 나오자, 적어도 사람들은 더 많은 책을 사는 것처럼 보였다. 영국에서는 첫 번째 국가 봉쇄가 내려지기 전주에 실제 도서 판매량이 6% 증가했으며, 페이퍼백 소설 판매량은 한 주 만에 35% 증가했으며, Waterstones는 온라인 판매는 한 주 만에 400% 증가했다고 보고했다. 도서관이 물리적으로 폐쇄되어 새로운 디지털 사용자가 크게 증가했다고 보고했으며, 예를 들어 Hampshire County 의회는 대여가 770% 증가했다. 덴마크에서는 가게들이 문을 닫았음에도 불구하고 2020년에 도서 판매량이 5.6% 증가했다는 것을 통계가 보여주었다. 게다가 이전보다 더 많은 사람들이 2020년에 도서 스트리밍 서비스에 가입했다.

VOCA

- human existence 인간 존재
- prior to ~에 앞서, 먼저
- lockdown (움직임 · 행동에 대한) 제재
- physically 자연 법칙에 따라, 물리적으로
- loan 대출[융자](금), 대여
- statistics 통계, 통계표, 통계학
- subscribe 구독하다, (인터넷 · 유료 TV 채널 등에[을]) 가입[시청]하다
- streaming 인터넷상에서 음성이나 동영상 등을 실시간으로 재생하는 기술

21 난도 ★★☆ 정답 ①

독해 > 대의 파악 > 추론

정답의 이유

첫 번째 문단의 두 번째 문장에서 '~ maintaining good relationships with your members, volunteers, and donors is critical to your success.'라고 했고, 두 번째 문단의 두 번째 문장에서 'the biggest reason that relationships matter to nonprofits is that the very nature of the operation relies on goodwill and volunteerism.'이라고 했으므로, 주어진 글에서 추론할 수 있는 것은 ① 'The success of a non-profit organization depends on the strength of its relationships with key stakeholders(비영리 단체의 성공은 주요 이해 관계자와의 관계의 강도에 달려 있다).'이다.

오답의 이유

② 비영리 단체의 역할은 사회의 생존과 성공을 위해 중요하다.
③ 사람들은 주요 기관들과의 공공 관계성을 바탕으로 많은 돈을 벌 수 있다.
④ 비영리 단체는 홍보를 위한 마케팅에 반드시 초점을 맞추는 것은 아니다.
⑤ 사람들은 그들 자신의 자기 효능감 향상을 위해 기부하고 자원하는 경향이 있다.

본문해석

관계는 모든 조직의 수익에 영향을 주지만, 비영리적인 세계에서는 관계가 훨씬 더 중요한 양상을 나타낸다. 여러분이 지역의 무료급식소를 운영하든지 토목 기사들을 위한 회원 조직을 운영하든지 간에 여러분의 회원들, 자원봉사자들, 그리고 기부자들과 좋은 관계를 유지하는 것이 여러분의 성공에 매우 중요하다.

부분적으로, 이것은 비영리 단체들이 그들 중 상당수가 수십억 달러의 예산을 가지고 있음에도 불구하고 종종 실제로는 사업체가 아닌 것으로 여겨진다는 사실에서 비롯된다. 하지만 관계가 비영리단체에게 중요한 가장 큰 이유는 운영을 선의와 자원봉사에 의존하고 있다는 바로 그 본질 때문이다. 관계는 여러분의 홍보 및 그 밖의 마케팅 노력이 쌓아온 평판과 인식의 기초이다. 그리고 그러한 관계가 없다면, 아마 누구도 어떤 것을 위해 기부하거나 자원봉사를 하지 않을 것이다. 따라서 지지층과 강력한 공동체적 관계를 맺지 않으면 조직은 곧 생존을 중단할 것이다. 이것이 바로 여러분의 관계의 본질과 효험에 대한 지속적인 측정이 중요한 이유이다.

VOCA

- impact 영향[충격]을 주다
- bottom line 수익, 핵심, 요점
- not-for-profit 비영리의
- take on 나타내다, 띠다
- run (사업체 등을) 운영[경영/관리]하다
- soup kitchen 무료급식소
- maintain 유지하다[지키다]
- donor 기부자, 기증자
- be critical to ~에 결정적이다
- be seen as ~으로 여겨지다
- rely on 기대다, 의존하다
- goodwill 친선, 호의
- volunteerism 자원봉사활동
- chances are (that) 아마 ~일 것이다, ~할 가능성이 충분하다
- communal relationships 공동체적 관계
- constituency (특정 인물 · 상품 등의) 지지층[고객층]
- cease 중단되다, 그치다, 중단시키다
- efficacy (특히 약이나 치료의) 효험

독해 > 대의 파악 > 제목, 주제

정답의 이유

세 번째 문장에서 'Roman concrete, in many cases, has proven to be longer-lasting than modern concrete ~'라고 했고, 마지막에서 두 번째 문장에서 연구팀이 로마 건축물의 콘크리트 안에 있는 하얀 덩어리들이 시간이 지나면서 생긴 콘크리트의 균열을 치료하는 능력을 제공한다는 것을 발견했다고 했으므로, 글의 제목으로 가장 적절한 것은 ② 'The Durability of Ancient Roman Concrete(고대 로마 콘크리트의 내구성)'이다.

오답의 이유

① 로마 공학의 역사
③ 현대 건축에서 콘크리트의 사용
④ 지진대 건축 구조물의 문제점
⑤ 고대 로마에서 새로운 유형의 콘크리트 발견

본문해석

고대 로마의 장엄한 건축물들은 수천 년 동안 살아남았다. 하지만 어떻게 그들의 건축 재료가 2,000년 이상 서 있는 판테온과 콜로세움 같은 거대한 건물들을 유지하는 것을 도왔을까? 많은 경우에, 로마의 콘크리트는 수십 년 안에 악화될 수 있는 현대의 콘크리트보다 더 오래 지속된다는 것이 입증되었다. 이제, 새로운 연구의 배후에 있는 과학자들에 따르면, 그들은 로마인들이 건축 자재의 내구성을 강하게 하여 부두, 하수도, 지진 지역과 같이 건축하기 힘든 장소에 정교한 구조물을 지을 수 있게 한 신비한 성분의 비밀을 알아냈다고 한다. 한 연구팀이 이탈리아 중부에 있는 도시의 벽에서 2,000년 된 콘크리트 표본을 분석했다. 그들은 콘크리트에 있는 하얀 덩어리들이 시간이 지나면서 형성된 콘크리트의 균열을 치료하는 능력을 제공한다는 것을 발견했다. 그 흰색 덩어리들은 이전에는 저품질 원료의 증거로 간과되었다.

VOCA

- majestic 장엄한, 위풍당당한
- structure 구조물, 건축물
- millennium 새로운 천년이 시작되는 시기(복수형: millennia)
- Pantheon (로마의) 판테온
- longer-lasting 더 오래 지속되는
- deteriorate 악화되다, 더 나빠지다
- uncover (비밀 등을) 알아내다[적발하다]
- mystery 신비스러운[수수께끼 같은] 사람[것]
- ingredient (특히 요리 등의) 재료[성분]
- durable 내구성이 있는, 오래가는
- sewer 하수관, 수채통
- chunk (두툼한) 덩어리
- crack (무엇이 갈라져 생긴) 금
- overlook 못 보고 넘어가다, 간과하다

독해 > 빈칸 완성 > 단어 · 구 · 절

정답의 이유

첫 번째 문장에서 '무리 행동'은 동물이 위험한 상황에서 포식자를 피할 때 무리지어 하는 행동에서 비롯되었다고 했으며, 네 번째 문장에서 이 용어는 인간에게도 적용된다고 했다. 빈칸 문장의 앞부분에서 '이것은 종종 ~을 가진다.'라고 했고, 빈칸 다음의 'as people's actions are driven by emotion rather than by thinking through a situation.'으로 미루어 문맥상 빈칸에는 부정적인 의미의 말이 들어가야 함을 유추할 수 있다. 따라서 빈칸에 들어갈 말로 적절한 것은 ⑤ 'implication of irrationality(불합리한 결과)'이다.

오답의 이유

① 합리적인 추론
② 동물과의 차이
③ 사물의 특징
④ 실증적 사건

본문해석

'무리 행동'이라는 용어는 특히 포식자를 피하는 것과 같은 위험한 상황에 있을 때 동물들의 집단적인 행위에서 유래했다. 모든 동물들은 하나의 그룹으로 긴밀하게 함께 뭉치고, 공포스러운 상태에서는 하나의 단위로 함께 움직인다. 무리의 일원이 무리의 이동에서 벗어나는 것은 매우 이례적인 일이다. 이 용어는 또한 인간의 행동에도 적용되며, 그것은 보통 대단히 많은 사람들이 동시에 같은 방식으로 행동하는 것을 묘사한다. 그것은 종종 불합리한 결과를 갖는데, 사람들의 행동이 상황을 통한 사유에 의하기보다는 감정에 이끌리기 때문이다. 인간의 무리 행동은 대규모 시위, 폭동, 파업, 종교 집회, 스포츠 행사, 그리고 폭도의 폭력 발생에서 목격될 수 있다. 무리 행동이 시작되면, 한 개인의 판단과 의견 형성 과정은 중단되는데, 그 또는 그녀가 자동적으로 무리의 움직임과 행동을 따라가기 때문이다.

VOCA

- herd behavior 무리 행동
- predator 포식자, 포식 동물
- in panic 당황하여
- unit 부대[단체]
- apply to ~에 적용되다
- implication 영향[결과]
- irrationality 불합리, 부조리
- large-scale 대규모
- demonstration 시위
- riot 폭동
- strike 파업
- religious gathering 종교 집회
- outbreak 발생[발발]
- mob violence 폭도의 폭력
- set in 시작하다[되다]
- judgment 판단, 심판, 심사

• opinion-forming 의견 형성의

24 난도 ★★☆   정답 ③

독해 > 대의 파악 > 제목, 주제

정답의 이유

첫 번째 문장에서 'California has been struck by a final round of storms, bringing more rain and snow to a state.'라고 한 다음에 폭풍의 피해를 설명하고 있다. 네 번째 문장에서 최근 캘리포니아를 강타한 폭풍으로 인해 지역사회가 침수되어 강제로 대피할 수밖에 없다고 했으며, 다섯 번째 문장에서 'The back-to-back deluges have eroded roads and felled trees, making each successive storm more liable to cause serious damage as soils weaken.'이라고 구체적인 피해 사례를 설명하고 있으므로 글의 제목으로 가장 적절한 것은 ③ 'Devastated California after a Series of Storms(일련의 폭풍 후 황폐해진 캘리포니아)'이다.

오답의 이유

① 캘리포니아 날씨의 가장 큰 패배자
② 비와 폭풍의 예측 불가능성에 대비하는 방법
④ 캘리포니아에서 홍수의 원인과 결과
⑤ 캘리포니아가 자초한 눈보라 재난

본문해석

캘리포니아는 마지막으로 한 차례 폭풍이 덮쳐서 주 지역에 더 많은 비와 눈이 내렸다. 월요일 밤 동안과 화요일 이른 아침까지 주 일부 지역에 비와 눈이 내릴 것으로 예상되었다. 이번 주에 날씨가 개선되었음에도, 현재 많은 지역이 홍수와 산사태의 위험에 처해 있다. 최근 몇 주 동안 폭풍이 캘리포니아를 강타하여 지역사회가 침수되어 강제로 대피하게 되었다. 연이은 홍수는 도로를 침식하고 나무를 쓰러뜨렸으며 연속적인 폭풍은 각각 토양이 약해지면서 심각한 피해를 받기 쉽게 만들었다. 지난 주말 캘리포니아 시에라 네바다 산맥 일부 지역에 1~3피트의 눈이 내렸다. 월요일 현재 캘리포니아 중부 해안에서는 8백만 명이 홍수의 영향권에 있으며, 월요일에 캘리포니아 주에서는 3만 8천 8백 명 이상의 고객들이 여전히 정전 상태다.

VOCA

• strike (재난·질병 등이 갑자기) 발생하다[덮치다]
• overnight 밤사이에, 하룻밤 동안
• at risk of ~의 위험에 처한
• landslide 산사태
• batter 두드리다[때리다/구타하다]
• evacuation 피난, 대피
• back-to-back 꼬리에 꼬리를 물고, 연이어
• deluge 폭우, 호우
• erode (비바람이[에]) 침식[풍화]시키다[되다]
• fell (나무를) 베어 넘어뜨리다
• successive 연속적인, 연이은, 잇따른
• liable ~의 영향을 받기[~당하기] 쉬운
• range 산맥

• as of ~현재
• remain 계속[여전히] ~이다

25 난도 ★★★   정답 ④

독해 > 글의 일관성 > 글의 순서

정답의 이유

주어진 글은 6월 9일 상하이에서 공산당 지도부에 대한 저항 시위가 일어나고 있다는 신문 기사이므로, 주어진 글 다음에는 'The demonstrators'로 시작하는 (C)로 이어지는 것이 자연스럽다. (C)는 상하이의 대학생들이 베이징 시위 당시 사망한 수천 명의 사람들을 애도하는 장송곡에 맞춰서 행진하고 있다는 내용이므로, 베이징 시위를 설명하는 (A)로 이어져야 적절하다. (A)의 마지막에서 민주화 운동에서 베이징과 상하이 두 도시의 모습이 대조적이라고 했는데, (B)에서 베이징의 분위기는 엄숙하고 두려운 반면, 상하이는 분노와 반항의 분위기라고 마무리 짓고 있다. 따라서 주어진 글에 이어질 글의 순서로 적절한 것은 ④ '(C) - (A) - (B)'이다.

본문해석

6월 9일 상하이 - 오늘 수만 명의 학생들과 사람들이 항의성 집회를 열었으며, 공산당 지도부에 대한 지속적인 반항 시위로 이 도시의 거리를 행진했다.

(C) 상하이의 많은 대학과 기술대학 학생들이 이끄는 시위자들이, 군대가 그곳에서 시위를 진압했을 때 베이징에서 사망한 수천 명의 사람들을 애도하는 녹음된 장례식 노래에 맞춰 행진했다.

(A) 기자들과 외교관들이 추정한 군중은 약 4만 명에서 10만 명 이상이었다. 보안 경찰이 베이징에서 민주화 운동 참가자들을 체포하고 있다는 보도가 나오는 가운데, 이번 집회는 두 도시 사이의 대비를 반영했다.

(B) 베이징의 분위기는 엄숙하고 무서운 반면, 상하이의 그날의 사건들은 중국의 가장 크고 경제적으로 가장 중요한 도시에서 계속되는 분노와 반항의 분위기를 나타낸다.

VOCA

• tens of thousands of 수만(萬)의
• protest rally 항의성 집회, 시위
• defiance 반항[저항]
• funeral 장례식
• lament 애통[한탄/통탄]하다
• crush (폭력으로) 진압[탄압]하다
• range from ~에서 (…까지) 걸치다
• amid 가운데[중]에
• report 발표하다, 전하다, 보도, 기록
• security police 보안(保安) 경찰
• democracy movement 민주화운동
• atmosphere 대기
• solemn 침통한, 근엄한

영어 | 2022년 국회직 8급

한눈에 훑어보기

✔ 영역 분석

어휘   01 02 14 16 18
5문항, 20%

독해   04 05 06 07 08 09 11 13 17 19 20 21
22 24 25
15문항, 60%

어법   03 10 12 15 23
5문항, 20%

✔ 빠른 정답

01	02	03	04	05	06	07	08	09	10
⑤	①	③	③	④	②	②	⑤	④	③
11	12	13	14	15	16	17	18	19	20
①	⑤	③	⑤	②	①	④	④	③	②
21	22	23	24	25					
④	⑤	②	①	③					

✔ 점수 체크

구분	1회독	2회독	3회독
맞힌 문항 수	/ 25	/ 25	/ 25
나의 점수	점	점	점

01 난도 ★☆☆ 정답 ⑤

어휘 > 단어

[정답의 이유]

밑줄 친 dispositions는 '(타고난) 기질 또는 성향'의 뜻으로 이와 의미가 가장 가까운 것은 ⑤ 'temperaments(기질)'이다.

[오답의 이유]

① 혐오감
② 배상금
③ 유인책
④ 미련, (사랑의) 열병

[본문해석]

사람들은 다른 사람들을 보는 방식과 다르게 자기 자신을 본다. 그들은 자기 자신의 감각, 감정 그리고 인지에 몰두하며 동시에 다른 사람들에 대한 그들의 경험은 외관상 관찰될 수 있는 것에 지배된다. 사람들이 자신과 다른 사람들을 인식할 때 가지게 되는 정보의 이러한 차이는 사람들이 자신과 다른 사람들의 행동을 평가하는 방식에 영향을 미친다. 사람들은 종종 자신의 행동을 상황적 제약으로 인한 것으로 보는 반면, 다른 사람들의 행동은 그들의 내부 성향으로 인한 것이라고 여긴다. 예를 들어 취업 면접에 늦게 도착한 사람이 지각을 교통 체증 탓으로 여기는 반면 면접관은 그것을 개인의 무책임 탓이라고 돌리는 경우가 있을 것이다.

VOCA

- immerse ～에 몰두하다
- sensation 느낌, 감각
- cognition 인지, 인식
- dominate 지배하다
- distinction 차이
- evaluate 평가하다
- situational 상황에 따른
- constraint 제약, 제한
- internal 내부의
- ascribe A to B A를 B의 탓으로 여기다

02 난도 ★☆☆
정답 ①

어휘 > 어구

정답의 이유

밑줄 친 hammered out은 '문제가 해결된, 타결된'의 뜻으로 이와 의미가 가장 가까운 것은 ① 'settled(해결된, 합의된)'이다.

오답의 이유

② 취소된

③ 비판받은

④ 단념된

⑤ ~에 대해 논쟁이 된

본문해석

최근 거래의 세부 사항은 미국 국무 장관과 러시아 국무 장관에 의해 타결되었다.

VOCA

• detail 세부 사항

• deal 거래

• counterpart 상대, 대응 관계에 있는 사람[것]

03 난도 ★★☆
정답 ③

어법 > 비문 찾기

정답의 이유

③ position은 '~를 어디에 두다'라는 뜻의 타동사로 그 뒤에 목적어가 있어야 한다. 현재 문장에서는 목적어가 없으므로 수동태인 'be positioned'라고 해야 한다.

오답의 이유

① 시간 또는 조건을 나타내는 부사절에서는 현재시제가 미래시제를 대신한다.

② 부대 상황을 나타낼 때는 전치사구, 'with+목적어+목적격 보어' 형태가 쓰이며, 목적어와 목적격 보어의 관계가 능동이므로 현재분사가 옳게 쓰였다.

④ '지각동사(see)+목적어+목적격 보어'는 '목적어가 목적격 보어하는 것을 보다'의 뜻인데, 'blotted' 뒤에 목적어가 없고 by the moon이 있으므로 '수동'의 의미인 과거분사(blotted)가 올바르게 사용되었다.

⑤ 동사 'appear'는 '~인 것 같다, ~ 처럼 보이다'의 의미로 쓰였고 형용사 보어 'bright'를 사용하는 것이 맞다.

본문해석

달이 하늘에 있는 태양의 원반 일부를 가리는 부분 일식은 2022년에 두 번 발생할 것이다. 첫 번째는 남아메리카 남부, 남극대륙 일부, 그리고 태평양과 남극해 일부에서 보일 것이다. 4월 30일, 달은 지구와 태양 사이를 지나갈 것이고, 최대 일식은 20시 41분 UTC*에 일어날 것이며, 그때 태양 원반의 64%까지 달에 의해 가려질 것이다. 그 일식의 최대치를 보기 위해, 관찰자들은 남극 반도의 서쪽인 남극해에 위치해야 할 것이다. 하지만 칠레와 아르헨티나의 최남단 지역에서 일식을 쫓는 사람들은 달에 의해 가려진 태양의 약 60%를 볼 수 있을 것이다. 부분 일식의 모든 단계를 안전하게 보기 위해서는 보호안경이 필요하다. 비록 태양이 하늘에서 밝게 보이지 않을지라도, 그것을 직접 응시하는 것은 당신의 눈을 심각하게 다치게 할 수 있다.

*UTC: 협정 세계시

VOCA

• visible 보이는

• occur 발생하다

• blot out 가리다

• phase 단계

• injure 다치게 하다

더 알아보기

부대 상황

• 부대 상황이란 주된 상황에 곁들여서 일어나는 상황을 말한다.

• 'with+목적어+목적격 보어'의 형태를 가진다. 목적격 보어에는 부사[부사구], 형용사, 현재분사, 과거분사가 들어갈 수 있다.

with+목적어 +부사[부사구]	예 I walked with both hands in my pockets. (나는 주머니 안에 양손을 넣고 걸었다.)
with+목적어 +형용사	예 Don't speak with your mouth full. (입을 가득 채우고 말하지 마라.)
with+목적어 +현재분사	예 He said "Yes" with his head nodding. (그는 머리를 끄덕이면서 "네"라고 말했다.)
with+목적어 +과거분사	예 She sat on the sofa with her eyes bandaged. (그녀는 눈을 붕대로 감은 채 소파에 앉았다.)

• with를 생략하여 나타낼 수도 있는데, 이때 생략된 with 앞에 쉼표(,)를 찍어 준다.

예 He sat on the chair with his legs crossed.

→ He sat on the chair, his legs crossed.

(그는 다리를 꼬고 의자에 앉았다.)

예 She told me the sad story with tears in her eyes.

→ She told me the sad story, tears in her eyes.

(그녀는 눈물을 글썽이며 나에게 슬픈 이야기를 하였다.)

독해 > 빈칸 완성 > 단어 · 구 · 절

정답의 이유

③ 'ignorant and ~'와 같은 병렬 구조에서는 ignorant(무지한, 무지막지한)와 같은 부정적 의미의 형용사가 와야 한다. 따라서 (A)에 알맞은 것은 '상스러운, 천박한'이라는 의미를 가진 'boorish'이다. 또한 (B)에도 'clown(광대)'과 상응하는 'vulgarity(천박함)'가 알맞다.

오답의 이유

① 근면 성실한 – 인기

② 합리적인 – 감각

④ 특이한 – 지성

⑤ 자랑하는 – 즉흥

본문해석

"그것 봐! 그것이 우리가 주도하는 삶이다. 이것은 사람을 울리기에 충분하다. 사람은 일하고 최선을 다하지만 사람은 지치고, 밤에 잠을 자지 못하고, 최선을 위해 무엇을 해야 할지에 대해 머리를 쥐어짠다. 그다음엔 무슨 일이 일어날까? 우선, 대중은 무지하고 (A) 상스럽다. 나는 그들에게 최고의 오페레타, 우아한 가극과 일류의 음악 홀 아티스트들을 선사한다. 하지만 그게 그들이 원하는 것이라고 생각하는가? 그들은 그런 종류의 어떤 것도 진가를 알지 못한다. 그들은 광대를 원한다. 그들이 요구하는 것은 (B) 천박함이다."

VOCA

• utmost　최대한

• appreciate　감상하다, 진가를 알다

독해 > 대의 파악 > 제목, 주제

정답의 이유

글의 서두에 주제를 제시하는 두괄식 형식의 글이다. 첫 번째 문장이 주제문으로 유동적인 재료들이 아이들의 감정 표현의 훌륭한 매체라는 내용을 언급하고 있다. 그 이후 그에 대한 구체적 사례들이 제시되고 있으므로 글의 제목은 ④ 'Developing Expressivity through Play(놀이를 통한 표현력 발달)'가 가장 적절하다.

오답의 이유

① 다양한 종류의 유동적인 재료

② 놀이에서의 개인적인 차이

③ 놀이에 대한 문화의 영향

⑤ 놀이에서 유동 재료를 사용하는 것의 장점과 단점

본문해석

점토나 핑거 페인트와 같은 유동적인 재료들은 아이들이 신체 부위와 기능에 대한 호기심뿐만 아니라 분노를 표현할 수 있는 훌륭한 매체이다. 아이들은 점토로, 무해하게 찢고 두드릴 수 있고, 그들은 또한 종종 해부학적으로 정확한 부분을 가진 사람의 형태를 만들 수도 있다. 점토, 모래 또는 블록으로, 그들은 안전하게 파괴적일 수 있고 그들 자신의 파괴적인 충동이 반드시 해로운 것만은 아니며 그들을 놀라게 해서는 안 된다는 것을 배울 것이다. 때때로 창조의 즐거움은 자신이 창조한 것을 파괴할 것이라는 기대감에 의해 강화된다. 인형으로, 아이들은 가족적인 장면을 연출하고 가족과 관련된 걱정거리를 탐구할 수 있다. 만약 그들이 손인형을 사용할 때 자유롭게 의사소통을 할 수 있도록 허락된다면, 의사소통을 하는 것은 그들이 아니라 손인형이기 때문에, 아이들은 그들의 가장 깊은 감정의 일부를 행동이나 말로 드러낼 수 있다.

어른들은 어린 아이들의 행동을 통제할 필요가 있으므로, 재료를 사용해서 자유롭게 표현하는 데 제한을 두어야 한다. 예를 들어, (아이들은) 점토를 두드리고, 잡아당기고, 납작하게 짓이길 수 있지만, (그것을) 벽이나 다른 아이들에게 던져서는 안 된다. 하지만, 어른들이 지나치게 제한을 둔다면, 그 놀이는 아이들을 위한 그 감정적인 가치의 일부를 잃을 것이라는 사실을 기억하려고 노력해야 한다. 그들은 또한 심지어 어린아이도 자신이 만든 블록 구조물을 넘어뜨리는 것과 교실에 있는 가구를 넘어뜨리는 것을 구별할 수는 있다는 사실을 알아차려야 한다.

VOCA

• curiosity　호기심

• function　기능

• destructive　파괴적인

• impulse　충동

• reveal　드러내다

• restrictive　제한적인

더 알아보기

빠른 독해 비법

대부분의 지문은 글의 서두에 주제를 제시하는 두괄식 형식의 글이기 때문에 주제 또는 제목을 찾는 문제에서는 지문의 앞부분을 공략하도록 하자. 정답을 찾을 때는 핵심 내용이 어떤 단어들로 표현되는지에 집중해야 한다. 핵심 내용은 핵심 키워드를 포함하면서도 본문의 요지를 담고 있어야 한다. 지나치게 광범위하거나 지나치게 세부적인 내용은 주제나 제목으로 적절하지 않다.

독해 > 글의 일관성 > 글의 순서

정답의 이유

내용 흐름에서 반복되는 단어들로 정답을 찾을 수 있는 문제이다. 주어진 글의 뒷부분에서 원인과 결과, 개연성과 우연의 복잡한 거미줄에 의해 각각의 상황과 사건들의 앞의 것과 뒤의 것들이 연결되어 있다고 했으므로 (B)의 현재가 사고의 결과일 수도 있고 거부할 수 없는 힘의 결과일 수도 있다는 내용으로 이어진다. (A)에서는 이 유일한 현재는 역사를 이해하지 않는 한 이해할 수 없으며, 역사의 사건들은 혼란(chaos) 그 이상이라고 하며, 이는 (C)의 첫 문장에 쓰인 과거의 혼란스러운(chaotic) 기록에 대한 언급과 이어진다. 따라서 정답은 ② '(B) – (A) – (C)'이다.

'역사의 교훈'은 정말로 친숙한 구절이기 때문에 가끔 그 교훈은 너무 잘 학습된다. 역사는 절대로 정확하게 반복되지 않는다. 어떠한 역사적 상황도 다른 것과 같지 않다. 심지어 두 가지의 유사한 사건들도 첫 번째 사건은 전례가 없는 반면 두 번째 사건은 전례가 있다는 점에서 다르다. 하지만 이런 점에서도, 역사는 교훈을 줄 수 있다. 다시 말해, 어느 것도 그대로 머물러 있지 않는다. 인간사에서 유일하게 변하지 않는 것은 변화 그 자체의 불변성이다. 역사의 과정은 유일무이하지만 그럼에도 불구하고 이해할 수 있다. 각각의 상황과 사건은 구별되지만, 각각은 원인과 결과, 개연성과 우연의 복잡한 거미줄에 의해 모든 앞의 것과 이후의 것들에 연결된다.

(B) 현재가 사고의 결과일 수도 있고, 거부할 수 없는 힘의 결과일 수도 있지만, 어느 경우든 과거 사건의 현재 결과는 현실적이고 되돌릴 수 없다.

(A) 과거의 각각의 독특한 지점과 마찬가지로, 그 독특한 현재도, 그것이 어떻게 생겨났는지에 대한 역사를 이해하지 않는 한 절대 이해할 수 없다. 역사는 독특한 사건들의 기록이지만, 그것은 혼란 그 이상이다.

(C) 과거 사건의 혼란스러운 기록에서 질서의 요소를 인식하는 것은 역사학자의 큰 임무이다. 사건, 사람, 집단, 기관은 적어도 부분적인 규칙성을 보이는 어떤 계층으로 나뉜다.

VOCA

- precedent 전례
- in this respect 이러한 점에서
- constancy 불변성
- intelligible 이해할 수 있는
- probability 개연성, 확률

07 난도 ★☆☆　　　　　　　　　　　　　정답 ②

독해 > 세부 내용 찾기 > 내용 (불)일치

정답의 이유

글의 주제인 분산 기억(transactive memory) 소스의 개념을 이해하면 쉽게 정답을 찾을 수 있는 문제이다. 본문은 인터넷과 기술이 수많은 정보를 우리의 뇌 대신 저장해 주고 있으므로 우리는 모든 것을 다 기억할 필요는 없다고 말하고 있다. 따라서 분산 기억 소스로 간주되기 어려운 것은 현대의 기술과는 거리감이 있는 ② 'A photo album of your childhood(어린 시절의 사진 앨범)'이다.

오답의 이유

① 다가오는 이벤트를 알려주는 알림 앱
③ 저장된 경로로 길을 찾는 것을 도와주는 GPS 장치
④ 다른 웹사이트의 비밀번호 서면 목록
⑤ 연락처 목록이 있는 휴대폰

검색 엔진은 우리가 인터넷을 사용하는 방식을 바꿔왔고, 클릭 몇 번만으로 방대한 정보 소스를 축적했다. 그러나 최근의 한 연구는 웹사이트와 인터넷이 기술 자체보다 훨씬 더 많이 변화하고 있다는 것을 보여준다. 그것들은 우리의 기억이 기능하는 방식을 바꾸고 있다. Dr. Wegner의 최근 연구인 'Google이 기억에 미치는 영향: 손끝에서 정보를 얻을 수 있는 것에 대한 인지적 결과'는 사람들이 검색 엔진에 접근할 때, 그들은 쉽게 사용할 수 있는 지름길로서 '검색'에 의존할 수 있다는 것을 알기 때문에 더 적은 사실과 더 적은 정보를 기억한다는 것을 보여준다. Wegner는 새로운 연구 결과들이 인터넷이 우리의 뇌가 정보를 구분하는 방법인 분산 기억 소스의 일부가 되었다는 것을 보여준다고 믿는다. 1985년에 Wegner에 의해 처음 가설된 분산 기억은 여러 형태로 존재하는데 이는 남편이 친척의 생일을 기억하기 위해 아내에게 의존하는 것과 같다. "이 기억의 전체 네트워크야말로 당신이 직접 세상의 모든 것을 기억할 필요가 없는 곳이다."라고 그는 말한다. "당신은 그저 누가 그것을 알고 있는지만 기억하면 된다." 이제 컴퓨터와 기술도 우리 기억의 가상 확장이 되고 있다.

VOCA

- cognitive 인지의
- consequence 결과
- rely on ~에 의존하다
- hypothesize 가설을 세우다, 가정하다

08 난도 ★★☆　　　　　　　　　　　　　정답 ⑤

독해 > 세부 내용 찾기 > 내용 (불)일치

정답의 이유

마지막 문장에서 'incubation period(=Latency)'란 충격적인 사고 이후 외상 후 신경증이 나타날 때까지의 잠복 기간이라고 말한다. 따라서 지문의 내용과 일치하는 것은 ⑤ 'Latency refers to the period when the impact of the shocking events remains dormant(잠재기란 충격적인 사고의 영향이 휴면 상태로 남아 있는 시기를 지칭한다).'이다.

오답의 이유

① 충격적인 사고 후 고통의 재발은 잘 알려진 사실이다. → 네 번째 문장에서 'This appears quite incomprehensible and is therefore a novel fact.'라고 했으므로, 글의 내용과 일치하지 않는다.

② '외상 후 신경증'은 바이러스에 감염되었을 때 생긴다. → 두 번째, 세 번째 문장에서 언급되었으므로, 글의 내용과 일치하지 않는다.

③ 잠복기라는 용어는 전염병과 관련이 없다. → 마지막에서 두 번째, 세 번째 문장에서 '~ "incubation period," a transparent allusion to the pathology of infectious disease. It is the feature one might term latency.'라고 했으므로, 글의 내용과 일치하지 않는다.

④ '외상 후 신경증'이란 사고 직후 느끼는 충격을 지칭한다. → 두 번째 문장에서 'In the course of the following weeks, however, he develops a series of grave psychical and motor symptoms, ~'라고 했으므로, 글의 내용과 일치하지 않는다.

본문해석

예를 들어 기차 충돌과 같은 충격적인 사고를 당한 장소에서 누군가 외관상으로는 상처를 입지 않고, 그곳을 벗어나는 일이 생길 수 있다. 그러나 그 후 몇 주 동안 그는 오직 쇼크 또는 사고 당시 발생한 다른 무언가 때문에 일련의 심각한 정신적, 운동적 증상을 나타낼 수 있다. 그는 '외상 후 신경증'을 앓게 된 것이다. 이것은 상당히 이해할 수 없는 것으로 보이므로 새로운 사실이다. 사고와 최초의 증상 발현 사이의 시간은 '잠복기'라고 불리는데, 그것은 병적인 측면으로의 투명한 암시이다. 그것은 소위 'latency(잠재기)'라고 칭하기도 하는 것의 특성이다.

VOCA

- apparently 겉으로는, 보여지기로는
- collision 충돌
- be ascribed to ~때문이다
- incomprehensible 이해할 수 없는
- elapse (시간이) 지나다
- infectious 전염되는

09 난도 ★☆☆ 정답 ④

독해 > 빈칸 완성 > 단어 · 구 · 절

정답의 이유

But 바로 앞 문장에서 우리가 다른 사람에게 기울이는 주의 깊은 관심이 그들의 표정과 단서들을 포착하여 우리들이 그 사람이 어떻게 느끼는지 동조하게 한다고 하였으므로 But 다음 문장에는 그와 반대의 내용이 와야 한다. 따라서 빈칸에 들어갈 적절한 것은 ④ 'we may miss those signals(우리는 그 신호를 놓칠지도 모른다)'이다.

오답의 이유

① 우리는 그 사람에게 더 관심을 기울일지도 모른다.
② 우리의 공감이 강화될 것이다.
③ 우리는 그 사람의 행동에 덜 동조된다.
⑤ 우리는 그 사람에게 무관심을 느낀다.

본문해석

다른 사람과 함께 있는 것은 지속적이고 배려하는 관심이며, 연민의 기본적인 형태로 볼 수 있다. 다른 사람에게 기울이는 주의 깊은 관심은 또한 공감을 증진시켜, 우리가 찰나의 표정과 그와 같은 다른 단서들을 더 많이 포착하게끔 하여 그 사람이 그 순간 어떻게 느끼는지 우리가 동조하게 한다. 하지만 만약 우리의 주의가 '깜빡'한다면, 우리는 그 신호들을 놓칠지도 모른다.

VOCA

- sustained 지속적인

10 난도 ★☆☆ 정답 ③

어법 > 비문 찾기

정답의 이유

③이 포함된 문장은 등위접속사 and로 연결된 병렬 구조로, and 앞에서 'Personality plays a big part in how you react'라고 현재시제 동사가 나왔다. 따라서 and 다음에도 주어(women)에 맞는 현재시제 동사가 나와야 하므로 tending → tend가 되어야 한다.

오답의 이유

① 선행사 people을 수식하는 관계사절이 and로 이어졌으며, 앞선 관계사절 'who express ~'와도 병렬 구조를 이루어 who recognize ~라고 했으므로 옳은 표현이다.
② know의 목적어인 명사절이 'how+형용사+주어+동사'의 구조로 바르게 사용되었다.
④ realizing은 명사절(주어부)을 이끄는 동명사이며, 이때 어순인 '동명사+주어(you)+동사(are)'가 바르게 쓰였다.
⑤ 동사 recommend는 동명사(-ing)를 목적어로 취하는 동사이므로 remaining은 어법상 옳은 표현이다.

본문해석

"너 자신을 사랑하고 그 경험에서 공통된 인간성을 인식하라."라고 연구원 David Sbarra는 말한다. 이것은 '자기 연민'이라고 불린다. 자기애를 표현하고 자신은 혼자가 아니며 다른 사람들도 그들이 느끼는 것을 느낀다고 인지하는 사람들은 이별에 대처할 때 더 많은 회복력을 가진다. 당신이 겁에 질렸을 때 누군가가 당신에게 "긴장을 풀라."라고 말하면 그것이 얼마나 실망스러운지 당신은 알고 있다. 그것은 이별 후 자기 연민을 배우는 문제의 일부이다. 불안은 당신이 스스로에게 친절하고 사랑하는 것을 막을 수 있지만 당신은 그 불안에서 스스로를 몰아낼 수 없으며 당신은 분명히 더 이상 스스로를 자책할 수 없다. 성격은 당신이 어떻게 반응하는지에 큰 역할을 하며 여자들은 남자들보다 더 자기 연민으로 그것을 다루는 경향이 있다. 긴 안목에서 당신의 경험을 유지하며, 이별 후에 스스로에게 더욱 친절해라. 많은 사람들이 고통스럽고 힘든 이별을 경험하고, 당신은 혼자가 아니다. 이별은 인간의 경험의 일부이며, 당신이 집단의 일부라는 것을 깨닫는 것은 당신의 인식을 더 건강한 곳으로 옮기는 데 도움을 줄 것이다. Dr. Sbarra는 또한 현재에 유념하고 현재에 남아있을 것을 제안한다. 당신이 분노와 질투를 느낄 때를 잘 알아차리고 그것을 받아들이고 발산해라. 당신이 그것을 발산하는 것이 힘들지라도 그것을 판단하지 마라.

VOCA

- self-compassion 자기 연민
- anxiety 불안
- in perspective 전체적인 관점에서, 긴 안목에서

- compassion 연민
- enhance 강화시키다
- fleeting 순식간의, 잠깐 동안의
- attune (악기를) 조율하다, (마음을) 맞추다, 조화시키다
- empathy 공감

- realize 깨닫다, 알다, 이해하다
- release 방출

11 난도 ★★☆ 정답 ①

독해 > 빈칸 완성 > 단어·구·절

정답의 이유

제시문은 과학이 이 세계를 조절할 수 있도록 과학적 이론을 구축할 수는 있지만, 인간의 여러 가지 중요한 감정의 면모들에까지 모두 적용하고 파악하는 것은 불가능하다는 내용이다. 첫 문장에서 과학적 방법론의 영구적인 진리에 도달할 수 없는 한계를 말한 다음에 (A) 앞부분에서 '이것은 또한 과학적 지식을 실존적, 본능적 본성 또는 인간의 삶에 ~하게 만들기도'라고 했고, (A) 다음의 '~which is unique and subjective and unpredictable'로 미루어 문맥상 빈칸 (A)에 들어갈 적절한 것은 'inapplicable(적용할 수 없는)'이다.

(B) 앞부분에서 'Science may provide the most useful way to organize empirical, reproducible data(과학은 경험적이고 재현 가능한 데이터를 구성하는 가장 유용한 방법을 제공할 수 있다)'라고 한 다음에 'but its power to do so is predicated on its (B) to grasp the most central aspects of human life'라고 했으므로, 빈칸에는 '부정'의 뜻을 가진 단어가 들어가야 함을 유추할 수 있다. 따라서 문맥상 빈칸 (B)에 들어갈 적절한 것은 'inability(무능함)'이다.

오답의 이유

② 무관한 – 혐오
③ 비슷한 – 나머지
④ 필수적인 – 현세, 속세
⑤ 일치된 – 장점

본문해석

그러나 역설은 과학적 방법론이 인간의 손의 산물이므로 어떤 영구적인 진리에 도달할 수 없다는 것이다. 우리는 세계를 조직하고 조종하기 위해, 현상을 다루기 쉬운 단위로 축소하기 위해 과학적 이론을 구축한다. 과학은 재현 가능성과 조작된 객관성에 기반을 둔다. 물질과 에너지에 대한 주장을 생성하는 능력이 강한 만큼, 그것은 또한 과학적 지식을 실존적, 본능적 본성 또는 인간의 삶에 (A) 적용할 수 없게 만들기도 하는데, 이는 독특하고 주관적이며 예측할 수 없다. 과학은 경험적이고 재현 가능한 데이터를 구성하는 가장 유용한 방법을 제공할 수 있지만, 그런 과학의 힘은 인간의 삶의 가장 중심적인 측면인 희망, 두려움, 사랑, 미움, 아름다움, 시기, 명예, 나약함, 노력, 고통, 미덕 등을 파악하는 과학의 (B) <u>무능함</u>에 근거한 것이다.

VOCA

- paradox 역설
- permanent 영구적인
- manipulate 조작하다
- manageable 다루기 쉬운
- unpredictable 예측할 수 없는
- empirical 경험적인

12 난도 ★☆☆ 정답 ⑤

어법 > 비문 찾기

정답의 이유

⑤ 문장의 주어인 Observations가 복수이므로 has been fitted → have been fitted가 되어야 한다.

오답의 이유

① to form은 to부정사의 형용사적 용법으로 명사 capability를 꾸며주고 있으므로 어법상 옳다.
② '~을 하는 것에 적응'의 의미로 adaptation to –ing 형태를 사용할 수 있으므로 오류가 없다. 이때 changing은 전치사 to의 목적어인 동명사로 사용되었다.
③ 선행사 observations를 꾸며 주는 현재분사 형태인 indicating이 사용되었다. 그 뒤에 that절이 indicating의 목적어로 사용되었다.
④ date back은 '~로 거슬러 올라간다'의 의미로 주어인 Observations가 복수 형태이므로 동사원형으로 사용하는 것이 맞다.

본문해석

기억을 형성하는 능력은 변화하는 환경적인 요구에 대한 유기체의 전략적 적응에 매우 중요하다. 수면이 기억력에 도움이 된다는 것을 나타내는 관찰은 초기의 실험적인 기억 연구로 거슬러 올라가며, 그 이후로 상당히 다른 개념들이 적용되었다.

VOCA

- strategic 전략적인
- adaptation 적응
- benefit 이롭다, 도움이 되다
- experimental 실험적인

13 난도 ★☆☆ 정답 ③

독해 > 글의 일관성 > 무관한 어휘·문장

정답의 이유

본문의 내용에서는 Oedipus가 자신이 왕의 살인자라는 것을 처음부터 알고 있지만 모르는 척하고 있다고 하였으므로 문맥의 흐름상 맞지 않는 것은 ③ 'innocent(결백한)'이다. ③의 바로 뒤따르는 문장에서 그가 그저 진실을 모르는 척하고 있다는 문장이 힌트가 된다.

본문해석

수년 동안 비평가들은 고대 그리스 연극 Oedipus Rex에 대해 논쟁해 왔다. 어떤 사람들은 Oedipus가 자신의 아버지를 살해했다는 사실이 밝혀지는 연극의 마지막까지 자신의 죄를 전혀 모른다고 주장해 왔다. 다른 사람들은 Oedipus가 그의 죄에 대해 모든 것을 알고 있다고 주장해 왔다. 이러한 관점으로 보면, 뛰어난 수수께끼 해결사인 Oedipus는 자신이 왕의 살인자라는 것에 대한 늘어나는 증거를 무시할 수 없었다. 단지 이 논쟁이 어떻게 또는 왜 그토록 오랫동안 격렬해졌는지는 미스터리로 남아 있다. 정확한 해석은 너무나 명백하다. Oedipus는 처음부터 자신이 결백한(→ 결백하지 않은)

것을 알고 있다. 그는 그저 진실을 모르는 척할 뿐이다. 예를 들어, 신하는 왕의 살해 이야기를 할 때, '노상강도들(bandits)'이라는 단어를 사용한다. 하지만 Oedipus가 그의 이야기를 반복할 때, 그는 단수형인 '노상강도(bandit)'를 사용한다. 소포클레스는 연극 내내 이와 같은 단서를 제공한다. 그러므로 왜 Oedipus가 자신의 범죄에 대한 진실을 몰랐다고 생각하는지 이해하기 어렵다.

VOCA
- evidence 증거
- murder 살해하다
- aware 알고 있다
- interpretation 해석
- ignorant 무지한
- bandit 노상강도

14 난도 ★☆☆   정답 ⑤

어휘 > 단어

정답의 이유

밑줄 친 inadvertently는 '무심코, 우연히, 부주의로'의 뜻으로 이와 의미가 가장 가까운 것은 ⑤ 'unintentionally(무심결에)'이다.

오답의 이유

① 고의로
② 모순되어
③ 부수적으로
④ 몰래, 부정하게

본문해석

재능은 나쁜 것인가? 우리는 모두 똑같이 재능이 있는가? 아니, 그렇지 않다. 어떤 기술의 학습 곡선을 빠르게 올라가는 능력은 분명히 매우 좋은 것이다. 그리고 좋든, 싫든 간에, 우리들 중 일부는 다른 이들보다 이것을 더 잘한다. 그렇다면 왜 '노력하는 자'보다 '타고난 자'를 선호하는 것이 그렇게 나쁜 것일까? *America's Got Talent, The X Factor, Child Genius* 같은 TV 쇼들의 부정적인 면은 무엇일까? 우리가 일곱 살에서 여덟 살 정도의 아이들을 두 그룹, 즉 '타고난 재능'을 지닌 소수의 아이들과 그렇지 않은 수많은 아이들의 그룹으로 나눠서는 안 되는 이유는 무엇인가? 탤런트 쇼가 '탤런트 쇼'로 명명되는 것이 실제로 무슨 해가 될까? 나의 견해로는 재능에 대한 집착이 해로울 수 있는 가장 큰 이유는 단순하다. 재능에 스포트라이트를 비춤으로써 우리는 다른 모든 것들을 그림자 속에 남겨둘 위험이 있다. 우리는 무심코 이러한 다른 요인들이—투지를 포함하여—실제로 그들이 하는 것만큼 중요하지 않다는 메시지를 보낸다.

VOCA
- separate 나누다, 분리하다
- preoccupation 집착

15 난도 ★☆☆   정답 ②

어법 > 비문 찾기

정답의 이유

② be held responsible for는 '~에 책임이 있다'의 뜻이므로 cannot hold → cannot be held가 되어야 한다. hold somebody responsible for something은 '~에게 …에 대한 책임을 지우다'의 뜻이다.

오답의 이유

① how 의문문으로 의문부사 how와 의문문의 어순인 '조동사(do)＋주어(we)＋동사(attribute)＋목적어(responsibility)'가 바르게 쓰였다.
③ since로 시작하는 부사절로써 주어 they와 동사인 lack 그리고 목적어 consciousness, free will, emotions, the capability to form intentions, and the like를 포함하는 어법상 옳은 문장이다.
④ 주어 humans와 동사 delegate, 목적어 agency 그리고 전치사구 to the machine이 오류 없이 사용되었다. delegate A to B는 'A를 B에게 위임하다'의 뜻이다.
⑤ 콤마(,)와 관계대명사 which를 사용한 계속적 용법의 관계대명사절이다. 관계대명사 which의 선행사는 앞 문장 전체이며 3인칭 단수 취급되므로 이어지는 동사는 gives가 사용되었다. 따라서 어법상 옳은 문장이다.

본문해석

만약 인공지능(AI)이 더 많은 대리권을 받고 인간이 하던 일을 맡게 된다면, 우리는 어떻게 도덕적 책임을 돌리겠는가? 인간이 AI에게 대리권과 결정을 위임할 때 기술의 해로움과 이로움에 대한 책임은 누구에게 있는가? 첫 번째 문제는 AI 시스템이 윤리적 결과를 가져오는 조치를 취하고 결정을 내릴 수 있지만, 무엇을 하는지 알지 못하고 도덕적인 사고를 할 수 없기 때문에 그것이 하는 일에 대해 도덕적으로 책임이 없다는 것이다. 기계는 의식, 자유의지, 감정, 의도를 형성하는 능력 등이 부족하기 때문에 대리인이 될 수는 있지만 도덕적 대리인은 될 수 없다. 예를 들어, 아리스토텔레스적 관점에서는 인간만이 자발적인 행동을 수행하고 자신의 행동에 대해 신중히 생각할 수 있다. 만약 이것이 사실이라면 유일한 해결책은 기계가 하는 일에 대해 인간이 책임을 지게 하는 것이다. 인간은 그러면 기계에 대리권을 위임하지만 그 책임은 유지한다. 그러나 이 해결책은 몇 가지 문제점에 직면한다. AI 시스템은 매우 빠르게 스스로 결정을 내리고 행동할 수 있는데 예를 들면 초단타매매 또는 자동차 자율주행에서 그러하며, 이 경우 인간이 최종 결정을 내리고 개입하기에는 시간이 부족하다. 이러한 행동과 결정에 있어서 과연 인간이 책임질 수 있을까?

VOCA
- take action ~에 대해 조치를 취하다
- voluntary 자발적인
- deliberate 신중히 생각하다
- delegate A to B A를 B에게 위임하다
- intervene 개입하다

16 난도 ★☆☆　　　　　　　　정답 ②

어휘 > 단어

정답의 이유

두 번째 문장에서 비(rain)와 눈(snow)을 언급한 것을 통해 빈칸에 적절한 것이 ② 'precipitation(강수량)'이라는 것을 쉽게 알 수 있다. 또한 그 뒤에 이어지는 문장 속의 습기(moisture)도 좋은 힌트가 된다.

오답의 이유

① 순환

③ 하수구

④ 가뭄

⑤ 관개

본문해석

사람들은 강수량이 전형적이고 예상되며 특이하지 않은 '정상적인' 양일 것이라고 기대한다. 정상적인 (양의) 비와 눈이 녹는 것은 지속적인 농업에 필수적인데, 이는 지구의 73억 명의 사람들을 먹여 살리기 위한 것이다. 모든 식물들과 동물들은 그들의 환경을 위한 정상적인 양의 습기에 적응한다. 하지만 '정상'이 항상 일어나는 것은 아니다.

VOCA

• consistent 지속적인

• agriculture 농업

17 난도 ★★☆　　　　　　　　정답 ④

독해 > 대의 파악 > 제목, 주제

정답의 이유

글의 서두에 주제를 제시하는 두괄식 형식의 글이다. 두 번째 문장에서 '~risk taking is not binary'라고 한 다음에 사람마다 감수하는 위험의 종류가 다르다고 했다. 사람들이 저마다 느낄 수 있는 위험의 출처로 비행기에서 뛰어내리는 스포츠와 많은 사람들 앞에서의 연설을 예로 들었다. 따라서 이 글의 주제는 ④ 'Perception of riskiness differs from person to person(위험에 대한 인식은 사람마다 다르다).'가 가장 적절하다.

오답의 이유

① 신체적 · 사회적 위험을 모두 감수하는 것은 우리에게 유익하다.

② 우리는 위험을 신체적 위험과 사회적 위험의 두 가지 범주로 분리해야 한다.

③ 신체적 위험을 감수하는 것은 저자에게 큰 도전을 제기한다.

⑤ 위험을 감수하려는 의지가 성공의 전제 조건이다.

본문해석

새로운 것을 시도하는 것은 위험을 감수하려는 의지가 필요하다. 하지만 위험을 감수하는 것은 이분법이 아니다. 나는 당신이 어떤 종류의 위험을 감수하는 것에는 편안함을 느끼고 다른 종류의 위험을 감수하는 것에 상당히 불편함을 느낄 것이라고 장담한다. 당신은 심지어 당신이 감당하기에 편안한 위험을 보지 못할 수도 있고, 그들의 위험을 무시할 수도 있지만, 당신을 더 불안하게 만드는 것들의 위험성을 증폭시키기 쉽다. 예를 들어, 당신은 번개처럼 빠른 속도로 스키 슬로프를 내려오거나 비행기에서 뛰어내리는 것을 좋아할 수 있으며, 이러한 활동을 위험하다고 여기지 않을 수도 있다. 만약 그렇다면, 당신은 상당한 신체적 위험을 감수하고 있다는 사실을 모르고 있는 것이다. 나처럼 신체적 위험을 감수하지 않는 사람들은 스키장에서 핫초코를 마시거나 스스로를 비행기 좌석에 단단히 묶어두고 싶어 한다. 그 대신, 많은 사람들에게 연설을 하는 것과 같은 사회적 위험에 대해서는 완전히 편안함을 느낄지도 모른다. 이것은 나에게 전혀 위험해 보이지 않는다. 하지만 비행기에서 뛰어내리는 것을 완벽히 행복해하는 다른 사람들은 파티에서 축배를 들어올릴 생각은 절대 하지 않을 것이다.

VOCA

• willingness 의지

• amplify 증폭시키다

• significant 상당한

• give a toast 축배를 들다

18 난도 ★☆☆　　　　　　　　정답 ①

어휘 > 단어

정답의 이유

① (A) 화자의 의견(a woman must have money and a room of her own if she is to write fiction)에 대한 부연 설명으로, 'they have some (A) upon women and some upon fiction(일부는 여성과 ~하고, 일부는 소설과 ~하다)'이라고 했으므로 문맥상 빈칸 (A)에는 'have bearing upon(~와 관련이 있다)'의 bearing이 적절하다. 또한 빈칸 (B) 앞의 the chance of와 (B) 다음의 목적어 '그들의 결론(their own conclusions)'으로 미루어 빈칸 (B)에는 '결론을 도출해내다'의 의미인 draw의 동명사형인 drawing이 적절하다. 빈칸 (C) 앞부분인 'making use of all the liberties and (C) of a novelist(소설가의 모든 자유와 ~을 이용해서)'와 (C) 다음의 'to tell you the story of the two days that preceded my coming here'로 미루어 문맥상 (C)에는 소설가의 자유와 자격(면허)을 의미하는 licenses가 적절하다.

오답의 이유

② 안도감 – 쓰기 – 상상력

③ 실력, 솜씨 – 익사 – 창의력

④ 관련성 – 던지기 – 의무

⑤ 기부 – 수집 – 직업

내가 할 수 있는 일은 당신에게 한 가지 사소한 점에 대한 의견을 제시하는 것뿐이었는데, 그것은 여성이 소설을 쓰려면 돈과 자기 방이 있어야 한다는 것이다. 나는 당신 앞에서 할 수 있는 한 완전하고 자유롭게 내가 그렇게 생각하게 된 일련의 생각을 발전시킬 것이다. 아마도 내가 이 진술의 이면에 있는 생각, 편견을 밝히면, 여러분은 그것들이 여성과, 일부는 소설과 (A) 관련이 있다는 것을 알게 될 것이다. 어쨌든, 어떤 주제가 매우 논란이 많을 때—그리고 성에 관한 질문이 있는 경우에—사람은 진실을 말하는 것을 바랄 수 없다. 그는 어떤 의견을 가지고 있든지 간에 자신이 어떻게 그런 의견을 갖게 되었는지 단지 보여줄 뿐이다. 그는 단지 청중들이 연설자의 한계와 편견, 그리고 특이한 성격을 관찰하면서 그들 스스로의 결과를 (B) 도출할 기회를 줄 따름이다. 이 지점에서 소설은 사실보다 더 많은 진실을 담고 있을 가능성이 높다. 그러므로, 나는 소설가의 모든 자유와 (C) 자격을 이용하여, 이곳에 오기 전 이틀 동안의 이야기를 당신에게 들려줄 것을 제안한다.

VOCA

• have bearing upon ~와 관련이 있다
• controversial 논란이 많은
• limitation 제한, 제약
• prejudice 편견
• idiosyncrasy 특이한 성격

19 난도 ★★★　　　정답 ③

독해 > 세부 내용 찾기 > 내용 (불)일치

정답의 이유

본문의 세부 내용을 묻는 문제이므로 모든 내용을 다 살펴봐야 한다. 본문 내용에 따르면 환경 옹호자들은 우리가 사는 이 시대의 명칭을 바꿈으로써 우리가 이 지구의 환경에 막대한 부정적인 영향을 끼치고 있음을 말하려고 하는 것이므로 정답은 ③ 'The environmental advocates believe that human beings will get aware of their rampant activities which cause destruction if the time period of the Earth is renamed(환경 옹호자들은 만약 지구의 시대가 다시 명명되면 인류가 파괴를 일으키는 만연한 활동에 대해 알게 될 것이라고 믿는다).'이다.

오답의 이유

① 지질학자들은 그 기간의 이름을 바꾸는 행동을 지지함으로써 환경보호론자들이 그들보다 우위에 서는 것을 원하지 않는다.
② 층서학자들은 지구의 시간대를 재명명함에 있어서 문화를 고려할 필요가 있다.
④ 지질학자들은 인간에 의해 야기된 변화가 짧은 시간 동안 계속되어 왔다고 믿는다.
⑤ 일부 인류세 지지자들은 진흙 속에서 표본을 발견하는 것이 어렵다는 층서학자들의 의견에 동의한다.

인류가 지구를 영구적으로 변화시켰는가? 겉보기에 단순한 질문은 우리가 살고 있는 기간을 무엇이라고 불러야 하는지에 대해 지질학자와 환경 옹호자들 사이의 새로운 싸움을 촉발시켰다. 국제 지질학 연합(International Union of Geological Sciences)에 따르면 우리는 공식적으로 마지막 주요 빙하기 이후 11,700년 전에 시작된 홀로세(Holocene epoch)에 살고 있다. 그러나 그 명칭은 구식이라고 일부 전문가들은 말한다. 그들은 '인류세(Anthropocene)'를 주장하는데—anthropo는 '인간'을 의미하고, cene는 '새로운'을 의미한다.—왜냐하면 인류가 다른 지속적인 영향들 중에서, 동식물종의 대량 멸종을 일으키고 바다를 오염시키고 대기를 변화시켰기 때문이다. 그러나 많은 층서학자(암층을 연구하는 과학자)들은 새로운 시대에 대한 명확한 증거가 존재하지 않는다고 하면서 이 아이디어를 비판한다. 그들에 따르면 지질학적 시간 용어에 이름을 붙이기 시작할 때, 우리는 그 경계가 정확히 무엇인지와 그것이 암석 지층에서 어디에 나타나는지를 정의해야 한다. 인류세는 자연 과학보다는 대중 문화에 관한 것이다. 중요한 질문은 인간이 언제 지구에 흔적을 남기기 시작했는지를 정확히 명시하는 것이다. 예를 들어, 원자력 시대는 지구상의 토양에 방사선의 흔적을 남겼지만, 반면에 더 깊은 암석층에서는 서기 900년까지 거슬러 올라가 유럽 농업의 특징이 발견될 수 있다. 한 층서학자는 "인류세는 눈길을 끄는 전문 용어를 제공하지만 지질학적 측면에서는 코드에 맞는 기본적인 사실이 필요하다."라고 말한다. 일부 인류세 지지자들은 그 어려움을 인정한다. 그러나 진흙탕에 빠지지 말고 날짜를 명시하고 넘어가라고 그들은 말한다. 호주국립대학교의 기후변화연구소 소장인 Will Steffen은 그 새 이름이 다음과 같은 메시지를 전달한다고 말한다. "우리가 현재 지구 전체의 규모에서 환경에 부정할 수 없는 영향을 주고 있어서 새로운 지질 시대가 시작되었다는 것을 일반적인 대중에게 강력하게 상기시켜 줄 것이다."

VOCA

• mass extinction 대량멸종
• boundary 경계
• stratigrapher 층서학자
• proponent 지지자
• undeniable 부정할 수 없는

20 난도 ★★★

독해 > 대의 파악 > 추론

정답의 이유

추론 유형은 지문의 모든 내용을 다 살펴봐야 한다. 지문 내용에 따르면 우리의 윤리적인 소비 패턴은 우리의 경제력과 교육 수준에 근거한다고 보여지며, 이는 존경과 지위를 불러온다고 한다. 반대로 윤리적 소비를 하지 못하는 사람은 환경을 향한 그의 관심과는 상관없이 무례함과 무시를 경험할 수도 있다고 한다. 따라서 정답은 ② 'What we buy is often related to our cultural and educational capital, and consumption patterns can reinforce existing social hierarchies(우리가 구매하는 것은 종종 우리의 문화적이고 교육적인 자본과 관련이 있고, 소비 패턴은 기존의 사회 계층을 강화할 수 있다).'이다.

오답의 이유

① 오염을 일으키는 디젤차를 하이브리드 모델로 교체하지 않는 사람은 윤리적인 소비자가 아니다.
③ 상품 소비를 늘리는 것은 윤리적 소비자의 바람직한 목표이다.
④ 소비는 진정한 윤리적인 삶을 실천하는 것의 수단이다.
⑤ 더 많은 문화적 자본을 가진 사람들이 더 낮은 수준의 문화적 자본을 가진 사람들보다 도덕적으로 더 우월할 가능성이 있다.

본문해석

전 세계의 많은 사람들은 글로벌 공급 체인을 괴롭히는 골치 아픈 상황들과 인간이 만든 기후 위기에 대응하여 소비자 윤리를 고려하고 일상 생활에서 윤리적인 소비자 선택을 하기 위해 일한다. 소비자 표시 체계에서 공정무역, 지역적으로 재배되고 지속 가능한 제품인 유기농 제품을 구매하기 위해 윤리적인 선택을 하는 사람들은 종종 이런 종류의 구매를 모르거나 신경 쓰지 않는 사람들보다 더 윤리적으로 우월한 것으로 보여진다. 소비재 분야에서 윤리적 소비자가 된다는 것은 다른 소비자에 비해 문화적 자본이 높고 사회적 지위가 높은 사람에게 수여되는 것이다. 예를 들어, 하이브리드 차량을 구입하는 것은 다른 사람들에게 환경 문제에 대해 염려하고 있다는 신호이며, 차도에서 그 차를 지나가는 이웃들은 심지어 그 차 소유자를 더 긍정적으로 볼 수도 있다. 그러나 20년 된 차를 교체할 여유가 없는 사람 역시 그만큼 환경에 관심을 가질 수도 있지만, 그것을 소비 패턴을 통해서 증명할 수는 없을 것이다. 그들이 만나는 사람들은 그들에 대해 가난하고 교육 수준이 낮다고 생각할 수도 있다. 그들은 그들이 타인에게 어떻게 행동하든 매일같이 무례와 무시를 경험할 수도 있다.

VOCA

- ethical 윤리적인
- morally 도덕적으로
- sustainable (환경 파괴 없이) 지속 가능한
- demonstrate 증명하다
- undereducated 교육을 받지 못한

더 알아보기

추론 유형 해결 비법

세부 정보 추론 유형은 본문의 내용을 전체적으로 이해해야 하고 반드시 본문에 근거하여 정답을 찾아야 한다. 추론 문제의 경우 보기를 먼저 읽고 나서, 그 후 지문을 바탕으로 추론할 수 있는 내용의 보기를 선택하는 것을 추천한다. 이때 본문의 핵심 어구를 그대로 언급하거나 의역을 바르게 한 것이 정답이 된다.

21 난도 ★★☆

독해 > 빈칸 완성 > 단어·구·절

정답의 이유

글의 서두에 주제를 제시하는 두괄식 형식의 글이며 그 주제가 글의 마지막에 한 번 더 반복된다. 첫 문장에서 계몽운동의 남성과 여성들의 철학적이고 지리학적인 프로젝트를 통해 동유럽을 발명했다고 했으므로 정답은 ④ 'an intellectual invention(지적인 발명품)'이다.

오답의 이유

① 허구적인 생각
② 무의식적인 투영
③ 지리적인 지도 제작
⑤ 헛된 꿈

본문해석

동유럽을 만들어낸 것은 계몽운동의 남성과 여성들에 의해 수행되었던 철학적이고 지리학적인 통합 프로젝트였다. 분명히, 동유럽의 땅은 본래 (상상력으로) 만들어진 가상의 것이 아니었다. 그 땅과 그곳에 살았던 사람들은 항상 전적으로 실제였고, 사실 상대적으로 서쪽에 있는 다른 땅들보다 상대적으로 동쪽에 있었다. 그러한 기부가 확실히 18세기에 번성했다고 해도, (동유럽을 만들어 낸) 발명 프로젝트는 단순히 진짜 땅이 발명되거나 신화적인 속성을 부여하는 문제가 아니었다. 계몽주의자들의 기록이 완전히 거짓이거나 허구인 것은 아니었다. 그와는 반대로, 야심을 품은 여행과 비판적인 관찰이 점점 더 증가한 시대에, 그 땅은 이전 어느 때보다 더 자주 방문되었으며 철저하게 연구되었다. 발명 작업은 동유럽의 일반적인 루브릭(rubric)을 생산하기 위해 사실과 허구를 이용하여 종합적인 토지 연합을 사들이는 것이었다. 그 루브릭은 다양한 영역의 땅과 사람들에 대한 일반적이고 연관적인 관찰의 집합체를 나타낸다. 바로 그런 의미에서 동유럽은 문화적 건설, 즉 계몽주의의 지적인 발명품이다.

VOCA

- Enlightenment 계몽운동
- attribute 자질, 속성
- synthetic 종합적인
- aggregation 집합체, 집합

22 난도 ★★☆　　　　　　　　　　　　　정답 ⑤

독해 > 글의 일관성 > 문장 삽입

정답의 이유

⑤ 주어진 문장에서 우리 인간이 타 동물들과는 다른 상징적 언어, 사회 제도, 종교 등을 가지고 있으며 기술의 발달을 통해 이동하고 소통한다고 말하고 있다. 본문의 마지막 문장에서 우리 인간이 유인원과 해부학적인 차이보다 행동과 제도의 차이가 훨씬 눈에 띈다고 했으므로 (E)에 문장을 삽입하는 것이 적절하다. 주어진 문장은 (E) 앞에서 언급한 행동과 제도의 차이의 예시가 된다.

오답의 이유

(A)~(D)의 앞뒤 내용에서는 인간과 침팬지 및 다른 종류의 동물들의 유사성에 대해 말하고 있으므로 인간의 독보적인 행동과 제도를 나타내는 주어진 문장이 삽입되기에는 적절하지 않다.

본문해석

침팬지는 우리 종인 호모 사피엔스의 가장 가까운 친척이다. 침팬지와 인간의 골격 사이에는 뼈 하나하나의 정확한 일치가 존재한다. 인간은 유인원과 다른 포유류처럼 새끼를 낳는다. 인간은 조류, 파충류, 양서류와 유사한 장기와 팔다리를 가지고 있다. 이 유사성은 척추동물의 공통된 진화적 기원을 반영한다. 하지만 우리 종의 뚜렷한 고유함을 알아차리는 데 많은 설명(묘사)이 필요하지는 않다. 인간과 침팬지 사이의 뚜렷한 해부학적 차이는 이족보행과 확대된 뇌를 포함한다. 해부학적인 차이보다 훨씬 더 눈에 띄는 것은 뚜렷이 구별되는 행동과 제도이다. 인간은 상징적 언어, 정교한 사회 및 정치 제도, 법전, 문학 및 예술, 윤리 및 종교를 가지고 있다. 인간은 도로와 도시를 건설하고 자동차, 배, 비행기로 이동하며 전화, 컴퓨터, 텔레비전을 통해 의사소통한다.

VOCA

• correspondence 유사성
• reptile 파충류
• amphibian 양서류
• vertebrate 척추동물
• conspicuous 눈에 띄는, 뚜렷한
• anatomical 해부학적인

23 난도 ★☆☆　　　　　　　　　　　　　정답 ②

어법 > 비문 찾기

정답의 이유

② etching은 타동사로서 그 뒤에 목적어가 와야 한다. 주어진 문장에서는 목적어가 없으며, '기억에 새겨진 ~'이라는 의미인 수동태로 쓰여야 하므로 etching → etched가 되어야 한다.

오답의 이유

① which is가 생략된 관계대명사절로 determined가 알맞게 사용되었다.
③ 동사 rule out의 목적어로써 동명사 playing이 바르게 사용되었다.
④ cater for는 자동사이며 현 문장에서 현재분사 catering이 바르게 사용되었다.
⑤ helping은 전치사 by의 목적어인 동명사 형태로 바르게 사용되었다.

본문해석

만약 당신이 스포츠를 좋아하지 않는다면, 당신은 아마도 전염병처럼 대학 스포츠팀을 피할 것을 계획하고 있을 것이며, 이것은 당신의 기억 속에 새겨져 있는 학교 스포츠 수업에서의 끔찍한 기억을 떠올리는 것을 피하기로 결심한 것이다. 하지만 어느 정도는 대학에서 스포츠를 하는 것을 배제하지는 마라. 대학에는 할 수 있는 다양한 스포츠가 있을 뿐만 아니라, 매우 활동적인 사람부터 완전한 초보자의 수준에 이르기까지 광범위하다. 만약 당신이 자신에게 맞는 클럽을 찾는다면, 단지 당신이 지난밤 먹은 피자를 해결하는 것을 돕는 것이 아니라 당신의 대학의 경험을 향상시킬 수 있는 몇 가지 방법들이 있다.

VOCA

• avoid 피하다
• determine 결심하다
• etch 새기다
• cater for ~에 맞추다, 부응하다

24 난도 ★★☆   정답 ①

독해 > 대의 파악 > 제목, 주제

정답의 이유

본문은 수면 시간의 증가와 감소에 대한 연구조사를 언급하고 있으므로 제목으로 적절한 것은 ① 'Are We Really Sleep-Deprived (우리는 정말 잠이 부족한가)?'이다.

오답의 이유

② 수면 장애는 어떻게 진단되는가?

③ 수면 장애의 다른 유형들은 무엇인가?

④ 왜 우리는 충분한 잠이 필요한가?

⑤ 수면 부족의 결과는 무엇인가?

본문해석

수면 패턴을 파악하는 것은 정기적인 고품질의 설문조사가 부족해서 어렵다. 그러나 2004년의 한 설문조사는 설문에 참여한 3분의 2의 사람들이 하룻밤에 5.5~8.5시간을 잔다고 답한 것을 통해서 평균 수면 시간이 7시간이라는 것을 알아냈다. 약 3분의 1은 대부분의 밤에 최소 한 번의 수면 장애를 경험했다고 보고했다. 수면 시간이 줄었는지 아닌지는 판단하기 어렵다. 한 연구(1983~2005)에 따르면 성인의 평균 수면 시간은 50분 증가했고, 짧은 수면(6시간 미만)의 발생은 15%에서 10%로 감소했으며, 긴 수면(9시간 초과)의 발생은 16%에서 28%로 증가했다. 어린이들의 수면 경향에 대한 증거는 결론을 내릴 수 없다. 그러나, 최근의 추가적인 연구는 아이들의 수면이 지난 1세기 동안 대략 1시간 정도 증가했음을 알아냈다. 비록 수면이 악화되지는 않았더라도, 전문가들은 충분하지 않은 수면 시간은 중요한 공중보건 문제라고 강조한다.

VOCA

• prevalence 유행, 횡행, 발생

• inconclusive 결정적이 아닌, 결론에 이르지 못하는

• emphasize 강조하다

• insufficient 불충분한, 부족한

25 난도 ★★☆   정답 ③

독해 > 글의 일관성 > 무관한 어휘 · 문장

정답의 이유

본문은 지도 제작에서 지켜지고 고려되어야 하는 사항들에 대한 내용이다. 지도는 사용자로 하여금 쉽게 사용하고 이해할 수 있도록 너무 지나친 세부 사항은 생략하며 지도의 용도에 맞게 정보를 단순화하는 작업이 필요하다고 했으므로 과거의 지도 제작 방식에 대한 ③ 'Until the 1970s, most maps were being drawn with ink pens and rulers, but now they are composed on computers and printed by machine(1970년대까지는 대부분의 지도가 잉크펜과 자로 그려졌으나 지금은 컴퓨터로 작성되고 기계로 인쇄된다).'은 전체적인 글의 흐름과 맞지 않는다.

본문해석

지도 제작은 수학과 공학의 도구와 그래픽 디자인의 도구를 결합한 고도로 기술적이며 어느 정도 예술적인 추구이다. 지도는 정확해야 하며, 왜곡되거나 부적절하게 위치하거나 정보가 잘못 표기된 것이 아닌 실제 존재하는 대로 상황을 묘사해야 한다. 그것들은 시각적으로 사용하기 쉬워야 하며, 불필요한 정보로 인한 혼란 없이 사용자가 필요로 하는 자료를 눈에 띄게 보여줘야 한다. 이것이 바로, 예를 들자면, 로드맵이 보통 가장 간단한 길을 제외하고는 산과 언덕을 표시하지 않는 이유이다. 1970년대까지는 대부분의 지도가 잉크펜과 자로 그려졌으나 지금은 컴퓨터로 작성되고 기계로 인쇄된다. 그렇게 하면 도로를 나타내는 선들로 이미 채워진 지도에 많은 선들을 추가할 것이다. 지리적인 데이터를 지표면의 원래 형태에서 지도 위의 단순화된 형태로 변환할 때, 우리는 이 정보가 어떻게 표현되어야 할지에 대해 많은 결정을 내려야 한다. 우리가 지도를 어떻게 그리든 우리는 세상의 모든 상세한 부분을 있는 그대로 정확하게 보여줄 수 없으며 또 그것을 원하지도 않을 것이다. 축척과 투영은 정보가 표현되는 방식을 결정하는 지도의 두 가지의 기본적인 속성이다.

VOCA

• accurate 정확한

• distorted 왜곡된

• prominently 눈에 띄게

• ways [단수 취급] (장)거리, 길

• convert 변환하다

• fundamental 기본적인, 핵심적인

영어 | 2021년 국회직 8급

한눈에 훑어보기

✓ 영역 분석

어휘 01 02 05 15
4문항, 16%

독해 06 08 09 10 11 12 13 14 19 20 21 22
23 24 25
15문항, 60%

어법 03 04 07 16 17 18
6문항, 24%

✓ 빠른 정답

01	02	03	04	05	06	07	08	09	10
①	③	④	③	④	④	①	③	①	④
11	**12**	**13**	**14**	**15**	**16**	**17**	**18**	**19**	**20**
②	⑤	③	④	②	⑤	②	①	⑤	⑤
21	**22**	**23**	**24**	**25**					
①	③	⑤	②	④					

✓ 점수 체크

구분	1회독	2회독	3회독
맞힌 문항 수	/ 25	/ 25	/ 25
나의 점수	점	점	점

01 난도 ★★★ 정답 ①

어휘 > 단어

[정답의 이유]
문맥상 프로 골퍼로서의 성공과 금전적인 부를 동시에 달성했다는 내용이 자연스러우므로 빈칸에 가장 적절한 것은 ① 'concomitant (수반되는)'이다.

[오답의 이유]
② 계속 오가는
③ 지겨운
④ 햇병아리, 풋내기
⑤ (책 속의 작은) 삽화

본문해석
Jack Nicklaus의 골프 코스에서의 성공과 그에 수반되는 그의 은행 계좌의 증가는 그를 모든 프로 골퍼들의 부러움의 대상이 되도록 하였다.

VOCA
• bank account (예금) 계좌
• envy 부러워하다, 부러움, 선망(의 대상)

02 난도 ★★☆ 정답 ③

어휘 > 단어

[정답의 이유]
빈칸 다음 문장에서 'reflects the fact that penalties laid down in the code were extremely severe'라고 했고, 좀도둑질을 살인과 같은 형벌인 사형으로 다스렸다고 했으므로 빈칸에 가장 적절한 말은 ③ 'harsh(가혹한)'이다.

[오답의 이유]
① 상냥한, 유순한
② 경계하는
④ 상서로운
⑤ ~에 좋은[유리한]

Draconian법은 아테네에서 만들어진 최초의 성문법전으로, 기원전 621년 또는 620년에 Draco라는 정치인에 의해서 도입되었다고 여겨진다. 비록 그 법의 세부 사항은 불분명하지만, 그 법들은 분명히 많은 범죄행위를 다루었다. 현대 형용사 'Draconian'은 지나치게 가혹함을 의미하는데, 그 법에 명시된 형벌들이 극도로 엄격했다는 사실을 반영한다. 좀도둑질이 살인과 동일한 형벌인 사형을 처벌받았던 것이다. 기원전 4세기의 한 정치인은 Draco가 그의 법들을 잉크가 아니라 피로 썼다고 비꼬았다.

VOCA

- written code of laws 성문법전
- draw up 만들다, 작성하다
- statesman 정치인
- obscure 어두운, 분명치 않은
- offence 위법 행위, 범죄, 모욕
- lay down (법칙 · 원칙 등을 지키도록) 정하다
- pilfering 좀도둑질
- quip 비꼬다, 풍자하다

03 난도 ★★☆　　　　　　　　정답 ④

어법 > 비문 찾기

정답의 이유

④ aspire(열망하다)는 to부정사를 목적어로 취하므로 becoming → to become이 되어야 한다.

오답의 이유

① 선행사(a person)가 단수이므로 주격 관계대명사(who) 다음에 단수동사(is skilled)가 올바르게 사용되었다.

② 주어(the term)가 단수이므로 3인칭 단수동사(originates)로 올바르게 사용되었다.

③ such as(예를 들어, ~와 같은) 다음에 명사구 Leonardo Da Vinci or Michelangelo가 올바르게 사용되었다.

⑤ 'People expected them to speak several languages, ~'의 수동태로 They were expected to speak(be expected to+동사원형)가 올바르게 사용되었다.

본문해석

르네상스적인 인물은 많은 분야에서 숙련되고, 많은 주제들에서 광범위한 학식을 가진 사람이다. '르네상스적인 인물'이란 용어는 Leonardo Da Vinci나 Michelangelo 같은 유럽의 르네상스 시대 예술가들과 학자들로부터 기원한다. 르네상스 시대에, 교육받은 사람들은 다재능한 사람이 되기를 열망하였다. 그들은 여러 언어들을 구사하고, 문학과 예술을 감상하고, 또한 훌륭한 스포츠맨이 될 것으로 기대되었다.

VOCA

- skilled 능한, 숙련된
- term 용어
- a broad range of 광범위한, 다양하고 폭넓은
- subject 주제, 과목, 분야
- originate from ~로부터 비롯되다, ~로부터 기원[유래]하다
- multi-talented 다재능한
- appreciate 감상하다, 이해하다, 평가하다, 고맙게 여기다

더 알아보기

to부정사를 목적어로 취하는 동사

주로 '미래' 또는 '긍정'의 뜻을 가진 동사들이 to부정사를 목적어로 취한다.

희망	want(원하다), wish(바라다), hope(희망하다), expect(기대하다), aspire(열망하다), desire(원하다), long(바라다) 예 You can't expect *to learn* a foreign language in a few months. (외국어를 몇 달 만에 배울 거라고 기대할 수는 없다.) 예 I wish *to speak* to the manager. (매니저와 이야기하고 싶어요.)
계획	plan(계획하다), intend(~하려고 하다), mean(의도하다), prepare(준비하다) 예 We intend *to go* to Australia next year. (우리는 내년에 호주에 갈 계획이다.)
시도 · 노력	try(노력하다), attempt(시도하다), seek(추구하다) 예 They sought *to reassure* the public. (그들은 대중을 안심시키려고 노력했다.)
그 외 빈출	decide(결정하다), agree(동의하다), offer(제공하다), manage(간신히 ~하다), afford(~할 여유가 되다), need(필요로 하다), demand(요구하다), ask(묻다, 요구하다), dare(감히 ~ 하다) 예 We managed *to get* to the airport in time. (우리는 간신히 시간 내에 공항에 도착했다.)

04 난도 ★☆☆　　　　　　　　정답 ③

어법 > 정문 찾기

정답의 이유

③ 현재 사실의 반대를 표현할 때는 가정법 과거, 과거 사실의 반대를 표현할 때는 가정법 과거완료를 사용한다. 가정법 과거완료는 '만약에 ~했다면, …했었을 텐데'의 뜻으로 'If+주어+had+p.p. ~, 주어+would[should/could/might]+have+p.p.'로 나타내므로 문법적으로 옳은 표현이다.

오답의 이유

① hold는 '열다, 개최하다'의 뜻으로 주로 수동태로 사용되므로 will held → will be held가 되어야 한다.

② hurt는 A-A-A 타입의 동사이므로 hurted → hurt가 되어야 한다.

④ 성품을 나타내는 형용사(kind)의 경우, to부정사의 의미상 주어는 'of+목적격'이므로 kind with him to invite → kind of him to invite가 되어야 한다.

⑤ 문맥상 '계획을 생각해냈다'는 과거의 시작된 일이 현재에 완료됨을 의미하므로 현재완료 시제를 써야 한다. 따라서 has came up with → has come up with가 되어야 한다.

① 제3차 국제지리학회가 서울에서 개최될 것이다.

② Susan이 나를 떠났을 때, 나는 너무나 상처받았다.

③ 만약 날씨가 더 좋았더라면, 나는 그가 도착했을 때 정원에 앉아 있었을 텐데.

④ 그의 80번째 생일파티에 나를 초대하다니 그는 정말 친절하다.

⑤ 그녀는 자신의 수입을 두 배로 늘릴 몇몇 놀라운 계획을 생각해 냈다.

05 난도 ★★★   정답 ④

어휘 > 단어

정답의 이유

(A) stupefaction(해리 포터에 자주 등장하는 주문 stupefy의 명사형)은 '망연자실, 깜짝 놀람'의 뜻으로 ①, ②, ④와 그 의미가 비슷하다. (B) congruence는 '일치, 합치'의 뜻으로 ③, ④, ⑤와 의미가 비슷하다. 따라서 밑줄 친 (A), (B)와 의미가 가까운 것은 ④ 'astonishment(깜짝 놀람) – accordance(일치, 합치)'이다.

오답의 이유

① 놀라움 – 불일치

② 경이(로운 것) – 독특함

③ 행복 – 조화

⑤ 만족 – 일치

본문해석

"한 장의 사진 속에서, 내가 그녀를 기억할 수 있기 전에, 나는 내 어머니가 입었던 옷으로부터 나의 부재를 읽을 수 있었다. 익숙한 존재가 다르게 옷을 차려입고 있는 것을 보았을 때 일종의 (A) 놀라움이 있다."라고 Roland Barthes는 *Camera Lucida*에서 자신의 출생 이전부터의 가족 사진을 훑어보면서 썼다. Barthes는 우리에게 말하기를, 한 장의 사진에서, 어머니가 목숨을 잃은 마지막 병을 앓는 동안 자신이 간호했던 늙고 허약한 노파와 그 어린아이가 재회하고 있다고 했다. "그녀는 나의 어린 딸이 되어, 나를 위해 첫 사진 속의 소중한 아이와 하나가 되었다." 거기서 그는 자기 어머니의 확신에 찬 온화함과 친절함을 발견한다. 거기서 그는 자신의 어머니뿐 아니라 그들 사이의 관계, 즉 '내 어머니의 존재와 그녀의 죽음에 대한 내 슬픔' 사이에서 (B) 일치를 발견한다.

VOCA

• non-existence 존재하지 않음

• stupefaction 망연자실, 크게 놀람

• search through ~을 철저하게 조사하다, ~을 찾아내다

• rejoin 재회하다

• frail 허약한

• assertive 적극적인, 확신에 찬

• gentleness 온화함, 관대함, 정다움

• congruence 일치

• amazement 놀람

• accordance 일치, 조화

06 난도 ★★☆   정답 ④

독해 > 글의 일관성 > 문장 삽입

정답의 이유

주어진 글의 'It eventually turned out that the signal was indeed a false alarm due to human error(결국 그 신호는 실제로 사람의 실수로 인한 잘못된 경보임이 판명되었다)'로 미루어 주어진 글 앞에는 신호(signal)가 선행한다는 것을 유추할 수 있다. 또 주어진 글의 뒷부분에 'by mistake inserted(실수로 주입했다)'가 있으므로 주어진 글은 문맥상 'But the general concluded that the signal was probably a false alarm ~'으로 시작하는 (C) 다음에 오는 것이 적절하다. 따라서 주어진 문장이 들어갈 위치로 적절한 곳은 ④ (D)이다.

본문해석

모든 복잡한 기술들과 마찬가지로, 미사일 감지 시스템은 오작동과 해석의 모호함에 영향받기 쉽다. 우리는 미국의 감지 시스템에 의해 주어진 최소한 세 번의 잘못된 경보를 알고 있다. 예를 들어, 1979년 11월 9일에, 미국 시스템 담당 당직사관으로 근무 중이던 미 육군 장군은 그 당시 국방부 차관인 William Perry에게 한밤중에 전화를 걸어, 말하기를, "제 감시 컴퓨터상에 소련에서 미국으로 날아오는 ICBM 200개가 보입니다."라고 했다. 그러나 그 장군은 그 신호가 아마 잘못된 경보일 것이라고 결론지었고, Perry 차관은 Carter 대통령을 깨우지 않았으며, Carter 대통령은 버튼을 누르지 않았고, 불필요하게 수백만의 소련인들을 죽이지도 않았다. 결국 그 신호는 실제로 사람의 실수로 인한 잘못된 경보로 판명되었다. 컴퓨터 운영자가 실수로 소련 ICBM 200대의 발사를 가정한 훈련 테이프를 미국 경보 시스템 컴퓨터에 삽입했던 것이다. 우리는 또한 러시아 감지 시스템에 의해 유발된 잘못된 경보가 최소 한 번 발생했다는 사실도 알고 있다. 1995년 노르웨이에서 떨어진 한 섬에서 북극으로 발사된 비군사용 로켓이 러시아 레이더의 자동 추적 알고리즘에 의해 미국 잠수함에서 발사된 미사일로 오인 식별되었다. 이 사건들은 중요한 점을 보여준다. 경고 신호는 분명하지 않은 것이다.

VOCA

• insert into ~에 삽입하다

• detection 발견, 간파, 탐지

• subject to ~하기 쉬운

• malfunction 오작동

• ambiguity 모호함

• watch office 당직 사관

• Under-Secretary of Defence 국방 차관

• ICBM 대륙간 탄도 미사일(Intercontinental Ballistic Missile)

• turn out ~임이 판명되다

• simulate 모의실험을 하다

• misidentify 오인하다

• algorithm 알고리즘, 연산 방식

• unambiguous 명백한

어법 > 비문 찾기

정답의 이유

① 접속사 as가 이끄는 절의 주어(dissatisfaction with working conditions or with the nature of the job)가 단수이므로 단수동사 mount → mounts가 되어야 한다.

오답의 이유

② 'so+형용사(bad)+that절' 구문은 '너무나 ~ 해서 결국 … 하다'의 뜻으로 어법상 올바르게 사용되었다.

③ those who were the most idealistic and driven은 '가장 이상적이며 의욕적인 사람들'의 뜻이다. 'those who ~'는 '~ 하는 사람들'의 뜻으로 복수동사로 받는다.

④ 감정유발동사의 경우, 주어가 감정을 일으키는 원인일 때는 현재분사를, 감정을 느끼는 대상(주로 사람)일 때는 과거분사를 쓴다. 주어(the realization)가 감정을 일으키는 원인이므로 현재분사 'disappointing and demoralizing'이 올바르게 사용되었다.

⑤ 선행사(idealism)를 수식하는 본래의 관계절은 'they may have entered a profession with the idealism'으로 전치사가 관계대명사 앞으로 이동하여 '전치사+관계대명사(with which)'로 올바르게 사용되었다.

본문해석

중년기의 직업 만족도는 보편적이지 않다. 어떤 사람들에게는 일이 점차 스트레스가 되어가고 있는데, 직장 여건이나 직업 특성에 대한 불만족이 커지기 때문이다. 어떤 경우에는 여건들이 너무 나빠져서 그 결과로 번아웃(극도의 피로) 또는 직업을 바꿀 결심을 하기도 한다. 번아웃은 근로자가 자신의 일에서 불만족, 환멸, 좌절, 권태를 경험할 때 발생한다. 번아웃은 타인을 돕는 일과 관련된 직종에서 자주 발생하며, 일 시작 초기에는 가장 이상적이며 의욕이 넘쳤던 그런 사람들에게 종종 타격을 가한다. 어떤 면에서, 그러한 근로자들은 자기 일에 지나치게 몰두해 있어서, 빈곤이나 의료 지원 같은 거대한 사회적 문제들에서 자신들이 단지 작은 영향을 줄 수밖에 없다는 것을 인식하면 실망하고 사기가 저하될 수 있다. 그로 인하여, 그들이 직업에 입문할 때 가졌던 이상주의는, 비관주의와 문제에 대한 의미 있는 해결책 제시가 불가능하다는 태도로 대체된다.

VOCA

- dissatisfaction　불만
- mount　늘다, 증가하다
- burnout　극도의 피로, 신경 쇠약
- disillusionment　환멸
- weariness　권태, 피로
- idealistic　이상적인
- driven　동기를 부여받은, 추진력을 갖춘, 의욕이 넘치는
- overcommitted　지나치게 헌신적인
- medical care　의료 지원
- make a dent in　~에 영향을 주다
- demoralize　사기를 저하시키다
- pessimism　비관론, 염세주의

독해 > 세부 내용 찾기 > 내용 (불)일치

정답의 이유

네 번째 문장에서 'Modern environments and experiences cut across all boundaries of geography and ethnicity ~'라고 한 다음, 'modernity can be said to unite all mankind(현대성이 모든 인류를 통합한다)'라고 했으므로 글의 내용과 일치하지 않는 것은 ③ 'Modernity separates mankind according to the different geographical locations(현대성은 인류를 다른 지리적 위치에 따라 분리시킨다).'이다.

오답의 이유

① 현대성은 전 세계 사람들에 의해 공유되는 경험의 한 방식을 의미한다. → 첫 번째 문장에서 'There is a mode of vital experience—experience of space and time, ~ shared by men and women all over the world today.'라고 했으므로 글의 내용과 일치한다.

② 현대성은 우리가 가진 모든 것을 파괴할 위협적인 환경에 처해 있다는 것을 발견한다. → 세 번째 문장에서 'To be modern is to find ourselves in an environment ~ that threatens to destroy everything we have, everything we know, everything we are.'라고 했으므로 글의 내용과 일치한다.

④ 현대성은 삶의 가능성과 위험을 포함하는 경험의 한 방식이다. → 첫 번째 문장에서 '~ experience of space and time, of the self and others, of life's possibilities and perils ~'라고 했으므로 글의 내용과 일치한다.

⑤ 현대성은 민족성, 국적, 그리고 관념의 경계들을 가로지른다. → 네 번째 문장에서 'Modern environments and experiences cut across all boundaries of geography and ethnicity ~'라고 했으므로 글의 내용과 일치한다.

본문해석

오늘날 전 세계의 남성과 여성에 의해 공유되는 필수적인 경험, 즉 공간과 시간, 나 자신과 타인들, 삶의 가능성과 위험성의 경험에 대한 한 가지 양식이 있다. 나는 이 경험을 '현대성'이라고 부를 것이다. 현대적으로 된다는 것은, 우리에게 모험, 힘, 기쁨, 성장, 우리 자신과 세상의 변형 등을 약속하며, 동시에 우리가 가진 모든 것, 우리가 아는 모든 것, 우리 자신을 파괴할 수 있는 위협을 가하는 환경에 놓인 우리 스스로를 발견하는 것이다. 현대의 환경과 경험은 지리와 민족성, 계층과 국적, 종교와 이념의 모든 경계를 가로지른다. 이런 의미에서, 현대성이 온 인류를 통합한다고 말할 수 있다. 그러나 그것은 역설적 통합, 즉 분열의 통합이다. 그것은 우리 모두를 끊임없이 계속되는 분열과 회복, 갈등과 모순, 모호함과 번민의 소용돌이 속으로 몰아넣는다.

VOCA

- vital　중요한, 생명유지에 필수적인
- peril　위험
- cut cross　~을 질러가다
- ethnicity　민족성

- paradoxical 역설적인
- disunity 분열
- maelstrom 대혼란, 큰 소용돌이
- perpetual 끊임없이 계속되는
- disintegration 붕괴
- contradiction 모순, 반박, 반대
- ambiguity 모호함
- anguish 고통, 번민
- traverse 가로지르다

09 난도 ★★☆ 정답 ①

독해 > 빈칸 완성 > 단어 · 구 · 절

정답의 이유

빈칸 앞 문장 '~ billed as the most radical such review since the end of the cold war'에서 존슨 정부의 국가정책에 대한 통합 평론지가 냉전 종식 이후 가장 급진적인 비평이라고 홍보되었다고 했고, 빈칸 다음 문장에서 'The text is free of the ebullient jingoism(그 글에는 맹목적 애국주의가 없는) ~'이라고 했으므로 빈칸에 가장 적절한 것은 ① 'it defies expectations(그것은 예상을 거스른다)'이다.

오답의 이유

② 그것은 인기를 얻는다
③ 그것은 브렉시트에 부합한다
④ 이것은 당의 추천을 동의한다
⑤ 이것은 그 나라의 경제적 상황을 간과한다

본문해석

'글로벌 영국'이라는 슬로건은, 2016년 EU(유럽연합)를 탈퇴하기 위한 국민투표 몇 개월 후에 처음 통용되었다. Theresa May는 수상으로서 처음으로 보수당 총회에서 연설할 때 이 표현을 다섯 번이나 사용하였다. 며칠 뒤 그것은 Boris Johnson이 May의 외무장관으로서 한 첫 번째 정책 연설의 제목이었다. 브렉시트가 경제적 자급자족을 의미하지 않는다는 것을 영국인들에게 안심시키기 위한 시도를 뛰어넘어, 그것이 실제로 의미하는 것은 모호한 상태로 남았다. 그 개념이 드디어 구체화되고 있다. 3월 16일, 존슨 정부는 '경쟁 시대의 글로벌 영국'이라는 제목으로 국가의 외교, 안보, 국방, 원조 정책에 대한 114페이지에 달하는 '통합 비평'을 출판했는데, 그것은 냉전 종식 이후 가장 급진적인 비평이라고 홍보되었다. 여러 가지 측면에서, <u>그것은 예상을 거스른다.</u> 그 글에는 Johnson과 그의 내각이 아주 좋아하는 맹목적 애국주의가 없다. 많은 관찰자들은 영국이 EU와 외교 참호전에 갇혀있는 유럽에서 벗어나 아시아의 떠오르는 강대국들을 향해 구심점을 옮길 것을 예상했다.

VOCA

- gain currency 퍼지다, 통용하기 시작하다
- deploy 배치하다, 효율적으로 사용하다, 전개하다
- Conservative Party 보수당
- in practice 실제로
- Brexit 브렉시트(영국의 유럽연합 탈퇴)

- autarky 경제적 자급 자족(self-sufficiency)
- hazy 흐릿한, 모호한
- flesh out ~을 더 구체화하다
- aid 원조
- ebullient 패기만만한, 사기충천한
- jingoism 맹목적 애국주의, 대외적 강경론
- cabinet 내각

10 난도 ★★☆ 정답 ④

독해 > 글의 일관성 > 글의 순서

정답의 이유

주어진 글에서 빅뱅 직후 뜨거운 우주의 상황이 제시되었으므로 다음에는 우주가 식는 상황이 이어져야 한다. 식는 상황은 (C)의 'Then, as time went on, we would see the Universe cool, ~'로 이어진 다음 (A)의 'As it continued to cool ~'로 연결되는 것이 자연스럽다. (D)에서 전자의 자유 활동으로 빛이 산란되어 우주가 불투명했다고 한 다음, (B)에서 전자가 원자 형성을 위해 흡수되면 빛 산란도 없어지므로 우주가 순간 투명해진다고 연결되는 것이 자연스럽다. 따라서 글의 순서로 알맞은 것은 ④ '(C) - (A) - (D) - (B)'이다.

본문해석

물리학 이론에 따르면, 만약 우리가 빅뱅 1초 후에 우주를 관찰한다면, 우리가 보게 되는 것은 중성자, 양성자, 전자, 반전자(양전자), 광자, 중성미립자들로 이루어진 100억 도의 바다이다.

(C) 그러고 나서 시간이 지남에 따라, 우리는 우주가 식어서 중성자가 양성자와 전자로 분해되거나, 또는 중수소(수소의 동위원소)를 만들기 위해 양성자와 결합하는 것을 보게 될 것이다.

(A) 우주가 계속 식어감에 따라, 전자가 원자핵과 결합하여 결국 중성 원자를 형성하는 온도에 이를 것이다.

(D) 이 '재결합'이 발생하기 전에, 우주는 불투명했을 것인데, 햇빛이 구름 속 물방울로부터 산란되는 방식으로, 자유 전자들이 빛(광자)의 산란을 초래했을 것이기 때문이다.

(B) 그러나 자유 전자가 흡수되어 중성 원자를 형성하게 되면, 우주는 갑자기 투명해진다.

이 동일한 광자들, 즉 우주의 배경 복사라고 알려진 빅뱅의 잔광이 오늘날 관측될 수 있다.

VOCA

- neutron 중성자
- proton 양성자
- electron 전자
- anti-electron 반전자
- positron 양전자
- photon 광자
- neutrino 중성미립자
- deuterium 중수소
- isotope 동위 원소
- nuclei 원자핵(nucleus의 복수형)

- neutral atom 중성 원자
- opaque 불투명한
- transparent 투명한
- droplet 작은 방울
- cosmic background radiation 우주 배경 복사

11 난도 ★★☆   정답 ②

독해 > 대의 파악 > 제목, 주제

[정답의 이유]

제시문의 서두에서는 인구 증가로 인해 식량 생산에 한계가 있음을 설명하고, 후반에서는 바다로부터 나오는 식량(해상 식량) 생산이 인류를 먹여 살리기 위해 필요하다는 것을 대안으로 제시한다. 따라서 글의 제목으로 적절한 것은 ② 'The Future of Food from the Sea(해상 식량 자원의 미래)'이다.

[오답의 이유]

① 세계 식량 수요의 증가
③ 기후 변화와 생물 다양성의 손실
④ 해양의 식량 생산 부문
⑤ 바다와 해양 문화에서 온 먹을 수 있는 음식

본문해석

인구 증가, 소득 상승, 선호도 변화는 향후 몇십 년간 영양가 있는 식품에 대한 세계적인 수요를 상당히 증가시킬 것이다. 영양실조와 기아로 인해 많은 나라들이 여전히 고통받고 있고, 2050년까지의 인구와 소득 추정치는 향후 인류의 소비 목적으로 해마다 최소 500 메가톤의 육류가 필요할 것이라고 제안한다. 육지 재배 식용작물의 생산량을 늘리는 것은 어려운 일인데, 그것은 수확률 감소, 부족한 토지와 수자원과의 경쟁 때문이다. 육지에서 생산되는 해산물(민물 양식과 내륙 포획 수산물을 의미하며, 우리는 모든 수중 식용작물과 해양 식량, 특히 해양자원을 나타내기 위해 해산물이란 용어를 사용한다)은 식량안보와 전 세계적인 공급에 중요한 역할을 하지만, 그것의 확장 역시 제한적이다. 육지 기반의 다른 생산물들과 마찬가지로, 육지 기반 수경재배의 확장은 물, 토양, 생물 다양성, 기후에 영향을 미치는 상당한 환경적 외부 영향을 초래했으며, 이는 환경의 식량생산능력을 위태롭게 했다. 수산물 생산에서 육지 수경재배의 중요성에도 불구하고, 많은 국가들(특히 최대 내륙 수경재배 생산국인 중국)은 이 목적으로의 육지와 물 사용을 제한하여, 그 확장을 제한하고 있다. 비록 내륙 포획 어업이 식량안보에 중요하지만, 전 세계 수산물 생산에서 차지하는 비중이 제한적이고, 생태계 제약으로 인해 그 확장이 방해받는다. 따라서 미래의 수요와 (육지 기반 어류 및 다른 식량 자원 역시 해결책의 일부라는 인식을) 충족하기 위해, 우리는 바다로부터 나오는 지속 가능한 식량 생산이 미래의 식량공급에서 중요한 역할을 하는지 여부를 묻게 된다.

VOCA

- shift 변화
- nutritious 영양가 있는
- malnutrition 영양실조
- plague 역병(에) 걸리게 하다

- projection 예상, 투사
- scale up 확대하다
- challenging 힘든
- scarce 부족한
- aquaculture 수경재배
- fishery 어장, 어업
- denote 표시하다, 나타내다
- aquatic 수생의
- compromise 위태롭게 하다
- terrestrial 육지의
- notably 현저히
- hamper 방해하다

12 난도 ★★☆   정답 ⑤

독해 > 빈칸 완성 > 단어 · 구 · 절

[정답의 이유]

(A) 다음에서 현존하는 Endangered Species Act는 멸종 위기종에 대한 보호를 목적으로 하는 법이고, 의회는 이를 저해할 수 있는 법안을 고려하고 있으므로 빈칸에는 Endangered Species Act에 대한 변화를 시작할 수 있다는 의미의 ①, ⑤가 적절하다.

(B) 다음의 'courts' power to overturn decisions to lift or loosen species protections'는 멸종 위기종 보호에 대한 결정을 뒤집는 법원의 힘을 뜻하므로 빈칸에는 법원의 힘을 제한한다는 의미의 ①, ⑤가 적절하다.

(C) 앞에서 'These bills discard science, increasing the likelihood of harm to species and habitat, create hurdles to protecting species'라고 하면서 이러한 법안들이 종들과 서식지에 대한 피해 가능성을 증가시키고 종들을 보호하는 데 장애물을 만든다고 했으므로 빈칸에는 법을 집행하는 시민의 능력을 약화시킨다는 의미의 ③, ④, ⑤가 적절하다.

따라서 빈칸에 가장 적절한 것은 ⑤ '(A) institute(시작하다) – (B) limit(제한하다) – (C) undermine(약화시키다)'이다.

[오답의 이유]

① 시작하다 – 방해하다 – 고치다
② 강화하다 – 채우다 – 바로잡다
③ 무효화하다 – 확대하다 – 망치다
④ 지시하다 – 넓히다 – 막다

본문해석

의회는, 만약 법으로 통과되면, 멸종 위기종의 법에 대한 변화를 (A) 시작하게 되어 보존방법에 대한 통제력을 주와 지역 정부로 이전하고, 종들의 보호에 대한 필요여부 결정을 가속화하고, 종 보호를 해제하거나 감소하는 결정을 뒤집는 법원의 힘을 (B) 제한시킬 일련의 법안들을 고려하고 있다고, Associated Press(AP) 통신은 보도한다. 많은 민주당원들과 야생생물 옹호자들은 제시된 변화들이 세계의 생물다양성을 위험에 빠뜨릴 것이라 주장한다. "야생생물 멸종 패키지는 멸종 위기종 보호법에 대한 극단적이고 포괄적인 공격이다."라고 비영리 환경 보호단체인 야생동물 보호단체 보호

프로그램의 수석부회장 Bob Dreher는 YubaNet.com에 게시된 성명문에서 말한다. "이 법안들은 과학을 버리는 것이고, 종과 서식지에 대한 위험성을 증가시키며, 위기종을 보호하는 것에 방해물을 만들게 되며, 법원에서 법을 집행할 수 있는 시민의 능력을 (C) 약화시키는 반면, 그것을 맡을 준비가 되지 않은 각 주, 심지어 기업이나 개인에게 종 관리에 대한 권한을 위임해버리는 것이다."

13 난도 ★★☆　　　　　　　　　정답 ③

독해 > 세부 내용 찾기 > 내용 (불)일치

[정답의 이유]

식수 회사에 의한 피해 보상은 제시문 어디에도 나와 있지 않으므로 글에 언급되지 않은 것은 ③ 'compensation for damage by the water company(식수 회사에 의한 피해보상)'이다.

[오답의 이유]

① 그 사건이 일어난 시간과 장소 → 첫 번째 문장에서 'In the first week of May 2000, unseasonably heavy rain drenched the rural town of Walkerton, Canada.'라고 했으므로 언급된 내용이다.

② 질병 발생의 주요 원인들 → 네 번째 문장에서 '~ the town's drinking water was contaminated with a deadly strain of E. coli'라고 했으므로 언급된 내용이다.

④ 그 마을의 사망자 숫자 → 마지막에서 두 번째, 세 번째 문장에서 '~ three adults and a baby died from their illnesses. ~ three more people succumbed'라고 했으므로 언급된 내용이다.

⑤ 그 마을의 인구 규모 → 마지막 문장에서 'In total, half of Walkerton's 5,000-strong population ~'라고 했으므로 언급된 내용이다.

14 난도 ★★☆　　　　　　　　　정답 ④

독해 > 빈칸 완성 > 단어 · 구 · 절

[정답의 이유]

빈칸 앞에서 '~ known as price fixing(가격 담합), is generally held to be an anticompetitive act.'라고 했고, 빈칸 다음에서 '~ in this manner are generally trying to ensure higher prices for their products ~'라고 했으므로 빈칸에 들어갈 적절한 것은 ④ 'collude(공모하다)'이다.

[오답의 이유]

① (법 등을 공공연히) 어기다
② 혹평하다
③ (능력 등을) ~에게 부여하다
⑤ 견책하다

대개의 경우, 둘 또는 그 이상 기업의 대표들이 비밀리에 그들의 제품에 대해서 비슷한 가격을 책정하는 것은 불법이다. 가격 담합으로 알려진 이 관행은, 일반적으로 반경쟁적인 행위로 간주된다. 이런 방식으로 공모하는 기업들은 그들의 제품에 대해 만약 시장이 자유롭게 기능할 경우, 일반적으로 이용 가능한 것보다 더 높은 가격을 확보하려고 노력한다.

VOCA

- competitive 경쟁적인
- ensure 확보하다, 보장하다
- function 기능하다

15 난도 ★☆☆ 정답 ②

어휘 > 어구

정답의 이유

밑줄 친 at large는 '아직 잡히지 않은'의 뜻이므로 이와 의미가 가장 가까운 것은 ② 'not yet confined(아직 붙잡히지 않은)'이다.

오답의 이유

① 분리되지 않은
③ 집단으로 변장한
④ 사람들과 함께 사라진
⑤ 은밀하게 위장한

본문해석

그 독약이 아직 잡히지 않고 공격을 실행하려고 단단히 결심한 다른 자들에 의해서, 우리가 알지 못하는 어딘가로 옮겨졌을 수도 있다는 심각한 우려가 있다.

VOCA

- poison 독, 독약
- at large (위험한 사람·동물이) 잡히지 않은[활개 치고 다니는]
- determined 단단히 결심한
- carry out 수행하다
- attack 폭행, 공격

16 난도 ★☆☆ 정답 ⑤

어법 > 비문 찾기

정답의 이유

⑤ 분사구문의 주어와 주절의 주어(the rules)가 같아 생략되었으며, 문맥상 분사구문의 주어(the rules)가 규정들이 '승인되다'라는 수동 의미이므로 If endorsing → If (being) endorsed가 되어야 한다.

오답의 이유

① are being은 진행 수동으로 '~되어지고 있는 중이다'의 뜻으로 올바르게 사용되었다.

② 주장 동사(state) 다음의 that절에는 '(should)+동사원형'이 오므로 should give가 올바르게 사용되었다.

③ preference(우선권, 선호도)는 수여동사(give)의 직접목적어로 쓰였으며, '~에 대한 우선권'의 뜻으로 전치사 for가 올바르게 사용되었다.

④ 'make+목적어+목적격 보어'가 '목적어가 ~하게 만들다'의 뜻으로 쓰였으며, 이때 it은 가목적어로, 진목적어(to fine the companies which ignore the rules)를 대신하고 있으므로 올바르게 사용되었다.

본문해석

유럽에서, 긍정적인 차별에 대한 규정들이 각 나라에서 논의되고 있다. 그 규정들은 여성들이 이사회 전체의 40%가 될 때까지, 더 나은 자격을 갖춘 남성 후보자가 없는 한, 기업들은 여성에게 비상임직에 대한 우선권을 주어야만 한다고 명시한다. 그 법률 초안은 그 규정을 무시하는 기업들에 대한 벌금 부과를 가능하게 만들었다. 만약 승인된다면, 규정이 시행되기까지는 7년이 걸릴 것이다.

VOCA

- discrimination 차별
- non-executive post 비상임직
- boardroom 이사회실
- endorse 보증하다, 승인하다
- come into force 시행되다, 효력을 발생하다

17 난도 ★★☆ 정답 ②

어법 > 비문 찾기

정답의 이유

② 'be likely to(~할 것 같다)'에서 likely는 형용사로, 조동사(would) 다음에 바로 올 수 없으므로 동사(be)를 추가하여 would likely to → would be likely to가 되어야 한다. 참고로 'would like to+동사원형(~ 하고 싶다)'은 현재의 소망을 나타낸다.

오답의 이유

① reach는 타동사로 다음에 목적어(them)가 바로 왔으므로 어법상 올바르게 사용되었다.

③ 접속사 Each time(~할 때마다) 다음에 절(they reached an island)이 왔으므로 어법상 올바르게 사용되었다.

④ 동사 posit(~라고 가정하다)의 목적어로 완전한 절(we might create ~ the same way)이 왔으므로 명사절 접속사 that이 올바르게 사용되었다.

⑤ 관계대명사 that의 수식을 받는 주어(rogue planets)와 동사가 '떠돌이 행성들이 추방되다'라는 의미의 수동 관계이므로 have been ejected from이 올바르게 사용되었다.

별들까지의 거리는 헤아릴 수 없을 정도로 어마어마하게 보일 수 있다. Princeton의 물리학자 Freeman Dyson은, 별에 도달하기 위해서 우리는 수천 년 전 폴리네시아인들의 항해로부터 무언가 배울 것이 있을지도 모른다고 시사한다. 시도했다면 재앙으로 끝났을 것 같은, 태평양을 가로지르는 한 번의 긴 여정을 시도하는 대신에, 그들은 이 섬 저 섬으로 가며, 광활한 그 대양의 대지를 한 번에 하나씩 가로질러 나아갔다. 그들이 섬 하나에 도착할 때마다, 그들은 영구 정착지를 세우고 나서 다음 섬으로 이동했다. 그는 우리가 같은 방식으로 먼 우주에 중간 단계의 집단 거주지를 만들 수 있을 것이라 가정한다. 이 전략의 핵심은 혜성들일 것인데, 이것들은 어떤 이유로 태양계로부터 추방된 떠돌이 행성들과 함께 별들에 이르는 경로를 어지럽힐 수 있다.

VOCA

- unfathomably 헤아릴 수 없을 정도로
- immense 거대한, 어마어마한
- island-hopping 이 섬 저 섬으로 여행 다니기
- landmass 광대한 대지(양)
- posit 가정하다, 단정하다
- rogue planet 떠돌이 행성
- somehow 어떻게든, 왜 그런지, 왠지
- eject 튀어나오게 하다, 추방하다
- litter 어지럽히다[어수선하게 만들다]

18 난도 ★★☆   정답 ①

어법 > 정문 찾기

정답의 이유

문맥상 '그의 탄생이 봄에 일어났을지도 모른다'라는 뜻으로, 과거의 불확실한 상황에 대한 추측을 나타내는 'may have＋p.p. ~(~했을지도 모른다)'가 되어야 하므로 빈칸에 들어갈 적절한 것은 ① 'may have occurred(일어났을지도 모른다)'이다.

본문해석

기독교 신앙의 초기에는 부활절이 주요 기념일이었고, 예수의 탄생은 축하받지 못했다. 4세기에 교회 성직자들이 예수의 탄생일을 기념일로 선언하기로 결정했다. 불행하게도 성경은 예수의 탄생일을 언급하지 않는다. (청교도들이 차후에 기념의 정당성을 부정하기 위해 지적한 사실이다.) 비록 몇몇 증거들이 그의 탄생이 봄에 일어났을지도 모른다고 (왜 양치기들이 한겨울에 양떼를 몰고 있겠는가?) 암시하고 있음에도 불구하고, 교황 Julius 1세는 12월 25일을 선택했다. 이것은 교회가 이교도들의 농신제 전통을 받아들이고 흡수하기 위한 노력으로 이 날을 선택했다고 흔히 믿어진다.

VOCA

- Christianity 기독교 신앙
- Easter 부활절
- declare 선언하다
- Puritan 청교도
- point out 지적하다
- legitimacy 정당성, 합법성, 타당성, 적법
- shepherd 양치기
- Pope 교황
- pagan 이교도
- Saturnalia festival 농신제(현재 크리스마스 무렵에 행해지던 고대 로마의 축제)

더 알아보기

조동사＋have p.p.

- 조동사＋have p.p.는 과거에 대한 '추측'과 '후회, 원망'을 나타낼 때 쓰는 표현이다.

추측	• would have p.p.: ~했을 것이다
	• must have p.p.: ~했음에 틀림없다
	  예 The garden is all wet. It <u>must have rained</u> last night.
	  (정원이 온통 젖어 있다. 어젯밤에 비가 왔음에 틀림없다.)
	• cannot have p.p.: ~했을 리가 없다
	  예 He <u>cannot have done</u> such a stupid thing.
	  (그가 그렇게 어리석은 짓을 했을 리가 없다.)
	• may[might] have p.p.: ~했을지도 모른다
	  예 Amy is very late. She <u>may have missed</u> her train.
	  (Amy는 매우 늦었다. 그녀는 기차를 놓쳤을지도 모른다.)
	• could have p.p.: ~했을 수도 있다

후회	• should[ought to] have p.p.: ~했어야 했는데 (하지 않았다)
	  예 Thomas <u>should have apologized</u> earlier.
	  (Thomas는 더 일찍 사과했어야 했다.)
	• shouldn't[ought not to] have p.p.: ~하지 말았어야 했는데 (했다)
	  예 He <u>ought not to have been driving</u> so fast.
	  (그가 그렇게 빨리 차를 몰아서는 안 되는 일이었다.)

- need have p.p. vs. need not have p.p.

필요	• need have p.p.: ~할 필요가 있었다 (그런데 하지 않았다)
	• need not have p.p.: ~할 필요가 없었다 (그런데 했다)
	  예 I <u>need not have watered</u> the flowers. Just after I finished it started raining.
	  (나는 꽃에 물을 줄 필요가 없었다. 내가 끝나자마자 비가 내리기 시작했다.)

19 난도 ★★☆ 정답 ⑤

독해 > 세부 내용 찾기 > 내용 (불)일치

정답의 이유

제시문 후반에 'Map these forms and conduits against each other, and you get what we think of as "the power structure" (이 형태들과 전달자들을 서로 매핑하면, 우리가 아는 '권력 구조'가 도출된다).'라고 했으므로 글의 내용과 일치하는 것은 ⑤ 'Relations between the forms and conduits of power help identify its structure(권력의 형태와 전달자들 사이의 관계들은 권력의 구조를 식별하는 데 도움이 된다).'이다.

오답의 이유

① 권력은 널리 환영받으며 편안하게 토론되는 단어이다. → 첫 번째 문장에서 'Power is something we are often uncomfortable naming and talking about explicitly.'라고 했으므로 글의 내용과 일치하지 않는다.

② 우리 시민들은 권력의 논리를 토론하고 이용할 권리가 없다. → 일곱 번째 문장에서 'Civic power is that capacity exercised by citizens in public, ~'라고 했으므로 글의 내용과 일치하지 않는다.

③ 시민 권력은 주로 정부 관리들이 행사하는 능력이다. → 일곱 번째 문장에서 'Civic power is that capacity exercised by citizens in public, ~'라고 했으므로 글의 내용과 일치하지 않는다.

④ 일상생활에서 사람들 대다수는 시민 권력을 능숙하게 매핑하는 경향이 있다. → 마지막에서 세 번째 문장에서 '~ too many people aren't able to draw, read or follow such a map.'이라고 했으므로 글의 내용과 일치하지 않는다.

본문해석

권력은 우리가 이름 붙이고 터놓고 말하기에 종종 불편한 어떤 것이다. 우리의 일상대화에서, 권력은 '권력에 미친', '권력에 굶주린', '권력의 과시' 등 도덕적으로 부정적인 분위기를 풍긴다. 그러나 권력은 본질적으로 불이나 물리학처럼 그 자체가 더 좋거나 나쁘지 않다. 권력은 그저 권력일 뿐이다. 유일한 질문은 우리가 그것을 이해하려고 노력하고 이용할 것인지 여부이다. 민주주의의 문화와 신화에서, 권력은 대중에게 귀속되어야 한다. 여기 권력에 대한 나의 간단한 정의가 있다. 그것은 여러분이 바라는 대로 타인이 하도록 보장하는 능력이다. 시민 권력은, 선거나 정부에서, 사회적 그리고 경제적 영역에서 시민에 의해 공개적으로 행사되는 능력이다. 시민 생활에서 권력은 강제력, 부, 국가배상, 이념, 사회적 규범, 수 등 여러 형태를 띠게 된다. 그리고 그것은 기관, 조직, 네트워크, 법과 규칙, 서사와 이념 같은 여러 전달자를 통해 흘러간다. 이 형태들과 전달자들을 서로 매핑하면, 우리가 아는 '권력 구조'가 도출된다. 오늘날의 문제는 너무 많은 사람들이 그런 지도를 그리거나 읽거나 이해하지 못한다는 점이다. 너무 많은 사람들이 권력에 대해 심각하게 문맹이다. 그 결과, 시민 생활에서 권력이 어떻게 작동하는지 이해하는 사람들이 불균형적인 영향력을 행사하고 다수의 무지에 의해 생겨난 빈틈을 채우는 것이 더욱더 쉬워졌다.

VOCA

• explicitly 숨김없이, 명쾌하게
• vibe 분위기, 느낌, 낌새
• inherently 선천적으로, 본래
• harness 이용하다
• reside 살다, 존재하다
• norm 기준, 규범
• conduit (정보나 물자의) 전달자[전달 기관/국가]
• map 지도를 만들다[그리다]
• profoundly 극심하게, 완전히
• illiterate 문맹의, 무식한
• wield 휘두르다
• disproportionate 불균형의
• void 빈틈

20 난도 ★★☆ 정답 ⑤

독해 > 글의 일관성 > 글의 순서

정답의 이유

주어진 글의 마지막 문장에 등장하는 hesitant는 현대 경제학자들의 주저함을 기술하고, (C)에서 그들의 내키지 않음(their reluctance)을 설명하는 것은 어렵지 않다고 이어가는 것이 자연스럽다. 표준 가정의 만족과 복지 후생의 결과가 생기는 모형(a model)을 제시하고, (B)에서 '그렇지 않으면(Otherwise)'으로 이어지는 흐름에서 the model로 연결되는 문맥과 (A)에서 추가적인 설명의 단어 moreover를 통해 경제학자의 또 다른 특성을 설명하는 것이 자연스럽다. 따라서 글의 순서로 알맞은 것은 ⑤ '(C) – (B) – (A)'이다.

본문해석

다른 분야에서 학자들의 수가 증가하는 것과는 대조적으로, 경제학자들은 상대적으로 소비 사회에 대한 최근의 비판에 거의 기여하지 못했다. 몇 가지 주목할 만한 예외가 있지만, 현대 경제학자들은 소비와 삶의 질 사이의 관계에 대해 질문하는 것을 주저해 왔다.

(C) 그들의 내키지 않음을 설명하기는 어렵지 않다. 대부분의 경제학자들은 일반적인 표준 가정이 충족되는 한, 소비는 틀림없이 복지를 양성한다는 모형을 지지한다.

(B) 그렇지 않으면 그런 일은 일어나지 않을 것이다. 실제로 우리가 보게 되겠지만, 그 모형의 영향은 훨씬 더 강력하다.

(A) 게다가, 경제학자들은 일반적으로 가치와 선호도에 대한 비판적 논의에 끼어들기를 주저한다. 그러한 논의가 없다면, 기존 소비자 선택의 형태가 최적이라고 쉽게 가정하게 된다.

VOCA

• critique 비판, 평론
• consumer society 소비 사회
• entertain (생각 · 희망 · 감정 등을) 품다
• reluctance 내키지 않음, 꺼려함
• subscribe to ~에 동의하다
• assumption 추정
• yield 굴복하다, 양성(산)하다

- implication 영향[결과], 함축, 암시
- unwilling 마지못해 하는
- preference 우선권
- in the absence of ~이 없을 때에, ~이 없어서
- existing 기존의, 현재 사용되는
- configuration 배치, 배열, 형태, 구성
- optimal 최적의

21 난도 ★☆☆　　　　　　　　　　　정답 ①

독해 > 빈칸 완성 > 단어 · 구 · 절

[정답의 이유]

빈칸 문장의 앞부분에서 흑사병 때문에 노동력이 급감하면서 지주들이 노동자들에게 임금 혹은 집세를 주게 되었고, 전반적인 임금 상승도 있었다고 했다. 또한, 빈칸 뒷부분의 'to the hitherto rigid stratification of society(지금까지 견고했던 사회 계층에)'로 미루어 보아 빈칸에 들어갈 말로 가장 적절한 것은 ① 'fluidity(유동성)'이다.

[오답의 이유]

② 폭력
③ 의학
④ 경계
⑤ 군주제

본문해석

1347년과 1351년 사이 유럽을 황폐화시킨 유행병인 흑사병은, 그 당시까지 알려진 다른 어떤 전염병이나 전쟁보다 비율적으로 더 많은 목숨을 앗아갔다. 이 끔찍한 대재앙의 결과는 엄청났다. 전쟁이 중단되고, 무역의 갑작스러운 침체가 즉시 이어졌지만, 단지 짧은 기간 동안 지속될 뿐이었다. 더 지속적이고 심각한 결과는 너무나 많은 노동자들의 사망으로 인한 경작지 면적의 급격한 감소였다. 이것은 많은 지주들의 몰락으로 입증되었다. 노동력 부족은 지주들이 소작인들을 유지하기 위한 노력으로 노동 서비스 대신에 그들의 임금 혹은 집세를 대체하도록 했다. 숙련공들과 소작농들에 대한 임금의 전반적인 상승도 있었다. 이러한 변화들이 지금까지 견고했던 사회 계층에 새로운 유동성을 가져왔다.

VOCA

- Black Death 흑사병
- pandemic 유행병
- ravage 파괴하다
- proportionately 비례해서
- toll of life 사망자 수(=death toll)
- catastrophe 재앙
- cessation 정지
- under cultivation 경작 중인
- money rent 집세
- in place of ~ 대신에
- tenant 소작인
- hitherto 지금까지

- stratification 계층화, 성층

22 난도 ★★☆　　　　　　　　　　　정답 ③

독해 > 빈칸 완성 > 단어 · 구 · 절

[정답의 이유]

(A) 다음의 'amounts of money ~'로 미루어 문맥상 (A)에는 선지 ①~⑤가 모두 가능함을 유추할 수 있다. 빈칸 (B) 다음 문장에서 'As humans, we evolved to respond more strongly to negative stimuli than positive ones.'라고 했고, (B) 다음의 'our worst tendencies(우리의 최악의 취향)'라고 했으므로 (B)에는 ③, ④가 가능하다. 빈칸 (C) 다음에서 이러한 알고리즘은 우리를 점점 더 부정적인 토끼 굴로 내려보내는 콘텐츠를 골라낸다고 했으므로 (C)에는 'reinforce(강화하다)'가 적절하다. 따라서 빈칸에 들어갈 적절한 것은 ③ '(A) staggering(엄청난) − (B) amplify(증폭시키다) − (C) reinforce(강화하다)'이다.

[오답의 이유]

① 엄청난 − 단축하다 − 과소평가하다
② 놀라운 − 압축하다 − 말하다
④ 놀라운 − 확대하다 − 개조하다
⑤ 경탄할 만한 − 압축하다 − 보강하다

본문해석

현대의 온라인 허위 정보는 우리가 현재 알고 있는 것처럼 대부분 인터넷을 동력으로 작동하는 관심 집중형 사업 모델을 이용한다. 구글과 페이스북 같은 플랫폼들은 우리의 관심을 끌고 사로잡아 우리에게 유료 광고를 보여줌으로써 (A) 엄청난 금액의 돈을 번다. 이러한 관심은 우리가 어떤 콘텐츠와 관련되는지 측정하고, 자동적으로 그와 유사한 더 많은 콘텐츠를 우리에게 보여주는 알고리즘을 이용해 조작된다. 문제는, 물론, 이러한 알고리즘이 자동적으로 우리의 최악의 취향을 추천하고 (B) 증폭시킬 때 나타난다. 인간으로서, 우리는 긍정적 자극들보다 부정적 자극들에 더 강하게 반응하도록 진화했다. 이런 알고리즘은 그것을 감지하고 (C) 강화하여, 우리를 점점 더 부정적인 토끼 굴로 내려보내는 콘텐츠를 골라낸다.

VOCA

- disinformation 허위 정보
- exploit 개발하다, 이용하다
- engage with 다루다, 관여하다, ~와 맞물리게 하다
- algorithm 알고리즘
- tendency 성향, 취향
- stimuli 자극
- detect 탐지하다
- rabbit hole 토끼 굴(헤어 나오기 힘든 어떤 것)

독해 > 글의 일관성 > 무관한 어휘 · 문장

정답의 이유

첫 문장에서 'a fluctuating proportion of the world's population has believed that the end of the world is imminent.'라고 한 다음, 제시문 전반에 걸쳐 종말론이 환경주의를 비롯해 여러 사상에 미친 영향을 서술하고 있는데, ⑤의 문장은 유라시아인들이 종말론을 항상 믿은 것은 아니라는 내용이다. 따라서 글의 흐름상 어색한 문장은 ⑤ 'Eurasians have not always believed that their world will end someday(유라시아인들은 그들의 세계가 언젠간 종말을 맞이하게 될 것이라고 항상 믿어온 것은 아니었다).'이다.

본문해석

최소한 3천 년 동안, 변동을 거듭해 온 세계 인구 비율은 세상의 종말이 임박했다고 믿어왔다. 학자들은 그 기원에 대해 논쟁하지만, 오늘날의 많은 환경주의를 굴절시킨 종말론적인 서술의 독특한 구조는 대략 기원전 1200년경, 조로아스터 또는 짜라투스트라로 알려진 이란의 예언자의 생각에서 시작했던 것처럼 보인다. 세상의 점진적인 쇠퇴의 개념은 고대 문명에서 널리 퍼졌다. 하지만 조로아스터는 유대교, 기독교 그리고 그 후 역사의 세속적 모형에도 세상의 종말에 대한 긴급함을 전파하였다. 로마 유대교의 광신도들로부터 다윗교 분파에 이르기까지, 아주 많은 신자들이 임박한 종말에 대한 공포와 희망 속에서 싸우고 죽어간 반면, 나치와 공산주의자를 포함한 몇몇 사람들은 위기와 분쟁에 대한 예언이 필연적으로 자신들을 충족시켜 주었기 때문에 파멸적인 결과를 가진 종말론적 수사법을 채택했다. 그러나 거의 틀림없이 비슷한 수사 전략들은 그것의 가장 눈에 띄는 성공들을 환경 운동에 제공했다. <u>유라시아인들은 그들의 세계가 언젠간 종말을 맞이하게 될 것이라고 항상 믿어온 것은 아니었다.</u> 이를 염두에 두면, 환경 보호적이고 급진적인 생태학적 담론에서 우리가 종말론적 이야기의 과거와 미래의 역할을 고려하는 것은 중요하다.

VOCA

- fluctuating 변동이 있는, 동요하는, 오르내리는
- imminent 긴박한
- distinctive 독특한
- apocalyptic 종말이 온 듯한, 종말론적인
- narrative 서술, 설화, 화술
- inflect 구부리다, 굴곡시키다
- prophet 예언자
- bequeath 물려주다, 유증하다, 계승하다
- secular 현세의, 세속의, 비종교적인
- urgency 긴급함
- demise 종말, 죽음, 사망
- catastrophic 참사의, 재난의
- inexorably 냉혹하게, 가차 없이
- arguably 주장하건대, 거의 틀림없이
- striking 현저한, 눈에 띄는
- with this in mind 이로 인하여

독해 > 빈칸 완성 > 단어 · 구 · 절

정답의 이유

빈칸 다음 문장에서 이러한 의존 관계는 상호 진화의 긴 역사를 시작했고, 바이러스는 숙주에 기생하여 살게 되면서 의존 관계를 형성했다고 했으므로 빈칸에 들어갈 말로 가장 적절한 것은 ② 'lost their autonomy as they evolved to thrive as parasites on other cells(그들이 다른 세포에서 기생충으로 자라도록 진화하면서 그들의 자율성을 잃었다)'이다.

오답의 이유

① 초기 세포의 원형들에게 많은 원시적인 특징들을 주입했다
③ 모기가 무는 것에서 침을 통해 인간에게 전해졌고 그것들로부터 독립되었다
④ 감각기를 이용해 세포막을 통해 전달되었고 지속적으로 변형되었다
⑤ 약해진 바이러스에 노출되었고 그런 특정 침입자를 인지했다

본문해석

세포는 생명의 기본으로 여겨지지만, 모든 유전적 다양성을 지닌 바이러스가 그 역할을 공유할지도 모른다. 우리 지구의 가장 초기 바이러스와 세포는 포식자와 먹이라는 뒤얽히고 때로는 공생하는 관계로 진화해왔을 것이다. 증거는 심지어 바이러스가 세포로 시작했지만 <u>그들이 다른 세포에서 기생충으로 자라도록 진화하면서 그들의 자율성을 잃었다</u>는 것을 시사한다. 이러한 의존 관계는 상호 진화의 긴 역사를 시작했다. 세포 안에 사는 바이러스는 그들의 숙주들이 적응하도록 만들고, 그런 변화들은 바이러스로 하여금 결코 끝나지 않는 한 수 앞서는 사이클에 적응하도록 야기시킨다.

VOCA

- genetic 유전의
- intertwine 뒤얽히다
- symbiotic 공생의
- lose one's autonomy 자율성을 잃다
- parasite 기생생물, 기생충 같은
- coevolution 상호 진화
- one-upmanship 한 발[한 수] 앞서기, 우월의식
- autonomy 자율성
- membrane 세포막
- receptor 감각기관
- invader 침입자

독해 > 대의 파악 > 제목, 주제

정답의 이유

첫 번째 문장에서 유전적 변이의 개념을 설명하고, 이를 입증하는 과정과 여러 예시들을 나열하면서 변이가 생기는 원인을 설명하고 있으므로 글의 제목으로 적절한 것은 ④ 'Inherited Causes of Variation(변이의 유전적 원인들)'이다.

오답의 이유

① 성별 차이의 원인들
② 자녀와 부모의 식별
③ 유전자 식별과 DNA
⑤ 사회적 유전성의 원인과 결과

본문해석

부모로부터의 유전적 정보의 결과물인 특질의 변이는 유전적 변이라고 불린다. 자녀들은 대개 아빠와도 약간 닮고, 엄마와도 약간 닮지만, 그들은 그들의 부모 중 어느 한쪽과도 똑같지는 않을 것이다. 이는 그들이 DNA 절반과 유전적 특징들을 각각의 부모로부터 받기 때문이다. 각각의 난자와 각각의 정자 세포는 개인에게 필요한 유전 정보의 절반을 포함하고 있다. 이것들이 수정 과정에서 합쳐질 때 새로운 세포는 개인에게 필요한 모든 유전 정보로 구성된다. 여기에 인간에게 유전된 변이의 몇 가지 예시가 있는데, 눈 색깔, 머리카락 색깔, 피부색, 귓불이 있거나 없는 귀, 혀를 말 수 있는 능력 등이다. 성별 역시 유전된 변이인데, 왜냐하면 당신이 남성인지 여성인지는 당신이 부모로부터 물려받는 유전자의 결과이기 때문이다.

VOCA

• variation 변화, 변동, 변이
• inherited 상속한, 유전의, 선천적인, 타고난
• egg cell 난자
• sperm 정자
• fertilization 수정
• lobe 귓불
• inheritance 유전성

당신이 저지를 수 있는 가장 큰 실수는, 실수를 할까 두려워하는 것이다.

— 앨버트 하버드 —

좋은 책을 만드는 길, 독자님과 함께하겠습니다.

2025 시대에듀 기출이 답이다 9급 공무원 영어 7개년 기출문제집

개정11판1쇄 발행	2024년 10월 15일 (인쇄 2024년 08월 14일)
초 판 발 행	2015년 06월 10일 (인쇄 2015년 05월 22일)
발 행 인	박영일
책 임 편 집	이해욱
편 저	시대공무원시험연구소
편 집 진 행	박종옥 · 정유진
표지디자인	박종우
편집디자인	박지은 · 곽은슬
발 행 처	(주)시대고시기획
출 판 등 록	제10-1521호
주 소	서울시 마포구 큰우물로 75 [도화동 538 성지 B/D] 9F
전 화	1600-3600
팩 스	02-701-8823
홈 페 이 지	www.sdedu.co.kr

I S B N	979-11-383-7438-5 (13350)
정 가	21,000원

시대에듀가 합격을 준비하는 당신에게 제안합니다.

성공의 기회! 시대에듀를 잡으십시오.
성공의 Next Step!

결심하셨다면 지금 당장 실행하십시오.
시대에듀와 함께라면 문제없습니다.

기회란 포착되어 활용되기 전에는
기회인지조차 알 수 없는 것이다.

－ 마크 트웨인 －

시대에듀의
지텔프 최강 라인업

1주일 만에 끝내는
지텔프 문법

10회 만에 끝내는
지텔프 문법 모의고사

답이 보이는 지텔프 독해

스피드 지텔프 레벨2

지텔프 Level.2
실전 모의고사

※ 도서의 이미지 및 구성은 변경될 수 있습니다.